"Here I am sitting at a comfortable table loaded heavily with books, with one eye on my typewriter and the other on Licorice the cat, who has a great fondness for carbon paper, and I am telling you that the Emperor Napoleon was a most contemptible person. But should I happen to look out of the window, down upon Seventh Avenue, and should the endless procession of trucks and carts come to a sudden halt, and should I hear the sound of the heavy drums and see the little man on his white horse, in his old and much-worn green uniform, then I don't know, but I am afraid that I would leave my books and the kitten and my home and everything else to follow him wherever he cared to lead. My own grandfather did this and Heaven knows he was not born to be a hero."

—HENDRIK WILLEM VAN LOON

"I am a fragment of rock thrown into space."

—NAPOLEON

A MILITARY HISTORY AND ATLAS OF
THE NAPOLEONIC WARS

Compiled for

THE DEPARTMENT OF MILITARY ART
AND ENGINEERING,
THE UNITED STATES MILITARY ACADEMY

WEST POINT, N.Y.

Prepared by

Brigadier General Vincent J. Esposito, *USA (Ret.)*
FORMER PROFESSOR AND HEAD OF DEPARTMENT

Colonel John Robert Elting, *Armor*
ASSOCIATE PROFESSOR AND DEPARTMENT RESEARCH OFFICER

FREDERICK A. PRAEGER, Publishers • New York • Washington

BOOKS THAT MATTER

Published in the United States of America in 1964
by Frederick A. Praeger, Inc., Publishers
111 Fourth Avenue, New York, N.Y. 10003

Third printing, 1968

© 1964 by Frederick A. Praeger, Inc.

Library of Congress Catalog Card Number: MAP 64-8

Printed in the United States of America

PREFACE

Although some 250,000 works have been written on the Napoleonic era, it is unlikely that a truly accurate account of Napoleon's campaigns ever can be compiled. The Emperor possessed the common human habit of embellishing his best exploits and blaming others for his reverses. He carried this behavior to extremes, even to the destruction of factual original documents. In such fashion, he developed the account of his mediocre Marengo campaign into a first-class epic romance. Napoleon's close followers, because of hero worship or personal considerations, also suppressed and invented. On the other hand, his enemies strove to portray him as a monster, and to present his best victories as lucky accidents. Kutusov's reports on the battles of Austerlitz and Borodino make both appear as Russian victories. National feeling also is reflected in the works of various authors. Read an English, a Prussian, a French, a Dutch, and a Belgian account of the Battle of Waterloo; you may easily be led to believe that you are reading about five different battles. Like all great historical periods, the Napoleonic era produced a flood of more-or-less spurious memoirs of dubious historical value—the so-called memoirs, for example, of Constant, Bourrienne, and Madame Junot. There is a multitude of old-soldier stories, such as Marbot's, which are a dangerous blend of facts and tall tales. Some writers, in unchecked pursuit of the picturesque, have scoured freely through these lower strata of Napoleonic history, and have emerged with plots and characterizations better fitted for comic opera. Likewise, some widely accepted historical novels—notably, Tolstoy's *War and Peace*—present a distorted picture of Napoleonic warfare.

Napoleon Bonaparte's battles, campaigns, and military theories have been studied by the cadets of the United States Military Academy since at least 1817. Even today, the Emperor stands as the exemplar of the great battle captain, eminently worthy of study, though not of uncritical emulation. Throughout the nineteenth century, the texts on the Napoleonic campaigns used by the cadets were either translations of French publications or books on strategy and tactics by American authors—principally heads of the forerunners of the present Department of Military Art and Engineering—who were deeply influenced by French military doctrine. In 1911, Gustave J. Fiebeger, then head of the department, prepared the Military Academy's first formal textbook dealing exclusively with Napoleon's campaigns: *Campaigns of Napoleon Bonaparte, 1796–97.* His successor, William A. Mitchell, included a section on Napoleon in his *Outlines of the World's Military History,* which was adopted in 1931. In 1939, the new department head, T. Dodson Stamps, introduced Baron Henri Jomini's *Life of Napoleon;* in 1942, he replaced this work with *Napoleon as a General* by Count Yorck von Wartenburg. In both instances, to facilitate study of the text, he directed the preparation of an atlas by department personnel.

Napoleon as a General and its accompanying atlas served the department's purpose well for many years. However, there came a time when the continual progression and expansion of the military studies that must be covered in the time available for the department's course in the History of the Military Art, and the development of new instructional objectives and techniques, demanded a simpler study medium. Since the method of integrated text and atlas used in *The West Point Atlas of American Wars* (published by Frederick A. Praeger in 1959) had proved successful in the conduct of the course, it was decided to develop a similar work for use in the study of Napoleon's campaigns.

All available original sources and the best secondary authorities were consulted during the compilation of the text for this new volume. The Wartenburg atlas maps were used as a basis, but all required at least some modification to conform to the new text, many had to be completely redone, and the number of full-page maps was increased from 125 to 169.

The maps for the Jomini atlas, from which the Wartenburg atlas plates originally were developed, were prepared by Edmund K. Daley, John C. B. Elliott, Philip F. Kromer, Jr., Thomas A. Lane, Kenneth D. Nichols, T. Dodson Stamps, and Horace F. Sykes, Jr., under the immediate direction of Theodore M. Osborne; those for the Wartenburg atlas were prepared by Allen F. Clark, Jr., Ellsworth I. Davis, John C. B. Elliott, Clayton S. Gates, Lawrence J. Lincoln, Alfred D. Starbird, and David H. Tulley, under the immediate direction of Vincent J. Esposito. All named are or were officers of the Corps of Engineers, United States Army. Mr. Edward J. Krasnoborski converted the basic map drafts for both atlases into production copy.

The narrative for this MILITARY HISTORY AND ATLAS OF THE NAPOLEONIC WARS was written by the undersigned, who also developed the accompanying maps. We are deeply indebted to Gerhard W. Schulz and Boyd T. Bashore, officers of this department, for their most valuable editorial assistance. Mr. Krasnoborski again applied his great talent to preparing the production copy. Mr. James Glover performed the tedious task of typing the manuscript in his usual steadfast manner.

VINCENT J. ESPOSITO
JOHN ROBERT ELTING

West Point, N.Y.
November 1963

Easy ys myne boke to rede and telleth of moche fyte
But then your easy rede is damned hard to wryte.
—Napier

1. DRAWS BACK FROM OTHERS, FROM PUBLICITY
2. PRESERVING AND CAREFUL IN WORK, HARDWORKING
3. UNREASONABLE DETERMINED TO HAVE ONES OWN WAY
4. THE ACT OF PROVING WRONG OR FALSE

INTRODUCTION

Napoleon and Modern Warfare

Why, in this age of nuclear weapons and guided missiles, should the student of military affairs be concerned with the campaigns of Napoleon? A simple answer would be: for historical or professional background. But there are more compelling reasons.

The conduct of war is an art based on ageless fundamental concepts that have remained valid irrespective of the prevailing means and methods of warfare. Furthermore, though weapons and tactics have changed continually in step with technological progress, the basic controlling element in war—man—has remained relatively constant. Napoleon reflected these views when he wrote: "The principles of warfare are those which guided the great captains [Alexander, Hannibal, Caesar, Gustavus, Turenne, Eugene, and Frederick] whose great deeds history has transmitted to us."

The Emperor did not imply that one must seek to memorize all the details of the campaigns of great captains of past wars. No two battles or campaigns have ever been exactly the same. Many fluctuating factors exert their influences: weather and terrain conditions, tactics, weapons, transportation facilities, training, morale, and leadership. The specific nature of all these factors is pertinent in a military study, but the subject of paramount importance is the skill with which the leader wielded the means available and exploited the victory, or, conversely, how through ineptitude, poor judgment, or other deficiencies he lost opportunities or suffered defeat.

Napoleon was truly a great captain, one who played a major role in the history and development of the military art. Few, if any, commanders, before or since, fought more wars and battles under more varied conditions of weather, terrain, and climate, and against a greater variety of enemies than the French Emperor. His understanding of mass warfare and his success in raising, organizing, and equipping mass armies revolutionized the conduct of war and marked the origin of modern warfare. By the very extent of his operations, he brought logistics into being as the necessary teammate of strategy. Through his own writings, and those of his quarreling disciples, Jomini and Clausewitz, he continues to influence the nature of war and peace today.

General Sir Archibald P. Wavell wrote: "If you discover how . . . [Bonaparte] inspired a ragged, mutinous, half-starved army and made it fight as it did, how he dominated and controlled generals older and more experienced than himself, then you will have learnt something." Follow this text, and you will find that the answers Wavell sought lie in Napoleon's professional competence and in his mastery of the art of leadership, that elusive characteristic that never becomes obsolete. He was a man for whom other men died willingly, whom the helpless dying cheered as he rode past; a man who knew the secrets of his soldiers' hearts, who could carry his soldiers with him despite the worst of prevailing conditions or future hopes. By the standards of his times, he took special care for the health of his troops, rewarded generously, forgave faults, shared hardships and danger, and dealt justly and patiently with the men in the ranks; yet, he could become heartless when necessary. The Emperor was a soldier's soldier, with full knowledge of every facet of military science and the art of war.

A study of Napoleon is more relevant than ever in this era of so-called tactical nuclear weapons. Gigantic operations of huge forces, such as were undertaken in World War II, are no longer feasible. Dispersion of forces and logistical facilities is essential to avoid appalling casualties and massive destruction. Dispersion results in a weakening of the control exercised by higher commanders, placing greater responsibility on subordinate unit commanders and requiring the highest degree of initiative of them. Over-all success in military ground operations will be dependent upon the aggregate of the individual tactical successes and failures of basic units, operating virtually independently. Such basic units must be of moderate size, highly mobile, compact and powerfully armed, self-sustaining, and bravely led—precisely the attributes that characterized a typical Napoleonic force. Napoleon was one of the major advocates of mobile warfare of the type that is necessary in an age of possible nuclear warfare. It matters not whether tactical nuclear weapons would or would not be used; the mere threat posed by their existence dictates a corresponding reorganization of forces and modification of tactics. There is no assurance that Napoleon's advice would not be taken literally: "It is a principle of war that when thunderbolts are available, they should be used in place of cannon."

Napoleon's Early Military Career

Napoleon Bonaparte was born at Ajaccio, Corsica, on 15 August 1769. His father, after having taken part in an unsuccessful revolt against French rule, had become one of its supporters. Consequently, Bonaparte, at the age of ten, was admitted to the Military Academy at Brienne, one of a series of provincial schools for poor nobility. In 1784, he entered the Military School of Paris for advanced training. In November 1785, after passing the artillery examination, he was commissioned a second lieutenant in the La Fere Artillery Regiment, at Valence. The Academy's evaluation of the new graduate showed keen insight; indeed, it proved to be a prophetic portrayal of Napoleon at the zenith of his career:

Retiring and diligent, he prefers study to amusements of any kind, and delights in the reading of good authors; he is devoted to abstract sciences, with little leaning to others, is well versed in mathematics and geography; is taciturn, loves solitude, is obstinate, proud, and exceptionally inclined to egotism; speaks little, is energetic in his answers, ready and severe in his refutations; possesses much love of self, is ambitious and hard-working. This young man deserves to be pushed on.

Bonaparte entered the military service during the beginnings of a period of strife, internal and external, which would soon burst out in the French Revolution and endure thereafter for some twenty years. The era was ideal for opportunism, an art that he soon mastered. While serving in the provinces, he applied himself to military studies and writings, but he found garrison life distasteful and avoided it whenever possible. Between 1785 and 1793, Bonaparte spent almost five years on various leaves and absences. During much of this time, he was in his native Corsica, striving futilely for self-aggrandizement in the obscure politics of the island.

Meanwhile, he had been promoted to first lieutenant of artillery in 1791, and in 1792, through intrigue, had got himself elected to an auxiliary post as lieutenant colonel of a Corsician volunteer battalion. That same year, his name had been removed from the Army rolls of regular lieutenants for absence without leave. He went to Paris to protest his dismissal and obtained not only his reinstatement but advancement to captain, with authority to return to his volunteer battalion in Corsica. There, he participated in a mismanaged and unsuccessful expedition against Sardinia, though his own battalion performed well. As a result of further machinations in the political affairs of Corsica, Bonaparte and his family were forced to flee to France. He then decided to seek his fortune as a French soldier and rejoined his regiment, which was engaged at the time in the siege of Toulon.

Here, Bonaparte's star began its ascension. At the time, "Representatives of the People, on Mission" (political commissars) accompanied the armies and wielded supreme power. One of these was Saliceti, a fellow Corsican. When the commandant of artillery at Toulon was wounded, Saliceti secured the post for Bonaparte. The siege was primarily a task for artillery, and Bonaparte applied the knowledge gained from seven years of study and contemplation. His plans were approved—no one present was capable of contesting them— and the siege was brought to a brilliant conclusion. The younger Robespierre, another of the Representatives, wrote with enthusiasm to his brother, then in power, of Bonaparte's achievements. The young, ambitious officer was immediately promoted to general of brigade and given command of the artillery of the French Army of Italy. In this position, he served with distinction.

In 1795, Bonaparte was assigned to the Army of the West (then operating against Royalists in the Vendee district) as commander of an infantry brigade. Disliking a task concerned only with civil war, and desiring to be at hand in Paris to exploit opportunities that might arise during the current period of political instability (Robespierre had fallen), he delayed reporting to his new command. Most of his energies were devoted to developing plans for the employment of the Army of Italy. His memorandum on the subject and the recommendations of Barras and others gained him a position on the planning staff of the Committee of Public Safety, where he came to the attention of Carnot, head of French military affairs. Bonaparte occupied his new post for only a short period. His refusal to proceed to Vendee had again endangered his career when a counterrevolutionary uprising broke out in Paris. Being readily available, he was selected by Barras to restore order. This he did with dispatch, receiving as reward promotion to general of division and soon thereafter the assignment as commander in chief of the Army of the Interior. Now, he devoted his full attention to the Army of Italy. His memoranda, critical of that

army's operations and urging new offensives, flowed freely and impressed his superiors. Scherer, commander of the Army of Italy, requested reinforcements and increased logistical support to meet the requirements of the new operational plans. At the same time, he complained to the Directory that the "eternal project mongers surrounded the Government," and that his army would "go to its destruction because some madmen are pleased to show you a map . . . how they could seize the moon with their teeth." Finally, he asked for a successor. An emissary, Saliceti, soon arrived in Italy. Scherer's resignation was accepted, and Bonaparte was appointed commander in chief of the Army of Italy.

(The chronicle of Napoleon Bonaparte is resumed from this point in detail in the atlas narrative.)

A Guide to Study

In compiling this work, the authors have made every effort to facilitate study. The reader will find his task much easier if he first becomes familiar with the references and time-saving devices employed, and with the background material provided. He should consult the table of symbols (p. xiv) used to describe the nature, size, location, and types of activity of military units; information concerning the weapons, tactics, and troop organization of the era—necessary to acquire proper perspective—can be found in the next section of this introduction.

Since the maps and the narrative are complementary, the reader must understand what a particular map is intended to portray before studying the accompanying text. Each map is provided with a title block indicating the situations and actions covered by the map *at a specific time or over a certain time period*. In addition, the title blocks contain direction arrows for geographical orientation, and distance scales. Troop dispositions at the particular time stated are shown in solid lines. On some maps, actions and movements, as indicated by appropriate route lines and symbols, will lead to the positions shown in solid lines; on others, the solid lines mark an initial location, and route lines emanating therefrom signify subsequent movements. The numbers that appear in parentheses under the names of commanders denote the numerical strength of their respective units. The narrative has been developed under the assumption that the reader is acquainted with the factual information depicted on the maps.

The conduct of every battle and campaign is strongly influenced by the topography of the area involved. Frequently, this topography dictates the course of action, and it often introduces significant hazards. An initial study of the ground over which the campaign was fought—mountains, roads, rivers, vegetation—will prove most helpful in understanding the reasons for many of the actions.

The text pertaining to each map is specially tailored to fit on the page opposite the map. Thus text and map are conveniently arranged side by side for joint study; only on rare occasions will it be necessary to turn back to another map. The narrative has been carefully designed to avoid involving the reader in a fruitless search for material not included on the map. Similarly, where places on the map are difficult to locate, the narrative includes direction guides. For this purpose, a map is divided vertically by tick marks into four lettered sections (A, B, C, and D) and horizontally into three numbered sections (1, 2, and 3). In keeping with military map-reading techniques, reference guides are read to the right and up. Thus a guide (*A1*) refers the reader to the lower left corner of the map; similarly, (*D3*) indicates the upper right corner.

The chronological charts (p. xii) provide a ready reference for checking the time relationship of events. Following the last map, there is a section devoted to short biographical sketches of Napoleon's marshals and other prominent figures. The volume closes with an extensive recommended reading list, prepared for those who desire to expand their investigation of particular aspects of this work or to delve into related fields of the Napoleonic era.

Names of individuals, towns, and cities throughout the work are used without accent marks in the interests of simplicity.

Organization, Weapons, and Tactics

BACKGROUND. The Royal French Army, before the Revolution, was a typical eighteenth-century force. Enlisted men were adventurers, ne'er-do-wells, or mercenaries. Commissioned rank was reserved primarily for the nobility. Discipline was ferocious, and morale poor. Tactics had been strictly copied from Frederick's rigid linear system.

The French Revolution brought war to the Continent. Fearing her aggressive foreign policies, monarchs throughout Europe joined against France. In 1792, every able-bodied Frenchman was declared liable for military service to meet this emergency; a National Guard was formed, and National Volunteers called up.

The rapid conversion of these masses of recruits into efficient fighting units was indeed a problem. Perhaps two-thirds of the officers of the pre-Revolutionary army had fled the country to escape the guillotine. In the new spirit of liberty and equality, the volunteers elected their officers, and discipline all but disappeared. During 1793–96, the infantry was reorganized into demi-brigades, each with a battalion of the old regular army and two of volunteers, in the hope of combining regular steadiness with volunteer enthusiasm. Initially, the result was that each element acquired the other's bad habits.

Tactics for the new armies had to be improvised, there being no time to drill the disorderly recruits into the robot steadiness and precision demanded by the Prussian linear system. What was needed was a method of rushing raw units up to deliver an effective attack before heavy losses broke their morale. An answer was found in a combination of skirmishers and columns of attack. On enemy contact, handfuls of brave skirmishers would move forward, take cover, and begin shooting, while the bulk of the command swayed in uneasy indecision as to whether to run or stand. If the skirmishers' fire was effective,

more men trickled forward; if the enemy wavered, the main body could usually be exhorted into advancing. The French conscripts and volunteers were men of higher intelligence than the enemy's "walking muskets." Some were fanatics, many had a fair idea as to why they fought. Even so, the first campaigns were touch-and-go. A little more determination and aggressiveness on the part of the Allies would have brought the French Revolution to a quick and bloody end. As usual, the supply of volunteers was soon exhausted; thereafter, various types of conscription were employed.

Conditions within the new French armies became intolerable. Until mid-1794, generals were haunted by Representatives of the People, on Mission, who accompanied the armies to see that all remained politically pure and to exact the death penalty for defeat. Losses from battle, starvation, and disease were enormous. By 1800, completely disillusioned with a Directory that lived in corrupt unconcern for their sufferings, the troops were ready to accept Bonaparte's *coup d'état*.

COMBINED ARMS. In the Napoleonic armies (after 1800), the corps was the smallest force of all arms. It was composed of two to four infantry divisions, a brigade or division of light cavalry, a company or two of corps artillery and engineers, and detachments of service troops. Basically, it was an infantry force with enough cavalry to scout for it.

The division consisted of two or more brigades, each of one or more regiments, and one or two attached companies of artillery.

Napoleon deliberately avoided standardization of his higher units, both because of the varying capabilities of his marshals and to confuse enemy intelligence. Along with the Imperial Guard, a large part of the cavalry (particularly the heavy cavalry) was held in reserve at the Emperor's personal disposal.

INFANTRY. Infantry was classified as *line* or *light*, the latter comprising about one-sixth of the infantry regiments. Organization and equipment were identical, but the light infantry maintained a tradition of dash and mobility. Initially, the typical infantry regiment consisted of three battalions, each of which had one elite company of *grenadiers* (*carabiniers,* in the light infantry) and eight of *fusiliers* (*chasseurs à pied,* in light infantry). Beginning in 1804, one of the fusilier companies in each battalion was converted into a new elite company—the *voltigeurs*. From 1805 through 1808, all infantry regiments were reorganized into four combat battalions of six companies each—one grenadier (*carabinier*), four fusiliers (*chasseur*), and one voltigeur—plus a depot (training) battalion of four companies. During 1809 and 1812, regimental cannon companies (with two to four light guns) were organized. The regiment also had a small headquarters, medical detachment, band, and train. A company at full strength had 140 officers and men; a regiment, 3,970.

The grenadiers, selected from the best and biggest men with at least two years' service, were excused from fatigue and guard duty, and drew extra pay. They were used for all missions requiring particular bravery and endurance. Voltigeurs were outstanding soldiers, too small to qualify as grenadiers. They specialized in scouting and skirmishing, and were supposed to be able to keep up with the cavalry at the trot.

CAVALRY. The French cavalry included *cuirassiers, carabiniers à cheval,* dragoons, *chasseurs à cheval,* and lancers. *Cuirassiers* were heavy cavalry— big men in steel helmets and cuirasses, mounted on big horses and armed with swords, carbines, and pistols. Their mission was the massed charge on the battlefield. The *carabiniers à cheval* were likewise heavy cavalry, but were not armored until 1810. *Dragoons* (originally mounted infantry, but now another type of cavalry) were armed with a light musket, sword, bayonet, and pistol, and wore brass helmets. They normally fought mounted, but were capable of effective dismounted action. The *chasseurs à cheval* and the *hussars* were light cavalry, armed with carbines, pistols, and sabers. (Their organization and employment were identical, but the hussars were more showily uniformed.) They usually engaged mounted with the saber, but were capable of mounted fire action and limited dismounted work. *Lancers* were also employed as light cavalry. Their long weapons gave them an advantage against infantry, especially in bad weather, when muskets were too wet to fire. Against other cavalry, lancers had to maintain a solid front, the lance being at a disadvantage against the sword in a melee.

Cavalry regiments varied in strength from 1,040 to 1,800 men. Heavy cavalry and dragoons were organized into homogeneous brigades and divisions; *chasseur à cheval,* hussar, and lancer regiments were frequently brigaded together.

ARTILLERY. This branch included foot artillery, horse artillery (in which each artilleryman was individually mounted and so able to accompany cavalry), coast artillery, and artillery for garrison duty in interior fortresses. Until 1800, the gun teams were driven by contract civilians with a violent aversion to glorious death. Their frequent cowardly behavior led to their replacement by military personnel. The artillery also included the *ponton* battalions. A company of foot artillery normally had six guns and two howitzers.

IMPERIAL GUARD. This was an elite organization under Napoleon's personal control. It grew from a strength of about 2,000 in 1800 to more than 60,000 in 1812. Its interior organization was complex. The original units, of all arms, were made up of tested veterans and collectively were titled the Old Guard. Other units, added between 1806 and 1815, formed the Middle Guard and Young Guard, according to their seniority. Beginning in 1809, the pick of the yearly call-up of conscripts went into the Young Guard.

The Old Guard drew special pay and always was fed, however hungry the rest of the army went. Its members had higher relative rank than other troops. These advantages, and its outstanding combat reputation, stimulated a feeling of emulation throughout the French Army, since admission to the Guard was open to any outstanding soldier. The principal advantage of the Guard was that it gave the Emperor a strong reserve of highly dependable troops and artillery at his immediate disposal, to be committed at the decisive time and place.

SUPPORTING TROOPS AND SERVICES. (1) *Engineers* were organized into separate battalions. Their work was largely confined to permanent and semipermanent bridges and fortifications. The *topographical engineers* were a small, separate staff of picked officers, charged with map-making and like duties. Engineer troops were employed in combat only in emergencies. (2) *Medical service* was provided by medical officers and assistants assigned to every headquarters from the regiment up. Medical evacuation roughly paralleled that of today—regimental dressing stations, ambulances (field hospitals), and base hospitals—but on a more limited and casual basis. (3) The *supply service* originally had been by contract, a practice that enriched the contractor and starved the army. To end these abuses, Napoleon formed battalions of supply-train troops. This was an improvement, but still left much to be desired. (4) *Communications* were represented by the Telegraph Service, which manned lines of semaphore signal towers connecting the major cities of the Empire and could transmit coded messages at the rate of 120 miles per hour in good weather. Another communications unit was the Military Postal Service, a relay system of messengers with the primary duty of keeping the army in contact with Paris. (5) *Military police* were provided by attaching a few gendarmes (national police) to a corps or division. These were backed up by the formidable elite gendarmerie of the Guard. (6) Frequently, *naval units* served with the army. These might be cadres, such as Napoleon employed in 1796 to form an improvised fleet on Lake Garda, utilizing local Italian sailors, or full battalions and regiments of sailors and naval artificers, such as were used in 1809 to patrol and bridge the Danube during the Wagram campaign. (7) The *National Guard,* organized at the beginning of the Revolution, furnished a general reserve. Its organization paralleled that of the regular army, though different terms were used— "legion" in place of regiment, and "cohort" for battalion. Eventually, it included all men from twenty to sixty years of age who had not served in the army.

FOREIGN TROOPS. Napoleon's foreign troops comprised three categories: (1) Those who enlisted in French units. (These became increasingly numerous as border districts of Italy and Germany were annexed by France.) (2) Entirely foreign units in the French service, such as the Swiss, the Hanoverian Legion, the Irish Legion, the Polish and Dutch Lancers of the Guard, and the Illyrian Regiment. Some of these—the Portuguese Legion, for example— were little better than forcibly impressed prisoners of war. In addition, there were special units that absorbed foreign volunteers and deserters. (3) Forces of allied or dependent states.

After 1806, about a third of the French Army were foreign; by 1812, more than half. These units varied greatly in effectiveness. The Poles, believing that Napoleon would re-establish a free Poland, were perhaps the best. The Swiss were well-trained mercenaries. Italians usually served well, doing some of the finest fighting of the Russian campaign. Germans were variable, Saxon cavalry and Württemberg infantry being thought the best. Neapolitans were frequently worthless.

COMMAND AND STAFF. During the Revolution, general officers were designated as "general of brigade" and "general of division." These were designations of grade and not necessarily of assignment. Napoleon added the grade of "marshal" with the establishment of the Empire. The few corps commanders who were not marshals were titled "general in chief," though by 1815 the term "lieutenant general" had come into common usage. Berthier's title as imperial chief of staff was "major general."

Napoleon's personal headquarters (the "Maison") was large, since he continued to govern France and direct all his armies, even when on campaign. He was assisted by a group of aides-de-camp, general officers capable of all missions from the negotiation of a truce to the command of a special task force. The Maison also handled intelligence matters.

Under the Maison came the general headquarters, headed by Berthier. In 1805, he had two principal subordinates: a "chief of the general staff," who handled all reports and returns and generally supervised all details; and a *"maréchal général des logis,"* in charge of all reconnaissance, marches, and everything pertaining to the movement of the army.

The general headquarters itself had four sections; roughly: (1) troop movements and intelligence (Berthier's "cabinet"); (2) records and personnel; (3) headquarters' functioning and security; and (4) prisoners, deserters, and legal matters. In addition, there were special staff sections—a topographic bureau, charged with map supply; artillery; engineers; military police; and a pool of unassigned officers. (Staff organization varied somewhat from year to year.)

Farther to the rear was the administrative headquarters, headed by the *Intendant,* who had responsibility for the army's logistics and administration.

Corps and division staffs followed the organization of the general staff, on a correspondingly reduced scale.

At best, staff work was difficult. Communication between units was by mounted messenger or aide. Orders had to be written out, one copy at a time, with quill pen and ink. Language difficulties increased with the number of foreign units. These conditions put great responsibilities on the aides-de-camp, who had to deliver, explain, and sometimes supervise the execution of orders.

SUPPLY. Napoleon's concept of supply was expressed in his phrase "Make war support war." French troops on campaign lived off the country. In peacetime, or in allied countries, this would be arranged beforehand by the staff. Soldiers were normally billeted on civilians and fed by them. Once the fighting began, much the same system might be followed, but there was no payment for food or lodging. In fact, the countryside was always stripped bare in any but the shortest campaigns; what authorized foraging parties did not take, undisciplined stragglers would plunder.

In theory, the troops were supplied in the field from magazines established in fortresses along the line of communication, but this was usually held to the minimum of bread and ammunition by the lack of transport. The loss of part of a command from hunger and fatigue was expected, and these losses became greater in the largely conscript armies of 1812–14.

This ramshackle system of supply put a heavy load on conscientious commanders. Farsighted ones, like Davout, took care to have qualified millers and bakers with each regiment. Much reliance was placed on local purchase, and many foreign businessmen made an excellent thing out of the Grand Army and its needs. Troops in outlying districts, especially in Spain, were usually short of food, clothing, and supplies of all kinds.

INFANTRY AND CAVALRY WEAPONS. The growing Industrial Revolution made the production of Napoleonic weapons easy and cheap, thus facilitating the organization of mass armies. Generally speaking, these weapons were muzzle-loading, smooth-bore, short-range, and inaccurate. Wet weather soon rendered them unserviceable. Small arms were all flintlocks; rifles, being slow to load, were little used. All weapons used black powder, which produced great clouds of smoke, frequently obscuring the battlefield.

The standard weapons of the French Army throughout the period 1790–1815 were: (1) The *musket,* used by most infantry units. Caliber varied from .69 to .71. Maximum range was 1,065 yards. Effective range against formed troops was 200–250 yards; against small groups, 150 yards; against individuals, 100 yards. Infantrymen carried about 50 cartridges. (2) The *dragoon musket,* issued to dragoons, engineers, foot artillery, voltigeurs, and other units. It was of standard caliber, but shorter and lighter than the infantry musket. (3) The *musketoon,* a sawed-off infantry musket, carried by some cavalry units. (4) The *carbine,* a short, light, standard-caliber weapon, carried by most of the cavalry and supply-train troops. It was effective only at short range. (5) *Pistols,* which came in several types, the standard caliber being .69. They were point-blank weapons, accurate up to 10 yards and heavy enough to make excellent clubs. (6) *Swords* varied greatly in design, the heavy cavalry carrying a long, straight thrusting sword and the light cavalry a heavy, curved saber. Grenadiers, voltigeurs, artillerymen, train troops, and Imperial Guard personnel likewise usually carried a sword of some type. (7) *Lances* were used increasingly after 1809, but their effective employment required careful training. (8) The *bayonet,* about 15 inches long.

The effectiveness of the Napoleonic small arms varied with the training and experience of the troops. The soldier pulled a cartridge from his pouch, bit off the end, primed his weapon's "pan" with some of the powder, closed the pan, poured the rest of the powder down the barrel, rammed the ball and cartridge paper home on top of the powder, withdrew the ramrod, took aim, pulled the trigger—and hoped the flint would spark and the musket fire.

Only well-drilled troops could deliver a sustained, reasonably accurate fire. Five rounds a minute were possible for short periods; after the muskets became fouled, four rounds in three minutes was a good average. Musketry training was sometimes neglected, many French commanders being too inclined to regard the musket as a handy handle for the bayonet. Since muskets were so inaccurate—one battalion firing at another at 100 yards might hit five men—the tendency was to hold fire until the enemy got within 30 or 40 yards. At such short range, massed fire was murderous, the soft lead slugs knocking over whole ranks, often with 50 per cent casualties. Some soldiers, by practice, got to be excellent shots and could pick a guerrilla from behind a rock at 300 yards.

ARTILLERY WEAPONS AND AMMUNITION. Artillery was smooth-bore and muzzle-loading. Its ammunition, like that of the infantry musket, seldom fit truly. Guns were traversed by shifting their trails. Since recoil mechanisms were unknown, it was necessary to re-lay the piece after each shot.

The approximate effective ranges, in yards, of the several types of artillery were:

Type	Solid Shot	Canister
12-pounder gun	920 to 1,050	600 to 700
6- or 8-pounder gun	820 to 920	500 to 600
4-pounder gun	820 to 920	400 to 500
6-inch howitzer	750 to 1,300 (shell)	450 to 600

Good gun crews could get off two rounds a minute from the lighter guns, one from a 12-pounder. Artillery commanders sought enfilade and ricochet fire whenever possible. Where swampy or muddy terrain prevented ricochet fire, as at Waterloo, artillery effectiveness was greatly reduced.

Artillery ammunition included: (1) *Solid shot,* a round iron ball fitting the gun's bore. (2) *Case-shot,* or *canister,* a tin can filled with musket balls. This ruptured on firing, giving a buckshot pattern. (Canister came in two types; one with larger balls, used for long-range fire, was sometimes termed "grapeshot.") (3) *Explosive shell,* a hollow, round shot filled with explosives. It was used primarily in howitzers. (4) *Shrapnel* (spherical case-shot), a round, hollow shot containing a bursting charge mixed with musket balls, and ignited by an adjustable fuse. Effective up to maximum range, it was the British "secret weapon" of the period. (5) *Hot shot,* ordinary solid shot heated in ovens for incendiary effect. Its use was generally limited to coastal batteries.

Generally, solid shot was used against troops and light buildings. Canister was for short-range, antipersonnel fire, double loads being employed when the enemy got near the guns. Shell was useful for destruction of buildings, but had only limited fragmentation effect.

Cannon were fired by means of a length of slow match (cord impregnated with gunpowder) wrapped around a short rod.

The British, in addition, used *rockets,* having learned their effectiveness in India. Their major faults were their inaccuracy and their tendency to boomerang. Employed as an area weapon against towns, they had excellent incendiary effect. In the field, they had decided psychological effect, usually stampeding the enemy's horses.

TACTICS. *Earlier Battles.* As mentioned previously, Napoleon's officers developed their tactics, as departures from the Prussian system of linear tactics, during the wars of the Revolution. The general pattern adopted was a line of battalion columns, covered by a thick swarm of skirmishers. Initially, this skirmish line was very thick, sometimes consisting of whole deployed battalions of light infantry. If there were enough troops to form two lines of battalion columns, the columns would be placed in checkerboard fashion, with the second line to the rear, out of range. Artillery and cavalry could move forward through the intervals. This, properly applied, was a highly flexible system. It avoided the frequent halts to dress the ranks and maintain alignment that were the constant curse of movements in line. There were no hard-and-fast rules. Units adapted their formations to their mission and the terrain—defending in line, attacking in line or column, forming squares against cavalry, as the situation demanded. A half-deployed, half-massed formation (the "mixed order," Napoleon's favorite) was developed, in which battalions were alternately in column and line. It was commonly employed in defensive missions, as at Austerlitz and Waterloo, but it was also used in decisive attacks at Arcola, Jena, and Friedland.

In the earlier battles, the swarming skirmishers, taking advantage of all possible cover, shot the enemy's line to pieces. The artillery seconded their work. Battalion columns meanwhile moved up rapidly, receiving little attention from an enemy already fixed by the skirmishers and artillery and blinded by smoke. Once within striking distance, the columns were hurled at the enemy line, crushing it by sheer impact and shock action. The skirmishers rallied in the intervals between the columns and continued to shoot. This continuous skirmisher action was important, for the columns had little available firepower and made big targets; therefore, it was essential that the enemy be kept under fire and distracted until the last possible moment.

If all went as planned, the columns caught enemy fire for only the last few minutes of their rush, and that fire probably was from a shaken line of tired men with fouled muskets. The supporting skirmishers were practically impossible to dislodge. They drifted away from infantry attacks, rallying in

INTRODUCTION

buildings and hedgerows to continue sniping. In open country, sudden cavalry charges might cut them up, yet veterans knew how to form into tight knots until their own cavalry arrived to free them.

Developments. The system changed gradually with the vast increase in the strength and technical skill of French artillery between 1796 and 1805. To a large extent, artillery took over the skirmishers' job of clearing the way for the attack columns.

On campaign, Napoleon's Grand Army moved with its different corps within mutually supporting distance. Ahead was a screen of light cavalry, from the Cavalry Reserve and the leading corps, with the mission of covering the Grand Army's advance and finding the enemy. Divisions of dragoons from the Cavalry Reserve might cover exposed flanks or stiffen the screen.

Once definite enemy contact was established, the entire army concentrated by forced marches. Initially, the advance guard seized the most favorable position available, striving to fix the enemy and to form a pivot of maneuver for the friendly troops in rear. While the advance guard spent itself, these fresh units went into action on its flanks, rather than reinforce it directly. First the light infantry probed in, developing weak spots and tying down hostile units in an incessant fire fight. Behind them, divisional and corps artillery moved aggressively forward into easy canister range. The light cavalry drove off the enemy's horsemen and dashed in on objectives of opportunity. Then large-scale infantry attacks were unleashed. Depending on the situation and the terrain, these attacks might be in line, "mixed order," or column—the last being preferred for assaults on defiles and strong points. The skirmishers advanced between the attacking units, still shooting to cut down the remaining enemy firepower. Some artillery likewise moved forward with the attack, cannoneers manhandling their guns where the ground was too rough for horses. Other batteries, on higher ground, provided overhead fire. If, despite all preliminary measures, the attacking units met severe resistance, they might deploy into line and begin a fire fight. The normal impulse, however, seems to have been to attempt to bull on through. Where the first line was checked, the second line, or the cavalry, might attack through it.

Massed Formations. In the latter years of the Empire, there was an increasing tendency toward massive formations. This commonly is attributed to the declining quality of the infantry, due to heavy losses; the large numbers of relatively untrained conscripts; and the greater number of foreign troops. Moreover, all units were growing larger, making it difficult for a division or corps commander to control his whole force, unless he kept them in larger formations. Probably the worst example was d'Erlon's corps at Waterloo.

Defensive Tactics. Defensive tactics were less well thought out. Normally, a line or "mixed order" formation was used, covered by skirmishers. The main line of resistance would be formed along the crest of a convenient ridge, or even on a forward slope, thus fully displaying the forces available.

Wellington's introduction of reverse-slope tactics was consequently baffling to French leaders.

The regulation line formation was three ranks deep, even though the middle rank could hardly fire effectively, and despite the demonstrated effectiveness of the English two-rank line. Napoleon, after grumbling for years about the uselessness of a third rank, finally abolished it in 1813 at Leipzig.

Cavalry Tactics. Cavalry tactics were based on shock action—mounted charges in mass with sword and lance. A mounted charge was made at progressively greater speeds. If the distance to be covered was 600 yards, the first 200 would be at a slow trot, the next 200 at the full trot, the next 150 (as the cavalry came into enemy musket range) at the gallop, and the last 50 yards at the dead run. Some commanders preferred to make the entire charge at a sharp trot because of better steadiness and control. Good judgment was required to prevent taking up the gallop too soon, so that the horses would not be nearing exhaustion by the time they struck the enemy. Leadership and discipline were equally necessary to rally a unit promptly after a charge.

Infantry formed squares when attacked by cavalry. Usually, the squares were by battalion, though Napoleon used division squares (with artillery and baggage inside them) in Egypt and Russia. Whenever possible, these squares formed in echelon to cover each other's flanks.

SUMMARY. To recapitulate, the Napoleonic battle was an affair of jarring local attacks all along the line, vigorous enough to pin the enemy to his position and break up his front line. As this attrition ripened the battle, Napoleon selected the point for his decisive attack and massed his artillery opposite it. Behind these guns, he concentrated the units selected for the blow. By that time, the battle-weary enemy was off balance and putting his reserves into the battle, usually piecemeal, as assault followed assault. The artillery fire intensified, masses of French cannon moving forward into musket range to literally blow holes in the enemy's line. By now, his shielding cavalry, assailed by French forces of all arms, had been driven in. Attacked everywhere, engulfed in smoke, and unsteady, the enemy was hit simultaneously by the full weight of fresh infantry and the rush of masses of the Cavalry Reserve—dragoons, cuirassiers, carabiniers—held ready for the moment. Breaking through, the French wheeled right and left, rolling up the line and driving its fragments against French secondary attacks elsewhere. Light cavalry poured through in pursuit, while infantry and artillery consolidated the victory.

Things could go wrong. At Maida, Reynier failed to use his skirmishers to soften the English positions; at Waterloo, Ney put in the heavy cavalry too soon, and without infantry support. But the successes of Napoleon's system were even more numerous and more impressive; their lessons on how wars are won are as vital today as at Austerlitz and Friedland.

Year	Events	Campaign
1796	10-15 Apr. -- Battles of Montenotte and Dego (Operations Against Colli and Beaulieu) 5 Aug. -- Battle of Castiglione (Würmser's First Advance) 8 Sept. -- Battle of Bassano (Würmser's Second Advance) 15-17 Nov. -- Battle of Arcola (Alvintzy's First Advance)	ITALIAN CAMPAIGNS
1797	14 Jan. -- Battle of Rivoli (Alvintzy's Second Advance) 10 Mar. -6 Apr. -- Operations Against Archduke Charles 17 Oct. -- Treaty of Campo Formio Between France and Austria	
1798	12 June-- Bonaparte Occupies Malta 21 July-- Battle of the Pyramids 1 Aug. -- Battle of the Nile: Nelson Destroys French Fleet	CAMPAIGN IN EGYPT AND SYRIA
1799	5 Feb. -- Bonaparte Invades Syria 17 Mar.-20 May -- Siege of Acre 25 July-- Battle of Aboukir 9-10 Nov. -- Bonaparte Becomes First Consul	
1800	18 Apr. -- Massena Besieged in Genoa 14 June-- Battle of Marengo 5 Sept. -- Vaubois Forced to Surrender Malta 5 Dec. -- Battle of Hohenlinden	MARENGO CAMPAIGN
1801	9 Feb. -- Peace of Luneville Between France and Austria 21 Mar. -- French Forces in Egypt Capitulate 15 July-- Concordat With the Pope	
1802	27 Mar. -- Treaty of Amiens Between France and England 1 Aug. -- Napoleon Made Consul for Life	
1803	30 Apr. -- Napoleon Sells Louisiana to the United States 18 May-- England Declares War 1 June-- Napoleon Begins Preparations for Invasion of England	
1804	21 Mar. -- Execution of the Duke of Enghien 2 Dec. --Napoleon Crowned Emperor of the French	
1805	26 May-- Napoleon Crowned King of Italy 17 Oct. -- Surrender of Mack at Ulm 21 Oct. -- Battle of Trafalgar 2 Dec. -- Battle of Austerlitz 26 Dec. -- Treaty of Pressburg Between France and Austria	ULM-AUSTERLITZ CAMPAIGN
1806	12 July-- Confederation of the Rhine Activated 14 Oct. -- Battles of Jena and Auerstädt	JENA CAMPAIGN
1807	8 Feb. -- Battle of Eylau 14 June-- Battle of Friedland 8 July-- Peace of Tilsit Signed by France, Russia, and Prussia 19 July-- Grand Duchy of Warsaw Instituted 30 Nov. -- Junot Occupies Lisbon	EYLAU-FRIEDLAND CAMPAIGN
1808	Feb. -- French Begin Occupation of Spain 2 May-- Insurrection in Madrid 22 July-- Dupont Surrenders at Baylen 26 Oct. -- Napoleon Goes to Spain to Direct Operations	NAPOLEON'S CAMPAIGN IN SPAIN
1809	17 Jan. -- Napoleon Returns to France 20-22 Apr. -- Battles of Abensberg, Landshut, and Eggmühl 21-22 May-- Battle of Essling 5-6 July-- Battle of Wagram 14 Oct. -- Treaty of Schönbrunn Between France and Austria	CAMPAIGN OF 1809
1810	1 Apr. -- Napoleon Marries Maria Louisa, Archduchess of Austria 26 Apr. -- Massena Begins Invasion of Portugal 10 Oct. -- Wellington Retires into the Torres Vedras Lines	
1811	5 Mar. -- Massena Withdraws from Portugal 20 Mar. -- Birth of Napoleon's Son, the King of Rome 3-5 May-- Battle of Fuentes de Onoro (Spain)	
1812	19 Jan. -- Wellington Captures Ciudad Rodrigo 6 Apr. -- Wellington Captures Badajoz 24 June-- Napoleon Invades Russia 7 Sept. -- Battle of Borodino 21 Oct. -- Wellington Repulsed at Burgos (Spain) 26-29 Nov. -- Crossing of the Beresina	RUSSIAN CAMPAIGN
1813	2 May-- Battle of Lützen 20-21 May-- Battle of Bautzen 21 June-- Battle of Vitoria (Spain) 26-27 Aug. -- Battle of Dresden 16-19 Oct. -- Battle of Leipzig 22 Dec. -- Allies Invade France	LEIPZIG CAMPAIGN
1814	31 Mar. -- Allies Enter Paris 11 Apr. -- Napoleon Abdicates 4 May-- Napoleon Reaches Elba 1 Nov. -- Congress of Vienna Opens	CAMPAIGN IN FRANCE
1815	1 Mar. -- Napoleon Lands in France 18 June-- Battle of Waterloo 15 July-- Napoleon Surrenders to British 16 Oct. -- Napoleon Arrives at St. Helena (Dies There 5 May 1821)	WATERLOO CAMPAIGN

FRENCH OPERATIONS IN SPAIN

CONTENTS

TABLE OF SYMBOLS

BASIC SYMBOLS

Regiment III	Cavalry . . . . ▨
Brigade x	Cavalry covering force . . . . . ●●●●●●●
Division xx	Artillery . . . . ▣
Corps xxx	Artillery in position . . . . ⊔⊔⊔
Army xxxx	(Does not indicate type or quantity)
	Engineers . . . . ▥
Infantry . . . . ⊠	Trains . . . . ⊡

Examples of Combinations of Basic Symbols

Small cavalry detachment . . . . ▨ Stengel	Arrighi's cavalry corps . . . . ▨ ARRIGHI (xxx)
Ledru's infantry division of Ney's corps ⊠ Ledru (NEY) (x x)	Massena's infantry division, less unit commanded by Brune . . . ⊠ Massena (−Brune) (x x)
Legrand's infantry division of Oudinot's II Corps . . . . ⊠ Legrand (II) (x x)	Milhaud's cavalry corps, with unit commanded by Domon attached ▨ MILHAUD (+Domon) (xxx)
Reynier's VII Corps . . . . ⊠ REYNIER (xxx) VII	

OTHER SYMBOLS

	Actual location	Prior location
Troops on the march	➡	⇢ (dashed)
Troops in position	⌣	⌣ (dashed)
Troops in bivouac or reserve . .	○	○ (dashed)

Troops displacing and direction . . .

Troops in position under attack . .

Route of march . . . . - ▸ - - ▸ - - ▸ - - ▸ - - ▸

Field works . . . . MWMW   ⋀⋀⋀⋀

The Italian Campaigns

"A consecutive series of great actions never is the result of chance and luck; it is always the product of planning and genius. . . . Is it because they are lucky that (great men) become great? No, but being great, they have been able to master luck. . . . What is luck? The ability to exploit accidents."
                                        —NAPOLEON

"There was an eye to see in this man, and a soul to dare and do. He rose naturally to be King. All men saw that he was such."
                                        —THOMAS CARLYLE

MAP 1: EARLY WARS OF THE REVOLUTION, 1792-94

The beginnings of the French Revolution (1789-92) had not particularly disturbed Europe. France had been an aggressive neighbor, and other nations were willing enough to see her weakened. Austria, Prussia, and Russia were preoccupied with the dismemberment of Poland. Though Prussia and Austria did form a defensive-offensive alliance against France in February 1792, they confined themselves largely to diplomatic pressure. But the following April, largely as a by-product of the savage struggles among its contending political parties, Revolutionary France declared war on Austria. So began twenty-three years of almost constant war.

The first French offensive, an invasion of the Austrian Netherlands (now Belgium), collapsed immediately. The new French armies, composed of demoralized regulars and untrained volunteers, refused to face the disciplined Austrian troops and were more dangerous to their own officers than to the enemy. Meanwhile, the Duke of Brunswick gathered an ill-organized army of some 100,000 Prussians, Austrians, Hessians, and French Royalists at Coblenz (*B2*) for a march on Paris (*B2*). He crossed the French border in late August, capturing Longwy (27 August) and Verdun (2 September). By 20 September, his deliberate advance reached Valmy, where 36,000 hastily assembled Frenchmen under Kellermann and Dumoriez blocked his path. Brunswick had outmarched his supplies; the weather was frightful; and sickness, desertion, and detachments to guard his line of communication had reduced his available force to approximately 34,000.

The ensuing Battle of Valmy was primarily a long-range artillery duel. The French infantry, steadied by Kellermann's personal courage, stood firm under heavy fire; the French regular artillerymen maintained their traditional reputation as the world's finest. Late in the day, the Prussian infantry advanced, but turned about as the French gunners got its range. Brunswick then gradually withdrew across the Rhine.

Valmy stimulated the French morale. To the south, when Sardinia declared war, the French promptly overran her mainland provinces of Savoy and Nice. On the Rhine, the French seized Mayence (Mainz) (*B2*) and raided to Frankfurt. In October, Dumoriez struck unexpectedly into Flanders (*B2*), defeated the Austrians near Jemappes, and swiftly occupied the whole country, including the port of Antwerp—a "pistol pointed at the heart of England." It was these successful offensives, rather than the execution of the French King, that brought England, Holland, Austria, Prussia, Spain, and Sardinia into the First Coalition against France. As the professional armies of these allies mustered, French volunteers, believing the war already won, swarmed homeward; the French supply system began collapsing; and the Belgians turned hostile.

The year 1793 found the French believing themselves already invincible. In March, Dumoriez invaded Holland, but was routed by the Austrians at Neerwinden (a victory that the Austrian army owed largely to its chief of staff, Colonel Mack, and its advance-guard commander, the Archduke Charles). Dumoriez thereupon attempted a counterrevolution, failed, and fled to the Austrians. These events sowed panic through the French armies in the Low Countries and the Rhineland. Discipline and morale collapsed, and the troops retreated in disorder behind their own borders. Terror and confusion ate out the French government, while Royalist revolts flared in Lyons (*B2*), Toulon (*B1*), and the Vendee district of northwest France (*A2*). At Royalist invitation, British forces occupied Toulon, the main French naval base on the Mediterranean.

In this crisis, a rapid Allied advance on Paris would have encountered little effective resistance. But the divergent political interests of the Allies, and the archaic strategy of their generals, saved France. Austria sought to occupy French Flanders; the British were concerned exclusively with the capture of the French channel ports. The Allied generals, devout students of Frederick the Great's short-range system of deliberate advances from secure bases, proceeded in step-by-step fashion to besiege the fortress towns of northern France—Valenciennes, Conde, Lille, Dunkirk.

While the Allies methodically conducted these minor operations, the executive authority of the French Government was taken over by the brutal, but efficient, Committee of Public Safety, dominated first by Danton, then by Robespierre and his clique of Jacobin fanatics. These men infused the French Army with something of their own demoniac energy. Untrained but enthusiastic volunteers filled its ranks. Government Representatives on Mission moved through the armies to hold officers and men alike to their duty. Unsuccessful generals went to the guillotine. Eventually, superior numbers smothered the Allied advance, and the internal revolts were bloodily put down or contained. Toulon was recaptured, in large part through the skill of the besiegers' young artillery commander, Captain Napoleon Bonaparte, who thereby earned promotion to general of brigade.

The Allies again had missed their opportunity; 1793 had been a year of crisis, but Revolutionary France had finally won its struggle for self-preservation. Now, it would seize the initiative and carry the Revolution into the hostile kingdoms of Europe.

For 1794, Carnot, the member of the Committee of Public Safety responsible for military operations, planned a two-pronged offensive in the north. This ran headlong into a renewed Allied invasion, which it beat down in a series of scrambling engagements, ending with the Battle of Fleurus (*B2*), where Jourdan's determination and Lefebvre's tactical skill saved a desperate day. The Allies then evacuated the Low Countries; Holland was overrun during the winter by a French army under Pichegru.

In the south, the French Army of Italy carried out a successful minor campaign; its chief of artillery, General Bonaparte (also unofficially its commander's brains), received the credit for this operation.

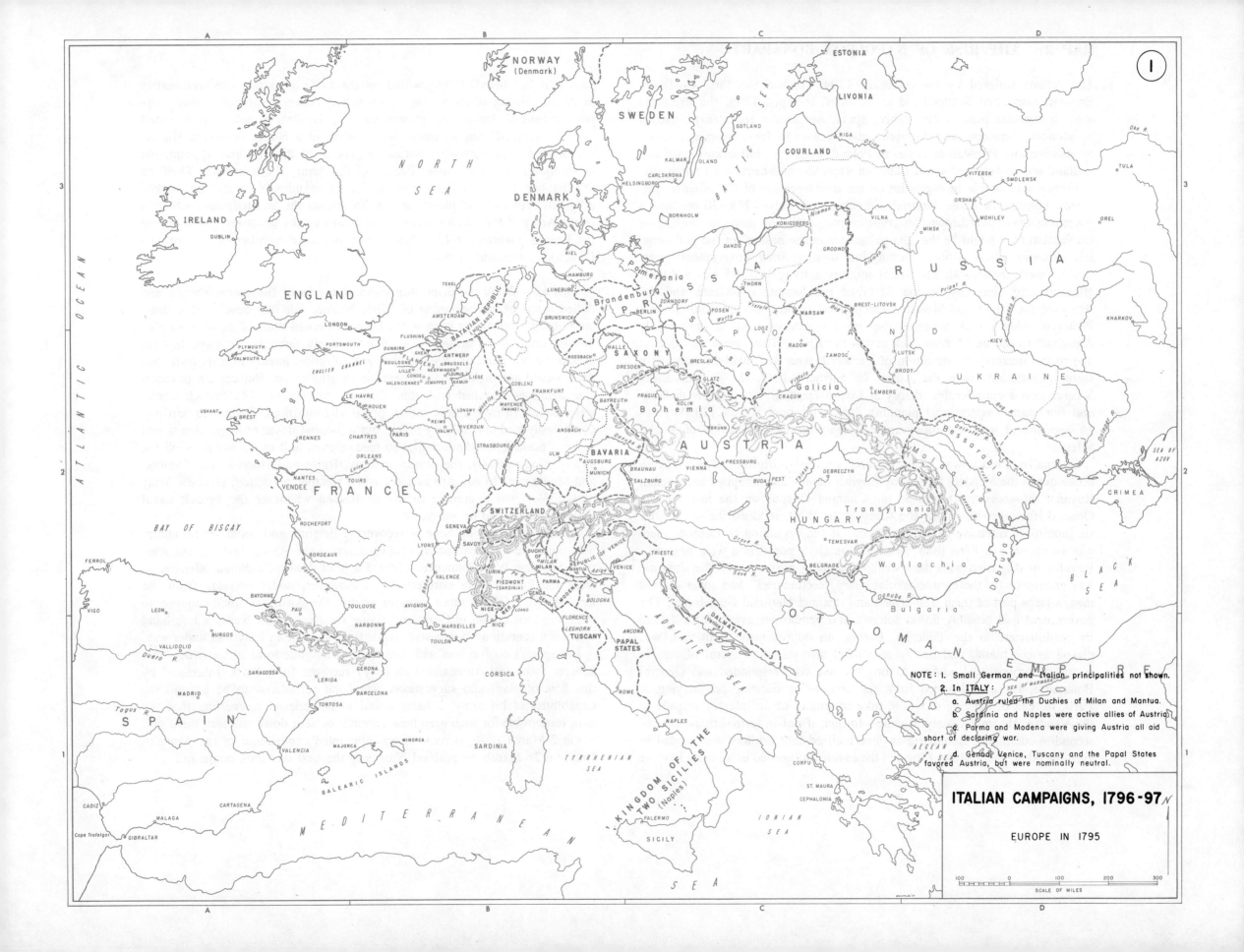

ITALIAN CAMPAIGNS, 1796-97

EUROPE IN 1795

NOTE: 1. Small German and Italian principalities not shown.
2. In ITALY:
   a. Austria ruled the Duchies of Milan and Mantua.
   b. Sardinia and Naples were active allies of Austria.
   c. Parma and Modena were giving Austria all aid short of declaring war.
   d. Genoa, Venice, Tuscany and the Papal States favored Austria, but were nominally neutral.

SCALE OF MILES
100   0   100   200   300

MAP 2: THE RISE OF NAPOLEON BONAPARTE

The defeats suffered by the Allies in 1794 wrecked the First Coalition. England suspended financial aid to its allies; in April 1795, the Prussians made a separate peace with France; Spain, her armies repeatedly defeated by Moncey, Perignon, and Augereau, did likewise in July; Austria, alarmed by Russian and Prussian activities in Poland, began to shift troops eastward. Holland was reorganized as the Batavian Republic, and became a French ally.

France was unable to capitalize on the disintegration of the alliance, primarily because of acute internal difficulties. In July 1794, Robespierre's government was overthrown, his constant purges having made his colleagues fearful that they might be the next to "sneeze in the basket" of the guillotine. His successors were more merciful, but weaker; their governments grew steadily more ineffectual. The major military activity in 1795 was a double offensive into Germany by the Army of the Sambre-and-Meuse and the Army of the Rhine-and-Moselle, commanded respectively by Jourdan and Pichegru. After initial successes, they were repulsed by Allied (principally Austrian) troops and forced back across the Rhine. This defeat was in part due to the inexplicable defection of Pichegru, who had involved himself in secret negotiations with the Allies. In northern Italy, the French under Scherer won a considerable victory at Loano (partially attributable to General Bonaparte's operational planning during his brief service [20 August–15 September] with the topographic bureau of the Committee of Public Safety).

Internally, France was bankrupt and wrung by disorder. Revolt again broke out in the Vendee, backed by English money and weapons and French Royalist refugees who recrossed the Channel to spur on the insurrection. General Hoche, commanding the Army of the West, subdued the revolt after six months of intensive campaigning, but at the beginning of October there was an uprising in Paris itself. Much of the city's population were now pro-Royalist or disgusted with their weak, tyrannical government. The situation was grim enough; the counterrevolutionary "sectionaries" had some 40,000 men, a large part of them well-armed and -trained National Guardsmen. The government had possibly 8,000 soldiers and gendarmes available to defend its headquarters in the Tuileries. Barras, an opportunistic politician, was placed in command, and hastily assembled all available general officers in search of professional advice. Among the five who responded was General Bonaparte, recently dropped from the service for insisting on tarrying in Paris, instead of obeying orders to take command of an infantry brigade in the Vendee. He immediately became—in fact, if not in formal title—Barras' second-in-command. Bonaparte at once realized that artillery was needed to even the odds, and a Major Murat of the cavalry succeeded in bringing in some

guns that had been left unguarded on the city's outskirts. The sectionaries made the mistake of attempting to storm the Tuileries without artillery support, instead of starving the government out. General Napoleon Bonaparte's expertly handled guns smashed the rebellion in a matter of hours. His rewards were immediate—promotion to general of division and appointment as second-in-command, under Barras, of the Army of the Interior. Then, on 26 October, he succeeded Barras as its commander. As such, he worked diligently, but still had plenty of time to discuss the unsatisfactory situation of the Army of Italy with Carnot, who, following the latest reorganization of the French government (27 October), was now a member of its five-man Directory, or executive body.

This map shows the dispositions and strengths of the major French and Allied forces at the beginning of 1796. Neither side had developed a clear-cut military strategy. In France, the Directory could think of no over-all plan beyond ordering its armies forward into enemy territory. In part, this reflected the last burst of revolutionary zeal: France, having won its own freedom, would now fight for the liberation of all Europe. But certain practical considerations marched with this idealistic conception: The French armies were unpaid, in rags, almost unfed, practically mutinous. Continued hardship could easily lead to a military revolt, but a successful war of aggression would make it possible for these armies to feed, clothe, and pay themselves off the enemy. Consequently, the armies of Italy, Rhine-and-Moselle, and Sambre-and-Meuse were to advance as soon as the weather permitted; Hoche's Army of the West would prepare to invade Ireland whenever the French naval units at Brest could be got ready.

Austria had given up hope of recovering Belgium and could see no attainable objective for a campaign westward across the Rhine. Instead, the Austrian Supreme War Council considered a joint Austro-Sardinian offensive to clear the French from northern Italy. However, under pressure from the English, who desired more decisive action, the Austrians finally agreed to reinforce their armies in Germany, giving the Archduke Charles a free hand to control operations in that area, while the campaign in Italy was under way.

Bonaparte's conferences with Carnot took tangible form in the orders that Scherer (who still commanded in Italy) received from Paris. Infuriated by this flow of plans and suggestions, which he considered to be beyond the capabilities of his army, Scherer asked to be relieved, suggesting that the man responsible for such grandiose schemes be sent down to carry them out.

On 2 March 1796, Bonaparte was appointed commander of the Army of Italy; on 26 March, he reached Nice, and the next day took command.

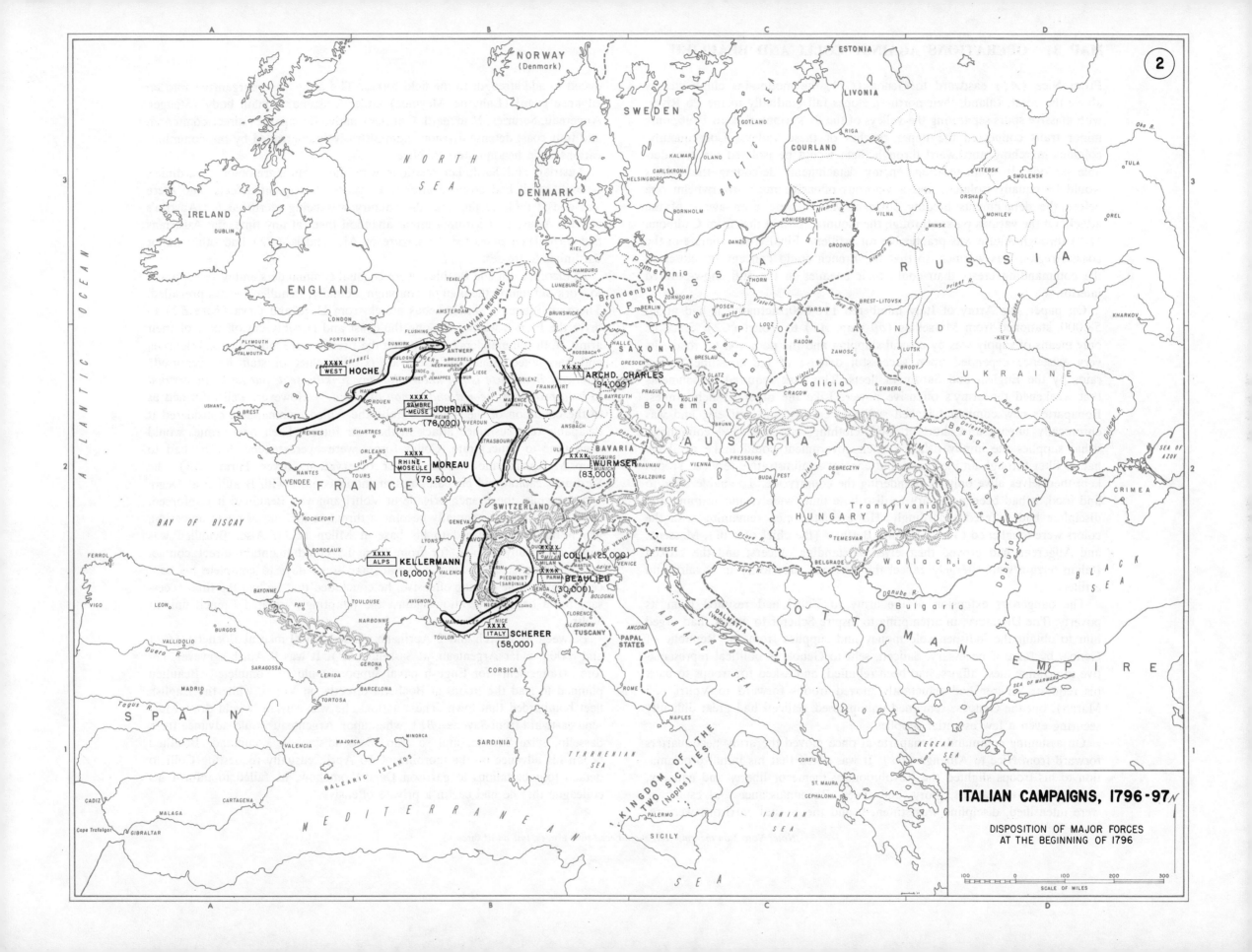

NORWAY
(Denmark)

SWEDEN

ESTONIA

LIVONIA

COURLAND

NORTH SEA

DENMARK

IRELAND

ENGLAND

ATLANTIC OCEAN

XXXX
WEST HOCHE

XXXX
SAMBRE-MEUSE JOURDAN
(78,000)

XXXX
ARCHD. CHARLES
(94,000)

XXXX
RHINE-MOSELLE MOREAU
(79,500)

BAVARIA

XXXX
WURMSER
(83,000)

FRANCE

SWITZERLAND

BAY OF BISCAY

XXXX
ALPS KELLERMANN
(18,000)

XXXX
COLLI (25,000)

XXXX
PARMA BEAULIEU
(30,000)

AUSTRIA

HUNGARY

SPAIN

XXXX
ITALY SCHERER
(58,000)

TUSCANY

PAPAL STATES

ADRIATIC SEA

OTTOMAN EMPIRE

BLACK SEA

CORSICA

SARDINIA

TYRRHENIAN SEA

KINGDOM OF THE TWO SICILIES
(Naples)

SICILY

MEDITERRANEAN SEA

AEGEAN SEA

IONIAN SEA

ITALIAN CAMPAIGNS, 1796-97

DISPOSITION OF MAJOR FORCES
AT THE BEGINNING OF 1796

100   0   100   200   300
SCALE OF MILES

From Nice (*A1*) eastward to Genoa (*C2*), the mountains climb steeply above the coast. Inland, their northern slopes fall gradually to the Po River, with massive spurs separating the valleys of the Po's tributaries. In 1796, only minor trails connected the upper reaches of these valleys. Consequently, columns marching northward through them would be isolated for considerable periods. In compensation, enemy detachments defending the valleys would be equally isolated, and a vigorous offensive might overwhelm one before the detachments holding adjacent valleys were even aware of the attack. Of the various passes through the mountains, only that from Cadibona (*B1*) through Altare was practicable for artillery. Finally, the climate in the coastal region was warmer, so that the French could concentrate closer to the commanding crests than could their enemies in the still snow-covered interior.

On paper, the Army of Italy numbered 116,000; actually, it had about 58,000, stationed from Marseilles (*off map, A1*) to Voltri (*C2*). Since its only means of supply was by coastal shipping and the poor coastal roads, its very existence depended upon successful defense of the coastline against raids by the English and Sardinian fleets. This task required detachments that weakened the army's offensive power. Like the other French armies, Bonaparte's new command lacked sufficient cavalry and artillery, and was chronically unpaid and short of food, clothing, weapons, and equipment. What supplies the impoverished French government could make available had to filter through an inefficient and corrupt administrative service. Troops kept themselves alive only by plundering the countryside. To enable them to find food, it had been necessary to distribute units widely, and training and discipline had suffered accordingly. However, the men remaining with the colors were toughened to all hardship; Berthier (the chief of staff), Massena, and Augereau had proved themselves outstanding officers; and the broken Italian terrain would largely cancel the Austrian superiority in cavalry and artillery.

The dangerous extension of the army to Voltri had resulted from its poverty. The Directory, in attempting to inspire Scherer to attack, had urged him to obtain the indispensable money and supplies from the Republic of Genoa, by force if necessary. Saliceti, sent to Genoa as political representative to arrange these affairs, had been rebuffed, and asked for troops to back his request. Scherer had reluctantly moved troops forward to Voltri (25 March), but the Genoese remained unimpressed. Saliceti had great difficulty securing even a few essential supplies.

On assuming command, Bonaparte at once moved the army headquarters forward from Nice to Albenga (*B1*). It was noted that his initial proclamation to his troops slighted the Revolutionary theme of liberty and equality, and stressed full rations, glory, and shoes. Reconnaissance and espionage were intensified, discipline was stiffened, and the coastal garrisons were re-duced to add strength to the field forces. The army was reorganized into an advance guard (Laharpe, Meynier) under Massena, a main body (Stengel, Augereau, Serurier, Macquard, Garnier) under Bonaparte's direct command, and four coast defense divisions administratively controlled by the communications zone headquarters at Nice.

Austrian and Sardinian relations were far from harmonious. Sardinia's national spirit had dropped after three years of frequent defeats, and there was considerable feeling that the country was being sacrificed for Austria's benefit. Aware that Sardinia might abandon them at any time, the Austrians had formulated plans for the seizure of Alessandria (*B2*) and other major Sardinian fortresses.

In theory, Colli and Beaulieu were coequal commanders and were supposed to work out jointly the plan of campaign; actually, Beaulieu's views prevailed. These envisioned a simultaneous attack from Dego and Ceva (*both B2*) to drive the French westward along the coast and possibly cut off part of their army. Both commanders believed that the French were mounting an offensive, and had noted Bonaparte's arrival. (Colli's chief of staff had reported: "*General Bonaparte is not known for any striking feat, but he is understood to be a profound theorist and a man of talent.*") However, well informed as to the condition of the Army of Italy, the Allied commanders considered it incapable of a sustained attack in the near future. Their own armies would need time to concentrate. Colli's forces were overextended, for he had to keep Macquard and Garnier under observation; cover Turin (*B2*), the Sardinian capital and his base; and maintain contact with Beaulieu at Dego.

Meanwhile, the French brigade at Voltri annoyed Beaulieu; if reinforced, these troops might eventually become a threat to his line of communication, which ran northeastward to his base at Milan (*C3*). Also, Beaulieu was eager to occupy Genoa, for from there he could maintain direct contact with the English fleet. Since it would take some days to complete his concentration for the coming offensive, he concluded that he had the time necessary for a limited operation against the temptingly isolated French unit at Voltri.

Between 31 March and 2 April, he massed 7,500 men at Bochetta (*C2*) and 8,000 under Argenteau, at Sassello (*B2*). It was 9 April, however, before arrangements for English naval support could be completed. Beaulieu planned to lead the troops at Bochetta directly on Voltri, while the English fleet bombarded that town. These actions, he was certain, would draw Massena eastward from Savona (*B1*), whereupon Argenteau would advance from Sassello, seize Savona, and so trap Massena's whole command. Beaulieu began his advance on the morning of 10 April, casually requesting Colli to detach four battalions to garrison Dego. Somehow, he failed to inform his colleague that he had begun a private offensive.

Note: Note 2 on the map (B3) should read four armies, *instead of* three.

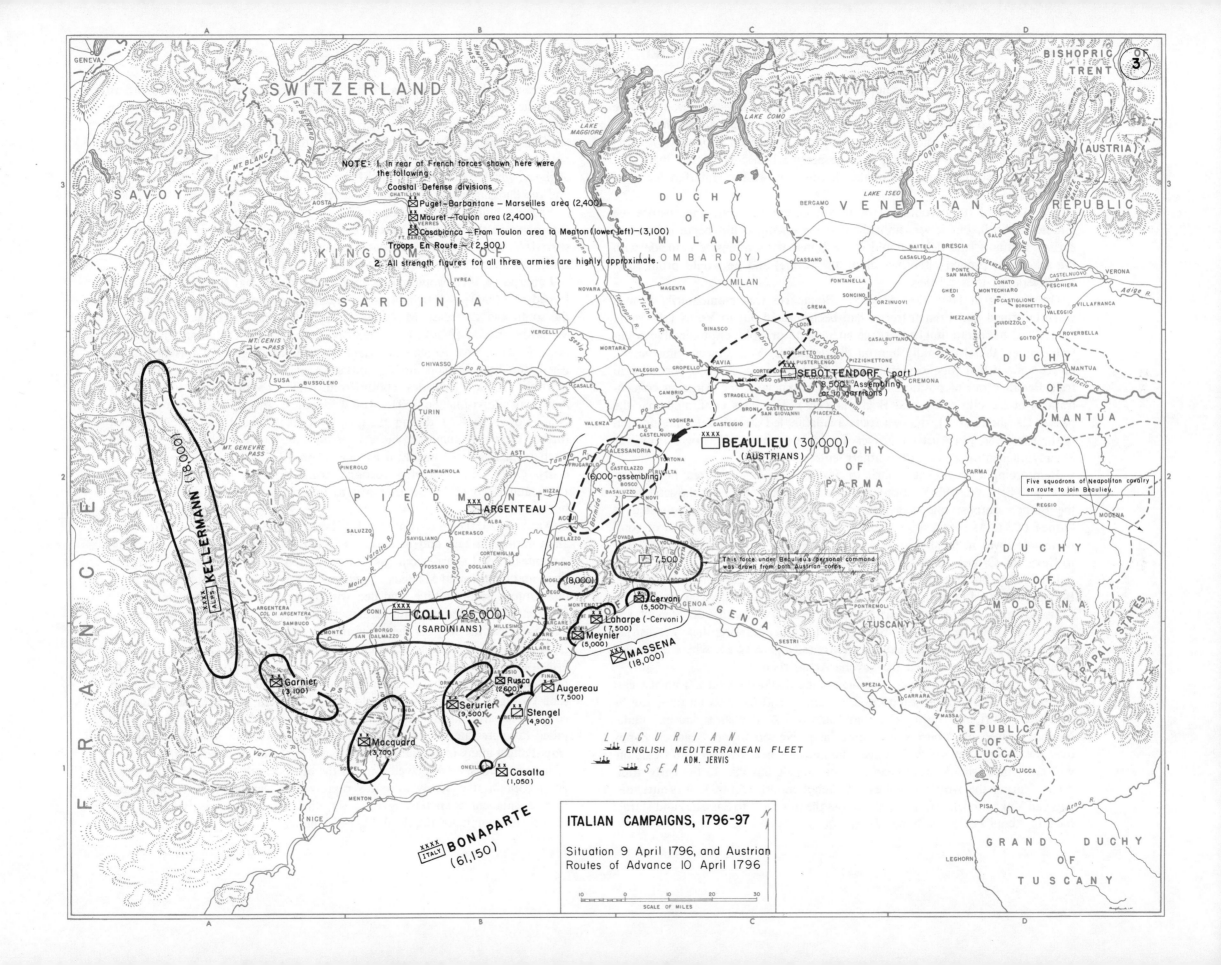

NOTE: 1. In rear of French forces shown here were
the following:

Coastal Defense divisions

⊠ Puget—Barbantane — Marseilles area (2,400)

⊠ Mouret—Toulon area (2,400)

⊠ Casabianca — From Toulon area to Menton (lower left)—(3,100)

⊠ Troops En Route — (2,900)

2. All strength figures for all three armies are highly approximate.

SWITZERLAND

SAVOY

KINGDOM OF

SARDINIA

PIEDMONT

FRANCE

DUCHY OF MILAN (LOMBARDY)

VENETIAN

REPUBLIC

BISHOPRIC OF TRENT

(AUSTRIA)

DUCHY OF MANTUA

SEBOTTENDORF (part) (8,500 Assembling or in garrisons)

BEAULIEU (30,000) (AUSTRIANS)

(6,000-assembling)

DUCHY OF PARMA

Five squadrons of Neapolitan cavalry en route to join Beaulieu.

DUCHY OF MODENA

(TUSCANY)

XXXX ALPS KELLERMANN (18,000)

XXX ARGENTEAU

XXXX COLLI (25,000) (SARDINIANS)

7,500

This force under Beaulieu's personal command was drawn from both Austrian corps.

(8,000)

⊠ Cervoni (5,500)

⊠ Laharpe (~Cervoni) (7,500)

⊠ Meynier (5,000)

XXX MASSENA (18,000)

GENOA

REPUBLIC OF LUCCA

⊠ Garnier (3,100)

⊠ Rusca (2,600)

⊠ Serurier (9,500)

XX Stengel (4,900)

⊠ Augereau (7,500)

⊠ Macquard (3,700)

XX Casalta (1,050)

LIGURIAN SEA

ENGLISH MEDITERRANEAN FLEET
ADM. JERVIS

GRAND DUCHY OF TUSCANY

XXXX ITALY BONAPARTE (61,150)

ITALIAN CAMPAIGNS, 1796-97

Situation 9 April 1796, and Austrian
Routes of Advance 10 April 1796

10   0   10   20   30
SCALE OF MILES

MAP 4: OPERATIONS AGAINST COLLI AND BEAULIEU

Bonaparte's general plan of campaign was based on his comprehension of the weaknesses of the Austro-Sardinian alliance. His offensive would strike between the two enemy armies, splitting them apart. That accomplished, he was certain that Colli and Beaulieu would be concerned primarily with the protection of Turin and Milan, their respective bases. He could then concentrate against and crush the weaker Sardinians, without interference from Beaulieu.

The Army of Italy would not be in any condition to advance before the middle of April, but it was unlikely that the enemy could begin operations earlier. Actually, the delay would make Bonaparte's offensive coincide with the scheduled French offensives along the Rhine, and he would profit from the diversions thus created.

On arriving at Nice (*see Map 3*), Bonaparte was momentarily furious when informed that French troops had been pushed out to Voltri (*this map, D2*). This, he feared, might alert the enemy and provoke unpredictable countermeasures, thereby forcing him on the defensive. Yet, almost immediately, he recognized that this accident might offer him an excellent opportunity to trick Beaulieu out of position. By 3 April, he knew of the Austrian concentrations at Sassello (*C2*) and Bochetta (*D2*). His spies confirmed that the pass at Cadibona (*C1*), the best route available, led directly into the junction of the Sardinian and Austrian armies. Fortunately, most of his own army was already concentrated near its southern entrance.

Reinforcing Cervoni, at Voltri, to 5,500, Napoleon ordered him, if attacked, to fight a delaying action back toward Savona (*C1*). At the same time, the French outpost line was reinforced. Supplies were to be collected at Ormea (*B1*). As soon as Ceva (*B2*) was captured, the French line of communication was to be shifted to run from the port of Oneille (*off map, B1*) to Ceva, via Ormea. (*For this road, see Map 3 [B1].*)

On 9 April, informed that Austrian patrols were heckling Cervoni's outposts, Bonaparte shifted his army headquarters forward to Savona. The same night, Massena sent (*action not shown*) Colonel Rampon (with 900 men of Laharpe's division) scouting toward Sassello. Encountering heavy Austrian forces, Rampon retired the next day to Monte Negino (*C2*), where a fortified French outpost commanded the Savona-Acqui road.

That afternoon (10 April), Beaulieu came down on Voltri from the east and north. Cervoni stood stubbornly; not until 1100 the next morning did he evacuate Voltri and retire to rejoin Laharpe. A British squadron, under Nelson, arrived off Voltri some hours later. Nelson found Beaulieu happy over his victory, yet worried because he had not heard Argenteau's cannon, which, by then, should have been echoing outside Savona. In the early afternoon, fearing the worst, Beaulieu left Sebottendorf (5,000) at Voltri, dispatched Vukassovich (over 2,100) across the hill trails to Sassello, and started back to Acqui (*C3*), via Novi (*D3*).

Argenteau had frustrations of his own. He had not received his orders until late on 9 April, and had needed the 10th to collect his troops. Early on the 11th, he had finally advanced with 4,500 men against Monte Negino, sending a flanking column (3,000) against Stella (*C2*). He drove in Rampon's outposts, but failed against the Monte Negino redoubt and halted to await his artillery, which had fallen behind. The attack on Stella likewise was repulsed, and the flanking column retired on Sassello.

From a hilltop north of Savona, Bonaparte had watched the smoke of Rampon's battle. Though Cervoni had been heavily attacked, Colli had not stirred. Toward evening, Bonaparte issued his final orders for the offensive. Berthier's muster rolls showed 40,520 men for duty in the five attack divisions.

Laharpe (4,500) would move up after dark and join Rampon (now reinforced to 3,000); at first light on the 12th, he would attack Argenteau from the south and southeast. Massena, the mountain-fighting expert, would lead Menard's brigade (3,500, Laharpe's division) through Cadibona and Montenotte (*C2*) against Argenteau's right rear. While Argenteau was thus abolished, the French main attack, consisting of Joubert's (2,000) and Dommartin's (3,000) brigades (both from Meynier's division), followed by Augereau's division (6,000), would advance from Finale through San Giacomo (*both C1*) during the night. Joubert would halt at Altare for further orders; Dommartin and Augereau—the point of the wedge to split Colli from Beaulieu—would drive ahead on 12 April to seize Carcare and Cairo (*both C2*), thereafter reconnoitering aggressively toward Millesimo (*B2*) and Dego (*C2*). Serurier was to immobilize Colli by demonstrations, but not to attack.

At about 2330 on 11 April, much delayed by the tardy issue of rations and ammunition, in rain and in darkness, the French marched. With morning, Argenteau saw Laharpe come up out of the fog like a cresting wave, tried to form and fight, found Massena's bayonets at his back, saw his command collapse into a fleeing rabble, and fled with them. Laharpe pursued him as far as Montenotte Inferior, while Bonaparte turned Massena westward toward Cairo to clear the way for the main attack.

This attack was behind schedule. The San Giacomo road was actually a fifteen-mile mule trail, alternately mud and sharp rocks, over a half-mile–high pass. Marching their hardest, Joubert and Augereau failed to overtake Massena by nightfall. Dommartin could not get beyond Montefreddo. Undoubtedly, Bonaparte, lacking previous service as an infantry commander, had failed to appreciate the difficulties of such a night march. It was a fault that would affect many of his future operations. On the other hand, in this the first of his campaigns, he displayed some of the attributes that were to make him a great captain: the ability to assess rapidly and clearly the advantages and hazards inherent in an existing situation, directness of purpose, vigorous execution, and simplicity and flexibility of planning.

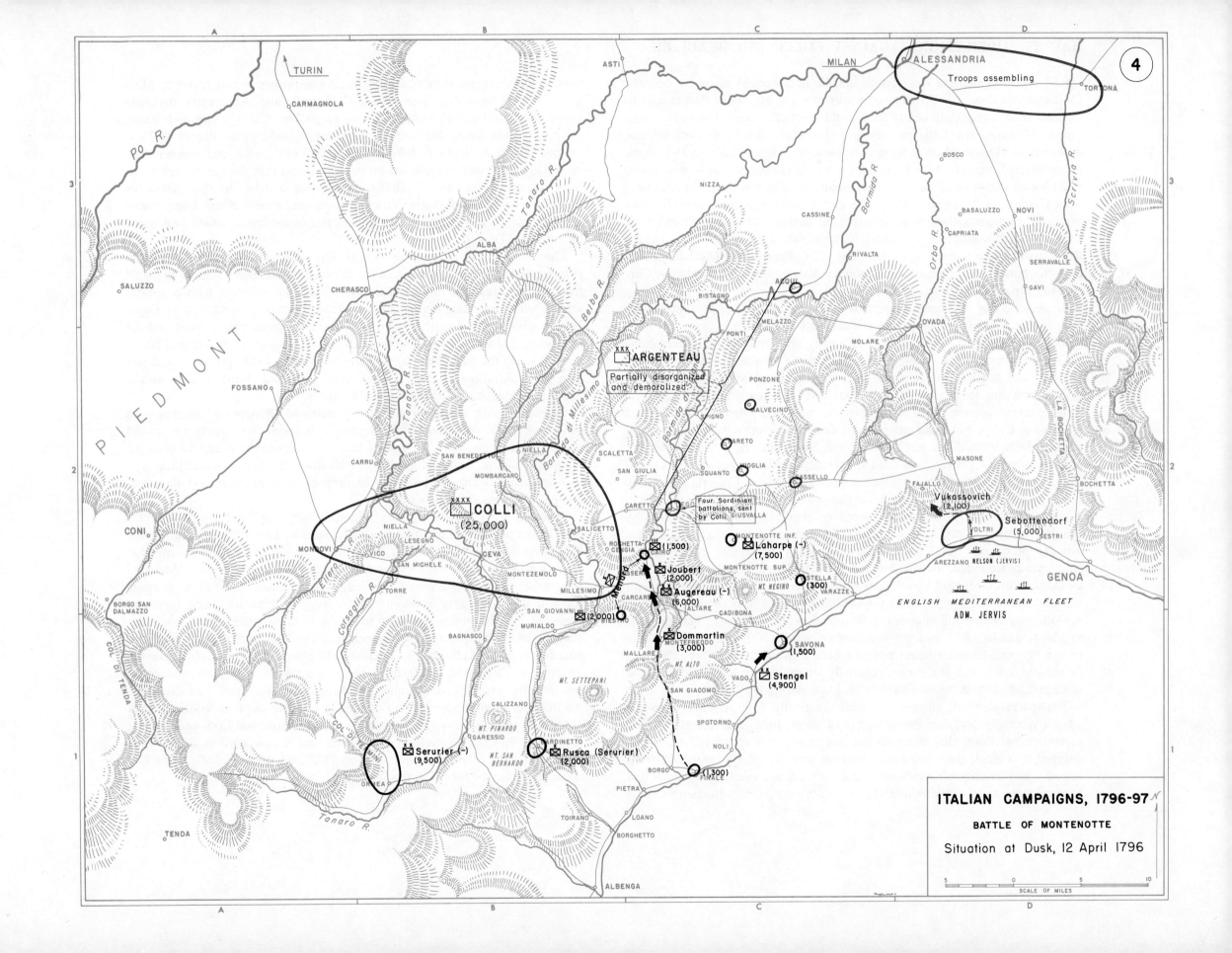

ITALIAN CAMPAIGNS, 1796-97

BATTLE OF MONTENOTTE

Situation at Dusk, 12 April 1796

On 13 April, Bonaparte was certain that he had wedged his army between Colli and Beaulieu. His problem now was to drive his wedge deeper and to separate them completely before they could react effectively. His orders were simple. Massena, with Laharpe's division (less Menard with his demi-brigade at Biestro [*C1*]), would drive Argenteau back on Spigno (*C2*). Its right flank thus protected, the rest of the French army would concentrate at Montezemolo (*B2*) for an attack on Ceva (*B2*). Augereau would follow the main road west from Carcare (*C2*), supported by Meynier with Dommartin's brigade. Joubert would advance along a secondary road farther south through San Giovanni; Menard would follow Joubert. Serurier would move down the Tanaro River, with Rusca advancing on his right via Calizzano and Murialdo (*both B1*). Six battalions, one from each infantry division, would assemble at Carcare to form a general reserve.

So began a day that again illustrated that sometimes "War is composed of nothing but accidents." (Napoleon's *Maxim XCV*.)

Colli, as requested by Beaulieu, had loyally sent four Sardinian battalions (1,700) to Dego (*C2*). These arrived in time to rally some of Argenteau's fugitives and begin organizing the town for defense. Massena had marched at once with only the elements of Laharpe's division already in Cairo (2,000). Finding Dego apparently held in strength, he reconnoitered it briefly and returned to Cairo. Augereau encountered units of Provera's Austrian auxiliary corps, which formed the left flank of the Sardinian army. Confronted by superior numbers, Provera sent most of his troops northward toward Rochetta-Cengia (*B2*), and threw himself into the ruined castle of Cosseria with some 1,000 picked men. Here, he dominated the main road. Surrounding the castle, Augereau fruitlessly demanded its surrender, then attacked it unsuccessfully. Reinforced by Joubert, he tried, and failed, again in the afternoon. These assaults produced 1,000 casualties—more than Bonaparte could afford. Joubert was wounded, and his brigade so riddled that it had to be replaced by Dommartin's. Menard had the day's only success: Bypassing Cosseria with his single demi-brigade, he drove the Sardinians out of Millesimo.

Colli, meanwhile, still unaware of Beaulieu's Voltri excursion, had galloped to Montezemolo (*B2*) and got together perhaps 1,700 men. Too weak to relieve Provera, he nevertheless put up a bold front and successfully deceived Bonaparte, who, with the enemy reputedly strong everywhere, held Laharpe in Cairo and made no second attempt on Dego during the 13th.

Bonaparte planned, however, to deal drastically with Argenteau on the 14th. Even the report that Provera—out of water, food, and cartridges—had capitulated at 0800 that morning did not change his objective. Augereau, stripped to a single demi-brigade of his own division, plus Joubert's battered brigade, was to skirmish westward and keep Colli occupied. Dommartin and Menard were to drive the remnants of Provera's corps from Rochetta-Cengia

toward Mombarcaro, then march on Dego, where they would revert to Massena's direct command. The rest of Laharpe's and Augereau's divisions (approximately 10,000) would move on Dego from Cairo, along both banks of the Bormida River. Meanwhile, Argenteau—huddling at Pareto (*C2*)—learned late in the night (13–14 April) that Vukassovich had reached Sassello. He immediately dispatched an urgent request that the latter push on to Dego "tomorrow morning." (Being a consistent bungler, he then dated his letter "14 April," to Vukassovich's thorough confusion.) Some hours thereafter, he finally roused himself to collect five battalions (3,000) and move back toward Dego.

The Dego garrison (possibly 4,000 Sardinians and Austrians) held a strong position on the east bank of the Bormida River, commanding the road from Cairo. Massena, on the east bank, fixed the garrison with a frontal attack, while extending his right flank along the high ground east of Dego. Here it surprised and easily routed Argenteau's approaching column. At the same time, Laharpe came down the west bank of the river and crossed below Dego, closing the trap. The bag was approximately 4,000 prisoners and sixteen guns. Argenteau betook himself hastily toward Acqui (*C3*), with a handful of French cavalry slashing at his heels.

Considering the Austrians sufficiently defeated, Bonaparte was ready to deal with Colli. Massena, with Meynier's division (less Joubert), would remain at Dego to cover the army's line of communication and reconnoiter vigorously toward Acqui; Augereau's division would be reassembled; Laharpe was ordered to Cairo, to be ready to support Augereau the next day; and Stengel was summoned forward.

Sundown of 14 April left three confused armies groping in the dark. Colli, with Rusca nibbling at his right flank and Serurier closing in, fell back from Montezemolo after nightfall; Augereau then groped forward to occupy that town. Carelessly leaving his troops at Dego to shift for themselves, Massena returned to the greater comforts of Cairo. His men had received no supplies for two days—the army's administrative personnel having been lazy and negligent, and the muddy mountain trails almost impassable for the few mule-pack trains. Consequently, the French in Dego scattered to seek food; no guards were posted. Eastward, Vukassovich, alarmed by heavy firing in the direction of Dego, had marched on his own initiative during the afternoon, but took the wrong road. Beaulieu, in Acqui since 13 April, had dismissed the Battle of Montenotte as minor compared to his triumph at Voltri. He had ordered Argenteau to hold Dego and Sassello, and requested Colli and Provera to attack. Now, he leisurely began to establish a new cordon from Voltri through Fajallo (*D2*) to Monte Negino (*C2*), as if the French army had taken root to await his pleasure.

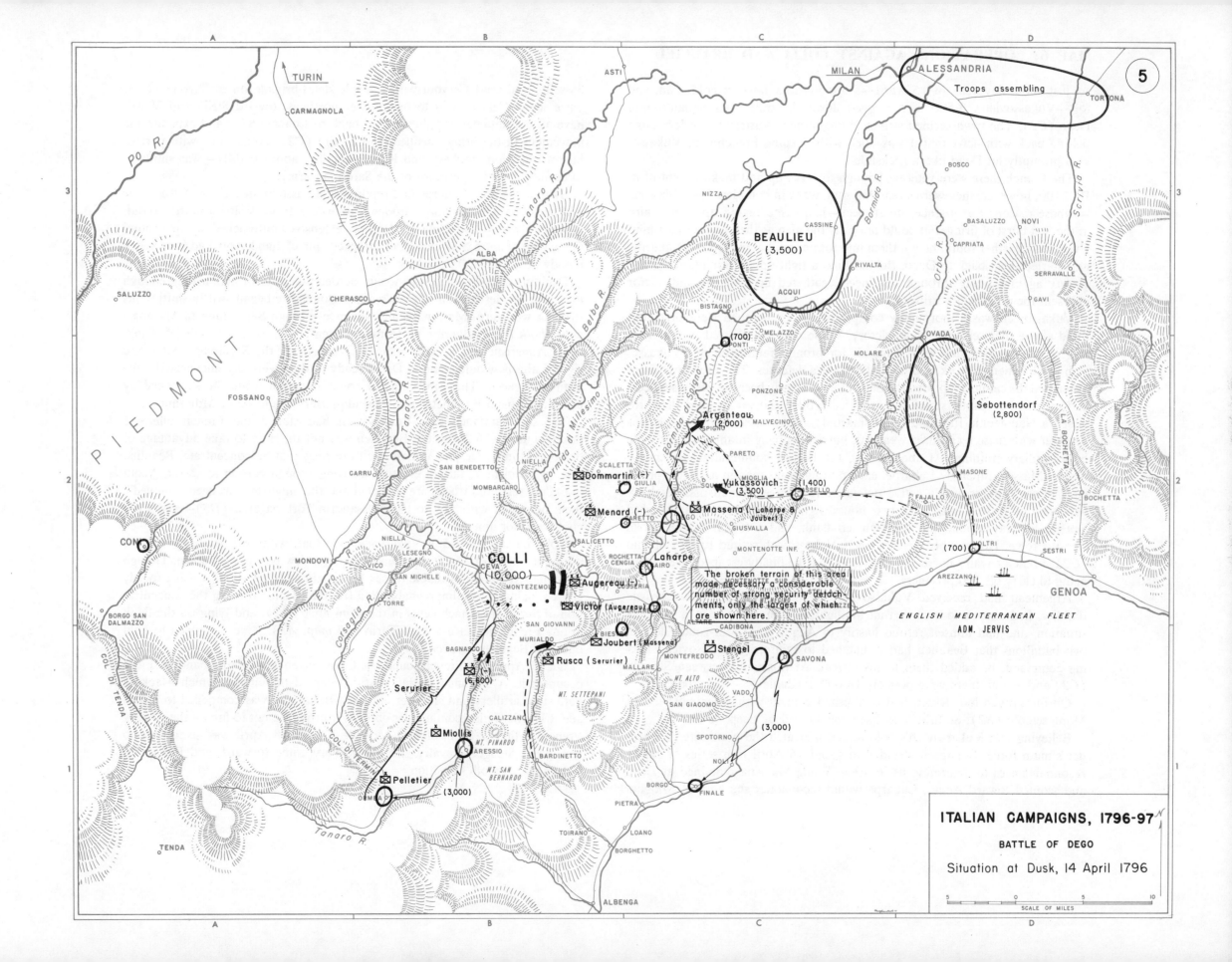

ITALIAN CAMPAIGNS, 1796-97

BATTLE OF DEGO

Situation at Dusk, 14 April 1796

MAP 6: OPERATIONS AGAINST COLLI AND BEAULIEU

At just about daybreak of 15 April—a disagreeable dawn of cold, rain, and fog—Vukassovich's 3,500 men slogged down the trail from Squanto into Dego (*C2*). The town seemed strangely unguarded; Austrian outriders came pelting back with news that it was filled with sleeping Frenchmen. Vukassovich promptly hit Dego like a rockslide.

The French there were veterans enough to wake up and make a fight of it. By 1100, however, they were streaming southward in complete rout. Massena —whose reasons for absence are suspect—had come racing up from Cairo at the first burst of firing, but could not rally the men as they poured past him. Eventually, farther south, he got them into formation, harangued them angrily, and started them back to Dego. Behind him, a tight-lipped Bonaparte, seeing victory again slipping through his fingers, gathered up Laharpe and Victor and sent them panting northward.

Vukassovich was a thoroughly competent officer; his men were tired, but lifted above themselves by their victory. While couriers spurred in search of Argenteau and Beaulieu with demands for prompt reinforcement, Vukassovich put his men to work improving the town's defenses. The French had not evacuated the cannon captured the day before—largely because various officers and men had promptly stolen the captured artillery horses (a deed that produced a Napoleonic fury and courts-martial). Vukassovich strengthened his defenses with these recaptured weapons, hurriedly giving infantry details some basic artillery training. At about 1400, the French counterattacks began— first by Massena, then by Laharpe, each putting in his men in a largely piece-meal effort. Vukassovich's active defense threw three French assaults back with serious losses. But, after two hours' fighting, numbers told; Menard worked his way around the Austrian left flank, and a fourth assault broke into the town. Holding his men together, Vukassovich retired toward Spigno (*C2*); French cavalry pursued him closely, but he finally escaped, even managing to carry off 200 prisoners.

Argenteau had received Vukassovich's report, but, with characteristic timidity, had chosen to assume that his fighting comrade was in a hopeless situation, and had himself retired hastily to Acqui (*C3*). En route, he met two battalions that Beaulieu had dispatched to reinforce Vukassovich. Taking command, he added them to his retreat. At this time, between Sassello (*C2*) and Acqui, there were possibly 14,000 available Austrian troops.

On the French left, Rusca had established contact with Augereau west of Montezemolo (*B2*); Serurier's advance was slowed by deep snow.

Believing that Vukassovich's bold attack indicated the proximity of Beaulieu's main force, Bonaparte decided to spend 16 April in a series of strong reconnaissances to determine its location. While Massena remained at Dego and scouted toward Acqui, Laharpe would reconnoiter the area of Mioglia-

Sassello, and send Cervoni with a single demi-brigade on to Savona (*C1*). Once there, Cervoni was to reconnoiter northeast toward Stella and Voltri, have all accumulated supplies moved back to Loano (*B1*), and expedite the movement of the army's artillery to Carcare (*C2*). Augereau—with part of his own division, Joubert, and Rusca (totaling about 6,400)—was similarly to develop the new positions of the Sardinian army.

By that evening, Laharpe had reported the Sassello area clear of Austrians and most of Sebottendorf's troops withdrawn from Voltri toward Acqui. Augereau had found Colli holding an extensive, entrenched camp around Ceva with some 6,500 men, had attacked out of hand, and had received a bloody nose and 600 casualties.

Deciding that Beaulieu now would be definitely out of action long enough to permit the destruction of Colli's army, Bonaparte began swiftly shifting his strength westward. Massena would advance through San Giulia to Mombarcaro (*both B2*), gathering up Dommartin en route, to turn Colli's left flank, while Augereau and Serurier attacked respectively the Sardinian center and right. Laharpe would stand at Dego, ready to deal with any unexpected Austrian resurgence. The army's line of communication would be shortened by using the Loano-Bardinetto route; headquarters would be at Millesimo.

The fact remained that Vukassovich had stalled the French offensive throughout 15–16 April; but Beaulieu was not the man to take advantage of this opportunity. Despite Vukassovich's urgings that he concentrate, Beaulieu saw his problem as that of erecting a strong enough cordon to screen Acqui until "my scattered troops are collected and the magazine has been removed"; then, he would withdraw to the Alessandria-Tortona area (*D3*)—and Colli could fend for himself.

Colli, having learned of Vukassovich's defeat, withdrew neatly from Ceva during the night of 16–17 April and took up a new position as shown. Though too extensive for his available forces (approximately 12,300), it was expertly chosen, being almost impregnable to a frontal attack, covering the concentration of Sardinian detachments in the Coni area (*A2*), and lying on the flank of any French advance toward Turin (*off map, A3*). Here, he hoped to hold out until Beaulieu recovered.

On 17 April, the French found the Ceva entrenched camp abandoned and occupied it. A Sardinian battalion still occupied the citadel, which—lacking both siege artillery and engineer officers—Bonaparte was compelled to block-ade. (The Sardinian commander obligingly promised not to fire on the passing French, if they left him alone.) Most of 17 and 18 April was given over to rest, while Stengel's cavalry and the artillery came forward, and Bonaparte reconnoitered Colli's position.

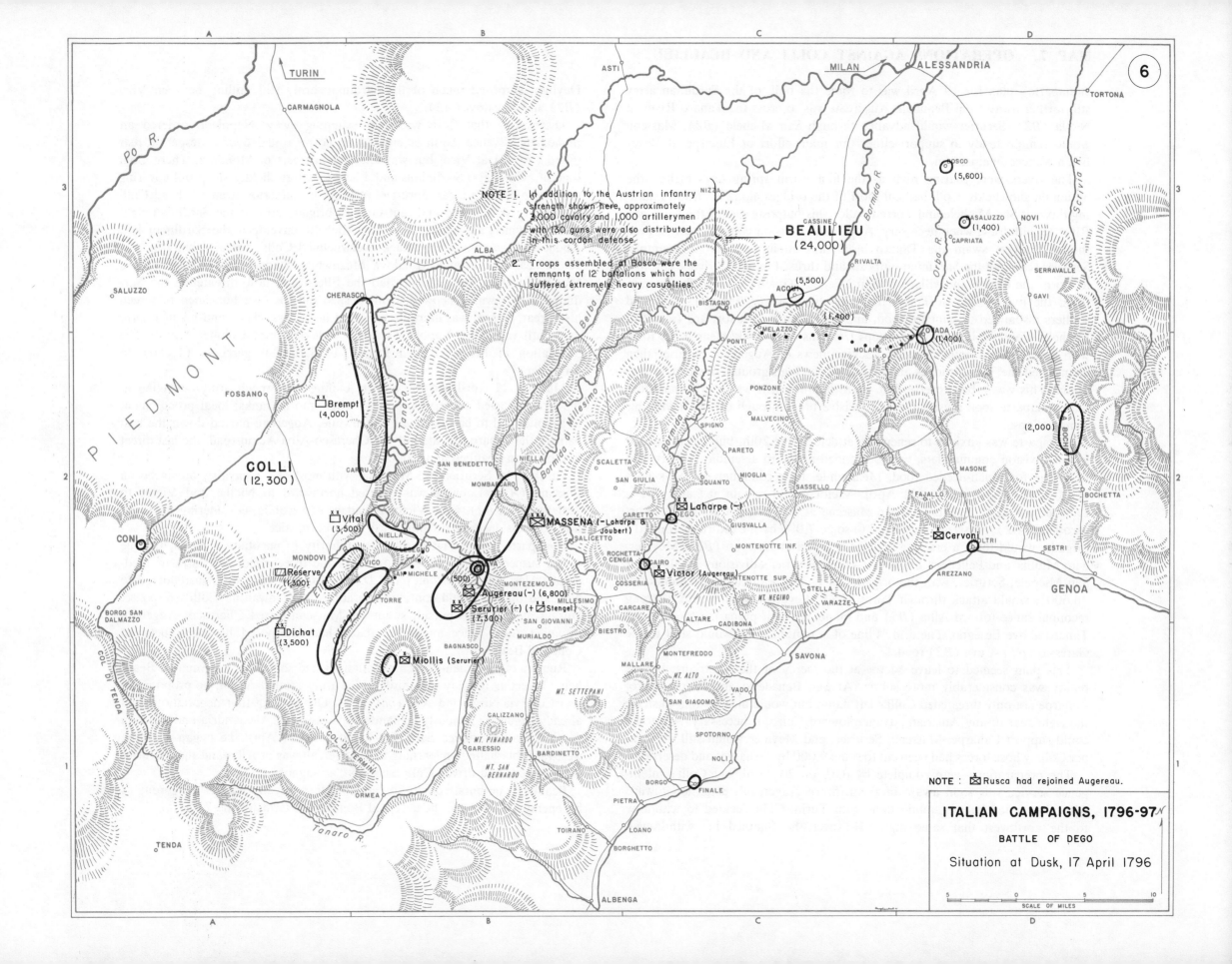

6

TURIN

PIEDMONT

COLLI
(12,300)

NOTE 1. In addition to the Austrian infantry
strength shown here, approximately
3,000 cavalry and 1,000 artillerymen
with 130 guns were also distributed
in this cordon defense.

2. Troops assembled at Bosco were the
remnants of 12 battalions which had
suffered extremely heavy casualties.

BEAULIEU
(24,000)

Bosco
(5,600)

Casaluzzo
(1,400)

(5,500)

ACQUI

(1,400)

(1,400)

Brempt
(4,000)

(2,000)

BOCHETTA

Vital
(3,500)

Laharpe (-)

MASSENA (-Laharpe &
Joubert)

Cervoni

Reserve
(1,300)

(500)

Victor (Augereau)

Augereau(-) (6,800)

Serurier (-) (+ Stengel)
(7,300)

GENOA

Dichat
(3,500)

Miollis (Serurier)

NOTE : ⊠ Rusca had rejoined Augereau.

ITALIAN CAMPAIGNS, 1796-97

BATTLE OF DEGO

Situation at Dusk, 17 April 1796

SCALE OF MILES

MAP 7: OPERATIONS AGAINST COLLI AND BEAULIEU

Bonaparte's plan for 19 April was to force the bulk of the Sardinian army still farther away from Beaulieu. Augereau was to cross the Tanaro River at Niella (*B2*); Serurier would advance through San Michele (*B2*); Massena would remain ready to support either this main effort or Laharpe, if Beaulieu advanced against him.

The rivers were roaring high as the first warm spring days melted the mountain snowfields. Colli had cut most of the bridges along his front, retaining those at San Michele and Torre to allow his outposts east of the Corsaglia River to withdraw, when necessary. Augereau's division could not cross, even though Joubert swam the Tanaro in a vain attempt to set an example. Serurier scattered the Sardinian outposts and thrust Fiorella's brigade through to storm the bridge and village of San Michele; Guieu's brigade finally captured the two bridges at Torre. Immediately, however, Fiorella's famished soldiers disbanded to hunt for food, and could not be got forward from San Michele. Colli, rapidly drawing troops from his right flank, cleared the town with a determined counterattack. Lacking news of Augereau, Serurier then abandoned the Torre bridges and retired to the high ground east of the Corsaglia. This was a bad reverse, but, more important, it was a grim reminder that Bonaparte soon must achieve a decisive breakthrough or risk having his army collapse.

Bonaparte was anxious to renew the attack on the 20th, but was dissuaded by his division commanders, who demanded a day to assemble artillery and to forage for much-needed food. Meanwhile, he reconnoitered Colli's lines and formed a new plan for 21 April: Victor would remain at Cairo (*C2*); Laharpe would immediately relieve Massena at San Benedetto and Mombarcaro (*both B2*); Massena, reinforced to some 7,000 by the return of Joubert's brigade, would force a crossing of the Corsaglia at Lesegno (*B2*); Meynier, with Miollis' and Pelletier's brigades (4,000, Serurier's division) would cover San Michele; Serurier, with the brigades of Guieu, Fiorella, and Dommartin (6,600), would attack through Torre (*B2*). Augereau would push a strong reconnaissance toward Alba (*B3*) and maneuver as if preparing to cross the Tanaro above Lesegno. The army's line of communication would shift to the Garessio (*B1*)–Ceva (*B2*) road.

This plan seemed to leave Victor at the mercy of the Austrians; but its reality was considerably more subtle. At San Benedetto and Mombarcaro, Laharpe not only threatened Colli's left flank, but would also be able to strike the right rear of any Austrian advance toward Cairo; if necessary, Augereau could support Laharpe. Massena, Serurier, and Meynier would still outnumber Colli, whose forces had been cut to some 9,000 by casualties and desertions.

The preparations were complete by dark on 20 April, but Colli's intelligence service was soon aware of them. Since Augereau's extension toward Alba threatened his communications with Turin, Colli decided to withdraw to the northwest that same night. However, he fumbled his withdrawal.

Daylight surprised much of the Sardinian army still milling between Vico (*B2*) and Mondovi (*A2*).

Discovering that Colli was again slipping away, Napoleon ordered an immediate advance. Serurier crossed at Torre, rolled over a desperate rear guard (2,000) at Vico, but was checked just east of Mondovi. There Colli himself, with 1,500 Sardinians and a heavy battery, held a steep hill covering the Ellero River bridges. Serurier, utilizing his superior strength, fixed Colli with heavy skirmishing and sent Guieu's brigade around the Sardinian right flank; Meynier, advancing from San Michele, enveloped the Sardinian left. About 1600, a converging attack overwhelmed Colli's force, driving its survivors headlong through Mondovi. Meanwhile, Stengel's cavalry, locating a ford below that town, had crossed the Ellero and now threatened the Sardinian withdrawal. Uncowed, Colli pushed out his own horsemen to screen his retreat. Stengel was mortally wounded in the first clash, and his men gave way until rallied by Napoleon's senior aide-de-camp, Colonel Murat. The population of Mondovi then forced its Sardinian garrison (1,250) to surrender.

Much of 22 April had to be spent cuffing the French army—reveling in the fat, unforaged country around it—back into its ranks; local procurement of supplies had to be organized. Meanwhile, Augereau moved down the east bank of the Tanaro, threatening the Cherasco-Alba-Acqui road, the last direct link between Beaulieu and Colli.

On the 23d, Serurier and Massena, with most of the cavalry, advanced on Fossano (*A2*); Laharpe was ordered northward to Niella, and Victor to Scaletta (*both B2*). King Victor Amadeus of Sardinia, considering his situation hopeless, instructed Colli to ask for an armistice.

Bonaparte replied that he had no authority to negotiate a peace, that he would suspend operations only if two of the three major fortresses of Piedmont (Alessandria, Tortona [*both D3*], and Coni [*A2*]) were surrendered to him, and that he would continue operations while awaiting Colli's response. During the 24th, his pursuit swept on. Massena seized Cherasco; Augereau occupied Alba. Once more, Bonaparte had interposed his army between Colli and Beaulieu.

Rumors of Sardinian-French negotiations had somewhat rejuvenated Beaulieu. Collecting roughly two-thirds of his army around Acqui, he proposed to join Colli via Nizza and Asti (*both C3*). On learning that negotiations had already begun, he furiously demanded possession of Alessandria and Tortona as pledges of continued Sardinian loyalty. On 24 April, he began crawling westward, but halted on learning that Augereau was at Alba and that Serurier and Massena had driven Colli back on Carmagnola (*A3*).

Beaulieu's outburst convinced the King that his ally was as dangerous as his enemy; on 26 April, he accepted Bonaparte's terms of the 23d.

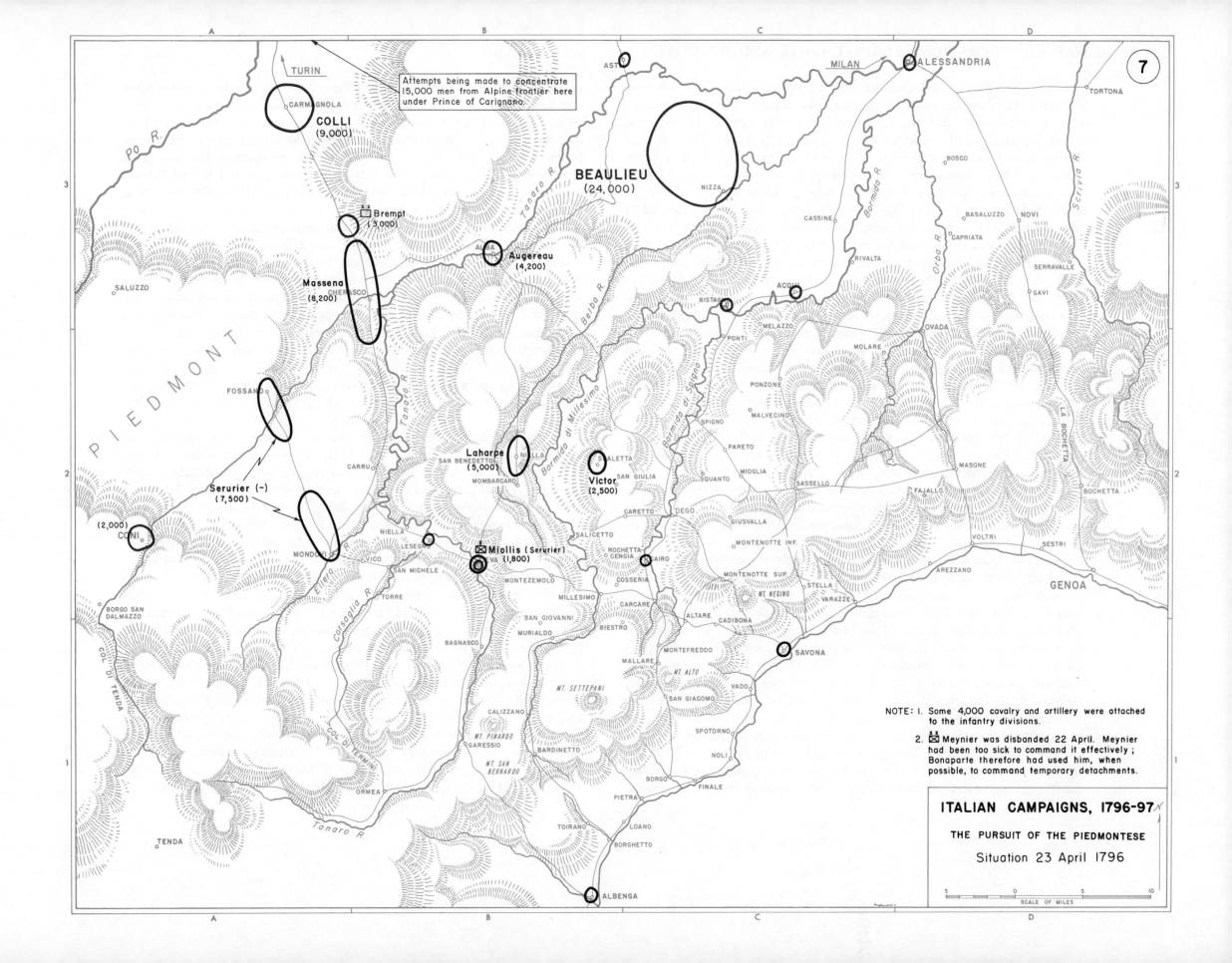

TURIN

CARMAGNOLA

COLLI
(9,000)

Attempts being made to concentrate
15,000 men from Alpine frontier here
under Prince of Carignano.

ASTI

MILAN

ALESSANDRIA

TORTONA

BOSCO

BASALUZZO   NOVI

Po R.

Tanaro R.

BEAULIEU
(24,000)

NIZZA

CASSINE

RIVALTA

SERRAVALLE

GAVI

Brempt
(3,000)

ALBA

Augereau
(4,200)

Massena
(8,200)

CHERASCO

SALUZZO

P I E D M O N T

FOSSANO

Tanaro R.

Serurier (-)
(7,500)

(2,000)

CONI

CARRU

NIELLA

MONDOVI

LESEGNO

SAN MICHELE

VICO

Laharpe
(5,000)

SAN BENEDETTO

MOMBARCARO

NIELLA

Victor
(2,500)

SAN GIULIA

SALETTA

CARETTO

Belbo R.

Bormida di Millesimo

Bormida di Spigno

Bormida R.

BISTAGNO

MELAZZO

ACQUI

PONTI

OVADA

MOLARE

PONZONE

MALVECINO

PARETO

SPIGNO

MIOGLIA

SQUANTO

SASSELLO

DEGO

GIUSVALLA

SALICETTO

Orba R.

CAPRIATA

MASONE

FAJALLO

BOCHETTA

VOLTRI

SESTRI

La Bochetta

Miollis (Serurier)
(1,800)

CEVA

MONTEZEMOLO

COSSERIA

ROCHETTA
CENGIA

MONTENOTTE INF.

MT. NEGINO

STELLA

CAIRO

MONTENOTTE SUP

VARAZZE

GENOA

Corsaglia R.

Ellero R.

BORGO SAN
DALMAZZO

TORRE

MILLESIMO

CARCARE

SAN GIOVANNI

BIESTRO

ALTARE

CADIBONA

MURIALDO

MALLARE

MONTEFREDDO

MT. ALTO

SAN GIACOMO

VADO

SAVONA

COL DI TENDA

BAGNASCO

CALIZZANO

MT. SETTEPANI

SPOTORNO

NOTE: 1. Some 4,000 cavalry and artillery were attached
to the infantry divisions.

2. ⊠ Meynier was disbanded 22 April. Meynier
had been too sick to command it effectively;
Bonaparte therefore had used him, when
possible, to command temporary detachments.

COL DI TERMINI

MT. PINARDO

GARESSIO

BARDINETTO

NOLI

MT. SAN
BERNARDO

ORMEA

FINALE

BORGO

PIETRA

ITALIAN CAMPAIGNS, 1796-97

THE PURSUIT OF THE PIEDMONTESE

Situation 23 April 1796

TENDA

Tanaro R.

TOIRANO

LOANO

BORGHETTO

ALBENGA

5   0   5   10
SCALE OF MILES

7

However, the situation had changed since 23 April. Colli's army was now shattered; Beaulieu obviously would not risk another beating. Serurier's advance to Fossano (*B2*) had uncovered the Col di Tenda (*B1*) and the Col di Argentera (*A2*), through which Bonaparte (27 April) called forward Macquard and Garnier. Possession of these passes gave Bonaparte an even shorter line of communication; consequently, he could also bring forward some of the troops guarding Savona and Albenga (*both B1*). Moreover, he now had direct contact with Kellermann, whom the Directory had ordered to reinforce the Army of Italy. Finally, he was methodically organizing and exploiting the local resources of the occupied territory to support his army.

Bonaparte's new demands on the Sardinians were harsh: Their army must retire north of the Stura River (*B2*); the fortresses of Demonte (*A1*), Coni (*B2*), and Tortona (*C2*) must be surrendered (if the Austrians seized Tortona, Alessandria [*B2*] would be substituted); the French army must have free passage through Piedmont (*B2*) and, specifically, be free to cross the Po River at Valenza (*B2*); the armistice would last until five days after the termination of future Franco-Sardinian peace negotiations. The Sardinian representatives accepted these terms at 0200 on 28 April.

In signing this armistice, Bonaparte knowingly violated the Directory's instructions that he was to take no diplomatic action. He had, however, the safety of his isolated army to consider; the Directory could give it little support, and might give it none. Therefore, he presented the Directory with this armistice as an accomplished fact, neatly wrapped in accounts of his latest victories, plus warnings that failure to ratify it would cripple future operations against Beaulieu. The Directory direly needed victories; finding Paris public opinion thoroughly pro-Bonaparte, it managed to swallow his insubordination with outward gratitude.

This campaign revolutionized the prevailing deliberate, chessboard concepts of the art of war. In four days of continuous battle, Bonaparte had hacked a bloody breach between Colli and Beaulieu, sending Beaulieu staggering northward to regroup. Then, wheeling westward, in fourteen days more he had crushed the Sardinians, shortened his line of communication, added most of his rear-area security detachments to his main army, re-established discipline among his troops, and organized the occupied territory to support them.

It had not been the clockwork campaign admiring historians would later make of it. Bonaparte was still learning the practical side of his trade; he occasionally anticipated events or assigned missions which overtaxed officers and soldiers alike. (That these missions were usually accomplished stands as a tribute to the general's inspiring leadership.) He had fought this campaign carefully and methodically. With fewer men than his opponents, he was always the stronger at the decisive point. If he had been fortunate in having Beaulieu

as an opponent, he had missed none of the opportunities Beaulieu thrust upon him. Luck had not favored him otherwise: The weather had clogged his operations; the indiscipline of his troops, the carelessness of his generals, and the ineptitude of his supply personnel had repeatedly invited disaster. His penetrating intelligence, his instinct for war, and his decisiveness had met every challenge. More than any earlier European general, he had looked beyond mere tactical victory on the battlefield to secure the overwhelming strategical success that would win the war itself.

Meanwhile, even as the armistice negotiations progressed, Bonaparte prepared his next blow at Beaulieu. Until he had definite information that peace had been established between France and Sardinia, Bonaparte would be compelled to operate with a potentially hostile Piedmont at his back. Consequently, he saw his problem as that of forcing Beaulieu to withdraw as far as possible without overextending his own forces. Fiorella (Serurier) was sideslipped to Borgo San Dalmazzo (*B1*) to establish liaison with Macquard's and Garnier's advancing divisions. Laharpe, reinforced with Victor's brigade, was to move (27 April) to a strong position near Cortemiglia (*B2*) and reconnoiter aggressively toward Acqui (*B2*). Massena, Serurier, and Augereau were summoned to army headquarters at Cherasco (*B2*) to receive their orders.

Shortly after signing the armistice, Bonaparte learned that Beaulieu had begun retiring on Valenza on 25 April. He at once ordered Laharpe to advance on Acqui; the rest of his army would follow. But, immediately, a hitch developed. Left to guard the French right flank in barren hill country, Laharpe's men had had neither supplies nor the chance for some quick, compensatory looting. Now, they were barefooted, starving, mutinous—and out of ammunition. It was the 30th before Laharpe could get them beyond Cortemiglia. He was, however, able to report that Beaulieu was continuing to withdraw.

Realizing that he could not overtake Beaulieu before the latter could cross the Po River, Bonaparte then advanced by easy stages. Strict discipline was maintained, the good will of the Piedmontese people being highly essential.

Meanwhile, in accordance with his secret instructions, Beaulieu had attempted to seize Tortona and Alessandria, but had found their Sardinian garrisons alert and unfriendly. His Neapolitan cavalry did occupy Valenza, but later evacuated it, following a French and Sardinian protest that he was violating the armistice. On 2 May, he completed crossing the Po at Valenza and spread his troops along the north bank, awaiting Bonaparte's next move. Though warned by Colli that the armistice had given Bonaparte the right to cross at Valenza, Beaulieu foresaw all the strategic possibilities of the French build-up around Alessandria and Tortona. On 4 May, worried about the security of his left flank, he dispatched Liptay to Corteolona (*C2*).

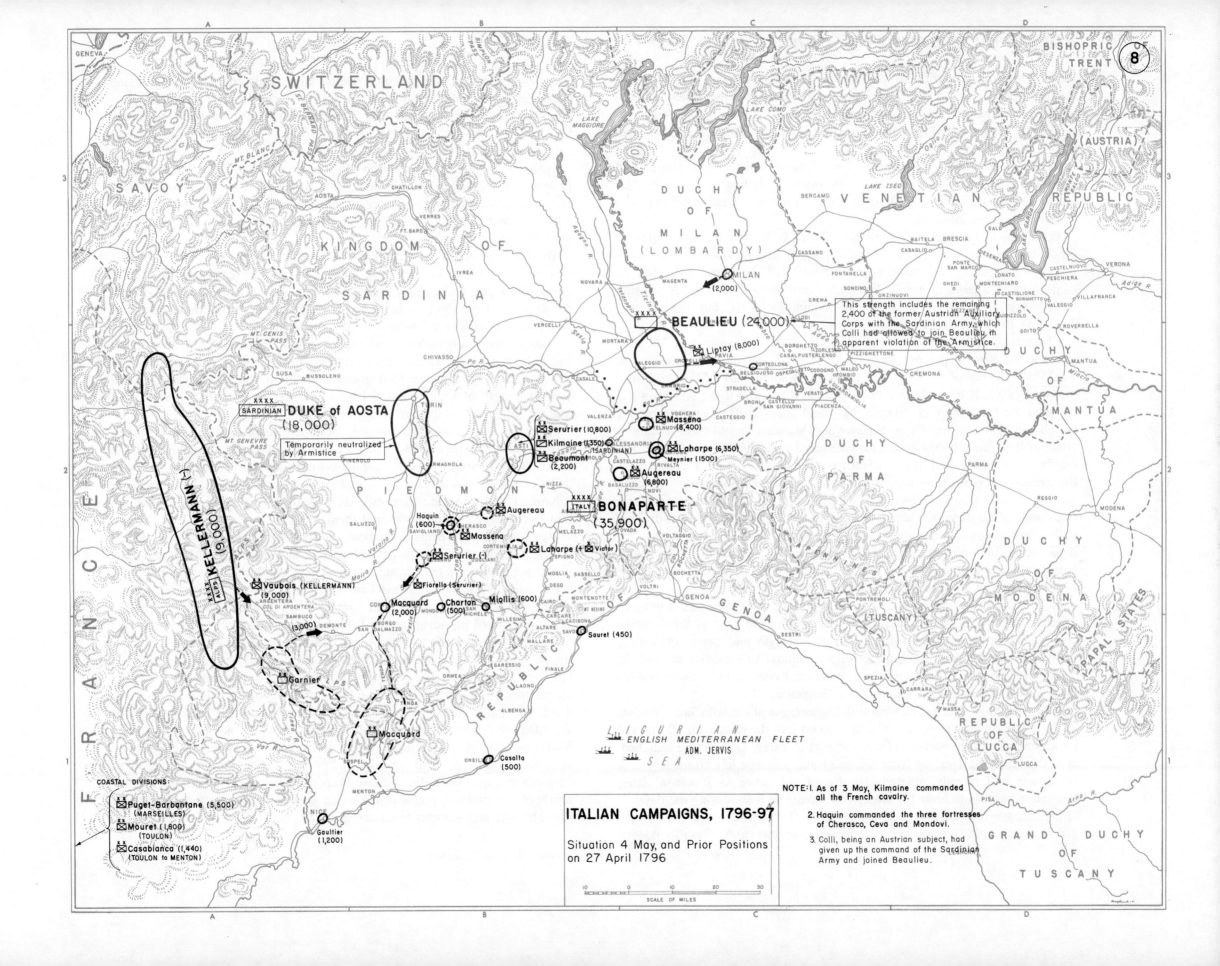

BISHOPRIC TRENT

8

SWITZERLAND

SAVOY

KINGDOM OF SARDINIA

DUCHY OF MILAN (LOMBARDY)

VENETIAN REPUBLIC

MILAN (2,000)

XXXX BEAULIEU (24,000)

This strength includes the remaining 2,400 of the former Austrian Auxiliary Corps with the Sardinian Army, which Colli had allowed to join Beaulieu in apparent violation of the Armistice.

Liptay (8,000)

XXXX SARDINIAN DUKE of AOSTA (18,000)

Temporarily neutralized by Armistice

Serurier (10,800)
Kilmaine (1,350)
SARDINIAN
Beaumont (2,200)
Meynier (1,500)
Massena (8,400)
Laharpe (6,350)
Augereau (6,800)

XXXX ITALY BONAPARTE (35,900)

DUCHY OF PARMA

DUCHY OF MANTUA

XXXX KELLERMANN (-) (9,000)
ALPS

Augereau
Haquin (600)
Massena
Serurier (-)
Fiorella (Serurier)
Laharpe (+ Victor)

Vaubois (KELLERMANN) (9,000)

Macquard (2,000)
Charton (500)
Miollis (600)
Sauret (450)

(3,000)

Garnier

GENOA

DUCHY OF MODENA

REPUBLIC OF LUCCA

Macquard

LIGURIAN
ENGLISH MEDITERRANEAN FLEET
ADM. JERVIS
SEA

Casalta (500)

REPUBLIC OF GENOA

PAPAL STATES

(TUSCANY)

COASTAL DIVISIONS:

Puget-Barbantane (5,500) (MARSEILLES)
Mouret (1,800) (TOULON)
Casabianca (1,440) (TOULON to MENTON)

Gaultier (1,200)

NICE

NOTE: 1. As of 3 May, Kilmaine commanded all the French cavalry.

2. Haquin commanded the three fortresses of Cherasco, Ceva and Mondovi.

3. Colli, being an Austrian subject, had given up the command of the Sardinian Army and joined Beaulieu.

GRAND DUCHY OF TUSCANY

ITALIAN CAMPAIGNS, 1796-97

Situation 4 May, and Prior Positions on 27 April 1796

10 0 10 20 30
SCALE OF MILES

FRANCE

Wishing to avoid serious operations until he knew the outcome of the French-Sardinian peace negotiations, Bonaparte limited his next objective to the occupation of Lombardy. That rich province possessed the resources necessary to support his ragged army; also, its occupation would force Beaulieu away from Piedmont's frontiers.

Beaulieu's defensive position was strong. The Po was in flood, and he had destroyed the bridges along his front. However, by failing to hold a bridge-head on the south bank he had condemned himself to a passive defense, and left Bonaparte the initiative.

Bonaparte had no ponton bridge train. To cross, he would have the double problem of maneuvering Beaulieu out of position and of securing a sufficient number of boats. If he crossed near Valenza (*B2*), he would thereafter be confronted by a series of highly defensible north-south river lines. A crossing farther east would threaten Beaulieu's communications, but risked over-extending the French army.

Characteristically, Bonaparte's plans were flexible. Serurier and Massena would ostentatiously prepare to cross at Valenza and Sale; meanwhile, he would take the rest of the army swiftly down the south bank of the Po toward Piacenza (*C2*). If he could find boats enough there, and if the Austrians did not hold the north bank in strength, he would cross. If Beaulieu detected his march and shifted to meet him, Serurier and Massena should then be able to cross on their front unopposed. This entailed dividing his forces, but he out-numbered Beaulieu, and the excellent road net south of the Po would allow the French to concentrate rapidly. For this operation, Bonaparte formed a special advance guard by detaching the grenadier and carabinier companies from most of his demi-brigades and forming them into a provisional division under Dallemagne, with Lanusse and Lannes as brigade commanders. To these picked infantrymen, Bonaparte added some 1,600 light cavalry and a battery of horse artillery. On 5 May, Dallemagne (5,200), Laharpe (6,600), and Augereau (7,100) moved out.

As previously noted, Beaulieu (now 26,000) had already sent Liptay to Corteolona, with orders to scout as far as Piacenza. On 6 May, the Austrian commander broke up his concentration at Valeggio and began organizing another cordon defense: Schübirz to support Liptay; Vukassovich to hold the Terdoppio River line; Sebottendorf to garrison Pavia; Colli to move toward Magenta. Beaulieu himself marched for Belgiojoso (*C2*).

Late on 6 May, Bonaparte, then with Dallemagne at Castello San Giovanni (*C2*), made his final plans. Lanusse trotted off into the dusk with 100 picked cavalrymen to secure boats. At 0400 the next morning, Dallemagne marched; at 0500, Kilmaine (just up from the rear) and Laharpe left Stradella (*C2*). Bonaparte had already ordered the rest of the army to Piacenza; later, Augereau was told to force his march so as to arrive there during the day.

Dallemagne reached Piacenza toward 0900. Two squadrons of enemy hussars showed a bold front on the north bank, some 500 yards of swiftly flowing water away. Lanusse had captured several large boats and a big ferry. Using everything that would float, the French surged across the river. Lannes reportedly was the first man ashore. The hussars left abruptly; by 1400, the north bank was firmly occupied, and French engineers were improvising a trail bridge.

About this time, Liptay, warned by his hussars, reached Guardamiglia. Despite his superiority in men and guns, he felt no urge to heroic action. Instead of attacking, he hastily organized a defensive position around Guardamiglia, Fombio, and Codogno (*all C2*), loopholing houses and planting his guns to sweep the roads.

By 0800 on 8 May, Laharpe had finished crossing. Augereau's leading elements, which had crossed from Verato on another commandeered ferry during the night, had already established contact with Laharpe, and French engineers were fortifying a bridgehead on the north bank. Bonaparte now sent Dallemagne forward to develop the situation.

Dallemagne's first rush cleared Guardamiglia. The Austrians in Fombio had to be pried loose with bayonets. As they broke, the French cavalry came down on them, bursting into Codogno with the fugitives. Lannes cut the roads west and north of Codogno, and Liptay, harried by French horsemen, fled into the little fortified town of Pizzighettone (*C2*).

After reconnoitering Pizzighettone, Bonaparte cautioned his subordinates to stay alert, and returned to Piacenza. Dallemagne halted at Maleo (*C2*); Laharpe, who had followed in support behind him, turned back to Codogno and Fombio. It was a black night and strange ground. Laharpe's men were exhausted, and some units neglected their local security, apparently assuming that Dallemagne's outposts covered them.

Beaulieu had left Belgiojoso about 0800 that morning; he had collected several detachments, including Schübirz, and had more than 7,000 men. His march was slow, and the accounts of it remain contradictory. Apparently, at about dark, he halted at Ospedaletto (*C2*) and pushed out several detachments, seeking contact with either Liptay or the French. Schübirz (1,600), who had formed his advance guard, pushed ahead through Casalpusterlengo (*C2*). Hereabouts, he stumbled over evidence of recent fighting, but continued cautiously on, entering Codogno about 2200. There was a sputter of fire from Laharpe's nodding sentries. Laharpe, galloping forward at the first alarm, was knocked from his saddle by a random bullet. Schübirz drove forward, and panic seized the leaderless French. Fortunately, Berthier was in Guardamiglia. Spurring up through the blackness, he got the fleeing men back into line. Menard brought the division reserve forward from Fombio. Astounded at the uproar his advance had produced, Schübirz retired hastily to Casalpusterlengo, while the shaken French blazed away spasmodically for much of the night. Liptay's contribution was to leave a small garrison in Pizzighettone and scamper to Cremona (*D2*).

Note: In Note 3 on this map (C1), Scandinavian should be Sardinian.

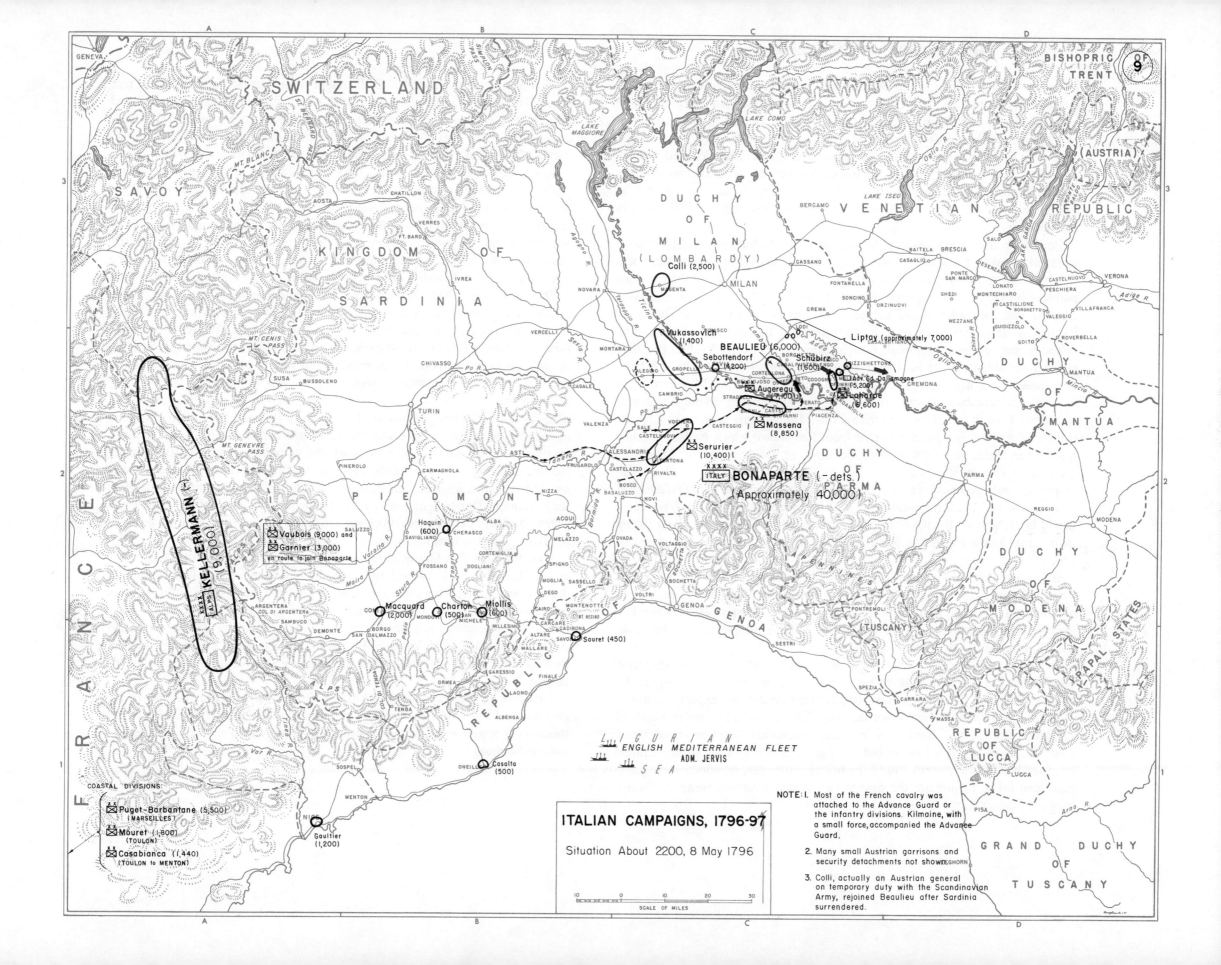

ITALIAN CAMPAIGNS, 1796-97

Situation About 2200, 8 May 1796

NOTE: 1. Most of the French cavalry was attached to the Advance Guard or the infantry divisions. Kilmaine, with a small force, accompanied the Advance Guard.

2. Many small Austrian garrisons and security detachments not shown.

3. Colli, actually an Austrian general on temporary duty with the Scandinavian Army, rejoined Beaulieu after Sardinia surrendered.

SCALE OF MILES
10   0   10   20   30

Early on 9 May, Berthier and Menard advanced grimly eastward. Beaulieu did not accommodate them; having at last comprehended the virtues of mobility, he was hastening up the road to Lodi (*C3*). Sebottendorf and Vukassovich had orders to rendezvous with him at Crema; Colli was to throw a garrison into the Milan citadel and retire on Cassano. Beaulieu had no idea of Liptay's fate until he picked up some scattered elements of that officer's division near Lodi; he thereupon sent Liptay orders to leave a garrison at Pizzighettone and retire to Cremona—orders that Liptay had already anticipated.

Bonaparte thereupon gave up the idea of an immediate pursuit. His troops were intermixed, ammunition was low, and the Po River ferries were still slowly bringing across Massena's cavalry and artillery. Also, he had serious political problems that required immediate solution. In using Piacenza as a crossing site, he had violated the pro-Austrian neutrality of the Duchy of Parma. Modena was likewise technically neutral, but definitely hostile. The armed forces of these two small principalities were inconsiderable, but they posed a possible threat to his line of communication. Therefore, he had Massena direct the army's regrouping, while he himself spent 10 May browbeating the representatives of the two duchies into submission. Menard was sent to relieve Dallemagne before Pizzighettone; Dallemagne was moved to the front at Zorlesco. Augereau reported from Borghetto, which he had reached during the night, somehow missing Schübirz in the process. As Massena's division trickled in, it was concentrated around Casalpusterlengo, where Kilmaine was ordered to collect all available cavalry except that with Dallemagne.

The road to Milan, the wealthy capital of Lombardy, was now free; but it would be dangerous for the French to move north so long as Beaulieu lay on their flank along the Adda River with an army still capable of offensive action.

Bonaparte left Menard to cover Pizzighettone against the chance that Liptay might attempt to debouch through that town to cut the French communications. Serurier would guard the area Piacenza-Ospedaletto, while Kilmaine swept the country toward Pavia. Dallemagne, Massena, and Augereau would march on Lodi.

Beaulieu, with most of his troops, was already at Crema. Sebottendorf (9,600) had crossed the Adda at Lodi and halted on the east bank to rest his exhausted troops. His dispositions indicate that he did not expect an attack. A rear guard of grenadiers blocked the road about three miles north of Zorlesco, and a small force was in Lodi, evacuating supplies stored there. Lodi itself was protected by an old rampart and ditch, and fourteen cannon were ready near the eastern end of the bridge. However, no effective measures had been taken to prepare the bridge (a wooden structure some 200 yards long) for destruction.

Moving out from Zorlesco, Dallemagne soon struck Sebottendorf's rear guard. The Austrian grenadiers died hard, but quickly. Their survivors poured into Lodi, the French at their heels, before the Austrians within the town could collect their wits. Dallemagne swept through Lodi and onto the bridge; there, a blast of artillery fire sent him back behind the town's ramparts.

It was about 1100. Bonaparte, who had ridden with the advance guard, got its two leading guns into action on the west bank, raking the length of the bridge, to the discouragement of any Austrian attempt to burn it. A ford was reported two miles upstream; Beaumont, with the advance guard's cavalry and a company of horse artillery, was sent to cross there and envelop the enemy's flank. As more guns came up, Bonaparte massed them along the river to pound the Austrian battery. Eventually, he had thirty guns in action.

Shortly before 1700, Massena arrived. Believing that Beaumont would attack at any moment, Bonaparte formed Dallemagne's infantry (3,000) behind the ramparts in one long column, six abreast. Massena's division formed behind the town. By then it was almost 1800, the sun was low, the Austrian battery had been badly mauled and forced to retire, but Beaumont had not appeared. Opportunity seemed to be slipping away.

The French artillery suddenly doubled its rate of fire. Out of the smoke, straight across the bridge, roared Dallemagne's column. With men dropping at each stride, it got to the center of the bridge before Austrian infantry fire smashed its head into a tangle of dead and wounded. Somehow untouched, red-bearded Major Dupas, commanding the leading battalion, shouted his men on. The column staggered, but Berthier seized a flag and went forward. Massena, Lannes, Dallemagne—a crowd of officers and men mixed together—followed. Some carabiniers, dropping from the bridge onto a sand bank in the river, gave the rush fire support.

Sebottendorf's first line went to pieces. His reserves counterattacked, shoving Dallemagne back toward the river in a savage melee. But Massena's division was up; Cervoni came into line on Dallemagne's right, Joubert on his left. Then, at last, Beaumont's leading squadron rode into Sebottendorf's right flank. Simultaneously, another regiment of cavalry, led by Rusca, swam the Adda below Lodi and hit the Austrian left; Augereau's infantry poured through Lodi. Sebottendorf retired in relatively good order, covered by his cavalry.

On 11 May, the French rested. On the 12th, Bonaparte marched down the east bank of the Adda and forced the surrender of Pizzighettone. Beaulieu, thoroughly cowed and harried by French cavalry, called in Colli and retired toward Mantua.

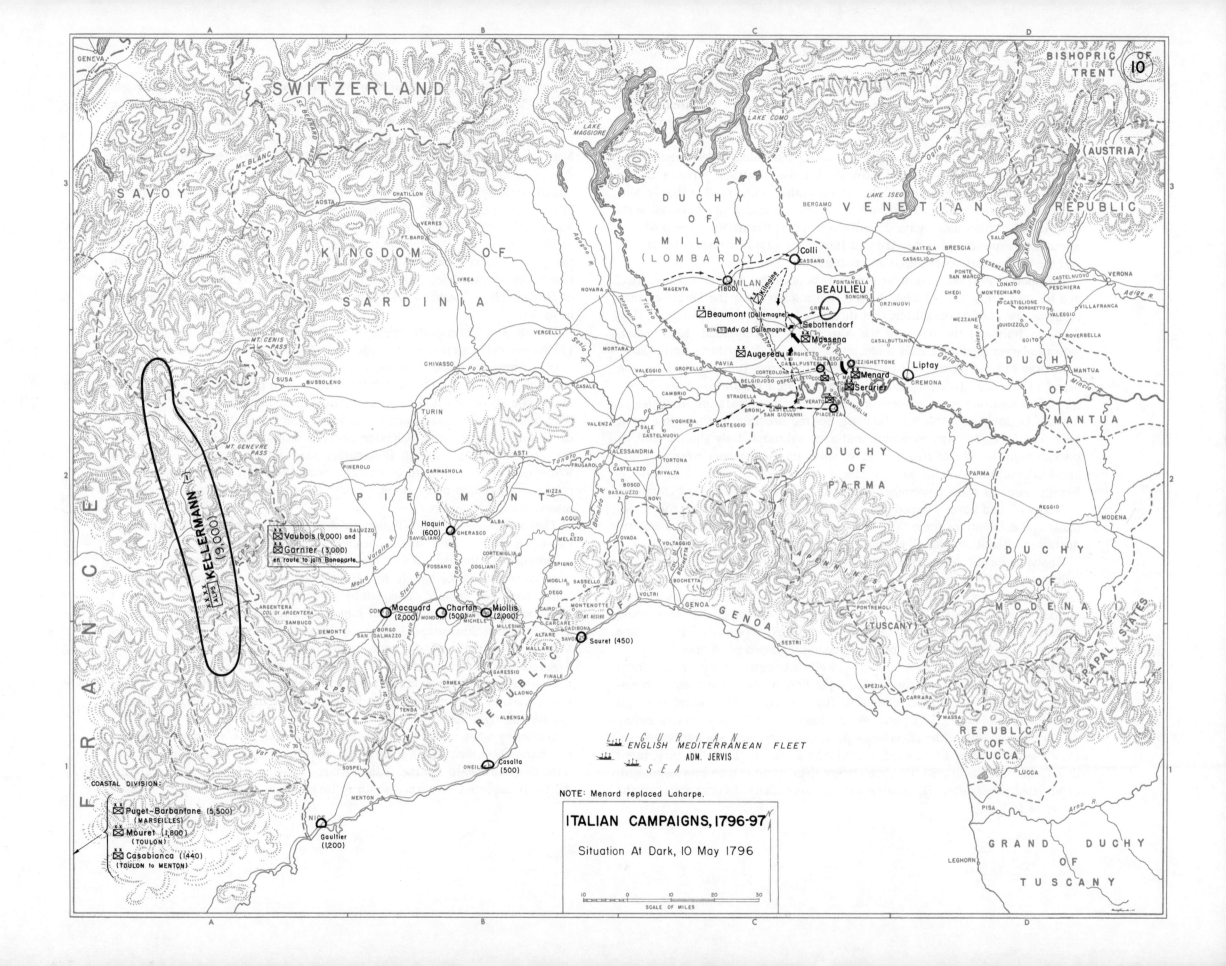

SWITZERLAND

GENEVA

BISHOPRIC OF TRENT

10

(AUSTRIA)

SAVOY

MT. BLANC

ST. BERNARD PASS

SIMPLON PASS

KINGDOM OF SARDINIA

LAKE MAGGIORE

LAKE COMO

LAKE ISEO

DUCHY OF MILAN (LOMBARDY)

VENETIAN REPUBLIC

Colli
CASSANO

MILAN (1800)

Killegagne

BEAULIEU

Beaumont (Dallemagne)

Sebottendorf

Adv Gd Dallemagne

Massena

Augereau

Menard

Serurier

Liptay
CREMONA

MT. CENIS PASS

MT. GENEVRE PASS

KELLERMANN (9,000)

ALPS

PIEDMONT

DUCHY OF PARMA

DUCHY OF MANTUA

Vaubois (9,000) and
Garnier (3,000)
en route to join Bonaparte.

Haquin (600)

Macquard (2,000)

Charton (500)

Miollis (2,000)

Sauret (450)

REPUBLIC OF GENOA

DUCHY OF MODENA

(TUSCANY)

REPUBLIC OF LUCCA

Casalta (500)

LIGURIAN

ENGLISH MEDITERRANEAN FLEET
ADM. JERVIS

SEA

COASTAL DIVISION:

Puget-Barbantane (5,500)
(MARSEILLES)

Mouret (1,800)
(TOULON)

Casabianca (1440)
(TOULON to MENTON)

NICE

Gaultier (1,200)

NOTE: Menard replaced Laharpe.

ITALIAN CAMPAIGNS, 1796-97

Situation At Dark, 10 May 1796

10   0   10   20   30
SCALE OF MILES

GRAND DUCHY OF TUSCANY

F R A N C E

Though only a small battle, Lodi had been highly dramatic, and Bonaparte's reports portrayed it as a minor epic. The sensation in Paris was tremendous. Later, Bonaparte would say that it was Lodi that made him certain he could be a man of high destiny.

After Lodi, he set up a defensive line along the Adda River, made a triumphant entry into Milan (*C3*), blockaded the Austrian garrison in the town's citadel, and then turned to administrative matters. Lombardy was given a new government; contributions in money and supplies of all sorts were levied (Milan alone gave 20 million francs); the troops were paid (an astounding experience for the Army of Italy); the supply services overhauled; and the whole army reorganized and refitted.

Bonaparte, however, had other problems besides the Austrians, Lombardy, and his own army. On 13 May, he received a letter from the Directory outlining a new plan of operations that threatened to clip short his career. The Army of Italy and the Army of the Alps would be combined. Kellermann, with the larger portion of this force, would operate in northern Italy; Bonaparte was to overrun the rest of Italy and even drive the English from the island of Corsica. This preposterous plan has been attributed to the Directory's fear that one of its generals might achieve enough stature to challenge its rule. Undoubtedly, this fear did exist, but the situation was far more complex. The Directory was bankrupt, and a raid through Italy should refill its pockets from the Papal treasury. Also, some of its members were violently anti-Catholic and anxious to sheer the Pope of power, as well as money. Finally, none of them comprehended strategy. Even Carnot, the "Organizer of Victory," had never grasped the essential principles of unity of command, mass, and economy of force. The two armies on the Rhine frontier were still operating without an over-all commander.

Replying on 14 May, Bonaparte served the Directory a dry lesson on military art. "If you weaken your power by dividing your forces . . . you will lose the finest opportunity to impose your rule in Italy. Everyone has his own method of waging war. General Kellermann has more experience and would do better than I, but the two of us together would do very badly." In the same vein, he wrote Carnot, "Better one bad general than two good ones."

These were blunt answers, but they were accompanied by an argument that even the Directory comprehended—the flow of the wealth which Bonaparte was collecting. Public opinion, deftly nudged by letters and bulletins from Italy, applauded Bonaparte. Also, Bonaparte was very understanding as to certain merits in the Directory's plan, and expressed willingness to execute it—if first given a free hand to deal with Beaulieu. The Directory, faced down and outmaneuvered by a man abler than its four members combined, capitulated. Thereafter, Bonaparte was the unchallenged commander of the Army of Italy.

Before this forced reconciliation had been achieved, General Bonaparte was back to the wars. On 21 May, he had learned that a Franco-Sardinian peace treaty had been signed. With the army's rear thus secure, Despinoy was left to blockade the Milan citadel, and Bonaparte departed for Lodi on 23 May, in preparation for an immediate offensive against Beaulieu. The next day, an insurrection exploded around Milan and Pavia (*C2*), sparked by pro-Austrian clergy and nobility, but fed by French greed and brutality. Bonaparte countermarched with 300 light cavalry and Lannes' grenadiers. Despinoy had kept Milan calm, but the insurgents had seized Pavia and were mustering at Binasco (*C3*). A whirlwind march ended with Pavia stormed and pillaged, Binasco burned, insurgents butchered, and dazed calm throughout Lombardy. Meanwhile, Berthier had massed the French army just south of Brescia (*D3*). Beaulieu lay behind the Mincio River, his forces disposed as shown.

On 28 May, Bonaparte began his offensive, leading with his left flank (Kilmaine and Augereau), while his right (Serurier) held back around Ghedi (*D3*). Augereau made some business of collecting boats, as if hoping to convince Beaulieu that the French intended to turn his right flank by a movement around, or across, Lake Garda. Beaulieu, unimpressed, saw this as a feint and waited for Bonaparte's next move. On the 29th, Serurier suddenly drove for Mezzane, while Kilmaine swerved south toward Castiglione (*both D3*). Confident that this was Bonaparte's main attack, Beaulieu brought his Roverbella force northward and established a defensive cordon, dropping a reinforced battalion or so at each bridge, and holding only a small cavalry reserve behind Valeggio.

That night (29–30 May), Bonaparte developed his actual attack: Augereau was to fix the Austrians around Peschiera; the rest of the army would strike at Borghetto. Kilmaine reached that town at about 0700, drove in the Austrian cavalry (thanks largely to Murat), and began repairing the bridge, which had been slightly damaged by the retreating Austrians. Gardanne's grenadiers, meanwhile, noting that some of the retreating Austrians had used a ford farther downstream, made an assault crossing there and attacked Valeggio from the south. By noon, the town was in French hands.

Augereau's fortunes against Peschiera remain obscure; later in the day, Bonaparte brought him south to cross at Borghetto and then to move against Peschiera from the south and east, while Kilmaine advanced on Castelnuovo to cover his right flank.

Gathering what troops he could, Beaulieu retired to Castelnuovo. He had lost barely 600 men, but his army was hopelessly split. By 1 June, he was retreating northward up the Adige River. Leaving Massena to watch the Adige, Bonaparte then turned south to invest Mantua (*D2*).

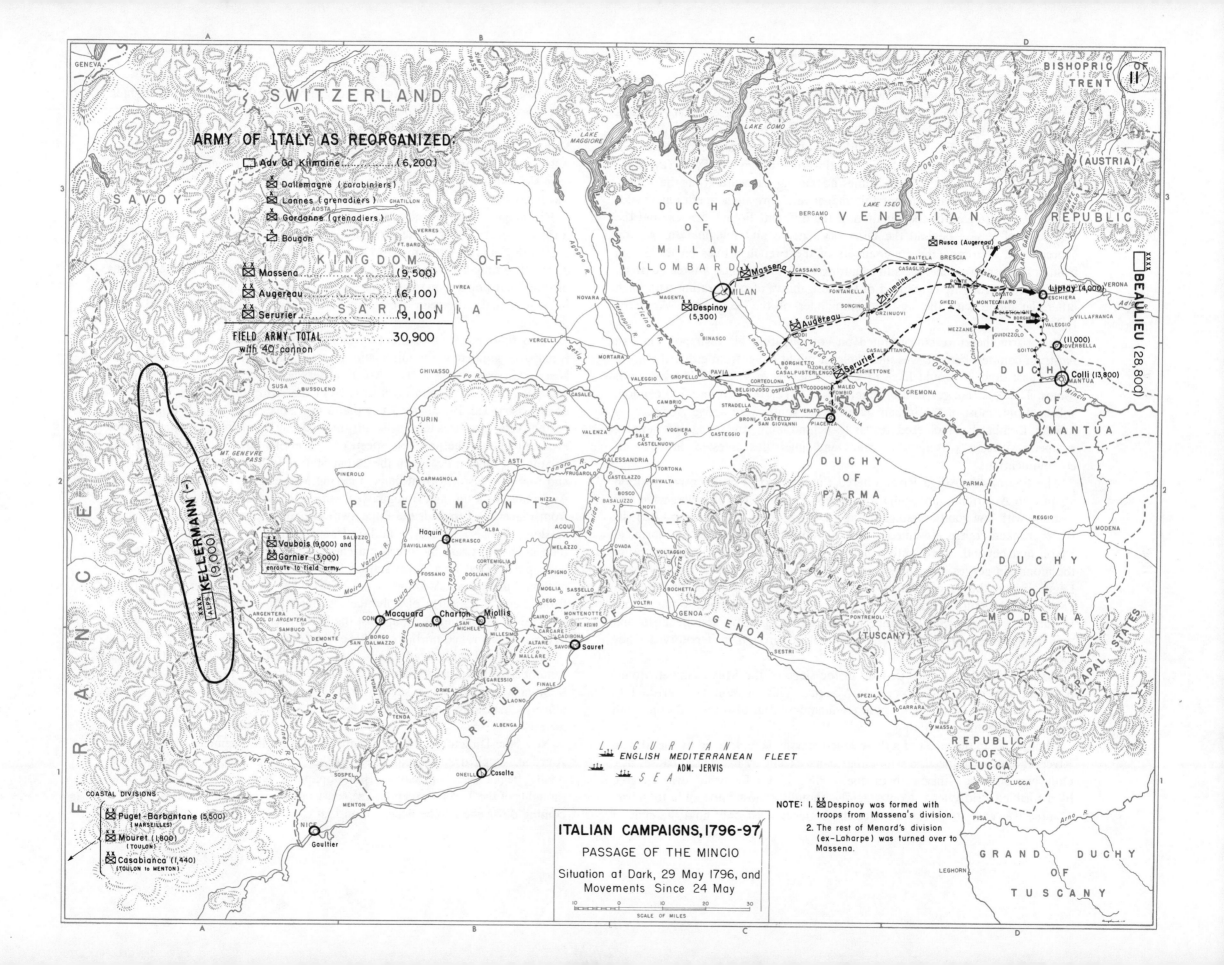

SWITZERLAND

GENEVA

SAVOY

ARMY OF ITALY AS REORGANIZED:

☐ Adv Gd Kilmaine .... (6,200)

⊠ Dallemagne (carabiniers)

⊠ Lannes (grenadiers)

⊠ Gardanne (grenadiers)

⊠ Bougon

⊠ Massena .... (9,500)

⊠ Augereau .... (6,100)

⊠ Serurier .... (9,100)

FIELD ARMY TOTAL 30,900
with 40 cannon

KINGDOM OF SARDINIA

⊠ Vaubois (9,000) and
⊠ Garnier (3,000)
enroute to field army.

XXXX KELLERMANN (-) ALPS (9,000)

FRANCE

PIEDMONT

DUCHY OF MILAN (LOMBARDY)

LAKE COMO
LAKE MAGGIORE
LAKE ISEO
LAKE GARDA

VENETIAN REPUBLIC

(AUSTRIA)

⊠⊠ Rusca (Augereau)

⊠⊠ Massena MILAN

⊠⊠ Despinoy (5,300)

⊠⊠ Augereau

⊠⊠ Kilmaine

Liptay (4,000)

XXXX BEAULIEU (28,800)

⊠⊠ Serurier

(11,000)

Colli (13,800)

DUCHY OF MANTUA

DUCHY OF PARMA

REPUBLIC OF GENOA

GENOA

DUCHY OF MODENA

(TUSCANY)

REPUBLIC OF LUCCA

⊠ Haquin
⊠ Macquard ⊠ Charton ⊠ Miollis
⊠ Sauret

L I G U R I A N   S E A

ENGLISH MEDITERRANEAN FLEET
ADM. JERVIS

COASTAL DIVISIONS:

⊠ Puget-Barbantane (5,500)
(MARSEILLES)

⊠ Mouret (1,800)
(TOULON)

⊠ Casabianca (1,440)
(TOULON to MENTON)

NICE

⊠ Gaultier

MENTON

⊠ Casalta

NOTE: 1. ⊠⊠ Despinoy was formed with troops from Massena's division.

2. The rest of Menard's division (ex-Laharpe) was turned over to Massena.

ITALIAN CAMPAIGNS, 1796-97

PASSAGE OF THE MINCIO

Situation at Dark, 29 May 1796, and
Movements Since 24 May

10 0 10 20 30
SCALE OF MILES

GRAND DUCHY OF TUSCANY

With Beaulieu on the run northward, Bonaparte reverted to a military conception which he had championed since 1794. Italy was a secondary theater; the war would necessarily be settled in Germany, probably by an offensive directed at Vienna. Therefore, the ultimate objective of a French victory in northern Italy should be an advance northward through the Tyrol (*off map, B3*) to link up with the French armies advancing eastward from the Rhine.

He was now ready to attempt this maneuver. Any such operation would, however, require careful coordination of the different French armies, and the very idea of it was beyond the Directory's nerve and imagination. As for Moreau and Jourdan (the commanders of the French armies on the Rhine frontier), those two generals, still squatting immobile in their winter quarters, were never thoroughly convinced of the desirability of cooperating with each other, let alone with the upstart commander of the second-rate Army of Italy.

Bonaparte therefore concentrated on consolidating his own position. An Austrian counteroffensive was inevitable; it might come from either the north or the east, and he would have to select a defensive line that blocked both routes. The Austrian garrison of Mantua (*B1*), 12,700 men and 500 cannon, still held out; most of the Italian states to the south were actively or secretly hostile, Lombardy smoldered restlessly behind him, and gangs of bandits, escaped Austrian prisoners of war, and guerrillas infested his line of communication.

The line of the Adige River offered the best possible defensive position against an Austrian counteroffensive. Below Legnago (*C1*), it was wide and swampy with few good crossings. From Legnago north to Pastrengo (*B2*), its swift, crooked course presented a serious military obstacle. Farther north, at Rivoli and beyond, there were a number of excellent defensive positions in the mountain gorges. Occupation of the Venetian cities of Verona (*B1*) and Legnago gave the French fortified bridgeheads on the east bank of the river. (Most of the territory from the Mincio River eastward belonged to the neutral Republic of Venice. Since Venice had no effective army, first Beaulieu and then Bonaparte marched and countermarched through its territory as they pleased.)

With his few heavy guns tied up in the siege of the Milan citadel, Bonaparte initially could only blockade Mantua. This mission he entrusted to Serurier, the slowest of his division commanders, but also the only one with the required technical training.

Mantua lay in the midst of a three-lobed marshy lake, formed by the Mincio River. It had no connection with either bank except by five raised causeways. Only one of these—the northern one, ending at La Favorita—was covered by a fortified bridgehead. Consequently, though almost impossible to storm, Mantua was easy to blockade, since the besieger need only hold the ends of the causeways, with the bulk of his strength opposite La Favorita. To tighten this blockade, Bonaparte soon organized a little squadron of light gunboats on the lakes. Meanwhile, the fevers produced by the marshy country around Mantua soon justified its reputation as one of the worst pestholes in Europe. A large proportion of the Austrian garrison, and of Serurier's division, were soon sick—the Austrians suffering much the worse because of foul water and short rations.

His major strategic and tactical problems thus disposed of, Bonaparte turned to his rear area. The civil administration of Lombardy was carefully overhauled, and an effort made to organize Italian troops for internal-security duties. The supply system was put on a better footing to avoid undue burdens on the local population, and some of his more thieving officers (Massena, Kilmaine, and Augereau were outstanding) and supply personnel were disciplined.

On 6 June, the King of the Two Sicilies (Naples) requested an armistice. Bonaparte granted it on fairly stiff terms, mainly to detach the excellent Neapolitan cavalry from the Austrian service. Shortly thereafter Vaubois reported with 12,000 reinforcements from the Army of the Alps, now practically disbanded. Bonaparte knew that a new Austrian army—Würmser with 25,000 veterans—was moving south through the Tyrol from Germany. However, calculating the probable speed of Würmser's advance, he decided that he still had time to deal with the Papal States, both to placate the Directory and to secure his own right flank. Leaving Massena along the Adige, he sent Augereau down through Bologna (*off map, C1*), while Vaubois moved south from Piacenza. Terrified, the Pope swiftly made considerable territorial concessions, and also yielded 34 million francs in treasure and supplies. Vaubois then swung westward by forced marches to seize Leghorn, which the English had appropriated as a naval station and commercial port. This yielded 20 million francs more. Vaubois, with 2,500 men, remained there in garrison. From Leghorn, a party of volunteers slipped through the British fleet and soon raised Corsica in revolt against the British occupation forces. Meanwhile, flying columns raked northern Italy to hunt down the bandit packs.

Milan citadel capitulated on 29 June, allowing the French siege train, plus a number of the citadel's heavy guns, to be shifted to Mantua. By 19 July, Mantua was under active siege, directed by Bonaparte's new army engineer officer, Chasseloup-Loubat; by the last of the month, its fall appeared imminent.

Now, the Directory refused Bonaparte more reinforcements. Moreau and Jourdan, supplied and re-equipped by the "earnings" of the Army of Italy, finally began their offensives. But Bonaparte had already postponed all thoughts of the Tyrol—except as the source of the Austrian storm of war now coming down the Alpine passes upon him.

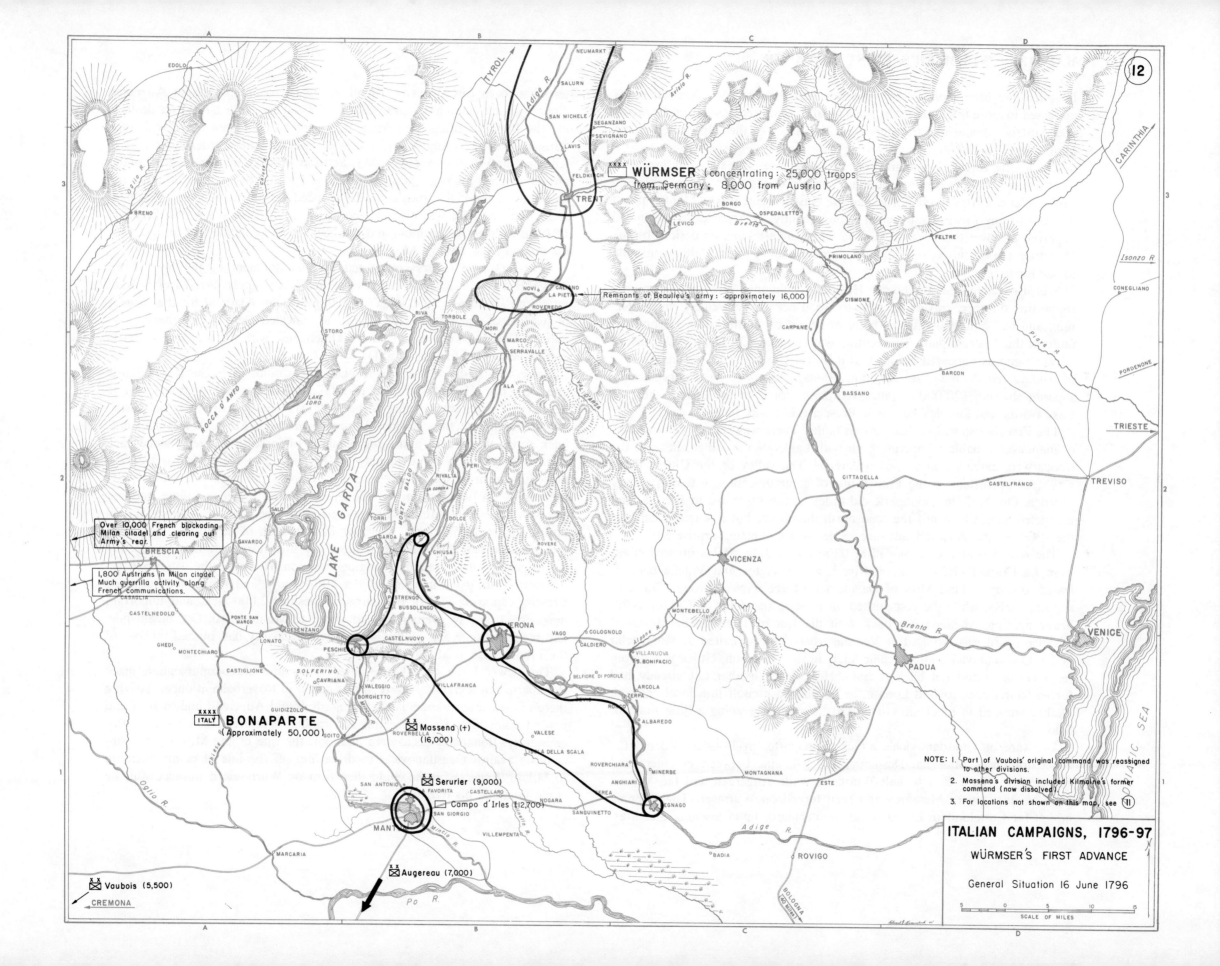

12

WÜRMSER (concentrating: 25,000 troops from Germany; 8,000 from Austria)

Remnants of Beaulieu's army: approximately 16,000

Over 10,000 French blockading Milan citadel and clearing out Army's rear.

1,800 Austrians in Milan citadel. Much guerrilla activity along French communications.

BONAPARTE (Approximately 50,000)

Massena (+) (16,000)

Serurier (9,000)

Campo d'Irles (12,700)

Vaubois (5,500)

Augereau (7,000)

NOTE: 1. Part of Vaubois' original command was reassigned to other divisions.

2. Massena's division included Kilmaine's former command (now dissolved).

3. For locations not shown on this map, see (11)

ITALIAN CAMPAIGNS, 1796-97

WÜRMSER'S FIRST ADVANCE

General Situation 16 June 1796

SCALE OF MILES

MAP 13: WÜRMSER'S FIRST ADVANCE

Beaulieu had been replaced by Würmser, and the dispirited Austrian army increased to more than 50,000 by the arrival of reinforcements from Germany and Austria. Meanwhile, transfers from the Army of the Alps raised Bonaparte's army to 42,600.

Conditions forced Bonaparte on the defensive. Greater reinforcement would be necessary before he could attempt a crossing of the formidable and easily defended Alps in the north, and the Austrian garrison at Mantua posed a threat to any forward movement. Consequently, Bonaparte had remained deployed to cover the siege of Mantua while undertaking, as desired by the Directory, the subsidiary operations to force the states of the Italian peninsula to sue for peace.

Würmser advanced as shown. His three columns were out of mutual supporting distance, traversing a limited road net over extremely rugged terrain, and had only a slight possibility of lateral communication. Despite the faults of the Austrian plan, its execution was vigorous. On 28 July, Würmser's advance guards appeared before Gavardo, La Corona, and Verona (*points of leading red arrows*). At this time, Bonaparte could have concentrated superior strength (30,000) against Würmser's force on the eastern shore of Lake Garda, but that day he was in Brescia (*A2*) with his wife.

The French dispositions had serious faults. There was no real central mass of maneuver capable of operating on both banks of the Adige; instead, the troops were extended in a cordon defense. The valley of the Chiese River (*A1*), an open door to the French line of communication, was only lightly guarded. On the 28th, Bonaparte did order Lanusse forward to Brescia, and instructed Sauret to guard the road north therefrom, but it was too late, for the speed of the Austrian advance came as a complete surprise.

The Austrian attack developed at 0300 on 29 July. Melas drove Joubert from La Corona (*B2*) back on Rivoli, where Victor and Valette concentrated to support him. Most of Davidovich's force moved through Dolce to support Melas, while the rest pushed on to seize the defile at Chiusa. After heavy fighting, Massena fell back with the loss of 1,600 men. Meszaros' advance guard was repulsed at Verona, whereupon he halted at Montebello (*C2*). Quasdanovich's attack came later. In the afternoon, Guieu was driven from Gavardo and fell back to Salo. Here, learning that Ott already had forced Sauret back toward Lonato, he barricaded himself in a local chateau. Ocskay stopped to blockade Guieu; Ott halted that evening a little south of Salo.

Unaware of Quasdanovich's attack, Bonaparte, in Brescia, ordered the concentration of Massena, Despinoy, and Kilmaine between Peschiera and Castelnuovo (*both B1*) to halt Würmser, while Augereau and the Verona garrison disposed of Meszaros and then turned on Würmser. That evening he left for Castelnuovo. En route, at Montechiaro, upon learning that Mas-

sena had been forced out of Rivoli, he issued counterorders to Augereau directing him to march to Roverbella, via Castellaro (*both B1*), after destroying the Legnago bridge and what munitions he could not carry with him. "Brigade Robert" (Augereau), at Zevio, received direct orders to report to Kilmaine at Villafranca (*both B1*). Serurier was ordered to send all of his artillery, except his siege guns, south of the Po, and to bombard Mantua immediately to see if the town could be reduced before the French might have to lift the siege. He was also to reconnoiter the line of the Molinella River (*B1*) as a defensive position, and to check on the condition of bridges over the Po and Oglio rivers (*A1*).

Actually, these orders constituted an abandonment of the line of the Adige. But they had hardly been dispatched when reports arrived of Sauret's retreat on Desenzano and Guieu's isolation at Salo. Alarmed for the security of his line of communication, Bonaparte canceled Despinoy's orders to remain at Castelnuovo and sent him to Desenzano, with the brigades of Bertin and Dallemagne (totaling 4,500).

Early on 30 July, Bonaparte reached Desenzano, where he found Sauret and Despinoy. He ordered them to retake Salo, and then continued on to Peschiera. During the morning of the 30th, Massena was driven in on Castelnuovo. Bonaparte then ordered Verona evacuated, Massena and Kilmaine back across the Mincio, and a regroupment of forces that strengthened each of their divisions to approximately 10,000 men. Augereau had arrived the preceding night at Castellaro, after a circuitous thirty-six–hour march. By evening of 30 July, the bulk of the French army formed a square between the Mincio and the Molinella rivers, covering the siege of Mantua and in position to strike Würmser, whatever his direction of advance.

Bonaparte had displayed great flexibility and resourcefulness in meeting the exigencies of the rapidly changing situation. However, the worst had yet to come. During the morning of the 30th, Spork and Reuss had surprised Brescia, capturing 700 of the garrison (besides 2,000 sick, and important magazines), and by evening had advanced to Montechiaro. Ott, meanwhile, had reached Ponte San Marco, and Austrian cavalry had pushed on toward the French base at Milan.

The news of the virtual severance of his line of communication upset Bonaparte considerably. Augereau was called to Roverbella at once. Arriving there himself several hours later, Bonaparte found Augereau undismayed and ready for anything. Upon receiving reports that Würmser was advancing very cautiously, Bonaparte decided to abandon the line of the Mincio and concentrate against Quasdanovich, to drive him off the line of communication to Milan. If successful, he could then turn on Würmser; if unsuccessful, he could continue his retreat.

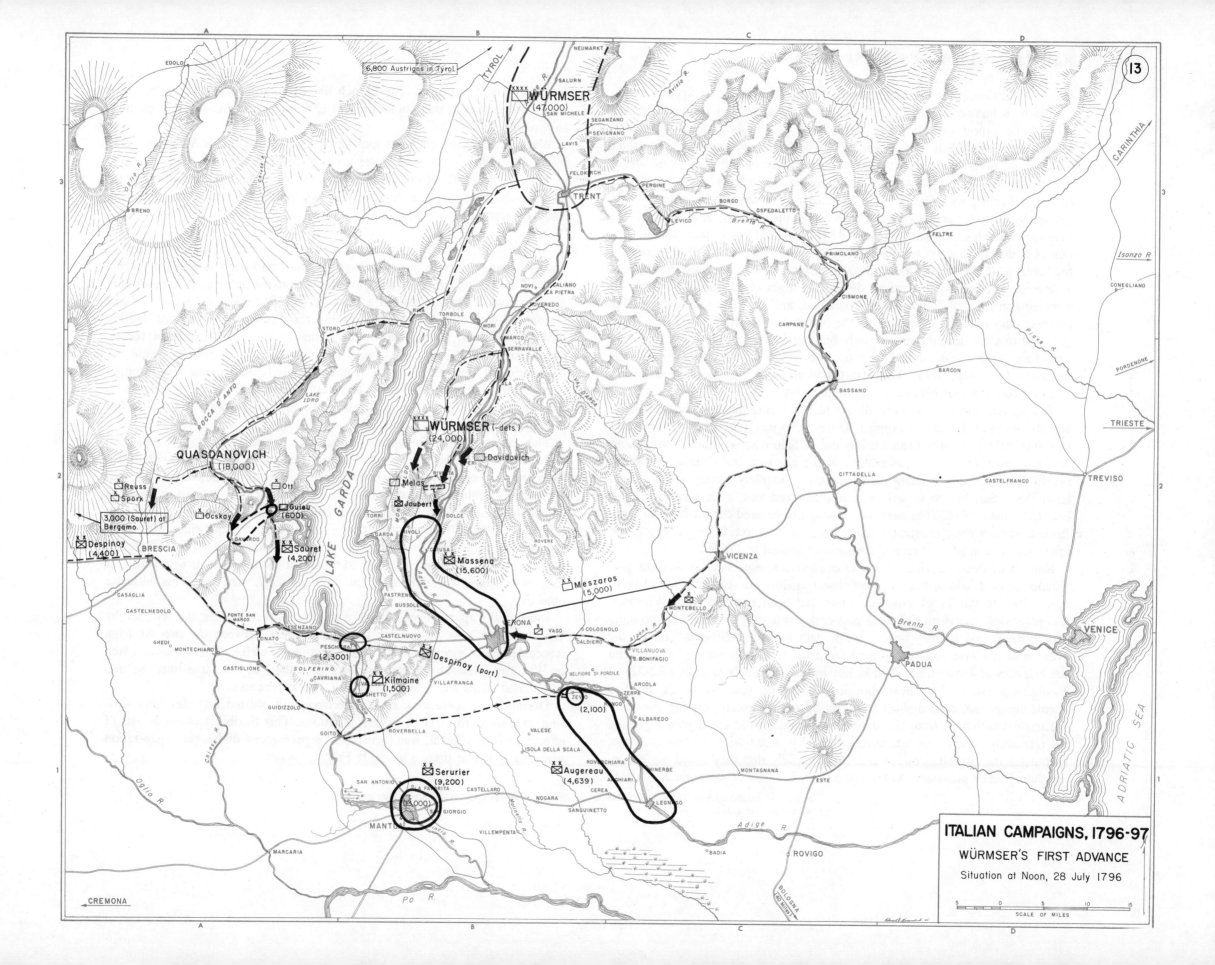

ITALIAN CAMPAIGNS, 1796-97

WÜRMSER'S FIRST ADVANCE

Situation at Noon, 28 July 1796

On 31 July, Bonaparte issued his orders for the concentration against Quasdanovich. Kilmaine would attack toward Montechiaro and Calcinato (*both A2*), while Sauret and Despinoy hit Salo, as previously ordered. If unsuccessful, they would fall back toward Pizzighettone (*off map, A1*). Massena would move on Lonato (*A2*) to support the attacks of Kilmaine or of Sauret and Despinoy (the last two were placed under his orders). Also, he would leave Guillaume, with 600 men, in Peschiera to command the highway and the bridge; throw out a cavalry screen along the Mincio; and send off his baggage through Cremona (*off map, A1*). Augereau would pick up the portion of Serurier's division stationed along the east bank of the Mincio (raising his force to 7,500), and move through Goito on Montechiaro to support Kilmaine. Serurier would destroy, during the night of 31 July–1 August, all siege equipment that could not be evacuated, and take the remainder of his division (those on the west bank of the Mincio) to Marcaria (*A1*) to cover the road to Cremona, the army's only remaining line of communication. He would also send a small detachment back to secure the bridge over the Po at Piacenza (*off map, A1*). These instructions were typical of Bonaparte's constant concern over his line of communication.

The movements ordered were all completed during the evening of 31 July and the night of 31 July–1 August. During this day (the 31st), Sauret and Despinoy attacked. Sauret ran Ocskay out of Salo without much trouble, and relieved Guieu from his incarceration in the chateau; but, fearing to be cut off, he fell back that evening on Desenzano. Despinoy, seeing Ott debouch from Ponte San Marco to seize Lonato, attacked and, after a furious fight, beat the Austrians off. The next day, Bonaparte ordered Sauret back to Salo. Encountering strong resistance along the road, Sauret failed to reach the town, was wounded, and turned over his command to Guieu.

Reports of these activities shook Quasdanovich, especially as Sauret's persistence against Salo seemed a direct threat against the Austrian line of communication to the Tyrol. Also, no news had been received from Würmser. Quasdanovich, therefore, fell back and concentrated at Gavardo, abandoning Montechiaro and leaving only a weak detachment at Brescia. During the evening of the 31st, Massena joined Despinoy at Lonato, bringing with him the brigades of Joubert and Victor, but leaving Valette's brigade (2,500) at Castiglione (*A2*). The next morning, Kilmaine and Augereau reached Montechiaro and, after a short rest, pushed on to Brescia, driving the weak Austrian detachment from the town. Augereau, an old cavalryman, pressed the retreating enemy with a handful of cavalry. According to some accounts, he hustled the Austrians out of Brescia so rapidly that they could not evacuate their French prisoners. At the same time, Lanusse brought his 3,000 men from Bergamo to Brescia. The French line of communication to Milan now was reopened, but it was not secure, for Quasdanovich was still in a position to threaten it.

Würmser's leading elements had advanced only as far as Valeggio (*B2*) by 31 July. Early on 1 August, he learned that Serurier had lifted the siege of Mantua the night before. He then wrote to Quasdanovich that he planned to cross the Mincio on 2 August, and proceeded toward Mantua, leaving small detachments at Valeggio and Goito.

At this point, it would be well to review the actions and aims of Würmser and Quasdanovich. It is not clear that the latter had been assigned a specific mission at the beginning of the advance. From his actions, it appears that his efforts were directed toward a juncture with Würmser just south of Lake Garda; not until then did he expect to undertake full-scale operations. During the past few days, he had had opportunities to concentrate superior forces, first against Sauret, and then against Despinoy. Their destruction would not have defeated Bonaparte, but it would have reduced his effective strength dangerously and made Würmser's task easier. Instead, he vacillated, assumed a defensive attitude, and accomplished little. Soon, he was to feel the full fury of the main French forces.

The opportunity for Bonaparte to deal with Quasdanovich alone had been provided by Würmser. On 1 August, upon learning of the French withdrawal from the siege of Mantua, he should have crossed the Mincio and advanced aggressively against Bonaparte. Instead, he deduced that, by lifting the siege of Mantua, the French had admitted defeat and were retreating. Actually, he had entertained this conception of French future actions since the beginning of the campaign. Now, on the 1st, he remained east of the Mincio, gloating over his success in freeing Mantua. At the moment, it appeared that this, rather than the defeat of the French army, had been his ultimate objective.

Indeed, Bonaparte feared most a rapid advance across the Mincio by Würmser, which would squeeze the French army between the two Austrian forces. He had concentrated his forces, hoping to strike either Quasdanovich or Würmser, without interference from the other; at the same time, he had formulated plans for retreat, should it become necessary.

During these operations, Bonaparte frequently shifted brigades from division to division to meet particular situations. This flexibility, without loss of effectiveness or control, was facilitated by permanent divisional organization and staffs—at that time, a uniquely French system.

Note: The suburb of San Giorgio (B1) was not fortified in 1796 (as incorrectly shown here and on Maps 15 and 16).

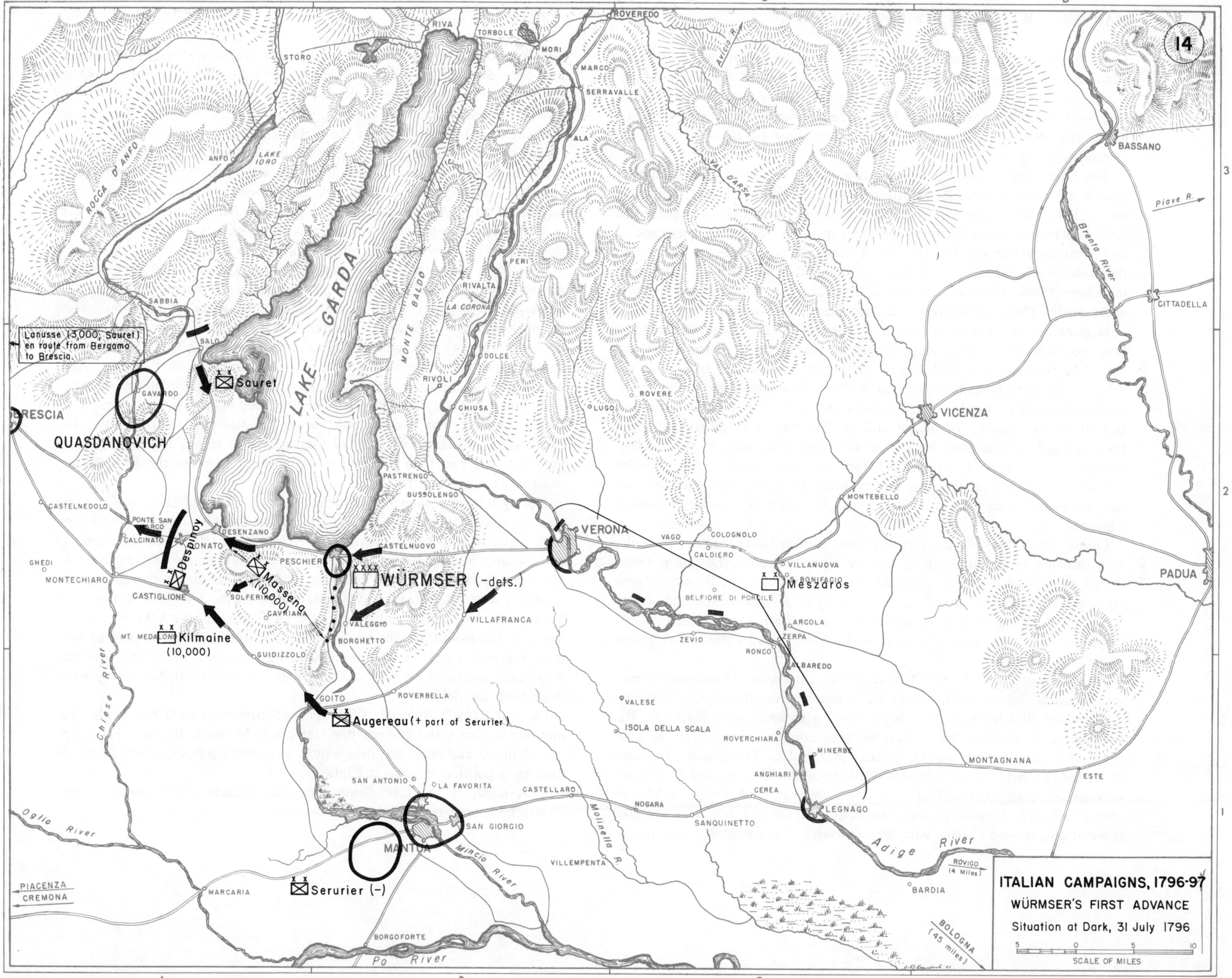

14

Lanusse (3,000, Sauret) en route from Bergamo to Brescia.

ROCCA D'ANFO

ANFO

LAKE IDRO

STORO

RIVA

TORBOLE

MORI

ROVEREDO

MARCO

SERRAVALLE

ALA

AVISIO R.

VAL D'ARSA

Piave R.

BASSANO

SABBIA

SALO

Sauret

LAKE GARDA

MONTE BALDO

PERI

CHIUSA

DOLCE

RIVALTA

LA CORONA

RIVOLI

ROVERE

LUGO

BRENTA RIVER

CITTADELLA

BRESCIA

QUASDANOVICH

GAVARDO

DESENZANO

PASTRENGO

BUSSOLENGO

CASTELNEDOLO

PONTE SAN MARCO

CALCINATO

Despinoy

PESCHIERA

CASTELNUOVO

VERONA

VAGO

COLOGNOLO

CALDIERO

VICENZA

MONTEBELLO

VILLANUOVA

GHEDI

MONTECHIARO

CASTIGLIONE

Massena (10,000)

SOLFERINO

CAVRIANA

WÜRMSER (-dets.)

VALEGGIO

VILLAFRANCA

BELFIORE DI PORCILE

Meszaros

PADUA

BONIFACIO

ARCOLA

ZERPA

MT. MEDALONE

Kilmaine (10,000)

GUIDIZZOLO

BORGHETTO

GOITO

ROVERBELLA

ZEVIO

RONCO

BAREDO

VALESE

ISOLA DELLA SCALA

ROVERCHIARA

MONTAGNANA

ESTE

Augereau (+ part of Serurier)

Chiese River

Oglio River

PIACENZA
CREMONA

MARCARIA

SAN ANTONIO

LA FAVORITA

CASTELLARO

MANTUA

Serurier (-)

SAN GIORGIO

Mincio River

Molinella R.

NOGARA

SANQUINETTO

CEREA

ANGHIARI

MINERBE

LEGNAGO

Adige River

VILLEMPENTA

ROVIGO (4 miles)

BARDIA

BOLOGNA (45 miles)

BORGOFORTE

Po River

ITALIAN CAMPAIGNS, 1796-97

WÜRMSER'S FIRST ADVANCE

Situation at Dark, 31 July 1796

SCALE OF MILES

MAP 15: WÜRMSER'S FIRST ADVANCE

On 2 August, Würmser became concerned over not having heard from Quas-danovich, and ordered Liptay to cross the Mincio at Goito (*B1*). Mean-while, he occupied himself by gathering such siege equipment as Serurier had not been able to destroy at Mantua, and began to arrange revictualing of the city. Not until the next morning did he start his main forces in the footsteps of Liptay.

The latter had pushed on toward Castiglione, where Valette stood with specific instructions from Bonaparte to hold the town at all cost. However, on the unfortunate advice of Augereau, Valette precipitately abandoned his post; Liptay thereupon occupied the town in force. Bonaparte was furious, and summarily relieved Valette. For a moment, he considered continuing the withdrawal—which a number of his generals approved—to gain more maneuver room. However, Augereau urged a fight, and the troops were enthusiastic. There are many stories that Bonaparte lost his nerve and was only sustained by Augereau's superior hardihood. These are undoubtedly false, for the orders subsequently issued by Bonaparte were too exact and logical to be those of a rattled man. (It is not unusual that in a crisis the subordinate appears more composed and optimistic than the commander. The responsibility is not his, nor is he fully aware of the over-all implications. But let the commander be absent and the full impact of decision descend upon the subordinate, and his confidence often evaporates.) Nevertheless, Bonaparte's morale was probably helped by Augereau's rough bravado. Finally, upon learning that the enemy force in Castiglione was only an advance guard, Bonaparte decided to attack Quasdanovich, while containing Liptay.

On the north flank, Guieu was to move up from Desenzano toward Salo, thus threatening Quasdanovich's line of communication; Despinoy (rein-forced by part of Lanusse's column) was to advance from Brescia against Gavardo. Both were to attack on the morning of 3 August. Massena was to move that morning from Calcinato to Lonato to form a central reserve. At the same time, Augereau, reinforced by Kilmaine, was to attack Castiglione to contain Würmser.

At about noon on 2 August, Quasdanovich (at Gavardo) received Würm-ser's message announcing his proposed advance across the Mincio that day, and decided that he had better begin moving to unite with Würmser. His advance (*only Ocskay shown*) was in three columns, which were to con-verge on Castiglione on the 3d: Ocskay marched on Desenzano; Ott came down the east bank of the Chiese toward Ponte San Marco; and Quasdano-vich himself, with Spork and Reuss, followed the west bank, aiming at Monte-chiaro (*all A2*). This march was soon disrupted. Ocskay, following the lake shore south, missed Guieu, who was following the mountain road to the west toward Salo. Ott, following the river, saw Guieu, concluded that Ocskay had been defeated, and bolted back to Gavardo, where he warned Quas-danovich. This general halted and dispatched Reuss, with a small force (*not shown*), to find Ocskay. Meanwhile, Ocskay had reached Desenzano, found it deserted, and halted there for the night.

The day of 3 August was, by all accounts, extremely hot. Ocskay moved early, heading for Lonato. Reaching that town, he surprised and routed Massena's advance guard. Then, seeing Massena's main body coming up, he formed up west of Lonato, extending his left flank in an attempt to con-tact Liptay, whom he knew was in the Castiglione area. Massena (11,500) immediately smashed Ocskay's center by a massed assault by Victor's brigade, and pushed cavalry through the gap in pursuit. Ocskay, badly broken, was almost enveloped. At the critical moment, Reuss—who seems at least to have possessed the soldierly virtue of marching to the sound of the guns—came up to cover the withdrawal of Ocskay's battered forces toward Salo and Gavardo. Meanwhile, Guieu and Despinoy, debouching from Salo and the Brescia area respectively, had attacked Quasdanovich at Gavardo. After initial success, Despinoy was seized by an "uncomprehensible inquietude," and retired suddenly on Brescia. Thus relieved, Quasdanovich turned on Guieu and drove him back on Salo, where he attempted to corner him. But that night, Quasdanovich heard of Ocskay's rout, leaped to the conclusion that Würmser had been defeated in his attempt to cross the Mincio, and ordered an immediate retreat to the Tyrol.

During this time, Augereau attacked Liptay, who had taken up a strong position straddling Castiglione. Augereau feinted at the strongly posted Aus-trian right, attacked the center, and enveloped the left, meanwhile holding out a sizable reserve. He was supported by artillery, under Bonaparte's aide, Marmont, borrowed for the occasion. After a hard fight, complicated by a lack of water, Augereau drove Liptay back on the hills east of the town. There, however, Liptay, reinforced by a small force under Schübirz (which had marched from Cavriana [*A2*]), made a stubborn stand, hoping to hold until Würmser came up. Not until Kilmaine's division came into line and Augereau committed his reserves against the Austrian left did Liptay with-draw from the field.

On that day (3 August), Würmser had crossed the Mincio in the late morning at Goito, and had reached Guidizzolo by noon. By then, his troops were fatigued and could advance only a scant three miles farther. There, he took up a position to support Liptay.

That night, in the Castiglione area, the French and Austrian armies bivouacked about two miles apart.

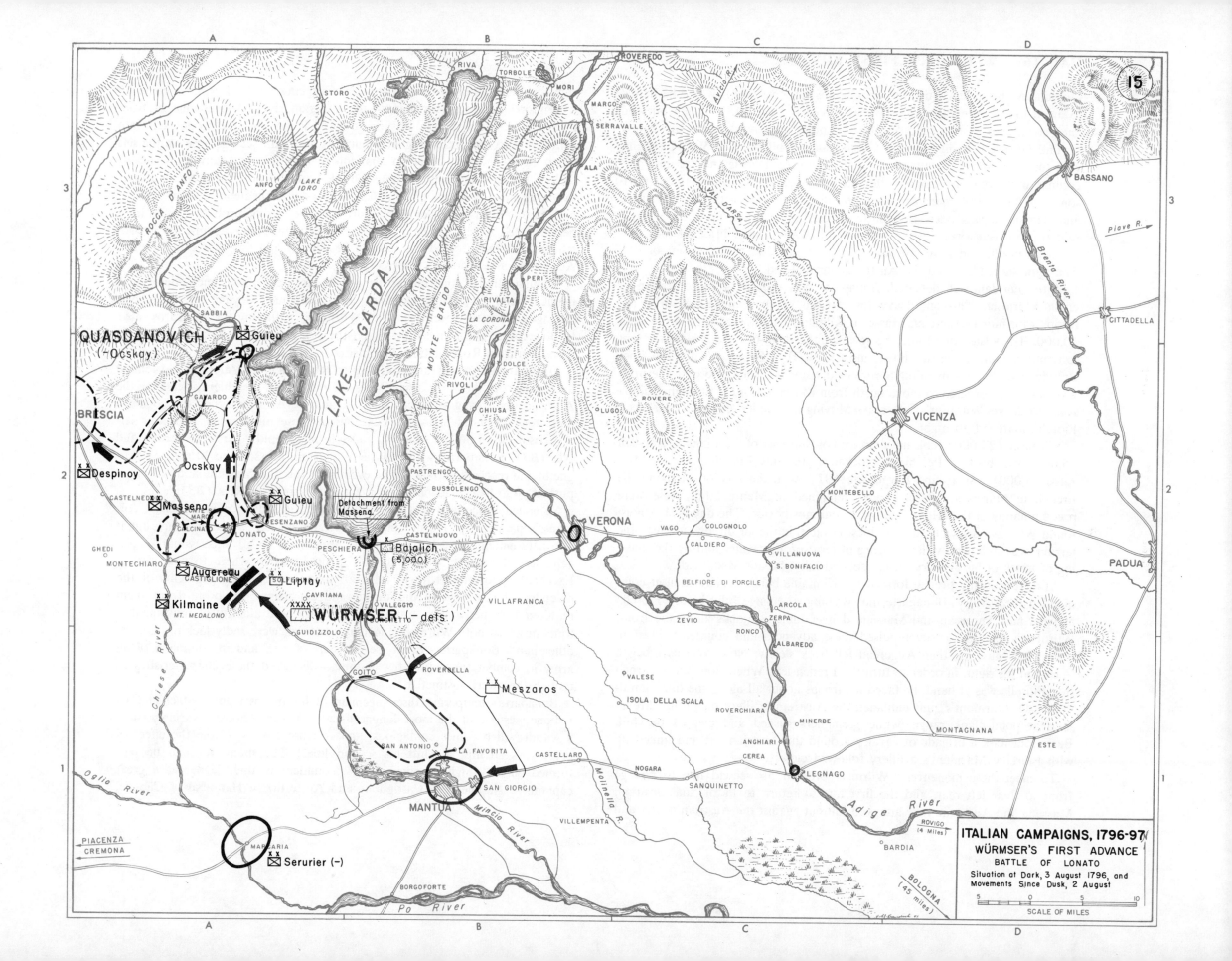

15

RIVA
TORBOLE
MORI
ROVEREDO
STORO
MARCO
SERRAVALLE
ALA
ANFO
LAKE
IDRO
ROCCA D'ANFO
SABBIA
PERI
VAL D'ARSA
Avisio R.
Piave R.
BASSANO
CITTADELLA
MONTE BALDO
LA CORONA
RIVALTA
DOLCE
RIVOLI
CHIUSA
PESCHIERA
LUGO
ROVERE
QUASDANOVICH
(−Ocskay)
⊠ Guieu

GAVARDO
BRESCIA
Ocskay
⊠ Despinoy

⊠ Massena
CASTELNEDO
MARCO
CALCINATO
LONATO
⊠ Guieu
PASTRENGO
BUSSOLENGO
CASTELNUOVO
Detachment from Massena.
Bajalich
(5,000)
⊠

VERONA
VAGO
COLOGNOLO
CALDIERO
MONTEBELLO
VILLANUOVA
S. BONIFACIO
VICENZA
ARCOLA
ZERPA
Brenta River

GHEDI
MONTECHIARO
⊠ Augereau
CASTIGLIONE
⊠ Kilmaine
MT. MEDALONO
GUIDIZZOLO
⊠ Liptay
50
CAVRIANA
VALEGGIO
VILLAFRANCA
WÜRMSER (−dets.)
XXXX
Chiese River

GOITO
ROVERBELLA
⊠ Meszaros
VALESE
ISOLA DELLA SCALA
ROVERCHIARA
RONCO
ALBAREDO
ZEVIO
ANGHIARI
CEREA
MINERBE
MONTAGNANA
ESTE
LEGNAGO

SAN ANTONIO
LA FAVORITA
CASTELLARO
NOGARA
SANQUINETTO
Molinella R.
SAN GIORGIO
MANTUA
Mincio River
VILLEMPENTA
Adige River
ROVIGO
(4 Miles)
BARDIA

PIACENZA
CREMONA
Oglio River

⊠ Serurier (−)
MARCARIA

BORGOFORTE
Po River
BOLOGNA
(45 miles)

ITALIAN CAMPAIGNS, 1796-97
WÜRMSER'S FIRST ADVANCE
BATTLE OF LONATO
Situation at Dark, 3 August 1796, and
Movements Since Dusk, 2 August

SCALE OF MILES
5   0   5   10

Quasdanovich, on 4 August, fell back almost to Riva (*B3*), where he halted to await events, keeping an outpost at Rocca d'Anfo (*A3*). Guieu pursued energetically to just beyond Sabbia. Despinoy advanced north to slightly beyond Gavardo. In his pursuit, Guieu had cut off about 2,500 Austrians, who turned south in an attempt to join Würmser. During the evening, this column wandered into Lonato, the site of Bonaparte's headquarters, garrisoned by only 1,000 men. An Austrian officer appeared with a flag of truce and demanded surrender. Bonaparte successfully worked up a fit of rage, said the Austrians were in the midst of his whole army, branded the summons an insult, and gave the Austrians eight minutes to surrender, or die. The bluff succeeded, and the Austrians surrendered.

With Quasdanovich defeated, Bonaparte now ordered a concentration to crush Würmser. Through heavy losses from combat and exhaustion, the troops with him (Augereau, Massena, Kilmaine) numbered little more than 20,000. To bolster this force, he recalled the demi-brigade previously sent to reinforce Guieu, and summoned most (5,000) of Despinoy's division from Brescia. Fiorella, commanding Serurier's division, now about 5,000 (Serurier was sick), was ordered to move north from Marcaria (*A1*), through Guidizzolo, to strike Würmser's left rear. Moving off under cover of darkness, Fiorella marched all night.

Würmser (24,000) took up a strong position east of Castiglione. Bajalich (5,000) was back at Peschiera, blockading the tiny French garrison; Meszaros (5,000) was around Borgoforte (*B1*), with the mission of fixing the French at Marcaria; 10,000 troops remained in Mantua, but these were predominantly of the original garrison, and mostly sick. The day of 5 August found Würmser drawn up in two lines. His left, in the air on low, unfavorable terrain, was stiffened by the presence of most of his cavalry and by the massing of much of his artillery on an isolated hill—Mount Medalono.

At daybreak, the French formed up. Kilmaine being sick, Beaumont commanded the cavalry. Bonaparte, not wishing to engage fully before Fiorella arrived, had Augereau and Massena deliver limited attacks along the front. Würmser's first line easily repulsed these advances and counterattacked in turn. First Massena, then Augereau fell back slowly. Now, Würmser began to extend his right, in order to turn the French left. When Bonaparte learned that Fiorella was at hand, he faced his troops about all along the line. Simultaneously, Marmont's guns enfiladed the Austrian artillery on Mount Medalono at point-blank range, while grenadiers rushed and cleared the hill. Beaumont took a brigade of cavalry around the Austrian left and linked up with Fiorella; Marmont's artillery followed closely.

To meet these maneuvers, Würmser ordered his second line to change front to their left rear, and the first line to return to its original position. Massena and Augereau now attacked full-out against the Austrian center and right, while Fiorella drove hard toward Cavriana (*A2*). Despinoy came up to reinforce Massena, threatening the Austrian right. The change of front of Würmser's second line was made too hastily, and the troops fell into confusion. Troops on the higher ground to the right, seeing those on the left fall back in disorder, began to abandon their positions. Many units, nevertheless, fought splendidly. Despite the odds and his advanced age, Würmser displayed great qualities of battlefield leadership, repeatedly charging at the head of his cavalry to cover the withdrawal. Even so, he probably would have been trapped, except for Bajalich's vigorous counterattack against the French left (made after a forced march from Peschiera) and the utter exhaustion of Augereau's and Fiorella's troops.

Though all the Austrian artillery was captured, the French victory remained incomplete. Only Despinoy advanced much beyond the battlefield, getting almost to Peschiera. But Würmser, gathering in Meszaros near Goito, crossed the Mincio, destroyed the bridges behind him, and took up a position from Roverbella to Peschiera.

On 6 August, Augereau moved up to the Mincio at Valeggio and feinted a crossing. At the same time, Massena moved on Peschiera, defeated the Austrians there, and advanced on Castelnuovo. Augereau then turned north and crossed behind Massena. Learning of these movements, Würmser left a garrison of 15,000 in Mantua, and fell back rapidly through Verona and Ala (*B3*). Bonaparte, with Serurier's division, crossed the Mincio at Borghetto and reached Verona on the evening of the 7th. Massena and Augereau pushed on to Roveredo (*B3*), Sauret and Despinoy to Riva (*B3*).

So ended Würmser's first offensive. His initial advance in dispersed columns, separated by high mountains and Lake Garda, was dangerous, but it also held enticing possibilities. In that area, such an advance would keep a defender off balance, dispersed, and in doubt as to where to concentrate. Excellent opportunities might arise to isolate and destroy segments of the defender's force. Several did during the campaign. To profit from them required keen perception, firmness of purpose, and alacrity of movement—traits in which both Würmser and Quasdanovich were sadly lacking. On the other hand, Bonaparte—twenty-seven years of age, and in command of an army in combat for only a few months—displayed these characteristics as though they were instinctive.

Bonaparte's temporary disengagement of his troops from contact at Castiglione was one of the most dangerous acts in war. Almost invariably, such a withdrawal becomes contagious, and collapse ensues. (Note the effect of Würmser's attempt to shift his second line.) The maneuver can be performed only by highly trained troops, confident in their leader as a great captain—a Napoleon of Castiglione and Austerlitz, a Hannibal of Cannae.

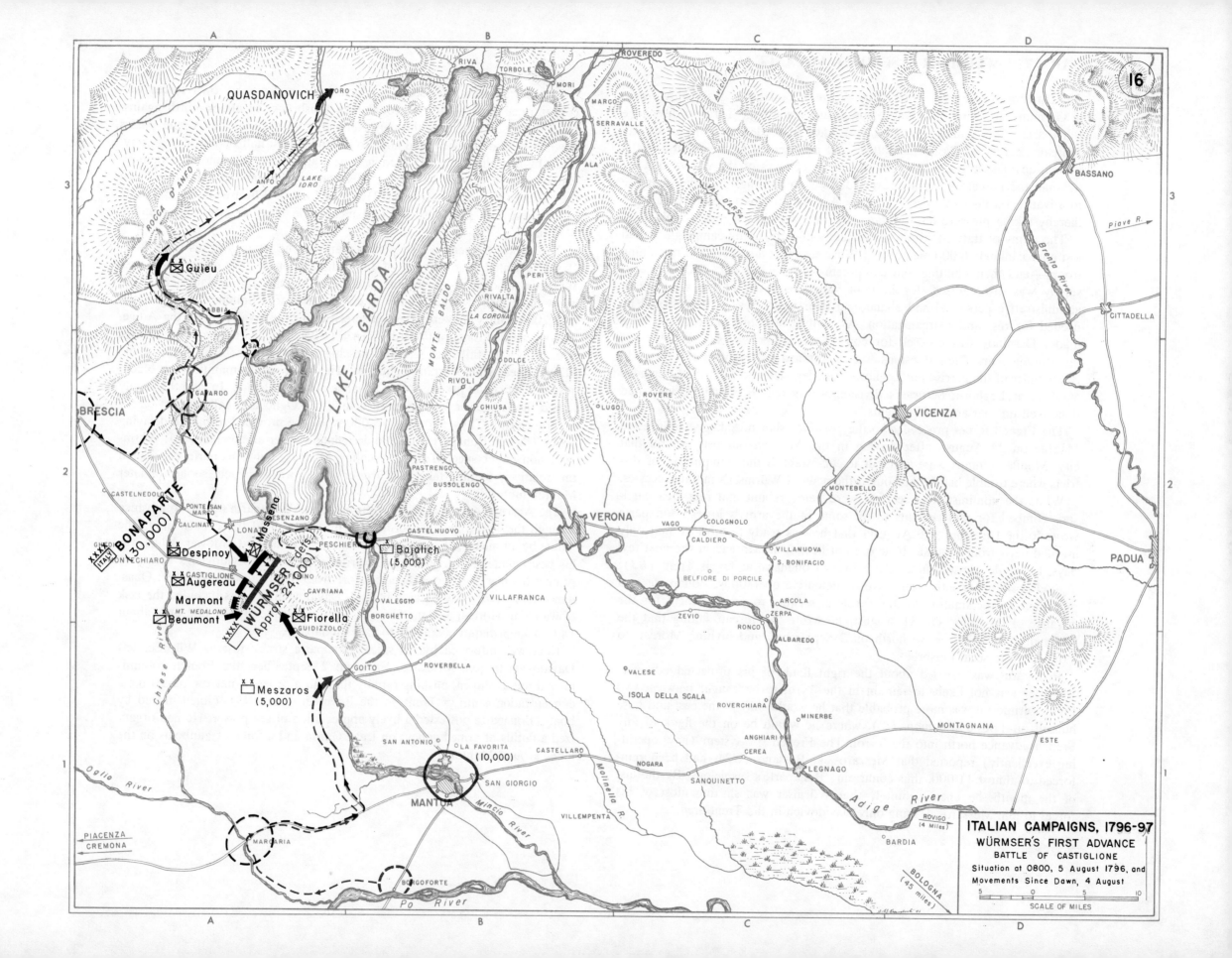

QUASDANOVICH

16

RIVA
TORBOLE
MORI
ROVEREDO

Piave R.

RIVA
MARCO
SERRAVALLE
ALA

Avicio R.

Val d'Arsa

BASSANO

⊠ Guieu

ROCCA D'ANFO
ANFO
LAKE IDRO

LAKE GARDA

PERI

PESCANTINA

MONTE BALDO

LA CORONA
RIVALTA

DOLCE

RIVOLI

CHIUSA

LUGO
ROVERE

Brenta River

CITTADELLA

VICENZA

GAVARDO

BRESCIA

MONTEBELLO

PASTRENGO

BUSSOLENGO

CASTELNUOVO

VERONA

VAGO
CALDIERO
COLOGNOLO

VILLANUOVA
S. BONIFACIO

PADUA

CASTELNEDOLO

PONTE SAN MARCO

BONAPARTE
(30,000)

Massena
CALCINATO
LONATO
DESENZANO

PESCHIERA

⊠ Bajalich
(5,000)

XXXX
ITALY
MONTECHIARO

⊠ Despinoy

⊠ Augereau
CASTIGLIONE

Marmont
MT. MEDALONO

⊠ Beaumont

WÜRMSER (deis.)
(Approx. 24,000)

SOLFERINO

CAVRIANA

VALEGGIO
BORGHETTO

VILLAFRANCA

BELFIORE DI PORCILE

ARCOLA
ZERPA
ZEVIO
RONCO
ALBAREDO

⊠ Fiorella
GUIDIZZOLO

GOITO
ROVERBELLA

VALESE

ISOLA DELLA SCALA

ROVERCHIARA
MINERBE

MONTAGNANA

ESTE

XX
Meszaros
(5,000)

Chiese River

Oglio River

PIACENZA
CREMONA

MARCARIA

SAN ANTONIO

LA FAVORITA
(10,000)

CASTELLARO

Molinella R.

NOGARA

SANQUINETTO

CEREA

LEGNAGO

SAN GIORGIO

Mincio River

VILLEMPENTA

ANGHIARI

Adige River

ROVIGO
(4 miles)

BARDIA

MANTUA

BORGOFORTE

Po River

BOLOGNA
(45 miles)

ITALIAN CAMPAIGNS, 1796-97
WÜRMSER'S FIRST ADVANCE
BATTLE OF CASTIGLIONE
Situation at 0800, 5 August 1796, and
Movements Since Dawn, 4 August

5 0   5   10
SCALE OF MILES

The Directory had been frightened by Würmser's offensive. It urged Moreau, in Germany, to swing his advance southward toward the Tyrol to disengage Bonaparte. This panicky, spontaneous idea succeeded only in confusing Moreau (never too elastic mentally), and contributed to the failure of the French advance into Germany. With receipt of news of the victory of Castiglione, the Directory rapidly reversed itself and strongly urged Bonaparte to advance through the Tyrol to draw Austrian troops to protect Bavaria, thereby taking pressure off Jourdan, who had got himself into trouble.

The Army of Italy could not immediately undertake any campaign. It had lost approximately 6,000 men during Würmser's first advance. The remaining troops—and their clothing and equipment—were worn out. The service of supply was disorganized, for in tight situations many of the semicivilian administrative personnel had abandoned their posts. Several days would be needed for rest and reorganization. A number of command changes were made: Despinoy was relieved for cowardice, Sauret was sick and so was sent to the rear. Their divisions were combined under Vaubois, formerly commander of the garrison at Leghorn. Serurier, sick and exhausted, replaced Vaubois at Leghorn; Serurier's division was given to Sahuguet, who had done well on rear-area assignments.

The French forces proceeded to the positions shown. Sahuguet reinvested Mantua on 24 August, after driving in the Austrian outposts around that city. Mobile columns were sent out to "re-establish the tranquillity" of districts where trouble had broken out at the news of Würmser's initial successes.

While the administrative services were being rebuilt and rear-area garrisons combed for replacements to fill some of the army's losses, Bonaparte wrote to the Directory (26 August) that he was ready to advance and only awaited news from Moreau. If he did not hear from Moreau in the next few days, he would himself undertake a limited offensive as far as Trent (B3), a good position for either offensive or defensive operations. Bonaparte also published a proclamation to the Tyrolese, seeking to prepare them for the advance of his army. On 31 August, he wrote to Moreau stating that the Army of Italy would move north on 2 September, and inviting Moreau to move south to seize Innsbrück.

Bonaparte was worried about the right flank of his projected advance. Würmser was not likely to remain in the Tyrol to be caught between two French armies; it was more probable that he would shift to the east and base himself on Trieste (off map, D2), where he would be on the flank of any French advance north into the Tyrol. The French spy system (now operating excellently) reported that Meszaros, at Bassano (C2), had been reinforced to almost 11,000, thus confirming Bonaparte's suspicions. By the last of the month, he knew definitely that Würmser was shifting most of his forces to join Meszaros, leaving only Davidovich in the Trent area.

Bonaparte's plan now seems to have been to keep his own forces well concentrated and, if Moreau could take Innsbrück, to attack north against Davidovich, driving him through Neumarkt (B3) and the Alpine passes beyond. In so doing, he could hope to cripple almost half of Würmser's army. Also, by first eliminating Davidovich, he could secure his line of communication through Brescia to Milan. This done, the French could strike down the valley of the Brenta River (C2), either forcing Würmser back on Trieste or catching him in rear if he had meanwhile tried to advance again on Mantua.

The critical element in Bonaparte's plan was the security of his right flank. It was essential that the line of the Adige be held long enough—in case Würmser attacked it—to enable Bonaparte to take appropriate action and allow the troops around Mantua to escape disaster. Kilmaine had a garrison of 1,200 infantry in Verona and a screen of 1,600 cavalry along the Adige, with scouts well forward toward Vicenza (C2). If forced to give up the Adige line, he was to fall back through Peschiera (B1) to the west bank of the Mincio, meanwhile warning Sahuguet. The latter would maintain the blockade of Mantua and place a strong advance post at Legnago. In case the enemy forced the Adige, he was to retire behind the Oglio and call on Serviez for reinforcements. Thus, a total of 15,000 would be provided to fight a delaying action (though Bonaparte failed to designate an over-all commander). Würmser again might succeed in revictualing Mantua, but Bonaparte considered this relatively unimportant; if Würmser's army was defeated, sooner or later Mantua must fall.

The Austrian government had information of Bonaparte's plans to advance through the Tyrol, and had ordered Würmser to hold the French along the Adige by all means. He had decided an offensive along the lower Adige was his best counterstroke. Placing unwarranted trust in Davidovich's ability to protect his rear, he started Sebottendorf from Trent on 1 September; Quasdanovich moved a day's march behind. Davidovich's orders included the task of watching Moreau and the Swiss frontier; consequently, he had only about 14,000 immediately available to face Bonaparte.

Kept well informed by his spies, Bonaparte struck just as Würmser left Davidovich to join Meszaros. Early on 2 September, the French columns moved out as shown, pushing rapidly through a series of narrow passes for a concentration south of Trent, in the Roveredo area (B3). Guieu moved by boat. (Bonaparte possessed a lively appreciation of sea power. He had organized a flotilla of armed galleys on Lake Garda and a force of gunboats on the lakes around Mantua.)

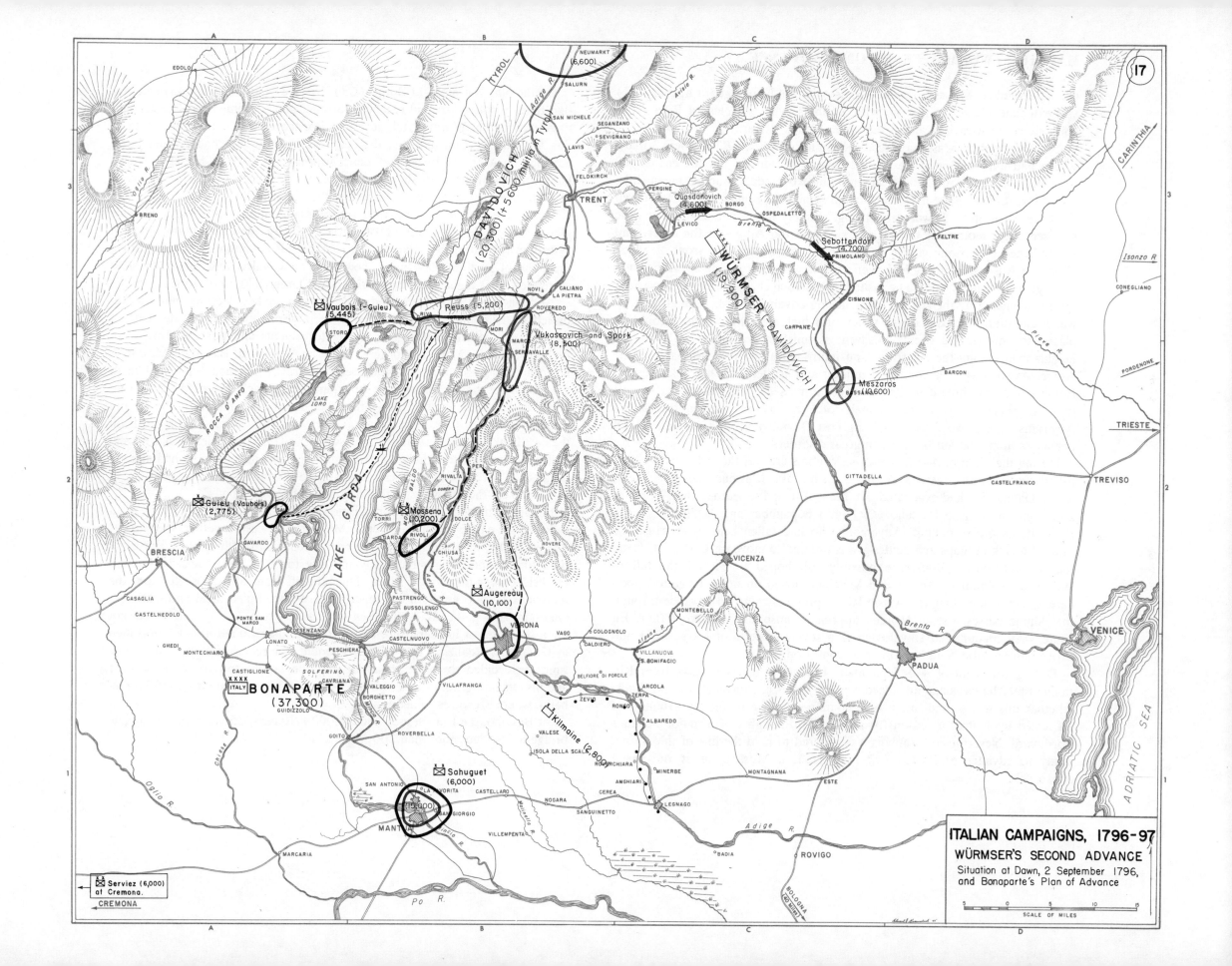

EDOLO

BRENO

OGLIO R.

NEUMARKT
(6,600)

TYROL

SALURN

DAVIDOVICH (20,300)(+5,600 militia in Tyrol)

SAN MICHELE

SEGANZANO

SEVIGNANO

LAVIS

FELDKIRCH

TRENT

PERGINE

Quosdanovich
(4,600)

BORGO

LEVICO

Brenta R.

OSPEDALETTO

CISMONE

CARINTHIA

Isonzo R.

Sebottendorf
(4,700)

PRIMOLANO

FELTRE

CONEGLIANO

CHIESE R.

LAKE IDRO

ROCCA D'ANFO

Vaubois (-Guieu)
(5,445)

STORO

Reuss (5,200)

RIVA

MORI

MARCO

SERRAVALLE

NOVI

CALIANO

LA PIETRA

ROVEREDO

Vukassovich and Spork
(8,500)

XXXX
WÜRMSER
(19,900)

WÜRMSER (19,900) (DAVIDOVICH)

CARPANE

Piave R.

BARCON

Meszaros
Bass (10,600)

PORDENONE

TRIESTE

CASAGLIA

CASTELNEDOLO

Guieu (Vaubois)
(2,775)

GAVARDO

BRESCIA

PONTE SAN MARCO

DESENZANO

LONATO

LAKE GARDA

BALDO

TORRI

GARDA

RIVALTA

LA CORONA

PERI

DOLCE

Massena
(10,200)

RIVOLI

CHIUSA

ROVERE

VICENZA

MONTEBELLO

Brenta R.

CITTADELLA

CASTELFRANCO

TREVISO

VENICE

GHEDI

MONTECHIARO

CASTIGLIONE
XXXX
ITALY
BONAPARTE
(37,300)

SOLFERINO

CAVRIANA

CASTELNUOVO

PASTRENGO

BUSSOLENGO

Augereau
(10,100)

VERONA

VAGO

COLOGNOLO

CALDIERO

Alpone R.

VILLANUOVA

S. BONIFACIO

ARCOLA

PADUA

GUIDIZZOLO

VALEGGIO

BORGHETTO

VILLAFRANCA

MINCIO R.

GOITO

ROVERBELLA

ZEVIO

ZERPA

RONCO

ALBAREDO

Kilmaine (2,800)

VALESE

ISOLA DELLA SCALA

PORCHIARA

MINERBE

MONTAGNANA

ESTE

ADRIATIC SEA

OGLIO R.

MARCARIA

SAN ANTONIO

LA FAVORITA

Sahuguet
(6,000)

CASTELLARO

NOGARA

CEREA

ANGHIARI

SANGIORGIO

(15,000)

MANTUA

VILLEMPENTA

Molinella R.

SANGUINETTO

Adige R.

BADIA

ROVIGO

Po R.

Tartaro R.

LEGNAGO

BOLOGNA
(TO MIRT)

ITALIAN CAMPAIGNS, 1796-97
WÜRMSER'S SECOND ADVANCE
Situation at Dawn, 2 September 1796,
and Bonaparte's Plan of Advance

SCALE OF MILES

Serviez (6,000)
at Cremona.

CREMONA

17

On 3 September, Massena routed Vukassovich's advance guard at Ala (*B2*) and extended his left to link up with Vaubois, who had cleared Riva (*B3*) and driven the Austrians across the upper Mincio River.

On 4 September, Massena forced the defile of Marco (*B2*), where Vukassovich had dug in. Bonaparte pushed cavalry in pursuit, but the enemy fell back in good order on Caliano, abandoning Roveredo. Vaubois, meanwhile, took Mori. Letting Massena's men snatch some rest, Bonaparte reconnoitered the Caliano position. It was very strong, scarcely more than 100 yards wide between sheer mountains on the one side and the Adige on the other, and strengthened by a stone village and a strong, old chateau, in front of which all of the Austrian artillery had been massed. Bonaparte judged the position impregnable—unless it could be rushed by a sudden charge while the Austrians were still shaken by the sight of their fleeing advance guard. A small plateau was found along the edge of the valley on which eight French guns could be placed to enfilade the enemy position; skirmishers scrambled up onto the heights overlooking the Austrians and infiltrated along the east bank of the Adige. As soon as their combined musket and artillery fire had taken effect, Bonaparte threw three demi-brigades into a massed charge which, in furious fighting, swept the position. A small force of cavalry pursued the fleeing Austrians. These two days of fighting cost Davidovich 6,000 casualties and twenty cannon, and left his army in great disorder.

During the night of 4–5 September, Vaubois crossed the Adige and established contact with Massena. At 0800 on the 5th, Massena occupied Trent, which Davidovich had evacuated. At Trent, Bonaparte learned that Würmser had begun moving to Bassano (*C2*) on 1 September and, without losing a moment, set out in pursuit. Augereau, who had fallen behind—because, he said, of a lack of maps and guides—was ordered to move on Levico (*C3*) by the shortest route. (Bonaparte possibly still hoped to cut off the tail of Würmser's column.) Vaubois and Massena moved on north to gain a good defensive position along the Avisio River, preparatory to an advance through the Alpine passes, should Moreau approach Innsbrück (*off map, B3*). En route, they encountered Davidovich in a strong position at Lavis (*B3*) and drove him back on Neumarkt in great confusion.

During the night of 4–5 September, Bonaparte received news from Kilmaine that Meszaros had advanced west of Vicenza. Bonaparte did not know whether this was an indication of a coming offensive or merely a feint, but he seized upon it as a reason for abandoning thoughts of a major advance northward. Nevertheless, Vaubois was ordered to hold the line of the Avisio, ready to advance to Botzen (*off map, B3*), if Moreau finally did reach Innsbrück.

On the 5th, Würmser, at Borgo (*C3*), learned of Bonaparte's advance. By that time, Sebottendorf had reached Bassano, and it seemed too late for him to countermarch. Würmser felt sure that Bonaparte would continue north to link up with Moreau, and that the best way to draw him back would be to advance on Mantua. Instead of concentrating, he ordered Meszaros (who had been sent forward to Vicenza to cover his advance) to attack Verona at once; meanwhile, he largely disregarded the threat to his own rear.

During the morning of the 7th, Lanusse, commanding Augereau's advance guard, struck three battalions of Croats (2,000 men, ten guns), which Würmser had left at Primolano (*C3*) to cover his communications. He drove them out of position, enveloped them with his cavalry, and forced them to surrender. That night, the weary French had largely closed up to Cismone.

Also on the 7th, Meszaros' advance guard attacked Verona, but was repulsed by Kilmaine. Meszaros then took position about two miles east of Verona, and called on Würmser for reinforcements and pontons. Instead of sending support, Würmser ordered him back toward Bassano. Meszaros, however, never got beyond Montebello. Würmser reached Bassano late in the evening of the 7th. Warned of Bonaparte's approach, he could think of no better action than to post strong rear guards on both banks of the Brenta north of Bassano, backed by Quasdanovich on a hill about a mile north on the east bank, and Sebottendorf in Bassano itself. At the time, he had barely 7,000 men immediately in hand. According to some accounts, he had already decided to retreat, and had sent his baggage off toward Cittadella (*C2*); it is more likely that he was still thinking and acting too slowly.

Bonaparte moved forward from Cismone at 0200 on 8 September. Augereau followed the east bank of the Brenta, Massena the west; together, their forces totaled 20,000 men. Both struck the enemy rear guards, flung them down the road to Bassano, fought their way into the town at their heels, and seized the bridge over the Brenta River. Thus cut off from Meszaros' division, the Austrians, despite stubborn resistance, were whipped piecemeal and scattered. Quasdanovich gathered 3,000 men at Castelfranco (*D2*), and stood not upon the order of his departure eastward. Würmser rallied about 1,000 men at Cittadella. Realizing that Meszaros could not reach him there for some time, he decided to move ahead to join the latter, and to throw himself and his remaining troops into Mantua. A forced march brought him to Montebello, where Meszaros joined him.

At Bassano, the French took some 3,000 prisoners, 35 cannon, 2 complete bridge trains, and more than 200 wagons.

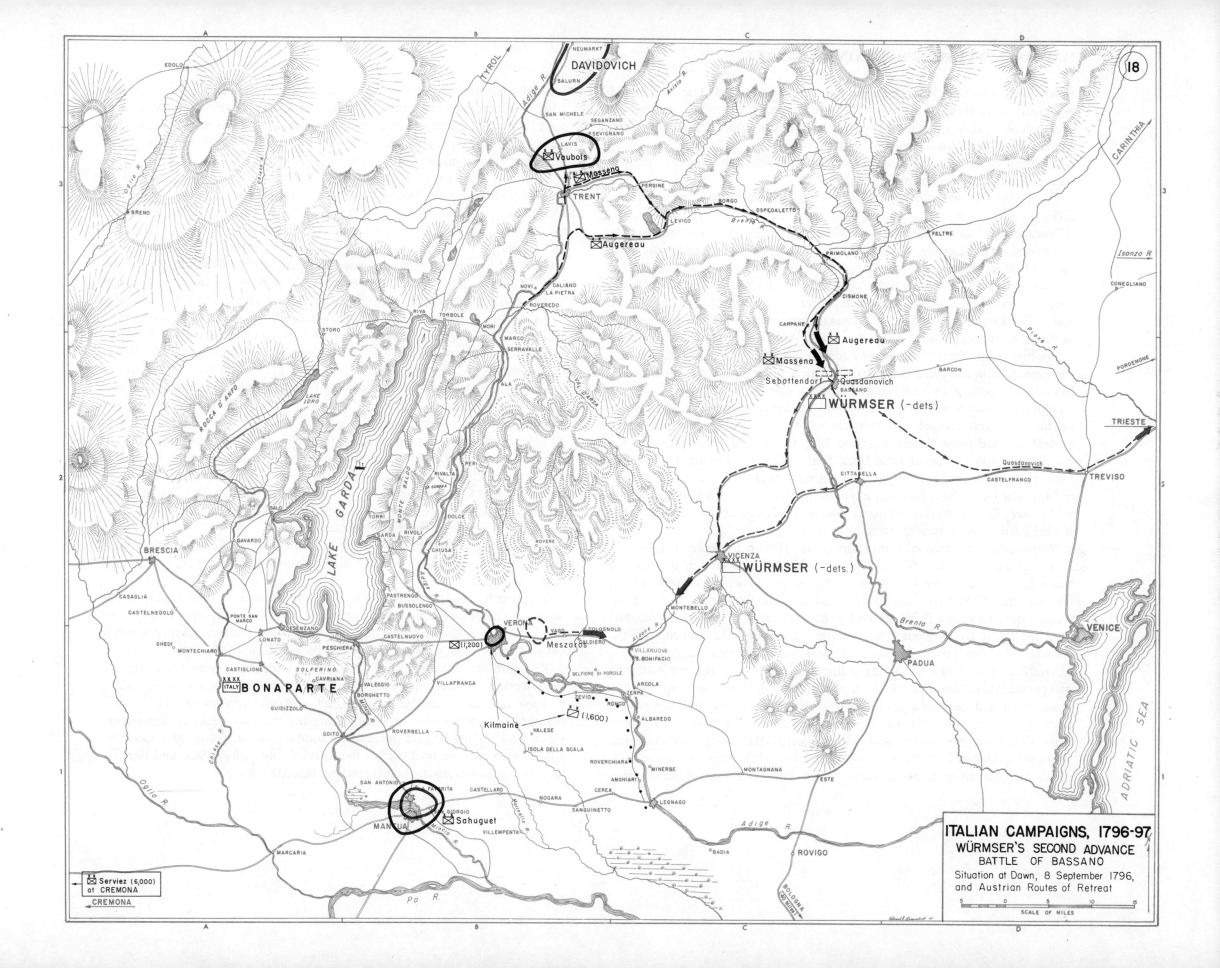

ITALIAN CAMPAIGNS, 1796-97
WÜRMSER'S SECOND ADVANCE
BATTLE OF BASSANO
Situation at Dawn, 8 September 1796,
and Austrian Routes of Retreat

Bonaparte, expecting Würmser to break eastward toward Trieste, ordered Augereau south through Padua (*D1*) to cut him off. Massena, meanwhile, was to push straight for Vicenza to maintain pressure on the retreating Austrians. His advance guard reached Vicenza during the night of 8 September; his division had marched about 100 miles and fought three battles—besides numerous minor engagements—in four days.

On the 9th, Augereau occupied Padua, Massena pushed toward San Bonifacio, and Würmser headed for Legnago (*C1*). Having lost his bridge trains, Würmser would have to seize a bridge over the Adige. Verona was strongly garrisoned, so the Legnago bridge seemed a logical choice. Würmser did have some 3,000 good cavalry. These seized the ferry at Albaredo and crossed two squadrons, which came down the west bank to reconnoiter Legnago. Here, they surprised and sabered some of the French garrison caught outside the walls. The French commander at Legnago, amazed to find Austrian cavalry in his rear, excitedly decided that the whole Austrian army had crossed the Adige higher up. Further alarmed by rumors among the local population that the French main army had been badly defeated, he promptly retreated toward Mantua—*forgetting, in his fright and haste, to destroy the Legnago bridge.*

Würmser, with some 10,000 to 12,000 exhausted men, reached Legnago on the 10th and crossed the river during the day. Meanwhile, Augereau pushed forward from Padua, reaching Este (*C1*), and Bonaparte directed Kilmaine to concentrate at Isola Della Scala (*B1*) and construct an improvised bridge at Ronco for Massena's division. Serviez was to advance rapidly to Marcaria (*A1*); Sahuguet was to guard the crossing of the Molinella River (*B1*). Very late in the day, Massena crossed the Adige at Ronco, apparently having been delayed by a shortage of boats.

Würmser finally departed from Legnago at 1100 on 11 September, leaving a rear guard of about 1,600 to delay pursuit. Always best in disaster, he seems to have been able to inspirit his beaten troops with something of his own hardihood. At Cerea, his advance guard, under Ott, struck that of Massena, under Murat and Pijon, which had been aiming for Sanguinetto but had been led astray by its guide. Ott's men broke through the French, and the Austrian columns pressed onward. Massena, with his men staggering from exhaustion, arrived on the morning of the 12th, only to find that the Austrians had passed. He followed resolutely in pursuit, but could not catch up.

Sahuguet had been charged to guard—and, if necessary, to destroy—the bridges over the Molinella. He, however, had concerned himself with those from Castellaro northward, and had neglected the bridges downstream. Würmser feinted at Castellaro, swung south, crossed the river at Villempenta, where he overran a do-or-die stand by an isolated French battalion that

Sahuguet had rushed—too late—to defend the Villempenta bridge. On the 13th, Würmser entered Mantua with more than 10,000 men and several hundred French prisoners, who had been picked up en route from Legnago. That same day, Legnago capitulated to Augereau, who then went on the sick list, after turning over his division to Bon.

Würmser, feeling more self-confident, now attempted to hold as wide an area as possible around Mantua, in order to subsist his troops. He had some 28,000 men, probably 18,000 to 20,000 of whom were fit, or could be spared, for service in the field. Thus, at the moment, he was almost as strong as Bonaparte, many of whose men had straggled from exhaustion. Bonaparte, on the other hand, wanted to hold Würmser as tightly within Mantua as possible, both to ensure that hunger and disease would shorten the siege, and to pen up the Austrians to prevent them from interfering with his future operations.

As a result of these conflicting aims, a series of clashes took place around Mantua. On 13 September, Würmser assaulted Sahuguet, driving him northward from La Favorita (*B1*). On the 14th, Massena advanced from the northeast, but was checked. Würmser, on the 15th, full of confidence, moved out to the east with most of his available forces, only to be trapped by Bonaparte. Massena, in the center, fell back, enticing Würmser forward; then Sahuguet closed in from the north and Bon from the south, largely masked by rolling terrain. Bon drove hard; Würmser shifted troops from his center to his right to stop him, whereupon Massena abruptly came down on the weakened center, seizing San Giorgio and splitting the Austrian army. The Austrian right was finally driven in by Bon, but Sahuguet failed to charge home against the Austrian left. Even so, Würmser lost some 4,000 men and twenty-five cannon during his short-lived sortie.

(Concurrently, Bonaparte learned that the major offensive of Jourdan and Moreau into Germany—which his operations had been designed to support—had been defeated.)

Würmser had approximately 24,000 men in Mantua, of whom some 9,000 were sick; rations were short, the water foul; 150 men a day were falling ill or dying. Confined almost within the city limits and without grazing ground, cavalry horses were starving and had to be killed for food.

Kilmaine, an "old army" man and thus presumably having knowledge of siege work, was placed in command of the siege force (originally Serurier's division, now temporarily under Sahuguet, and reinforced to 9,000). Numerous Austrian sorties were repulsed during the last two weeks of September. For a while, Würmser held the outlying southern suburbs, but, on 1 October, Kilmaine forced him back within the fortified city proper. Sick and hungry, the Austrians remained almost inactive through October.

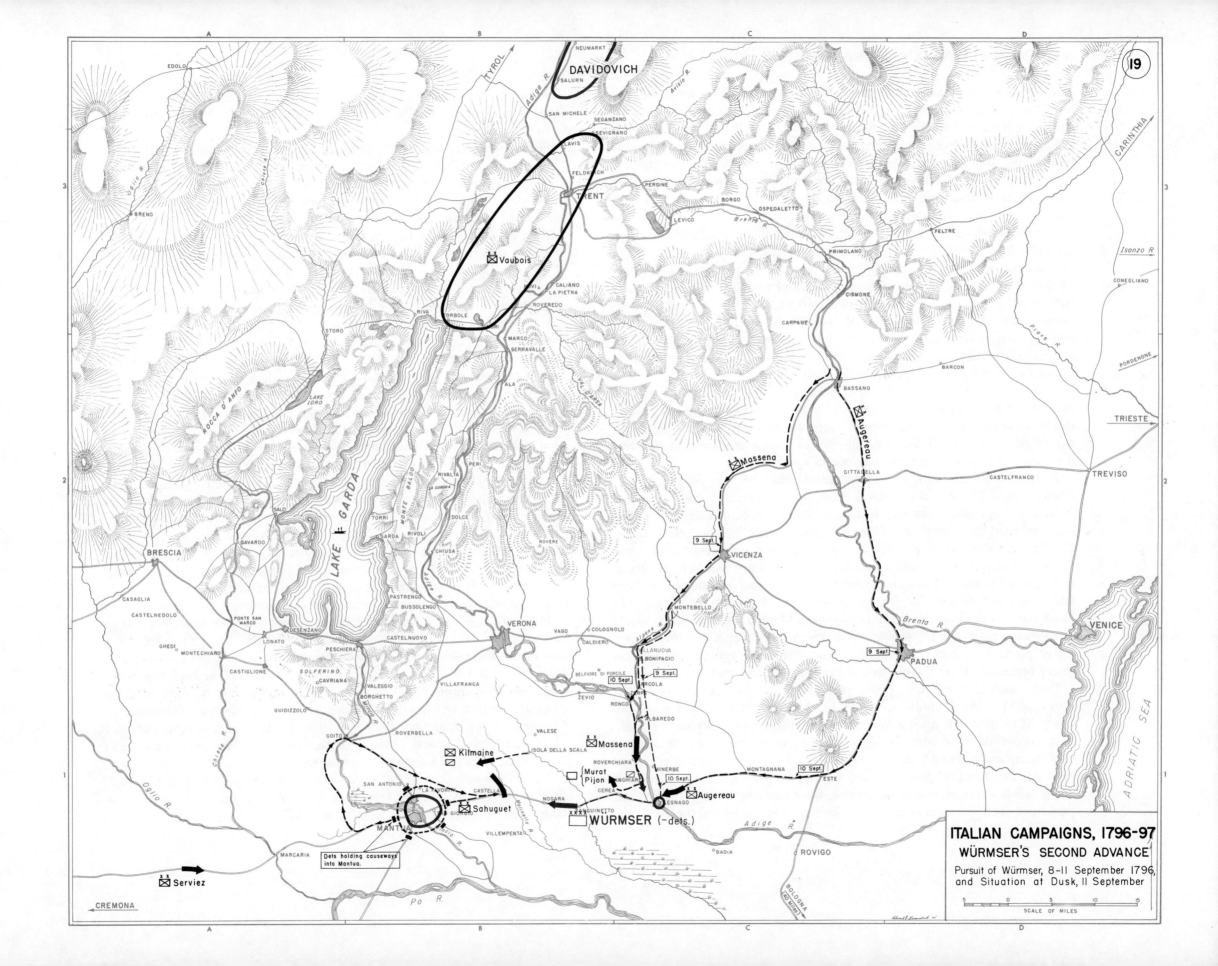

ITALIAN CAMPAIGNS, 1796-97
WÜRMSER'S SECOND ADVANCE
Pursuit of Würmser, 8-11 September 1796,
and Situation at Dusk, 11 September

SCALE OF MILES
5   0   5   10   15

After the operations against Würmser, the French Army of Italy required rest. It was isolated, due both to the retreat of the French armies in Germany and the approach of winter, which had begun to block the Alpine passes. On 2 November, the troops were in position as shown. Vaubois and Massena covered the approaches to Mantua (*B1*) from the north and east, respectively; Augereau and Joubert formed a centrally located reserve. Bonaparte could therefore concentrate rapidly when the direction of the expected Austrian advance was determined.

The rolls of the army showed 41,500 men immediately available. However, the unhealthy climate around Mantua did not affect only Austrians. Some 14,000 sick and 4,000 wounded French were in hospitals, leaving barely 24,000 fit for duty. The large number of sick and wounded officers left many staffs weak and regiments shaky. Bonaparte had demanded 20,000 replacements, but the Directory promised only 16,000. As of early November, these had only begun to trickle in; most of the promised reinforcements did not arrive until January. They had been in the Vendee, accustomed only to irregular warfare; their officers were especially unskilled.

In the Directory, there was considerable envy of Bonaparte, some concern over the independence of this successful general, and even talk of sending Hoche to relieve him. These attitudes were undoubtedly inflamed by Bonaparte's attempts—largely unsuccessful—to restrict the wholesale looting that the Directory's agents were carrying out in northern Italy.

Political considerations complicated the situation of the Army of Italy. France was sick of war and internal disorder, and was eager for peace. The Directory was aware of its own feebleness; the series of defeats in Germany had weakened its prestige and caused it to lose its taste for a war of conquest. The Directory wanted peace, but naturally did not want to treat with a victorious Austria. The complete conquest of northern Italy was therefore necessary in order to give it a bargaining point, and Austrian possession of northern Italy could not be considered extinguished until Mantua fell. On the other hand, the Austrians were determined to relieve Mantua. Such a success would threaten the entire French position in northern Italy, would put Austria in a better position in future negotiations, and would release the considerable forces blockaded there for use in any necessary future operations.

Under such circumstances, Bonaparte's liberty of maneuver was somewhat restricted. He could hardly raise the blockade of Mantua and maneuver freely, as he had done against Würmser's first advance. Local political conditions also added to his concern. Many elements in northern Italy were hostile to France, and a French defeat would result in serious insurrection in his rear. Already bandits (Barbets) were raiding supply lines in the Nice area, and English warships, based on Corsica, were harrying the coastline. Bonaparte took such measures as he could: Garnier, commanding in the Nice area,

was sent against the Barbets; the expedition launched from Leghorn on 19 October finally drove the English out of Corsica; and an alliance with Piedmont was negotiated.

Following instructions of the Directory, he organized Lombardy into the "Transpadane Republic," and the provinces of Modena, Reggio, Bologna, and Ferrara (all south of the Po, taken from territory of the Papal States and the Duchy of Modena) into the "Cispadane Republic," both under the protection of France and responsible for raising their own troops.

With the defeat of the French armies in Germany, a new major Austrian offensive in Italy was certain. Not having the strength for a major offensive of his own, Bonaparte would have to take full advantage of the terrain and try to wage a war of limited defensive-offensive operations. Meanwhile, he strengthened his defenses along the rivers and established posts in depth to guard his line of communication and to serve as pivots for future maneuvers.

Alvintzy had been given command of the Austrian forces in Italy. Davidovich had been reinforced to 18,400; 20,000 conscripts and other reinforcements had been sent to Quasdanovich's force in front of Trieste, raising his strength to 28,700. The quality of the troops was very mixed. Most of Davidovich's were probably veterans from Germany; part of Alvintzy's main body were unwilling Poles and poorly trained conscripts, and part exceptionally good Hungarian and Croat regiments. Some units were not completely trained, and were short of qualified cadres and equipment. Würmser, as noted, had about 24,000 in Mantua, possibly 14,000 of them effective. Despite these deficiencies, the Austrian Supreme War Council insisted that the troops advance on 1 November. Their plan contemplated simultaneous advances from the north and east, designed to link up near Verona and move together to relieve Mantua. Since each of the separated columns was superior to the French forces that could be committed against it, the plan was sound. However, the council's insistence that Alvintzy and Davidovich advance simultaneously reduced their chances of surprising or confusing Bonaparte.

Bonaparte was aware of the Austrian preparations and ordered Massena to retire on Vicenza, if attacked. Between 25 and 30 October, he received false information that many of Davidovich's troops had been transferred to Alvintzy's main force, and that Davidovich's remaining command around Neumarkt (*B3*) was outnumbered by Vaubois. This led him to plan to have Vaubois drive Davidovich well north of Neumarkt, and then shift 3,000 troops to Massena. In the meantime, Bonaparte would bring up Augereau and part of Joubert to give himself a mobile striking force. On 30 October, he issued appropriate orders to Vaubois and Massena.

Davidovich advanced in full strength on 1 November; on the 2d, he collided with Vaubois, likewise coming forward. At this time, Alvintzy's main body had just crossed the Piave (*D2*), as shown.

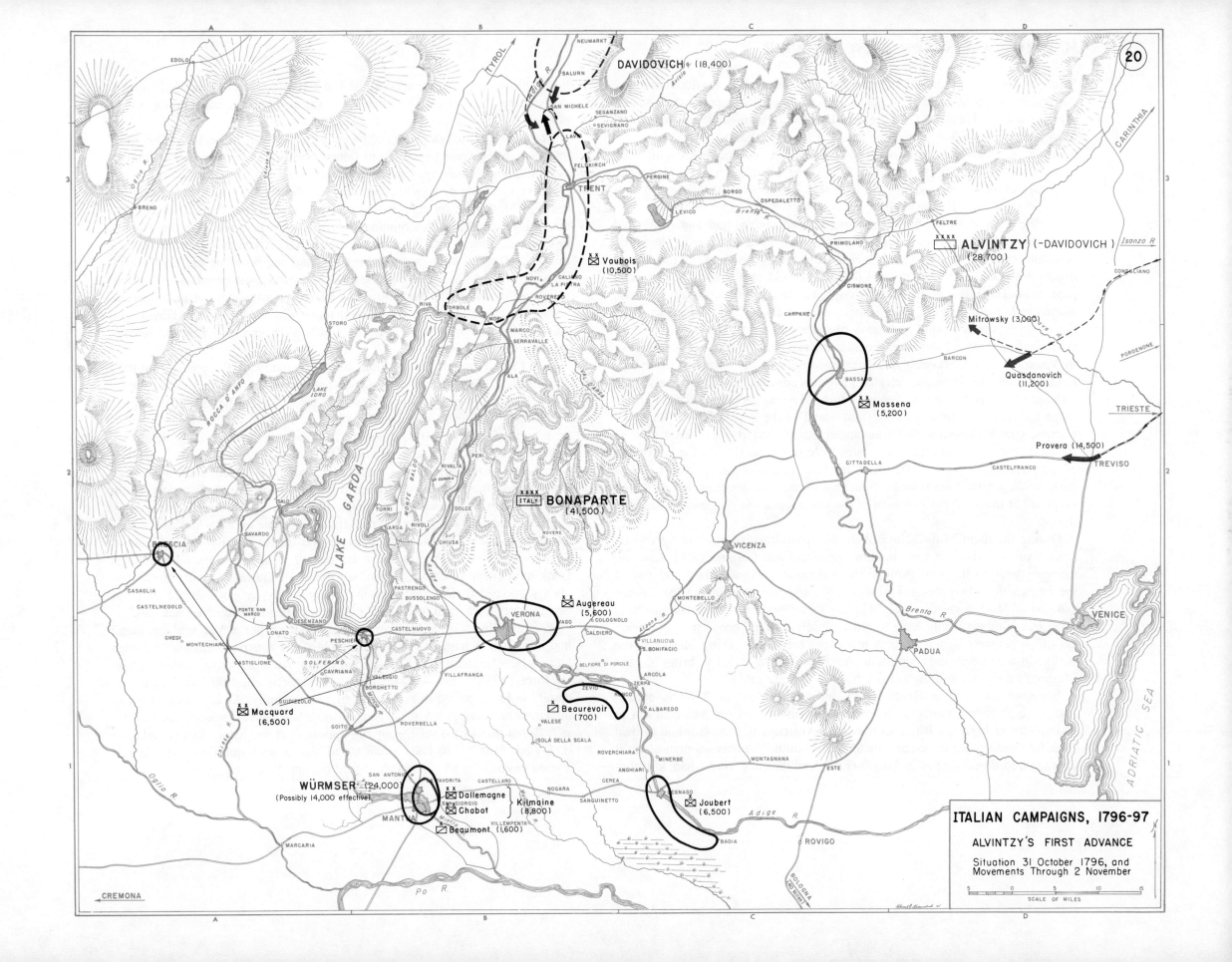

ITALIAN CAMPAIGNS, 1796-97

ALVINTZY'S FIRST ADVANCE

Situation 31 October 1796, and
Movements Through 2 November

SCALE OF MILES

Vaubois emerged second best from the encounter with Davidovich on 2 November. After a hard fight, he was outflanked by superior forces and driven back on Trent (*B3*). Threatened with envelopment there, he retired during the night of 3–4 November to the defile of Caliano.

Alvintzy, meanwhile, advanced in two columns of equal strength: one, under Provera, moving on Cittadella (*C2*); the other, under Quasdanovich, on Bassano (*C2*). Quasdanovich had sent Mitrowsky (3,000) to Feltre (*D3*) to watch the Brenta Valley and link up with Davidovich.

During 3 and 4 November, Bonaparte realized that he had underestimated Vaubois' opposition. On the 3d, he sent Berthier north to examine the situation, and ordered Joubert to advance on the 5th to disengage Vaubois and organize a position at La Corona (*B2*), to be held at all costs. At the same time, confident in the quality of his troops and noting that Alvintzy's advance guards were well ahead of their respective main bodies, he decided to strike the advance guards a rapid and heavy blow, hoping to destroy them.

Accordingly, on 5 November, he moved Beaumont's cavalry and Augereau to Vicenza (*C2*). (Massena had already withdrawn to that town from Bassano.) On the 6th, Massena defeated Provera's advance guard; Provera moved forward to its aid, but was driven in in turn. Massena, however, could not dislodge the Austrians from an important island in the Brenta River. Augereau likewise struck Quasdanovich's advanced guard, and drove it back toward Bassano, but could not clear the Austrians from the heights on the west bank of the river. After losing 1,000 men in these indecisive engagements, Bonaparte broke off the action and retired that evening to Vicenza. He had been surprised at the good performance of the unseasoned, heterogeneous Austrian troops.

During the night of 6–7 November, Bonaparte received disturbing reports from Vaubois, who had been holding successfully at Caliano (*B3*). Laudon, swinging wide to the west through the mountains, had surprised and routed the French demi-brigade at Torbole (*B3*), and was threatening the French position at Mori. Simultaneously, Ocskay threatened Mori from the north. If Mori fell, Vaubois would have to retire rapidly on La Corona to avoid being cut off. Bonaparte hastened north to the troubled area, taking Massena (the mountain-warfare expert) with him. Augereau was directed to bring his and Massena's divisions and the cavalry back to Verona (*B1*).

Bonaparte arrived at Rivoli (*B2*) during the night of 7–8 November, and there he found Vaubois' troops in some disorder. They had held out at Caliano throughout the 7th, until rumors of Austrians in their rear had thrown them into sudden panic, sending them fleeing south. Vaubois—a man of great courage and firmness, but lacking mental flexibility and *élan*—had lost control of his troops. Bonaparte administered a severe rebuke to the shaken men, and directed Massena and Joubert to restore order and to organize a new position.

From the 2d through the 6th of November, the French had lost 5,000 men, and their morale was beginning to falter. Fortunately for Bonaparte, Davidovich did not advance aggressively to exploit his initial successes.

There was little activity on the 9th. Davidovich had taken up a position south of Mori, with his right flank near Riva and his left flank extended into the Val d'Arsa (the valley running southeast from Roveredo), in an attempt to establish contact with Alvintzy. There, he sat. Alvintzy—whose skill, flexibility, and moral courage were limited—had lumbered as far as Vicenza, showing little inclination to push beyond. Mitrowsky was near Bassano. Bonaparte took advantage of this lull to give his troops a few days of much-needed rest, while awaiting the Austrians' next move. On the 9th, seeing Davidovich still inactive, he transferred part of Vaubois' troops to Verona, leaving Vaubois about 8,500.

The French actions thus far had been exemplary of Bonaparte's military philosophy: "Take advantage of all your opportunities. Fortune is a woman; if you let her slip one day, you must not expect to find her again the next." Yet, rather than await opportunities, he had tried to create them. Assailed by superior forces from two directions, he had avoided a passive defense—into which refuge most generals would have fled—and instead had attacked both forces. Alvintzy, he had calculated, could be forced back across the Brenta; then, the French would rush to bolster Vaubois and eliminate Davidovich. Inferiority in numbers he confidently brushed aside, perhaps thinking, as he later wrote: "There are no great and memorable events which are merely the work of chance and luck; they are always due to forethought and genius. Great men are rarely seen to fail, even in their most hazardous undertakings. Look at Alexander, Caesar, Hannibal, the great Gustavus, and others; they always succeeded. Did they become famous only by good luck? No, but because they were great, and they knew how to bend Fortune to their will."

True, the obstinacy of Alvintzy's troops and the flight of Vaubois' command had frustrated Bonaparte's plan; nevertheless, the Austrian columns had been halted. Now he stood disposed to counter any Austrian move, with his striking force (13,000 men—Massena, part of Augereau, and the cavalry) immediately in hand, poised to exploit the first opportunity. As he waited, we can imagine him musing: "A great general must say several times a day to himself, 'What should I do if the enemy appeared in my front, on my right, or on my left flank?' If he finds it difficult to answer such questions, he is not in a good position, or all is not as it should be, and he must alter it."

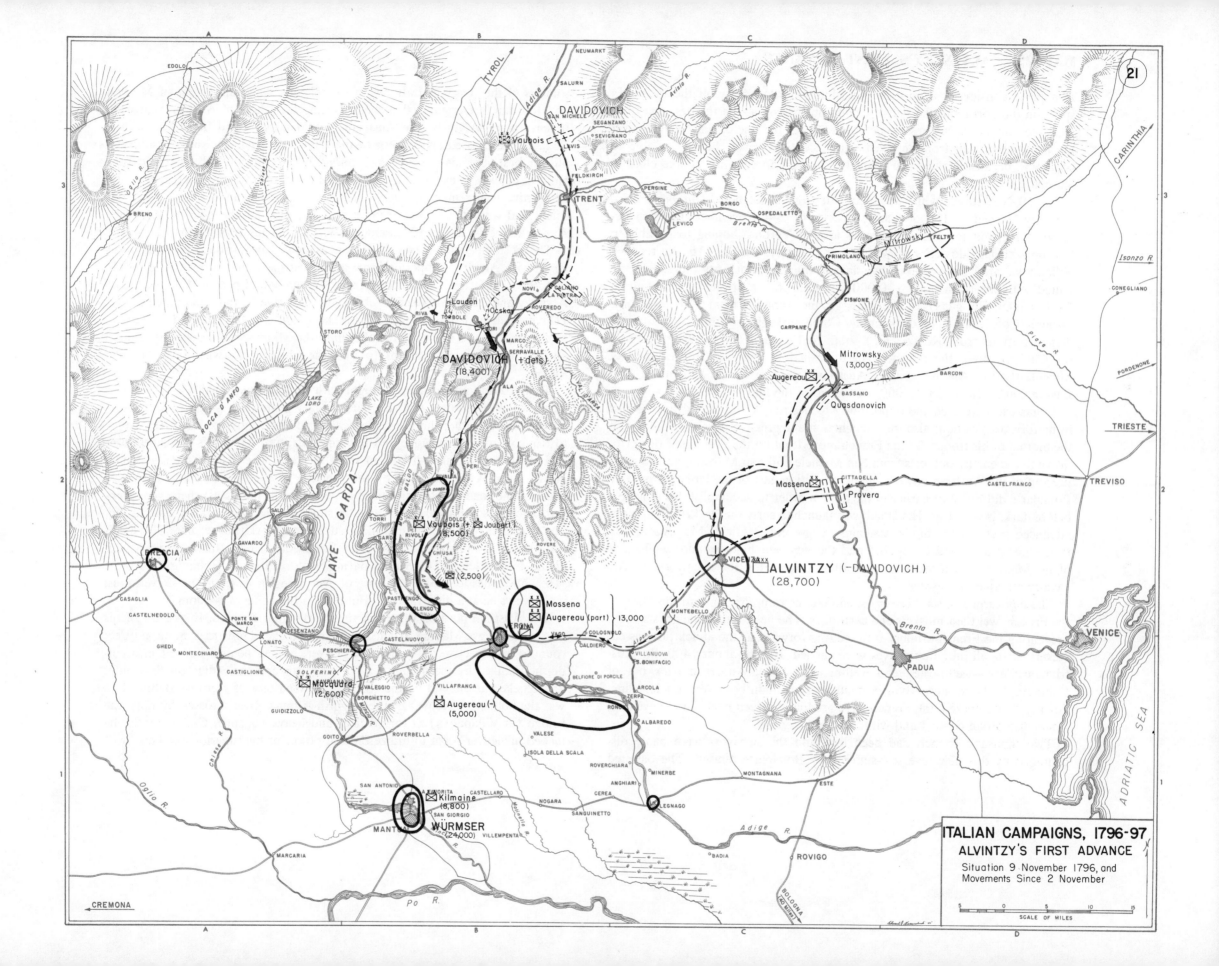

ITALIAN CAMPAIGNS, 1796-97
ALVINTZY'S FIRST ADVANCE
Situation 9 November 1796, and
Movements Since 2 November

SCALE OF MILES

Bonaparte considered a position at Caldiero (*B2*)—between the mountain spurs on the north and the Adige swamp on the south—as the best one from which to conduct an aggressive defense to cover the line of the Adige against an army advancing from the east. At present, however, he was unable to occupy it, because Davidovich's threat to his rear forced him to hold close to Verona (*A3*).

On 10 November, while advancing through Montebello (*off map, D3*), Alvintzy learned of Davidovich's successes of 2–4 November. He then decided to feel out the French defenses around Verona, hoping to be able to link up with Davidovich somewhere near that city. On the 11th, he reached Villanuova, after having taken five days to march about forty miles. Here he halted with his main body (10,000), sending out a strong advance guard (8,000 men, 26 guns) to the high ground running from Caldiero north through Colognolo, and dispatching Colonel Brigido (3,000) to conduct demonstrations from Ronco (*C1*) south to Legnago (*off map, D1*). From the Caldiero area, the advance guard pushed its outposts forward to San Michele (*A3*). Another 6,000 Austrians were between Villanuova and Bassano, and Mitrowsky (3,000) remained in the latter town.

Bonaparte perceived the opportunity to destroy Alvintzy's advance guard in its forward position; also, he thought some aggressive fighting would raise the morale of his troops. So the French moved out on the evening of the 11th, drove in the enemy outposts from San Michele and San Martino, and camped in front of the Austrian advance guard's position east of the latter town. Why Bonaparte did not start earlier in the day, in order to accomplish his objective before dark, is not clear. His attack was launched early on the 12th. Augereau advanced south of the highway against Vago and Caldiero. Massena moved to the north to attack Colognolo and the adjacent high ground, while part of his force started around through Illasi, to envelop the enemy right. The cavalry remained in reserve.

The day turned miserable very soon. Winter rain, driving into the faces of the French, wet their muskets and cartridges. The flat countryside grew boggy, preventing the French artillery from getting forward as the attack progressed. Nevertheless, all initial objectives were carried. But, at about 1400, the Austrian artillery—well-posted and well-handled—shot Augereau back out of Caldiero. An hour later, Alvintzy finally got his main body forward into line. Greatly outnumbered, the French were gradually forced back. In the evening, Bonaparte broke contact and withdrew into Verona.

Two thousand French had been lost, and the survivors were badly discouraged by this new reverse—suffered by Bonaparte himself. The battered soldiers of the Army of Italy began to feel that, since the defeat of Moreau and Jourdan in Germany, they were fighting the whole of Austria; that even if they routed Alvintzy, the Austrians would merely send in another army. Bonaparte expressed his concern to the Directory: "All our superior officers, all our best generals are *hors de combat*. The Army of Italy, reduced to a handful of men, is exhausted. . . . We are abandoned in the interior of Italy. The brave men remaining regard death as inevitable amid chances so continual and with forces so inferior in number. Perhaps the hour of the brave Augereau, of the intrepid Massena, of Berthier, of my own death is at hand."

The position of the Army of Italy was indeed precarious. To lock horns again with Alvintzy's superior force and its artillery in the open field would be to invite disaster. To withdraw from Verona would permit the juncture of Alvintzy and Davidovich and a subsequent offensive by their combined forces. (Davidovich had not yet moved, but he could not be expected to remain forever motionless.) A withdrawal behind the Mincio would uncover Mantua and permit Würmser's troops to join the already overwhelming Austrian forces.

This growing predicament, fraught with uncertainty, failed to shake Bonaparte; rather, it brought forth his true military genius. He would reduce forces everywhere to gather the greatest strength possible, move south of the Adige to Ronco, cross there, move to Villanuova, capture Alvintzy's baggage trains and artillery park, and strike him from the rear. The field of combat would be the swampy area formed by the junction of the Alpone and the Adige. Most of the roads ran along raised dikes, through morasses; there were very few patches of solid ground. Action in such an area would favor French tactics—column rushes along the dikes, supported by skirmisher fire. There was little room for the regular Austrian formations, and artillery employment would be restricted. This was a daring venture, but, in Bonaparte's words, "He who wishes to make quite sure of everything in war, and never ventures, will always be at a disadvantage. Boldness is the acme of wisdom."

The Austrian position was favorable to Bonaparte's plan. In pursuit of his mission to relieve Mantua, Alvintzy had moved ahead toward Verona, a direct route to his objective. In so doing, however, he had penned himself in a cul-de-sac, flanked by the mountains on the north and the Adige on the south, and blocked at the end by the strongly fortified city of Verona. Behind him was the bottleneck formed by the sluggish Alpone River, crossed by only one bridge (at Villanuova) fit for artillery and heavy baggage. Consequently, he lacked maneuver room to utilize the full power of his superior numbers.

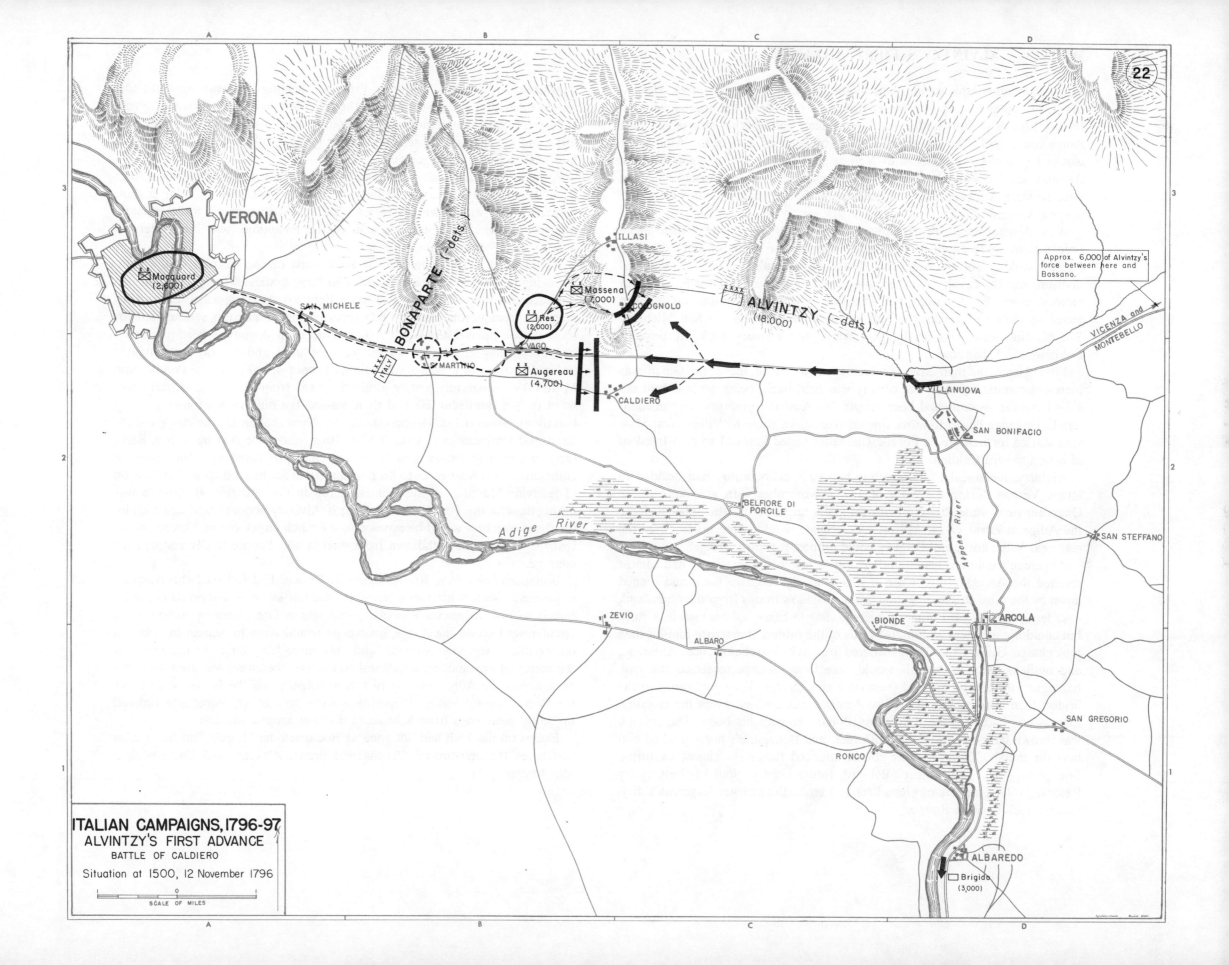

22

ILLASI

Approx. 6,000 of Alvintzy's force between here and Bassano.

⊠ Macquard (2,600)

VERONA

SAN MICHELE

BONAPARTE (-dets.)

⊠ Massena (7,000)

COLOGNOLO

⊠ Res. (2,000)

XXXX ALVINTZY (-dets)
(18,000)

VICENZA and MONTEBELLO

VAGO

XXXX ITALY

S. MARTINO

⊠ Augereau (4,700)

CALDIERO

VILLANUOVA

SAN BONIFACIO

BELFIORE DI PORCILE

Adige River

Alpone River

SAN STEFFANO

ZEVIO

ALBARO

BIONDE

ARCOLA

SAN GREGORIO

RONCO

ALBAREDO

□ Brigido (3,000)

ITALIAN CAMPAIGNS, 1796-97
ALVINTZY'S FIRST ADVANCE
BATTLE OF CALDIERO
Situation at 1500, 12 November 1796

0
SCALE OF MILES

Bonaparte had completed his plans by the morning of 13 November. He had decided to make a main crossing at Ronco (*C1*). There, the approaches of a former French ponton bridge still were intact, and another bridge over the Adige could readily be constructed. Also, by keeping west of the Alpone, he would be in closer contact with Verona and better able to keep between Alvintzy and Davidovich. According to Bonaparte's latest information, there were no large Austrian units around Arcola, though enemy hussars were outposting Albaredo (*D1*).

A small detachment quietly moved up to Ronco late on the 13th to make preparations to re-establish the bridge. During the night of the 14th, the French striking force (Augereau, Massena, Guieu's brigade of Vaubois' division, and the cavalry reserve) moved out along the river road with great secrecy, especially as to objective. That day, Alvintzy had pushed his advance guard up close to Verona; the bulk of his forces were in the San Michele–San Martino area; and his baggage trains and artillery park sat between Caldiero and Villanuova.

First Augereau, then Massena crossed at dawn on the 15th; Guieu was then still coming forward; the cavalry was held back, being useless until the exits from the swamps had been seized. No Austrian outposts were encountered. Augereau began to move toward Arcola, en route to Villanuova; Massena started for Belfiore de Porcile (hereafter called Porcile) to gain freedom of action toward Caldiero.

Alvintzy, meanwhile, after wasting two days deliberating, had decided to attack Verona during the night of 15–16 November with a column under Quasdanovich, while Provera, with a slightly larger force, attempted to force the Adige at Zevio (*B1*). Mitrowsky's brigade would come up to cover the rear near Villanuova, and Brigido would outpost the lower Adige.

Augereau's column, encountering only a few scattered shots, had almost reached the Arcola bridge when it was suddenly taken in flank and pinned down by the musketry and cannon fire of Brigido's troops from the other bank —at less than 100-yard range. Augereau, flag in hand, led his men in a rush, but could not get them within 200 yards of the bridge. Bonaparte himself then took charge. Guieu (3,000) was ordered to cross by boat below, near Albaredo, and outflank Arcola. As this would take time, Bonaparte seized the flag, harangued the troops, and led them on a new charge. They got almost to the bridge, then were broken up by two Austrian guns, which swept the crossing. Lannes was badly wounded covering Bonaparte with his body. The column was thrown back in considerable disorder, and Bonaparte's horse pitched him into the marsh. The Austrians counterattacked furiously, almost capturing Bonaparte, but a staff officer (Belliard, future chief of staff of the Cavalry Reserve) rallied a party of grenadiers and broke the charge. Augereau's division then fell back on Ronco.

Massena, meanwhile, had met Provera's leading elements near Bionde, routed them, and rushed them back through Porcile. There, Provera, apparently reinforced, counterattacked vigorously. The struggle swayed back and forth, but at sundown Massena still held the village. Bonaparte then recalled him to Ronco to join Augereau.

At about 1900, after dark, Guieu struck the exhausted Austrians in Arcola from the south, and cleared the town in his first rush, without firing a shot. Augereau had withdrawn, so Guieu, finding his own small force isolated, returned to Ronco. (Bonaparte had, in the meantime, sent him orders to do so.)

Alvintzy had heard firing in his left rear early on the morning of the 15th. Believing the marshes there impassable to large bodies of troops, he had disregarded the firing as a feint by French light troops, designed to distract his attention from Verona. Brigido had reported the situation as serious, but for some reason his message—or its consideration in Alvintzy's headquarters— had been delayed. At any rate, it was not until about 1100 that Alvintzy ordered Provera to detach six battalions (about 4,500 men) to Porcile, and Mitrowsky (apparently loafing along the road from Bassano) to hurry forward to San Bonifacio. He had then massed the bulk of his forces (twenty battalions, about 15,000) opposite Zevio. Now shaken by the day's events, he moved ten battalions (some 7,500) back across the Alpone to San Bonifacio, where they joined Mitrowsky, who had just come up. The Austrian commander was worried as to his position. In order to accomplish his mission of relieving Mantua, he must somehow regain the initiative. Bonaparte was on his flank in the Porcile-Arcola area; if Alvintzy concentrated against him there, his own rear would be exposed to a French attack out of Verona. News that the French had withdrawn from Arcola and Porcile finally restored his courage.

Bonaparte, observing from a tower in Ronco, had followed the Austrian movements. He had his own worries. He did not know how soon he might be forced to rush to rescue Vaubois, about whose fate alarming rumors were circulating. Beyond the Adige, his troops would have to remain in columns on the dikes (eleven yards wide, and only three feet above the marshes), at the mercy of any sudden, accidental panic. He, therefore, withdrew his army back across the Adige, leaving two demi-brigades on the far bank to cover the Ronco ponton bridge. Preparing for the final effort, Bonaparte ordered up 3,000 more men from Kilmaine's division around Mantua.

Events on the 15th had not gone as Bonaparte had hoped, but he at least had taken the pressure off Verona and drawn Alvintzy and Davidovich a little farther apart.

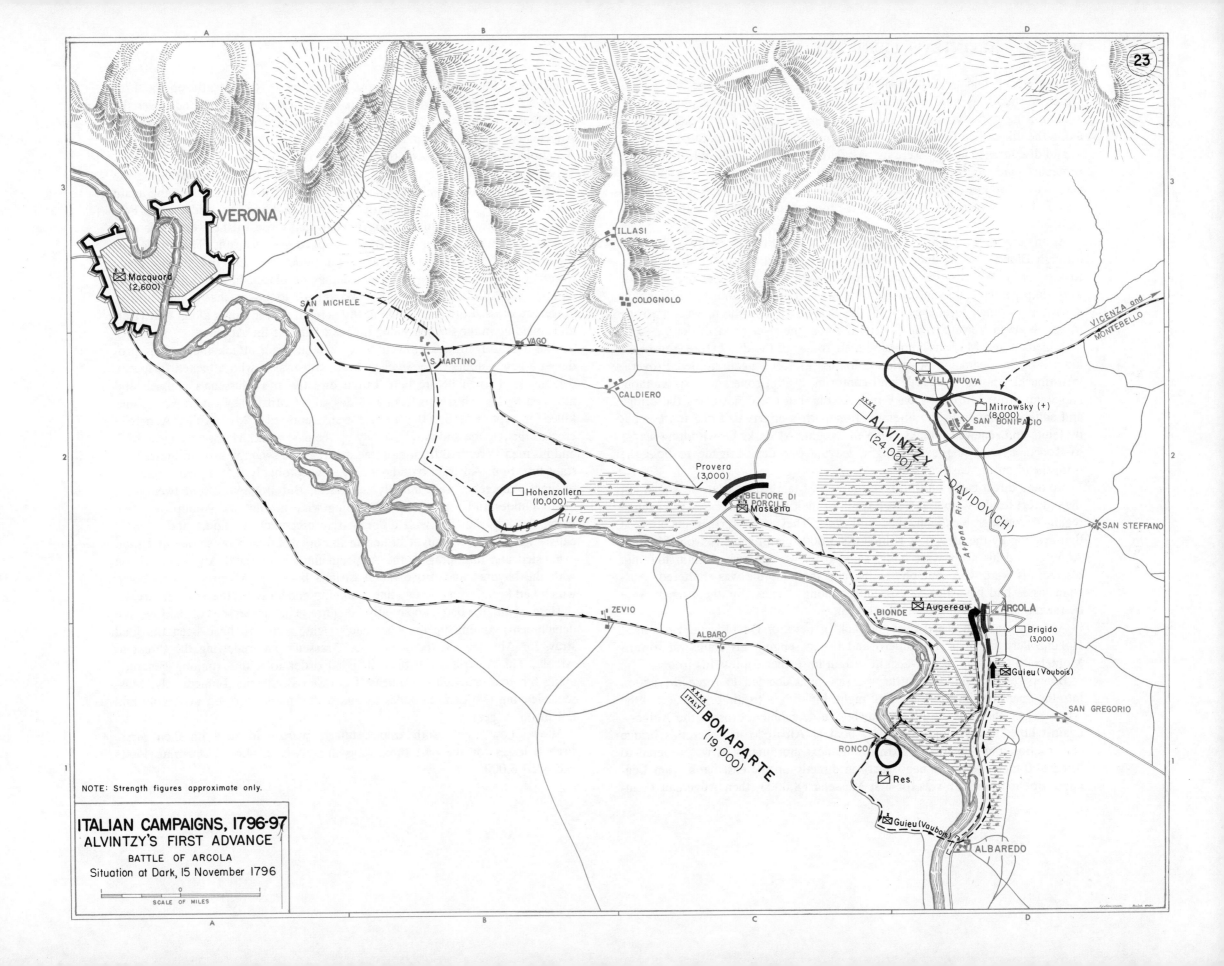

23

VERONA

Macquord
(2,600)

SAN MICHELE

S. MARTINO

VAGO

ILLASI

COLOGNOLO

CALDIERO

VICENZA and
MONTEBELLO

VILLANUOVA

Mitrowsky (+)
(8,000)
SAN BONIFACIO

XXX
ALVINTZY
(24,000)

Provera
(3,000)

Hohenzollern
(10,000)

Adige River

BELFIORE DI
PORCILE
Massena

(-DAVIDOVICH)

San Steffano

ZEVIO

ALBARO

BIONDE

Augereau

ARCOLA

Brigido
(3,000)

Guieu (Vaubois)

XXXX
ITALY
BONAPARTE
(19,000)

RONCO

Res.

SAN GREGORIO

Guieu (Vaubois)

ALBAREDO

NOTE: Strength figures approximate only.

ITALIAN CAMPAIGNS, 1796-97
ALVINTZY'S FIRST ADVANCE
BATTLE OF ARCOLA
Situation at Dark, 15 November 1796

0   1
SCALE OF MILES

On the second and third days of the Battle of Arcola, Bonaparte's actions (often mistaken as pure obstinacy) actually had two specific purposes: to maintain the initiative, and to wear down the enemy in a battle of attrition along the dikes. The French fought best when they had the initiative; without it, and discouraged as they were by past defeats, they might have lost all heart. Bonaparte had already detected a slowness and hesitancy in Alvintzy's maneuvers; and it had not escaped his keen, battle-wise eyes that the Austrian forces were full of raw recruits, poorly fitted for the irregular fighting in the swampy area.

At an early hour on 16 November, Alvintzy sent Provera (*Map a*) forward through Bionde (*A1*), and Mitrowsky from Arcola along the dike toward Ronco (*A1*). Whether these moves were made with offensive intentions, or were simply a reconnaissance in force, is not certain. One aim, at least, was to destroy the French bridgehead opposite Ronco. Hohenzollern, with a strong force, observed Verona from a position across the river from Zevio.

Augereau and Massena, retracing their routes of the day before, ran headlong into the advancing Austrian columns. Massena again routed Provera, thrusting him north of Porcile and capturing 800 prisoners and six cannon. Augereau drove Mitrowsky back into Arcola, but could not carry the bridge and suffered heavily in the attempt. Bonaparte's efforts to force the combat by feints and renewed attacks came to naught. At dark, he withdrew across to Ronco, as on the previous night, leaving one demi-brigade to hold the bridgehead on the east bank.

Nothing direct came of all this in the way of tactical or strategic gains, but the indirect results were great. As a result of their partial successes, the French regained considerable confidence and *élan*. They were further encouraged that evening by the arrival of Kilmaine's 3,000 reinforcements from Mantua. Alvintzy and his army were badly shaken by two days of constant fighting; his recruits were worn out physically, and their morale was shattered. Austrian losses had been heavy, especially among officers, for the French were by far the better skirmishers and marksmen.

Alvintzy was concerned over the lack of news of Davidovich. He moved Hohenzollern north near Caldiero and began sending his trains off toward Montebello (*off map, B3*)—a sight certain to further depress his troops.

Bonaparte now felt the battle was ripe, and decided to force the action into the open. Engineers worked all night, building a trestle bridge across the Alpone, just above its mouth. Meanwhile, a detachment crossed the Adige— against little, if any, opposition—by boat at Albaredo to cover this bridge construction and Augereau's crossing the next morning. Vial was ordered to bring 800 men of the Legnago garrison directly up the east bank from Legnago. Bonaparte's plan was for first Massena (8,000), then Augereau (rein-

forced to 12,000–14,000) to recross the Adige at Ronco early on the 17th (*Map b*). Massena would then threaten Arcola from the west and cover the French left against any Austrian offensive from the direction of Porcile. Augereau would proceed across the new bridge over the Alpone and attack Arcola from the south, along the east bank of the river.

As Massena began his crossing at Ronco, one of the boats supporting the bridge sank; at that same moment, Mitrowsky's advance guard, coming again from Arcola, struck the French demi-brigade holding the bridgehead. Fortunately, the French artillery was concentrated close to the west bank near Ronco. It went into action rapidly and stopped the Austrians. The bridge was repaired, and Massena crossed at about 0900. He sent one demi-brigade toward Porcile, one toward Arcola; another he placed in ambush in a grove east of the Arcola dike, holding two others to cover the Ronco bridge. Augereau crossed the Adige behind this screen, moved down along that river, and coiled up in the thickets along the west bank of the Alpone.

The demi-brigade sent toward Arcola feinted an attack there. This produced a new outburst (*not shown*) from Mitrowsky, who attacked furiously, driving the French before him. Lured directly into Massena's ambush and attacked by French troops from all sides, all of Mitrowsky's men were either killed or captured (3,000 prisoners were reported). Meanwhile, Augereau crossed the Alpone and moved slowly up the east bank. The weather was foul, and his men were tired from movement across the swampy ground under constant fire. Four Austrian battalions (by now, probably 2,500 men), sent out to block Augereau, were initially successful. But Bonaparte sent twenty-five of his Guides and four trumpeters riding wide around the swamp, to come in on the Austrian left with a "great reinforcement of shouts and trumpet calls." Thus startled, caught in line in the open, blinded by smoke and rain, exhausted and discouraged, the Austrian flank crumpled. Augereau fell on with the bayonet and drove the Austrians back on Alvintzy's main body, which had been formed in two lines, running generally southeast from Arcola.

Here, again, the battle apparently hung fire. The appearance of the Legnago detachment, coming up on Augereau's right, seems to have been the final straw for Alvintzy. At the same time, Massena was renewing the threat to Arcola. The Austrians fell back in good order to a line running generally along the road extending southeast from San Bonifacio. Immediately, Massena, leaving two demi-brigades to guard the marsh, crossed at Arcola and fell in on Augereau's left.

It was now night. Both armies, utterly worn out, slept on their arms. French losses for the past three days are given as 4,600; Austrian losses exceeded 6,000.

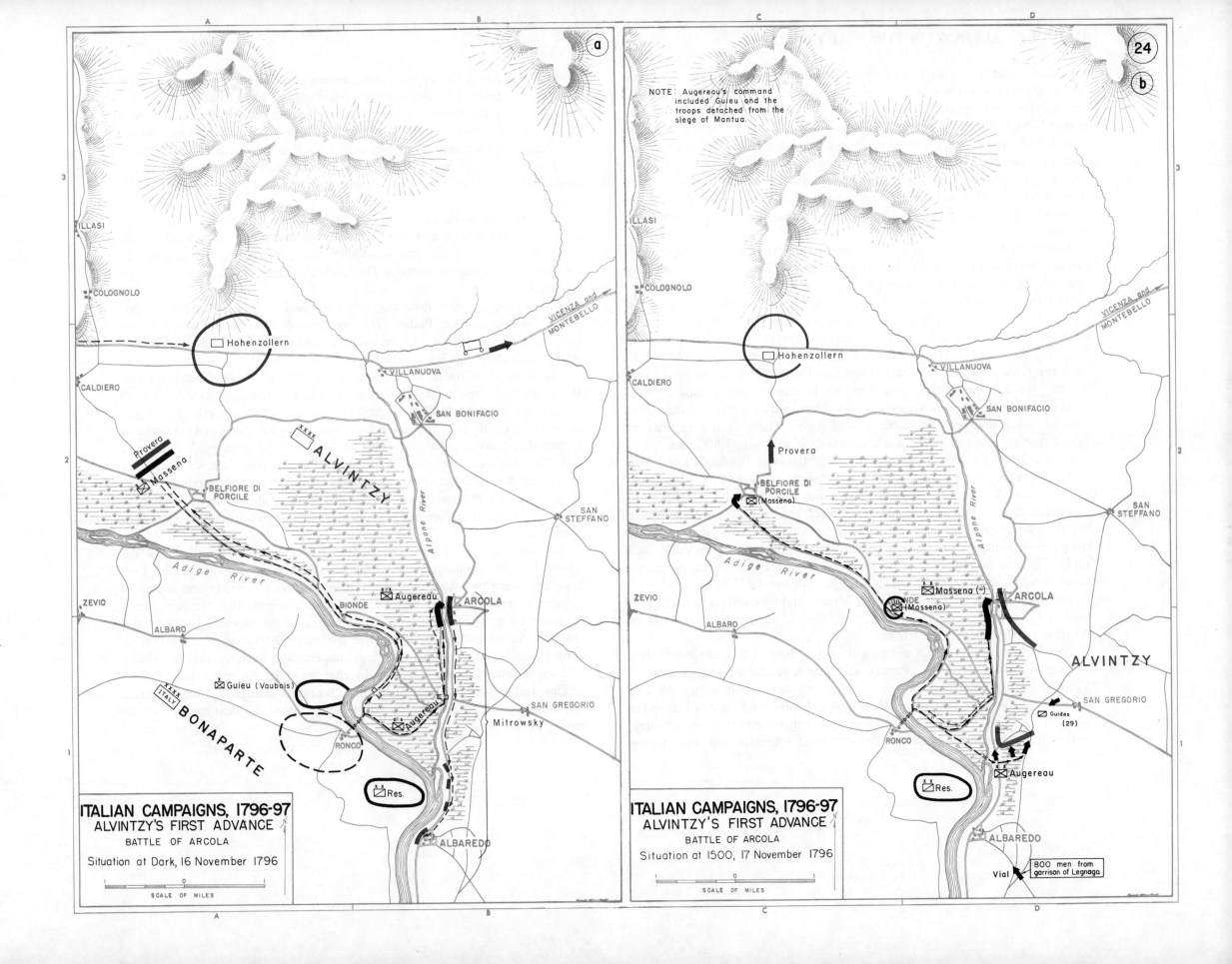

(a)

ILLASI

COLOGNOLO

Hohenzollern

VICENZA and MONTEBELLO

CALDIERO

VILLANUOVA

SAN BONIFACIO

Provera

Massena

ALVINTZY

BELFIORE DI PORCILE

Alpone River

SAN STEFFANO

Adige River

BIONDE

Augereau

ARCOLA

ZEVIO

ALBARO

Guieu (Vaubois)

ITALY

BONAPARTE

Augereau

SAN GREGORIO

Mitrowsky

RONCO

Res.

ALBAREDO

ITALIAN CAMPAIGNS, 1796-97
ALVINTZY'S FIRST ADVANCE
BATTLE OF ARCOLA

Situation at Dark, 16 November 1796

SCALE OF MILES

(b) 24

NOTE: Augereau's command included Guieu and the troops detached from the siege of Mantua.

ILLASI

COLOGNOLO

Hohenzollern

VICENZA and MONTEBELLO

CALDIERO

VILLANUOVA

SAN BONIFACIO

Provera

BELFIORE DI PORCILE (Massena)

ALVINTZY

Alpone River

SAN STEFFANO

Adige River

ZEVIO

ALBARO

NDE (Massena)

Massena (-)

ARCOLA

ALVINTZY

Guides (29)

SAN GREGORIO

RONCO

Res.

Augereau

ALBAREDO

Vial

800 men from garrison of Legnago.

ITALIAN CAMPAIGNS, 1796-97
ALVINTZY'S FIRST ADVANCE
BATTLE OF ARCOLA

Situation at 1500, 17 November 1796

SCALE OF MILES

Bonaparte must have thought of Arcola when he wrote: "The fate of a battle is a question of a single moment, a single thought; . . . the decisive moment arrives, the moral spark is kindled and the smallest reserve force settles the matter." And again: "There is a moment in engagements where the least maneuver is decisive and gives the victory; it is the one drop of water which makes the vessel run over." The Austrian commander and his men, exhausted, discouraged, and harassed, had been psychologically vulnerable to the "one drop of water"—that tiny, but noisy and energetic, detachment of Guides and trumpeters that had set off a chain reaction of fear and despair among the Austrians.

Hohenzollern had been pulled back across the Alpone on 17 November. On the morning of the 18th, having no news of Davidovich, and morally crushed, Alvintzy retired on Montebello.

The reason for the constant lack of news from Davidovich remains a puzzle. It may have been a failure to set up a courier route, though Austrian staffs were usually very efficient in such matters. Davidovich, meanwhile, after languidly scouting the French positions at La Corona and Rivoli (both B2) since the 13th, finally moved south in force and struck Vaubois on the 17th— the day the decisive struggle was going on in the marshes around Arcola. Vaubois had evacuated La Corona on the 15th, and concentrated the 3,500 men he had immediately available around Rivoli. There, he put up a determined resistance, retiring on Castelnuovo only after losing 1,800 men.

On the 18th, Vaubois fell back across the Mincio at Peschiera and began gathering in the troops he had had to leave along the Adige (from Bussolengo south toward Verona) to guard against a possible attempt by Alvintzy to cross that river north of Verona. Davidovich did not, however, advance beyond Pastrengo (B2). On that same day, Bonaparte sent Guieu and the troops from Kilmaine's command back through Ronco (C1) to Villafranca (B1). He also dropped Massena at Villanuova (C1) to watch Alvintzy's future actions, and started Augereau through Caldiero (B1) to Verona.

Vaubois, on the 19th, recrossed the Mincio and concentrated some 8,000 men at Castelnuovo. Simultaneously, Davidovich, having received word of Alvintzy's retreat, retired on Rivoli.

Bonaparte called Massena northward on the 20th. The latter established small garrisons at Albaredo, Ronco, and Zevio; reinforced the garrison of Verona; and then moved up on Pastrengo. Augereau advanced up the east bank of the Adige on Peri (B2). Davidovich, falling back on Ala before the advance of Vaubois and Massena, now received a message from Alvintzy, stating that Alvintzy had strength for one more offensive and was moving toward the Adige. (This appears to be the first Austrian message that definitely got through rapidly.) Davidovich then countermarched to Rivoli.

On the 21st, Davidovich suddenly realized that the entire French army was upon him. He started rapidly northward, but Joubert broke up his rear guard, and Augereau's advance guard cut across his line of retreat at Peri. Davidovich broke through just in time, but lost 2,000 men during the day, plus a considerable part of his supply trains. The rest of his troops were badly disorganized.

Alvintzy, meanwhile, came forward again to Caldiero, pushing the French cavalry—left to observe and delay any such renewed offensive—ahead of him. There, on the 23d, in the same blind alley before Verona from which he had just been ejected, he got news of Davidovich's defeat, and rapidly withdrew eastward.

The opposing armies now mutually collapsed. Alvintzy's forces stopped along the Brenta, from Padua (D1) northward; Davidovich halted at the north end of Lake Garda, in the Ala-Roveredo-Riva area; and the French rested along the Adige River, from Rivoli south.

And what of Würmser, in Mantua, during the past several weeks? Twice Bonaparte had severely pared Kilmaine's blockading forces to provide strength for his offensive. On the 23d Würmser finally undertook a sortie, which was easily repulsed. By then the troops borrowed from Kilmaine had returned. It is doubtful, however, that an earlier sortie would have enjoyed a different fate. The only exits from the fortress were along narrow causeways, covered by French fire; and Bonaparte's gunboats patrolled the surrounding waters. It is likely that Würmser knew little, if anything, about affairs outside of Mantua; what little information might have trickled in from spies was sure to be late.

The campaign of Alvintzy's first advance is somewhat reminiscent of the Chancellorsville campaign in the American Civil War. Bonaparte, like Lee, caught between two superior forces, utilized superior mobility and a central position to exploit enemy delays and to seize the initiative. Similarly, both campaigns were largely battles between the wills of the opposing commanders. As Lee did with Hooker, Bonaparte overcame Alvintzy and Davidovich through determination, superior energy, impetuosity, tenacity, and the ability to analyze situations and calculate the chances under the most difficult conditions. In the words of General Patton: "Weapons change, but man changes not at all. To win battles, you do not beat weapons—you beat the soul of the enemy man."

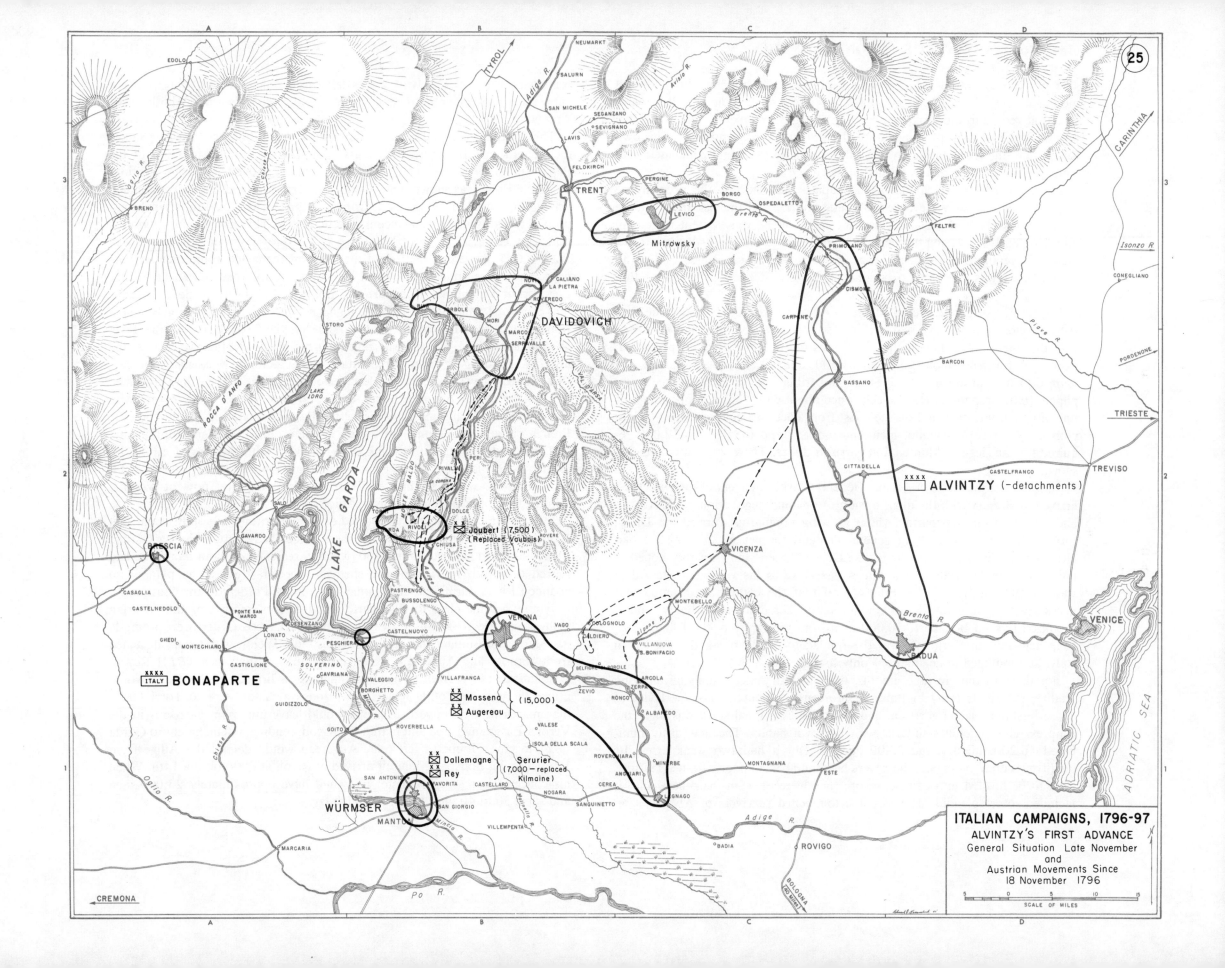

CARINTHIA

TYROL

NEUMARKT

SALURN

SAN MICHELE

SEGANZANO

SEVIGNANO

LAVIS

FELDKIRCH

PERGINE

TRENT

BORGO

OSPEDALETTO

LEVICO

Mitrowsky

FELTRE

PRIMOLANO

CONEGLIANO

CALIANO

LA PIETRA

NOVE

ROVEREDO

DAVIDOVICH

MORI

MARCO

SERRAVALLE

CISMONE

CARPANE

BASSANO

BARCON

PORDENONE

ISONZO R.

PLAVE R.

Adige R.

Brenta R.

Avisio R.

EDOLO

BRENO

OGLIO R.

Chiese R.

LAKE IDRO

ROCCA D'ANFO

STORO

VAL D'ARSA

TRIESTE

GAVARDO

SALO

LAKE GARDA

MONTE BALDO

TORBOLE

RIVA

RIVALTA

LA CORONA

RIVOLI

CHIUSA

PER

DOLCE

XX Joubert (7,500)
(Replaced Vaubois)

CITTADELLA

CASTELFRANCO

TREVISO

XXXX ALVINTZY (-detachments)

BRESCIA

CASAGLIA

CASTELNEDOLO

PONTE SAN MARCO

GHEDI

MONTECHIARO

LONATO

DESENZANO

CASTELNUOVO

PESCHIERA

PASTRENGO

BUSSOLENGO

VICENZA

Brenta R.

MONTEBELLO

VENICE

XXXX
ITALY BONAPARTE

SOLFERINO

CAVRIANA

GUIDIZZOLO

VALEGGIO

BORGHETTO

VILLAFRANCA

VERONA

VAGO

CALDIERO

COLOGNOLO

VILLANUOVA

S. BONIFACIO

ARCOLA

ZERPA

BELFIORE

PORCILE

Alpone R.

Adige R.

XX Massena
XX Augereau } (15,000)

ZEVIO

RONCO

ALBAREDO

GOITO

ROVERBELLA

VALESE

ISOLA DELLA SCALA

ROVERCHIARA

MONTAGNANA

ESTE

XX Dallemagne
XX Rey

Serurier
(7,000 - replaced Kilmaine)

SAN ANTONIO

FAVORITA

CASTELLARO

NOGARA

CEREA

ANGIARI

MINERBE

LEGNAGO

SANGUINETTO

WÜRMSER

MANTUA

SAN GIORGIO

VILLEMPENTA

Mincio R.

Tartaro R.

MARCARIA

Po R.

BADIA

ROVIGO

Adige R.

ADRIATIC SEA

BOLOGNA
(27 MILES)

CREMONA

GALO

ITALIAN CAMPAIGNS, 1796-97
ALVINTZY'S FIRST ADVANCE
General Situation Late November
and
Austrian Movements Since
18 November 1796

SCALE OF MILES
0   5   10   15

PADUA

The gradual arrival of reinforcements promised by the Directory several months before filled some of the gaps left by the Arcola campaign. Bonaparte slaved at reorganization and resupply. In the midst of plenty, and while furnishing immense sums of money to the Directory, he frequently found his own forces suffering from shortages due to the venality of supply personnel, over whom he had only extremely limited authority.

From the preceding campaigns, Bonaparte had learned the necessity of watching the Chiese Valley, west of Lake Garda, and the risk of extending his positions north of that lake. For the moment, he was content to remain on the defensive, pressing the siege of Mantua and awaiting further reinforcements. By retaining bridgeheads over the Adige at Verona, Ronco (*C1*), and Legnago, he was prepared to operate offensively, if necessary, east of that river.

Intercepted dispatches revealed that the Pope and Austria had come to a secret understanding, and that the former was covertly gathering an army, with the intention of intervening as soon as the military situation permitted. Bonaparte formed a mobile column (3,300, under Lannes) at Bologna (*off map, C1*) to overawe the Papal States and stiffen the forces of France's new puppet Italian republics. He also echeloned about 6,000 more troops along his line of communication and on the coast from Nice to Leghorn. This left him with 47,000 troops at hand, including the sick and the 10,000–12,000 required for the siege of Mantua and garrison duties. These were distributed as shown.

Shortly after the battle of Arcola, General Clarke, an agent of the Directory, arrived in Brescia with the dual mission of opening negotiations with Austria and reporting on Bonaparte (whose growing popularity worried the Directory). There seemed to be a general demand for peace; an armistice had already been declared along the Rhine. Defeated there, the Directory hoped to indemnify itself in Italy. Bonaparte won Clarke to his view that the Adige was the natural frontier for France, and that the capture of Mantua was necessary to ensure it. Clarke convinced the Directory accordingly, and it promised to send Bonaparte 30,000 men from the Army of the Rhine. Austria, victorious in Germany, was determined to finally break the French in Italy, and indulged in negotiations only to gain time.

For the fifth time in nine months, the Austrian state, displaying amazing vitality, rebuilt its army in Italy. Reinforcements poured in—new levies of conscripts, the Vienna garrison, and volunteers. National spirit was high; the Empress embroidered standards with her own hands. The new army numbered 46,200 infantry and 2,800 cavalry. But it had two weaknesses. Its quality was uneven—again, there were large numbers of poorly trained recruits, soon to be hustled into combat before they were fit. (On the other hand, it included some splendid regiments, the toughened survivors of Alvintzy's re-cent debacle.) Worse, Alvintzy was left in command. It probably was not appreciated in Vienna that it was Alvintzy, more than his army, who had lost Arcola.

The Austrian plan had been carefully worked out, but was based on incorrect reports that Bonaparte was massing at Bologna for an invasion of the Papal States. On 7 January 1797, their columns moved out from positions along the Brenta, as shown. On the 8th, Provera made the first direct contact, driving in Augereau's outposts in front of Legnago. On the 9th, French outposts detected Bajalich's advance near Villanuova. That day, Joubert reported no enemy contacts. On the 10th, a part of Provera's column appeared before Badia (*C1*). Augereau reinforced the garrison there, left some men in Legnago, and concentrated (7,500) at Ronco, ready to cross and strike toward Legnago or Villanuova. Bonaparte, at Bologna, but aware of developments, sent most of Lannes' force from Bologna north to Badia. Leaving Bologna, Bonaparte arrived in Roverbella (*B1*) late on the 11th. Early on the 12th, he concluded that Alvintzy was repeating his previous offensive against the lower Adige, and gave orders for an attack in that sector by Massena, Augereau, Rey, and the cavalry reserve. (Bonaparte's espionage service had informed him on the actual Austrian plans, but he always viewed such reports with great distrust.) That same day (the 12th), Bajalich advanced boldly upon the French outposts at Verona, provoking Massena into a sudden eruption that sent the Austrians streaming back on Villanuova with the loss of 1,000, including 600 prisoners. That day, also, Joubert reported light attacks at La Corona (*B2*), which he had easily repulsed. Bonaparte, now at Verona, awaited developments on the lower Adige front.

Late on the 13th, Augereau reported only light skirmishing on his front, but Joubert sent alarming news. He had been under heavy attack at La Corona since 0900; had held out until 1400, when, threatened on both flanks, he had retired to Rivoli. In view of the enemy's superior strength, he planned to abandon Rivoli during the night, unless he received orders to the contrary.

It now became clear to Bonaparte that his spies' reports of the Austrian plans were correct—Alvintzy's was the main attack force. Orders were promptly issued for a maximum concentration against him. Victor, with troops detached from Serurier and Augereau, would move up to Villafranca (*B1*); Rey to Castelnuovo (*B1*); Murat (now commanding a brigade under Rey) would utilize the gunboat flotilla to ferry the troops at Salo (*A2*) to Torri (*B2*), then march to join Joubert. Massena would leave minimum garrisons in the Verona-Bussolengo area and march for Rivoli, sending a detachment to Garda (*B2*) to cover Joubert's left rear. Augereau would defend the Adige from Verona south. Bonaparte himself arrived at Rivoli at 0200 on the 14th. When his concentration was complete, he would have approximately 23,000 men and some 30 to 40 guns to engage Alvintzy.

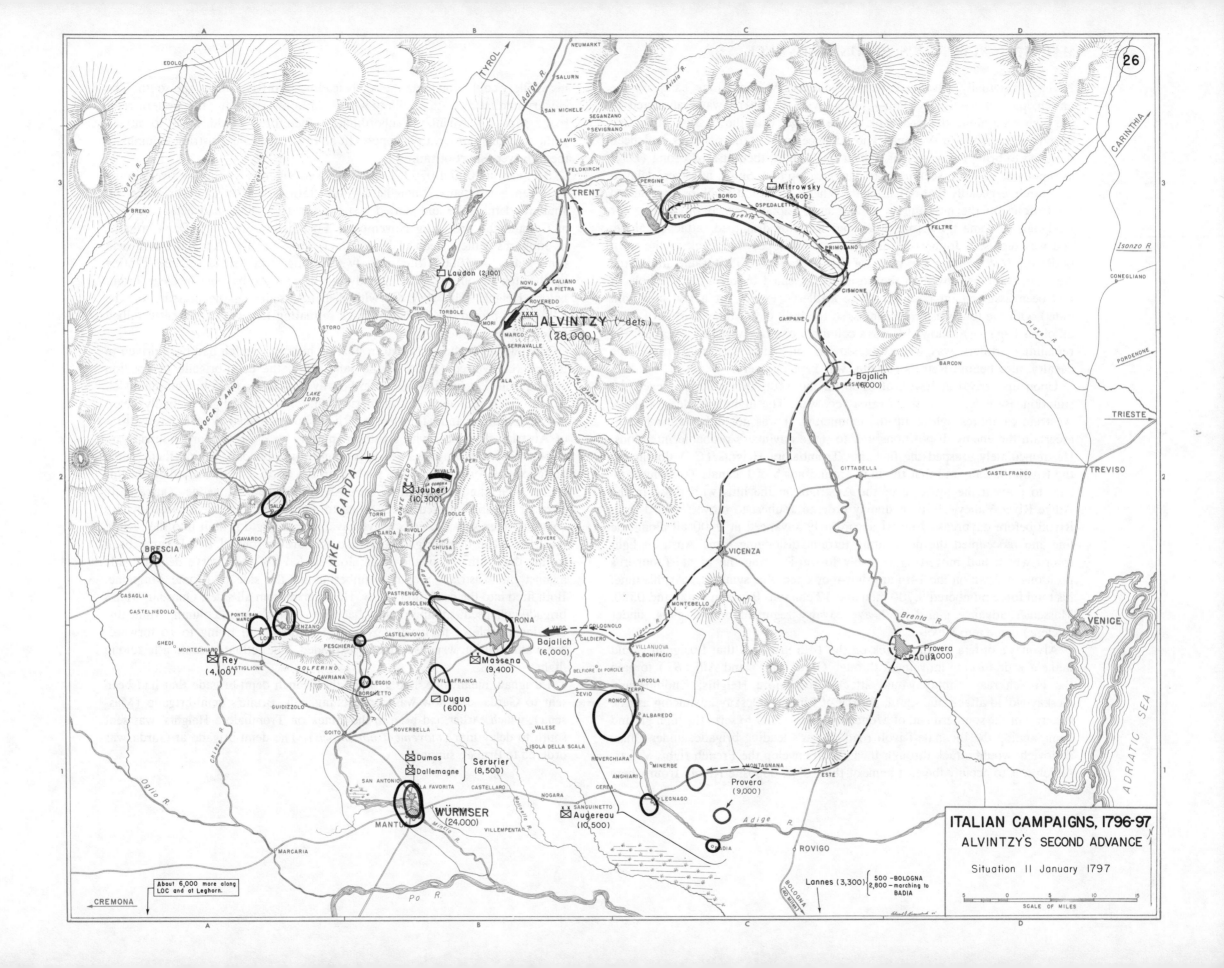

ITALIAN CAMPAIGNS, 1796-97

ALVINTZY'S SECOND ADVANCE

Situation 11 January 1797

Alvintzy originally advanced in five columns. At some time early on the march, part of Reuss's column—Vukassovich (2,900)—was transferred to the high road along the east bank of the Adige, with the mission of linking up with Bajalich near Verona. The advance in multiple columns had been designed to bring major weight to bear on Joubert, then at La Corona (*D3*), as rapidly as possible, seeking to fix and envelop him. Snow, however, delayed the march, especially that of Lusignan. When Liptay and Knöblös approached La Corona on the morning of 12 January, Liptay insisted on waiting for Lusignan to come up before attacking; Knöblös disagreed, attacked alone, and was repulsed. Joubert, afraid of being enveloped, fell back to the town of Rivoli (*C1*) during the night of 13–14 January. That same night, the Austrian columns moved to the positions indicated by open red symbols. It had been assumed impossible to take artillery (except for a few mountain guns) with the four western columns, so the bulk of Alvintzy's artillery (and all of his baggage) followed Reuss's column along the western river road; the remaining artillery was with Vukassovich, on the eastern river road. The cavalry, also behind Reuss's column, was kept in reserve.

Upon his arrival at Rivoli at 0200 on the 14th, Bonaparte surveyed the situation. By now, he knew this area very well. The night was clear, and the Austrian campfires lighted up the mountains. It was not difficult for him to ascertain the enemy dispositions and to sense Alvintzy's probable intentions. He immediately grasped the fact that Trombalora Heights (*C2*) dominated the Rivoli plateau, and that the high ground north of Incanale (*C2*) must be held to prevent the juncture of the Austrians in the hills with those in the Adige River Valley. He immediately ordered Joubert to move forward from Rivoli before daybreak. Joubert accordingly advanced at 0400 all along the line and reoccupied the dominating terrain, dislodging some Austrian light troops which had moved aggressively forward during the night. (Joubert's positions at dawn on the 14th are shown by open blue symbols.) At this time, his total force numbered 9,700 men and 12 cannon. Between 0400 and 0500, Massena's advance guard (a heavy cavalry regiment and 6 guns, under Leclerc) came into Rivoli.

Alvintzy's orders for the attack on the 14th provided that Lusignan would make a wide turning movement through Garda (*A1*) and Affi (*B1*) to gain the French rear; Liptay would attack Trombalora Heights; Knöblös and Ocskay would attack due south, abreast of Liptay—Ocskay advancing astride the crest of the southern end of Monte Magnone (*C2*) to seize the high ground commanding the Incanale-Rivoli road. Reuss's leading brigade, under Quasdanovich, would attack through Incanale to envelop the French right; Vukassovich was to occupy the east bank of the Adige, opposite Rivoli, from where

his artillery could dominate the roads leading into Rivoli from the south. The cavalry and much of the artillery were held in reserve along the western river road. Most of Alvintzy's subordinates, therefore, would have to attack without artillery or cavalry support. In addition, the four Austrian columns in the hills were short of rations.

Between 0600 and 0700, Liptay attacked vigorously, slightly overlapping the French left flank. Immediately, the 85th and 29th Demi-brigades, on Joubert's left, broke and started a stampede. (The 85th had acted similarly at Caliano the preceding November.) Fortunately, the 14th Demi-brigade, in Joubert's center, steadied by Berthier, drew back its left flank and held firm. Now (at 1000) Massena's two leading demi-brigades came panting up through Rivoli, and were quickly put in with the bayonet to clear Trombalora Heights. This they did with dispatch, relieving the pressure on the 14th Demi-brigade. Most of Joubert's retreating left wing apparently rallied to join them.

Meanwhile, Joubert had had trouble on his right, which had been driven in toward San Marco (*C2*). At the same time, the demi-brigade in position around Della Dogana Inn (*C1*) was heavily attacked in front by Quasdanovich and raked by Vukassovich's artillery from across the Adige. It finally abandoned its position and retired toward Rivoli, hotly pursued by several squadrons of Austrian dragoons, with Austrian infantry in close support. Spurring up the hill road, the dragoons won a footing on the plateau; behind them, three battalions of Austrian infantry pushed up the north side of the valley. In this crisis, with the French rear seriously threatened, someone (apparently Berthier) hastily massed fifteen guns to smash the head of Quasdanovich's column—then sent Leclerc's heavy cavalry charging downhill into the reeling Austrians. The demi-brigade that had withdrawn toward Rivoli came back to line the south rim of the defile; Joubert led his one reserve demi-brigade against the Austrian infantry clambering up the side of Monte Magnone. Both fired into the confusion below. Hammered from all sides, Quasdanovich's brigade collapsed, spilling rapidly back into Reuss's main column. Amid this growing jumble of fleeing troops and of artillery still trying to go forward, some ammunition wagons suddenly exploded. The retreat became a headlong flight.

Lusignan, meanwhile, had avoided the French demi-brigade that had been sent to Garda, and now was approaching Affi. Brune's demi-brigade (Massena), which earlier had been in the attack on Trombalora Heights, was sent south to delay him (*movement not shown*). The demi-brigade at Garda was ordered to Brune's support.

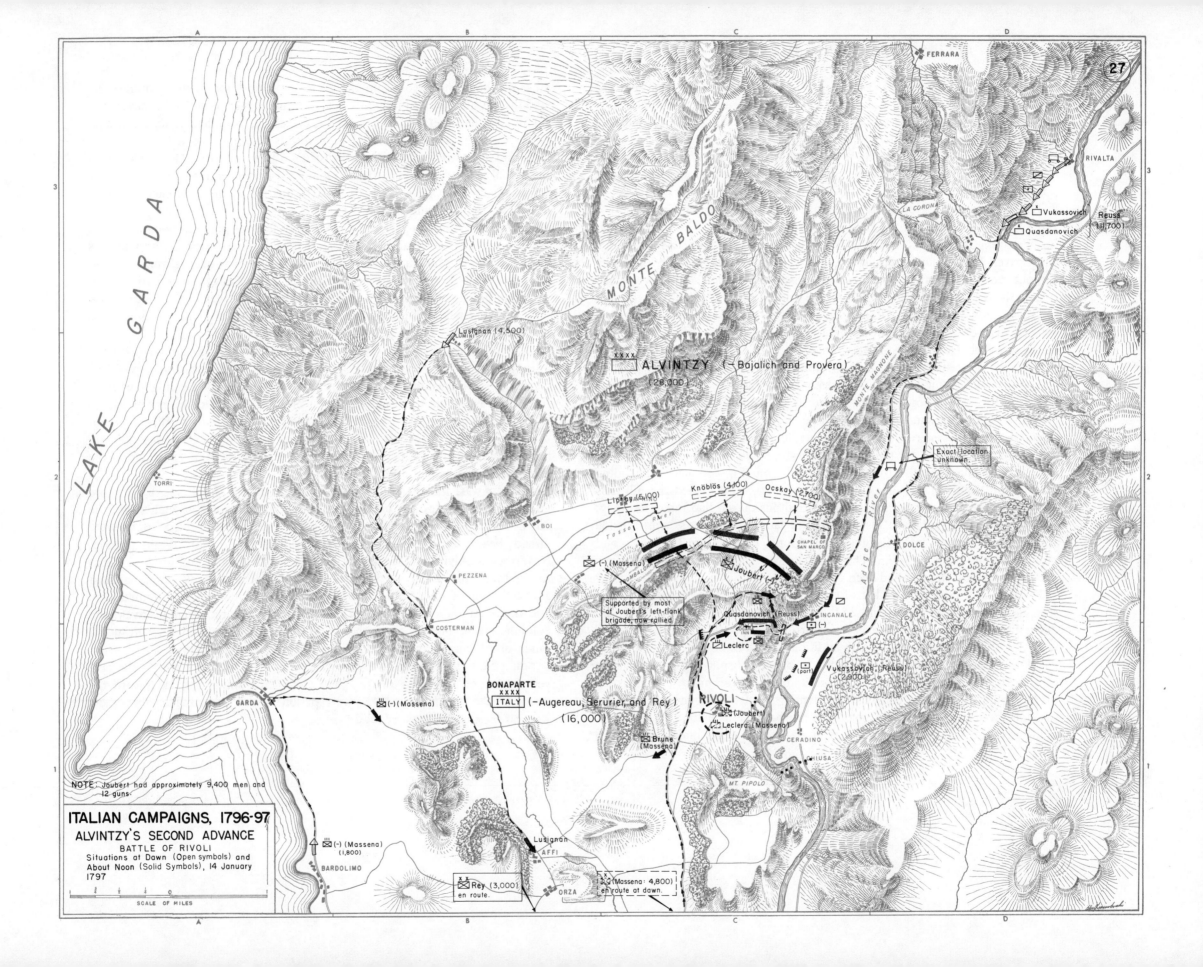

RIVALTA

FERRARA

LA CORONA

Reuss
Vukassovich (11,700)

Quasdanovich

MONTE BALDO

LAKE GARDA

TORRI

Lusignan (4,500)
LUMINI

$\times\times\times\times$
□ ALVINTZY (~Bajalich and Provera)
(28,000)

MONTE MAGNONE

Adige River

Exact location
unknown.

BOI

Lipthay (5,100)   Knöblös (4,100)   Ocskay (2,700)

CHAPEL OF
SAN MARCO

DOLCE

Tosso River

PEZZENA

✕ (-) (Massena)

TOMBALOR

Joubert (-)

COSTERMAN

Supported by most
of Joubert's left-flank
brigade, now rallied

Quasdanovich (Reuss)

INCANALE

Leclerc

(-)
(part)

Vukassovich (Reuss)
(2,000)

GARDA

✕ (-) (Massena)

BONAPARTE
$\times\times\times\times$
ITALY (~Augereau, Serurier, and Rey)
(16,000)

RIVOLI

(Joubert)
Leclerc (Massena)

CERADINO

CHIUSA

✕ Brune
(Massena)

MT. PIPOLO

NOTE: Joubert had approximately 9,400 men and
12 guns.

✕ (-) (Massena)
(1,800)

Lusignan
AFFI

ITALIAN CAMPAIGNS, 1796-97
ALVINTZY'S SECOND ADVANCE
BATTLE OF RIVOLI
Situations at Dawn (Open symbols) and
About Noon (Solid Symbols), 14 January
1797

BARDOLIMO

✕✕ Rey (3,000)
en route.

ORZA

(Massena: 4,800)
en route at dawn.

SCALE OF MILES

Having routed Quasdanovich and the remainder of Reuss's column, and sent troops to delay Lusignan, Bonaparte now gathered all forces immediately available for an attack on the center Austrian columns. Vial (commanding the French right flank, while Joubert attended personally to Quasdanovich) had already rallied the troops there and halted the advance of Knöblös and Ocskay; at the same time, Massena had forced Liptay back, and now threatened Knöblös' right flank.

The principal effort of Bonaparte's attack was directed against Knöblös and Ocskay. The French infantry was strongly supported by artillery and further strengthened by a small body of light cavalry, under Lasalle, which had arrived from Mantua during the day. The Austrian infantry, operating without adequate artillery and cavalry support, nevertheless performed splendidly against the French infantry and guns, charging repeatedly through the snow. However, the handful of French cavalry, furiously led, appears to have created several small panics. Knöblös and Ocskay were driven in disorder back across the Tasso River; Liptay, under pressure from Massena and afraid of being cut off, retired behind the town of Caprino.

To the south, Brune had gradually been driven back by Lusignan's superior numbers. In the afternoon, he was joined by the demi-brigade called in from Garda. At about the same time, the head of Rey's column reached Orza. Rey—another Vendee general—had started late; finding Lusignan between himself and Bonaparte, he had paused to await developments. Lusignan, meanwhile, strictly following orders, moved to occupy Monte Pipolo, the commanding high ground south of Rivoli. A little before 1500, he occupied the hill. His mission had been accomplished, but his circuitous march had taken too long; by now the battle had been lost. Bonaparte launched Brune's demi-brigade and the demi-brigade from Garda against Monte Pipolo from the north, and ordered Rey up from the south. The Austrians, caught between two fires, were broken up; by 1700, most had been captured.

Rivoli was a curious and hard-fought battle. The forces engaged in the struggle were 19,000 French and 25,000 Austrians. Of the latter, some 6,000 did not really come to grips, except for artillery support. The French losses were 2,200; the Austrian, 3,300, in addition to 7,000 men taken prisoner or listed as missing in action. In this battle, Bonaparte displayed his generalship at its best. One glimpse at the Austrian campfires in the night, and his keen insight could forecast the course of the coming battle: Lusignan, meandering through the mountains, would not reach the battlefield in time; Reuss's column, advancing along the western river road, posed the major threat and

must not be permitted to gain the plateau; against the center columns, he held the advantages of superior artillery, and maneuver room for his cavalry to exploit. He had met the Austrian attacks calmly, confidently, and courageously. From his central position, he skillfully concentrated a superiority of men and firepower against each Austrian threat in turn. Despite over-all numerical inferiority, Bonaparte had managed to concentrate, for the decisive action on the plateau, a force (15,000) superior to the combined columns of Liptay, Knöblös, and Ocskay (12,000).

During the afternoon, while giving orders for the pursuit, Bonaparte was advised that Provera had eluded Augereau along the lower Adige and was on the march to Mantua. Leaving Rey's force and Massena's strongest demi-brigade with Joubert, he moved south with Massena's cavalry and two remaining demi-brigades, picking up Victor's force on the way. (Rey, sternly rebuked for not having pushed forward to the sound of the guns, was relieved and given the duty of escorting Austrian prisoners to the rear.)

Joubert collected all his forces—possibly 15,000—and, at dawn on the 15th, started in energetic pursuit of the Austrians. Vial's brigade moved forward along the crest of Monte Magnone to envelop the retreating Austrians from the east; Vaux's brigade advanced along the slope of Monte Baldo to cut off the enemy at La Corona; Joubert led the main body in direct pursuit up the central valley. Murat, who had landed at Torri (A2) during the evening of the 14th with a demi-brigade of light infantry from Salo, across the lake, marched cross-country all night.

Alvintzy was, after all, soldier enough to feel that he should make one more attempt to break through to Mantua. Also, ignorant of Lusignan's fate, he did not want to abandon him. Actually, the Austrian central columns were already beaten; the men were disheartened, hungry, and short of ammunition. Nevertheless, Alvintzy reorganized them as best he could, and ordered Reuss to reinforce him through La Corona. The Austrian attack, made against Joubert's center, rapidly broke down; Joubert counterattacked immediately and drove Alvintzy up the valley. In the meantime, the French enveloping columns made good progress; their trap closed near La Corona, cutting off much of Alvintzy's command and throwing the rest into panic.

Some 28,000 men had advanced with Alvintzy from Roveredo as the new year began; on the 16th, a bare 7,000 streamed frantically back toward the town. Of the remainder, 13,000 were prisoners in French hands; the others were stragglers, deserters, or dead.

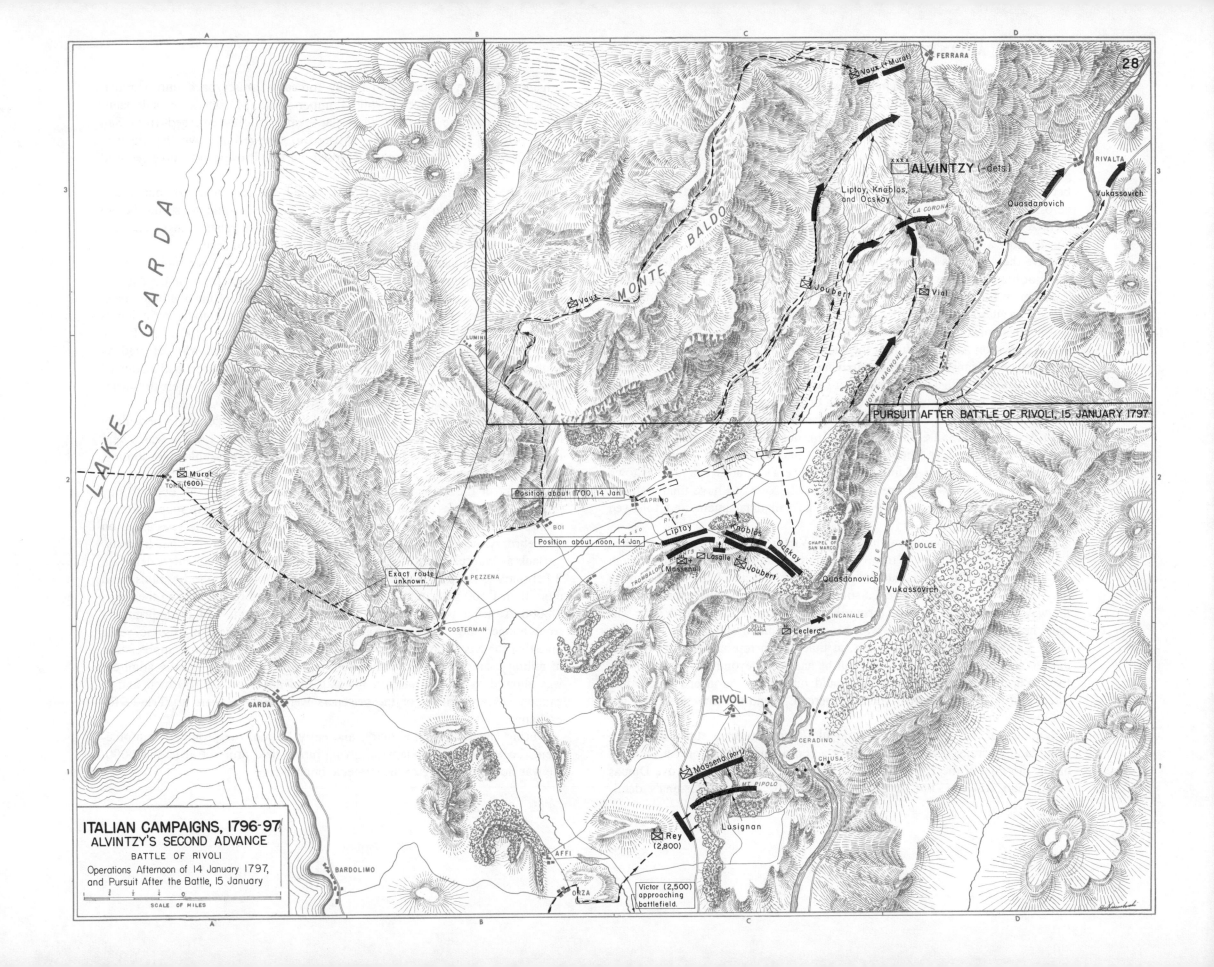

28

ALVINTZY (-dets)

Liptay, Knablos,
and Ocskay

LA CORONA

RIVALTA

Quasdanovich

Vukassovich

FERRARA

Vaux (-Murat)

MONTE BALDO

Vaux

Joubert

Vial

MONTE MAGNONE

LUMINI

PURSUIT AFTER BATTLE OF RIVOLI, 15 JANUARY 1797

Murat
(600)

TORRI

Position about 1700, 14 Jan

CAPRINO

BOI

Position about noon, 14 Jan

Liptay

Knablos

Ocskay

CHAPEL OF
SAN MARCO

DOLCE

Lasalle

Massena

Joubert

Quasdanovich

Vukassovich

Exact route
unknown.

PEZZENA

TROMBALORA

ADIGE River

INCANALE

COSTERMAN

DELLA
DOGANA
INN

Leclerc

GARDA

RIVOLI

CERADINO

CHIUSA

Massena (part)

PIPOLO

Lusignan

ITALIAN CAMPAIGNS, 1796-97
ALVINTZY'S SECOND ADVANCE
BATTLE OF RIVOLI
Operations Afternoon of 14 January 1797,
and Pursuit After the Battle, 15 January

Rey
(2,800)

AFFI

BARDOLIMO

SCALE OF MILES

ORZA

Victor (2,500)
approaching
battlefield.

LAKE GARDA

While the French and Austrian armies clashed in the north, Provera spent three days considering the situation on his front along the lower Adige. His delay, however, had the probably unintended result of lulling his opponent, Augereau. When Bonaparte had moved north and left Augereau to his own devices, the latter had taken up a cordon defense west of the river. Provera got Bajalich to make a feint at Arcola (C2) on 13 January, and made a number of similar moves himself. That evening, he pushed an advance guard across the river in boats at Anghiari, driving out the small garrison of 200 men. A bridgehead was established, and the night of 13–14 January spent in constructing a bridge. Guieu (1,400) rushed down from Ronco on the 14th to drive the Austrians back across the river, but was repulsed by their greatly superior forces. On the evening of the 14th, Provera marched for Mantua with 7,000 men; for some unknown reason, he left 2,000 men and 14 guns (*not shown*) to guard his bridge at Anghiari. That night he halted at Nogara.

Augereau, meanwhile, recalled his troops along the lower Adige to Legnago, and marched on Anghiari during the evening of the 14th—apparently hoping to find the Austrians still there. On arriving at the town, he wasted time attacking the Austrian bridge guard, killing or capturing the whole of it and burning the bridge. Moving westward in the path of Provera, he came upon the Austrian rear guard near Cerea, inflicting considerable losses upon it.

Provera reached San Giorgio on the 15th, but failed to surprise the French garrison (1,500) under Miollis, which held that suburb as a strong point in the French lines around Mantua. All of Provera's attacks against the town were repulsed. The cannon fire from this battle seems to have finally stirred Augereau; he sent Lannes forward with a small detachment and followed later, reaching Castellaro.

On the 15th, Bonaparte—with Massena, Victor, and the cavalry—reached Roverbella (B1). Massena's troops had marched north to Rivoli all through the night of the 13th–14th, had fought in that battle all of the 14th, and on the night of the 14th had marched south for more than thirty miles, much of the way by rough hill tracks. During the night of the 15th–16th, Victor was sent ahead toward La Favorita, with his own command and two of Massena's weary demi-brigades. Bonaparte has, at times, been reproached for this mad dash to catch Provera's small force. But he had seen beyond this simple objective: Würmser and Provera united would outnumber Serurier's blockading forces and might well destroy them; Augereau, it had become clear, was not the man to save the situation.

Ignorant of the ring closing around him, Provera got a staff officer into Mantua and arranged with Würmser for a coordinated attack on La Favorita on the morning of the 16th. The attack was vigorous; Würmser drove Dumas out of San Antonio, but Serurier, supported by one of Massena's demi-brigades, held La Favorita and finally forced Würmser back into Mantua. Victor then struck Provera, while Rampon, with Massena's second demi-brigade, turned the Austrian right flank, and Miollis emerged from San Giorgio to hit Provera's left rear. Augereau, swaggering down the highway from Castellaro, now appeared and closed the net. Provera, his force reduced to some 5,000 men, surrendered.

Würmser's fate in Mantua was now sealed. He still held out, but it was obvious that he could hardly do so much longer. It would be spring before Austria could assemble and dispatch another army of relief; hunger and disease, Würmser's immediate foes, would triumph before then.

The French immediately drove forward in exploitation (*not shown*). Massena pushed through Ronco to Vicenza; Augereau sped through Legnago to Padua (D2) and then to Cittadella (D3). Bajalich had meanwhile fallen back toward Bassano (D3); he was caught between the two converging columns on the 24th and driven north in disorder, with the loss of 1,000 men. To the west, Laudon moved south to cover Alvintzy's retreat, but was defeated by Joubert north of Peri (B3) on the 27th. By 2 February, Joubert had advanced to the Avisio River, twenty miles north of Roveredo (B3). Augereau, meanwhile, had pushed on to Treviso, twenty-five miles east of Cittadella.

On 1 February, Bonaparte marched to deal with the Pope. He personally led the detachment (8,600, including 4,000 Italian troops), for it was a venture that required tact and judgment amid wonderful opportunities for looting. Under such circumstances, neither Massena nor Augereau could be trusted. The object of the invasion was largely financial—to force the Pope to pay promised indemnities and to extract additional amounts to help support Bonaparte's subsequent military operations. The Pope offered little resistance; on 19 February, he acceded to Bonaparte's demands and signed a harsh treaty.

Back at Mantua, Würmser, in desperate straits, finally had surrendered on 2 February to Serurier. Some 16,000 men (including 6,000 in hospitals) and more than 1,500 guns of various calibers fell to the French. During the siege, 18,000 Austrian troops and 6,000 civilian inhabitants had died, primarily from hunger and disease. Reportedly, 7,000 French died of disease while investing the city. This experience left Bonaparte with a lifelong appreciation of military sanitation. Würmser, whose courage the French greatly admired, was allowed to march out with his staff and an escort of 500 men and 6 cannon. The remainder of the prisoners were sent eastward to Trieste for exchange.

During late January, February, and early March, the promised reinforcements began to reach Bonaparte, giving him a field army of at least 40,000. He was now ready to seize the strategic offensive.

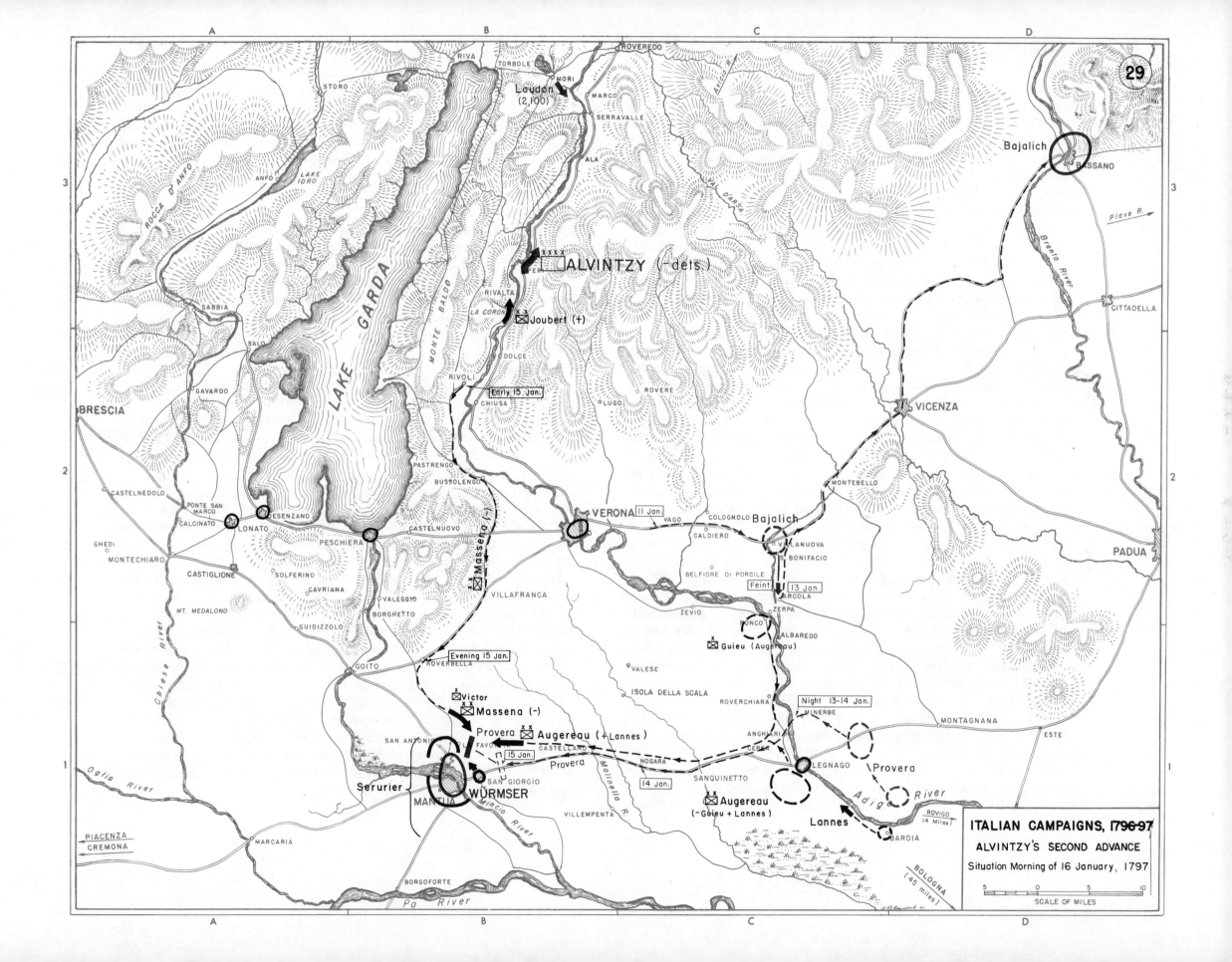

29

ROVEREDO

RIVA
TORBOLE
MORI
Laudon
(2,100)
MARCO
SERRAVALLE
ALA

STORO

LAKE
IDRO

ANFO

ROCCA D'ANFO

Bajalich
BASSANO

Piave R.

Brenta River

LAKE GARDA

MONTE BALDO

ALVINTZY (-dets)

RIVALTA
LA CORONA
Joubert (†)
DOLCE
RIVOLI
Early 15 Jan.
CHIUSA
LUGO
ROVERE

SABBIA

SALO

CITTADELLA

PASTRENGO
BUSSOLENGO

VICENZA

MONTEBELLO

CASTELNEDOLO

PONTE SAN MARCO
CALCINATO
LONATO
DESENZANO

PESCHIERA

CASTELNUOVO

Massena (-)

VERONA
11 Jan.
VAGO
COLOGNOLO
Bajalich
CALDIERO
VILLANUOVA
S. BONIFACIO
BELFIORE DI PORCILE

PADUA

GHEDI
MONTECHIARO

CASTIGLIONE

SOLFERINO

CAVRIANA

VILLAFRANCA

VALEGGIO

BORGHETTO

MT. MEDALONO

GUIDIZZOLO

GOITO

ROVERBELLA

ZEVIO

Feint
13 Jan.
ARCOLA
ZERPA
RONCO
ALBAREDO
Guieu (Augereau)

VALESE

ISOLA DELLA SCALA

ROVERCHIARA

MINERBE

MONTAGNANA

ANGHIARI

ESTE

Chiese River

Oglio River

Evening 15 Jan.

Victor
Massena (-)
Provera
Augereau (+Lannes)

SAN ANTONIO
FAVORITA
15 Jan.
Provera
CASTELLARO
NOGARA
SANQUINETTO

14 Jan.

Night 13-14 Jan.

Provera

LEGNAGO

Adige River

Serurier
MANTUA
WÜRMSER
SAN GIORGIO

Molinella R.

VILLEMPENTA

Augereau
(-Guieu + Lannes)

Lannes

BARDIA
ROVIGO
(4 Miles)

MARCARIA

Mincio River

PIACENZA
CREMONA

BORGOFORTE

Po River

BOLOGNA
(45 miles)

ITALIAN CAMPAIGNS, 1796-97
ALVINTZY'S SECOND ADVANCE
Situation Morning of 16 January, 1797

5   0   5   10
SCALE OF MILES

Bonaparte had won Rivoli at a moment when the Directory, shaking under new defeats along the Rhine and growing political opposition at home, had been willing to make peace on bargain terms. Now, its members saw unlimited prospects of further conquest and loot, and all thoughts of peace were discarded. The main French effort would be shifted from the Rhine to northern Italy; Bonaparte would be reinforced and given a free hand for an advance on Vienna; Moreau would advance into southern Germany to clear the Tyrol and cover Bonaparte's left flank.

Believing that a decisive victory over Bonaparte would completely capsize the reeling French war effort, the Austrians decided to stand on the defensive in Germany and concentrate an army of 90,000 in northern Italy. The Archduke Charles, conqueror of Jourdan and Moreau, was placed in command. When he reached Italy in February 1797, he found some 44,000 regulars and militia on hand—mostly survivors of recent defeats inflicted by Bonaparte, and too disorganized and demoralized for another offensive. As the promised reinforcements slowly trickled in, the Archduke, forced on the defensive, disposed his troops as shown to cover the routes leading to the heart of Austria.

Since intelligence reports placed the bulk of the Austrian forces to the east, Bonaparte decided to make his main effort there. Joubert, meanwhile, would protect his left flank until Moreau's promised advance cleared the Austrians from the Tyrol. Of the 50,000 reinforcements promised by the Directory, 23,000, mostly seasoned troops, had arrived by early March. A series of skirmishes soon gave Bonaparte a clear picture of the Austrian positions and the low state of Austrian morale. Also, reports disclosed that the reinforcements from Germany had been delayed and that the Austrian frontier fortresses had not yet been put on a war footing. Because of these favorable circumstances, Bonaparte decided to attack at once with the troops at hand. On 11 March, he moved forward in echelon, with the left wing (Massena) leading, in an effort to cut the Austrians off from Tarvis Pass (*C2*).

As Massena advanced against Lusignan, Joubert sent Baraguay to Primiero (*B2*), while Serurier thrust a brigade toward Serravalle (*B2*). Lusignan withdrew, and it was not until the 14th that Massena caught up with him at Longarone (*B2*). Lusignan, a good soldier, if no general, sacrificed a rear guard and himself to allow his disorganized column to escape. Massena was then called in on Aviano, but snow-choked roads forced him to detour through Serravalle and thus lose time. Meanwhile, on 12 March, Serurier had defeated Hohenzollern and advanced to Conegliano (*B2*). Here he halted, while Guieu and Dugua, with his cavalry, pursued Hohenzollern, and Bernadotte came forward at top speed.

Bonaparte now advanced against the Archduke. Intending to fight only a delaying action, Charles had spread his 27,000 men behind the Tagliamento (*B2*), from Latisana north almost to Gemona. On the 16th, the French attacked on a front of about two miles near Codroipo, their troops moving with magnificent steadiness as if on the parade ground. Avoiding a serious engagement, the Archduke retired on Palmanova. Here, he sent his trains north under escort of Bajalich (5,000), while his main force moved toward Laibach (*D2*) through Gradisca (*C2*), where he left 2,500 men. His intention seems to have been to draw Bonaparte away from Bajalich and the trains and to entice him as far eastward as possible, thus increasing the French supply problems.

Bonaparte had expected the Archduke to retire through Tarvis Pass, and had sent Massena toward the pass to cut off the Austrian retreat. He was, therefore, surprised and disturbed when the Archduke moved eastward. Nevertheless, on the 17th, Massena was ordered to continue to Tarvis, while Bonaparte himself pursued the Archduke. At the same time, Joubert was ordered to advance northward to Brixen (*A3*), as added flank protection. On the 18th, at Palmanova, Bonaparte learned of Bajalich's northward move, and sent Guieu in pursuit. The next day, Gradisca surrendered to Bernadotte and Serurier. Gorizia (*C2*) fell on the 20th.

Now convinced of the futility of following in the Archduke's tracks, Bonaparte decided to concentrate toward Klagenfurt (*C3*), on the direct route to Vienna. First, however, he again felt out the Austrian dispositions: Bernadotte and Chabot (who had replaced the sick Serurier) moved toward Laibach, defeating the Archduke's rear guard at Czernitza (*C2*), while Dugua took the cavalry ahead to occupy Trieste (*C1*) on 23 March.

During this same period, Massena had driven Ocskay's brigade (1,900) back to Wurzen (*C2*) and had got his advance guard into Tarvis Pass on the 21st. But the next afternoon, Bajalich's advance guard appeared unexpectedly from the south and retook the pass. Also, the Archduke, learning of Massena's advance and Guieu's pursuit of Bajalich, rushed in person to Wurzen, gathered what troops he could, and advanced through Tarvis against Massena. The result was a furious and bloody battle at Malborghetto on 23 March. The French, superior in numbers and better mountain fighters, were victorious, and the Archduke was thrown back to Villach. Two days later, Bajalich, trapped between Guieu and Massena, surrendered twenty-five cannon, 300 wagons, and 2,000 men. To date, the Archduke had lost some 15,000 men (not counting many stragglers and deserters) in a series of piecemeal encounters, without inflicting any appreciable delay on Bonaparte's advance.

To the west, Joubert had beaten the Austrians along the Avisio River on the 20th, reaching Neumarkt on the 21st and Botzen on the 22d. When Laudon (covering Davidovich's withdrawal) retired to an excellent flanking position at Meran, Joubert left Baraguay to contain him while he himself skillfully fought his way on, entering Brixen on the 24th.

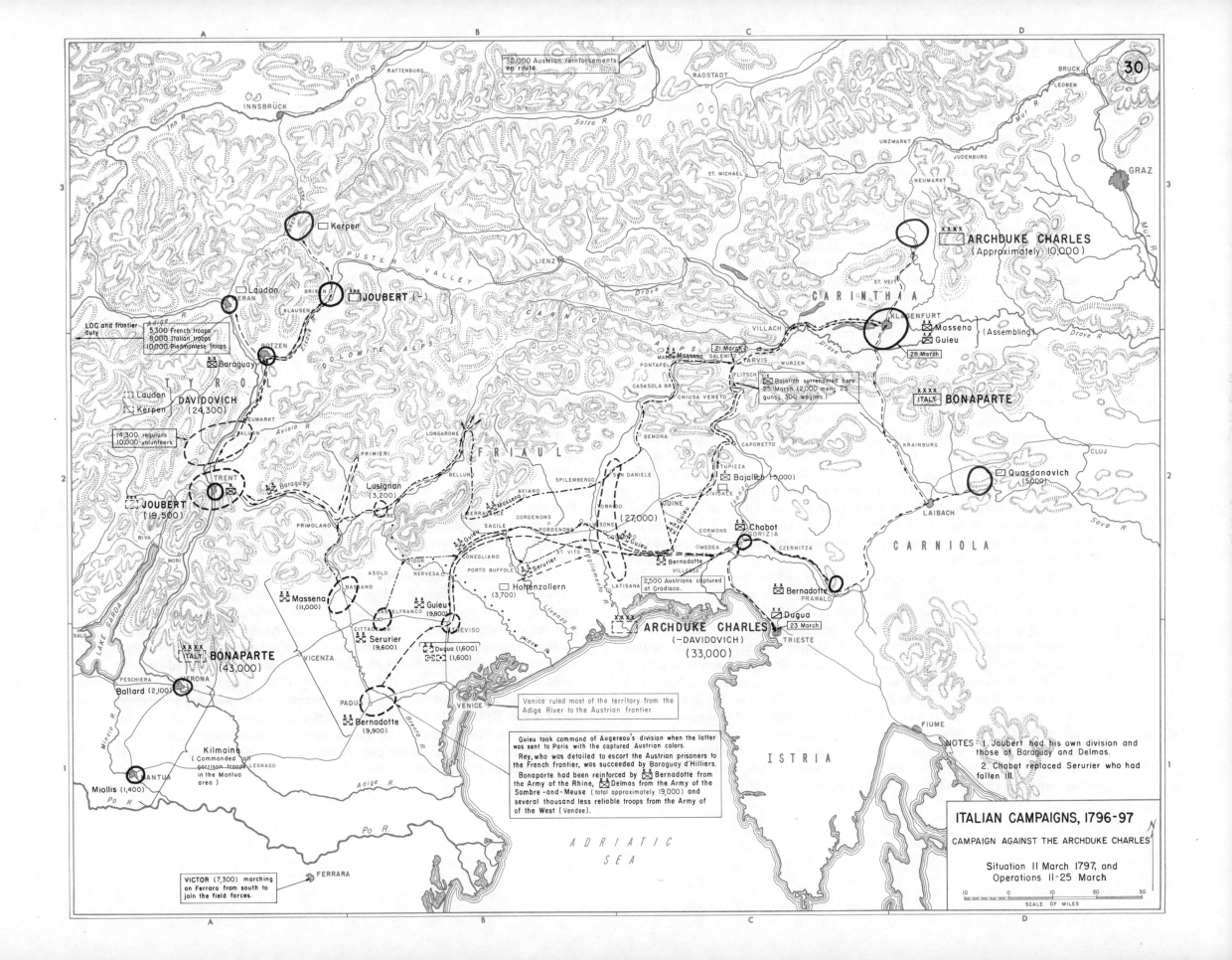

30,000 Austrian reinforcements en route

ARCHDUKE CHARLES (Approximately) 10,000

LOG and frontier duty
5,300 French troops
8,000 Italian troops
10,000 Piedmontese troops

JOUBERT (−)

Kerpen

Laudon

Masséna

Baraguay

DAVIDOVICH (24,300)

Laudon
Kerpen

Massena SALENITZ 21 March

Bajalich surrendered here 25 March (2,000 men; 25 guns; 300 wagons.)

Klagenfurt 28 March
Massena
Guieu (Assembling)

ITALY BONAPARTE

14,300 regulars 10,000 volunteers

TRENT

JOUBERT (19,500)

Baraguay

Lusignan (3,200)

FRIAUL

Bajalich (5,000)

(27,000)

Quasdanovich (5,000)

Laibach

CARNIOLA

Massena

Chabot GORIZIA

Bernadotte

Guieu

Masséna (11,000)

Guieu (9,800)

Bernadotte

2,500 Austrians captured at Gradisca.

Bernadotte PRAWALD

Serurier (9,600)

Hohenzollern (3,700)

Dugua
23 March

ITALY BONAPARTE (43,000)

Verona

Dugua (1,600)
(1,600)

ARCHDUKE CHARLES (−DAVIDOVICH) (33,000)

TRIESTE

Ballard (2,100)

Kilmaine (Commanded all garrison troops in the Mantua area)

FIUME

Miollis (1,400)

Mantua

Bernadotte (9,900)

ISTRIA

Venice ruled most of the territory from the Adige River to the Austrian frontier.

Guieu took command of Augereau's division when the latter was sent to Paris with the captured Austrian colors.
Rey, who was detailed to escort the Austrian prisoners to the French frontier, was succeeded by Baraguay d'Hilliers.
Bonaparte had been reinforced by Bernadotte from the Army of the Rhine, Delmas from the Army of the Sambre-and-Meuse (total approximately 19,000) and several thousand less reliable troops from the Army of of the West (Vendee).

NOTES: 1. Joubert had his own division and those of Baraguay and Delmas.
2. Chabot replaced Serurier who had fallen ill.

ADRIATIC SEA

FERRARA

VICTOR (7,300) marching on Ferrara from south to join the field forces.

ITALIAN CAMPAIGNS, 1796-97

CAMPAIGN AGAINST THE ARCHDUKE CHARLES

Situation 11 March 1797, and Operations 11-25 March

10 0 10 20 30
SCALE OF MILES

By 28 March, Bonaparte had concentrated around Klagenfurt (*D3*); Bernadotte remained behind to organize fortified depots at Palmanova and Gradisca (*both C2*) and to watch Quasdanovich, whom the Archduke had detached east of Laibach. Joubert, after repeatedly defeating Kerpen, had occupied a position north of Brixen (*A3*), from which he could protect Bonaparte against any Austrian advance down the Puster Valley (*B3*) and also assist Moreau's contemplated advance toward Innsbrück (*A3*).

Since mid-March, Bonaparte had repeatedly urged the Directory to start Moreau's eastward advance, but to no avail. His situation now was highly delicate. The French forces were spread along a front of some 200 miles, and their communications ran back through Tarvis (*C2*) to Verona (*A1*). Bernadotte and Joubert could not be called forward without leaving his flanks exposed to Quasdanovich and Laudon. Though the forces confronting Bonaparte were weak, there were still 80,000 Austrians along the Rhine. If the French there remained motionless, the Austrians could easily shift troops from the Rhine, overwhelm Joubert, and drive down the Adige to cut the Army of Italy from its roots.

To gain time, Bonaparte requested an armistice; but, to dispel any conception of the offer as a sign of weakness, he presented it on the point of his sword by renewing his advance. The Archduke replied that he had no authority to negotiate and would refer the offer to his government; meanwhile, he had called in Kerpen and Quasdanovich, hoping with their help to hold a series of good defensive positions south of Vienna against Bonaparte's offensive. His hopes were futile. Massena, the wily mountain fighter, led the French advance, utilizing his superior numbers to maneuver and batter the Archduke back through Neumarkt (*D3*, 1 April), Unzmarkt (3 April), and Leoben (7 April), inflicting heavy losses. Guieu's detached brigade, meanwhile, blocked Kerpen's advance guard.

On 2 April, Bonaparte ordered Bernadotte and Joubert to join him (the latter to leave two divisions in the Tyrol). Bernadotte easily frightened Quasdanovich away, but the fanatical, sharpshooting Tyrolese had risen in mass, blocking all direct communications between Bonaparte and Joubert. Worse, Laudon drove Baraguay out of Botzen, cutting Joubert off from Verona. Learning, through energetic reconnaissance, that Bonaparte was near Klagenfurt, Joubert moved suddenly down the Puster Valley, collecting Baraguay's division, repulsing Laudon, and scattering the assembling Tyrolese levies en route. On 8 April, he reached Villach (*C3*) with 12,000 men and 7,000 prisoners. The day before, Austrian representatives had appeared at Leoben and concluded a five-day truce, but Bonaparte had received news from the Directory (sent 31 March) that Moreau was still not ready—news which he read as an oblique warning that he was entirely on his own.

On the 13th, the truce was extended for another five days. Meanwhile, Venice (*B1*) had turned openly hostile; French stragglers were frequently bushwhacked. Bonaparte placed Victor at Kilmaine's disposal and, on 11 April, ordered Baraguay southward. On the 17th, insurrection burst out violently at Verona; at the same time, Laudon brushed aside the brigade Joubert had left in the Trent (*A2*) area, and advanced on Verona. Only the firmness of Kilmaine and the timely arrival of Victor and Baraguay saved the day. Augereau, returning from leave in France, was placed in command of the area between the Adige and the Piave, and put down the disorders with a heavy, acquisitive hand.

Bonaparte concluded that the only way to save his army and his own reputation was to gain an armistice long enough to enable even Moreau to ready himself. To do this, it was necessary to begin negotiations for a peace treaty. News that Bonaparte might bring France peace having aroused potent popular feeling in his favor, the Directory reluctantly gave him full powers to treat. Negotiations, begun on 18 April at Leoben, were much influenced by a series of crises in Paris which several times almost toppled the Directory and which drove Carnot, its only member with integrity and military knowledge, into exile. Meanwhile, the French troops withdrew from Austrian territory, and Bonaparte ruled northern Italy from his headquarters in Milan.

The treaty was of the usual cynical eighteenth-century type: France got Austrian territory in Belgium and on the west bank of the Rhine, and established the Cisalpine Republic—made up of part of the Papal States and the former Austrian or Austrian vassal-state territories of Lombardy, Mantua Province, and Modena. Austria received the mainland possessions of Venice up to the Adige, including the cities of Verona and Legnago. She regarded the treaty as "only a truce" which would enable her to renew the war when she wished, and with a better base in Italy than she had previously held.

While the negotiations progressed, the Directory began to assemble an "Army of England" along the English Channel, to complete its victories by subduing its last opponent. Bonaparte was given command—probably to get him out of Italy, where he seemed all-powerful. At the same time, to keep its armies occupied, maintain external tension to reduce internal opposition, and gain money by international plundering, the Directory embarked on new ventures in Italy and Switzerland. In January 1798, it ordered troops into Switzerland (then a loose confederation), establishing a Swiss Republic after fairly severe fighting. In Italy, tortuous plot and counterplot ended with an attack on the French embassy in Rome. Berthier, commanding the French troops in Italy, marched on the city. A republic was proclaimed (February 1798), and the Pope retired to Pisa.

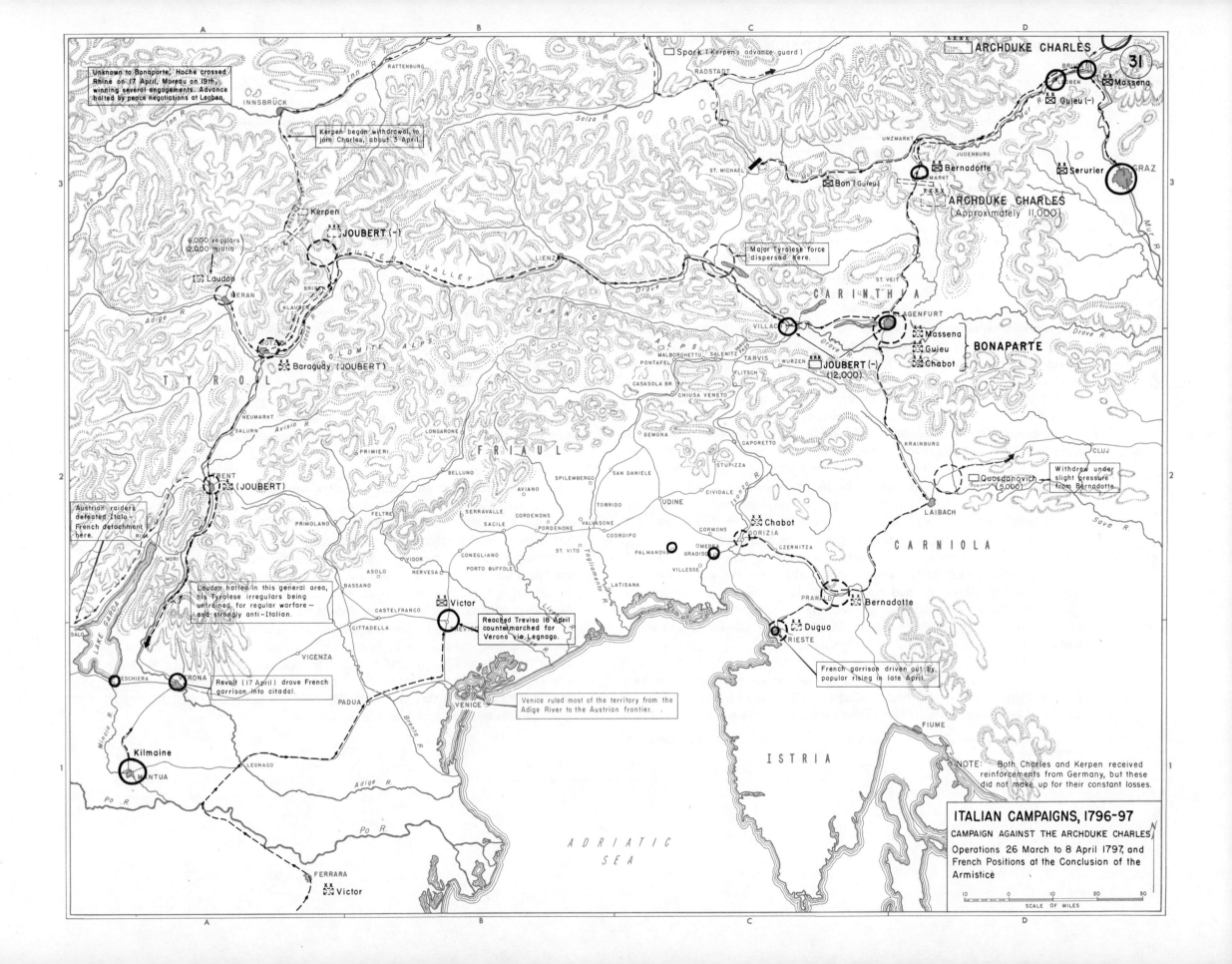

Unknown to Bonaparte, Hoche crossed Rhine on 17 April, Moreau on 19th, winning several engagements. Advance halted by peace negotiations at Leoben.

Kerpen began withdrawal to join Charles, about 3 April.

□ Spork (Kerpen's advance guard)

⌧XXXX ARCHDUKE CHARLES

RADSTADT

RATTENBURG

INNSBRÜCK

Salza R.

Inn R.

St. MICHAEL

BRUCK

OBEN

⌧XX Massena

⌧XX Gujeu (-)

Mur R.

JUDENBURG

UNZMARKT

MARKT

⌧XX Bernadotte

⌧XX Serurier

GRAZ

□ Kerpen

⌧JOUBERT (-)

PUSTER VALLEY

LIENZ

Drave R.

ARCHDUKE CHARLES (Approximately 11,000)

Major Tyrolese force dispersed here.

6,000 regulars 12,000 militia

□ Laudon

MERAN

KLAUSEN

BRIX

Eisack R.

BOTE

⌧ Baragudy (JOUBERT)

□ □ □ MITE ALPS

CARINTHIA

ST. VEIT

VILLACH

⌧ Bon (Gujeu)

□ □

⌧JOUBERT (-) (12,000)

CARNIC ALPS

MALBORGHETTO SALENITZ

PONTAFEL

TARVIS WURZEN PASS

FLITSCH

CASASOLA BR.

CHIUSA VENETO

AGENFURT

⌧XX Massena

⌧XX Gujeu

⌧XX Chabot

BONAPARTE

Withdrew under slight pressure from Bernadotte

□ Quosdanovich (5,000)

NEUMARKT

SALURN

Avisio R.

LONGARONE

FRIAUL

GEMONA

CAPORETTO

KRAINBURG

CLUJ

TRENT

⌧XX (JOUBERT)

PRIMIERI

BELLUNO

AVIANO

SPILEMBERGO

SAN DANIELE

CIVIDALE

Isonzo R.

STUPIZZA

LAIBACH

Sova R.

Austrian raiders defeated Italo-French detachment here.

FELTRE

SERRAVALLE

SACILE

CORDENONS

PORDENONE

VALVASONE

UDINE

CORMONS

⌧ Chabot

GORIZIA

CZERNITZA

CARNIOLA

Laudon halted in this general area, his Tyrolese irregulars being untrained for regular warfare — and strongly anti-Italian.

MORI

PRIMOLANO

BASSANO

ASOLO

NERVESA

CONEGLIANO

ST. VITO

CODROIPO

Tagliamento R.

PALMANOVA

MEDEA

GRADISCA

VILLESSE

PRAWALD

⌧ Bernadotte

SALO

BASSANO

CASTELFRANCO

CITTADELLA

OVIDOR

PORTO BUFFOLE

Livenza R.

LATISANA

Reached Treviso 18 April countermarched for Verona via Legnago.

⌧XX Victor

TREVISO

Dugua

RIESTE

French garrison driven out by popular rising in late April

PESCHIERA

VERONA

Revolt (17 April) drove French garrison into citadel.

VICENZA

PADUA

VENICE

Venice ruled most of the territory from the Adige River to the Austrian frontier.

FIUME

Mincio R.

Kilmaine

MANTUA

LEGNAGO

Adige R.

Po R.

ISTRIA

NOTE: Both Charles and Kerpen received reinforcements from Germany, but these did not make up for their constant losses.

ADRIATIC SEA

FERRARA

⌧XX Victor

ITALIAN CAMPAIGNS, 1796-97

CAMPAIGN AGAINST THE ARCHDUKE CHARLES

Operations 26 March to 8 April 1797, and French Positions at the Conclusion of the Armistice

10   0   10   20   30

SCALE OF MILES

31

COMMENTS ON THE ITALIAN CAMPAIGNS

At the end of his first year of independent command, Bonaparte stood at Leoben, less than 100 miles from Vienna, the Austrian capital. Far from his bases and without hope of assistance from the French armies along the Rhine, his military position was precarious. Yet, through political astuteness and unhesitating assumption of responsibility, he extricated himself by forcing the Austrians to a truce and then a peace, however tenuous. During his campaigns he had defeated seven armies, captured 160,000 prisoners of war, 170 flags, and more than 2,000 cannon, and extorted untold millions of francs in contributions.

How did this young man, twenty-seven years of age, achieve such astounding and continued success in his first experience as commander in chief of an army on campaign—a task Desaix described as the most difficult on earth; the one above all others that requires the display of the greatest number of qualities in a given time? General Clarke, the Directory's emissary in Italy, gave a partial explanation when, after the Battle of Arcola, he wrote of Bonaparte to his superiors: "Here all regard him as a man of genius. He has great power over the soldiers of the Republican Army. His judgment is sure; his resolutions are carried out with all his powers, his calmness amidst the most stirring scenes is as wonderful as his extraordinary rapidity in changing his plans if obliged to do so by unforeseen circumstances."

Throughout this first campaign, Bonaparte had displayed an inordinate ambition, a lust for power and fame, political as well as military. To these ends, he had pressed his ventures craftily and with an indomitable will. *"I hold the immortality of the soul to be the remembrance which we leave behind in the minds of men. This thought is an inspiring one; it were better not to have lived at all than to leave no trace of one's existence behind."** The successes of his Army of Italy had placed him in the center of the stage, a position he had been quick to exploit. Scintillating day-by-day accounts of his operations, embellished and cleverly written for the public eye, had flowed into Paris. Soon he had become the idol of all Frenchmen and his name a household word. It is no wonder that the Directory, sustained in its teetering position largely by funds acquired through Bonaparte's victories, looked upon the young general with trepidation.

No sudden spark of genius had launched Bonaparte in his rapid rise to prominence. From his first cadet days, he had recognized knowledge as a basic element of power and had applied himself assiduously to the study of war in all its aspects. *"Knowledge of the higher fields of war is acquired only by the study of the history of the wars and battles of the great captains and from experience. . . . Read and reread the campaigns of Alexander, Hannibal, Caesar, Gustavus Adolphus, Turenne, Eugene, and Frederick; model yourself on them; it is the only way to become a great captain and to discover the secrets of the art."*

For three years, he had meditated on the conduct of war in Italy. Consequently, when he gained the chief command of the Army of Italy, he was able to proceed confidently and with a broad and thorough appreciation of the political and military situation of his adversaries and of the topography of the theater of war. *"If I seem always ready to meet any difficulty, to face any emergency, it is because before undertaking any enterprise I have spent a long time thinking it out, and seeing what might happen. It is not a guardian spirit that reveals to me suddenly and in secret what to say or to do in circumstances unexpected by others, it is my meditations, my thinking things out. I am always at work: at dinner, at the theater; in the night I get up to work."*

Perhaps the most outstanding attribute possessed by the young general was that of a perfect balance of perception and moral courage. *"If courage preponderates too much, a general will undertake things above his grasp and commit errors, and on the other hand, if his character or courage is much inferior to his perception, he will not dare to execute what he has conceived."*

The mass armies, fed by conscription, which the French Revolution had spawned, had made the accepted eighteenth-century tactics, strategy, and logistics obsolete. Foreign military leaders were slow to break away from these concepts and lacked imagination to fill the void. Bonaparte, however, saw the opportunity for the exercise of originality in the application of the fundamental truths governing the conduct of war—those truths which prevail irrespective of the nature of the military means available, and which, for want of a better name, are termed the principles of war. By maintenance of the initiative, rapidity of maneuver, concentration of superior forces at the decisive place and time, and vigorous prosecution of the attack and pursuit, he had confounded and overwhelmed his less viable adversaries in Italy; through his political acumen he had gained the fruits of victory. Meanwhile, by his successes and his understanding of the forces motivating men, he had won the admiration and confidence of his troops and had inspired them to heroic deeds despite severe privations. By now, his fame and reputation had spread across the length and breadth of Europe.

* The italicized quotations on this page are extracts from Bonaparte's later writings or conversations.

"The first quality of a soldier is consistency in enduring fatigue and hardship. Poverty, privation, and want are the school of a good soldier." —NAPOLEON

"A conqueror should know how to employ by turns severity, justice, and leniency in suppressing or preventing disturbances." —NAPOLEON

Bonaparte convinced the Directory that the contemplated invasion of England could not succeed until French naval strength had been greatly expanded. Meanwhile, he insisted, it would be best to strike at English possessions in India, through Egypt. In such a venture, Bonaparte saw an opportunity to be out of the country, acquiring new renown, while the Directory ruined itself. (Many influential Frenchmen had urged an Egyptian expedition to strengthen France's position in the eastern Mediterranean.)

His expedition sailed secretly from Toulon on 19 May 1798. Before reaching the island of Malta, it was joined by convoys from Genoa, Corsica, Marseilles, and Civita Vecchia. The combined fleet totaled 100 warships and 400 transports; the troops aboard numbered about 36,000, mostly the best regiments of the Army of Italy. Only 1,230 horses were taken—700 for the cavalry and the remainder for the artillery and staff. Considering his mission one of civilization as well as conquest, Bonaparte took along a large group of scientists and artists.

The English, meanwhile, were principally concerned with unrest in Ireland and the threat of invasion of their homeland. In late April, suspecting that the French intended some major operation in the Mediterranean, Lord Nelson sailed from Gibralter with a small fleet to see what the French were about.

Under pressure from French commercial interests to capture Malta as a link in the trade route to the Middle East—and suspecting that Austria and Russia had similar designs—the Directory had ordered Bonaparte to seize that island. (He himself had urged this.) Malta was ruled by the international Order of the Knights of Malta. The Order, sadly degenerated from its earlier days, had become unpopular with its Maltese subjects; many of its French members had entered the pay of the French government. Consequently, when Bonaparte's troops landed on 10 June, they encountered little resistance. After reorganizing the local government and resupplying his fleet, Bonaparte left Vaubois with 3,500 men to garrison the strongly fortified island, and set out for Egypt, taking with him 500 of the Knights' best troops.

The expedition reached Alexandria late on 1 July, in bad weather. Three days previously, Nelson had scouted that city; finding the harbor empty, he had turned northwest, but missed the approaching French fleet. Aware of Nelson's proximity, Bonaparte began landing near Marabout, despite the lateness of the hour and the perilous high seas. Because of shoals, the transports had to anchor well out. Many Frenchmen became wretchedly seasick in the resulting six-mile row to shore.

Egypt, then nominally part of Turkey's empire, was actually ruled in a semifeudal fashion by a turbulent warrior caste known as the Mamelukes. The military leader was Murad Bey; Ibrahim Bey was the civil head, insofar as one existed. Bonaparte presented his invasion as a liberating campaign to restore the authority of the Turkish Sultan and free the people from the oppression of the Mamelukes, whom he charged, as an excuse for the whole affair, with mistreating French merchants.

Leaving Reynier to cover the disembarkation, Bonaparte formed some infantry elements (4,500 men) into three columns and marched through the night across the desert to Alexandria. Early on the morning of the 2d, he stormed and captured the city. Menou then advanced and occupied Rosetta, while Desaix headed for Damanhur, on the road to Cairo.

On the 5th, the army followed in the wake of Desaix, while a flotilla of light river boats, chiefly impressed, ascended the Nile to serve as gunboats and supply craft. In the march across the desert, the troops suffered severely from heat, sickness, and thirst. Arabs haunted the columns, robbing, torturing, and killing stragglers. Disillusionment and discontent spread among the troops, but Bonaparte maintained discipline with a firm, cold hand. On 21 July, after skirmishes with the Mamelukes at Rahmaniya and Shubra Khit, Murad's main force was encountered in a strong position at Embabeh, just north of the Pyramids. Across the Nile, Ibrahim had several thousand additional troops, but, possessing more head and less heart than Murad, he had already massed his treasures, harem, and slaves for rapid evacuation eastward.

Murad had converted Embabeh into an entrenched strong point, bristling with heavy fortress guns (*inset sketch*). His Mamelukes—some 6,000 fierce individual fighters, splendidly mounted and armed, each accompanied by several retainers—were his only reliable troops. Possibly 20,000 ragtag "infantry" (mostly Egyptians, stiffened by a few Turks) held Embabeh; some unstable Arab levies hovered around Gizeh. In all, Murad had approximately 40,000 men, over half of whom would be useful only for mop-up operations, if the Mameluke horsemen succeeded in breaking the French. The French army (approximately 25,000) advanced in echeloned division squares—artillery at the corners and between the battalions, the cavalry, trains, and headquarters inside—ready to move or fight in any direction. Bonaparte held his left flank (Bon and Vial) back out of range of the artillery in Embabeh and moved forward with his right (Desaix and Reynier), intending to envelop Murad's left and pocket him against the river. Murad, divining Bonaparte's intent, charged Desaix and Reynier furiously, but without success. This repulse of the Mameluke cavalry demoralized Murad's infantry; when Bon and Vial deployed into columns and stormed Embabeh, the town quickly fell. Meanwhile, the French right continued its inexorable advance. Large numbers of the enemy were cut off, the French suffering very light losses (300 reported). Bonaparte's troops picked up enormous amounts of loot—the Mamelukes carried their wealth, in gold, on their persons—and, more important, many much-needed horses. Murad retired unmolested to the south; Ibrahim, after frustrating the French pursuit by strong rear-guard action at El Salhiya (*B2*) on 11 August, began his eastward trek into Syria.

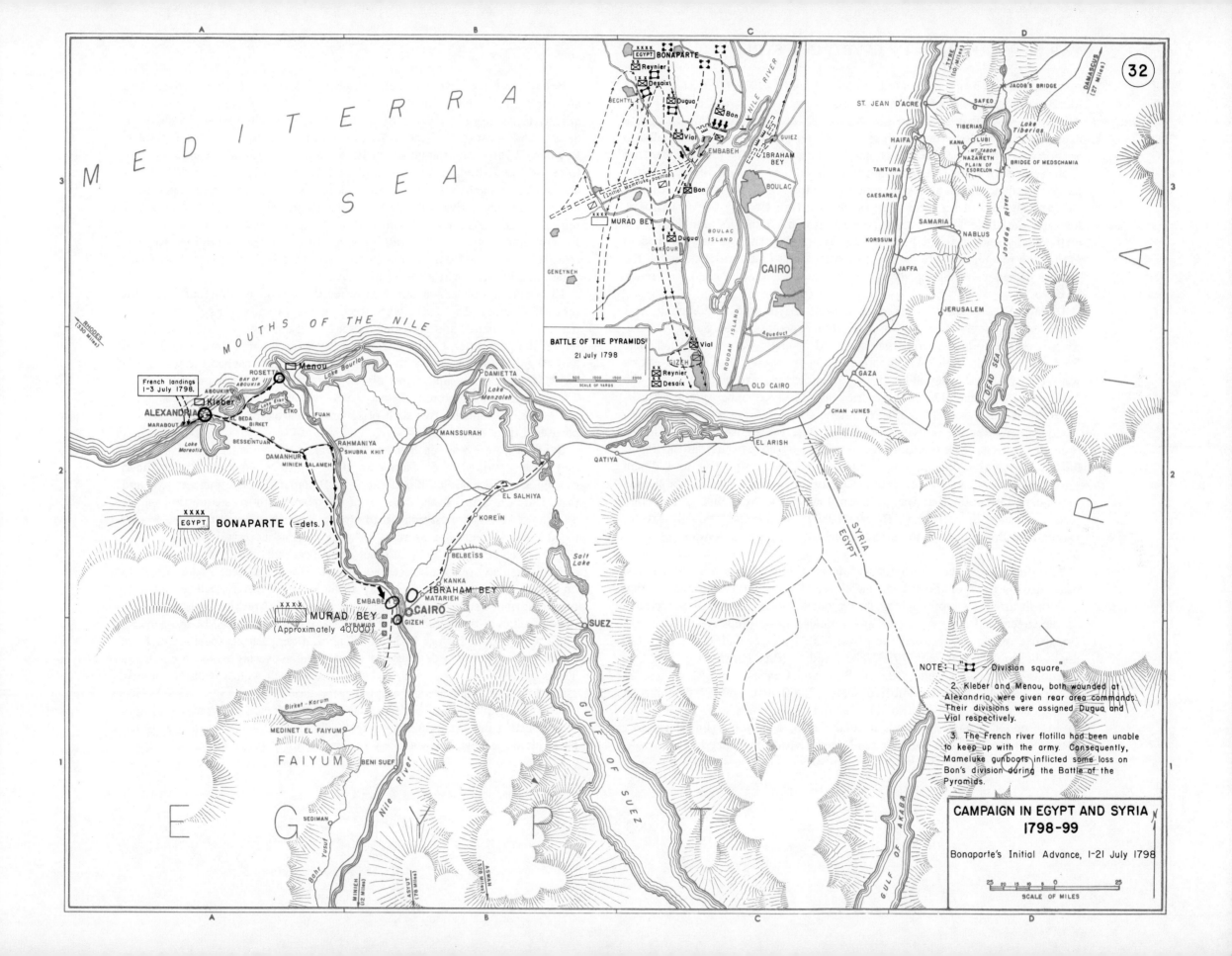

MEDITERRANEAN SEA

RHODES
(350 MILES)

MOUTHS OF THE NILE

BATTLE OF THE PYRAMIDS
21 July 1798

XXXX
EGYPT BONAPARTE

Reynier
Desaix
Dugua
Bon
Vial
EMBABEH
IBRAHAM BEY

Initial Mameluke position

XXXX
MURAD BEY

Dugua
DAKROUR

GENEYNEH

BOULAC ISLAND

BOULAC

CAIRO

Aqueduct

ROUDAH ISLAND

Vial

GIZEH

Reynier
Desaix

OLD CAIRO

SCALE OF YARDS
500 1000 1500 2000

SYRIA

DAMASCUS
(27 Miles)

TYRE
(10 Miles)

JACOB'S BRIDGE

ST. JEAN D'ACRE

SAFED

TIBERIAS
KANA   Lake Tiberias
LUBI
HAIFA   MT. TABOR
NAZARETH   PLAIN OF
ESDRELON
TANTURA   BRIDGE OF MEDSCHAMIA

CAESAREA

SAMARIA
KORSSUM   NABLUS

Jordan River

JAFFA

JERUSALEM

DEAD SEA

GAZA

CHAN JUNES

EL ARISH

French landings
1-3 July 1798.

ROSETTA
BAY OF
ABOUKIR
ABOUKIR
Menou
Lake Bourlos

Kleber
ALEXANDRIA
MARABOUT
EL BEDA
BIRKET
BESSEINTUAN
Lake
Mareotis

DAMANHUR
MINIEH SALAMEH

ETKO   FUAH
Lake Etko
RAHMANIYA
Shubra Khit

DAMIETTA
Lake
Menzaleh

MANSSURAH

QATIYA

SYRIA
EGYPT

XXXX
EGYPT BONAPARTE (-dets.)

EL SALHIYA

KOREIN

BELBEISS

Salt
Lake

KANKA

EMBABE
IBRAHAM BEY
MATARIEH

XXXX
MURAD BEY
(Approximately 40,000)

CAIRO
GIZEH
PYRAMIDS

SUEZ

GULF OF SUEZ

NOTE: 1 "⊡ – Division square"

2. Kleber and Menou, both wounded at
Alexandria, were given rear area commands.
Their divisions were assigned Dugua and
Vial respectively.

3. The French river flotilla had been unable
to keep up with the army. Consequently,
Mameluke gunboats inflicted some loss on
Bon's division during the Battle of the
Pyramids.

E G Y P T

Birket - Karum

MEDINET EL FAIYUM

F A I Y U M

BENI SUEF

SEDIMAN

Nile River
Bahr Yusuf

MINIEH
(32 Miles)

ASYUT
(78 Miles)

ASWAN
(528 Miles)

GULF OF AKABA

**CAMPAIGN IN EGYPT AND SYRIA
1798-99**

Bonaparte's Initial Advance, 1-21 July 1798

25 20 15 10 5 0   25
SCALE OF MILES

32

Bonaparte set up headquarters in Cairo on 24 July 1798. On the 31st, Nelson found the greater part of the French fleet at anchor in Aboukir Bay (*A2*). Admiral Brueys had anchored his ships close to shore, planning to fight a defensive action. However, the ships at the outer end of the line had failed to anchor near enough to the shoals, and the inshore guns of the fleet had not been readied for firing. Nelson, with thirteen ships of the line, drove into the harbor as night fell and attacked immediately, trusting to the superior seamanship and gunnery of his force. Part of his fleet thrust boldly between Brueys' line and the shore. Thus caught between two fires, the French ships were methodically knocked out. Four of the seventeen French vessels escaped to Malta; the remainder were captured or destroyed. Thus, with one blow, the English gained naval superiority in the Mediterranean and isolated the French in Egypt.

Undaunted, Bonaparte worked to convert Egypt into a French protectorate and a supply base for his projected expedition into Syria. The resources of the country were organized, and arsenals were established. The French even made their own gunpowder. On the whole, Bonaparte's efforts were broad and statesmanlike. If he attempted to exploit Egypt for the benefit of the French, he at least tried to introduce some system of self-government and more equitable taxation.

Concerned over the activities of Murad Bey, Bonaparte, in late August, ordered Desaix to seek him out. Desaix moved by boat from Cairo as far as Siut (now Asyut; *off map, B1*), returning by the Bahr Yusuf to Sediman (*A1*), where he found Murad. On 7 October, Desaix attacked, employing the square formation that was so frustrating to the Mamelukes, and completely defeated his opponent. Reinforced by 1,000 cavalry under Davout, Desaix then drove beyond the first cataracts of the Nile, at Aswan (*off map, B1*).

The French advance into Syria was delayed. On 22 October, the natives, heartened by news of the French naval defeat at Aboukir and rumors that a Turkish army was approaching, broke out in open revolt. All Frenchmen on the streets and even those sick and wounded in hospitals were butchered. Bonaparte quickly suppressed the revolt with equal brutality. The advance finally began on 6 February 1799. The invading force consisted of four lean divisions—those of Reynier, Kleber, Bon, and Lannes—and Murat's small cavalry unit. All told, it numbered some 13,000 men and 52 field pieces. Siege guns were to go by sea to Jaffa. About 16,000 men were left in Egypt in four major groups: Dugua's around Cairo, Marmont's in Alexandria, Menou's at Rosetta, and Desaix's reinforced division in upper Egypt.

Bonaparte knew that one Turkish army was being formed in Syria and another on the island of Rhodes (*off map, A3*). He could only hope to strike quickly to destroy the army in Syria, for it was obvious that he would soon have to shift most of his forces back to Egypt to meet the army from Rhodes. Reynier (2,150) took the village of El Arish on 10 February from a Turkish force of equal strength, after a hard and costly fight. About 1,500 Turks took refuge in the fort. Reynier, too weak to assault it, began siege operations and awaited the arrival of Kleber. In the meantime, enemy troops (8,000 reported) advanced from Gaza and took up a position threatening the French supply line. (*Action not shown.*) In a brilliant operation, Reynier attacked this force from the rear after dark on 14–15 February and stampeded it, with very light losses to his division.

El Arish capitulated on the 20th, after the arrival of Bonaparte and his remaining forces. The Turks were freed, under promise not to serve again; the fort was repaired and garrisoned, as a link in the French supply line. Gaza fell on the 25th, after a short skirmish, but the garrison of Jaffa (4,000 men and 40 guns) fought stubbornly. French guns finally breached the walls, and on 7 March Lannes' and Bon's divisions stormed the place outright. Some 2,000 Turks were captured, almost half of whom had been previously freed at El Arish. Unable to trust such prisoners on parole or to feed them, Bonaparte had them all shot.

St. Jean d'Acre was reached on 18 March. Its fortifications were old, but they were supported by Sir Sidney Smith's English squadron, which included two ships of the line. Smith had captured Bonaparte's siege guns at sea, and these had been added to the defenses of the town. With the sea on three sides, St. Jean d'Acre was most difficult to attack. The siege lasted from 17 March to 20 May, with repeated assaults and sallies, all unsuccessful.

In the meantime the Turkish relief army (perhaps 20,000 men, and more a horde than an army) advanced southward. Bonaparte sent Kleber (3,000) on 9 April to hold this force away from St. Jean d'Acre. Kleber tried to repeat Reynier's surprise night maneuver on 15–16 April but, miscalculating the difficulties of the march, found himself at dawn surrounded by the Turkish army at the southern foot of Mount Tabor. Bonaparte, suspecting such an event, had advanced with a second column, maneuvering so as to catch the Turks between his troops and Kleber's. The French won a decisive victory; much loot and badly needed supplies were seized.

Meanwhile, plague had begun to decimate the French army, and Marmont was reporting increasing enemy activity off Alexandria. Accordingly, Bonaparte lifted the siege and withdrew during the night of 20 May.

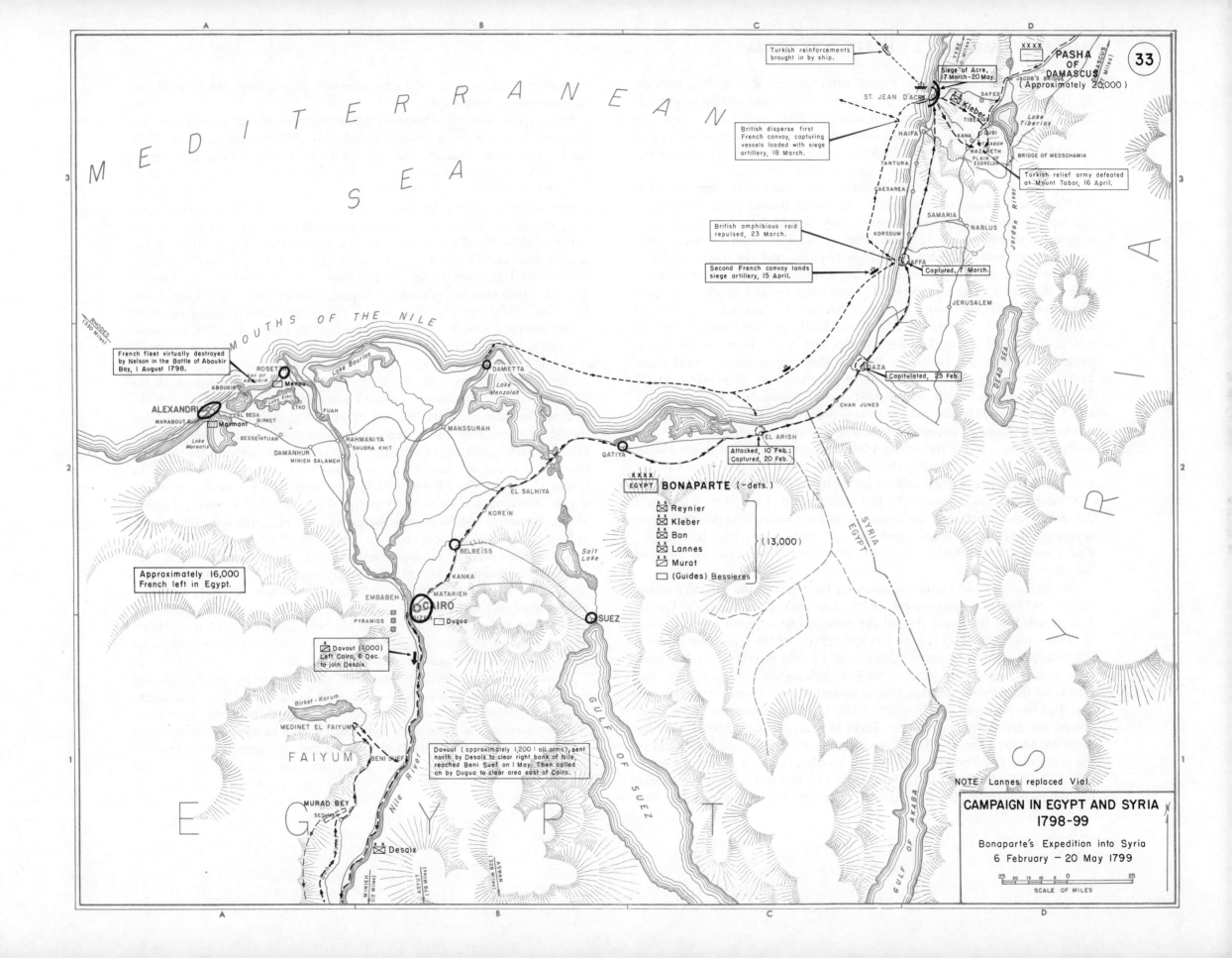

MEDITERRANEAN SEA

MOUTHS OF THE NILE

RHODES
(350 Miles)

Turkish reinforcements brought in by ship.

PASHA OF DAMASCUS
(Approximately 20,000)

Siege of Acre, 17 March-20 May.

ST. JEAN D'ACRE

Kleber

TYRE

SAFED

DAMASCUS (190 Miles)

Lake Tiberias

TIBERIAS

KANA

MT. TABOR

BRIDGE OF MEDSCHAMIA

British disperse first French convoy, capturing vessels loaded with siege artillery, 18 March.

HAIFA

TANTURA

CAESAREA

NAZARETH

PLAIN OF ESDRELON

Turkish relief army defeated at Mount Tabor, 16 April.

SAMARIA

NABLUS

Jordan River

British amphibious raid repulsed, 23 March.

KORSSUM

Second French convoy lands siege artillery, 15 April.

JAFFA

Captured, 7 March.

JERUSALEM

DEAD SEA

French fleet virtually destroyed by Nelson in the Battle of Aboukir Bay, 1 August 1798.

ROSETTA

Menou

Lake Bourlos

DAMIETTA

Lake Menzaleh

CHAN JUNES

GAZA

Capitulated, 25 Feb.

ALEXANDRIA

Marmont

ABOUKIR
BAY OF ABOUKIR

AL BEDA
BIRKET
ETKO
Lake Etko

FUAH

MANSSURAH

MARABOUT

Lake Mareotis

BESSEINTUAN

DAMANHUR
MINIEH SALAMEH

RAHMANIYA
SHUBRA KHIT

EL ARISH

Attacked, 10 Feb.; Captured, 20 Feb.

QATIYA

XXXX
EGYPT BONAPARTE (−dets.)

Approximately 16,000 French left in Egypt.

EL SALHIYA

KOREIN

BELBEISS

KANKA

Salt Lake

MATARIEH

EMBABEH

CAIRO

Dugua

GIZEH

PYRAMIDS

Davout (4,000) Left Cairo, 6 Dec. to join Desaix.

Davout (approximately 1,200: all arms), sent north by Desaix to clear right bank of Nile, reached Beni Suef on 1 May. Then called on by Dugua to clear area east of Cairo.

Birket-Karum

MEDINET EL FAIYUM

FAIYUM

BENI SUEF

MURAD BEY

SEDMEN

Nile River

Desaix

MINIEH (72 Miles)

ASYUT (178 Miles)

ASWAN (528 Miles)

Reynier
Kleber
Bon
Lannes
Murat
(Guides) Bessieres

(13,000)

SUEZ

GULF OF SUEZ

SYRIA

EGYPT

GULF OF AKABA

SYRIA

EGYPT

33

NOTE Lannes replaced Vial.

CAMPAIGN IN EGYPT AND SYRIA 1798-99

Bonaparte's Expedition into Syria
6 February – 20 May 1799

25 20 15 10 5 0   25
SCALE OF MILES

The Turks failed to pursue the French from St. Jean d'Acre, but, even so, the retreat involved great hardship. Bonaparte's army had lost approximately 2,200 dead (including 1,000 from disease) in Syria; 2,300 more were sick or wounded. Lannes and Bon had received severe wounds, Bon later dying from his. Leaving an outpost at El Arish, Bonaparte took Bon's (now Rampon's) division to Cairo and sent Kleber to Damietta (*B2*).

On 11 July 1799, Marmont reported more than 100 ships (British, Turkish, and Russian) off Alexandria (*A2*)—the Rhodes force had arrived. Mustapha Pasha disembarked his troops (between 15,000 and 18,000 men) without opposition on 15 July. By noon of the 17th, Fort Aboukir, commanding the head of the bay, had been reduced, and the Turks began to dig in to await the arrival of their cavalry, transport, and a division of janissaries. Bonaparte's reaction was swift: Desaix was ordered to abandon upper Egypt temporarily and move to Cairo; Kleber, at Damietta, was ordered forward to Birket, as were all other immediately available troops; Reynier was to guard against any Turkish invasion from Syria. From Birket, Bonaparte could attack the Turks' left flank, if they moved north toward Alexandria, or their right flank, if they advanced toward the Nile. When, by 24 July, the Turks had made no offensive move, Bonaparte advanced to the attack before daylight the next morning, hoping to catch them off guard.

Mustapha Pasha's forward position was concave, extending from the Hill of the Sheik back to the Hill of the Vizar, and then southward to the Hill of Puits (*inset sketch*). Actually, there was no continuous defensive line, for only the hills were occupied, and no fortifications connected them.

Some 8,000 Turks manned the first "line"; another 6,000 to 7,000 held the second line, which centered around an old redoubt. About 30 field pieces supported these two positions, and Turkish gunboats covered both flanks. The reserve (4,000–5,000) occupied Aboukir Village and the Fort of Aboukir.

Bonaparte deployed Lannes' division on the right, Murat's cavalry in the center, and Destaing's brigade on the left. Lanusse's division and the Guides (commanded by Bessieres) formed the reserve; Davout, with a small group of cavalry and dromedary troops, covered the rear of the army (*not shown*). All told, Bonaparte had about 7,700 men, 17 field pieces, and a few siege guns (which were to do yeoman work in driving off the gunboats). The attack on the forward position was swift and brutal. Lannes and Destaing assaulted the principal hills frontally, while Murat drove up the center, then veered left and right to catch the Turks in rear. Already thrown into disorder by artillery fire, the Turks were driven into the sea on both sides of the peninsula. The Turkish center moved forward from the Hill of the Vizar to aid their hapless comrades, but Murat caught them in flank and rear, while Lanusse struck their front. The Turks tried to break out on either side

to reach the sea; most who did were drowned. In one hour, the forward line had been utterly destroyed.

Immediately, Bonaparte attacked the strongly entrenched second line (*action not shown*). From a small peninsula, his artillery managed to enfilade the left end of this position. The battered Turks abandoned that point, leaving a 200-yard gap next to the shore. The French attack along the front of the position was generally repulsed, and the Turks poured out to kill the wounded and decapitate the dead for a promised bounty. Thus exposed, they were caught by the French infantry counterattack, which broke into the redoubt, while Murat pushed through the gap on the left and rolled up the second line. The French then pressed up the peninsula, killing or driving most of the Turks into the sea. Some 3,000–4,000 held out in Fort Aboukir and the neighboring villages until 2 August. Turkish losses were 2,000 killed in action, 10,000 to 11,000 drowned, and 3,000 taken prisoner; possibly 1,200 escaped. French losses were small—150 killed and 750 wounded. Bonaparte said later that the Turks were brave, but lacked proper organization, could not maneuver easily, and had no idea of tactics.

During negotiations with Sir Sidney Smith over the disposition of the Turkish wounded, Bonaparte obtained newspapers that told of French defeats in Germany and Italy. He had informed the Directory repeatedly that should the situation in Europe become dangerous, he would return. Actually, two recall orders had been dispatched to him by the Directory. One had been intercepted at sea by Nelson; the other Bonaparte received later, when he landed in France. On 22 August 1799, he embarked for France in a fast frigate, accompanied by a select party which included Berthier, Lannes, Murat, Bessieres, and Marmont. Kleber was left in Egypt with instructions to hold out if at all possible until the conclusion of a general peace.

Kleber again defeated the Turks, but was assassinated. The command then passed to the incapable Menou, who finally succumbed to a major English effort under Sir Ralph Abercromby during the summer of 1801. His army was returned in English ships to France, free to serve again, in accordance with the terms of an earlier convention. Vaubois, similarly isolated on Malta, had surrendered to the English, Russians, and Neapolitans in September 1800, when his troops faced starvation.

Bonaparte's venture in Egypt and Syria was strategically meaningless and costly in military resources. It pulled some of France's best troops and generals away from the Continent when they were needed most, and brought on the destruction of the French Mediterranean fleet. The work of the scientists —such as the discovery of the Rosetta Stone and the subsequent deciphering of Egyptian hieroglyphics—proved to be the only enduring value of the expedition.

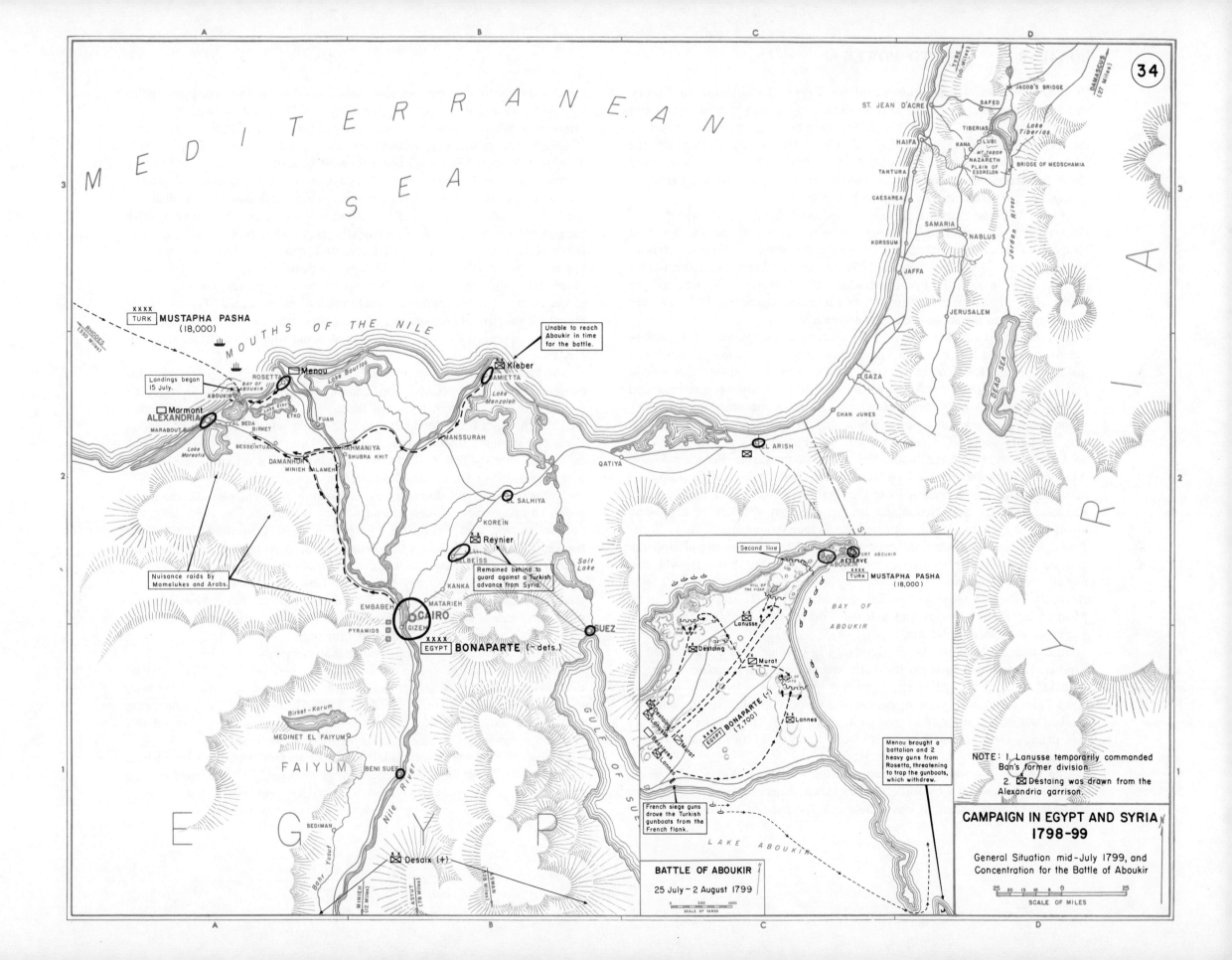

MEDITERRANEAN SEA

34

MUSTAPHA PASHA (18,000)

Unable to reach Aboukir in time for the battle.

Landings began 15 July.

Menou

Kleber

Marmont
ALEXANDRIA

MOUTHS OF THE NILE

Nuisance raids by Mamelukes and Arabs.

Reynier

Remained behind to guard against a Turkish advance from Syria.

CAIRO

BONAPARTE (~ dets.)

SUEZ

Desaix (+)

BATTLE OF ABOUKIR
25 July – 2 August 1799

SCALE OF YARDS

Second line

MUSTAPHA PASHA (18,000)

Lanusse

Destaing

Murat

BONAPARTE (+) (7,700)

Lannes

BAY OF ABOUKIR

Menou brought a battalion and 2 heavy guns from Rosetta, threatening to trap the gunboats, which withdrew.

French siege guns drove the Turkish gunboats from the French flank.

LAKE ABOUKIR

NOTE: 1. Lanusse temporarily commanded Bon's former division
2. Destaing was drawn from the Alexandria garrison.

CAMPAIGN IN EGYPT AND SYRIA
1798-99

General Situation mid-July 1799, and Concentration for the Battle of Aboukir

SCALE OF MILES

BONAPARTE'S RISE TO POWER

Even as Bonaparte's expedition sailed for Egypt, the situation in Europe had again become critical. Incensed by French aggression in Switzerland and Italy, the powers of Europe began to organize in a concerted effort to throttle the French and restore the "old order." Under English pressure, the Second Coalition—England, Russia, Austria, Turkey, Portugal, Naples, and the Papal States—was formed. (Sardinia planned to join, but the French—noting her preparations—reoccupied Piedmont.)

In late 1798, the British and Neapolitans combined in an attempt to clear the French from central Italy. Though initially successful, the raw, ignorant Neapolitans were soon outclassed by smaller numbers of French veterans. Naples capitulated in early January 1799, leaving the French in control of all of Italy. In 1798 also, the French invaded Ireland. However, storms and the British Navy prevented the landing of their main body, and the 1,100 Frenchmen who reached the shore eventually surrendered.

In 1799, the Coalition opened several campaigns against the French—the Austrians and Russians attacking in northern Italy and Switzerland, and the English and Russians in Holland. There were also minor offensives in Naples and the Adriatic. (Allied forces in northern Italy were commanded by the famous Russian general, Suvorov.) At the same time, the Directory began offensives along the upper Rhine and in Italy and Switzerland, but with no more decisive objective than to get French troops into enemy or neutral territory, where they could live off the country. The French offensive into Germany was beaten back by the Austrians, who failed to follow up their advantage. Operations on this front then stabilized into minor local actions. Russian, Austrian, and Neapolitan troops, aided by the British fleet—and errors of the French generals—cleared the French from most of Italy. Under Brune, however, the French defeated the Anglo-Russian invasion of Holland, and the Austro-Russian armies in Switzerland (including Suvorov, who had moved north from Italy) were routed by Massena. These defeats disrupted the Austro-Russian alliance, and Suvorov returned to Russia with his army. Meanwhile, Turkish troops and a Russo-Turkish fleet captured the French garrisons in the Ionian Islands.

Such was the situation on 9 October 1799, when Bonaparte landed at Toulon. He reached Paris on the 16th, where, with his stunning victory at Aboukir fresh in the public mind, he was greeted as a returning hero. By now, France was in a state of near-anarchy and collapse. To the country, already war-weary, the war seemed endless, for it was obvious that Massena's and Brune's victories had merely temporarily staved off an ultimate invasion by the overwhelming forces of the Second Coalition.

The French also were exasperated with the Directory. Weak and corrupt, it had utterly resisted—by force and fraud when necessary—any change in its system of government. It was widely believed that its members continued the war merely to keep themselves in office and for personal pecuniary gain. The Army viewed it with outright hostility. As Bonaparte neared Paris, the Minister of War reported, "For four months the service for the war is null. Hospitals, pay, subsistence, ammunition, clothing, armaments, all is blocked, every sort of service is abandoned, all credit is destroyed."

Politically, the Directory was pinched between the Jacobins, the underground Royalists, and a moderate group (which included two members of the Directory itself—Sieyes and Roger-Ducos) whose aim was to reorganize the government on the basis of greater efficiency and stability. Also, the legislative body (currently the Corps Legislatif) was reasserting its powers in opposition to the Directory and had caused a deadlock. Thus, as public order deteriorated and the government lost confidence and power, the importance of the Army, the one remaining stable institution, increased. This naturally magnified the national importance of the leading generals. The Directory had long been apprehensive over the danger of being supplanted through a military *coup d'état*.

Not finding a suitable man of action among themselves, Sieyes and his moderate group sought their "sword" among the military leaders. Bonaparte's arrival proved a godsend, for, until then, their search had failed. Nevertheless, if it had not been Bonaparte then, it would have been another general later. The intrigues leading to the fall of the Directory are beyond the scope of this account. Suffice it to say that a provisional government was set up with Sieyes, Roger-Ducos, and Bonaparte as consuls, and a hasty revision of the constitution begun. Immediately, it became apparent that the moderate group had acquired a master instead of a sword. Sieyes was gently elbowed into retirement, and Bonaparte emerged as First Consul—a position he theoretically was to hold for ten years. *Thus, only thirty-three days after landing at Toulon, Bonaparte had become master of France.*

The people, looking for any promise of reasonably honest and competent government, were generally happy with the change. The initial Army reaction was one of casual acquiescence—spiked with some hostility—but this would turn to enthusiasm after the Marengo campaign.

It would be almost six months before that campaign could be undertaken. During that period, Bonaparte did some of his greatest work: The constitution was rewritten; local governments were regularized; law and order were re-established; finances were placed on a sound basis; and the armies were reorganized and prepared for operations in the spring. Many changes of this period still remain part of the internal organization of France.

In short, Bonaparte made himself into a symbol of both the triumph and the end of the Revolution. Any successful general could have carried out the *coup d'état,* some probably more smoothly than Bonaparte, but to make himself First Consul and then to remake France required genius.

The Marengo Campaign

As the year 1800 opened, France's position, both politically and militarily, was grim indeed. Bonaparte's offer of peace to the Second Coalition had been rebuffed, and the English and Royalists had again sparked the Vendee into revolt. France could count as allies only unenthusiastic Spain, Holland, and Switzerland. Vaubois was blockaded on Malta, and Kleber was isolated in Egypt. French armies on the Continent supposedly numbered 280,000, but desertion had drained this total to a possible 150,000. Because of the semicollapse of local government, only one-third of the conscripts levied ever reported. Until Bonaparte could find means to remedy the neglect of the Directory in providing food, pay, clothing, and replacements for the armies, they could live only by forced requisitions on the unlucky localities where they were stationed. Since Kray's army represented a direct threat to French territory, Moreau's Army of the Rhine was given priority on the scanty funds and supplies available.

On 25 January, Bonaparte secretly ordered Berthier, his minister of war, to organize a Reserve Army of 60,000 around Dijon (*A2*). He intended eventually to lead this force himself; for the time being, he made Berthier its commander. (Carnot replaced Berthier as war minister.) As troops dribbled in from Holland, Paris, and the Vendee, supply shortages made it necessary to billet them by small units over a wide area. Enemy spies, who had soon learned of the Reserve Army's activation, consequently had trouble locating it. Troops actually seen at Dijon included many raw conscripts; all were ragged and half-disciplined. Allied headquarters therefore dismissed the existence of the Reserve Army as an obvious fraud.

Bonaparte's main preoccupation was to ensure the coordination of *all* French armies in any forthcoming campaign. Through the winter, St.-Cyr won several seemingly hopeless actions around Genoa (*B1*); tenuous negotiations with Austria continued; and it became increasingly evident that the Reserve Army would be ready by the time Moreau was. Planning went slowly and jarringly. His power far from consolidated, Bonaparte could not deal abruptly with Moreau, who preferred his own deliberate fashion of making war and had strong support among politicians and generals alike. Bonaparte began by proposing that he himself command the Reserve and Rhine armies in a combined spring offensive through the Schaffhausen area (*B2*), to split Kray and Melas apart. That achieved, he would lead the Reserve Army south through the Splügen Pass (*B1*) to deal with Melas, while Moreau disposed of Kray. Moreau had endless objections—incomplete preparations, bad weather, insufficient supplies. Also, he would resign rather than have Bonaparte command the Army of the Rhine, even temporarily. Bonaparte modified his plan in order to placate Moreau, but the latter still found fault. Finally, Bonaparte issued a general order: The campaign would open in mid-April; Moreau, after detaching approximately 25,000 men to defend Switzerland and occupy the St. Gothard Pass (*B1*), would advance to turn Kray's south flank and cut his direct communications with Melas. Once Moreau's offensive was well developed, the Reserve Army—reinforced by the corps Moreau was to leave in Switzerland—would drive through the St. Gothard and Simplon passes (*both B1*) to link up with Massena.

Moreau still vacillated, but finally promised limited cooperation. He would attack on 25 April, so as to separate Kray and Melas. Originally, he would leave only Moncey (about 5,500) in Switzerland. Once Kray had been defeated, Moncey's strength would be at least doubled.

It was clear to Bonaparte that the negotiations with Austria were collapsing and that an Austrian offensive could be expected momentarily. It was also clear that Moreau would neither act decisively nor cooperate wholeheartedly. To relieve him, however, might incite a national crisis. If France was to have the early, major victory that its still-shaky government needed, Bonaparte must win it himself.

Bad news from Italy hurried his decisions. Melas had attacked on 6 April; by the 24th, Massena's army had been split and driven back on Genoa and Nice (*A1*). The Reserve Army would have to advance immediately, both to relieve Massena and to take advantage of the fact that he was still engaging most of Melas' army.

Berthier had reached Dijon on 18 April to find only some 30,000 troops available, and these short of everything. Under instructions to advance as soon as possible, he recommended (26 April) using either the Simplon (*B1*) or the St. Bernard Pass (*A1*), preferably the latter. Concurrently, since the Reserve Army would have to march with only the rations it could carry, he requested that Bonaparte correct the supply situation. On 27 April, Bonaparte approved the St. Bernard route, and the Reserve Army began to shift toward Geneva. Bonaparte's hard-riding aides-de-camp (Duroc, Lauriston, Lefebvre-Desnoëttes) hunted out weapons, transportation, and supplies.

About 1 May, learning that Massena was penned up in Genoa, Bonaparte ordered Berthier's improvised army forward. His plan was risky, but quick action was imperative. Bonaparte was depending on Moreau, who had France's finest army, for little or nothing; on Massena to somehow keep Melas occupied until at least 30 May; on himself for virtually everything else.

The plans of the Allies were based on Anglo-Austrian cooperation. (Czar Paul, angered over the 1799 campaign, had withdrawn the Russian troops.) While Kray defended the Rhine frontier, Melas would seize Genoa and establish contact with the English fleet. Using Genoa as a base, he would then advance down the coast to Toulon (*A1*). An English expeditionary force was waiting on Minorca, in the Balearic Islands (*off map, A1*), to join him. Meanwhile, the English would carry out diversionary amphibious raids along the French coasts. Once Melas' operations had forced Bonaparte to transfer troops from Moreau, Kray would take up the offensive.

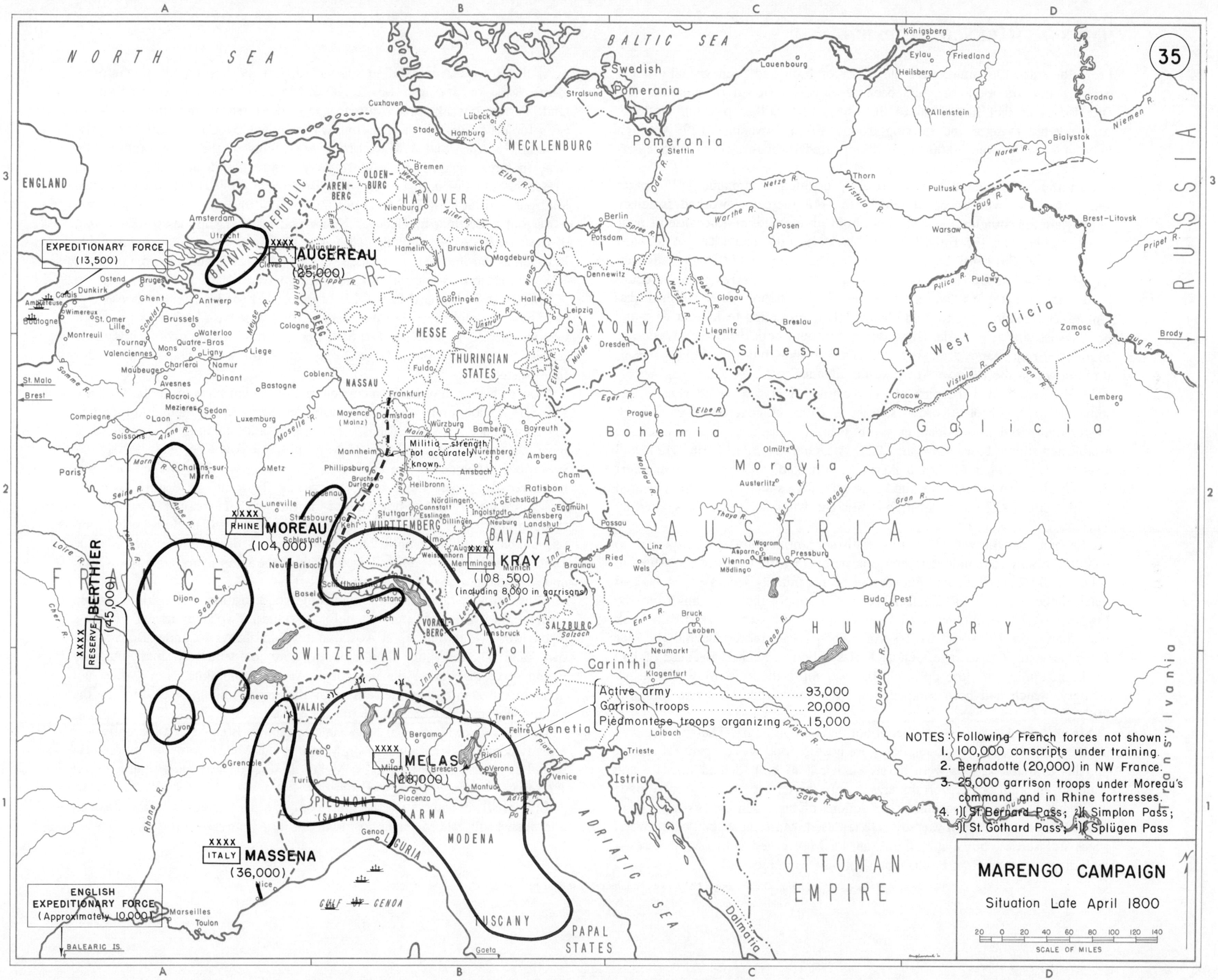

35

NORTH SEA
BALTIC SEA

ENGLAND

RUSSIA

Königsberg
Eylau
Friedland
Heilsberg
Grodno
Niemen R.
Allenstein

Swedish Pomerania
Stralsund
Lauenbourg
Narew R.
Bialystok

MECKLENBURG
Pomerania
Stettin
Thorn
Brest–Litovsk
Vistula R.

Cuxhaven
Stade
Hamburg
Lübeck
Bremen
HANOVER
Berlin
Potsdam
Posen
Warsaw
West Galicia
Zamosc
Brody
Pulawy
Pripet R.
Pilica R.
Bug R.

Amsterdam
Utrecht
BATAVIAN REPUBLIC
OLDEN-BURG
AREM-BERG
Nienburg
Hamelin
Brunswick
Magdeburg
Dennewitz
Spree R.
Aller R.
Weser R.
Elbe R.

EXPEDITIONARY FORCE (13,500)

XXXX AUGEREAU (25,000)

Ostend
Bruges
Ghent
Antwerp
Cleves
Wesel
Münster
Lippe R.
Rhine R.
BERG
Halle
Göttingen
Leipzig
SAXONY
Dresden
Breslau
Liegnitz
Glogau
Silesia
Cracow
Lemberg
Galicia

Calais
Dunkirk
Ambleteuse
Wimereux
St. Omer
Boulogne
Lille
Brussels
Waterloo
Quatre-Bras
Ligny
Liege
Namur
Cologne
Coblenz
NASSAU
Frankfurt
HESSE
THURINGIAN STATES
Fulda
Erfurt
Mulde R.
Eger R.
Bohemia
Prague
Elbe R.
Moravia
Olmütz
Austerlitz

St. Malo
Brest
Tournay
Valenciennes
Mons
Charleroi
Maubeuge
Avesnes
Rocroi
Mezieres
Sedan
Dinant
Bastogne
Luxemburg
Mayence (Mainz)
Darmstadt
Würzburg
Bamberg
Boyreuth
Amberg
Cham

Compiegne
Laon
Soissons
Aisne R.
Marne R.
Chalons-sur-Marne
Metz
Moselle R.
Phillipsburg
Bruchsal
Durlach
Mannheim
Heilbronn
Nuremberg
Ansbach
Ratisbon
Amberg
Regen R.

Paris
Seine R.
Aube R.
Luneville
Haguenau
Strasbourg
Kehl
WÜRTEMBERG
Stuttgart
Cannstatt
Esslingen
Dillingen
Nördlingen
Neuburg
Ingolstadt
Landshut
Passau
Linz
Wels

Militia — strength not accurately known.

XXXX RHINE MOREAU (104,000)

Schlestadt
Neuf Brisach
Basel
Schaffhausen
Constance
Weissenhorn
Memmingen
Augsburg
Munich
Ried
Braunau
Mödling
Vienna
Asparn
Essling
Wagram
Pressburg

FRANCE

XXXX RESERVE BERTHIER (45,000)

Loire R.
Cher R.
Dijon
Saone R.
Lyon
Geneva

XXXX KRAY (108,500) (including 8,000 in garrisons)

Zürich
SWITZERLAND
VORARL-BERG
Innsbruck
Tyrol
Isar R.
Lech R.
Inn R.
SALZBURG
Salzach
Carinthia
Klagenfurt
Neumarkt
Leoben
Bruck
Enns R.
Raab R.
Danube R.
HUNGARY
Buda
Pest
Thaya R.
March R.
Waag R.
Gran R.

Active army 93,000
Garrison troops 20,000
Piedmontese troops organizing 15,000

Grenoble
Valais
Turin
Ivrea
Milan
Bergamo
Brescia
Verona
Rivoli
Mantua
Trent
Feltre
Venetia
Laibach
Trieste
Istria
Venice
Adige R.
Po R.
Piave R.
Drave R.
Save R.

XXXX MELAS (128,000)

NOTES: Following French forces not shown:
1. 100,000 conscripts under training.
2. Bernadotte (20,000) in NW France.
3. 25,000 garrison troops under Moreau's command and in Rhine fortresses.
4. 1)(St. Bernard Pass; 2)(Simplon Pass; 3)(St. Gothard Pass; 4)(Splügen Pass

Rhone R.
PIEDMONT (SARDINIA)
Piacenza
PARMA
MODENA
Genoa
LIGURIA
TUSCANY
PAPAL STATES
Gaeta

XXXX ITALY MASSENA (36,000)

Nice
GULF OF GENOA

ENGLISH EXPEDITIONARY FORCE (Approximately 10,000)

Marseilles
Toulon
BALEARIC IS.

ADRIATIC SEA
Dalmatia
OTTOMAN EMPIRE

Transylvania

MARENGO CAMPAIGN

Situation Late April 1800

20 0 20 40 60 80 100 120 140
SCALE OF MILES

N

MAP 36: MARENGO CAMPAIGN

From the start, the situation of the Army of Italy had been virtually hopeless. Its area of operations had been repeatedly stripped of supplies. The Directory had sent little food to the army, and neither pay nor clothing. An epidemic ravaged the starving troops. From November 1799 through February 1800, some 30,000 men disappeared through sickness and desertion.

Conditions demanded a tough-souled, talented commander. Bonaparte chose Massena, who accepted reluctantly, but thereafter worked furiously to alleviate the situation. Supplies were built up at Nice, but, because of poor roads, winter, and the English naval blockade, little could be got forward to the troops. In April 1800, Massena's remaining 36,000 men had been largely on half-rations for two months, and the few surviving horses could hardly move his guns. Nevertheless, he had somehow re-established discipline. His mission was to hold Genoa (B1), attracting to himself as many of the Austrians as possible. By so doing, he could both delay the invasion of southern France and draw the Austrians away from the Alpine passes, through which the Reserve Army would advance.

Melas commanded the pick of the Austrian Army. A sound general, responsible for much of Suvorov's success in 1799, he covered his right flank by fortifying the passes leading south from France and Switzerland, and established supply bases at Milan (B2), Alessandria (B2), Turin (A2), and Leghorn (off map, C1). On 6 April, he attacked, making his main effort through Montenotte (B1). (Kaim launched a diversionary attack that cleared Mount Cenis [A2] on 8 April, but was thrown back three days later by Turreau.)

Massena, caught with his army half-reorganized and still dispersed to facilitate supply, was unable to concentrate against the heads of the Austrian columns. By 7 April, he and Suchet had been definitely separated, Melas had reached the sea, and the English fleet could supply the Austrians from the Leghorn base. Despite repeated counterattacks, Massena was driven back into Genoa on 20 April. By 10 May, Suchet had retired behind the Var River. Leaving Ott to take Genoa, Melas followed Suchet. Because of bad roads, he could not close up along the Var until about 14 May. His heavy artillery, which had been shipped down the coast, did not arrive until the 20th.

Meanwhile, Massena grimly set about defending Genoa. The city was well fortified, but most of the population were hostile, food was desperately scarce, and his available troops were barely sufficient to both defend the city and maintain internal order. Fortunately, the broken terrain around Genoa made it difficult for Ott to coordinate the actions of his columns. His attempt to storm Genoa on 30 April was severely repulsed. Massena replied with several successful sorties, but a major one on 13 May failed with heavy losses—including the competent Soult, wounded and captured.

As the Reserve Army shifted southward, Bonaparte scraped up reinforcements: Swiss and Italian troops; 2,100 of Moreau's men in southeast Switzerland; Turreau's weak corps. Moreau again interfered, demanding that Moncey's force be released to him, but was rebuffed by Carnot. (Surprisingly, between 25 April and 8 May, Moreau had crossed the Rhine and beaten Kray in three engagements.) Word from Massena indicated that he could stretch his supplies until late in May. Bonaparte replied that Massena must hold out until at least 30 May, and Suchet until 4 June. On 9 May, Bonaparte joined Berthier at Geneva. Nonarrival of vital supplies forced a halt of the Reserve Army until the 13th, but this time was employed profitably in organization and reconnaissance. On 14 May, as Melas closed up to the Var, Lannes moved out with the advance guard.

The Great St. Bernard Pass (A3) was selected for logistical reasons. Supplies could be moved easily from Geneva to Villeneuve (both A3) by water, whereas the use of the better Little St. Bernard road by the main army would require the organization of large supply trains, for which neither means nor time existed.

Moncey had been ordered to concentrate at the entrance to the St. Gothard Pass (B3), maintaining constant pressure on enemy forces there and threatening an advance on Milan. Short of transport and supplies, he promised to have 2,800 men at the pass on 21 May, but would not be ready for serious action before the end of the month. In Simplon Pass (B3), Bethencourt was to "make the enemy think he had a strong force and to disturb them by attacks on their outposts, but without imprudence." Turreau was to debouch through Susa (A2) and join the main army at Ivrea (B2). He reported himself unable to advance until 21 May. Chabran's division was sent via the Little St. Bernard as a feint. It would rejoin the main army at Aosta (A3), and so would not be in any danger.

Thus, through rapid planning and some good fortune, five columns would advance on a front of approximately 115 miles. Two, comprising the mass of the army, would link up at Aosta, and would always be under Bonaparte's own hand. The remaining three columns were comparatively small, but they would serve to confuse the defenders. At the same time, they would not actually move into open terrain until the main column was through the mountains, and therefore would run little risk.

Despite his recognition of Massena's extremity, Bonaparte apparently was already considering an advance on Milan, to cut Melas' communications. He would fight for the highest stakes: Melas' destruction was his primary object; the rescue of Massena was secondary.

But speed was imperative; he must complete his maneuver while Massena and Suchet still held Melas in position, and they were hard-pressed.

Note: On this map, Loison's command (A3) should be labeled XX instead of XXX.

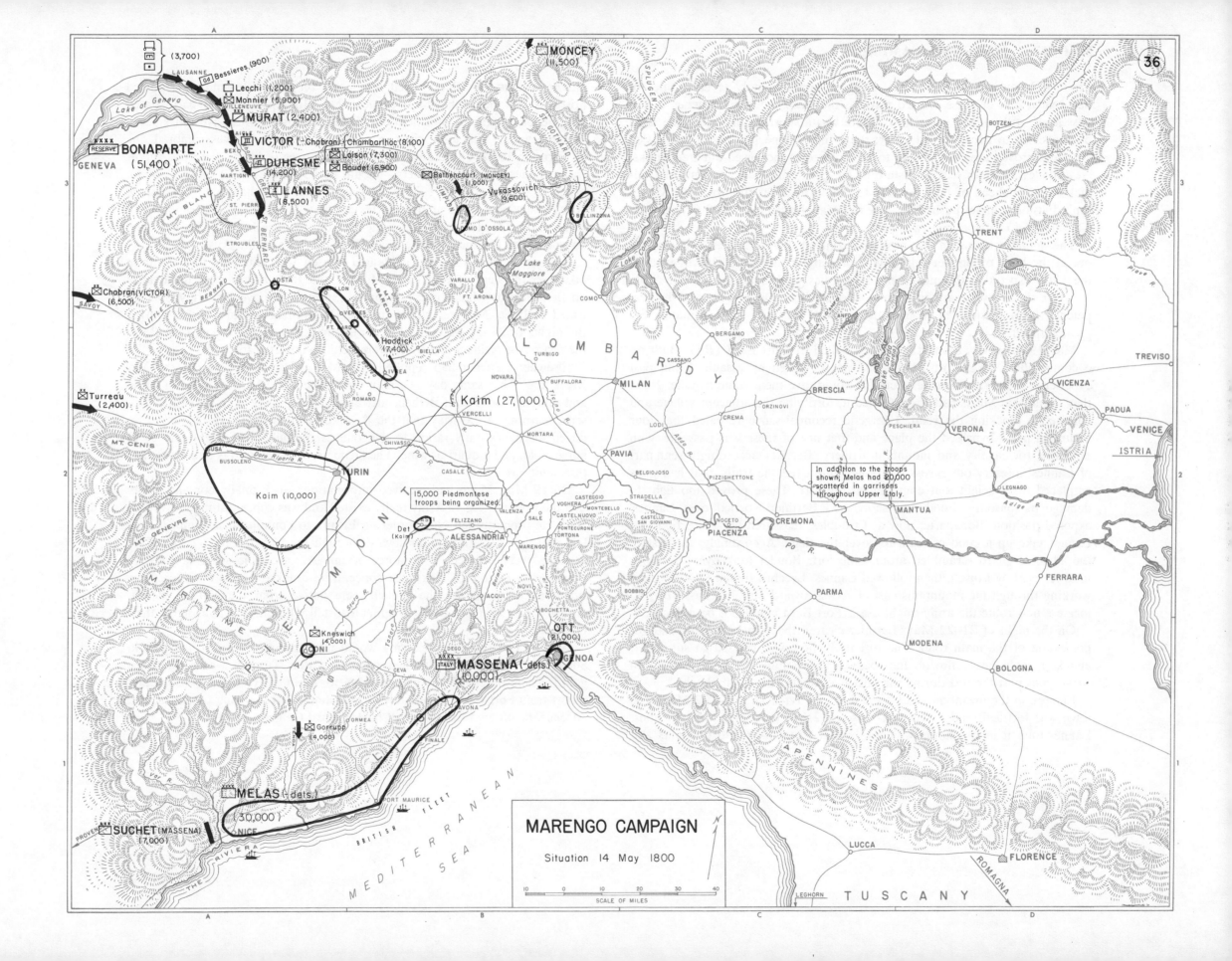

MARENGO CAMPAIGN

Situation 14 May 1800

10   0   10   20   30   40
SCALE OF MILES

From Villeneuve to Aosta (*both A3*) was approximately seventy miles of bad roads. Ten of these twisted through the steep mountain reaches of the pass itself, still banked with snow. There was a shortage of mules; the local peasants fled to avoid forced labor; the artillery's specially constructed sled carriages proved useless and had to be replaced by hollowed-out tree trunks. Nevertheless, Lannes seized Aosta on 17 May, flushing detachments of Haddick's Croats ahead of him. After a brief halt to cover the arrival of Chabran's division, Lannes pushed on. The next day, he cleared 1,200 Croats from Chatillon (*A3*), capturing two guns.

The actual crossing of the pass was controlled by Berthier, who moved out at the head of Boudet's division. Bonaparte remained at Martigny until the 19th, expediting the movement of supplies, and arranging for the Swiss to cover the army's rear until Brune arrived from Dijon. Alarmed by dispatches from Suchet, he constantly prodded Berthier with demands for greater speed.

May 19, however, found the French halted by Fort Bard (*B3*). Built on a commanding crag, Fort Bard could not be taken by assault. From past experience, the French had expected it would give them some trouble. Now, they found that Melas had strengthened it, fortifying the adjacent village and completely blocking the road. Energetic reconnaissance revealed that four mountain paths bypassed the place and that one of these was passable, with difficulty, for cavalry and mountain artillery. Berthier accordingly sent part of Lannes' infantry out across the ridges, improved the trails, and had guns emplaced on a height that commanded the fort. These proved too light to damage its masonry. Food was short, and Berthier worried over Lannes' exposed position. Bonaparte, now at Etroubles, reassured him, directing that Lannes take up a good position to cover the siege. Accordingly, the rest of the advance guard scrambled around the fort. Boudet took over the siege, until relieved by Loison, then followed Lannes. Lecchi's Italian Legion began working through the mountains east of Aosta toward Simplon Pass (*B3*) to locate a new route the army might use if Fort Bard could not be reduced.

On the night of 21–22 May, Berthier cleared the village of Bard and got possession of the main road. The fort itself, however, refused to surrender, and kept up a heavy fire on the roadway, preventing its use. Attempts to sneak guns past the fort during the next two nights failed completely.

Lannes, in the meantime, had come down on Ivrea (*B2*) on 22 May. The town was fortified, and garrisoned by some 2,500 men with fourteen guns. Lannes took it in two hours with the bayonet, snatching 300 prisoners and

all the artillery. Berthier joined him early on the 24th, and interrogated prisoners and local inhabitants exhaustively. His report to Bonaparte stated that Genoa apparently still held out; Haddick was reported five miles south of Ivrea with 5,000 men, but appeared confused; Melas was rumored due at Turin on the 23d; there was no news of Turreau. Attached to this report was a request for further orders—should he now turn right to join Turreau, or left to contact Moncey? Since, as long as Fort Bard held out, the Reserve Army's artillery and ammunition trains were blocked, it was essential to strike at once to clear one of the other passes. Any artillery required for such an operation, Berthier observed, could be taken from the Austrians.

Bonaparte, then at Aosta, contented himself with directing that Chabran take over the siege of Fort Bard. Moncey and Bethencourt were to advance on the 27th, at which time Bonaparte expected to have his army concentrated at Ivrea. Monnier would replace Chabran in Victor's corps. During the nights of 24–26 May, the French finally got six cannon past Fort Bard; the rest of the artillery and trains were held up until the fort fell.

Elsewhere, Suchet had repulsed (22 May) Elsnitz's attack on the Var River line. That same day, Turreau had forced the Austrians out of Susa, and marched on Turin; Bethencourt and Moncey were almost ready. Massena, learning on 20 May that the Reserve Army would soon advance, reduced his men's daily ration to five ounces of foul bread, eight ounces of horse meat, and a quart of wine. The Genoese were eating rats and grass, and threatening revolt.

On 19 May, Melas had received information which finally convinced him that the French Reserve Army really existed and was concentrating in Switzerland. He promptly left Nice, ordering Elsnitz to contain Suchet until Genoa fell, and then to withdraw northward through the Col di Tenda (*A1*). Two brigades were ordered to reinforce Kaim. All available reserves were to assemble at Turin; Haddick must concentrate quickly. Melas considered the situation confusing, for the French were active from the Var to the St. Gothard Pass (*B3*), and it was difficult to tell where they would make their main effort.

Judging that the Reserve Army would take the most direct route to join Suchet and Massena, Melas first concluded that Turreau was its advance guard. Then, on 24 May, while en route to Turin, he received a disquieting report from Fort Bard: Thousands of Frenchmen were moving past that post. At once, he ordered Elsnitz to fall back toward Genoa.

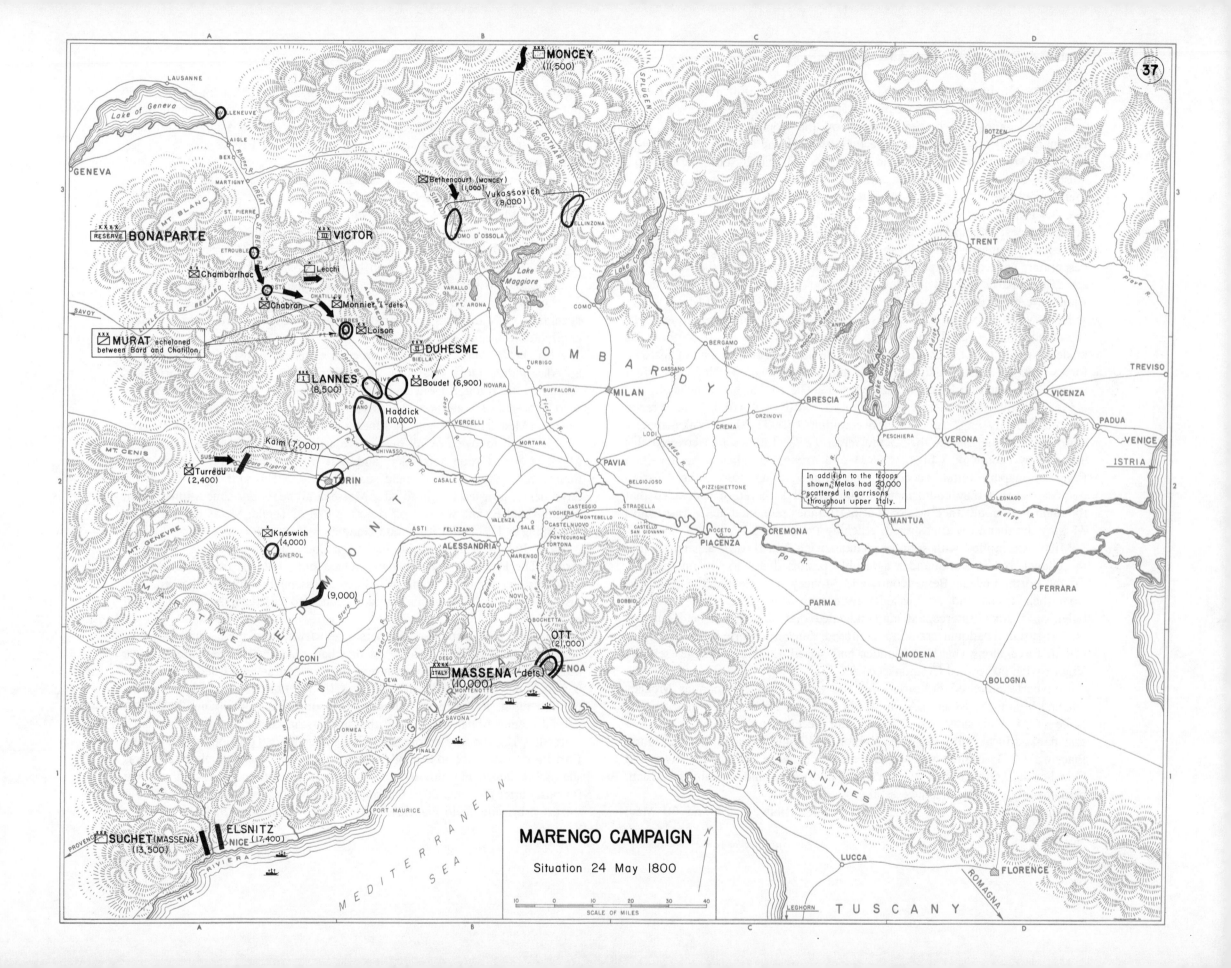

MARENGO CAMPAIGN

Situation 24 May 1800

Except for Chabran's division, the Reserve Army (32,000 men and 8 cannon) assembled around Ivrea by 26 May. Murat was scouting toward Vercelli, and Lannes had driven Haddick off the Romano heights (*all B2*). Bonaparte now ordered an advance on Milan. He had two reasons for this decision: Milan was Melas' major base; its fall would cut the principal Austrian line of communication and shake Allied morale. More important, Melas would be forced either to withdraw quickly from western Italy or to risk his army's destruction. But these military reasons were reinforced by personal ones: Bonaparte required a quick, spectacular victory that would immediately confirm him as France's ruler and outstanding general; France desperately needed a competent government which could end the war. In this crisis, Bonaparte showed absolute conviction that his fortune and that of France were inextricable.

He saw his opportunity, but his generalship still had not matured. His roundabout maneuver through Milan offered Melas time to concentrate; his anxiety to trap the still-undefeated Austrians led him to overextend his own forces in an attempt to plug every possible hole through which Melas might escape. The resulting lesson in strategy would be rough, but beneficial.

Accordingly, the Reserve Army moved swiftly on Milan. The French entered that city on 2 June, after overcoming (30–31 May) Vukassovich's effort to hold the line of the Ticino River (*B2*). Lannes had covered this advance by occupying Chivasso (*B2*) and driving Haddick over the Orco River. (Bonaparte initially accompanied Lannes, riding close to the Austrian outposts, so that they could identify him. Haddick therefore concluded that the main French advance was on Turin.) Lannes remained at Chivasso until 31 May; he then moved eastward, reaching Pavia on 2 June.

Milan was stuffed with supplies. Vukassovich had thrown a garrison into the citadel, but its commander agreeably promised not to fire on the city. To the north, Lecchi, Bethencourt, and Moncey had cleared the Austrians from their fronts and established liaison with Bonaparte. Fort Bard had fallen on 1 June. Intercepted mail indicated that Genoa still held out and that Austrian headquarters were confused. Suchet reported the Austrians still in force along the Var. Boudet had seized Lodi on 4 June, sending Vukassovich off toward Cremona (*both C2*).

Bonaparte prepared his orders for the next move. As soon as Moncey reached Milan, the Reserve Army would cross the Po and seize the Stradella defile (*C2*). Duhesme (less Boudet) and Lecchi would screen the army's east flank; Murat, with Boudet's division and some cavalry, would capture Piacenza (*C2*); Lannes would cross the Po between the Ticino River and Castello San Giovanni; Chambarlhac's division would remain in Milan, ready to reinforce the first successful crossing.

Melas, at this moment, had many troubles. Between 27 and 30 May,

Kaim's reinforced command had pushed Turreau back on Susa, but could not exploit this success because of Haddick's reverses. Melas momentarily considered (29 May) advancing with the forces he had available, crushing Lannes, and attacking Bonaparte from the rear. But Elsnitz was in danger, and Ott was pinned to Genoa.

Elsnitz, with British frigates providing gunfire support, had made a determined attack on Suchet's position (26 May), but had been repulsed. Receiving Melas' order to retire toward Genoa, he tried to screen his withdrawal with another attack. But Suchet was already moving to turn Elsnitz's right flank. Only fragments of Elsnitz's rear guard (Gorrupp's brigade) reached Coni (*A1*); Elsnitz's main body was painfully hustled.

In Genoa, his men almost too weak to lift their weapons and his hospitals overflowing, Massena made a last futile sortie (31 May) before finally accepting Ott's demand for a parley. Even then, he would not consider capitulation on any terms.

Also on 31 May, Melas had ordered a general Austrian concentration at Alessandria (*B2*). Haddick and Kaim were to move via Turin and Asti; Elsnitz, through Coni and Asti; Ott, via Novi. Ott must immediately send a brigade to reinforce the garrison of the fortified bridgehead at Piacenza. (Melas himself, on 1 June, started O'Reilly's reinforced brigade for Piacenza, followed by all his reserve artillery.) Ott objected, stating that Massena would soon surrender, and that if the Austrians withdrew now, their greedy English allies would seize the city. Melas authorized Ott a few days' delay, instructing him to offer Massena all necessary concessions. Then, learning that Elsnitz was cut off from the Col di Tenda, Melas himself chose to remain in Turin with Kaim and Haddick.

By 4 June, the anxious Ott had been coerced into accepting Massena's terms: The French would evacuate Genoa, but would be free to serve once they were again within their own lines. Massena promptly embarked with his artillery and 2,200 of his soundest men, and sailed for Antibes (*just off map, A1*).

Both opposing army commanders knew frustration on 5 June. Moncey began entering Milan, but reported that bad roads had forced him to leave most of his artillery and ammunition behind. Murat and Boudet spent the day in futile efforts to take the weakly defended Piacenza bridgehead. (During the night, its garrison retired to the south bank, breaking the bridge behind them.) Bonaparte learned that an Austrian detachment had occupied Vercelli (*B2*) the day before, and that his artillery (previously delayed by Fort Bard) could not go beyond Ivrea for lack of an escort. Only Suchet was successful, destroying almost half of Elsnitz's retreating forces and pushing furiously after the remainder. Ott solemnly took possession of Genoa, but did start one brigade off to Piacenza and another to Tortona (*B2*).

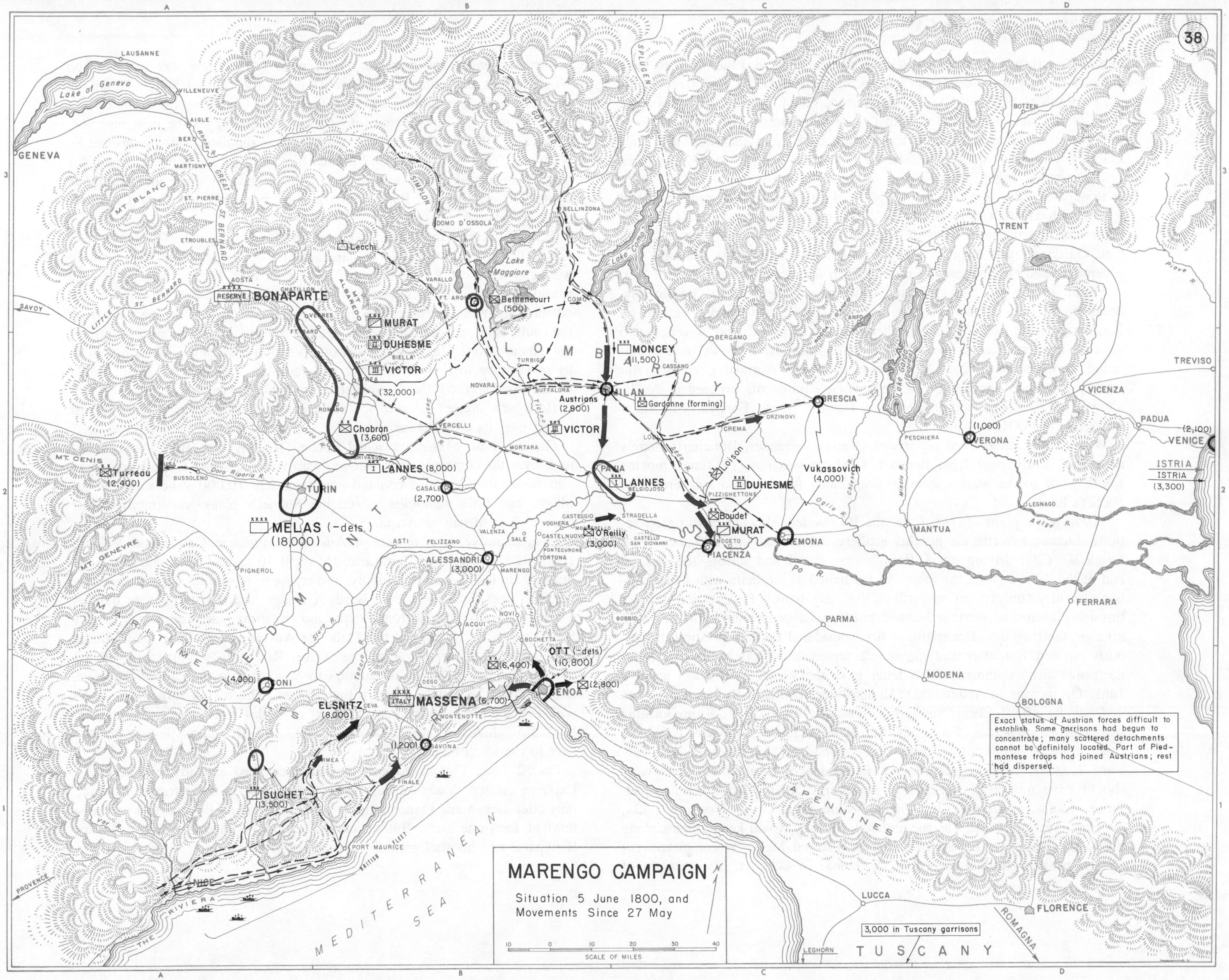

38

MARENGO CAMPAIGN

Situation 5 June 1800, and
Movements Since 27 May

LAUSANNE

Lake of Geneva

VILLENEUVE

GENEVA

AIGLE

MT. BLANC

MARTIGNY

ST. PIERRE

GREAT ST. BERNARD

SAVOY

LITTLE ST. BERNARD

AOSTA

Lecchi

DOMO D'OSSOLA

Lake
Maggiore

BELLINZONA

SPLUGEN

COMO

TRENT

VARALLO

FT. ARO

Bettencourt
(500)

RESERVE BONAPARTE

ETROUBLES

MURAT

DUHESME

VICTOR

(32,000)

Chabran
(3,600)

BIELLA

NOVARA

TURBIGO

BUFFALORA

MILAN

Austrians
(2,800)

BERGAMO

LOMBARDY

MONCEY
(11,500)

CASSANO

Gardanne (forming)

BRESCIA

ORZINOVI

CREMA

PESCHIERA

(1,000)

VERONA

VICENZA

PADUA

VENICE
(2,100)

VERCELLI

VICTOR

MT. CENIS

Turreau
(2,400)

BUSSOLENO

CHIVASSO

LANNES (8,000)

MORTARA

CASALE
(2,700)

LANNES

BELGIOJOSO

Loison

Vukassovich
(4,000)

DUHESME

PIZZIGHETTONE

MISTA
ISTRIA
(3,300)

OLEGNAGO

TURIN

MELAS (-dets.)
(18,000)

ASTI

FELIZZANO

VALENZA

SALE

CASTEGGIO

MONTEBELLO

O'Reilly
(3,000)

VOGHERA

Boudet

MURAT

CREMONA

MANTUA

PIGNEROL

ALESSANDRIA
(3,000)

MARENGO

TORTONA

CASTELNUOVO

PONTECURONE

CASTELLO
SAN GIOVANNI

NOCETO

PIACENZA

Po R.

NOVI

BOBBIO

PARMA

FERRARA

ACQUI

BOCHETTA

(4,000)

ELSNITZ
(8,000)

ORMEA

MASSENA (6,700)

ITALY

MONTENOTTE

DEGO

OTT (-dets.)
(10,800)

(6,400)

GENOA

(2,800)

MODENA

BOLOGNA

APENNINES

(1,200)

SAVONA

FINALE

SUCHET
(13,500)

PORT MAURICE

BRITISH FLEET

NICE

PROVENCE

THE RIVIERA

MEDITERRANEAN SEA

LIGURIA

LUCCA

ROMAGNA

FLORENCE

TUSCANY

LEGHORN

Exact status of Austrian forces difficult to
establish. Some garrisons had begun to
concentrate; many scattered detachments
cannot be definitely located. Part of Piedmontese troops had joined Austrians; rest
had dispersed.

3,000 in Tuscany garrisons

10   0   10   20   30   40
SCALE OF MILES

O'Reilly's advance guard reached Piacenza early on 6 June, only to have a battle explode to its left rear. Lannes had improvised a trail ferry across the Po south of Belgiojoso (*C2*); his advance guard, moving inland to cover the crossing site, had collided with O'Reilly's column. The Austrian units under attack managed to keep the French back from the highway, while O'Reilly frantically countermarched the rest of his brigade and the Austrian reserve artillery behind them.

Bonaparte, busy in Milan with high-level political-military problems, had left operational matters to Berthier. Victor had started for Lodi (*C2*) with Chambarlhac's division. Berthier countermarched them—followed by Monnier, Gardanne, and Lapoype's cavalry—to Lannes' support; Duhesme was ordered to seize a bridgehead at Cremona, then advance on Piacenza (*both C2*).

Murat, meanwhile, had collected boats near Noceto (*C2*). Before daybreak on 7 June, Boudet's division crossed the Po and quickly carried all Piacenza, except the citadel. Furthermore, it surprised and wrecked two Austrian reinforcements: the brigade Ott had sent from Genoa and a battalion from Parma (*C2*). Downstream, Duhesme stormed Cremona. But Lannes' crossing, because of its improvised equipment, proceeded slowly, allowing O'Reilly to withdraw across Lannes' front. Forewarned, Melas ordered Ott to O'Reilly's aid.

When Murat intercepted reports of Genoa's surrender, Bonaparte merely demanded more speed from Berthier. Chabran was now (7 June) moving south, while to the west scarecrow Frenchmen from Genoa staggered into Suchet's lines.

Through the night of 7–8 June, the Po flooded, slowing crossing operations. Lannes nevertheless got his artillery across and at 0200 moved on Stradella (*C2*), driving out O'Reilly's rear guard and seizing the western end of the defile beyond the town. Victor halted at Stradella with Chambarlhac's infantry (his artillery was still on the north bank). Berthier sent cavalry through Piacenza to overtake Lannes, but it was appropriated by Murat, who sat tight there all day. Bonaparte at first considered Lannes' position dangerously exposed. But, after studying an intercepted letter from Melas to Vienna, he turned airily optimistic. This letter gave the Austrian situation as of 5 June: Ott moving to Acqui (*B2*); Hohenzollern detached to garrison Genoa and Savona (*B1*); Elsnitz retreating through Ormea (*B1*); Kaim jousting with Turreau on 4 June. From this, Bonaparte deduced that Melas could not concentrate at Alessandria before 12–13 June—and then could have only some 22,000. Therefore, Lannes was in no danger, and the Reserve Army should have numerical superiority. Bonaparte ordered an immediate advance. Lannes, supported by Victor, would push on to Voghera (*B2*), knocking over any Austrians encountered. Moncey would keep abreast along the Po's north bank. Bonaparte's reports pictured Melas as completely cut off and probably forced to retreat to Genoa. In sad fact, his estimates of

Austrian strength and marching speed were far too low. Ott had reached Voghera late on 8 June; except for delays at the flooded Scrivia River, he might have caught Lannes still astride the Po. Gathering up O'Reilly, Ott (17,000 men, 35 guns) went into position at Casteggio the next morning. Lannes (5,400, 4 guns) met him head on, was repulsed, but—reinforced by Victor (6,000)—broke Ott and hunted him through Montebello. There, for lack of cavalry, Lannes' pursuit ended. Meanwhile Monnier and Gardanne completed crossing the Po; Murat, relieved by a brigade from Cremona, moved westward.

Having secured the Stradella defile and received word of Suchet's successes, Bonaparte issued orders for the advance on Alessandria (*B2*). Moncey would guard the area between the Po, Oglio, and Ticino rivers. Duhesme would hold the vital Piacenza crossing with Loison's division. Lapoype would advance along the north bank of the Po, keeping abreast of the main army on the south bank; if Melas advanced against him, he would defend the line of the Tincio River. The main army would keep one division a day's march in its rear, ready to recross the river and reinforce Lapoype. A small flotilla would move up the Po, to be available for such an emergency.

Bonaparte himself rejoined the army at Stradella late on 9 June, at last taking over its direct command.

On the coast, Massena reached Finale (*B1*) by boat from Antibes and took over the command from Suchet, who was preparing to push inland to join Bonaparte. Massena counted approximately 10,000 valid men, no artillery, and little ammunition. Judging Suchet's plans too ambitious, he ordered him to halt at Acqui.

Ott's offensive, plus reports of Austrian activity at Casale and Valenza (*both B2*), had sobered Bonaparte. He spent 10 and 11 June concentrating, building up his ammunition supply, and trying to hasten forward the artillery that had been delayed by Fort Bard. A bridge and trail ferry were built at Voghera. Desaix arrived from Egypt, and the army was reorganized to give him a corps. By evening of the 11th, the Austrians remaining quiet, Bonaparte ordered his army toward the Scrivia River (*B2*), apparently on the assumption that Melas would attempt to break out to the east on 12 June, and so could be caught crossing that stream. The march formation shown was designed for a surprise envelopment of Melas' north flank, forcing him back through Acqui on Genoa and Suchet. At 2230, Lapoype was ordered over to the south bank.

On 12 June, Victor's advance flowed unchecked around Tortona (*B2*). Lapoype crossed slowly on trail ferries established near Casteggio, finishing only after dark. Some French artillery caught up, giving Bonaparte a probable total of forty-one guns. But no contact could be established with Melas; Bonaparte and his staff grew increasingly worried.

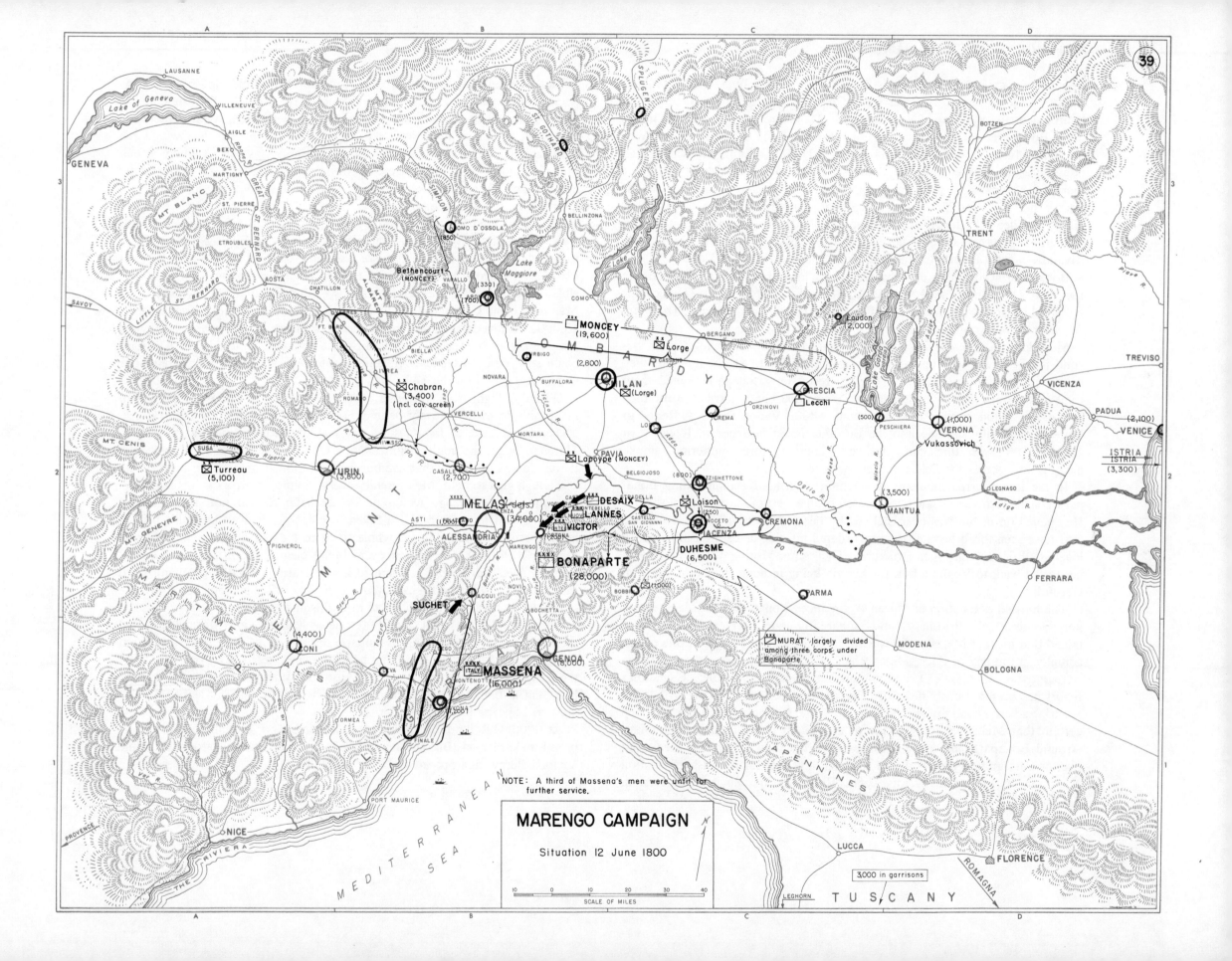

MARENGO CAMPAIGN

Situation 12 June 1800

NOTE: A third of Massena's men were unfit for further service.

MURAT largely divided among three corps under Bonaparte.

3,000 in garrisons

SCALE OF MILES
10   0   10   20   30   40

Bonaparte's anxiety grew through the morning of 13 June. Melas avoided contact; a letter dated 11 June from Chabran reported the Austrians assembling boats at Casale (*off map, A3*). To determine the enemy's intentions, Bonaparte (at 0530, at Voghera [*off map, D3*]) ordered Lannes, Victor, and Murat across the Scrivia River (*D1–D3*). Riding forward three hours later, he learned that they had still failed to contact Melas. The fact that Melas apparently was giving up the Marengo plain, which seemed to offer a fine field for his numerous cavalry, caused Bonaparte to revert to his earlier idea that the Austrian commander did not wish to risk battle, and that he was either shifting north through Casale or retiring on Genoa. Rivaud's cavalry reported no enemy activity along the Po.

Bonaparte accordingly directed Desaix to leave Lapoype at Pontecurone (*off map, D3*), and to send Monnier to Torre di Garofoli (*D2*). Desaix himself would march with Boudet, via Rivalta (*D1*), toward Serravalle (*off map, 20 miles southeast of Alessandria*).

Meanwhile, Lannes and Victor had found the supposedly level plain beyond the Scrivia so cut up that scouting was difficult. At about 1300, they halted abreast of San Giuliano (*C2*) to rest. Here Bonaparte joined them some two hours later with all available cavalry, but a terrific storm then halted all action until 1630. At about 1800, Victor found O'Reilly in Marengo; O'Reilly scuttled into the Bormida River bridgehead. It was then almost 2100, with thickening darkness, another storm muttering, smoke hanging low across the fields, and everyone exhausted.

In the last, blurred moments of daylight, Marmont (commanding Bonaparte's artillery reserve) saw Ott's ponton bridge west of Castel Ceriolo (*B3*). He opened on it, but was overwhelmed by heavier Austrian guns. Bonaparte may have seen this bridge; at least he ordered his aide-de-camp, Lauriston, to locate and destroy any such structures. Then, after visiting Victor's outposts, he started back to Voghera but, the Scrivia being in flood, halted at Torre di Garofoli.

The hurried evacuation of Marengo convinced Bonaparte that Melas would not counterattack. Prisoners (and, apparently, one or more spies) maintained that most of Melas' army was still at Alessandria. However, one agent, actually in the pay of Zach, Melas' chief of staff, insisted that the Austrians were moving on Casale. Chabran now reported Casale quiet. Lauriston's report has been variously described, but Bonaparte took it to mean that the Austrians had no additional bridges over the Bormida. He went to sleep certain that Melas was only trying to escape, in one direction or another. Around Bonaparte, his army bivouacked in the mud and rain where night overtook its units. From both the strategic and tactical aspects, its position was poor. Its local security was worse, Victor having shown no interest in the matter.

Melas, fortunately, had been slow to comprehend, and slower to act. As he saw his situation, a move down the north bank of the Po would be no better than a flight across a series of river lines, with Moncey on his left and Bonaparte on his right. A retreat to Genoa and the British fleet would run the risk of being pocketed between Bonaparte and Massena. Anyhow, Melas preferred to fight: He was at least as strong as Bonaparte, with more cavalry and artillery. A victory over the First Consul of France would change the entire course of this campaign.

He had ordered O'Reilly to retire slowly, *but to hold Marengo*; Zach's spy was briefed; and Ott built his ponton bridge. The Austrians would attack in three columns: Ott (7,600) to make a secondary attack on the left along the axis Castel Ceriolo–Sale (*off map, D3*) to engage as many French as possible; Melas to lead the center (20,200) down the main highway from Marengo to San Giuliano, then turn left and roll up the French line; O'Reilly (3,000) to cover the right flank. Success would drive Bonaparte northward into the corner between the Po and Scrivia rivers; if repulsed, the Austrians could still retire on Genoa. All units would be deployed behind Fontanone Creek at daylight on the 14th.

O'Reilly's flight from Marengo on the 13th crippled this plan. Instead of being able to form leisurely behind Fontanone Creek for his main attack, Melas would have to fight his way across that stream line and then clear Marengo before he could deploy. Since Ott's bridge appeared endangered, it was floated upstream that evening and reinstalled behind the bridgehead.

Though glad to fight, Melas made several thumping errors in his planning. Assuming that Marengo would be lightly held, he did not designate any particular unit to capture it. He failed to construct new gates in his bridgehead, thereby condemning his whole force to file out by a single road and forcing Ott to wait until O'Reilly and Melas cleared the bridgehead. He did not add Alessandria's big garrison to his field army. Finally, receiving word that Suchet's cavalry had seized Acqui (*off map, A2*), he detached a brigade of cavalry from his center column to meet this movement.

Bonaparte did no better. At 0800, one of Murat's aides warned him that the Austrians were advancing. Bonaparte dismissed this movement as a feint. Desaix's aide, Savary, reported that he had reconnoitered Novi (*off map, C1*) the previous afternoon and found no Austrians. Bonaparte refused to believe him, and at 0900 directed Desaix to march as previously ordered. He also ordered Lapoype back across the Po.

At 0900, O'Reilly fell gently upon Gardanne who, though somewhat surprised, held him off. But Melas' main column was swarming forward, while Victor's sleepy men groped for their weapons.

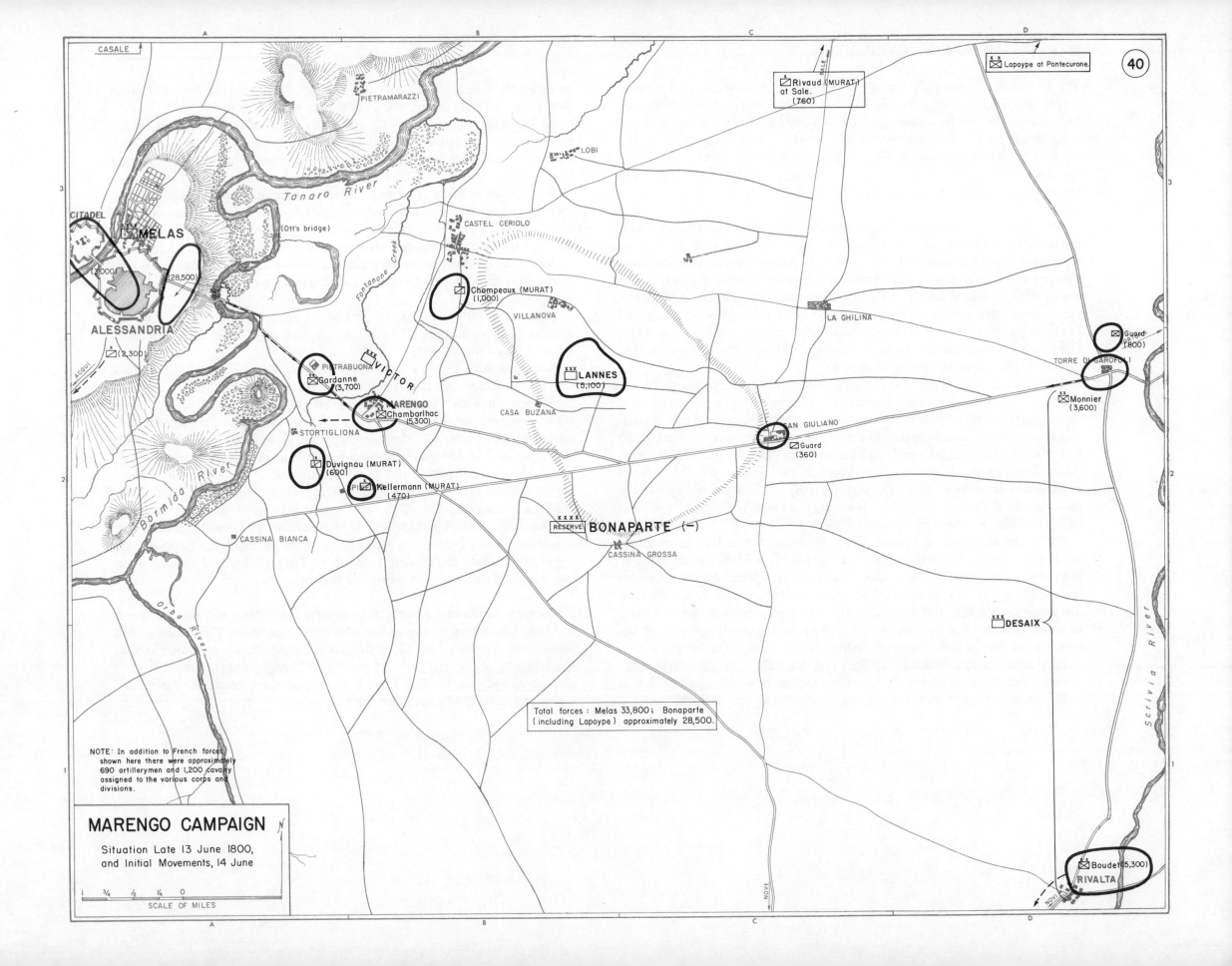

CASALE

PIETRAMARAZZI

Tanaro River

(Ott's bridge)

LOBI

Lapoype at Pontecurone.

40

Rivaud (MURAT)
at Sale.
(760)

CASTEL CERIOLO

CITADEL

MELAS
(3,000)
(28,500)

ALESSANDRIA
(2,300)

Champeaux (MURAT)
(1,000)

VILLANOVA

LA GHILINA

Guard
(1800)

TORRE DI GAROFOLI

PIETRABUONA
VICTOR
Gardanne
(3,700)

LANNES
(5,100)

Monnier
(3,600)

Fontanone Creek

MARENGO
Chambarlhac
(5,300)

CASA BUZANA

STORTIGLIONA

SAN GIULIANO

Guard
(360)

Duvignau (MURAT)
(600)

Kellermann (MURAT)
(470)

Bormida River

RESERVE BONAPARTE (−)

CASSINA BIANCA

CASSINA GROSSA

DESAIX

Orba River

Scrivia River

Total forces : Melas 33,800 ; Bonaparte
(including Lapoype) approximately 28,500.

NOTE: In addition to French forces
shown here there were approximately
690 artillerymen and 1,200 cavalry
assigned to the various corps and
divisions.

MARENGO CAMPAIGN

Situation Late 13 June 1800,
and Initial Movements, 14 June

1   ¾   ½   ¼   0
SCALE OF MILES

N

ACQUI

NOVI

NOVI

Boudet (5,300)

RIVALTA

The terrain here, seemingly "open" at first glance, was so cut up by roads, fences, and ditches that it favored the defense. Numerous stone farmhouses, each surrounded by its walled garden, orchard, and vineyards, were ready-made strong points. The ground was still waterlogged from the rains, hindering cavalry movements and making it difficult for the artillery to get far off the roads. Fontanone Creek, normally a minor obstacle at Marengo, now ran deep between muddy, slippery banks.

Gardanne quickly halted O'Reilly's hesitant advance on Pietrabuona (*A2*); repulsed, O'Reilly fell off to the south, giving over the assault to Frimont with Melas' advance guard (1,200). Massing sixteen guns astride the road, Frimont drove in furiously, with Haddick's division in close support. It was a spectacular, gallant attack. (Melas had issued new uniforms and equipment—also extra rations of meat, rice, and wine.) Austrian officers of all grades exposed themselves recklessly to set their men an example. By 0930, Gardanne had been pushed back on Marengo. Utilizing the elbowroom thus gained, Melas began deploying as shown.

Chambarlhac meanwhile had gone into position behind Fontanone Creek, with his center in Marengo. Gardanne's withdrawal into the town thus scrambled Victor's formation, intermixing his two divisions from the start.

As soon as the first Austrian line was formed (sometime between 0930 and 1000), Haddick personally led Bellegarde's brigade against Marengo, colors flaunting, bands playing. The Austrians came on bravely, but French resistance was savage. Haddick was mortally wounded and his attack smashed. As Bellegarde's riddled brigade sagged back, Kaim took command of the first line, and brought up more guns.

Off to the southeast at Rivalta (*D1*), daybreak found Boudet resuming the task of getting his division across the still-swollen Scrivia River. Thanks to the discovery of a leaky boat, which his artificers repaired during the night, the operation was finished by 1000, and the division stood ready to march on Serravalle as ordered. But Desaix, a shy man who lived only for the glory of serving France, had been listening to the increasing rumble of guns in the direction of Alessandria. Sometime before 1000, he had sent Savary with a cavalry detachment to reconnoiter Novi (*off map, D1*) for the second time. Savary again found it empty of Austrians. Desaix promptly dispatched him to Bonaparte to report that fact and request further orders. Desaix's decision

to delay his march south saved the Reserve Army; it probably also saved Bonaparte's military career, and changed the shape of history.

At Marengo, Victor's corps began to show some unsteadiness as the vastly stronger Austrian artillery gained fire superiority and pounded the French infantry. Duvignau's cavalry brigade, left leaderless when Victor sent that general to the hospital at 0512 (Duvignau had been badly hurt during the night when his horse fell on him), failed to work as a unit, though its individual regiments seem to have behaved well enough. Worse, at this time or a little later, Chambarlhac panicked when his orderly was killed beside him, and fled the field, abandoning his troops. Still, Victor managed to hold out on both sides of Marengo. Behind him, Lannes—as a result of either his own alertness or of an appeal from Victor—began to get his troops under arms and into line.

Meanwhile, with both O'Reilly and Melas finally out of the way, Ott was able to begin debouching from the bridgehead for his delayed blow from Castel Ceriolo toward Sale.

Bonaparte initially almost ignored the fighting, believing that Melas' attack could be nothing more than a feint, designed to throw the French back on their heels while the Austrian army withdrew from Alessandria. At about 1000, however, the growing uproar at last convinced him that the situation might be serious after all. Mounting, he rode forward to the only available "high ground," a low ridge running generally from Cassina Grossa (*C2*) through Casa Buzana (*B2*) to a point slightly east of Castel Ceriolo. Reaching it at about 1100 (apparently somewhere to the northwest of San Giuliano), he saw a panorama which rapidly apprised him of his errors. His reaction was as quick, and perfectly calm; Monnier and the Consular Guard were to come forward; Desaix and Lapoype were to be recalled. (Lapoype, engaged in recrossing to the north bank of the Po, probably had some interesting, unofficial comments on receipt of that order.)

Marengo was so vital a battle to Bonaparte that, unlike his usual behavior, he showed no mercy to any officer who failed him there. Chambarlhac and Monnier disappeared from the active list. (Chambarlhac's own men shot at him when he reappeared the next morning.) Duvignau also found himself a scapegoat, and was forcibly retired, even over the protests of Victor and various medical officers, the following August.

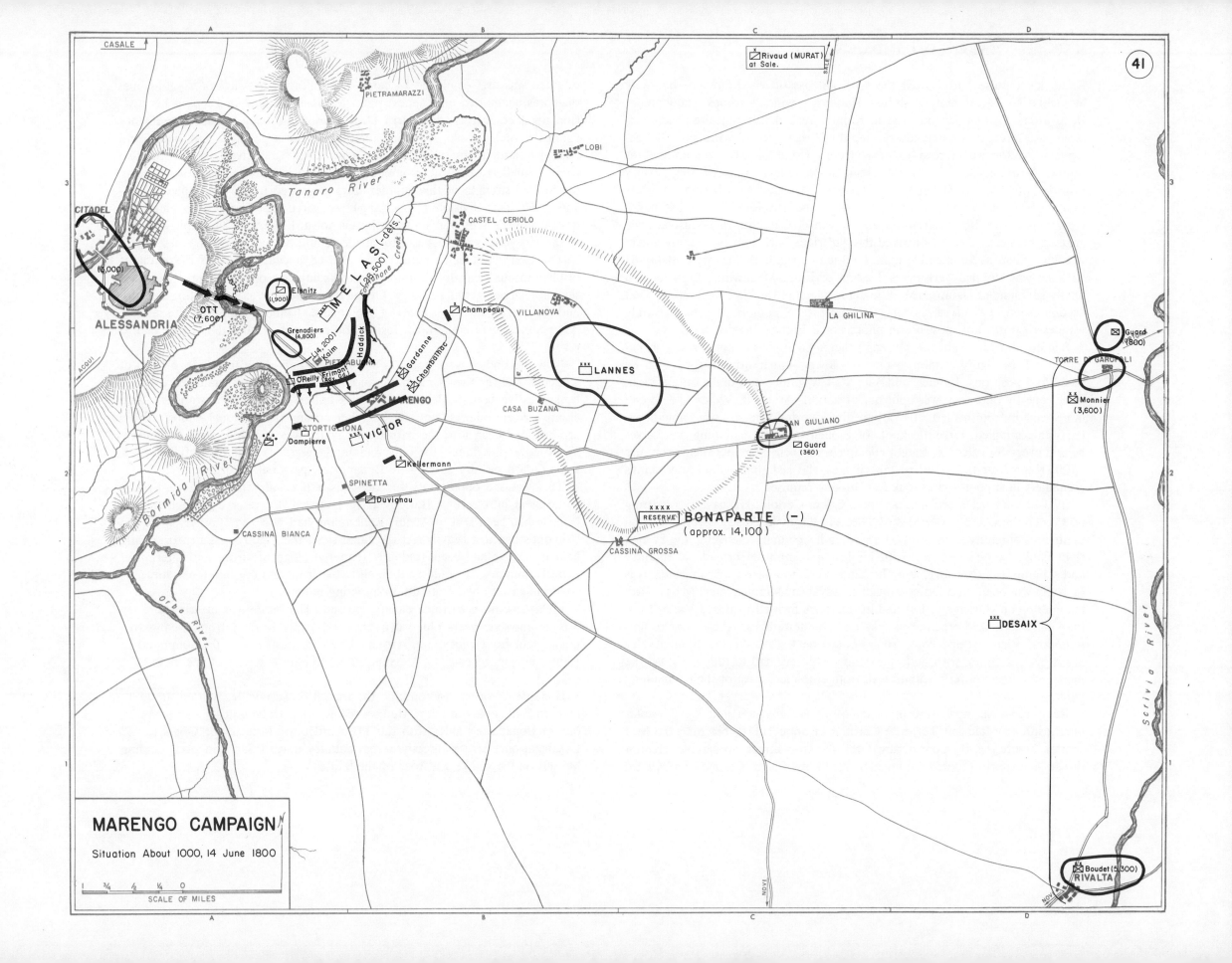

CASALE

41

Rivaud (MURAT)
at Sale.

PIETRAMARAZZI

LOBI

Tanaro River

CASTEL CERIOLO

CITADEL

LA GHILINA

(3,000)

MELAS (-dets.)
(29,500)

Elsnitz
(1,900)

Champeaux

VILLANOVA

Guard
(800)

OTT
(7,600)

ALESSANDRIA

TORRE DI GAROFOLI

Grenadiers
(4,800)

Kaim
(4,200)

Haddick

Gardanne

Chambarlhac

LANNES

Monnier
(3,600)

ACQUI

PIETRABUONA

O'Reilly Friman
(Adv. Gd.)

MARENGO

CASA BUZANA

SAN GIULIANO

Guard
(360)

STORTIGLIONA

VICTOR

Dampierre

Bormida River

Kellermann

SPINETTA

Duvignau

BONAPARTE (-)
(approx. 14,100)

RESERVE

CASSINA BIANCA

CASSINA GROSSA

Orba River

DESAIX

Scrivia River

MARENGO CAMPAIGN

Situation About 1000, 14 June 1800

1   ¾   ½   ¼   0
SCALE OF MILES

Boudet (5,300)
RIVALTA

NOVI

Haddick's repulse had slowed the Austrian assault on Marengo, but only momentarily. Melas simply shifted Haddick's winded troops (now under Bellegarde) to their left and fed in Kaim's fresh division. Kaim's men battered at Marengo; though always repulsed, they slowly wore out the defenders. Victor was forced to draw troops from his left to reinforce his center. Noticing this movement about noon, Melas ordered the cavalry brigade attached to Bellegarde's (formerly Haddick's) division to cross Fontanone Creek to the south of Marengo and envelop Victor's left flank. Kellermann saw this Austrian cavalry advance. Catching them just as they crossed, his heavy cavalry knocked the Austrians back into the muddy creek, wrecking them as an effective unit. To Victor's right, Bellegarde's attempted advance was stopped by Lannes' leading division. Meanwhile, O'Reilly had finally surrounded Dampierre's little detachment in the Cassina Bianca. That accomplished, he left a cavalry detachment to contain it, and leisurely wandered southward, possibly in pursuit of a French cavalry regiment.

Behind him, the fight for Marengo increased in fury. Melas had concentrated at least eighty cannon against the town—apparently all for which he could find positions. Lannes' and Victor's few guns could make only a weak reply; one by one, they were put out of action. At 1300, Victor had to call more units in from his left. His various divisions and brigades were now hopelessly intermingled, but little knots of French infantry, clamping themselves behind every bit of cover, fought effectively on their own. Between noon and 1400, Kaim four times rushed the village—the last time with Lattermann's grenadiers in support—and took four bloody repulses.

By 1400, however, Ott had occupied Castel Ceriolo. His cavalry reporting no French force of any size toward Sale, and the main Austrian column being in obvious difficulty to his south, Ott swung his column to envelop the French right flank, Lannes met him with his last uncommitted brigade of infantry and Champeaux's cavalry, but the odds were too heavy. Champeaux was mortally wounded, and Ott continued to advance. Minutes later, Melas' grim hammering at Marengo at last had its effect: A fifth effort drove Victor from the village in a wild series of attacks and counterattacks. Almost out of ammunition, Victor reeled back from Fontanone Creek, the Austrian cavalry at his heels. Lannes, with both flanks now exposed, had to follow, though he managed a fairly orderly withdrawal. Both corps lost most of their remaining guns.

Reinforcements now were at hand. Monnier's division and the Consular Guard infantry had left Torre de Garofoli at about 1130, reaching the field shortly before 1400. Considering Ott's flanking attack to be the greatest threat, Bonaparte ordered Monnier to recapture Castel Ceriolo. The Guard infantry was first employed to carry cartridges up to Victor's sagging line, then was committed on Lannes' right. Monnier, instead of keeping his division together, merely sent Carra St.-Cyr with one demi-brigade (regiment) against Castel Ceriolo, detached another to cover St.-Cyr's left flank, and held the third in reserve. Though Carra St.-Cyr quickly took his objective from a small Austrian detachment left to hold it, Ott—apparently realizing the limited strength of this counterattack—ignored it and continued his advance. His rear division (Vogelsang) recovered the village as it came up, and Monnier's scattered units withdrew toward Torre di Garofoli, keeping to the vineyards so that Austrian cavalry could not get at them.

The Consular Guard infantry had also advanced, supported by remnants of Champeaux's cavalry. Forming square southwest of Villanova, it repulsed several charges by Ott's cavalry. Ott met this check by concentrating infantry and artillery against two faces of the square. Frimont supported his attack. After a game half-hour stand, losing 260 men out of 800, the Guard had to retire.

Now the French went back on San Giuliano all along the front, a froth of wounded and fugitives scrambling on ahead. Lannes' corps managed to retire by successive bounds; Victor's line was only a collection of stubborn little clumps, where officers kept men together around their colors. Almost all the artillery had been lost; the hard-used cavalry was spending itself maneuvering to cover the flanks; the only remaining reserve was the handful of Consular Guard cavalry serving as Bonaparte's personal escort.

This was the opportunity for the Austrian cavalry to harry the French withdrawal into a rout. But Melas had no cavalry reserve available: One brigade had been sent to Acqui; Kellermann had wrecked another; Ott's and Frimont's had lost heavily. At the same time, the 1,900 horsemen originally held in reserve had been gradually scattered along the front and intermixed with the infantry. It would be difficult to extricate and regroup them; anyway, Austrian cavalry had no tradition of acting in mass.

Melas saw no need for a cavalry pursuit. The battle was clearly won. He was seventy-one years old, worn out, and badly bruised from having two horses shot from under him. Around 1500, he turned over the command to Kaim and jogged back to Alessandria to prepare a report of his victory.

Bonaparte's orders to continue the march to Serravalle, written at 0900, had reached Desaix at noon. He moved out, only to be quickly overtaken by one of Bonaparte's aides with the 1100 order to "Return, for God's sake." Desaix at once struck directly across country toward San Giuliano, guiding himself on the smoke and roar of the battle.

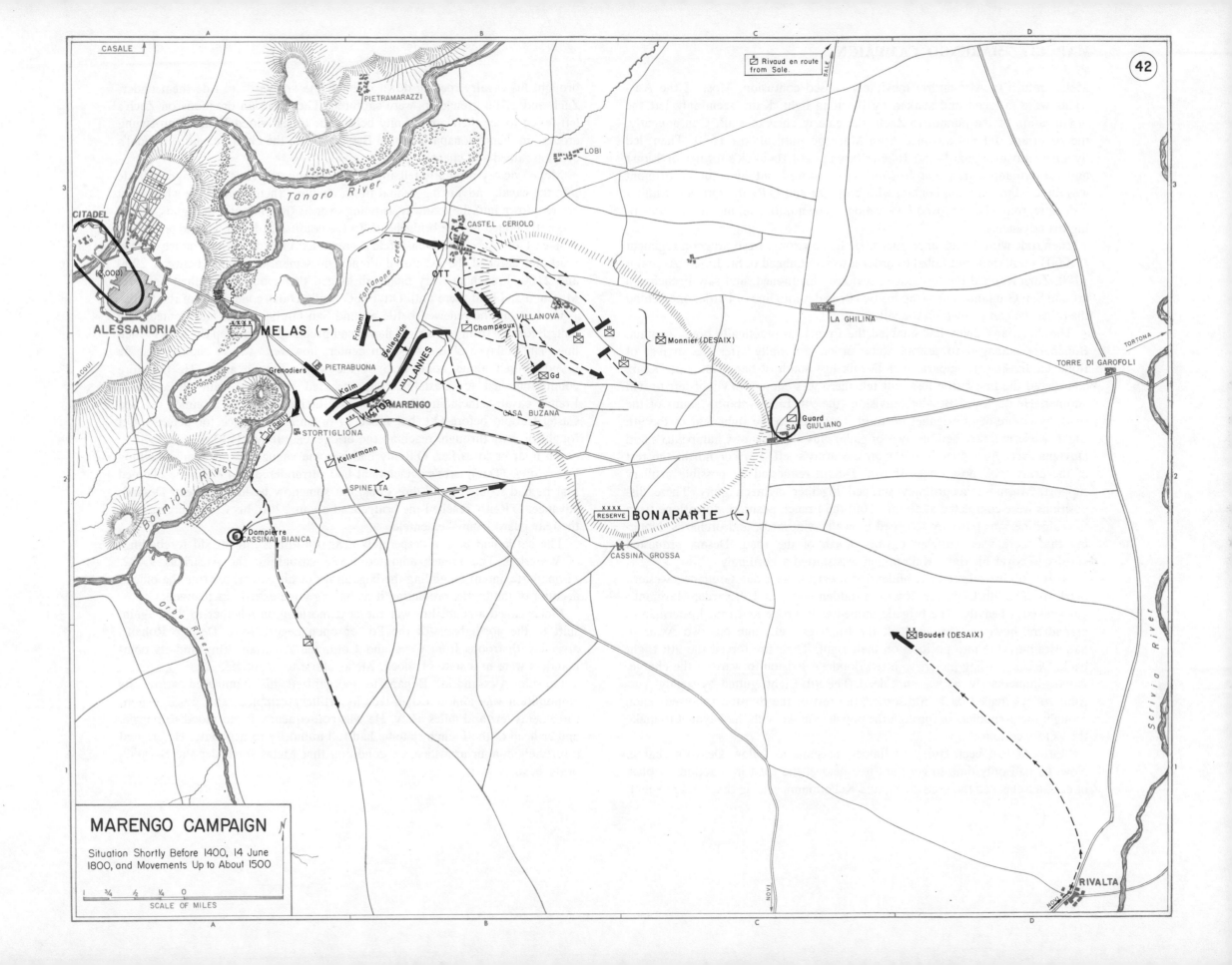

42

CASALE

PIETRAMARAZZI

Tanaro River

LOBI

Rivaud en route
from Sale.

SALE

CITADEL

(3,000)

ALESSANDRIA

CASTEL CERIOLO

OTT

VILLANOVA

LA GHILINA

XXXX
MELAS (−)

Frimont

Bellagarde

Champeaux

Monnier (DESAIX)

TORTONA

TORRE DI GAROFOLI

Grenadiers

PIETRABUONA

LANNES

Kaim

VICTOR MARENGO

Gd

O'Reilly

STORTIGLIONA

CASA BUZANA

Guard
SAN GIULIANO

Bormida River

Kellermann

SPINETTA

XXXX
RESERVE BONAPARTE (−)

Dampierre
CASSINA BIANCA

CASSINA GROSSA

Boudet (DESAIX)

Orba River

Scrivia River

N

RIVALTA

NOVI

NOVI

MARENGO CAMPAIGN

Situation Shortly Before 1400, 14 June
1800, and Movements Up to About 1500

1 ¾ ½ ¼ 0
SCALE OF MILES

Melas' return to Alessandria inevitably caused confusion. Most of the Austrians were fatigued and shaken by the long fight. Kaim seemingly left the organization of the pursuit to Zach, the elderly chief of staff. Consequently, the Austrians did not advance from Marengo until almost 1630. Then, led by a new advance guard—St. Julien's brigade (of Haddick's former division) and Lattermann's grenadier brigade—they moved out in column. Frimont was directed to maintain contact with both Ott and O'Reilly. Ott, left without orders, regrouped and moved forward on his own initiative, his cavalry screening his advance.

Zach rode with the advance guard. He had a strong, fresh dragoon regiment (1,000) on his left, but failed to order it to scout ahead of St. Julien. At about 1700, Zach reached the low ridge previously mentioned, and saw Frenchmen around San Giuliano. Throwing his two brigades into line of battle, one behind the other, he came down on the village.

The Austrians' delay had enabled the French to practically break contact. Bonaparte managed to restore some order, especially after the arrival of Boudet's division. Bonaparte met Desaix just south of San Giuliano; Desaix considered the first battle lost, but felt there was enough daylight left to win another. He deployed Boudet's division: the 9th Light Infantry south of the road, two more demi-brigades north of it, slightly to the right rear of the 9th Light. Kellermann rallied his own brigade, plus elements of Champeaux's and Duvignau's (approximately 650) on the army's left. Farther north, the rest of the army took position as shown. Desaix requested all possible artillery support; Marmont accordingly scraped together eighteen guns. These dispositions were completed at about 1700; the French position, downslope from the ridgeline, was partially screened by walls, vineyards, and orchards. Noticing that there was Austrian cavalry north of the road, Desaix requested cavalry to cover his right. Kellermann was shifted accordingly.

St. Julien's brigade came confidently forward toward San Giuliano's western outskirts. The 9th Light met it with a sudden volley at 100 yards; Marmont's guns raked it heavily. The brigade immediately broke and ran. Lattermann's grenadiers, however, shrugged off the fugitives and came on, two Austrian batteries hurrying into position on their right. Their fire forced the 9th Light back. Desaix, sensing the crisis, lifted Boudet's division forward at the charge. Almost immediately, he was shot dead. The 9th Light, gutted by steady Austrian volleys, reeled back in disorder; the rest of the division followed. Zach brought the grenadiers in through the powder smoke with the bayonet to make the victory certain.

Marmont had been trying to limber his guns to follow Desaix's charge. Now, he had only time to get the three nearest the road into action. A blast of canister checked the grenadiers, and Kellermann, seizing that vital moment, brought his cavalry roaring down through the vineyards to ride them under. Zach and 1,700 grenadiers were captured. The Austrian dragoons on Zach's left failed to see their opportunity before the quick-witted Kellermann swung around on them. Bonaparte loosed Bessieres with the Guard cavalry; Boudet's division rallied and charged again.

Melas' victory promptly fell apart. Stampeding, the Austrian dragoons rode into the cavalry advancing behind them, carrying them away. The whole rout poured down into the roadway, running over its own infantry and guns, which promptly bolted for the bridgehead. In the confusion, Kaim was ridden down. Just east of Marengo, Weidenfeld's grenadier brigade formed north of the road and checked the exhausted French horsemen. Sometime between 2000 and 2100, French infantry finally dislodged them, but they rallied again in Marengo and held there until Ott and O'Reilly could come in from the flanks.

On hearing the renewed battle around San Giuliano, Ott had immediately halted, formed front to his right flank, and prepared to envelop the new French line. The collapse of the Austrian center, however, was so sudden that he found himself alone, confronted by the whole French army. He therefore countermarched for Castel Ceriolo, heckled by Murat with all available French cavalry, including Rivaud's newly arrived brigade. Monnier reached Castel Ceriolo before Ott, but failed to organize the place for defense. Ott fought his way through, reaching the bridgehead about 2130.

An hour or so earlier, O'Reilly had become vaguely aware that something was wrong. (Dampierre's detachment had surrendered at 1900.) He claimed that he had scouted in all directions, but somehow he had not seen Desaix's advance. O'Reilly reached the bridgehead about 2200, his Croats taking over the rear guard from Weidenfeld.

The battle had been a desperately near-run affair, full of odd forebodings of Waterloo. The French admitted 5,835 casualties; the Austrians 9,402. (Bonaparte, intent on gilding the beginnings of his career, rewrote the official account of the battle, presenting it as having gone exactly as planned.)

Melas called a council of war the next morning on whether to fight again, shift to the north bank of the Po, or open negotiations. Despite Rohan's arrival with troops from Ceva and Coni, the Austrian army and its commanders were in a state of shock. Melas chose to negotiate.

Outside Alessandria, Bonaparte reorganized his hammered army. Its ammunition was almost exhausted, its artillery crippled, and possible reinforcements few and miles away. He was consequently in no mood to haggle, and as head of the French state he had full authority to negotiate. He granted a forty-eight–hour armistice, on condition that Melas surrender the Bormida bridgehead.

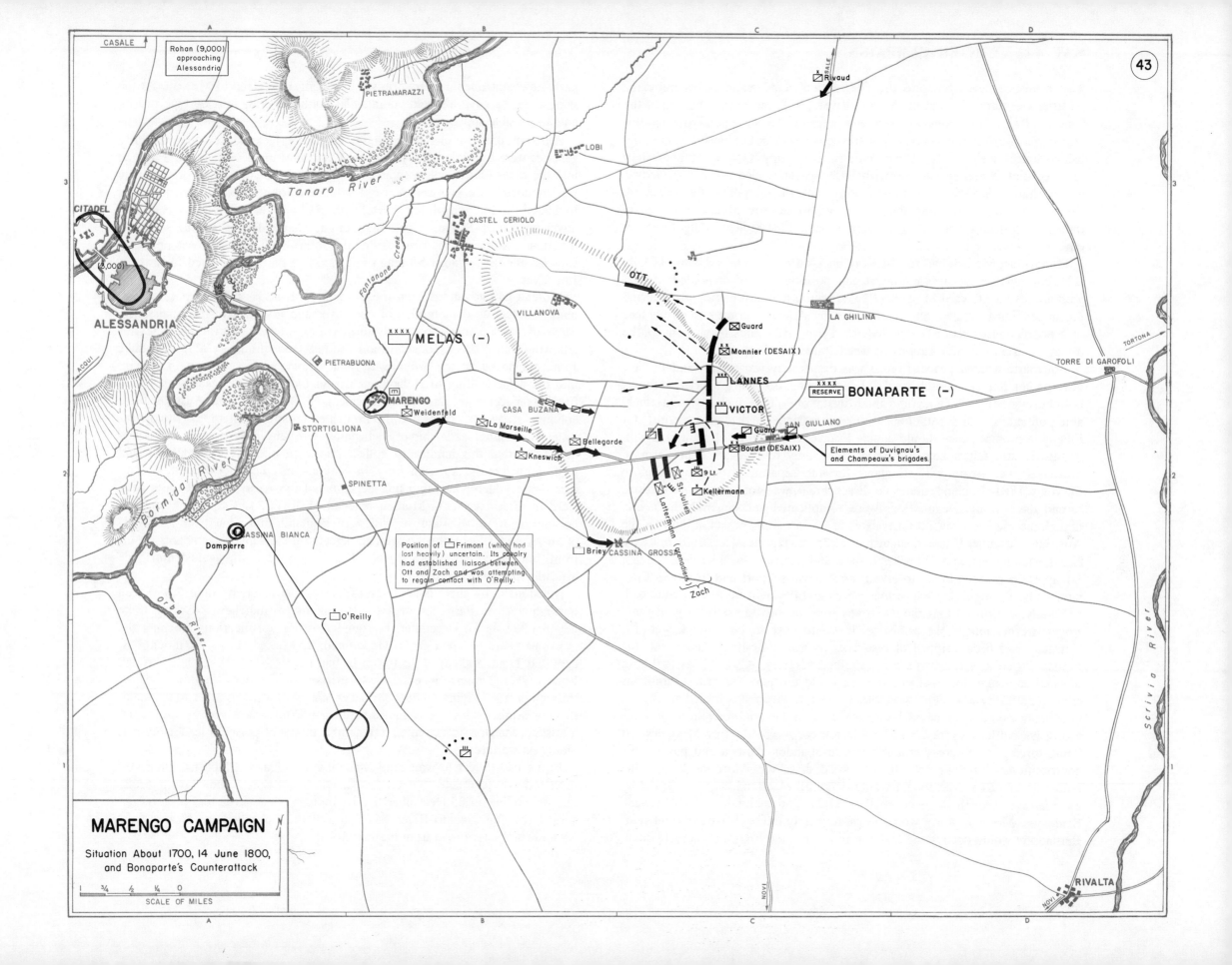

CASALE

Rohan (9,000)
approaching
Alessandria

PIETRAMARAZZI

Tanaro River

CITADEL

(3,000)

ALESSANDRIA

PIETRABUONA

CASTEL CERIOLO

LOBI

VILLANOVA

XXXX
MELAS (—)

Fontanone Creek

MARENGO

Weidenfeld

CASA BUZANA

STORTIGLIONA

La Marseille

Kneswich

Bellegarde

Bormida River

SPINETTA

CASSINA BIANCA

Dampierre

Position of Frimont (which had
lost heavily) uncertain. Its cavalry
had established liaison between
Ott and Zach and was attempting
to regain contact with O'Reilly.

Briey CASSINA GROSSA

St. Julien

Lattermann (Grenadiers)

Zach

9 Lt.

Kellermann

OTT

Guard

Monnier (DESAIX)

LANNES

VICTOR

XXXX
RESERVE BONAPARTE (—)

Guard SAN GIULIANO

Boudet (DESAIX)

Elements of Duvignau's
and Champeaux's brigades.

RIVAUD

LA GHILINA

TORRE DI GAROFOLI

TORTONA

O'Reilly

Orbo River

Scrivia River

NOVI

RIVALTA

NOVI

MARENGO CAMPAIGN

Situation About 1700, 14 June 1800,
and Bonaparte's Counterattack

1   ¾   ½   ¼   0
SCALE OF MILES

43

This armistice developed into the Convention of Alessandria, whereby the Austrians withdrew behind the Mincio River (*B1*), the French halting at the Chiese (*B1*). Operations in Germany were to be suspended during this armistice. The Austrians carried out the convention scrupulously; when English Admiral Keith showed inclinations to occupy Genoa, Hohenzollern rebuffed him. Marengo had been what Bonaparte needed—a showy victory, which established him as a man of destiny. But, though politically successful, Bonaparte's Marengo campaign had failed to destroy Melas' army. Sixty thousand Austrians, with 300 guns, retired behind the Mincio, to fight another day.

Meanwhile, Moreau had forced Kray back on his entrenched camp at Ulm (*B2*) but, unable to capture that strong position, finally contented himself with an advance toward Munich (*B2*) to secure a good billeting area during the impending truce. He had neither destroyed Kray's army nor (from fear of a popular insurrection) occupied the Tyrol (*B2*), thus leaving intact the direct Austrian communications between Italy and Germany.

Bonaparte wanted peace. France was desperately war-weary, and its new government not yet consolidated. (Even during Bonaparte's brief absence, both Foreign Minister Talleyrand and Minister of Police Fouche, two extremely able politicians with a pathological itch for intrigue, had plotted against it.) Finally, a prompt peace should enable France to hold both Malta and Egypt.

Austria still felt unbeaten, wanted time only to reorganize her armies. Moreover, her treaty with England forbade separate negotiations before February 1801. England, under no direct threat, was not particularly anxious to end the fighting. Negotiations were complicated and generally insincere, though the truce was several times extended—once, only on condition that the Austrians surrender Ulm and Ingolstadt (*B2*). Bonaparte successfully re-established friendly negotiations with Russia and Prussia. Berthier and Lucien Bonaparte persuaded Spain to give France naval support and to attack England's ally, Portugal. French armies were carefully built up and re-equipped.

Finally, convinced that the Austrians were negotiating only to gain time, Bonaparte denounced the armistice. It would have to be a quick war, for Germany had been stripped of resources by the contesting armies, and the French logistical system would be strained severely. Also, it was to be an unusual campaign for, realizing that he could not play the general until his civilian authority was unquestionable, Bonaparte directed it from Paris.

Moreau would advance on Vienna (*C2*)—an operation certain to produce a decisive battle. Augereau's Franco-Dutch corps would cover Moreau's left flank, forcing the minor German states to abandon Austria and pay sizable contributions to the French. Brune would drive the Austrians behind the Adige River (*B1*). Macdonald would defend Switzerland, support Brune by an offensive through the Splügen Pass (*B2*), and maintain liaison between Brune and Moreau. Murat would move into Italy to cover Brune's right rear; Bernadotte would occupy the Vendee and watch the English Channel. Bona-

parte now controlled matters firmly; he no longer deferred to Moreau. At the same time, he gave his field commanders only general, mission-type orders, and all possible support.

Austrian preparations were characteristically lackadaisical. Some thirty generals were indiscriminately dismissed, and untrained recruits were packed into the ranks. There was a shortage of artillery, and the Army of Germany was confided to the eighteen-year-old Archduke John. The Austrian plan was to defend the Inn and Mincio rivers, with the hope that an Anglo-Neapolitan advance against Brune's right flank might enable Bellegarde to seize the initiative. At the last moment, Archduke John's staff planned a complicated surprise offensive against Moreau's left flank, as the latter moved toward the Inn River.

Moreau had advanced from the Munich area in six widely separated columns. He had no definite plan of maneuver and no effective reconnaissance. The Austrian advance accordingly surprised him, forcing him to pull back his left wing and order a concentration around Hohenlinden (*B2*). Archduke John, convinced he was winning a great victory, plunged his main column into the defile leading to Hohenlinden from the east. The result was a confused, semiaccidental meeting engagement (3 December), as Austrian flank columns tried to catch up, and the French commanders attempted to concentrate. The combat leadership of Richepanse, Grouchy, Ney, and Decaen somehow converted this haphazard collision into an effective envelopment and rout of much of the Austrian army. Moreau advanced cautiously on 8 December; then, suddenly catching fire, he hounded the Austrians 189 miles eastward in fifteen days. As Moreau reached Mölk (*C2*), Emperor Francis II became ready to negotiate, regardless of England, and signed the Armistice of Steyer on 25 December. Augereau defeated the enemy detachments on his front, but was almost trapped when Klenau moved north against him. The armistice probably saved him.

Macdonald, by sheer courage and force of character, brought 7,000 men through Splügen Pass, despite snow storms and avalanches. Reaching Lake Como (*B2*) on 12 December, he found Austrian fortifications blocking the passes eastward to Trent (*B1*). Undaunted, he worked across the mountains, captured Trent, and called the troops he had left in Switzerland south through Botzen (*B2*). Though one entrapped Austrian commander (Laudon) escaped through energetic lying (telling Moncey, sent northward to meet Macdonald, that an armistice had been signed) and a second was saved by the actual armistice, Macdonald's campaign remains a model of personal leadership and mountain warfare.

Brune had orders to wait until Macdonald's advance made itself felt. He soon proved incompetent; nevertheless, Dupont, Suchet, and Davout broke the Mincio line on 25 December. By 16 January, Bellegarde had been driven behind the Tagliamento River (*B1*). Miollis had checked the Neapolitans, whom Murat later drove from the Papal States.

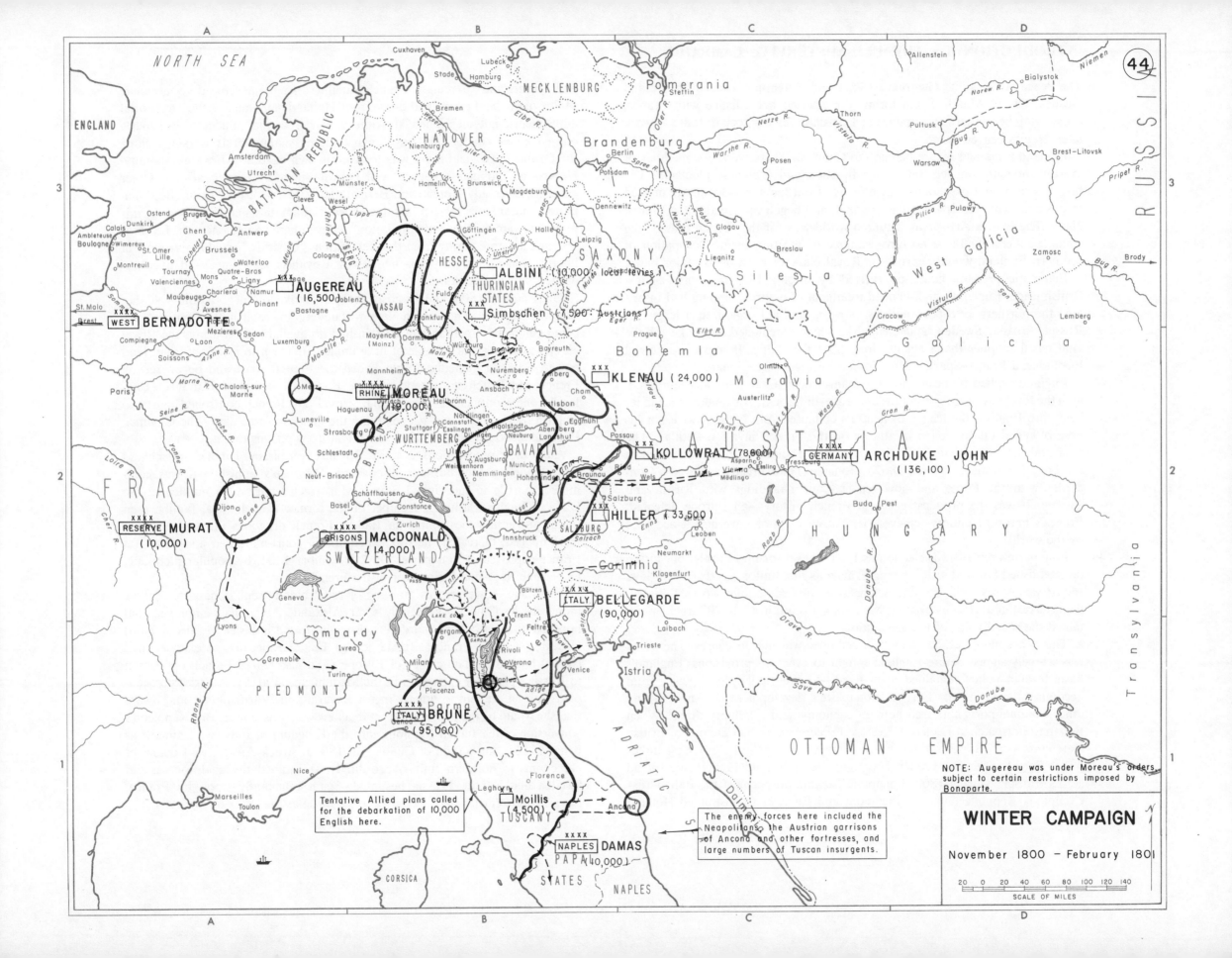

NORTH SEA

ENGLAND

RUSSIA

44

MECKLENBURG Pomerania

Brandenburg

HANOVER

PRUSSIA

SAXONY

Bohemia

MORAVIA

West Galicia

Galicia

xxxx WEST BERNADOTTE

AUGEREAU (16,500)

HESSE NASSAU

ALBINI (10,000 local levies)

THURINGIAN STATES

xxx Simbschen (7,500 Austrians)

xxx KLENAU (24,000)

xxx RHINE MOREAU (19,000)

WURTTEMBERG

BAVARIA

xxx KOLLOWRAT (78,000)

xxxx GERMANY ARCHDUKE JOHN (136,100)

AUSTRIA

HUNGARY

xxx HILLER (33,500)

xxxx RESERVE MURAT (10,000)

FRANCE

xxxx GRISONS MACDONALD (14,000)

SWITZERLAND

Tyrol

Carinthia

xxxx ITALY BELLEGARDE (90,000)

Lombardy

PIEDMONT

Venetia

NOTE: Augereau was under Moreau's orders subject to certain restrictions imposed by Bonaparte.

xxxx ITALY BRUNE (95,000)

Parma

OTTOMAN EMPIRE

ADRIATIC

Tentative Allied plans called for the debarkation of 10,000 English here.

Moillis (4,500)

TUSCANY

Ancona

The enemy forces here included the Neapolitans, the Austrian garrisons of Ancona and other fortresses, and large numbers of Tuscan insurgents.

WINTER CAMPAIGN

November 1800 – February 1801

CORSICA

xxxx NAPLES DAMAS PAPAL (40,000) STATES

NAPLES

20 0 20 40 60 80 100 120 140
SCALE OF MILES

INTRODUCTION TO THE ULM-AUSTERLITZ CAMPAIGN

The Peace of Luneville (February 1801) ended fighting between France and Austria. On 21 March, Spain formally reasserted her alliance with France, exchanging her American province of Louisiana for territory in Italy. A week later, Naples begged peace.

England remained secure behind the Channel. There were two methods of exerting pressure on her: threatened invasion and economic blockade. The first was risky, but psychologically effective from the start. Bonaparte massed troops and light vessels along the Channel, and began resurrecting the French Navy. The British Army was scattered world-wide; if the French crossed the Channel, there would be no force capable of meeting them. Occupation of southern England would deprive the Royal Navy of most of its major bases.

Economic pressure could be exerted by closing Europe's ports against British trade. England's high-handed treatment of neutral shipping had infuriated the northern European nations. Now, Czar Paul organized a league of Russia, Prussia, Sweden, and Denmark, which threatened to choke off the vital naval supplies that England drew from the Baltic. Bonaparte occupied Piedmont; a Franco-Spanish army forced Portugal to capitulate.

England replied by destroying the Danish fleet. Czar Paul was murdered, with the foreknowledge—if not the consent—of his heir, Alexander. Alexander being pro-English, the league of neutrals collapsed. But Nelson twice got his nose bloodied off Boulogne in attacks on the French invasion flotilla. "The tiger and the shark" had reached a stalemate. Tedious negotiations ended in the Treaty of Amiens (March 1802). Bonaparte had already achieved a Concordat with the Pope, and now reached understandings with Russia and Turkey. It was the proudest peace in French history—all Europe defeated, France's natural frontiers achieved, its chosen form of government accepted by the world.

Bonaparte's reward was election as First Consul for life. Firmly, but justly, he established law and order, giving France its first uniform code of civil law. Industry was revived, arts and sciences stimulated, public works initiated, finances restored. His government was strongly centralized, but it largely maintained the social gains of the Revolution.

This peace, however, had merely ended open war, not its causes. The treaty was scarcely signed before England sought to evade its provisions. England's basic foreign policy remained unchanged—to prevent any one power from becoming the master of Europe. Bonaparte's development of Antwerp and other Channel ports appeared both an economic and a military threat. When Bonaparte dispatched Leclerc to restore French rule in San Domingo, British merchants worried over future French competition for the British West Indies trade. Furthermore, the French Navy grew steadily, and French rule spread across Europe: During 1802, Bonaparte became president of the Italian (ex-Cisalpine) Republic; annexed Piedmont and Elba; and constrained Holland and Switzerland to remain French satellites. England refused to evacuate Malta until the French withdrew from Holland and made other territorial adjustments, not mentioned at Amiens. Angered and reluctant, Bonaparte offered minor concessions, but began building shallow-draft warships along the Channel. To yield more was to risk his own head and France's stability. He was not popular—or even well known—in most French armies. Other generals, especially Moreau and Bernadotte, were envious of "Comrade Bonaparte" and anxious to step into his shoes. Bonaparte's major support at this period was among the civil population, yet even here he had enemies. Jacobins resented any trend away from the Revolution. "Liberals," speaking vaguely of liberty, wanted authority for themselves. Royalists, in France and overseas, plotted Bonaparte's murder.

On 12 May 1803, the English abruptly broke off negotiations. Neither side was prepared. The French Navy was undergoing rebirth, the French Army being completely reorganized. Britain had no available field army; the Royal Navy was strong, but capable of little immediate harm to a self-sufficient land power. England immediately blockaded the French coast and began seizing French and Dutch ships and colonies. Bonaparte occupied Hanover (England's one Continental possession), closed all French-controlled ports to English trade, and began reassembling the invasion force along the Channel. England anxiously sought allies who might draw off this threat.

Amid these preparations, a major Royalist conspiracy, hatched in England and entangling Moreau, was discovered. (Moreau's punishment was commuted to exile in the United States.) Incorrect reports also implicated the Duke of Enghien, a junior member of the former French royal family, then living just across the frontier in Baden. French dragoons plucked Enghien from his bed; thereafter, he was expeditiously court-martialed and shot. But France approved of Bonaparte: On 2 December 1804, by popular plebiscite, he became Napoleon I, Emperor of the French.

Elsewhere, however, this "spilling of royal blood" sent Bonaparte's fellow monarchs into shock—especially Czar Alexander, who had employed and honored his own father's murderers. England found it easier to raise a Third Coalition against France. Russia joined England because Alexander had elected himself the conscience of Europe (and also feared French opposition to Russia's plans for expansion in the Mediterranean area). Austria, preoccupied with an attempt to quietly ingest Bavaria and Württemberg, and aware that she would be the probable target in a new war, was slower. But Napoleon's conversion of the Italian Republic into the Kingdom of Italy, with himself as King, and his annexation of Genoa (all 1805), struck Austria as a denial of her claims to northern Italy. Accordingly, she joined the coalition, as did Sweden and Naples. Prussia hesitated. Spain reluctantly stood by France. Bavaria and Württemberg secretly chose France as the lesser of two evils.

The Ulm-Austerlitz Campaign

"There are many good generals in Europe, but they see too many things; as for me, I see only one: masses. I seek to destroy them, knowing well that the accessories will then fall of their own accord." —NAPOLEON

"The man who cannot look upon a battlefield dry-eyed will allow many men to be killed uselessly."—NAPOLEON

Napoleon wanted a French Navy capable of ruling the seas. By 1805, its bases had been improved, strengthened, and linked by semaphore telegraph. Large numbers of excellent warships of all classes, generally superior to their English counterparts in design and construction, had been commissioned. However, there had not been time to develop a new naval officers' corps. Professional pride and skill had dwindled during the Revolution; worse, the defeatist traditions of the old Royal Navy, with its "prudence to conserve matériel," still survived. Too many officers still lacked necessary skills as seamen, shipmasters, and gunnery officers.

The British declaration of war (1803) found the invasion flotilla only begun and the French Navy badly dispersed. The British Royal Navy, wise from much experience, held its strongest units in the Channel to watch Brest, the major French base, and Boulogne (*both D3*), the center of French invasion preparations. Smaller units cruised off Spain and patrolled the Mediterranean.

Napoleon had few illusions as to the difficulty of invading England. Some historians have doubted that he ever intended to attempt it, seeing his preparations for the invasion as merely a means of satisfying public opinion while reorganizing, training, and gaining personal ascendancy over his army. Yet it is impossible to believe that, if he could have secured command of the Channel, he would not have crossed with his veterans in a neck-or-nothing try at conquering England—the ultimate glory for a French ruler.

Initial operations were of an exploratory nature. By November 1804, Napoleon had 177,000 men and more than 2,000 light craft along the Channel, with another troop concentration at Toulon (*D3*) to threaten Egypt and Sicily. He began by optimistically assuming that, given a few hours of dead calm or fog, he could make a rapid, surprise crossing. Rehearsals soon showed that it would take several days just to embark and form his forces for the operation, and that no fluke of weather could be trusted to last so long. Meanwhile, the British blockade penned the invasion flotilla within its harbors, but British attempts to raid these harbors failed. The stalemate continued.

Napoleon saw a solution. Brest was tightly blocked, but Toulon was less closely watched. He assigned Latouche-Treville, his best admiral, the Toulon squadron, with orders to slip past Nelson, pick up the Rochefort squadron, swing wide around Brest, and come into the Channel. Thereafter, he was expendable, so long as he smothered the British Channel fleet while the invasion flotilla crossed.

Latouche-Treville, however, died suddenly in August 1804. In October, the British, for unknown reasons, seized a Spanish treasure fleet. This brought Spain into the war on the side of France. His naval strength thus increased, Napoleon expanded the scope of his planning. He was well informed as to the strength and general locations of the British squadrons, but unaware of one standing instruction issued to all blockading units: If the French force under blockade escapes and evades pursuit, sail immediately for the Channel.

Napoleon's final plan was theoretically excellent. The Toulon squadron (now under Villeneuve) would embark 6,500 troops, elude Nelson, pick up Spanish squadrons at Cartagena and Cadiz (*both D2*), and sail for the West Indies. The Rochefort squadron (Missiessy) would rendezvous with him there. The Brest squadron (Ganteaume) would likewise escape, break the blockade of Ferrol, pick up the Spanish ships there, and join the others. Once this concentration was complete, Ganteaume would lead the whole force into the Channel, avoiding any unnecessary fighting en route.

After one false start, Villeneuve got to sea. Nelson, fearful for Sicily and Egypt, moved south of Sardinia and lost contact. At Cartagena, Villeneuve found the Spanish there had no orders to join him. Orde's squadron dodged northward (*movement not shown*), and Villeneuve picked up Admiral Gravina's squadron at Cadiz. Villeneuve reached Martinique (*A1*), only to find that Missiessy already had been mistakenly recalled after a brilliant campaign (*not shown*) in the West Indies. Orders from France instructed Villeneuve to wait until 20 June for Ganteaume; if he did not appear, Villeneuve was to return, pick up the Ferrol squadron, unblock Brest, and clear the Channel.

Meanwhile, Nelson had reached Gibraltar. After ascertaining that Villeneuve had not turned north, Nelson (as usual) ignored his standing orders and sailed in pursuit. News of his arrival in the West Indies led Villeneuve to depart early. Returning, he again outmaneuvered Nelson, shifting northward, while the latter, supposing the French would return to Toulon, pushed for Gibraltar.

However, a British brig, carrying Nelson's dispatches to London, sighted Villeneuve heading for the Bay of Biscay. The British Admiralty ordered strong forces detached from the concentration off Ushant to intercept him. A chance encounter in heavy fog with the Ferrol blockaders cost Villeneuve's worn-down fleet two ships. The British, somewhat hammered, retired north; Villeneuve made for Cadiz, but was blown back on Ferrol by contrary winds.

Roughly urged on from Paris, he finally sailed for Brest, but his courage failed. Turning about, he made for Cadiz, arriving there to find history had bypassed him. Enemy concentrations beyond the Rhine had left Napoleon not even time for a hit-and-run raid on England. He had only odd jobs now for Villeneuve: Disembark his troops at Naples, then return to Toulon to overhaul his worn ships and reorganize them into commerce-raiding squadrons.

Nelson had taken over the Cadiz blockade. On 21 October, he intercepted and destroyed Villeneuve's fleet off Cape Trafalgar.

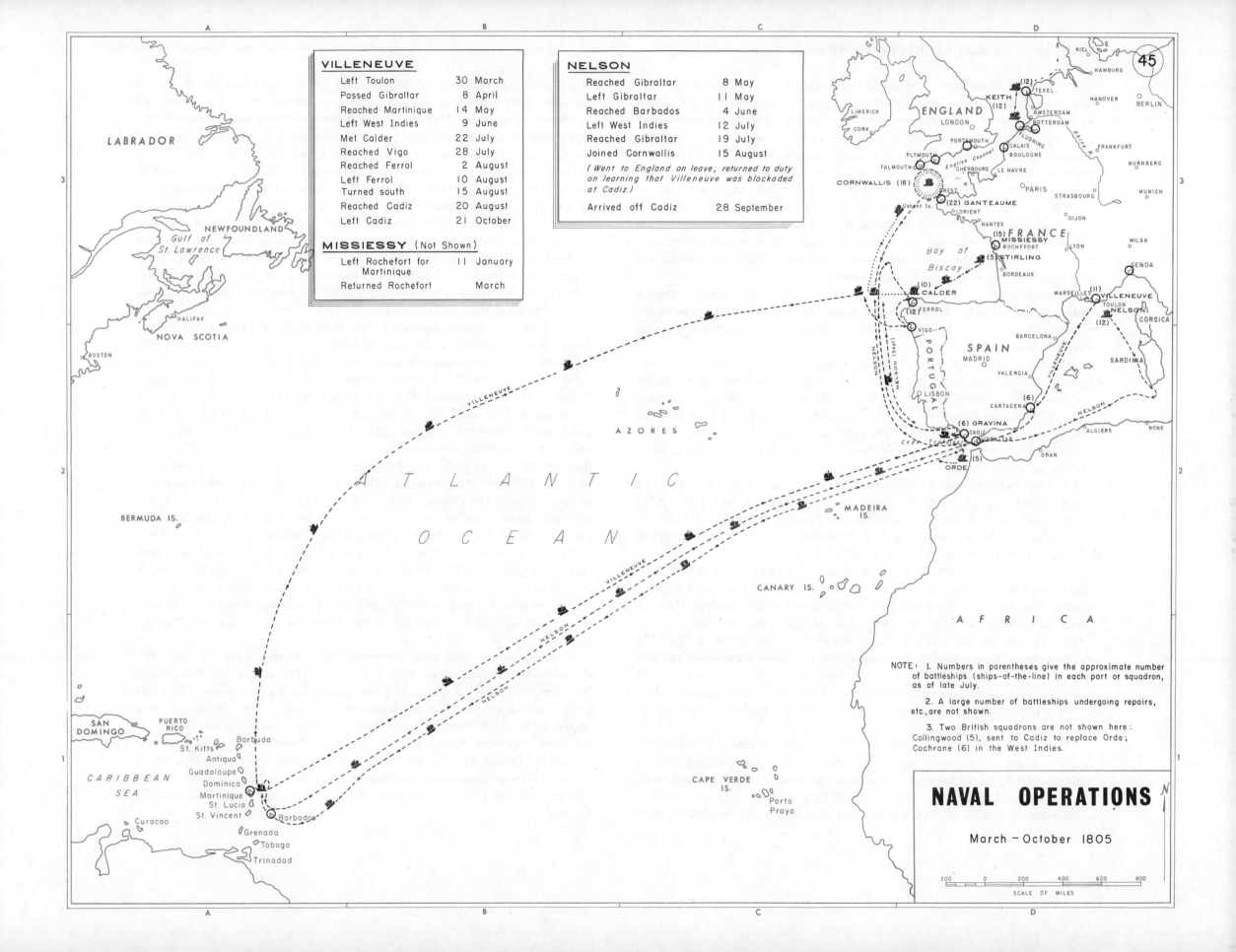

45

VILLENEUVE

Left Toulon	30 March
Passed Gibraltar	8 April
Reached Martinique	14 May
Left West Indies	9 June
Met Calder	22 July
Reached Vigo	28 July
Reached Ferrol	2 August
Left Ferrol	10 August
Turned south	15 August
Reached Cadiz	20 August
Left Cadiz	21 October

MISSIESSY (Not Shown)

Left Rochefort for Martinique	11 January
Returned Rochefort	March

NELSON

Reached Gibraltar	8 May
Left Gibraltar	11 May
Reached Barbados	4 June
Left West Indies	12 July
Reached Gibraltar	19 July
Joined Cornwallis	15 August

(Went to England on leave; returned to duty on learning that Villeneuve was blockaded at Cadiz.)

Arrived off Cadiz	28 September

NOTE: 1. Numbers in parentheses give the approximate number of battleships (ships-of-the-line) in each port or squadron, as of late July.

2. A large number of battleships undergoing repairs, etc., are not shown.

3. Two British squadrons are not shown here: Collingwood (5), sent to Cadiz to replace Orde; Cochrane (6) in the West Indies.

NAVAL OPERATIONS

March – October 1805

SCALE OF MILES

The Third Coalition had the initiative in choosing war, but squandered time in negotiations. England, the Coalition's paymaster, demanded quick action to draw the French concentration from the Channel—and to cut costs. Austria, impoverished by eight years of defeats, had neglected her army. Quartermaster General Mack was now attempting to modernize it. His ideas were generally sound, but too revolutionary to be accepted willingly. Austrian strategy was complicated by conflicting interests. England urged an offensive in central Germany to bring Bavaria and Prussia into the Coalition; Austrian statesmen wanted to conquer northern Italy. There was general realization that Russian reinforcements were necessary, but also a general mistrust of Russia. Russia likewise was impoverished; between official ineptitude and long distances, its mobilization went slowly.

The final Allied plan was more of a collection of these viewpoints than a compromise. Archduke Charles would attack in northern Italy to seize the Milan area (*B1*), then halt until Russian reinforcements had reached Archduke Ferdinand.

Ferdinand (with Mack to do his thinking) meanwhile would move into Bavaria as far as the Iller River (*B2*) to force that nation into the Coalition and cover the northern exits of the Tyrol. He was not to become seriously engaged before the arrival of Russian reinforcements; if superior French forces advanced against him, he was to fight a delaying action.

Archduke John would remain on the defensive in the Tyrol until Charles crossed the Adda River.

Once the Russians joined Ferdinand, their combined forces would advance toward Strasbourg (*B2*), seeking a decisive battle. Charles, with John on his right, would move through Switzerland into France. If the Austro-Russians were defeated, Charles would stand on the defensive along the Mincio River (*B1*) and detach a strong force northward.

Much reliance was placed on two diversionary attacks: English and Russian forces would land at Naples, unite with the Neapolitan Army, and advance against Massena; an Anglo-Russian-Swedish army would land in Hanover (*B3*), threaten Holland, and encourage Prussia to join the Coalition.

In personnel, morale, and training, Napoleon's Grande Armee of 1805 was the finest he ever commanded. Its organization combined maximum flexibility and maximum control. However, a shortage of horses left the army with insufficient transportation and a third of its dragoons without mounts. (This shortage is possibly the best indication that he really intended to invade England rather than Austria.)

On 23 August, Napoleon decided to turn eastward—not because Villeneuve had failed him, but rather because of the growing Austrian concentrations in Italy and the Tyrol. In his usual fashion, he had studied the probable theaters of operation and had roughed out a general plan. Though the main Austrian concentration was in Italy, Germany was obviously more important, since it was there that the Austrian and Russian forces would link up. He would therefore move directly on Vienna, surprising and destroying Ferdinand and the Russians in detail. Massena would defend northern Italy; Gouvion St.-Cyr would cover Massena's flank; Brune would guard the Channel coast with newly raised battalions, Italian units, coast artillery, and naval troops.

On 24 August, French cavalry began forming a screen along the middle Rhine. The next day, Murat and Bertrand—followed by Savary—went into Germany incognito to reconnoiter the terrain between the Rhine and Lech (*B2*) rivers, with special attention to the Ulm area. On the 27th, the Grande Armee moved out. To becloud its movements, Napoleon personally returned to Paris from Boulogne; the cavalry screen spread upstream to Basel; newspapers were forbidden (12 September) to publish anything concerning troop movements; the frontiers were sealed (22–28 September); bridge materials were collected at Neuf-Brisach (*B2*).

The Austrian offensive began on 2 September. Bavarian Elector Maximilian-Joseph was directed to put his army at Ferdinand's disposition, but spun out negotiations until it could withdraw northward. Mack meanwhile pushed rapidly ahead to the Iller River and began fortifying Ulm and Memmingen. However, the half-organized Austrians were considerably disordered by this short march. Ferdinand became nervous and demanded a withdrawal eastward. Mack considered their position excellent: Napoleon undoubtedly would follow the traditional invasion route through the Black Forest (*B2*); after detaching troops to guard the Channel and control Paris, he would have barely 70,000 men. Any major French stroke from the northwest would have to come through the Prussian enclave of Ansbach (*B2*), and France would not dare violate Prussian territory. Mack intended to strike the heads of the French columns as they emerged from the Black Forest.

Kutusov marched ten days late, in less strength than promised, and very slowly. At Lemberg (*D2*), his rear division was detached toward the Turkish frontier. On 22 September, he reached Teschen (*C2*), where the Austrian authorities provided wagons to transport part of his troops. Even so, bad roads still slowed his march. Buxhöwden and Bennigsen were awaiting Prussian permission to cross Silesia (*C2–C3*).

Napoleon as yet knew little concerning the Austrian forces in Germany. Accordingly, he planned to mass his army in the area Brisach-Mayence-Würzburg (*all B2*), out of reach of the opening enemy operations, and await more exact information. On 13 September, a dispatch from Murat told him of the invasion of Bavaria; succeeding dispatches gave a good picture of Ferdinand's advance, though information on the Russians remained scant and inaccurate. Franco-Austrian diplomatic relations were broken off, and, on 20 September, Napoleon issued his final orders, leaving Paris four days later. Lannes, followed by most of the Cavalry Reserve, crossed the Rhine on 25 September.

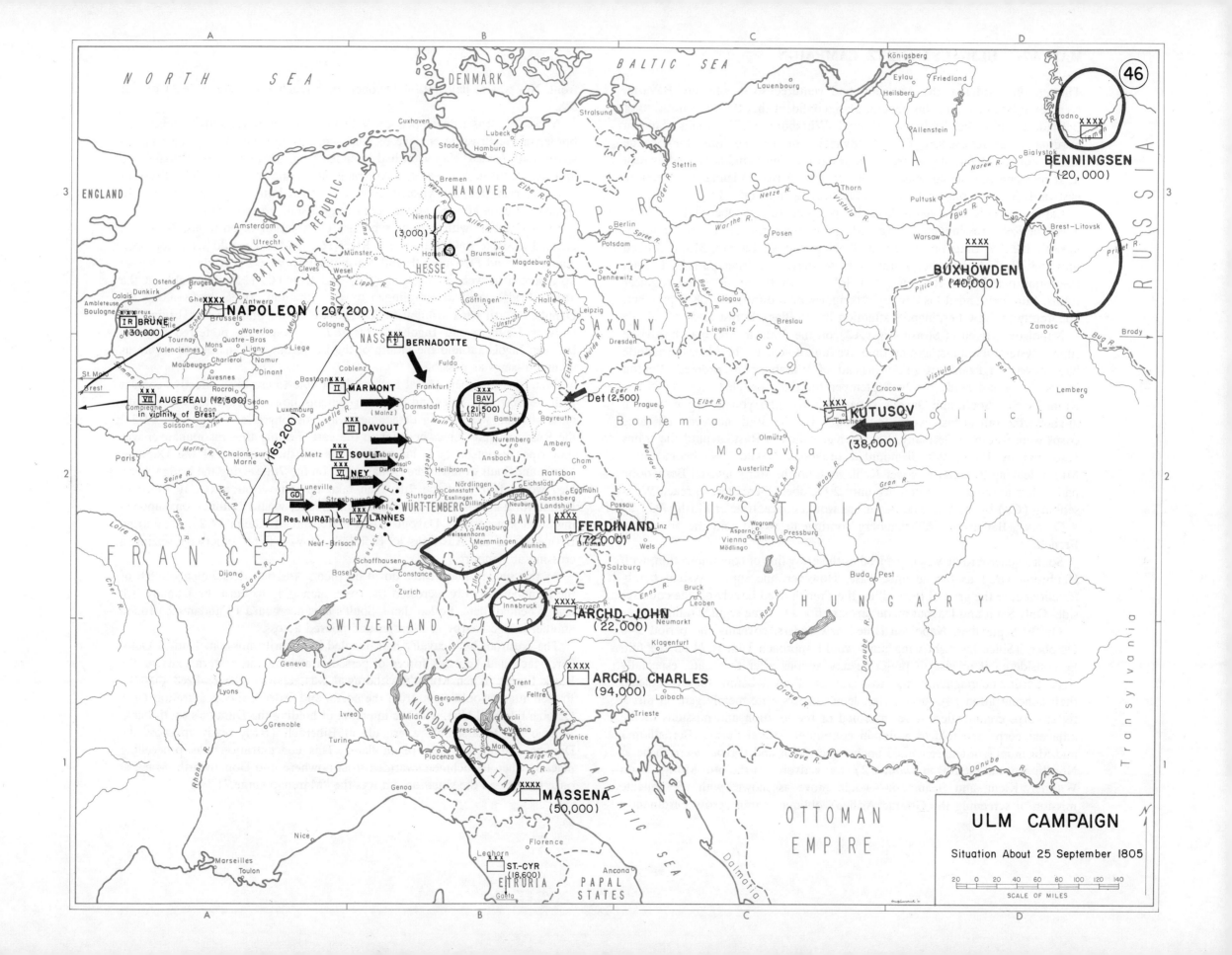

NORTH SEA
BALTIC SEA
DENMARK
HANOVER
P R U S S I A
RUSSIA

BENNINGSEN
(20,000)

BUXHÖWDEN
(40,000)

NAPOLEON (207,200)

IR BRUNE
(30,000)

BERNADOTTE

NASSAU

MARMONT
(Mainz)

AUGEREAU (12,500)
in vicinity of Brest.

BAV
(21,500)

Det (2,500)

KUTUSOV

(38,000)

DAVOUT

SOULT

NEY

GD

Res. MURAT

LANNES

WÜRT-TEMBERG

(165,200)

BAVARIA

FERDINAND
(72,000)

SWITZERLAND

ARCHD. JOHN
(22,000)

ARCHD. CHARLES
(94,000)

Tyrol

F R A N C E

HUNGARY

KINGDOM OF ITALY

MASSENA
(50,000)

OTTOMAN
EMPIRE

ULM CAMPAIGN

Situation About 25 September 1805

ST-CYR
(18,600)

ETRURIA
PAPAL
STATES

20 0 20 40 60 80 100 120 140
SCALE OF MILES

46

Though surprised that the Austrians had ventured so deeply into Bavaria, Napoleon did not change his general plan, confident that the concentration of Bernadotte and the Bavarians around Würzburg (*C3*) would dampen Ferdinand's aggressiveness. Though advancing on a broad front, the Grande Armee could concentrate in three or four days, if Ferdinand advanced against it. If he stood fast, its advance would cut him off from Vienna. If he retired eastward, it could pursue him, possibly heading him off.

Lannes initially occupied a defensive position west of Oberkirch (*A2*) to cover the Kehl crossing; he was warned against premature action, which might unsettle the Austrians into a retreat. Passing through Lannes, Murat probed into the Black Forest, but found only scattered Austrian patrols. Lannes thereupon marched to Rastadt (*A2*), followed by the artillery and engineer trains. Murat extended his cavalry reconnaissances during 26–28 September, apparently to draw Ferdinand's attention to the Black Forest area.

Napoleon arrived at Strasbourg (*A2*) on the 26th, to find his improvised supply system in a mess, and no time available to correct it. Also, Bernadotte had moved on Frankfurt (*B3*) instead of Würzburg, as ordered. Ponton bridges were not ready on 26 September for the scheduled crossing of the Rhine by Ney, Soult, and Davout. Davout, utilizing ferryboats, began crossing anyhow; the others lost twenty-four hours. By the 30th, however, all three corps were well into Germany. Lannes had halted at Rastadt until the trains (escorted by Baraguay's dismounted dragoons) could pass behind him. Murat, leaving Bourcier to cover Kehl, rode north. Marmont and Bernadotte had orders to remain at Würzburg until 2 October; thereafter, to reach Weissenburg (*C2*) by the 9th. The Bavarians would concentrate at Fürth (*D3*) by 4 October. Baden and Württemberg contingents would join the advancing French.

Soult's general route was organized as the army line of communication, with Heilbronn (*B2*) as the advance base. However, the supply system barely functioned; to the grief of their allies, the French lived largely off the countryside. Only Soult and Davout made serious efforts to issue regular rations.

On 30 September, Napoleon issued new orders, covering the period 2–6 October. (Since his right wing units would approach Ulm [*C1*] on the 6th, he considered it unwise to prescribe any actions after that date, especially since Ferdinand might attempt to strike the French before they completed their concentration.) As usual, Napoleon's orders were merely general directives; corps commanders were informed of the location and missions of the adjacent corps and told to maintain continuous lateral liaison. Bernadotte's and Marmont's orders remained unchanged. Soult and Davout were to be at Nördlingen and Oettingen (*both C2*), respectively, on the 6th. Murat—with Walther, Klein, and Beaumont—would move as shown, with the delicate mission of screening the Grande Armee's oblique march across Ferdinand's front. Ney was to halt until 4 October, then reach Heidenheim (*C2*) on the 5th.

A possible crisis developed on 3 October when Bernadotte reached the border of the Prussian enclave of Ansbach, through which the major north-south roads passed. Napoleon had intended from the first to risk Prussia's ire and march through it (as the Austrians had done in 1800). The Prussian governor protested, but yielded in view of Bernadotte's superior strength. In revenge, Prussia allowed (6 October) the Russians to cross Silesia.

By 4 October, with a clearer picture of Austrian dispositions, Napoleon decided to strike toward the Lech River (*C1*). Murat would scout the open country around Donauwörth and Nördlingen (*both C2*), while Bourcier set up a screen between Geislingen (*C2*) and Ulm (*C1*). Soult would get the army's bridge train to Nördlingen by the 7th, and collect boats along the Danube's north bank tributaries. Bernadotte would find the best bridge site between Neuberg and Ingolstadt (*both D2*). Napoleon preferred to cross between Ingolstadt and the mouth of the Lech, but was anxious to secure as many crossings as possible.

Even by 5 October, Murat had not been able to establish effective contact with the Austrians. Spies and Bavarian civilians, however, reported Ferdinand's mass at Ulm, with strong detachments at Nördlingen and Eichstädt (*D2*); the Russians were somewhere far to the east. Feeling that his maneuver was now ripe, Napoleon gave his final orders for the crossing of the Danube: Murat and Soult would strike Donauwörth on the 7th, seizing the bridge there. Ney would halt until the 7th, then take up a position next day to cover Donauwörth against an attack from Ulm. Lannes would continue on, supporting Soult if necessary. Davout would march on Monheim (*C2*), supporting Bernadotte if the Austrians at Eichstädt showed fight, otherwise seizing a crossing at Neuburg.

As this sudden flood came down on them, Austrian detachments north of the Danube hurriedly recrossed the river, managing to burn the Donauwörth bridge behind them. Foiled there, Soult's advance guard (Vandamme) found another bridge nearby at Münster and poured across.

The Austrian light cavalry had bungled its security mission. Until 3 October, Mack had kept his forces dispersed, watching the eastern exits of the Black Forest. When Murat's withdrawal was reported, he realized that the French attack would come from the north, and ordered a concentration (4–8 October) around Ulm, with the intention of holding the Danube's south bank. Jellacic was to assemble a brigade at Biberach (*B1*), ready to cross the Danube and attack the French flank. This concentration was proceeding placidly when Frenchmen swarmed from nowhere into Donauwörth. Mack at once recognized the situation—it was the "Marengo game."

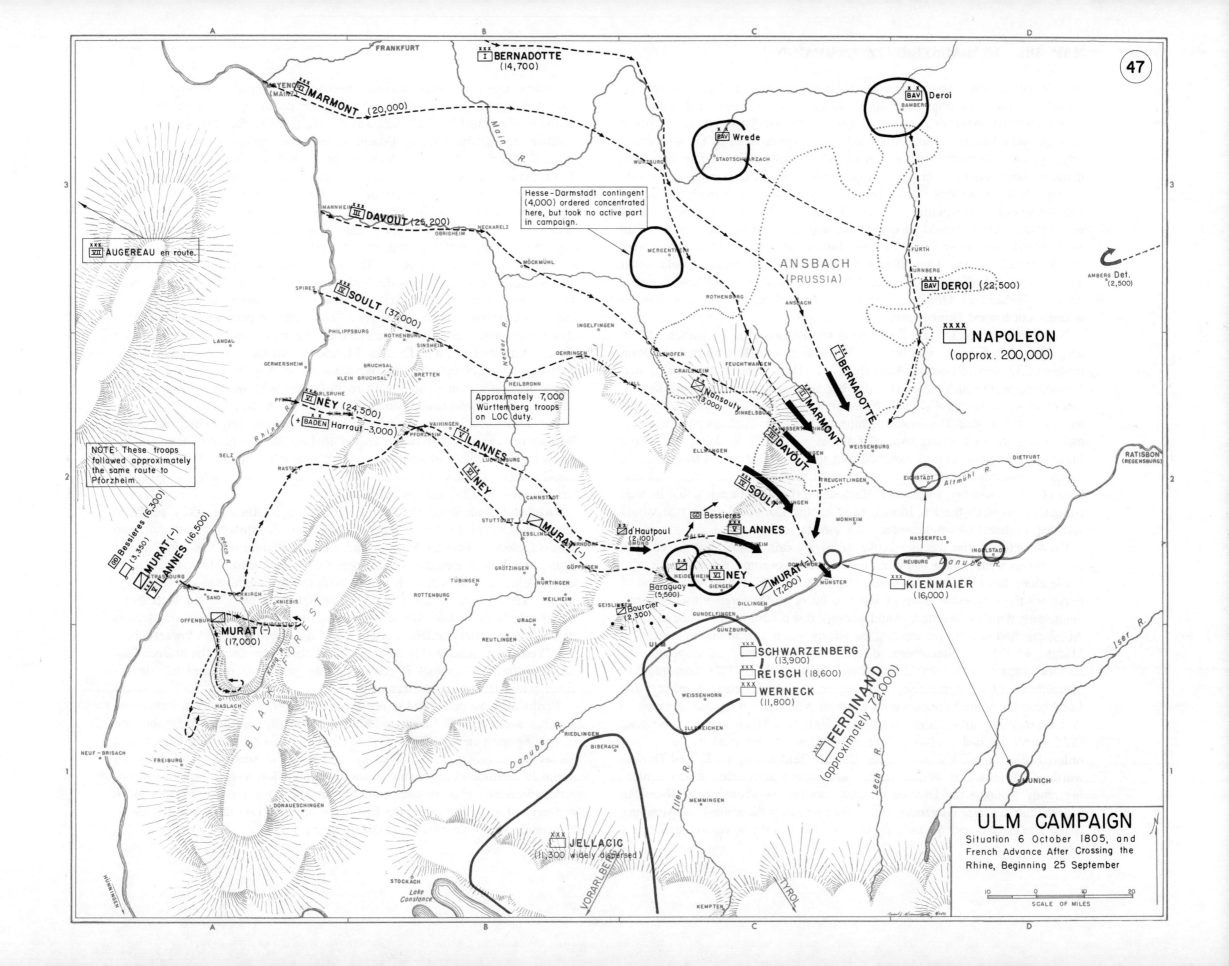

47

FRANKFURT

XXX
I BERNADOTTE
(14,700)

XXX
II MARMONT (20,000)

MAYENCE
(MAINZ)

Main R.

BAV Deroi

BAV Wrede
STADTSCHWARZACH

WÜRTBURG

ANSBACH
(PRUSSIA)

XXX
AUGEREAU en route.

Hesse-Darmstadt contingent
(4,000) ordered concentrated
here, but took no active part
in campaign.

MERGENTHEIM

ROTHENBURG

FÜRTH

NÜRNBERG

XXX
BAV DEROI (22,500)

AMBERG Det.
(2,500)

XXX
III DAVOUT (25,200)

MANNHEIM

OBRIGHEIM

NECKARELZ

MÖCKMÜHL

ANSBACH

XXXX
NAPOLEON
(approx. 200,000)

SPIRES

XXX
IV SOULT (37,000)

Neckar R.

INGELFINGEN

FEUCHTWANGEN

XX
I BERNADOTTE

PHILIPPSBURG

ROTHENBURG

SINSHEIM

OEHRINGEN

ILSHOFEN

CRAILSHEIM

DINKELSBÜHL

II MARMONT

GERMERSHEIM

BRUCHSAL

HEILBRONN

HALL

Nansouty
(3,000)

XX
III DAVOUT

KLEIN BRUCHSAL

BRETTEN

Approximately 7,000
Württemberg troops
on LOC duty.

ELLWINGEN

WEISSENBURG

XX
IV SOULT

LANDAU

KARLSRUHE

XXX
VI NEY (24,500)

PFORZHEIM

+ BADEN Harraut -3,000

VAIHINGEN

PFORZHEIM

XXX
V LANNES

LUDWIGSBURG

TREUCHTLINGEN

RATISBON
(REGENSBURG)

Altmühl R.

DIETFURT

NOTE: These troops
followed approximately
the same route to
Pforzheim.

Rhine R.

SELZ

RASTATT

XXX
VI NEY

CANNSTADT

EICHSTÄDT

XX
GD Bessieres

NASSENFELS

INGOLSTADT

Bessieres (6,300)

Reuss R.

XXX
V LANNES (6,500)

STUTTGART

ESSLINGEN

XXX
MURAT (-)

d'Hautpoul
(2,100)

GMUND

XXX
V LANNES

MONHEIM

NEUBURG

Danube R.

GD Bessieres (3,350)

XXX
MURAT (-)

STRASBOURG

XXX
V LANNES (16,500)

GRÖTZINGEN

GÖPPINGEN

XX
VI NEY

Baraguay
(5,500)

HEIDENHEIM

GIENGEN

MURAT (-)

DONAU (-)

MÜNSTER

XXX
KIENMAIER
(16,000)

KEHL

KNIEBIS

TÜBINGEN

NÜRTINGEN

WEILHEIM

XX
MURAT
(7,200)

DILLINGEN

XXX
MURAT (-)
(17,000)

OFFENBURG

EBERSTADT

SAND

OBERKIRCH

HASLACH

ROTTENBURG

REUTLINGEN

URACH

GEISLINGEN

Bourcier
(2,300)

GUNDELFINGEN

ULM

GÜNZBURG

NEUF-BRISACH

FREIBURG

BLACK FOREST

Kinzig R.

XXX
SCHWARZENBERG
(13,900)

XXX
REISCH (18,600)

XXX
WERNECK
(11,800)

XXX
FERDINAND
(approximately 72,000)

Iser R.

WEISSENHORN

DONAUESCHINGEN

Danube R.

RIEDLINGEN

BIBERACH

ILLEREICHEN

Iller R.

Lech R.

MUNICH

HÜNINGEN

JELLACIC
(11,300 widely dispersed)

STOCKACH

Lake Constance

VORARLBERG

MEMMINGEN

KEMPTEN

TYROL

ULM CAMPAIGN

Situation 6 October 1805, and
French Advance After Crossing the
Rhine, Beginning 25 September

SCALE OF MILES
10   0   10   20

Mack's immediate reaction was to strike the French as they crossed the Danube, at the same time ordering Kienmaier to attack westward. The Austrian command, however, was a split personality. Mack, an officer of proven courage and initiative (if somewhat pedantic), was scorned by his aristocratic colleagues as a Protestant ranker. Ferdinand, dutifully echoed by his corps and division commanders, wanted a prompt retreat. (Exact responsibility for subsequent Austrian actions cannot be determined. Mack was made the scapegoat—archdukes, no matter how chuckleheaded, being sacrosanct.) Mack urged that a retreat would be disastrous, that it would be better to wage an aggressive defense around Ulm until reinforcements arrived. Final orders were to concentrate in the Ulm-Günzburg area (A2); Kienmaier could cover Vienna. One detachment (d'Aspre, 2,600; not shown) would hold a north-bank bridgehead at Günzburg; another (Auffenberg, 4,800; not shown) would scout toward Donauwörth (C3).

Napoleon reached Donauwörth during the afternoon of 7 October. Murat, with Walther's division, was bullying Kienmaier, who had burned the Rain bridge (C3) and retired on Aichach (C2). That night, only Walther and Vandamme were south of the Danube, but most of Soult's corps and Klein's, Beaumont's, d'Hautpoul's, and Nansouty's divisions of Murat's Cavalry Reserve were around Donauwörth. Information from civilians and prisoners indicated only that strong Austrian forces were still at Ulm. As before Marengo, Napoleon eagerly assumed that the Austrians would think only of escape—probably through Augsburg (C2); if blocked there, through Landsberg (C1) or, possibly, southward. He doubted that Ferdinand "could be mad enough to cross to the left [north] bank of the Danube," since that would sacrifice his direct communications with Vienna and the Tyrol.

On 8 October, the weather broke in an icy rain, sometimes mixed with snow. Roads went rapidly to pieces, fields became swamps. Expecting a major battle along the Lech by 9 October, Napoleon sent Mathieu-Dumas (one of Berthier's three assistant chiefs of staff) to hurry up the three left-flank corps. Soult, with Walther attached, would advance down both banks of the Lech on Augsburg, first making certain that the enemy was not in strength at Aichach. Murat (with Klein, Beaumont, d'Hautpoul, Nansouty, and a brigade of Lannes' corps cavalry) would march on Zusmarshausen (B2), continuing to Mindelheim (B1) if possible, and cutting the roads from Augsburg and Landsberg to Ulm. Lannes would cross at Münster (B3) and advance to Wertingen (B2) to support Murat. At 0600, Ney (then around Höchstadt [B2], where he had captured three bridges) was reinforced as shown and ordered to cover all the roads from Ulm to Heidenheim (A3) and Donauwörth (C3), attacking without hesitation as opportunity offered, and remaining ready to cross the Danube on short notice. At about noon, Napoleon ordered him to seize Günzburg (A2), thus blocking the main Ulm-Augsburg road. The Guard and Suchet's division would remain in reserve at Donauwörth.

Orders were one thing, execution another. Overeager, Marmont took the Eichstädt-Neuburg road (C3), thinking he could clear Eichstädt before Bernadotte reached it. The result was a three-corps traffic jam; none of them reached the Danube that day. Davout surprised the bridge guard at Neuburg, crossed, and pushed hard for Aichach. Soult, however, had found more than 5,000 Austrians there and so halted short of that town. Ney did not move until 1400. Lannes and Murat destroyed half of Auffenburg's detachment (action not shown), but St. Hilaire—tugged in contrary directions by Soult's orders and Murat's demands for support—spent the day countermarching.

Napoleon remained overoptimistic. Despite prisoner reports that the enemy was massed along the Iller River, he sent Ney an amazing order: Get Gazan and Baraguay to Augsburg by the 10th; send a division to Ulm to chase away the 3,000–4,000 Austrians there; if they prove stronger, move against the city with your whole force and make a "nice catch of prisoners." Having thus thoroughly miscomprehended the situation, he proceeded to concentrate for the expected battle: Soult, Davout, Marmont, and the Guard would mass at Augsburg; Lannes between Zusmarshausen and Augsburg; Bernadotte and Deroi, leaving a strong garrison in Ingolstadt, would march immediately on Munich (D1) to constitute a covering force against the Russians.

The actual positions reached, as shown, fell considerably behind his plans. Bernadotte was slow; Marmont halted to feed his exhausted men. On the north bank, Malher had smashed d'Aspre's detachment near Günzburg, but could not save the bridge from destruction. Ney, uncertain of actual Austrian strength around Ulm, did not release Gazan.

October 9 had found Ferdinand's army around Burgau (B2) ready to advance eastward on Zusmarshausen. However, Auffenberg's rout indicated that Napoleon had cut the Vienna road. Ferdinand and the corps commanders again urged an immediate retreat, preferably southward. Mack faced them down: Ulm was a strong, well-stocked position; two could play the "Marengo game." He ordered an advance north through Günzburg to cut Napoleon's communications. While Mack, according to Austrian routine, personally drafted the necessary orders, word came of d'Aspre's disaster. Schwarzenberg and Werneck marched to Günzburg, and set about rebuilding the bridge. That accomplished, Malher took it from them, also seizing an incompletely demolished bridge farther downstream.

Ferdinand now demanded either a retreat into the Tyrol or an immediate advance north through Elchingen. Mack, thoroughly disheartened by the lack of fighting spirit among officers and men alike, ordered a return to Ulm, where he set about reorganizing the army. (This would seem to have been an untimely measure, but probably was a desperate effort to get the better troops grouped under the more competent commanders.) Darkness brought more bad news: Loison had seized the Elchingen bridge. (Loison later withdrew to Langenau; the whole episode remains obscure.)

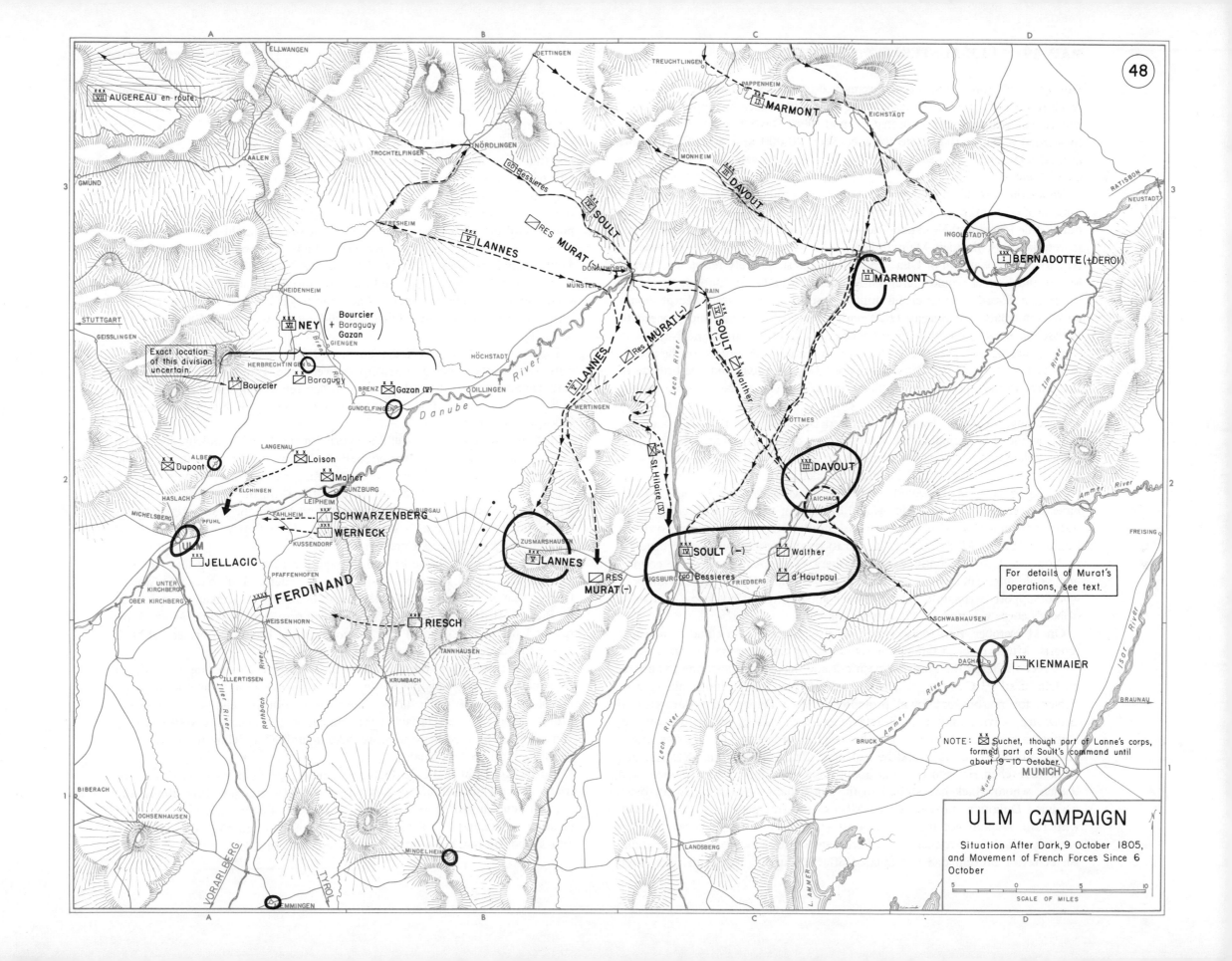

48

ULM CAMPAIGN

Situation After Dark, 9 October 1805, and Movement of French Forces Since 6 October

NOTE: ⊠ Suchet, though part of Lanne's corps, formed part of Soult's command until about 9–10 October.

For details of Murat's operations, see text.

SCALE OF MILES

During 10 October, the French remained relatively stationary. Napoleon received an early message from Ney, requesting assurance of support since the enemy was stronger than expected around Ulm. Davout, at Aichach (C2), forwarded a report that there were between 40,000 and 50,000 Austrians around Ulm, and (erroneous) that Russians were expected in Munich (D1) on 16 October.

Napoleon was now willing to admit that Ferdinand had a considerable force around Ulm, but—committing the folly of trying to guess enemy intentions while ignoring their capabilities—insisted that the Austrians were about to retreat south through Memmingen (A1). At 1800 that day, he ordered Ney to "take possession of Ulm" and pursue the supposedly retreating enemy. Murat and Lannes would march on Mindelheim (B1). He himself would go to Munich. Shortly thereafter, his military instinct asserted itself: Murat should move immediately to Burgau (B2) with a force of all arms, and proceed to Weissenhorn (A1) on the 11th to connect and control Lannes and Ney.

Ney, accepting Napoleon's intelligence estimate, issued orders for the investment of Ulm on the 11th. Dupont, supported by Baraguay and one brigade of Bourcier, would operate on the north bank, the rest of Ney's force on the south.

Reaching Augsburg, Napoleon received complete reports of Ney's operations on the 9th, including the interrogation of the captured d'Aspre. This made it plain that both Ferdinand and Mack were near Ulm with approximately 40,000 troops; that they had intended to operate on the north bank; that—cornered or not—Mack would fight. Murat, with Ney and Lannes, should have men enough to overwhelm Mack, but only if he kept his forces concentrated and maneuvered carefully and skillfully. Napoleon therefore ordered Lannes to follow Murat to Burgau and to remain within supporting distance of Ney. Soult would continue to Landsberg (C1); Augereau (now coming up) would intercept any Austrians escaping westward. Davout and d'Hautpoul would support Bernadotte. The Emperor apparently did not know that most of Ney's corps was now on the south bank.

On 11 October, Bernadotte halted short of Munich in a cloud of alarmist reports. Murat reached Günzburg (A2) during the morning, conferred with Ney, reconnoitered the Austrian position, and decided to postpone the attack on Ulm until 13 October. Meanwhile, he left Ney's dispositions unchanged.

Ney, for reasons unknown, promptly ordered Dupont and Baraguay to Günzburg, leaving only a small detachment near Albeck (A2). Meanwhile, Dupont had marched according to his original orders for 11 October. Baraguay's orders arrived late, and he lost more time collecting his detachments. Dupont reached Haslach (A2) at about noon and found Schwarzenberg and Riesch, whom Mack had shifted to the north bank. Austrian cavalry overwhelmed Dupont's, pursued it into Albeck, and stampeded his trains. Faced with ruin, Dupont got his back against Haslach and fought savagely. Fortunately, Mack was wounded, and Ferdinand's and Schwarzenberg's amateurish behavior prevented a coordinated attack. Dupont held until dark, then

retired on Baraguay, who had secured Albeck. At about midnight, Dupont received Ney's order to move to Günzburg, but instead made a disorderly retreat toward Brenz (B2).

The jubilant Austrians had captured orders showing Ney's dispositions, and thus knew the road north was open. Mack accordingly planned a prompt advance to link up with the Russians at Ratisbon (off map, D3), wrecking Napoleon's communications en route. Werneck, however, insisted that his troops were too weary. Ferdinand supported Werneck, and escape was postponed until the 13th. The evening of 12 October brought surprising reports of French forces west of Weissenhorn. Mack changed his plan: Werneck would march northeast via Heidenheim (A3)–Nördlingen (B3); Riesch would cover the army's right flank, moving through Gundelfingen and Höchstadt (both B2); Schwarzenberg would feint toward Weissenhorn on the 13th, turn northward on the 14th; Jellacic would withdraw through Biberach (A1) to the Tyrol.

Early on the 13th, as Ferdinand moved out, numerous French columns were reported advancing westward between the Danube and the Landsberg-Memmingen road, while an intelligence report suggested a major crisis in France. Mack thereupon decided that Napoleon simply might be taking the shortest road home.

Instead, after a study of Murat's reports for the 11th, Napoleon had finally comprehended the actual situation and was moving westward with the II and IV Corps and the Guard. Now overestimating Ferdinand's strength, he had ordered Murat to postpone his attack until the 14th, throw a bridge south of Albeck to improve contact with Dupont, and spend the 13th preparing his troops for a major battle. Soult was to have his infantry advance guard at Memmingen by 0200, 13 October.

Bad weather plagued the French through the 12th. Learning that Ney had recalled Dupont to the south bank, Murat ordered him back to Albeck. Dupont sent back only a small detachment, marching his shaken command on to Brenz. (He had reported a glorious victory, and did not mention his retreat.) Murat also ordered Ney to reoccupy the Elchingen bridge (A2), if it could be done without a major engagement.

Also on 12 October, Bernadotte reached Munich, and promptly confused the situation by reporting that Ferdinand had been there until late on the 11th. Napoleon could only order further investigation. Fortunately, he soon received Murat's report of the Haslach fight, indicating the enemy was still around Ulm. He then ordered Soult to move "like lightning" for Ulm, if enemy forces at Memmingen proved small.

During the night of 12–13 October, Lannes' outposts intercepted an Austrian courier whose dispatches showed Ferdinand's strength, dispositions, and plans. Lannes urged Murat to reinforce Dupont. Fearing such action might disorganize Napoleon's plans, Murat merely forwarded this information to him. Napoleon reached Günzburg early on the 13th.

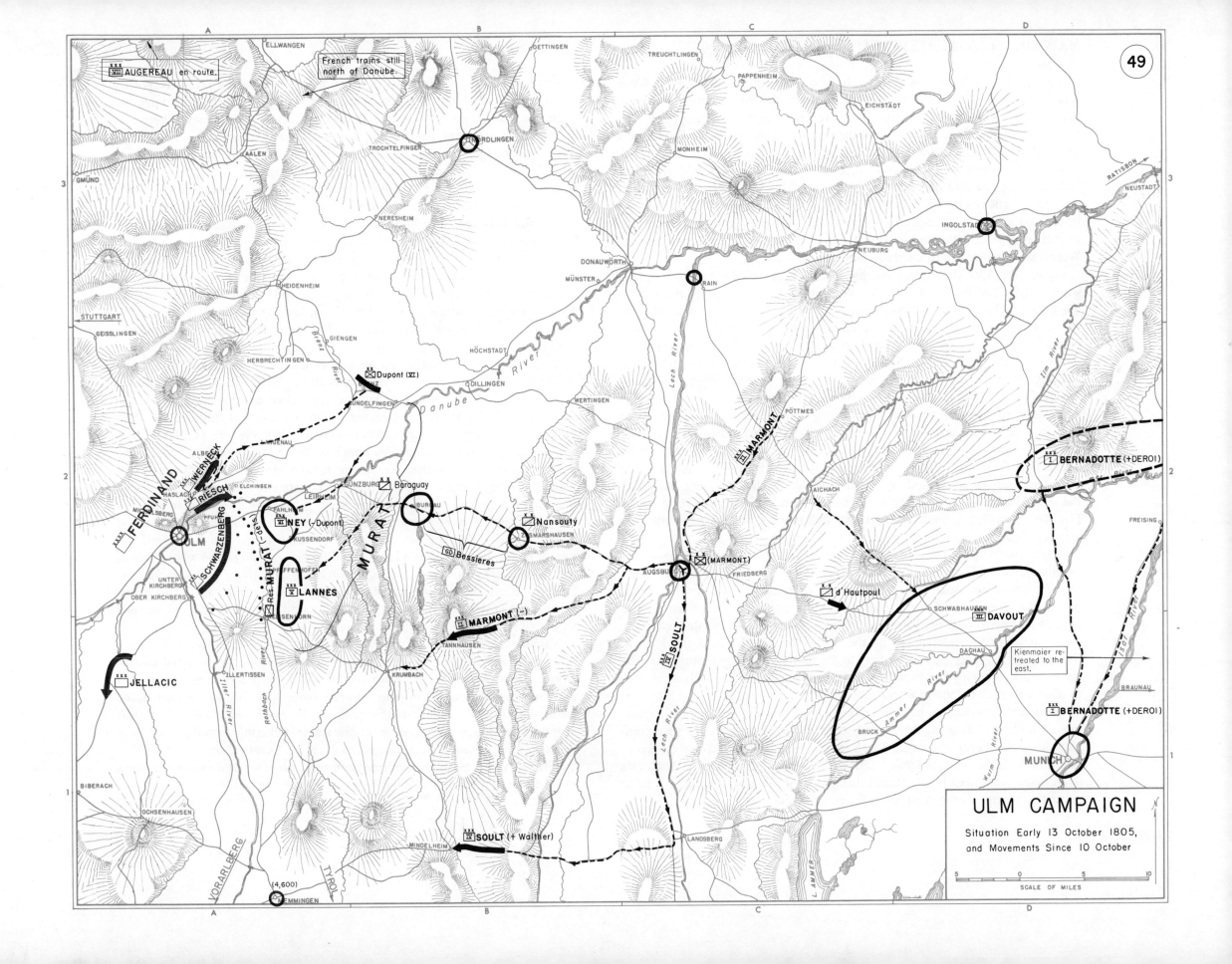

49

XXX VII AUGEREAU en route.

French trains still north of Danube.

ELLWANGEN
OETTINGEN
TREUCHTLINGEN
PAPPENHEIM
EICHSTÄDT
RATISBON
NEUSTADT

NÖRDLINGEN
TROCHTELFINGEN

GMÜND

AALEN

MONHEIM

INGOLSTADT

NERESHEIM

STUTTGART

GEISSLINGEN

HEIDENHEIM

DONAUWÖRTH
MÜNSTER
NEUBURG
RAIN

HERBRECHTINGEN
GIENGEN

HÖCHSTADT
Danube River

XX Dupont (VI)
DILLINGEN
WERTINGEN

PÖTTMES

XXX MARMONT

XXX I BERNADOTTE (+DEROI)

ALBECK
WERNECK
GÜNZBURG XX Baraguay
LEIPHEIM
BURGAU
ELCHINGEN
AICHACH

FERDINAND
RIESCH
HASLACH

FAHLHEIM
XX VI NEY (-Dupont)
XX Nansouty
ISMARSHAUSEN

ULM
PFUHL
RUSSENDORF
GD Bessieres
XX (MARMONT)
AUGSBURG
FRIEDBERG

SCHWARZENBERG
Res. MURAT (-dels.)
XXX V LANNES
XX d'Hautpoul

UNTER KIRCHBERG
SENDEN
XXX II MARMONT (-)
SCHWABHAUSEN
XXX III DAVOUT

OBER KIRCHBERG
TANNHAUSEN
XXX IV SOULT
DACHAU

JELLACIC
KRUMBACH
Kienmaier retreated to the east.

ILLERTISSEN
BRUCK
BRAUNAU

XXX I BERNADOTTE (+DEROI)

BIBERACH
LANDSBERG
MUNICH

OCHSENHAUSEN

VORARLBERG
TYROL
(4,600)
MEMMINGEN
XXX IV SOULT (+ Walther)
MINDELHEIM
L. AMMER

ULM CAMPAIGN

Situation Early 13 October 1805, and Movements Since 10 October

SCALE OF MILES

Napoleon's first concern was to strengthen his forces on the north bank. Considerable searching was necessary to find Dupont. Ney was ordered to capture the Elchingen bridge (*A2*) before dark. He gave this mission to a reinforced battalion, which found the heights on the north bank swarming with Austrians and withdrew hurriedly (*action not shown*).

These Austrians were Riesch's corps, which had been shifted from the Gundelfingen route to one through Elchingen. This latter road lay in a belt of slippery, sticky clay. Riesch could barely wallow a mile an hour through it, but did arrive at Elchingen in time to thwart Ney. Finding considerable French strength on the south bank, he requested new orders. On his left, Werneck's advance guard entered Heidenheim.

During the 13th, Soult had blockaded and bypassed Memmingen (*A1*), while Lannes had occupied Ober Kirchberg (*A2*). Ney's negligence concerning both the bridge and Dupont brought him an imperial rebuke, plus an emphatic order to seize Elchingen Heights on the morning of the 14th. Napoleon pulled Lannes northward to support Ney; ordered Marmont to replace Lannes; and directed Soult to cut the Ulm-Biberach (*A1–A2*) road.

Early on the 14th, Riesch began shifting back to the Langenau-Gundelfingen road, but was interrupted by reports that Elchingen was under attack and that a French column was approaching from Brenz. The column was Dupont's; it bolted back to Gundelfingen after a brief clash with Riesch's advance guard. Ney's attack, launched across the stringers of the partially demolished Elchingen bridge, eventually drove Riesch westward toward Ulm after ten hours of hard fighting. Lannes prodded Schwarzenberg back into the Austrian bridgehead on the south bank; Marmont's cavalry reached the Danube above Ulm; Soult reached Ochsenhausen (*A1*), barely failing to intercept Jellacic.

Mack, meanwhile, concluded that Napoleon's inexplicable actions—the evacuation of the Danube's north bank and the massed march westward south of the river—confirmed the supposition that the Emperor was heading home because of troubles in France. Mack therefore announced that the French were retreating toward the Rhine, and began issuing orders to intercept them. These dreams were interrupted by the arrival of Riesch's decimated corps. Mack then summoned Schwarzenberg to the north bank to garrison Ulm. The heavy artillery having followed Werneck, Schwarzenberg had only field guns to emplace in the defensive works.

Ferdinand now decided he must "deprive the French of the glory of capturing a Hapsburg." Schwarzenberg and others deserted their troops to accompany his flight. Ferdinand urged Mack to join them, but Mack, determined to buy time for other Allied armies, refused. Jellacic had got clear; Werneck's main body had halted in the Herbrechtingen (*A2*)–Neresheim (*B3*) area to cover the passage of the Austrian artillery and trains.

Determined to complete the destruction of Ferdinand's army, Napoleon ordered most of his troops across to the north bank to pen the Austrians into Ulm. As yet, he was unaware of Werneck's escape. The crossing began at 0200 on the 15th, but went slowly, the whole army having to defile over the Elchingen bridge. The Austrians fought gamely, but were finally driven out of their field works around Ulm and into the city proper.

Meanwhile, Dupont had advanced again from Gundelfingen. Between Langenau and Albeck, a strong force of Austrian cavalry, coming from the *north,* suddenly fell upon him. Werneck had taken the soldierly decision to countermarch and attack the French rear. Sending his cavalry ahead, he had divided his infantry into two columns, one to move due south, the other via Brenz-Langenau. This latter column bogged down in the previously mentioned clay belt; Werneck waited for it. Meanwhile, his unsupported cavalry had Dupont in desperate straits, when Klein, hearing the firing to the French rear, rode to the rescue. That night (15 October), Ferdinand reached Aalen (*A3*).

This attack on Dupont jarred Napoleon into acute awareness that strong Austrian forces were across his communications. His siege guns, ammunition trains, and army treasure were somewhere between Ellwangen (*A3*) and Nördlingen (*B3*). He ordered Murat off in pursuit, and directed the Rain (*C3*) and Augsburg (*C2*) garrisons to reinforce Donauwörth (*C3*).

Werneck planned to resume his attack on the morning of 16 October, but was halted by an order from Ferdinand to join him at Aalen. Just short of Aalen, a second order directed that he countermarch through Neresheim and establish contact with Kienmaier. Klein gobbled Werneck's rear guard at Neresheim that evening, and caught Werneck and his exhausted infantry at Trochtelfingen (*B3*) the next day. The Austrian trains and heavy artillery were pinched out between Ellwangen and Oettingen (*B3*). The whole French rear area was by now in a high state of confusion, trains and detachments being captured and recaptured. Murat kept up his pursuit until 21 October, rejoining the army by way of Neustadt (*D3*) on the 25th. Ferdinand escaped with approximately 3,500 exhausted cavalry.

Napoleon had demanded the surrender of Ulm on 15 October. Mack refused; he was short of food, but had a strong position and plenty of ammunition. He knew that Werneck was across the French communications, that the countryside around Ulm was foraged bare, and that the French siege train was still far to the rear. His generals, however, mutinied and opened negotiations with Napoleon. After considerable dickering (some possibly not to Napoleon's credit), Mack surrendered on 20 October, on condition that the French VI Corps be immobilized until the 25th. The total bag of prisoners so far in the campaign numbered between 50,000 and 60,000.

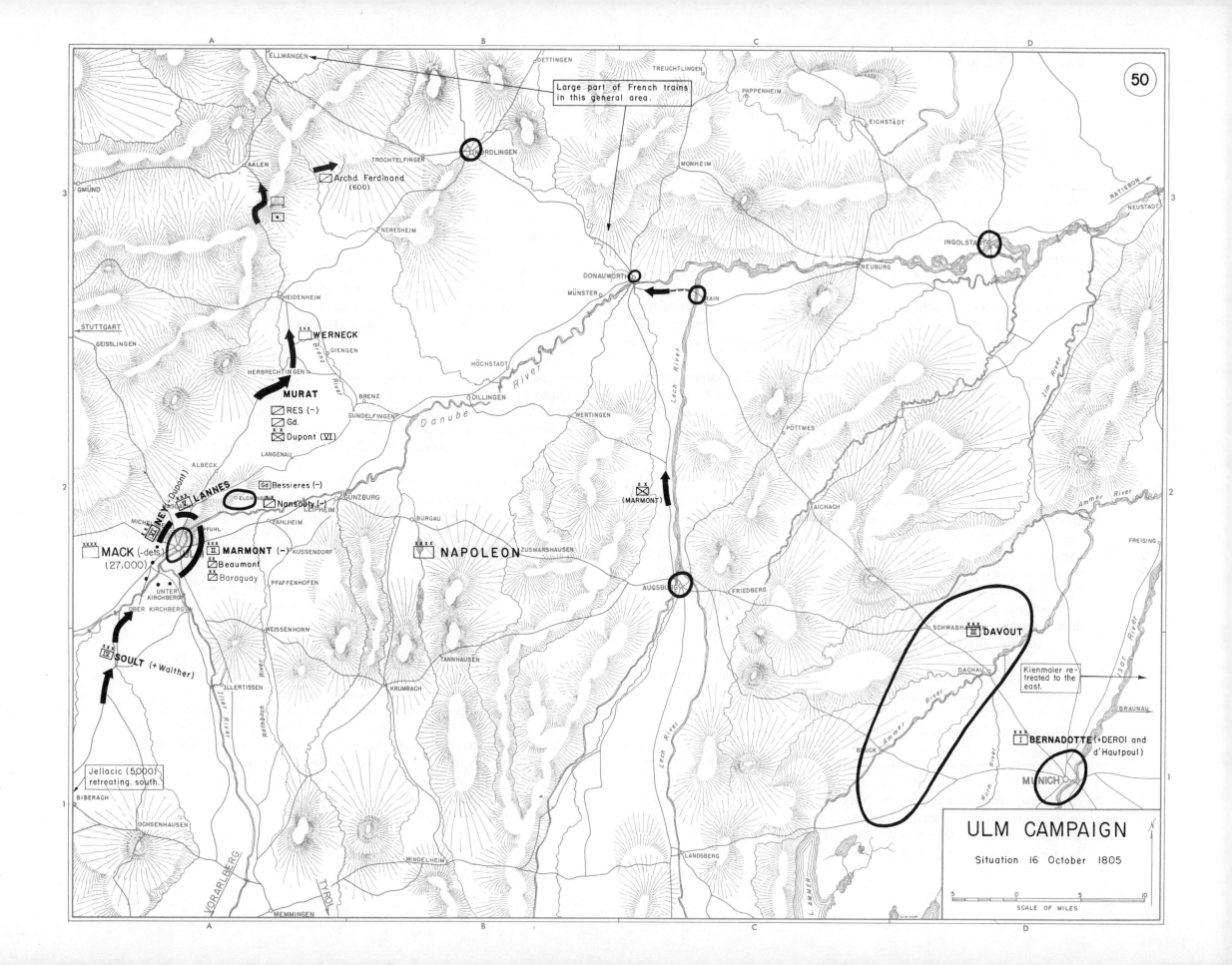

50

Large part of French trains in this general area.

ELLWANGEN

OETTINGEN

TREUCHTLINGEN

PAPPENHEIM

EICHSTÄDT

NÖRDLINGEN

TROCHTELFINGER

AALEN

Archd. Ferdinand (600)

NERESHEIM

MONHEIM

RATISBON

NEUSTADT

GMÜND

HEIDENHEIM

DONAUWÖRTH

NEUBURG

INGOLSTADT

MÜNSTER

RAIN

STUTTGART

WERNECK

GIENGEN

HÖCHSTADT

Danube River

Lech River

GEISSLINGEN

HERBRECHTINGEN

BRENZ

DILLINGEN

WERTINGEN

PÖTTMES

Amper River

MURAT

RES (–)
Gd.
Dupont (VI)

BRENZ

GUNDELFINGEN

LANGENAU

ALBECK

NEY (–Dupont)

LANNES

Bessieres (–)

Nansouty (–)

GÜNZBURG

BURGAU

(MARMONT)

AICHACH

FREISING

ELCHINGEN

PFUHL

PFAFFENHOFEN

MICHELSBERG

MACK (–defs.) (27,000)

MARMONT (–)

Beaumont
Baraguay

KUSSENDORF

ZUSMARSHAUSEN

NAPOLEON

AUGSBURG

FRIEDBERG

Ilm River

UNTER KIRCHBERG

OBER KIRCHBERG

WEISSENHORN

TANNHAUSEN

SCHWABH

DAVOUT

SOULT (+Walther)

KRUMBACH

DACHAU

Kienmaier re-treated to the east.

Isar River

ILLERTISSEN

Iller River

Rothbach River

BRAUNAU

Lech River

BRUCK

Amper River

BERNADOTTE (+DEROI and d'Hautpoul)

Jellacic (5,000) retreating south.

BIBERACH

Wurm River

MUNICH

OCHSENHAUSEN

MINDELHEIM

LANDSBERG

L. AMMER

ULM CAMPAIGN

Situation 16 October 1805

VORARLBERG

TYROL

MEMMINGEN

SCALE OF MILES

It had been an astounding, swift campaign—but also an improvised one. Bad weather, ruined roads, and scant food had littered the French rear with stragglers, marauders, and deserters. Only Napoleon's innate ability to lead and inspire, plus the tough fiber of his soldiers, had made it possible.

Time pressed Napoleon: The Russians were approaching, new Austrian armies were mustering, and Prussia was mobilizing. Yet, as his forces massed between Munich and Landshut (both B2), he gave first priority to organizing his communications. Relays of impressed wagons brought forward essential supplies—chiefly ammunition and shoes. Augsburg (A2) became the army's advanced base: Its defenses were improved; workshops, bakeries, and hospitals were established. Stragglers were ruthlessly rounded up and hurried forward.

Napoleon arrived at Munich at 0900 on 24 October. He overestimated Kutusov's forces, then astride the Inn River (B2), at 100,000, with 60,000 Austrian reinforcements soon available. His aim was to destroy Kutusov before these could join him.

Kutusov had closed up along the Inn between 12 and 25 October (the very period that Mack had expected him on the Iller). He had barely 36,000 exhausted Russians and Meerfeldt's 22,000 Austrians (Kienmaier's corps, plus reinforcements originally intended for Ferdinand). Of these, 3,000 were blockading Passau's (C2) citadel, which the Bavarians still held. No major reinforcements could be expected in the near future.

Learning on 23 October of Mack's capitulation, Kutusov withdrew behind the Inn River and burned its bridges. His plan apparently was to retire rapidly into Moravia (D3), where he expected Buxhöwden, and possibly the Prussians, to reinforce him. Emperor Francis of Austria finally persuaded him to attempt to delay the French invasion, explaining that the Danube's south-bank tributaries would offer a series of defensive positions, and that Charles and Buxhöwden might be able to join him in time to save Vienna.

Napoleon's plan, as illustrated here, was an advance in three strong columns, roughly echeloned from the right. Murat's cavalry screen covered the center column; directly behind Murat marched a strong engineer detachment with the army bridge train. Ney and Augereau would drive John away from the main army's right rear. Baraguay would collect horses for his dismounted dragoons. Unfortunately, orders for Dupont, Dumonceau, and Klein were delivered a day late.

The advance began on 26 October; two days later, the French were crossing the Inn. Kutusov abandoned the fortress city of Braunau (B2), which was stocked with large stores of food and munitions, on the 29th. Napoleon made it his new advanced base. Bernadotte entered the city of Salzburg (B2) on the 30th against minor opposition. Napoleon then ordered Marmont forward on Bernadotte's left to envelop any enemy force attempting to defend the Traun River (C2). Deroi was detached with one Bavarian division to move against Innsbrück (B2), in cooperation with Ney.

Murat found the enemy rear guard elusive. Kutusov's delaying tactics were confined to burning bridges and stripping the countryside of food. Winter was a worse enemy: heavy snows, dissolving roads, empty bellies, cold.

To gain time, Francis repeatedly attempted to open negotiations. That failing, he ordered the steep-banked Enns River (C2) held as long as possible. Kutusov refused, claiming the headlong French pursuit had disorganized his men. A council of war on 3 November decided to withdraw behind the Traisen River (C2). Thereafter, unless reinforcements arrived, Kutusov would cross the Danube at Krems (C2) while Kienmaier retired on Vienna. To cover the withdrawal, Kutusov dropped Bagration's Russian division (not shown) in a strong position at Amstetten (C2).

East of Enns, the open plain south of the Danube narrows suddenly. Napoleon accordingly reshuffled his columns, shifting the divisions of Gazan (V Corps), Dupont (VI Corps), and Dumonceau (II Corps) to the north bank to form a provisional corps under Mortier which would threaten Kutusov's communications. If the Russians turned on Mortier, Napoleon planned to transfer his main army rapidly to the north bank. For such service (and to transport supplies), a flotilla of approximately 250 boats was organized to follow the army down the Danube. But Napoleon forgot, in his driving impatience, that the delay in Dupont's and Dumonceau's original orders had left them well to the rear. Initially, Mortier would have to advance with Gazan alone.

On 5 November, Bagration checked Murat and Oudinot's division (V Corps) at Amstetten until dark. Napoleon therefore eagerly expected a decisive battle around Saint Pölten (C2). On the 7th, however, Murat easily cleared Neumarkt (C2), and intercepted messages indicated that the enemy planned to retreat across the Danube at Krems. Napoleon accordingly sent Klein across the river to scout for Mortier and ordered Murat and Soult to collect all available boats. Mortier would take over the pursuit of Kutusov; Marmont would turn southeast to Leoben (C2) to block Charles and John.

To cover his left rear, Napoleon previously had sent Baraguay raiding into Bohemia (C3). Ney had moved southeast on 26 October, catching John's scattered forces as they began concentrating toward the Brenner Pass (B1). Blocked in the mountains south of Salzburg, Deroi had sent a brigade off to the southwest against the mountain fortress of Kufstein (B2).

As for Italy, Napoleon had changed Massena's original orders, directing him to attack Charles to prevent his sending reinforcements to other Austrian armies. Charles, aware of Mack's capitulation and preparing to withdraw from Italy, planned a spoiling attack to cripple Massena enough to prevent pursuit. The resulting brawl at Caldiero (A1) on 29–30 October was discreditable to both. Subsequently, Charles expertly slipped away, halting behind the Tagliamento River (B1) to cover John's withdrawal.

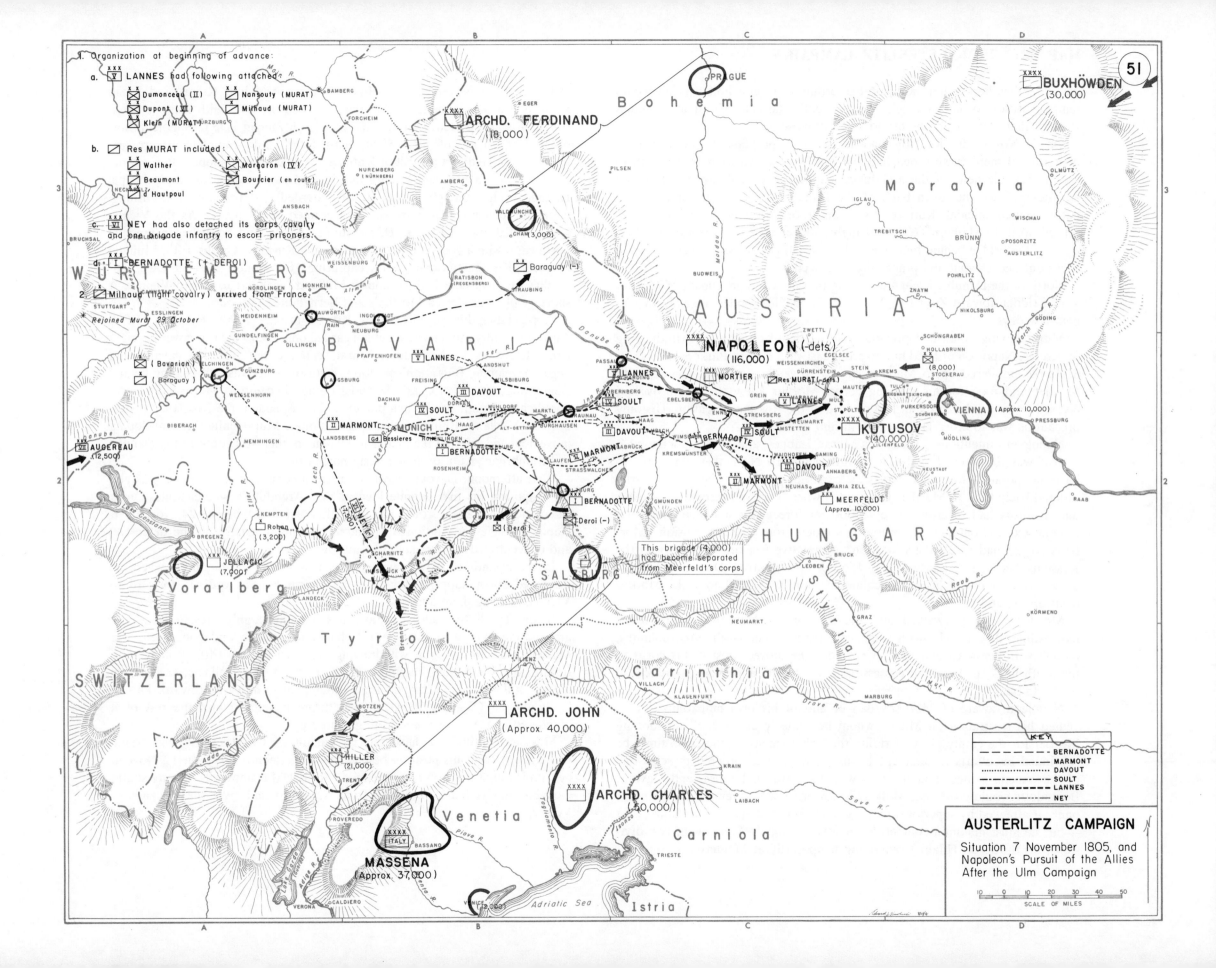

51

1. Organization at beginning of advance:

a. ☒☒☒ LANNES had following attached:
- ☒ Dumonceau (II)   ☒ Nansouty (MURAT)
- ☒ Dupont (VI)   ☒ Milhaud (MURAT)
- ☒ Klein (MURAT)

b. ☒ Res MURAT included:
- ☒☒ Walther   ☒☒ Margaron (IV)
- ☒☒ Beaumont   ☒☒ Bourcier (en route)
- ☒☒ d'Hautpoul

c. ☒☒☒ VI NEY had also detached its corps cavalry and one brigade infantry to escort prisoners.

d. ☒☒☒ I BERNADOTTE (+ DEROI)

2. ☒ Milhaud (light cavalry) arrived from France.

* Rejoined Murat 29 October

BUXHÖWDEN (30,000)

ARCHD. FERDINAND (18,000)

NAPOLEON (-dets.) (116,000)

KUTUSOV (40,000)

VIENNA (Approx. 10,000)

MEERFELDT (Approx. 10,000)

AUGEREAU (12,500)

NEY (7,500)

Rohan (3,200)

JELLACIC (7,000)

This brigade (4,000) had become separated from Meerfeldt's corps.

HILLER (21,000)

ARCHD. JOHN (Approx. 40,000)

ARCHD. CHARLES (50,000)

ITALY

MASSENA (Approx. 37,000)

KEY
- — — — — BERNADOTTE
- — · — · — MARMONT
- ············ DAVOUT
- — — — — SOULT
- —— —— —— LANNES
- — —— — NEY

AUSTERLITZ CAMPAIGN

Situation 7 November 1805, and Napoleon's Pursuit of the Allies After the Ulm Campaign

SCALE OF MILES
10   0   10   20   30   40   50

Napoleon had hoped that the favorable terrain near Saint Pölten (*C2*) would tempt Kutusov to halt and fight. Consequently, he held Murat and Lannes short of that area during the 8th to let Soult close up.

On 7 November, Kutusov had available approximately 40,000 half-demoralized men. Buxhöwden had not reached the Austrian frontier; there was no reliable news of the archdukes; and a French column was reported advancing down the north bank of the Danube. Under such conditions, a battle seemed suicidal. Kutusov rested his troops for most of 8 November, retired north to Mautern (*C2*) that night, and crossed to Krems on the 9th, burning the bridge behind him. Meerfeldt was caught (8 November) between Marmont and Davout and practically destroyed.

North of the Danube, Klein—assuming that he was independent of Mortier—had ridden toward Zwettl (*C2*), where he would wander uselessly for the next few days.

Murat having confirmed previous reports that Kutusov was withdrawing on Krems, Napoleon ordered him to scout eastward toward Purkersdorf (*D2*). Soult reconnoitered up to Mautern on 10 November, seeking contact with Mortier and food for his starving corps. Mortier knew that Kutusov had crossed to the north bank, but had no idea of the Russians' location. His only precaution was to order Dupont to join him on the 11th.

Napoleon's intention—at least, as Murat, Lannes, and Soult understood it—now was to march directly on Vienna. Until 10 November, he seems to have temporarily forgotten Mortier's exposed position. Then, he angrily ordered Klein back to Mortier. His sudden worry was well inspired, but overdue. Kutusov had received some 10,000 reinforcements and had somewhat reorganized his command. Captured marauders from Gazan's division (Mortier's corps) had revealed its location and relative weakness (6,000) to the Russians. Seeing his chance to trap Mortier in the narrow Dürrenstein (*C2*) defile, Kutusov dispatched three columns (almost 15,000) to strike Mortier front, flank, and rear.

Mortier obligingly walked into the trap on 11 November, but proved indigestible, driving off—with some help from Dupont—all three columns, though with heavy casualties. The next day, he moved most of his corps to the south bank, maintaining possession of only Spitz and Weissenkirchen on the north bank.

Napoleon, aware of Mortier's danger and of his own culpability for it, vented his frustration on Murat, whom he unjustly accused of abandoning Mortier for the empty glory of riding through Vienna. At the same time, he continued his efforts to intercept Kutusov. Murat was ordered to seize one of the Vienna bridges and to cross with the cavalry, Lannes, and Davout. Bernadotte would cross near Mölk (*C2*). Mortier would remain on the north bank; if attacked by superior forces, he might retire as far west as Linz (*C2*)—but he must maintain contact. Soult was to support Murat with two divisions, his third (St. Hilaire) remaining temporarily at Mautern.

Early on 13 November, St. Hilaire got a patrol into Krems and found Kutusov evacuating the town. Mortier recrossed the river with Dupont's division and later reported the Russians retiring on Znaym (*D3*). Napoleon now ordered St. Hilaire off after Soult. Bernadotte would complete his crossing and take up the direct pursuit of Kutusov; Mortier would support Bernadotte.

Meanwhile, Murat and Lannes had bluffed their way across the principal Danube bridge, though it was heavily guarded and prepared for burning, under the pretense that Napoleon had granted an armistice. As the Vienna garrison fled toward Brünn (*D3*), Murat, Lannes, and Soult began pressing northward, with a good chance of intercepting Kutusov. On the 14th, Milhaud overtook Kienmaier's rear guard, capturing 180 cannon. Davout (less Caffarelli's division, detached to support Milhaud) was left to secure Vienna. A shortage of boats slowed Mortier's and Bernadotte's crossings.

Appreciating his peril, Kutusov left Bagration (8,000 Russians, 1,500 Austrian cavalry) in a narrow defile near Schöngraben (*D2*) to cover his right flank. Early on 15 November, Murat scattered the Austrian cavalry and began developing Bagration's position. Kutusov, who was still passing behind Bagration, sent one of Czar Alexander's aides-de-camp to Murat with a proposed capitulation: the French pursuit to be suspended, the Russians to withdraw into Poland. Biting on that specious offer, Murat halted his enveloping movement and referred the matter to Napoleon, then still south of the Danube at Schönbrünn. Kutusov made haste northward.

That afternoon, Davout's cavalry caught a courier from Charles, thus giving Napoleon his first definite idea of that Archduke's whereabouts. Quick calculation showed he could not reach Leoben (*C2*) before 24 November. Napoleon therefore cautioned Marmont to remain strictly on the defensive, and concentrated on overhauling Kutusov.

In the meantime, Baraguay had raided as far as Pilsen (*B3*), where he destroyed major supply depots. On his return he was ordered forward to Vienna, arriving there during 2–7 December.

In the Tyrol, Ney and the Bavarians had thoroughly broken up John's army. John, out of contact with Rohan and Jellacic and concerned over Massena's advance, began withdrawing eastward on the 14th. Rohan, infiltrating southward along mountain trails, escaped Ney. Jellacic, considering himself still part of Ferdinand's army, attempted to move northward. Part of his command (Wartensleben) slipped through; Jellacic and the rest of it blundered into Augereau and were gathered up.

Massena continued a lackadaisical pursuit of Charles, who had begun withdrawing from his position behind the Tagliamento (*B1*) on 12 November, on learning that John had escaped and that Marmont was moving south. Gouvion St.-Cyr had come north from Naples to take over the blockade of Venice.

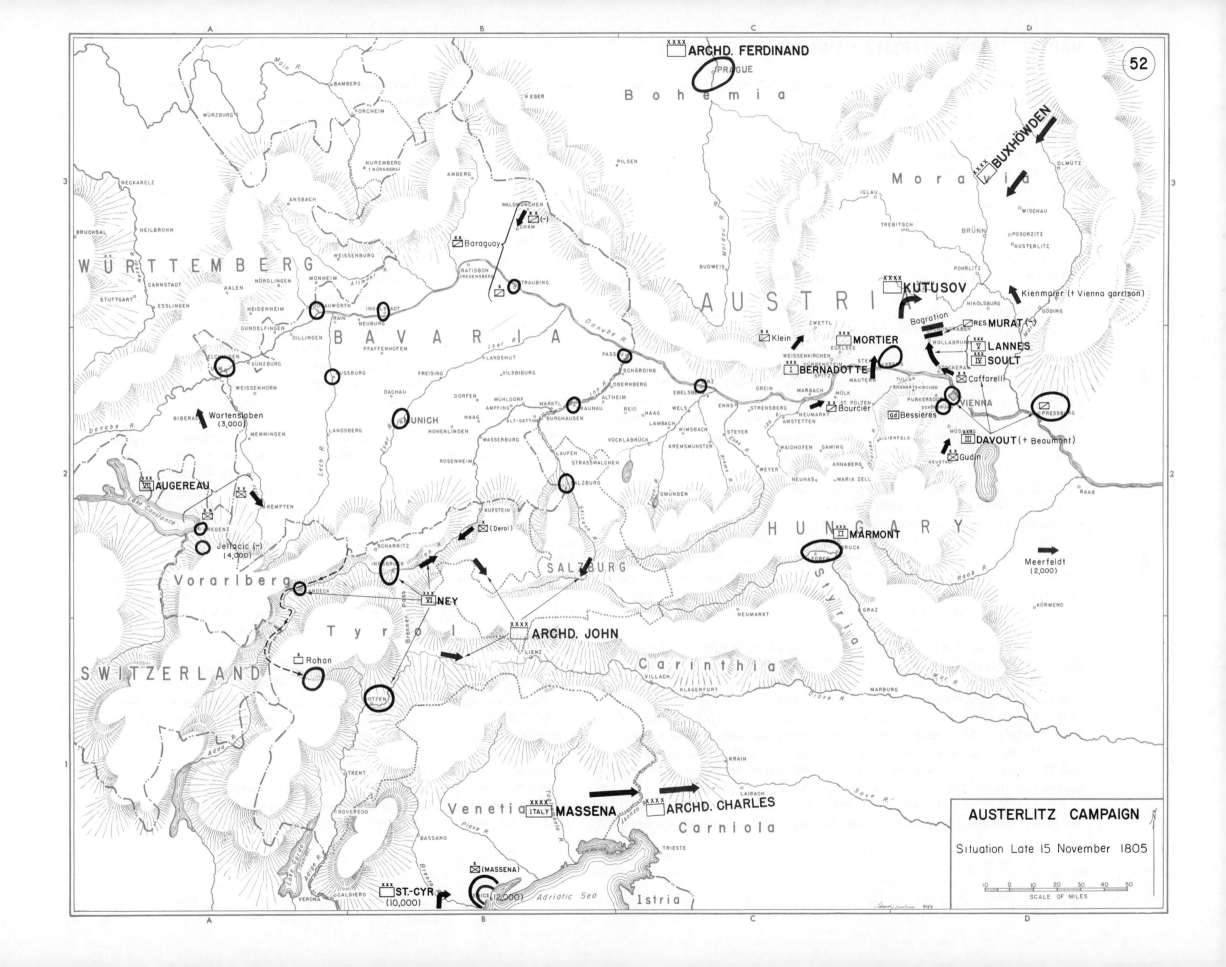

52

XXXX ARCHD. FERDINAND

Bohemia

PRAGUE

Moravia

XXXX BUXHÖWDEN

WÜRTTEMBERG

Main R.

BAMBERG
FORCHHEIM
NUREMBERG (†NÜRNBERG)
AMBERG
PILSEN
TREBITSCH
IGLAU
BRÜNN
OLMÜTZ
WISCHAU

WÜRZBURG
BRUCHSAL
NECKARELZ
HEILBRONN
ANSBACH
EGER
BUDWEIS
POHRLITZ
POSORZITZ
AUSTERLITZ
GÖDING

WEISSENBURG
WALDMÜNCHEN
XX (-) CHAM
XX Baraguay

NEUMARKT
NIKOLSBURG
Kienmaier (+ Vienna garrison)

STUTTGART
ESSLINGEN
CANNSTADT
AALEN
NÖRDLINGEN
MONHEIM
RATISBON (REGENSBURG)
STRAUBING
X

XXXX KUTUSOV
Bagration
ZWETTL
RES MURAT (-)

HEIDENHEIM
GÜNDELFINGEN
RAIN
NEUBURG
XX Klein
WEISSENKIRCHEN
MORTIER
EGELSEE
XXX V LANNES
XXX IV SOULT

BAVARIA
Danube R.
Iser R.
LANDSHUT
PFAFFENHOFEN
VILSBIBURG
SCHÄRDING
OBERNBERG
XXX I BERNADOTTE
SPITZ
MAUTERN
XX Caffarelli

ELCHINGEN
M
GÜNZBURG
DILLINGEN
AUGSBURG
FREISING
DACHAU
DORFEN
MÜHLDORF
Inn R.
GRIEZ
MÖLK
MARBACH
KREMS
TULLN
SIEGHARTSKIRCHEN
PURKERSDORF
SCHÖNBRUNN
VIENNA

WEISSENHORN
BIBERACH
Wartensleben (3,000)
MEMMINGEN
LANDSBERG
HAAG
AMPFING
BRAUNAU
REID
WELS
STRENGBERG
ST. PÖLTEN
XX Bourcier
NEUMARKT
Gd Bessières
XXX III DAVOUT (+ Beaumont)
PRESSBURG

Danube R.
ROSENHEIM
WASSERBURG
ALT-OETTING
BURGHAUSEN
LAMBACH
WIMSBACH
STEYER
KREMSMÜNSTER
WAIDHOFEN
GAMING
LILIENFELD
MÖDLING
HEUSTADT
Gudin

XXX VII AUGEREAU
XX KEMPTEN
KUFSTEIN
XX (Derol)
SCHARNITZ
SALZBURG
Salzach R.
SALZBURG
GMÜNDEN
STEYER
ANNABERG
MARIA ZELL
NEUHAS
HUNGARY
XXXX II MARMONT
ÖDENBURG

Lake Constance
XX
BREGENZ
Jellacic (-) (4,000)
Vorarlberg
INNSBRUCK
Inn R.
Brenner Pass
XXX VI NEY
SALZBURG
Meerfeldt (2,000)

Tyrol
XXXX ARCHD. JOHN
LIENZ
Carinthia
VILLACH
KLAGENFURT
Drave R.
GRAZ
Styria
MARBURG
KÖRMEND
Raab R.
RAAB

SWITZERLAND
X Rohan
BOTZEN
Adda R.
Adige R.
TRENT
KRAIN
Save R.
LAIBACH

ROVEREDO
BASSANO
Piave R.
XXXX ITALY MASSENA
XXXX ARCHD. CHARLES
Isonzo R.
Carniola
TRIESTE
Istria

ST-CYR (10,000)
XX (MASSENA)
(12,000)
Venetia
CALDIERO
VERONA
Adriatic Sea

AUSTERLITZ CAMPAIGN

Situation Late 15 November 1805

10 0 10 20 30 40 50
SCALE OF MILES

November 16 was filled with imperial wrath. Napoleon received the "capitulation" forwarded by Murat, and emphatically ordered him to attack at once. Bernadotte was harshly rebuked for his slowness in crossing the Danube. Augereau had not established contact with the Imperial headquarters: A letter to Ney directed him to "Find out whether he [Augereau] is alive or dead." For the rest, Ney was to turn the occupation of the Tyrol (*B1*) over to the Bavarians and join Marmont.

Napoleon then considered his logistical problems: His line of communication was reorganized as Strasbourg–Freudenstadt–Rottenburg–Ulm (*A2*)–Augsburg (*A2*)–Braunau (*B2*)–Vienna (*D2*). Vienna proved to be so crammed with weapons, ammunition, food, and equipment that only shoes and overcoats had to be brought forward from France. These were ordered expedited.

On receiving Napoleon's angry message, Murat attacked Bagration with his cavalry, the V Corps, and one division of the IV. Bagration fought a magnificent delaying action, finally breaking away after dark with about half of his division.

Napoleon joined his advance guard early the next morning (17 November), entering Znaym (*D3*) shortly after Murat had taken it (along with important supply depots). It was evident that Kutusov had escaped. The Grande Armee had been marching steadily since it left Boulogne. Its shoes, clothes, and weapons were in bad shape. The hungry marches eastward from the Inn River had left behind another swarm of stragglers and marauders that must be gathered up. Further pursuit could only draw him deeper into central Europe, without any certainty that he could force the enemy to give battle. Meanwhile, Prussia was taking an increasingly threatening attitude.

Napoleon decided to halt in a good position to resupply, reorganize, and rest. Brünn (*D3*) was his choice—a fortified road center, which would make a good offensive base. To put the best possible face on this decision, he took advantage of a letter just received from the Emperor Francis, then in Brünn. The French, Napoleon wrote in reply, would delay their advance so that Francis might evacuate Brünn unhurriedly.

Accordingly, the pursuit slowed, Lannes' corps even getting a day's rest. Bernadotte, leaving Rivaud's division at Znaym, turned northwest to watch Ferdinand. Mortier brought Gazan's and Dupont's battered divisions to Vienna, leaving Dumonceau at Krems. Murat mauled the Russian rear guard at Pohrlitz (*D3*) on the 18th, entering Brünn the next day. (Brünn, too, was full of supplies.) Momentarily, resistance stiffened. Scouting toward Olmütz (*D3*), Walther was almost overwhelmed by enemy cavalry. However, Murat and Bessieres came up with reinforcements, Bessieres personally leading a charge that rushed the enemy back through Wischau in disorder.

Reaching Wischau (*D3*) on 19 November, Kutusov had found Buxhöwden's advance guard and Lichtenstein's Austrian corps. Still considering his army too weak for a counteroffensive, he continued on to Olmütz, where Francis and Alexander had established their headquarters. These loyal allies were hardly brothers-in-arms. Russians sneered at Austrian skill and valor, and foraged and looted as if in enemy territory. Alexander was urging Prussia to honor a tentative agreement, which he recently had made with its King, Frederick William, whereby the Prussians would drive south through Bamberg (*A3*), while Charles advanced north through Munich (*B2*). Prussia, however, was at loggerheads with England over Hanover, sobered by Allied defeats, and anxious to learn what Napoleon would offer her *not* to fight. The Allies should have had little to lose by waiting until early December to see if Prussia actually would join them, since their own armies would increase steadily in the meantime. However, the Olmütz area was quickly "eaten up." No food could be secured from Hungary, because the Russians had stripped the country of horses. Furthermore, Kutusov held his troops in the open around Olmütz, allowing only headquarters in the city. Disease rapidly spread through the cold, hungry army. Kutusov then proposed retiring eastward into unforaged country, but was overruled by the Austrians and Alexander's staff.

A council of war (24 November) decided on an immediate counteroffensive. On 27 November, the Allies moved against Brünn, while Ferdinand advanced southward from Prague (*C3*).

Napoleon's central position between Iglau (*C3*) and Leoben (*C2*) gave plenty of maneuver room, allowing him to concentrate against either the archdukes or Kutusov—though it could become desperate if Prussia turned against him. However, he knew that the Prussian foreign minister, Haugwitz, was en route to see him, and so felt certain that Prussia was not yet ready for war. His immediate worry was the archdukes. On 22 November, he sent Massena specific orders to pursue Charles "without relaxation"; on the 24th, he sent Dumonceau to rejoin Marmont.

On 25 November, Austrian representatives presented themselves to Napoleon, professing a desire for serious negotiations. Suspecting that espionage was more likely to be their objective, he sent them to Vienna to consult Talleyrand. In return, he dispatched Savary to negotiate with the Czar—and to look over Olmütz.

On 28 November, during discussions with Haugwitz, Napoleon was informed that Bagration had driven Murat out of Wischau and that Soult's outpost line was under attack. He rode immediately to the outposts, where Savary brought him Alexander's reply (insultingly addressed to the "head of the French government"), and news that the whole Allied army was swarming down the road from Olmütz.

Elsewhere, Deroi took over the occupation of the Tyrol. Rohan had broken through Ney's screen at Bötzen (*B1*), but had been rounded up by St.-Cyr. Archdukes John and Charles had united on the 26th at Marburg (*D1*), where, thanks to Massena's lack of energy, they were able to rest and reorganize.

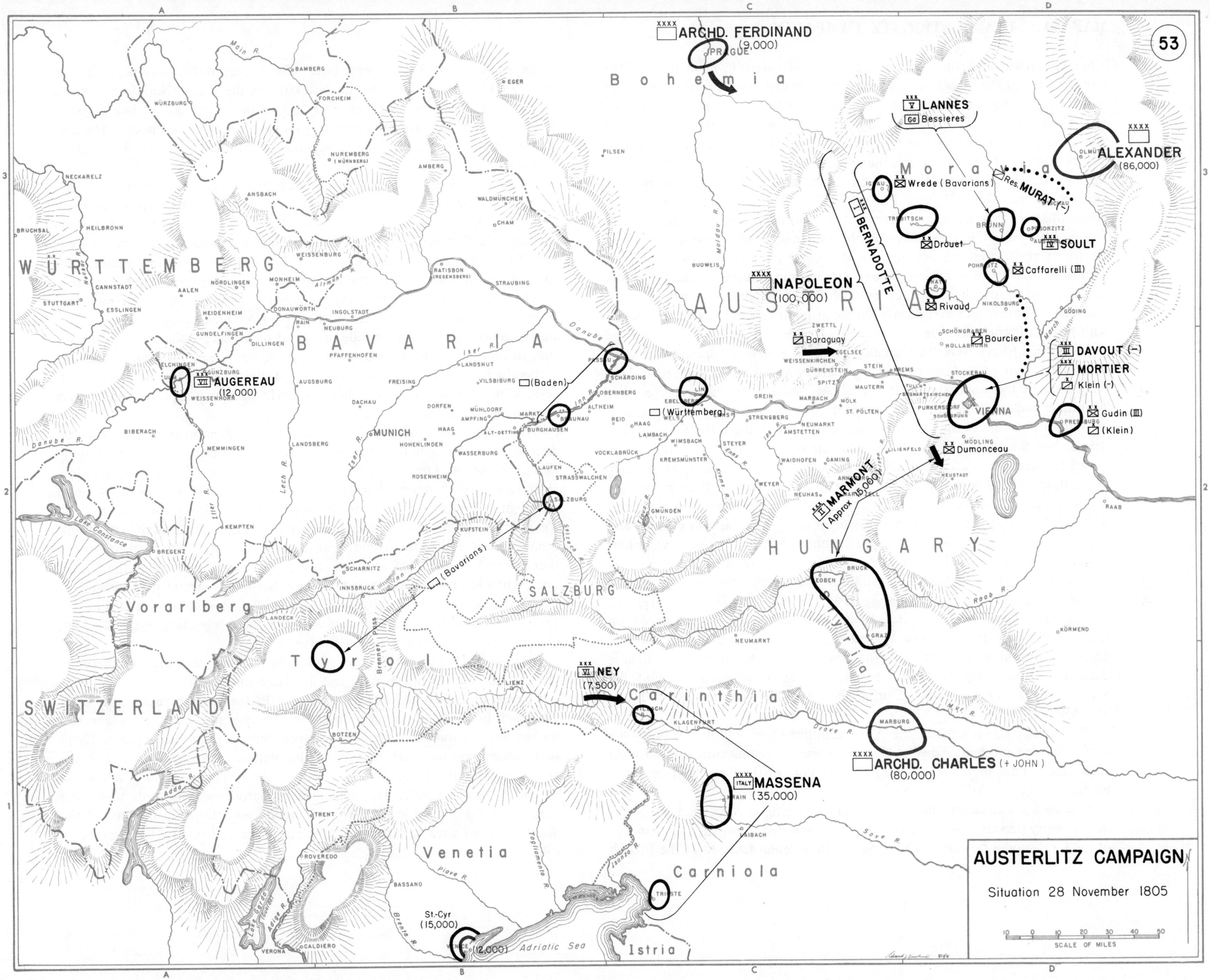

53

XXXX □ ARCHD. FERDINAND
PRAGUE (9,000)

B o h e m i a

XXX ▣ V LANNES
Gd Bessieres

XXXX ◯ ALEXANDER
OLMÜ (86,000)

M o r a v i a

☒ Wrede (Bavarians)   ▢ Res. MURAT (-)

XX
▣ II BERNADOTTE

☒ Drouet   BRÜNN   ☒ Caffarelli (III)

XXX
▣ IV SOULT

XXXX □ NAPOLEON
(100,000)

A U S T R I A

☒ Rivaud

XX
☒ Baraguay   ☒ Bourcier

SCHÖNGRABEN
HOLLABRUNN   NIKOLSBURG

XXX
▣ III DAVOUT (-)

XXX
▣ MORTIER

☒ Klein (-)

W Ü R T T E M B E R G

B A V A R I A

Danube

XXX ▣ VII AUGEREAU
GÜNZBURG (12,000)

□ (Baden)

SCHÄRDING   ☒ (Württemberg)

OBERNBERG   EBELSBERG   LINZ

MUNICH   BRAUNAU   BURGHAUSEN

VIENNA

☒ Gudin (III)
PRESBURG
☒ (Klein)

☒ Dumonceau

XXX
▣ MARMONT
(Approx 15,000)

H U N G A R Y

S A L Z B U R G

□ (Bavarians)

V o r a r l b e r g

T y r o l

S W I T Z E R L A N D

I l l y r i a

GRAZ

XXX ▣ VI NEY
(7,500)

C a r i n t h i a

KLAGENFURT

MARBURG

XXXX □ ARCHD. CHARLES (+ JOHN)
(80,000)

V e n e t i a

C a r n i o l a

XXXX ITALY MASSENA
(35,000)

TRIESTE

I s t r i a

St-Cyr
(15,000)

(2,000)   Adriatic Sea

AUSTERLITZ CAMPAIGN

Situation 28 November 1805

10 0 10 20 30 40 50
SCALE OF MILES

Since his arrival at Brünn (*A3*), Napoleon had carefully reconnoitered the terrain as far east as Wischau (*off map, D3*). He had not expected so early an Allied counteroffensive, but was determined to meet it. After receiving Savary's report, he sent him back—ostensibly, to request a personal interview with Alexander; actually, to observe the enemy. (The overconfident Allies allowed Savary to come and go through their lines.) That done, Napoleon ordered Murat and Soult to fall back behind Goldbach Brook (*B1–B2*), leaving only an outpost line along Pratzen Plateau (*C2*). Dumonceau was ordered to countermarch for Vienna, and Marmont warned to be ready to move north. It was 1900 on 28 November before Murat's and Soult's reports confirmed Savary's warning that this actually was the Allied counteroffensive. Napoleon then ordered Davout (divisions Friant, Gudin, and Bourcier) and Klein forward by forced marches; Mortier would hold the Vienna area with Dupont and Gazan; Bernadotte would leave Wrede at Iglau (*off map, A3*), and rejoin with his two French divisions.

The Allied forces were theoretically under the supreme command of Czar Alexander, who knew little of military matters and cared considerably less. Kutusov had the approximate status of Alexander's executive officer, but Alexander preferred the advice of the ignorant young members of his personal entourage, plus that of the Austrian staff officer, Weyrother. The French withdrawal had filled these empty heads with the conviction that Napoleon was afraid to accept battle and would fall back on Vienna. Consequently, they claimed, the Allied army should maneuver to its left, cut the French off from Vienna, and then drive them northward into the Bohemian mountains. The Allies had a slight degree of numerical superiority, especially in cavalry and artillery. Most of the Austrians (approximately 15,700), however, were new recruits, and few of the Russians had seen any serious service.

The Allies spent 29 November shifting their army south of the Brünn-Olmütz highway, Bagration standing fast at Raussnitz (*D3*) to cover the movement. Napoleon reconnoitered, and ordered a battery emplaced on Santon Hill (*C3*). He knew that Bernadotte and Davout could not rejoin him before 1 December. If attacked before they arrived, he intended to fight a delaying action along Goldbach Brook, retiring if necessary behind the Schwarzawa River (*A1–A3*). During the day, Caffarelli arrived and was attached to Lannes.

Throughout 30 November, the Allies continued their crablike sidle to the south. Roads were bad; Allied staff work worse. Columns continually fouled each other. That night, Kollowrat's corps—supposedly the Allied center—bivouacked on the Allies' extreme left.

Napoleon watched this movement carefully, riding even beyond his outermost cavalry pickets. During the day, Savary returned, bringing with him one of the Czar's aides-de-camp, whom Napoleon ordered detained at the French outposts. Alexander's terms were brief: The French might have peace if they evacuated Italy, Belgium, and the west bank of the Rhine. Napoleon rejected this offer, at the same time managing to give the impression of being deeply worried. Later, he gave the order to evacuate the Pratzen Plateau. His aim was the destruction of the Allied army, not an "ordinary" victory. The plateau was the bait to draw the Allies into his trap.

As he had calculated, the Allies—unable to resist the temptation to occupy this dominating terrain—halted their move to the south and turned westward, occupying the positions shown between 1500 and 0200. This change in direction further scrambled their formation: Kollowrat halted on Lichtenstein's right instead of his left; Kienmaier, blocked by converging columns, did not get into line until 2100—too late to reconnoiter the terrain to his front.

The French concentration was progressing rapidly. Napoleon now had more than 60,000 men massed on the left of his line, ready to maneuver in any direction. When Davout rode in, ahead of his corps, Napoleon instructed him to hold it well to the rear at Raigern Abbey (*A1*). The night was disturbed by Kienmaier's fruitless probings at Tellnitz (*B1*). Napoleon and Soult rode along the whole front, once narrowly escaping capture, but always acclaimed by their waiting troops.

The Allies had noted the fortification of the Santon, and had observed Bernadotte's arrival on the French left. Only a thin outpost line showed along Goldbach Brook. Obviously, Napoleon feared an attack down the Olmütz-Brünn highway; therefore, their plan to turn his right flank was sound. Around midnight, verbal attack orders were issued. At 0700, Docturov would attack Tellnitz; Langeron would advance between Tellnitz and Sokolnitz; Prschibitschewski and Kollowrat would seize Sokolnitz Castle. All of them would thereafter wheel half-right, attacking toward Turas (*B2*) to roll up the French line. When Docturov had cleared Tellnitz, Kienmaier would pass through to block the Vienna-Brünn highway. Meanwhile, Bagration would pin the French left in position; Lichtenstein would connect Bagration and Kollowrat; Constantine would constitute the reserve.

Because of language difficulties, this plan probably was only indifferently understood. Written orders were not available until 0800.

The terrain here is dominated by Pratzen Plateau, which rises gently from Goldbach Brook to fall rather abruptly into the Littawa River. Napoleon had his headquarters on an isolated hill between Bellowitz and Schlappanitz (*both B2*), which gave an excellent view of the plateau. The northern part of the area was generally favorable for cavalry action. There was a small wood around Sokolnitz Castle, and numerous orchards and vineyards along the streams. A slight thaw left the ground muddy and slippery, and turned the marshy-banked streams into obstacles. The lakes and ponds, however, were still frozen.

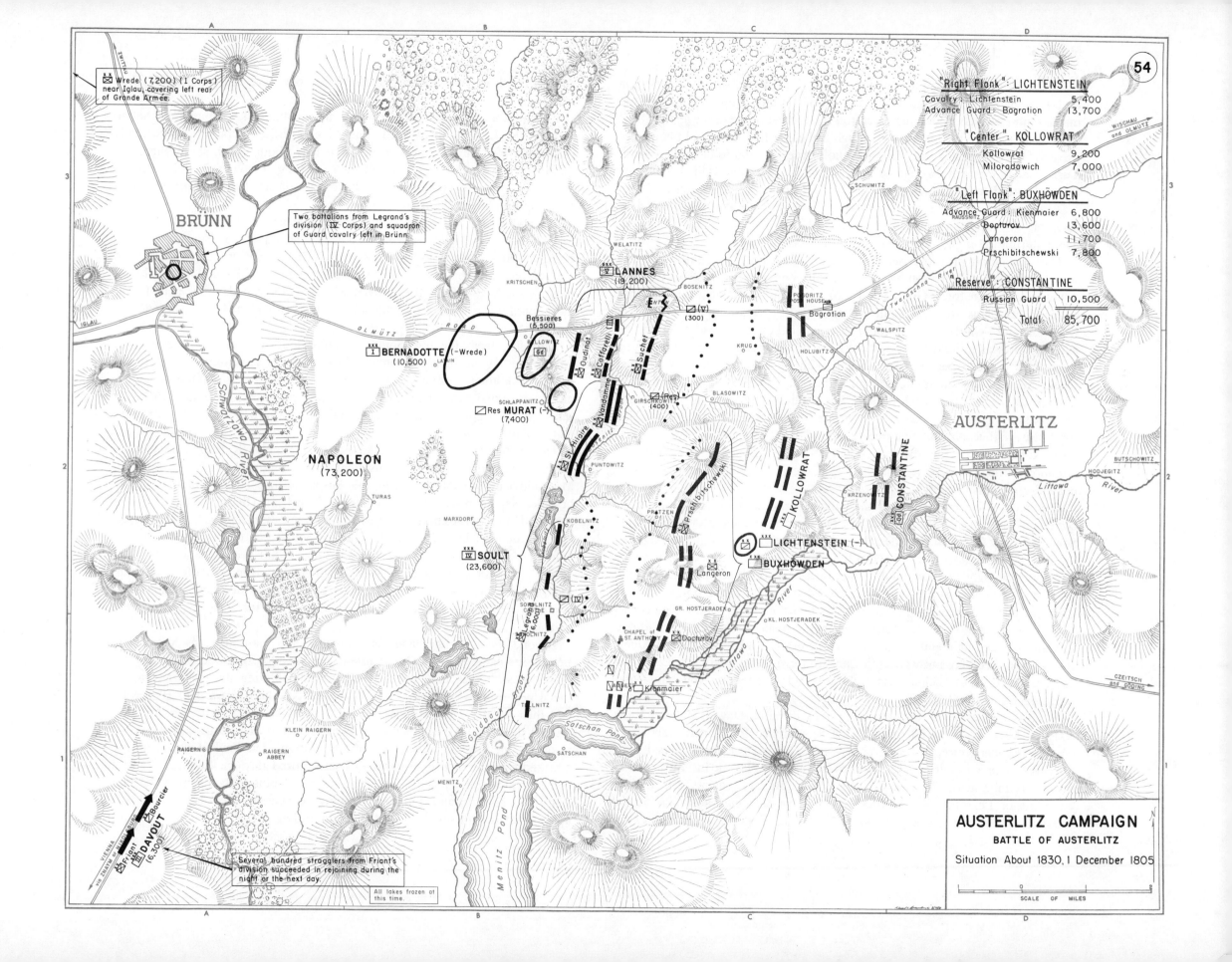

54

"Right Flank" LICHTENSTEIN

Cavalry: Lichtenstein — 5,400
Advance Guard: Bagration — 13,700

"Center" KOLLOWRAT

Kollowrat — 9,200
Miloradowich — 7,000

"Left Flank" BUXHÖWDEN

Advance Guard: Kienmaier — 6,800
Docturov — 13,600
Langeron — 11,700
Prschibitschewski — 7,800

"Reserve" CONSTANTINE

Russian Guard — 10,500

Total — 85,700

BRÜNN

Two battalions from Legrand's division (IV Corps) and squadron of Guard cavalry left in Brünn.

LANNES (19,200)

Bessieres (5,500)

BERNADOTTE (-Wrede) (10,500)

Res MURAT (-) (7,400)

NAPOLEON (73,200)

SOULT (23,600)

AUSTERLITZ

KOLLOWRAT

CONSTANTINE

LICHTENSTEIN (-)

BUXHÖWDEN

Langeron

Docturov

Kienmaier

Several hundred stragglers from Friant's division succeeded in rejoining during the night or the next day.

DAVOUT (6,300)
Bourcier
Friant

All lakes frozen at this time.

AUSTERLITZ CAMPAIGN

BATTLE OF AUSTERLITZ

Situation About 1830, 1 December 1805

SCALE OF MILES

Napoleon's original conception of the Allies' plan—based on his observation that they had left a strong force astride the Brünn-Olmütz highway and massed most of their remaining forces on the Pratzen Plateau—was that their enveloping attack would be made through Kobelnitz (*B2*). He had planned to leave only one brigade in the Tellnitz-Sokolnitz sector, and to move Davout to Turas (*B2*), where he would be well placed to strike the Allied left flank as it advanced from Kobelnitz. Napoleon's orders had been issued at 2030, 1 December. The marshals (except Davout, who must be at Raigern) were to assemble at Napoleon's headquarters at 0730 on the 2d, in case developments during the night made new orders necessary.

The precaution proved wise. Kienmaier's fumblings at Tellnitz, and the sound of troops shifting southward, gradually convinced Napoleon that the Allies intended to force Goldbach Brook south of Kobelnitz. He therefore changed his plans slightly. Soult would leave Legrand's division between Kobelnitz and Tellnitz. Davout would march on Sokolnitz instead of Turas; his new mission was to hold the lower crossings of Goldbach Brook, and he was warned he could expect no help. Soult, with his two remaining divisions, would make the the main effort toward Pratzen, with Bernadotte in support. Lannes (less Oudinot) would deliver a secondary attack along the Brünn-Olmütz highway. Murat would form an elastic link between the two attacks, supporting either one as required. Legrand's left brigade would advance from Kobelnitz to cover the right flank of Soult's attack. The Guard and Oudinot formed the reserve. The plan was nicely calculated; success would depend upon exact timing.

Daybreak, 2 December, found the valleys curtained with fog, which concealed the advance of the French left and center to their attack positions. Sometime after 0630, Buxhöwden thrust Kienmaier's Austrian infantry against Tellnitz. An hour later, the French still held the village. Soult's corps cavalry, screening the right flank of Soult's still-concealed corps, advanced down the east bank from Kobelnitz against Buxhöwden's right flank, but was overwhelmed and driven back. Its commander had the wit to send an officer to warn Davout. At 0830, Docturov put in a Russian brigade, which drove Legrand's defending regiment back across the brook. Unhappily for the Allies, Buxhöwden then chose to wait until Langeron had taken Sokolnitz. Langeron had been blocked by Lichtenstein (who was trying to detour Kollowrat) and could not attack until 0800.

Because of the exhausted state of Friant's division, Davout did not leave Raigern Abbey until about 0630. Then he marched for Turas, Napoleon's change of orders, directing him on Sokolnitz, having somehow missed him. However, Soult's cavalry officer soon overtook him; Davout instantly turned toward Tellnitz at the double. Friant's leading brigade regained the village, but some of Legrand's troops fired into it from the rear, mistaking it for Russians in the fog. In the resulting confusion, Docturov and Kienmaier regained Tellnitz and got across the brook, but were again halted by Buxhöwden.

Langeron and Prschibitschewski had finally attacked Sokolnitz and Sokolnitz Castle. Legrand held hard, but Allied artillery superiority eventually made itself felt. Both places were carried at about 0900. Even then, the jamming of Allied columns slowed their crossing. Leaving Bourcier and an infantry brigade to contain the Tellnitz bridgehead, Davout hurried north, breaking into Sokolnitz at about 1000.

Meanwhile, the battle was being won elsewhere. At 0730, Soult, Lannes, Murat, and Bernadotte were at Napoleon's headquarters. Sunrise—a little before 0800—confirmed Napoleon's judgment. Though fog and smoke filled the low ground, the hilltops were clear, and he could see Allied columns moving southward from the Pratzen Plateau. He waited about a half-hour more, until it was evident that the Allies were well engaged. Then he released Soult.

Emerging from the fog, Soult's two divisions moved up the slope: St. Hilaire guiding on the high ground behind Pratzen, Vandamme on the dominating peak about a mile north. Kollowrat was following Prschibitschewski, his forces in two parallel columns: Austrians on the left, Miloradovich's Russians on the right. For security, he had sent two battalions into Pratzen. Kutusov rode with him.

The battalions in Pratzen collapsed immediately. Kutusov shouted for Miloradovich to form front to his right flank, for the Austrians to form on Miloradovich's left. Momentarily, the Austrians checked St. Hilaire's leading brigade. Napoleon sent six 12-pounders forward; St. Hilaire's second brigade appeared. Kollowrat charged with his Austrians, was repulsed, and charged again, supported by a Russian brigade from the rear of Prschibitschewski's column. For a moment, the decision swayed—5,000 French to 8,000 Allies. Then, Vandamme plowed through Miloradovich's division. The Russians ran; the Austrians followed. The French offensive swept forward again, Vandamme's left-flank brigade swinging wide around the central peak of the plateau.

Beyond them, Lannes and Bagration sparred cautiously, as Murat and Bernadotte came forward. Lichtenstein, entangled with Kollowrat and Langeron, was late reaching his assigned position. Noting the resulting gap in the Allied front, Constantine had hurried a battalion forward to Blasowitz, and then led the entire Russian Guard forward to support it, thereby committing the whole Allied reserve. Lichtenstein, hurrying northward, now had to detour the Russian Guard to reach Bagration's left flank. Once there, he attacked some French light cavalry. These retired through Lannes' infantry, which formed squares and wrecked his charge. Kutusov then summoned him south to oppose Vandamme's enveloping movement. He obeyed, but left approximately half his command with Bagration.

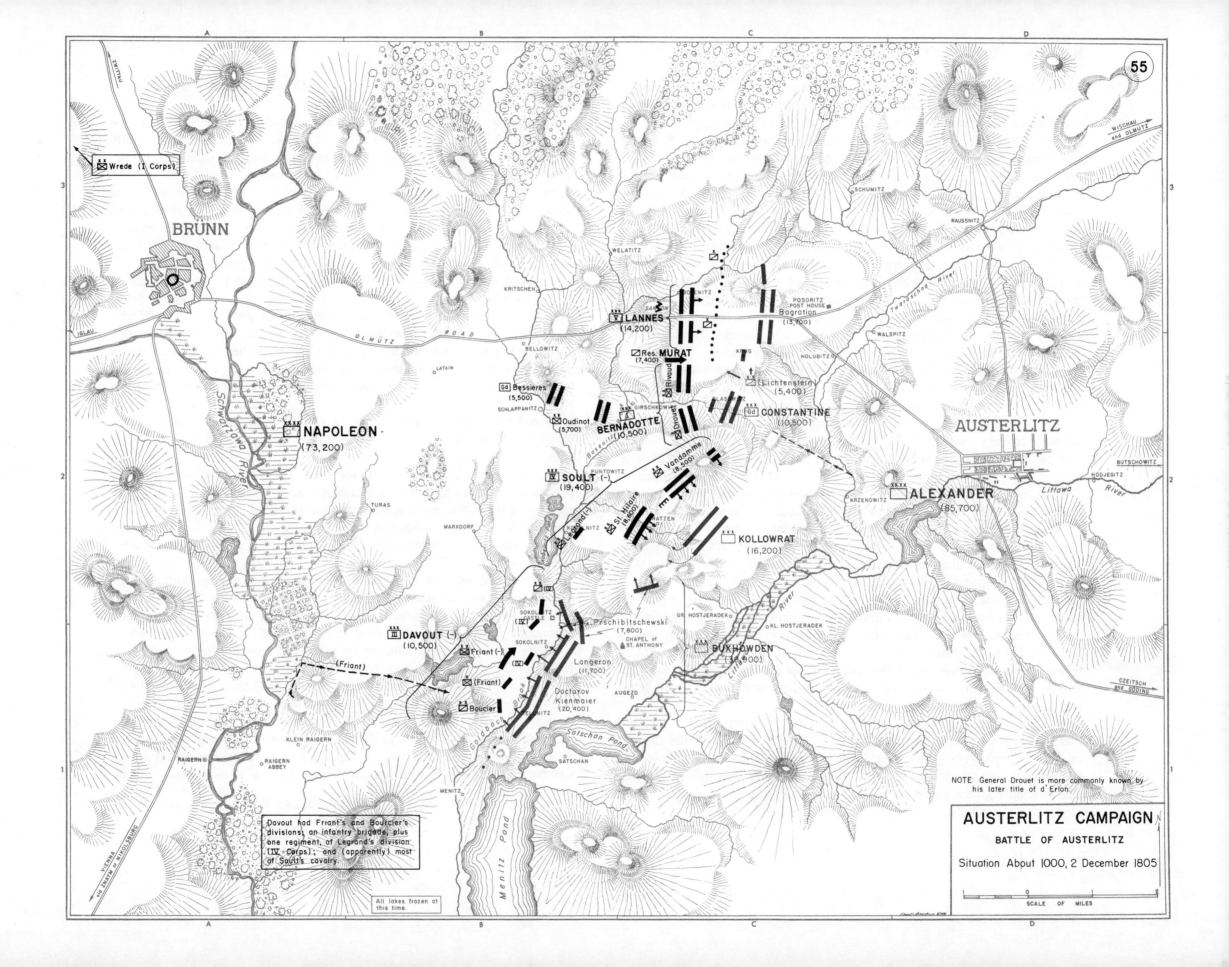

55

Wrede (I Corps)

BRUNN

XXX V LANNES
(14,200)

Bagration
(13,700)

Res. MURAT
(7,400)

Rivaud

(Lichtenstein)
(5,400)

Gd Bessieres
(5,500)

Gd CONSTANTINE
(10,500)

Oudinot
(5,700)

BERNADOTTE
(10,500)

AUSTERLITZ

NAPOLEON
(73,200)

Vandamme
(8,500)

XXX IV SOULT (-)
(19,400)

ALEXANDER
(85,700)

Legrand(-)
St. Hilaire
(8,500)

XXX KOLLOWRAT
(16,200)

(IV)

DAVOUT (-)
(10,500)

SOKOLNITZ
CASTLE (IV)

Przibitschewski
(7,800)

XXX BUXHÖWDEN
(29,000)

Friant (-)
SOKOLNITZ (IV)

CHAPEL OF
ST. ANTHONY

(Friant)

Langeron
(11,700)

(Friant)

Docturov
Kienmaier
(20,400)

Bourcier

Satschan Pond

NOTE: General Drouet is more commonly known by
his later title of d'Erlon.

Davout had Friant's and Bourcier's
divisions; an infantry brigade, plus
one regiment, of Legrand's division
(IV Corps); and (apparently) most
of Soult's cavalry

AUSTERLITZ CAMPAIGN

BATTLE OF AUSTERLITZ

Situation About 1000, 2 December 1805

All lakes frozen at
this time.

SCALE OF MILES

On the French right flank, Davout fought Langeron and Prschibitschewski to a standstill around Sokolnitz, the town changing hands repeatedly. The one definite result was that the Allied left wing—though outnumbering the defenders by more than four to one—remained jammed in the Sokolnitz and Tellnitz crossings, unable to deploy and exploit its superiority.

In the center, Soult's attack and Lichtenstein's wanderings had left the Russian Guard unsupported, to be roughly heckled by Caffarelli's skirmishers. (Being parade troops only, they were too stiff to meet such tactics.) Rivaud's division then stormed Blasowitz; the Russian Guard counterattacked, but was defeated by Rivaud and Caffarelli. At about 1100, Kutusov ordered the guard infantry toward the center of the plateau, but here it met Vandamme, who drove it off toward Krzenowitz. The Russian Guard cavalry, however, pounced on and scattered Vandamme's isolated left-flank brigade.

This success was only momentary. Napoleon had already sent Bernadotte forward to clear Vandamme's left flank. Now he dispatched Bessieres with the cavalry of the Imperial Guard to rescue the broken brigade. After several charges, a final one—led by Rapp, one of Napoleon's aides-de-camp—rode over the Russian horsemen, capturing their commander and their horse artillery. Lichtenstein was caught in the debacle; at the sight of Bernadotte's bayonets, the guard infantry went streaming back through Austerlitz, while Rivaud's artillery bombarded them from the eastern edge of Pratzen Plateau.

Around 1000, Bagration had attempted to turn Lannes' left flank. (Despite their great superiority in light cavalry, the Allies failed to mass it here.) The Russians got into Bosenitz, but were stopped there by the Santon battery, French skirmishing tactics, and the resolute action of French light cavalry. Galled by the heavier Russian artillery, Lannes counterattacked. Bagration's cavalry and the squadrons left by Lichtenstein repeatedly, but unsuccessfully, assailed Caffarelli's division. Murat then threw Nansouty's cuirassiers against their flank, stampeding them into the rout pouring through Austerlitz. Bagration fought stoutly, but eventually retired just beyond Posoritz, where he stood off an attack by Murat. Lannes then rapidly mounted a coordinated attack, massing eighteen guns north of the highway to enfilade Bagration's line. The Russians broke, and could not be rallied short of Raussnitz (D3). It was now dusk; uncertain of the results of the main attack, Murat halted pursuit. Bagration retired south through Austerlitz, leaving the Olmütz highway and the Allied trains unguarded.

The main assault, meanwhile, had swept to the south edge of Pratzen Plateau by 1100. Here, Napoleon halted it until the results of the fighting on his left flank were clear. Shortly after 1300, he ordered its resumption: St. Hilaire would attack toward Sokolnitz Castle; Vandamme toward Augezd. The interval between their two divisions would be filled by a regiment from Legrand, one of Oudinot's brigades, and Beaumont. (Oudinot's other brigade

apparently was sent down the west bank of Goldbach Brook.) The Imperial Guard massed near Saint Anthony's Chapel.

This attack came down irresistibly on the milling Allies. Almost at the same time, Davout counterattacked all along his front. In less than thirty minutes, Prschibitschewski's and Langeron's divisions were shattered, Prschibitschewski being captured with most of the survivors. Buxhöwden concentrated on saving himself. A crowd of fugitives fell back on Docturov and Kienmaier, who checked Soult momentarily by massing thirty-six guns around Tellnitz and showing a firm front. The only escape route left was the strip of land between Satschen and Menitz ponds. Kienmaier crossed first with his cavalry, taking a position east of Satschen Pond to oppose any further advance by Vandamme. The infantry began to follow, but the massed artillery of the IV Corps and the Imperial Guard literally blew them away. Many were drowned when the ice of Menitz Pond broke under them. St. Hilaire ended this last stand by storming Tellnitz, while Davout pushed through Menitz. Only some 7,500 Allied troops could be rallied, with the greatest difficulty, on this wing, even though Kienmaier's cavalry covered their retreat gallantly. (Generally speaking, the Austrian recruits did better than the Russian veterans.)

French losses were approximately 2,000 killed and 7,000 wounded. The Allies lost 15,000 killed and wounded, 11,000 prisoners, 45 flags, and 180 guns.

The battle ended in snow, extreme cold, and early darkness, with the French too exhausted for an immediate pursuit. Furthermore, the complete collapse of the Allied army made its principal line of flight uncertain, especially as the snow soon blurred its tracks.

Napoleon spent the night at Posoritz (C3). Francis and Alexander halted briefly at Hodjegitz (D2), then fled southeast into Hungary. Before daybreak on 3 December, an Austrian representative reached Napoleon with Francis' request for a personal interview. Napoleon granted it for 4 December, and immediately launched a pursuit. Murat and Lannes took the Olmütz road; Bernadotte and Soult moved on Göding (off map, D1); Davout marched on the same town by a road more to the south, picking up Gudin and Klein en route. On reaching Wischau (off map, D3), Murat decided that he was following a cold trail and turned south, sending Walther on toward Olmütz to gather up the Allied trains. On the 4th, Napoleon and Francis agreed on an armistice, which would be extended to the Russians on condition that they withdrew to their own territory. (Meanwhile, Davout overtook the shattered Russian army. He spared it only on Kutusov's pledged word and Alexander's written statement—both undoubtedly false—that the Russians had already concluded an armistice.)

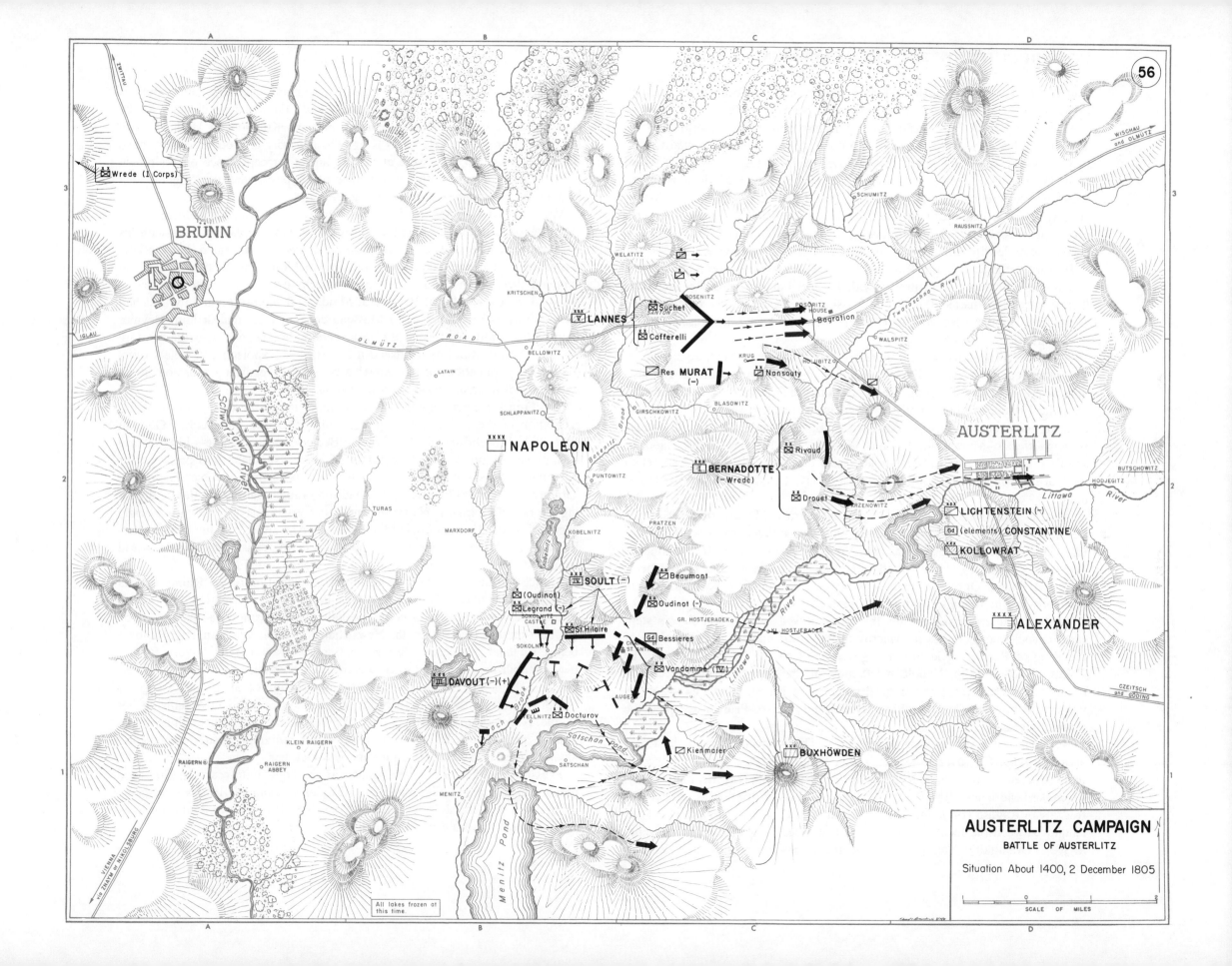

56

BRÜNN

ZWITTAU

WISCHAU and OLMÜTZ

WELATITZ

☒ Suchet

LANNES

☒ Cafferelli

Res MURAT (-)

KRUG

☒ Nansouty

☒ Bagration

PÖSORITZ HOUSE

TWORSCHNA River

WALSPITZ

RAUSSNITZ

SCHUMITZ

OLMÜTZ ROAD

KRITSCHEN

BELLOWITZ

LATEIN

SCHLAPPANITZ

BOSENITZ

ROSENITZ

HOLUBITZ

BLASOWITZ

GIRSCHKOWITZ

PUNTOWITZ

NAPOLEON

BERNADOTTE (-Wrede)

☒ Rivaud

☒ Drouet

STERZENOWITZ

AUSTERLITZ

Littawa River

BUTSCHOWITZ

HODJEGITZ

☒ LICHTENSTEIN (-)

Gd (elements) CONSTANTINE

☒ KOLLOWRAT

TURAS

MARXDORF

KOBELNITZ

Kobelnitz Pond

Bosenitz Brook

PRATZEN

GR. HOSTJERADEK

Kl. HOSTJERADEK

ALEXANDER

☒ Beaumont

SOULT (-)

☒ (Oudinot)

☒ Legrand (-)

SOKOLNITZ CASTLE

☒ St. Hilaire

SOKOLNITZ

☒ Oudinot (-)

Gd Bessieres

☒ Vandamme (IV)

Littawa River

DAVOUT (-)(+)

Goldbach Brook

TELLNITZ

☒ Docturov

AUGER

MENITZ

Satschan Pond

SATSCHAN

☒ Kienmaier

BUXHÖWDEN

CZEITSCH and GÖDING

SCHWARTZAWA River

IGLAU

KLEIN RAIGERN

RAIGERN

RAIGERN ABBEY

Menitz Pond

VIENNA via ZNAIM or NIKOLSBURG

Wrede (1 Corps)

All lakes frozen at this time.

AUSTERLITZ CAMPAIGN

BATTLE OF AUSTERLITZ

Situation About 1400, 2 December 1805

SCALE OF MILES

INTRODUCTION TO THE JENA CAMPAIGN

The Franco-Austrian armistice relieved Wrede, who had been driven out of Iglau (*C2*) on 5 December. (*Map references pertain to Map 57.*)

Meanwhile, the Allies' diversionary operations had trailed miserably away. The French had evacuated Hanover (*B3*), except for a few garrisoned towns. Prussia, which had long lusted for Hanover, immediately occupied it. Gustavus IV, the insane King of Sweden, withdrew his contingent in anger over Prussian interference. The British largely confined their activity to enlisting Hanoverians—which incensed the Prussians. The Russians came late and proved useless. The French garrisons held out. An improvised Franco-Dutch army, assembled in Holland for emergencies, saw little service.

In Naples, the British and Russians had been received as liberators, Naples denouncing her treaty of neutrality with France. Lack of transport and conflicting objectives halted this Anglo-Russian offensive slightly north of the Neapolitan frontier. Here and in Hanover, news of Austerlitz caused a hasty re-embarkation.

While peace negotiations continued, Napoleon strengthened, re-equipped, and retrained his army, making lavish use of Austrian resources. He also negotiated a Franco-Prussian treaty of alliance (Treaty of Schönbrünn) with the Prussian foreign minister (then in Vienna), providing for Prussia to have Hanover, but to cede Ansbach to Bavaria and two tiny Rhineland principalities to Murat and Berthier. France was to have a free hand in southern Germany and Italy. Napoleon also promoted his allies: The "electors" of Bavaria and Württemberg became kings; the Duke of Baden, a grand duke.

Austria protestingly accepted Napoleon's terms (Treaty of Pressburg). Besides paying a huge war indemnity, she was obliged to cede the Tyrol (*B1*) and minor enclaves to Bavaria; Venetia, Friaul (*both B1*), Dalmatia, and Istria (*both C1*) to the Kingdom of Italy; and minor areas to Württemberg and Baden. Once the treaty was signed, the French evacuated Austria gradually, as the treaty's provisions were executed.

Political-military developments thereafter moved swiftly. Napoleon's stepson Eugene, who served as his viceroy in Italy, was married to a daughter of the King of Bavaria. The Prussian government having refused to ratify the Treaty of Schönbrünn, Napoleon left most of the Grande Armee in central Germany, where it put psychological pressure on Prussia, and the cost of its upkeep on his own German allies. By February 1806, Prussia accepted the original terms.

Relations with Austria soon deteriorated. The Austrians turned the Kotor area (*off map, C1*) over to Russia, rather than to France. Napoleon accordingly ordered Berthier to halt along the Inn River and hold Braunau (*B2*). To make head against the Russian expansion in the Adriatic, he ordered the free city of Ragusa (*off map, C1*), occupied. The French in Ragusa were soon caught between the local tribes and a Russian fleet, but held until Marmont arrived. Eventually, Talleyrand negotiated a peace treaty with a Russian ambassador.

Meanwhile, a change of government in England increased hopes for an Anglo-French peace, although Napoleon badly damaged its chances at the start by converting the Dutch Republic into the Kingdom of Holland, with his younger brother, Louis, as its King. The sincerity on both sides may have been imperfect, but both were at least willing to accept peace on their own terms. Unfortunately, both were expanding empires, and the original idea became lost in wrangles over Sicily and colonies.

Massena had been sent to deal with Naples, where Napoleon decreed that the degenerate Bourbon rulers had "ceased to reign," replacing them with his older brother, Joseph. The regular Neapolitan forces evaporated, but the lawless interior provinces soon broke out in rebellion. The British armed and supplied them, even landing an expeditionary force under Stewart. Stewart defeated the overconfident Reynier at Maida (*off map, C1*) in July, but had to withdraw in September when Massena concentrated against him. Reynier then methodically suppressed the insurrection, but vicious guerrilla warfare smoldered until Murat extinguished it in 1808–9. Napoleon completely overlooked the implications of this guerrilla resistance, regarding it as something to be put down harshly by second-line troops.

The French Emperor's interest that summer lay in the creation of a "Confederation of the Rhine"—a major grouping of south and central German states, which would be allied to France. Because most of these—like Bavaria—had been originally under Austria's influence, Napoleon was prepared for Austrian protests, but Francis bowed to the temporarily inevitable. The nation actually angered was Prussia, which had long-range plans of gradually digesting the rest of Germany. Napoleon knew that his Prussian "ally" was already negotiating secretly with England and Russia. Alexander, sulking over Austerlitz, and developing the theory that he had a divine mission to free the world from despotism, refused to ratify the peace treaty with France.

France had invited Saxony to join the Confederation of the Rhine. Prussia demanded that it become part of a "league of north German states," which Prussia was setting up as a counterweight. The Prussian war party, led by Queen Louise, gained strength. News that Napoleon was dangling Hanover before England as a peace offering was the last straw. On 10 August, Prussia began mobilizing, intending to coax Saxony into alliance by overrunning her. On 26 September, Prussia threw down an ultimatum: all French troops to withdraw west of the Rhine; Prussia to have a free hand in organizing her league; Napoleon to evacuate several disputed Rhineland principalities immediately; negotiations to begin at once on all remaining issues; Napoleon's answer to reach Prussian headquarters by 8 October.

Prussia knew her ultimatum meant war, without quite realizing she stood alone. England might offer money, but England's available troops were being squandered unsuccessfully in Buenos Aires. The Royal Navy could not help. Russian support would be calculated—and slow.

The Jena Campaign

"A general should say to himself many times a day: If the hostile army were to make its appearance to my front, on my right, or on my left, what should I do? And if he is embarrassed, his arrangements are bad; there is something wrong; he must rectify his mistake." —NAPOLEON

"The art of war is like everything else that is beautiful and simple. The simplest moves are the best." —NAPOLEON

Prussia's ultimatum finally reached Napoleon on 7 October at Bamberg (*B2*). He had been slow to believe that Prussia would deliberately choose war. Since Frederick the Great's death, Prussian foreign policy had resembled the buzzard more than the eagle. Consequently, Napoleon had calculated that Prussia would appraise the world situation realistically and give up Hanover. Napoleon could then use Hanover to buy peace with England, indemnifying Prussia with other German territory.

Prussia, however, still suffered an uneasy, periodic hangover from the glories of Frederick the Great. Avid of further territorial expansion and prestige, her rulers reacted with unthinking arrogance. King Frederick William III was young and well intentioned, but mentally slow and irresolute. His vigorous wife, Louise, had long demanded war. Prussian national spirit, however, had ebbed. The army had become completely detached from the civilian population, which was concerned only with its own comforts.

The army itself was largely a parade-ground façade, composed in large part of mercenaries, both officers and men. Prussian enlisted men were drafted exclusively from the lower classes; for reasons of economy, they were placed on leave most of the year, being recalled only for emergencies or minimum training. Pay, food, and clothing were scant; discipline harsh; training little more than close-order drill. The supply system depended on an elaborate system of depots and supply trains. Soldiers were accustomed to regular delivery of rations and firewood; units were encumbered by amazing amounts of baggage. The officers generally were educated and hard-working, but old for their grades, drowned in inconsequential minutiae, and disdainfully ignorant of modern warfare. The few who had observed French operations had misinterpreted the lessons involved. For example, just as the campaign opened, the army was organized into divisions—but these were divisions of all arms, such as the French had abandoned in 1800. A few young officers, led by Scharnhorst, had urged reforms, but these had usually been squelched in the sacred names of economy and Frederick the Great.

Prussia's greatest weakness was the complete lack of unity of command. In theory, nothing could be done except on the King's order or with his consent. Frederick William, however, had exaggerated respect for his aging generals. The generals had a weakness for frequent councils of war, at which each aired his views at great length. Sometimes it became difficult to discover who was actually in command and what plan had been adopted.

Finally, the Prussian plan for mobilization was unrealistic. On paper, including garrison troops and militia, 225,000 men were available. Prussia was the aggressor and so had the initiative. Her flanks were covered by neutral Austria and the sea. At her back were Sweden and Russia. Therefore, she should have been able to mass 200,000 men for her offensive. Instead, the routine dispositions shown here were followed. Some 90,000 men were immobilized in various garrisons, yet no effort was made to put these fortresses on a wartime footing. Thoughtful officers remembered that the Prussian Army had performed poorly even during Frederick the Great's last campaigns, and again in 1792–93.

During early 1806, Napoleon had concentrated on his administrative and diplomatic problems, leaving army matters largely to Berthier and the marshals. Early reports of Prussian fury he disregarded. But Alexander's rejection of the Franco-Russian peace treaty suggested grimmer possibilities. Accordingly, he notified Berthier on 5 September to prepare orders for a concentration around Bamberg, and to dispatch engineer officers to reconnoiter roads leading toward Berlin (*B3*). There was no urgency in this order: "I have no operation planned against Berlin," he wrote. On 13 September, however, Napoleon warned Prussia that an invasion of Saxony would be cause for war. Six days later, learning that the Prussians had moved anyhow, he started his Guard eastward from Paris, he himself following on the 25th.

He now commanded the forces of France, Holland, the Confederation of the Rhine, and most of Italy. Spain was still an ally, though increasingly ready to stab France in the back at the first opportunity. Confronting him were England, Prussia, Russia, Sweden, and Portugal. Austria declared herself neutral, but would be quick to take advantage of a French defeat. Hence, she was to be neither irritated nor trusted. Saxony had been clubbed into becoming Prussia's ally. Hesse-Kassel favored Prussia, but stayed fearfully neutral. Turkey, angered by constant Russian aggression and English hostility, had left the Allies. (Aided by General Sebastiani, the French ambassador, the Turks were to inflict a humiliating defeat on a British fleet in the Dardanelles during February 1807. A British attempt to occupy northern Egypt later that same year also failed.)

The Grande Armee had been repeatedly alerted for return to France, only to have some new emergency postpone this anticipated event. Consequently, except for Davout and Soult, the marshals had paid little attention to discipline and training. Morale was good, but there were serious shortages of equipment, money, and transportation. Napoleon's secondary theaters were held by minimum forces. Louis was to defend Holland, keep Hesse-Kassel neutral, and distract the Prussian command. Eugene would watch Austria; Marmont would check Russian operations in Dalmatia. The Rhine fortresses and the coasts were held by elite National Guard units, limited-service veterans, and naval troops.

During this period, Napoleon was extremely careful to avoid actions which might enable the Prussians to accuse him of aggression. His real thoughts remain unknown, but he gave every indication of hoping to prevent this war.

Note: On the map, Ruchel *(B3) should be* Rüchel.

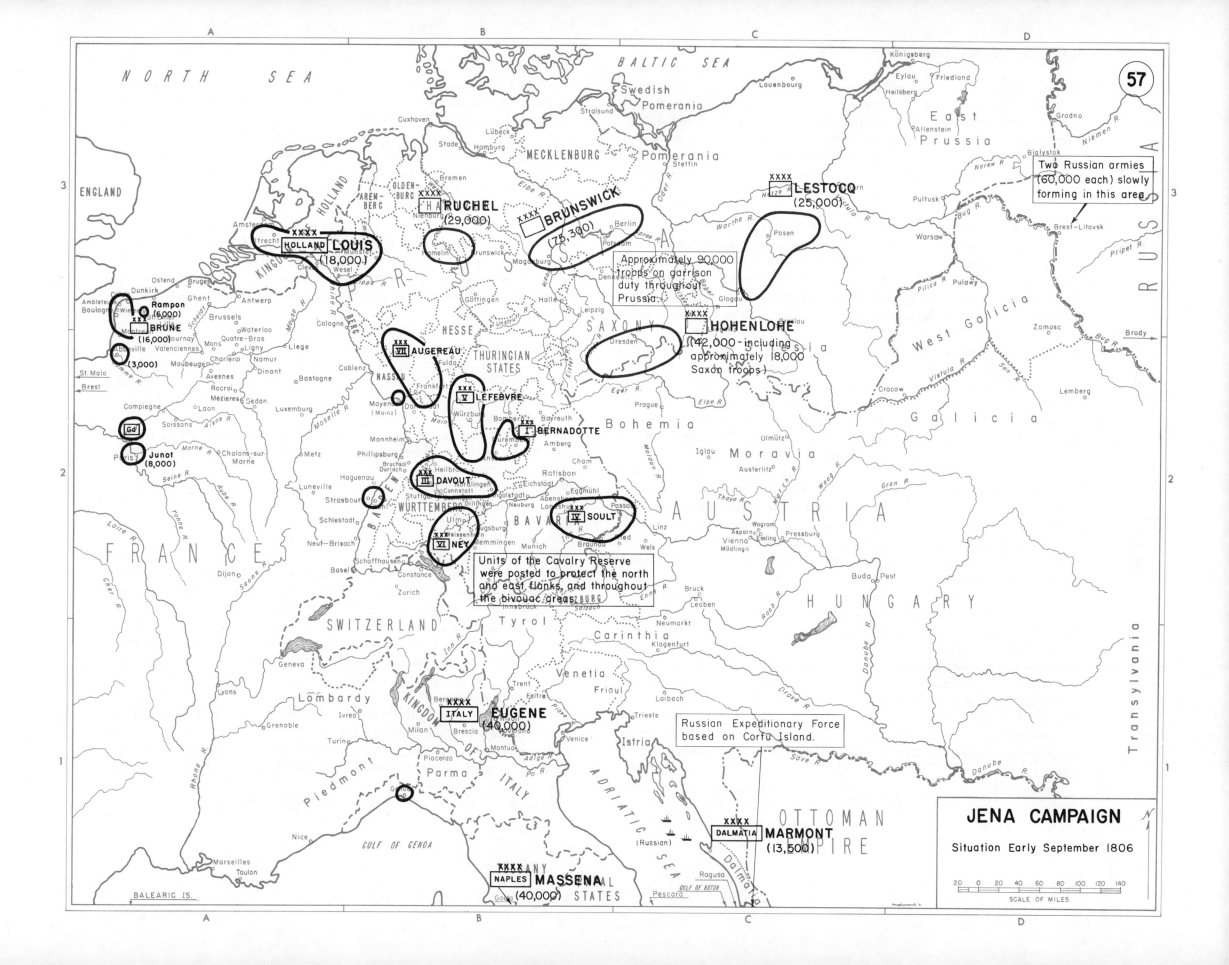

NORTH SEA

BALTIC SEA

ENGLAND

Two Russian armies (60,000 each) slowly forming in this area.

XXXX **LESTOCQ (25,000)**

XXXX **'HA.. RUCHEL (29,000)**

XXXX **BRUNSWICK (75,300)**

Approximately 90,000 troops on garrison duty throughout Prussia.

XXXX **HOHENLOHE (42,000 - including approximately 18,000 Saxon troops)**

Rampon (6,000)
XXX **BRUNE (16,000)**
(3,000)

Gd
Junot (8,000)

XXX VII **AUGEREAU**

XXX V **LEFEBVRE**

XXX I **BERNADOTTE**

XXX III **DAVOUT**

XXX IV **SOULT**

XXX VI **NEY**

Units of the Cavalry Reserve were posted to protect the north and east flanks, and throughout the bivouac areas.

XXXX **ITALY EUGENE (40,000)**

Russian Expeditionary Force based on Corfu Island.

XXXX **DALMATIA MARMONT (13,500)**
(Russian)

XXXX **NAPLES MASSENA (40,000)**

JENA CAMPAIGN

Situation Early September 1806

20 0 20 40 60 80 100 120 140
SCALE OF MILES

57

Prussia had decided to strike without waiting for the Russians. A swift offensive would catch the French in detail; the resulting victory would win all north Germany, and possibly Austria, as allies. Executed with decision and skill, by a better army, under competent commanders, this plan might have succeeded.

But Prussian mobilization was slow. Frederick William's determination wavered. The order to occupy Saxony (*D2*) was given only on 30 August; it was 6 September before the Prussians could cross the frontier, and 12 September before Dresden (*D2*) was occupied. Thereafter, the Prussian and Saxon armies were to mass around Erfurt (*C2*), but the Saxons proved oddly unenthusiastic about mobilizing. No espionage system having been organized, there was extensive ignorance as to French dispositions. Hohenlohe urged an advance through Hof (*C2*); Brunswick, one through Gotha (*C2*) on Würzburg (*C1*). It was decided to adopt both plans, in the belief this would compel Napoleon to split his forces. These movements began, but, on 27 September, Brunswick abruptly ordered Hohenlohe to move to Jena (*C2*), leaving detachments at Hof to simulate an advance by that route. Brunswick and Rüchel would advance through the Thuringian Forest on 11 October, debouching on Meiningen and Hildburghausen (*all C2*). By 4 October, the Prussians had reached the general locations shown. Information concerning the French was now available: Napoleon reportedly was at Würzburg, where his forces were concentrating; the Imperial Guard was at Mayence (*B2*); Königshofen (*C2*) was being fortified. At this news, Brunswick's nerve broke. He called a council of war, which considered a variety of plans for three days. The final decision was to stand on the defensive. The Prussian army now covered the two best invasion routes available to the French: Fulda-Erfurt and Hof-Gera. Brunswick would concentrate against the French as they emerged from the Thuringian passes, Four reconnaissance parties were dispatched southward to learn which routes the French would follow. Considering this risky, Frederick William canceled three of them.

Napoleon's first definite orders to Berthier (13 September) had been to concentrate the Cavalry Reserve; the III, VI, and VII Corps; and Dupont's division at Würzburg, as soon as Berthier learned that the French ambassador had left Berlin. (The ambassador had instructions to do so immediately should the Prussians invade Saxony.) Two days later, still hopeful of a peaceful settlement, he drastically restricted Berthier's initiative—the concentration should not begin until the ambassador informed him that diplomatic relations had been broken off. Against a different enemy, this could have been dangerous. Berthier knew on the 19th that the invasion had begun, but the ambassador did not write until 21 September. His letter reached Berthier on the 26th.

Napoleon had already formed a general plan: a direct advance on Berlin (*D3*) from the Bamberg-Würzburg area. The Bamberg-Würzburg position covered both his primary (Mayence-Frankfurt), and secondary (Bamberg-

Augsburg) lines of communication. His only worry was that the Prussians might advance before he had completed his concentration. However, previous studies had convinced him that the Prussian Army would mobilize slowly; that Louis' threat to the Prussian flank would inhibit any rash advance; and that the Prussians would stand on the defensive behind the Elbe River. Informed of the invasion of Saxony on 18 September, he first considered it a limited movement. On the 19th, he directed Berthier to form the VII, V, and III Corps along the Main River (*between C1 and C2*); and I, IV, and VI between Amberg and Ansbach (*both C1*); the cavalry on the right flank. (These orders incorrectly named Bamberg, instead of Nüremberg [*C1*], as Bernadotte's objective.) However, a letter from Berthier (written 19 September, received the 24th) reported that the Prussians had reached Hof. Napoleon thereupon ordered an immediate concentration around Bamberg and Würzburg.

The result was a confused scramble, the exact developments of which are hard to untangle. Berthier already had begun the concentration ordered on the 19th. Overly cautious, despite his excellent intelligence system, he failed to occupy Kronach (*C2*), and left much of the cavalry far to the rear. Napoleon's mistake in Bernadotte's orders resulted in the latter's blocking Davout's advance.

While this concentration was proceeding, Napoleon reached Mayence (28 September) and began showering orders: Bernadotte would occupy Kronach; all leading corps would push cavalry reconnaissances; Murat would go to Würzburg to supervise the collection of enemy information; an VIII Corps would be formed under Mortier at Mayence; the Cavalry Reserve would come forward.

In the late afternoon of 29 September, with all available intelligence at hand, his plan took shape. From 2200 until into the following morning, he dictated fifteen letters that laid the groundwork for subsequent operations. Screened by a mist of cavalry actions, the French would shift to their right, leaving the entire space between the Rhine and Bamberg ungarrisoned. Napoleon hoped that the Prussians would believe that his front stretched thinly from Bohemia to the Rhine, covering his communications. He intended to seize the initiative by a swift, massive blow into the heart of Prussia, along the line Gera (*C2*)–Leipzig (*D2*). Meanwhile, to deceive Prussian spies, Berthier was to fortify Würzburg.

Reaching Würzburg on the evening of 2 October, Napoleon continued his work on logistical problems, though the lack of time and trained assistants made for mediocre results. As more information on the enemy and terrain came in, he further refined his plan. Thanks to the Prussians' indecision and their three-day halt—and his own heroic efforts—his army was ready. It would advance on 7 October, entering Prussian-occupied territory the next day.

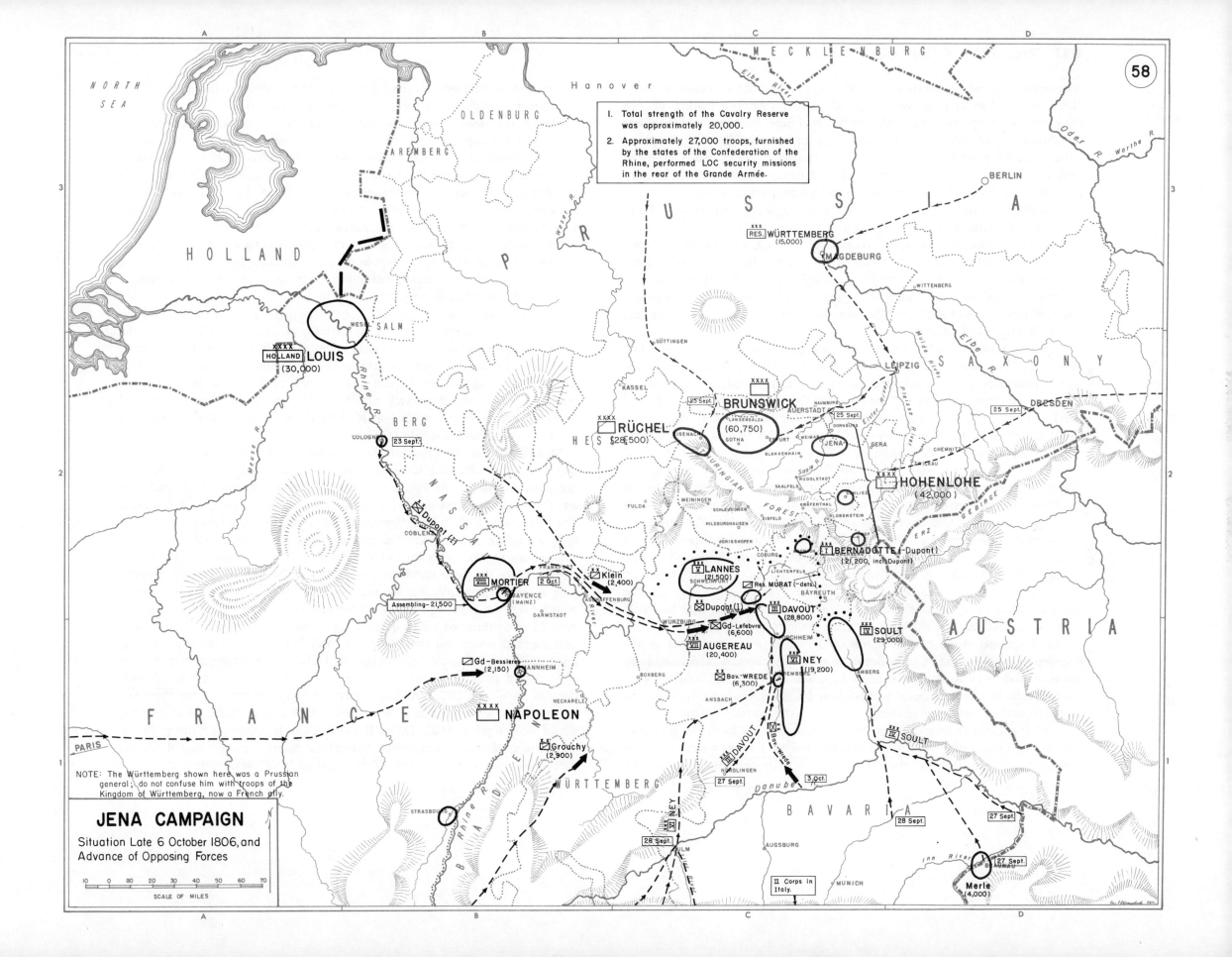

58

1. Total strength of the Cavalry Reserve was approximately 20,000.

2. Approximately 27,000 troops, furnished by the states of the Confederation of the Rhine, performed LOC security missions in the rear of the Grande Armée.

NOTE: The Württemberg shown here was a Prussian general; do not confuse him with troops of the Kingdom of Württemberg, now a French ally.

JENA CAMPAIGN

Situation Late 6 October 1806, and Advance of Opposing Forces

SCALE OF MILES

Napoleon's plan was based on a relatively clear picture of the enemy situation. No Prussians had approached Fulda (*B2*), and therefore neither his left flank nor his Mayence (*A1*)–Würzburg (*B1*) line of communication was immediately threatened. The principal enemy forces were reported still around Erfurt and Naumburg (*both C2*). The southeastern end of the Thuringian Forest (*C1*) would not be a serious barrier: Its roads were good, the streams fordable, and the country fertile enough to feed his passing army.

In addition to his Mayence-Würzburg and Augsburg-Ulm-Ansbach-Bamberg lines of communication, a third one (Strasbourg-Mannheim-Würzburg) had been organized (*see Map 58*). Würzburg, Kronach, and Forchheim (*this map, C1*)—which would constitute his initial advance bases—had been fortified sufficiently to resist raids by Prussian light troops. Stores of food and ammunition had been accumulated, hospitals and repair shops established, and furnaces built to bake bread. Schweinfurt (*B1*), considered indefensible, had been stripped of supplies.

Napoleon now had under consideration a massed advance on Dresden (*off map, D2*). The capture of their capital should knock the Saxons out of the war immediately, and a continued advance in this direction could cut the Prussians off from Berlin, or at least from the Oder River (*Map 58, D3*) and the Russians. This, however, must wait upon events. As usual, he had no detailed plan; once the two armies were in motion, his actions would depend upon the opportunities offered him by the enemy. "First, one must see . . ." He had no preconceived idea of how the Prussians would react, but felt that they might fall back on Magdeburg (*this map, C3*) to cover Berlin; should the Prussians take the offensive, he expected it to be against his left wing. If they did so, he felt confident of being able to "throw them into the Rhine."

Meanwhile, he would advance with the Grande Armee so disposed that it could concentrate on any one of its component corps within forty-eight hours. As in 1805, the march was preceded by a cavalry screen. This time, however, the screen was a comparatively weak force of light cavalry only. (In the broken terrain of the Thuringian Forest, a mass of cavalry could be easily checked, and would then block the advance of the rest of the army.)

Murat scouted ahead of the central column with six regiments from the Cavalry Reserve and the I Corps, Bernadotte having orders to keep an infantry advance guard well forward to support him. The right and left columns were covered only by the corps cavalry of Soult and Lannes, respectively, while the dragoons and cuirassiers were held well back in the central column.

The left column (Lannes, Augereau) was considered a flank guard against a possible Prussian offensive. If attacked in strength, Lannes was to retire on Coburg (*C1*), thus drawing the enemy between Augereau and the rear ele-ments of the central column. As a final deceptive measure, Lannes was told to leave the usual cavalry patrols north of Königshofen (*B1*).

During the passage of the mountains, lateral communications would be difficult, if not impossible. Therefore, once they reached the northern slope, the first consideration of the leading corps commanders must be to re-establish contact. Lannes and Soult were told, emphatically and at length, of the importance of keeping the Emperor constantly informed as to themselves and the enemy. Napoleon expected the various Prussian armies to become moving targets, once they realized the direction of the French advance.

The entire French formation was at once massive and wonderfully flexible, putting the whole army under Napoleon's direct control "like a battalion in the hands of a good commander, ready for anything." (Napoleon accordingly nicknamed it his "battalion square.")

Early on 8 October, the French pushed across the Saxon frontier, meeting little opposition except for a cavalry skirmish at Saalburg (*C1*), where the bridge was captured intact. Tauenzien, finding himself under growing pressure from two directions, recalled his detachment from Hof, thus opening the door for Soult. By nightfall, the French had reached the positions shown. French intelligence reported Brunswick at Erfurt, Hohenlohe at Jena, a force of 30,000 (actually barely 9,000) at Rudolstadt (*C2*), and 3,000 (actually a few outposts) around Saalfeld (*C2*).

Meanwhile, the one Prussian reconnaissance party (commanded by Captain Müffling), which the King had permitted, had scouted as far as Königshofen on the 7th; on the 8th, it sent in a startling report that the French had left the Würzburg area and were advancing through Coburg and Kronach. The threat was clear, but the Prussian headquarters at once instituted another long wrangling session over the proper measures to be taken to meet it. Scharnhorst (Brunswick's chief of staff) proposed to mass the Prussian-Saxon army between the Saale and Elster rivers, to bar the route to Leipzig. Hohenlohe agreed in principle, but wanted the concentration farther south toward Auma (*D2*) for a prompt attack on the advancing French. During this dispute, Müffling returned with a detailed report which indicated that the French advance had uncovered their Mayence-Würzburg communications. Seizing upon this news, Brunswick dispatched the Duke of Saxe-Weimar with a force of 11,000 of all arms (drawn from both his and Rüchel's armies) to advance through Meiningen (*B2*) on Schweinfurt and Fulda. The rest of the Prussian-Saxon forces would concentrate around Blankenhain (*C2*); Württemberg would move south to Halle (*D3*). Brunswick's orders, however, did not state the purpose of this concentration. Hohenlohe coolly assumed that it was to execute his own plan, and accordingly prepared for a counteroffensive.

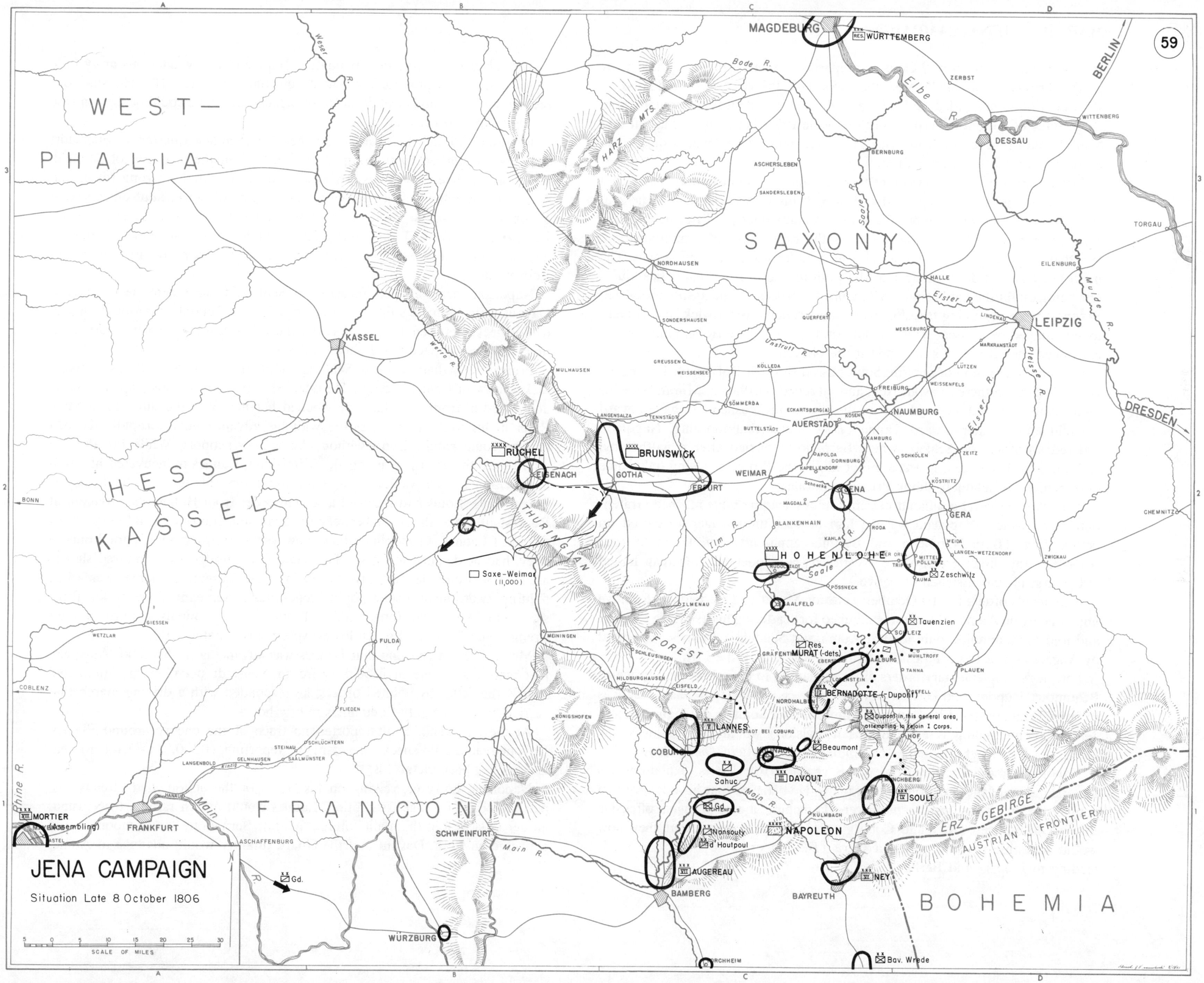

JENA CAMPAIGN

Situation Late 8 October 1806

SCALE OF MILES

5 0 5 10 15 20 25 30

59

WEST-PHALIA

HESSE-KASSEL

FRANCONIA

SAXONY

BOHEMIA

MAGDEBURG

RES. WÜRTTEMBERG

ZERBST

BERNBURG

DESSAU

WITTENBERG

TORGAU

ASCHERSLEBEN

SANDERSLEBEN

NORDHAUSEN

HALLE

EILENBURG

LEIPZIG

SONDERSHAUSEN

QUERFERT

MERSEBURG

MARKRANSTÄDT

LÜTZEN

WEISSENSEE

GREUSSEN

KÖLLEDA

FREIBURG

WEISSENFELS

KASSEL

MULHAUSEN

LANGENSALZA

TENNSTÄDT

SÖMMERDA

BUTTELSTÄDT

ECKARTSBERG(A)

KÖSEN

NAUMBURG

AUERSTÄDT

DRESDEN

RÜCHEL

BRUNSWICK

EISENACH

GOTHA

WEIMAR

APOLDA

DORNBURG

KAPELLENDORF

JENA

GERA

KÖSTRITZ

ZEITZ

SCHÖLEN

KAHLA

HOHENLOHE

MITTEL PÖLLNITZ

Zeschwitz

LANGEN-WETZENDORF

ZWICKAU

CHEMNITZ

Saxe-Weimar (11,000)

BLANKENHAIN

RODA

WEIDA

ILMENAU

SAALFELD

PÖSSNECK

Tauenzien

SCHLEIZ

MEININGEN

GRÄFENTHAL

Res. MURAT (-dets)

EBERSDORF

SAALBURG

MÜHLTROFF

PLAUEN

FULDA

HILDBURGHAUSEN

EISFELD

NORDHALBEN

LOBENSTEIN

TANNA

BERNADOTTE (+Dupont)

Dupont in this general area, attempting to rejoin I Corps.

KÖNIGSHOFEN

NEUSTADT BEI COBURG

LANNES

HOF

COBURG

Sahuc

Beaumont

DAVOUT

KRONCHBERG

SOULT

SCHWEINFURT

Gd.

Nansouty

d'Hautpoul

NAPOLEON

KULMBACH

ERZ GEBIRGE

AUSTRIAN FRONTIER

BAMBERG

AUGEREAU

BAYREUTH

NEY

MORTIER (Assembling)

FRANKFURT

HANAU

ASCHAFFENBURG

Gd.

WÜRZBURG

FORCHHEIM

Bav. Wrede

Hohenlohe therefore spent 9 October preparing to concentrate his whole army in the Triptis-Auma (*D2*) area the next day. Prince Louis Ferdinand of Prussia, who commanded Hohenlohe's advance guard, was ordered to hold Rudolstadt (*C2*) and the crossing of the Saale River between Rudolstadt and Saalfeld until relieved by Brunswick's advance guard. Louis would then move eastward through Pössneck and rejoin Hohenlohe.

Instead, Prince Louis, a sworn enemy of Napoleon, immediately dispatched troops to Saalfeld, following on the 10th with his whole command. The reasons for this apparently impulsive action remain unclear. Elsewhere, Saxe-Weimar groped southward, vainly seeking the French line of communication; Württemberg was slow to march and, once under way, marched slowly. The main body moved deliberately into the positions shown, the royal headquarters being established at Weimar. Many units—especially the hastily mobilized Saxons—were beginning to suffer from short rations. Brunswick and Hohenlohe wrangled by messenger; it was late on the 9th before Hohenlohe became convinced that Brunswick intended to be obeyed.

During the morning of the 9th, Soult passed through Hof (*D1*), leaving St. Hilaire's division there to await Ney, and marched on Plauen. Murat, once his light cavalry reached the north side of the mountains, pushed a brigade toward Saalfeld and another toward Tanna (*D1*). Later that morning, Napoleon ordered an attack on Schleiz, which Bernadotte carried after a halfhearted resistance by Tauenzien. It was a minor affair, the Prussians losing only some 400 men, yet it definitely shook Prussian morale.

That evening, after a difficult march, Lannes' leading units reached Gräfenthal (*C1*), where Napoleon warned him to wait until Augereau closed up behind him. (Both Napoleon and Berthier apparently had failed to send Augereau any direct orders since 5 October; consequently, Augereau halted at Coburg, his last assigned objective.)

Napoleon's orders for 10 October were for Murat and Bernadotte to move immediately on Auma. (Murat was rebuked for scattering his available cavalry, and told to reconnoiter only toward Auma and Saalfeld.) Lannes, supported by Augereau, was to be in position to attack Saalfeld on the 11th.

Berthier's supplementary orders directed Lannes to urge Augereau forward; Beaumont, Dupont, and Davout were to advance rapidly to Schleiz; Ney was to be at Tanna on the 12th, ready to support either Soult or the main column; Jerome (commanding Wrede's Bavarian division) would take or invest the fortress of Külmbach, thereafter continuing to Lobenstein (*both C1*).

Napoleon now wrote Soult one of his characteristic letters, explaining his understanding of the situation and his plans. He believed that his advance had caught the Prussians just as they were launching a two-pronged offensive through Meiningen (*B2*) and Coburg (*C1*). He anticipated that they now would scramble to concentrate at Gera (*D2*) in order to block the roads leading to Leipzig and Berlin.

Though anxious for a decisive battle, Napoleon first wanted his army fully closed up, and so proposed to halt during the 10th and 11th. His staff was reconnoitering a good position north of Schleiz, which he could occupy in case of an unexpected Prussian attack.

Between 1000 and 1100 on 10 October, Imperial headquarters at Ebersdorf (*C1*) was disturbed by the thunder of battle from the direction of Saalfeld. Reaction was lively—Lannes obviously had encountered a strong force, and Augereau probably was not yet within supporting distance. Staff officers went galloping with orders: Augereau to join Lannes by forced marches; Davout, Lefebvre, Nansouty, Klein, and d'Hautpoul to move on Schleiz; Soult to advance through Weida on Gera; Jerome to advance to Hof instead of Lobenstein.

Napoleon then galloped forward to Schleiz, from where he dispatched Davout, with Milhaud's light cavalry brigade and Dupont's division attached, to Pössneck. Between 1500 and 1600, the firing ceased; from its short duration, Napoleon judged that Lannes had won.

Prince Louis had reached Saalfeld at about 0900, to find his outposts bickering with Lannes' scouts. He selected a position on low, open ground, dominated in front and flank by wooded heights, with the unfordable Saale River at his back. Lannes, riding with his advance guard, rapidly decided that he could handle Louis without Augereau's support. While his advance guard fixed the enemy by energetic skirmishing, Lannes maneuvered his leading division to turn Louis' right flank and drive him into the Saale River. (Meanwhile, Louis had received a second order from Hohenlohe: Remain at Rudolstadt, cover the space between the Saale and Inn rivers, and keep out of trouble.) Lannes' enveloping attack, however, moved too swiftly for Louis to obey, had he deigned to do so. The Saale River bridge was captured shortly after 1300. Louis, leading his cavalry in a last, desperate charge, was killed fighting, sword against saber, by a French hussar sergeant. Some 9,000 Prussians and Saxons had fought 5,500 French, losing roughly a third of their strength and 27 guns; French losses were approximately 200.

Meanwhile, on learning that Lannes was advancing on Saalfeld, Augereau had merely sent one division forward to Neustadt bei Coburg. Stimulated shortly thereafter by pointed orders, he responded with a driving march that carried his corps eighty-three miles in fifty hours.

At the day's end, Soult reported no trace of the enemy around Plauen. Davout reached Pössneck late at night, reporting (0200, 11 October) that Lannes had been victorious.

Napoleon, however, relying on his "feel" of the action, had already dispatched orders on that assumption. Lannes would march rapidly to Neustadt an der Orla to join the main column; Murat, Bernadotte, and Dupont would converge on Gera; Davout and the Guard infantry would advance to Auma.

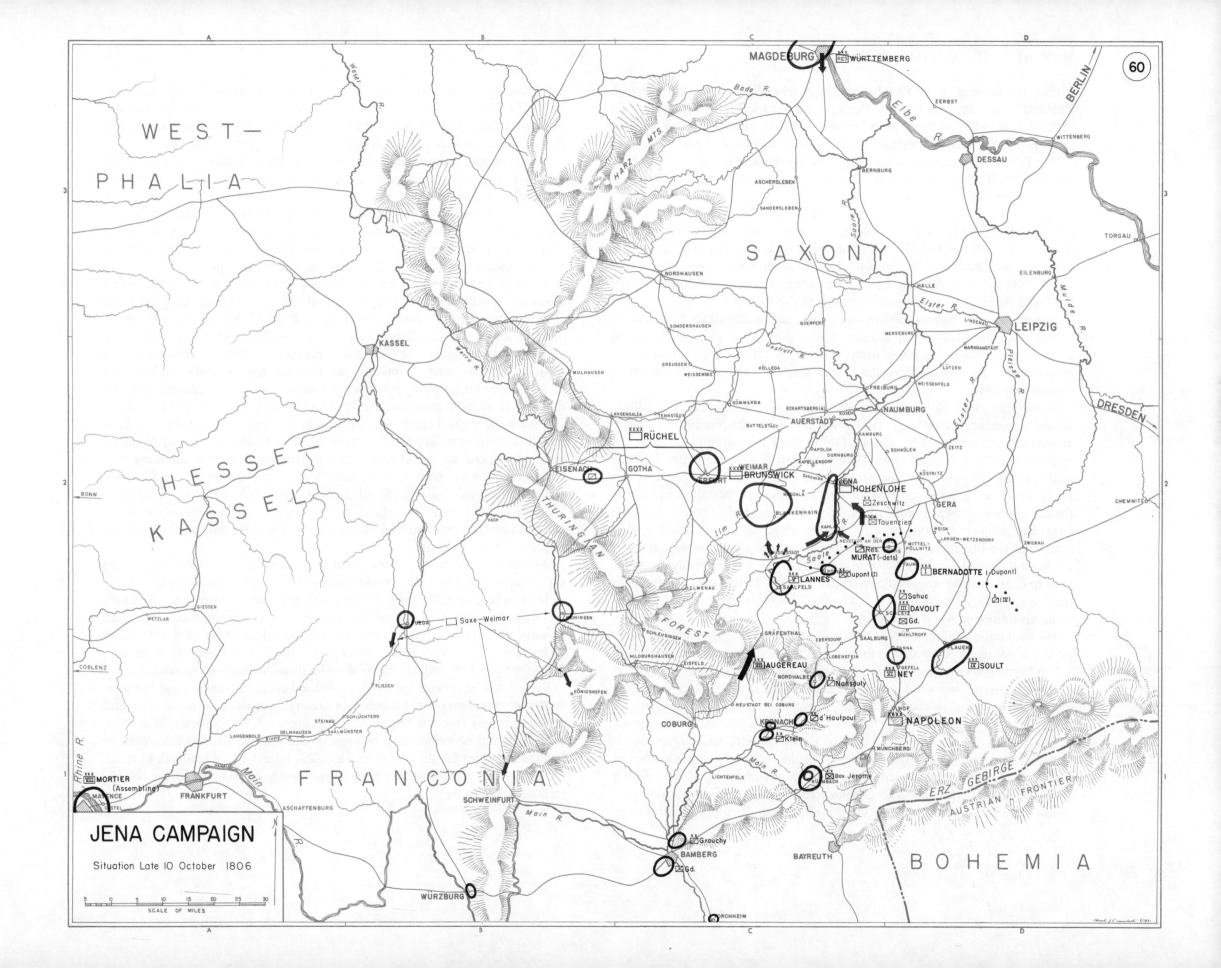

WEST-PHALIA

HESSE-KASSEL

FRANCONIA

BOHEMIA

SAXONY

THURINGIAN FOREST

MAGDEBURG

WÜRTTEMBERG

BERLIN

ZERBST

DESSAU

WITTENBERG

TORGAU

EILENBURG

LEIPZIG

DRESDEN

HALLE

MERSEBURG

LÜTZEN

WEISSENFELS

FREIBURG

NAUMBURG

AUERSTÄDT

RÜCHEL

WEIMAR

BRUNSWICK

GOTHA

EISENACH

ERFURT

HOHENLOHE

Zeschwitz

GERA

Tauenzien

MURAT (-dets)

Res.

LANNES

Dupont (I)

BERNADOTTE (-Dupont)

SAALFELD

Sahuc

DAVOUT

Gd.

SOULT

NEY

PLAUEN

AUGEREAU

Nansouty

d'Houtpoul

NAPOLEON

KRONACH

Klein

Bav. Jerome

MÜNCHBERG

HOF

ERZ GEBIRGE

AUSTRIAN FRONTIER

MORTIER

(Assembling)

FRANKFURT

Saxe-Weimar

Grouchy

BAMBERG

Gd.

BAYREUTH

SCHWEINFURT

WÜRZBURG

JENA CAMPAIGN

Situation Late 10 October 1806

SCALE OF MILES

During the evening of 10 October, fugitives from Saalfeld flooded through Kahla (*C2*), so demoralized that Hohenlohe had to send them to Jena (*C2*) to reorganize. Most of them were Saxons, unwilling allies who now felt that incompetent Prussian leadership had deliberately sacrificed them.

The Prussian command itself was appalled by this second defeat and Louis' death. Both Rüchel and Saxe-Weimar were ordered to join Brunswick as quickly as possible.

October 11 was a day of hard marching. Early in the morning, Lasalle's light cavalry brigade swept into Gera, capturing Hohenlohe's supply train. Napoleon himself reached Gera by noon; by dark, he had Bernadotte, Lasalle, Milhaud, and Beaumont's dragoon division around that town. Soult had reached Weida; Ney, Schleiz. Lannes was already north of Neustadt an der Orla, and Augereau was pounding through Saalfeld.

Hohenlohe—his Saxons almost mutinous, and Tauenzien's Prussians in considerable disorder—reached Jena. There, during the evening, a sudden panic flamed through his whole army, throwing it into complete disorder for several hours. He finally rallied the Saxons north of Jena, leaving Tauenzien around that town.

During the night of 11–12 October, Napoleon re-examined all available intelligence reports. There were no signs of an enemy concentration on Gera; prisoners stated that the King and most of his army were around Erfurt (*C2*); there was evidence of uncertainty in the Prussian headquarters and demoralization in the Prussian army; the French were already between the enemy and Dresden. The time appeared ripe for him to swing his "battalion square" to the left and attack. Accordingly, he ordered Ney forward to Neustadt an der Orla. But additional information received at about 0800, 12 October, indicated that the Prussians were preparing to withdraw along the west bank of the Saale River to Leipzig (*D3*) or Magdeburg (*C3*). Consequently, he would have to continue his own advance northward to cut those routes. At the same time, a secondary thrust toward Jena would be necessary to fix the enemy while his turning movement developed.

His final orders redirected Ney to Mittel-Pöllnitz (*D2*). Davout, reinforced by Sahuc's dragoon division, was to march as rapidly as possible to Naumburg (*C2*), keeping his cavalry well out to the front and his corps ready for combat. Murat and Bernadotte would advance to Zeitz (*D2*); if the enemy remained at Erfurt, they were to continue on to Naumburg, reconnoitering vigorously toward Leipzig. Lannes would advance on Jena, while Augereau moved through Kahla to join him. Soult and the Guard infantry were summoned to Gera; cavalry and ammunition trains still in the rear were to press forward. All commanders were reminded of the need for accurate enemy information, speedily delivered. Enemy units encountered (unless occupying strong positions) were to be attacked, thus upsetting Prussian attempts to concentrate and breaking down enemy strength and morale piecemeal. Should the Prussians advance from Erfurt on Saalfeld, Lannes was to join Augereau and strike their flank. Finally, Napoleon wrote to the King of Prussia, warning him that he was already as good as defeated and urging him to make peace.

Napoleon was primarily interested in the situation north of Gera; the direction and progress of any enemy withdrawal; the location of Württemberg's force, of which he had only vague knowledge; and the execution of his own efforts to cut the direct roads to Berlin. He gave little attention to the one major weakness of his plan: Lannes and Augereau, moving up the west bank of the Saale River, were dangerously isolated and exposed to an attack by the whole Prussian army, should Brunswick recognize his opportunity.

Through 12 October, the French advance moved swiftly. Murat picked up a French spy at Zeitz, who reported that the main enemy army was still around Erfurt. Murat therefore continued north with his cavalry and Bernadotte, halting across the direct routes to Leipzig. Davout's corps cavalry galloped through Naumburg at 1530 and immediately seized a bridgehead on the west bank of the Saale, capturing the Prussian army's bridge train in the process. After interrogating prisoners, deserters, and local inhabitants, Davout reported all in agreement that the Prussians were massing at Weimar (*C2*).

During the night, Lannes' cavalry patrols, probing toward Jena, had been told that there were 80,000 Prussians between Gotha (*C2*) and Weimar. Prisoners picked up en route to Jena stated that the Prussian army was encamped between Jena and Weimar, with a strong outpost in a village approximately two miles south of Jena. Lannes at once sent his advance guard forward to clear the place, before bivouacking for the night. From Kahla, Augereau reported that Hohenlohe was retiring to Weimar and that Brunswick was at Erfurt.

As was his custom, Napoleon issued his orders for 13 October during the early morning hours: Auma would become the army's advance base; Jerome would continue to Schleiz; the Baden contingent would move from Bamberg to Bayreuth (*both C1*); Deroi would bring his newly mobilized Bavarian division to Bayreuth and relieve Jerome's detachments at Hof (*D1*) and Külmbach (*C1*); Ney would advance to Roda (*C2*); Klein, Nansouty, d'Hautpoul, and the artillery trains would halt at Auma to await orders.

Rüchel and Brunswick achieved a confused concentration around Weimar. Staff work had been poor: Units fought among themselves for camp sites, and many regiments received neither food nor firewood. Headquarters was absolutely ignorant of the location of most of the Grande Armee. Saxe-Weimar had taken a short cut through Ilmenau (*C2*), intending, he claimed, to strike the French left rear. However, he marched slowly, possibly to let his detachments rejoin him.

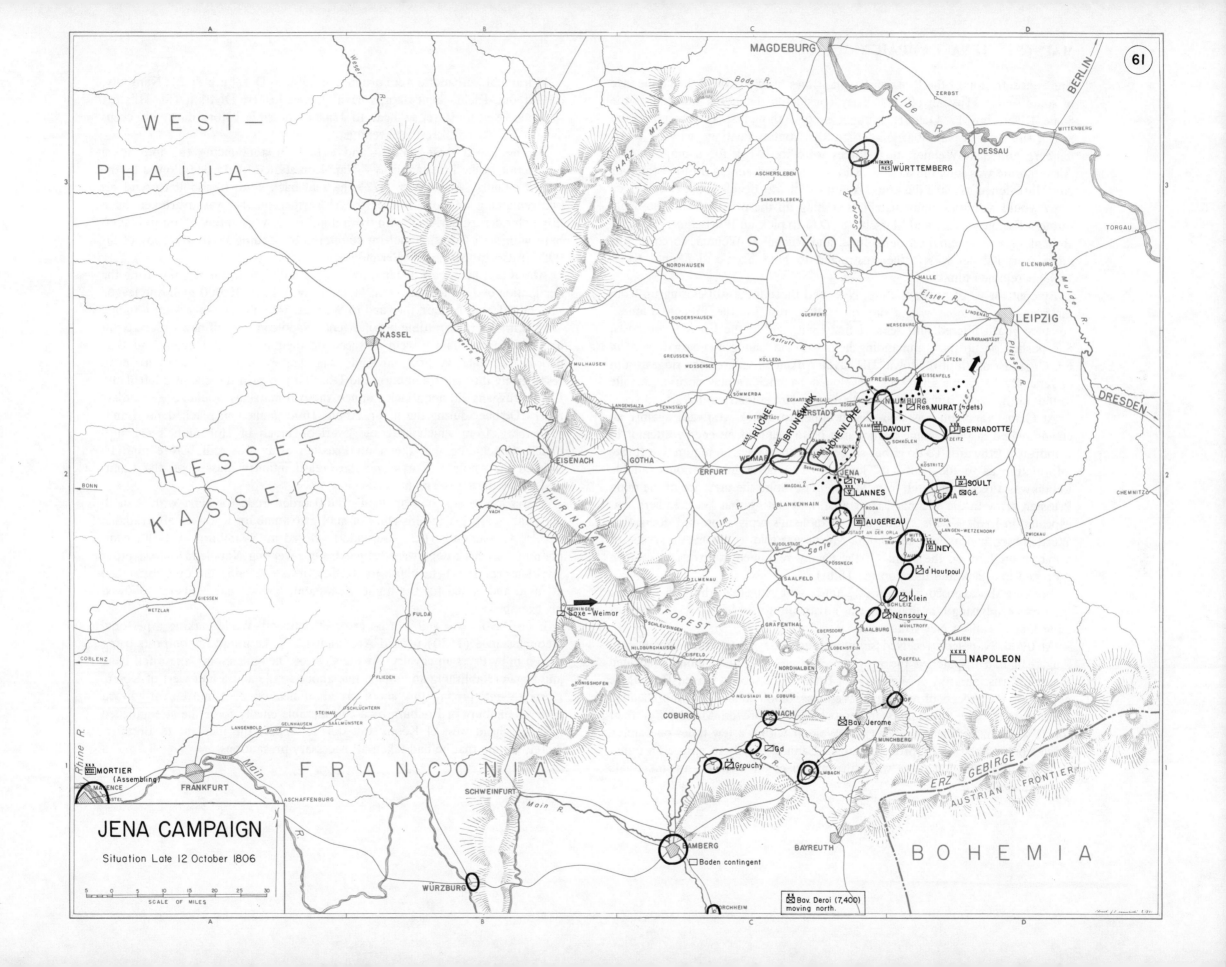

61

MAGDEBURG

WEST-
PHALIA

SAXONY

WÜRTTEMBERG

LEIPZIG

DRESDEN

HESSE-

KASSEL

Res MURAT (+dets)

DAVOUT

BERNADOTTE

RÜCHEL

BRUNSWICK

HOHENLOHE

WEIMAR

SOULT

JENA

Gd.

LANNES

AUGEREAU

NEY

d'Hautpoul

Klein

MEININGEN
Saxe-Weimar

Nansouty

NAPOLEON

THURINGIAN

FOREST

MORTIER
(Assembling)

FRANKFURT

Bav. Jerome

FRANCONIA

Gd

Grouchy

JENA CAMPAIGN

Situation Late 12 October 1806

5   10   15   20   25   30
SCALE OF MILES

Baden contingent

WÜRZBURG

BAYREUTH

BOHEMIA

Bav. Deroi (7,400)
moving north.

The concentration of the Prussian-Saxon armies briefly revived the confidence of some senior Prussian officers. They considered defending the line of the Saale River, but 13 October brought second thoughts: Davout's position astride the Saale at Naumburg imperiled their communications; without Württemberg and Saxe-Weimar, their forces were too weak for a major battle. Also, morale was low; the Saxons, who had received almost no food for four days, threatened to leave the army. A council of war decided that Brunswick's army would withdraw immediately, marching up the west bank of the Saale through Freiburg (*C2*) and Merseburg (*D3*) to pick up Württemberg's corps. Hohenlohe would remain around Jena, and Rüchel at Weimar, to cover this movement; Rüchel was further instructed to hold his position until Saxe-Weimar rejoined him.

By contrast—except for Lannes, Ney, and those units still closing up from the rear—13 October was a day of relative rest for the French. Lannes' advance guard filtered into Jena at first light, ousted the Prussian outposts, and pushed on up the commanding height of the Landgrafenberg (*see Map 63, C1*), just north of the town. His cavalry likewise secured the ridges south of Jena. By 1300, his scouts had developed Tauenzien's new position, a mile to the north, where it was covering the rest of Hohenlohe's army.

At Gera, Napoleon was well placed either to attack westward against an enemy halted in the Weimar-Erfurt area or to head off an enemy attempt to withdraw northward. To do either successfully, however, he required accurate information as to the Prussians' location. The latest information available to him was a recent dispatch from Murat, confirming the presence of the main Prussian army in the Weimar-Erfurt area, and stating that Württemberg was expected in Leipzig with 25,000 men. Napoleon's reply expressed doubt that Württemberg had more than 10,000; Murat was told to rest his dragoons for a march on Jena on the 14th. (If the enemy remained at Erfurt, Napoleon proposed to attack him there on the 16th.)

Noticing the exposed position of Lannes and Augereau, he also wrote to the former, advising him that Ney was advancing to Roda (*C2*), and authorizing him to call on Ney if attacked.

At 0900, Napoleon received simultaneously the reports that Davout and Augereau had dispatched the previous evening. The first definitely located the main Prussian army at Weimar, not Erfurt. The second placed Hohenlohe at Jena, in the process of retiring on Weimar. Napoleon swiftly comprehended the situation. The Prussians were preparing to retire on Magdeburg; their forces were massed between Jena and Weimar within a few miles of Lannes' single corps. They would probably attack Lannes, if only to ensure an unimpeded withdrawal, but there was still time to catch them by an immediate advance westward.

Murat and Bernadotte were ordered at 0900 to Dornburg (*C2*); Nansouty, d'Hautpoul, Klein, Soult's corps cavalry, and his 1st Division (St. Hilaire) to Roda. Ney must get as near to Jena as possible before dark; his corps cavalry should be there that evening.

Having issued these orders—and a bulletin announcing the impending destruction of the Prussian army—Napoleon started for Jena, followed by the Guard infantry. At Köstritz (*D2*), he sent back word for Soult to send his two remaining divisions to that town. Further on, he was overtaken by a dispatch rider from Murat, with word that Murat was continuing on to Naumburg with the I Corps. Napoleon countered by sending Davout a copy of his 0900 orders for Murat and Bernadotte.

About four miles east of Jena, he met a courier from Lannes, reporting the occupation of Jena and also that "the enemy has . . . 30,000 men one league [2½ miles] from here on the road to Weimar. He will probably want a fight." With skirmisher fire rattling beyond Jena, Napoleon sent off new orders. Soult and the Guard infantry were to speed up their march. If Davout and Bernadotte heard heavy firing around Jena that evening, they were to move respectively through Naumburg and Dornburg to turn the enemy's left flank. If the Prussians did not attack Lannes, the two marshals would receive orders for 14 October during the night. About 1600, Napoleon reached the Landgrafenberg, from which he could overlook much of Hohenlohe's encampments. Concluding that the main Prussian army was still before him, he ordered the whole V Corps and the Guard infantry massed on the Landgrafenberg during the night.

Murat, on receipt of Napoleon's 0900 order, rode for Jena with a small personal escort, leaving his chief of staff at Naumburg to direct all available cavalry to Kamburg (*C2*). Bernadotte closed at Naumburg at 1400, complaining that his troops were fatigued. On receiving Napoleon's latest order (written near Jena), he chose to consider it as canceling the one dispatched at 0900 and halted for the night. Beaumont, Sahuc, and Milhaud followed his example.

Even Davout was guilty of an error of omission. While making a personal reconnaissance (1630) toward Auerstädt (*C2*), he found his outposts being driven in by Prussian cavalry. At the sight of Davout's escort, these fell back and began establishing an outpost line about a mile and a half west of Kösen. Correctly interpreting this action as an indication of a movement toward either Naumburg or Freiburg by a considerable enemy force, he strengthened his bridgehead west of Kösen, but did not report the incident to Berthier, merely stating that he had taken all necessary precautions.

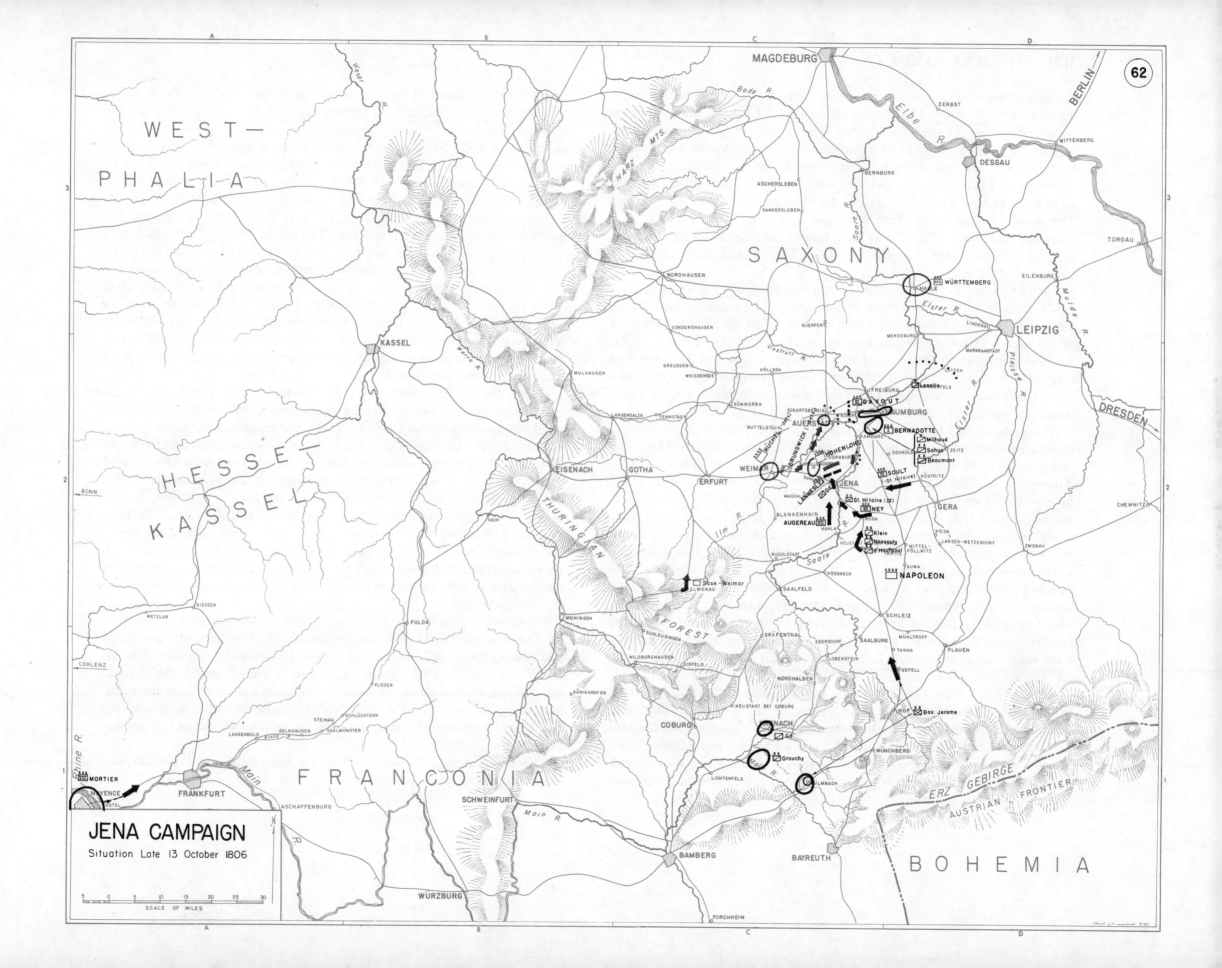

WEST-PHALIA

HESSE-KASSEL

SAXONY

FRANCONIA

BOHEMIA

MAGDEBURG

ZERBST

BERLIN

DESSAU

WITTENBERG

TORGAU

LEIPZIG

EILENBURG

DRESDEN

CHEMNITZ

WÜRTTEMBERG

HALLE

KASSEL

NORDHAUSEN

ASCHERSLEBEN

SANDERSLEBEN

BERNBURG

MERSEBURG

LINDENAU

MARKRANSTÄDT

SONDERSHAUSEN

QUERFERT

WEISSENFELS

GREUSSEN

WEISSENSEE

KÖLLEDA

FREIBURG

Lasalle

DAVOUT

NAUMBURG

BERNADOTTE

Milhaud

Sahuc

Beaumont

ZEITZ

SÖMMERDA

LANGENSALZA

TENNSTÄDT

BUTTELSTÄDT

AUERSTÄDT

BRUNSWICK (Adv)

HOHENLOHE

DORNBURG

SCHKÖLN

EISENACH

GOTHA

ERFURT

WEIMAR

MAGDALA

LANNES

JENA

SOULT (-St. Hilaire)

St. Hilaire (Div)

NEY

KÖSTRITZ

GERA

BLANKENHAIN

AUGEREAU

RODA

KAHLA

Klein

Nansouty

d'Hautpoul

WEIDA

LANGEN-WETZENDORF

ZWICKAU

VACH

MEININGEN

Saxe-Weimar

ILMENAU

RUDOLSTADT

NEUSTADT

POSSNECK

AUMA

NAPOLEON

MITTEL-POLLNITZ

SCHLEIZ

THURINGIAN FOREST

SCHLEUSINGEN

GRÄFENTHAL

EBERSDORF

SAALBURG

MÜHLTROFF

PLAUEN

HILDBURGHAUSEN

EISFELD

LOBENSTEIN

TANNA

GEFELL

NORDHALBEN

NEUSTADT BEI COBURG

HOF

Bav. Jerome

MÜNCHBERG

COBURG

NACH

Gd

Grouchy

LICHTENFELS

KULMBACH

BAYREUTH

ERZ GEBIRGE

AUSTRIAN FRONTIER

MORTIER

MAYENCE

FRANKFURT

HANAU

ASCHAFFENBURG

SCHWEINFURT

BAMBERG

WÜRZBURG

FORCHHEIM

Harz Mts

Elbe R.

Bode R.

Saale R.

Elster R.

Mulde R.

Pleisse R.

Unstrut R.

Werra R.

Ilm R.

Saale R.

Main R.

Rhine R.

Weser R.

JENA CAMPAIGN

Situation Late 13 October 1806

SCALE OF MILES
5   0   5   10   15   20   25   30

62

Because of assorted delays and misunderstandings, Brunswick did not begin withdrawing until 0900, 13 October. He then moved out in a single column, without bothering to send an advance guard ahead to secure the Pass of Kösen (*D3*). The security of his right flank was left to Hohenlohe. Blücher, with approximately half of Rüchel's army, formed the rear guard.

Brunswick's march was a crawl. His leading division (Schmettau) covered eight miles in nine hours; Blücher did not close up until 0200, 14 October. The sound of gunfire near Jena did cause a brief halt, but this was soon dismissed as a minor affair. It was cold; rations and firewood were still lacking; the Prussians were skimpily clad. Discipline cracked, and neighboring villages were looted.

For 14 October, Brunswick ordered Schmettau to occupy the Kösen Heights (*D3*), forming a flank guard while Wartensleben and Orange defiled through Kösen Pass. Kuhnheim's and von Arnim's divisions (grouped under Kalkreuth as the army's "reserve") would take the road through Eckartsberg (*C3*). Brunswick specified in detail the positions to be occupied at Freiburg (*off map, D3*), but said nothing about French dispositions—though Schmettau's cavalry had reported that the French held Kösen in strength, and prisoners stated that there were 30,000 French in Naumburg (*D3*).

Hohenlohe spent 13 October in a state of advanced confusion, the details of which are still disputed. The greater part of his army seems to have been facing to the southwest, toward Magdala (*B1*) and Saalfeld (*off map, A1*). Afterwards, he claimed to have advanced to attack Lannes, only to be halted by a verbal order from Brunswick, supposedly transmitted by Massenbach, his own chief of staff. This claim, however, appears to be a mendacious afterthought. Hohenlohe is known to have accompanied Holtzendorf's detachment, which he dispatched to the Dornburg (*C2*)–Kamburg (*D2*) area during the afternoon—either in reaction to a report that the French had ordered 12,000 rations prepared there, or as a belated move to screen Brunswick's waddle northward. (This expedition found no French except the aide carrying Napoleon's letter to the King of Prussia.) Leaving Holtzendorf there, Hohenlohe returned to his headquarters at about 2200. It is noteworthy that he had not reinforced Tauenzien, though Lannes had steadily driven Tauenzien back for the past thirty-six hours.

After dark, the French began massing on the Landgrafenberg (*C1*). Napoleon, impatient over the nonarrival of Lannes' artillery, went looking for it, and found that, in the gloom, it had mistaken a ravine leading toward Cospeda (*C1*) for the trail leading up the cliff. The lead piece had jammed itself between two rocks; those behind it could neither bypass it nor turn around. Artillerymen and horses were worn out; the officers responsible for the column had gone off in search of supper. Quietly swallowing his fury, the Emperor became once more the captain of artillery and skillfully got the column moving. The French massed steadily, Augereau and Lefebvre coming up shortly after dark. Ney's advance guard appeared somewhat later; the rest of his corps halted at 2000, to resume their march at about 0300 on 14 October. St. Hilaire and the IV Corps cavalry arrived at about midnight; Soult's other two divisions halted at 1800, to rest until 0200. Nansouty, d'Hautpoul, and Klein reached Roda (*D1*) at 1800. Here they rested, prepared to resume their march at 0100. The whole V Corps and the Guard infantry bivouacked in squares on the southern slopes of the Landgrafenberg. (Contrary to popular accounts, they were not jammed into a dense mass.)

The only French bivouac fires visible to the enemy were a relatively small group on the Landgrafenberg; the rest were concealed by the depth of the Saale Valley and the glare from the burning buildings in Jena, part of which had caught fire. The French had orders to be quiet, but noise could not be entirely avoided in moving guns up the Landgrafenberg. But, whatever noise was made, Hohenlohe ignored.

During the day, Napoleon had been able to see only part of the terrain held by the Prussians—an undulating plateau cut up by streams, villages, and small woods—because the Dornberg (*C2*), the highest point on the plateau, blocked much of his view. The night, however, was very clear, and the extent of the Prussian campfires convinced him that the whole Prussian army—more than 100,000 men—was before him. He himself had approximately 55,000 men in hand; 40,000 more should reach him by noon of the 14th, but the troops around Naumburg could not arrive before midafternoon. The tame Prussian withdrawal from Jena had reinforced his deduction that the enemy was seeking to retreat on Magdeburg. Nevertheless, should the Prussians realize his relative weakness and attack promptly in the morning, they might very well be able to drive Lannes and Lefebvre into the Saale, and thereby abort his whole offensive.

Napoleon resolved to keep the initiative: "There are moments in war when no consideration should override the advantage of anticipating the enemy and striking first." At 2200, he sent Davout his orders for the 14th: The III Corps was to advance on Apolda (*B2*) to strike the left rear of the Prussian army, which by then should be fixed by Napoleon's advance from the Landgrafenberg. Berthier added a postscript: "If . . . Bernadotte is with you, you can march together, but the Emperor hopes that he will be in the position assigned him at Dornburg."

This order reached Davout at 0300. He immediately gave Bernadotte a written copy.

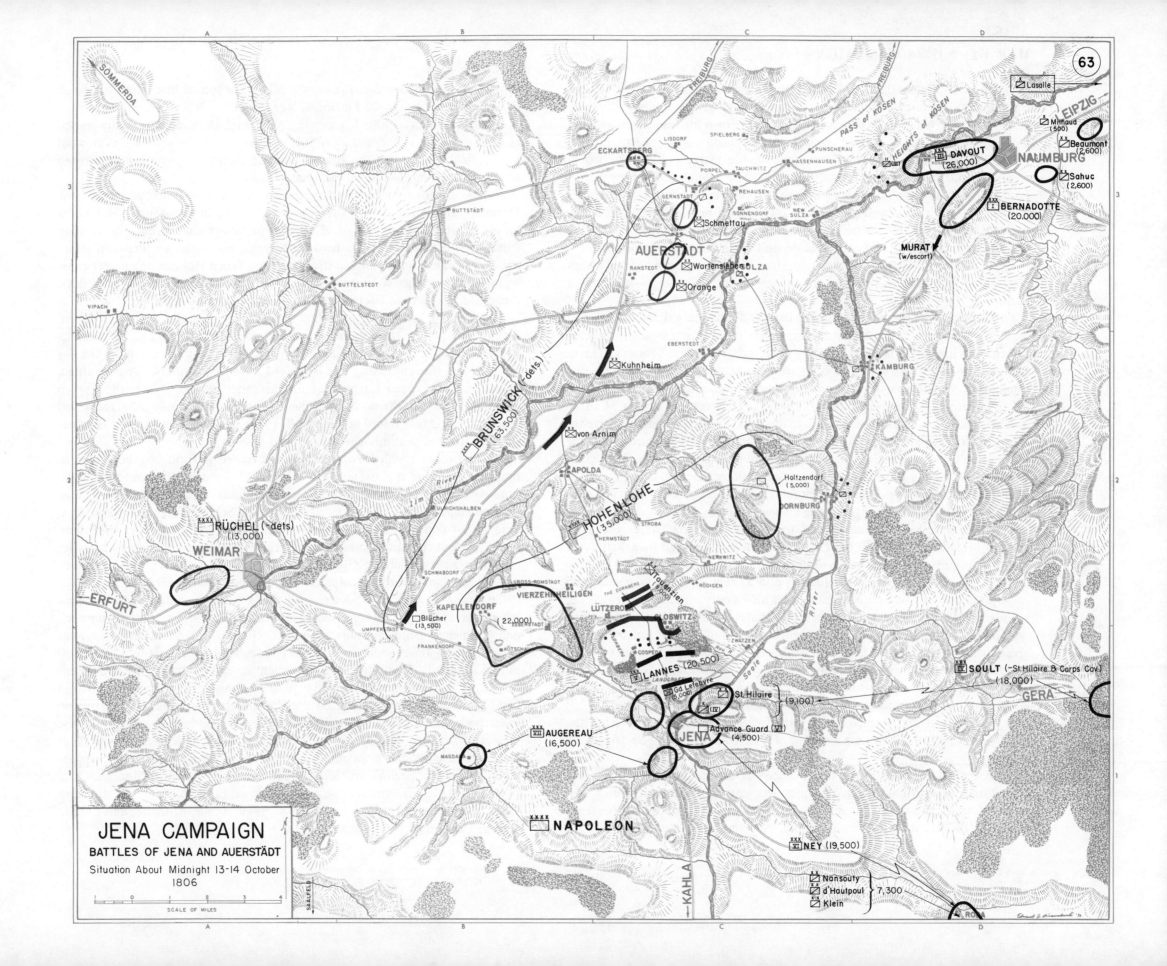

JENA CAMPAIGN

BATTLES OF JENA AND AUERSTÄDT

Situation About Midnight 13-14 October
1806

SCALE OF MILES

Between 0300 and 0400, 14 October, Napoleon dictated his orders for the coming battle. Lannes would attack, on order, about dawn, with both divisions abreast, to take Closwitz (*C2*). Augereau would form his leading division on the Jena-Weimar road, its head opposite the Cospeda ravine (*C1*). As soon as Lannes had secured deployment room on the plateau, Augereau would debouch onto it and form on Lannes' left. Ney would come forward on Lannes' right as soon as Closwitz was taken. Soult would constitute the army's right flank. The Guard and the heavy cavalry, as it arrived, would form the reserve. Napoleon's immediate objective was to gain room to deploy on the plateau. Subsequent maneuvers would depend on the enemy's reactions.

Early morning brought thick, clinging fog. Napoleon postponed his attack until about 0630, when—fearing the enemy might strike first—he ordered Lannes forward anyhow.

Groping between the ravines north of the Landgrafenberg, Lannes advanced on Closwitz. Fog-blinded, his attack strayed to its left, striking and breaking Tauenzien's line about halfway between Lützeroda (*C2*) and Closwitz. Thereafter, as the fog drained from the higher ground, Lannes found his leading elements in considerable disorder and almost out of ammunition, with Prussian cavalry forming on the Dornberg. Always an expert drillmaster, Lannes quickly passed his second line through to the front, and advanced on Vierzehnheiligen (*B2*), efficiently smashing a counterattack from Lützeroda against his left flank. His renewed attack carried Vierzehnheiligen and the Dornberg, but lost its crest and the village to a Prussian counterattack. Lannes, however, clung to the lower slopes, while his left flank cleared Lützeroda. Concurrently, some Prussian units, dislodged from Closwitz by St. Hilaire's advance, attempted to drive across Lannes' rear to Kapellendorf, but were routed by Vedel's brigade. From 0730 on, Lannes had been supported by a battery of twenty-five guns that Napoleon had collected on the Landgrafenberg.

Soult, personally directing St. Hilaire's attack, rapidly cleared Closwitz and its adjoining wood. After a brief halt to let his cavalry and artillery catch up, he advanced on Rödigen, but almost immediately collided with Holtzendorf, who had marched to the sound of the guns. Checking Holtzendorf by aggressive skirmishing, Soult turned his left flank, chased him off in disorder (1015), and then moved toward Hermstädt.

Augereau, apparently misunderstanding his orders, had crammed his whole corps into the Cospeda ravine. It was 0930 before his leading division struggled onto the plateau and formed up beyond Lützeroda. Then, discovering the enemy in strength in the woods east of Isserstadt, it changed front and attacked.

Ney reached the plateau with his advance guard to find that St. Hilaire had closed on Lannes' right, but that Lannes' left was open. He therefore crossed behind Lannes and came into action on his left, just as Lannes lost Vierzehnheiligen (0930). Attacking immediately, Ney recovered the village and the

south end of the Dornberg. Prussian artillery fire forced him back, but some of his infantry clung to the blazing village.

It was now about 1000. The capture of Vierzehnheiligen had finally roused Hohenlohe, who so far had dribbled in small reinforcements to meet what he seemingly considered the French advance guard. He now began massing all available troops to retake Vierzehnheiligen.

Napoleon called on Lannes for another effort. The V Corps cleared the Dornberg and linked up with Ney just as Hohenlohe made his major effort at about 1030, advancing in Potsdam parade-ground order, in echelon from the left, artillery moving forward between his battalions. Prussian infantry, however, had no training in street fighting. When Hohenlohe's center came within musket range of Vierzehnheiligen, it halted and began to fire volleys. Augereau finally took Isserstadt (1100) and linked up with Ney's left.

Meanwhile, Davout had marched at 0630 to seize the defile at Hassenhausen (*C3*), preparatory to an advance on Weimar (*A2*). His leading squadron caught the Prussian advance guard, marching carelessly in the fog just beyond Hassenhausen, and snatched several prisoners. Thus warned, Davout at once seized Hassenhausen. Thereafter, it was a race; the French defiling across the Kösen bridge, the Prussians becoming badly entangled around the bridge and ford at Auerstädt. (This jam grew worse when Blücher, pushing forward with his cavalry, shoved into it.)

Once in contact with Davout, Schmettau halted to form up, then stood in the open, volleying at Hassenhausen. At 0800, Blücher finally got to the front, but was roughly beaten off after a series of clumsily furious charges against the French flank. By 0830, under attack by both Schmettau and Wartensleben, Gudin's division began to waver, but was opportunely reinforced by Friant, whom Davout committed on his right. Friant drove one of Orange's brigades out of Spielberg, enabling Gudin to shift troops to reinforce his own hard-pressed left flank. Davout's corps cavalry arrived at about 0900.

Brunswick finally made a determined attack with Schmettau's and Wartensleben's divisions. At Hassenhausen, this assault collapsed, both Brunswick and Schmettau being mortally wounded. Gudin's left flank, however, was driven back against the highway when Orange's other brigade was also committed against it. This retrograde movement spread to the troops in Hassenhausen, who began abandoning the place. In this crisis, Morand's division came into action at the double on the French left. Hassenhausen was recovered. Swinging forward through heavy fire, Morand beat off the frantic masses of Prussian cavalry and wrecked Wartensleben. King Frederick William then sent Blücher's infantry, the Prussian Guard infantry, and, apparently, part of Kuhnheim's division through Sonnendorf against Morand.

Bernadotte had interpreted the orders received through Davout as directing him to the village of Dornburg (*C2*); Beaumont, Sahuc, Milhaud, and Lasalle marched according to Murat's orders.

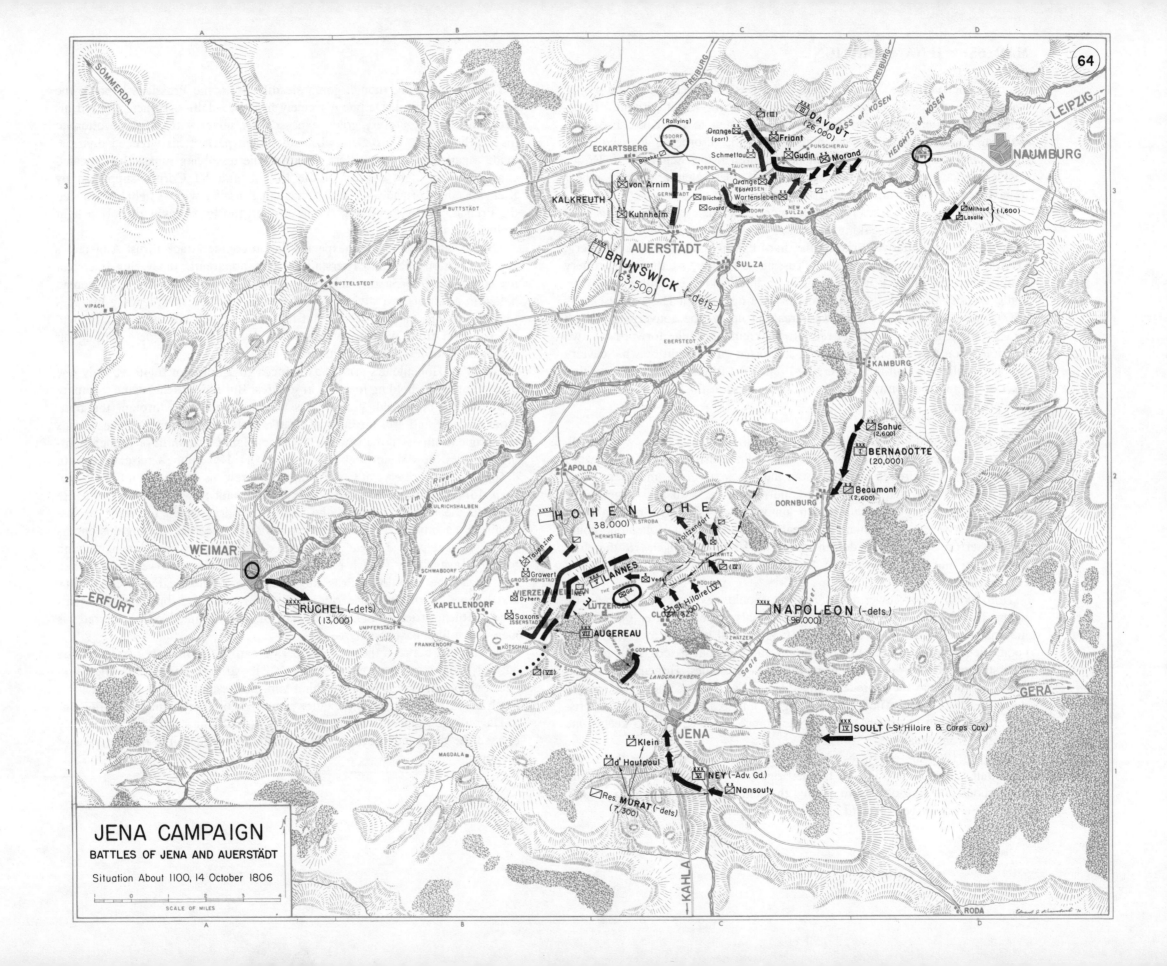

JENA CAMPAIGN

BATTLES OF JENA AND AUERSTÄDT

Situation About 1100, 14 October 1806

SCALE OF MILES

Around Auerstädt, the main Prussian army was coming apart at the seams, even as it made its last effort. Brunswick's fall having left it without a designated commander, command responsibility reverted to the King. Frederick William, however, had involved himself with the disordered Prussian right flank—displaying great bravery, but no comprehension. Scharnhorst, Brunswick's chief of staff, was with the sagging Prussian left. Neither of them appear to have been promptly advised of Brunswick's wound.

Morand crushed the last Prussian counterattack; then, pivoting on his right flank, he swung inward, taking the whole Prussian line in enfilade. Davout now gripped the initiative. Friant, after hard fighting, had retained Spielberg; Davout sent him down across the Prussian left flank, so that his artillery could sweep the whole Prussian front in an interlocking cross fire with Morand's. Gudin's battered division came forward again from Hassenhausen. By 1300, the whole Prussian front was breaking up, as the converging French attack threatened to cut off its retreat. Kalkreuth brought forward his two divisions (von Arnim and Kuhnheim), supported on the right by what cavalry Blücher could rally, but the converging French fire forced him to retire behind Gernstadt, and the continuing French advance soon flushed him out of this new position.

At Jena, Hohenlohe's assault on Vierzehnheiligen had come to a standstill, the Prussian infantry standing in tight-ranked lines, firing volleys at the word of command. The French infantry, from the wrecked village and every bit of cover to either side of it, responded by individual fire "as if at a target." The French artillery, though dueling with almost twice as many Prussian guns, eventually won the upper hand by greater skill and dash. Hohenlohe could not muster the courage to order an assault on Vierzehnheiligen. He therefore decided to put off any definite action until reinforced by Rüchel and Holtzendorf.

Holtzendorf, now cowering in Apolda, would never come. Rüchel—on whom Hohenlohe had called for reinforcements sometime after 0800—had marched for the battlefield at 1000, leaving a small garrison in Weimar. His good intentions and courage were beyond question, but it took him, for reasons still unknown, four hours to march those six miles. Hohenlohe's unfortunate infantry was therefore left ranked in the open for two hours, to be shot down steadily, without inflicting any significant loss in return. Not surprisingly, they began to waver; "extreme measures" were required to keep some regiments from breaking.

Between 1200 and 1230, Napoleon judged the battle ready for the plucking. Soult had come into line on Lannes' right; Ney's two divisions and Klein, d'Hautpoul, and Nansouty were nearing the field. He ordered a general attack, and the French surged forward all along the front.

For the first hour, though going steadily back, the Prussians kept up the semblance of a front. Despite extremely heavy casualties, Hohenlohe and his Prussian officers of every grade exposed themselves with great devotion to inspire their men. Tauenzien, who had rallied part of his wrecked division, made a gallant, but vain, effort, to stiffen the dissolving ranks. But repeated charges by the light cavalry of the IV, V, and VI Corps—supported by Klein's leading brigade—at last broke the Prussian will to fight. Murat led the French cavalry in person, riding through the Prussians with only a light whip in his hand.

On the extreme left, an unexpected Saxon counterattack thrust Augereau's leading division back into Isserstadt Woods, apparently recovering Isserstadt itself. Finding the Saxons solidly established around Kötschau, Augereau halted to await his rear division, renewing his advance as its leading brigades joined him. The Saxons, seeing that the main French advance was about to cut them off from Weimar, withdrew in relatively good order, fighting off Augereau's not-too-energetic pursuit.

By 1430, Hohenlohe's army was reduced to a horde of fugitives, only one or two battalions holding together in squares. But now Rüchel came tramping onto the lost battlefield, plowing his way with difficulty through the rout. Stout of heart and arm (if thick of head), certain that Frederick the Great's teaching encompassed the whole art of war, highly disdainful of French fighting qualities, he did not seek merely to cover Hohenlohe's retreat. Instead, dropping a small reserve at Frankendorf, he threw his little army into a wedge-shaped formation and marched on Gross Romstadt to win his own battle. He repulsed the initial attacks of the French cavalry, which fell back on the leading French infantry, throwing them into some disorder. Seizing this opportunity, Rüchel pushed ahead and secured a footing on the plateau, though battered savagely by French horse artillery. Once there, however, he halted and began the traditional Prussian volley fire. Within a half-hour, Soult's and Lannes' skirmishers had riddled his line. Wounded, but clinging to his saddle, Rüchel tried to fight back, until St. Hilaire and Vedel scattered his men with a final bayonet charge.

Meanwhile, between these two desperate battles, Bernadotte had sauntered leisurely from Naumburg to Dornburg (*C2*). All during the march, he could hear the roar of Davout's fight behind him, but resolutely kept his back to it, firmly silencing Sahuc when the latter proposed countermarching his dragoons to Davout's assistance. Reaching Dornburg at 1100, he slowly and awkwardly crossed the river and got his artillery up the hill road to the plateau west of the town.

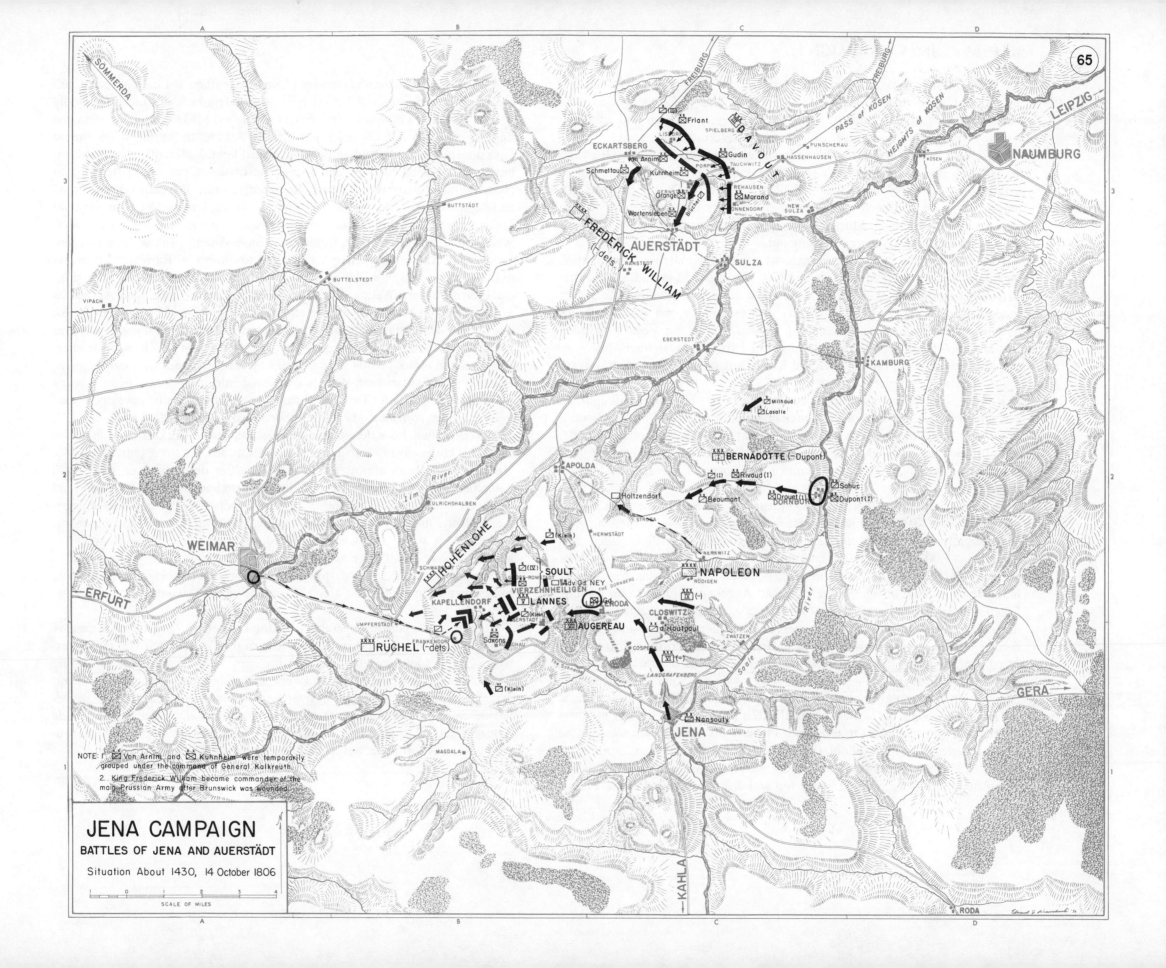

SOMMERDA

FREIBURG

PASS OF KÖSEN

FREIBURG

LEIPZIG

Friant

DAVOUT

Gudin

HEIGHTS of KÖSEN

NAUMBURG

ECKARTSBERG

von Arnim

Schmettau

Kuhnheim

PORP

SPIELBERG

HASSENHAUSEN

PUNSCHERAU

KÖSEN

TAUCHWITZ

REHAUSEN

Orange

Morand

NEW SULZA

Buchel

SONNENDORF

XXX
FREDERICK

Wartensleben

BUTTSTÄDT

WILLIAM
(-dets.)

AUERSTÄDT

RANSTEDT

SULZA

BUTTELSTEDT

VIPACH

EBERSTEDT

KAMBURG

ULRICHSHALBEN

Milhaud

Lasalle

River

Ilm

APOLDA

XXX
BERNADOTTE (-Dupont)

(I)
Rivaud (I)

Sahuc

Holtzendorf

Beaumont

Drouet (I)

DORNBURG

Dupont (I)

WEIMAR

HOHENLOHE

(Klein)

HERMSTÄDT

SCHWABS

XXX
HOHENLOHE

SOULT

(IV)

RÖDIGEN

XXXX
NAPOLEON

ERFURT

KAPELLENDORF

ROMSTEDT

VIERZEHNHEILIGEN

Adv Gd NEY

THE DORNBERG

XXX
IV (-)

UMPFERSTÄDT

(V)
LANNES

(Klein)

ISSERSTEDT

Roda

CLOSWITZ

XXXX
RÜCHEL (-dets)

FRANKENDORF

Saxons

AUGEREAU

d'Hautpoul

ZWATZEN

SCHWABHAUSEN

XXX
VII

XXX
VI (-)

LANDGRAFENBERG

Saale River

GERA

MAGDALA

(Klein)

Nansouty

JENA

KAHLA

RODA

NOTE: 1. ⊠ Von Arnim and ⊠ Kuhnheim were temporarily grouped under the command of General Kalkreuth.

2. King Frederick William became commander of the main Prussian Army after Brunswick was wounded.

JENA CAMPAIGN
BATTLES OF JENA AND AUERSTÄDT
Situation About 1430, 14 October 1806

SCALE OF MILES

As Rüchel's men broke, Murat came down on them again with Klein's dragoons, d'Hautpoul's cuirassiers, and the IV, V, and VI Corps light cavalry. For six miles of driving pursuit, the French horsemen sabered and trampled the mob of fugitives, riding over every attempt to form a rear guard.

Marchand, Vedel, and Augereau followed close behind Murat. Soult swung St. Hilaire's division to the right to intercept those Prussians attempting to withdraw toward Apolda and Ulrichshalben (*both B2*). On the extreme left, the Saxons, who had been withdrawing successfully from Augereau's front, were suddenly caught by Murat. Several thousand surrendered on the spot, though a handful of cavalry cut its way out.

Exhaustion finally halted the French, who had been marching and fighting for hours. Reaching Weimar at about 1800, Murat halted in and around that city, Klein continuing the pursuit some three miles farther along the Erfurt road. Augereau and Ney's light cavalry also pushed beyond Weimar; Ney's infantry halted on the heights east of it. Lannes (except for Vedel's brigade) was at Umpferstädt. Soult spent the night at Ulrichshalben, where his other two divisions rejoined him. The Guard had halted at Gross Romstadt, returning to Jena with Napoleon that night.

By now, Napoleon was certain of only one thing: He had not fought, as he had supposed, the bulk of the Prussian-Saxon forces. Half-audible sounds of a major battle to the northeast indicated that either Davout or Bernadotte, or both, were seriously engaged, but no report had as yet been received from them. Consequently, he had to reckon on the possibility of another, greater battle on the 15th.

Jena had seen approximately 48,000 Prussians and Saxons matched against 96,000 French (40,000 of whom were not actually engaged). French losses were slightly over 5,000; the enemy's approximately 11,000 killed and wounded, 15,000 prisoners; 200 cannon, and 30 flags. It had been a battle of accident and incident, in which most of Napoleon's initial plan had rapidly fallen apart because of weather, terrain, and Augereau's stupid troop leading. Like Grant fifty-seven years later at Chattanooga, Napoleon seems to have at times lost control of the battle; he intervened frequently, but usually only to correct or exploit an accomplished fact. Had the whole Prussian-Saxon army faced him, the struggle would have been desperate. As it was, the day was won largely through Lannes' stark fighting qualities, Soult's imperturbable conduct, and the initiative and ardor of the subordinate officers and soldiers.

Hohenlohe fought his battle piecemeal. Even when he had superior numbers of men and guns, he failed to use them. Possibly his basic failure was that he knew practically nothing about the French, and apparently did nothing to enlighten himself. The entire Prussian army seems to have been dazed by the complete failure of its vaunted volley fire and drill against the flexible French tactics.

At Auerstädt, Kalkreuth, dislodged from his position behind Gernstadt, fell back to another just east of Eckartsberg (*C3*). Here he was attacked frontally by part of Gudin's division, while Friant enveloped his left flank. At the same time, Davout massed his howitzers against Auerstädt, setting it on fire to flush out the Prussians holding it. After a hard fight, Kalkreuth was dislodged, but he had gained time enough to get the divisions previously defeated at Hassenhausen fairly well in hand. Reportedly, some Prussian officers urged an attempt to renew the battle. The King, however, ignorant of events around Jena, not unreasonably decided that the better course was first to retire on Weimar and rally Hohenlohe, Rüchel, and Saxe-Weimar. In the dusk and confusion, with Kalkreuth making a last stand southwest of Ranstedt, his orders did not reach some units, which retired through Buttelstedt (*A3*). The principal retreat toward Weimar initially was orderly enough, but near Apolda its leading elements met fugitives who reported that town held by the French. An attempted countermarch ended in a confused milling of weary, disheartened troops in the dark, as Kalkreuth retired from Ranstedt. Hungry soldiers straggled and looted; roads were blocked by long files of abandoned wagons. Fugitive groups from both defeats blundered into each other, compounding the existing confusion. Two main currents of flight finally developed: one toward Erfurt (*off map, A2*), the other toward Sömmerda (*off map, A3*).

Davout halted his exhausted infantry southwest of Eckartsberg at about 1630; his corps cavalry pursued as far as Buttstädt, where it halted at 1930. His losses had been almost 8,000 men; Gudin's division alone had 3,500 casualties. But the Prussians had lost approximately 12,000 killed and wounded, 3,000 prisoners, and 115 guns! Auerstädt was a model engagement; always in the thick of the most critical fighting, Davout had never lost control of the battle as a whole, and had executed a double envelopment of an army of more than twice his strength.

Bernadotte reached Apolda toward 1600, but did nothing except to write to Berthier, claiming that his arrival there had saved Davout.

To sum up, Napoleon's operations during the period 7–13 October deserve to be called masterly. Working always to turn the Prussian left and cut Brunswick's line of communication, he kept his army well concentrated, regulating its marches to avoid confusion and unnecessary fatigue. At the last moment, when Brunswick's unexpected retreat and Bernadotte's near-treasonous behavior upset his calculations, the fighting spirit and efficiency of his Grande Armee nevertheless won him the rewards of his careful planning and maneuvering. He was fortunate, but he had earned his good fortune.

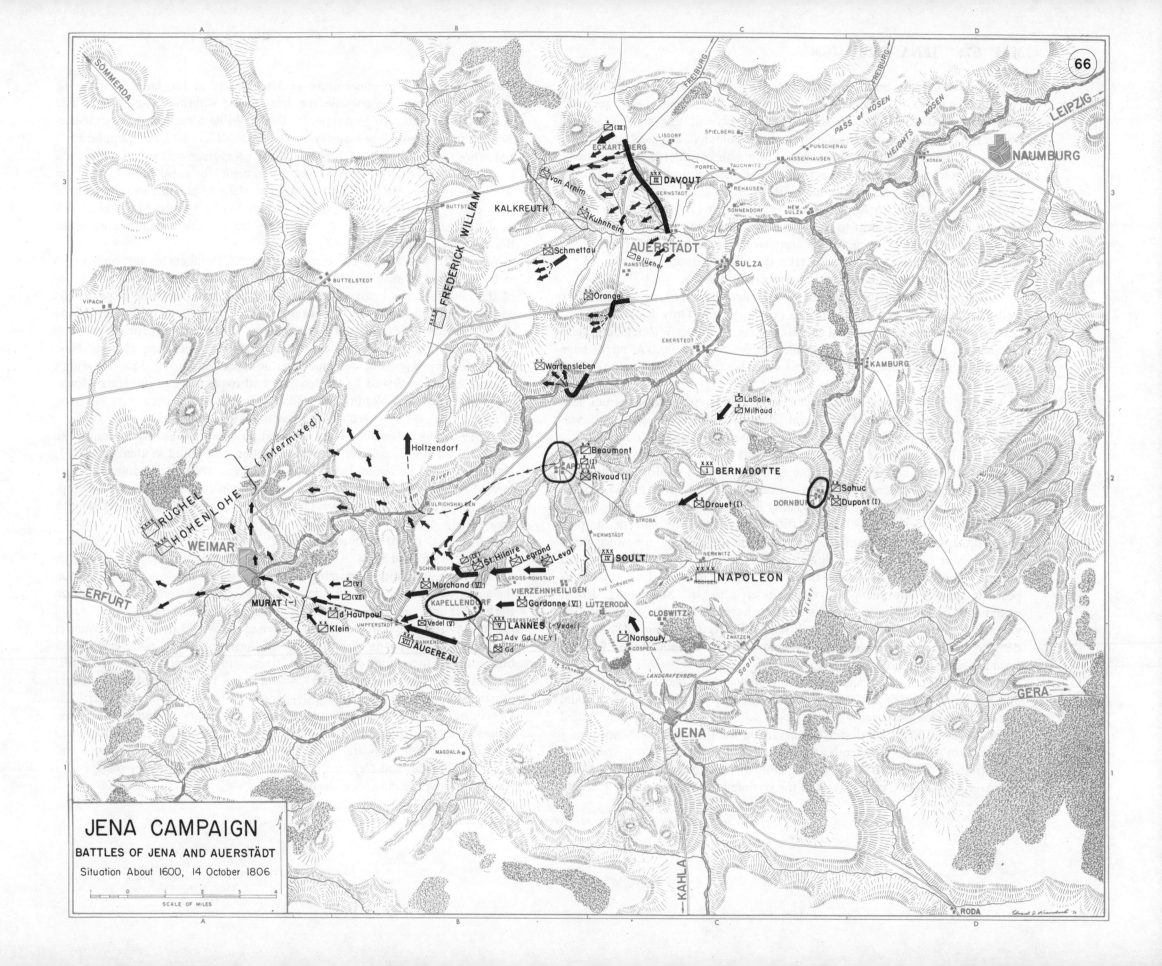

JENA CAMPAIGN
BATTLES OF JENA AND AUERSTÄDT
Situation About 1600, 14 October 1806

SCALE OF MILES

Napoleon issued his initial orders concerning the pursuit of the defeated Prussians at 0500, 15 October; the troops around Weimar (*A1*) received them at about 0700. There was still no news of Davout, and no clear indication of the direction of the Prussian retreat, the complete fragmentation of the Prussian armies having littered the countryside with bewildered enemy detachments. Napoleon reasoned, however, that the Prussians probably would retire toward Magdeburg (*B2*) to unite with Württemberg's corps. Therefore, Murat, supported by Ney, should push toward Erfurt (*A1*), where the enemy might be expected to collect to follow the main highway through Weissensee (*A1*) to Magdeburg. The rest of the army would stand fast until the situation was clarified. Thereafter, it would take the shortest route to Berlin (*C2*), keeping between the Prussians and their Russian allies.

The King of Prussia spent the night at Sömmerda (*A1*), remaining there well into the 15th, in a vain effort to rally fugitives. Only Kalkreuth's two battered divisions remained intact. Had Saxe-Weimar, Württemberg, and troops from nearby garrisons been called in, an army of 60,000 might have been assembled, but demoralization and weak leadership prevented any effective action.

At about 0900, Napoleon received Davout's first report, which struck him as practically unbelievable. Consequently, he maintained a cautious readiness until noon, when a second dispatch from Davout removed all doubt. Murat meanwhile had bluffed the fortress city of Erfurt into surrender under the very nose of Saxe-Weimar, who, fearing the arrival of French reinforcements, soon retired. Napoleon ordered all Saxon prisoners released, as a prelude to the negotiations by which he converted Saxony into an ally.

Napoleon's orders at 0200 on the 16th gave the general plan for the pursuit: Murat, with Ney in support, was to pursue the enemy, "his sword point at their kidneys," in whatever direction the information he received should indicate. Bernadotte was to cut the Erfurt-Halle (*B1*) road as quickly as possible, driving any enemy force encountered toward Magdeburg. Erfurt would now be the Grande Armée's advance base; its line of communication would run through Frankfurt-Fulda-Eisenach-Erfurt (*see Map 62*). Security detachments were shifted accordingly, and Mortier was summoned forward from Mayence to Fulda.

Late on the 16th, Klein and Lasalle intercepted detachments under Blücher and Kalkreuth (*action not shown*), but allowed them to pass on their claim that an armistice had been—or was about to be—signed. (Napoleon noted Klein and Lasalle in his dispatches as an outstanding pair of simpletons.) Soult caught up with Kalkreuth at Greussen (*this map, A1*), capturing part of his trains. Frederick William, finding Hohenlohe at Nordhausen (*A1*) with approximately 15,000 men, gave him the command of the remaining Prussian

forces. These were to concentrate at Magdeburg, in the hope of covering Berlin. If that proved impossible, the army would withdraw into East Prussia to join the Russians. To gain time, Frederick William requested an armistice, then left the army—where his bravery at Auerstädt had won him popularity—and retired to the fortress of Küstrin (*C2*). (Napoleon refused the requested armistice on 19 October.) Hohenlohe optimistically considered turning on Soult, in order to gain time for as many Prussians as possible to rally to him, but—finding Soult hot on his heels—retired hastily toward Magdeburg. To clear the roads, Hohenlohe sent his artillery trains, with a small escort under Blücher, toward Brunswick (*A2*).

Württemberg had received no orders since 13 October, his last ones being to hold himself in readiness at Halle (*B1*). He had learned on 15 October of the defeat of the Prussian-Saxon army, and had therefore disposed his corps (approximately 17,000) in a remarkably poor defensive position astride the Saale River. Bernadotte attacked and routed him on the 17th.

On the 18th, Napoleon had had no news from his left wing (Murat, Ney, Soult) for two days, but continued his advance on Berlin. The left wing's advance had been slowed by the few and bad roads through the Harz Mountains (*A1*), between Nordhausen and Halberstadt. That same day, the head of Hohenlohe's disorganized column reached Magdeburg.

On 19 October, Davout having reported no important enemy forces on the west bank of the Elbe River between Dresden (*C1*) and Wittenberg (*B1*), Napoleon issued his orders for the crossing of that river. Bernadotte was sent toward Aschersleben (*B1*) to establish liaison with the left wing and to support it if necessary. Murat was rebuked for not having scouted the Eisenach area (*A1*).

Before dawn on 20 October, the French Emperor had the reports of Murat (of 17 October) and Soult (18 October). Noting that the enemy was retiring on Magdeburg without attempting to make a stand, he decided to clean up the south bank of the Elbe as quickly as possible, then continue his push on Berlin. No time would be lost besieging Magdeburg, "a mousetrap, where all the [enemy stragglers] would collect." Bernadotte would drop one division at Aschersleben, march on either Calbe or Bernburg (*both B1*), establish a bridge across the mouth of the Saale River, and attempt to force the Elbe. Davout (who had a bridge train) would seize Wittenberg; Lannes would cross at Dessau (*B1*) as previously ordered. (Lannes having reported the Dessau bridge burned, Napoleon had sent him additional pontoniers and the sailors of the Imperial Guard.) Murat, if his present position permitted, was to scour the country toward Magdeburg. If not, he was to leave Klein and Sahuc to aid Soult and Ney, and move on Calbe with the rest of the Cavalry Reserve to join the march on Berlin.

Note: *In the title block of this map (and similarly on Map 68), Aüerstadt should be* Auerstädt.
On the map (and similarly on Map 68), Württemburg (B1) should be Württemberg.

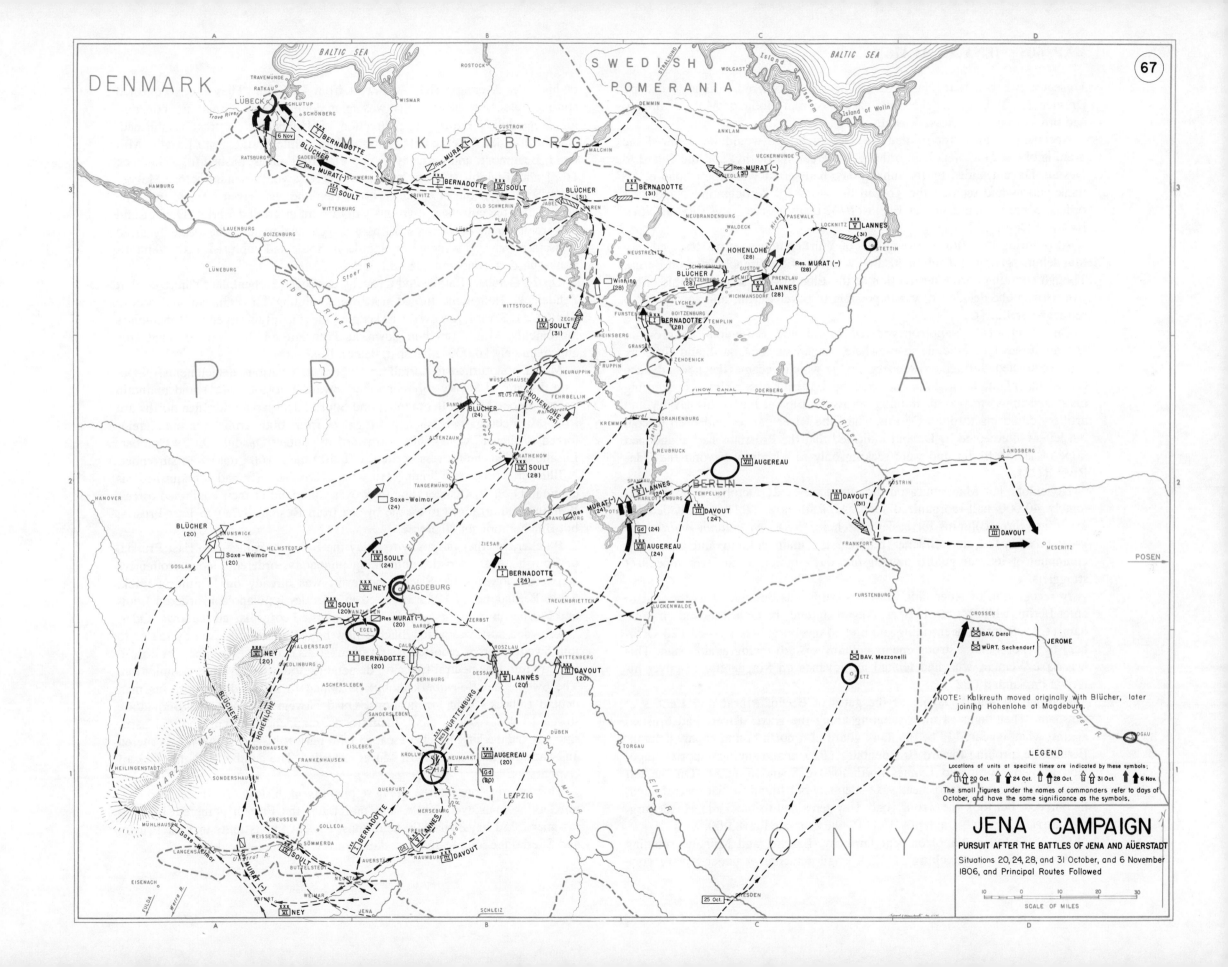

NOTE: Kalkreuth moved originally with Blücher, later joining Hohenlohe at Magdeburg.

LEGEND

Locations of units at specific times are indicated by these symbols:

20 Oct.   24 Oct.   28 Oct.   31 Oct.   6 Nov.

The small figures under the names of commanders refer to days of October, and have the same significance as the symbols.

JENA CAMPAIGN

PURSUIT AFTER THE BATTLES OF JENA AND AÜERSTADT

Situations 20, 24, 28, and 31 October, and 6 November 1806, and Principal Routes Followed

SCALE OF MILES

To secure his right rear, Napoleon (20 October) ordered Jerome to occupy Dresden (*C1*). Louis would move eastward from Holland; Mortier already had orders to occupy Hesse-Kassel.

Receiving Lannes' report that the Dessau bridge would be repaired the evening of the 21st, Napoleon ordered Augereau, Grouchy, and the Guard to Dessau. Davout, aided by the inhabitants, had seized Wittenberg; one of his flank patrols had secured the Torgau bridge (*B1*). Anticipating Napoleon's orders, Murat was massing at Egeln (*B1*), ready to cross the Elbe at either Barby or Dessau.

Also during the 20th, the remnants of Württemberg's corps straggled into Magdeburg, giving Hohenlohe his first warning of the French drive on Berlin. Though counting on the destruction of the Elbe bridges to trip up this offensive, Hohenlohe decided it was impossible to cover Berlin, and so ordered a retreat to Stettin (*C3*).

On 21 October, Napoleon ordered Murat and Bernadotte to cross at Dessau, if they had not done so elsewhere. Augereau, the Guard, and Grouchy were redirected through Wittenberg (*B1*), which became the new advance base. That night, Bernadotte (spurred by Imperial observations concerning his sluggishness) ferried his infantry across the Elbe at Barby, his cavalry and artillery detouring through Dessau. The Elbe River barrier had been forced, but letters intercepted by Davout indicated that the Prussians had abandoned hope of saving Berlin and were seeking only to withdraw beyond the Oder River (*C2*).

Hohenlohe left Magdeburg on the afternoon of 21 October with approximately 40,000 half-reorganized men. At Rathenow (*B2*), he divided his army into three columns for easier marching (*left-hand column omitted for greater clarity*). Later, Blücher rejoined the main column and was given command of its rear guard, moving one day's march to the rear to collect stragglers.

In recognition of Auerstädt, Davout's corps was designated as the first to enter Berlin, while Murat, Lannes, Augereau, and the Guard moved on Potsdam (*C2*). Soult, concentrating south of Magdeburg, was startled (23 October) by reports that a strong enemy column was advancing against him. This was Saxe-Weimar, who had feinted an advance on Magdeburg to cover his retreat on Sandau (*B2*).

October 24 found Davout at the gates of Berlin, Murat and Lannes at Potsdam. Their light cavalry, scouting along the Havel River, had brushed against what appeared to be the flank guard of a north-bound enemy column. Bernadotte, probing toward Brandenburg (*B2*), made similar reports. Napoleon hustled Murat and Lannes north toward Spandau (*C2*). On the left flank, Soult moved out to meet Saxe-Weimar, but found he had been bilked; he pursued, but took the wrong road. Ney remained to blockade Magdeburg, the garrison of which—actually 16,000—he estimated as 8,000.

On 25 October, Napoleon sent Grouchy, Lasalle, and Milhaud scouting northward from Oranienburg (*C2*); a small detachment under Savary (one

of his aides-de-camp) rode northwest from Potsdam. These units collected considerable information, which was again confirmed by Bernadotte, concerning Hohenlohe's retreat. The direction of Hohenlohe's retreat established, Napoleon ordered Bernadotte to follow him, while Murat (with Lasalle, Milhaud, Beaumont, and Grouchy), supported by Lannes, pushed for Zehdenick (*C2*) and Templin (*C3*) to head him off. Ney would remain before Magdeburg; Soult, now out of contact with Hohenlohe, was given a free hand. The Guard and the cuirassier divisions would remain around Berlin. Davout and Augereau would move eastward as a screen against any unexpectedly rapid Russian advance. Unknown to Napoleon, Soult had captured Saxe-Weimar's flank guard at Tangermünde (*B2*) on the 25th.

On 26 October, Lasalle and Grouchy destroyed Hohenlohe's flank guard at Zehdenick. Hohenlohe turned northward, aiming for Prenzlau and Stettin (*both C3*). Savary, however, was keeping the pursuit informed of Hohenlohe's movements. Murat ran him down at Prenzlau on 28 October, capturing approximately 16,000 exhausted, demoralized men.

Murat now turned to corralling Hohenlohe's various detachments. Napoleon dispatched Savary to reconnoiter toward Wittstock (*B3*) and maintain liaison among Murat, Bernadotte, and Soult. Klein would advance northward from Magdeburg, sweeping up stragglers from both armies. Jerome (reinforced as shown) would shift northward to contact Davout. On 29 October, Lasalle bluffed the fortress of Stettin (5,500 men, 160 guns) into surrender.

Blücher retired on Winning (to whom Saxe-Weimar had relinquished his command) on 30 October, and took over command of their combined forces. Winning had arranged to escape by sea from Rostock (*B3*) to East Prussia, but Blücher thought otherwise.

Blücher, whether purposely to delay the French advance into East Prussia, or from his characteristic, unthinking pugnacity, ordered a counteroffensive across the lower Elbe. Savary, however, was already on Winning's track. Soult, Bernadotte, and Murat closed in relentlessly; Napoleon ordered Louis and Mortier in from the west. Lannes' exhausted corps barred the lower Oder.

Crowded northwestward, Blücher now hoped either to escape by sea or to join Swedish forces reported near Lübeck (*A3*). On 5 November, he forced his way into that neutral free city, demanding food, money, and ammunition. The Swedes had re-embarked, but he hoped to rest and resupply his men behind Lübeck's light fortifications. On 6 November, Soult and Bernadotte stormed Lübeck out of hand; their troops, maddened by long-endured hardship, sacked the city. Blücher escaped with part of his army, but was cornered and captured the next day. In Murat's words, "The combat ends for lack of combatants."

This remains one of the greatest pursuits of history. In three weeks of unrelenting maneuver, battle, and marching, the French gathered 140,000 prisoners, 250 flags, and 800 field guns. Except for its units in East Prussia and Silesia, the long-feared Prussian Army was completely destroyed.

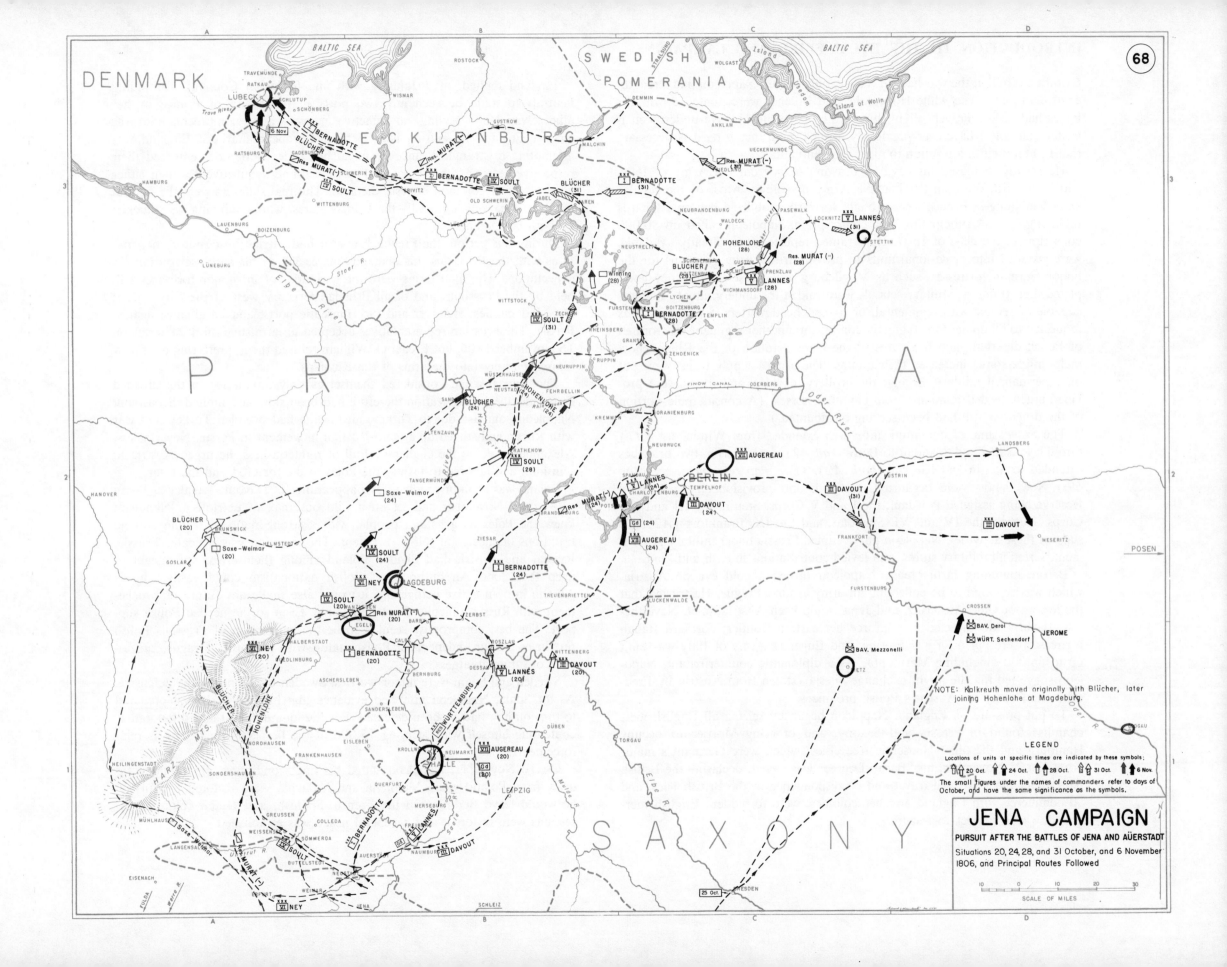

JENA CAMPAIGN

PURSUIT AFTER THE BATTLES OF JENA AND AÜERSTADT

Situations 20, 24, 28, and 31 October, and 6 November 1806, and Principal Routes Followed

NOTE: Kalkreuth moved originally with Blücher, later joining Hohenlohe at Magdeburg.

LEGEND

Locations of units at specific times are indicated by these symbols:

20 Oct.   24 Oct.   28 Oct.   31 Oct.   6 Nov.

The small figures under the names of commanders refer to days of October, and have the same significance as the symbols.

SCALE OF MILES

INTRODUCTION TO THE EYLAU-FRIEDLAND CAMPAIGNS

Grimly aware that the war had, in reality, only begun, Napoleon had strengthened his forces, even while Hohenlohe and Blücher were hunted down. His losses had been relatively slight, but—"the plan which I have undertaken is vaster than any I have ever previously formed, and, therefore, it is necessary that I put myself in a position to meet all eventualities."

He greatly increased his cavalry, drawing units from the Army of Italy, which, in turn, drew on the inactive Army of Naples. Most of the regular units remaining in France were brought forward, mobilized National Guards replacing them. "Anticipating" the conscription, Napoleon called up 80,000 conscripts of the class of 1807. Half-trained replacements, already available, were grouped into provisional units to provide trustworthy garrisons for the major German fortresses, such as Magdeburg and Kassel, while they completed their training. Military schools were raided for undergraduate students capable of service with regimental, or higher, headquarters. Switzerland was requested to fill up her four-regiment contingent; another regiment was formed of Polish deserters; and the states of the Confederation of the Rhine (now including Saxony) increased their quotas. The army's supply trains were put on a permanent military footing; the artillery, cavalry, and trains were provided much-needed remounts from captured horses. (A considerable portion of the dragoons still had been serving dismounted.)

The army's line of communication was extended from Wittenberg (*A1*) through Potsdam and Spandau to Berlin (*all A2*); from Berlin, two branches extended to Stettin and Küstrin (*both A2*). (*For map references, see Map 69.*) New depots were organized, fortified, and provisioned, the Cavalry Reserve being assigned Potsdam; the I and V Corps, Stettin; the III and VII Corps, Küstrin; the IV and VI, Spandau; and the IX, Frankfort (*A2*). To support these activities, Napoleon put occupied Prussia under military government, seized all military stores, and levied contributions in cash and kind.

Before marching farther east, Napoleon turned a cold eye on Austria, which was reported to be collecting an army around Prague. He trusted that the lessons of Ulm, Austerlitz, and Jena would keep Austria quiet. Nevertheless, Bavaria was directed to reinforce her eastern frontier; northern Italian fortresses were put on a war footing; and Eugene's Army of Italy was built up to 64,000 (including Marmont). As a diplomatic counterirritant, Napoleon suggested that he might exchange Silesia (stolen from Austria by Frederick the Great) for Austria's Polish provinces.

To put pressure on England, Napoleon began by seizing all English merchandise found in Prussia and Saxony, and ordering Mortier to occupy Hamburg and the other Hanseatic free cities, which were Germany's major ports. On 21 November, his "Berlin Decree" was issued, declaring the British Isles under blockade. All travel and correspondence to the British Isles, and all commerce with England and her colonies, were forbidden; English merchandise was subject to seizure.

England replied on 7 January with an "Order in Council," forbidding neutrals to trade between any two ports in possession of France or her allies. Napoleon—having no effective navy—was waging economic war against England by cutting her off from European markets; England was attempting to strangle France by naval blockade. Both sides enforced their respective decrees with a great deal more zeal and acquisitiveness than either legal nicety or common honesty dictated. The real sufferers were the neutral mercantile nations, especially the United States, whose shipping was plucked by both belligerents.

During this period, the French Emperor had carried on desultory negotiations with the Prussians, his demands increasing as his successes outran his expectations. His final terms were the surrender of all major fortresses still held by the Prussians, and of all Prussian territory west of the Elbe (*A1*); large indemnities; Hanover and the Hanseatic ports; and an alliance against Russia. The Prussian representatives accepted an armistice on these terms on 16 November 1806, but Frederick William refused them, preferring to "throw himself entirely into the arms of the Russians."

The Russians had considered themselves only auxiliaries to the dreaded Prussians; their mobilization therefore had been slow and limited. Sebastiani, Napoleon's ambassador to Turkey, meanwhile had prodded Turkey into war with Russia and stirred up an anti-Russian movement in Persia. Nevertheless, Alexander took up the challenge. Full of righteousness, he urged Austria to join him, and labored to inspire the Poles to die for God and the Czar.

Poland was a major problem. The appearance of Davout's cavalry at Posen (*B2*) on 4 November had set off a wild outbreak of patriotism. Napoleon knew the Poles as a gallant people, with a strong national feeling and no traditions of successful self-government. The situation was delicate: Prussia, Russia, and Austria had divided Poland among themselves, and meant to keep their loot. An outbreak of Polish nationalism could easily convert Austria into an active belligerent; it would also make any future rapprochement with Russia difficult, if not impossible. Even so, he needed Polish support. The best compromise seemed to be the conversion of Prussia's Polish provinces into an independent Polish state—with plentiful, if vague, suggestions of future greatness.

Sweden and Spain were minor worries. Sweden had gone on the defensive. As for Spain, Napoleon now had evidence that his ally had been prepared to turn on him had he been defeated. For the moment, he feigned ignorance, contenting himself with securing 15,000 of the best Spanish troops as reinforcements.

On 10 November, Napoleon stated his final conditions: He would withdraw from Poland when Moldavia and Valachia were restored to Turkey; he would leave Berlin when the French, Spanish, and Dutch colonial possessions were restored, and a general peace was established.

The Eylau-Friedland Campaigns

"A general-in-chief should never allow any rest either to the conquerors or the conquered." —NAPOLEON

"I received your letter in a tumble-down farm house, where I have the mud, the wind, and some straw for my bed." —NAPOLEON

Bennigsen had advanced from Grodno (*D3*) on 3 November 1806, but was checked by news of Jena and subsequent orders not to cross the Vistula River (*C3 to D1*). He then turned south through Ostrolenka (*D2*) to cover Warsaw, which he guessed would be the next French objective, hoping to delay Napoleon until Buxhöwden could come up. Buxhöwden, however, was still concentrating: Essen had far to march; the Russian Guard, and other units in Russia's interior, were only beginning to mobilize; one strong corps (30,000) was required to oppose the Turks.

Beside Lestocq's corps, the Prussians had strong garrisons in Warsaw and their fortresses in Silesia and along the Baltic seacoast. The total manpower of these garrison troops was considerable, but their isolated units lacked mobility. An attempt to call up all available reservists failed because of the swift French occupation of most of Prussia.

Once he had become master of Berlin, Napoleon's first objective to the east had been the occupation of the line of the Oder River (*C1 to A2*), to ensure the undisturbed destruction of Hohenlohe and Blücher. This was easily accomplished, the key fortresses of Frankfort, Stettin, and Küstrin surrendering tamely.

Napoleon then sought to gain control of as much territory as possible between the Oder and Vistula rivers, thereby halting Prussian mobilization in that area and encouraging insurrection in Prussia's Polish provinces. The best plan, he felt, was to occupy the line of the Vistula—with bridgeheads on its east bank to permit quick offensive action—and then to put his army into good winter quarters behind it, while preparing for a decisive spring campaign. However, only Davout, Lannes, Augereau, Jerome, and part of the cavalry were available east of the Oder; Bernadotte, Soult, Ney, and the remaining cavalry were still around Lübeck or Magdeburg (*off map, A2*). Whether intentionally or accidentally, Blücher's retreat westward had pulled two French corps and considerable cavalry some fifteen or twenty marches to the rear. With only approximately half of his army available, and uncertain of the location of the Russians, Napoleon chose to advance by successive bounds as enemy information was secured.

The choice of his axis of advance was a serious problem. Possession of Warsaw, Poland's ancient capital and major road center, would be immensely important in converting Poland into an effective ally. Seizure of the Warsaw area would isolate Silesia (*B1*) and give him possession of a deep salient from which an advance northward would threaten the communications of any enemy force remaining on the lower Vistula. However, this advance involved grave disadvantages—chiefly, that of thrusting his head into a sack, with unsubdued Silesia to his rear, unfriendly Austria on his right, and an enemy concentration on his left. His badly stretched line of communication would run parallel to the Vistula for some distance. Finally, to cross the Vistula

near Warsaw would lead him into difficult country around the junction of the Bug, Narew, and Wkra rivers (at *C2–D2* dividing line).

Balancing his responsibilities as a commanding general and as a chief of state, Napoleon chose to advance initially on Warsaw, while at the same time bringing one of his rear corps forward on Thorn (*C2*). Information available on 7 November indicated that the Russians had not reached Warsaw on 30 October. He therefore ordered Davout to move his whole corps forward to Posen (*B2*), take up a position covering the roads from Thorn and Warsaw, and reconnoiter the country thoroughly. If the Russians advanced, he would fight them there. Informed later that Bennigsen could not reach Thorn before 7 November, he ordered Lannes, Augereau, Jerome, the Guard, Klein, and Nansouty to concentrate on Davout, hoping they could pause at Posen until Murat, Soult, and Bernadotte reached Berlin.

Davout occupied Posen on the 9th—the same day that Napoleon learned of the captures of Blücher and Magdeburg. On the 10th, Napoleon recalled Ney, Soult, Grouchy, and d'Hautpoul to Berlin; Bernadotte would remain in the Lübeck area until relieved by Mortier.

By 12 November, reports agreed that the Russians were not yet west of the Vistula. The Posen area had proved short of food and forage. (Lannes said the country reminded him of Egypt, except that the roads were worse.) Napoleon therefore decided to push his leading elements forward to the Vistula, between Thorn and Warsaw. Warsaw was the main objective, but the march was organized to permit a rapid concentration, if necessary, toward Thorn. Napoleon recalled Bernadotte to Berlin on 14 November; two days later he ordered Jerome to leave part of his corps to blockade Glogau, and advance toward Breslau (*both B1*). Lannes arrived opposite Thorn on the 17th. The bridge there had been burned, but he did learn that no Russians had reached that area.

Informed by spies on 18 November that Bennigsen was advancing on Warsaw, Napoleon placed Murat in command of all forces east of the Oder River, with orders to renew the offensive if the armistice agreed upon with the Prussians on the 16th were not ratified. On reaching Sompolno (*C2*), Davout learned that the Russians had entered Praga (*D2*) on the 15th. On 19 November, Milhaud reported a Russian division, which Bennigsen had sent forward to forage, in Sochaczew (*C2*). He clashed with its patrols at Lowicz (*C2*) on the 22d. Expecting increasing resistance, Davout began concentrating at Klodawa (*C2*); Lannes occupied Brzesc (*C2*) to cover Davout's left. Joining Davout, Murat ordered the advance renewed on 24 November.

Deciding that he could not hold the line of the Vistula, Bennigsen began evacuating Warsaw on the 26th. Two days later, Murat made a triumphal entry.

Note: On the map, Scherozk (D2) should be Serock, and Sakrotschin (C2) should be Zakroczym.

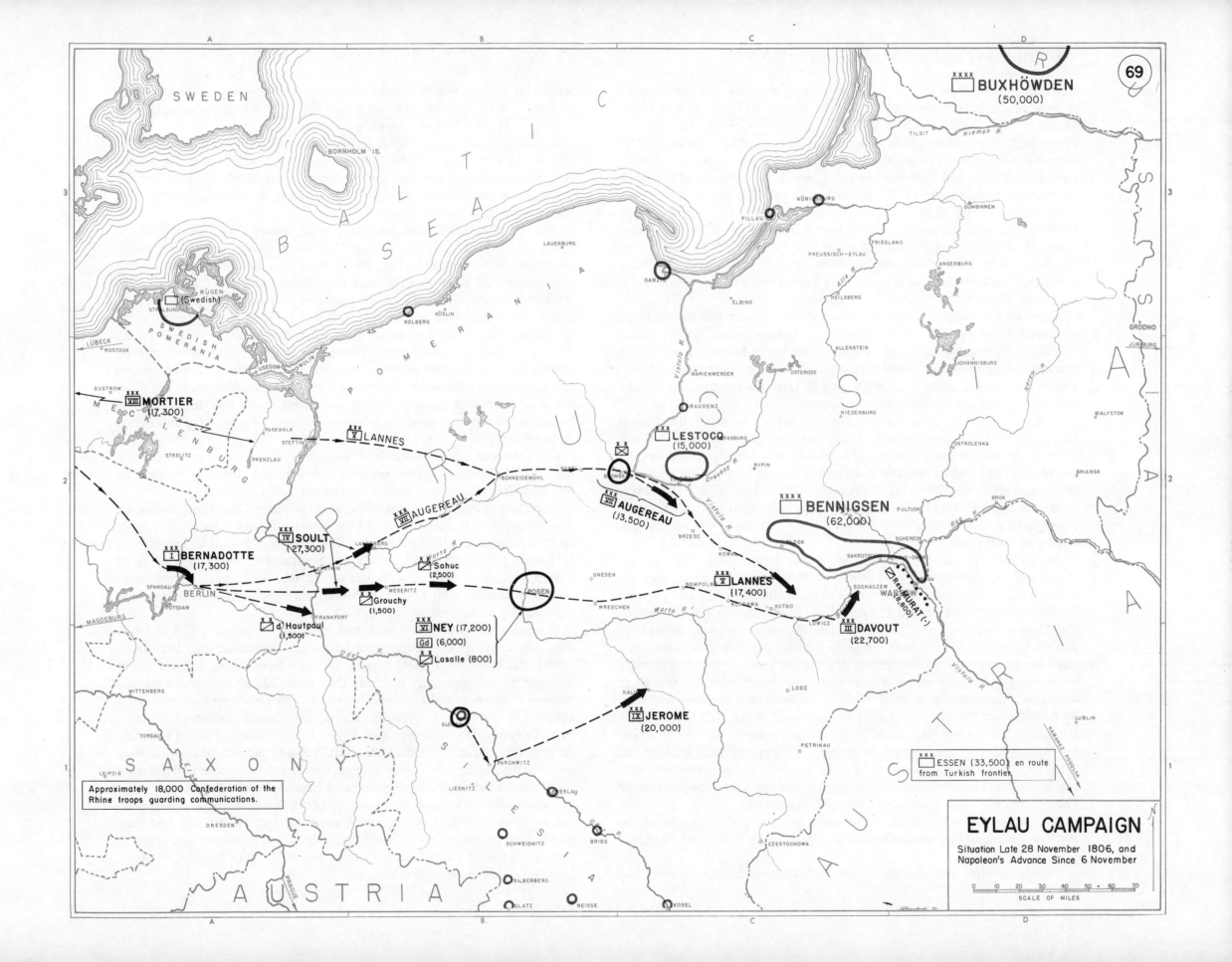

SWEDEN

BALTIC SEA

BORNHOLM IS.

RÜGEN
(Swedish)
STRALSUND

SWEDISH
POMERANIA

XXXX BUXHÖWDEN
(50,000)

69

TILSIT   Niemen R.

KÖNIGSBERG

GUMBINNEN

PILLAU

PREUSSISCH-EYLAU   FRIEDLAND

Alle R.   ANGERBURG

HEILSBERG

XXX LESTOCQ
(15,000)

XXX BENNIGSEN
(62,000)

XXX MORTIER
(17,300)

XXX LANNES

XXX AUGEREAU

XXX AUGEREAU
(13,500)

XXX SOULT
(27,300)

XXX BERNADOTTE
(17,300)

x Sahuc
(2,500)

x Grouchy
(1,500)

POSEN

XXX LANNES
(17,400)

R. & MURAT (-)

XXX DAVOUT
(22,700)

XXX NEY (17,200)
Gd (6,000)
x Lasalle (800)

x d'Hautpoul
(1,500)

XXX JEROME
(20,000)

Approximately 18,000 Confederation of the
Rhine troops guarding communications.

XXX ESSEN (33,500) en route
from Turkish frontier

EYLAU CAMPAIGN

Situation Late 28 November 1806, and
Napoleon's Advance Since 6 November

0 10 20 30 40 50 60 70
SCALE OF MILES

AUSTRIA

Reaching Posen (*off map, A1*) on 27 November, Napoleon initially intended to hold Soult, Bernadotte, and the Guard there—ready to support either Murat or Ney—while he dealt with his logistical problems. Learning (1 December) of the liberation of Warsaw, he ordered Praga (*Map a, B1*), occupied if the enemy evacuated it. Augereau would halt opposite the junction of the Vistula and Narew rivers (*B1*), where a crossing would outflank any Russian attempt to defend the line of the Bug and Narew.

Bennigsen, fearful of being cut off from Buxhöwden, began withdrawing (2 December) into the easily defended terrain between the Wkra and Narew rivers. He also required the protesting Lestocq to retire (5 December) on Strasburg (*A1*). Davout's leading regiment entered Praga on the 3d; three days later, Ney's advance guard crossed the Vistula and stormed Thorn (*A1*). Westward, Glogau surrendered (2 December).

Napoleon now ordered Jerome to besiege Breslau, meanwhile leaving Deroi at Kalisch (*both off map, A1*). Informed (5 December) of the occupation of Praga, he became impatient, preparing to order his whole reserve to Warsaw as soon as Davout crossed the Narew. His hopes outran his marshals. Floating ice and a shortage of boats slowed Davout's crossing. Unfriendly Austrians would sell neither boats nor urgently needed food.

Bennigsen now began a counteroffensive, hoping to catch the French astride the Vistula. Cooperating, Lestocq countermarched on Thorn, but was driven back toward Lautenburg (*A1*). Buxhöwden blandly halted east of Ostrolenka (*B1*). Better weather had enabled Davout to establish a fortified bridgehead over the Narew at Pomichowo (*B1*) early on 10 December. Bennigsen attacked it on 11 December, was repulsed, and thereafter organized a defensive position behind the Wkra, Narew, and Bug. Augereau began linking up with Davout.

At Posen, Napoleon had received reports to include only 9 December. Concluding that Bennigsen would defend the Narew, he reversed his previous plans, ordering Ney toward Strasburg, and Soult, Bernadotte, Bessieres, and the Guard from Thorn toward Pultusk (*B1*). Informed on 13–14 December that Davout was across the Narew, he again changed his plan: Bernadotte and the Guard would remain at Posen; Ney, Soult, and Bessieres would continue as ordered. By 15 December, Napoleon's spies reported the roads northeast of Pultusk jammed with advancing Russians. Concluding that there would be a major battle north of Warsaw, he ordered Bernadotte to Thorn by forced marches. Ney would turn south toward Rypin (*A1*) to support Bessieres until Soult could arrive. That night, Napoleon left for Warsaw, followed by the Guard. Increased estimates of enemy strength between the Wkra and Narew led him to group Ney and Bessieres under Bernadotte, who was to threaten the enemy right flank. Soult would cross the Vistula at either Zakroczym (*B1*) or Warsaw (later changed, as shown).

Meanwhile, the aging Marshal Kamenski had assumed command of the Russian armies, and ordered an offensive toward Plock (*A1*) and Graudenz (*A2*).

Though attempts to bridge the Vistula at Zakroczym failed, Augereau had ferried his corps across, establishing contact with Bessieres on 20 December at Plonsk (*B1*). Grouchy and Sahuc had driven in the enemy outposts near Biezun (*A1*), and Soult was crossing the Vistula.

Increasingly impatient, Napoleon planned a general offensive for 23 December. Davout, supported by Lannes and Murat, would attack across the Narew River. Augereau would advance from Plonsk; Soult would extend this movement northward, linking up with Bernadotte, whose advance, by then, should have unsettled the Russians.

Thaws had turned Poland into soupy mud; troops were spread widely to find food. Augereau's orders arrived late; Soult was barely beyond Plock. Bernadotte had advanced timidly, falling three days behind schedule.

Napoleon had noted that Davout's Pomichowo bridgehead was ringed by Russian batteries. Accordingly, he launched a coordinated night surprise attack across the mouth of the Wkra (*Map b, D1*), employing feints farther upstream, a heavy artillery preparation, and smoke screens. One of Davout's divisions (Morand) seized the dominating plateau at Czarnowo, splitting Bennigsen's line. On 24 December, another of his divisions (Friant) passed through Morand, followed by Murat and Lannes. Meanwhile, Augereau made a skillful wide-front crossing around Kolozomb; Soult was delayed by his bogged-down artillery; Bessieres halted at Biezun (*C1*), but Ney and Bernadotte pushed on.

His attempted offensive shattered, Kamenski ordered a retreat on Ostrolenka (*D1*), then, collapsing, resigned his command. Lestocq, battered by Ney and Grouchy, retired toward Neidenburg (*D2*).

Uncertain as to the direction of the Russian retreat, and eager to link up with Bernadotte, Napoleon started Davout toward Nowemiasto (*D1*) early on 25 December, but rerouted him through Strzegocin toward Golymin (*both D1*) when he learned of Augereau's and Soult's progress. Lannes advanced toward Pultusk. Napoleon, with Murat and the Guard cavalry, continued toward Nowemiasto. At Lopaczyn, Murat destroyed a Russian column and reported the enemy retiring on Pultusk.

Bennigsen had halted at Pultusk that morning. Docturov rallied at Golymin, but Lestocq was retiring northeastward. Unfortunately, Bernadotte lacked the courage to push beyond Biezun. Increasingly anxious about Bernadotte, and apparently believing that some 20,000 Russians were still between Ciechanow and Golymin, Napoleon (26 December) ordered Soult against Ciechanow, and Augereau, Murat, and Davout against Golymin.

At Golymin, Docturov repulsed Augereau and Murat. Davout's leading division then began enveloping the town, but—by stout fighting—the Russians escaped after dark. Soult entered Ciechanow unopposed. Bernadotte and Bessieres did not budge. Ney defeated Lestocq beyond Soldau.

Lannes (20,000) found Bennigsen (37,000, 50 guns) in a strong position covering Pultusk. Lannes knew himself isolated; his artillery had been unable to get forward, but he immediately attacked. Bennigsen attempted to envelop his right flank, but was stopped by one of Davout's divisions (5,000). Darkness ended the indecisive struggle.

70

EYLAU CAMPAIGN
PULTUSK CAMPAIGN
Situation 22 December 1806

SCALE OF MILES

EYLAU CAMPAIGN
PULTUSK CAMPAIGN
Situation Late 25 December 1806

SCALE OF MILES

Map a (left):

BALTIC SEA

KURISCHES HAFF

Niemen R.

TILSIT

KÖNIGSBERG

PILLAU

FRISCHE NEHRUNG

FRISCHES HAFF

Pregel R.

TAPIAU

WEHLAU

GUMBINNEN

WITTENBERG

KREUZBURG

ZINTER

WACKERN

GRAVENTIN

ALLENBURG

FRIEDLAND

ROSITTEN

ALTHOF

SCHLODITTEN

PREUSSISCH-EYLAU

SERPALLEN

DANZIG

KOLBERG

BRAUNSBERG

Passarge R.

ORSCHEN

ENGELSWALDE

LANDSBERG

HOF

ANGERBURG

ELBING

SPANDEN

MEHLSACK

WORMDITT

FREIMARKT

Alle R.

BARTENSTEIN

HEILSBERG

BISCHOFSTEIN

PREUSSISCH-HOLLAND

LIEBSTADT

ARENSDORF

GUTTSTADT

SEEBURG

RHEIN

ROSTENBURG

MOHRUNGEN

WALTERSDORF

HEILIGENTHAL

SCHLITT

SPIEGELBERG

BERGFRIED

WARTENBURG

BISCHOFSBURG

DEPPEN

JONKOWO

VISTULA R.

MARIENWERDER

FINKENSTEIN

OSTERODE

ALLENSTEIN

GRODNO

FREISTADT

PASSENHEIM

GRAUDENZ

HOHENSTEIN

DEMBEN OFEN

WILLENBERG

ORTELSBURG

JOHANNISBURG

BIALLA

LÖBAU

Pisa R.

KOLNO

GILGENBURG

NEIDENBURG

KOSCHEVO

Omulew R.

MYSZYNIEC

NOWOGROD

LOMZA

MALY PLOCK

STRASBURG

LAUTENBURG

SOLDAU

XXX VI NEY

XXX LESTOCQ

XXXX KAMENSKI (approximately 50,000)

MILAWA

CHORZELE

PRZASNYSZ

KRASNOSIELSK

OSTROLENKA

BROMBERG

THORN

Drewenz R.

RYPIN

XXX I BERNADOTTE

BIEZUN

LIPNO

XXX BESSIERES

SIERPC

Narew R.

XXXX BENNIGSEN

GOLYMIN

MAKOW

ROZAN

XXX BUXHÖWDEN

XXXX NAPOLEON

WOCLAWEK

Vistula R.

LOPACZ

STRZEGOCIN

SONSK

PRZASNYSZ

MOSZYN

PULTUSK

BRANSK

BROK

XXX VII AUGEREAU

KOLOZOMB

NOWEMIASTO

NASIELSK

WYSKOW

Bug R.

WYSZOGROD

MICHOWO

XXX III DAVOUT

OKUNIN MODLIN

ZAKROCZYM

SEROCK

XXX V LANNES

Res MURAT (-)

AUSTRIA

POSEN

LECZYCA 5 Miles

3 Miles

WARSAW PRAGA

Gd.

GALICIA

Map b (right):

BALTIC SEA

KURISCHES HAFF

Niemen R.

TILSIT

KÖNIGSBERG

PILLAU

FRISCHE NEHRUNG

FRISCHES HAFF

Pregel R.

TAPIAU

WEHLAU

GUMBINNEN

WITTENBERG

KREUZBURG

ZINTER

WACKERN

GRAVENTIN

ALLENBURG

FRIEDLAND

ROSITTEN

ALTHOF

SCHLODITTEN

PREUSSISCH-EYLAU

SERPALLEN

DANZIG

BRAUNSBERG

Passarge R.

ORSCHEN

ENGELSWALDE

LANDSBERG

HOF

ANGERBURG

ELBING

PREUSSISCH-HOLLAND

SPANDEN

MEHLSACK

WORMDITT

FREIMARKT

Alle R.

BARTENSTEIN

HEILSBERG

BISCHOFSTEIN

LIEBSTADT

ARENSDORF

GUTTSTADT

SEEBURG

RHEIN

ROSTENBURG

MOHRUNGEN

WALTERSDORF

HEILIGENTHAL

SCHLITT

SPIEGELBERG

BERGFRIED

WARTENBURG

BISCHOFSBURG

DEPPEN

JONKOWO

VISTULA R.

MARIENWERDER

FINKENSTEIN

OSTERODE

ALLENSTEIN

GRODNO

FREISTADT

PASSENHEIM

GRAUDENZ

HOHENSTEIN

DEMBEN OFEN

WILLENBERG

ORTELSBURG

JOHANNISBURG

BIALLA

LÖBAU

Pisa R.

KOLNO

GILGENBURG

NEIDENBURG

KOSCHEVO

Omulew R.

MYSZYNIEC

NOWOGROD

LOMZA

MALY PLOCK

STRASBURG

LAUTENBURG

SOLDAU

MILAWA

XXX LESTOCQ

XXXX KAMENSKI

XXX VI NEY

BROMBERG

THORN

Drewenz R.

RYPIN

XXX I BERNADOTTE

XXX BESSIERES

BIEZUN

LIPNO

SIERPC

Narew R.

CIECHANOW

PRZASNYSZ

KRASNOSIELSK

ROZAN

OSTROLENKA

XXXX NAPOLEON

WOCLAWEK

Vistula R.

Res. MURAT (-)

Docturov

XXX VII AUGEREAU

XXX IV SOULT

SONSK

XXX III DAVOUT

XXX BUXHÖWDEN

XXXX BENNIGSEN

MOSZYN

PULTUSK

WYSKOW

BRANSK

BROK

KOLOZOMB

NOWEMIASTO

NASIELSK

XXX V LANNES

Bug R.

PLOCK

DOBRZYKOW

MICHOWO

OKUNIN

ZAKROCZYM

SEROCK

WARSAW PRAGA

AUSTRIA

GALICIA

LECZYCA 5 Miles

3 Miles

Hastily reporting a victory over 60,000 French, led by Napoleon himself, Bennigsen bolted for Ostrolenka—adding that only Buxhöwden's failure to support him had saved the French from destruction. Covered by aggressive cavalry actions, the Russian retreat continued as shown (*Map a*). Eventually, Buxhöwden and Bennigsen agreed to move nearer Königsberg (*B3*). On 11 January 1807, in recognition of his "victory," Bennigsen received command of both armies and began concentrating them around Bialla (*B2*).

Napoleon had intended only to gain elbowroom east of the Vistula, though he obviously had hoped to cripple the Russian armies in the process. Brutal weather, the few wretched roads, and the boggy, barren terrain had made it impossible for the French to move swiftly and in mass. His commanders were calling his attention to the condition of their troops—hungry, exhausted, ragged. Sickness was increasing; the supply system had collapsed. The soldiers themselves were loudly discontented. Without rest and resupply, his army would soon be incapable of serious action.

Realizing on 27 December that the Russians had escaped, Napoleon feinted an advance on Grodno (*off map, B2*) by ordering Bernadotte and Bessieres toward Willenberg (*B2*); Murat, supported by Soult, would pursue Bennigsen cautiously. The army thereafter would go into winter quarters.

After some reshuffling, the army was distributed as shown. Supply depots were moved west of the Vistula; corps' assembly areas were designated; bridgeheads were organized along the Vistula and Narew at Thorn, Modlin, Praga, Serock, and Pultusk. Since Poland could not feed his army, Napoleon reorganized his logistical system along conventional lines.

His final dispositions left Bernadotte to cover the sieges of Danzig (*A3*), Graudenz (*A2*), and Kolberg (*off map, A2*), which would be carried out by Polish, Baden, and Hessian units. (Some of these were grouped, under Victor, into the new X Corps. Victor being promptly captured by partisans from Kolberg, Napoleon sent Lefebvre to replace him.)

Early January was quiet, except for minor skirmishes with Bennigsen's and Essen's outposts. Mortier drove the Swedish army into Stralsund (*see map 69, A3*). In Silesia, Breslau (*B1*) surrendered, after Vandamme (serving under Jerome) broke up an attempted Prussian concentration. Bernadotte had almost settled into winter quarters when he received (23 January) a message from Ney, requesting support against an all-out Russian offensive.

Despite orders against any offensive action during the winter, Ney had continually edged to the northeast, dispersing his corps over the area indicated (*this map, dot-dash blue line*) and planning a dash on Königsberg. Rebuked by Napoleon, he begrudgingly ordered (20 January) a return to his assigned area.

The Russian plan, concocted by Buxhöwden and Bennigsen, supposedly was to cover Königsberg, restore communications with Danzig and Graudenz, and take up winter quarters on the lower Vistula and Passarge rivers (*A2*). Spurred by Ney's nibblings toward Königsberg, Bennigsen advanced on 10 January, ordering Essen to move against Ostrolenka. Bennigsen for-

feited all chance of surprise by turning his cavalry loose two days ahead of his main body, thereby alarming the French without doing them any appreciable damage. Apparently unaware of the actual French dispositions, he merely struck the head of Ney's overextended corps, instead of cutting it in two.

Though Ney's outnumbered cavalry was attacked on 18 January and roughly handled, Ney seemingly did not comprehend his danger until the 23d. He then warned Berthier and Bernadotte, and ordered a concentration toward Neidenburg (*B2*), planning to hold the line Hohenstein–Gilgenburg (*both A2*)–Neidenburg as long as possible in order to protect Bernadotte's advance toward Osterode (*A2*). By 28 January, he had shaken off his pursuers and reached Gilgenburg (*Map b, C2*).

Bennigsen meanwhile had turned on Bernadotte, who was coming south by forced marches. His leading elements intercepted Bernadotte at Mohrungen (*C2*) on 25 January, but were thoroughly beaten. Without orders, and afraid of being cut off from Thorn, Bernadotte retired through Löbau (*C2*), where d'Hautpoul joined him, and finally halted at Strasburg (*C1*).

Napoleon had lost contact with Bennigsen shortly after the latter's departure from Bialla, regaining it only during January 21–24, when prisoners disclosed the Russian march westward. Believing this move a reaction (possibly limited) to Ney's activities, Napoleon merely issued warning orders. On 27 January, having studied Ney's and Bernadotte's latest reports, he decided that Bennigsen had launched a major offensive toward the lower Vistula, and so issued orders for an immediate counterblow. Ney and Bernadotte would take up defensive positions at Hohenstein and Osterode, respectively, to fix the enemy. (If they were forced to retire further, this would only draw Bennigsen deeper into a trap.) Davout, Soult, most of the Cavalry Reserve, and the Guard would strike north along the axis Ortelsburg-Bischofsburg-Bischofstein (*all D2*), to cut Bennigsen off from Königsberg. Savary (replacing Lannes, who was sick) and Beker would contain Essen. Lefebvre would defend the lower Vistula with a patchwork concentration of second-line troops; Oudinot would guard the army's line of communication north from Warsaw. Every effort was to be made to maintain secrecy.

Napoleon left Warsaw early on 30 January to rejoin his advance guard. At Przasnysz (*D1*), he learned that Bernadotte had withdrawn to Löbau, and Ney to Gilgenburg. Deciding that the Russian advance was becoming a threat to his own left flank, he shifted his axis of advance westward through Allenstein-Guttstadt (*both D2*), ordering Bernadotte to cover Thorn until Lefebvre arrived, then to join the main army. On the 31st, however, he directed Bernadotte to attempt to rejoin immediately via Gilgenburg.

Bennigsen had halted at Mohrungen on 27 January to rest his troops and await Napoleon's reactions. The next day, learning of French movements along the Narew, he turned his left corps eastward, shifted his reserve corps to support it and cover Königsberg, and continued the advance of his center. Lestocq, meanwhile, had forced Rouyer to lift the blockade of Graudenz.

Map (a)

EYLAU CAMPAIGN

Winter Quarters of the French, and Movements of Both Sides, 1-23 January 1807

SCALE OF MILES
10   0   10   20   30

LEGEND
★ – Designated corps assembly area.

a

BALTIC SEA

KURISCHES HAFF

Niemen R.

TILSIT

KÖNIGSBERG

TAPIAU   Pregel R.   WEHLAU

GUMBINNEN

FRISCHE NEHRUNG

PILLAU

WITTENBERG

KREUZBURG   ALLENBURG   FRIEDLAND

ZINTER   WACKERN   ALTHOF   SCHLODITTEN

ROSITTEN   SCHLODITTEN

FRISCHES HAFF

DANZIG
KOLBERG

BRAUNSBERG   ORSCHEN   PREUSSISCH-EYLAU   SERPALLEN

ENGELSWALDE   LANDSBERG   HOF

ELBING   MEHLSACK   WORMDITT   FREIMARKT   ARENSDORF   BARTENSTEIN

[XXX] **LESTOCQ**

23 Jan.

PREUSSISCH-HOLLAND   LIEBSTADT   SCHLITT   BISCHOFSTEIN   PAKENBURG

[XXXX] **BENNIGSEN**

WALTERSDORF   HEILIGENTHAL   SPIEGELBERG   DEPPEN   SEEBURG   RHEIN

VISTULA R.

MARIENWERDER   FINKENSTEIN   OSTERODE   BERGFRIED   BISCHOFSBURG   GRODNO

[XXX] I **BERNADOTTE**
[XX] Sahuc
FREISTADT

JONKOWO   ALLENSTEIN   WARTENBURG

PASSENHEIM

HOHENSTEIN   LÖBAU   DEBEN OFEN   SEELSBURG   JOHANNISBURG

BIALLA

[circle] BRAUDENZ

[XXXX] **BUXHÖWDEN**

LESTOCQ

STALL

[XX] **Rouyer** (Hessian)

GILGENBURG   SOLDAU

[XXX] VI **NEY**
[XX] Grouchy

Omulew R.

STRASBURG   LAUTENBURG   KOSCHEN   MALY PLOCK

[XXXX] **BENNIGSEN**

BROMBERG   RYPIN   CHORZELE   NOWOGROD   LOMZA

★ MLAWA

PRZASNYSZ

[XX] **Lasalle** (-)
[XX] **Milhaud** (-) (MURAT)

THORN

[XX] Res. **MURAT** ( )
   [XX] (Milhaud)
   [XX] (Lasalle)
   [XX] Klein
   [XX] d'Hautpoul

[XXX] IV **SOULT**

ROZAN

PLOCK   BIEZUN   CIECHANOW   MAKOW

[XXX] III **DAVOUT**
[XX] Beker

PULTUSK   ★   BRIANSK

WOCLAWEK   DOBRZYKOW   LOPACZYN   SONSK   STRZEGOCIN   NASIELSK

★   WYSKON

[XXX] **ESSEN**
(approaching)

[XXX] VII **AUGEREAU**

NOWEMIASTO   ZEBROWSKI   SEROCK   Bug R.

POMICHOWO

[XXXX] V **LANNES**

OKUN   MOLIN

[Gd] **Nansouty** (MURAT)
[XX] **Suchet** (V) (part)
[XX] **Reille** (III)

WARSAW   PRAGA

GALICIA   AUSTRIA

POSEN   LECZYCA 5 Miles   LOWICZ 3 Miles

Map (b)

EYLAU CAMPAIGN

Situation 31 January 1807

SCALE OF MILES
10   0   10   20   30

NOTE: Lannes was gravely ill; replaced by Savary.

71

b

BALTIC SEA

KURISCHES HAFF

Niemen R.

TILSIT

KÖNIGSBERG

TAPIAU   Pregel R.   WEHLAU

FRISCHE NEHRUNG

PILLAU

WITTENBERG

KREUZBURG   GRAVENTIN   ALLENBURG

ZINTER   WACKERN   ALTHOF   FRIEDLAND

ROSITTEN   SCHLODITTEN

(6,000)

DANZIG

BRAUNSBERG   ORSCHEN   PREUSSISCH-EYLAU   SERPALLEN

ENGELSWALDE   HOF   LANDSBERG

ELBING   WORMDITT   MEHLSACK   FREIMARKT   HEILSBERG   BARTENSTEIN

[XXXX] **BENNIGSEN**
(77,000)

PREUSSISCH-HOLLAND   LIEBSTADT   BISCHOFSTEIN   ROSTENBURG

WALTERSDORF   HEILIGENTHAL   SPIEGELBERG   DEPPEN   SEEBURG   RHEIN

BERGFRIED   WARTENBURG   BISCHOFSBURG

MARIENWERDER   JONKOWO   GRODNO

[XXX] **LESTOCQ**
(13,000)

OSTERODE   HOHENSTEIN

[XX] **Lasalle** (2,200)
GÖRTELSBURG
[XX] **Milhaud** (3,000)   **MURAT**

(3,000) BRAUDENZ

LÖBAU   DEBEN OFEN   SEELSBURG   JOHANNISBURG

BIALLA

[XX] **Grouchy** (1,900)
WILLENBERG

[XX] **Rouyer** (7,000)

GILGENBURG   ORDENBURG

[VI] **NEY** (15,000)

[XXX] Finkenstein
[XX] Sahuc

[IV] **SOULT**
KOSCHEVO
(27,800)

[XXX] **Sedmoratzki**
(18,000)

MYSZYN   MALY PLOCK   ROMOGROD   LOMZA

[Gd] **Gd** (6,200)

STRASBURG   LAUTENBURG   SOLDAU

[XXX] III **DAVOUT** (20,700)

[XXX] I **BERNADOTTE** (18,000)
[XX] **Sahuc** (2,100)
RYPIN
[XX] **d'Hautpoul** (1,700)

MLAWA

OSTROLENKA

[XXX] VII **AUGEREAU** (14,600)

PRZASNYSZ   KRASNOSIELSK

THORN

[XXX] X **LEFEBVRE**
(Approx. 25,000, assembling along lower Vistula)

BIEZUN   LIPNO   ROZAN   MAKOW

[XXX] V **SAVARY** (16,000)
[XX] **Beker** (2,100)

[XX] **Klein** (MURAT) (2,100)

WOCLAWEK   LOPACZYN   SONSK   STRZEGOCIN   GOLYMIN   PULTUSK

Wkra R.   Narew R.   BRIANSK

PLOCK   NOWEMIASTO   NASIELSK   Bug R.

[XXX] **ESSEN** (18,000)

DOBRZYKOW   PLONSK   KOLOZOMB   ZEBROWSKI   SEROCK   WYSKON

[XX] **Nansouty** (MURAT) (2,900)

Oudinot (6,000)

WARSAW   PRAGA   **Lemarois** (approx. 6,000)

GALICIA   AUSTRIA

LECZYCA 5 Miles   LOWICZ 3 Miles

Early on 1 February, Bennigsen received an intercepted copy of Napoleon's orders of 30 January to Bernadotte, announcing the French offensive. He therefore ordered a general concentration at Jonkowo (*Map a, A2*), with the announced intention of advancing southeast through Allenstein to meet Napoleon. That night, he received an intercepted copy of Napoleon's latest (31 January) orders to Bernadotte.

These orders explained Napoleon's plans in considerable detail. For some reason, they were in clear text. Berthier had sent eight separate messengers by different routes, but the first seven were caught by Cossacks. One captured courier, a newly commissioned officer, failed to destroy his copy. Bagration, now commanding Bennigsen's advance guard, read the intercepted message before forwarding it, and immediately retired northward.

The French offensive meanwhile made a straggling start. Napoleon committed his frequent error of failing to allow for the state of the local roads while computing the time necessary for his concentration. His striking force, therefore, was never as tightly grouped as he wished, and the rapidity with which he pushed the offensive did not give the rearmost units an opportunity to close up. Murat drove the Russian cavalry out of Passenheim (*B2*) on 1 February; on the 2d, Napoleon pushed Murat and Soult on Allenstein, with orders to attack vigorously if they encountered no more than 12,000–15,000 Russians. Murat cleared the town with little trouble, but developed large enemy forces at Jonkowo.

Also on 2 February, Napoleon ordered Savary to maintain pressure on Essen, without engaging himself too deeply. If forced to act defensively, he should take position at Ostrolenka (*B1*); Oudinot, at Pultusk (*B1*), would form his reserve. Davout's detachment at Myszyniec (*B2*) would serve as a connecting link with Savary.

After a study of Murat's reports, Napoleon decided (3 February) that Bennigsen would actually concentrate at Guttstadt (*B2*), since Jonkowo could be easily turned from the east. Murat would push vigorously forward with the available cavalry (Milhaud, Lasalle, and Grouchy); Soult would advance up the right bank of the Alle River on Guttstadt; Ney would close up on Murat's left; Davout would force his march on Wartenburg. By 0600, however, Murat reported more than 30,000 Russians on the Jonkowo heights, seemingly determined to stay there. Napoleon now ordered Murat to act with prudence: Should the Russians suddenly advance on Allenstein, the dispersed French corps might be in a vulnerable situation. Davout was to hold Morand at Passenheim, and Gudin at Ortelsburg until the situation cleared.

After personally reconnoitering the Russian position, Napoleon ordered Murat to advance on it, with St. Hilaire's (IV Corps), Lasalle's, and Milhaud's divisions. Ney would continue as ordered; Augereau and the Guard would support them. Soult, with his two remaining divisions and Grouchy's dragoons, would turn the Russian left flank. The main attack was scheduled to coincide with Augereau's expected arrival, at about 1300.

Though forewarned, Bennigsen had been taken aback by the speed of the French offensive. Renouncing the idea of an advance, he decided to "wait until he could determine the movements of the enemy." At Murat's first advance, the Russian outposts retired; Napoleon thereupon ordered Soult to cut in through Bergfried, and launched a holding attack against Bennigsen's front. Soult struck a Russian division at Bergfried; it was dark by the time he had forced a crossing of the Alle River there, though his corps cavalry captured Bennigsen's supply depot at Guttstadt. Augereau had been late; Napoleon therefore could not convert his holding attack into a solid blow. Bennigsen hurriedly withdrew after dark.

Napoleon pursued on the 4th (*Map b*), but difficult ground and the superior numbers of Russian cavalry slowed his progress. On 5 February, scouts reported a strong enemy column (Lestocq's corps) on the left flank of the French advance. Napoleon sent Ney against it with Lasalle and Grouchy, warning him not to go too far west in pursuit. Lestocq escaped, but only by sacrificing his flank guard and abandoning his rear guard. Recalling Lasalle and Grouchy, Napoleon ordered Ney to pursue the column he had just beaten, maneuvering so as to keep it from rejoining Bennigsen. (He also ordered that the army's base be shifted to Thorn, Warsaw having become too distant.)

Murat had kept heavy pressure on the Russian rear (commanded by Barclay) through 5 February. The next day, he overtook it near Hof (*D2*), breaking Barclay after a short, violent battle. Morand and Friant (both III Corps) battered the Russians out of Heilsberg. These clashes convinced Napoleon that Bennigsen would be brought to bay on the 7th.

If Bennigsen continued eastward, he must sacrifice Königsberg; if he retired on Königsberg, he would be pocketed there. Finally, the French could outmarch him, whichever way he went. Napoleon accordingly ordered Davout to Landsberg; Ney would move generally on Kreuzburg, pushing Lestocq toward the sea.

Reaching Preussisch-Eylau (hereafter referred to as Eylau) after an all-night retreat, Bennigsen posted Bagration (approximately 15,000 men) west of the town to cover his withdrawal through it, and began forming up on the plateau to the east. Encountering Bagration, Murat and Soult finally outflanked him and drove him back into Eylau about dark. Napoleon was thereupon ready to halt: The hills west of Eylau offered a good position, and neither Davout nor Ney was with him. Both armies, however, wanted the town for shelter against the February night. After several hours of confused night fighting, Soult cleared Eylau.

Convinced that a major battle was imminent, Napoleon ordered Davout to march at dawn for Serpallen. For unknown reasons, he did not summon Ney until 0900 on 8 February. Lestocq had received orders at 0330 that day to rejoin Bennigsen.

72

EYLAU CAMPAIGN

Situation Late 3 February 1807

SCALE OF MILES

EYLAU CAMPAIGN

Pursuit From Jonkowo to Preussisch-Eylau
4-7 February 1807

SCALE OF MILES

LEGEND

Situation Late 5 February

Situation Late 7 February

Map (a) — Situation Late 3 February 1807

BALTIC SEA

KURISCHES HAFF

Niemen R.

TILSIT

KÖNIGSBERG

FRISCHE NEHRUNG

FRISCHES HAFF

Pregel R.

TAPIAU

WEHLAU

GUMBINNEN

WITTENBERG

Frisching River

KREUZBURG

ALLENBURG

FRIEDLAND

ZINTER

WACKERN

GRAVENTIN

ALTHOF

ROSITTEN

PREUSSISCH-EYLAU

SERPALLEN

BRAUNSBERG

ORSCHEN

DANZIG

KOLBERG

Passarge R.

ENGELSWALDE

LANDSBERG

ELBING

MEHLSACK

HOF

Alle R.

BARTENSTEIN

ANGERBURG

SPANDEN

WORMDITT

HEILSBERG

BISCHOFSTEIN

PREUSSISCH-HOLLAND

FREIMARKT

ARENDSDORF

GUTTSTADT

ROSTENBURG

LIEBSTADT

SEEBURG

RHEIN

MARIENWERDER

MOHRUNGEN

WALTERSDORF

HEILIGENTHAL

SCHLITT

SPIEGELBERG

BERGFRIED

IV SOULT

BISCHOFSBURG

DEPPEN

BENNIGSEN

WARTENBURG

JONKOWO

Res. MURAT

ALLENSTEIN

III DAVOUT

GRODNO

VI NEY

AUGEREAU

Gd

FINKENSTEIN

FREISTADT

OSTERODE

LESTOCQ

PASSENHEIM

HOHENSTEIN

Res. MURAT (-)

MORTELSBURG

JOHANNISBURG

GRAUDENZ

DEMBEN OFEN

BIALLA

LÖBAU

VI NEY

GILGENBURG

WILLENBERG

III DAVOUT

VII AUGEREAU

NEIDENBURG

IV SOULT

Gd

PYNIEC

KOSCHEVO

Omulew R.

MLAWY PLOCK

MÖRTELSBURG

Visula R.

STRASBURG

LAUTENBURG

SOLDAU

KOLNO

NOWOGROD

OMZA

BROMBERG

LEFEBVRE

BERNADOTTE

Drewenz R.

THORN

RYPIN

MILAWA

CHORZELE

OSTROLENKA

ESSEN

BIEZUN

PRZASNYSZ

ARASNUSIELSK

Narew R.

LIPNO

ROZAN

CIECHANOW

MAKOW

SAVARY

LOPACZYN

SONSK

GOLYMIN

PLOCK

STRZEGOCIN

MOSZYN

PULTUSK

BRIANSK

WOCLAWEK

Visula R.

NASIELSK

WYSKOW

Oudinot

DOBRZYKOW

NOWEMIASTO

ZEBROWSK

SEROCK

Bug R.

POMICHOWO

CZARNOWO

Narew R.

WYSZOGROD

ZAKROCZYM

OKUNIN MODLIN

AUSTRIA

WARSAW

PRAGA

GALICIA

Lemrois

POSEN

LECZYCA 5 Miles

LOWICZ 3 Miles

Map (b) — Pursuit From Jonkowo to Preussisch-Eylau, 4-7 February 1807

BALTIC SEA

KURISCHES HAFF

Niemen R.

TILSIT

KÖNIGSBERG

FRISCHE NEHRUNG

FRISCHES HAFF

Pregel R.

TAPIAU

WEHLAU

GUMBINNEN

WITTENBERG

Frisching River

KREUZBURG

ALLENBURG

ZINTER

WACKERN

GRAVENTIN

FRIEDLAND

Res. MURAT (-)

LESTOCQ

BENNIGSEN

ROSITTEN

PREUSSISCH-EYLAU

SERPALLEN

IV SOULT

VII AUGEREAU

Gd

BRAUNSBERG

ORSCHEN

VI NEY

LANDSBERG

III DAVOUT

DANZIG

ENGELSWALDE

MEHLSACK

Alle R.

BARTENSTEIN

ANGERBURG

ELBING

SPANDEN

Res. MURAT (-)

IV SOULT

HEILSBERG

BISCHOFSTEIN

PREUSSISCH-HOLLAND

FREIMARKT

ARENDSDORF

ROSTENBURG

NEIDSTADT

VI NEY

III DAVOUT

SEEBURG

RHEIN

MARIENWERDER

FINKENSTEIN

WALTERSDORF

HEILIGENTHAL

SCHLITT

BERGFRIED

VII AUGEREAU

BISCHOFSBURG

MOHRUNGEN

DEPPEN

WARTENBURG

JONKOWO

ALLENSTEIN

FREISTADT

BERNADOTTE

OSTERODE

PASSENHEIM

GRAUDENZ

HOHENSTEIN

DEMBEN OFEN

Sedmoratzki

LÖBAU

JOHANNISBURG

BIALLA

GILGENBURG

WILLENBERG

PYNIEC

KOLNO

NEIDENBURG

KOSCHEVO

Omulew R.

Piza R.

MLAWY PLOCK

Visula R.

STRASBURG

LAUTENBURG

SOLDAU

NOWOGROD

OMZA

BROMBERG

LEFEBVRE

THORN

Drewenz R.

RYPIN

MILAWA

SAVARY

KRAENOBIELSK

ESSEN

BIEZUN

CHORZELE

OSTROLENKA

Narew R.

LIPNO

CIECHANOW

ROZAN

SONSK

SAVARY

PULTUSK

BRIANSK

LOPACZYN

GOLYMIN

MOSZYN

Oudinot

PLOCK

STRZEGOCIN

NOWEMIASTO

WYSKOW

KOLOZOMR

NASIELSK

DOBRZYKOW

ZEBROWSKI

SEROCK

Bug R.

POMICHOWO

CZARNOWO

Narew R.

ZAKROCZYM

OKUNIN MODLIN

AUSTRIA

WARSAW

PRAGA

GALICIA

Lemrois

LECZYCA 5 Miles

LOWICZ 3 Miles

The Eylau area is generally open and rolling, broken in summer by multitudes of small lakes, marshes, and creeks—all of which were now frozen solid and invisible beneath one to three feet of snow. The only conspicuously high ground east of Eylau is the knoll where that town's church and cemetery were located, and a slightly higher ridge north of Serpallen (C1).

February 8 was cold and dark; a high north wind whirled frequent, heavy snow squalls into the Frenchmen's faces. Davout later noted that this battle had many of the characteristics of night combat.

This open countryside offered Bennigsen opportunities to exploit his superior numbers, especially of cavalry, by maneuver. His plan, however, remains unknown. He later claimed that he had hoped to tempt Napoleon to attack his center. Other Russian accounts claim that he planned to attack Napoleon's center after an artillery preparation. His general dispositions were careless: Both flanks were in the air, and most of his army stood massed on forward slopes, perfect targets for French gunners.

Outnumbered and outgunned, Napoleon had a simple and effective plan. He would grip the terrain around Eylau, deploying only the IV Corps, supported by available light cavalry and most of his artillery. Two-thirds of the French army would thus be massed under cover behind his right flank. As Davout struck Bennigsen's left, he would commit this reserve, rolling up Bennigsen's left flank and driving him against the sea. If Bennigsen attacked the French left, he could be checked by committing the reserve there while Ney struck his rear and Davout his left.

At daylight, the Russian artillery opened all along the front. The French replied. Soult's corps was partially covered by buildings and hillocks, but the sheer weight of the Russian bombardment caused considerable losses. (Bennigsen may have mistaken Soult's movement into position for a threatened attack; anyhow, he reported repulsing one which never occurred.) About 0900, Tutchkov attempted—and failed—to take the Windmill Knoll (B2). Napoleon refrained from following up this minor success, since Davout had not yet arrived.

Shortly thereafter, Friant pushed Bagavout out of Serpallen, beat off a heavy counterattack, and drove the enemy toward Klein-Sausgarten (D2). Russian artillery, overpowering Friant's lighter divisional guns, covered this withdrawal effectively.

It was now about 1000. Considering Davout's progress, and the heavy loss Soult was enduring, Napoleon decided to seek a quick decision. Augereau would pass through the IV Corps and attack the enemy's center. St. Hilaire (now acting under Napoleon's direct orders) would advance on Augereau's right, maintaining contact with Davout.

St. Hilaire advanced under murderous artillery fire. Augereau, so sick he could hardly ride, brought his two divisions forward, deploying them abreast as they cleared Soult's line. Then, a sudden, dense snowstorm came down, blinding men and wetting muskets. Augereau's open formation could not be controlled in this blizzard; its attack strayed off to its left, presenting its flank to seventy-two Russian guns, which raked it mercilessly. (The Russians, having the storm at their backs, could dimly distinguish the struggling mass, some 300 yards away.) Worse, this error brought Augereau's men under the fire of the French center's artillery, which was maintaining a blind bombardment through the storm.

Bennigsen loosed his reserve cavalry, supported by at least a division (not shown) of infantry. Breaking in between Augereau and St. Hilaire, the Russian horsemen rode through the fugitives, though certain die-hard French regiments retired in solid order, partially protecting the rest. At this point, the storm lifted, showing Napoleon the wreckage of Augereau's corps, now streaming back on Eylau. It had lost, in a half-hour, approximately 929 killed and 4,271 wounded, including Augereau and both division commanders; many survivors could not be rallied.

The situation was critical: Gudin's division (III Corps) was not yet up, Augereau was shattered and being smothered by Russian cavalry, Soult was badly mauled, the Russian infantry was beginning to advance. Napoleon calmly ordered Murat forward with the Cavalry Reserve.

Murat rode out, in column of divisions—Grouchy, d'Hautpoul, Klein, Milhaud, and Bruyere's brigade. Grouchy cleared the Russian cavalry from the retreating French infantry, driving it off to the northwest. Coming up on his right, d'Hautpoul smashed through the first line of Russian infantry, shattered the second line, and drove the Russians confronting him into the woods south of Anklappen. Bennigsen quickly committed his reserve—horse, foot, and guns. Grouchy had broken through the first line, but apparently had been checked by the second. Part of the Russian first and second lines now toughly re-formed and began firing wildly to the rear; Murat's leading divisions seemed hopelessly trapped.

Instead, the cavalry of the Guard burst forward, trampling the Russian infantry flat and cutting Murat loose. During this melee, a column (4,000) of Russian grenadiers, following the retreating VII Corps, blundered blindly up to the Eylau cemetery knoll (action not shown). Calm amid his startled staff, Napoleon paused to trap and exterminate them between his nearest Guard infantry and Bruyere.

His left-flank units badly hurt, St. Hilaire had retired, uncovering Morand's left. (Morand had, in the meantime, pushed well north of Serpallen.) The Russian cavalry now pounced upon him, hustling him back into Serpallen. Klein saw the danger and swung a brigade against the flank of the Russian cavalry, scattering it. Davout personally lifted Morand's infantry forward to regain the ground they had lost. Friant's leading brigade had stormed Klein-Sausgarten (action not shown), forcing Bennigsen to divert Kamenski to save Bagavout and regain the town.

Note: On the map (C2), Bennigsen's total strength should be 60,000 instead of 6,000.

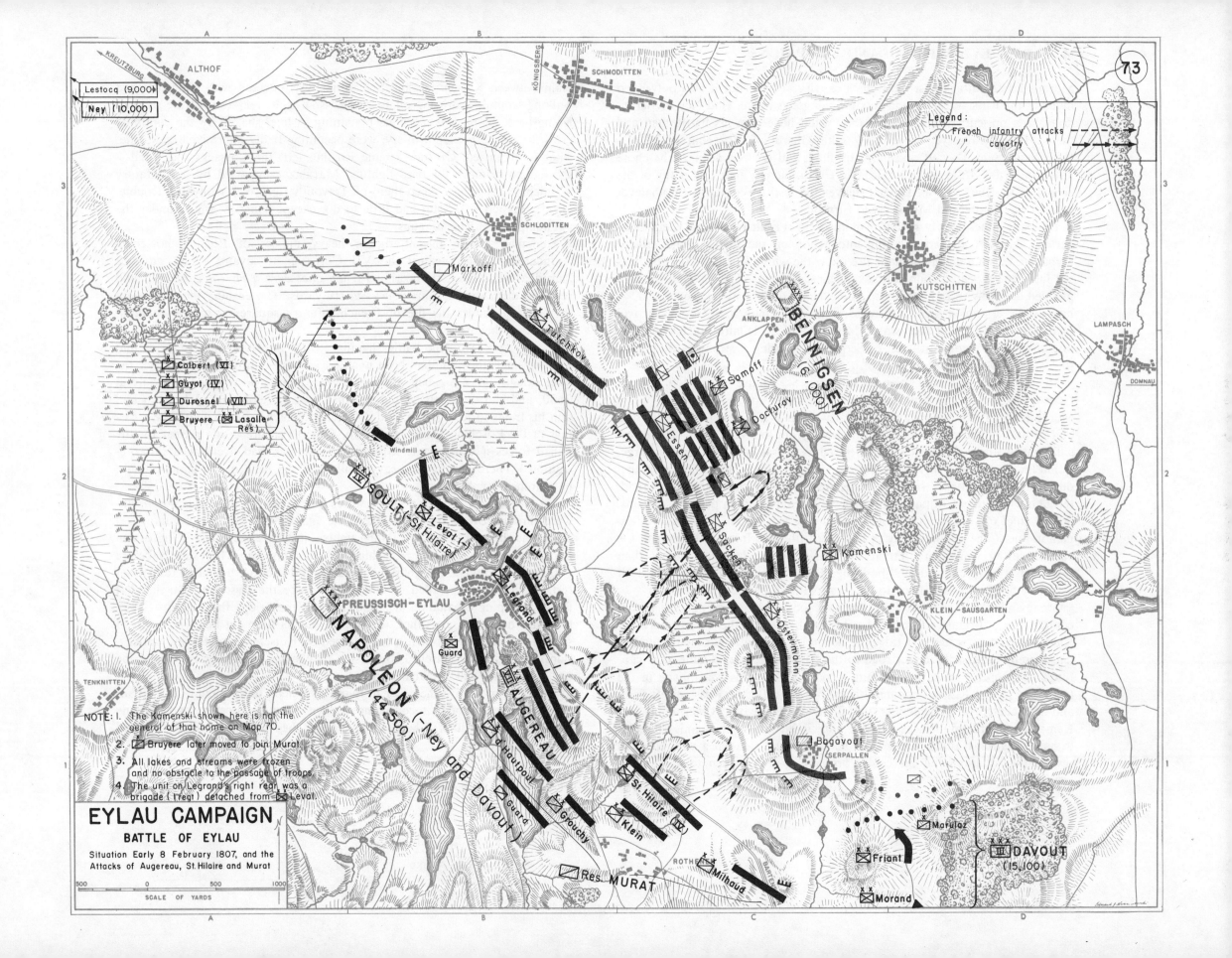

KREUTZBURG

ALTHOF

Lestocq (9,000)

Ney (10,000)

Legend:
French infantry attacks – – – –
"   "   cavalry

73

KÖNIGSBERG

SCHMODITTEN

KUTSCHITTEN

SCHLODITTEN

Colbert (VI)
Guyot (IV)
Durosnel (VII)
Bruyere (Lasalle Res)

Markoff

Tutchkov

ANKLAPPEN

BENNIGSEN
(6,000)

Samoff

Dochturov

LAMPASCH

Essen

DOMNAU

Windmill

SOULT (-St Hilaire)

Leval (-)

Sacken

Kamenski

Ostermann

KLEIN-SAUSGARTEN

PREUSSISCH-EYLAU

Legrand

NAPOLEON (-Ney and Davout)
(44,500)

Guard

TENKNITTEN

AUGEREAU

d'Hautpoul

Guard

Bagavout

SERPALLEN

St. Hilaire (IV)

Grouchy

Klein

Marulaz

NOTE: 1. The Kamenski shown here is not the
general of that name on Map 70.
2. Bruyere later moved to join Murat.
3. All lakes and streams were frozen
and no obstacle to the passage of troops.
4. The unit on Legrand's right rear was a
brigade (1 regt) detached from Leval.

ROTHE

Milhaud

Friant

DAVOUT
(15,100)

Res. MURAT

Morand

EYLAU CAMPAIGN
BATTLE OF EYLAU
Situation Early 8 February 1807, and the
Attacks of Augereau, St. Hilaire and Murat

500   0   500   1000

SCALE OF YARDS

Murat's driving attack cost the French cavalry heavily, but it also pulverized much of the Russian center and shook Bennigsen's nerve. Had Ney or Bernadotte been present, Napoleon probably would have won his battle then and there. His only reserve, however, was his Guard infantry (barely 3,500). With Ney absent, Davout's position still fluid, and Lestocq at large, he chose not to hazard it. Instead, he would hold Eylau, thereby fixing as many of the enemy as possible, and let Davout deliver the decisive attack with whatever support St. Hilaire and Murat could furnish.

Davout's attack slowly gathered momentum. Friant recovered Klein-Sausgarten; Davout's artillery, coming into action on the high ground around Serpallen, began a deadly enfilade fire along the whole Russian front. Bennigsen launched repeated counterattacks against Morand. The Russian infantry plodded doggedly through the deep snow "heads down, bayonets extended"— but always crumbled away before Morand's marching fire. Gudin's arrival increased the weight of the assault. Morand and St. Hilaire pinched out the line of small mounds northwest of Serpallen, securing a strong position that thereafter served Davout as a pivot.

His line thus shortened, Napoleon shifted St. Hilaire to the left and attached Milhaud's relatively fresh dragoon division to the III Corps. While Murat reorganized his exhausted cavalry behind the cemetery knoll, staff officers and gendarmes rounded up fugitives from the VII Corps. There was still fight in some of Augereau's men; even as Murat began his great charge, a thin line of battered regiments and individual soldiers had rallied spontaneously along the line of small mounds just north of the Bartenstein road, through which they had passed on their advance. Napoleon placed Compans, Soult's chief of staff, in command of them; by evening, he had some 3,000 men in line. (The popular story of how the 14th Line Infantry Regiment was cut off during Augereau's retreat and fought to the last man rather than surrender is a typical cock-and-bull tale. That regiment did distinguish itself —but by fighting its way back to the road, with 50 per cent casualties.)

Meanwhile, Morand's left-flank regiment took Anklappen, but lost it to a counterattack. Friant, supported by Milhaud, cleared the woods north of Klein-Sausgarten, seized the ridgeline beyond, and finally stormed Kutschitten, thereby cutting the direct road to the Russian frontier. Gudin now captured Anklappen and its neighboring woods. These gains were made in the teeth of repeated Russian counterattacks, but by 1700 the Russian left flank and left center were beginning to fall apart. Bagavout, Ostermann, and Kamenski committed their last reserves, only to be outfought. Bennigsen seems to have withdrawn some troops from his center and right in a vain effort to restore the situation, but his center probably had few men to spare. The plain between Kutschitten and Schloditten was covered with stragglers and walking wounded, drifting off to the Russian right rear toward the road to Königsberg. Those Russian units remaining in line, shaken by the continual cross fire of the French artillery, were becoming badly intermixed and somewhat disorganized. On the extreme Russian left, the Cossacks—as usual— showed no stomach for hard fighting. Marulaz (supported by one infantry regiment) was able to keep them off Davout's right rear with little trouble. On the French left, Soult had little to do, except hang on grimly under the pounding of the Russian guns.

Sometime during the afternoon, heavy masses of Russian horsemen floundered forward against the VII Corps' light cavalry. Their advance lacked Murat's dash; the jeering French *chasseurs à cheval* closed up and received them with carbine volleys at six yards. The ensuing melee brought the Russians under the fire of French infantry squares near the windmill, completing their rout.

It was now—with the battle shaping swiftly into a French victory—that Lestocq intervened. He had been unable to march until 0800 because of the utter exhaustion of his men. His former rear guard had rejoined him only at 0600, and had to be left behind. (It managed to rejoin later.) Lestocq had sent his trains to Königsberg, and dispatched detachments to guard the crossings of the Frisching River (*Map 72b, D3*), to ensure a safe retreat for the Allied forces if worse came to worst. (Bennigsen had overlooked this precaution.) Then, putting his heavy artillery at the head of his main column, he marched for Althof.

En route, Ney's advance guard struck him, forcing him to detour northward through Graventin. At Wackern, he again sacrificed a flank guard, and —in a hairbreadth series of running fights—just barely escaped being drawn into a general engagement. Reaching Althof (*this map, A3*) shortly before 1400 with his remaining 7,600 men and 30-odd cannon, he halted for a brief rest. Bennigsen now called on him to reinforce the dissolving Russian left flank. Dropping a battalion at Althof to hold the bridge there against Ney's pursuit (the stream at Althof was frozen, but its deep-cut bed—now full of snow—remained an obstacle), he marched on Kutschitten, gathering up Russian fugitives as he marched. By design or chance, his attack enveloped the end of Davout's widely extended line.

Ney did not receive the order to rejoin Napoleon until about 1030. Abandoning his pursuit of Lestocq, he moved swiftly by the shortest road, the one leading through Althof. There, Lestocq's detached battalion initially blocked his advance guard.

Note: On this map, Milhaud's division (D3) should be shown as cavalry instead of infantry.

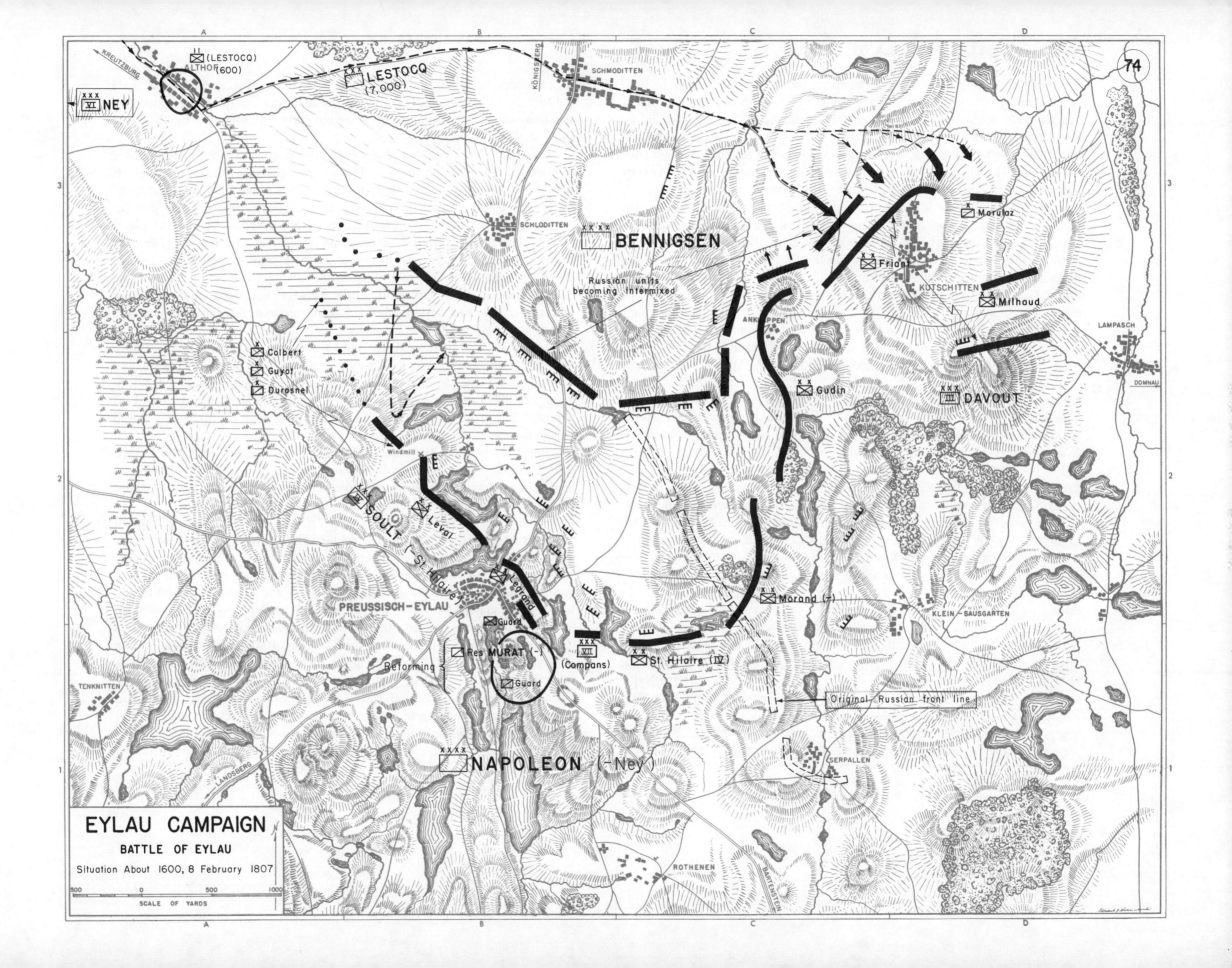

74

KREUTZBURG

⊠ (LESTOCQ)
ALTHOF (600)

XXX
VI NEY

XX
LESTOCQ
(7,000)

KÖNIGSBERG   SCHMODITTEN

SCHLODITTEN

XXXX
BENNIGSEN

Marulaz

Russian units
becoming intermixed

XX
Friant

KUTSCHITTEN

⊠ Milhaud

⊠ Colbert

⊠ Guyot

⊠ Durosnel

ANKAPPEN

LAMPASCH

XX
Gudin

DOMNAU

Windmill

XXX
III DAVOUT

XXX
SOULT
(~ St. Hilaire)

⊠ Leval

PREUSSISCH-EYLAU

⊠ Legrand

⊠ Guard

Res MURAT (~)

Reforming

⊠ Guard

XXX
VII
(Compans)

⊠ St. Hilaire (IV)

XX
⊠ Morand (~)

KLEIN-SAUSGARTEN

Original Russian front line

TENKNITTEN

XXXX
NAPOLEON (~Ney)

SERPALLEN

LANDSBERG

EYLAU CAMPAIGN
BATTLE OF EYLAU
Situation About 1600, 8 February 1807

500   0   500   1000
SCALE OF YARDS

ROTHENEN

BARTENSTEIN

Lestocq's enveloping attack on Kutschitten found the place held by only twelve weary companies of French infantry, with Marulaz in support. Marulaz was soon driven southward; the infantry held on too long in the town, were practically surrounded, and lost heavily while breaking out. As the Russian left flank rallied and joined in Lestocq's advance, the situation became highly confused. After repeated assaults, the Allies regained Anklappen and the woods south of Kutschitten. But Davout, massing all available guns on the high ground north of Klein-Sausgarten, rallied Friant's and Gudin's divisions in a splendid display of personal courage. Three successive Allied attacks were shot into the ground as they advanced southward out of the woods. Morand held his position on the III Corps left flank with equal firmness. Having broken the Allied attack, Davout again shouldered forward, one of Gudin's brigades achieving considerable success after dark. Night and exhaustion finally ended the battle at about 2100. The final positions held here are uncertain, but there can be no doubt that Davout was within a relatively short distance of Kutschitten and the road leading to the Russian bases east of the Niemen River. Around 1900, while Davout's fight raged in almost complete darkness, Ney rushed Althof, swept aside the detachment Lestocq had left there, and pushed his leading brigade toward Schloditten. The light cavalry on the French left immediately linked up with him. About 2000, he took Schloditten after a warm little fight, thereby cutting the Königsberg road behind Bennigsen.

Feeling a trap closing in on him, Bennigsen, at about 2200, committed five battalions of relatively fresh grenadiers. Ney's men held their fire until the Russians were at point-blank range, then blew them back downhill.

Ney, however, felt too weak to risk trying to defend Schloditten to the bitter end. (Only approximately half of his corps had reached the field.) Shortly after its capture, he wrote to Berthier, stating that he would not attempt to hold the village after 0200 the next morning should the enemy continue in force on his front. Now, uncertain of the general situation, he retired to Althof for the rest of the night.

Bennigsen ordered a retreat. Some of his commanders protested, claiming that they had just won the battle, but Bennigsen could not share their optimism. Both of his flanks had been turned, and his rear was threatened. He had put in his last man and gun against a smaller force, only to have Napoleon retain the initiative throughout the day. The next morning, Napoleon would have Ney and the Guard infantry—and possibly Bernadotte and Nansouty—at his disposal. Furthermore, the Russians (though not the Prussians) were without food, almost out of ammunition, disorganized, and weakened by casualties, straggling, and desertion. Ostermann, for example, had only 2,170 men with his colors. Bennigsen himself was exhausted. Accordingly, the Russians began withdrawing at about midnight, followed by the Prussians at 0200.

Meanwhile, Napoleon remained uncertain as to whether he would have to continue the battle on the 9th. There is no reliable evidence that he ever considered retreating. From the positions of Ney's and Davout's campfires, he could see that he had the enemy half-surrounded, but he knew that his losses had been very heavy. The French were ordered to bivouac in place, without leaving their ranks; ammunition would be replenished (Davout's caissons were already busy with this work). Napoleon himself stayed awake, checking reports from his subordinates until 0300, when Soult reported the enemy thinning out on his front. Later, Davout reported sounds indicating that the enemy was withdrawing. Morning showed the battlefield empty, except for a few last Cossack patrols.

The French held the battlefield, and so claimed a victory, but it had been rather fruitless and extremely costly. Napoleon lost between 20,000 and 25,000 men, including a considerable number of senior officers. Approximately 11,000 Russians were left dead on the field. The Russians carried off almost 1,200 prisoners and 5 eagles. The French held approximately 2,500 prisoners (mostly wounded), 23 guns, and 16 flags.

After victories like Austerlitz and Jena, Eylau seemed almost a French defeat. Allied propaganda rapidly began magnifying it as such. (Bennigsen began the process by requesting religious services of thanksgiving throughout Russia for his second great victory over Napoleon.)

Napoleon took this battle deeply to heart. He may have been impressed by the stubbornness of the Russian soldier. He certainly felt a sincere grief and responsibility for the heavy French losses. (There is a most unusual note of humility in his correspondence of this period.) But, above all, he was impressed with the difficulty of waging war along the eastern edge of Europe. With approximately 300,000 men under arms in Germany and Poland, he had with difficulty assembled 70,000 for a decisive battle, which might have ended in the destruction of his empire. Of these, 10,000 had arrived so late as to have little effect. Obviously, he had employed insufficient forces; just as obviously, his logistical support was insufficient for even the forces he had employed. Reorganization and rest were essential. This pause might add weight to enemy propaganda, discourage his allies, and set restless heads in Paris to buzzing, but it would also restore the morale and condition of the Grande Armee.

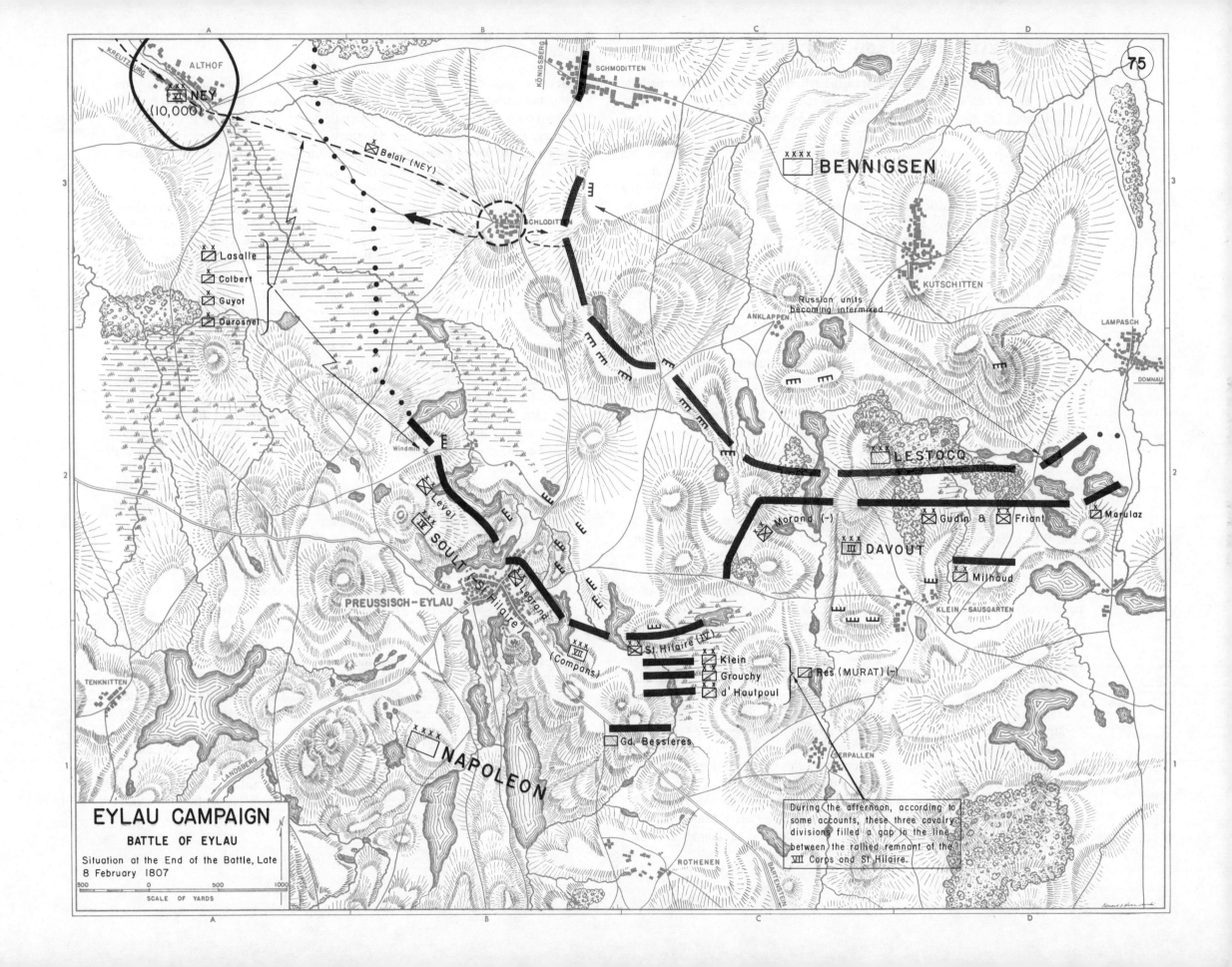

ALTHOF

KREUTZBURG

XXX
VII NEY
(10,000)

75

X⊠ Belair (NEY)

XXXX
BENNIGSEN

SCHMODITTEN

KÖNIGSBERG

SCHLODITTEN

KUTSCHITTEN

XX⊠ Lasalle
X⊠ Colbert
X⊠ Guyot
X⊠ Durosnel

LAMPASCH

DOMNAU

Russian units
becoming intermixed

ANKLAPPEN

Windmill

E

XX⊠ Leval
IV SOULT
(St. Hilaire)

XXX
LESTOCQ

X Marulaz

XX⊠ Gudin & ⊠ Friant

⊠ Morand (−)

III DAVOUT

PREUSSISCH-EYLAU

Legrand

⊠ Milhaud

KLEIN-SAUSGARTEN

XXX
VII
(Compans)

XX⊠ St. Hilaire (IV)
X⊠ Klein
X⊠ Grouchy
X⊠ d'Hautpoul

⊠ Res (MURAT) (−)

TENKNITTEN

XXXX
Gd Bessieres

XXXX
NAPOLEON

SERPALLEN

EYLAU CAMPAIGN
BATTLE OF EYLAU
Situation at the End of the Battle, Late
8 February 1807

During the afternoon, according to
some accounts, these three cavalry
divisions filled a gap in the line
between the rallied remnant of the
VII Corps and St. Hilaire.

500   500   1000
SCALE OF YARDS

LANDSBERG

ROTHENEN

BARTENSTEIN

Murat, supported by Ney, had followed the Allies on 9 February. Bernadotte reached Eylau on the 10th; Napoleon now sent him to Kreuzburg (*Map a, B3*), Davout to Friedland (*B3*), and Soult to Schmoditten (*B3*). Murat had halted on an east-west line through Wittenberg (*B3*), Ney some eight miles north of Eylau. Behind this demonstration, Napoleon worked to ensure the success of his next campaign. The army would go into winter quarters around Osterode (*A2*); Thorn (*A1*) would be its new advance base; the Vistula would be bridged at Marienwerder and Marienburg (*both A2*). On 17 February, the Grande Armee began its withdrawal.

Meanwhile, Russian cavalry had raided the French right rear near Willenberg (*B2*), and Sedmoratzki (*see Map 72b*) had made an almost successful attempt (*action not shown*) to capture the French detachment at Myszyniec (*this map, B2*). Bennigsen now ordered Sedmoratzki to rejoin him, and Essen to create a diversion in Napoleon's rear. Essen obediently advanced along both banks of the Narew River against Ostrolenka (*B1*). French cavalry captured a copy of his orders. Summoning Oudinot forward, Savary utilized the fortified Ostrolenka bridgehead to concentrate against each of Essen's columns in turn, defeating them both. On 24 February, Massena assumed command of the V Corps.

In Silesia, the French campaign was hampered by Napoleon's demands for reinforcements for the main theater. (Napoleon was willing to abandon all of Silesia except Glogau [*off map, A1*] if necessary.) However, Vandamme (acting under Jerome's theoretical leadership) managed to continue the steady reduction of the Silesian fortresses. Their cannon went to strengthen Napoleon's positions along the Vistula and Passarge rivers.

Covered by Ney, the French moved methodically into their winter quarters. When disposed as shown, the army could be supplied via Magdeburg-Posen-Bromberg (*see Map 69*). Moreover, this position would cover the French forces engaged in the siege of Danzig (*this map, A3*)—an operation necessary to clear the French rear, since that seaport offered a ready-made beachhead into which the Allies could pour reinforcements.

The French were still occupying their assigned areas when the Allies reappeared. The French withdrawal had rather surprised Bennigsen, who had retired to Königsberg in some disorder. Only on 19 February did he begin moving westward, apparently to discover how badly the French were hurt. Enlightenment came painfully: Bennigsen lost a flank guard at Braunsberg (*A3*) and a weak division at Guttstadt (*B2*). But Ney, believing himself faced by an overwhelming force, retired from Guttstadt to Deppen (*A2*).

Napoleon began concentrating at Osterode, intending to offer battle there if Bennigsen pressed his pursuit. Interviews with captured Russian officers soon convinced him that Ney had withdrawn prematurely. To meet fresh Russian movements toward Willenberg, the Emperor ordered Zajonczek's newly organized Polish division to Neidenburg (*B2*). On 1 March, learning that Bennigsen had reached Queetz (*A2*), he decided to launch a limited

offensive against him. Ney, followed by Davout, would advance directly on Guttstadt, while Soult maneuvered against Bennigsen's flank, and Bernadotte moved on Mehlsack (*A2*). Neither Bennigsen nor his famished troops wanted another battle; at the first clash (Launau, 4 March), Bennigsen immediately retreated into winter quarters. Napoleon then turned to his right flank, ordering both Murat and Massena against Willenberg. This proved to be a wild goose chase, only a few Russian cavalry being found.

All through March, Napoleon—living in miserable quarters at Osterode—struggled to feed and reorganize his army. After 1 April, conditions slowly improved. The VII Corps was broken up, the Reserve Cavalry sent to the rear to recuperate, the line of the Passarge River organized for defense.

Meanwhile, Lefebvre had cleared the country around Danzig (1–11 March) and had begun siege operations. Wishing to retain Danzig, the Allies planned the two-pronged amphibious relief expedition shown here, which was to be combined with diversionary attacks on Massena and Davout. Napoleon's intelligence service soon reported this general plan; the Emperor began organizing a "Reserve Corps" under Lannes in the Marienburg-Danzig area. Kamenski arrived on 10 May to find Lefebvre holding most of the islands between Danzig and the sea. Attacking energetically on the 15th, Kamenski was heavily repulsed and penned in his beachhead. Bülow arrived a day late, to be completely defeated. Lefebvre was preparing to storm the city when Marshal Kalkreuth requested terms. Eager to settle the affair quickly, Napoleon was generous. Kalkreuth surrendered the city (crammed with all sorts of supplies) on 27 April; Kamenski had evacuated his survivors two days previously. In Pomerania, after some minor scufflings, Mortier forced the Swedes to conclude an armistice.

Napoleon planned to open his spring offensive on 10 June. But, during the morning of 5 June, Bernadotte reported his outposts under attack; later, Ney reported the enemy assailing Altkirch (*Map b, D2*).

Alexander and Frederick William had hoped to deliver a major offensive across the Passarge River, while some 60,000 Allied troops broke out of Stralsund (*see Map 69, A3*) into the French rear, and Austria entered the war. Austria, however, chose to remain neutral; England had no available troops; and the Swedes had been defeated. Nevertheless, Bennigsen decided to attack. Lestocq would fix Bernadotte; Bennigsen, advancing in six columns, would block Soult and Davout and cut off Ney. This offensive was scheduled for 4 June; various delays caused Bennigsen to postpone it until the 5th. Lestocq was not informed in time, and consequently delivered an abortive attack that merely alerted Bernadotte. Attacking again on the 5th, Lestocq failed to penetrate Bernadotte's front, his right wing being driven back on Mehlsack, his left wing (Kamenski) checked at Lomitten. Bennigsen drove Ney back with considerable (2,500) losses, but Ney's knack for rear-guard fighting halted the Russians at Queetz (*this map, C2*).

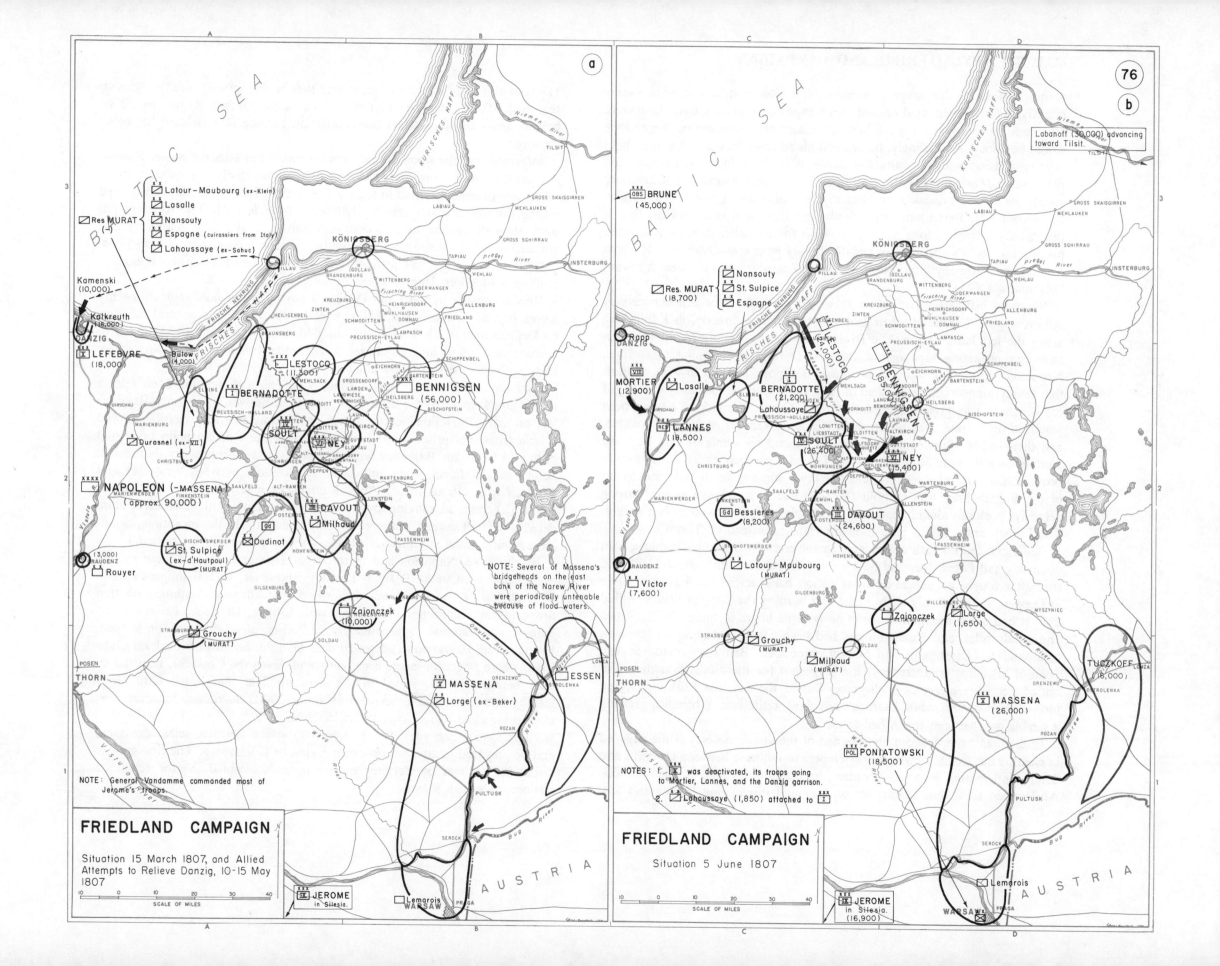

A quick study of his maps convinced Napoleon that any serious enemy offensive would be directed against Ney's exposed position around Guttstadt. Now that Danzig was in French hands, a major operation against Bernadotte would be idiocy. Accordingly, he ordered his reserves forward: Lasalle's light cavalry division and the cuirassier divisions of Nansouty, St. Sulpice, and Espagne to Marienburg (*Map a, A2*); Lannes and Mortier to Christburg (*A2*); the dragoon divisions of Grouchy, Milhaud, and Latour-Maubourg to Osterode (*A2*). Bernadotte, Ney, Soult, and Davout would hold the line of the Passarge River as long as they could; if forced back, they were to retire to the line of Preussisch-Holland–Saalfeld–Liebemühl–Osterode. Massena would immobilize anything confronting him; Zajonczek was to close in toward Gilgenburg (*A2*).

Napoleon estimated that his army would be sufficiently concentrated by the evening of 7 June. He then proposed to advance directly on Königsberg along the left bank of the Alle River, thus cutting Bennigsen off from his base and pocketing him against the sea. During the morning of 6 June, Napoleon's continuing study of his marshals' reports led him to write to Paris that "everything would be finished in eight days." Victor (recently exchanged for Blücher) was given command of the I Corps, Bernadotte having been wounded on 5 June. Ney was to hold out at Ankendorf as long as possible, and then—since Napoleon's plans would depend on whatever line Ney and Soult eventually were able to hold—to fall back on Deppen as slowly as was prudent. Davout, who would form the pivot for any retrograde movement of the French line, was to hold the Osterode area (where several strong defensive positions already had been reconnoitered) and to cover Ney's right. The French army would base itself on Danzig, instead of Thorn.

Bennigsen felt no such confidence; by the end of 6 June, his complex plan obviously had failed. Ney had held around Ankendorf until about 1100, and thereafter fought an expert delaying action back across the Passarge River at Deppen, suffering only slight losses and burning the Deppen bridge behind him. It had taken the main Russian army three hours to force him back two and a half miles, and Russian losses had been heavy, including two division commanders (Ostermann and Somoff) wounded. Bennigsen made Sacken (one of his corps commanders) the scapegoat for the affair, hounding him out of the Russian service in disgrace. During the day, the Russians massed toward their center, while Lestocq's left flank retired on Wormditt, creating a sizable gap between the Allied armies.

In the meantime, Davout had learned of the attack on Ney while engaged in clearing out Cossacks who had attempted to infiltrate between his corps and Soult. Anticipating Napoleon's orders, he promptly massed in the Ostrode–Alt-Ramten area, thus closing up on Ney and threatening Bennigsen's left.

(Davout also sent Ney a message, stating that he was moving into the Russian rear with 40,000 men and that the whole of the Grande Armee would be behind him—and dispatched the courier by a route that ensured his being captured.)

Informed that the whole French army seemed to be on the move, Bennigsen decided on 7 June that discretion was undoubtedly the better part of valor, and ordered a retreat to the great entrenched camp he had constructed during the winter and spring at Heilsberg (*Map b, D2*). The Russians fell back through Queetz in considerable disorder, with much marching and countermarching. Bennigsen apparently (accounts are contradictory) decided to make a stand at Guttstadt, and called on Lestocq to support him by striking Soult's left flank.

Reconnaissance by the I and IV Corps having found no significant enemy forces beyond Spanden and Elditten, Napoleon ordered a general advance on Deppen for the 8th, attaching Latour-Maubourg to Soult and Milhaud to Davout, and summoning Zajonczek to Osterode. For some unknown reason, Davout's orders reached him late.

Arriving at Deppen early on 8 June, Napoleon had Ney and Soult feint a major attack to force the enemy to "show themselves." The only Russians still present—Bagration's corps, serving as Bennigsen's rear guard—showed a bold front, but prisoners soon disclosed that the Russian main body had retired on Guttstadt. Bagration withdrew slowly and was not seriously pressed, Soult's cavalry having been ambushed by Cossacks between Wolfsdorf and Altkirch with serious losses. Also, Kamenski's and Rambow's divisions of Lestocq's command, rallying toward Bennigsen's north flank as ordered, blundered into Soult instead and were roughly handled. (In the meantime, deciding against a stand at Guttstadt, Bennigsen was continuing his retreat.)

By this time, Napoleon had learned that Davout could not close on the main army until 0600, 9 June. Deciding, however, that Bennigsen's main body should be near Guttstadt, he ordered the advance continued on that town. Murat accordingly moved out with Lasalle, Grouchy, Nansouty, St. Sulpice, and Espagne (approximately 12,700 cavalrymen) early on 9 June. Encountering Bagration's rear guard near Glottau, he drove it back on Guttstadt, where Bagration made a gallant stand. Even the Cossacks, inspired by their hetman, Platov, joined in the stand-up fight that lasted until Ney's leading infantry stormed the town at about 2000. Bagration, however, was able to burn the bridges over the Alle River.

Napoleon's orders to Victor had been to attack Lestocq, seize Mehlsack, and be prepared to advance on either Eylau or Königsberg. The first courier dispatched to him by Berthier having been intercepted, Victor remained stationary through 9 June.

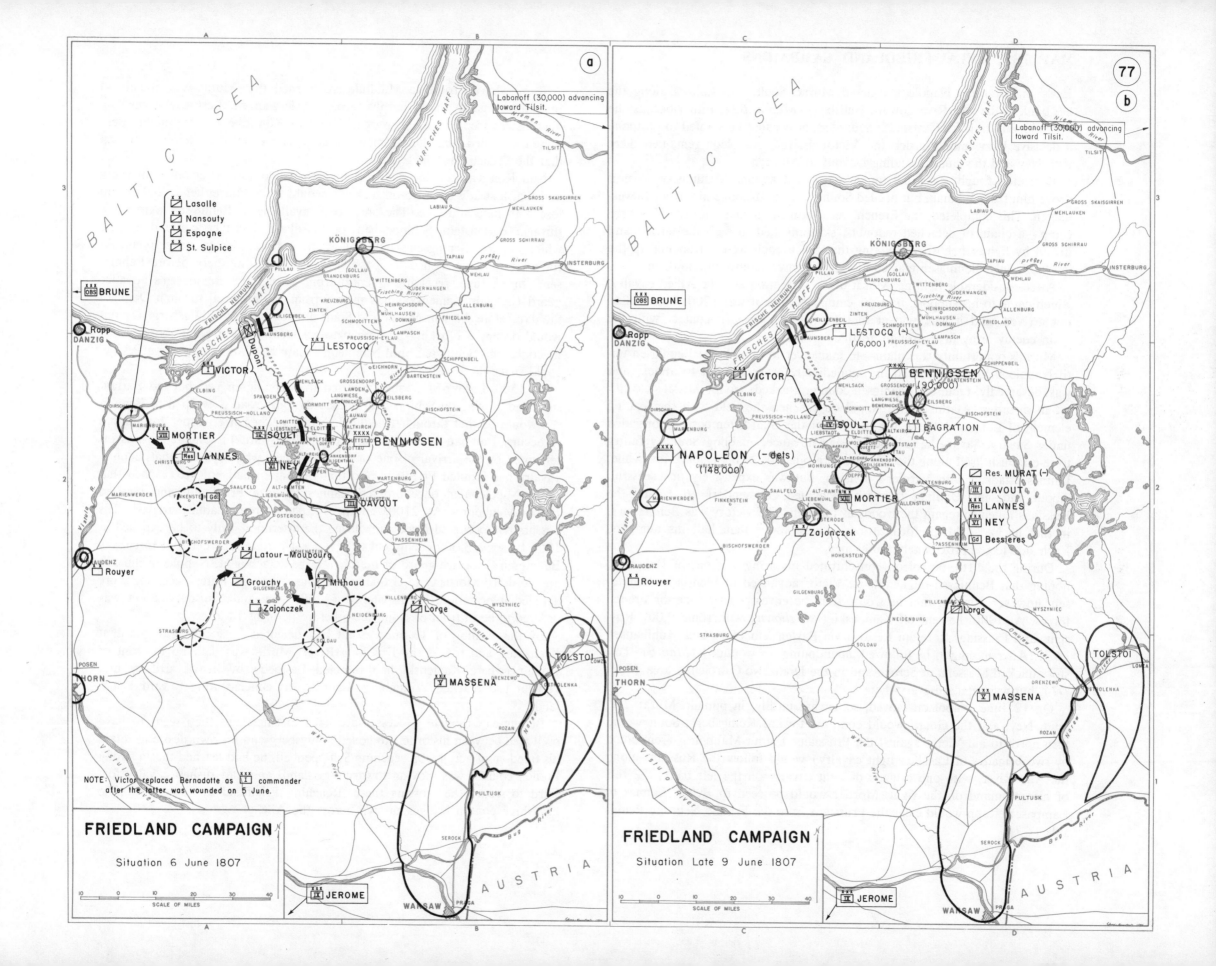

FRIEDLAND CAMPAIGN

Situation 6 June 1807

FRIEDLAND CAMPAIGN

Situation Late 9 June 1807

Early on 10 June, Napoleon ordered Murat, Soult, and Lannes along the left bank of the Alle River toward Heilsberg (*Map a, B2*). Either because he was reluctant to leave Guttstadt unguarded, or because he wanted to postpone a decisive blow until Mortier and Victor arrived, Napoleon remained there with Ney and the Guard, sending Davout to Altkirch.

Bagration fought his usual tough rear-guard action. About noon, Murat drove him from Launau, but needed Soult's help to dislodge him from Bewernicken. This completed, the French were soon in contact with the Heilsberg camp—a chain of detached redoubts, skillfully tied in with the terrain and linked by lighter fieldworks. Noting that the French were advancing up the left bank only, Bennigsen massed his whole army there to oppose them.

After considerable fighting, Murat drove Bagration and the Allied cavalry, which came to his support, into the camp. By then it was 1700; Lannes had not arrived, and it was evident that the French were in contact with the main enemy army in a strongly fortified position.

Murat's opportunity was plain—to maneuver to immobilize Bennigsen until Napoleon arrived. Instead, he immediately ordered Soult to attack, and was, deservedly, repulsed. Bennigsen counterattacked, driving Murat's cavalry off in disorder. At this point, Napoleon reached the field with the leading element of Lannes' column, the fusiliers of the Guard, temporarily brigaded under Savary. Savary halted the Russian advance, enabling Soult's infantry to re-establish itself along the southwestern outskirts of the camp. Meanwhile, Lannes attacked with Verdier's division, but was expensively unsuccessful. About midnight, Oudinot (Lannes) occupied Grossendorf (*B2*), and the Russians failed to regain the woods at Lawden. The victory was Bennigsen's, in that he had held his fortifications against fewer than half his numbers. Each side lost approximately 8,000 men.

During the 11th, Napoleon concentrated his army in front of Heilsberg, hoping that Bennigsen might attack. Victor advanced to Mehlsack. Bennigsen, however, foresaw that he would soon be enveloped by superior French forces. At 1800, he sent off Kamenski (*not shown*) with some 9,000 Russians and Prussians to rejoin Lestocq via Bartenstein (*B2*) and Mühlhausen (*B3*). After midnight, he followed, abandoning his wounded (*Map b*). Tolstoi attacked Massena at Serock and in the Drenzewo-Ostrolenka area (*both D1*), but was repulsed everywhere.

On 12 June, Napoleon moved, somewhat tardily, in pursuit. Murat, Davout, Ney, and the Guard would continue toward Königsberg; Soult would turn north to aid Victor against the Prussians. Latour-Maubourg (reinforced by two brigades of Lasalle's light cavalry) would follow the Russians along the Alle River, with one brigade of light cavalry on the left bank, the rest of his command on the right. Mortier would proceed to Eylau, Lannes to Lampasch. Rapp would clear the Prussians from the Frische Nehrung Peninsula (*C3*).

Kamenski, en route to Mühlhausen, learned that Murat was already in that town, and detoured hastily through Uderwangen. Lestocq, warned by Victor's intercepted orders, retreated toward Königsberg. That night, Bennigsen informed him that Kamenski had been detached to rejoin him, but that the French were in Eylau.

Napoleon was convinced that Bennigsen would seek to cover Königsberg and that a steady advance on that city would force him either to fight or to lose both base and face. The only roads available to Bennigsen were those through Bartenstein, Schippenbeil, or Friedland. Until he could determine which of these Bennigsen would follow, he did not wish to leave Eylau. At the same time, he wished—if possible—to reach Königsberg before Bennigsen. On 13 June, receiving a report from Murat that Bennigsen's advance guard (actually Kamenski) had moved from Schippenbeil through Domnau the day before, he sent Murat and Soult directly against Königsberg. Davout would occupy a blocking position between Domnau and Königsberg, where he could stop Bennigsen until Napoleon's main body, now massing at Eylau, could strike the Russian flank.

At 1500, Latour-Maubourg reported that Bennigsen was beyond Bartenstein and moving on Schippenbeil. Since the only road now open to Bennigsen would be that through Friedland, Napoleon began an order for Lannes to occupy Domnau and reconnoiter carefully toward Friedland. He was interrupted by the arrival of one of Lannes' aides, who reported that Lannes' cavalry had scouted Friedland and that Bennigsen had not yet reached that town. Napoleon at once ordered Lannes to seize Friedland, and recalled Latour-Maubourg. At 2100, another dispatch from Lannes arrived: His hussars had occupied Friedland during the afternoon, only to be expelled at 1800 by some 3,000 enemy cavalry. Not yet certain whether that force was Bennigsen's advance guard or merely a large detachment, Napoleon immediately ordered Mortier and Grouchy to Lannes' support. Later, receiving more detailed information, he dispatched (2200) Ney and Nansouty. Soult was ordered to be in front of Königsberg before noon of 14 June.

By the evening of 13 June, Soult had defeated Lestocq's rear guard at Kreuzburg and forced the Frisching River. Murat was held up in front of Gollau (where Kamenski had rejoined Lestocq) by heavy artillery fire. Davout had reached Wittenberg; Lannes was concentrating toward Friedland.

Bennigsen's thought processes are hard to trace, but they seem to have oscillated between his orders to cover Königsberg and his own desire to retain his freedom of action. On reaching Schippenbeil, he had learned that a strong French column was moving toward Friedland, and had rushed cavalry forward to secure the crossing there. Reaching Friedland at about 2300, he had three ponton bridges thrown across the Alle.

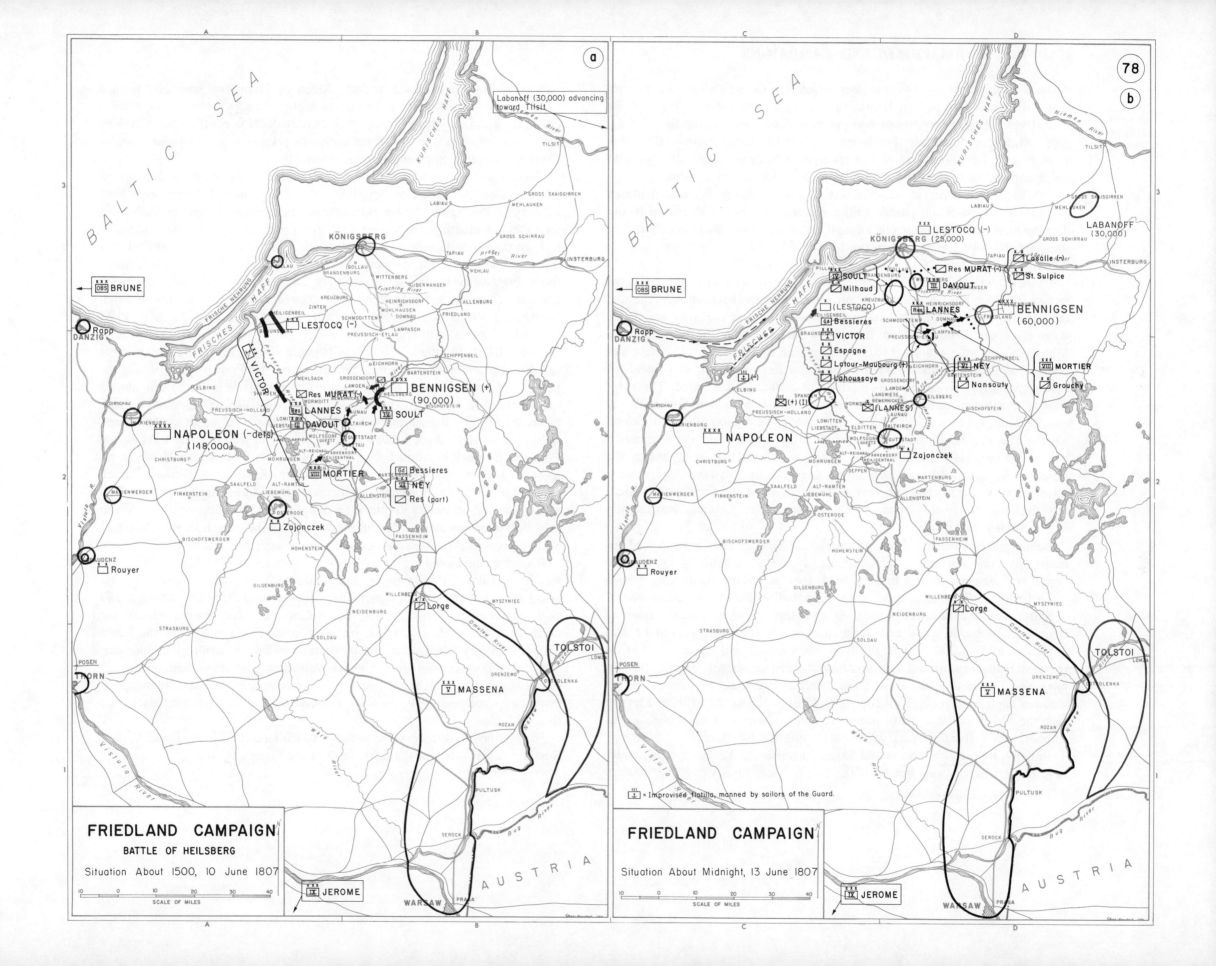

a

BALTIC SEA

Labanoff (30,000) advancing toward Tilsit

TILSIT

KURISCHES HAFF

Niemen River

Pregel River

KÖNIGSBERG

OBS BRUNE

Rapp
DANZIG

LESTOCQ (−)

VICTOR

FRISCHES HAFF

Res MURAT (−)

LANNES

DAVOUT

SOULT

BENNIGSEN (+)
(90,000)

NAPOLEON (−dets)
(148,000)

MORTIER

Gd Bessieres
VI NEY
Res (part)

Zajonczek

Rouyer

Lorge

TOLSTOI

Omulew River

V MASSENA

THORN
POSEN

Bug River

Visiula River

WARSAW

AUSTRIA

IX JEROME

FRIEDLAND CAMPAIGN
BATTLE OF HEILSBERG
Situation About 1500, 10 June 1807

SCALE OF MILES

b

BALTIC SEA

KURISCHES HAFF

Niemen River

GROSS SKAISGIRREN

LABANOFF
(30,000)

LESTOCQ (−)
(25,000)

KÖNIGSBERG

Lasalle (−)

V SOULT
Milhaud

Res MURAT (−)

III DAVOUT

St. Sulpice

OBS BRUNE

(LESTOCQ)

Gd Bessieres

Res LANNES

BENNIGSEN
(60,000)

Rapp
DANZIG

FRISCHES HAFF

I VICTOR

Espagne

Latour-Maubourg (+)

Lahoussaye

VI NEY

VIII MORTIER

III (+)(I)

Nansouty

Grouchy

± (−)

(LANNES)

NAPOLEON

Zajonczek

Rouyer

Lorge

TOLSTOI

Omulew River

V MASSENA

THORN
POSEN

± = Improvised flotilla, manned by sailors of the Guard.

Bug River

Visiula River

WARSAW

AUSTRIA

IX JEROME

FRIEDLAND CAMPAIGN
Situation About Midnight, 13 June 1807

SCALE OF MILES

Around midnight of 13–14 June, Bennigsen had Galitzin's cavalry, two infantry divisions, and part of Bagration's command on the west bank of the Alle River. These weary troops had not moved far beyond Friedland (*C2*); only cavalry outposts held Posthenen (*B1*) and Heinrichsdorf (*B3*). For some reason, Bennigsen had placed his ponton bridges so that they led into the cramped area of the town itself, thus greatly slowing his crossing.

Reaching Posthenen at about 0100, Lannes' leading brigade scattered Bennigsen's outposts and pushed to the western outskirts of Friedland before developing Russian forces strong enough to force it back. By 0200, there was sufficient light for Lannes—then on the low ridge east of Posthenen—to see the Russians still flowing steadily across the Alle into Friedland.

Lannes' tactical dispositions mark him as a general who could make the terrain fight for him. Friedland lay on a narrow ridge between the Alle and the Mühlen Fluss (Mill Stream); there were only two roads by which the Russians could debouch from its narrow streets. Both the Alle and the Mühlen Fluss were major obstacles, steep-banked and deep, with few and poor fords. North of the Mühlen Fluss lay a large open plateau, ideal for cavalry action; to its south, the country was broken and wooded. The ridge west of Posthenen commanded the whole area. Lannes had Oudinot's big elite division, his own corps cavalry, and Grouchy's dragoon division. Selecting the hills around Posthenen as a handy cork to the Friedland bottleneck, he massed most of his infantry and guns there, with two battalions in the Forest of Sortlack (*B1*) to threaten the flank of any Russian advance westward from Friedland. His left flank was anchored on the small woods south of Heinrichsdorf, covered by most of his corps cavalry. Grouchy was initially in reserve near Posthenen.

Bennigsen had learned from prisoners that he had only a reinforced infantry division confronting him. Apparently, being completely ignorant of Napoleon's dispositions, he decided to destroy it. (Many reasons have been given for his actions here; none of them, including the above, make sense.)

Skirmisher fire began about 0300 and rapidly grew violent, spurring Bennigsen to hustle more and more men across the bridges until he had approximately 45,000 west of the Alle. Such of his artillery as was left on the east bank was massed into several batteries, as shown. (Since the east bank was higher than the west, these batteries had excellent fields of fire.) Russian engineers hastily built four light bridges across the Mühlen Fluss to link the halves of their army. Bennigsen's plan seems to have been to fix Lannes with a frontal attack while enveloping his left flank.

Initially, the French hussars and Saxon cuirassiers of Lannes' corps cavalry kept his left flank clear, but by 0600 Uvarov's cavalry, with some infantry

and guns, broke into Heinrichsdorf. Aided by Nansouty, who had pushed ahead of the French infantry during the night, Grouchy promptly beat them out again with heavy losses. (As senior cavalry division commander, Grouchy acted as chief of cavalry in Murat's absence.) Lannes now detached one of Oudinot's brigades to defend Heinrichsdorf.

There was little action in the center, but Bagration made a determined effort to clear the Forest of Sortlack, committing most of Bennigsen's light infantry in that effort. Better skirmishers, the French *voltigeurs* stalled his attack in a fluctuating tree-to-tree fight. All along the front, Lannes managed to keep the general initiative through fierce local counterattacks, shifting his troops rapidly from point to point to give the impression of a much stronger force. Fighting in swarms of skirmishers, and utilizing every scrap of cover and concealment, the French infantry offered few targets to the Russian gunners. In comparison, the Russians were largely massed in the open, clear marks for Lannes' artillery.

About 0700, Mortier's VIII Corps began arriving, led by its Dutch corps cavalry. These were immediately committed on the French right, where the handful of Lannes' corps cavalry originally posted there had been almost overwhelmed in their fight to keep Bagration's cavalry off Oudinot's flank. Next came Dupas' French division, which Lannes posted north of Posthenen, leaving most of Oudinot's division in front of that village. The fight in the Forest of Sortlack continued to ebb and flow. Four times, the Russians almost cleared it, but were always driven out. One French counterattack stormed the village of Sortlack, but was soon forced back into the forest. The rest of Lannes' infantry (Verdier's French division and, apparently, a Saxon brigade) came up about 0745. Lannes sent one brigade into the Forest of Sortlack, where Bagration's superior numbers were beginning to tell.

Bennigsen attempted a general attack at about 0900, with his major weight on his right flank. Hard fighting and skillful troop leading repulsed him all along the line—Grouchy, in particular, displaying outstanding courage and skill against odds of two to one. Some Cossacks (*not shown*) circled far north and west of Heinrichsdorf, but were caught by elements of the I and VI corps cavalry. Thereafter, the battle relaxed into a desultory cannonade. This suited both commanders: Lannes wanted to gain time; Bennigsen—his troops sagging from night marches on empty bellies, his artillery ammunition dwindling—had seemingly decided to stand on the defense until dark and then withdraw.

For nine hours, with never more than 26,000 men, Lannes had held 60,000 Russians at bay—one of the finest feats in the history of war.

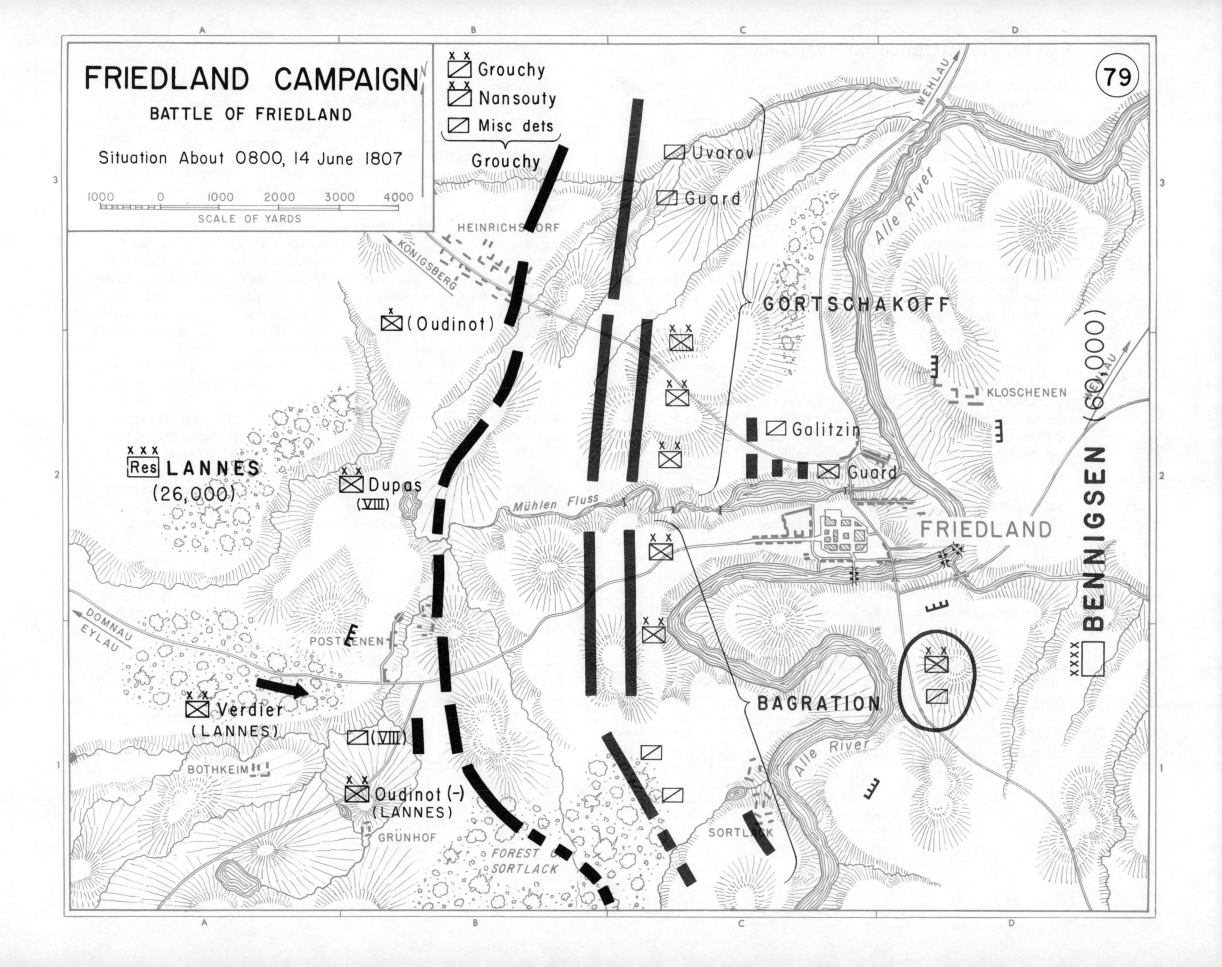

FRIEDLAND CAMPAIGN

BATTLE OF FRIEDLAND

Situation About 0800, 14 June 1807

SCALE OF YARDS
1000 0 1000 2000 3000 4000

Grouchy
Nansouty
Misc dets
Grouchy

Uvarov

Guard

GORTSCHAKOFF

KLOSCHENEN

HEINRICHSDORF

KÖNIGSBERG

(Oudinot)

Galitzin

Guard

FRIEDLAND

Alle River

WEHLAU

Res LANNES
(26,000)

Dupas
(VIII)

Mühlen Fluss

BENNIGSEN (60,000)

DOMNAU
EYLAU

POSTHENEN

Verdier
(LANNES)

(VIII)

Oudinot (-)
(LANNES)

BOTHKEIM

GRÜNHOF

FOREST OF
SORTLACK

SORTLACK

BAGRATION

Alle River

79

About noon, Napoleon rode into Posthenen, a flood of reinforcements at his heels. Before leaving Eylau (0400), he had renewed his orders for Murat to take Königsberg: Murat was to employ Soult's whole command (the IV Corps, plus Milhaud's dragoon division), but to use Davout only if absolutely necessary. He was not to "amuse himself" with frontal attacks on Lestocq. Berthier added the information that a major battle seemed to be developing at Friedland; consequently, once Königsberg had been taken, Murat was to move to support the left flank of the main army with his cavalry and Davout's corps.

Arriving at Posthenen, Napoleon and his staff began a deliberate reconnaissance of Bennigsen's position. (Napoleon's first reaction was complete disbelief that even Bennigsen could have got himself into such a fix—his second that such a chance to destroy an enemy never came twice.) He at once detected the crucial weakness of Bennigsen's dispositions: The Russian army was pinned against the Alle River, with no visible line of retreat except the Friedland bridges. Furthermore, the Russians were split roughly in two by the Mühlen Fluss. To exploit this opportunity, Napoleon decided to attack with his right flank to capture Friedland, thus pocketing Bennigsen on the west bank of the Alle. To make this attack more effective, it would strike the extreme left of the Russian line, rolling it up, instead of advancing directly on Friedland from the southwest. The French right wing would be able to assemble for this attack in relative secrecy behind the Forest of Sortlack.

To deliver this attack, he selected Ney and his VI Corps, which had missed Austerlitz and played only a minor part at Jena and Eylau. Lannes would now form the army's center from Posthenen to a point just south of Heinrichsdorf. He would reform his corps into two lines, shifting Oudinot slowly northward in order to distract the Russians, and remaining ready to advance on order, once Ney's attack was well developed. Mortier would defend Heinrichsdorf and the Königsberg road; his corps would form the pivot for the eventual general French advance. Beyond him, Grouchy—with his own division, Espagne's cuirassiers, and the light cavalry of the I, VI, and VIII Corps—would cover the army's left flank and maneuver so as to do the enemy as much damage as possible. Victor and the Guard would remain in reserve, ready to support Ney if necessary. Latour-Maubourg was attached to Ney, Nansouty to Lannes, Lahoussaye to Victor. When Ney attacked, all French artillery would double its rate of fire.

As his troops arrived and moved into their assigned positions, Napoleon wrote Murat to expedite his operations and rejoin, since the battle at Friedland might last two days if the Russians proved to be in great force—in which

case Napoleon might content himself for the 14th with an artillery duel while awaiting Murat's arrival. This order was impossible to execute, since Friedland was almost thirty miles from Königsberg, and Napoleon knew it. Actually, he had no intention of postponing his attack until the 15th, since Bennigsen undoubtedly would attempt to slip away during the night. In all probability, this message was merely intended as a thoroughly backhanded method of stimulating Murat to make himself available during 15 June for the pursuit.

Meanwhile, there were minor cavalry bickerings on both flanks, the Russians winning several small successes, but always being driven back by French countercharges. Shortly after 1600, the Guard infantry and Victor reached the field, giving Napoleon approximately 80,000 available men. Even so, he took time to personally put them into position, giving them a few minutes to catch their breath, while he checked on the army's ammunition supply. Satisfied, at 1700, he gave an order; the twenty-gun battery behind Posthenen fired three salvos—the signal for Ney to advance.

Bennigsen had no forewarning of Ney's coming attack, but his observers in the Friedland church steeple had cautioned him that the French were constantly being reinforced. At some undetermined point he seems to have decided that it would be well to withdraw as quickly and quietly as possible. As a preparatory measure, he began shortening his front, resting his left flank on Sortlack and his right on a brickworks beside the Alle. However, his order to withdraw to the east bank—if ever actually issued—had to be canceled when Ney's attack pushed out of the Forest of Sortlack. Instead, Bennigsen ordered all of the cavalry and most of the infantry still on the east bank across the Friedland bridges to reinforce his battle front. Some detachments, including Platov's Cossacks, which he had sent ahead toward Wehlau on 13 June to secure crossings over the lower Alle, also were now returning to Friedland.

Ney's attack came on in echelon, Marchand's division leading on the right along the river. Both divisions were in cramped formations, just as they had assembled along the roads in the Forest of Sortlack, but Ney did not pause to deploy. Guiding on the Friedland church steeple (the only part of the town not hidden from him by a swell of the intervening ground), Marchand quickly drove the Russians holding Sortlack village into the river. Bagration threw a mass of cavalry against Marchand's left flank, but these were routed by Latour-Maubourg, who had moved into the interval between Marchand and Bisson.

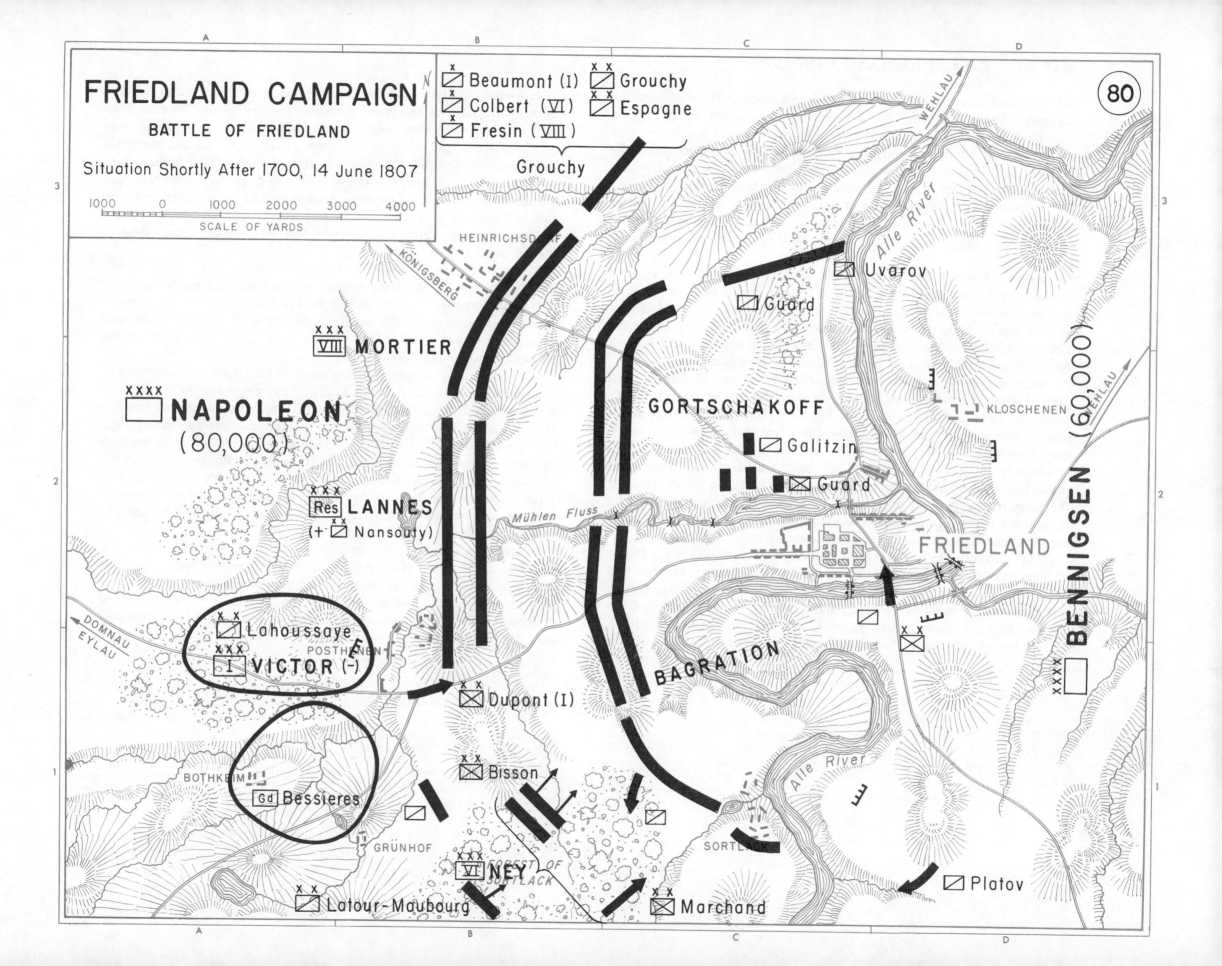

FRIEDLAND CAMPAIGN

BATTLE OF FRIEDLAND

Situation Shortly After 1700, 14 June 1807

1000   0   1000   2000   3000   4000
SCALE OF YARDS

Beaumont (I)   Grouchy
Colbert (VI)   Espagne
Fresin (VIII)
Grouchy

80

WEHLAU

Alle River

Uvarov

Guard

HEINRICHSDORF

KÖNIGSBERG

MORTIER

NAPOLEON
(80,000)

GORTSCHAKOFF

Galitzin

KLOSCHENEN

Guard

LANNES
(+ Nansouty)

Mühlen Fluss

FRIEDLAND

BENNIGSEN
(60,000)

WEHLAU

DOMNAU
EYLAU

Lahoussaye

POSTHENEN

VICTOR (-)

Dupont (I)

BAGRATION

Alle River

Bisson

BOTHKEIM

Bessieres

GRÜNHOF

Platov

NEY

FOREST OF SORTLACK

SORTLACK

Latour-Maubourg

Marchand

As Marchand (his ten battalions formed into a single column of battalion columns) rounded the projecting loop of the Alle and moved directly on Friedland, he was raked by hastily massed Russian guns on the far bank of the river. At the same time, Bagration concentrated his own guns against the heads of both French divisions, riddling their deep ranks. Staggered by this cross fire, Ney's advance halted. On his left, Bisson (whose division was formed in two lines of battalion columns) attempted to deploy, but was caught in the act by more Russian cavalry and sent to the rear, dragging Marchand with him. Only three regiments were able to form square and stand firm amid the rout.

Napoleon, however, had begun moving Victor forward as soon as Ney's advance began. Now, on his own initiative, Dupont, commanding the I Corps' leading division, came smartly forward on Bisson's left. Latour-Maubourg charged again, riding down the Russian cavalry that was pursuing the VI Corps. Behind him, Ney's artillery went into action, smashing the Russian battery across the Alle. But the heaviest blow was yet to come.

Senarmont, Victor's chief of artillery, already had moved forward with twelve guns to support Dupont. Judging these insufficient, he secured Victor's permission to take the I Corps' remaining twenty-four guns. Leaving six of these in reserve, he formed the remaining thirty into two fifteen-gun batteries, one on each flank of Dupont's division, and accompanied its advance. Approximately 150 yards from Bagration's front, the narrowing terrain compelled him to combine the two batteries. At 120 yards, he halted. Ignoring the heavy Russian artillery fire, Senarmont blasted Bagration's infantry with canister for twenty-five minutes, knocking over 4,000 of them and sending the rest streaming back into Friedland's choked streets.

In this bloody respite, Ney—fairly frothing at the mouth in his fury—damned and led his corps back in a howling assault. Dupont had followed Senarmont. As he came abreast of the end of the Mühlen Fluss lake, Bennigsen desperately committed his last reserve, putting in the infantry of the Russian Imperial Guard against Dupont, and ordering the Guard cavalry against Senarmont's flank. Senarmont swiftly changed front, blowing the

Czar's picked cavalrymen off the battlefield with two quick volleys. Simultaneously, Dupont met, and broke, the Russian Guard infantry with the bayonet, seizing the temporary bridges across the Mühlen Fluss. Crossing to its north bank, he surged down the Königsberg road into Friedland, supported by the guns from Senarmont's reserve. Senarmont pushed closer to the village, raking its streets and bridges, both of which were jammed with retreating Russians. Other French artillerymen, meanwhile, had concentrated howitzers south of Friedland, supporting the infantry attacks with high-angle fire into the Russian masses. Berthier moved with this final assault, coordinating its different elements.

The combined efforts of the French artillery soon set the Friedland bridges afire. (Apparently the Russians also set one or more of these bridges afire while their troops were still crossing.) Packed into the village, their means of escape going up in flames, the Russians formed a big target with little protective firepower. Their plight became worse as their batteries on the east bank were gradually knocked out.

In the meantime, Gortschakoff had renewed his attack on Heinrichsdorf, his artillery setting the town afire, and his cavalry attempting to work around the French left flank. Lannes, Mortier, and Grouchy had no difficulty beating off this advance, but Napoleon took the precaution of sending Savary, with the two regiments of fusiliers of the Guard, to reinforce Mortier. Napoleon's application of economy of force was almost as noteworthy here as at Austerlitz. Lannes, Mortier, and Grouchy together were probably outnumbered by Gortschakoff until the end of the battle—at best, they had no more than equal forces of infantry and inferior numbers of cavalry and guns. Meanwhile, Napoleon crushed Bagration's outnumbered force.

On the French right, there was a minor flurry as Platov's Cossacks appeared on the east bank of the Alle, considerably in rear of Ney's advancing corps. Platov made a gesture at attempting to ford the river there, but was easily discouraged, and took no further part in the battle. (Cossacks dreaded artillery fire, and Platov—though described as personally brave—probably could not get them to face it.)

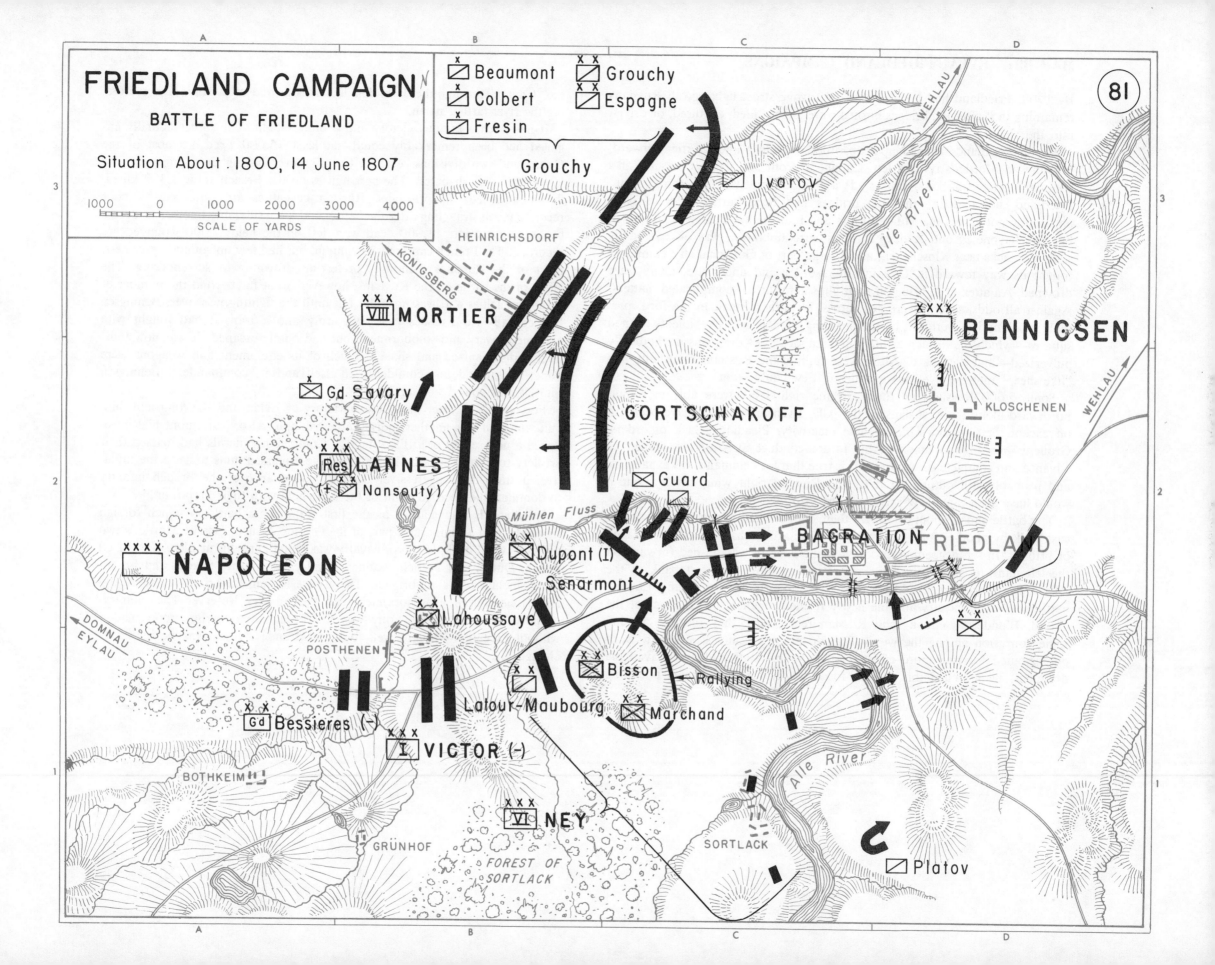

FRIEDLAND CAMPAIGN

BATTLE OF FRIEDLAND

Situation About 1800, 14 June 1807

1000 0 1000 2000 3000 4000
SCALE OF YARDS

x	Beaumont	xx	Grouchy
x	Colbert	xx	Espagne
x	Fresin		

Grouchy

x Uvarov

WEHLAU

Alle River

xxxx BENNIGSEN

KLOSCHENEN

WEHLAU

HEINRICHSDORF

KÖNIGSBERG

xxx VIII MORTIER

GORTSCHAKOFF

x Gd Savary

Mühlen Fluss

xx Guard

Res LANNES
(+ xx Nansouty)

xxxx NAPOLEON

xx Dupont (I)

Senarmont

BAGRATION

FRIEDLAND

DOMNAU
EYLAU

xx Lahoussaye

POSTHENEN

Rallying

xx Bisson

Gd Bessieres (-)

Latour-Maubourg

xx Marchand

xxx I VICTOR (-)

BOTHKEIM

xxx VI NEY

SORTLACK

Alle River

GRÜNHOF

FOREST OF
SORTLACK

x Platov

81

By 1900, Friedland had been cleared by savage street fighting; all Russians remaining in it after the bridges burned were either killed, captured, or driven into the river.

Seeing Friedland taken, Napoleon ordered Lannes and Mortier forward, pivoting on Mortier's refused left. Caught in front and flank, Gortschakoff's command broke up. Some units made a game attempt to break through into Friedland, not realizing that the bridges had been burned. One division apparently got across the Mühlen Fluss and into the north edge of the town, but was bayoneted out. A deep ford, hitherto unknown, was discovered by some Cossacks near Kloschenen, and a large part of Gortschakoff's command fought its way toward it. Crossing in disorder and under fire, many were drowned. An attempt to bring off their guns here further complicated matters. Against all odds, several were got across, but others stuck in the ford, partially blocking it. Overtaken by the pursuing French, many regiments formed squares—which the French artillery and Lahoussaye's dragoons methodically pulverized—and died hard. All bravery failing, the Russians eventually fled "like sheep" into the river or surrendered. Few could swim.

Some 5,000 Russians on their extreme right flank were able to retreat northward along the west bank of the Alle. Even these would have been cut off except for Grouchy's inexplicable inactivity. Pleading a lack of orders, Grouchy—in an odd omen of his future conduct at Waterloo—failed to advance and complete the victory. (It is true that his command was exhausted, and probably still outnumbered by the Russian right wing cavalry, but it would have been capable of one more charge.)

The battle ended about 2230. By then, Mortier had begun crossing to the east bank by another ford, but the rest of the army was blocked by the lack of bridges. In the deepening darkness, some cavalry was pushed forward on the left flank to pursue the Russians retreating down the west bank of the Alle. The units dispatched, however, were poorly chosen, being Lannes' hard-used Saxon cavalry and the newly formed regiment of dragoons of the Guard. Blundering into a solid Russian rear guard, they retired, creating some confusion among the weary French infantry. Lannes, sick and worn out, shouted for one more effort. Collecting his staff and every available drummer, he marched this scratch force boldly forward, drums pounding the "Charge" through the dark. The Russians moved off hastily, later recrossing the river farther north.

It had been a famous victory and a bloody fight. The forces actually engaged had been remarkably equal—at least 15,000 French (most of the Guard and two divisions of the I Corps) never having been engaged. The losses are much disputed. The best figures on the French show 1,372 killed, 9,108 wounded, 55 prisoners. Russian casualties are obscured by poor records, much straggling after the battle, and a considerable number of deaths by drowning. Some 11,000 dead were left on the field; 7,000 wounded are recorded. The French captured 80 cannon, but had few unwounded prisoners, most of the Russians seemingly preferring drowning to surrendering. The effect of the battle on the Russians, however, went far beyond the number of actual casualties and was not fully felt until the fighting was over. Bennigsen had casually led Russia's best field army into a trap; it had fought with extreme bravery and stubbornness, but had barely escaped. It was now thoroughly disorganized and shaken; much of its equipment and weapons were gone; and it had lost confidence in itself and its commanders. Bennigsen himself was cowed and broken.

For Napoleon, after the dubious victory of Eylau and the long and difficult winter, it was another indisputable triumph. Also, Senarmont had introduced a new school of artillery tactics. Competent generals had massed their artillery for years; Senarmont had used these massed guns to seize the initiative, pushing them aggressively forward in advance of the French infantry to dominate the decisive point of the battlefield with their firepower.

Friedland is also notable as the first Napoleonic battle in which foreign troops formed an important part of the Grande Armee. One of Mortier's two divisions was Polish; his corps cavalry was Dutch; and his artillery was mixed Polish, Dutch, and French. Lannes' cavalry was mostly Saxon, and his infantry included a Saxon brigade. There were Italian, Bavarian, Württemberg, and Hohenzollern light horsemen with the Cavalry Reserve. The infantry-artillery backbone of the army was still French, the foreign troops had—without exception—fought well, but the Grande Armee was beginning to change.

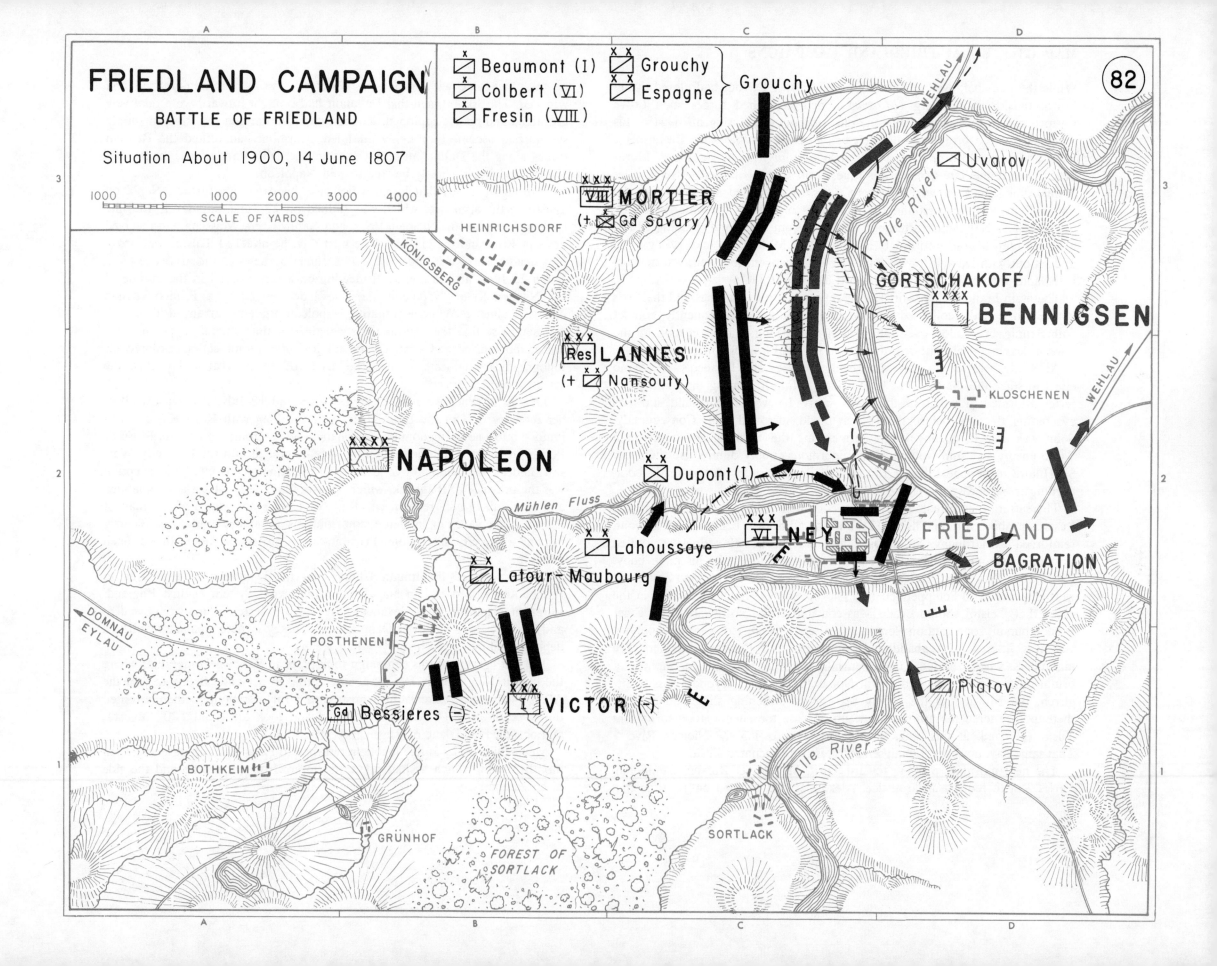

FRIEDLAND CAMPAIGN

BATTLE OF FRIEDLAND

Situation About 1900, 14 June 1807

1000 0 1000 2000 3000 4000

SCALE OF YARDS

x Beaumont (I)
x Colbert (VI)
x Fresin (VIII)
xx Grouchy
Espagne

Grouchy

WEHLAU

VIII MORTIER
(+ x Gd Savary)

Uvarov

HEINRICHSDORF

KÖNIGSBERG

Alle River

GORTSCHAKOFF

BENNIGSEN

Res LANNES
(+ xx Nansouty)

KLOSCHENEN

WEHLAU

NAPOLEON

Mühlen Fluss

Dupont (I)

xx Lahoussaye

VI NEY

FRIEDLAND

xx Latour-Maubourg

BAGRATION

DOMNAU EYLAU

POSTHENEN

Platov

Gd Bessieres (-)

I VICTOR (-)

Alle River

BOTHKEIM

GRÜNHOF

SORTLACK

FOREST OF SORTLACK

82

MAP 83 : EYLAU-FRIEDLAND CAMPAIGNS

While the guns bellowed at Friedland on 14 June, Davout had closed up on Murat outside Königsberg (*Map a*). Their combined forces soon drove Lestocq out of the suburbs into the old fortress city, cutting off most of his rear guard and a brigade he had left behind earlier to blockade Braunsberg. Soult and Milhaud arrived early the next morning. As at Heilsberg, Murat ordered an immediate assault; this time, Soult bluntly refused. After a brief bombardment had shown Königsberg to be well fortified and defended, the marshals decided to surround the city. This maneuver was interrupted by the arrival of Napoleon's afternoon dispatch from Friedland, bidding Murat to rejoin him. Murat accordingly left Soult and Milhaud to take Königsberg, and set out with Davout for Domnau. At Uderwangen, they received news of Friedland, with orders to march toward Tapiau (*B3*).

The main French army, worn out by repeated forced marches and the day's battle, had virtually collapsed after winning Friedland. Consequently, contact with Bennigsen was lost overnight. The next morning, Napoleon took up the pursuit, leaving Ney's battered division on the field to reorganize.

At Königsberg, Soult—his force being weaker than Lestocq's—made no effort to surround the city, but began bombarding it. During the 15th, a deserter informed him that Lestocq had received news of Friedland and was evacuating the city before the French could surround him. Consequently, Soult was able to occupy Königsberg during the 16th, finding more than 7,000 enemy sick and wounded, and enormous supply dumps. He then sent St. Hilaire to besiege Pillau (*A3*), which Rapp's forces were already bombarding from across the channel.

Thereafter, the retreat and pursuit continued (*Map b*). Bennigsen and Lestocq pushed hard for Tilsit (*D3*), burning all bridges behind them. Davout, reinforced by Grouchy, St. Sulpice, and part of Lasalle's division, routed Lestocq's rear guard at Labiau, but was unable to overtake his main body. On 17 June, Ney seized Insterburg. Dombrowski (VIII Corps) and Zajonczek were dispatched to Schippenbeil (*D2*) to cover the French right rear in the event that Tolstoi should evade Massena and strike northward. The eager French pursuit soon told on Bennigsen's already-exhausted men; the countryside was littered with abandoned equipment and Russian stragglers and marauders, whom the local inhabitants—hating the Russians for months of brutal mistreatment—hunted down. Not until 18 June, beyond Gross Skaisgirren, did Murat find the enemy rear guard stiffening slightly. Napoleon thereupon ordered the army to close up, in case the enemy stood to fight at Tilsit. (He had, at this time, no intention of crossing the Niemen River.) That same day, however, Bennigsen and Lestocq evacuated Tilsit.

The next morning, probing toward Tilsit, Murat met Russian plenipotentiaries sent to request an armistice. Alexander had decided on 16 June that he must negotiate with Napoleon. Bennigsen's army was demoralized and wrecked. The 30,000 men that Labanoff had brought forward were relatively untrained and poorly equipped. Russian mobilization and the Russian supply system had become thoroughly muddled. Marmont had routed the Russian forces along the Dalmatian coast; Jerome (actually Vandamme) had swept Silesia, and would shortly be free to join Napoleon.

Thoroughly happy that he need not push his campaign further, Napoleon agreed to the armistice, which was ratified on 23 June, stipulating the line of demarcation as the Niemen, Bobr, and Narew rivers. Massena had received news of Friedland on 21 June. The next day, he attacked Tolstoi and drove him steadily eastward, until halted (28 June) by news of the armistice.

On 25 June, after a theatrical meeting on a raft moored in the middle of the Niemen River, Napoleon and Alexander agreed to a Franco-Russian defensive alliance. While negotiating, Napoleon prudently arranged his army's rest camps so that the various units remained within mutual supporting distance; reorganized and strengthened his line of communication; ordered his topographical engineers to map the newly occupied area; and pushed the fortification of Warsaw.

Treaties of peace were finally signed on 9 and 12 July. Prussia lost all of her territory west of the Elbe River, which—along with Hesse-Kassel—was lumped into a new Kingdom of Westphalia, under Jerome Bonaparte. Prussia's Polish provinces, with one exception, were combined into the Duchy of Warsaw, under the traditional overlordship of the King of Saxony. The exception was the province of Bialystok, which Prussia's loyal ally—Russia—demanded and received. Prussia recognized all of Napoleon's alterations of the map of Europe, and gave up immense contributions in money and kind. Danzig became a free city, under joint Prussian-Saxon protection, but with a French garrison.

Russia returned the Ionian Islands and the Dalmatian coastal area to France and agreed to join Napoleon's Continental System against England. In return, Napoleon gave Alexander a free hand to seize Finland from Sweden, and territory along the lower Danube from Turkey (where a palace revolt had deposed and murdered his ally Sultan Selim).

The last fighting of this campaign took place in Swedish Pomerania, where the lunatic King Gustav IV—after attempting to persuade Brune to join the Allies—denounced the existing armistice on 3 July. Brune immediately routed the Swedish army (6 August); besieged and took Stralsund (20 August); and occupied the Island of Rugen (*see Map 69*).

Meanwhile, on 27 July, Napoleon returned to Paris, after an absence of ten months, during which he had ruled his empire from his saddle and the side of his campfires.

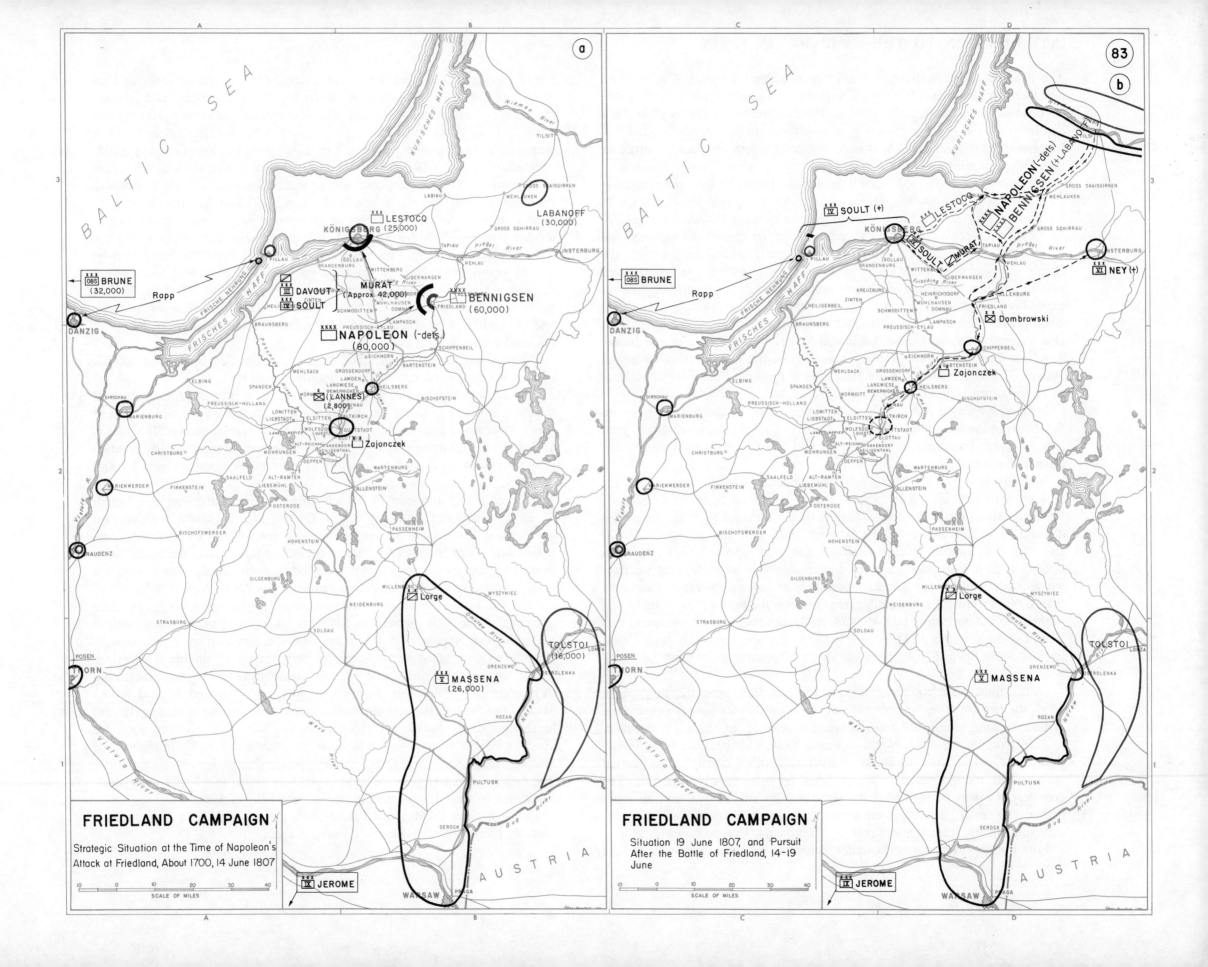

a **83** **b**

FRIEDLAND CAMPAIGN

Strategic Situation at the Time of Napoleon's
Attack at Friedland, About 1700, 14 June 1807

SCALE OF MILES

FRIEDLAND CAMPAIGN

Situation 19 June 1807, and Pursuit
After the Battle of Friedland, 14-19
June

SCALE OF MILES

INTRODUCTION TO THE CAMPAIGN IN SPAIN

The Peace of Tilsit shattered the existing structure of central Europe. The new German kingdoms (Westphalia, especially) would require years of peace to consolidate their enlarged territories. The creation of the Duchy of Warsaw had inflamed the Poles' ambition to restore their ancient kingdom—and had frightened the Russians and Austrians, neither of whom intended to surrender their Polish provinces.

Napoleon now demanded that England make peace, or have the remaining ports of Europe (in Sweden, Denmark, Austria, the Papal States) closed to her trade. Czar Alexander attempted to mediate between France and England, but England—convinced that Napoleon must be destroyed—ignored his efforts. Both France and England demanded that Denmark declare itself; the Danes, doubtful of England's will or ability to protect them against a French invasion, chose France. The British retaliated with an expert amphibious expedition (August–September 1807), which ravaged Copenhagen and destroyed the Danish fleet. This made the Danes firm allies of Napoleon; it also angered Alexander, who considered himself the guardian of the Baltic. The Czar then joined Napoleon in persuading Austria to enter the Continental System. The Emperor began concentrating a Franco-Spanish corps in Denmark for an invasion of Sweden.

In Italy, Napoleon had the secondary objective of establishing a territorial link between the Kingdom of Italy and Naples. An agreement with Spain gave him Tuscany. Thereafter, it was easy to find pretexts for occupying the disorderly Papal States.

Portugal attempted to evade Napoleon's demands through drawn-out negotiations. Irritated, Napoleon proposed a joint Franco-Spanish invasion of Portugal, which was to be divided into two Spanish satellite states. Junot was dispatched on this mission on 19 October 1807 with approximately 23,000 men. But the promised Spanish reinforcements and supplies did not materialize; his maps proved faulty; and his conscripts collapsed under foul weather, worse roads, and hunger. On 23 November, he entered Portugal with fewer than 6,000 exhausted men. Undaunted, he took the best 1,500 of them and pushed straight on Lisbon (*see Map 84, A2*), stampeding the government into a panicky flight to Brazil. During early December, the rest of his army closed up and some Spanish troops appeared, enabling him to occupy the entire country.

At this time, Napoleon's intentions as to Spain itself were still fluid. Since 1795, the two countries had been friends or allies, France always demanding, Spain increasingly resentful and evasive. Aware of Spain's intended treachery in 1806, Napoleon knew it would be unsafe to turn his back on Spain in any future war. Spain itself—with its degenerate royalty, corrupt, disorganized government, and ignorant and impoverished population—disgusted him. The conquest of Spain tempted alike his ambition, his love of war, and his sense of law and order. The occasion seemed propitious: England was his only surviving enemy; from fear or favor, all Continental Europe was with him.

Forming a provisional corps under Dupont, who appeared ready for the test of independent command (the full extent of his erratic behavior at Ulm was as yet unknown), Napoleon gradually fed it into north-central Spain, on the excuse of establishing a secure line of communication with Junot. This done, a second corps under Moncey was eased in behind Dupont, and a third corps, under Duhesme, moved into northeast Spain. In early February 1808, a detachment of the Guard and Napoleon's campaign equipment were sent to Bayonne (*C3*). Napoleon himself apparently intended to follow, but was detained (possibly fortunately) in Paris throughout March. His alliance with Russia already was proving deceptive: Napoleon wanted an ally; Alexander wanted time to rebuild his armies. The impressionable Alexander may have been momentarily dazzled by Napoleon, yet it must be remembered that he was an expert dissembler, reared amid the desperate plots and counterplots that formed the childhood environment of every czar. Now, when the French Emperor wished to discuss the possibilities of marrying a Russian princess and of securing the cooperation of the Russian Mediterranean fleet, he found Alexander unexpectedly coy.

Compelled to remain in Paris, Napoleon gave Murat the Spanish command, with instructions to occupy Madrid "without hostilities."

A "Reserve Corps" was formed under Bessieres to protect Murat's rear. Of the approximately 118,000 men Napoleon had allotted for the occupation of Spain, only some 34,000 were from the regular French Army. The rest—aside from 15,000 foreign troops—were almost-raw conscripts, hastily huddled into temporary units that were short of officers, equipment, morale, and discipline.

Between 6 February and 18 March, using a variety of ruses, the French seized the Spanish frontier fortresses. On 14 March, Murat marched on Madrid with Dupont and Moncey, calling Bessieres forward to hold his communications from Burgos (*B3*) north. Initially, Murat's advance caused little excitement, but heavy requisitions for food and the rowdy behavior of his troops soon aroused considerable resentment. Popular feeling, still fearful of the French, turned on the Spanish government. Prince Ferdinand, the heir apparent, utilized this outburst to force his father to abdicate—concurrently requesting that Napoleon grant him any available female relative in marriage. The ousted King called on Napoleon for help against his undutiful offspring. The latter summoned the whole Spanish royal family to Bayonne, ostensibly to mediate their differences. Meanwhile, Murat had entered Madrid on 23 March. On 2 May, the city revolted against his rule, but was quickly and harshly put down. Napoleon thereupon ordered King and Prince to abdicate, directing Murat to reorganize the Spanish government and demobilize the Spanish Army. Surprisingly, the country remained calm for almost a month. The national Junta (legislative body) submissively requested that the French Emperor's brother, Joseph Bonaparte, become King of Spain.

Then—between 20 May and 5 June—Murat fell gravely ill, and an enthusiastically bloody revolt exploded all across Spain.

"It is very necessary to attend to detail, and to trace a
biscuit from Lisbon into a man's mouth on the frontier, and to provide for its removal from place to
place, by land and by water, or no military operations
can be carried on."
—ARTHUR WELLESLEY, FIRST DUKE OF WELLINGTON

"A general in the power of the enemy has no orders to
give: Whoever obeys him is a criminal."
—NAPOLEON

Spain and Portugal form a high plateau, seamed by mountain chains and deep-cut rivers. Land communication with France in the early nineteenth century was limited virtually to the highways at either end of the Pyrenees. Since the eastern roads led only into the blind alley of Catalonia (*D2–D3*), Bayonne (*C3*) became the principal French base. In Spain, the major highway ran directly from Vitoria (*C3*) through Burgos (*B3*) to Madrid (*B2*). From Madrid, neglected roads radiated to other major cities. This limited road net and the rough terrain made possession of certain fortified road centers essential. San Sebastian and Pampeluna (*both C3*) commanded the Bayonne-Vitoria highway; Figueras and Gerona, the highway from Perpignan (*all D3*). Badajoz (*A2*) and Ciudad Rodrigo (*B2*) barred the major passes into Portugal.

Except for the provinces of Andalusia (*B1–C1*) and Catalonia, most of Spain produced barely enough to keep a thinly spread population alive. Wood and water were scarce, disease-carrying insects plentiful. During the hot summer, extensive operations were extremely difficult.

Spanish resistance developed sporadically, beginning in the outlying provinces and gathering in scattered elements of the partially disbanded Spanish Army. Napoleon's orders to Murat had been based on their Egyptian experience: Leave no small garrisons or detachments; hold the capital in strength; handle any revolts by sending out strong mobile columns to "make examples." Working from faulty maps, Napoleon did not realize that much of Spain is vertical; certainly he never foresaw a massive national uprising. In early April, he had come forward to Bayonne. Receiving (beginning 30 May) vague reports of revolts, he initially attempted to deal with them piecemeal. Lefebvre-Desnoëttes marched from Pampeluna against Tudela and Saragossa (*both C3*); Bessieres sent Verdier's division to subdue Logrono (*C3*) and then join Lefebvre-Desnoëttes at Saragossa; Moncey moved on Cuenca and Valencia (*both C2*) with a reinforced French division and a Spanish brigade; Duhesme dispatched Chabran's division south to meet Moncey (*movement not shown*); Reille mustered a division at Perpignan to clear Duhesme's endangered communications. On Joseph's arrival, Napoleon briefed him carefully: The original plan was obviously incorrect; Joseph must concentrate his forces around Madrid and strike the Spanish armies in succession as they advanced, meanwhile maintaining his communications with France. This would demand coolness, patience, and calculation (qualities Joseph had *not* shown in Naples), but would give Joseph the prestige necessary for a new King. Napoleon then left for Paris: Austria was rearming, and a strong expeditionary force had sailed from England.

Dupont had left Toledo (*B2*) on 24 May for Cadiz (*A1*); his command included a Swiss brigade (2,400) formerly in the Spanish service. On 7 June, he routed a Spanish army at Alcolea and stormed and pillaged Cordova (*both B1*). Learning that his communications with Madrid were cut (detachments

and sick he had left en route were brutally butchered), and that the small French fleet at Cadiz had been forced to surrender, he retired (16–19 June) to Andujar (*B1*).

Moncey left Madrid on 4 June, following a route laid down by Napoleon, but marching leisurely to avoid exhausting his conscripts. Expecting Moncey to take the longer, easier route through San Clemente (*C2*), Cervellon concentrated most of his army there. Moncey, however, understood mountain fighting and Spaniards. By an unexpectedly quick dash over a difficult secondary road, he broke through to Valencia, routed a hastily collected army outside its walls, but failed in two attempts to storm the city. Short of ammunition, encumbered by his wounded, and without word from Duhesme (Chabran had been unable to break through), he retired through Albacete (*C2*), thereby completely confusing Cervellon. Maintaining strict discipline, and employing strong flank guards, he drove Spanish detachments out of a series of seemingly impregnable positions, and reached San Clemente (and Frere's division) on 9 July, subsequently retiring to Madrid.

Meanwhile, Murat's illness had paralyzed the central command at Madrid. On 14 June, Savary arrived with Napoleon's new plan. (Murat turned over the command to him and left Madrid on the 29th.) However, finding that Moncey and Dupont were deeply committed already, and that the latter had become isolated, he acted on his own initiative, ordering Frere to Madridejos (*B2*) and sending Vedel south to extricate Dupont.

Momentarily, the situation stabilized. Vedel reached Baylen (*B1*) and re-established liaison with Dupont. In the north, Bessieres routed Cuesta and Blake, and captured Zamora, Benavente, and Leon (*all B3*). Thus reassured, Joseph proceeded to Madrid. Lefebvre-Desnoëttes drove Palafox into Saragossa, which Verdier later began besieging against fanatical resistance.

Unfortunately, one of Napoleon's last orders (19 June), based on unreliable maps, shifted Frere to San Clemente. This allowed the Spanish to again cut the Madrid-Andujar road (*B1–B2*). Dupont demanded Frere's division be sent south to him; instead, Savary stationed Gobert between Madridejos and Baylen, with orders to remain in contact with Madrid. On 19 July, increasingly worried over Dupont's position, Savary sent him a firm order to withdraw north of the Sierra Morena.

Joseph's first actions on reaching Madrid (20 July) were to countermand this order and to direct Gobert to join Dupont. Immediately thereafter (23–28 July) came news that Dupont had been overwhelmed at Baylen (*see text, Map 85*). Joseph instantly demanded a retreat northward. Savary agreed, believing it imperative to get Joseph out of Madrid before his cowardice produced a second, worse disaster. The retreat began on 1 August, Joseph abandoning his sick and ordering Verdier to lift the siege of Saragossa. About two weeks later, having received reinforcements, Joseph halted north of the Ebro River (*C3*). It took the Spaniards two months to catch up with him.

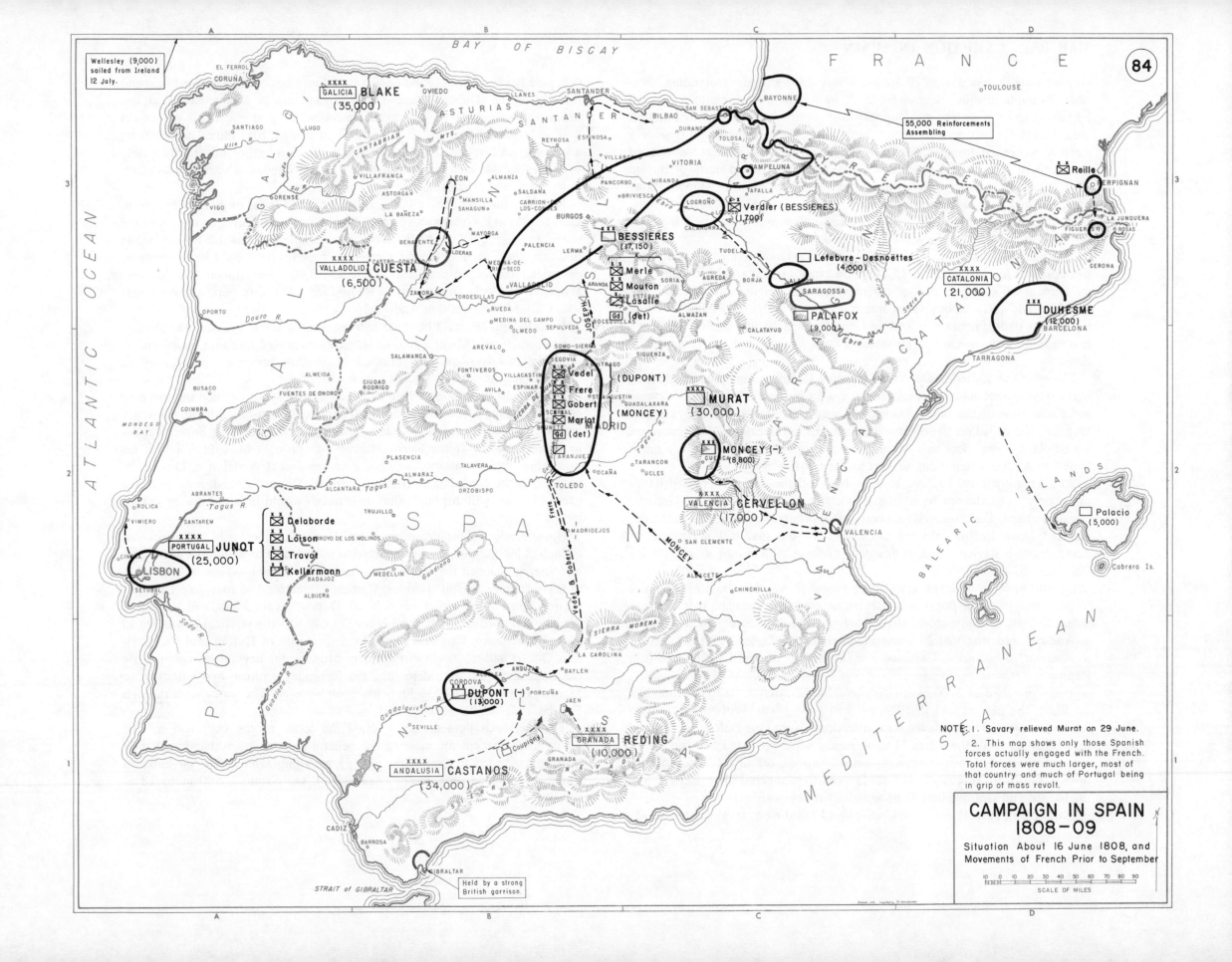

BAY OF BISCAY

FRANCE

84

Wellesley (9,000)
sailed from Ireland
12 July.

55,000 Reinforcements
Assembling

xxxx
GALICIA BLAKE
(35,000)

xxxx
VALLADOLID CUESTA
(6,500)

xxx
BESSIERES
(17,150)

⊠ Verdier (BESSIERES)
(1,700)

☐ Lefebvre - Desnoëttes
(4,000)

⊠ Merle
⊠ Mouton
⊠ Lasalle
Gd (det)

☐ SARAGOSSA
▨ PALAFOX
(9,000)

xxxx
CATALONIA
(21,000)

xxx
DUHESME
(12,000)
BARCELONA

⊠ Vedel   (DUPONT)
⊠ Frere
⊠ Gobert   (MONCEY)
⊠ Marlat
Gd (det)
☐

☐ MURAT
(30,000)

xx
MONCEY (-)
(8,800)

xxxx
VALENCIA CERVELLON
(17,000)

☐ Palacio
(5,000)

Delaborde
Loison
Travot
Kellermann

xxxx
PORTUGAL JUNOT
(25,000)

LISBON

xx
DUPONT (-)
(13,000)

☐ Coupigny

xxxx
GRANADA REDING
(10,000)

xxxx
ANDALUSIA CASTANOS
(34,000)

NOTE: 1. Savary relieved Murat on 29 June.
2. This map shows only those Spanish
forces actually engaged with the French.
Total forces were much larger, most of
that country and much of Portugal being
in grip of mass revolt.

Held by a strong
British garrison.

CAMPAIGN IN SPAIN
1808–09
Situation About 16 June 1808, and
Movements of French Prior to September

10 0 10 20 30 40 50 60 70 80 90
SCALE OF MILES

Dupont's operations during 19 June–23 July 1808 are an outstanding "horrible" example for any commander faced by a popular insurrection. Ordered by Savary to exercise caution, Dupont clung inertly to the unhealthy Andujar area, except for two raids on Jaen (*B1*) to seize food. Hunger and dysentery steadily weakened his men. Vedel remained at Baylen, which commanded the southern end of the Sierra Morena passes. Gobert halted north of Baylen (7 July), after leaving garrisons along the road from Madrid; Dupont, however, ordered half of Gobert's remaining troops to Andujar. In early July, receiving reports of an impending Spanish offensive, he warned his subordinates to be alert, but took no further action.

Completing his concentration (8–11 July), Castanos divided his army into five columns for an attack on 15 July. Castanos himself would maneuver to fix Dupont at Andujar; one of his divisions (Coupigny) would cross the Guadalquivir (*B1*) about seven miles upstream and join Reding; Reding would cross still farther east and advance through Baylen against Dupont's rear; a small force would operate on each flank against Dupont's communications.

The offensive started badly. Vedel repulsed Reding's attempted river crossing; Coupigny got across, but immediately went into hiding; one flank detachment was routed, the other blocked. However, Castanos' feinting alarmed Dupont, who called on Vedel for reinforcements. Overzealous, Vedel marched his whole division (less two battalions outposting the Guadalquivir's north bank) to Andujar, requesting Gobert to occupy Baylen.

Attacking again on 16 July, Reding drove off the two unsupported battalions, only to be thrown back from Baylen by the furious rush of Gobert's advance guard. Unfortunately, Gobert was mortally wounded; his successor, Dufour, drove Reding into the Guadalquivir—but marched northward at 2200, leaving Baylen again unguarded, because of a minor attack on La Carolina (*B1*).

Dupont now knew the enemy's general dispositions. He could either retire to the strong, central position at Baylen or cross the Guadalquivir through his south-bank bridgehead and strike Castanos. Instead, he remained passively at Andujar, ordering Vedel to sweep the country to Baylen—and then return to Andujar! By contrast, Castanos was inspired to compel Coupigny to join Reding.

Vedel marched at 2100 on 16 July, reaching Baylen at 0830. Dufour had vanished; the natives said that Reding had gone north. Without pausing to reconnoiter, Vedel bolted in the same direction. Overtaking Dufour, he ordered him ahead to scout the Sierra Morena passes while he rested his own weary troops. Informed of this, Dupont not only approved, but urged Vedel to push farther north. It was night before Dupont remembered that Baylen was unguarded and sent two battalions to hold that key position.

Early on 18 July, Reding and Coupigny (17,000 men, 16 guns) peacefully occupied Baylen. Vedel found he was on a fool's errand, but decided to spend the day resting. Dupont, warned that Baylen was in enemy hands, at last decided to retreat. Hoping to avoid detection, he postponed this movement until 1800, and did not destroy the Andujar bridge. His column was split by a wagon train carrying some 1,200 sick; more than half of his approximately 9,700 serviceable men marched in rear of these wagons. The march was hot, dusty, slow, and exhausting.

Reaching Baylen at about 0300, Dupont made a series of blundering, piecemeal attacks as his troops came up, failing either to maneuver or to exploit the successes of his cavalry. At the crisis of the battle, his Spanish-Swiss brigade deserted, and Castanos' leading elements struck his rear. By 1300, casualties, desertion, and exhaustion had left barely 3,000 Frenchmen still fighting. Wounded and sick, Dupont asked Reding for a truce, to permit negotiations with Castanos (then still at Andujar).

Even though he could hear the fighting around Baylen, Vedel had strolled slowly southward. About 1700, he stumbled over Reding's rear guard and—suddenly effective—quickly smashed it. Reding protested indignantly to Dupont; Dupont ordered Vedel to cease hostilities.

Early on 20 July, Dupont held a council of war which decided that his own command, trapped without food or water, could only capitulate. Castanos agreed that Vedel was free to retire. Then the officer carrying Savary's order to withdraw north of the Sierra Morena was brought in, captured with his dispatches intact. Castanos at once demanded that Vedel and Dufour be included in the capitulation. His spirit broken, Dupont agreed, provided (the exact terms are still disputed) that their troops would be sent back to France by sea.

However, during the preceding night, Dupont momentarily had recovered enough of his one-time famous courage to warn Vedel to withdraw, and Vedel had already reached the foothills of the Sierra Morena, where he was practically safe from pursuit. Furious, Castanos threatened to massacre Dupont's encircled men unless Vedel was recalled. Dupont recalled him, and Vedel had the moral cowardice to obey the order Dupont had the physical cowardice to give. Furthermore, Castanos exacted the surrender of Dufour and the garrisons Gobert had left north of the Sierra Morena, far beyond his reach. Only the commander at Madridejos had the fortitude to refuse and withdraw to Madrid. In all, some 17,635 Frenchmen surrendered. The shock went through Europe.

The Spaniards immediately violated the terms of the capitulation. The whole force (except for most of the general officers, who abandoned their men and returned to France on parole), was imprisoned, first on hulks in Cadiz harbor, later on Cabrera Island (*D2*). Only some 2,500 managed to survive.

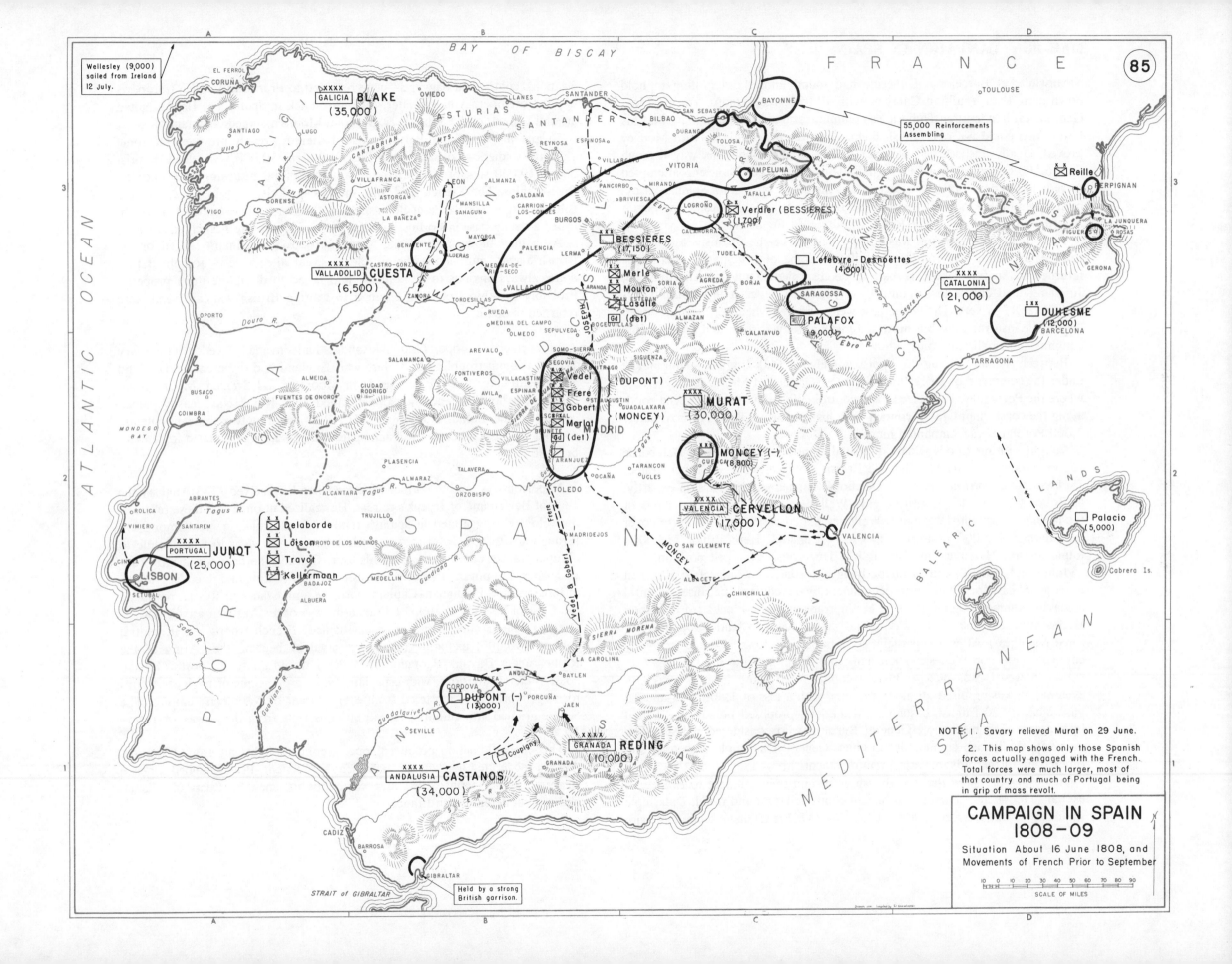

BAY OF BISCAY

FRANCE

85

Wellesley (9,000)
sailed from Ireland
12 July.

55,000 Reinforcements
Assembling

XX Reille

GALICIA BLAKE
(35,000)

XXXX
VALLADOLID CUESTA
(6,500)

BESSIERES
(17,150)

Verdier (BESSIERES)
(1,700)

Lefebvre-Desnöettes
(4,000)

Merle
Mouton
Lasalle
Gd (det)

SARAGOSSA
PALAFOX
(9,000)

CATALONIA
(21,000)

DUHESME
(12,000)

Vedel
(DUPONT)
Frere
Gobert
Morlot
(MONCEY)
Gd (det)

MURAT
(30,000)

MONCEY (-)
(8,800)

VALENCIA CERVELLON
(17,000)

Palacio
(5,000)

ATLANTIC OCEAN

Delaborde
Loison
Travot
Kellermann

XXXX
PORTUGAL JUNOT
(25,000)

LISBON

DUPONT (-)
(13,000)

Couplgny

GRANADA REDING
(10,000)

XXXX
ANDALUSIA CASTANOS
(34,000)

Held by a strong
British garrison.

STRAIT of GIBRALTAR

MEDITERRANEAN SEA

NOTE: 1. Savary relieved Murat on 29 June.

2. This map shows only those Spanish
forces actually engaged with the French.
Total forces were much larger, most of
that country and much of Portugal being
in grip of mass revolt.

CAMPAIGN IN SPAIN
1808-09

Situation About 16 June 1808, and
Movements of French Prior to September

10 0 10 20 30 40 50 60 70 80 90
SCALE OF MILES

Meanwhile, at Barcelona, Duhesme had found himself attempting to hold down more than a million Catalans with 12,000 green troops. During May, Gerona revolted, cutting Duhesme's communications with Perpignan, and his best efforts could not re-establish them. His attempt to link up with Moncey proved equally unsuccessful. About 24 July, Reille fought his way through with 6,500 conscripts from Perpignan. Thus reinforced, Duhesme attempted to reduce Gerona, but was attacked and defeated by a new Spanish army, built around regulars brought from the Balearic Islands. Duhesme thereupon retired into Barcelona, while Reille withdrew on Figueras.

In Portugal, the situation was equally bad. Once the Spanish insurrection had begun, Junot was completely isolated. Some of his Spanish auxiliaries returned to Spain; the others had to be disarmed. Thus left shorthanded, Junot retained only a loose control over the area between the Douro (A3) and Sado (A1) rivers. The Portuguese were scattered whenever they attempted large-scale insurrections, but most of Junot's army was soon tied up in mobile columns and small garrisons.

Between 1 and 5 August, approximately 14,000 English—temporarily under the command of Sir Arthur Wellesley—landed at Mondego Bay (A2), where the Portuguese had seized local control. Wellesley then advanced south along the coast, maintaining contact with his supporting fleet. Approximately 2,000 Portuguese accompanied him.

Caught with his troops widely dispersed, Junot could only send Delaborde (approximately 5,000) to delay the British advance, while he concentrated. (Subsequent actions not shown.) Delaborde carried out his mission expertly; at Rolica (A2) on 15 August he gave Wellesley one of the hardest fights of the latter's career. On 19 August, Wellesley halted at Vimiero (A2) to cover the landing of 5,000 reinforcements from England. Here, Junot (13,000) found him on 21 August in a strong but dangerously cramped position.

Junot had failed to call in his outlying garrisons, and had left 6,500 men to control Lisbon. (This last detachment was required because Admiral Seniavin, commanding the Russian Mediterranean fleet—blockaded in Lisbon Harbor by the British on its way home—had refused to land troops to reinforce his allies.) After a superficial reconnaissance, Junot decided, correctly enough, to envelop Wellesley's left flank and drive him into the sea. His execution, however, was puerile, his enveloping force being far too weak. By evening, he was repulsed all along the line, with a loss of 1,800 men and 13 guns against 720 English casualties. Wellesley's proposed pursuit was halted by the arrival of his senior, General Burrard, who considered it risky. The next day, the British commander in chief, General Dalrymple, appeared and ordered no further advance until reinforcements arrived.

Junot now proposed that the British grant him free shipment to France, in exchange for such of Portugal as he still controlled. Old and timid, Dalrymple snatched at this easy conquest. In all, 25,747 Frenchmen—complete with

weapons, colors, and baggage—were returned to France in English transports by 10 November. A month later, they were back in Spain. The British halted around Lisbon; on 25 September, Sir John Moore assumed command.

Events in Spain and Portugal had battered French prestige. Of some 130,000 soldiers who had begun this campaign, 30,000 were dead or prisoners, 20,000 sick or wounded, and almost 26,000 returning to France on British ships. The French held only the besieged city of Barcelona, and the Bilbao-Burgos-Tudela-Pampeluna area in the north. The British had established a strong base in Portugal, on the flank of any future French advance.

As a final blow, most of the Spanish troops in Denmark, egged on by British agents, mutinied on being told to swear allegiance to Joseph. Bernadotte, always anxious to be popular, had failed to discipline them properly. Probably two-thirds of them escaped to waiting British warships, and were returned to Spain.

In northern Europe, Czar Alexander had invaded Sweden (February 1808), without troubling to declare war. England had dispatched a fleet and an expeditionary force under Sir John Moore to aid Sweden. Moore could accomplish nothing, and was soon recalled. The Royal Navy easily gained control of the Baltic, but—as in 1715–21—could only parade impotently without seriously hindering Russian operations. Sweden capitulated in September 1809.

Napoleon was touring northern France when he received (1–5 August) the news of Baylen and of Joseph's retreat. He realized at once that these reverses, marvelously exaggerated in Spanish reports, would make a great impression throughout Europe. Infuriated, but clear-headed, he went to work, while to all appearances coolly continuing his tour. Clarke (the new minister of war) was ordered to put the Pyrenees fortresses on war footing and to collect rations at Bayonne and Perpignan. Caulaincourt, the ambassador to Russia, reminded the Czar of his duty to support France in case of an Austrian attack. On 12 October, the Grande Armee was inactivated. French troops left in central Europe (90,000, including the heavy cavalry) became the "Army of the Rhine" under Davout. Bernadotte (12,000) would guard the north German coast. Veteran divisions, with especially large proportions of engineer troops for siege work, were mustered from every corner of Napoleon's empire. The Senate granted him authority to call up conscripts from the classes of 1806–10.

This energetic action produced sober second thoughts all around Europe. Austria moderated her language and her rearmament; Prussia signed a peace treaty on French terms; Alexander was happy to renew his treaty of alliance and mutual defense with France.

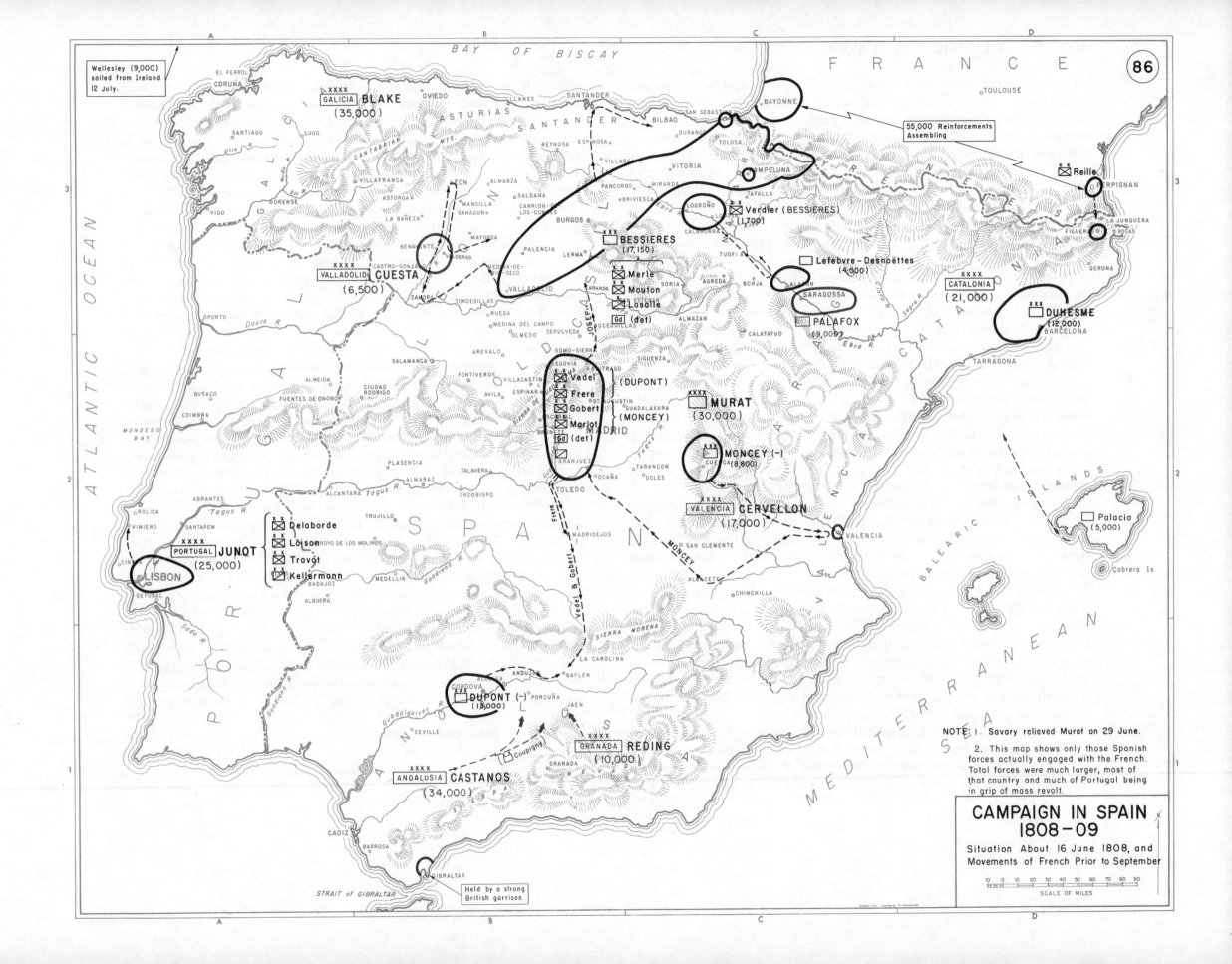

BAY OF BISCAY

FRANCE

86

TOULOUSE

Wellesley (9,000)
sailed from Ireland
12 July.

BAYONNE

55,000 Reinforcements
Assembling

Reille

PERPIGNAN

EL FERROL
CORUNA

OVIEDO

SANTANDER

SAN SEBASTIAN

LA JUNQUERA

ROSAS

XXXX GALICIA BLAKE
(35,000)

ASTURIAS

SANTANDER

LLANES

BILBAO

TOLOSA

PAMPELUNA

FIGUERAS

GERONA

SANTIAGO

LUGO

ASTURIAS

REYNOSA

ESPINOSA

DURANGO

VITORIA

MIRANDA

LOGROÑO

Verdier (BESSIERES)
(1,700)

VIGO

VILLAFRANCA

LEON

SALDANA

CARRION DE
LOS CONDES

BURGOS

BRIVIESCA

CALAHORRA

Ebro

XXXX CATALONIA
(21,000)

ORENSE

ASTORGA

MANSILLA

SAHAGUN

PALENCIA

LERMA

BESSIERES
(17,150)

TUDELA

Lefebvre-Desnoëttes
(4,000)

XXX DUHESME
(12,000)

LA BAÑEZA

BENAVENTE

MAYORGA

MEDINA DE
RIO SECO

VALLADOLID

Merle

Mouton

SORIA

AGREDA

BORJA

SARAGOSSA

BARCELONA

XXXX VALLADOLID CUESTA
(6,500)

CASTRO-GONZALO

ZAMORA

TORDESILLAS

VALLADOLID

Lasalle

Gd (det)

ALMAZAN

PALAFOX
(9,000)

Ebro R.

TARRAGONA

RUEDA

MEDINA DEL CAMPO

SALAMANCA

OLMEDO

SEPULVEDA

SEGOVIA

ARANDA

SIGUENZA

CALATAYUD

ATLANTIC OCEAN

OPORTO

Douro R.

ALMEIDA

BUSACO

CIUDAD
RODRIGO

AREVALO

VILLACASTIN

ESPINAR

Vedel

Frere

Gobert

Marlot

(DUPONT)

GUADALAXARA

MURAT
(30,000)

COIMBRA

FUENTES DE ONORO

AVILA

Gd (det)

(MONCEY)

MADRID

MONCEY (-)
(8,800)

MONDEGO BAY

PLASENCIA

SIERRA DE GUADARRAMA

ESCORIAL

ARANJUEZ

TALAVERA

TOLEDO

TARANCON

UCLES

VALENCIA CERVELLON
(17,000)

BALEARIC ISLANDS

Palacio
(5,000)

ABRANTES

Tagus R.

ALCANTARA Tagus R.

ORZOBISPO

Frere

MADRIDEJOS

SAN CLEMENTE

MONCEY

VALENCIA

ROLICA

VIMIERO

SANTAREM

TRUJILLO

ARROYO DE LOS MOLINOS

Delaborde

Loison

Travot

Kellermann

Vedel & Gobert

ALBACETE

Cabrera Is.

CINTRA

XXXX PORTUGAL JUNOT
(25,000)

LISBON

SETUBAL

MEDELLIN

BADAJOZ

ALBUERA

Guadiana R.

CHINCHILLA

Sado R.

Guadiana R.

MEDELLIN

SIERRA MORENA

MEDITERRANEAN SEA

LA CAROLINA

CORDOVA

ALCOLEA

ANDUJAR

PORCUNA

BAYLEN

NOTE: 1. Savary relieved Murat on 29 June.

DUPONT (-)
(13,000)

JAEN

Guadalquivir R.

SEVILLE

Coupigny

XXXX GRANADA REDING
(10,000)

2. This map shows only those Spanish
forces actually engaged with the French.
Total forces were much larger, most of
that country and much of Portugal being
in grip of mass revolt.

XXXX ANDALUSIA CASTANOS
(34,000)

GRANADA

SIERRA NEVADA

PORTUGAL

CADIZ

BARROSA

GIBRALTAR

STRAIT of GIBRALTAR

Held by a strong
British garrison.

CAMPAIGN IN SPAIN
1808-09

Situation About 16 June 1808, and
Movements of French Prior to September

10 0 10 20 30 40 50 60 70 80 90
SCALE OF MILES

Napoleon reached Bayonne on 3 November, to be confronted by an outstanding logistical snarl. Spain had not been an active theater since 1795, and the existing administrative system had been hard put to take care of Joseph's defeated army. Now, the lack of proper food, clothing, and medical service—combined with Spain's harsh climate, strong wines, and general filth—soon resulted in an average sick rate exceeding 20 per cent. The new French army of invasion was far superior to the first one, but of most uneven quality. Foreign contingents formed a fourth of its strength; its French regiments had been filled up with half-trained conscripts. Aside from the Guard, its best elements were Ney's and Victor's veteran corps, but these soon proved poorly disciplined. Joseph's troops were now down to a tough, battle-tested core, but were thoroughly disgusted and insubordinate. Officers and men alike seem to have disliked this new campaign, but to have wanted revenge for Baylen.

Spain was an outburst of confused vanity, her regiments proclaiming themselves the "conquerors of the conquerors of Austerlitz." The squabbling provincial juntas, however, would not agree on either a national government or a unified military command. Their various commanders were equally vainglorious and uncooperative. Nevertheless, large numbers of new troops were raised, and Romano returned from Denmark with approximately 9,000 veterans. On 5 September, a council of war in Madrid decided on a double envelopment of Joseph's position in northern Spain (*not shown*). Further plans, revisions, and clashes of authority used up October. In early November, Blake was ready to attack the French right flank; Castanos and Palafox would strike the French left near Pampeluna.

Meanwhile, General Moore had begun an advance into the interior. Accepting dubious Portuguese advice that the Salamanca (*B2*)–Valladolid (*B3*) route was impractical for artillery, he sent his cavalry and most of his guns by the long southern route, as shown. Baird would land at Coruna (*A3*) and march inland to meet him at Valladolid.

Napoleon had hoped that Joseph would hold the Douro River between Valladolid and Tudela (*C3*). When Joseph, instead, retired to the Ebro River, Napoleon remarked that he made war like a postal inspector, and urged him to hold Burgos and Tudela and to build up the morale of his men through offensive action. Hurt by such disrespectful language, Joseph proposed abandoning his communications and marching straight on Madrid with 50,000 men. His shocked younger brother retorted that any commander who would so ignore the principles of war deserved to be shot.

As the Spanish offensive developed, Blake took Bilbao (*C3*) on 20 September, lost it on 26 September, and retook it on 11 October. Bessieres gave up Burgos and Briviesca; Moncey was forced out of Tudela. Joseph ordered marches and countermarches, while his generals did as they pleased. Napoleon wished the Spanish left undisturbed as long as possible so that he could "finish the war at one blow." However, Blake attacked again on 23 October, pushing almost to Durango (*C3*). This annoyed Lefebvre, who on 31 October suddenly knocked him back through Bilbao. Joseph sent Victor to support Lefebvre, in hopes of trapping Blake. Both marshals insubordinately ignored Joseph's plans, and Victor slipped away, abandoning Lefebvre, whose rear guard was almost trapped when Blake and Romano counterattacked.

Blake was now alerted, and Napoleon's striking force scattered by Joseph's spasmodic reactions, but the other enemy commanders showed no alarm. Napoleon decided to split the enemy front by an advance on Burgos, then maneuver according to circumstances. After reorganizing his army (Soult received the II Corps, Bessieres the Cavalry Reserve) and his supply system, he paused until informed that Lefebvre had again routed Blake (7 November) west of Bilbao. He then advanced on 9 November with Soult, Bessieres, Ney (less two divisions), and the Guard, warning Moncey that—once Burgos was taken—the action would probably shift to the French left flank.

Napoleon's advance met (10 November) Belveder, who was slowly moving into the empty Spanish center. The Spanish broke at the first sight of French bayonets, and were harried for ten miles by Bessieres' horsemen. (Spanish losses, 3,400; French, less than 200.) Burgos fell immediately; French cavalry fanned out to the west; Soult moved on Reynosa to get into Blake's rear. Victor crushed Blake at Espinosa on 11 November, while Lefebvre destroyed another Spanish detachment near that town. Reaching Reynosa on 14 November, Soult caught part of Blake's fleeing army. Blake reached Leon (*B3*) with only a handful of men.

Learning on 14 November of Blake's defeat and the occupation of Valladolid by French cavalry, Napoleon ordered Soult to occupy the port of Santander (*B3*), called Victor to Burgos, and sent Bessieres and Ney (with only two divisions) to Aranda (*B3*) to begin the envelopment of the Spanish right flank. He himself remained in Burgos with his Guard, awaiting Victor and hoping to obtain news of Moore's progress. This pause has been criticized by some writers, but the collection of intelligence during a national uprising always has been a difficult task. Meanwhile, Bessieres and Ney reached Aranda (16 November), and Milhaud's patrols could find no organized enemy southwest of Valladolid. On 18 November, Napoleon gave Lannes (until then, without a command) the III Corps, two of Ney's divisions which Joseph had mislaid at Logrono, and a brigade of dragoons, with orders to attack the Spanish right flank. Bessieres would halt at Aranda, patrolling well to the south; Ney would advance on either Soria or Almazan (*both C3*), as circumstances dictated, to intercept Castanos' retreat.

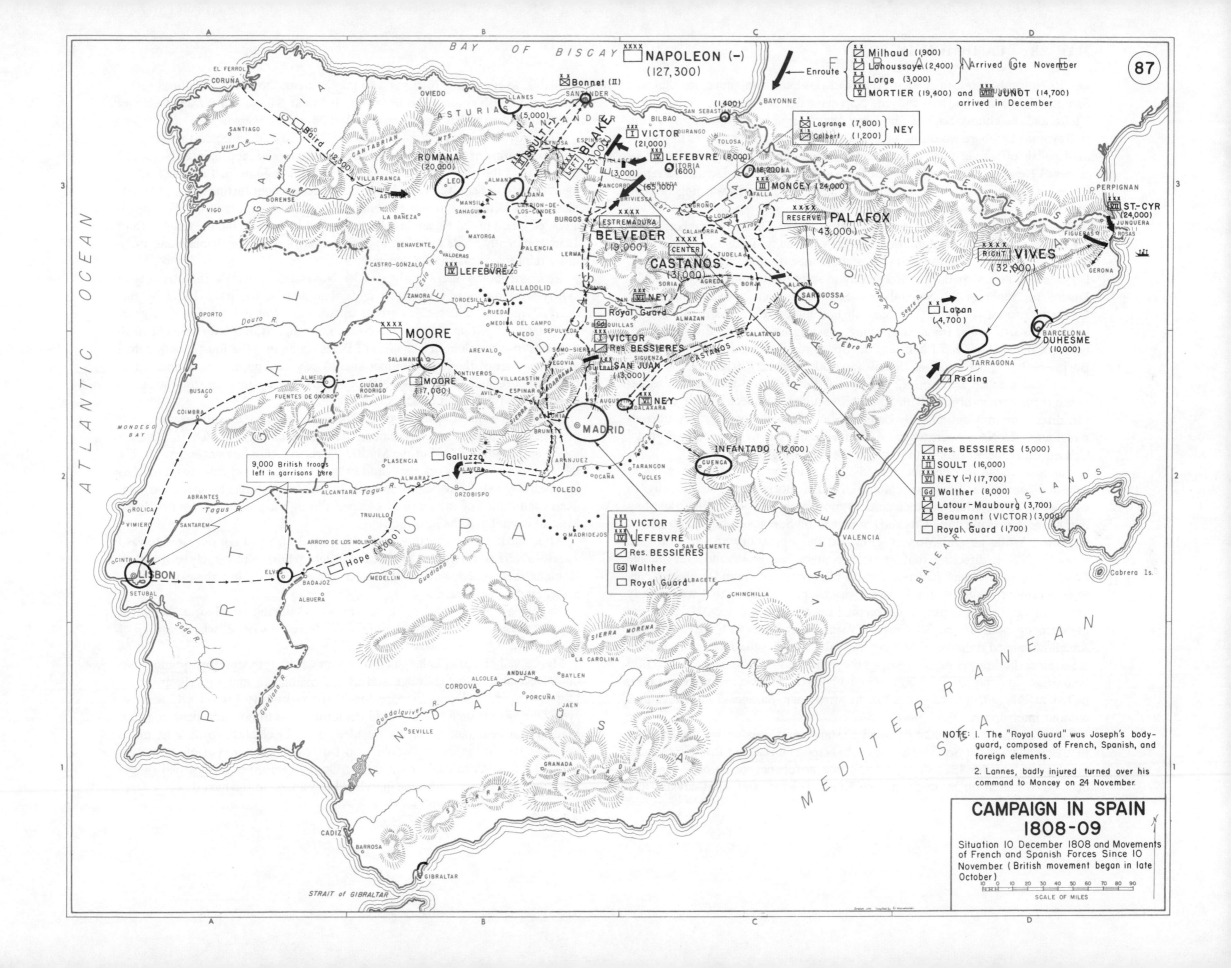

CAMPAIGN IN SPAIN
1808-09

Situation 10 December 1808 and Movements of French and Spanish Forces Since 10 November. (British movement began in late October)

On 20 November, informed that Soult had occupied Santander and that the Spanish right wing had not moved, Napoleon decided to support Ney with Victor and the Guard. Soult would leave one division in Santander and return to Reynosa; Lefebvre would move to Carrion-de-los-Condes (*B3*). In case of an English offensive, they would support each other. The rear echelon of Imperial Headquarters would stay in Burgos under Mathieu-Dumas (a senior officer of Berthier's staff) to handle intelligence and the forwarding of reinforcements. Ney was ordered on to Agreda (*C3*).

Castanos and Palafox had done little but squabble. On 21 November, learning that Ney had reached Almazan, Castanos retired to Tudela, warning Palafox to do likewise. Palafox delayed, and Lannes, though crippled when his horse fell on an icy road, came on swiftly to seize the heights west of Tudela. During the night of 22 November, a Spanish council of war voted, over Castanos' protest, to fight. The Spanish had almost twice Lannes' strength, but Lannes struck first the next morning, massing his corps against the Spanish right flank. After hard fighting, the Spaniards fled toward Saragossa and Borja (*both C3*). (Casualties: Spanish, 6,000; French, 700).

Ney had reached Soria on 22 November, but, because the mountains between them were swarming with Spanish irregulars, had been unable to establish direct communication with Lannes. Sticking to his orders, Ney did not budge until 25 November, when he received the order to proceed to Agreda. Consequently, he was too late to catch the retreating Spaniards.

Lannes, unable to ride, had turned the pursuit over to Moncey. Moncey split his forces, sending one column through Borja and subsequently to Calatayud (*C2*), while another column moved on Saragossa. Ney, learning that Moncey was pursuing Castanos, marched on Saragossa, hoping to take it by storm. While he and Moncey discussed this operation, an order arrived from Napoleon, directing that Moncey contain Saragossa and Ney pursue Castanos. Lannes (who had not yet left his former command) advised Ney to start promptly with the force (two divisions, plus cavalry) that was already at Calatayud, but Ney insisted on keeping his own corps intact. He therefore gathered up both of the VI Corps divisions that were with Moncey—and somehow carried off most of Moncey's cavalry, leaving the latter only 15,000 men. Since he knew that Saragossa now contained 35,600 regulars, 10,000 volunteers, and possibly 20,000 armed civilians, Moncey with his 15,000, halted at Alagon, allowing Palafox to strengthen Saragossa's fortifications without interruption. Ney's pursuit was unsuccessful.

Learning that Lannes had defeated Castanos and Palafox on the 23d and that Ney had not left Soria until the 25th, Napoleon realized that his planned envelopment of the Spanish right flank had no chance of success. He then decided to march on Madrid with the Guard, Victor, and what cavalry was available, to cut off any fugitives who might attempt to reach Andalusia (*B1*). Since an English column had been reported near Salamanca (*B2*), Lefebvre and Milhaud would advance through Valladolid to Segovia (*B2*).

The provisional Spanish government in Madrid had collected the debris of Belveder's army at Segovia and had sent San Juan with approximately 13,000 men to hold the vital Somo-Sierra Pass (*B2*). San Juan, in turn, sent 4,000 men forward to Sepulveda and began constructing light fortifications at Somo-Sierra. The detachment sent to Sepulveda repulsed an attack by the French advance guard on 28 November, but withdrew to Segovia the next night. (San Juan apparently made no effort to regain control over this detachment, or to draw reinforcements from Segovia.)

Reaching Somo-Sierra early on 30 November, Victor's infantry began slowly working its way up the heights that flanked the pass. Irked by this delay, Napoleon launched his escort squadron of the Polish light cavalry of the Guard straight up the pass in a column of fours. Riding over three Spanish batteries in succession, this handful of Poles broke into the fourth, entrenched at the summit of the pass. Another small body of Guard cavalry spurred to their support, and the Spanish infantry—terrified by this amazing stroke— broke up and fled in all directions.

Sending Lasalle toward Segovia, Napoleon pushed ahead, reaching the outskirts of Madrid on 2 December. The government had fled to Badajoz (*A2*) and Seville (*B1*), but the Madrid garrison refused to surrender. During the 3d, French artillery opened—and French infantry occupied—two breaches in Madrid's walls, but Napoleon then halted the fighting to spare the city. That night, most of the garrison escaped through a gap in the French lines. Madrid capitulated the next morning.

After making a faint gesture at relieving Madrid, San Juan retreated toward Talavera (*B2*). En route, his men murdered him, and largely disbanded. Romana had rallied some 20,000 men at Leon (*B3*), but these were half-armed and half-naked.

Napoleon now called Ney, Lefebvre, and Milhaud to Madrid. While at Segovia, Lasalle and Milhaud had failed to ferret out Hope, who, learning of their presence, retired toward Avila (*B2*).

Moore had closed at Salamanca on about 23 November, Hope joining him on 5 December. Practically ignored by the Spaniards, and vaguely aware of Lannes' victory at Tudela, Moore considered retiring to Lisbon (*A2*). However, fearing that such action would demoralize his troops, and believing that Madrid still held out, he finally decided, on 6 December, to at least make a demonstration toward Valladolid and Burgos. If he were cut off from Lisbon, he would retire on Coruna (*A3*). On 10 December, he learned of the fall of Madrid. Nevertheless, he marched for Valladolid the next day.

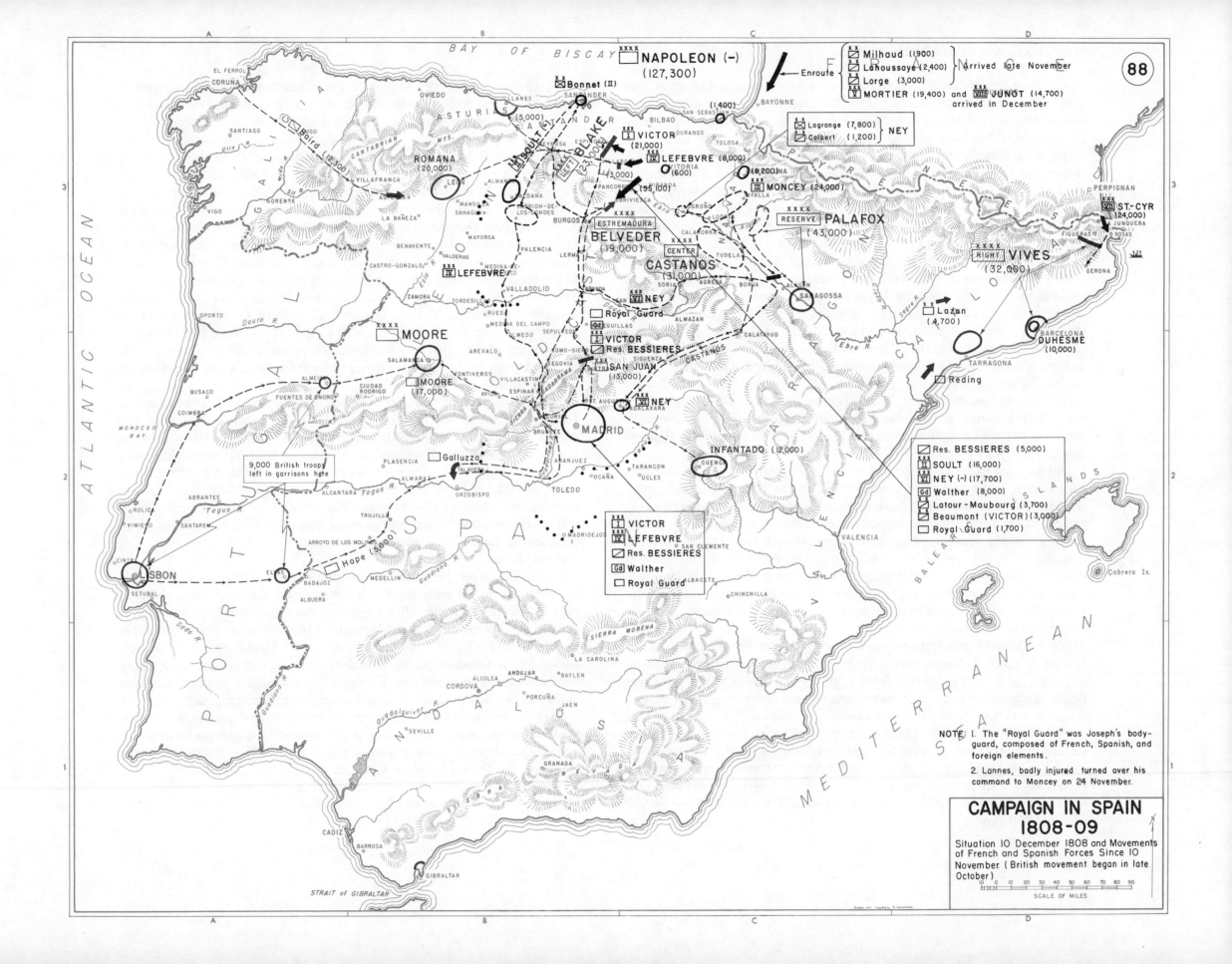

BAY OF BISCAY

XXXX NAPOLEON (-) (127,300)

Enroute
XX Milhaud (1,900)
XX Lahoussaye (2,400)
XX Lorge (3,000)
V MORTIER (19,400) Arrived late November
VIII JUNOT (14,700) arrived in December

XX Lagrange (7,800)
XX Colbert (1,200) NEY

88

XX Bonnet (II)
(5,000)
SANTANDER

ROMANA (20,000)

SOULT
BLAKE
(23,000)

XXX I VICTOR (21,000)
XXX IV LEFEBVRE (8,000)
(3,000) (600)

XXX III MONCEY (24,000)

(55,000)

XXXX RESERVE PALAFOX (43,000)

XXXX ST-CYR (24,000)

LEÓN

ESTREMADURA
XXXX BELVEDER (19,000)

CENTER
CASTAÑOS (31,000)

RIGHT VIVES (32,000)

XXX VI NEY
Gd Royal Guard
XXX I VICTOR
Res BESSIERES
XXX SAN JUAN (13,000)

XX Lazan (4,700)

DUHESME (10,000)

VALLADOLID

MOORE

MOORE (17,000)

XXX VI NEY

Reding

MADRID

INFANTADO (12,000)

CUENCA

Res. BESSIERES (5,000)
XXX SOULT (16,000)
XXX VI NEY (-) (17,700)
Gd Walther (8,000)
XX Latour-Maubourg (3,700)
XX Beaumont (VICTOR) (3,000)
Royal Guard (1,700)

LISBON

Galluzzo

9,000 British troops left in garrisons here

Hope (5,000)

XXX I VICTOR
XXX IV LEFEBVRE
Res. BESSIERES
Gd Walther
Royal Guard

VALENCIA

Cabrera Is.

ANDALUSIA

NOTE: 1. The "Royal Guard" was Joseph's body-guard, composed of French, Spanish, and foreign elements.

2. Lannes, badly injured turned over his command to Moncey on 24 November.

STRAIT of GIBRALTAR

MEDITERRANEAN SEA

ATLANTIC OCEAN

CAMPAIGN IN SPAIN 1808-09

Situation 10 December 1808 and Movements of French and Spanish Forces Since 10 November (British movement began in late October)

0 10 20 30 40 50 60 70 80 90
SCALE OF MILES

If Napoleon had not ended Spanish resistance at one stroke, he had at least made an impressive start. Holding Madrid, he would be able to strike at each still rebellious province in turn. Meanwhile, as his army closed up around him, he forced Madrid's inhabitants to petition for the return of their "well-loved" King Joseph, and began the work of regenerating Spain. The Inquisition, feudal rights, provincial custom barriers, and other relics of medievalism were all abolished. Napoleon's reforms were excellent and civilizing ones, but they took little account of the average Spaniard's aloof pride in his own institutions. (Monks and smugglers whom the new laws left unemployed went to swell guerrilla bands.)

Napoleon knew that the English had reached Salamanca (B2), but felt certain that they would soon retire into Portugal—a matter that he proposed to settle by marching down the Tagus River to Lisbon. To prepare for this offensive, he sent Victor to destroy a Spanish force that had rallied at Guadalaxara (C2); built a fortified camp outside Madrid to dominate that city and give him a secure advance base; sent Mortier to cover the siege of Saragossa; and pushed Lasalle and Milhaud westward to Talavera (B2) to form the nucleus of his future advance guard. On 10 December, he directed Soult (reinforced by one brigade of Milhaud's dragoons) to cover Burgos (B3) while the main army marched on Lisbon; after Moore retired into Portugal, Soult was to seize Leon, Benavente, and Zamora (all B3), and drive Romana into Galicia (A3).

Old Marshal Kellermann was summoned to Bayonne to serve as rear-area commander, as he had done previously along the Rhine. The high road, Bayonne–Miranda–Pancorbo–Burgos–Aranda–Somo-Sierra–Madrid, was organized as the army's line of communication. The major towns along it were strongly fortified, and entrenched halting places constructed between them at intervals of an average day's march. The supply services began to function with fair regularity, a convoy system was organized to thwart guerrilla raids, forward depots were filled, and replacements and reinforcements brought up. During this period, Napoelon rested his troops as much as possible, but took severe measures to restore discipline.

His methodical preparations were interrupted on 10 December, when Lasalle occupied Talavera, picked up some stragglers from Hope's column, and reported a strong Spanish force south of the Tagus River. At once, Bessieres started for Talavera to take command of the advance guard; Lefebvre followed with two of his divisions (Sebastiani, Valence), leaving the third (Leval) in Madrid. Victor, likewise leaving a division (Lapisse) in Madrid, marched his other two (Ruffin, Villatte) to Toledo (B2). Ney left a division (Dessoles) at Guadalaxara, and pushed for Madrid. Cavalry reconnaissances probed vigorously in all directions. When ready, Napoleon thus could move on Lisbon with Victor, Lefebvre, Ney, Bessieres, and the Guard—some 54,500 men and 150 guns.

December 19 came with ill tidings. Three deserters (Frenchmen, captured at Trafalgar and enlisted in the British Army) reached the French outposts with news that Moore had been in Salamanca as late as 13 December and had made no preparations for a retreat. That afternoon, a message from Soult (written on 16 December) reported that his outposts at Tordesillas and Rueda (both B3) were under attack by British cavalry, and that Romana was moving eastward. Moore's offensive appeared at first glance so foolhardy that Napoleon felt it must be merely a feint designed to draw him away from Lisbon. If so, it should be ignored; if not, the opportunity to destroy Moore must not be missed. Napoleon ordered Ney to advance across the Guadarrama Mountains (B2) with his corps cavalry and two available infantry divisions (Marchand, Maurice-Mathieu). Lahoussaye (then apparently north of Madrid) would scout westward toward Arevalo (B2) and Salamanca. Dessoles was called to Madrid. Mathieu-Dumas (still in Burgos) was advised of the situation and Napoleon's plans. The VIII Corps (Junot would relieve Moncey in command of the III Corps) and Lorge's dragoon division were assigned to Soult, who was instructed to maneuver to fix the English while Napoleon cut them off from Salamanca.

On 20 December, Napoleon recalled Ruffin from Toledo to relieve Lapisse. Lefebvre-Desnoëttes led the Guard cavalry in Ney's wake. Napoleon had decided that the appearance of British infantry in Valladolid (B3) would be a good indication that Moore was in earnest, and he therefore would remain in Madrid until this was reported. When the report reached him that afternoon, he ordered Lapisse to march at once, the Guard infantry the next morning, and Dessoles (Ney) on the 22d, as soon as relieved by Ruffin. It seemed obvious that Moore had changed bases and that Soult might be in considerable danger. However, by hard marching, he hoped to overtake and destroy Moore.

On 22 December, he completed his preparations. Lefebvre, with Lasalle and Milhaud, would cross the Tagus River on the 23d and chase Galluzzo back to Trujillo (B2); thereafter, Lefebvre would stand ready to move toward either Ciudad Rodrigo (B2) or Madrid, as subsequent developments might require. Victor (Villatte, Ruffin, Leval, Latour-Maubourg, and two battalions left at Guadalaxara by Dessoles) received the mission of covering Madrid from the south and east. Finally, wishing to ensure unity of command in the Madrid area (and also to regild Joseph's tarnished prestige), he left his brother in command of both Lefebvre and Victor, with one mission—to hold Madrid. Various stray cavalry detachments around Madrid were formed into a provisional brigade under d'Avenay and sent after Ney. Quite late in the afternoon, the French Emperor followed.

BAY OF BISCAY

FRANCE

89

ATLANTIC OCEAN

EL FERROL
CORUÑA
SOULT
MOORE
NEY
ROMANA (4,000)
VIGO
ORENSE
SANTIAGO

OVIEDO
LLANES
SANTANDER
ASTURIAS
SANTANDER
REYNOSA
ESPINOSA
VILLARCAYO
LEON
ALMANZA
ROMANA (23,000)
SOULT (+ most of VIII and Lorge)
BURGOS

BAYONNE
SAN SEBASTIAN
BILBAO
DURANGO
TOLOSA (Elements of VIII)
VITORIA
MIRANDA
PANCORBO
LOGROÑO
PAMPELUNA
TAFALLA

TOULOUSE

PERPIGNAN

LA JUNQUERA
FIGUERAS
ROSAS
GERONA

PALAFOX (45,000)
JUNOT
MORTIER (-)
LANNES (35,000)
ST-CYR

BARCELONA

Suchet (MORTIER)

TARRAGONA
REDING

MOORE
LEFEBVRE
Lasalle
Milhaud
MADRID
(14,000)
ST. AUGUSTIN (2 bns - NEY)
GUADALAXARA

INFANTADO (21,000)

CUENCA
TARANCON

VICTOR (+)

VALENCIA

(9,000 British)

Galluzzo

LISBON
SETUBAL

NAPOLEON (42,000)
NEY (-)
Gd Walther
Lahoussaye
Lapisse (VICTOR)
(provisional) d'Avenay

Ruffin (VICTOR)
Leval (LEFEBVRE)
Royal Guard (Approximately 12,500)

VICTOR (-)
Latour-Maubourg (9,000)

SAN CLEMENTE
ALBACETE
CHINCHILLA

BALEARIC ISLANDS

Cabrera Is.

ANDALUSIA
DEL PALACIO (6,000)

SEVILLE

GRANADA
NEVADA

CADIZ
BARROSA
GIBRALTAR

STRAIT of GIBRALTAR

MEDITERRANEAN SEA

NOTE: VIII was deactivated, 2 January. Most of its units were transferred to Soult.

CAMPAIGN IN SPAIN
1808-09

Situation 22 January 1809, and Movements of Opposing Forces Since 11 December 1808.

SCALE OF MILES
10 0 10 20 30 40 50 60 70 80 90

MAP 90: CAMPAIGN IN SPAIN

Until 19 December, the weather had been favorable; thereafter, it steadily worsened. A blizzard and subzero cold caught Ney and the Guard cavalry in the Guadarrama Mountains; the troops following them found the icy roads almost impassable. Napoleon walked eight and a half miles up the steepest part of the pass, arm in arm with Savary and Duroc, without halting. Lapisse's division, "exasperated by fatigue," shouted insults and menaces as he passed. Under such conditions, the French advance became badly strung out, losing the equivalent of a half-day's march.

Napoleon now missed Lasalle and Milhaud. Ney's corps cavalry lacked the strength for long-range reconnaissance through this broken country. Though it found Salamanca evacuated (thus confirming Napoleon's deduction that Moore had given up Lisbon for another base, farther north), it also reported the English no farther ahead than Valladolid. In this case, a swift advance might still envelop them. Napoleon felt so hopeful that—while ordering Ney to seize the Tordesillas bridge (B3) and exerting himself to get the column closed up—he wrote to Joseph to have the Madrid papers publish the news that "20,000 English are cornered and doomed."

The actual situation was considerably different. Soult had taken position at Saldana (B3) on 4 December, with some 13,000 weary men. Hearing that Romana had more than 25,000 Spanish around Leon, and that some English had appeared at Astorga (B3), he posted Debelle's brigade of cavalry at Sahagun (B3) and Franceschi's around Valladolid (not shown). On 13 and 14 December, British cavalry began forcing Franceschi northward; Moore was reported nearing Valladolid, and Romana advancing from Leon. Soult's mission was to cover Napoleon's communications; accordingly, he decided to hold his present position as long as possible, calling on Mathieu-Dumas for whatever reinforcements might be available. Mathieu-Dumas at once began sending units of the VIII Corps and Lorge's dragoon division westward as rapidly as they became available. Thus reinforced, Soult (18–20 December) considered a spoiling attack toward Leon, even though Franceschi had been forced back to Palencia (B3). On the 21st, however, British cavalry surprised and defeated Debelle at Sahagun. Soult then concentrated at Carrion-de-los-Condes, awaiting Loison's division (VIII Corps), which could not reach Burgos until the 25th. However, learning during the night of 25–26 December that Ney had reached Tordesillas, Soult changed his plans and ordered an advance through Sahagun on the 27th to fix the enemy, while Ney came in on their flank and rear.

Moore, meanwhile, though fully aware that his plan was dangerous, reckoned the French strength in Spain at only 85,000. Consequently, he expected that Burgos would be only lightly garrisoned and that an advance

against it would force Napoleon to evacuate Madrid and countermarch to protect his communications. On 13 December, his cavalry picked up a copy of Napoleon's 10 December order to Soult, taken from the body of a murdered French officer. Thus advised as to the location of the various French units, and probably undeceived as to the total French strength, Moore still decided that he had time for a hit-and-run attack on Soult. Swinging his columns to the left, he linked up with Baird at Mayorga (B3) on 20 December. Here also, he established contact with Romana, whom he had persuaded to join his attack on Soult. (Only 7,000 of Romana's 23,000 men proved fit for action.) During 22–23 December, Moore massed at Sahagun to prepare his attack, but was warned late on the 23d by Romana that Napoleon had been advancing northward from Madrid "since 18 December." Moore began withdrawing the next morning, his rear guard remaining at Sahagun until the 25th and his cavalry making a feint at Carrion before retiring.

During the afternoon of 26 December, Napoleon received Soult's report of his plans for the 27th, with his request that Ney support him by advancing through Benavente. Napoleon already knew of Moore's presence in the Leon-Sahagun area, but his own troops were so exhausted (they had averaged fifteen miles a day, over primitive tracks, in heavy rains) that he had allowed them to rest most of the 26th. Now, hoping to trap Moore between his army and Soult, he sent his whole force forward at daybreak, Ney leading. Unfortunately, worried that Soult might be too weak to resist a major offensive, he directed Ney toward Medina-de-Rio-Seco, instead of Benavente (both B3). Consequently, 27 December was a day of frustrated scrambling. Moore apparently had evaporated, but, finally, reports from Ney's corps cavalry (which had found English cavalry in Mayorga late on the 26th) led Napoleon to change Ney's objective to Valderas (B3). By the 28th, with English infantry reported in Benavente, it was evident that Moore was retreating. Still hopeful of striking Moore's flank, Napoleon drove his troops forward along roads knee-deep in mud, galloping ahead of them with a small escort in his anxiety to determine whether Moore were retiring through Astorga or Zamora. During the 28th and 29th, he checked his infantry along the flooded Esla River, awaiting the outcome of his cavalry reconnaissances—which proved disappointing. Ney's cavalry could not find a ford. Lefebvre-Desnoëttes swam the river at Castro-Gonzalo with a detachment of Guard cavalry, but probed too deeply and recklessly, and was overwhelmed and captured. Franceschi, however, caught Romana astride the river at Mansilla and smashed his advance guard. Romana had planned to withdraw northward into Asturias. Now, finding the passes there blocked with snow, he turned toward Astorga, crowding in on Moore's withdrawal.

90

BAY OF BISCAY

FRANCE

CAMPAIGN IN SPAIN
1808-09

Situation 22 January 1809, and Movements of
Opposing Forces Since 11 December 1808.

NOTE: VIII was deactivated, 2 January. Most
of its units were transferred to Soult.

SCALE OF MILES
10 0 10 20 30 40 50 60 70 80 90

Ruffin (VICTOR)
Leval (LEFEBVRE)
Royal Guard
(Approximately 12,500)

NAPOLEON (42,000)
NEY (-)
Walther
Lahoussaye
Lapisse (VICTOR)
(provisional) d'Avenay

VICTOR (-)
Latour-Maubourg
(10,000)

ANDALUSIA DEL PALACIO
(6,000)

PALAFOX (45,000)

JUNOT
MORTIER (-)
LANNES
(35,000)

ST-CYR

Suchet (MORTIER)

REDING

INFANTADO
(21,000)

VICTOR (+)

SOULT

MOORE

NEY
ROMANA
(4,000)

ROMANA
(23,000)

SOULT (+ most of VIII and Lorge)
(25,000)

(Elements of VIII)

Baird
(29,000)

MOORE

LEFEBVRE
Lasalle
Milhaud

(14,000)

MADRID

(2 bns - NEY)

(9,000 British)

Galluzzo

LISBON

On 30 December, the main French army began crossing the Esla River at Castro-Gonzalo; Soult entered Leon. All through the next day, Napoleon pushed forward, but the cares of his empire were plucking at his coattails: Dessoles must be sent back to reinforce Joseph; Clarke (the minister of war) ordered to call up the class of 1810 "if Austria budges." On 1 January, the Emperor left Benavente, still hopeful that Moore would stand at Astorga to gain time for his trains to get through the mountains. Some distance from Astorga, a messenger from Paris overtook him: Austria seemed on the verge of declaring war; Fouche and Talleyrand were deep in intrigues against him; he was urgently needed in France. Joseph's dispatches also arrived: Lefebvre was insubordinately marching away from Madrid; the Spanish were massing to the southeast. Napoleon spent the night at Astorga, which the English had thoroughly sacked. All reports indicated there was little chance of intercepting Moore. The next morning, he announced his decisions: The Guard, Lapisse, and d'Avenay would return to Benavente; Ney would concentrate at Astorga; Soult, with three infantry divisions, his corps cavalry, and two dragoon divisions, would continue the pursuit. This force was weak for the mission assigned it. Possibly, Napoleon overestimated the demoralization of Moore's army; more likely, he realized that even this force would have difficulty finding food in a barren region, already stripped by the English and the Spanish.

Moore's army had been eager to fight, but many units' morale cracked once the retreat began. Sullen, avid for drink and loot, indifferently disciplined, they treated Galicia like a hostile country. A tough rear guard always fought, but most of the army reached Coruna (11 January 1809) little better than a mob. Soult, with only 16,000 infantry and 3,500 cavalry, pressed Moore hard, but ran no unnecessary risks, not venturing an attack when Moore paused beyond Lugo. Moore sent his light troops through Orense to Vigo (*movement not shown*), where they embarked on the 17th. Romana fled southward.

There were supplies at Coruna, but no transports—the British fleet having been unable to round the tip of Portugal against unfavorable winds. Moore fed his men and waited. The transports came on 14 January; Moore hastily embarked his sick, wounded, cavalry, and guns. Soult, delayed by blown bridges, appeared the next day. Moore had 16,000 infantry and 9 guns in a strong position; Soult, 12,000 infantry, 20 guns, and 3,200 largely useless cavalry. He apparently had little hope of success, but, feeling duty-bound to try, attacked the next afternoon. The only result was about 900 casualties on each side. Moore, mortally wounded, died that night, while Hope pressed the embarkation. He had almost finished by morning, when Soult's guns came into action from cliffs overlooking the bay. Six transports ran ashore in the resulting confusion, but British warships finally silenced Soult's battery. The

expedition reached England between 21 and 23 June, having lost some 8,800 men.

Soult then took Coruna and the great naval base of El Ferrol. Ordered to reoccupy Portugal, he promptly marched on Santiago (*A3*). Meanwhile, at Soult's request, Ney sent a division to Orense; en route, it destroyed Romana's rear guard. Later, Ney occupied all of Galicia.

During this period, Infantado had marched on Madrid in three columns, aided by Del Palacio's feeble demonstration toward Madridejos (*B2*). After some maneuvering, Victor destroyed the strongest enemy column at Ucles (*C2*), killing and capturing 11,000 out of 12,800. (Here, Senarmont, caught in a defile with his unescorted guns by Spanish guerrillas, routed them with point-blank canister.) Victor thereafter chased Infantado beyond Chinchilla (*C2*), capturing all his artillery.

Joseph had ordered Lefebvre to return to Madrid once he had disposed of Galluzzo. But Lefebvre, somehow conceiving himself ordered to pursue Moore, stubbornly pushed north to Avila (*B2*), where, on 8 January, a stinging letter from Berthier started him back to Madrid.

Moncey, reinforced by Mortier, had renewed the siege of Saragossa on 20 December. (Mortier took Suchet's division to Calatayad to cover the besieger's communications with Madrid.) Moncey was later relieved by Junot, who in turn was relieved, on 22 January, by Lannes, who had returned briefly to France for medical attention. Operating carefully and methodically, substituting artillery fire and mining for infantry assaults, Lannes broke Palafox's incompetent—if fanatical—resistance by 20 February.

In Catalonia (*D3*), Gouvion St.-Cyr's mission was to save Barcelona "at any price" and resume the siege of Gerona (*both D3*); otherwise, he had a free hand. He began, on 5 December, by taking the little seacoast fortress of Rosas (*D3*), to remove a possible beachhead from his flank. The coastal road from Rosas south being under the fire of an English fleet, he left his artillery in Figueras and moved inland across the hills with 15,000 infantry and 1,500 cavalry. A feint toward Gerona screened his departure (9 December). Knocking out Spanish units in detail as they hurried to intercept him, capturing the artillery he needed from the enemy, he reached Barcelona on 17 December. Three days later, he drove Vives' remaining forces into Tarragona.

Napoleon paused at Valladolid, where he issued final orders. Berthier and the Guard would remain there until it was certain that the English had reembarked. Lefebvre was relieved, and his corps given to Jourdan; Joseph was named commander in chief of the Army of Spain. Then, on 17 January, the Emperor began a breakneck ride for Paris, arriving there on the 24th.

BAY OF BISCAY

FRANCE

91

ATLANTIC OCEAN

EL FERROL
CORUNA
SOULT
MOORE
SANTIAGO
VIGO
ORENSE
VILLAFRANCA
ASTORGA
LA BANEZA
NEY
ROMANA
(4,000)
BENAVENTE
CASTRO-GONZALO
ZAMORA
TORDESILLAS

OVIEDO
LLANES
SANTANDER
ASTURIAS
SANTANDER
CANTABRIAN MTS.
REYNOSA ESPINOSA
VILLARCAYO
LEON
ALMANZA
ROMANA
(23,000)
MANSILLA
SAHAGUN
LOS-LANOES
MAYORGA
(29,000)
VALDERAS
MEDINA-DE-RIO-SECO
VALLADOLID
ARANDA
SAN ESTEBAN

BILBAO
DURANGO
TOLOSA
(Elements of VIII
VITORIA
MIRANDA
PANCORBO
SOULT (+ most of VIII)
and Lorge)
BURGOS
LERMA
SORIA

SAN SEBASTIAN
BAYONNE
PAMPELUNA
TAFALLA
LOGRONO
LODOSA
CALAHORRA
AGREDA
BORJA
TUDELA
ALMAZAN

TOULOUSE

PERPIGNAN

PALAFOX (45,000)
JUNOT
ZARAGOSSA
MORTIER (-)
LANNES
(35,000)

ST-CYR

FIGUERAS
ROSAS
GERONA
BARCELONA

DOURO R.
OPORTO
SALAMANCA
MOORE
CIUDAD RODRIGO
FUENTES DE ONORO
COIMBRA
BUSACO

RUEDA
MEDINA DEL CAMPO
OLMEDO
AREVALO
SEPULVEDA
SEGOVIA
BUITRAGO
SIGUENZA
SOMO-SIERRA
AVILA
ESPINAR
SIERRA DE GUADARAMA
ESCORIAL
ST. AUGUSTIN (2 bns.-NEY)
GUADALAXARA

SUCHET (MORTIER)
CALATAYUD
EBRO R.

TARRAGONA
REDING

MONDEGO BAY

ABRANTES
ROLICA
VIMIERO
SANTAREM
CINTRA
LISBON
SETUBAL

(9,000 British)

PLASENCIA
ALMARAZ
ALCANTARA
Tagus R.
TRUJILLO
Gallazzo
ARROYO DE LOS MOLINOS
BADAJOZ
ELVAS
MEDELLIN
MEDELLIN

VILLACASTIN
LEFEBVRE
Lasalle
Milhaud
(14,000)
BRUNETE
MADRID
TALAVERA
ORZOBISPO
TOLEDO
ARANJUEZ
OCANA
MADRIDEJOS

TARANCON
CUENCA
INFANTADO
(21,000)

MEDITERRANEAN SEA

BALEARIC ISLANDS

Cabrera Is.

VALENCIA

SAN CLEMENTE
ALBACETE
CHINCHILLA

VICTOR (+)

Ruffin (VICTOR)
Leval (LEFEBVRE)
Royal Guard
(Approximately 12,500)

NAPOLEON (42,000)
NEY (-)
Walther
Lahoussaye
Lapisse (VICTOR)
(provisional) d'Avenay

VICTOR (-)
Latour-Maubourg
(10,000)

BAYLEN
ANDUJAR
ALCOLEA
PORCUNA
JAEN
ANDALUSIA
DEL PALACIO
(6,000)

LA CAROLINA
SIERRA MORENA

CADIZ
BARROSA
GIBRALTAR
STRAIT of GIBRALTAR

SEVILLE
GRANADA

NOTE: VIII was deactivated, 2 January Most of its units were transferred to Soult.

CAMPAIGN IN SPAIN
1808-09

Situation 22 January 1809, and Movements of
Opposing Forces Since 11 December 1808.

SCALE OF MILES

As Napoleon spurred northward, the conquest of Spain seemed assured. Spanish patriotism, however, was merely stunned, not crushed; guerrilla resistance steadily increased. Given time, this could be put down, as it was in Naples. But the presence of an English army in Portugal kept the French from consolidating their position. By invading Spain, Napoleon had saddled himself with a continuous second front.

Summary of Succeeding Events in Spain, 1809–14

1809.   Victor advanced on Badajoz (*A2*), defeating Cuesta at Medellin (*B2*). Soult occupied northern Portugal, but halted at Oporto (*A3*) to refit his battered army before advancing on Lisbon. In April, Wellesley took command of the British forces in Portugal, plus a new, British-trained Portuguese army. Striking north, Wellesley surprised Soult and drove him into the interior. With Portugal in revolt all around him, Soult seemed doomed, but escaped by a daring march through the mountains to Orense (*A3*). Wellesley then turned on Victor and advanced up the Tagus River together with Cuesta. Victor retired to Talavera (*B2*), where Joseph joined him with the French reserves. Cuesta fled at the first clash; Wellesley repulsed Victor in a two-day battle, but had to retreat hurriedly when Soult, Ney, and Mortier emerged from the mountains to his left rear. In Aragon (*C2–C3*), Blake defeated Suchet, who had just taken over Junot's neglected III Corps. Reorganizing his forces, Suchet soon drove Blake out of Aragon. In Catalonia (*D2–D3*), Augereau (who had replaced St.-Cyr) captured Gerona.

1810.   Having crushed Austria at Ratisbon and Wagram, Napoleon planned to finish off Spain. Massena, with Ney, Junot, and Reynier, would advance from Salamanca (*B2*) against Wellesley (hereafter Wellington, from the title granted him after Talavera); Soult, with Victor, Mortier, and Sebastiani, was to occupy Andalusia (*B1–C1*) and seize Badajoz and Elvas (*both A2*). Soult rapidly cleared all of southern Spain except Cadiz (*A1*), which he left Victor to blockade. Massena took Ciudad Rodrigo (*A2*), and forced Wellington back through Almeida to Busaco (*both A2*), where Wellington offered battle. Goaded by his headstrong corps commanders, Massena made an unsuccessful frontal attack. The next day, he turned Wellington's flank, and the latter thereupon retired—devastating the countryside as he went—into a previously fortified position (the "Lines of Torres Verdes") around Lisbon. Augereau and Suchet continued the conquest of Catalonia.

1811.   Napoleon, foreseeing war with Russia, could spare Joseph no reinforcements. Rather, he soon began withdrawing the best units and individual soldiers from his Spanish armies, a process that continued into 1814. Massena grimly held his starving army before Lisbon for a month, then fell back to Santarem (*A2*), where Wellington did not choose to attack him. In March, with supplies utterly exhausted, Massena managed a skillful retreat on Salamanca (*B2*), with Ney again displaying a savage talent for rear-guard fighting. Soult, meanwhile, had captured Badajoz (*A2*). Victor was defeated at Barrosa (*B1*) by Graham, but the cowardice of the Spanish commander, La Pena, made it a fruitless success, and Victor soon renewed the blockade.

In April, Wellington besieged Almeida (*A2*). Massena advanced to its relief, attacking Wellington at Fuentes de Onoro. Outgeneraled, Wellington was saved only by the innate toughness of his troops and (apparently) Bessieres' failure to support Massena. After this battle, the Almeida garrison escaped through the British lines by a night march. Part of Wellington's army, under Beresford, had besieged Badajoz, until Soult forced it to retire on Albuera (*A2*). There, Soult outmaneuvered Beresford, but could not quite win the battle, and so retired to Seville (*B1*). Wellington joined Beresford and unskillfully renewed the siege of Badajoz. Marmont (who had replaced Massena) joined Soult, and Wellington retired—but soon appeared before Ciudad Rodrigo (*A2*). In September, Marmont crowded him back and reprovisioned that fortress. Gerard's French division allowed itself to be surprised and routed west of Trujillo, at Arroyo de los Molinos. Suchet took Tarragona (*D2*) and hunted Blake into Valencia (*C2*). Macdonald recovered Figueras (*D3*), which Spanish irregulars had surprised earlier in the year.

1812.   Perfecting his logistical system (which gave him an immense advantage over the French, who lived largely off the country) and his cooperation with the Spanish irregulars (who were an excellent source of information), Wellington seized the initiative. In this, he made costly captures of Ciudad Rodrigo and Badajoz (*both A2*), and destroyed the Almaraz bridge (*B2*), which formed the main link between Marmont and Soult. Marmont now reacted; he and Wellington maneuvered expertly and cautiously through the Salamanca area, Marmont usually having the initiative because the French soldier was the better marcher. Finally, the eager Marmont let his army become momentarily overextended. Wellington instantly struck and defeated him, thereafter pushing ahead through Madrid to Burgos (*B3*). Here his assaults were costly failures. Soult evacuated Andalusia (*B1*) and marched north, while Clausel rallied the army defeated at Salamanca. Wellington made a competent, if somewhat costly, withdrawal to Ciudad Rodrigo. Suchet drove Blake into Valencia (*C2*), capturing that city and Blake's whole army.

1813.   Wellington advanced boldly against Joseph and Jourdan (then commanding in central Spain), routing them at Vitoria (*C3*), but failing to pursue effectively. He now shortened his communications by shifting his base of operations to the northern Spanish coast, and began operations against San Sebastian and Pampeluna (*both C3*), at first unsuccessfully. Soult (now given command of all French forces in Spain) advanced through the western Pyrenees, but was finally repulsed. Wellington then stormed San Sebastian, later invading southern France as far as Bayonne (*C3*). Suchet, now almost isolated, evacuated Valencia, but defeated two British expeditions from Sicily.

1814.   Wellington forced Soult away from Bayonne toward Toulouse (*D3*), where Soult fought—and almost won—the last battle of the war, unaware that Napoleon had already abdicated at Fontainebleau. Suchet had recrossed the Pyrenees in March, but most of his troops had previously been drawn off to other armies.

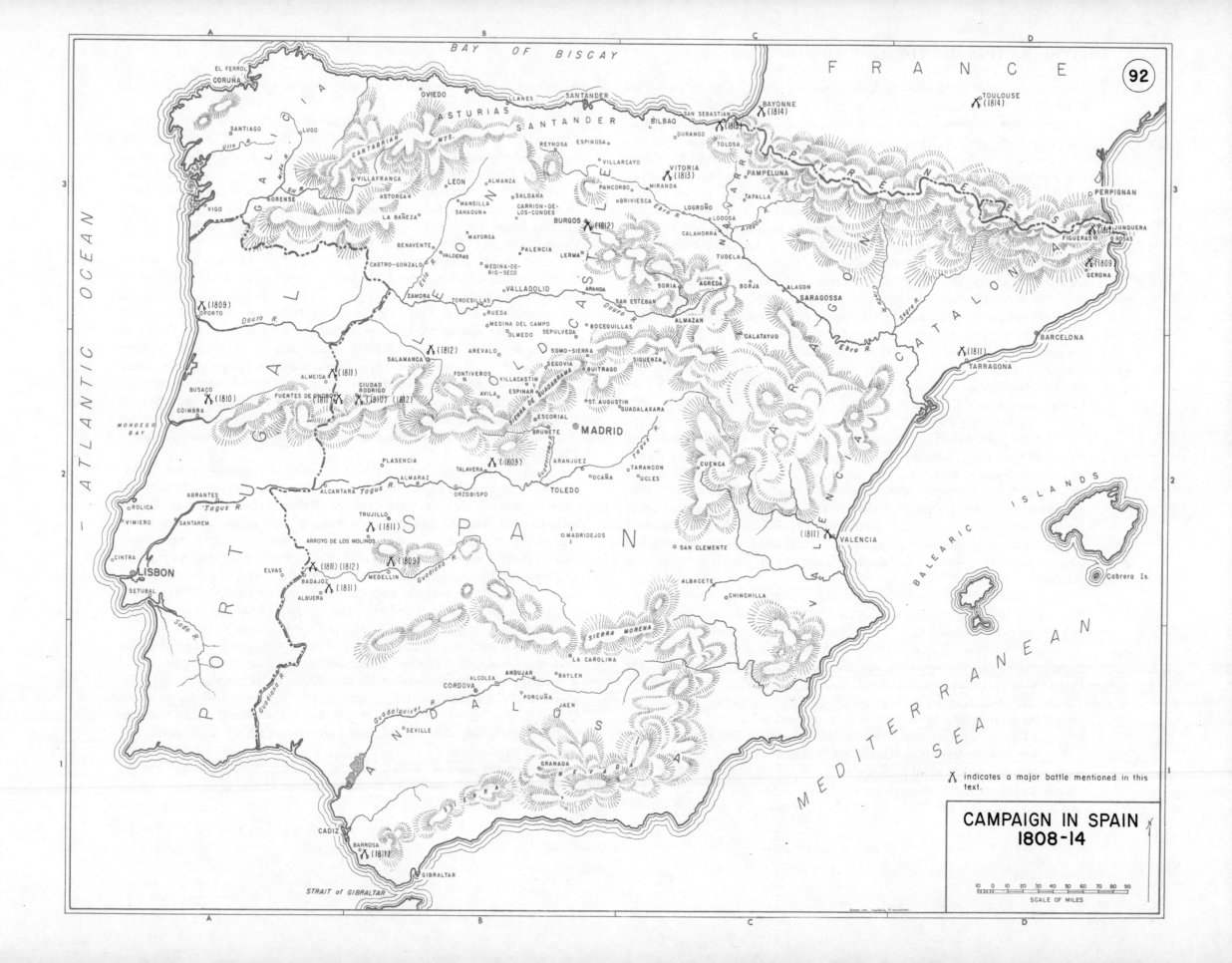

92

BAY OF BISCAY

FRANCE

ATLANTIC OCEAN

EL FERROL
CORUÑA
SANTIAGO
LUGO
VIGO
ORENSE
VILLAFRANCA
ASTORGA
LA BAÑEZA
BENAVENTE
CASTRO-GONZALO
ZAMORA

OVIEDO
LLANES   SANTANDER
ASTURIAS   SANTANDER
CANTABRIAN MTS.
REYNOSA   ESPINOSA
VILLARCAYO
LEON   ALMANZA
MANSILLA   SALDAÑA
SAHAGUN   CARRION-DE-
MAYORGA   LOS-CONDES
VALDERAS   PALENCIA
MEDINA-DE-   LERMA
RIO-SECO   BURGOS ⚔(1812)
VALLADOLID   ARANDA
TORDESILLAS   SAN ESTEBAN
RUEDA

SAN SEBASTIAN
BILBAO   BAYONNE
DURANGO   ⚔(1814)
TOLOSA
⚔(1813)
PANCORBO   VITORIA
BRIVIESCA   (1813)
MIRANDA
EBRO R.   LOGROÑO
CALAHORRA   PAMPELUNA
TAFALLA
LODOSA
TUDELA

TOULOUSE
(1814)

PERPIGNAN
⚔(1814) JUNQUERA
FIGUERAS   ROSAS
⚔1809
GERONA

OPORTO ⚔(1809)
Douro R.
COIMBRA
BUSACO ⚔(1810)
MONDEGO BAY
ABRANTES
ROLICA
VIMIERO
SANTAREM
CINTRA
LISBON
SETUBAL
Sado R.

SALAMANCA ⚔(1812)
ALMEIDA
CIUDAD ⚔(1811)
RODRIGO
FUENTES DE ONORO
(1810) (1812)
(1811)
PLASENCIA
ALCANTARA
ALMARAZ
TRUJILLO
⚔(1811)
ARROYO DE LOS MOLINOS
ELVAS
BADAJOZ ⚔(1811)(1812)
ALBUERA ⚔(1811)
MEDELLIN ⚔(1809)

AREVALO
FONTIVEROS
VILLACASTIN
AVILA
ESPINAR
SIERRA DE GUADARRAMA
ESCORIAL
BRUNETE
MADRID
TALAVERA ⚔(1809)
Tagus R.
ORZOBISPO   TOLEDO
ARANJUEZ
OCAÑA
Guadiana R.
MADRIDEJOS

MEDINA DEL CAMPO
OLMEDO   SEPULVEDA
SOMO-SIERRA
SEGOVIA   BUITRAGO
ST. AUGUSTIN   GUADALAXARA
BOCEQUILLAS
SORIA   AGREDA
ALMAZAN   BORJA
CALATAYUD   ALAGON
SIGUENZA   SARAGOSSA
CUENCA

TARANCON
UCLES
SAN CLEMENTE

VALENCIA ⚔(1811)

⚔(1811)
TARRAGONA
BARCELONA

BALEARIC ISLANDS

ALBACETE
CHINCHILLA
Cabrera Is.

OLD CASTILE
NEW CASTILE
SPAIN
ARAGON
CATALONIA
VALENCIA

ANDALUSIA
SIERRA MORENA
ALCOLEA   ANDUJAR   BAYLEN
CORDOVA   PORCUÑA
JAEN
LA CAROLINA
SEVILLE
Guadalquivir R.
GRANADA
SIERRA NEVADA

CADIZ
BARROSA ⚔(1811)
GIBRALTAR
STRAIT of GIBRALTAR

MEDITERRANEAN SEA

⚔ indicates a major battle mentioned in this text.

CAMPAIGN IN SPAIN
1808-14

10 0 10 20 30 40 50 60 70 80 90
SCALE OF MILES

INTRODUCTION TO THE CAMPAIGN OF 1809

In 1809, the effect of Napoleon's Spanish venture was part of an unguessed future. The French defeat at Baylen, and Joseph's subsequent panic, had given France's enemies an ecstasy of hope, all the dearer for having been completely unexpected. Then, an aghast Europe saw Spain's armies run whimpering at the first glimpse of Napoleon's advance guard, and knew only that England's army had been driven into the sea, its commander killed.

Austria, however, had committed herself too thoroughly to easily draw back. She had always intended to fight again: to avenge her defeats of 1796–1797, 1800, and 1805; to regain the territories those defeats had cost her; to re-establish herself as an expanding empire. The Archduke Charles had toiled for three years to create the mightiest army Austria had ever put into the field, organizing it carefully in the image of the Grande Armee. To support this regular army, Charles developed a national guard—the "Landwehr"—throughout Austria proper; in Hungary, a similar organization, called the "Hungarian Insurrection," already existed. By the end of March 1809, Austria had mobilized approximately 306,600 regulars with 791 guns, backed by some 230,000 second-line troops. Even so, her preparations were far from complete; the organization and training of the Landwehr and the Insurrection were still rudimentary, and Charles hoped eventually to bring his total strength to 700,000.

The principal question was *when* to strike. Charles preferred to wait until his forces were fully mustered. The war party urged haste, while the greater part of the French Army was still entangled in Spain. England promised assistance; Czar Alexander was surprisingly benevolent; Talleyrand murmured that Napoleon's popularity was waning in France. By December 1808, the war party had won out; the government decided on war in the coming spring. National morale—except in Galicia, where the Polish population was sullenly pro-French—was relatively high, especially in the German-speaking provinces.

Once more in Paris, Napoleon tried diplomatic pressure, calling on his Russian ally for support. Alexander exuded vague goodwill and sweet evasiveness. Prussia was smoldering; the Tyrol was on the verge of revolt against Bavarian rule. Popular discontent over conscription and the presence of French troops ran through Italy and the Confederation of the Rhine. And France was, as Talleyrand had noted, wearying of constant wars.

Militarily, Napoleon's task was enormous. He did not want war, yet it plainly lay in his path. More than half of his veteran troops, including the Imperial Guard, were in Spain. He would have to create a new army—swiftly, yet without furnishing Austria the pretext for striking before he was ready. He recalled the Guard from Spain; increased the strength of his Young Guard; called on the Confederation of the Rhine to ready its contingents; and began forming a new IV Corps at Ulm. Hopefully, he estimated that the Austrians would not be able to move before the end of April, and that he would be ready a month before that.

He was too hopeful; the crisis outran his preparations. On 2 March 1809, Metternich, the Austrian ambassador to France, served notice that the Austrian Army was being placed on war footing "as a simple precautionary measure." On the 21st, Napoleon learned that Archduke Charles had issued a proclamation, summoning his troops to "break their German brothers' chains." Napoleon was further angered two days later to learn that the Austrians had arrested a French diplomatic courier. He ordered Austrian couriers stopped wherever the writ of the French Empire ran.

On 30 March, a dispatch (dated 22 March) from Davout, who—besides supervising the organization of the Duchy of Warsaw—had developed an excellent intelligence network throughout central Europe, reported that the Austrian Army was moving. The next day Napoleon sent Berthier off to Strasbourg. He himself remained in Paris, undoubtedly to press the French mobilization, possibly to increase the appearance of unprovoked Austrian aggression. On 10 April, Metternich demanded his passports. Intercepted Austrian diplomatic dispatches revealed that an Austrian offensive was impending. Next, on the evening of 12 April, came a telegraphic message from Berthier: Neglecting the customary formality of declaring war, the Austrians had struck into Bavaria on the 9th, with 209,400 troops under Archduke Charles.

Napoleon had immediately available in southern Germany approximately 170,000 men and more than 350 guns. Of this force, 50,000 were Germans from the states of the Confederation of the Rhine. Almost half of the French were recently inducted conscripts; too many of their officers were the scrapings of the retired list, or mere boys plucked prematurely from the military schools. Even the available Guard units were mostly conscripts, well trained and with excellent cadres, but completely untried. Except in Davout's command, there was a shortage of weapons, clothing, and transport. The medical service was half-organized, and even the artillery lacked equipment. It was an improvised army, caught half-ready, like the Prussians in 1806.

This army, furthermore, missed many of the fighting commanders of earlier campaigns. Soult, Ney, Mortier, Victor, and Suchet were held in Spain; Murat was entangled in the problems of his new Kingdom of Naples. Lannes, Bessieres, and Augereau were riding north from Spain, but had far to come. Consequently, Davout would have to handle a corps twice the size of any he had ever previously commanded. The inexperienced Eugene must lead the Army of Italy.

Napoleon left Paris at 0400, 13 April, with only "his little conscripts, his name, and his long boots."

"Begin by seizing what your opponent holds dear; then he will be amenable to your will."
—SUN TZU

"When ignorance has gotten ten men killed where it should have cost only two, is it not responsible for the blood of the other eight?"
—NAPOLEON

Archduke Charles initially had planned to advance with six corps from Pilsen (C3) directly on Bamberg (B3), catching Davout's forces in their peacetime cantonments. Thereafter, he could either march down the Main River against Mayence (A3) or turn south toward Ulm (A2). Two more Austrian corps would advance along the south bank of the Danube. It was a daring plan and could have had decisive results—if launched about 20 March and carried through with speed and decision.

During March, however, the Austrians noted a developing French concentration around Augsburg (B2). The more conservative members of the Austrian high command became fearful that this force might crush the two Austrian corps south of the Danube and threaten Vienna (D2) before the main offensive could make its weight felt. (Also, Charles may have decided that Bohemia [C3] was not a suitable base for a major offensive.) Eventually, he reversed his plan. Bellegarde's two corps would attack out of Bohemia toward Nüremberg (B3); Charles himself would advance south of the Danube with the other six. The two forces would link up between Ratisbon and Ingolstadt (both B3), thereafter moving up the Danube abreast, ready to concentrate on either bank. Though less risky, this plan could not promise decisive success unless the Austrians moved swiftly and in mass. Moreover, hostilities were postponed until about 10 April to allow complete mobilization.

Two secondary operations were planned: Archduke Ferdinand would invade the Duchy of Warsaw (off map, C3) in the hope that success here would lead Alexander to change sides. (Alexander already had hinted that he would not protect Poland.) In Italy, Archduke John had a triple mission: Contain Marmont, raise the Tyrol (B2) in revolt, and gain as much territory as possible.

Napoleon had decided that, if he must fight, he would seize the initiative as soon as possible. His preliminary plan (about 20 March) was for Davout to occupy the general area Bayreuth-Bamberg-Nüremberg-Ratisbon (all B3), screening the Würzburg area (A3), where the Confederation of the Rhine contingents would concentrate. Likewise, Lefebvre's Bavarians would cover the concentration of Lannes and Massena, who would form the nucleus of Napoleon's future mass of maneuver. In case of an unexpectedly early Austrian attack, Davout was to retire southward. As usual in Napoleon's planning, his intendant general (Daru) received (28 March) the first exact orders: Donauwörth (B3) would be the advance base; the build-up of rations there must be expedited. Should the Austrians attack before 10 April, the French would concentrate behind the Lech River (B2); otherwise, they would remain in their present dispersed positions for greater convenience in living off the country.

Napoleon's instructions (30 March) to Berthier showed little urgency. Berthier was to pause at Metz to inspect a Westphalian division. If the situation did not worsen, he was to remain at Strasbourg (A3). By day, in good weather, a semaphore telegraph message could reach Strasbourg from Paris in six minutes. A courier took two days between Paris and Strasbourg, some thirty-four hours between Strasbourg and Donauwörth. While at Strasbourg, Berthier was to deal with a mass of administrative preparations. He did not command the French forces in Germany; as usual, he simply would transmit the Emperor's orders to the marshals, supervise their execution, and issue all necessary supplementary orders.

Strategically, Napoleon's instructions to Berthier were deceptively simple: An Austrian declaration of war, followed by an offensive from Bohemia, was likely on or after 15 April. Between 1 and 15 April, unless attacked sooner, Davout should concentrate at Nüremberg; Lannes (St. Hilaire, Oudinot) and Bessieres (Montbrun, Nansouty, Espagne) at Ratisbon; Massena at Augsburg. Army headquarters would be at Ratisbon. If the Austrians attacked before the 15th, the French would concentrate behind the Lech. No alternate courses of action were authorized.

Once again, Napoleon was estimating troop movements too optimistically. Berthier could hardly reach Strasbourg before 4 April; the more distant detachments could not receive his orders until the 7th; Lannes would have difficulty reaching Ratisbon much before the 15th. Also, Napoleon largely ignored the enemy's capabilities. Charles had the initiative; the mountains would screen his initial movements; and, from Pilsen, he could reach Ratisbon in five days.

About 1 April, Napoleon received vague indications that the Austrian main offensive might be directed against Lefebvre or into the Tyrol. Consequently, he sent officers from his personal staff to Innsbrück (B2), Kufstein (B2), and Passau (C3) to collect information, and ordered Eugene to send an aide to Brixen (B2) for the same purpose. Berthier was told to spread the III Corps from Bayreuth south to Ratisbon—leaving it a perfect target for a major offensive out of Bohemia. Five days later, suddenly aware of this danger, Napoleon ordered the whole corps brought nearer Ratisbon. On 7 April, he ordered the Saxon Army concentrated at Dresden (off map, C3). By 8 April, he had information that the Austrians were shifting south of the Danube, but apparently concluded they were bound for the Tyrol.

When, on 10 April, intercepted Austrian diplomatic messages indicated an imminent Austrian offensive across the Inn against Lefebvre, Napoleon telegraphed Berthier that, if the enemy attacked before the 15th, he was to go forward to Augsburg and concentrate the army at Augsburg and Donauwörth. Unhappily, a storm blocked telegraph transmissions; Napoleon was told the next morning that his message had been delayed, but he disregarded this notice. Some hours after preparing the telegraphic message, he had written to Berthier radically changing his previous orders.

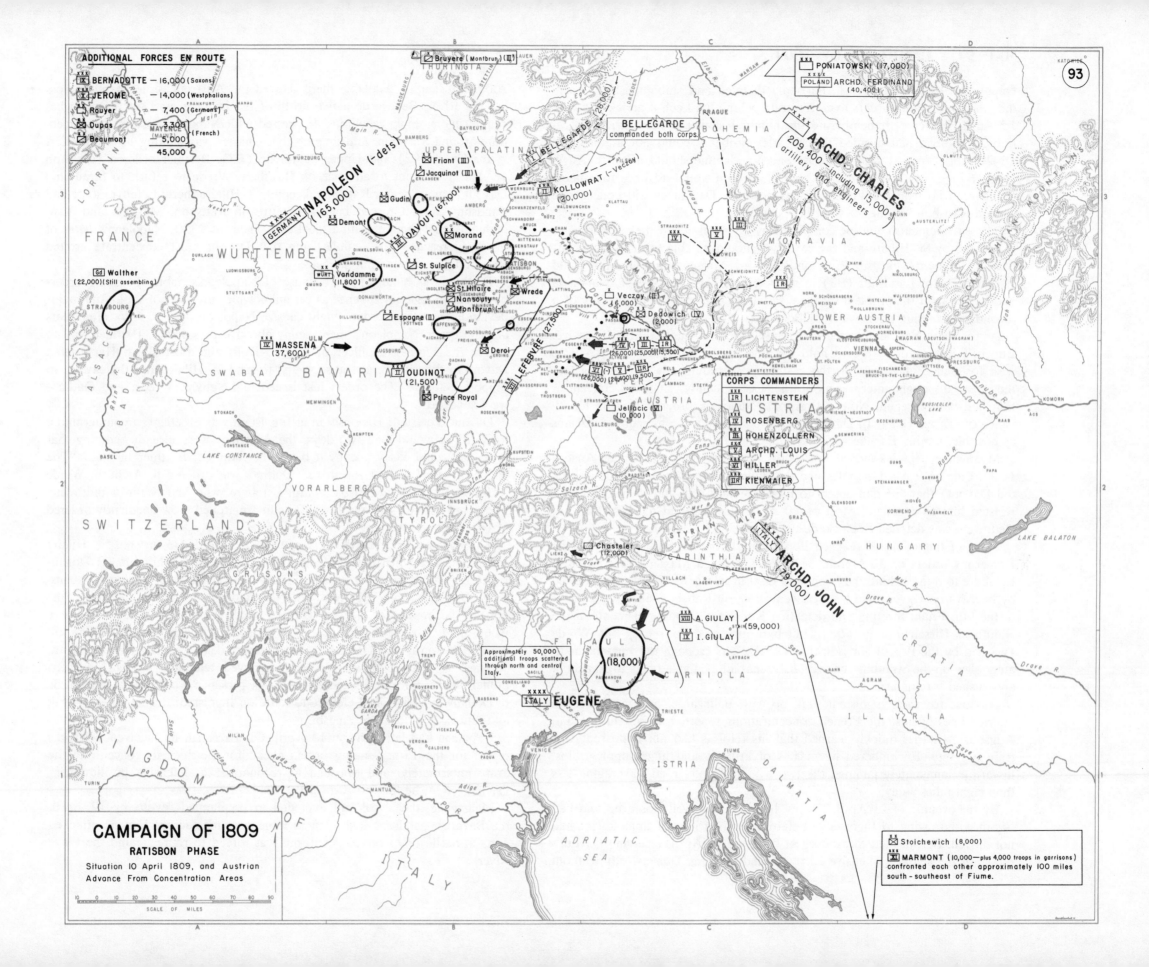

93

ADDITIONAL FORCES EN ROUTE

BERNADOTTE — 16,000 (Saxons)
JEROME — 14,000 (Westphalians)
Rouyer — 7,400 (Germans)
Dupas — 3,300 (French)
Beaumont — 5,000

45,000

MAYENCE

NAPOLEON (-dets)
(165,000)

GERMANY

Bruyere (Montbrun) (III?)

THURINGIA

II BELLEGARDE (28,000)

BELLEGARDE
commanded both corps.

PONIATOWSKI (17,000)

POLAND ARCHD. FERDINAND
(40,400)

WARSAW

BOHEMIA

PRAGUE

ARCHD. CHARLES
(209,400 — including 5,000
artillery and engineers)

UPPER PALATINATE

Friant (III)

Jacquinot (III)

II KOLLOWRAT (-Veczay)
(20,000)

MORAVIA

FRANCE

LORRAINE

FRANKFURT

Gudin

Demont

DAVOUT
(67,000)

Morand

FRANCONIA

St. Sulpice

BAVARIA

RATISBON

V

AUSTERLITZ

WÜRTTEMBERG

Walther
(22,000) (Still assembling)

STRASBOURG

Vandamme
(WÜRT) (11,800)

St. Hilaire
Nansouty
Montbrun (-)

Wrede

Veczay (II)
(16,000)

Dedowich (IV)
(2,000)

LOWER AUSTRIA

VIENNA

Espagne (II)

Deroi

Affenhofen

LEFEBVRE (27,500)

IV (-) III IR
(26,000)(25,000)(5,500)

ULM

MASSENA
(37,600)

AUGSBURG

OUDINOT
(21,500)

VI (-) V IR
(26,000)(26,400)(9,500)

VIII

Jellacic (VI)
(10,000)

Prince Royal

AUSTRIA

CORPS COMMANDERS

IR LICHTENSTEIN
IV ROSENBERG
III HOHENZOLLERN
V ARCHD. LOUIS
VI HILLER
IR KIENMAIER

SWABIA

BAVARIA

SWITZERLAND

VORARLBERG

SALZBURG

HUNGARY

LAKE CONSTANCE

TYROL

INNSBRUCK

STYRIAN ALPS

LAKE BALATON

GRISONS

CARINTHIA

Chasteler
(12,000)

ARCHD. JOHN
(79,000)

ITALY

A. GIULAY
(59,000)
I. GIULAY

FRIAUL

Approximately 50,000
additional troops scattered
through north and central
Italy.

UDINE
(18,000)

CARNIOLA

CROATIA

KINGDOM OF ITALY

ITALY EUGENE

VENICE

ISTRIA

DALMATIA

ILLYRIA

ADRIATIC SEA

CAMPAIGN OF 1809

RATISBON PHASE

Situation 10 April 1809, and Austrian
Advance From Concentration Areas

SCALE OF MILES
10 0 10 20 30 40 50 60 70 80 90

Stoichewich (8,000)

MARMONT (10,000—plus 4,000 troops in garrisons)
confronted each other approximately 100 miles
south-southeast of Fiume.

Napoleon's letter of 10 April, hurriedly dictated and ambiguously phrased, did confirm previous orders to concentrate behind the Lech if attacked before 15 April. However, remembering the habitual slowness of Austrian operations, Napoleon had decided that Charles probably could not attack until 16–20 April. In that case, Massena and Vandamme should move to Augsburg (*B2*); Nansouty, Montbrun, and St. Hilaire would advance to support Lefebvre, who would hold his present position. Davout should concentrate around Ratisbon "no matter what happens."

These movements could be completed by 15 April. Thereafter, Lefebvre—reinforced by St. Hilaire and the cavalry—should be able to delay any Austrian attack across the Isar River until Davout, Massena, and Oudinot could advance toward Landshut (*B3*) to support him. Again, however, Napoleon had not thought the problem through, failing to consider the probability of a secondary Austrian offensive from Bohemia.

As for Italy, Napoleon expected Archduke John to stand on the defensive. Eugene's instructions were to hold the line of the Adige River (*B1–B2*), with fortified bridgeheads on the east bank, avoiding any movements that the Austrians might interpret as hostile. Consequently, Eugene's concentration had barely begun. Now (10 April), Napoleon ordered Eugene to advance on Tarvis (*C2*). In Dalmatia, Marmont was to fix as many Austrians as possible, joining Eugene when he could.

Meanwhile, Charles moved four corps from Bohemia into Upper Austria (*C2*). Late on 9 April, he informed the Bavarian government (as Bellegarde did Davout) that "he had orders to move forward . . . and to treat all who resisted him as enemies." Most of 10 April was required to cross the Inn; Dedowich was detailed to blockade the Passau (*C3*) citadel.

News of this offensive reached Berthier early on 11 April. Following the Emperor's orders of 30 March, he at once ordered Massena to Augsburg, Lefebvre to retire behind the Lech, and Davout to mass at Ingolstadt. Alerted by his cavalry, Davout had been concentrating on Ratisbon since the evening of the 9th, Friant meeting and defeating Kollowrat's leading elements in the Hahnback-Hirschau area (*B3*). Lefebvre prepared to retire, but Wrede (warned by the Passau garrison that Charles was crossing the Inn) immediately blew up the Straubing bridge (*B3*), sent all available boats to Ratisbon, and rushed for Ingolstadt.

Anxious to reach Ingolstadt, link up with Bellegarde, and maneuver on interior lines against the French concentrations reported at Nüremberg and Augsburg, Charles quickly learned that his reforms had not improved Austrian mobility. Encumbered by masses of artillery and huge supply trains, his army immediately jammed the two available good roads, averaging less than eight miles a day.

By the evening of 11 April, Davout had his corps well closed up and had begun withdrawing to Ingolstadt. Lefebvre, finding himself unmolested, had not moved. Berthier left Strasbourg at 0100 on 12 April, receiving Davout's report of Bellegarde's offensive en route, and reaching Donauwörth at about 2000. Information available there showed the Austrian center barely across the Inn River, Bellegarde active north of the Danube, and the Tyrolese becoming increasingly rebellious. Impressed with Napoleon's desire to concentrate around Ratisbon, and judging that Charles was making his main effort in the Tyrol (*B2*) and Upper Palatinate (*B3*), Berthier ordered (early on 13 April) Oudinot to advance on Ratisbon; Wrede to return to Straubing; Davout to move nearer Ratisbon, keeping St. Hilaire there; Lefebvre to defend Landshut and—if forced back—to retire on Ratisbon. Massena and Vandamme would remain behind the Lech. Then, at 2330, Napoleon's *letter* of 10 April reached him, emphasizing that Davout must concentrate around Ratisbon "no matter what happens."

Berthier was handicapped because of Napoleon's habit of issuing orders based on strategic intelligence as yet unknown to his chief of staff. Any major deviation from these orders might capsize Napoleon's plans. Also, after years of exposure to Napoleon's increasingly abrasive personality, Berthier was no longer the aggressive officer of Lodi, Rivoli, and Fort Bard. He ordered Davout to concentrate at Ratisbon and to send St. Hilaire and the cavalry to support Lefebvre. The orders just issued to Lefebvre, Wrede, and Oudinot were canceled.

Davout protested: His position at Ingolstadt was excellent; a countermarch to Ratisbon would take two days; the Austrians were already scouting that town and could easily occupy it before he returned. Berthier insisted: "The Emperor wishes to find you there." Oudinot was ordered to Aichach, Wrede to Ingolstadt, Lefebvre to Augsburg. Lefebvre, who had begun withdrawing northward on the 14th, and had just countermarched, now obediently ordered a retirement westward.

Through the 15th, Berthier's confusion increased. He ordered St. Hilaire to Ingolstadt, countermanded Oudinot's last orders, and himself left Donauwörth for Augsburg. Wrede marched and countermarched, ending at Abensberg; Davout reoccupied Ratisbon. Next morning, Berthier developed the possible beginnings of a plan: Davout would retain St. Hilaire, Lefebvre would hold Geisenfeld, Oudinot would mass at Aichach. The Austrians still crawled forward, and Deroi fought an expert delaying action at Landshut.

Then, as a final blow, Napoleon's delayed telegram arrived! Berthier, politely blunt, informed Napoleon that his presence would be helpful; rode to Donauwörth to order Lefebvre to retire on Ingolstadt during 17–18 April; and returned anxiously to Augsburg.

Napoleon had left Paris on 13 April. On 16 April, he received Berthier's report for the 13th. Sending orders ahead for Berthier to concentrate the army immediately, and Massena to reconnoiter a defensive position near Dachau (*B2*), he hurried eastward.

Meanwhile, the Tyrol had exploded in preplanned revolt; by 12 April, the Bavarian garrisons had been in large part massacred. Eugene attacked John at Sacile (*B1*) on 16 April, but was forced to retire behind the Piave River.

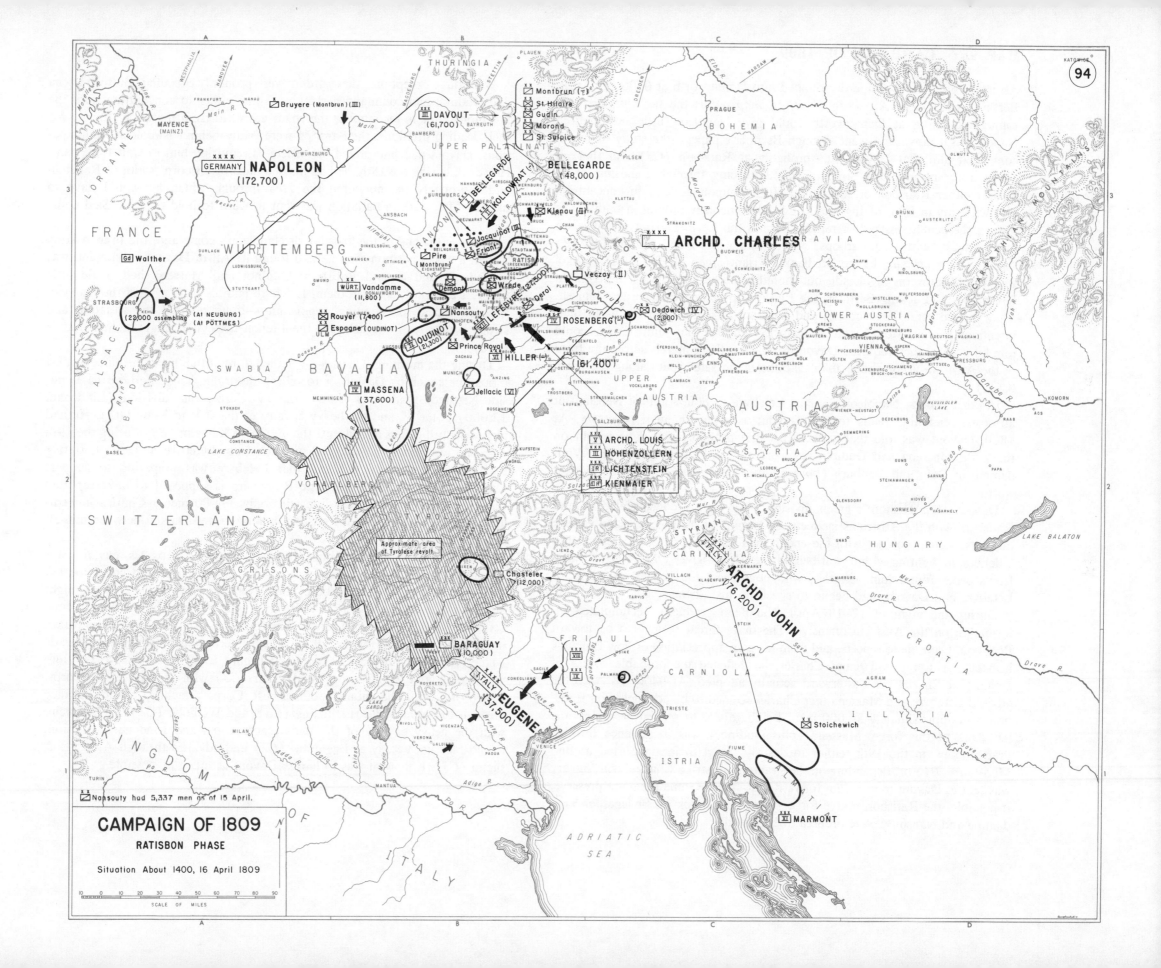

94

CAMPAIGN OF 1809

RATISBON PHASE

Situation About 1400, 16 April 1809

SCALE OF MILES

An irate and anxious Emperor pounded into Donauwörth at 0500, 17 April. Berthier was still at Augsburg (*both off map, A2*); the headquarters personnel remaining at Donauwörth could give Napoleon little information. Napoleon sat down and went through Berthier's papers, the study of which convinced him that Davout was probably at Ratisbon (*C3*) and that an enemy force of unknown strength was advancing through Landshut (*C1*) against either Ratisbon or Ingolstadt. He thereupon decided to concentrate his own army in front of Ingolstadt, by simultaneously pulling in both wings toward the center, instead of retiring behind the Lech. Davout would move to Ingolstadt "with all his troops," via Neustadt (*B2*) and Geisenfeld (*A2*) "without ever crossing to the left bank." Friant (then at Hemau [*B3*]) likewise would retire on Ingolstadt, but should leave outposts along the Altmühl River (*B3*). (Lacking Berthier, the Emperor prepared these orders himself. They proved rambling, unclear, and far from urgent. Uncertain as to their intention, Davout would wait at Ratisbon another day until Friant could join him. Also, they required Davout to make a flank march across the front of the Austrian army, rather than take the much safer route along the north bank.)

In other orders, Napoleon directed Lefebvre to hold south of Neustadt at all costs, remaining ready to give Davout a helping hand if necessary. At 1800, Davout was told that a decisive battle probably would be fought on the 19th; Massena and Oudinot were ordered to Pfaffenhofen (*A1*), Vandamme to Rain and Neuburg (*both off map, A2*), and Rouyer to Donauwörth.

Davout (less Demont's green division) was tightly concentrated around Ratisbon, with the Austrians ineffectively tapping at his northern and eastern outposts. Actual contact with the enemy had quickly steadied Lefebvre into a deliberate, fighting withdrawal behind the Abens River (*B2*), where Napoleon's order found him. Charles, who now knew the general positions of Lefebvre and Davout, had begun to speed up his advance.

During the night of 17–18 April, Napoleon gradually accumulated information on the Austrian offensive. The main threat seemed to be toward Ratisbon. From these reports, and from his own appreciation of how Davout's isolated position would tempt Charles, he deduced the probable course of action that Charles soon afterward actually adopted. At 0400, 18 April, he advised Lefebvre and Massena that Charles seemed to be advancing on Ratisbon with approximately 80,000 men. Lefebvre was to maneuver against the left flank of this force. Massena (plus Oudinot) was to advance through Pfaffenhofen on the 19th, either to destroy the Austrians reported around Moosburg (*B1*) or, depending on the situation, to strike Charles' rear. Savary was sent to Davout to urge him forward, but—at the same time—to preserve, if possible, the Ratisbon bridge for a subsequent attack on Bellegarde. Vandamme and Nansouty were ordered to Ingolstadt.

With three exceptions, these orders were promptly executed. Both Massena and Oudinot had commanded slackly, failing either to concentrate until the last moment or to reconnoiter the roads eastward from the Lech. Except for their leading divisions, their troops were badly behind Napoleon's anticipations. Davout had interpreted his orders as requiring him to wait for Friant. However, during the 18th, he had massed most of his corps south of Ratisbon and thoroughly reconnoitered the area through which he would have to march. After dark, a battalion was sent forward to hold the vital Saal defile (*B3*).

Thus, at the end of the first day of Napoleon's command, the French army was in a worse position than he had found it: All of Davout's command was actually in and around Ratisbon; Oudinot and Massena had made little progress eastward; between them, Lefebvre had his back against the Danube. Charles had an outstanding opportunity—if he realized the situation and struck promptly. If he delayed, the French dispersion might tighten into a trap.

During the morning, Charles—whether to reinforce his right flank against a possible attack by Davout or to relieve the traffic congestion on the Landshut-Neustadt road—had shifted the IV Corps, one division (Lindenau, 12,000) of the V, and the heavy cavalry of the II R to Rohr (*B2*). He had already issued orders to continue the march on Kelheim (*B3*) during the 19th when he received an intercepted dispatch from Lefebvre to Davout, stating that Napoleon had arrived and that Lefebvre was preparing to support Davout. (Also, at about this time Rosenberg is supposed to have reported that Davout was still in Ratisbon with only 33,000 men.) Charles immediately decided to turn toward Ratisbon, hoping to trap Davout between himself and Kollowrat.

Hiller and the Archduke Louis (to whom the II R Corps, less cavalry, was attached) would fix the Bavarians along the Abens River and cover the left flank of the attack on Ratisbon. They were warned that Lefebvre might attack; if defeated, they were to retire on Landshut, and Hiller would assume command of their combined forces. The force massed at Rohr would advance on Ratisbon at 0600 on the 19th. Hohenzollern would detach one brigade (Thierry, 6,000) toward Kirchdorf and Biburg (*both B2*) to serve as a link with Louis, and would move on Abbach (*C3*) with the rest of his corps. Rosenberg, with the infantry of the I R Corps attached, would advance through Langquaid (*C2*), Dinzling (*C3*), and Weillohe (*C3*). Lichtenstein, with the heavy cavalry of the two reserve corps and Lindenau's division, would pick up Veczay at Eggmühl (*C2*) and advance through Alt Egglofsheim (*C3*). Kollowrat was to harass Davout as much as possible.

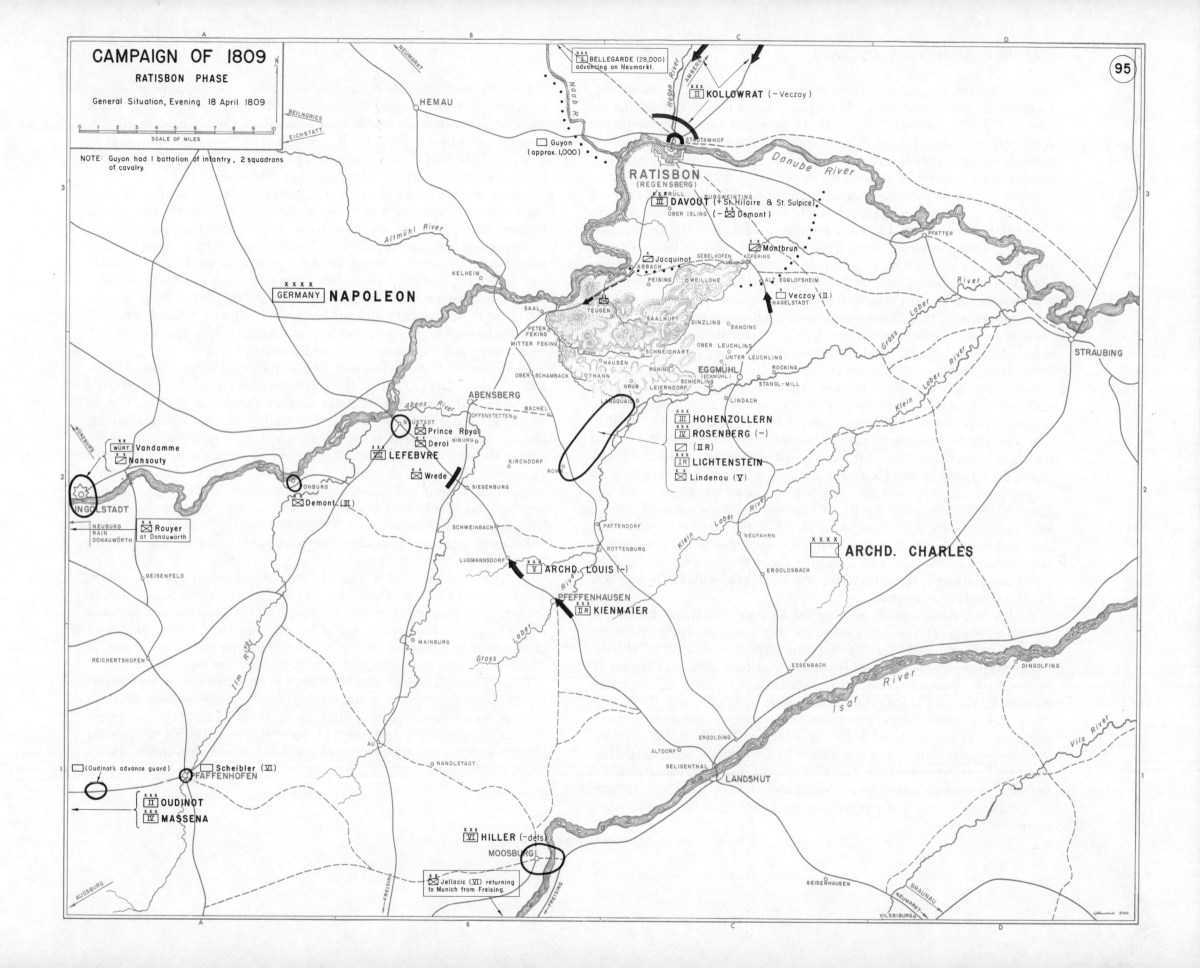

95

CAMPAIGN OF 1809

RATISBON PHASE

General Situation, Evening 18 April 1809

SCALE OF MILES
0 1 2 3 4 5 6 7 8 9 10

NOTE: Guyon had 1 battalion of infantry, 2 squadrons
of cavalry.

BELLEGARDE (28,000)
advancing on Neumarkt.

KOLLOWRAT (−Veczay)

Guyon
(approx. 1,000)

RATISBON
(REGENSBERG)

STADTAMHOF

Danube River

DAVOUT (+St. Hilaire & St. Sulpice)
(−Demont)

Montbrun

Jacquinot

Veczay (II)

GERMANY NAPOLEON

STRAUBING

ABENSBERG

EGGMUHL
(ECKMÜHL)

Prince Royal

Deroi

LEFEBVRE

WÜRT Vandamme
Nansouty

Wrede

HOHENZOLLERN

ROSENBERG (−)

(IIR)

LICHTENSTEIN

Lindenau (V)

Demont (III)

INGOLSTADT

Rouyer
at Donauwörth

NEUBURG
RAIN
DONAUWÖRTH

ARCHD. CHARLES

ARCHD. LOUIS (−)

PFEFFENHAUSEN

KIENMAIER

Scheibler (VI)

Oudinot's advance guard)

PFAFFENHOFEN

OUDINOT

MASSENA

LANDSHUT

HILLER (−dets)

MOOSBURG

Jellacic (VI) returning
to Munich from Freising.

Charles did not assign any specific missions in his orders to Rosenberg, Lichtenstein, and Hohenzollern. He obviously hoped to trap Davout, but his plan was poorly designed. Davout would have free use of the Ratisbon-Abensberg road during most of the 19th; only Hohenzollern's advance on Abbach would directly threaten it, and this at a point halfway to Davout's junction with Lefebvre. Moreover, the move toward Ratisbon would open a considerable gap between the Austrian center and left wing. Besides exposing the Austrians to defeat in detail, this would expose the Austrian line of communication, running from Landshut eastward, to a French counteroffensive.

Davout was up and marching at 0500 on 19 April, an hour before Charles stirred. He had left the 65th Regiment of Line Infantry (Coutard) in Ratisbon to screen his departure from Kollowrat as long as possible, intending to withdraw it once the III Corps cleared the Saal defile. (Apparently considering the situation still too fluid for such drastic action, he did not blow up the massive Ratisbon bridge before his departure.) As shown, the III Corps marched in four columns, its trains and heavy artillery on the best road. The other roads were difficult dirt tracks, winding from village to little village, through broken and wooded country. The critical point was the narrow defile just east of Saal. According to certain sources, Charles had somehow secured a copy of Davout's march order. If so, he failed to make use of it.

At about 0930, Rosenberg's advance guard clashed briefly with Morand's in the woods above Schneidhart, but was checked until the latter passed. Charles halted the infantry of the I R Corps at Grub, waiting for Hohenzollern to come up on his left. Hohenzollern, leaving—Austrian fashion—another detachment (Pfanzelter) at Bachel to link him to Thierry, crawled through Hausen at about 1030. He then found French skirmishers (apparently Morand's and St. Hilaire's flank guards) along the wooded ridge north of Hausen, and had considerable difficulty dislodging them. Some of his jaegers infiltrated down a tongue of timber southwest of Teugen, striking Gudin's rear guard, but were soon mopped up.

At the first shots, Davout had hurried Morand and Gudin forward to occupy the defiles at Saal and Feking. He then swung St. Hilaire's division by the left flank into line, recapturing the high ground north of Hausen. Though delayed by the abominable roads, Friant soon came into line on St. Hilaire's left. Thereafter, the battle became a large-scale bushwhacking between St. Hilaire (11,000) and Hohenzollern (18,000), with elements of Friant and Rosenberg likewise involved. Rosenberg, scattering detachments broadcast as he advanced, had finally come down on Montbrun near Dinzling. With the odds at least two to one against him, Montbrun nevertheless kept the whip hand throughout the day. Charles remained a spectator at Grub, uncertain as to where and when to commit his reserve of grenadiers. Lichtenstein collected Veczay and promenaded northward, ignoring all the vulgar uproar on his left.

Lefebvre, meanwhile, had marched with about half his corps to Abensberg, leaving Wrede to hold the bridges at Biburg and Siegenburg. About 1030, he heard Davout's cannon, and immediately thrust eastward, encountering and defeating Thierry. Louis, noting that his "orders did not speak of attacking," did little except cannonade Wrede at long range. To the west, Oudinot scattered Scheibler's detachment at Pfaffenhofen (A1).

Napoleon remained all morning at Ingolstadt (with Vandamme, Demont, and Nansouty), prepared if necessary to support Lefebvre. He had ordered Massena to push Oudinot toward Au (B1) and Freising (off map, B1), and to concentrate his own corps around Pfaffenhofen, ready to move at once toward either Neustadt, Freising, or Au. Ignorant as to Davout's fortunes, Napoleon was mainly concerned with getting Massena and Oudinot into a position from which they could envelop Charles' left flank—which, by sundown, might be anywhere between Landshut (C1) and Neustadt (B2). If possible, he intended to seize Landshut, cut Charles' communications, destroy his left wing, and drive him against the Danube.

Shortly before 1800, Davout sent two of Friant's regiments against Hohenzollern's right flank, and two of Gudin's against his left, achieving local superiority and driving the Austrians back in disorder on Hausen. Charles counterattacked with four battalions of grenadiers, but was repulsed. Having covered the withdrawal of his corps, Davout halted his advance along the edge of the woods above Hausen. A violent storm ended the fighting at about 1900. Davout bivouacked around Teugen with St. Sulpice (less Clement's brigade), St. Hilaire, and Friant. Montbrun withdrew deliberately to Peising, unpursued by Rosenberg—who reported that he had "defeated the enemy's left wing." Lichtenstein halted at Alt Egglofsheim.

Kollowrat attacked Stadtamhof, the north-bank suburb of Ratisbon, but was repulsed after a hot fight.

By 2100, Lefebvre had linked up firmly with Davout. Morand, Gudin, Jacquinot, and Clement bivouacked near Abensberg. Vandamme and Nansouty reached Neustadt; Demont, Vohburg (A2). Oudinot halted southeast of Pfaffenhofen, later sending one of his divisions back through that town to take position astride the road to Neustadt. Massena had three divisions in Pfaffenhofen, with the fourth some twelve miles to the rear.

Hiller, worried about his own left flank, had halted all day at Au, advancing to Mainburg only late in the evening. Louis, though ordered at about 1900 to rejoin Charles via Rohr (B2), decided that such a move was impossible, and sent merely a detachment of the II R Corps. Thierry had planned to retire to Rohr, but, when informed that Louis would support him, rallied south of Offenstetten (B2).

Note: On this map, Kienmaier's corps (B2) should be IIR instead of IR.

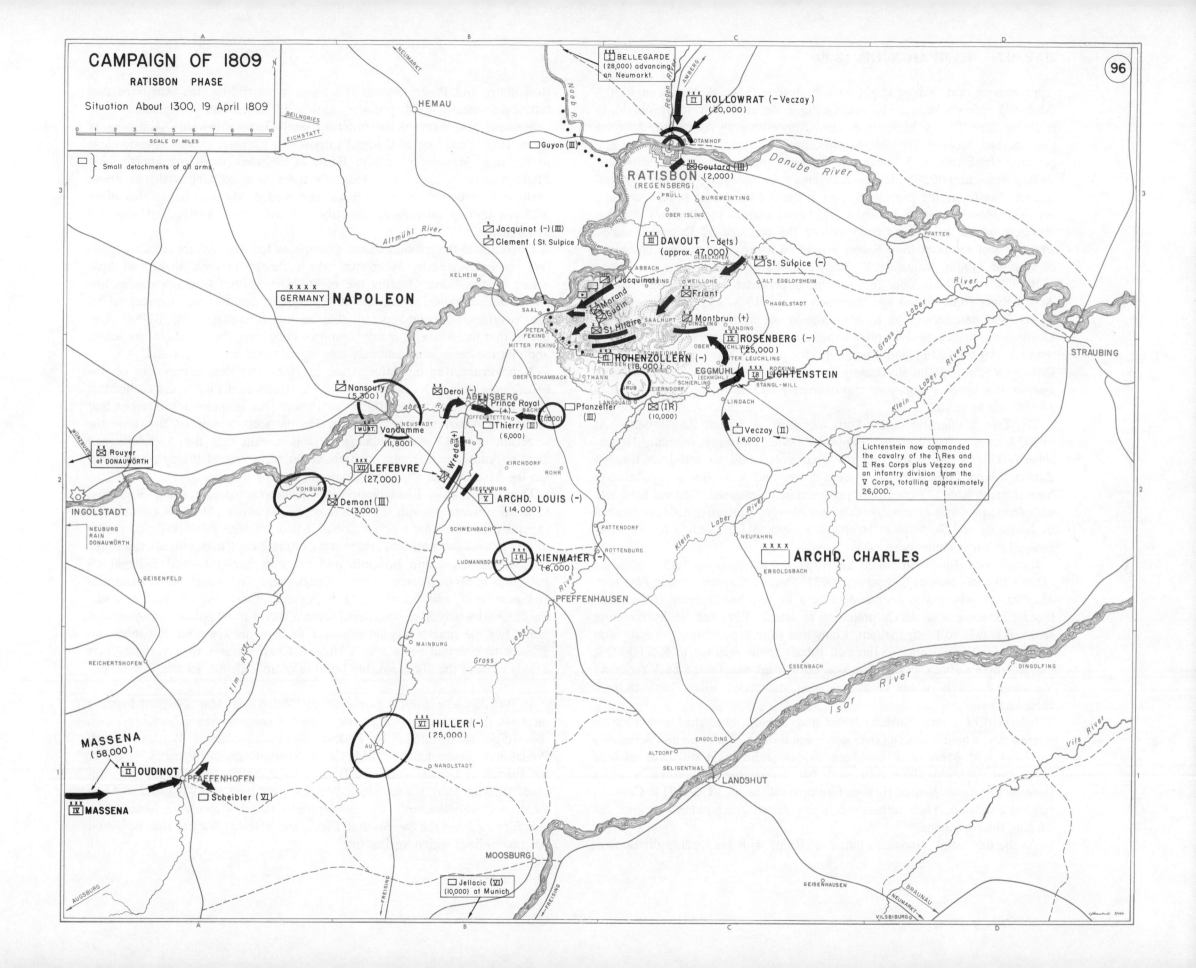

CAMPAIGN OF 1809

RATISBON PHASE

Situation About 1300, 19 April 1809

SCALE OF MILES
0 1 2 3 4 5 6 7 8 9 10

☐ — Small detachments of all arms.

BELLEGARDE (28,000) advancing on Neumarkt.

KOLLOWRAT (–Veczay) (20,000)

Guyon (III)

Goutard (III) (2,000)

RATISBON (REGENSBERG)

Jacquinot (–)(III)
Clement (St. Sulpice)

DAVOUT (–dets) (approx. 47,000)

St. Sulpice (–)

GERMANY NAPOLEON

(Jacquinot)
Morand
Gudin
Friant
St. Hilaire
Montbrun (+)

ROSENBERG (–) (25,000)

HOHENZOLLERN (–) (18,000)

EGGMÜHL LICHTENSTEIN

Nansouty (5,300)

Deroi (–)

ABENSBERG
Prince Royal (–)
Pfanzelter (III)

(IR) (10,000)

Thierry (III) (6,000)

Veczay (II) (6,000)

Rouyer at DONAUWÖRTH

WÜRT. Vandamme (11,800)

Lichtenstein now commanded the cavalry of the I Res and II Res Corps plus Veczay and an infantry division from the V Corps, totalling approximately 26,000.

LEFEBVRE (27,000)

Wrede

Demont (III) (3,000)

VOHBURG

ARCHD. LOUIS (–) (14,000)

INGOLSTADT

NEUBURG
RAIN
DONAUWÖRTH

KIENMAIER (–) (6,000)

ARCHD. CHARLES

STRAUBING

DINGOLFING

MASSENA (58,000)

HILLER (–) (25,000)

OUDINOT

PFAFFENHOFEN

Scheibler (VI)

MASSENA

LANDSHUT

Jellacic (VI) (10,000) at Munich

96

Apprehensive that Davout might have been overwhelmed, Napoleon (0300, 20 April) ordered Massena to send Oudinot, via either Au or Geisenfeld, to reinforce the left wing. Massena was to advance through Au to seize a bridge over the Isar between Freising and Moosburg. On learning that Davout had defeated Hohenzollern, however, the Emperor became extremely optimistic. Telling Massena (0630) that the Austrians were retreating and that he himself was beginning the pursuit, he now ordered Massena to seize a crossing between Moosburg and Landshut. Lefebvre, with Vandamme's division attached, would advance at once to take the pressure off Davout. Lannes, who had just returned from Spain, was given a provisional corps composed of Morand, Gudin, Nansouty, St. Sulpice, and Jacquinot.

By this time, Napoleon knew—from a personal reconnaissance of the Abens River front during the afternoon of the 19th, and from spies, prisonsers, and deserters—that he had nothing to his immediate front except Louis' two weak corps. He now planned to split the Austrian left wing from the main Austrian army and drive it into the net that Massena was spreading. Davout would contain any enemy forces confronting him. Napoleon had assembled a mass of maneuver approximately 66,000 strong, with Oudinot's 14,000 still en route.

The French offensive of 20 April was more of a hunt than a battle. At 0900, Lannes surged forward. Pfanzelter bolted eastward, rejoining Hohenzollern. Thierry, still expecting reinforcements, tried to withdraw through Bachel, found French troops already there, and was chased in confusion back through Rohr. There, Louis' promised help appeared: General Schustek, with four squadrons of cavalry. Schustek charged gallantly, but was crushed by Nansouty and St. Sulpice. Thierry was captured, and only a few fugitives escaped through Rottenburg (B2).

Meanwhile, Hiller had halted his corps at Pfeffenhausen (B2), while he himself joined Louis at Siegenburg (B2). Despite Charles' orders (see text, Map 95), Louis was in no mood to be a loyal subordinate to Hiller, even though Lefebvre was clearly preparing to attack. Rebuffed, Hiller therefore returned slowly to Pfeffenhausen. Louis had shifted (this map) one division to his right that morning to threaten Biburg. Now recalled to Kirchdorf, it met Lefebvre's attack stoutly, but was outflanked and routed by Wrede and Vandamme. Louis' whole command soon stampeded wildly back through Pfeffenhausen.

Informed of Lannes' attack, Hiller had already dispatched a division to Rottenburg, where it was run over and swept away by Thierry's and Schustek's survivors, with Morand at their heels. Although he could still have rejoined Charles at Eggmühl, Hiller decided that his overriding mission was to cover the direct route to Vienna. He therefore ordered the V, VI, and II R Corps to rally at Landshut. Their retreat was highly disorderly, hundreds of men discarding their weapons.

At the day's end, Napoleon halted at Rohr, with his leading divisions at Rottenburg and Pfeffenhausen. His losses were trifling; the Austrians had lost approximately 4,000 prisoners and 2,700 killed and wounded.

Massena had received the order to send Oudinot toward Abensberg at about 1000. Since one of Oudinot's divisions (Claparede) was already close to Freising, Massena gave him Boudet's division (then just approaching Pfaffenhofen) in exchange. Oudinot's corps reached Geisenfeld at about 1600, only to be informed that it was not needed. Massena halted that night with his leading infantry at Freising and his corps cavalry just short of Moosburg.

Davout held the position shown throughout the day. Except for an aggressive reconnaissance by Montbrun, which cleared Hausen, there was little action on this front. (During the night, learning that Coutard was almost out of ammunition, Davout sent him a supply, but this was intercepted by the Austrians.) Davout reported that he was in contact with 30,000 Austrians, that the smoke of many campfires hung over the forests to his south, and that the enemy was definitely moving eastward across his front.

Napolon received this information at 2000 with loud expressions of disbelief, even though Nansouty seems to have reported four hours earlier this same Austrian shift toward Ratisbon. In turn, the Emperor told Davout that all of the Austrians were in flight. He particularly wanted to know the whereabouts of Charles, claiming he was certain that the Archduke had already retired on Eggmühl in preparation for a retreat through Landshut. On the 21st, Davout was to seek out and destroy the enemy.

During the day, Lichtenstein and Kollowrat had attacked Ratisbon. Coutard surrendered with the honors of war at about 1800, his ammunition expended and half his men casualties. Unfortunately, he lacked the means to first destroy the Ratisbon bridge. Its capture gave Charles an alternate line of communication into Bohemia and the opportunity to add Bellegarde's two corps to his own army. Instead, Charles sent Kollowrat toward Beilngries (off map, A3), and did not recall Bellegarde. Their mission remains undefined; Charles may have considered them a threat to Napoleon's communications. For the time being, he intended to base his army on Ratisbon and attempt to maintain contact with Hiller. (Charles seems to have been inert during most of the 20th, possibly because of an epileptic seizure.)

In Italy, Eugene threw a garrison into Venice (see Map 94) and began a methodical withdrawal behind the Adige. Chasteler was advancing down the Adige on Roveredo. In Poland, Ferdinand reached Warsaw, which Poniatowski evacuated on 21 April. A Russian army—by treaty, allies of the French and Poles—watched from the far bank of the Vistula (as another Russian army would watch Warsaw destroyed in 1944). Czar Alexander was simultaneously telling Napoleon that his available forces were committed against the Swedes and Turks, and assuring Austria that he would not take serious action against her.

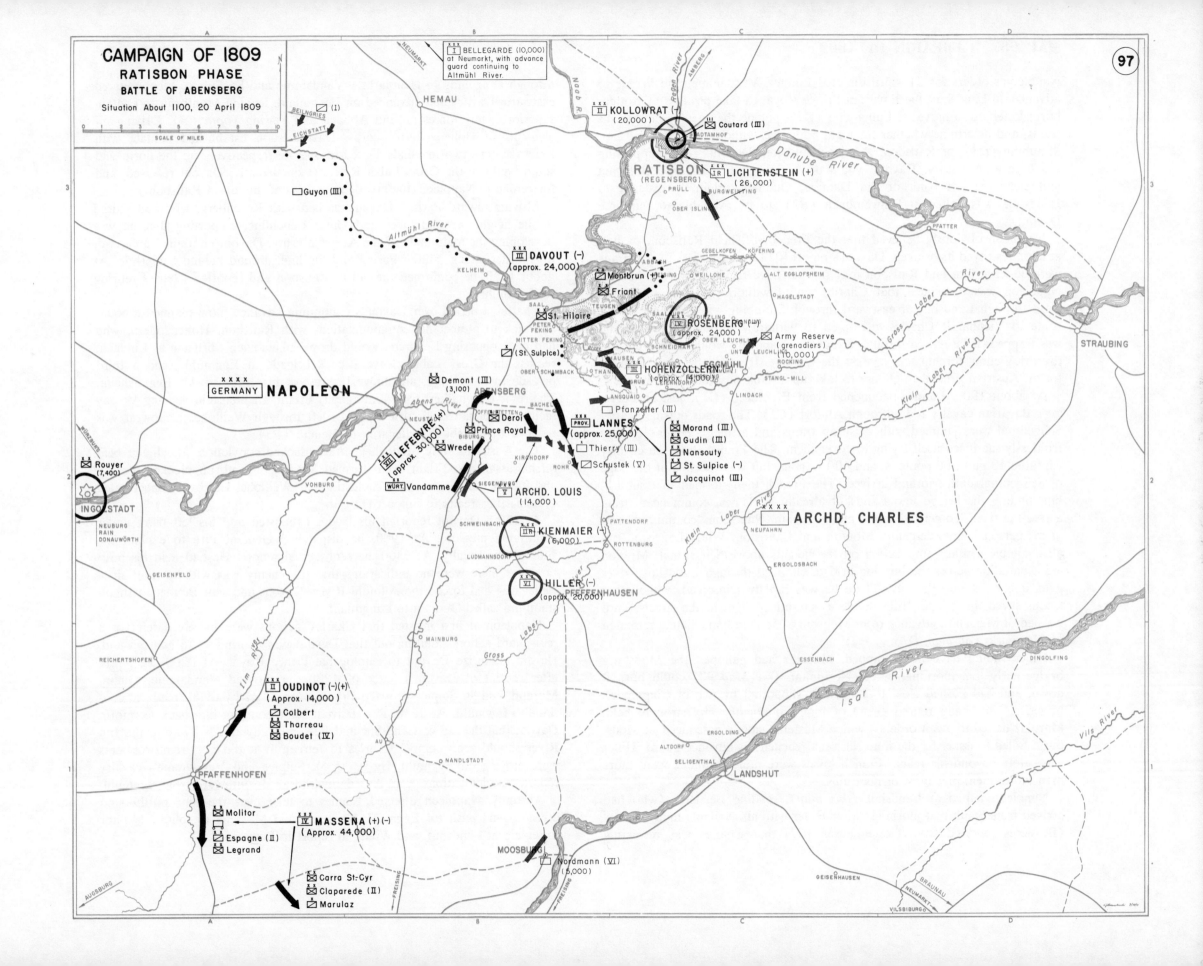

97

CAMPAIGN OF 1809
RATISBON PHASE
BATTLE OF ABENSBERG

Situation About 1100, 20 April 1809

SCALE OF MILES

BELLEGARDE (10,000)
at Neumarkt, with advance
guard continuing to
Altmühl River.

KOLLOWRAT (−)
(20,000)

Coutard (III)

RATISBON
(REGENSBERG)

LICHTENSTEIN (+)
(26,000)

Guyon (III)

DAVOUT (−)
(approx. 24,000)

Montbrun (+)
Friant

St. Hilaire

(St. Sulpice)

ROSENBERG (−)
(approx. 24,000)

Army Reserve
(grenadiers)
(10,000)

STRAUBING

HOHENZOLLERN
(approx. 4,000)

EGGMÜHL

GERMANY NAPOLEON

Demont (III)
(3,100)

ABENSBERG

Pfanzetter (III)

LANNES
(approx. 25,000)

Morand (III)
Gudin (III)
Nansouty
St. Sulpice (−)
Jacquinot (III)

Deroi
Prince Royal
Wrede

LEFEBVRE (+)
(approx. 30,000)

Thierry (III)

Schustek (V)

WÜRT. Vandamme

ARCHD. LOUIS
(14,000)

ARCHD. CHARLES

Rouyer
(7,400)

INGOLSTADT

NEUBURG
RAIN
DONAUWÖRTH

KIENMAIER (−)
(6,000)

HILLER (−)
(approx. 20,000)

PFEFFENHAUSEN

OUDINOT (−)(+)
(Approx. 14,000)

Colbert
Tharreau
Boudet (IV)

LANDSHUT

PFAFFENHOFEN

Molitor

MASSENA (+)(−)
(Approx. 44,000)

Espagne (II)
Legrand

MOOSBURG

Nordmann (VI)
(5,000)

Carra St.-Cyr
Claparede (II)
Marulaz

Napoleon's orders for 21 April directed Lannes, Vandamme, and Wrede to advance on Landshut; the Bavarian Prince Royal to take position at Rotten-burg; Lefebvre to move on Langquaid (C2), pursue the enemy, capture his trains, and determine whether his main body was withdrawing on Landshut, Straubing (D3), or Ratisbon. Boudet would join Davout. After supporting Lefebvre as necessary, Davout would drive Bellegarde back into Bohemia and clear the left bank of the Danube. Oudinot, originally ordered to Landshut, was halted at Schweinbach (B2), to be available to reinforce Davout.

Napoleon obviously believed that the French still held Ratisbon, or had at least destroyed its bridge. (Davout's report [0230] that masses of Austrians were between him and Ratisbon may not yet have reached him.) Likewise, Napoleon was convinced that Charles would withdraw—either southeast-ward through Landshut or eastward through Straubing—to cover the direct route to Vienna. If Charles attempted to withdraw through Landshut, he was trapped. If he retired through Straubing, Napoleon would outmarch him toward Vienna, forcing him against the Danube. It would be most unlikely for an Austrian general to choose to take up a flank position at Ratisbon.

At about 1900, Lannes debouched from Ergolding (C1), just as Prays-ing's Bavarian cavalry rode through Altdorf (C1). The roads outside nearby Seligenthal were jammed with Austrian trains and artillery. Hiller's cavalry fruitlessly sacrificed itself trying to cover them. The Franco-Bavarian cavalry captured 13 guns, 60 pontons, and 600 wagons, but was checked at the edge of Seligenthal until Morand arrived. The French then stormed that suburb, but, finding the bridge into Landshut already in flames, commenced firing across the river. To get the attack moving again, Napoleon "committed" two of his personal aides-de-camp, Mouton and Lauriston. While Lauriston put all available artillery into action on the heights above Seligenthal, Mouton led a battalion across the burning bridge, chopped through Landshut's river gate, and burst into the city. There he was rapidly reinforced, while other troops saved the bridge. Hiller made a determined fight in the streets, until warned of Massena's advance from Moosburg. He then immediately retreated on Neumarkt (off map, D1).

Hiller should have been trapped. Marulaz had galloped the Moosburg bridge early that morning, before Nordmann (see Map 97) could burn it down, and had pushed close to Landshut, supported by two of Claparede's brigades. Nordmann retired ahead of him. Finding the city strongly held, Marulaz halted to await orders—which Massena, snugly ensconced in Moos-burg, failed to issue. By the time Massena reached his advance guard, Hiller was safely beyond his reach. French losses were minor; Hiller's were more than 9,000 men, plus most of his trains.

Napoleon halted at Landshut (this map), sending Bessieres (who had arrived from Spain that morning) after Hiller with all available light cavalry. (Bessieres reported from Geisenhausen [C1] that Charles was retreating

through Dingolfing to Neumarkt.) Vandamme and St. Sulpice reconnoitered eastward. Davout had advanced on Langquaid, leaving Montbrun to contain superior enemy forces around Abbach and Peising (both C3). Driving off elements of Hohenzollern's corps, Davout soon established contact with Lefebvre. The two marshals agreed to operate respectively on the north and south banks of the Gross Laber River. (Concurrently, Davout received, and forwarded to Napoleon, the first definite news of the fall of Ratisbon.)

Moving toward Paring, Davout clashed with Rosenberg, who had retired to the heights around Ober and Unter Leuchling. Reporting that he was developing the main body of the Austrian army, Davout continued a careful, open-order attack, taking Paring and the high ground behind Schierling. At about 1430, he confirmed the fall of Ratisbon and reported Charles retiring on Eggmühl.

Charles, worried over Davout's continuing advance, now planned a coun-terattack to protect his communications with Ratisbon. Hohenzollern, who had been opposing Lefebvre, would drop Vukassovich's brigade at Lindach, recross the Gross Laber, leave Biber's brigade at Eggmühl, send a third brigade to Rosenberg, and move the rest of his corps to Alt Egglofsheim. The reserve grenadiers were sent against Friant. Lichtenstein, leaving Veczay facing Abbach, would turn Davout's left through Weillohe. Kollowrat was recalled to Ratisbon, Bellegarde to Hemau (B3).

The Austrians were tired; their attacks lacked conviction. St. Hilaire beat off his assailants; Friant even stormed Sanding. Montbrun blocked Veczay and fought Lichtenstein to a standstill near Weillohe. Lefebvre concentrated at Schierling, ready to support Davout.

At 1700, Davout reported his troops exhausted and his left flank under continuing pressure. At 1900, he dispatched General Pire to explain the situation personally. At 2300, he sent a final report: He had held his posi-tion, but there were no indications that the enemy was withdrawing; since Bellegarde had forced the Altmühl River, Davout had sent Boudet to Ingol-stadt and called Oudinot to Langquaid.

Napoleon at first insisted that Charles' actions were merely a feint or a rear-guard action, pointing out that Davout was continuing to gain ground. He did authorize Davout to employ the Prince Royal. At 0200, 22 April, after receipt of Davout's letter of 1700, he ordered Vandamme, Gudin, Morand, and St. Sulpice to reach Ergoldsbach (C2) by 0900, ready to con-tinue to Eggmühl. At 0230, Pire arrived; Napoleon sent him back to inform Davout that the fall of Landshut and Bessieres' advance halfway to the Inn River should soon compel Charles to retreat. If it did not, reinforcements were moving on Eggmühl. By 0300, St. Sulpice and Vandamme's cavalry reported no indications of an Austrian withdrawal southward from Eggmühl.

Abruptly, Napoleon directed Lannes to take over the four northbound divisions and push for Eggmühl, Nansouty and Massena to follow, Molitor to remain at Landshut, and Wrede to report to Bessieres.

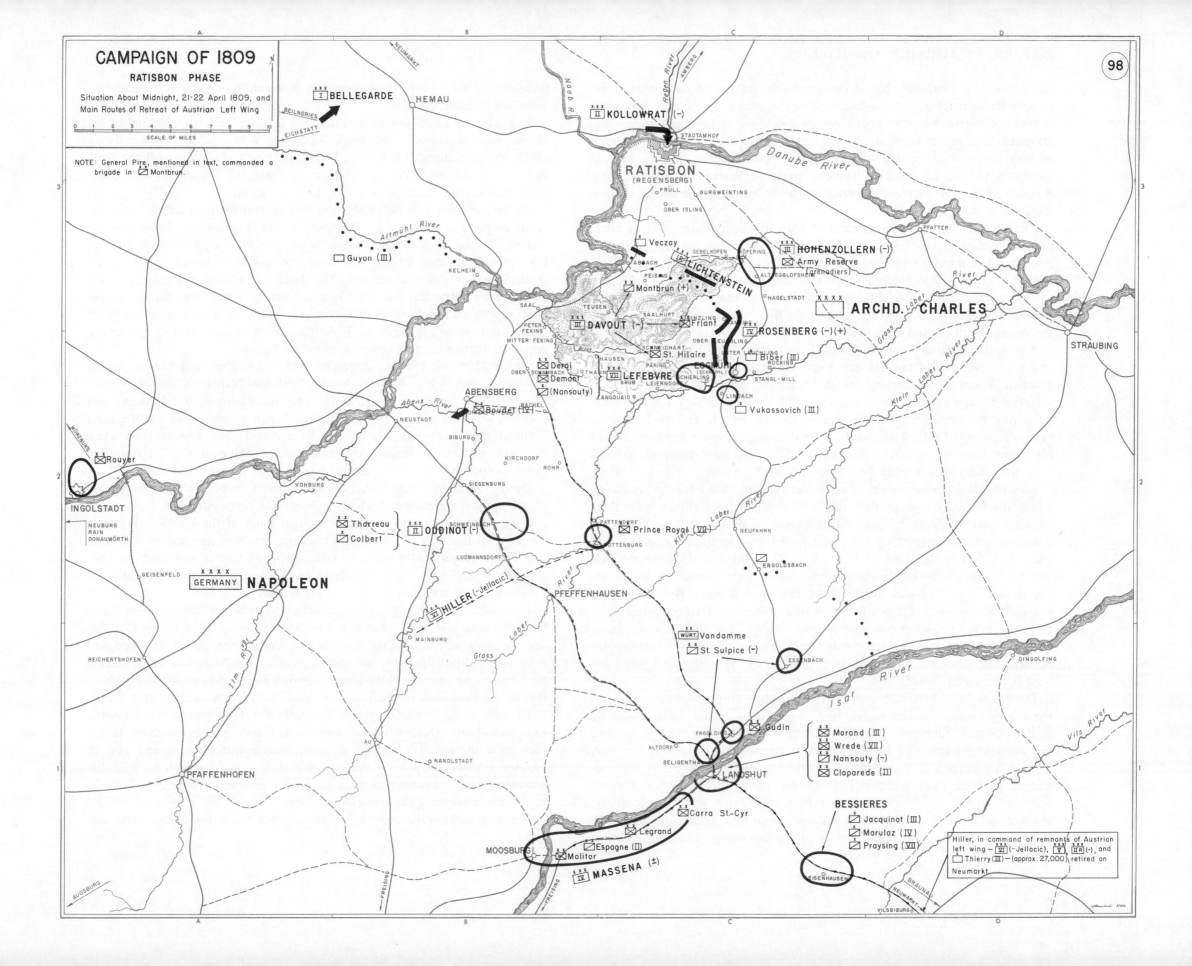

CAMPAIGN OF 1809

RATISBON PHASE

Situation About Midnight, 21-22 April 1809, and
Main Routes of Retreat of Austrian Left Wing

SCALE OF MILES

NOTE: General Pire, mentioned in text, commanded a
brigade in ▯ Montbrun.

98

After reaching Landshut, Napoleon—probably influenced by rumors concerning Bellegarde's activities—had ordered the army's line of communication shifted southward so as to pass through Augsburg rather than Ingolstadt. Davout's final report seems to have given the Emperor his first clear idea of how far west Bellegarde had penetrated. Consequently, before leaving Landshut (0600, 22 April), Napoleon wrote to Rouyer authorizing him, if endangered by Bellegarde's advance, to call in his detachments and destroy the Danube bridges.

Charles now had a good estimate of Davout's actual strength and comparative isolation. His general plan remained the same—to turn Davout's left, thus (he thought) threatening Napoleon's communications, while protecting his own escape hatch at Ratisbon. Kollowrat would pick up Veczay and advance on Abbach; Lichtenstein and Hohenzollern would attack toward Peising. Rosenberg would fix Davout, while Biber and Vukassovich covered the Austrian left around Eggmühl.

Again, the Austrians moved slowly. Rosenberg waited for the enveloping attack to develop. Lichtenstein and Veczay waited for Kollowrat. Kollowrat dawdled. When the enveloping attack finally did get under way, Montbrun stalled it by aggressive skirmishing. By 1000, the Prince Royal brought his perspiring division into Schierling. The French and Bavarians held firm everywhere until 1300; then, slowly, overwhelming numbers began to crowd Montbrun back and threaten Friant's left flank. By then, however, massed French artillery was already bellowing around Eggmühl.

At 0400, Württemberg light infantry had run the Austrian outposts out of Ergoldsbach (C2) and pressed on northward, Lannes riding with their advance guard. The march was difficult—nine divisions in a twenty-three-mile-long column slogging up the single road from Landshut. Between 1300 and 1400, Vandamme cleared Lindach (C2). Behind him, Napoleon galloped onto the nearby heights, which gave an excellent view of the surrounding terrain. Eggmühl was quickly captured, Vandamme's Württembergers storming across the bridge, while Gudin forded the river farther downstream, and Lefebvre sent Demont against it from the west. St. Sulpice's and Nansouty's cuirassiers now passed to the front through Eggmühl, forming up between that town and Schierling. A strong force of Bavarian and Württemberg light cavalry joined them.

Davout and Lefebvre had already attacked, their corps pivoting on Friant. Rosenberg (whom Charles merely told to get out of his fix the best way he could) resisted stubbornly, until St. Hilaire stormed Unter Leuchling, and the mass of French and German cavalry began moving across his rear, routing his cavalry and capturing his artillery. He then (1600–1700) retreated in good order on Alt Egglofsheim. However, Davout, Lefebvre, Lannes, and the cavalry pressed after him. Initially, it was slow business: the weather hot, the terrain rough, and the troops near exhaustion. Then the Austrians collapsed into a mob of fugitives that swept away all but two

battalions of the reserve grenadiers and blocked Hohenzollern's attempt to withdraw through Köfering.

At the first news of Napoleon's attack on Eggmühl, Charles had halted his envelopment of Davout's left flank. Kollowrat was ordered to Ober Isling (C3), the grenadiers to Köfering, Lichtenstein to Gebelkofen. All available cavalry was massed at Alt Egglofsheim to check the French pursuit. Bellegarde was urgently ordered to rejoin the main army.

As darkness fell (about 1900), the French and German cavalry met the Austrian horse and deployed—Nansouty in the first line, St. Sulpice in the second, Bavarians on the right, Württembergers on the left. The mounts of the French cuirrasiers being too weary to gallop, Nansouty charged the Austrian heavy cavalry at the trot. The shock was terrific, the ensuing melee momentarily desperate; but the French, better armored and better swordsmen, rapidly outfought their opponents. St. Sulpice got into action only for the pursuit, sweeping clear to Köfering, riding down the two remaining grenadier battalions, and almost capturing Charles.

About 2200, the French, staggering with exhaustion and hunger, halted along the general line Abbach–Alt Egglofsheim. Napoleon has been criticized for failing to push his advance home on Ratisbon, but Massena and Oudinot were not yet up, the converging French advance had left the units in hand too intermixed for a night engagement, and Charles had some 50,000 comparatively fresh troops available. Casualties during 22 April are dubious—possibly 6,000 French, and more than 12,000 Austrians.

During the night, Napoleon ordered Massena to march immediately on Straubing, seize a ponton bridge the Austrians reportedly had built there, and intercept the retreating enemy on either bank of the Danube. Bessieres would seize Braunau (off map, D1), calling Molitor forward to join him. The Prince Royal would move to Landshut, Vandamme and Oudinot concentrate at Eggmühl, and Boudet join Massena. Lannes, Davout, and Lefebvre would continue the pursuit on Ratisbon.

Likewise, during the night, Charles had a ponton bridge thrown downstream from Ratisbon and moved much of his army to the far bank of the Danube, leaving his cavalry outside the town as a covering force. At an undetermined hour on 23 April (possibly at around 1100, after Nansouty had defeated his cavalry), he abandoned the idea of offering battle and evacuated Ratisbon, leaving six battalions in the place to delay the French as long as possible. Ratisbon's medieval walls were half-ruined, but 12-pounders were needed to breach them. (During this bombardment, Napoleon was wounded in the foot by a spent ball.) Finally, a small breach was opened, and two of Lannes' aides-de-camp led a party of grenadiers over the wall to seize the Straubing gate. Attacking through it, Gudin seized the bridge and north-bank suburb, trapping the Austrian garrison.

Massena, meanwhile, occupied Straubing, but found the bridge there cut.

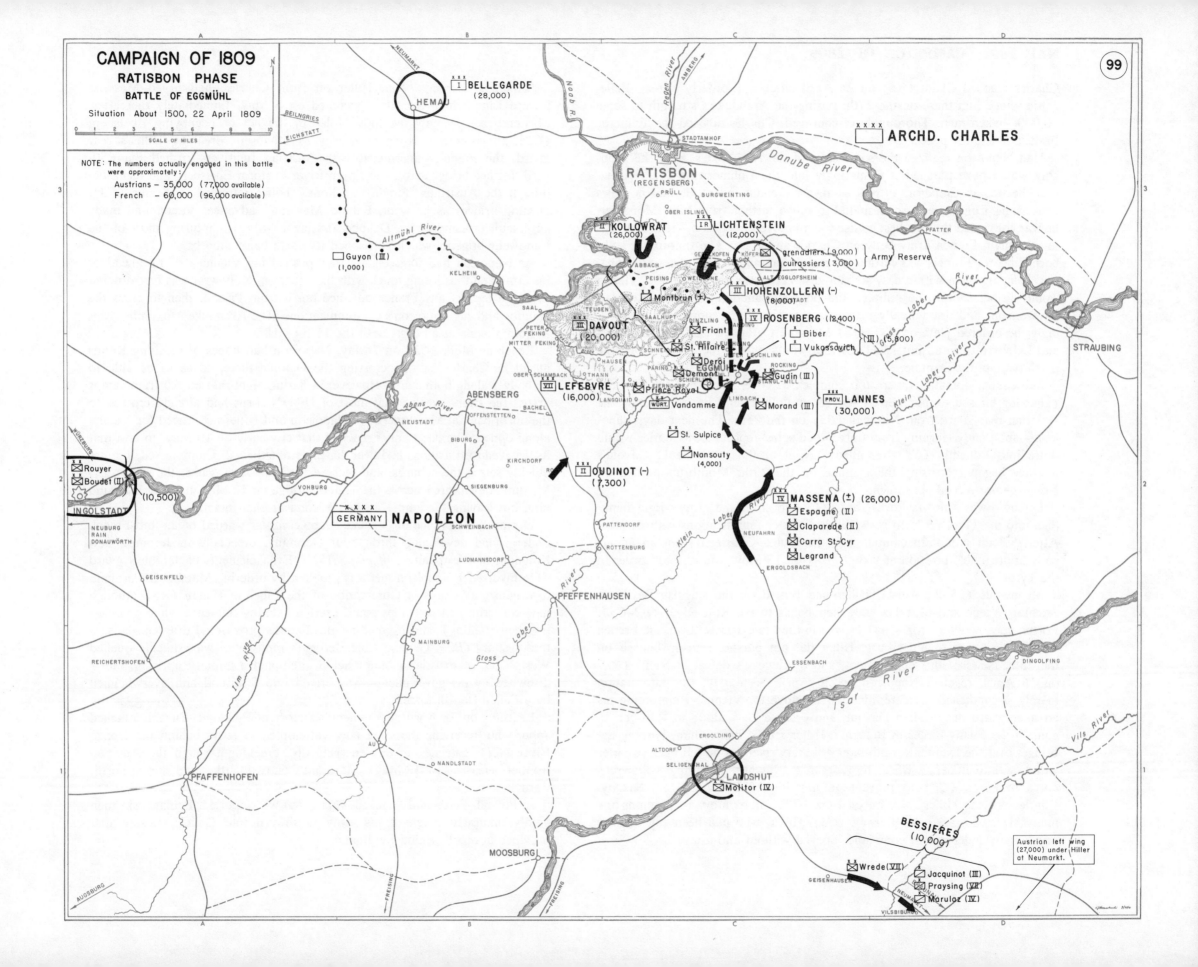

CAMPAIGN OF 1809
RATISBON PHASE
BATTLE OF EGGMÜHL

Situation About 1500, 22 April 1809

0 1 2 3 4 5 6 7 8 9 10
SCALE OF MILES

NOTE: The numbers actually engaged in this battle were approximately:

Austrians – 35,000 (77,000 available)
French – 60,000 (96,000 available)

XXXX ARCHD. CHARLES

99

I BELLEGARDE (28,000)

HEMAU

☐ Guyon (III) (1,000)

II KOLLOWRAT (26,000)

IR LICHTENSTEIN (12,000)

grenadiers (9,000)
cuirassiers (3,000)
Army Reserve

☐ Montbrun (†)

III HOHENZOLLERN (-) (8,000)

III DAVOUT (20,000)

IV ROSENBERG (12,400)

☐ Friant

☐ Biber
☐ Vukassovich

(III) (5,800)

☐ St. Hilaire

☐ Deroi
☐ Demont
EGGMÜHL
☐ Gudin (III)

VII LEFEBVRE (16,000)

☐ Prince Royal

WÜRT. Vandamme

☐ Morand (III)

PROV LANNES (30,000)

☐ St. Sulpice

☐ Nansouty (4,000)

☐☐ Rouyer
☐ Boudet (II)
(10,500)
INGOLSTADT

II OUDINOT (-) (7,300)

GERMANY NAPOLEON

IV MASSENA (±) (26,000)
☐ Espagne (II)
☐ Claparede (II)
☐ Carra St-Cyr
☐ Legrand

LANDSHUT
☐ Molitor (IV)

BESSIÈRES (10,000)

Austrian left wing (27,000) under Hiller at Neumarkt.

☐ Wrede (VII)

☐ Jacquinot (III)
☐ Praysing (VII)
☐ Maruloz (IV)

Charles reached Cham (*B3*) on 24 April, after a disorderly retreat. Belle-garde joined him there on the 27th, raising the Archduke's strength to some 90,000 shaken men. Thoroughly discouraged, Charles advised the Emperor Francis to sue for peace.

Had Napoleon realized the sorry state of the Archduke's army, he prob-ably would have pursued it unsparingly into the Böhmerwald (*C3*). How-ever, he was an Emperor, as well as an army commander: He had no news concerning Eugene, and so hesitated to move farther from him. Moreover, he was convinced that his best course was to move directly on Vienna, thrust-ing the main French army between Charles and John. The timorously stub-born Emperor Francis was certain to recall both archdukes to defend Vienna, thus bringing them within easy striking distance. Also, the capture of Vienna would dislocate both the military and political functioning of the Austrian government, and dramatically reassert his own military supremacy. Accord-ingly, he ordered (late on 23 April) Massena to Passau (*C3*), and Lannes and Lefebvre to Landshut (*B3*). Davout would pursue the enemy along the north bank of the Danube.

Subsequent operations were too complex to cover here in detail. Davout (knowing himself outnumbered) moved carefully after Charles, evicting the Austrian rear guard from Nittenau (*B3*) on the 25th. The next day, Napo-leon—apparently learning from unrecorded spies' reports that Charles would retire into Bohemia (*C3*)—recalled Davout to the south bank. Davout's infantry began recrossing the Danube on the 29th; Montbrun pushed on along the north bank as shown.

Lefebvre was sent first to Salzburg (*C2*) to cover the army's right flank, then into the Tyrol (*B2*) to re-establish direct communications with Eugene. After difficult mountain campaigning, he routed Chasteler from an appar-ently impregnable position at Wörgl (*B2*) on 13 May, and restored order in the Tyrol.

Meanwhile (23–24 April), Hiller had turned on the sluggish Bessieres, catching Wrede and Marulaz with their backs to the Rott River (*B2–C3*). Fortunately, Molitor (Massena) arrived in time to extricate them, the French thereafter retiring to Vilsbiburg. Hiller did not pursue, retiring himself on the 25th. News of this engagement, and of Eugene's defeat at Sacile (*B1*) on 16 April, reached Napoleon on 26 April. Seemingly, this information merely strengthened his determination to move on Vienna. Reinforcing his advance guard, he recalled Davout, and ordered Bernadotte to Ratisbon to contain the enemy forces in Bohemia. Hiller retired before him, burning the bridges over the Danube's south-bank tributary rivers as he fell back. Charles withdrew into Bohemia where he reorganized his army, sending Kollowrat's corps to Pilsen (*C3*) to prevent an invasion of Bohemia from Saxony. Charles ordered Hiller to retire on Linz (*C2*), preparatory to rejoining the main Austrian army near Budweis (*C3*). Hiller, who had been enjoying his accidentally independent command, obeyed without enthusiasm.

Napoleon, hoping to cut Hiller off from Charles, had urged Massena toward Linz, which the latter occupied on 3 May. Immediately thereafter, Massena unexpectedly overtook Hiller in the act of occupying Ebelsberg (*C2*), to cover a crossing at nearby Mauthausen. Breaking Hiller's rear guard, the French—intermixed with Austrian fugitives—rushed the 650-yard fortified bridge across the Traun River to storm Ebelsberg and its castle, though the Austrians "fought like lions." Hiller retreated to Krems (*C3*), burning bridges as he went. Behind Massena's advance, Vandamme made an assault crossing of the Danube at Linz (5 May), capturing most of the Landwehr brigade, which garrisoned its north-bank suburbs.

As Napoleon had foreseen, Charles pushed for Vienna—riding ahead of his army and thus losing touch with the situation. Kollowrat was first ordered to guard against any French advance north from Passau, then to cross the Danube and cut Napoleon's communications. The Archduke Maximilian was to hold Vienna at all costs until the 17th or 18th.

Reaching Mölk (*C2*) on 7 May, Napoleon had hopes of reaching Krems ahead of Charles, and of crossing the Danube there, so as to be able to maneuver along both banks. However, a daring night raid on Austrian camps across the river revealed that most of Hiller's corps had already crossed to the north bank at Mautern (*C3*). Napoleon and Hiller now raced for Vienna along opposite banks. Lannes reached that city early on 10 May, to find that its decayed fortifications had been hastily strengthened. Unimpressed, Lannes quickly seized the suburbs, and massed his howitzers against the inner city. Maximilian withdrew across the Thabor bridge on 12 May, burning it behind him, but leaving the amply-stocked Vienna arsenal intact.

During this advance on Vienna, Napoleon was warned of an anti-French underground developing throughout Germany, especially in Jerome's new Kingdom of Westphalia (*off map, A3*). (Even elements of Jerome's guard were involved.) Napoleon met this problem by ordering Marshal Kellermann to organize a "Corps of Observation of the Elbe" at Hanau (*A3*) (though new conscripts, these troops could exert a calming influence while complet-ing their training), and by sending Beaumont's provisional dragoon division to Augsburg (*B2*). General Eble, Jerome's minister of war, quickly quelled Westphalia. In Prussia, a Major Schill attempted a military uprising, but—disowned by his government—was driven into Stralsund and overwhelmed by a Dutch-Danish force.

Learning on 28 April of Napoleon's victory at Eggmühl, Eugene attacked John, who, receiving the same news, attempted to retire behind the Isonzo River (*C1*). Eugene pursued energetically, breaking through the Austrian frontier defenses (14–18 May). Marmont won two battles, and started north-ward.

In Poland, Ferdinand attacked Thorn, but was repulsed. Poniatowski then boldly infiltrated much of his army southward into Galicia, raising that province in revolt behind Ferdinand.

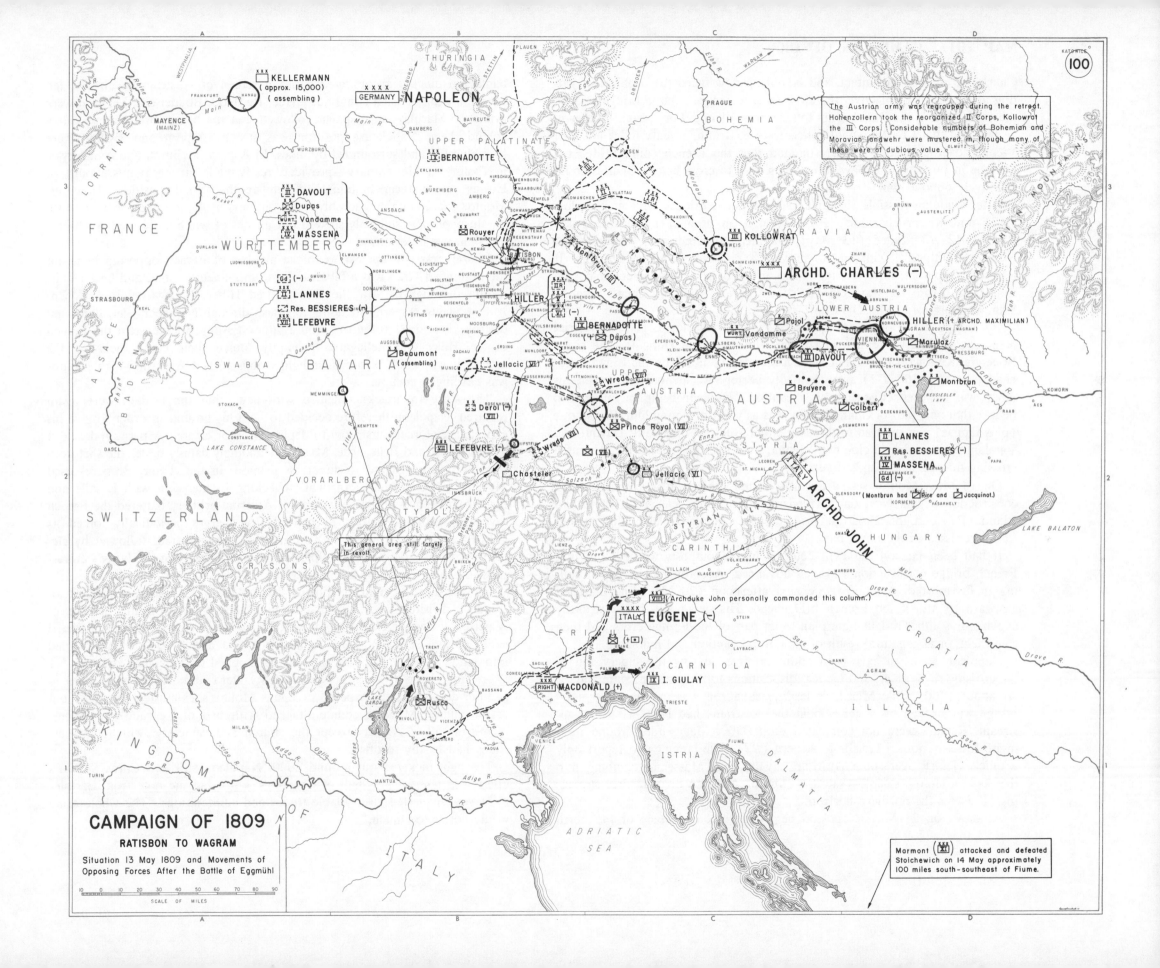

100

KELLERMANN
(approx. 15,000)
(assembling)

GERMANY NAPOLEON

The Austrian army was regrouped during the retreat. Hohenzollern took the reorganized II Corps, Kollowrat the III Corps. Considerable numbers of Bohemian and Moravian landwehr were mustered in, though many of these were of dubious value.

BERNADOTTE

DAVOUT
Dupas
Vandamme
MASSENA

KOLLOWRAT

ARCHD. CHARLES (−)

LANNES
Res. BESSIERES (−)
LEFEBVRE

HILLER

Rouyer

Bernadotte (+ Dupas)

Vandamme

Pajol

HILLER (+ ARCHD. MAXIMILIAN)

VIENNA

Marulaz

DAVOUT

Beaumont
(assembling)

Jellacic (VI)

Wrede

Bruyere

Colbert

Montbrun

Derol

Wrede

Prince Royal (VII)

LANNES
Res. BESSIERES (−)
MASSENA

(Montbrun had Pire and Jacquinot.)

LEFEBVRE (−)

Chasteler

Jellacic (VI)

This general area still largely in revolt.

ARCHD. JOHN

(Archduke John personally commanded this column.)

ITALY EUGENE (−)

RIGHT MACDONALD (+)

I. GIULAY

Rusca

Marmont attacked and defeated Stoichewich on 14 May approximately 100 miles south-southeast of Fiume.

CAMPAIGN OF 1809

RATISBON TO WAGRAM

Situation 13 May 1809 and Movements of Opposing Forces After the Battle of Eggmühl

10   0   10   20   30   40   50   60   70   80   90
SCALE OF MILES

Charles' army was still intact, and Napoleon now faced the problem of getting at it. His first objective, therefore, was to secure a large bridgehead on the north bank of the Danube, not too far from Vienna. For reasons unknown, he believed that Charles would concentrate at Brünn, seventy miles north of Vienna; overoptimistically, he estimated that the French could bridge the Danube in three or four days, thus being able to cross before Charles could effectively oppose him.

After studying possible sites, Napoleon ordered bridges built at Nussdorf (A2) and Kaiser-Ebersdorf (B1). Though an attempt to seize Jedelsee Island (A2–A3) failed (13 May), Napoleon ordered work continued at Nussdorf, both as a feint and to provide a possible secondary crossing. It was soon apparent, however, that the Kaiser-Ebersdorf bridge could not be completed before 19 May. On 16 May, Charles' leading elements reached Stammersdorf (A3) and Gerasdorf (B3).

By taking up a position opposite Vienna, Charles hoped to restrict Napoleon's initiative, remain in contact with John and Hungary, and cover Bohemia. Kollowrat (17 May) made a blundering attack on the Linz bridgehead (see Map 100, C2) and was badly beaten. Accidentally, however, his intent was more effective than his execution, Napoleon being encouraged to believe that only part of Charles' army was as yet confronting him. Bernadotte (plus Dupas) was ordered to threaten either Budweis or Zwettl; Davout and Vandamme were drawn closer to Vienna; the forces designated for the initial crossing massed near Kaiser-Ebersdorf.

On 18 May, Molitor seized the Lob-Grund (this map, B1), and bridge construction began. Next day, Austrian outposts were cleared from Lobau Island (B1); on the 20th, the bridges were completed, and Molitor and Lasalle crossed to the north bank.

It had been late on the 19th before Charles' outposts warned him that French bridge construction was well advanced. Accordingly, he began calling in his most distant corps; the next afternoon (20 May), he marched eastward to attack the French bridgehead. His delay has been variously explained as either a deliberate plan to let part of the French cross and then trap them, or as a natural result of his normal caution and indolence.

Napoleon seems to have been oddly carefree, leaving the supervision of the crossing to Berthier, and tactical dispositions to his division commanders. At about 1700, while Marulaz's leading squadron was crossing, the main bridge was broken by a heavy boat the Austrians had launched from upstream. Repairs were not completed until 0300. Meanwhile, around midnight, Massena joined Lasalle at Aspern (B2). The latter could report only a quick victory over some Austrian cavalry, but Massena—climbing into the Aspern church steeple—saw the glow of Austrian bivouac fires stretching all across the northern horizon.

At dawn on 21 May, Napoleon began his reconnaissance of the north bank, but quickly encountered a heavy screen of Austrian cavalry, which Lasalle's weak division could not pierce. By 0900, Boudet and Legrand were available; Marulaz and Espagne followed, but the bridge broke immediately behind them. Napoleon's position was strong: Aspern and Essling were strongly built and surrounded by dikes. In Aspern, a church and cemetery—in Essling, a big granary—provided ready-made strong points. South of Essling, stone farm buildings offered another good position. However, Molitor unaccountably had only a few outposts in Aspern itself. About 1430, the dusty horizon suddenly spewed out masses of white-uniformed Austrians, less than two miles away.

Charles was still unclear as to the number of French opposing him, but the Marchfeld (B2) was a favorite Austrian maneuver area, and he knew its terrain thoroughly. Now, he concentrated Hiller, Bellegarde, and Hohenzollern against Aspern, intending to smash through Napoleon's left flank and destroy his bridge. Rosenberg would attack Essling; Lichtenstein the French center. Hiller and Bellegarde promptly fouled their corps, delaying the attack. It was 1500 before their light troops rushed Aspern, which Molitor was hustling to occupy.

The Austrian attack coincided with news that the bridges were again repaired. Napoleon therefore decided to hold his ground in order to give his expected reinforcements room to deploy. Molitor cleared Aspern, and held it against Hiller and Bellegarde, Massena standingly calmly under the shell-torn trees of the churchyard to direct his defense. In the center, Bessieres used Marulaz to fix Hohenzollern, while checking Lichtenstein with Lasalle and Espagne. The overwhelmingly superior Austrian artillery battered the French savagely, though desperate French cavalry charges periodically forced its guns to withdraw. Toward 1800, Carra St.-Cyr appeared, followed by elements of Nansouty's and St. Sulpice's divisions. Putting in the latter's cuirassiers, Bessieres drove off Lichtenstein.

On the French right, Napoleon had placed Lannes in command of Boudet's division, so that Massena could concentrate on the defense of Aspern. Having carefully organized Essling for defense, Lannes inflicted a bloody repulse on Rosenberg's tardy (1630) attack. Dedowich straggled into action at 1800, but was immediately stopped by Espagne's division.

An hour later, Charles personally led Hiller's and Bellegarde's corps in a do-or-die attack on Aspern, sweeping Molitor's exhausted survivors out of the village. Massena counterattacked with two of Legrand's regiments, recovering all of Aspern except the church and cemetery, which the Austrians had hastily fortified.

The fight flickered out around 2000. Napoleon still had Carra St.-Cyr's division in reserve, plus half of Legrand's, but a laconic note from Berthier to Davout requested all available troops and ammunition: "The whole army would not be too much."

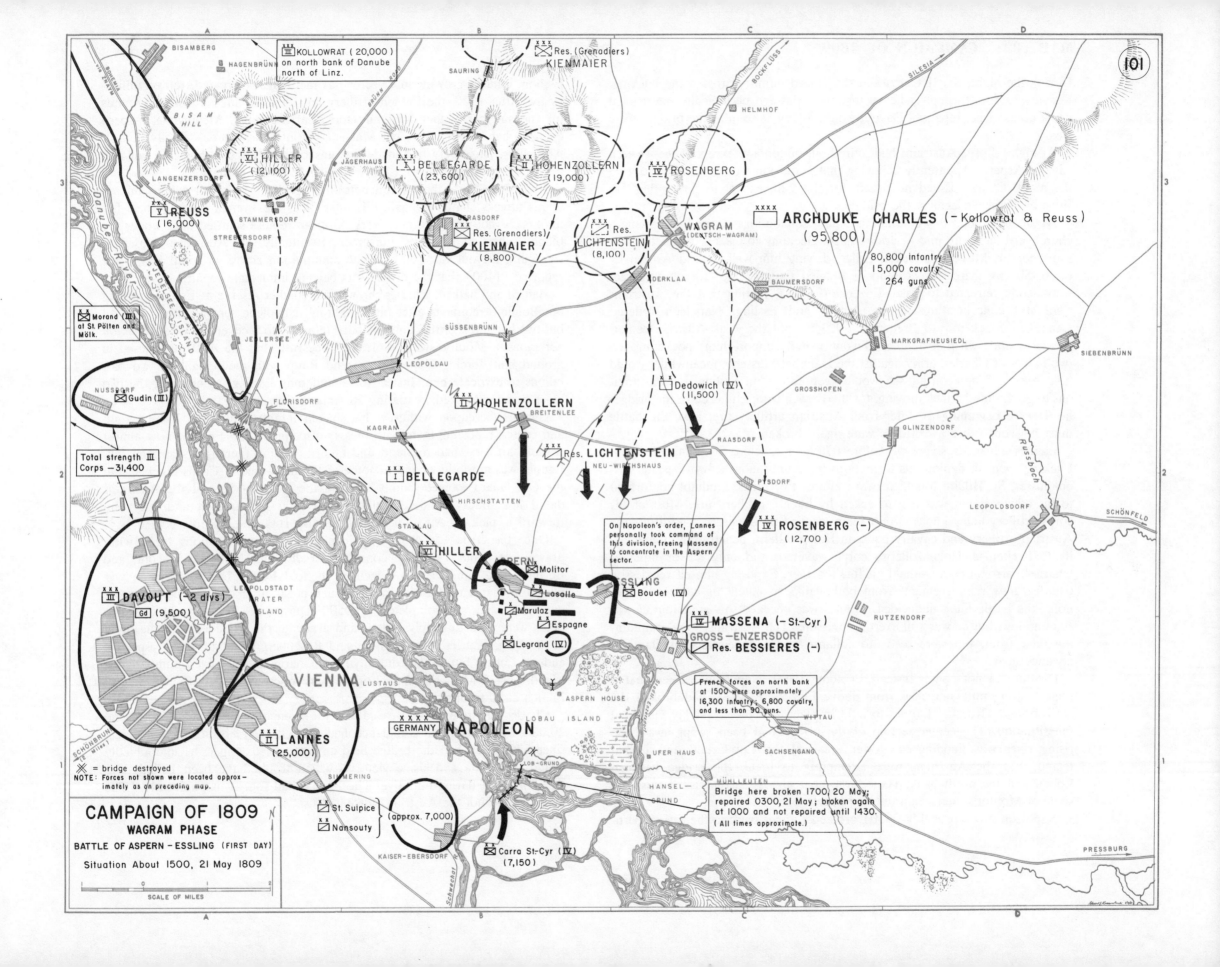

101

KOLLOWRAT (20,000) on north bank of Danube north of Linz.

Res. (Grenadiers) KIENMAIER

BISAMBERG

HAGENBRÜNN

SAURING

HELMHOF

BOCKFLUSS

SILESIA

BISAM HILL

VI HILLER (12,100)

JÄGERHAUS

I BELLEGARDE (23,600)

II HOHENZOLLERN (19,000)

IV ROSENBERG

ARCHDUKE CHARLES (- Kollowrat & Reuss) (95,800)

LANGENZERSDORF

STAMMERSDORF

KRASDORF

Res. (Grenadiers) KIENMAIER (8,800)

Res. LICHTENSTEIN (8,100)

WAGRAM (DEUTSCH-WAGRAM)

80,800 infantry 15,000 cavalry 264 guns

V REUSS (16,000)

STREBERSDORF

DERKLAA

BAUMERSDORF

Morand (III) at St. Pölten and Mölk.

JEDLERSEE

SÜSSENBRÜNN

LEOPOLDAU

Dedowich (IV) (11,500)

MARKGRAFNEUSIEDL

SIEBENBRÜNN

NUSSDORF

Gudin (III)

FLORISDORF

II HOHENZOLLERN

BREITENLEE

GROSSHOFEN

GLINZENDORF

Russbach

Total strength III Corps — 31,400

KAGRAN

Res. LICHTENSTEIN NEU-WIRTHSHAUS

RAASDORF

I BELLEGARDE

HIRSCHSTATTEN

PYSDORF

LEOPOLDSDORF

SCHÖNFELD

STADLAU

VI HILLER

ASPERN

Molitor

On Napoleon's order, Lannes personally took command of this division, freeing Massena to concentrate in the Aspern sector.

IV ROSENBERG (-) (12,700)

LEOPOLDSTADT KRATER ISLAND

III DAVOUT (- 2 divs) Gd (9,500)

Lasalle

ESSLING

Boudet (IV)

Marulaz

Espagne

IV MASSENA (- St.-Cyr)

RUTZENDORF

VIENNA

LUSTAUS

Legrand (IV)

GROSS - ENZERSDORF

Res. BESSIERES (-)

II LANNES (25,000)

French forces on north bank at 1500 were approximately 16,300 infantry; 6,800 cavalry, and less than 90 guns.

ASPERN HOUSE

LOBAU ISLAND

UFER HAUS

WITTAU

SCHÖNBRUNN (1/2 MILE)

GERMANY NAPOLEON

SIMMERING

HANSEL- GRUND

SACHSENGANG

= bridge destroyed
NOTE: Forces not shown were located approx- imately as on preceding map.

St. Sulpice

Nansouty

(approx. 7,000)

LOB-GRUND

MÜHLLEUTEN

Bridge here broken 1700, 20 May; repaired 0300, 21 May; broken again at 1000 and not repaired until 1430. (All times approximate.)

PRESSBURG

CAMPAIGN OF 1809
WAGRAM PHASE
BATTLE OF ASPERN - ESSLING (FIRST DAY)
Situation About 1500, 21 May 1809

KAISER-EBERSDORF

Carra St-Cyr (IV) (7,150)

Schwechat

SCALE OF MILES

During the night, the II Corps and the Guard infantry crossed the bucking, weaving bridges through a heavy fog, their passage periodically interrupted while breaks were repaired. Davout would follow as soon as the bridges were clear.

At nightfall, the Austrians had retired out of contact, except at the western edge of Aspern. Apparently believing that Napoleon would withdraw during the night, Charles issued no orders for the 22d, except to direct that fire ships be launched against the bridges.

At about 0300, the continuous small squabblings around the Aspern churchyard flared up into a serious clash. Deciding to clean out this troublesome corner, Massena attacked Hiller, driving him well beyond Aspern by 0500. Shortly thereafter, Rosenberg assailed Essling, but—for obscure reasons—soon retreated to Gross-Enzersdorf (*C1*). Noting that the Austrians were still concentrating against Aspern and Essling, Napoleon ordered Lannes to attack toward Breitenlee (*B2*) to split the weak Austrian center. Bessieres and, when available, Davout would support him, pocketing the two halves of Charles' army against the Danube. Massena, meanwhile, would hold Aspern; Napoleon himself would keep an eye on Essling. He was anxious to get Lannes' attack moving, for the French troops, massed in the bridgehead, were beginning to suffer from Austrian artillery fire; also, the battle must be won before his bridges were again broken.

Lannes advanced sometime before 0700, in echelon, St. Hilaire leading. Lacking room to deploy, his formations were unusually heavy. Despite serious losses, St. Hilaire fought forward almost two miles. Oudinot conformed to his advance, but was then checked by intense artillery fire. Most of his corps artillery being knocked out, Lannes called on Bessieres, who drove the Austrian artillery and cavalry back on Hohenzollern, penetrating momentarily to Breitenlee. Hohenzollern's corps wavered, and only the example of Charles' personal courage held his line together. Exposing himself recklessly, Charles drew reinforcements from both flanks to patch his center. For an hour, the battle hung undecided. Lannes was checked; his ammunition was running low, but he was still exerting pressure. The Austrians were maintaining their front, but were ready to collapse at the appearance of Davout's advance guard.

Davout did not come. Instead, at about 0800, Napoleon learned that a huge floating mill, launched from above Florisdorf (*A2*), had broken the main bridge. Ordering Lannes to hold in place, Napoleon quickly inspected the situation. The center section of the bridge had been swept away, the rising river was flooding the lower areas of the Lob-Grund and Lobau Island, and the Austrians were attempting to break the bridge between Lobau and the north bank. (One large boat almost accomplished this, but some of Molitor's men swam out and beached it.)

Napoleon now (probably 0930) ordered Lannes back to the line Aspern-Essling. Lannes, growing more serene as the danger increased, retired unhurriedly. After 1000, the French artillery fell silent, saving its last few rounds for the emergency that was only too clearly coming. Meanwhile, Aspern changed hands four times, but Massena—grim as at Genoa—finally held it. At Essling, Rosenberg had made five unsuccessful attacks; his sixth got into the village, but could not dislodge Boudet from the granary.

By 1330, Charles began concentrating against the French center, but all of his attacks shattered against Lannes' line, the French holding their fire until each shot would count. Every Austrian repulse scuttled back under the bloody sabers of Bessieres' horsemen. Eventually, the Austrians refused to try again. Davout was getting some ammunition across in small boats, but reported (1400) that the bridge was beyond immediate repair.

Baffled and balked, Charles threw his grenadier reserve at Essling, forcing out Boudet's remnants after bitter fighting. Napoleon sent Mouton, with all but two battalions of the Young Guard infantry, to recover the village (*action not shown*). Mouton swept it clean in one rush, but the Austrians closed in around him, forcing Napoleon to send Rapp with the remaining two battalions to extricate him. Instead of abandoning Essling, as ordered, the two aides counterattacked, scattering Rosenberg's corps.

Charles thereupon withdrew his shaken infantry from the French right and center, replacing them with masses of cannon. The French, now almost without artillery, had to stand and take it, closing their ranks as men fell. Lannes was mortally wounded, some of the hard-used II Corps flinched, but the Old Guard loomed calmly through the worst of it, and the Austrians dared not attack. Bessieres rallied some light infantrymen and led them forward to pick off Austrian cannoneers. By 1600, the fighting ceased.

Once the crisis was over, Napoleon began his preparations for a withdrawal. At about 1900, he consulted briefly with Massena, Davout, and Berthier, and announced his decision to hold Lobau Island. Massena was placed in charge of the withdrawal, which began after dark, in perfect order and quiet, and was completed by 0500. During 23–24 May, all available boats were used to supply Lobau and evacuate the wounded. On the night of the 24th, Charles ordered Hiller and Rosenberg to attack their respective ends of Lobau, but neither did anything. Charles did not even bombard the island. On 27 May, the main bridges were re-established by newly arrived French naval troops.

Charles admitted 23,400 casualties; the French lost between 19,000 and 20,000. Napoleon's self-confidence had brought him his first actual defeat since 1796. Yet, had the bridge held an hour or so longer, he undoubtedly would have won a decisive victory—which would have been hailed as a masterpiece of daring initiative. The French had fought magnificently. "The Danube, and not the Austrians, defeated us."

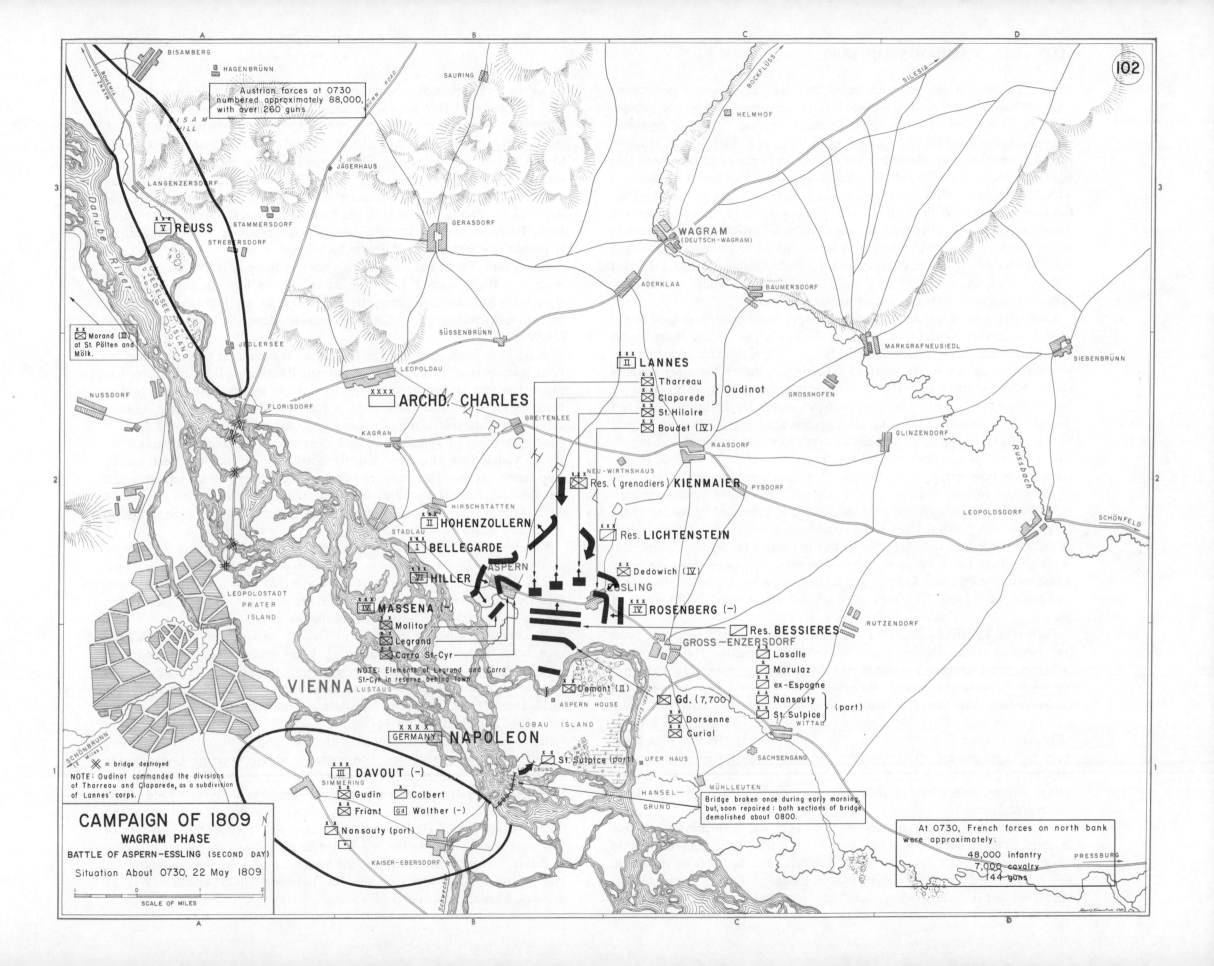

102

Austrian forces at 0730 numbered approximately 88,000, with over 260 guns.

BISAMBERG

HAGENBRÜNN

SAURING

BOCKFLÜSS

SILESIA

HELMHOF

BISAM HILL

LANGENZERSDORF

JÄGERHAUS

V REUSS

STAMMERSDORF

GERASDORF

WAGRAM
(DEUTSCH-WAGRAM)

STREBERSDORF

ADERKLAA

BAUMERSDORF

Danube River

JEDLERSEE

XX Morand (III) at St. Pölten and Mölk.

FLORISDORF

KAGRAN

LEOPOLDAU

MARKGRAFNEUSIEDL

SIEBENBRÜNN

GROSSHOFEN

NUSSDORF

ARCHD. CHARLES

BREITENLEE

II LANNES

Tharreau

Claparede

St. Hilaire

Boudet (IV)

Oudinot

RAASDORF

GLINZENDORF

Russbach

NEU-WIRTHSHAUS

Res. (grenadiers) KIENMAIER

PYSDORF

LEOPOLDSDORF

SCHÖNFELD

HIRSCHSTATTEN

II HOHENZOLLERN

Res. LICHTENSTEIN

STADLAU

I BELLEGARDE

VI HILLER

ASPERN

Dedowich (IV)

ESSLING

LEOPOLDSTADT PRATER ISLAND

IV MASSENA (-)

Molitor

Legrand

Carra St-Cyr

IV ROSENBERG (-)

Res. BESSIERES

GROSS-ENZERSDORF

Lasalle

Marulaz

ex-Espagne

Nansouty

St. Sulpice

(part)

RUTZENDORF

NOTE: Elements of Legrand and Carra St-Cyr in reserve behind town.

VIENNA

LUSTAUS

Demont (II)

ASPERN HOUSE

Gd. (7,700)

Dorsenne

Curial

LOBAU ISLAND

SCHÖNBRUNN

= bridge destroyed

GERMANY NAPOLEON

St. Sulpice (part)

UFER HAUS

SACHSENGANG

MÜHLLEUTEN

NOTE: Oudinot commanded the divisions of Tharreau and Claparede, as a subdivision of Lannes' corps.

III DAVOUT (-)

SIMMERING

Gudin   Colbert

Friant   Gd Walther (-)

Nansouty (part)

GRUND

HANSEL-GRUND

PRESSBURG

Bridge broken once during early morning, but, soon repaired: both sections of bridge demolished about 0800.

At 0730, French forces on north bank were approximately:

48,000 infantry
7,000 cavalry
144 guns

KAISER-EBERSDORF

Schwechat

CAMPAIGN OF 1809

WAGRAM PHASE

BATTLE OF ASPERN-ESSLING (SECOND DAY)

Situation About 0730, 22 May 1809

SCALE OF MILES

Napoleon's army might feel undefeated, but Austria stridently proclaimed an overwhelming victory. The wish to believe was strong throughout Europe. Even in France, where Napoleon's position appeared far more desperate than it was, the usual rash of plotting again broke out. Anti-French agitation spread across Germany; Russian nonassistance to Poniatowski developed into downright interference. Prussia was rearming and opening secret negotiations with Austria. In northern Italy, pro-Austrian factions began to stir. An English fleet was heckling the Italian coast, pinning down Murat in Naples and French forces in central Italy. A strong amphibious expedition was known to be organizing in England; its objective was rumored to be some point along the Channel or the north German coast. Finally, Napoleon had quarreled with the Pope, and occupied the Papal States. The Pope replied with a carefully noncommittal decree of excommunication.

Confronting these problems, Napoleon kept a cool head, and used to the utmost his terrible capacity for work. If the fate of his empire hung on his next battle, none knew it better than he. The principal threat confronting him was still Charles' army. He intended to destroy it before his other enemies could intervene effectively. His immediate tasks, he felt, were to mass an overwhelming force under his own command, secure his flanks and rear, and prepare for a successful Danube crossing. Since his present position should fix Charles, he began shifting available reinforcements forward. Vandamme would defend the Danube's south bank from Mölk (C2) to Vienna; Bernadotte would concentrate at St. Pölten (C2); Lefebvre, leaving Deroi in the Tyrol, would advance to Linz (C2). For greater freedom of maneuver, additional north-bank bridgeheads were established at Enns and Ebelsberg (both C2). Junot was recalled from Spain to command the Corps of Observation of the Elbe; together with Jerome, he was to protect the upper Danube and contain partisan bands operating out of Bohemia. Fortresses along the lower Rhine were put on a war footing, and additional national guard units mobilized for coast defense. The Pope was arrested and hustled off to northern Italy.

Following Lefebvre's departure, news of Aspern-Essling sent the Tyrol into renewed revolt, forcing Deroi to withdraw hurriedly. Raiding out of Bohemia, Am Ende and Brunswick seized Dresden (off map, C3) and Leipzig while Radivojevich entered Bayreuth (B3) on 14 June, and advanced on Nüremberg. However, few Saxons joined them. Jerome recovered Leipzig and Dresden on 1 July; Junot, advancing with his one available division (Rivaud) reached Bayreuth on the 7th. Unfortunately, Jerome and Junot were too light-minded to cooperate. Kienmaier joined Radivojevich with reinforcements, defeated Junot on 9 July, and drove him toward Amberg (B3). Jerome then retreated westward, pursued by Brunswick. Am Ende reoccupied Dresden.

To the south, Eugene's pursuit of John went on, both armies suffering severely from hunger, cold, and hardship. (Charles had ordered John to advance on Linz from the south while Kollowrat attacked it from the north, but John judged the order impossible to execute.) On 25 May, Jellacic blundered into Eugene's column and was destroyed; the next day, Eugene

linked up with Lauriston. (Napoleon had sent Lauriston to Semmering [C2] with two brigades [not shown] to screen the Grande Armee's right rear.) Marmont meanwhile made an expert march through difficult, almost roadless country, infested with Austrian irregulars, but showed no zeal whatever to join Eugene. Consequently, Chasteler was able to push back Rusca and escape eastward to join I. Giulay on 13 June. Thus strengthened, Giulay evaded both Marmont and Broussier (not shown), whom Macdonald had detached to establish liaison with Marmont, and attacked Graz (C2) on 25 June. Here, in an epic fight, he was bloodily repulsed by 1,200 French. Napoleon now summoned Marmont to Vienna.

Northward, Ferdinand—discovering Galicia in open revolt behind him—evacuated Warsaw on 1 July. Poniatowski drove him steadily southward, though the Russians made energetic efforts to limit any Polish gains. Charles had difficulty withstanding Emperor Francis' demands that Ferdinand be reinforced.

Anxious to keep John and the Hungarian Insurrection from troubling his right rear, or from joining Charles through Pressburg (D2), Napoleon had meanwhile sent Davout against that city. Davout seized the Austrian bridgehead on the south bank and, later, a fortified island in the river, causing Charles considerable alarm. Eugene overtook and badly defeated John at Raab (D2) on 14 June. (John had expected strong reinforcements from Hungary, but that kingdom—latently hostile to Austria and bemused by Napoleon's psychological warfare—largely failed him.) John retired across the Danube; Eugene halted to cover the siege of Raab, which fell on 25 June. After two unsuccessful attempts to recross the Danube, John moved to Pressburg, where he remained fixed by Davout's operations.

Charles had strengthened his army by recalling Kollowrat and by incorporating some 60,000 Landwehr as filler replacements. An inexplicable shortage of horses, however, prevented his cavalry and artillery from regaining their former effectiveness. Charles fortified the Aspern–Gross-Enzersdorf area, but did little to extend these defenses farther east.

By contrast, Napoleon drove at the task of concentrating every available man, horse, and gun. He utilized the whole resources of occupied Austria to feed, clothe, and equip his troops, concurrently building up their morale and maintaining strict discipline. Various small islands around Lobau were captured and fortified, increasing Napoleon's command of the river, and confusing the Austrians as to his future crossing site. Lobau itself was a well-organized entrenched camp, the river around it patrolled by a strong squadron of French gunboats. The ponton bridge connecting Lobau to the south bank had been rebuilt, and a trestle bridge begun alongside it. Additional pontons, rafts, portable bridges, and special landing craft were ready. Deciding, inspecting, and correcting everything, Napoleon showed himself an officer "of all arms." He had hoped to cross on 15 June, but—because of Marmont's delays—it was 28–29 June before his orders were out for an attack on 5 July. Davout would reach Kaiser-Ebersdorf on 3 July. Eugene, Marmont, and Broussier would arrive on the 4th. Lefebvre would send him Wrede's division. Vandamme would hold Vienna.

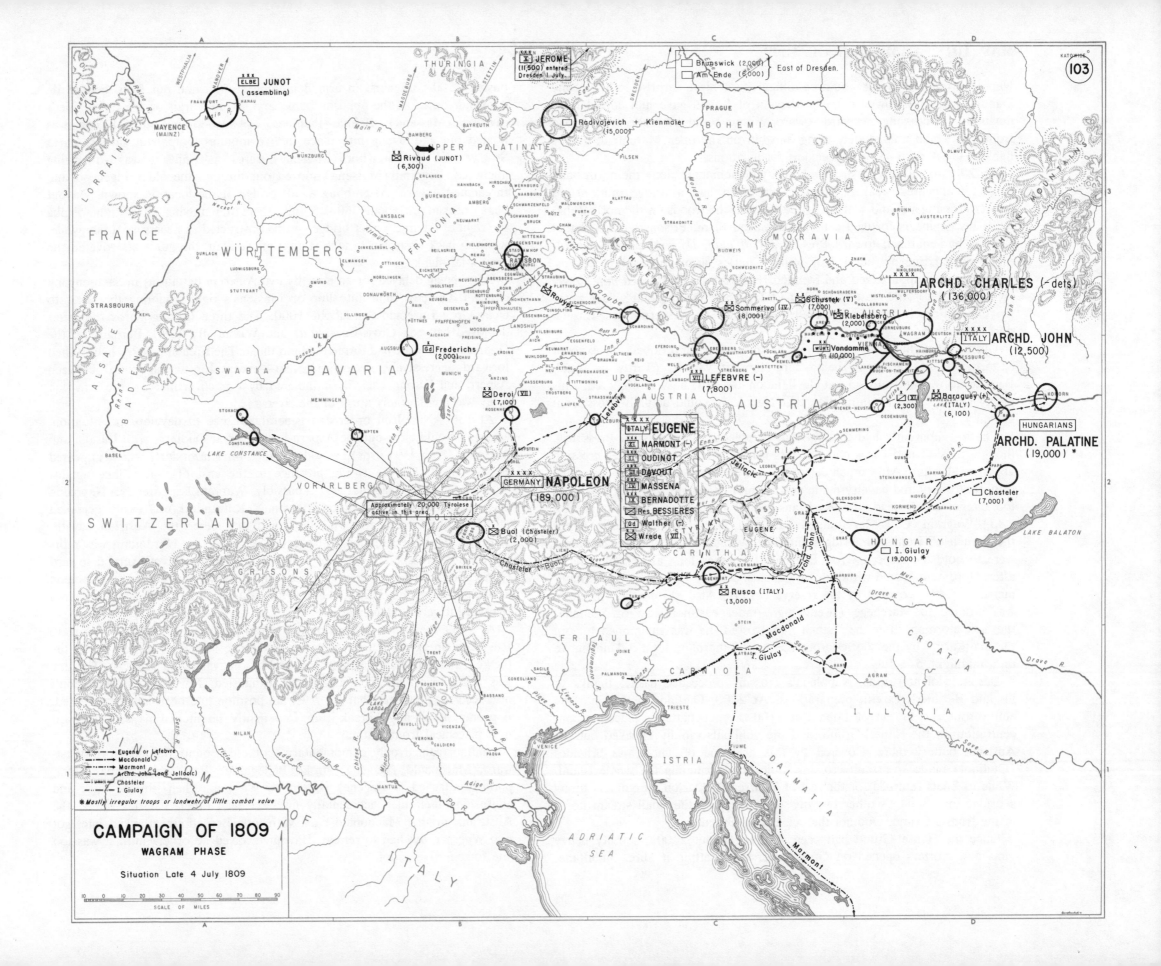

CAMPAIGN OF 1809

WAGRAM PHASE

Situation Late 4 July 1809

Napoleon realized that it would be difficult to achieve surprise in his second Danube crossing. However, the possession of Lobau gave him considerable flexibility. A crossing eastward toward Wittau could be made on a broad front and would immediately bring him out on the open Marchfeld, on the flank of the Aspern–Gross-Enzersdorf fortifications.

On 29 June, however, Austrian security detachments along the north bank suddenly appeared weaker. Puzzled, Napoleon had a bridge built at his former crossing site and sent a brigade to scout the woods on the north bank, while his engineers fortified a new bridgehead there. Prisoners claimed that Charles had marched toward Pressburg (off map, D1). Napoleon accordingly warned Eugene, but 1 July found Charles' army in its old positions. Napoleon thereupon seized and fortified Ile Bessieres (see boxed note, lower right) and the island west of Stadlau (B2), while shelling that village heavily. Other French batteries gradually beat down the Aspern–Gross-Enzersdorf defenses.

During the night of 3–4 July, troops began moving onto Lobau, the exposed eastern side of the island being carefully left vacant. (Tardy as usual, Bernadotte was still crossing at daylight on the 4th; he was observed, thus giving Charles his first intimation that Napoleon would actually cross from Lobau.)

Charles apparently had thought that Napoleon might cross at Pressburg, though his staff and corps commanders generally expected another crossing at Aspern-Essling. After much debate, it was decided that the French superiority in artillery and cavalry made any attempt to defend the river line itself too dangerous. Instead, the Austrians would occupy the line Bisam Hill (A3)–Wagram (C3)–Markgrafneusiedl (C2), thereafter maneuvering to cut the French off from their bridges and destroy them. Klenau and Nordmann were to hold the Aspern–Gross-Enzersdorf lines as long as possible; thereafter, Nordmann would withdraw on Glinzendorf (D2) and Klenau on Stammersdorf (A3), covered by the reserve cavalry. At 1900 on the 4th, John was ordered to Marchegg (twenty-eight miles east-northeast of Vienna); the next morning, after the French had crossed, he was summoned to join the main army by the shortest route. Ever the marplot, John did not move until midnight, 5–6 July.

Despite violent storms, Napoleon's crossing proceeded easily, thanks to his and Berthier's careful preparations. At 2000, Oudinot moved into the empty southeast corner of Lobau; at 2100, French batteries placed a concentration on the Hansel-Grund, and the gunboats rapidly knocked out the Austrian battery there. Covered by this fire, one of Tharreau's brigades (Oudinot) made an assault crossing, quickly overrunning the whole island. While its boats returned for the rest of Tharreau's division, pontoniers threw a bridge for Oudinot's other two divisions. Bridging the small stream north of the Hansel-Grund, Oudinot then cleared Mühlleuten.

Once the Hansel-Grund had been secured (about 2300), seventy heavy guns and mortars opened on Gross-Enzersdorf, setting it afire. Simultane-

ously, 1,500 voltigeurs, in armed landing craft, came out from behind Ile Alexandre, cleared the opposite bank, and set up a trail bridge for Boudet's division (Massena). Behind them, a 179-yard-long ponton bridge was floated out and swung into place in five minutes. Napoleon started Carra St.-Cyr and Molitor (both Massena) across it while it was still being anchored. Legrand (Massena) moved out through the old bridgehead and threatened Aspern. Assembling a raft bridge at the location shown, Davout began crossing at about 0600, 5 July, thereafter moving on Wittau to take the right of the line. Other bridges were constructed as necessary. Meanwhile, working back upstream to take station off Stadlau, the gunboats covered the army's left flank.

After being delayed for an hour by two Austrian battalions in Sachsengang chateau, Oudinot came into line on Massena's right, enabling the latter to clear Gross-Enzersdorf at about 1000. The three leading corps thereafter deployed between Gross-Enzersdorf and Wittau. By 1230, Bernadotte, the Guard, and Eugene had formed behind them. The French cavalry had pushed forward aggressively, discovering that—except for a rear guard between Aspern and Essling (heavily hammered by French artillery)—the Austrian army was considerably north of the river.

At 1300, Napoleon ordered a general advance to develop the situation. Massena would clear out the Aspern-Essling area; Oudinot, with Lasalle and Marulaz (both IV Corps), would advance on Rutzendorf, which appeared strongly held; Davout would advance to the east of that village against "Prince Charles' headquarters" (possibly Wagram; apparently, Napoleon originally intended to pivot on Massena). Rutzendorf was easily occupied at 1400, but Lasalle and Marulaz could not pierce the Austrian cavalry screen, leaving the situation still obscure. Finding that Nordmann was retiring toward Grosshofen, Oudinot followed him, while Davout turned toward Glinzendorf. This opened a gap between Massena and Oudinot; Napoleon accordingly sent first Bernadotte and then Eugene into it. Klenau scampered rearward toward Stammersdorf.

At 1800, the army was well placed for an attack on the Wagram plateau. Russbach Brook, to its front, was no obstacle to infantry but, because of the thickets along its course, almost impassible to cavalry and artillery. The day was nearly over; the men and horses exhausted. Nevertheless, Napoleon's practiced eye could see that the Austrian position had been hastily occupied. A prompt attack might break it up. Impatiently, he pitched his corps forward in a piecemeal frontal attack.

Oudinot gained only a momentary foothold around Baumersdorf. Westward, Macdonald (Eugene) broke Bellegarde's line, while Dupas (temporarily attached to Eugene) penetrated Wagram. Then—in the dusk and confusion—their men accidentally fired on each other. Charles rallied the Austrians, driving Macdonald back with loss. Bernadotte attacked late, got into Wagram, but had to retreat. Davout received no orders until it was too late for effective action.

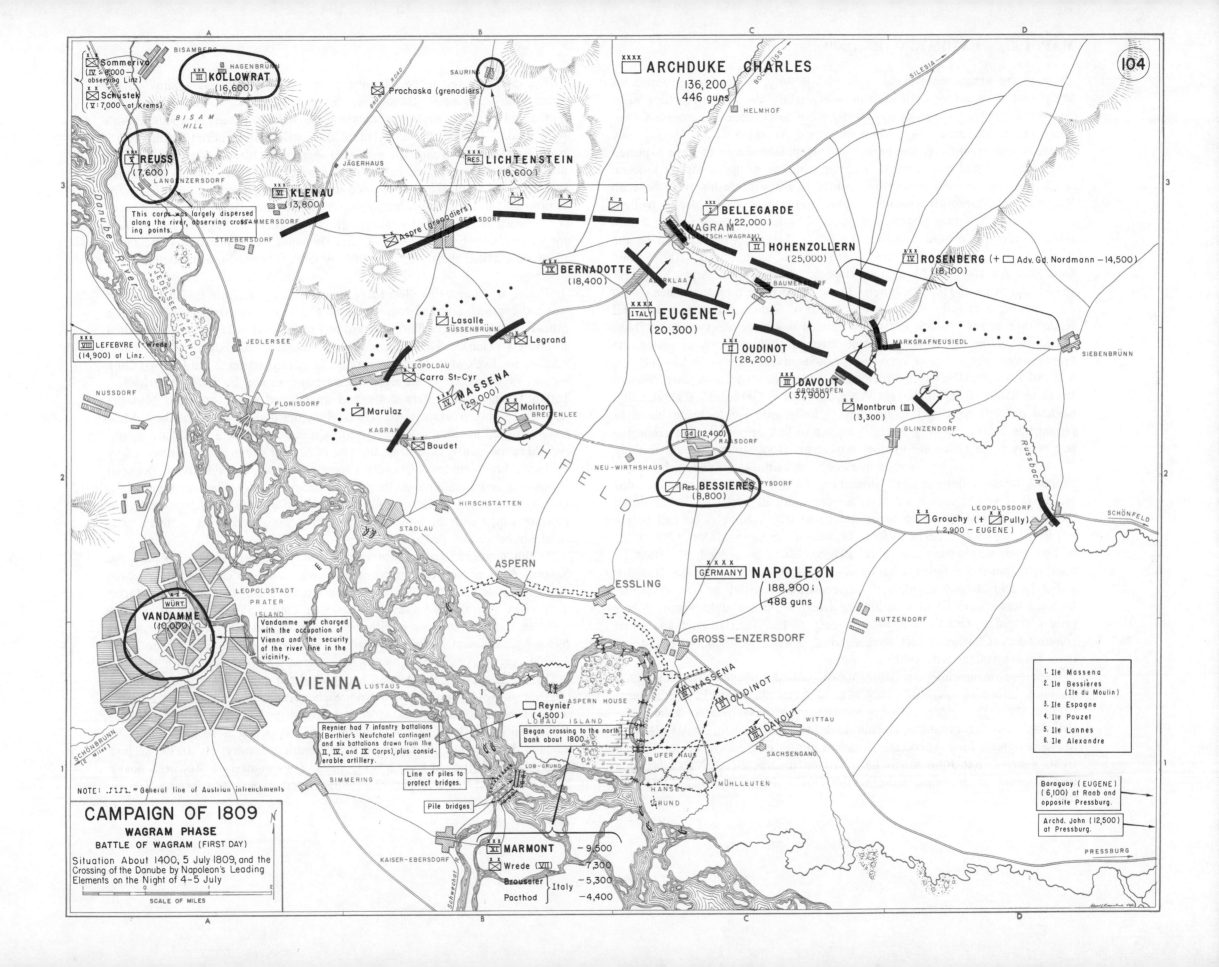

104

Sommeriva (IV : 8,000 — observing Linz)

Schustek (V : 7,000 at Krems)

XXX III KOLLOWRAT (16,600)

HAGENBRUNN

BISAMBERG

BISAM HILL

XX Prochaska (grenadiers)

SAURIN

XXXX ARCHDUKE CHARLES (136,200 446 guns)

SILESIA

BOCKFLIES

HELMHOF

X V REUSS (7,600)
LANGENZERSDORF

This corp was largely dispersed along the river, observing crossing points.

JÄGERHAUS

RES LICHTENSTEIN (18,600)

XXX V KLENAU (13,800)

HAMMERSDORF

STREBERSDORF

XX Aspre (grenadiers)

XX XX

GERASDORF

XXX I BELLEGARDE (22,000)

WAGRAM (DEUTSCH-WAGRAM)

XXX II HOHENZOLLERN (25,000)

XXX IV ROSENBERG (+ Adv. Gd. Nordmann — 14,500)

XXX IX BERNADOTTE (18,400)

ADERKLAA

BAUMERSDORF

XXXX ITALY EUGENE (-) (20,300)

XX Lasalle SÜSSENBRUNN

XX Legrand

XXX II OUDINOT (28,200)

MARKGRAFNEUSIEDL

SIEBENBRUNN

XXX VIII LEFEBVRE (-Wrede) (14,900) at Linz.

JEDLERSEE

LEOPOLDAU

XX Carra St-Cyr

IV MASSENA (29,000)

XXX III DAVOUT (37,900)

GROSSHOFEN

FLORISDORF

X Marulaz

XX Molitor
BREITENLEE

XX Montbrun (III) (3,300)

GLINZENDORF

NUSSDORF

KAGRAN

XX Boudet

Gd (12,400)

RAASDORF

RUSSBACH

STADLAU

NEU-WIRTHSHAUS

Res BESSIERES (8,800)

PYSDORF

HIRSCHSTATTEN

LEOPOLDSDORF

SCHÖNFELD

XX Grouchy (+ XX Pully) (2,900 — EUGENE)

ASPERN

ESSLING

XXXX GERMANY NAPOLEON (188,900; 488 guns)

RUTZENDORF

LEOPOLDSTADT PRATER ISLAND

WÜRT.

VANDAMME (10,000)

Vandamme was charged with the occupation of Vienna and the security of the river line in the vicinity.

GROSS-ENZERSDORF

VIENNA LUSTAUS

SCHÖNBRUNN

Reynier (4,500)

ASPERN HOUSE

MASSENA

OUDINOT

DAVOUT

WITTAU

1. Ile Massena
2. Ile Bessières (Ile du Moulin)
3. Ile Espagne
4. Ile Pouzet
5. Ile Lannes
6. Ile Alexandre

SIMMERING

Reynier had 7 infantry battalions (Berthier's Neufchatel contingent and six battalions drawn from the II, IV, and IX Corps), plus considerable artillery.

LOBAU ISLAND

Began crossing to the north bank about 1800.

UFER HAUS

SACHSENGANG

Line of piles to protect bridges.

Pile bridges.

LOB-GRUND

HANSEL GRUND

MÜHLLEUTEN

Baraguay (EUGENE) (6,100) at Raab and opposite Pressburg.

Archd. John (12,500) at Pressburg.

PRESSBURG

NOTE: [hatching] = General line of Austrian intrenchments

CAMPAIGN OF 1809
WAGRAM PHASE
BATTLE OF WAGRAM (FIRST DAY)

Situation About 1400, 5 July 1809, and the Crossing of the Danube by Napoleon's Leading Elements on the Night of 4-5 July

KAISER-EBERSDORF

XXX XI MARMONT — 9,500

XX Wrede (VII) — 7,300

Broussier — 5,300
Italy
Pacthod — 4,400

SCALE OF MILES

Through the unseasonably cold night of 5–6 July, Napoleon regrouped his army toward its center until its front was slightly less than five miles wide. His verbal orders to Davout apparently were to concentrate around Grosshofen (C2). Massena was to close in toward Aderklaa (C3), leaving only Boudet (4,600) to cover the French left. Napoleon seems to have expected that Charles would mass around Wagram, the key to the Austrian position.

Charles had, in fact, previously planned to concentrate his army between Wagram and Markgrafneusiedl. However, the failure of Napoleon's twilight attack on the Wagram plateau convinced Charles that the Austrian forces already there could hold it against the renewed assaults he expected on the morning of the 6th. He therefore ordered Klenau to march at 0100, 6 July, from Stammersdorf (A3) against Aspern. At the same hour, Kollowrat would march from Hagenbrünn (A3) on Leopoldau and Breitenlee (both B2), leaving a brigade on the heights north of Stammersdorf. Klenau's and Kollowrat's attack—which Charles estimated would develop at about 0400 —was thereafter to be pushed home through Essling "without giving the enemy time to recover." Lichtenstein would advance between Süssenbrünn and Aderklaa, first sending Prochaska's grenadier division against Süssenbrünn at 0300. (Charles thought Prochaska was at Gerasdorf [B3]; actually, he had not left Sauring.) Concurrently, Bellegarde would bring his right forward at 0400 from Wagram to Aderklaa to link up with Lichtenstein, the rest of his corps following up the movement. Hohenzollern would initially remain on the defensive; as soon as Bellegarde's attack developed, he would debouch through Baumersdorf. Rosenberg (whose command now included Nordmann) would attack whatever French were in front of him at 0400, to create a diversion for the main attack. At 0200, John (who had barely left Pressburg) was ordered to force his march via Leopoldsdorf (D2).

This plan was daring and ably designed. If it succeeded, it would be another Cannae; if it failed, Charles would probably be cut off from Hungary —but he had already decided, if unsuccessful, to withdraw into Bohemia. Its weaknesses were Charles' failure to assemble all available troops, John's proven stupidity, and the innate inefficiency of the Austrian staff and corps commanders. Charles' orders were delayed; Klenau and Kollowrat did not leave their bivouacs until 0400.

Napoleon, meanwhile, up before dawn, visited Eugene, Bernadotte, and Oudinot, informing them that they were to renew their attacks on the same front as the night before. (His intentions seem to have been to develop the situation before committing Davout and Massena.) Then, at 0400—with Massena approaching Aderklaa—a violent uproar broke loose on the French right. Fearing that John might have arrived unannounced, Napoleon rode to the sound of the guns, ordering the Guard, Nansouty, and Arrighi to follow.

The cause proved to be Rosenberg, attacking as ordered against Grosshofen and Glinzendorf. Davout was already in motion westward; now he halted and hit back, while Nansouty's horse artillery blazed into Rosenberg's right flank. By 0600, the badly mauled Austrians had retired behind Russbach Brook. Reinforcing Davout with Arrighi's cuirassiers and additional artillery, Napoleon ordered him to seize Markgrafneusiedl. Davout demanded two hours to mount the attack, since he would have to countermarch toward Glinzendorf to find a suitable crossing over Russbach Brook.

Napoleon then returned to Raasdorf (C2), where he began issuing orders for an attack by Eugene, Oudinot, and Bernadotte to support Davout. These plans were halted shortly before 0900 by news that the French left flank was in danger.

There, at about 0400, Bernadotte had suddenly decided that his position was too exposed, and had retired almost a mile east of Aderklaa. Bellegarde quickly swung his right flank forward to occupy that village, but then halted to await Prochaska. The latter appeared around 0730, but also hung back, waiting for Kollowrat. Massena arrived first. Injured on 2 July by a falling mount, he now rode in an elaborate carriage, drawn by four white horses. Instantly sensing that Bernadotte had abandoned a key position, Massena sent Carra St.-Cyr against Aderklaa. Momentarily, the attack stalled; Massena launched his shining vehicle into its midst and cursed it forward again. Aderklaa was swiftly recovered, but two of St.-Cyr's regiments—carried away by battle fury—advanced too far beyond it. Charles caught them between Prochaska and Lichtenstein, then burst back into Aderklaa on their heels, and soon regained it. Bernadotte now ordered an advance, but his Saxon infantry (apparently held too long in massed formation under artillery fire) suddenly broke and fled.

At this moment, Napoleon arrived, his very presence serving to rally the Saxons. After a brief conference with Massena, he ordered him to recover Aderklaa in order to anchor the French left until Davout's attack produced a decision. Nansouty's cuirassiers deployed facing Süssenbrünn to contain Prochaska; the Saxons were withdrawn to Raasdorf for reorganization. At 0945, Massena sent Molitor forward; his division (already reduced to some 3,000) carried Aderklaa in one swoop, thereafter organizing it for defense.

On the French right, Davout had completed his preparations at about 0930, clearing Austrian cavalry from Siebenbrünn, and placing his artillery so as to secure a cross fire on Markgrafneusiedl and the heights behind it.

On the other flank, Boudet lost his artillery when a reckless effort to enfilade the Austrian lines exposed it to Austrian cavalry. By 1030, he had been driven into the old French bridgehead. Thus unmasked, Reynier's heavy batteries opened fire, sweeping the plain around Aspern and forcing Klenau to keep his distance.

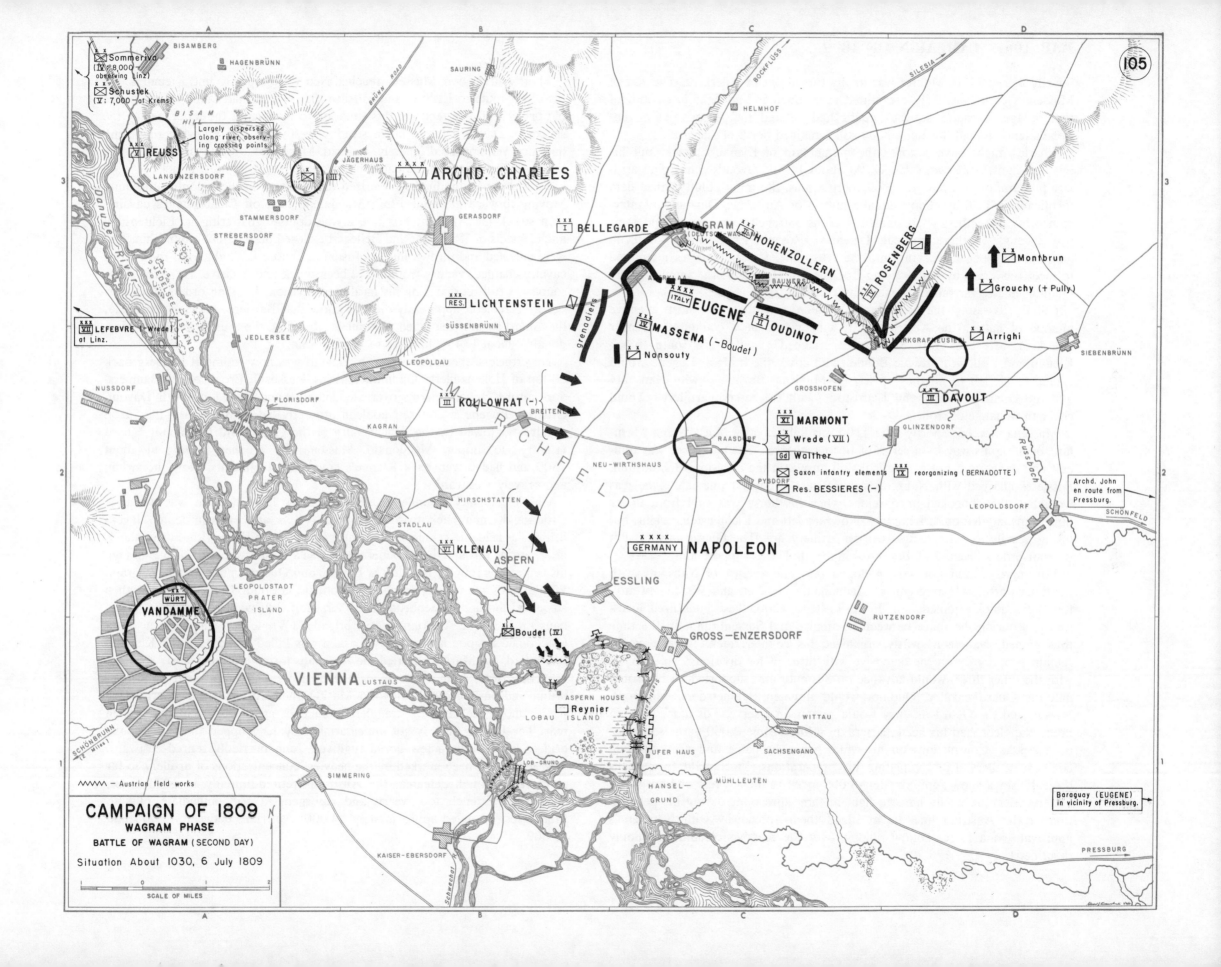

105

Sommeriva
(IV: 8,000 –
observing Linz)

Schustek
(V: 7,000 – at Krems)

Largely dispersed
along river, observ-
ing crossing points.

BISAMBERG

HAGENBRÜNN

BISAM HILL

SAURING

HELMHOF

BOCKFLUSS

SILESIA

REUSS

LANGENZERSDORF

JÄGERHAUS

ARCHD. CHARLES

STAMMERSDORF

GERASDORF

WAGRAM

HOHENZOLLERN

ROSENBERG

STREBERSDORF

BELLEGARDE

Montbrun

Grouchy (+ Pully)

LEFEBVRE (–Wrede)
at Linz.

RES. LICHTENSTEIN

grenadiers

ITALY EUGENE

OUDINOT

Arrighi

JEDLERSEE ISLAND

JEDLERSEE

SÜSSENBRUNN

MASSENA (–Boudet)

Nansouty

SIEBENBRUNN

NUSSDORF

LEOPOLDAU

GROSSHOFEN

FLORISDORF

KOLLOWRAT (–)

Danube River

BREITENLEE

III DAVOUT

KAGRAN

NEU-WIRTHSHAUS

RAASDORF

XI MARMONT

Wrede (VII)

GLINZENDORF

Russbach

Gd Walther

Saxon infantry elements IX reorganizing (BERNADOTTE)

Res. BESSIERES (–)

LEOPOLDSDORF

Archd. John
en route from
Pressburg.

HIRSCHSTETTEN

PYSDORF

SCHÖNFELD

STADLAU

GERMANY NAPOLEON

VI KLENAU

ASPERN

ESSLING

RUTZENDORF

WÜRT.
VANDAMME

LEOPOLDSTADT
PRATER
ISLAND

Boudet (IV)

GROSS-ENZERSDORF

WITTAU

ASPERN HOUSE

Reynier

VIENNA

LUSTAUS

LOBAU ISLAND

SACHSENGANG

SCHÖNBRUNN
(8 miles)

LOB-GRUND

UFER HAUS

MÜHLLEUTEN

HANSEL-
GRUND

Baraguay (EUGENE)
in vicinity of Pressburg.

SIMMERING

Schwechat

KAISER-EBERSDORF

PRESSBURG

~~~~ – Austrian field works

CAMPAIGN OF 1809
WAGRAM PHASE
BATTLE OF WAGRAM (SECOND DAY)
Situation About 1030, 6 July 1809

N

0

SCALE OF MILES

Shortly before 1100, Molitor was finally forced out of Aderklaa. The rest of Massena's corps was fully committed in a touch-and-go fight just south of that village. Klenau's advance guard had entered the Aspern-Essling entrenchments, though his main body still remained north of Aspern.

Charles might have restored the momentum of Klenau's attack, but his own left flank was now in danger. At about 1100, Davout's converging artillery preparation overpowered Rosenberg's guns. Storming uphill against field fortifications, held by almost equal numbers of Austrians, Davout's infantrymen drove Rosenberg's left flank out of its entrenchments and fought their way through Markgrafneusiedl. Defeating Rosenberg's cavalry, Montbrun and Grouchy began working into the Austrian left rear. Charles attempted to meet this crisis by withdrawing troops from Hohenzollern, against whom Oudinot had so far failed to exert any pressure.

Calmly assessing the situation, Napoleon saw that the most effective method of halting the Austrian right wing would be a counterattack near Aderklaa. Massena (with St. Sulpice attached) would turn south, block Klenau and Kollowrat, rescue Boudet, and cover the bridges. Eugene would extend to his left to fill the gap left by Massena. Bessieres (with Nansouty and the Guard cavalry) and Lauriston (with the reserve artillery) would cover this change of front.

Massena marched shortly after 1100, his light cavalry (Lasalle and Marulaz) opening his way by a series of furious charges. His maneuver was difficult and dangerous, but his tactical skill answered the occasion. Behind him, Bessieres charged with Nansouty's cuirassiers. Almost immediately, he was wounded, then knocked unconscious when his horse was shot from under him. Nansouty led on, driving in Kollowrat's left and Lichtenstein's right, but losing heavily to converging Austrian artillery fire. The Guard cavalry, left without orders because of Bessieres' injury, failed to support him.

Fortunately, Lauriston now galloped into line abreast of Nansouty with the Guard artillery (sixty guns). Macdonald's eighteen and Wrede's twenty-four guns quickly joined him. From 1130 to 1200, these guns fired incessantly, scouring the space between Breitenlee and Süssenbrünn. In the time thus gained, Napoleon swiftly organized his counterattack. Eugene would remain temporarily on the defensive with three of his divisions; Macdonald, with the other three, would advance on Süssenbrünn, supported by Nansouty and the Guard cavalry. Oudinot would threaten Baumersdorf. Marmont, Wrede, and the Guard infantry would remain in reserve. For more than an hour, Napoleon had his headquarters on a knoll some 2,000 yards southeast of Aderklaa. Conspicuous on his white horse, he came and went through constant artillery fire, completing his preparations. Macdonald formed his three divisions (now approximately 8,000 men) to the left rear of Lauriston's battery. Since he would have to fight in three directions during his penetration of the Austrian line, he arranged them—obviously with Napoleon's approval—in a large, hollow oblong (*not* the massive column commonly described).

Shortly after noon, Massena reached Neu-Wirthshaus to find Klenau across the direct route to Essling, and to learn that Boudet had taken refuge in the old bridgehead. He reported this situation to Napoleon; the latter, seeing the smoke of Davout's battle move steadily westward, and knowing that John had not yet appeared, merely ordered Macdonald to advance. Then he informed Massena that the battle was won, and that he must attack.

Lauriston had gradually pulverized the Austrian artillery confronting him. Moving forward at about 1230, Macdonald beat off Lichtenstein's cavalry, then struck the Austrian first line at the double, shattering it. Lichtenstein and elements of Kollowrat and Bellegarde closed desperately around him, but were defeated and thrown into confusion in a close fire fight. Had the French cavalry charged, victory would have been quick and decisive. However, Nansouty was still reorganizing his hard-used division. Lacking orders from Bessieres (Napoleon apparently did not know that Bessieres had left the field), the Guard cavalry remained motionless. Rallying, the Austrians halted Macdonald (about 1345), halfway to Süssenbrünn.

Nevertheless, the battle was won. Davout was now rolling Rosenberg back on top of Hohenzollern. Oudinot, crossing Russbach Brook below Baumersdorf, broke Hohenzollern's overextended line and linked up with Davout. Ordering Eugene to attack, Napoleon promptly fed in Wrede and the Saxon cavalry—followed by the light cavalry of the Guard and the Young Guard infantry—to support Macdonald. Massena had reached Essling at about 1300 and had driven back Klenau's advance detachments. Now, he swung aggressively westward.

Charles, slightly wounded, had realized by 1300 that he was defeated. Ordering Klenau back to Stammersdorf (*A3*) and Bellegarde to Hagenbrünn, he held his center tightly engaged to cover their withdrawal, thereafter retiring through them. Generally, it was a masterful performance, though his center was roughly handled as Eugene and Oudinot pinched out Wagram. Wrede and some cavalry reached Macdonald at about 1440. The latter then advanced through Süssenbrünn and Gerasdorf, but was checked near Jägerhaus (*A3*) by the Austrian reserve brigade. (Wrede had slipped away from Macdonald as soon as possible.) Lasalle was killed while pursuing Klenau's rear guard, but Marulaz harried the Austrians through Strebersdorf.

About 1600, John (though warned by Rosenberg) appeared at Siebenbrünn and pushed cavalry toward Markgrafneusiedl, creating a large-scale panic among the mass of stragglers, wounded, and foragers in the French rear. The French quickly got under arms; Reynier stopped the rush for the bridges by shooting a few dozen fugitives. John hurriedly retired eastward.

Wagram had been marked by the heaviest concentrations of artillery so far employed. Though defeated, the Austrians retired initially in good order, leaving the French too weary and disorganized for immediate pursuit. French losses totaled approximately 34,000; Austrian, between 40,000 and 43,000.

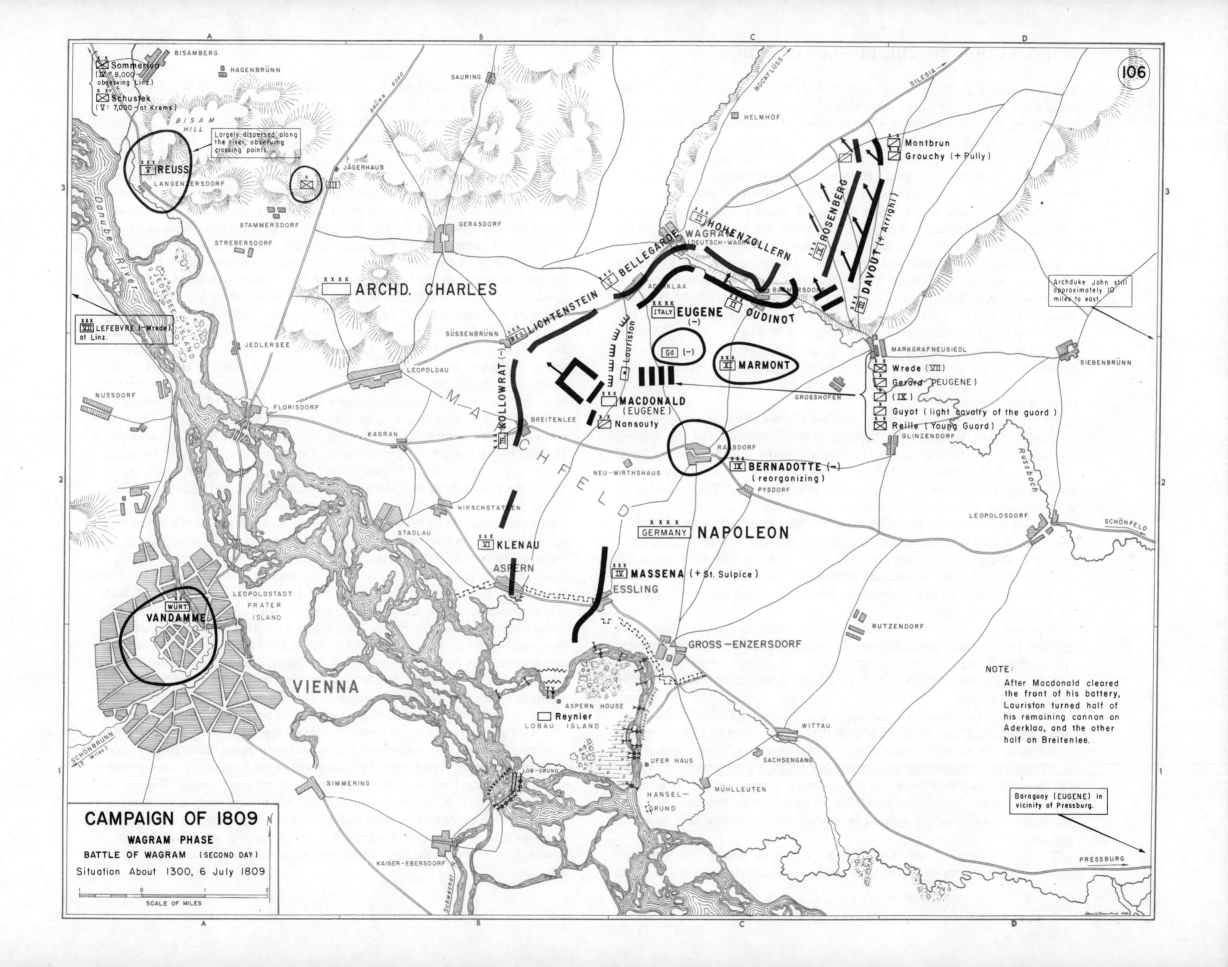

106

Sommeriva
(IX) 8,000 →
observing Linz.)
Schustek
(V) 7,000 at Krems

BISAM HILL

BISAMBERG

HAGENBRÜNN

Largely dispersed along the river, observing crossing points.

REUSS
LANGENZERSDORF

(III)

JÄGERHAUS

SAURING

STAMMERSDORF

STREBERSDORF

GERASDORF

BRÜNN ROAD

HELMHOF

BOCKFLÜSS

SILESIA

Montbrun
Grouchy (+ Pully)

ROSENBERG

HOHENZOLLERN

WAGRAM
(DEUTSCH-WAGRAM)

DAVOUT (+ Arrighi)

ARCHD. CHARLES

BELLEGARDE

LICHTENSTEIN

ADERKLAA

BAUMERSDORF

Archduke John still approximately 10 miles to east.

SÜSSENBRUNN

RES.

ITALY EUGENE (–)

Lauriston

OUDINOT

LEFEBVRE (–Wrede) at Linz.

JEDLERSEE

LEOPOLDAU

FLORISDORF

Gd (–)

MARMONT

MARKGRAFNEUSIEDL

SIEBENBRÜNN

Wrede (VII)
Gerard (EUGENE)
(IX)
Guyot (light cavalry of the guard)
Reille (Young Guard)

NUSSDORF

KOLLOWRAT (–)

BREITENLEE

KAGRAN

MACDONALD (EUGENE)

Nansouty

GROSSHOFEN

GLINZENDORF

STADLAU

NEU-WIRTHSHAUS

RAASDORF

BERNADOTTE (–)
(reorganizing)

PYSDORF

LEOPOLDSDORF

SCHÖNFELD

HIRSCHSTATTEN

GERMANY NAPOLEON

KLENAU

ASPERN

WÜRT.
VANDAMME

LEOPOLDSTADT PRATER ISLAND

MASSENA (+ St. Sulpice)

ESSLING

RUTZENDORF

GROSS-ENZERSDORF

WITTAU

SCHÖNBRUNN
(2 miles)

VIENNA

ASPERN HOUSE

Reynier
LOBAU ISLAND

NOTE:
After Macdonald cleared the front of his battery, Lauriston turned half of his remaining cannon on Aderklaa, and the other half on Breitenlee.

SACHSENGANG

MÜHLLEUTEN

UFER HAUS

HANSEL-GRUND

LOB-GRUND

SIMMERING

Baraguay (EUGENE) in vicinity of Pressburg.

KAISER-EBERSDORF

PRESSBURG

CAMPAIGN OF 1809
WAGRAM PHASE
BATTLE OF WAGRAM (SECOND DAY)
Situation About 1300, 6 July 1809

SCALE OF MILES

MARCHFELD

RUSSBACH

INTRODUCTION TO THE RUSSIAN CAMPAIGN

The Austrians initially withdrew in good order and morale, but an energetic French pursuit (though never quite able to bring Charles to bay) soon wore them down. On 10 July 1809, Charles asked for an armistice. Meanwhile, Eugene, reinforced by the IX Corps (now under Reynier, Bernadotte having been relieved for incompetence and insubordination) and Vandamme, cleared the country south from Vienna. Lefebvre countermarched on the Tyrol.

Francis, though now a refugee in Hungary, considered this armistice only as a chance to rebuild the Austrian Army and secure effective foreign intervention. For a while, he knew hope. The Tyrolese repulsed Lefebvre, and the British launched a major amphibious expedition against Antwerp.

A sudden stroke against Antwerp might have succeeded, but the senior British commanders were individually incompetent and mutually incompatible. Nevertheless, their appearance sowed confusion in Paris. Clarke (minister of war) and Decres (navy) lost such small wits as they had. Fouche (interior), seizing the chance to pose as the savior of France, energetically assembled troops and mobilized National Guard units, even in southern France and Piedmont. He entrusted their command to Bernadotte. By interfering with the regular army and navy commanders, Fouche produced complete confusion—possibly intentionally.

Knowing the unhealthy nature of the Dutch coast, Napoleon was not particularly alarmed. By telegraph, he directed the organization of the defense, but quickly found Fouche and Bernadotte unreliable, and therefore replaced the latter with Bessieres. The English captured Flushing with suspicious ease, but—their forces gutted by malaria—thereafter retired to Walcheren Island, which they evacuated on 23 September.

Meanwhile, Napoleon prepared his army for renewed hostilities. Austria could not match it, especially since much of the money and materials expended by Napoleon were appropriated from Austrian sources. Francis sullenly signed a costly and humiliating peace on 14 October, cynically betraying the Tyrolese, whom he had promised to protect. (Eugene completely pacified the Tyrol by early 1810.)

Napoleon now confronted the three basic obstacles to the consolidation of his rule: Spain, where popular insurrection and Wellington's army supported one another; Russia, technically still an ally, but plainly a treacherous one; and the state of his dynasty, which remained embodied in his own person, since he had no heir.

The Spanish problem appeared capable of prompt solution. Wellington's army was excellent, but small; without it, the Spanish could be brought to heel by the same antiguerrilla methods that had succeeded in Vendee and Naples and, against more formidable opponents, in the Tyrol. Furthermore, this army was England's last field force; its defeat should bring England to accept a Napoleonic peace. Napoleon turned this problem over to Massena, of all his marshals the one most experienced in independent command and mountain warfare.

The French Emperor hoped to keep the peace with Russia. Needing Alexander's support for his Continental System, he had put off with soft words all Polish pleas that he transform their semi-independent Duchy of Warsaw into a free Kingdom of Poland. This, Alexander insistently demanded that he promise never to do. Napoleon had already blocked the constant, lemming-like westward expansion of the Russian empire. But Poland had been the traditional keeper of Europe's eastern borders against Asian barbarism; worse, Poles could remember that Smolensk once had been a Polish frontier fortress.

As a countermove against Napoleon's influence in Poland, in 1810 Alexander pushed a propaganda campaign throughout the Duchy of Warsaw, urging the reunification of Poland under his own personal rule. Russian troops concentrated along the Duchy's eastern frontier, ready to advance if any sort of popular support could be aroused for Alexander's proposed client kingdom. No demand whatever developed, but the concentrations remained.

Also, there was the matter of Napoleon's second marriage. (Josephine, whom he had married in 1796, had given him no children.) To ensure the continuity of his dynasty, Napoleon needed a wife who could give him an heir. He suggested that one of Alexander's sisters might satisfy all requirements. Alexander temporized, and Napoleon decided to marry Maria Louisa, daughter of the Emperor Francis. Alexander chose to consider this a species of insult; moreover, the implications of a Franco-Austrian alliance shook him.

Finally, the Continental System bore increasingly heavily upon England and continental Europe alike. To tighten its enforcement, Napoleon annexed Holland (1810) and various minor north German states. The latter included Oldenburg, a minuscule principality, the heir-apparent of which had married Alexander's favorite sister. Alexander protested; Napoleon retorted that he would recompense the displaced ruling family, but would keep its territory. Alexander (prodded by his merchants) raised his tariff on French wines and opened his ports to "neutral" (actually English) shipping. England, desperate for allies, labored to capitalize on every Russian resentment against France.

In 1811, Napoleon's empire nevertheless seemed assured. In March, his young wife gave birth to the long-desired heir, the "King of Rome." But Napoleon was studying all available books on Russia, French garrisons remained in the Prussian fortresses, French troops quietly massed between Hamburg and Danzig, and spies came and went. As for Alexander, he had decided on war sometime early in 1810. Taught by defeat, he had decided to remain on the defensive militarily, but to employ diplomacy, subversion, and economic pressure aggressively everywhere. This threw the onus for any open hostilities completely onto Napoleon—hence the popular "historical" picture of a lovable, liberal Czar, subjected to unprovoked assault by a squat little Corsican bounder. Alexander also was considering peace with Turkey, and negotiating gingerly with England and Sweden. Bernadotte, now Crown Prince (and actual ruler) of Sweden, would join any alliance against France, if promised Norway. Napoleon remained oddly passive to these shifts, neither making a real effort to conciliate Bernadotte nor supplying the money and weapons needed to support Turkey's war effort. He did not want war with Russia, but, as before, the thrill of an impending campaign was beginning to grip him.

The Russian Campaign

"A man has his day in war as in other things; I myself shall be good for it another six years, after which even I shall have to stop." —NAPOLEON (1805)

"But when the Tsar of all the Russias, the commander-in-chief of three million horse-guards, foot-guards, life-guards and Cossacks, begins to talk sweetly of brotherly love, it is time for decent people to look to their guns." —HENDRIK WILLEM VAN LOON

"Understand that the foundation of an army is the belly. It is necessary to procure nourishment for the soldier wherever you assemble him and wherever you wish to lead him. This is the primary duty of a general." —FREDERICK THE GREAT

Through early 1812, the armies mustered, while last-ditch diplomatic missions scurried to and fro. Russia demanded exorbitant subsidies from England; Napoleon wrung auxiliary armies from Prussia and Austria. Prussia and Austria negotiated secretly with Russia and England. Napoleon still hoped his massive preparations might overawe Alexander. Alexander spoke nobly of peaceful intentions and abused friendship, but demanded that the French evacuate Prussia and Swedish Pomerania as the price of serious negotiations.

Napoleon had studied eastern Europe: Poland, Lithuania, and Russia were poor and thinly settled, incapable of feeding large armies; roads were few and primitive; the climate marked by violent extremes. An advance south of the Pripet Marshes (*B1–C1*) via Kiev (*D1*) would pass through the relatively rich Ukraine, but would threaten only Moscow (Russia's traditional capital), and must be based largely on Austria. An offensive from Königsberg (*B3*) through Tilsit (*B3*), Mitau (*B3*), and Riga (*C3*) must pass through difficult country, and would threaten only St. Petersburg (Russia's political capital). The traditional invasion route—Grodno (*B2*)–Vilna (*C2*)–Minsk (*C2*)–Orsha (*D2*) –Smolensk (*D2*)—offered a good axis of advance, securely based on Poland and threatening both capitals. The French intelligence service had located all major Russian units, except some in lower Volhynia (*B1–C1*), but had overestimated their strength, reporting that Barclay and Bagration together had 200,000 men.

Napoleon accordingly decided to strike through Kovno and Vilna with the major part of his army, hoping to catch and destroy Barclay in detail west of the Dwina River. Should all or most of Barclay's forces manage to evade his initial attack and mass to the south toward Grodno, Napoleon proposed to swing to his right and drive them into the Pripet Marshes. In the meantime, he initially would hold back his right flank to tempt Bagration to advance on Warsaw—or at least to stand fast. However, should Bagration begin withdrawing, Jerome was immediately to attack and fix him.

Eugene, though part of the main attack, was echeloned to its right rear, both to maintain contact with Jerome and to block Bagration, should the latter advance to the northwest. On Jerome's right, Reynier had a similar mission in respect to Schwarzenberg and Tormassov. Macdonald would threaten St. Petersburg, and seize Riga to provide the army with an advanced base. Oudinot would move generally north, once the Niemen was crossed, so that his advance would converge with Macdonald's, freeing the Niemen and Vilia rivers, and possibly trapping Wittgenstein. Schwarzenberg would cover the French right rear and be available to support Jerome.

A year's study of the logistical problems involved had convinced Napoleon that he must use the pre-Revolutionary system of depots and trains. Vast supplies were accumulated in Warsaw, Modlin, Plock, Thorn, Graudenz (*all A2*), Marienburg, and Danzig (*both A3*). The Navy provided special units to handle coastal and river craft. A large number of transportation battalions were activated, some of them specially equipped. Davout's corps was well supplied with food and transport. The other marshals, with less talent and opportunity, ended by stripping East Prussia and Poland to procure the required reserve rations. The principal line of communication would run from Königsberg to Labiau, then up the Niemen and Vilia rivers to Kovno and Vilna. (The Vilia proved largely unnavigable.) A second route would be by sea from Danzig to Königsberg, thence up the Pregel River to Insterburg.

After considering an assortment of plans, including diversionary operations in the Mediterranean and a pre-emptive invasion of Prussia, Alexander finally adopted one drafted by Phull, a refugee Prussian officer. Under it, Barclay would cover the main roads to the two Russian capitals. After meeting the first shock of the French offensive, he would retire slowly to the fortified camp at Drissa (*C3*). Theoretically, the French army would arrive before that camp considerably weakened by casualties and detachments left behind to protect its communications. It would then be forced either to attack Barclay's entrenched army or to retreat. Meanwhile, Bagration, reinforced by all available Cossacks, would strike into the French right rear. Tormassov would protect Kiev against a possible Austrian advance; if not attacked, he would move north.

This plan must have been based on the assumption that the reorganization of the Russian Army (begun in 1806) would give Alexander a numerical equality with Napoleon. However, the general inefficiency of the Russian government produced only some 420,000 men out of a paper strength of 600,000. (Barclay, for example, supposedly had 153,000 men; of his actual 127,000, several thousand Poles and Lithuanians promptly deserted.) The Drissa camp was so poorly located that it could easily become a trap. (Phull, a thorough pedant, seems to have intended it to fill the role of Frederick the Great's famous entrenched camp at Bunzelwitz in 1761.) Riga had been fortified, but the defenses of Dünaburg (*C3*), Borisov (*C2*), and Bobruisk (*C2*) were far behind schedule.

The Russian command was in a comparable state of confusion. Alexander insisted on leading his troops in person, but knew nothing of war and was suspected of personal cowardice. Bagration envied Barclay, and constantly intrigued against him—with the aid of Barclay's own staff, who hated their chief as a "foreigner."

By 22 June, through a generally overlooked feat of staff planning and execution, the French were massed along the frontier as shown. The next day, disguised as a Polish cavalryman, Napoleon selected his bridge sites. At 2200 that night, three companies of Morand's voltigeurs crossed the Niemen in boats. Behind them, Eble's pontoniers began assembling three bridges.

Note: On this map (and similarly on Maps 108–10), Nowo-Minsk (A2) should be Minsk Mazowiecki. Novo-Alexandria (A1) should be Pulawy (on this map and similarly on Maps 108–10, 115, and 119).

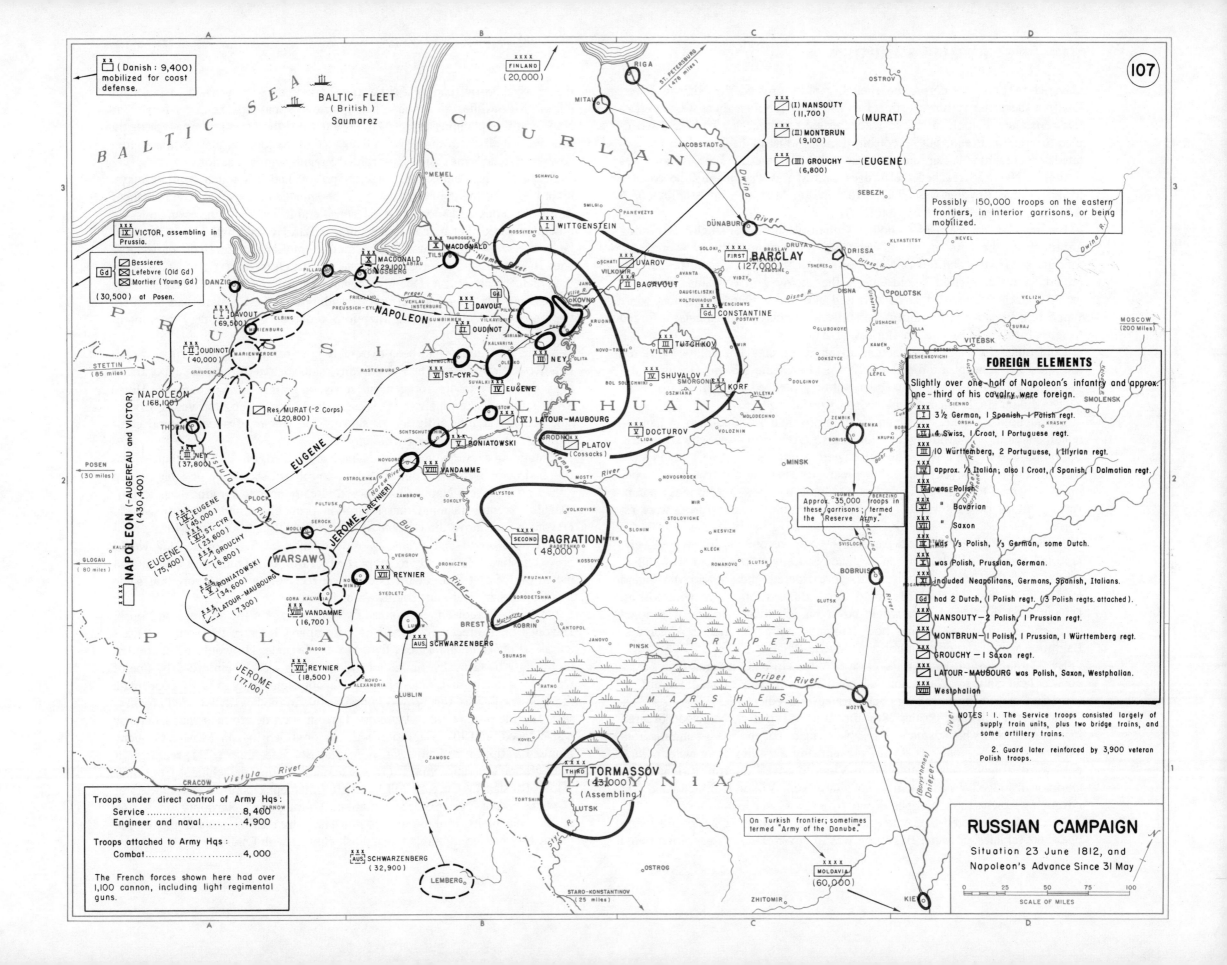

RUSSIAN CAMPAIGN

Situation 23 June 1812, and
Napoleon's Advance Since 31 May

107

Covered by Davout's corps, the French rapidly crossed the Niemen River, Oudinot thereafter turning north across the Vilia. Though there was no effective resistance, Napoleon moved with unusual caution. Ney had been scheduled to cross at Prenn, but Napoleon, deciding this might leave him too isolated, ordered him to the main crossing site. By late 24 June, Kovno was occupied, Ney had reached the bridges, and Murat was beating the country toward Vilna. Reynier was ordered to garrison Warsaw and Modlin (*both A2*), and advance toward Bialystok (*B2*).

Barclay did not learn of Napoleon's offensive until that night. Expecting an attack on the 25th, he already had issued his orders. Platov would concentrate at Grodno and attack Napoleon's right flank. "If circumstances permitted," Barclay himself would engage the enemy west of Vilna; if not, he would concentrate around Svencionys and offer battle there. Bagration, while supporting Platov, must conform generally to Barclay's movements; if forced to retreat, he should move via Borisov (*C2*).

Confronted by Napoleon's actual advance, Barclay immediately ordered the rearward concentration at Svencionys. (For some reason, Docturov did not receive these orders.) Alexander publicly pledged himself not to make peace while a single enemy remained on Russian soil.

Throughout 25 June, Napoleon—with more than 120,000 men in hand—remained cautious, awaiting developments. (According to Schwarzenberg, Bagration had begun a forced march toward Vilna on 17 June.) Macdonald was ordered to Rossiyeny (*B3*), Napoleon stressing the importance of opening the Niemen River as a supply line. Oudinot and Ney were to make a converging attack on Janow (*B3*), where considerable Russian forces were reported.

Janow was found empty on the 26th; Murat, reconnoitering aggressively, reported Barclay withdrawing on Svencionys. Only Wittgenstein was still in contact with the French. Napoleon therefore ordered Oudinot and Macdonald to deal with him. He himself would move directly on Vilna with Murat, Davout, and the Guard. Ney would cover his left flank; Eugene was urged to hurry his march. Knowing how ferocious noises impressed Alexander, Bagration was demanding authority to invade Poland.

By 27 June, Murat had pushed close to Vilna. Jerome, learning that Grodno was held only by Platov, moved on that town, and ordered Reynier to seize Bialystok. Schwarzenberg concentrated at Syedletz (*B2*).

Entering Vilna early on the 28th after a brief skirmish, Napoleon ordered its organization as his advanced base. Ney was to cut the roads running from Vilna north to Vilkomir (*C3*), to prevent any Russians from withdrawing northward; Eugene was summoned to Vilna to cover the army's right flank. Oudinot dislodged Wittgenstein's rear guard from Vilkomir. Macdonald was advancing slowly, though opposed only by a few Cossacks.

Barclay now ordered Platov to join him via Smorgonie (*C2*), burning supplies and vehicles en route. Bagration was to cover Barclay's south flank and the Minsk-Borisov road (*C2*); he and Tormassov were warned to maintain liaison. Meanwhile, Alexander's headquarters, apparently beset by fears that Napoleon was planning to cut Barclay off from the Drissa camp, repeatedly ordered Bagration to move via Vileyka (*C2*) to join Barclay, while Platov covered Barclay's movement and raided French communications.

Because of his cautious advance, Napoleon had lost touch with Barclay's main body. During the 29th, therefore, he launched energetic reconnaissances in all directions and soon amassed considerable information. From this, he quickly realized that he had overestimated Barclay's strength. Unfortunately, he confused Docturov (who had remained motionless, for lack of orders) with Bagration, and so ordered Jerome toward Oszmiana (*C2*). (That same day, realizing his danger, Docturov began a forced march to Swir [*C2*]). Also, Napoleon made the greater error of deciding that the Russians had no effective forces in Volhynia, and therefore ordered Schwarzenberg to Slonim (*C2*).

So far, the weather had been extremely hot and dry. On the 29th, it broke in a five-day rainstorm. The Russian dirt roads melted into mud; supply trains bogged; hungry troops foraged ruthlessly, angering the Lithuanians. Horse losses mounted alarmingly, and sickness developed among the young troops. The artillery could hardly move, slowing the whole advance. Lateral communications grew increasingly difficult.

Examining captured messages, Napoleon decided, on 30 June, that Bagration had not moved north until the 20th and that it should be possible to trap him. Jerome, whom Napoleon supposed already beyond Grodno, was to pursue him, keeping in mind that Bagration probably would retire on Minsk. Davout would move directly on Minsk to head Bagration off. Murat, reinforced by Morand and Friant, would advance on Svencionys. Ney would move on Murat's left, ready to support either Murat or Oudinot. (Eugene had halted on the east bank of the Niemen on receiving a false report that some 35,000 Russians were just southwest of Kovno.)

On 1 July, Napoleon reorganized Davout's corps for the advance on Minsk. Davout would directly command only Compan's infantry division, Valence's cuirassier division, and Pajol's light cavalry brigade. He would be supported on his right by Grouchy, on his left by Nansouty—each reinforced by one of Davout's infantry divisions. Though Davout supposedly was to coordinate these three columns, this proved impracticable in the heavily wooded countryside. Moving promptly on Oszmiana, Davout soon determined that Docturov had escaped, and that Bagration was rumored retiring on Minsk. Grouchy repulsed a Russian column (*not shown*) at Bol Solechniki (*C2*), reporting it as Bagration's advance guard. (It was actually a stray detachment from Shuvalov's Russian IV Corps.) Still hoping to intercept Docturov and careless of Davout's increasingly exposed situation, Murat pulled Nansouty off to the north. That night, Murat reported the Russians retiring toward the Dwina River. Ney had been unable to establish contact with Oudinot.

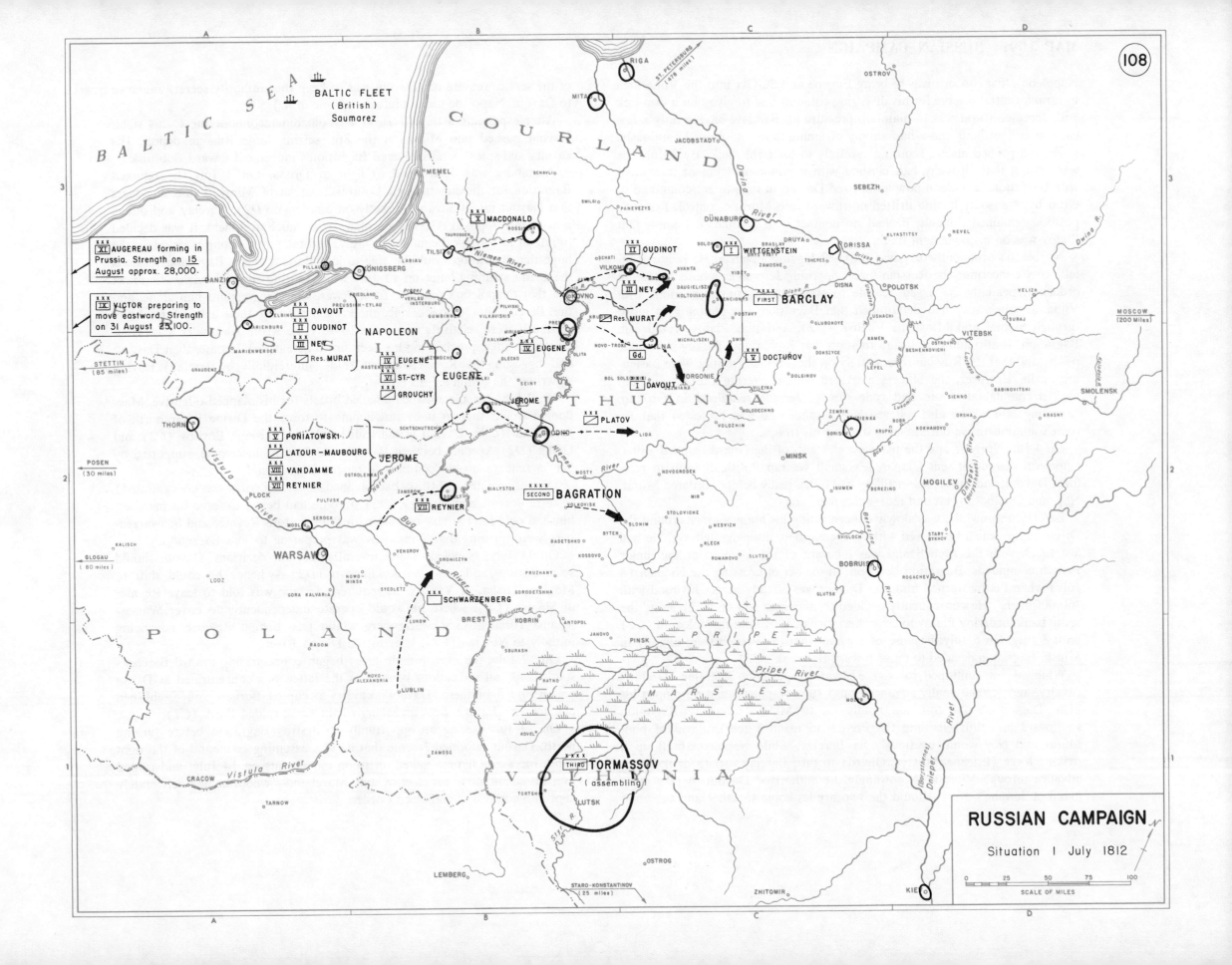

108

BALTIC SEA

BALTIC FLEET
(British)
Saumarez

COURLAND

XI AUGEREAU forming in
Prussia. Strength on 15
August approx. 28,000.

IX VICTOR preparing to
move eastward Strength
on 31 August 25,100.

MOSCOW
(200 Miles)

XXX MACDONALD

XXX II OUDINOT

XXX I WITTGENSTEIN

XXXX FIRST BARCLAY

XXX III NEY

Res. MURAT

XXX NAPOLEON

I DAVOUT
II OUDINOT
III NEY
Res. MURAT

NAPOLEON

XXX IV EUGENE

Gd.

XXX IV EUGENE
VI ST-CYR
GROUCHY

EUGENE

XXX I DAVOUT

XXX V DOCTUROV

LITHUANIA

JEROME

XXX PLATOV

V PONIATOWSKI
V LATOUR-MAUBOURG
VIII VANDAMME
VII REYNIER

JEROME

XXXX SECOND BAGRATION

XXX VII REYNIER

XXX SCHWARZENBERG

POLAND

PRIPET

MARSHES

Pripet River

VOLHYNIA

XXXX THIRD TORMASSOV
(assembling)

RUSSIAN CAMPAIGN

Situation 1 July 1812

N

0   25   50   75   100
SCALE OF MILES

Napoleon's first concern was to bring Eugene and St.-Cyr into the Vilna area to form a central reserve for his diverging columns and to give him a firm link with Jerome. Murat was to maintain pressure on Barclay; having only a few cannon and an hour-and-a-half supply of ammunition, he moved cautiously.

Davout pushed ahead, scouting carefully to his right flank. By 3 July, he was certain that Grouchy had clashed with a minor detachment instead of with Bagration. Napoleon now authorized Davout to take direct command of Grouchy, Nansouty having drifted northward into Murat's control. Davout's position remained difficult; he had no contact with Jerome, but knew that Platov was on his own right flank.

Napoleon's principal worry was Jerome's lagging advance. He required intelligence concerning the Russian forces opposing Jerome as a basis for future orders. Repeatedly, he urged Jerome to open lateral communications with Vilna. Jerome's staff had determined that Bagration was planning to move through Slonim and Minsk to Vitebsk (D2), and that Platov would join Bagration. It also had certain information that Russia and Turkey had made peace, and that the Russian forces lately on the Turkish frontier were hastening north. However, the officers entrusted with delivering this information took a roundabout route and rode slowly. Jerome remained in Grodno, "awaiting orders"; he also relieved Vandamme, who had protested that Jerome's administrative officers were starving his troops.

On 4 July, Eugene and the rearmost elements of the Guard reached Vilna. Napoleon thereupon sent Claparede's small veteran Polish division to reinforce Davout; and, since their artillery had fallen badly behind, ordered Murat, Ney, and Oudinot to rest and reorganize their units.

Barclay, meanwhile, was slowly concentrating his hungry army around the Drissa camp, which he viewed with an increasingly disenchanted eye. He had lost touch with the French and was ignorant of the location of the major French commands. Bagration had been in the act of crossing the Niemen (4 July) when Platov warned him that Davout was already across his road with "60,000 men." He consequently decided to march to Minsk (C2) along the south bank, ordering Platov to cover his movement by holding Volozhin (C2) until 8 July. On 6 July, because of a rumor that the French were already in Minsk, Bagration decided to move toward Bobruisk (C2).

While Murat continued to edge eastward, repeatedly defeating Barclay's cavalry, and Jerome finally advanced on 5 July, Napoleon had developed his plan. Davout should continue boldly on to Minsk, crowding Bagration southward and thus enabling the French to reach Vitebsk ahead of him. Murat and Ney would cautiously fix Barclay, while Napoleon built up a striking force (Eugene, St.-Cyr, Guard) to turn Barclay's south flank by an advance through Vitebsk. Accordingly, he authorized Davout to take command of Jerome's army, should the two armies come together and the good

of the service require it. (Davout was to keep this authority secret; unknown to Davout, Napoleon did not inform Jerome of it.)

After expending a day (7 July) at Volozhin reconnoitering to his right, Davout pushed into Minsk on the 8th, seizing large Russian depots. His cavalry and spies soon discovered Bagration's movement toward Bobruisk.

Alexander was determined to fight at Drissa. On 8 July, he rebuked Bagration for moving through Bobruisk instead of Minsk, expressing fears that Davout might advance directly on Smolensk (D2). Barclay and others now openly opposed Alexander's plan. After much argument, it was decided to retreat to Vitebsk, beginning 14 July, and take up a strong position, in the hope that Bagration would be able to join Barclay there. Bagration received the Czar's scolding letter on 11 July while retiring from Nesvizh. His retort was that "Napoleon's principal forces" were operating against him alone, and that Barclay should attack, since the French pursuing the Russian First Army obviously were relatively weak. On 13 July, he wrote Alexander a fire-and-slaughter letter, proclaiming his decision to defeat first Jerome, then Davout, and suggesting that Russia had been "sold" (inferentially, by Barclay). Having so written, he continued his retreat.

On 9 July, Napoleon issued detailed orders for his planned offensive. Macdonald would support it by threatening to force the Dwina River north of Jacobstadt (C3). Davout would shift northward through Borisov (C2) and Orsha (D2), keeping between Barclay and Bagration. Jerome, supported by Schwarzenberg, would continue to pursue Bagration.

Davout, isolated at Minsk, had planned (once his corps was concentrated) to seize Borisov and Mogilev (D2). Jerome had begun to force his marches, but had only intermittent contact with Platov. Both Reynier and Schwarzenberg were warning that Tormassov was preparing to join Bagration.

On 11 July, Napoleon made several important decisions. Davout should seize Borisov and move to Kokhanovo (D2)—whence he could shift to Mogilev, Orsha, or Vitebsk, as required. Jerome was told to leave Reynier at Slonim (C2), where he would operate independently to cover Warsaw against Tormassov. Schwarzenberg would pass behind Reynier, advancing initially to Nesvizh (C2), later to the Dwina River.

On 12 July, the French main army began concentrating toward Barclay's south flank, all indications being that the latter was concentrated at Drissa and would fight there. Davout's cavalry occupied Borisov and established contact with Jerome. Schwarzenberg's light horse raided Pinsk (C1).

On 13 July, seeing an opportunity to destroy Bagration before turning north, Davout informed Jerome that he was assuming command of the right wing. Incensed, Jerome halted all troop movements on 14 July, and turned over his command to his chief of staff, Marchand—whom he had deliberately kept in ignorance of Napoleon's orders.

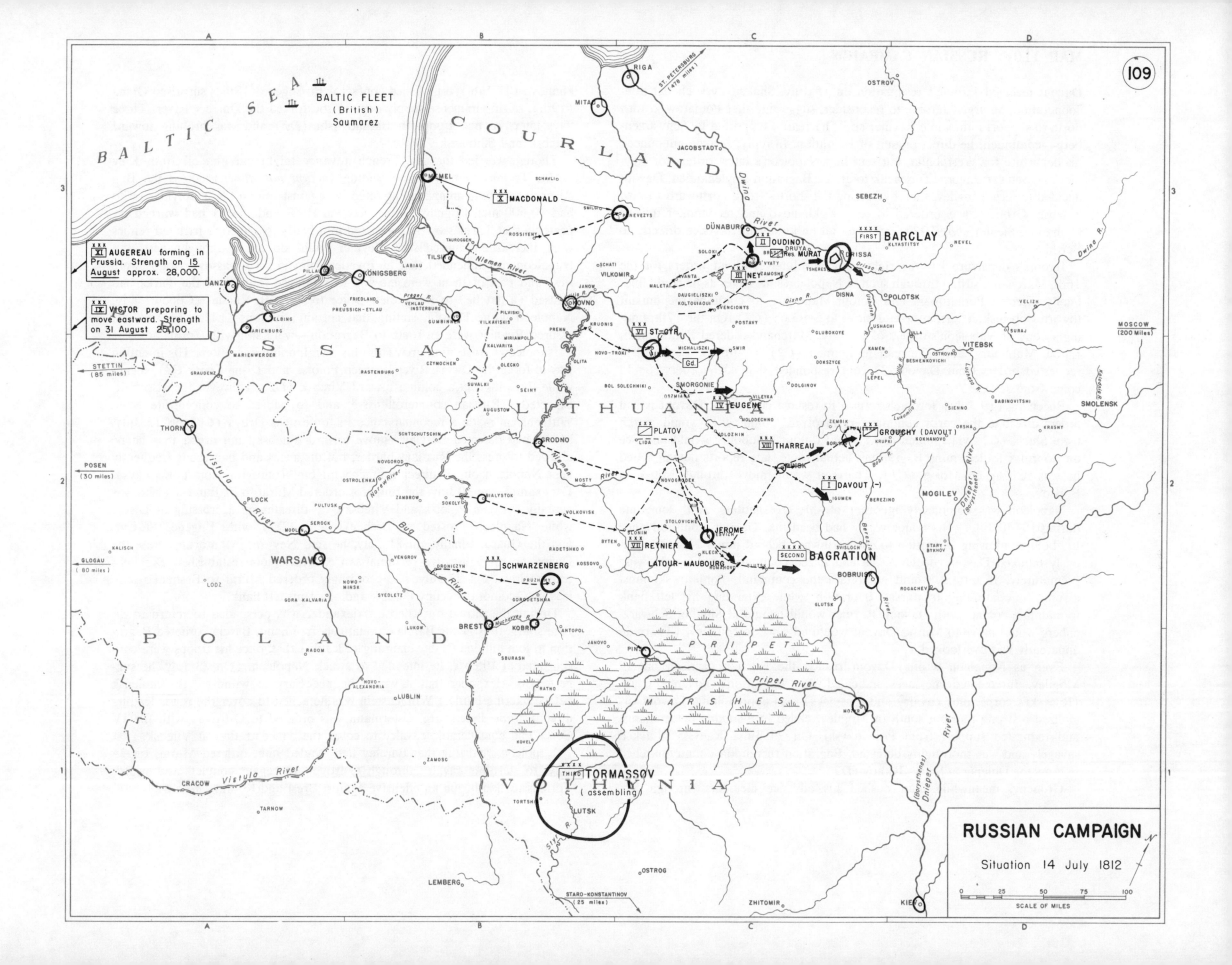

BALTIC SEA

COURLAND

BALTIC FLEET
(British)
Saumarez

109

RIGA

ST. PETERSBURG
(478 miles)

OSTROV

MITAU

JACOBSTADT

SCHAVLIO

SEBEZH

MEMEL

XXX
X MACDONALD

SMILUTO

NEVEZYS

DÜNABURG

Dwina River

KLYASTITSY

NEVEL

XXX
XI AUGEREAU forming in
Prussia. Strength on 15
August approx. 28,000.

XXX
IX VICTOR preparing to
move eastward. Strength
on 31 August 25,100.

TAUROGGEN

ROSSIENY

VILKOMIR

JANOW

KOVNO

XX
II OUDINOT
DRUYA
Res. MURAT

XXX
III NEY

VYATY
ZAMOSNE

SOLOKI

DRISSA
BARCLAY
FIRST

DISNA

POLOTSK

VELIZH

MOSCOW
(200 Miles)

TILSIT

Niemen River

LABIAU

PILLAU

KÖNIGSBERG

DANZIG

FRIEDLAND

PREUSSICH-EYLAU

Pregel R.

Vehlau

VEHLAU
INSTERBURG

GUMBINNEN

PILVISKI

VILKAVISKIS

MARIENBURG

ELBING

MARIENWERDER

STETTIN
(85 miles)

CZYMOCHEN

RASTENBURG

SUVALKI

OLECKO

SEINY

KALVARIA

MIRIAMPOL

PRENN

OLITA

KRUONIS

NOVO-TROKI

XXX
VI ST-CYR

Gd.

MICHALISZKI

SWIR

SMORGONIE

VILKOMIR

DAUGIELISZKI

KOLTOUIAOUI

SVENCIONYS

POSTAVY

VILEYKA

XXX
IV EUGENE

GLUBOKOYE

DOKSZYCE

DOLGINOV

KAMEN

LEPEL

VITEBSK

OSTROVNO

BESHENKOVICHI

SIENNO

BABINOVITSHI

SMOLENSK

THORN

GRAUDENZ

POSEN
(30 miles)

GLOGAU
(80 miles)

PLOCK

KALISCH

Vistula River

MODLIN

SEROCK

Narew River

OSTROLENKA

NOVGOROD

ZAMBROW

WARSAW

PULTUSK

LOOZ

NOWO-MINSK

GORA KALVARIA

RADOM

LUBLIN

NOVO-ALEXANDRIA

CRACOW

Vistula River

TARNOW

AUGUSTOW

GRODNO

BOL SOLECHNIKI

OSZMIANA

Niemen River

MOSTY

SOKOLYO

BIALYSTOK

SCHTSCHUTSCHIN

NOVOGRODEK

VOLKOVISK

STOLOVICHE

SLONIM

BYTEN

Bug River

Muchavez R.

SEROCK

VENGROV

SYEDLETZ

DROHICZYN

KOSSOVO

RADETSHKO

LUKOW

XXX
SCHWARZENBERG

PRUZHANY

GORODETSHKA

BREST

KOBRIN

ANTOPOL

SBURASH

RATNO

KOVEL

POLAND

LEMBERG

ZAMOSC

TORTSHIN

KOSZ

XXXX
THIRD TORMASSOV
(assembling)

LUTSK

Styr R.

STARO-KONSTANTINOV
(25 miles)

VOLHYNIA

OSTROG

ZHITOMIR

PLATOV

LIDA

VOLOZHIN

KOLOZHIN

ZEMBIK

XXX
VIII THARREAU

BOBR

XXX
I DAVOUT (-)

IGUMEN

MOGILEV

STARY BYKHOV

GROUCHY (DAVOUT)

KRUPKI

KOKHANOVO

KRASNY

Berezina River

BEREZINO

Dnieper (Borysthenes) River

XXX
VII REYNIER

LATOUR-MAUBOURG

JEROME

KLECK

NESVIER

SLUTSK

NOVOGRADEK

SECOND
XXXX
BAGRATION

SVISLOCH

BOBRUISK

ROGACHEV

GLUTSK

MARSHES

PRIPET

Pripet River

PINSK

JANOVO

MOZIR

KIEV

Dnieper River

Berezina River

RUSSIA

RUSSIAN CAMPAIGN

Situation 14 July 1812

N

0   25   50   75   100
SCALE OF MILES

Davout received Jerome's resignation on 15 July. Shaken by such flat non-cooperation, he urged Jerome to reconsider, suggesting that Poniatowski turn north to support him, while Reynier and Tharreau—supported by Schwarzenberg—continued the direct pursuit of Bagration. In reply, Jerome announced his departure for Westphalia, but sent him Napoleon's latest orders for Reynier and Schwarzenberg. Too weak to attack Bagration singlehanded, Davout decided to seize Mogilev, thereby barring the shortest road northward toward Vitebsk. Grouchy was ordered to seize Kokhanovo and reconnoiter toward Orsha and Sienno (both D2), reporting all important intelligence directly to Berthier.

Jerome's departure left the right wing absolutely without orders for the 16th. Marchand, sifting through such of Napoleon's messages as he could find, finally directed Poniatowski and Latour-Maubourg to continue the pursuit toward Bobruisk; Tharreau would move to Svisloch (C2). On the 17th, finding a copy of Napoleon's orders of 11 July, Marchand ordered Poniatowski, Latour-Maubourg, and Tharreau to Igumen (C2). Confused, Poniatowski requested orders from Davout; Davout responded that such orders should come from Jerome.

Receiving (19 July) Jerome's refusal to resume command, Davout issued orders direct to the corps commanders involved. Poniatowski would march from Slutsk (C2) via Igumen to Mogilev; Latour-Maubourg would advance on Bobruisk to determine Bagration's actual route, late reports having stated he was retiring on Mozyr (C1); Tharreau would move through Minsk to Borisov.

Napoleon was completely ignorant of this crosshauling until sometime during 19–20 July. (His major worry had been that Davout would advance too boldly, allowing Bagration to cut northward behind him.) Now, he furiously rebuked Davout, declaring he had seized command of the right wing prematurely. If Jerome would not retain the command, Poniatowski must assume it, continuing to pursue Bagration, while extending his left flank to maintain contact with Davout. Reynier would remain at Slonim, Schwarzenberg would move to Minsk; Davout would advance to Mogilev. (Tharreau apparently was overlooked.)

Even as Napoleon wrote, Davout rushed the Russian garrison out of Mogilev. Intercepted messages indicated that Bagration's advance guard (Raevski's corps, plus cavalry and Cossacks) was approaching. Davout organized a strong position south of Mogilev, called in available detachments, and requested support from Poniatowski. On 23 July, Raevski attacked savagely and was thoroughly defeated. Bagration thereupon countermarched to cross the Dnieper at Stary-Bykhov (D2).

Grouchy, meanwhile, had pushed his advance elements through Ko-khanovo (17 July); established contact with Eugene (18th); surprised Orsha (19th), seizing immense supply depots; and forced the Dnieper River. Three days later, he had troops in Babinovitshi (D2) and was probing toward Vitebsk and Smolensk.

Though worried that the French advance might cut him off from Kiev (D1), Tormassov now began raiding (action not shown) across the Bug River, threatening an impending offensive against Lublin (B1). Reynier (who had 10,600 men to guard a line between Brest and Pinsk) had warned repeatedly that Tormassov outnumbered him badly. Napoleon's irritated replies were increasingly unrealistic: Reynier could do as he thought best, but Napoleon recommended that he invade Volhynia; Tormassov's troops were raw, and part of them were moving to reinforce Bagration; the Turks had refused (a flat lie) to ratify their peace treaty with Russia. (Concurrently, Napoleon wrote Davout, stating that certain divisions—which he had just assured Reynier were en route to Bagration—were still with Tormassov.)

Napoleon's frustration grew from his own limping operations. His intention was to force the Dwina River between Polotsk and Disna (both C3), meanwhile throwing out a column toward Vitebsk (D2). However, he also half-expected a Russian counteroffensive, and so paused to concentrate when Wittgenstein made a reconnaissance in force near Druya (C3) on 15 July. Murat had detected Barclay's move toward Vitebsk, and urged that he be allowed to press the Russians harder, but distances and bad roads frequently kept Napoleon out of direct contact with him (once for almost two days). For example, on 20 July, the Emperor ordered Murat to fix Barclay (who was actually between Polotsk and Vitebsk) by threatening a crossing at Disna, while Napoleon crossed at Beshenkovichi (D2) with Eugene, St.-Cyr, and the Guard. Finally, on 21 July, he sent Ney and Montbrun across the Dwina on an aggressive reconnaissance, which soon established Barclay's true position. On 23 July, he accordingly ordered Murat to Beshenkovichi, leaving Oudinot to occupy Polotsk and cover his left flank.

During the retreat on Vitebsk, Alexander was persuaded to return to St. Petersburg, thus giving Barclay a relatively free hand. Barclay ordered Bagration to join him via Orsha, claiming (21 July) that, once his troops were concentrated at Vitebsk, he intended to attack Napoleon. (On 23 July, he suggested to Alexander that it would be necessary to withdraw to Smolensk before offering battle.) Wittgenstein was detached to cover the roads leading directly to St. Petersburg. Ostermann was ordered to Ostrovno with the IV Corps and considerable cavalry to cover the concentration at Vitebsk.

Napoleon, realizing that Barclay had evaded him, ordered Murat, on 24 July, to start his cavalry through Ostrovno to regain contact. Southward, Tormassov had begun an offensive against Brest and Kobrin (both B2).

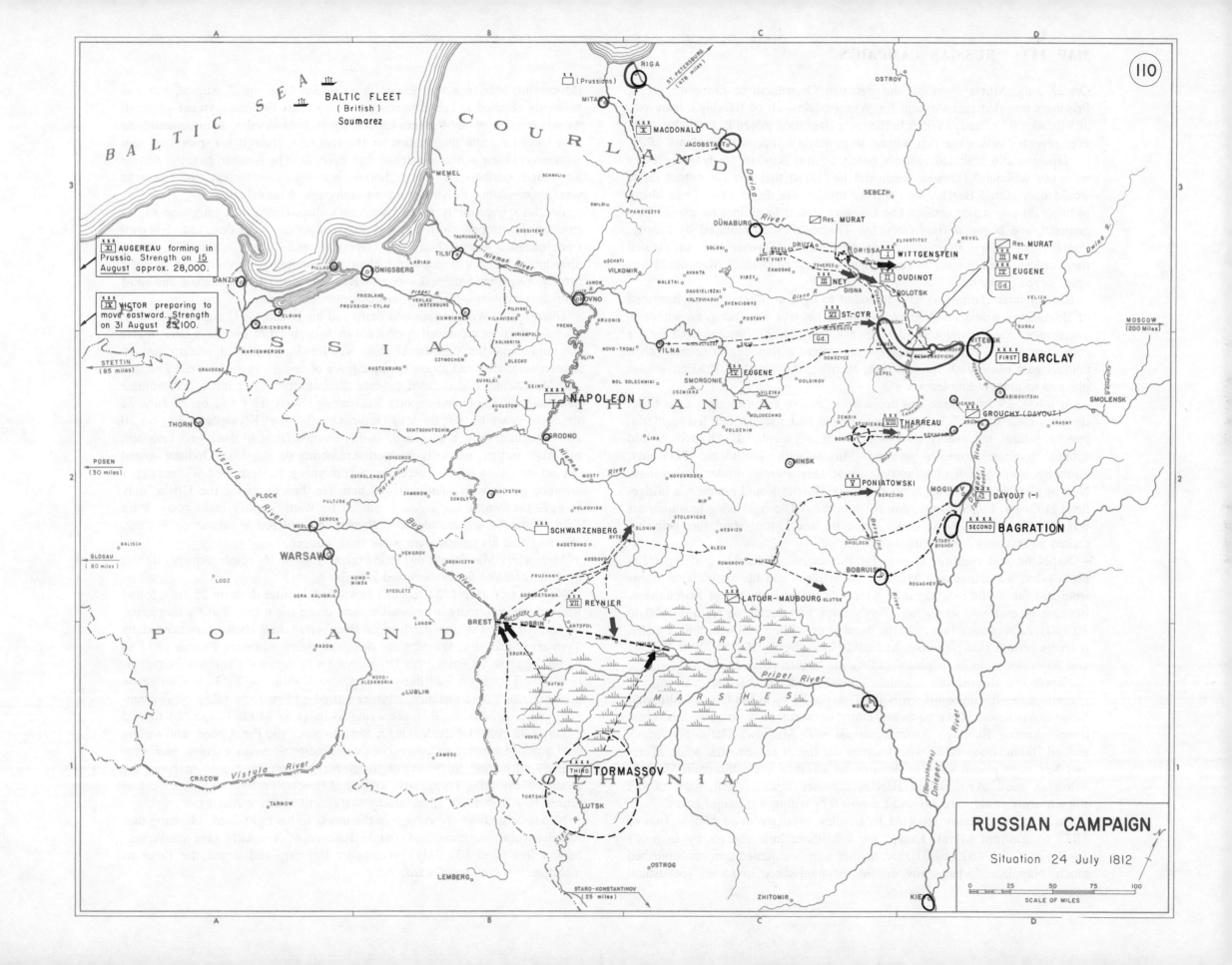

BALTIC FLEET
(British)
Saumarez

XXX
XI AUGEREAU forming in
Prussia. Strength on 15
August approx. 28,000.

XXX
IX VICTOR preparing to
move eastward. Strength
on 31 August 25,100.

STETTIN
(85 miles)

POSEN
(30 miles)

GLOGAU
(80 miles)

BALTIC   SEA

COURLAND

C O U R L A N D

RIGA

ST. PETERSBURG
(478 miles)

(Prussians)

MITAU

XXX
X MACDONALD

JACOBSTADT

MEMEL

SCHAVLI

OSTROV

SEBEZH

NEVEL

Dwina   River

DÜNABURG

Res. MURAT

DRISSA

KLYASTITSY

XXX
I WITTGENSTEIN

Res. MURAT

XXX
III NEY

XXX
IV EUGENE

Gd.

MOSCOW
(200 miles)

XXX
III NEY

XXX
II OUDINOT

XXX
VI ST-CYR

Gd.

VELIZH

SMOLENSK

XXXX
FIRST   BARCLAY

VITEBSK

TILSIT

Niemen   River

KÖNIGSBERG

DANZIG

PILLAU

FRIEDLAND
PREUSSICH-EYLAU

ELBING

MARIENBURG

MARIENWERDER

GRAUDENZ

THORN

VILKOMIR

KOVNO

VILNA

SMORGONIE

XXX
IV EUGENE

SMOLENSK

GROUCHY (DAVOUT)

XXXX
NAPOLEON

L I T H U A N I A

XXX
VIII THARREAU

GRODNO

MINSK

XXX
V PONIATOWSKI

MOGILEV

DAVOUT (-)

BOBRUISK

XXX
SCHWARZENBERG

WARSAW

Vistula   River

SECOND   BAGRATION

P O L A N D

Bug   River

Berezina   River

XXX
VII REYNIER

BREST

KOBRIN

XXX
LATOUR-MAUBOURG   GLUTSK

P R I P E T

Pripet   River

M A R S H E S

V O L H Y N I A

XXXX
THIRD   TORMASSOV

LUTSK

(Borysthenes) Dnieper River

KIEV

ZHITOMIR

LEMBER

CRACOW

Vistula   River

TARNOW

OSTROG

STARO-KONSTANTINOV
(25 miles)

RUSSIAN CAMPAIGN

Situation 24 July 1812

0   25   50   75   100
SCALE OF MILES

On 25 July, Murat overtook and defeated Ostermann at Ostrovno (*A2*). Prisoners revealed that—except for Wittgenstein—all of Barclay's army was at Vitebsk (*B2*), ready to offer battle once Bagration joined it. Grouchy, however, reported indications that Barclay soon would withdraw to Smolensk (*B2*).

Napoleon still hesitated to move boldly against Barclay, for his own forces were not sufficiently concentrated, and he feared that any premature move would only startle Barclay into further retreat. He therefore forbade Murat to bring on any major action. The Emperor ordered Oudinot to attack Wittgenstein, and began shifting Grouchy, Tharreau (soon replaced by Junot), Poniatowski, and Latour-Maubourg northward. (Davout had anticipated these orders, maneuvering to keep Bagration east of Orsha.) Macdonald was again urged forward.

Barclay later claimed to have intended to fight at Vitebsk, until informed of Bagration's defeat at Mogilev. Whatever his true intentions, he withdrew (*movement not shown*) toward Smolensk early on 27 July, covered by the rough terrain and Pahlen's competent rear-guard action. Murat re-established contact east of Vitebsk on the 28th, learning that the two Russian armies planned to unite at Smolensk.

At 0400, 29 July, Napoleon decided to "devote seven to eight days to let the army close up. . . ." Troops were to be put under shelter and fed regularly; reserve rations for twenty days were to be accumulated. All units would submit accurate strength returns. Murat—with Montbrun, Nansouty, Grouchy, and some light infantry—would keep Barclay under observation. Ney, at Lezno (*B2*), would support Murat. Davout would establish a bridgehead at Orsha; Eugene one at Suraj (*both B2*). The right wing headquarters was abolished, Poniatowski, Junot, Grouchy, and Latour-Maubourg being attached to Davout's command.

Napoleon had plentiful reasons for this pause. His army, and especially his cavalry, was exhausted. Much of his artillery and his ammunition trains were still far to the rear; some of Murat's cavalry were out of ammunition. Because of excessive straggling (Ney's corps had decreased from 37,800 to 20,700), he was uncertain as to the number of soldiers still with him. Finally, it seems certain that Napoleon had cold-bloodedly decided to allow Barclay and Bagration to unite, hoping that they might then risk a battle.

Napoleon's dispositions around Vitebsk indicate that he was already planning to shift southward, cross the Dnieper River in the Orsha-Dubrovna-Rosasna area, and strike eastward along its south bank to seize Smolensk, thereby cutting Barclay's communications with Moscow. The dense forests around Babinovitshi (*B2*) would screen his initial movements, while Murat and Ney were placed so as to threaten an advance along the main Vitebsk-Smolensk road. And, should Barclay advance against them, most of the French army could mass around Lezno (*B2*) within forty-eight hours.

On 1 August, Platov reported to Barclay, who stationed him at Inkovo (*B2*) to confront Murat. Except for a brilliant little success by Eugene's cavalry at Velizh (*B2*) on 31 July, neither army's mounted arm accomplished much. Napoleon forbade any distant reconnaissance in force. (Sebastiani

[Montbrun] rode to within fifteen miles of Smolensk on 2 August, but was promptly recalled.) The Emperor had forbidden the employment of small patrols because of the Russian superiority in light cavalry. Consequently, he now lacked definite information of the Russians, though his spies kept him informed of their general locations and strength. The Russian cavalry, despite its greater numbers and better horses, was highly inefficient; the Cossacks were accomplished hecklers but poor collectors of information.

Barclay's uncertainty as to Napoleon's dispositions was only one of his troubles. His troops, worn out and poorly supplied, were deserting. His own staff intrigued against him as a "German" and "traitor" who had tamely abandoned Russia's Polish and Lithuanian conquests. Any attempt to retire farther, giving up Smolensk—one of Russian imperialism's earliest and most cherished trophies—plainly would endanger his career.

Hearing that Wittgenstein had destroyed his Drissa (*A3*) supply depots on 25 July, Oudinot advanced northward on Sebezh (*A3*) two days later, under the impression that Wittgenstein was withdrawing. But Wittgenstein, though relatively isolated and aware of the danger of being caught between Oudinot and Macdonald, had decided to seize the initiative. (A panicky subordinate had destroyed the Drissa depot.) Evacuating Dünaburg (*A3*) on 27 July, he suddenly struck the left flank of Oudinot's column at Klyastitsy (*A3*) on 30 July. Oudinot, though surprised, swiftly formed front to flank and beat him off. After further, mutually inexpert scrambling on the 31st, Oudinot retired behind the Drissa River. There, the next morning, he destroyed Wittgenstein's advance guard, which had pursued him. He then recrossed the Drissa, only to have his own advance guard mauled by Wittgenstein's main body. With that, Oudinot's self-confidence collapsed; he ordered a retreat to Polotsk, claiming that his troops were weak from hunger.

Meanwhile, Macdonald did little except to whine for reinforcements. It was 31 July before he finally occupied Dünaburg.

Reynier (*see Map 115*) reached Janovo (*B1*) after dark on 25 July, found Russians unexpectedly in possession, and drove them out. Shortly thereafter, he learned that the tiny garrison of Brest (*B1*) had been overwhelmed by Tormassov's cavalry. Warning the Saxon regiment guarding Kobrin (*B1*) to be on the alert, he pushed for Drohiczyn (*A2*), but soon learned from fugitives that Tormassov had likewise captured Kobrin on 27 July. Calling on Schwarzenberg for assistance, Reynier retired on Pruzhany (*B2*). Schwarzenberg (then at Nesvizh [*B2*], preparing to move to Minsk) marched toward Slonim (*B2*) on 31 July, leaving a force to block the Pinsk road, and calling on Latour-Maubourg to cover Nesvizh. Finding Russian cavalry near Pruzhany, and fearing to be cut off from Warsaw, Reynier, too, marched for Slonim. Meanwhile, Tormassov, advised of Barclay's retreat to Smolensk, had retired to Antopol (*B1*), remaining there until about 9 August.

Napoleon was slow to recognize the threat to his right flank, claiming that Reynier was strong enough to contain Tormassov. He finally gave Schwarzenberg a free hand (31 July) to support Reynier, and urged the Poles to mobilize their National Guard.

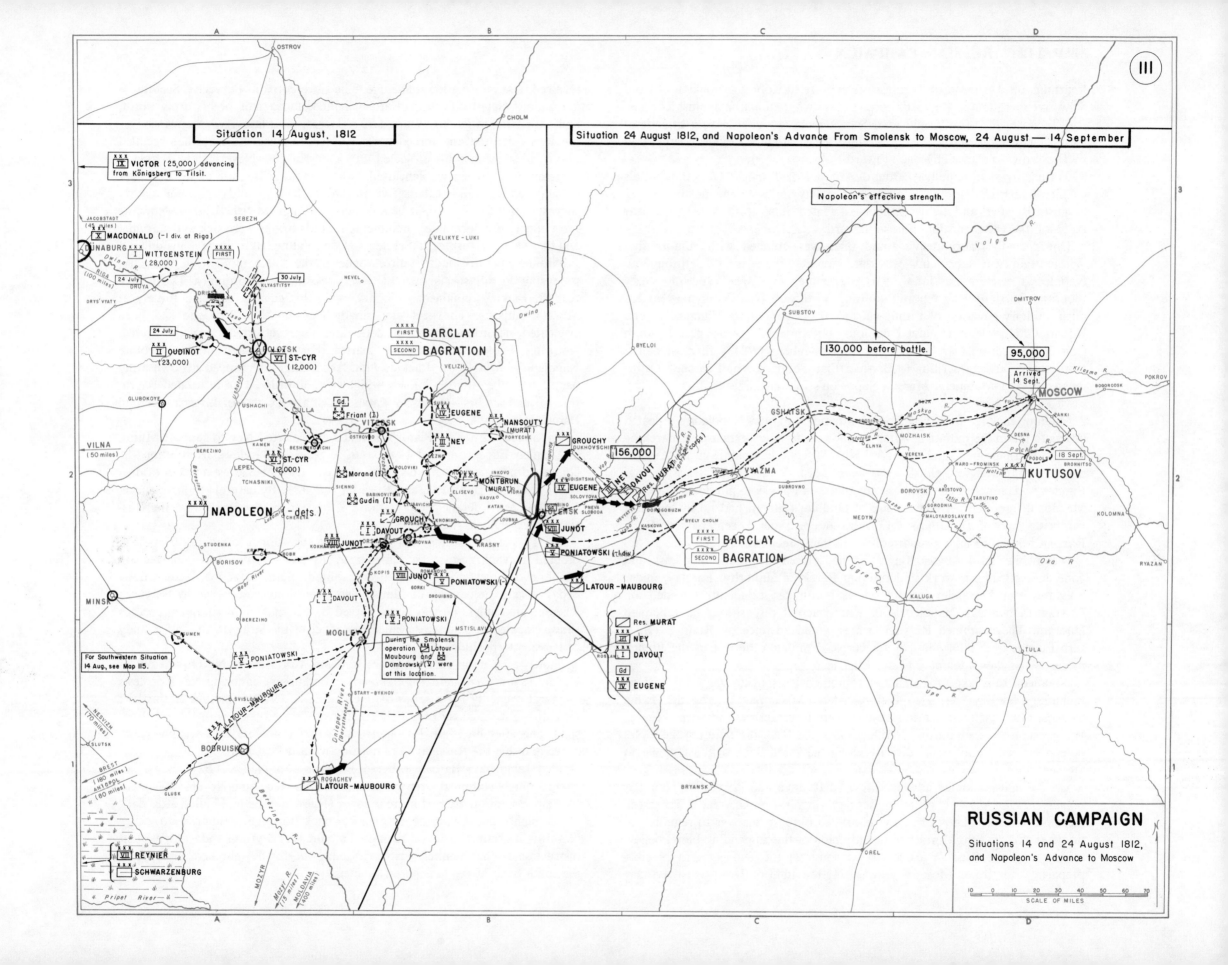

III

Situation 14 August, 1812

Situation 24 August 1812, and Napoleon's Advance From Smolensk to Moscow, 24 August — 14 September

XXX IX VICTOR (25,000) advancing from Königsberg to Tilsit.

OSTROV

CHOLM

Napoleon's effective strength.

Volga R.

JACOBSTADT (45 miles)
SEBEZH

X MACDONALD (-1 div. at Riga)

VELIKYE - LUKI

SUBSTOV

DMITROV

DÜNABURG
XXX I WITTGENSTEIN (FIRST) (28,000)
RIGA (100 miles)
24 July
DRUYA
DRYS'VYATY

Dwina R.
KLYASTITSY

NEVEL

VELIZH

BYELOI

130,000 before battle.

95,000

Kliazma R.

POKROV

30 July

24 July

VILNA (50 miles)

II OUDINOT (23,000)

XXX VI ST-CYR (12,000)

POLOTSK

Dwina R.

XXXX FIRST BARCLAY
XXXX SECOND BAGRATION

Arrived 14 Sept.

MOSCOW

BOGORODSK

GLUBOKOYE

USHACHI

Gd
XXX Friant (I)

VITEBSK

XXXX IV EUGENE

NANSOUTY (MURAT)
PORYECHE

GROUCHY
DUKHOVSHCHI

156,000

GSHATSK

MOZHAISK

Moskva R.

FILI

DESNA

BERESINO
KAMEN

VI ST-CYR (12,000)

XXX III NEY

VYAZMA

VEREYA

NARO-FROMINSK

18 Sept.
BRONNITSO

LEPEL
TCHASNIKI

Morand (I)

MONTBRUN (MURAT)

NEY DAVOUT
IV EUGENE
Res. MURAT

DUBROVNO

KUTUSOV

NAPOLEON (-dets.)

SIENNO
Gudin (I)

SMOLENSK

FIRST BARCLAY
SECOND BAGRATION

BOROVSK

Oka R.

RYAZAN

STUDENKA

GROUCHY
I DAVOUT

VIII JUNOT

MEDYN

MALOYAROSLAVETS

BORISOV

KRASNY

V PONIATOWSKI (1div)

KALUGA

MINSK

VIII JUNOT
V PONIATOWSKI (-)

LATOUR-MAUBOURG

TULA

I DAVOUT

DROUIBNO

V PONIATOWSKI

MOGILEV

MSTISLAV

Res. MURAT
III NEY
I DAVOUT
Gd
IV EUGENE

During the Smolensk operation Latour-Maubourg and Dombrowski (V) were at this location.

BRYANSK

For Southwestern Situation 14 Aug, see Map II5.

XXX V PONIATOWSKI

SVISLOCH
STARY-BYKHOV

Dnieper River (Borysthenes)

NESVIZH (70 miles)

LATOUR-MAUBOURG

BOBRUISK

BREST (180 miles)
ANTEOPOL (80 miles)

GLUSK

ROGACHEV
XXX LATOUR-MAUBOURG

OREL

MOZYR R.
MOZYR R. (115 miles)
MOLDAVIA (400 miles)

Pripet River

XXX VII REYNIER

SCHWARZENBURG

N

RUSSIAN CAMPAIGN

Situations 14 and 24 August 1812, and Napoleon's Advance to Moscow

10 0 10 20 30 40 50 60 70
SCALE OF MILES

Learning, on 2 August, of Tormassov's capture of Kobrin, Napoleon ordered Schwarzenberg to add Reynier's corps to his own, and march against Tormassov. To cover the army's right rear, Schwarzenberg would leave a brigade at Nesvizh (*off map, A1*); Davout would order Latour-Maubourg (supported by Dombrowski's division) back toward Bobruisk (*A1*).

Tormassov had remained around Antopol (*off map, A1*), though his cavalry had raided as far as Bialystok, ninety miles to the north. On 12 August, Reynier and Schwarzenberg defeated him at Gorodetshna, near Antopol, thereafter hustling him southward.

Unexpectedly, Tormassov's timid offensive—coupled with rumors that Wittgenstein was advancing westward—created consternation throughout Napoleon's rear area, as far west as Gumbinnen (*see Map 110, B3*). Sixty thousand Russians were reported pouring northward from Volhynia. Hogendorp, military governor of Lithuania, talked of abandoning Vilna (*C2*) and Kovno (*B3*). Victor remained dubious, but ordered cavalry patrols south from Tilsit. Loison marched hotfoot for Rastenberg (*B2*) with most of the Königsberg garrison, writing to Berthier that Tormassov had reached Ostrolenka (*B2*). Fortunately, Maret (Napoleon's foreign minister, then in Warsaw) kept his head.

Oudinot, now reinforced by St.-Cyr, attempted to obey Napoleon's repeated orders to retain the initiative. After a minor clash, much exhausting marching and countermarching, and a quarrel with St.-Cyr, he again, on 14 August, droopingly retired to Polotsk (*this map, A2*). Wittgenstein, learning that Barclay had launched an offensive, advanced on Polotsk to pin down Oudinot. Macdonald, though perfectly aware of Oudinot's plight, had no intention of venturing east of Dünaburg (*A3*), his interests being centered on Riga. Russian forces in Finland reportedly were being recalled.

Meanwhile, on 4 August, Bagration had closed up around Smolensk and gone energetically to work undermining Barclay's authority. Barclay, under pressure from Alexander and his own subordinates, reluctantly decided, on 6 August, to attack Napoleon—of whose actual dispositions he remained ignorant. The combined Russian armies would advance on Rudnya (*B2*), turn Eugene's left flank, destroy his corps, then catch the rest of the French piecemeal as they attempted to aid Eugene.

Napoleon fully expected that the combined Russian armies would attack him after a few days' rest. He therefore ordered Macdonald to cross the Dwina to assist Oudinot; Oudinot and St.-Cyr were to retain the initiative, keeping Wittgenstein from supporting Barclay. Once the Russians were checked, Napoleon himself would strike directly along the south bank of the Dnieper at Smolensk.

On 7 August, Barclay advanced toward Rudnya and Poryeche (*both B2; movements not shown*), ordering Bagration against Katan (*B2*). To screen these movements, Platov's heavily reinforced outpost line was to remain motionless until the 8th. Murat had no suspicion of this impending blow, believing most of the Russian armies to be south of the Dnieper and possibly preparing to retire on Moscow. But, during the night of 7–8 August, Barclay

received false information that Eugene had two corps in Poryeche. Scenting a horrendous Napoleonic trap, Barclay halted, faced half of his army north, and called Bagration to Widra (*B2*). He forgot Platov, who advanced as previously ordered and forced back Murat's outposts. Barclay then recalled Platov, to strengthen his projected attack on Eugene. Nevertheless, Barclay's aggressiveness (never wholehearted) was wobbling. Bagration, worried over the exposed Russian left flank (which Barclay had ignored), had maliciously suggested that Davout might be advancing through Mstislavl (*B1*). Now, he grew openly insubordinate, announcing that his troops were sick and starving, and that he was returning to Smolensk. Capitulating, Barclay gave his difficult subordinate permission to retire whenever the latter thought it necessary, promising to adjust his own tactical dispositions accordingly. During 11 August, Barclay remained stationary, while his cavalry fumbled futilely at Murat's outposts. The next day, finally learning that Poryeche had been evacuated, he ordered Platov to determine the exact direction of the French "retreat"—but suddenly became fearful that the French might celebrate Napoleon's birthday by attacking *him*. Accordingly, he moved his own army back astride the Vitebsk-Smolensk highway and ordered an infuriated Bagration to send his light troops to Katan and mass the rest of his army behind Barclay's left flank.

Napoleon, warned by Platov's advance, had alerted Ney to support Murat, and pulled Eugene toward Lezno (*B2*). Sensing Barclay's irresolution, he continued preparations for his own offensive. Davout had established bridgeheads at Orsha, Dubrovna, and Rosasna (*all B2*). By careful reconnaissance, he had amassed detailed information on the terrain, the roads, and the Russian forces south of the Dnieper.

On 12 August, seeing that Barclay was unwilling to attack, Napoleon ordered Davout across the Dnieper to Rosasna, while Junot moved on Romanovo. Murat, Ney, and Eugene shifted south, as shown, screened by Sebastiani's light cavalry division. There were only rumors as to Barclay's whereabouts; unless he was better served by his spies than surviving records show, Napoleon's plan was more the product of his intuition than of a study of Russian dispositions.

Shortly after noon on 14 August, Ney and Murat drove Neverovski out of Krasny (*subsequent action not shown*). Thereupon—ignoring Ney's protests—Murat excitedly led a series of uncoordinated cavalry charges against the retreating Russians. By hard fighting, Neverovski escaped with several thousand men after nightfall. Prisoners stated that Smolensk was weakly garrisoned and that the Russians were massing toward Poryeche.

That same day, Barclay ordered Bagration to Nadva (*B2*). Bagration complainingly complied, arriving after midnight. Receiving Neverovski's pleas for help, Bagration ordered his rear corps (Raevski, who had halted after dark about eight miles west of Smolensk) back through Smolensk to cover Neverovski's retreat. Raevski requested a cuirassier division and more explicit instructions. When neither was forthcoming, he finally marched, crossing to the south bank of the Dnieper at Smolensk.

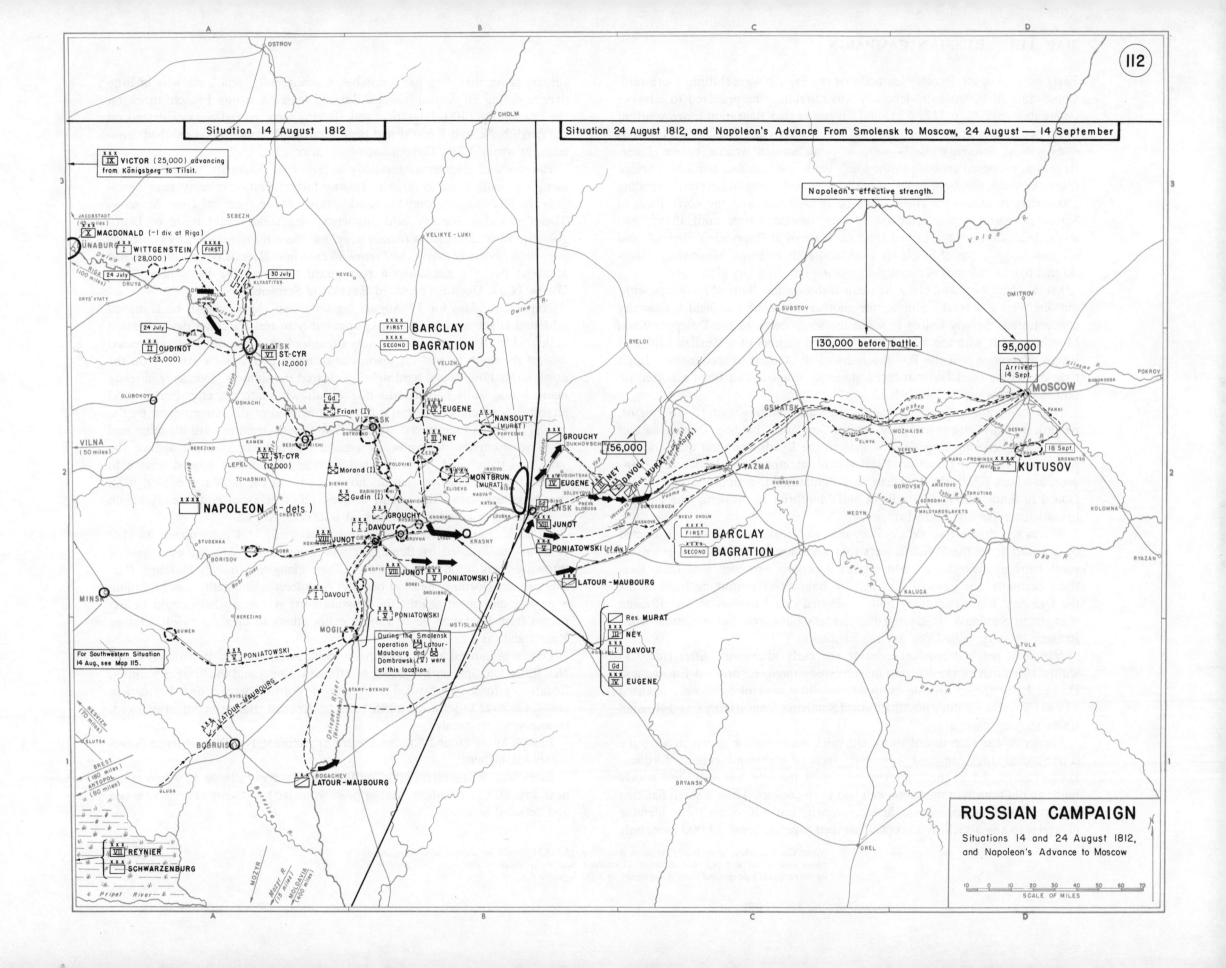

Situation 14 August 1812

Situation 24 August 1812, and Napoleon's Advance From Smolensk to Moscow, 24 August — 14 September

IX VICTOR (25,000) advancing from Königsberg to Tilsit.

Napoleon's effective strength.

130,000 before battle.

95,000

Arrived 14 Sept.

X MACDONALD (-1 div. at Riga)

I WITTGENSTEIN (FIRST) (28,000)

24 July

30 July

DMITROV

MOSCOW

POKROV

24 July

II OUDINOT (23,000)

VI ST-CYR (12,000)

FIRST BARCLAY
SECOND BAGRATION

18 Sept.

KUTUSOV

VILNA (50 miles)

Gd Friant (I)

VITEBSK

V EUGENE

NANSOUTY (MURAT)

GROUCHY

56,000

GSHATSK

III ST-CYR (12,000)

III NEY

IV EUGENE

III NEY

NAPOLEON (-dets.)

Morand (I)

MONTBRUN (MURAT)

VYAZMA

Gudin (I)

FIRST BARCLAY
SECOND BAGRATION

I DAVOUT

GROUCHY

VII JUNOT

VII JUNOT

V PONIATOWSKI (-1 div.)

LATOUR-MAUBOURG

MINSK

VIII JUNOT

V PONIATOWSKI (-1)

I DAVOUT

Res. MURAT

III NEY

I DAVOUT

V PONIATOWSKI

MOGILEV

During the Smolensk operation Latour-Maubourg and Dombrowski (V) were at this location.

Gd EUGENE

For Southwestern Situation 14 Aug, see Map 115.

BOBRUISK

V PONIATOWSKI

LATOUR-MAUBOURG

ROGACHEV

LATOUR-MAUBOURG

VII REYNIER

SCHWARZENBURG

RUSSIAN CAMPAIGN

Situations 14 and 24 August 1812, and Napoleon's Advance to Moscow

10 0 10 20 30 40 50 60 70
SCALE OF MILES

Early on 15 August, Barclay learned that the French were shifting southward. Concluding that Napoleon definitely was retreating, he prepared to advance on Vitebsk (*see Map 112, B2*), and suggested that Bagration move south of the Dnieper. Bagration, protesting that Neverovski's and Raevski's commands —as well as Smolensk itself—were in peril, wanted written orders. Later, Bagration proposed crossing to the south bank at Katan and building a bridge there. As usual, this bold project rapidly shriveled—Bagration merely sending a few cavalry across the river, while he himself followed the north bank to Smolensk. Barclay was reluctant to take drastic action until Platov had scouted farther west, but placed Docturov's corps at Bagration's disposal, and warned the governor of Smolensk to evacuate his archives. Meanwhile, Raevski had halted just west of Smolensk, retiring into that city after dark.

Murat (Nansouty and Grouchy) halted three miles short of Smolensk without discovering Raevski. Hoping for another battle, he had held his cavalry concentrated, thereby failing to scout the south bank of the Dnieper. When Montbrun (left with the main body) reported rumors of a Russian bridge at Katan, Napoleon sent the Polish lancers of the Guard to reconnoiter. Junot took the wrong road and wandered aimlessly. Eugene and Pajol reported no hostile contacts on the north bank.

Napoleon somehow turned hesitant. Just after midnight of 15–16 August, he ordered only Murat and Ney against Smolensk, holding Davout east of Krasny and ordering Eugene to remain in the Lyadi-Khomino area and improve the bridges at Khomino. Pajol was to attempt to locate Barclay. However, at about 0700, the Emperor sent Poniatowski, Junot, and part of the Guard to Smolensk, ordering Pajol and Montbrun to move up the Dnieper toward the reported Katan bridge.

Murat had driven Raevski's cavalry into Smolensk, but had been distracted by a report from the Polish lancers that a strong Russian force was on the south bank opposite Katan. Montbrun's approach, however, sent these Russians (actually, the cavalry detached by Bagration) swimming back across the Dnieper. Ney (*this map*) had committed one battalion to test Russian strength in Smolensk. It cleared the citadel's outworks, but withdrew when Russian infantry sallied out against its flanks.

Napoleon reached Smolensk during the early afternoon. After riding to within 100 yards of the Russian lines to study them, he ordered Eugene and Davout forward. An aide-de-camp, on a hilltop west of Smolensk, reported (1530) Russian infantry pushing toward Smolensk from Rudnya, and Russian trains shifting eastward.

Smolensk was surrounded by an old brick wall, outside of which were the conventional ditch, covered way, and glacis of eighteenth-century fortifications. The citadel at the southwest corner of the city was new, but poorly built; an old breach in the south wall had been converted into a small flanking battery. These defenses were in poor repair, but still offered considerable obstacles to any attack. Raevski had scraped together some 13,000 men, only slightly fewer than Ney had available. Consequently, Smolensk was in little danger during 16 August, though Raevski feared a strong French attack on the citadel. By 1700, Bagration and Barclay were partially concentrated on the north bank, and Raevski had been reinforced. Poniatowski reached Smolensk at about 1700; Davout sometime after dark.

Barclay and Bagration seemingly agreed that Napoleon would continue along the south bank to seize a crossing farther east—probably near Dorogobuzh, fifty miles beyond Smolensk—thus cutting them off from Moscow. Therefore, while Barclay held Smolensk, Bagration would retire to Dorogobuzh. Their actual ideas remain hazy, *but there is no trace of any conscious plan to deliberately decoy the French deeper into Russia.* Bagration marched at about daylight, detaching a rear guard to watch the fords near Shein Ostrov (*C2*). Docturov replaced Raevski in Smolensk.

Napoleon's plans for 17 August are unknown. About 1230, he launched a limited attack against Smolensk, apparently to test Barclay's determination to defend it. His assault was shrewdly organized, its main effort being directed against the south face of the town, out of reach of Barclay's artillery on the north bank. Four hours' hard fighting cleared the suburbs. Docturov, already mauled, was badly hammered while withdrawing into the city. Poniatowski almost carried one of the gates, but was thwarted at the last moment by the arrival of Eugen's reinforced division. The French seem to have made no real effort to storm the old walls, their main efforts being directed against the gates and the citadel. When massed French 12-pounders proved unable to breach the wall, Davout used his howitzers to set the buildings behind it on fire. Napoleon halted the assault at about 2000. Davout had already begun preparing for a coordinated attack at 0200, 18 August.

At 2300, Barclay ordered Smolensk evacuated. This precipitated another generals' mutiny, led by Bennigsen and Constantine, who accused him of throwing away a "glorious victory." Their clamoring merely stiffened Barclay's spine: Docturov had lost heavily; Napoleon undoubtedly was beginning a turning movement against the Russian First Army; no help could be expected from Bagration beyond more exhortations to fight for "Holy Mother Russia and the Czar."

Detecting indications of Docturov's withdrawal, Davout, Poniatowski, and Ney thrust into Smolensk at 0230, but found it empty and the bridges burning. Locating a ford, Ney hustled a column of Württembergers and Portuguese across the river to seize the north-bank bridgehead. Barclay counterattacked, furiously but fruitlessly.

French losses around Smolensk were approximately 9,000; Russian losses somewhat higher.

Elsewhere, Wittgenstein attacked Polotsk unsuccessfully on 17 August; the next day, St.-Cyr (Oudinot having been wounded) suddenly counterattacked and defeated him.

Note: On this map, Docturov's force in Smolensk (A2–B2) should be shown as a reinforced corps instead of a reinforced division. (Docturov had three infantry divisions, the survivors of Neverovski's command, and a regiment of light infantry.)

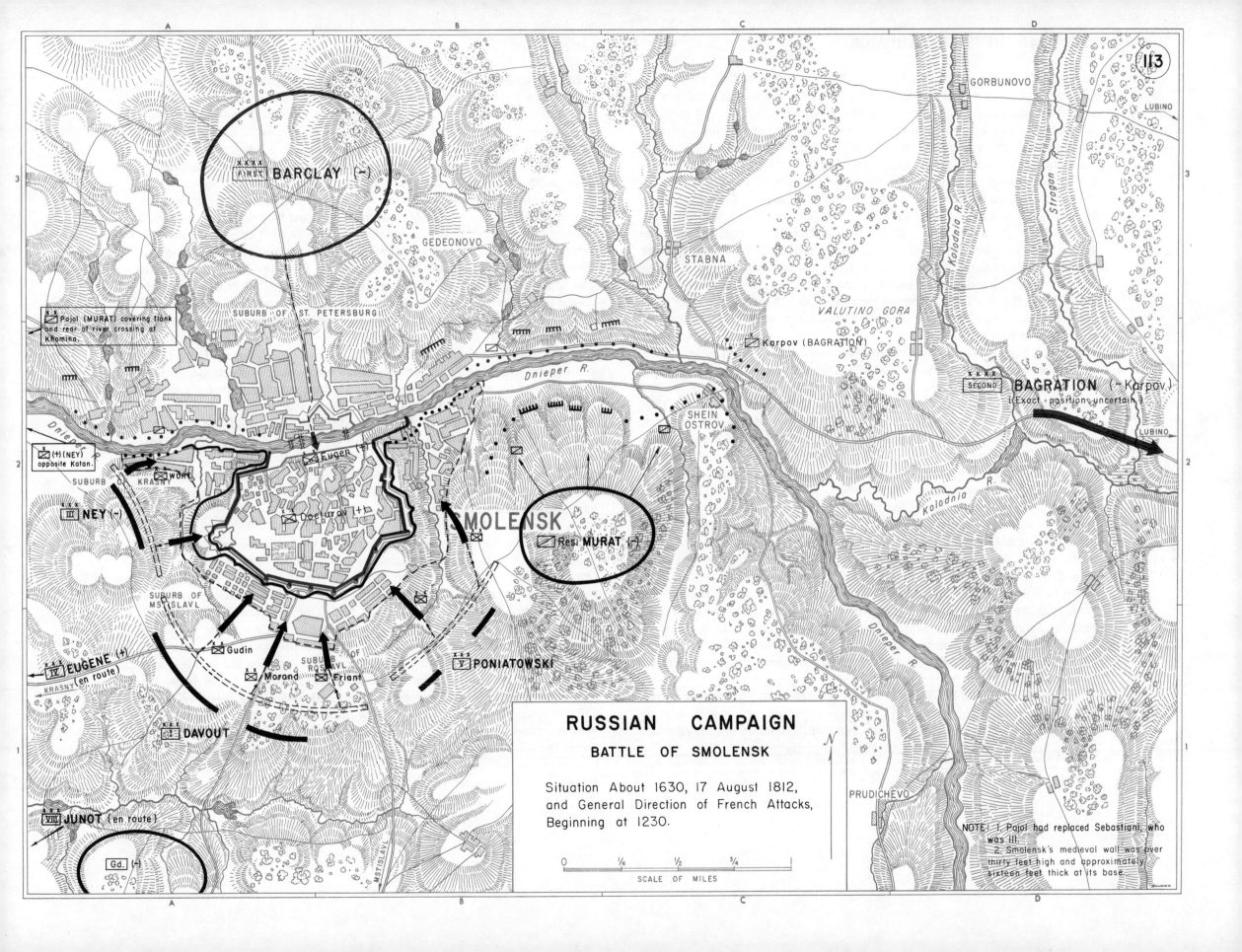

113

GORBUNOVO

LUBINO

XXXX
FIRST | BARCLAY (—)

GEDEONOVO

STABNA

VALUTINO GORA

Kolodnia R.

Stragan R.

SUBURB OF ST. PETERSBURG

Dnieper R.

Karpov (BAGRATION)

XX
Pajol (MURAT) covering flank
and rear of river crossing at
Khomina.

SHEIN
OSTROV

XXXX
SECOND | BAGRATION (—Karpov)
(Exact position uncertain)

LUBINO

Dnieper R.

X
(+)(NEY)
opposite Katan.

Kolodnia
R.

Euger (+)

SUBURB OF KRASN

WÜRT

XXX
III | NEY (—)

X
Docturov (+)

SMOLENSK

X
Resi MURAT (—)

SUBURB OF
MSTISLAVL

X
Gudin

SUBURB OF
RQSLAVL

XXX
V | PONIATOWSKI

XXX
IV | EUGENE (+)
(en route)

KRASNY

X
Morand

X
Friant

Dnieper R.

XXX
I | DAVOUT

RUSSIAN CAMPAIGN

BATTLE OF SMOLENSK

N

VIII | JUNOT (en route)

MSTISLAVL

Gd. (—)

Situation About 1630, 17 August 1812,
and General Direction of French Attacks,
Beginning at 1230.

PRUDICHEVO

NOTE: 1 Pajol had replaced Sebastiani, who
was ill.
2 Smolensk's medieval wall was over
thirty feet high and approximately
sixteen feet thick at its base.

0   1/4   1/2   3/4

SCALE OF MILES

Barclay held his discouraged army on the heights across the Dnieper through 18 August, withdrawing after dark. Since only two roads were available, he sent about half of his command northward through Prudishtsha (*off map, 15 miles northeast of Smolensk*). The other half, under his own immediate command, would detour along country roads through Gorbunovo (*D3*) to gain the main Smolensk-Moscow highway east of Shein Ostrov (*C2*). Fearing that a French crossing at Shein Ostrov might cut this route, he sent forward a strong advance guard under Tutchkov to reinforce Karpov's Cossacks, whom Bagration had left in that area. Korf, with a sizable rear guard, was to remain in position until late at night, then follow Barclay. The retreat quickly developed into a nightmare. Roads had not been reconnoitered; no guides were available; bridges collapsed; the various corps lost contact. Missing its road, the rear half of Barclay's column marched in circles, pursued by Korf. At about 0600, Barclay finally emerged from the woods, expecting to enter Gorbunovo—but, instead, discovered himself at Gedeonovo (*B3*), nose-to-nose with Ney's outposts.

Ney had begun crossing the Dnieper about 0400, with the double mission of covering the crossing of the rest of the army and of determining the extent and direction of the Russian withdrawal. Probing the heavy woods on the north bank went slowly, and Ney seems to have felt little need to hurry. (That Barclay might manage to mislay himself for the night, within three miles of one of Russia's major cities, could hardly have occurred to the French.) Just before 0600, Ney had requested more explicit orders. Napoleon replied that if the enemy had retired behind a strong rear guard, Ney was to follow it; if the Russians had withdrawn in several columns, Ney was to advance through Stabna (*C3*), reconnoitering to the north.

Barclay met this unexpected crisis calmly and firmly. The ground—cut up by woods, marshes, and steep-banked streams—was favorable for a rearguard action; the woods would conceal the extent of his predicament from Ney. Posting Eugen's division across the Gedeonovo-Gorbunovo road with orders to hold to the last, he hurriedly countermarched the rest of his column. From 0800 to 0930, Ney's attack developed slowly against Eugen's aggressive delaying action. Nansouty (Murat) began moving eastward along the Moscow highway, but was driven back by Korf's and Tutchkov's cavalry. Korf's infantry then disengaged Eugen, and their two commands retired at 1100 on Gorbunovo.

Reporting that he had chased away a small rear-guard, and that the enemy was retiring along the Moscow highway, Ney urged that a corps be sent up the south bank of the Dnieper to cut them off. Napoleon meanwhile had steadily fed Davout and the rest of Murat's cavalry across the Dnieper. At 0500, he had ordered Junot to cross at Prudichevo (*C1*) to cover the construction of a ponton bridge.

Little is known of Napoleon's whereabouts during much of the day. Seemingly lulled by Ney's optimistic reports, he devoted considerable time to administrative matters. He wrote sharply to Oudinot that his tactics would destroy his troops' morale: "Military reputation is everything in war, and equivalent to actual military strength." The bridges at Khomino and Rosasna were ordered taken up, and the route Warsaw-Minsk-Orsha-Smolensk designated as the new line of communication.

Meanwhile (about 1100), Tutchkov had occup d a position between the Kolodnia and Stragan rivers (*D2*). Karpov reported Ney advancing eastward along the Moscow highway; a German deserter told Tutchkov of Junot's movement. Deciding to fight where he was, Tutchkov ordered Karpov to cover his left and massed his guns to sweep the highway. Ney's leading division attacked at about 1330. After an hour's sluggish fighting, Tutchkov retired behind the Stragan River, where Barclay—with much of his command still between Gorbunovo and Lubino—was concentrating troops for a do-or-die stand.

At the sound of the firing, Napoleon had appeared at Valutino Gora (*D2*) and ordered Gudin to Ney's assistance. His appearance, however, coincided with Tutchkov's withdrawal. Napoleon therefore concluded that the action had been only a minor rear-guard squabble, and returned to Smolensk. (Grouchy was later ordered toward Prudishtsha, but could not penetrate Platov's screen). Following up Tutchkov, Ney developed Barclay's new position (*D2*) at 1600, and attacked after an hour's artillery preparation, trying to work around both flanks. Barclay counterattacked repeatedly. Ney forced the Stragan, but could not clear the crest beyond it. A marsh on the Russian left thwarted Murat.

At approximately this same time, Junot reached, in his own words, a "superb position in rear of the left of the enemy," and immediately pulled back, though nothing confronted him but Orlov Denisov's light cavalry. Contemporary accounts agree only that Murat twice tried desperately to get Junot to advance, but that Junot refused. *There is no indication that either Junot or Murat reported the existing situation to Napoleon.* It is possible that Murat did not fully appreciate the opportunity before him, since he soon shifted to Ney's left, searching for terrain where his cavalry could operate.

At 1900, with dusk blinding the Russian gunners, Ney put in his whole force for one last effort. Gudin was mortally wounded, but his division, led by Gerard, finally cleared the crest around 2230. Barclay withdrew behind a stiff rear-guard fight. Junot had made a futile demonstration (about 1700) with his cavalry; thereafter, his frustrated subordinates eventually crowded Orlov Denisov off the field by unauthorized local attacks. But Junot, pleading lack of orders, refused to initiate the general advance that could have crushed Barclay.

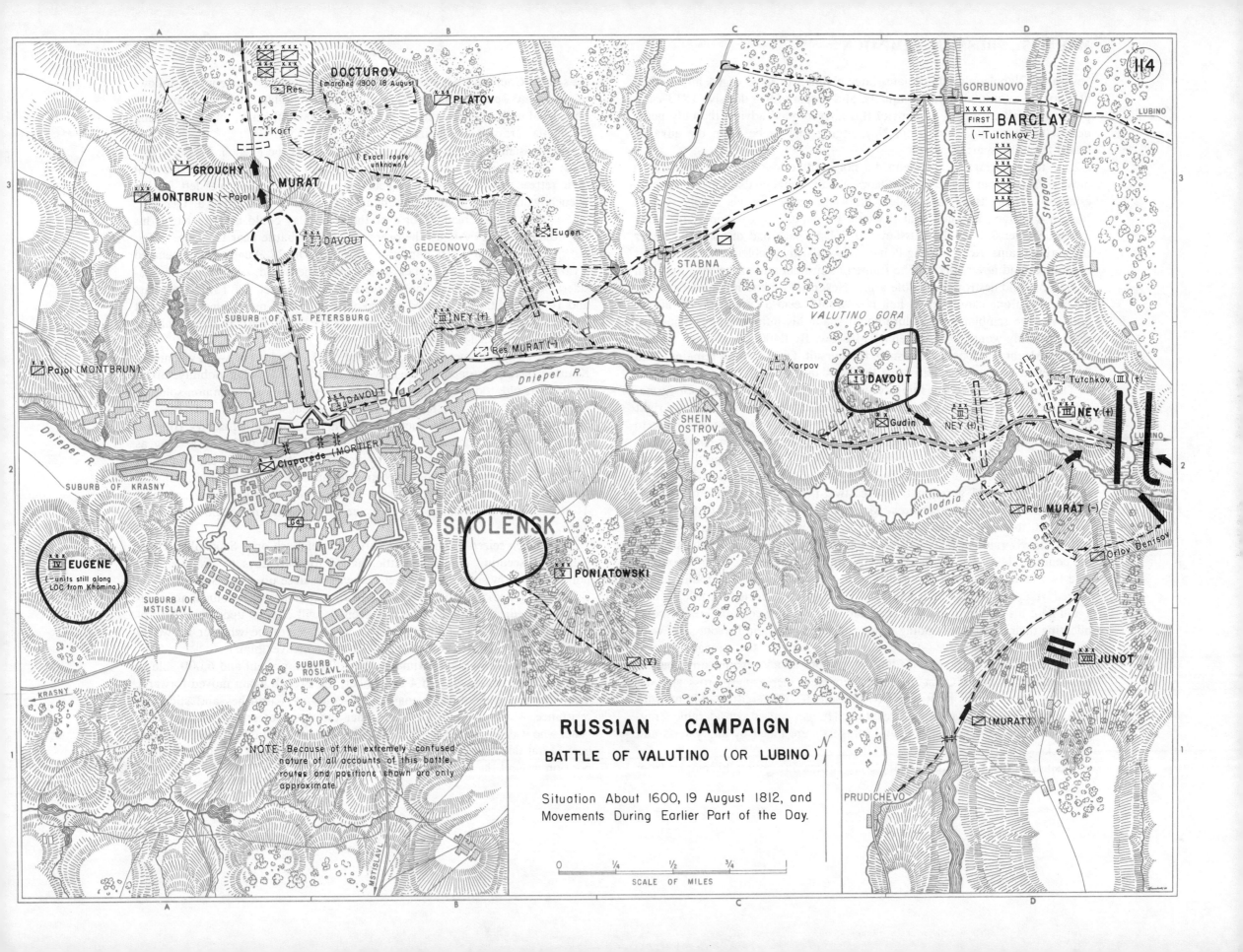

114

DOCTUROV
(marched 1900 18 August)
Res.
PLATOV
Korf
GROUCHY
MURAT
(Exact route unknown)
MONTBRUN (-Pajol)
GORBUNOVO
LUBINO
FIRST BARCLAY
(-Tutchkov)
DAVOUT
GEDEONOVO
Eugen
STABNA
VALUTINO GORA
SUBURB OF ST. PETERSBURG
NEY (†)
Res. MURAT (-)
Pajol (MONTBRUN)
Karpov
DAVOUT
Tutchkov (III) (†)
Dnieper R.
DAVOUT
Gudin
NEY (†)
NEY (†)
Claparede (MORTIER)
SHEIN OSTROV
LUBINO
Dnieper R.
SUBURB OF KRASNY
Gd
Res. MURAT (-)
SMOLENSK
Kolodnia
Orlov Denisov
EUGENE
(-units still along LOC from Khomino)
PONIATOWSKI
SUBURB OF MSTISLAVL
Dnieper R.
KRASNY
(V)
JUNOT
SUBURB ROSLAVL
MSTISLAVL

NOTE: Because of the extremely confused nature of all accounts of this battle, routes and positions shown are only approximate.

RUSSIAN CAMPAIGN

BATTLE OF VALUTINO (OR LUBINO)

Situation About 1600, 19 August 1812, and Movements During Earlier Part of the Day.

N

PRUDICHEVO

(MURAT)

0   ¼   ½   ¾
SCALE OF MILES

Several of Napoleon's subordinates later claimed to have urged him to halt at Smolensk, consolidate his conquests, and prepare for a decisive 1813 campaign. No written record remains of this alleged good advice; the only pertinent letter surviving is one from Ney, urging that he be given the advance guard for an unsparing pursuit.

One thing is certain: Napoleon did not hesitate long over his decision to move forward from Smolensk. In theory, a halt would enable him to regroup, establish Poland as an independent ally, and reorganize his supply system. But, in cold fact, he knew that it would be impossible to support his army around Smolensk once the Russian and Polish roads had disappeared under the autumn rains. Reorganizing Poland was a thorny problem which the Poles themselves had never solved. The Emperor's instinct and experience told him to seek out and destroy the hostile army. Never before had he failed to defeat his enemy in one campaign. A halt now would seem a confession of failure, and even the semblance of failure could shake his infant empire. The Russians certainly would fight to defend Moscow. By 0400, 20 August, he had ordered Murat and Davout to resume the pursuit. One question remains: Had he forgotten how he once had lured the Russians to attack him at Austerlitz?

The French advanced in three columns (see Map 112 for French formations and routes). Latour-Maubourg was directed to fall in on the army's right flank via Roslavl (this map, C2), meanwhile sending Dombrowski back to cover Mogilev (C2) and Minsk (B2). Pino, Pajol, and Guyon (not shown) were to clean out the Vitebsk-Smolensk area (C2) before joining the pursuit. Thoroughly sensible of his lengthening line of communication, Napoleon shifted reserves and garrison troops eastward, and ordered Victor to take command of the army's rear area. Macdonald was authorized to take Riga.

At first, the weather was hot and dusty, with wells and streams going dry. Later, nightly rains helped. Astride the main highway, the Russians stripped the countryside as they retreated, leaving little for the center French column. The two flank columns, though slowed by poor roads, usually found undisturbed villages and sufficient supplies. Hoping for a decisive battle, Murat again kept his cavalry massed at the head of the center column, greatly complicating their problem of finding water and forage. He and Davout soon were thoroughly at loggerheads—Davout trying to conserve the strength of men and horses, Murat constantly leading impromptu attacks against any chance-encountered group of Cossacks. Napoleon grew increasingly cross and demanding, heckling his most devoted subordinates unmercifully. Siding with Murat, he accused Davout of overcaution. Hunger caused considerable straggling, and numbers of stragglers and foragers were killed by angry serfs and Cossacks.

Despite all these difficulties, Napoleon continued to govern his empire from his saddle. Couriers from Paris came and went regularly; the convoys following the army were seldom troubled; supplies accumulated in the advance depots; local military governments gradually became effective; and a promising Lithuanian army was organized.

The Russian armies suffered at least as much as the French. Morale dwindled; sickness and desertion increased. Russian commanders protested that their retreat was so poorly managed that everything edible was left for the French, while their own men went hungry! Constantly damned as a "German" and a "traitor," and blamed for everything, Barclay could no longer trust his subordinates. On 21 August, he proposed offering battle near Usvyatye (C2), but quickly gave in when Bagration objected. On 27 August, he evacuated Vyazma (D2), burning supplies accumulated there and, accidentally, a considerable part of the city. Shortly thereafter, reinforced by 15,000 regulars and 10,000 militia, he decided to make his fight in a preselected position at Tsarevo Zaimishche (D2). Reaching it on the 29th, Barclay found that he had been superseded by Kutusov.

Kutusov's appointment had been forced on Alexander (between whom and Kutusov there was open dislike) by the frightened Russian nobility. Sixty-seven years old, too fat to mount a horse, popular with the common soldiers, crafty, lazy, and greedy, Kutusov was still a realist. He had little hope of defeating Napoleon, yet he knew he must fight to defend Moscow. To get a better grip on his command and to postpone that day of battle as long as possible, he risked his popularity by continuing the retreat. He confirmed Barclay and Bagration in their respective commands, and saddled himself with Bennigsen as chief of staff. Kutusov's one positive measure was to order Tormassov and Tshitshagov to renew the offensive against Napoleon's south flank.

The French seized Gzhatsk (D2) after a brief clash on 1 September. Here, Napoleon, scenting imminent battle, halted for two days to rest men and horses, and allow stragglers and detachments to close up. On 2 September, he called for immediate and careful musters of available men, mounts, ammunition, and medical supplies—"for my decision will depend upon them." (Apparently, the number of men available would determine whether he would move directly against Kutusov or seek to outmaneuver him.)

The returns showed approximately 128,000 men present and 6,000 able to close up within five days. On 4 September, the French again moved forward. That day and the 5th were marked by constant skirmishes and stiffening resistance, which initially dissolved under the threat of envelopment by Eugene, who was advancing north of the highway. At about 1400 on 5 September, Murat developed the main Russian army, occupying a hastily fortified position around the little town of Borodino (D2).

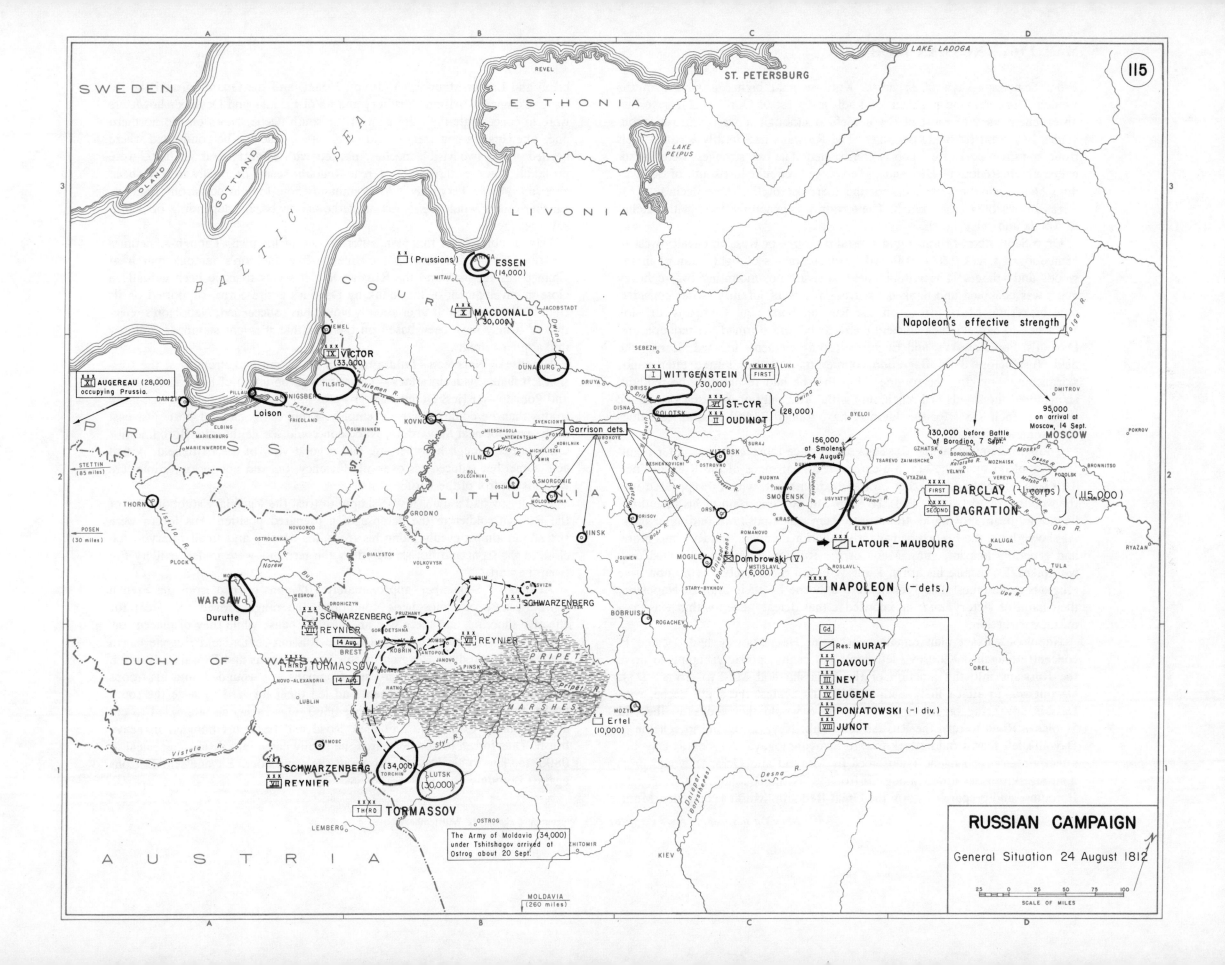

RUSSIAN CAMPAIGN

General Situation 24 August 1812

From Semyonovskaya (*C2*) north, Kutusov held higher ground than the French. His command post, on the knoll just west of Gorki (*C2*), gave him an excellent view of most of the battlefield (though it was to prove inconveniently distant from the fighting). The Russians had hastily fortified their front, but their works were poorly constructed. The two strongest were the so-called Great Redoubt (*C2*) and the advanced redoubt just south of Schivardino (*B1*). All the works, except the rearmost of the three flèches (*C1*), were fully visible to the French. The terrain was generally open, with patches of woods and thick brush.

On 5 September, Murat found several divisions of Russian cavalry west of Semyonovka Creek (*B2*), stiffened by detachments of light infantry in the woods and villages. The redoubt near Schivardino, mounting twelve heavy guns, was occupied and flanked by strong forces of infantry. After considerable bickering, Murat drove off the Russian horsemen. Compans' division (attached to Murat) then efficiently enveloped and stormed the redoubt, and Davout's, Poniatowski's, and Eugene's leading elements finished clearing the field. Just before dark, Bagration counterattacked, but retired after minor skirmishing—making the routine claim that he had recaptured the redoubt, slaughtered thousands of French, and withdrawn only on Kutusov's emphatic orders. French losses for the day may have totaled 2,000; Russian casualties were somewhat greater.

Though anxious that the Russians might once more slip away after nightfall, Napoleon spent the 6th in a careful reconnaissance of the Russian lines. This was relatively easy except on their extreme left, which disappeared into the woods around Utitza (*C1*). To keep Kutusov uncertain of his intentions, he did not begin moving his troops into their attack positions until after dark. As shown here, the French had slightly superior numbers; the Russians more, and generally heavier, guns. Many of the Russian militia were armed only with pikes. To inspire his army, Kutusov began 6 September with impressive religious ceremonies. The French were upborne by their faith in Napoleon, their habit of victory, *and* the knowledge that defeat—deep within Russia—meant destruction.

Napoleon's exact plan remains uncertain. He obviously had decided to concentrate against Kutusov's left flank and center, possibly hoping to drive the Russians into the junction of the Kalatsha and Moskvo rivers (*D3*). Davout was to attack first, sending Compans against the south flèche, with Dessaix advancing on his right. Poniatowski would then move up the Old Smolensk Road to turn the Russian left flank; Ney, advancing in echelon to Davout's left rear, would attack toward Semyonovskaya. As soon as Davout's attack developed, Eugene (reinforced by Morand and Gerard) would press a strong skirmisher attack along his front to fix the Russian right wing, take Borodino, and prepare to storm the Great Redoubt. Murat (Nansouty, Mont-

brun, and Latour-Maubourg), Junot, Friant, and the Guard formed the reserve. Compan's divisional artillery and all of Friant's and Dessaix's howitzers were to concentrate their fire against the south flèche; Ney's on the northern one. The Guard's howitzers would be grouped, ready to be committed where needed. (The two visible flèches, packed with infantry and artillery, were profitable howitzer targets; the Great Redoubt seems originally to have been garrisoned by artillery only.) All commands were to hold out strong reserves. Further orders would be issued after the action began, depending on Kutusov's reactions.

Davout objected to this plan, offering one of his own. Though sometimes described as a wide turning movement—like Jackson's famous march at Chancellorsville—around the Russian left, it seems to have been actually a close-in envelopment of that flank by Davout's entire corps, supported on its right by Poniatowski. It undoubtedly would have succeeded; Napoleon's rejection of it may have been based on the fear that it might stampede Kutusov into a quick retreat.

Because of Napoleon's failure to learn the extent and strength of the Russian left flank, his main attack—Davout (with only two of his five divisions) and Poniatowski (less Dombrowski)—was too weak, while Eugene had more troops than he could effectively employ. From his command post, just east of the redoubt near Shivardino, Napoleon could see neither the Borodino nor Utitza areas, though he otherwise had a good view of the battlefield. A bad cold somewhat reduced his over-all efficiency, but did not seriously interfere with his control of the battle.

If Kutusov had a plan, it was simply to trust the legendary stubbornness of the Russian soldier in the defense of a prepared position. His forces were spread out almost evenly along his front; his cavalry and small reserve—too close to the front and not sheltered by the terrain—were under artillery fire from the start.

At 0600, 7 September, approximately 102 guns opened from the French right. Because of atmospheric conditions, the range proved too great for effective shooting, and there was an enforced pause while they displaced forward. Ney's artillery then opened on the Russian center, and Eugene began bombarding Borodino. Covered by this fire, Compans and Dessaix advanced, but met massed Russian artillery fire. Compans was wounded, and his troops wavered until Davout rallied them and led them forward to seize the south flèche. Poniatowski had moved out at 0500. Overeager, he attempted to cut across country to the Old Smolensk Road and became entangled in heavy brush. Thus forced to countermarch, he finally came into action piecemeal at 0800, too late to aid Davout. At about the same hour, Eugene sent Delzons against Borodino.

Note: On this map, in Ney's corps (B1–B2), Würtemberg should be Württemberg.

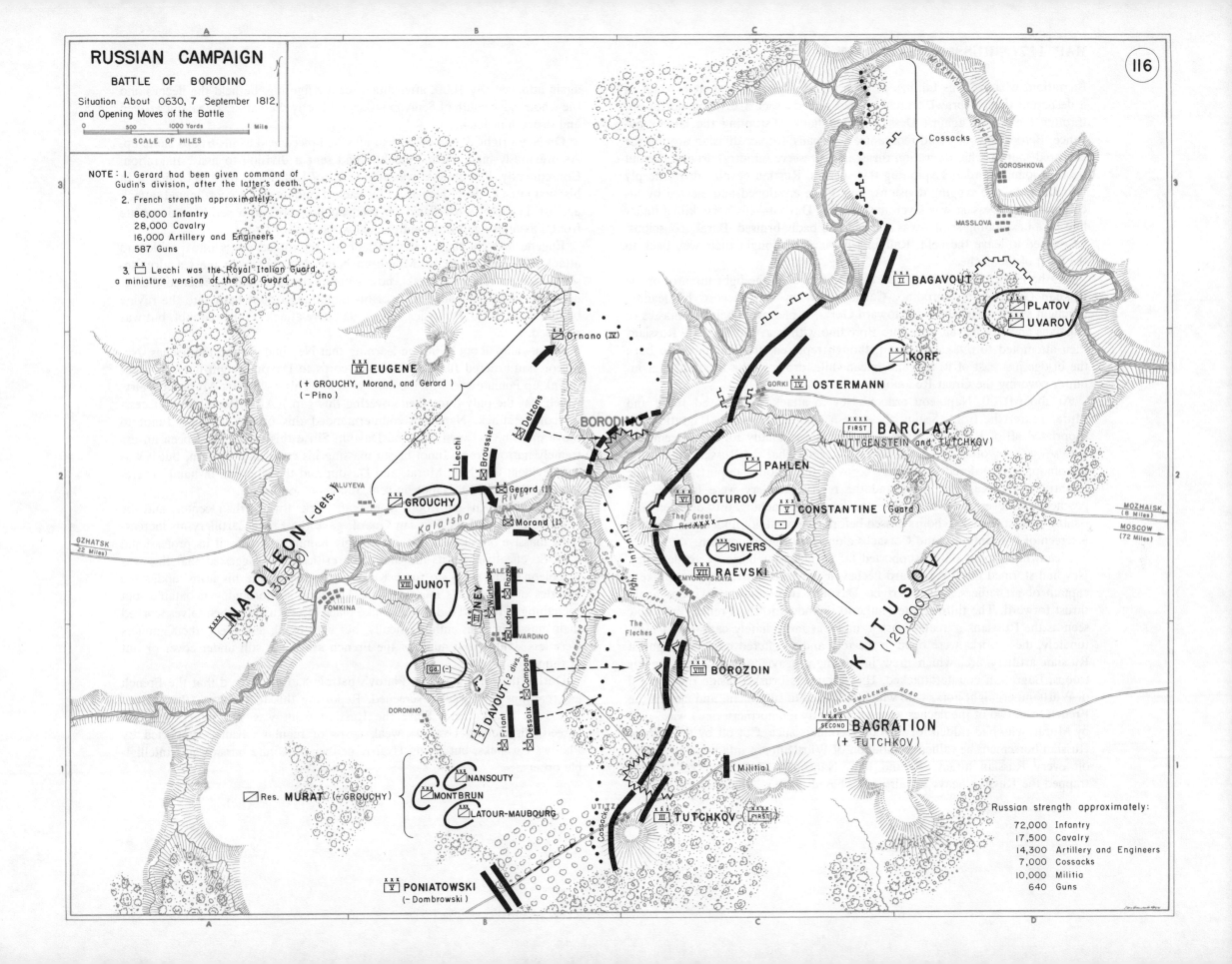

116

RUSSIAN CAMPAIGN

BATTLE OF BORODINO

Situation About 0630, 7 September 1812,
and Opening Moves of the Battle

0   500   1000 Yards   1 Mile

SCALE OF MILES

NOTE: 1. Gerard had been given command of
Gudin's division, after the latter's death.

2. French strength approximately:
86,000 Infantry
28,000 Cavalry
16,000 Artillery and Engineers
587 Guns

3. ▢ Lecchi was the Royal Italian Guard,
a miniature version of the Old Guard.

Cossacks

GOROSHKOVA

MASSLOVA

II BAGAVOUT

PLATOV

UVAROV

KORF

Ornano (IV)

IV EUGENE
(+ GROUCHY, Morand, and Gerard)
(− Pino)

Delzons

GORKI IV OSTERMANN

BORODINO

FIRST BARCLAY
(+ WITTGENSTEIN and TUTCHKOV)

Lecchi   Broussier

PAHLEN

GROUCHY   Gerard (I)   River

Kalatsha   Morand (I)

VALUYEVA

VI DOCTUROV

V CONSTANTINE (Guard)

The Great Redoubt

SIVERS

VII RAEVSKI

MOZHAISK
(8 Miles)

MOSCOW
(72 Miles)

GZHATSK
22 Miles

NAPOLEON
(130,000)

VIII JUNOT   III NEY   SALEZKI   Razout   Wurtemberg   Ledru

FOMKINA

SEMYONOVSKAYA

KUTUSOV
(120,800)

Light infantry

Semyonovka Creek   Kamenka Creek

The Fleches

Gd. (−)

Shevardino

VIII BOROZDIN

DAVOUT (2 divs.)   Compans

DORONINO   Friant   Dessaix

OLD SMOLENSK ROAD

SECOND BAGRATION
(+ TUTCHKOV)

(Militia)

Res. MURAT (− GROUCHY)
NANSOUTY
MONTBRUN
LATOUR-MAUBOURG

UTITZA

Cossacks

III TUTCHKOV   FIRST

V PONIATOWSKI
(− Dombrowski)

Russian strength approximately:
72,000 Infantry
17,500 Cavalry
14,300 Artillery and Engineers
7,000 Cossacks
10,000 Militia
640 Guns

Bagration, whatever his failings as an army commander, was at his best in a desperate tactical brawl. Tutchkov had already sent a division northward through the woods against Dessaix's right flank, disrupting the latter's advance. Before Davout could reorganize Compans' former division around the captured south flèche, Bagration thrust in his reserve infantry, driving Davout back in some disorder. Exploiting this success, Russian cavalry drove deeply into Davout's two sagging divisions, only to be enveloped and ejected by his corps cavalry. Dessaix was severely wounded; Davout—his horse killed under him by an exploding shell—was stunned and badly bruised. Barely conscious, he refused to leave the field. Rallying, his infantry fought their way back to the front of the flèche.

On the French left, Delzons had quickly dislodged the light infantry of the Russian Guard from Borodino. Carried away by this success, his leading regiment swept on up the ridge toward Gorki. It met overwhelming masses of Russians and was driven back into Borodino with heavy losses. The Russians then attempted to retake the town; though repulsed, they managed to burn the bridge just east of it. Morand, meanwhile, drove in the Russian light infantry covering the Great Redoubt.

At about 0700, Napoleon ordered Ney to attack, and moved Junot and Murat nearer the front. Seeing these fresh troops advancing, Bagration appropriated all of Raevski's reserves and clamored loudly for reinforcements. Kutusov (or, by other accounts, Barclay), seeing that the Russian right wing was unopposed, ordered Bagavout's corps to Bagration's support; part of the infantry of the Russian Guard and the reserve artillery were likewise dispatched. However, time had been consumed in reaching this decision and issuing orders; some two hours passed before Bagavout got under way, leaving a screen of light infantry and Cossacks along his original position.

Meanwhile, about 0800, supported by an incessant blaze of artillery fire, Ney had stormed the two forward flèches, leading his corps in person "like a captain of grenadiers." On his right, Davout's two battered divisions again thrust forward. The third flèche (hitherto unknown to the French) was now seen as the Russians retreated past it, and was immediately captured. Unfortunately, these works were open in the rear and so offered no shelter against Russian artillery fire, which grew increasingly heavier. Swiftly rallying his troops, Bagration counterattacked. His cuirassiers brushed aside the handful of Württemberg light horse with which Ney tried to stop them, and ejected the French from two of the flèches. One (apparently the northern one) was saved by Murat, who had ridden forward on reconnaissance. Cut off by the rush of Russian horsemen, he rallied a battalion of Württemberg infantry and fought off every Russian attack. Behind him, Nansouty's Polish lancers mousetrapped the Russian heavy cavalry and chased it back. Thus supported, Ney

again attacked. By 1000, after much seesaw fighting, he held the flèches and the whole ridge south of Semyonovskaya. Shortly thereafter, Bagavout arrived and drove him back.

On Ney's right, Poniatowski had attacked piecemeal as his troops came up. As previously mentioned, Tutchkov had sent a division to assist Bagration. Consequently, Poniatowski was able to carry Utitza and the hill behind it in his first attack. But thereafter, instead of mounting a coordinated attack against Tutchkov's left flank, he used up his corps in a series of desperate frontal assaults against the entrenched wood east of Utitza.

Eugene had got the greater part of his reinforced corps into position to attack the Great Redoubt, Montbrun being detached from the Cavalry Reserve to support him. Raevski, now without reserves, had garrisoned the redoubt strongly and pulled most of his remaining troops back into the ravine behind it. At 1000, Broussier made a tentative attack on the redoubt, but was repulsed.

Meanwhile, about 0900, on learning that Ney had carried the flèches, Napoleon had ordered Junot to move his corps to Davout's right flank in order to link up Poniatowski with the main attack. (This would free Murat's cavalry, which was the only force then covering this gap.) After Bagration's successful counterattack, Napoleon countermanded this order, directing Junot to move into line between Ney and Davout. Since this would have been an extremely narrow front, Junot began massing his corps into column, but it was soon evident that Ney, Murat, and Davout had the situation in hand. Therefore, at about 1000, Napoleon sent Junot on southward.

The shift of Russian troops from both flanks toward their center, and the advance of part of the Russian Guard, gave the French artillery an increasingly massive target, which it unceasingly hammered with all its professional skill. So effective was its fire that some critics have suggested that this was Napoleon's real plan—to force Kutusov to concentrate his army under the muzzles of Napoleon's massed guns. The idea is thoroughly debatable, but something of the sort did actually take place. The Russians themselves worked their masses of guns enthusiastically, but with much less effect; their gunners were less skillful, and much of the French army was still under cover or out of range.

During the early morning, Platov's patrols had discovered that the French left rear was only weakly screened. Reporting this to Kutusov, Platov suggested an attack there. Since the Russian front was still intact, Kutusov agreed, dispatching Uvarov's weak corps of regular cavalry, supported by Platov's Cossacks, but giving Uvarov neither a definite mission nor intelligible orders.

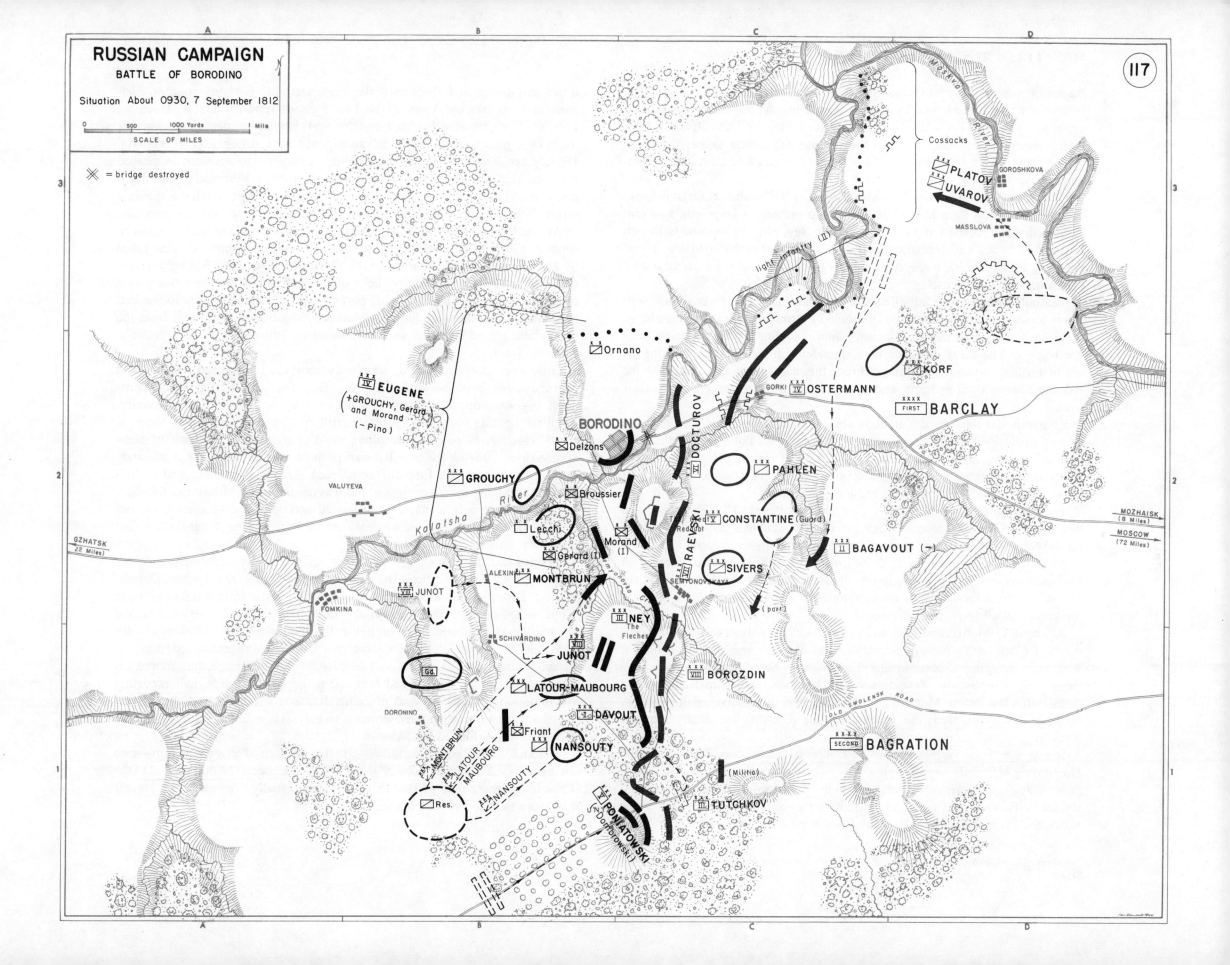

117

RUSSIAN CAMPAIGN
BATTLE OF BORODINO

Situation About 0930, 7 September 1812

0   500   1000 Yards   1 Mile
SCALE OF MILES

⊠ = bridge destroyed

MOSKVA RIVER

Cossacks

GOROSHKOVA

XXX
PLATOV
XX
UVAROV

MASSLOVA

light infantry (II)

⊠ Ornano

XXX
IV
EUGENE
(+GROUCHY, Gerard,
and Morand)
(– Pino)

BORODINO

⊠ Delzons

XXX
⊠ GROUCHY

⊠ Broussier

XXX
DOCTUROV
VI

GORKI XXX
IV OSTERMANN

⊠ KORF

XXXX
FIRST BARCLAY

XXX
⊠ PAHLEN

Redoubt

XXX
IV CONSTANTINE (Guard)

MOZHAISK
(8 Miles)

MOSCOW
(72 Miles)

⊠ Lecchi

XX
Morand
(I)

RAEVSKI

VII

⊠ Gerard (I)

SEMENOVSKAYA

XXX
⊠ SIVERS

XXX
II BAGAVOUT (–)

(part)

VALUYEVA

River Kalatsha

GZHATSK
(22 Miles)

ALEXINKI
XXX
⊠ MONTBRUN

XXX
VIII JUNOT

FOMKINA

SCHIVARDINO

XXX
III NEY
The
Fleches

XXX
VIII JUNOT

XXX
VIII BOROZDIN

Gd.

XXX
⊠ LATOUR-MAUBOURG

XXX
I DAVOUT

OLD SMOLENSK ROAD

DORONINO

XX
⊠ Friant

XXX
⊠ NANSOUTY

XXXX
SECOND BAGRATION

MONTBRUN
LATOUR-
MAUBOURG
NANSOUTY

(Militia)

XXX
III TUTCHKOV

⊠ Res.

XXX
⊠ PONIATOWSKI
(+Dombrowski)

Bagration was mortally wounded, and the French retook the flèches at 1100, but were again thrown out by a last, despairing counterattack. Attacking again at 1130 with his whole corps, Ney, supported by Davout, once more swiftly overran the flèches, driving the Russian left center across the creek behind them. Here, the Russians rallied, repulsing Ney's first attack on Semyonovskaya.

Murat now conferred with Ney and Davout. (Half-stunned, Davout could do little more than keep his saddle and set an example.) Napoleon had sent Friant's division forward at 1100 to reinforce Ney; Murat proposed to launch Latour-Maubourg and Nansouty, supported by all available artillery, across the creek on either side of Semyonovskaya to open the way for an attack by Friant on that village itself.

Nansouty crossed first; initially successful, he was finally forced back with heavy losses. Latour-Maubourg was delayed by rough terrain, but his charge broke up the Russian infantry opposing him, enabling Friant to storm Semyonovskaya. The three marshals now shouldered forward, concentrating an arc of artillery around that village. From this high ground, it enfiladed the Russian lines to right and left, and pounded the disorganized enemy to their front.

Bagavout had reinforced Tutchkov about noon, holding Junot at bay and driving Poniatowski back into Utitza. Now the riddled Poles, seeing the Russian center cave in, made a gasping, final assault. Junot got his indifferent Westphalian infantry moving. The Russian left wing cracked and almost broke before exhaustion finally halted its assailants.

The Russian left and left center now were shattered. Though smoke and dust obscured the full extent of their success, the marshals sensed the opportunity. Napoleon must come forward and deliver the finishing blow.

At his distant command post, Napoleon had lost his usual fine sensing of the battle's ripening. He sent only one division of the Young Guard—to provide a reserve if the Russians counterattacked. From Semyonovskaya south, the battle fell off into an artillery duel.

At about 1100, Morand's leading brigade suddenly overran the Great Redoubt. Unluckily, Yermolov (Barclay's chief of staff) was passing behind it with two companies of horse artillery, en route for Semyonovskaya. Wheeling these guns into position, Yermolov rallied fugitives, called up Raevski, and counterattacked before Morand could get the rest of his division forward. A confused brawl followed; the French lost the redoubt, but finally repulsed Raevski.

It was now noon. While Kutusov dawdled on his hilltop, Barclay shifted Docturov southward, improvising a new line, though the guns around Semyonovskaya raked this new position cruelly. Seventy-six cannon bombarded the Great Redoubt as Eugene organized another assault. Then, a loud panic seized the camp followers behind the French left flank as Uvarov and Platov

drove in Ornano and threatened the French trains. Forming squares, Delzon's infantry blocked Uvarov; the train's escort repulsed Platov. Even so, Eugene countermarched with Grouchy and Lecchi to determine whether these were mere raiders or the advance guard of a strong Russian column. Largely accidentally, Kutusov thus gained an hour. Ostermann was pushed into line to stiffen Raevski. All the Russian corps now were badly intermixed and jammed into a shorter front than the French occupied, making a splendid target. For all their stoic endurance, many units grew increasingly unsteady.

At last Eugene came on again, Broussier leading, Gerard and Morand in support. General Caulaincourt* (replacing Montbrun, who had been killed by a stray cannon ball) charged to the south of the redoubt. Riding over the remnants of Raevski's infantry, he routed the Russian reserve cavalry that sought to stop him. Then, swinging part of his cuirassiers abruptly to the left, he scattered the Russian infantry behind the redoubt and stormed it from the rear—falling dead as he did so. Simultaneously, Broussier's infantry broke in from the front.

Ostermann counterattacked, was badly shot up, and retired. Gerard and Morand came into line with Broussier. Grouchy pursued the fleeing Russians, but was stopped by Kutusov's last reserve, the Russian Guard cavalry. Then the fighting paused as Eugene's artillery displaced forward to the captured ridgeline. Napoleon rode along the French outpost line east of Semyonovskaya, studying the new Russian position that Barclay was desperately cobbling together. The Emperor considered sending Claparede and a division of the Young Guard against it, but was dissuaded by Murat and Berthier, who urged that only a major, coordinated attack would be certain of success. Napoleon then decided against committing the Old Guard ("my last reserve").

In hard fact, he had some 30,000 fresh or practically fresh men ready for action. Except for its artillery, the Guard had not fired a shot. Lecchi, Delzon, Gerard, Broussier, Grouchy, and Junot had done little serious fighting, while Kutusov had committed every available man. The French artillery dominated the battlefield. A possible explanation is that Napoleon himself—between his cold and the strain of this long campaign—was more exhausted than his army. Noting the Russians waiting stolidly on the next ridge, he ordered his artillery to increase its fire, and returned to his headquarters, half-expecting to continue the battle the next morning. Kutusov wrote to the Czar, reporting that he had won another glorious victory. Then, in the small hours of 8 September, he bolted for Moscow.

Borodino has been magnified—largely through Tolstoy's fiction—into an apocalyptic struggle. Losses *were* heavy—between 28,000 and 31,000 French, and more than 45,000 Russians—but actually Wagram was a greater and more sternly contested battle.

---

* General Caulaincourt was a brother of Napoleon's Master of Horse. See the Biographical Sketches.

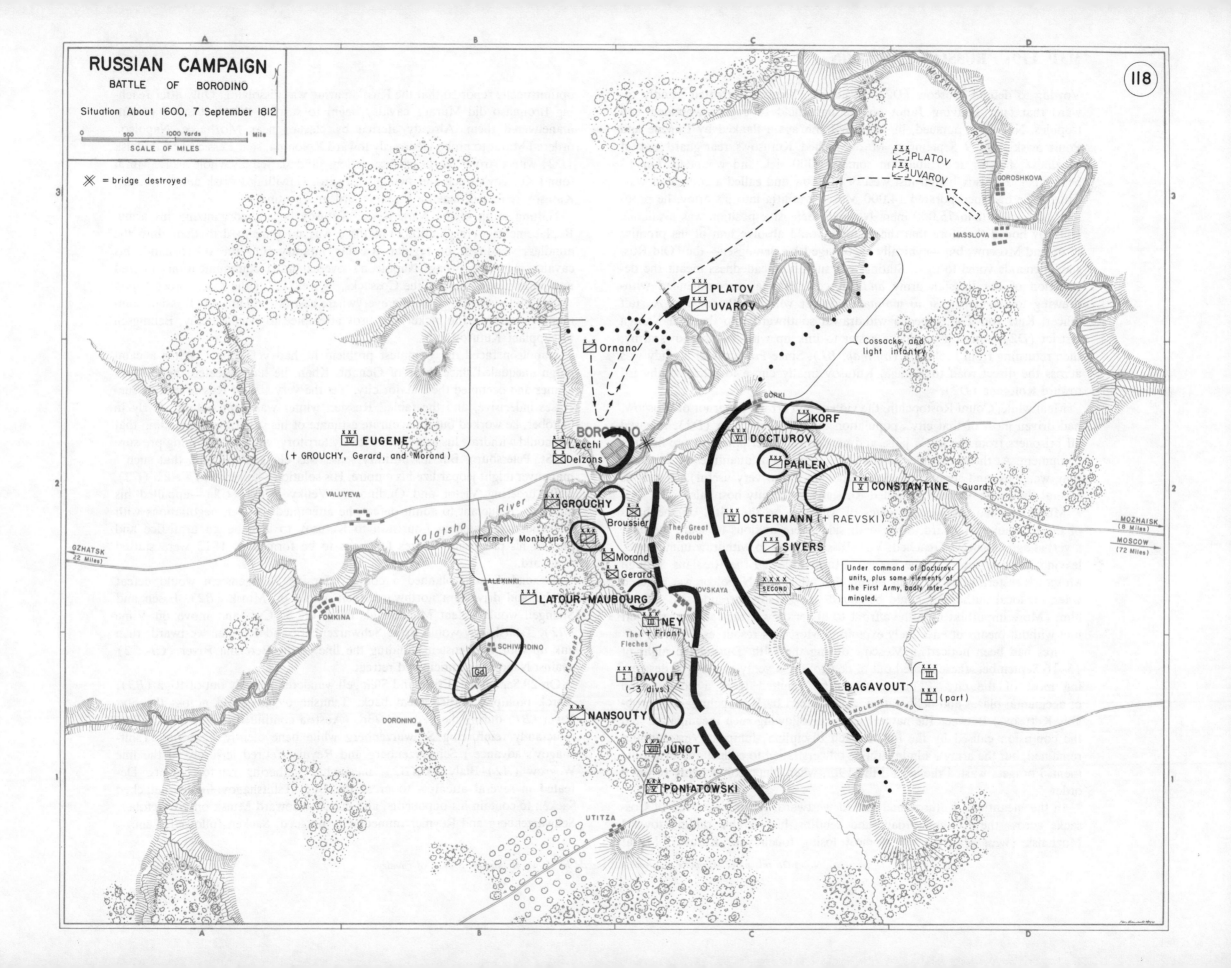

RUSSIAN CAMPAIGN
BATTLE OF BORODINO

Situation About 1600, 7 September 1812

SCALE OF MILES

✕ = bridge destroyed

118

PLATOV
UVAROV

GOROSHKOVA

MASSLOVA

Cossacks and
light infantry

Ornano

GORKI

BORODINO
Lecchi
Delzons

KORF

DOCTUROV

PAHLEN

CONSTANTINE (Guard)

EUGENE
(+ GROUCHY, Gerard, and Morand)

River Kalatsha

GROUCHY

Broussier
The Great Redoubt

(Formerly Montbrun's)

VALUYEVA

MOZHAISK
(8 Miles)

MOSCOW
(72 Miles)

OSTERMANN (+ RAEVSKI)

SIVERS

Morand
Gerard

ALEXINKI

GZHATSK
(22 Miles)

LATOUR-MAUBOURG

SECOND

Under command of Docturov:
units, plus some elements of
the First Army, badly intermingled.

FOMKINA

NEY
(+ Friant)
The
Fleches

SCHIVARDINO

Gd

DAVOUT
(~3 divs.)

DORONINO

BAGAVOUT

(part)

OLD SMOLENSK ROAD

NANSOUTY

JUNOT

PONIATOWSKI

UTITZA

Vowing to defend Moscow (*D2*) to the last, Kutusov retreated rapidly toward that city. Leaving Junot on the battlefield to collect wounded and trophies, Napoleon pursued, his main column again flanked by Eugene and Poniatowski. On 9 September, Murat rushed Kutusov's rear guard out of Mozhaisk, forcing it to abandon some 10,000 sick and wounded. On 13 September, Kutusov halted just west of Moscow and called a council of war. Though he had incorporated 14,000 Moscow militia into his army, he probably had fewer than 75,000 men. No good defensive position was available. Kutusov hoped therefore that the council would absolve him of his promise to defend Moscow, but—cynically encouraged by Bennigsen—the "Old Russian" generals voted to fight. Stating that such bullheadedness meant the destruction of the Russian army *and* Moscow, Barclay recommended withdrawing to the northeast to maintain contact with St. Petersburg. A staff officer, Karl von Toll, urged a withdrawal southward into the rich Kaluga district (*D2*), where it would be easier to link up with Tshitshagov's army, then returning from Moldavia (*off map, B1*). Since Poniatowski already was across the direct road to Kaluga, Kutusov finally chose to retire southward toward Kolomna (*D2*).

Meanwhile, Count Rostopchin, the violent and erratic governor of Moscow, had driven most of that city's population off toward Ryazan (*D2*), released all prisoners from the city's jails, and carried off or crippled all fire-fighting equipment. At the same time, he abandoned enormous quantities of ammunition, weapons, and supplies (which Napoleon found very useful), as well as several thousand sick and wounded Russians in the city hospitals.

Murat reached the western gates of Moscow on the 14th, on the heels of the Russian rear guard. Since both sides were anxious to spare the city, a verbal agreement was reached: The Russians were to withdraw unmolested, leaving Moscow intact to the French. Murat followed the Russians through Moscow's eastern gates. Arriving during that afternoon, Napoleon was angered when no local authorities could be found to formally surrender the city to him. (More important than the affront to his pride was the fact that this left him without means of effectively exploiting Moscow's resources.)

Fires had been noticed in Moscow during the 14th. During the night of 15–16 September, these flamed out of control for seventy-two hours, destroying most of the city. (This conflagration resulted from a combination of accidental blazes and deliberate arson, planned by Rostopchin—and probably Kutusov.) Between the natural letdown following such a campaign, and the confusion caused by the fire, French discipline slumped. Vast supplies remained, but the army's administrative officers failed to collect and distribute them. Foragers wasted them until the 19th, when Napoleon roughly restored order.

In the meantime, Kutusov had turned westward, leaving a screen of Cossacks across the Kolomna road, and sending his cavalry raiding toward Mozhaisk (*west of Moscow*). Almost losing touch with Kutusov, Murat

optimistically reported that the Russian army was dissolving. Only after reaching Bronnitso did Murat's cavalry begin to suspect that Kutusov had outmaneuvered them. Already alerted by clashes near Mozhaisk, Napoleon ordered Murat to probe vigorously toward Kolomna, sent Bessieres to Podolsk (*D2*) with a strong "corps of observation," and alerted his whole army. Murat found Kutusov's track and swung westward. Unwilling to risk another battle, Kutusov retreated, leaving a rear guard at Tarutino.

Halting south of the Nara River, Kutusov began reorganizing his army. Replacements were plentiful, but there was no time to drill them into the mindless steadiness of regular Russian infantry. On the other hand, his cavalry remained strong. Napoleon's overextended communications offered an appropriate target for the Cossacks, as well as for the local forces (*opolcheni*) and guerrillas gathering everywhere east of the Dnieper. Russian commanders continued to bicker: Kutusov attempted to evict Barclay, Bennigsen to supplant Kutusov.

Napoleon faced the grimmest problem he had yet known. After a campaign unequaled since those of Genghis Khan, he had defeated the Russian armies and occupied their major city. Yet the very size of Russia left his successes indecisive, and the fabled Russian winter was approaching. Early in October, he worked out an accurate estimate of his situation, concluding that he should withdraw his army into friendly territory, while maintaining pressure on St. Petersburg. But his military sense was clogged by fears that such a maneuver might jeopardize his empire. His solution—to retire to Velizh (*C2*), while ordering Victor and Oudinot to Velikye Luki (*C2*)—appalled his marshals. Reluctant to admit defeat, he attempted to open negotiations with Alexander, dispatching Lauriston to Kutusov to arrange an armistice and present his proposals. Cadres for units to be formed in 1813 were started westward.

Alexander's staff planned a counteroffensive. Wittgenstein would defeat St.-Cyr and drive him northward, then march on Minsk (*B2*). Essen and Steingell would defeat Macdonald, finish off St.-Cyr, and move on Vilna (*B2*). Tshitshagov would drive Schwarzenberg and Reynier westward, then link up with Wittgenstein, holding the line of the Berezina River (*C1–C2*) against Napoleon's anticipated retreat.

On 29 September, Essen and Steingell wandered vaguely out of Riga (*B3*). Yorck promptly herded them back. Tshitshagov advanced across the Styr River (*B1*) during the 22d and 23d. (Austria continued her double-dealing, reluctantly reinforcing Schwarzenberg while benevolently observing Tshitshagov's advance.) Schwarzenberg and Reynier retired leisurely to the line Wegrow (*A2*)–Bialystok (*B2*), meanwhile gathering reinforcements. Defeated in several attempts to cross the Bug, Tshitshagov finally detached Sacken to contain his opponents, and marched toward Minsk on 29 October. Schwarzenberg and Reynier immediately pursued; Sacken followed them.

Note: On this map, Morand's division (A2) should be shown as infantry instead of cavalry.

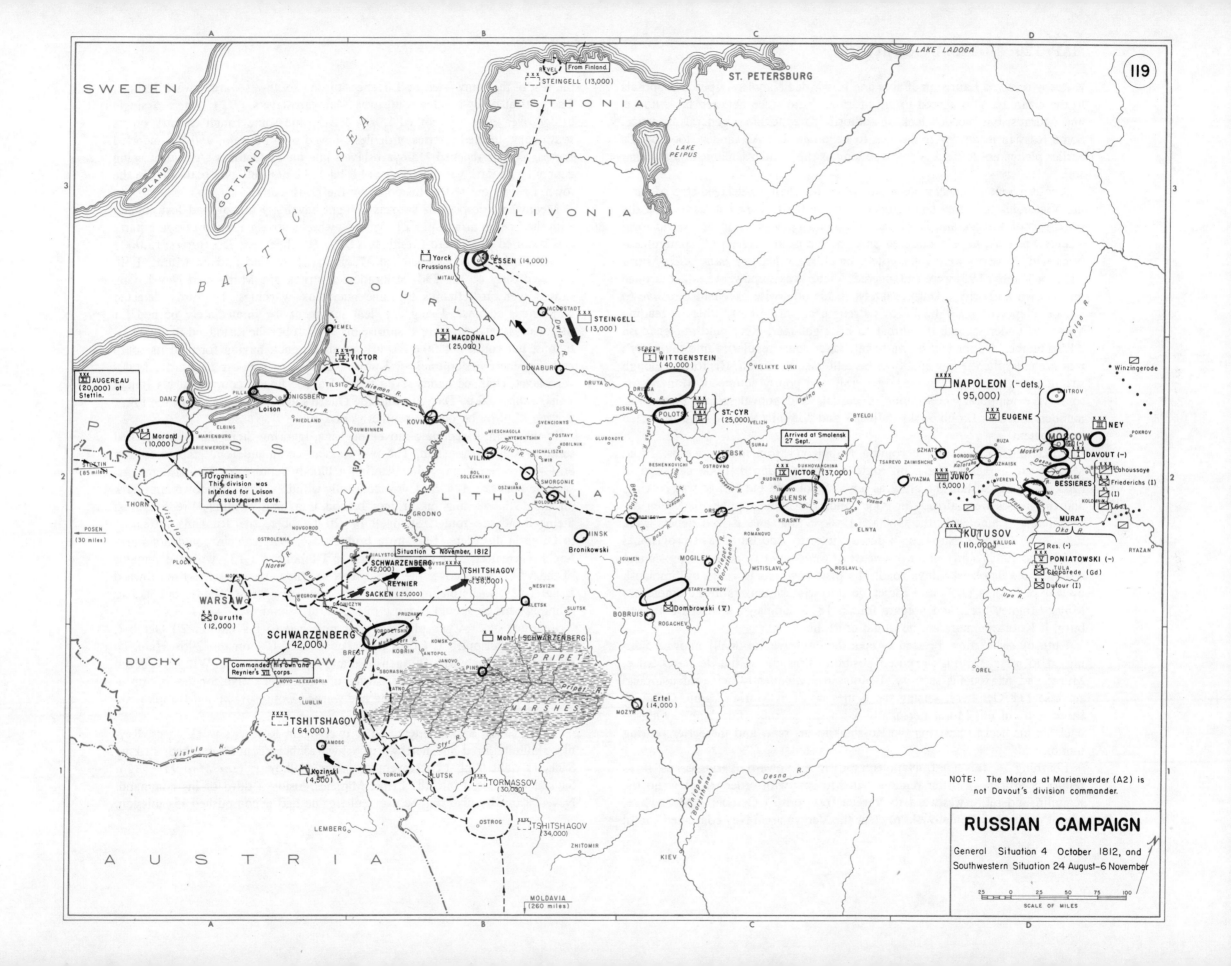

RUSSIAN CAMPAIGN

General Situation 4 October 1812, and
Southwestern Situation 24 August–6 November

NOTE: The Morand at Marienwerder (A2) is
not Davout's division commander.

Kutusov received Lauriston affably and forwarded Napoleon's peace proposals to the Czar. He also agreed to an informal, local truce between his outposts and Murat's, but pleaded lack of authority to conclude a general armistice. Some Russian leaders were anxious to negotiate, but Alexander stood by his earlier pledge not to discuss peace so long as the French remained on Russian soil.

About 6 September, Napoleon had taken the too-long-delayed step of naming Victor his rear-area commander, with authority over Lithuania and the provinces of Vitebsk and Smolensk. Strategically, Victor's forces would form a central reserve, to be committed only on Napoleon's orders. (If communications with Moscow were interrupted, or either Vilna [off map, A2], Minsk [A2], or Vitebsk [B2] were endangered, Victor was empowered to act at once on his own authority.) Unfortunately, in his otherwise excellent directive to Victor, Napoleon set Tshitshagov's strength at only 40,000, thereby leading Victor to underestimate the threat to his right rear. Reaching Smolensk on 24 September, Victor had begun to introduce some regularity into the army's rear area, despite the low quality of his administrative staff. His forces, though strong enough on paper, were largely raw and poorly equipped. Many garrisons were temporary collections of casuals and convalescents; their commanders, such as Bronikowski (Minsk) and Jomini (Vilna), were too often incompetent.

Food and forage were becoming Napoleon's principal concerns. From Moscow to Smolensk, the main route had been stripped. Food captured in Moscow would sustain the army as far as Smolensk, but forage was lacking, and the horses were already in poor condition. Some supplies had been accumulated in Smolensk; the Orsha, Minsk, Vilna, and Kovno depots were full. On 17 October, Napoleon ordered Victor to send Baraguay's provisional division to Elnya (fifty miles southeast of Smolensk) to collect supplies and organize the Smolensk-Elnya road. His plan now was to retire on Smolensk by way of Kaluga (D2) and Elnya, go into winter quarters in the Smolensk-Minsk-Mogilev area, and prepare for an 1813 campaign against St. Petersburg. If Kutusov interfered, he would crush him.

Kutusov struck first. Pressed to take the offensive, he finally allowed Bennigsen to attack Murat's exposed position. Trusting to the de facto truce, Murat had relaxed his security. Bennigsen consequently achieved complete surprise (18 October), seizing the defiles north of Murat's camp. Outnumbered and cut off, Murat personally led a savage rally, knocking Bennigsen back on his heels, scattering the Russians in his rear, and thereafter retiring unmolested.

Learning of this fight, Napoleon advanced toward Tarutino, as if to reinforce Murat. (Mortier remained in Moscow with orders to blow up the Kremlin and retire westward to Vereya [D2] on 23 October.) Meanwhile, Murat dispatched Poniatowski to clear the Vereya area. Ney continued south;

the rest of the army—led by Eugene—turned southwestward toward Kaluga. The critical point on this route was Maloyaroslavets (D2), where a single bridge over the steep-banked Luzha River, and some rough country on its south bank, formed a series of defiles. Slowed by mud, rain, and his underfed horses, Eugene reached Maloyaroslavets late on 23 October. Afraid of being caught in the dark with the river at his back, he put only two battalions in the town, holding the rest of his corps on the north bank.

Meanwhile, despite his swarms of light cavalry, Kutusov had lost contact with the French army until 22 October, when a strong French foraging party was reported near Naro-Frominsk (D2). He then sent Docturov (15,000) to drive it back, and dispatched Miloradovich to find and fix Murat. Both marched early on the 23d. Miloradovich struck air, Murat and Ney having shifted westward; thanks to some guerrillas' warnings, Docturov detected Napoleon's advance. Using excellent judgment, he immediately pushed for Maloyaroslavets. Arriving at sunrise on 24 October, he dislodged the two battalions, but could not take the bridge, the French having fortified its south end. Eugene counterattacked; Kutusov arrived to support Docturov; Maloyaroslavets changed hands seven times. Eugene finally committed his Italian units. Supported by Davout's and the Guard's artillery, these swept the town, driving Kutusov beyond its southern outskirts.

In the north, Macdonald moved on Riga, ignoring Steingell, who marched south to join Wittgenstein. The two Russian commanders attempted to trap St.-Cyr between them. Administering a bloody repulse to Wittgenstein's assault on Polotsk (A2), St.-Cyr successfully withdrew from that town after dark on the 19th, burning his bridges behind him, and sending Wrede against Steingell. Wrede routed Steingell on 20 October, the Russians retreating to Disna in disorder. (Lacking a bridge train, Wittgenstein could not interfere.) Thereafter, St.-Cyr sent Wrede to Glubokoye (A2) with the remains of the VI Corps to cover the direct road to Vilna. He himself retired toward Lepel (A2), to be on the flank of any advance against Wrede, but had to relinquish his command because of a painful wound.

Learning of St.-Cyr's plight, Victor marched to his aid on 20 October, reaching the crippled II Corps near Tchasniki (A2) on the 29th. Here, he clashed indecisively with Wittgenstein, and retired on Sienno. Wittgenstein did not pursue. Victor had already learned of Alexander's plan for the link-up of Wittgenstein and Tshitshagov, and had warned Dombrowski and Bronikowski to send out scouts and spies.

To the south, Sacken attempted to overwhelm Reynier's weak corps. Reynier skillfully lured him northward; Schwarzenberg countermarched, striking Sacken's right flank (16 November) near Volkovisk (see Map 110, B2). Sacken was chased into the Pripet Marshes, losing a third of his command. Nevertheless, by diverting Schwarzenberg, he had accomplished his mission.

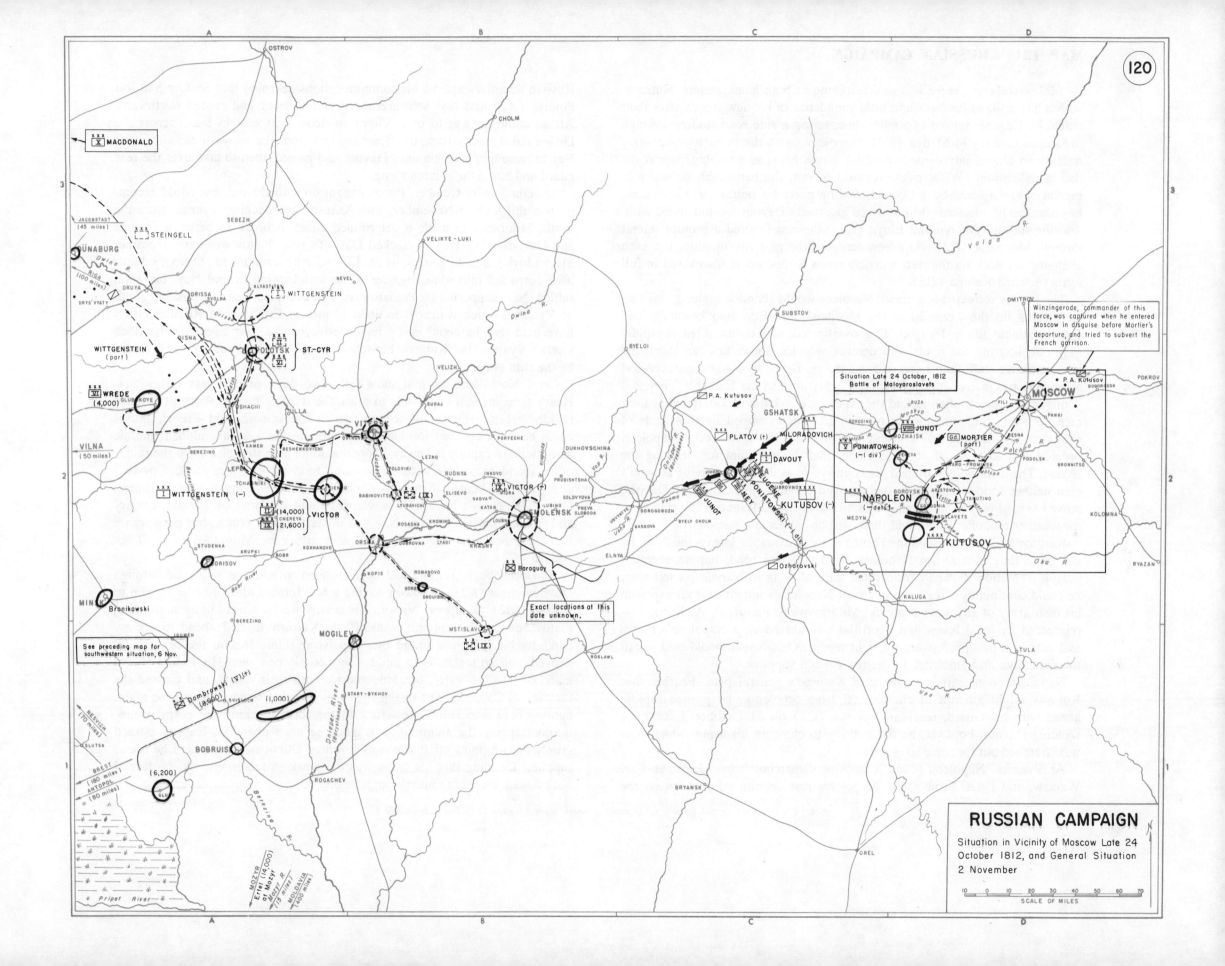

MACDONALD

Situation Late 24 October, 1812
Battle of Maloyaroslavets

Winzingerode, commander of this
force, was captured when he entered
Moscow in disguise before Mortier's
departure, and tried to subvert the
French garrison.

STEINGELL

WITTGENSTEIN
(part)

WITTGENSTEIN

ST.-CYR

WREDE
(4,000)

VILNA
(50 miles)

WITTGENSTEIN (-)

II (14,000)
IX CHEREYA (21,600)
VICTOR

VICTOR (-)

SMOLENSK

MOSCOW

P. A. Kutusov

PLATOV (+)

MILORADOVICH

DAVOUT

EUGENE
NEY
PONIATOWSKI (-1 div)
KUTUSOV (-)

JUNOT

VIII JUNOT

V PONIATOWSKI
(-1 div)

MORTIER
(part)

NAPOLEON
(-dets)

KUTUSOV

Baraguay

Exact locations at this
date unknown.

Ozharovski

See preceding map for
southwestern situation, 6 Nov.

Dombrowski (V)(+)
(8,000)

(1,000)

(6,200)

MINSK

Bronikowski

BOBRUISK

MOGILEV

MSTISLAVL

IX

RUSSIAN CAMPAIGN

Situation in Vicinity of Moscow Late 24
October 1812, and General Situation
2 November

SCALE OF MILES

At Maloyaroslavets, there was soul-searching in both headquarters. Kutusov, with a hill defile at his back and little confidence in his new troops after their defeat by Eugene, retired two miles, uncovering a side road leading through unforaged country to Medyn (*C2*). Napoleon, with the main Russian army holding an almost impregnable position across his road to Kaluga, spent the day in indecision. (While riding forward to visit the battlefield, he was momentarily endangered by a Cossack raiding party.) Contrary to his custom, he consulted his marshals. Murat urged an attack; Davout recommended withdrawing through Medyn and Elnya (*C2*); the rest favored a prompt retreat through Mozhaisk (*C2*). Napoleon accepted the majority opinion, not even changing his decision the next morning when Kutusov was discovered in full retreat toward Kaluga (*D2*).

The French retreated at a crawl. Napoleon would abandon nothing, insisting on picking up the wounded in the Mozhaisk and Borodino hospitals, and every available gun and wagon. Thus overloaded, his exhausted teams rapidly gave out, littering the roads with derelict vehicles. Provisions ran short; the administrative staff almost ceased functioning. Bored by a hard, unsuccessful campaign, too many senior officers left everything to the Emperor; energetic younger officers too often lacked the experience or habit of looking after their men. Davout, commanding the rear guard, was swamped by thousands of stragglers and lagging artillery and wagons from the main body. Napoleon ordered him to herd all of these along, then blamed him for delaying the retreat. The main body scorched the countryside as it passed, leaving Davout's men neither food, forage, nor shelter. And Eugene, just ahead of Davout, moved very slowly in his anxiety to spare his men and animals. Fortunately, the weather remained good, and there was no immediate pursuit.

Kutusov had again mislaid the French army. Advancing late on the 27th, he lost more time looking for Napoleon on the Medyn road, but his eventual pursuit formation showed considerable skill. Moving to Napoleon's left rear, he could continually threaten to intercept Napoleon's retreat without exposing his own army to any sudden attack. Miloradovich, Platov, P. A. Kutusov—reinforced by local levies and guerrillas—would envelop Napoleon's flanks and rear in a mosquito swarm of light troops. Ozharovski would raid ahead toward Elnya and Smolensk to destroy French supplies.

Napoleon soon learned or deduced Kutusov's general plan. Fearing that Kutusov might attempt to cut him off from Smolensk, he pushed rapidly ahead with his Guard, reaching Vyazma (*C2*) on 31 October. Except for scolding Davout, however, he did nothing to close up his army, which now was stretched out for some sixty miles.

At Vyazma, Napoleon found a mass of dispatches from Victor, St.-Cyr, Warsaw, and Paris. From these, he got his first definite information on the Russian offensives against his communications, learning that St.-Cyr had lost Polotsk (*A2*) and that Schwarzenberg and Reynier had retired northward. All he could do was to urge Victor to drive Wittgenstein back across the Dwina River; recall Baraguay (*not shown*) from the Elnya area; and order Ney to remain in Vyazma until Davout had passed, then to take over the rear guard and hustle the column along.

Sometime on 31 October, Platov caught up with Davout, but could accomplish nothing. On 3 November, with Kutusov approaching Vyazma from the south, Miloradovich made a determined effort to break in between Eugene and Davout, while Platov attacked Davout's rear. Platov was early repulsed; Miloradovich had to retreat when Eugene countermarched. Davout's hard-used corps fell into some disorder while withdrawing behind Ney, but soon rallied. Ney, supported by Poniatowski, had occupied a strong position south of Vyazma, which Kutusov declined to attack. English and Russian critics have held that he could easily have destroyed the four French corps then around Vyazma, but Kutusov himself obviously felt that such a battle would be the ruin of his army.

On 4 November, the first snow fell. Two days later, it was full winter. Heavy snow made it impossible to graze the starving horses. Worse, the roads rapidly became ribbons of ice, on which the smooth-shod French horses could hardly keep their footing. Guns and wagons were abandoned; morale and discipline rapidly fell away. More and more men straggled from the ranks, often abandoning their weapons, seeking food off to either flank. Cossacks and guerrillas hunted them; those who were killed outright were fortunate. One of Baraguay's brigades was surprised and captured by Russian cavalry and irregulars west of Elnya. Ney was under frequent attack, but pressure on him slackened after he repulsed a major attack by Miloradovich at Dorogobuzh (*C2*).

At Dorogobuzh, Eugene had been ordered to take the side road through Dukhovschina (*B2*), Napoleon having a half-formed idea of ordering him to Vitebsk (*B2*) to support Victor. His march was a horse-killing nightmare; Platov hounded his column, while P. A. Kutusov dashed ahead to occupy Dukhovschina. Eugene found the Vop River thinly frozen, the bridges destroyed, and no materials to build a serviceable new one. His Italian Guard marched into the water, breaking the ice with their chests, and cleared the far bank of Cossacks. The rest of the corps followed slowly through the night, fighting flank and rear. Guns stuck in the ford, blocking the corps' trains. Booby-trapping the ammunition wagons he must abandon, Eugene pushed grimly on, whipping off Platov and storming Dukhovschina, where he found supplies. Deciding that his corps was too weak to reach Vitebsk, he turned back toward the main route through Smolensk.

Note: On this map, in the French force moving north from Mogilev (A1), Svitloch *should be* Svisloch.

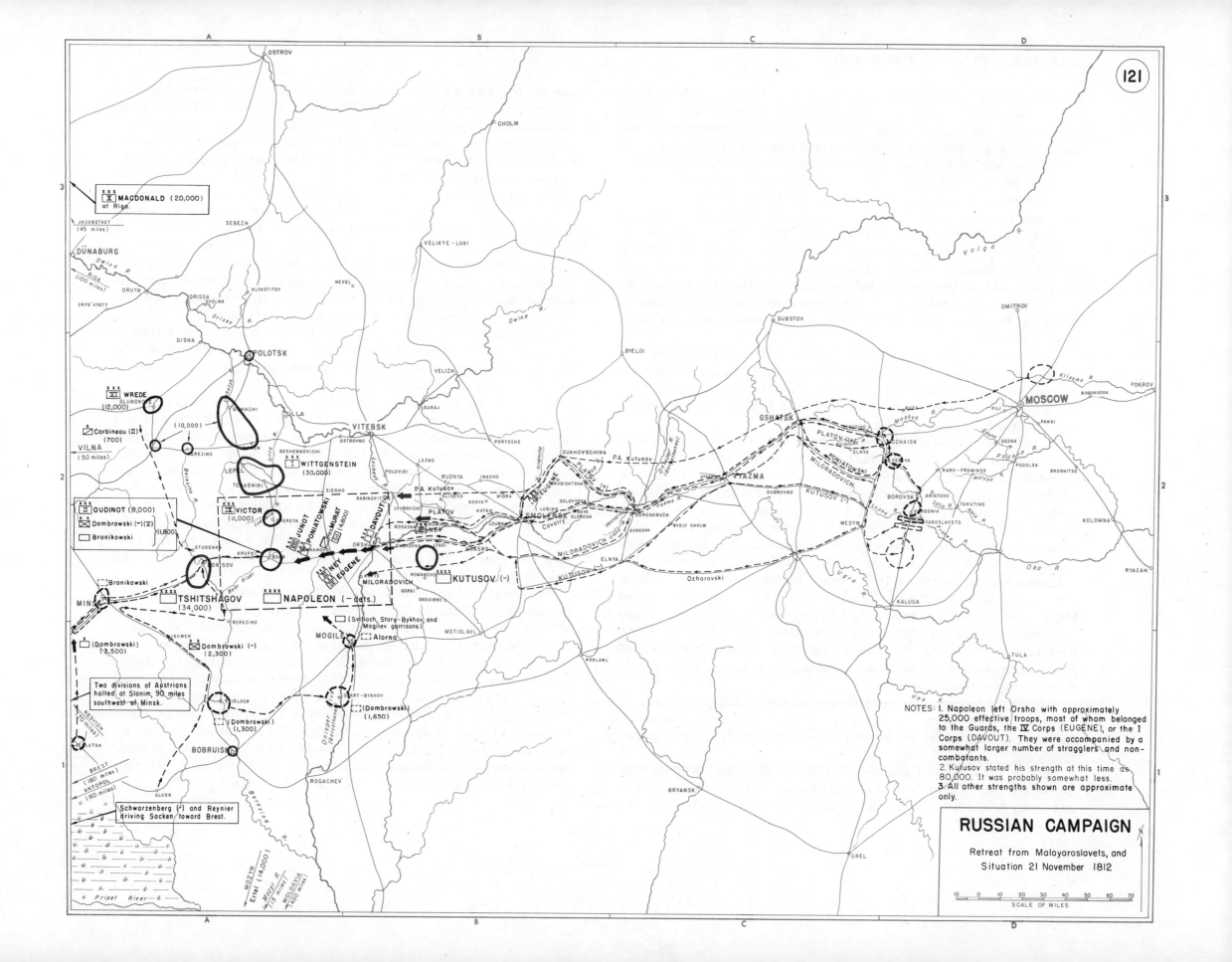

121

MACDONALD (20,000) at Riga.

MACDONALD (20,000) at Riga.

WREDE (12,000)

Corbineau (II) (700)

OUDINOT (8,000)
Dombrowski (-)(V)
Bronikowski (1,800)

VICTOR (11,000)

WITTGENSTEIN (30,000)

Bronikowski

TSHITSHAGOV (34,000)

NAPOLEON (-dets.)

(Dombrowski) (3,500)

Dombrowski (-) (2,300)

(Svisloch, Stary-Bykhov and Mogilev garrisons)
Aloma

Two divisions of Austrians halted at Slonim, 90 miles southwest of Minsk.

(Dombrowski) (1,300)

(Dombrowski) (1,650)

Schwarzenberg (-) and Reynier driving Sacken toward Brest.

Ertel (14,000)

KUTUSOV (-)

PLATOV
PONIATOWSKI
MILORADOVICH

MILORADOVICH

KUTUSOV (-)

NOTES: 1. Napoleon left Orsha with approximately 25,000 effective troops, most of whom belonged to the Guards, the IV Corps (EUGENE), or the I Corps (DAVOUT). They were accompanied by a somewhat larger number of stragglers and non-combatants.
2. Kutusov stated his strength at this time as 80,000. It was probably somewhat less.
3. All other strengths shown are approximate only.

RUSSIAN CAMPAIGN

Retreat from Maloyaroslavets, and Situation 21 November 1812

SCALE OF MILES

As a soldier, Napoleon had touched his lowest ebb. Traveling near the head of the army, in the middle of his Guard, he at times seemed to have abdicated his command. He warned neither Victor, Macdonald, Schwarzenberg, nor Maret of his plight, and made no effort to coordinate their operations. (It was 7 November when he finally advised Victor that the main army was exhausted and its situation critical.) And, by isolating himself from his army, he completely neglected its still-deep resources of morale and devotion.

Napoleon reached Smolensk on 9 November, and found bad news: the loss of Baraguay's brigade; Wittgenstein's capture of Vitebsk (7 November); sickness among Victor's young conscripts. He grouped his remaining cavalry under Latour-Maubourg, warned Dombrowski to cover Minsk, ordered the Guard issued fifteen days' rations and other units six. The Smolensk administrative staff fumbled the situation, either demanding formal requisitions or panicking. Stragglers began looting, other troops joined them, and many supplies were wasted.

Instead of leaving Smolensk with his 50,000 effective troops well closed up, Napoleon proceeded as if the Russians did not exist. Junot and Poniatowski marched on 12–13 November; the Guard on the 14th; Eugene on the 15th. Davout and Ney were to march on the 16th—and Ney was to delay another day, if necessary, to blow up Smolensk's walls.

On 15 November, Napoleon overtook Junot near Krasny (B2), ordered a halt to await Eugene, and sent back word for Davout and Ney to march immediately. Somewhere along that road—possibly during a running fight in which Mortier had cuffed Miloradovich aside—Napoleon had become himself again. On learning that Russians held the villages south of Krasny in strength, he delivered a vicious night attack, scattering or destroying Ozharovski's corps. Prisoners reported Kutusov nearby. (Kutusov actually had got within two miles of Krasny, but retired on learning that Napoleon was there.)

Eugene was intercepted on 16 November by Miloradovich at a difficult defile seven miles east of Krasny. Repulsed, he waited until dusk, then turned Miloradovich's left flank, and reached Krasny—aided by a Young Guard detachment that made a demonstration toward Miloradovich's rear. Shortly thereafter, Davout reached Miloradovich's position. He already had warned Ney to hurry, since the situation was worsening; now, he concentrated for a desperate attack the next morning.

Early on 17 November, contemptuous of his enemy, Napoleon seized the initiative. Sending Eugene toward the vital Orsha bridges (B2), and leaving Claparede to hold Krasny, he marched eastward with the Guard and Latour-Maubourg.

Kutusov reportedly had planned a holding attack against Krasny, while Tormassov (now Kutusov's chief of staff) cut the highway between Krasny and Orsha. Miloradovich was to let Davout pass, damaging him as much as possible, then reclose the highway behind him to stop Ney. Thrown off balance by Napoleon's move, Kutusov halted Tormassov. His attack on Krasny failed; Miloradovich, caught between Napoleon and Davout, retired immediately.

That afternoon, fearing that Kutusov's supineness might mask a Russian dash on Orsha, Napoleon reluctantly resumed his retreat. Tomassov immediately attacked. Hoping that Ney would appear, Davout delayed until so hard pressed that he had to sacrifice his rear-guard regiment to extricate himself.

Ney, in an umbrageous temper, had scorned Davout's warning, deliberately remaining at Smolensk until the morning of the 17th. The next day, he ran into Kutusov's army, formed across the highway in Miloradovich's former position. Summoned to surrender, he attacked head on, but was repulsed after a short, savage fight. Favored by the early dusk, he then retired eastward and camped. After dark, leaving his fires burning, he turned north and crossed the Dnieper over treacherous ice, abandoning his guns and baggage.

Platov attacked him the next morning, but was fought off in a running battle through the woods bordering the river. Alerted by a Polish officer who had slipped through to Orsha, Eugene marched eastward and brought Ney in—with 900 survivors out of 6,000.

Meanwhile, on 16 November, Tshitshagov had captured Minsk with its immense depots. Despite repeated warnings, the feckless Bronikowski had neither fortified the city nor organized an intelligence network to report Tshitshagov's progress. Learning (18 November) of this new misfortune, Napoleon finally ordered Dombrowski, Oudinot, and Victor to Borisov (A2), the site of his one bridge across the Berezina River. His plan now was to fight his way back through Minsk, pick up Schwarzenberg, and hold the line of the Berezina. Pausing briefly at Orsha to reorganize, he likewise marched on Borisov. Because of time lost trying to trap Ney, Kutusov had fallen behind; only some Russian cavalry and horse artillery remained in contact with Davout, who again formed the rear guard.

Bronikowski had retired into the bridgehead guarding the west end of the Borisov bridge. Here, on 21 November—though warned by prisoners of Tshitshagov's approach—he allowed himself to be surprised. Dombrowski arrived too late to restore the situation, and the bridge and Borisov were lost.

During 11–13 November, Oudinot and Victor had skirmished indecisively with Wittgenstein near Tchasniki (A2). Wrede (considerably reinforced through Maret's efforts) had offered to aid them by an advance on Wittgenstein's rear, but had been ignored—except for a demand that he return Corbineau's brigade of light cavalry, which St.-Cyr had loaned him after the evacuation of Polotsk. Released on 17 November, Corbineau moved skillfully across country toward Borisov, only to find it held by the enemy. Friendly civilians, however, directed him to a ford at nearby Studenka.

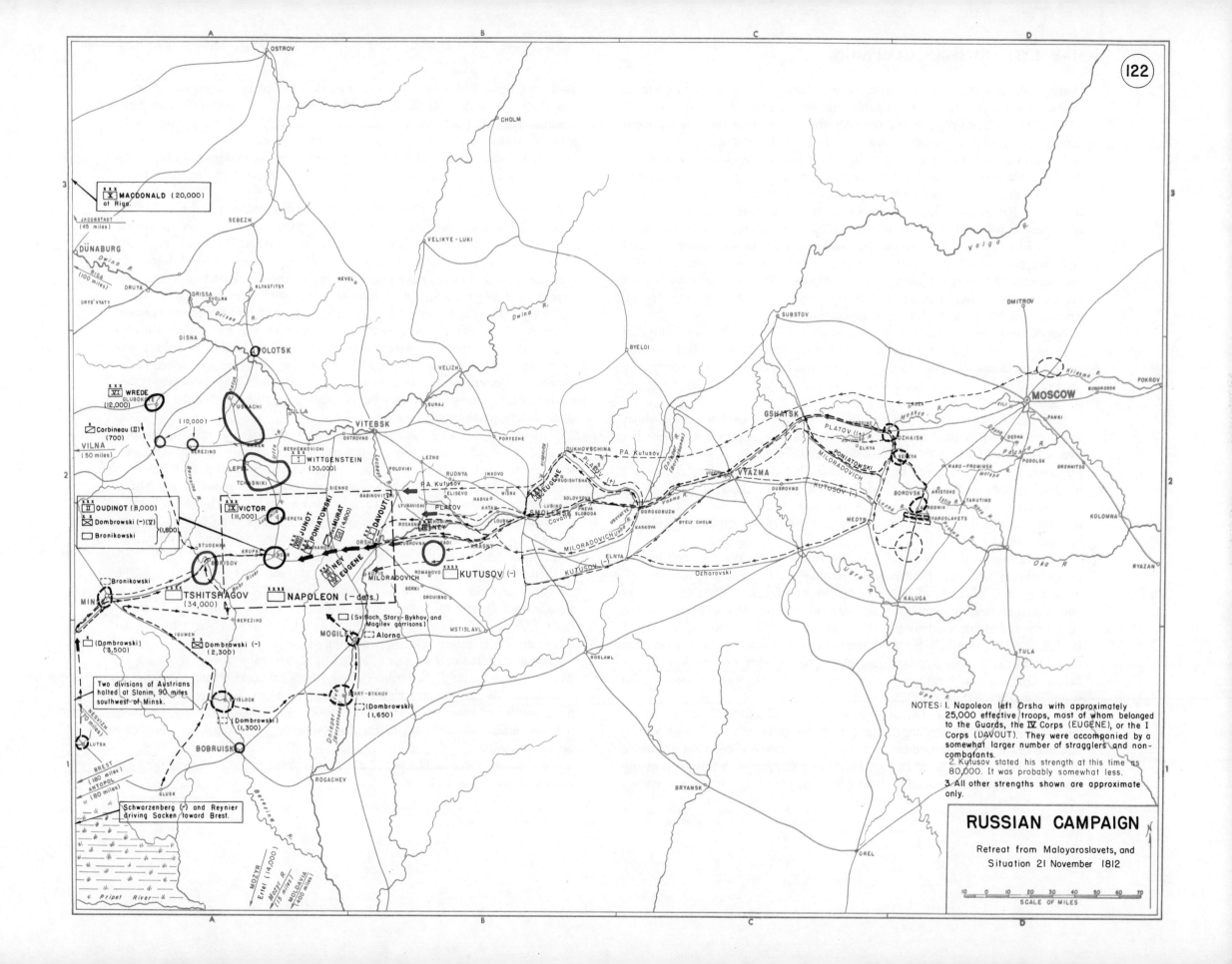

122

XXX
X MACDONALD (20,000)
at Riga.

JACOBSTADT
(45 miles)

DÜNABURG

RIGA
(100 miles)

XXX
VI WREDE
GLUBOKOE
(12,000)

(10,000)

VILNA
(50 miles)

XXX
IX VICTOR
(11,000)

XXX
II OUDINOT (8,000)
⊠ Dombrowski (-)(V)
□ Bronikowski
(1,800)

I WITTGENSTEIN
(30,000)

PA Kutusov

PLATOV

P.A. Kutusov

PONIATOWSKI
MURAT
(4,800)

JUNOT
NEY
DAVOUT

EUGENE

□ Bronikowski

XXXX
TSHITSHAGOV
(34,000)

EUGENE
NEY

MILORADOVICH

XXXX
NAPOLEON (-dets.)

XXXX
KUTUSOV (-)

X (Dombrowski)
(3,500)

⊠ Dombrowski (-)
(2,300)

□ (Svitloch, Stary-Bykhov, and
Mogilev garrisons)

□ Alorna

MILORADOVICH

KUTUSOV (-)

Two divisions of Austrians
halted at Slonim, 90 miles
southwest of Minsk.

Dombrowski)
(1,300)

□ (Dombrowski)
(1,650)

BREST
(180 miles)
ANTOPOL
(80 miles)

Schwarzenberg (-) and Reynier
driving Sacken toward Brest.

MOZYR (14,000)
Ertel

MOZYR R.
(75 miles)

MOLDAVIA
(400 miles)

Pripet River

NOTES: 1. Napoleon left Orsha with approximately
25,000 effective troops, most of whom belonged
to the Guards, the IV Corps (EUGENE), or the I
Corps (DAVOUT). They were accompanied by a
somewhat larger number of stragglers and non-
combatants.
2. Kutusov stated his strength at this time as
80,000. It was probably somewhat less.
3. All other strengths shown are approximate
only.

RUSSIAN CAMPAIGN

Retreat from Maloyaroslavets, and
Situation 21 November 1812

10 0 10 20 30 40 50 60 70
SCALE OF MILES

Orsha had been the salvation of the French army. Its commanding officer and administrative staff were capable and determined, and had taken all possible measures to receive and resupply the troops from their well-stocked magazines. Insofar as possible, stragglers had been sent back to their units and rearmed. In a belated effort to lighten his army, Napoleon ordered all surplus vehicles burned, and their horses transferred to the artillery. He himself set the example, destroying most of his papers and personal baggage. Counting, somewhat overoptimistically, on being able to use the Borisov bridge, he even burned his ponton bridge train, over the objections of its commander, General Eble. (However, Eble quietly managed to retain two field forges and eight wagons loaded with coal and tools. Each of his pontoniers carried a tool, spikes, and clamps.) Though it was impossible to give the army what it needed most—a short rest—it pulled itself together to a surprising degree. The news of Ney's escape further raised morale.

Napoleon received Oudinot's report of the loss of the Borisov bridge at Tolochin (*D3*) on 22 November. Oudinot's report added that he would advance on Borisov to develop the situation, was pessimistic about recovering the bridge, but knew of a good ford at Veselovo (*A2*), about ten miles upstream.

Napoleon's first reaction was a hasty message that Oudinot must either recover the Borisov bridge or locate another crossing point somewhere between Berezino (*twenty-five miles south*) and Veselovo. If it were toward Berezino, it must be secured by the 24th, so that the main army could turn south from Bobr (*C2*) without losing time. Later, after checking his maps, he decided for the Veselovo crossing and ordered (0100, 23 November) Oudinot to seize that crossing, build two bridges, and construct fortified bridgeheads to protect them.

Oudinot meanwhile had marched on Borisov with the II Corps and part of Dombrowski's division. Tshitshagov, learning that Napoleon might be approaching, had left most of his army on the west bank of the Berezina, but had moved his headquarters and trains into Borisov, and sent a strong advance guard toward Bobr. Oudinot's cavalry struck this force two miles west of Loshnitsa (*B2*), smashing it into a panicked mob that went scampering back through Borisov. The Russians just managed to burn the Borisov bridge before Oudinot could rush it, but left him some 350 wagons loaded with supplies and more than 1,000 prisoners.

Oudinot had learned of two other fords: one at Studenka (from Corbineau, who joined him after crossing there during the night of 21–22 November), and one nearer Borisov, used by a Polish regiment that had been cut off on the 21st. He and his staff appear to have been fairly familiar with this area; at any rate, Oudinot quickly decided to use the Studenka crossing. Not as well known

as the Veselovo ford, it was less likely to be watched by the enemy. Also, it was shallower, and so would need less preparation. As soon as it was dark, Oudinot sent off Corbineau, a regiment of infantry, and his pontoniers to seize it. At the same time, he pressed reconnaissances for additional crossing points and began a study of the road net from Bobr to Studenka. In reporting these actions, Oudinot added that Tshitshagov appeared to be shifting troops southward toward Berezino.

Napoleon's orders of 20 November to Victor directed that he be in Borisov on the 26th to form the rear guard for the army during its march on Minsk. Retiring on the 23d, Victor marched due south to Bobr, thus uncovering the Chereya (*C3*)–Veselovo road and Oudinot's right rear. Had Wittgenstein been alert, he still might have been able to bar the Berezina line against the French. But Wittgenstein (according to Clausewitz, who was on his staff) had only the vaguest idea of the existing situation. For unknown reasons, Tshitshagov's recent efforts to establish liaison with him had failed. He also had no idea of Kutusov's whereabouts, but he *had* heard that Napoleon was approaching with an army of 60,000. (Note that Napoleon's presence is beginning to dominate the situation. While Wittgenstein and Tshitshagov become hesitant, Oudinot suddenly begins operating efficiently for the first time since the campaign began.)

Napoleon's actions during the next few days are only partially understood because of the subsequent loss of vital records and certain key subordinates. It is certain that he studied routes other than the Studenka and Veselovo crossings. Bronikowski's staff was questioned about the roads in the Minsk area and the supply situation between Borisov and Minsk. The roads leading southward to Berezino were likewise checked. Another plan reportedly considered was that of concentrating all available troops, defeating Wittgenstein, and returning to Vilna through Lepel (*see Map 122, A2*).

Victor was ordered to be in Kholopenichi (*this map, B3*) on the night of the 23d to cover Oudinot against an advance through Barany (*B3*). If Wittgenstein moved against Oudinot, Victor must attack him vigorously. Unfortunately, Victor had already, as previously noted, got too far south to execute this order. Wittgenstein was following him gingerly.

Davout reported that he was followed by considerable forces of Cossacks, with a few pieces of light artillery. The Cossacks heckled him periodically and shelled his camps every night. His major problem, however, was an "infinite number of stragglers," who clung close to his troops for safety, but—on the least alarm—would rush to the rear, spreading confusion and breaking up his formations.

Northward, Wrede had launched a reconnaissance in force, driving the local Russian forces back on Lepel.

Note: In the title block of this map (and similarly on Maps 124–25), Beresina should be Berezina. In the note on this map (D1), oniatowski should read Poniatowski.

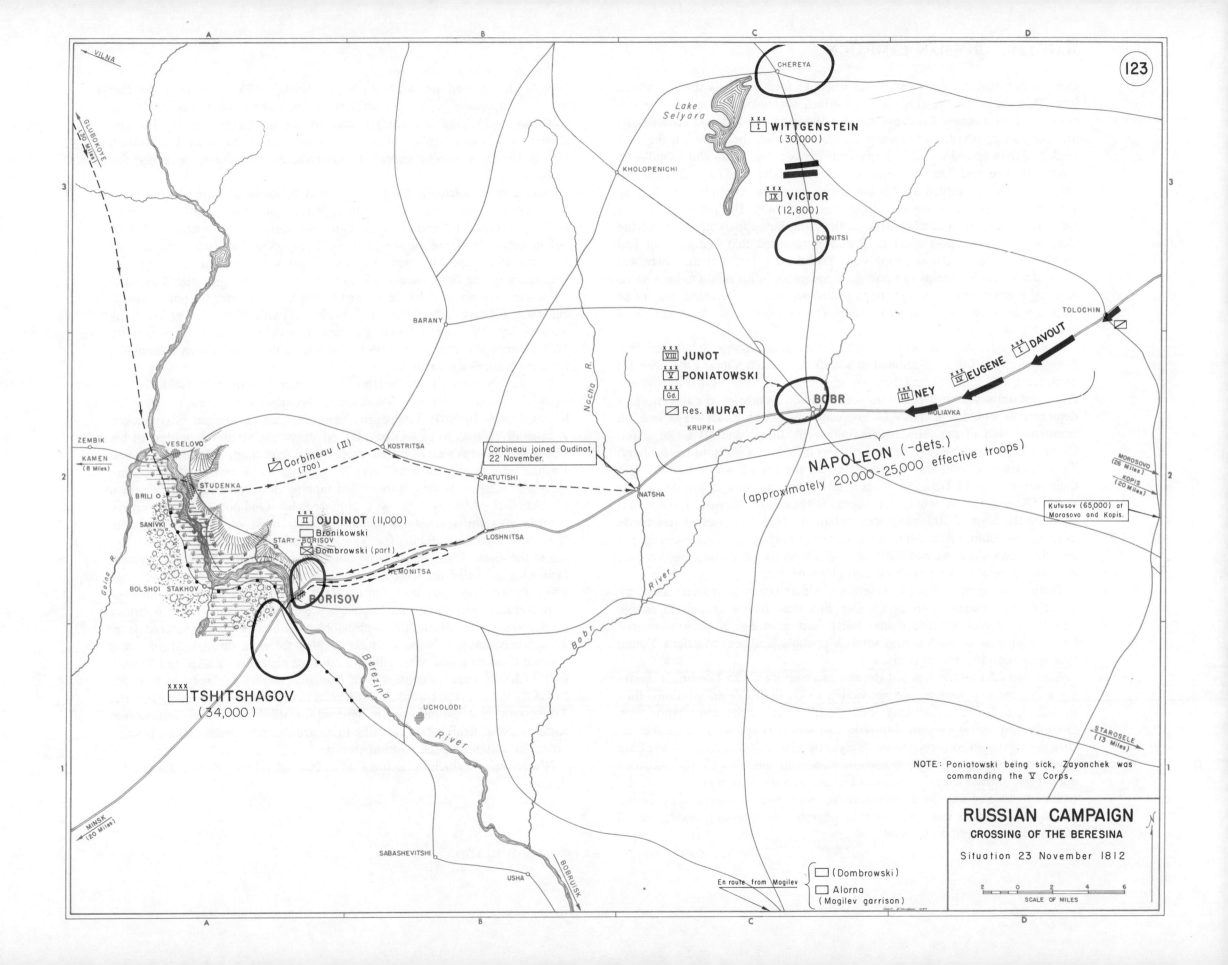

123

VILNA

Lake Selyara

CHEREYA

XXX
I WITTGENSTEIN
(30,000)

KHOLOPENICHI

XXX
IX VICTOR
(12,800)

DOKNITSI

GLUBOKOYE
(20 Miles)

TOLOCHIN

BARANY

Nacha R.

XXX
VIII JUNOT

XXX
V PONIATOWSKI

Gd.

Res. MURAT

KRUPKI

BOBR

XXX
I DAVOUT

XXX
IV EUGENE

XXX
III NEY

MOLIAVKA

MOROSOVO
(26 Miles)

KOPIS
(20 Miles)

ZEMBIK

KAMEN
(8 Miles)

VESELOVO

Corbineau (II)
(700)

KOSTRITSA

RATUTISHI

Corbineau joined Oudinot,
22 November.

NATSHA

NAPOLEON (-dets.)

(approximately 20,000-25,000 effective troops)

Kutusov (65,000) at
Morosovo and Kopis.

STUDENKA

BRILI

SANIVKI

STARY BORISOV

XXX
II OUDINOT (11,000)

Bronikowski

Dombrowski (part)

LOSHNITSA

NEMONITSA

Gaina R.

BOLSHOI STAKHOV

BORISOV

Bobr River

TSHITSHAGOV
(34,000)

Berezina

UCHOLODI

STAROSELE
(13 Miles)

MINSK
(20 Miles)

NOTE: Poniatowski being sick, Zayonchek was
commanding the V Corps.

SABASHEVITSHI

USHA

River

BOBRUISK

En route from Mogilev

(Dombrowski)

Alorna
(Mogilev garrison)

RUSSIAN CAMPAIGN
CROSSING OF THE BERESINA

Situation 23 November 1812

2   0   2   4   6
SCALE OF MILES

Corbineau found the west bank of the Studenka ford held by a strong Russian force. Moreover, the weather having warmed somewhat during the last few days, the ford was now five feet deep, the Berezina had widened accordingly, and the current was full of floating ice cakes. Worse, the marsh on the west bank had thawed and would be impassable for vehicles. Meanwhile, Oudinot's reconnaissance had located fords at Bolshoi-Stakhov (*A2*) and Ucholodi (*B1*). Both were guarded by Russian detachments, but Oudinot was carrying out demonstrations at every ford from Veselovo south. He had issued orders for a march on Studenka after dark on the 24th, but, apparently on receiving Corbineau's report, postponed it. Prisoners reported that Wittgenstein had finally established communication with Tshitshagov, but that the latter was worried about Schwarzenberg's possible appearance in his rear. Oudinot noted that Tshitshagov was sending troops southward toward Berezino, but in so open a manner that he suspected a feint. Oudinot had as yet been unable to contact Victor.

Concurrently, lacking any reliable information as to Schwarzenberg, Napoleon appears to have decided to withdraw through Vilna. Eble, with his pontoniers, and Chasseloup (the army engineer), with the available engineer and naval units, were ordered to support Oudinot. Dombrowski's and Alorna's detachments would join the V Corps, which would be under Ney's over-all command. Half of the vehicles remaining with the V and VIII Corps and Claparede's division were to be burned, and their horses given to the artillery. Since Oudinot's dispatches made it plain that the French would have to fight their way across the Berezina, Napoleon wanted his guns as mobile as possible. The main army would move gradually toward Borisov, Davout still covering the mass of straggling noncombatants. Napoleon viewed this horde as men who could, given a little food and breathing space, once more be got into the ranks. Also, he had the true soldier's horror of abandoning his own wounded and, always an artilleryman, of losing guns.

During the night of 23–24 November, winter began to reassert itself; by the 25th, the marshes west of the Berezina were frozen enough to enable infantry to deploy off the roads. Early that morning, Napoleon ordered Oudinot to cross at Studenka as soon as possible, and sent Mortier's Young Guard division forward to Borisov.

Eble and Chasseloup reached Borisov at about 0430, 25 November. Leaving a detachment there to add conviction to Oudinot's demonstrations, they pushed on to Studenka, arriving about 1630. After a brief consultation with Oudinot and Murat (whom Napoleon had sent forward with impossible instructions to begin constructing the bridges by 2200), it was decided that Eble would construct two trestle bridges, Chasseloup one. At 1800, Oudinot's main body slipped silently northward from Borisov, leaving only small detachments to continue the demonstrations. Work went on desperately during the night. Studenka was torn down to provide the necessary wood; needed iron work was forged on the spot.

Victor had moved out two hours before daylight (25 November), but had found it impossible to get his artillery through the back roads leading to Kostritsa (*B2*), and accordingly had to detour farther south. He and Davout had begun burning all bridges behind them, to delay the Russian regular troops. Cossacks appeared intermittently, but could be easily dispersed.

Napoleon intended—if the bridges could be finished during the night of 25 November—to cross with Oudinot, Victor, and the Guard, and, "with the help of God," to clear the right bank and carry out an operation "which will influence the rest of the campaign." (He expected that Victor would reach Kostritsa during the 25th, and so be available.) Victor was to leave one division north of the Bobr-Borisov highway to contain Wittgenstein. The other corps were to gradually close in toward Borisov; if successful, Napoleon would call them forward across the river, beginning with Ney. The gendarmerie were to halt all stragglers and dismounted cavalrymen east of Nemonitsa (*B2*). During the 25th, Napoleon reconnoitered the Borisov area thoroughly, reaching Studenka after midnight.

Thoroughly nervous at the thought of facing Napoleon "with 70,000 French" (like other Russian commanders, he mistook the mass of stragglers for serviceable troops), Tshitshagov easily became submerged in confusion. A third of his own force was cavalry, which would be almost useless in the woods and swamps west of the Berezina. More important, Schwarzenberg and Reynier were in his rear with forces far superior to his own, and Napoleon's army was massing around Borisov and tapping at every ford from Veselovo to Ucholodi. Although he was confused by Oudinot's demonstrations, Tshitshagov's initial dispositions were sound: most of his army opposite Borisov, a division watching the Veselovo-Studenka fords, and detachments out to the south. Then, on 24 November, came a dispatch from Wittgenstein expressing the belief that Napoleon was attempting to retire through Borisov and Bobruisk (*off map, B1*). On the 25th, Tshitshagov received a message from Kutusov, suggesting that Napoleon was moving toward either Bobruisk or Berezino. This information—probably a garbled version (secured from French prisoners) of Napoleon's earlier plan to retire through Minsk—was the best Kutusov could offer. His own advance elements (Platov and Yermolov) had only tenuous contact with Davout. Interested chiefly in loot, the Cossacks and irregulars were almost useless at collecting intelligence. To date, Tshitshagov had enthusiastically ignored or disobeyed every order from Kutusov. Now, deliberately choosing to regard this hazy message as a positive order, he shifted into the position shown.

Wittgenstein, detaching a force of 6,000 to follow Victor, started for Barany.

Note: On this map, Zayonchek (B2) should be Zajonczek.

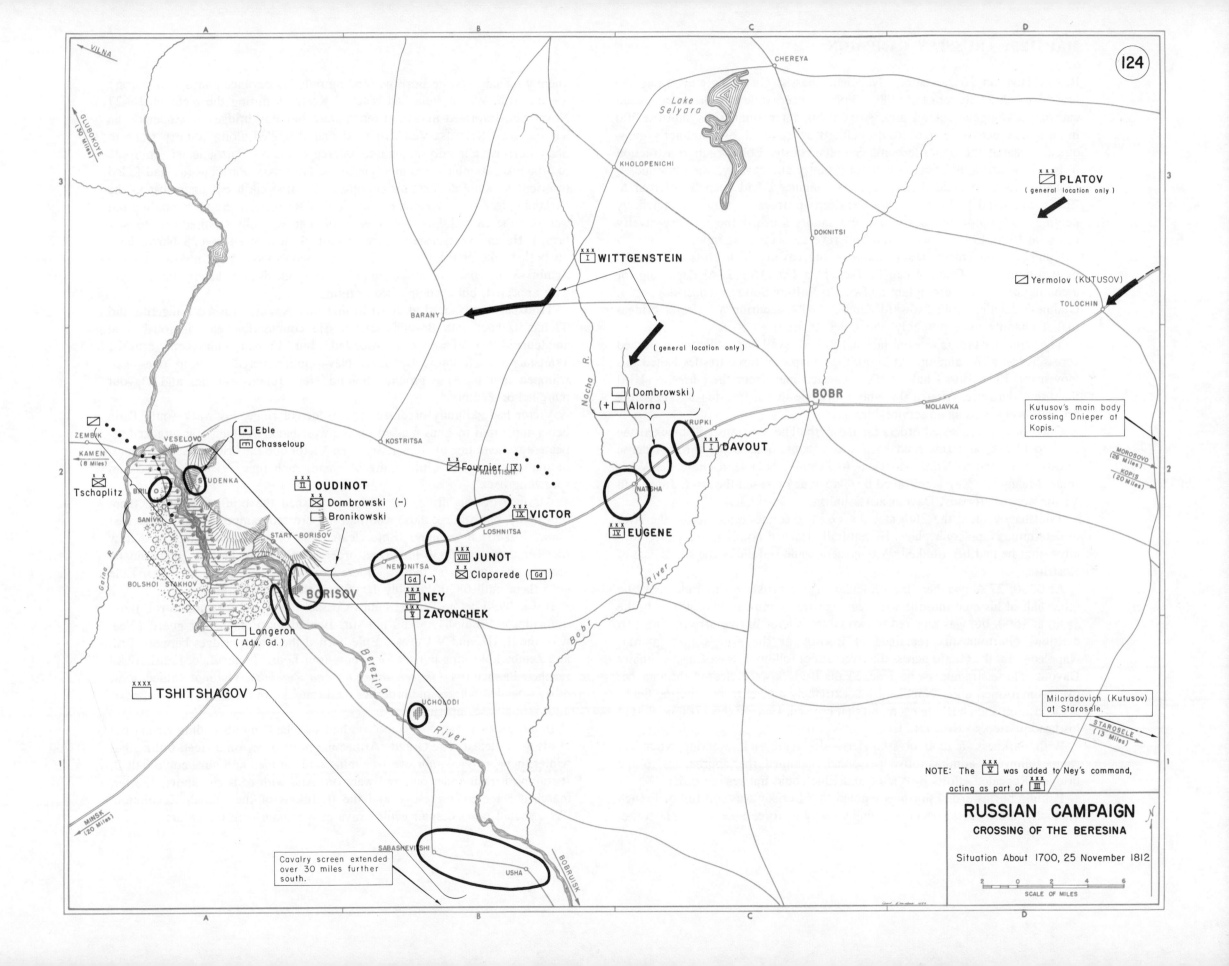

RUSSIAN CAMPAIGN
CROSSING OF THE BERESINA

Situation About 1700, 25 November 1812

Before dawn on 26 November, Napoleon massed Oudinot's guns along the low ridge behind Studenka. At 0800, Polish lancers rode into the stream, each carrying a voltigeur behind him. After them, three small rafts shuttled 300 infantrymen across. These troops, efficiently covered by Oudinot's guns, quickly cleared the opposite bank. Simultaneously, Eble began construction of two 105-yard-long bridges—one for infantry and cavalry, one for vehicles. (Lacking tools to build their bridge, the engineers had been transferred to Eble's command.) Working shoulder-deep in freezing water, buffeted by floating ice, pontoniers, engineers, and sailors finished the infantry-cavalry bridge at 1300. Eble, austere and deeply revered, set the example.

Oudinot's and Dombrowski's infantry and cavalry then crossed, followed by two light guns. Oudinot caught Tschaplitz (see Map 124) deploying for a counterattack, and drove him halfway to Bolshoi-Stakhov (this map, A2). Oudinot's cavalry pushed toward Zembik (A2), securing a series of bridges that Tschaplitz unaccountably had failed to destroy.

The vehicular bridge was finished at 1600; all available artillery was pushed across as fast as it came up. At 2000, the collapse of three trestles halted this movement. Eble roused half of his exhausted men from their fires, and led them into the river. After a three-hour struggle in the freezing darkness, the artillery bridge was again serviceable.

Oudinot now requested orders for the 27th. The Russians still blocked the road to Minsk, and this road itself was a continuous defile through dense forests. The road to Vilna was clear to Zembik. Napoleon chose the Vilna route. Meanwhile Ney (reinforced by Claparede) crossed the river. Junot and Victor were at Borisov, Davout at Loshnitsa.

Tshitshagov spent the 26th at Usha (B1), reconnoitering across the river to determine Napoleon's plans. He naturally learned nothing, except—gradually—that he had been bilked. Wittgenstein wallowed along the roads east of Kostritsa.

At 0200, 27 November, the vehicular bridge broke again; Eble took the other half of his men into the wreckage, got traffic moving by 0600. It broke again at 1600, but was repaired in two hours. Victor having arrived with two divisions (Partouneaux remained at Borisov as the army's rear guard), Napoleon sent the Guard across the river. Junot followed, then Eugene, finally Davout. Those stragglers who reached the bridges were cleared through between the formed units. Napoleon was extremely active, reconnoitering Oudinot's position and checking each unit that crossed. Late on the 27th, he shifted his headquarters to Brili (A2).

With darkness, a mob of stragglers—deserters, sick, walking wounded, camp followers, administrative personnel—jammed the approaches to the bridges. Repeated efforts by Victor and Eble could not restore order.

Panting northward, Tshitshagov noted that Borisov was still full of French (actually, mostly stragglers), seemingly ready to force a crossing. He conse-quently halted opposite Borisov, sending only his advance guard (Langeron) toward Brili. Wittgenstein had reached Kostritsa during the night of 26–27 November. Informed that the French were building bridges at Studenka, he left the good Kostritsa-Veselovo road and struggled along country trails to Stary-Borisov, allegedly hoping to intercept Victor. Partouneaux, en route to Studenka, stumbled into him late in the afternoon. Partouneaux had failed to orient his subordinates; his capture at the first clash left them lost in the darkening forests. Nevertheless, they fought savagely, some units holding out well into the 28th. Tshitshagov meanwhile had sketchily repaired the Borisov bridge. He and Wittgenstein agreed to attack next morning (28 November) on both banks of the river, while Tshitshagov's cavalry (Lanskoi) cut the Zembik-Vilna road. Yermolov came up and joined Tshitshagov. Platov likewise appeared, but accomplished nothing.

Tshitshagov advanced at dawn to find that Ney had rushed Langeron and Tschaplitz back into Bolshoi-Stakhov. He counterattacked, vigorously and amateurishly. Oudinot was wounded, but French cuirassiers crushed Tshitshagov's left flank. By dark, Ney—outnumbered three to one—had whipped him into the ground. Behind Ney, Junot, Eugene, and Davout marched on Zembik.

Victor had skillfully organized the Studenka ridge, his weak south flank being supported by guns massed on the west bank. Wittgenstein attacked repeatedly, attempting to break in between Victor and the bridges. Several times, he managed to place artillery fire on them; each time, Victor knocked him sprawling back.

Alarmed by this firing, the stragglers rushed the bridges, blocking them repeatedly, but at dusk those who had not crossed camped again on the east bank, deaf to all warnings. Eble cleared the bridges, and Victor withdrew between 2100 and 0630 in perfect order. The sight of his rear guard finally aroused the stragglers; though ordered to burn the bridges at 0700, Eble gave them until 0830. Possibly 10,000 of them did not escape.

It was 0900 before Wittgenstein's Cossacks ventured forward to rob those unfortunates. Tshitshagov did not stir. Behind the French rear guard (Ney, with the II, III, and V Corps), Eble burned the major bridges between Brili and Zembik, blocking pursuit for twenty-four hours. Meanwhile, Lanskoi had reached Pleshenitisy (sixteen miles beyond Zembik). Oudinot rallied some other wounded officers and orderlies, and fought him off until Junot's appearance sent him scampering.

In more senses than one, Napoleon had snatched an outstanding victory out of his worst defeat. The Grande Armee might be dying on its feet, but neither winter, hunger, rivers, nor overwhelming odds in men and guns could halt it. It trampled them underfoot, and went on. And with it, borne above disaster, marched Napoleon's prestige and the traditions of the French Revolution. "You should never despair while brave men remain with the colors."

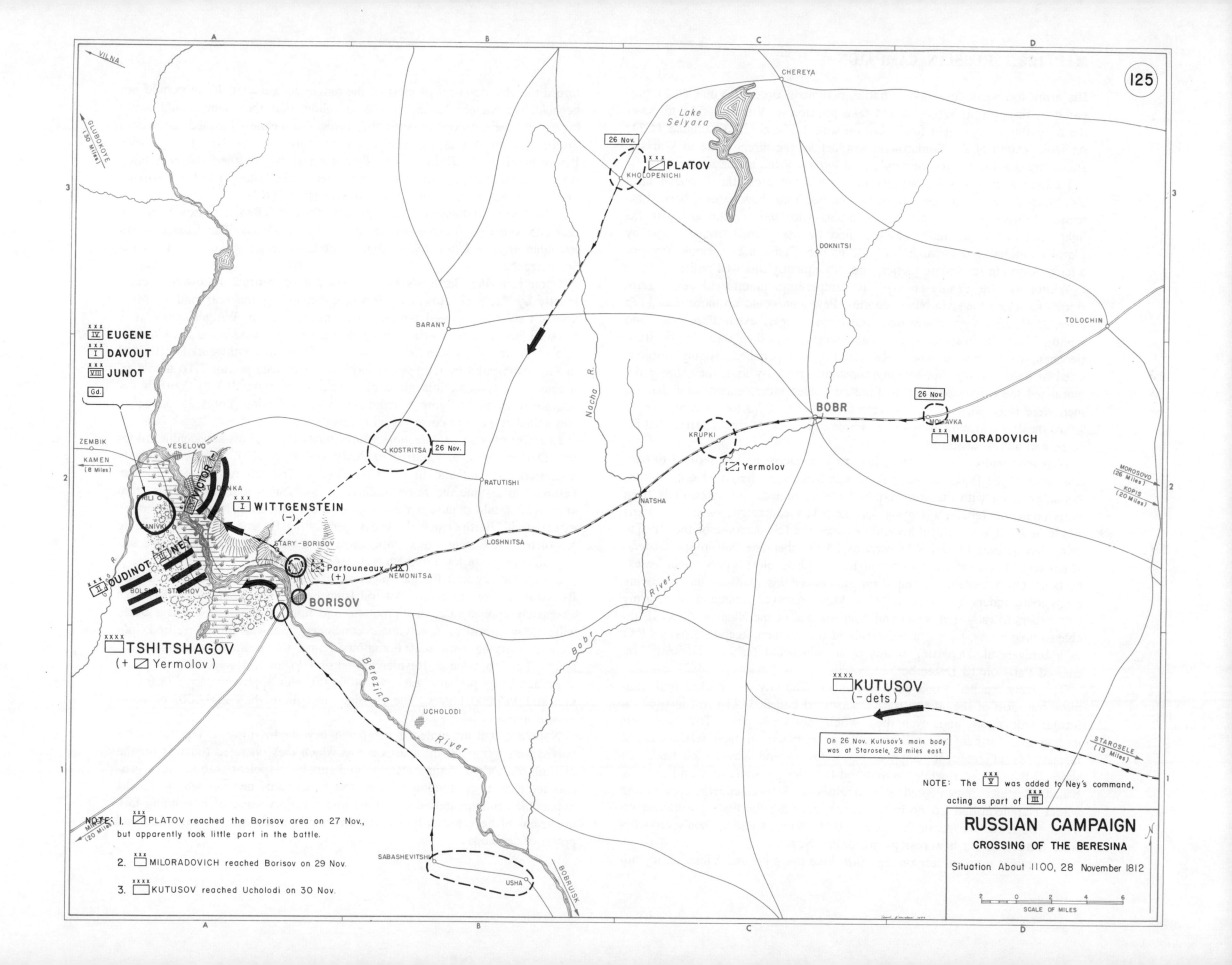

125

VILNA

GLUBOKOYE
(30 Miles)

CHEREYA

Lake Selyara

26 Nov.

xxx
◿ PLATOV
KHOLOPENICHI

DOKNITSI

TOLOCHIN

xxx
IV EUGENE
xxx
I DAVOUT
xxx
VIII JUNOT
Gd.

BARANY

BOBR

26 Nov.
MOHAVKA

xxx
MILORADOVICH

ZEMBIK

KAMEN
(8 Miles)

VESELOVO

DONKA

26 Nov.
KOSTRITSA

KRUPKI

◿ Yermolov

MOROSOVO
(26 Miles)

KOPIS
(20 Miles)

xxx
VICTOR

xxx
I WITTGENSTEIN
(—)

RATUTISHI

NATSHA

STARY-BORISOV

NEY

Partouneaux (IX)
(+)
NEMONITSA

LOSHNITSA

Nacha R.

xxx
OUDINOT
II

BOLSHOI STAKHOV

BORISOV

xxxx
TSHITSHAGOV
(+ ◿ Yermolov)

Bobr River

Berezina River

UCHOLODI

xxxx
KUTUSOV
(— dets)

On 26 Nov. Kutusov's main body
was at Starosele, 28 miles east.

STAROSELE
(13 Miles)

MILES
(20 Miles)

River

SABASHEVITSHI

USHA

BOBRUISK

NOTE: The ⊠ was added to Ney's command,
acting as part of III
xxx

NOTE: 1. ◿ PLATOV reached the Borisov area on 27 Nov.,
but apparently took little part in the battle.

2. ☐ MILORADOVICH reached Borisov on 29 Nov.

3. ☐ KUTUSOV reached Ucholodi on 30 Nov.

RUSSIAN CAMPAIGN

CROSSING OF THE BERESINA

Situation About 1100, 28 November 1812

SCALE OF MILES
2   0   2   4   6

His army too weak for another battle, Napoleon ordered Vilna (*C2*) prepared to resupply it. Wrede would take position at Vileyka (*C2*) to cover the retreating army's right flank; Loison would advance to Oszmiana (*C2*). At Molodechno (*C2*), Poniatowski would take the direct route to Warsaw. Junot and the dismounted cavalry would bypass Vilna to the south.

Lacking a bridge train, Wittgenstein could not cross the Berezina until Tshitshagov loaned him the necessary pontons. Tshitshagov's own belated attempt at direct pursuit—sending Tschaplitz (*not shown*) forward with his light troops—was promptly blocked, first by the burned bridges, next by Platov's wandering command. On 2 December, Tschaplitz overtook Ney, got a harsh lesson in rear-guard tactics, and subsequently followed politely.

Winter was the deadly enemy. The temperature plummeted below zero; storms scourged the shambling columns. Few men could do more than keep alive. Both armies gradually dissolved from hunger, exhaustion, cold, and typhus. Now, the irregulars and Cossacks came into their own: Hardy frontiersmen, they endured where Russian regulars perished. Highly disinterested in hard fighting, but hunting constantly for easy loot, they slowly demoralized the exhausted French. Late on 2 December, announcing that his men were fatigued, Ney coolly scrambled ahead of Victor, leaving him to guard the disintegrating army's rear. Three days later, Victor reported that his corps had almost dissolved.

Napoleon had decided to leave his army, a course he had refused to consider east of the Berezina. Now there was little more he could do; his continued presence with the army exposed him to unnecessary risks. Only from Paris could he rebuild his army for the 1813 campaign; only from Paris would he be able to control his empire, once the full outcome of the Russian campaign became known. (As early as 24 October, the half-insane General Malet had almost seized Paris through a fantastic plot; others might be expected.) On 5 December, Napoleon announced his plans to his approving corps commanders at Smorgonie (*C2*). Murat received command of the army with orders to rally it at Vilna and hold the line of the Niemen River. If unable to hold Vilna, he might retire behind the Niemen, keeping Kovno (*B3*) as a bridgehead. Departing in his usual whirlwind fashion, Napoleon reentered Paris on 18 December.

The army reached Vilna on 9 December. The city was packed with supplies, but most of the administrative personnel had fled. The rest insisted on formal requisitions and, even then, would not be hurried. The result was looting and further demoralization; large numbers of men refused to go farther. Murat's courage snapped, but Lefebvre and Ney rallied troops to shoo off the Cossacks, while Davout and Berthier got some food and clothing issued. Berthier remembered Macdonald and Schwarzenberg (concerning whom Napoleon had left no instructions), ordering the first to withdraw on Tilsit (*B3*), the second on Bialystok (*B2*). Wrede's and Loison's survivors were formed into a new rear guard, under Ney.

The retreat resumed late on the 10th. Five miles beyond Vilna, an icy hill

forced the abandonment of most of the remaining vehicles. Kovno could not be held, the Niemen having frozen so solidly that the enemy could easily bypass it. Again, troops pillaged the stores; drunkenness finished the army's disorganization. Murat left Kovno on the 13th, just as Ney arrived with Platov at his heels. Rallying odd detachments, Ney burned the remaining stores and the bridges, withdrawing after dark—the last man to leave Russia. On 19 December, the French reached Königsberg (*B3*).

Tshitshagov established winter quarters west of Vilna; Kutusov halted in that city, ordering Wittgenstein to intercept Macdonald. The Cossacks and irregulars were to follow the French as far as possible; Sacken was to watch Schwarzenberg.

Upon receiving Berthier's orders, Macdonald retired, followed circumspectly by Paulucci. However, Yorck, commanding the rear half of Macdonald's column, allowed himself to be intercepted by Wittgenstein's weak advance guard. Instead of pushing it aside, he coyly concluded the Convention of Tauroggen, which "neutralized" his Prussian contingent. He justified this act as inspired by the "purest motives" of a "true patriot." To a soldier, it remains a contemptible piece of treachery, compounded by Yorck's deliberate delay in notifying Macdonald, who—believing Yorck in danger—had halted at Tilsit to cover his withdrawal.

Learning of Yorck's defection, Murat threw most of his serviceable troops into Danzig (*A3*), and retired to Posen (*off map, A2*). He then suddenly abdicated his command in favor of Eugene, and left for Naples. Eugene hesitated to assume the responsibility; no marshal would take orders from another; it would require ten days to get a decision from Napoleon. Though extremely ill, Berthier met the crisis, persuading Eugene to accept, warning Napoleon that Eugene's new status must be confirmed immediately, and setting an example of loyal and energetic subordination.

Schwarzenberg and Reynier meanwhile went into winter quarters around Bialystok. Hoping to detach Austria from her French alliance, the Russians alternately applied discreet diplomatic and military pressure. Austria being willing, an armistice finally was concluded: Schwarzenberg retired into Galicia, carrying with him Poniatowski and the partially reorganized V Corps. Thus abandoned, Reynier retired on Glogau (*off map, A2*).

French losses probably exceeded 400,000, plus approximately 1,000 cannon and 175,000 horses. The Russians lost more than 250,000, plus unknown numbers of irregulars.

Napoleon had attempted a campaign beyond his means. The forces involved were too great, the spaces across which they operated too vast for the existing methods of communication and supply. Napoleon's ability as a general and a ruler, outstanding as it proved to be, could not compensate for the impossible demands imposed by time and space. A sense of impending failure seems to have seized him early, frequently muffling his clear mind and power of decision.

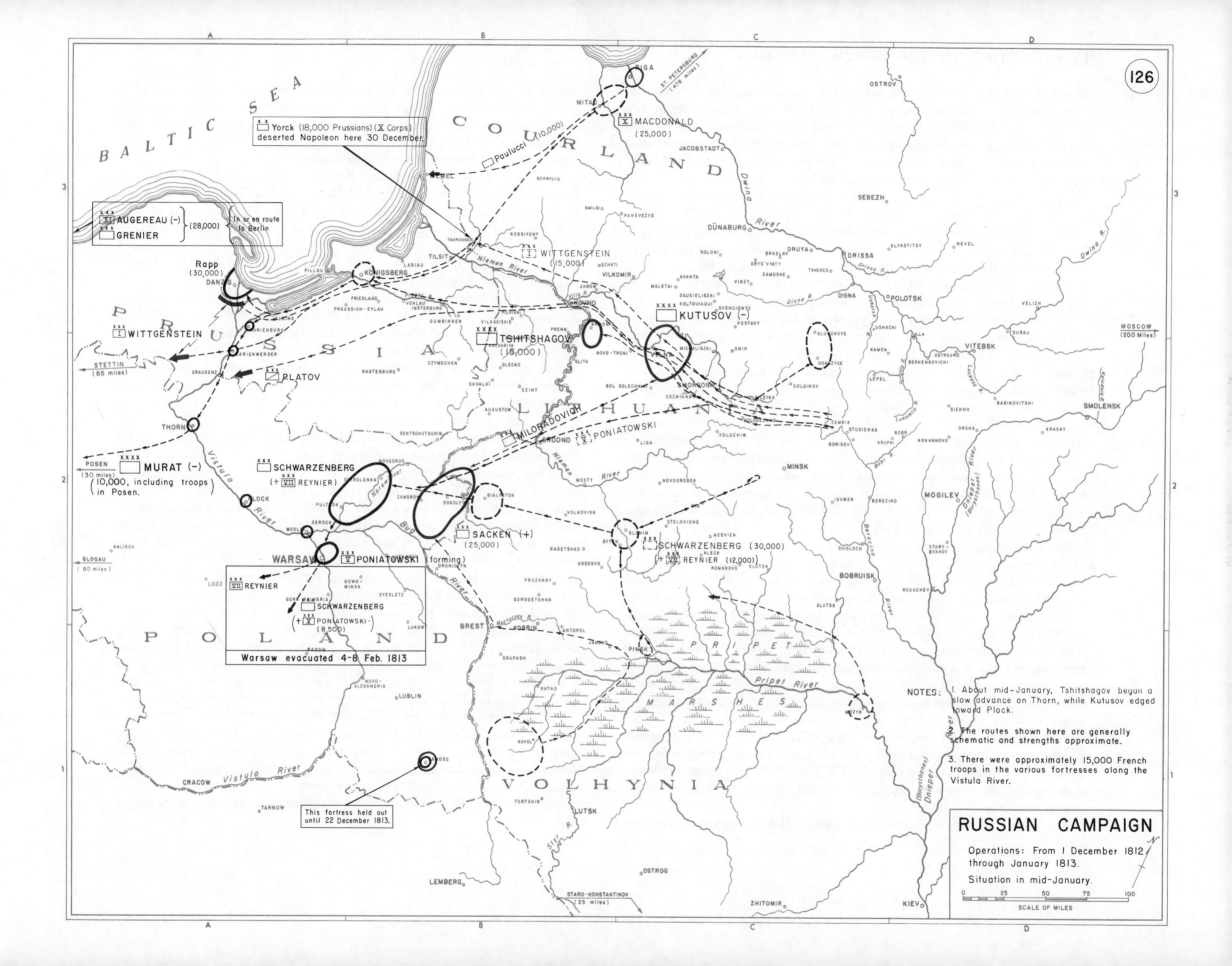

126

BALTIC SEA

COURLAND

Yorck (18,000 Prussians) (X Corps)
deserted Napoleon here 30 December.

XXX
XI AUGEREAU (-)   (28,000)   (In or en route
XXX   to Berlin)
GRENIER

Rapp
(30,000)
DANZIG

XXX
I WITTGENSTEIN

STETTIN
(85 miles)

XXX
PLATOV

THORN

POSEN
(30 miles)   XXXX
               MURAT (-)
(10,000, including troops)
(in Posen.)

GLOGAU
(80 miles)

XXX
SCHWARZENBERG
(+ XXX
   VII REYNIER)

XXX
SACKEN (+)
(25,000)

WARSAW   XXX
           V PONIATOWSKI (forming)

XXX
VII REYNIER

SCHWARZENBERG
(+ XXX
   V PONIATOWSKI -)
(8,500)

Warsaw evacuated 4-8 Feb. 1813

P O L A N D

This fortress held out
until 22 December 1813.

CRACOW

LEMBERG

P R U S S I A

L I T H U A N I A

MILORADOVICH   XXX
GRODNO   V PONIATOWSKI

XXXX
TSHITSHAGOV
(15,000)

XXXX
I WITTGENSTEIN
(15,000)

XXXX
KUTUSOV (-)

KOLTOUIAQUI

SMORGONI

ST. PETERSBURG
(476 miles)

XXX
X MACDONALD
(25,000)

Paulucci
(10,000)

DWINA River

DÜNABURG

DRISSA

POLOTSK

MOSCOW
(200 miles)

VITEBSK

SMOLENSK

SCHWARZENBERG (30,000)
(+ XXX
   VII REYNIER (12,000)

MINSK

MOGILEV

BOBRUISK

B U G River

BREST   KOBRIN

P R I P E T

PINGK

M A R S H E S

Pripet River

V O L H Y N I A

LUTSK

Vistula River

TARNOW

STARO-KONSTANTINOV
(25 miles)

ZHITOMIR

KIEV

NOTES:
1. About mid-January, Tshitshagov began a
slow advance on Thorn, while Kutusov edged
toward Plock.

2. The routes shown here are generally
schematic and strengths approximate.

3. There were approximately 15,000 French
troops in the various fortresses along the
Vistula River.

RUSSIAN CAMPAIGN

Operations: From 1 December 1812
through January 1813.

Situation in mid-January.

0   25   50   75   100
SCALE OF MILES

INTRODUCTION TO THE LEIPZIG CAMPAIGN

Napoleon had lost an army; with spring and another campaign only months away, he created a new one. He found 120,000 half-trained conscripts already available, drew 80,000 men from the National Guard, and called up 100,000 more who had escaped service between 1809 and 1812. The Navy furnished infantrymen, artillerymen, and engineers. Troops were summoned from Spain and Italy; retired veterans were recalled; the gendarmerie and other security units were screened. A surprisingly high proportion of officers and NCO's had survived the Russian campaign. Those not needed with the wrecked Grande Armee, now rallying in Germany, formed cadres for new units. The Imperial Guard was re-formed and enlarged from veterans and the pick of the conscripts. Because most of his infantry would be facing their first campaign, Napoleon likewise sought to strengthen his artillery. This took longer, but by mid-August 1813, he had 1,300 serviceable guns.

The men of this new army were young and full of spirit, but lacking in physical toughness. There was a shortage of officers (which Napoleon solved by stripping the military schools and promoting veteran noncommissioned officers) and a similar lack of qualified noncommissioned officers. The cavalry was handicapped by a shortage of suitable horses; the average cavalryman was a poor rider. There was not time to reorganize the administrative services, and these would prove the worst enemy of the new soldiers, who, lacking experience in foraging for themselves, required regular issues of supplies.

As the extent of Napoleon's Russian debacle became known in France, resistance to conscription increased, and some imperial officials began to moderate their zeal. Royalists felt renewed hope, and Talleyrand—still a member of Napoleon's council—was in the pay of Napoleon's enemies. The general public spirit, however, remained good.

Spain continued to absorb roughly 175,000 seasoned French troops. Half of these in Germany, as Berthier urged, would have crushed the exhausted Russian spearheads and brought Prussia to heel. But Napoleon would not give up any part of his conquests to save the rest.

The prospect of continued war appalled the states of the Confederation of the Rhine. They had pledged Napoleon loyalty; in return, he had increased their territory and prestige (at the expense of Austria and Prussia), and left their internal affairs alone. But now the Russians were moving westward, while Yorck's and Schwarzenberg's defections hinted that Prussia and Austria were about to again switch sides. Prussian "liberation," Russian occupation, and French vengeance seemed equally dreadful. Eventually, each did what seemed safest. Baden, Hesse, Nassau, Westphalia, and Frankfort—being under the guns of French fortresses—promptly raised new contingents for Napoleon. His country partially overrun, the King of Saxony fled to Bavaria, ordering his army to remain neutral. At Austria's urging, Bavaria and Württemberg considered neutrality.

The Russians were momentarily exhausted. Happily convinced he was truly a military genius, Alexander felt a divine mission to become the liberator of Europe and the champion of its "legitimate" rulers. At the same time, strictly in the interests of international justice, he would extend Russia's frontiers. Kutusov favored letting England fight France. He had much popular support, and temporarily restrained Alexander.

Bernadotte, dreaming of becoming King of France, had edged Sweden into the Allied camp, but with an eye toward the greatest possible gain for the least possible risk. England and Russia bought him with the promise of Norway (then part of Denmark). As paymaster to the Allied powers, England was willing to make extreme exertions for the victory she now considered quickly attainable. However, the growing war in America somewhat limited her contribution, especially in manpower.

Though reluctant to move openly while the French still held Berlin, Prussia soon secretly joined Russia (Treaty of Kalisch, 28 February 1813) in a pledge to liberate—and divide—Germany. The Prussian Army was energetically strengthened despite considerable difficulties. Popular legends aside, though the Prussians may have hated Napoleon, remarkably few of them volunteered to risk getting shot. In some areas, military force was required to put conscription into effect. As the French forces in Germany retired, Prussia declared war, on 16 March.

Much depended on Austria's attitude. Napoleon naïvely hoped that his marriage to an Austrian princess would be a firm link between their two countries. His Austrian in-laws regarded Maria Louisa only as a temporary sacrifice, tossed to the Corsican ogre. However, Austria had never recovered from her financial and military losses in 1809 and knew that another defeat could destroy her. Her foreign minister, Metternich, was aristocratic, courageous, devious as a basket of snakes, and a sworn foe of the French Revolution—"a gangrene which must be burnt out with a hot iron." He chose to prepare Austria for war, while remaining ostensibly neutral, thus hoping to force both sides to bid high for Austrian support. He further planned to then demand such humiliating concessions from France that Napoleon would automatically reject them. Meanwhile, he briskly pretended friendship, sending Schwarzenberg to Paris "to the side of his commander in chief." (En route, Schwarzenberg would urge Napoleon's German allies to send the Emperor as few troops as possible—and especially to send no cavalry, which Napoleon particularly needed.) Metternich himself intrigued murkily with Murat.

Napoleon still retained one advantage. With almost absolute control over his own empire, he stood against a league of wrangling, jockeying monarchs, each of whom, for excellent reasons, mistrusted the others. Their negotiations were laborious; Austria required secrecy; messages passed slowly across a Europe wracked by winter, war, and typhus.

By early April 1813, Napoleon was ready enough; the Allies were not.

The Leipzig Campaign

"Principal load {of a commanding general} is standing disappointment and upsetting of plans. Everything conspires against him—dumb execution, weather, breakdowns, misunderstandings, deliberate obstructions, jealousies, etc. Must be prepared to accept fifty per cent results in twice the time calculated."
—GENERAL JOSEPH W. STILWELL

"No one should imagine that sound heads are common in armies. Offensive generals are rare among us; I know only a few, and, nevertheless, it is only to these that . . . a detachment can be entrusted."
—FREDERICK THE GREAT

Napoleon had hoped that Eugene would hold Warsaw (*C2*) and Posen (*B2*), and relieve Danzig (*C2*). Ney (later, St.-Cyr) was to organize a new "advance guard" (from Italian reinforcements and various garrisons in Prussia) at Posen to support him, while new corps were organized in the various German fortresses. If forced to retire from the Posen area, Eugene was to hold Magdeburg (*A2*) and the line of the Elbe River. At the worst, he must protect Hanover (*A2*) and Kassel (*A1*).

A competent corps commander, Eugene was cool, resilient, and convinced that "Glory costs too much." To protect the Empire's eastern frontier, he had 14,000 men: exhausted veterans, rattled conscripts, and sullen allies. He could lose Napoleon's empire in one afternoon.

Realizing that the French were incapable of effective action, the Allies planned to advance to the Elbe on a broad front, then mass to their left near the Austrian frontier, hoping in that way to encourage Austria to join them. Wittgenstein dispatched three small "free corps" (Czernitchew, Benkendorf, and Tettenborn) raiding westward across Pomerania (*B2*) to create confusion.

Eugene soon judged his Posen position too dangerous. The Prussian government evaded his orders, the population was restless, Schwarzenberg's withdrawal southward exposed his right flank. Reynier had been overtaken and defeated at Kalisch (*C1*). Communications with France were shaky, and Berthier had collapsed from sickness and overwork. Accordingly, Eugene retired, on 12 February 1813, to Frankfort (*B2*), where St.-Cyr joined him, increasing his strength to 30,000. Ignoring the fact that the rivers were still frozen and thus worthless as barriers, Napoleon scolded him for not concentrating east of Küstrin (*B2*), claiming that this would have forced the enemy to do likewise before attempting to cross the Oder. After two days at Frankfort, where he learned that Berlin (*B2*) was threatened, Eugene resumed his retreat. Berlin appearing indefensible, he finally halted at Wittenberg (*A2*) on 6 March, and set up a cordon defense behind the Elbe. His rear guards (Gerard at Frankfort, Rechberg's Bavarians at Crossen) had to fight their way out. Rebuffed by Thielmann (commanding the Saxon garrison [*not shown*]) when they attempted to retire through Torgau (*B1*), they finally joined Reynier, whose Saxons had deserted him, at Dresden (*B1*). Poor staff work (probably Augereau's) resulted in Morand's division being forgotten in Pomerania; Morand attempted to break out, but was overwhelmed near Hamburg (*A2*).

By evacuating Berlin, Eugene left Prussia free to declare war. (Napoleon insisted this could have been considerably delayed had Eugene concentrated east of Berlin as if ready to give battle.) Eugene's dispositions behind the Elbe produced more imperial scoldings (2–15 March) on the art of war: Eugene must concentrate most of his available troops in an entrenched camp east of Magdeburg. Victor should hold bridgeheads at Torgau, Wittenberg, and Dessau; Reynier should guard the Elbe from Torgau to the Austrian

frontier, Davout from Magdeburg to Hamburg. Jerome's Westphalians would support either Davout or Eugene. If Eugene were attacked, Davout and Victor should cross the Elbe and strike the enemy's flanks. Unfortunately, this excellent plan overestimated Eugene's strength, underestimated the enemy's, and assumed that the mutinous Westphalians and the now neutral Saxons were still loyal allies.

Before these orders reached him, Eugene further scrambled his foster father's chessboard by ordering Davout to Dresden. Napoleon wrote again: Dresden was important, but Hanover and Bremen were more so. Then, uncertain if Eugene had received his orders, he ordered Lauriston to establish an entrenched camp east of Magdeburg and circulate rumors of an impending French offensive.

In the north, meanwhile, the Russian free corps had created a fog of war through which Lauriston got reports of Bernadotte's appearance in northern Germany (true), Danish mobilization against France (probable), imminent British landings (false), and a Russian offensive (false). Lauriston combined these into an imagined Allied plan to seize Hamburg and strike south to cut Eugene's communications. His alarmist reports startled Carra St.-Cyr into evacuating Hamburg, which Tettenborn promptly occupied.

This news, and Napoleon's repeated orders, finally led Eugene to mass around Magdeburg and order Davout to Hamburg. Believing that his division (3,000) was too weak to hold Dresden, Durutte (Reynier being ill) then retired westward, allowing Blücher to occupy that city on 27 March.

Having reached the Elbe, the Allies squabbled over their next step. The Prussians wanted to push ahead; Alexander agreed; Kutusov preferred to reorganize. He ordered Wittgenstein to leave a detachment to mask Magdeburg, and come south to join Blücher. Objecting that this would leave Berlin unprotected, Wittgenstein asserted that he could assist Blücher best by crossing at Rosslau (*A2*) to fix Eugene.

Learning of Wittgenstein's advance, Eugene moved up and engaged him (3–5 April) in a sprawling clash around Möckern (*A2*), but retired to the west bank of the Elbe on receiving a false report that another enemy column was crossing at Rosslau. Wittgenstein was too battered to interfere, but proclaimed that he had defeated a major French offensive against Berlin.

With Blücher massing around Dresden, the Elbe River was no longer a tenable line of defense. Eugene therefore swung his right flank back behind the lower Saale River. He had neither held as much ground nor gained as much time as Napoleon had desired, but he had built up an effective army and now occupied a strong position.

Wittgenstein crossed at Rosslau and linked up with Blücher. Nevertheless, the Allies found themselves considerably overextended. They had had to leave detachments to besiege the various Polish and German fortresses, and Kutusov (now dying) stubbornly held most of the main Russian army at Kalisch (*C1*). On 19 April came a rumor that Napoleon was advancing.

Note: On this map, Lubeck (*A2*) *should be* Lübeck.

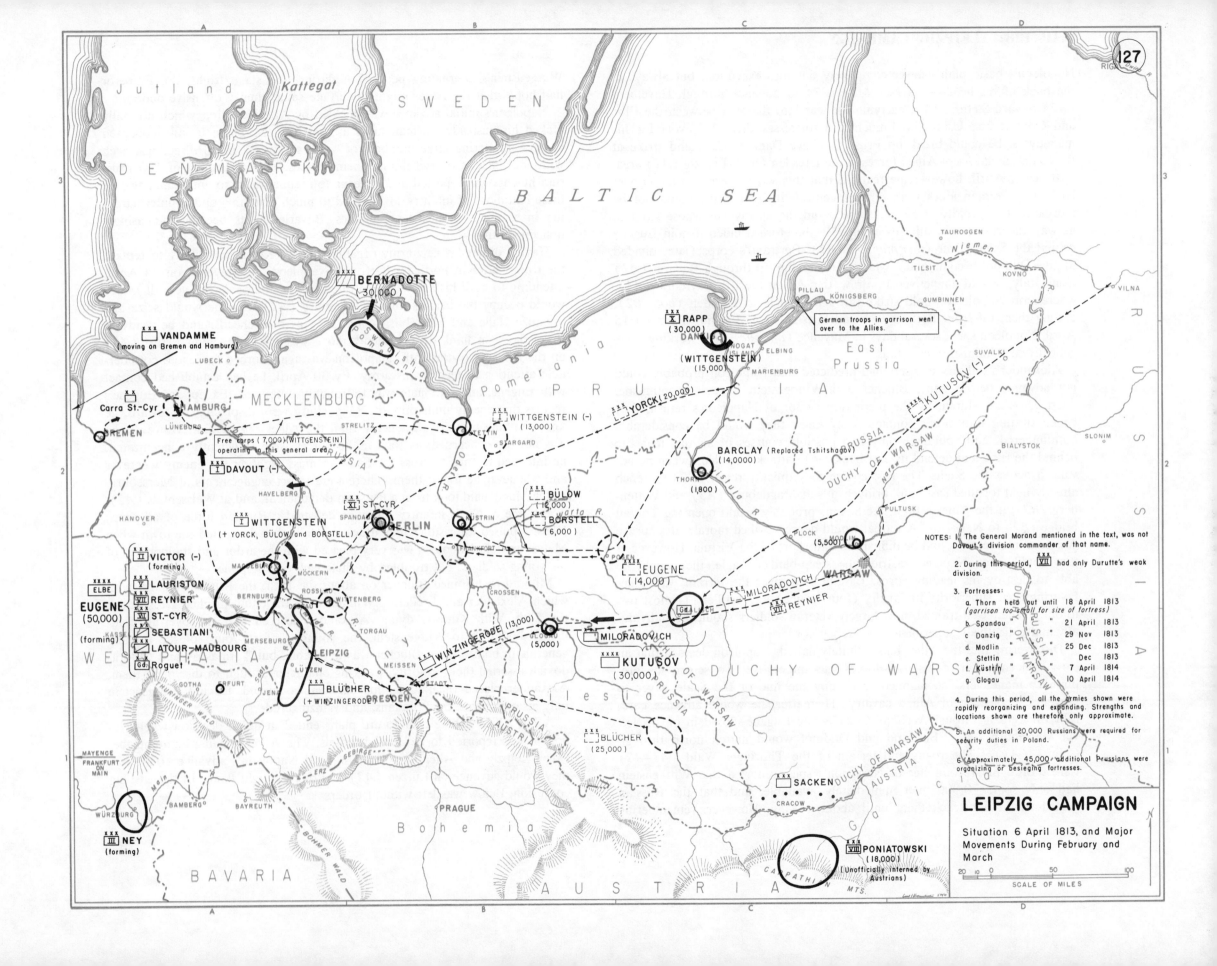

127

LEIPZIG CAMPAIGN

Situation 6 April 1813, and Major Movements During February and March

SCALE OF MILES
20 10 0   50   100

NOTES: 1. The General Morand mentioned in the text, was not Davout's division commander of that name.

2. During this period, VII had only Durutte's weak division.

3. Fortresses:
a. Thorn held out until 18 April 1813 (garrison too small for size of fortress)
b. Spandau   " 21 April 1813
c. Danzig   " 29 Nov 1813
d. Modlin   " 25 Dec 1813
e. Stettin   "   Dec 1813
f. Küstrin   "   7 April 1814
g. Glogau   " 10 April 1814

4. During this period, all the armies shown were rapidly reorganizing and expanding. Strengths and locations shown are therefore only approximate.

5. An additional 20,000 Russians were required for security duties in Poland.

6. Approximately 45,000 additional Prussians were organizing or besieging fortresses.

BERNADOTTE (30,000)

VANDAMME (moving on Bremen and Hamburg)

Carra St.-Cyr

RAPP (30,000)

German troops in garrison went over to the Allies.

(WITTGENSTEIN) (15,000)

I WITTGENSTEIN (-) (13,000)

YORCK (20,000)

BARCLAY (Replaced Tshitshagov) (14,000)

(1,800)

Free corps (7,000)(WITTGENSTEIN) operating in this general area

I DAVOUT (-)

XI ST.-CYR

I WITTGENSTEIN (+ YORCK, BÜLOW and BORSTELL)

BÜLOW (12,000)

BORSTELL (6,000)

(5,500)

EUGENE (14,000)

II VICTOR (-) (forming)

ELBE

EUGENE (50,000) (forming)

V LAURISTON

VII REYNIER

VI ST.-CYR

SEBASTIANI

LATOUR-MAUBOURG

Gd Roguet

MILORADOVICH

VII REYNIER

WINZINGERODE (13,000)

MILORADOVICH (5,000)

KUTUSOV (30,000)

BLÜCHER (+ WINZINGERODE)

BLÜCHER (25,000)

NEY (forming)

SACKEN

PONIATOWSKI (18,000) (Unofficially interned by Austrians)

Napoleon's basic plan—never completely put into execution, but always in the back of his head—was (see Map 127) to advance through Havelberg (A2) toward Stettin (B2), carrying the war into the area between the Elbe and Oder rivers. Using the French-held fortresses there as pivots for his maneuvers, he could break up Prussia, relieve Danzig (C2), and strike at the communications of Allied forces in the Dresden (B1)–Leipzig (A1) area.

By early April, however, he realized that this scheme was too ambitious: His south German allies were turning neutral, his own army could not be reorganized as rapidly as he had hoped, and the enemy (of whose strength he was uncertain) was still advancing. He therefore decided to join Eugene behind the Saale River (this map, A2–A3). Bertrand's corps (later divided to give Oudinot a command), which was moving up through Bavaria (A1) from Italy, would maneuver to draw the Allies toward Bayreuth (A1), whereupon Napoleon would strike through Leipzig to Dresden (both B2), cutting them off from Berlin (B3) and Silesia (D2). Leaving Paris on 15 April, Napoleon spent several days in Mayence (off map, A1), working energetically at administrative details.

Alexander's military advisers had predicted that Napoleon probably could not advance before June. Blücher and Wittgenstein were less optimistic. Alerted, on 19 March, by the premature rumor of Napoleon's return, they began shifting into closer contact. They knew they would be considerably outnumbered, and could see only two possible courses of action: to retire behind the Elbe and defend its east bank, or to attack Napoleon when he advanced across the Saale. The first course they quickly rejected. The French already held fortified east-bank bridgeheads at Magdeburg (A3) and Wittenberg (B3); if the Allies retired, the Saxons probably would open the Torgau bridge (B2) to Napoleon. A retreat would depress Allied morale, discourage Austrian intervention, and be difficult to halt short of the Vistula. However, if they could catch Napoleon astride the steep-banked Saale, they might be able to destroy his leading corps. East of that river the terrain was open, favoring their superiority in cavalry (four to one) and artillery (almost two to one). Their well-trained, now largely veteran soldiers should be individually and collectively superior to the French conscripts.

Discovering that the Allies had definitely halted, Napoleon decided that an early concentration of his own forces was imperative. To screen his preliminary maneuvers, he planned to occupy the line of the Saale River to prevent the passage of Allied cavalry. Thereafter, he would advance carefully on Leipzig through Weimar (A2), while Eugene closed in on his left via Merseburg (A2). Bertrand and Oudinot would march north through Coburg (A1). The roads and terrain of the Thuringer Wald (A1–A2) were thoroughly reconnoitered. Napoleon's spies reported that Wittgenstein had only some 70,000 men immediately available, and that the Russian Guard would not reach them until about 1 May. However, remembering

Wittgenstein's alternating periods of daring and stage fright, the Emperor had hopes that the Allies might undertake some clumsy offensive action.

Napoleon's initial advance was heckled by Allied cavalry, which normally picked his unsteady German units as their targets. These usually collapsed at once, scattering large numbers of "only survivors" in all directions, each with wild tales of overwhelming enemy forces. (A detachment of 150 Prussian hussars was reported as "three or four squadrons, six guns, and two or three battalions of infantry"!) This led to much marching and countermarching in search of nonexistent enemies. Bavarian units became increasingly noncooperative.

Having ordered a new army organized in his Kingdom of Italy to replace the troops brought north by Bertrand, Napoleon left Mayence on 24 April, intending to have his army concentrated behind the Saale the next day. Ney would occupy the heights above Naumburg (A2); Eugene would seize and organize Halle and Merseburg (both A2) as bridgeheads, and be ready to strike the right flank of any enemy move westward. Reaching Erfurt (A2) on the morning of the 25th, Napoleon was again forced to devote considerable attention to feeding his army. By 30 April, he had established contact with Eugene, and the Saale was thoroughly outposted. Except for Eugene's reports that enemy units opposite Magdeburg were displacing southward, he knew nothing more of the enemy than the Allies did of him. However, he was not too concerned; as soon as his forces were sufficiently concentrated, he intended to thrust across the Saale in mass, fighting the enemy wherever and whenever he found them. There were smart engagements at Merseburg, which Macdonald took from a Prussian detachment, and at Weissenfels (A2), where one of Ney's infantry divisions defeated a Russian force of all arms. Kleist repulsed Lauriston's first attack on Halle, but evacuated the town when Merseburg fell. Napoleon was very pleased with the ardor and staunchness of his young soldiers, but troubled by their lack of discipline.

Miloradovich joined Blücher on about the 19th; the Russian Guard, with which Alexander and Frederick William were traveling, reached Dresden on the 24th. With Kutusov dying, Alexander decreed that the over-all command should go to Wittgenstein, the youngest (forty-four) of the ranking generals in both armies. Blücher was agreeable, but Tormassov and Miloradovich asserted their seniority. Lacking character enough to discipline them, Alexander placed them under his personal command, leaving Wittgenstein only his own corps, the Prussians, and Winzingerode.

A hot Allied debate over future plans ended in quick decision when Napoleon was reported to be at Weissenfels. The Allies began assembling between Leipzig and Altenburg (both B2). If Napoleon's advance continued, they would advance on Lützen (A2) to strike his right flank. In the ensuing confusion, Bülow was left without orders.

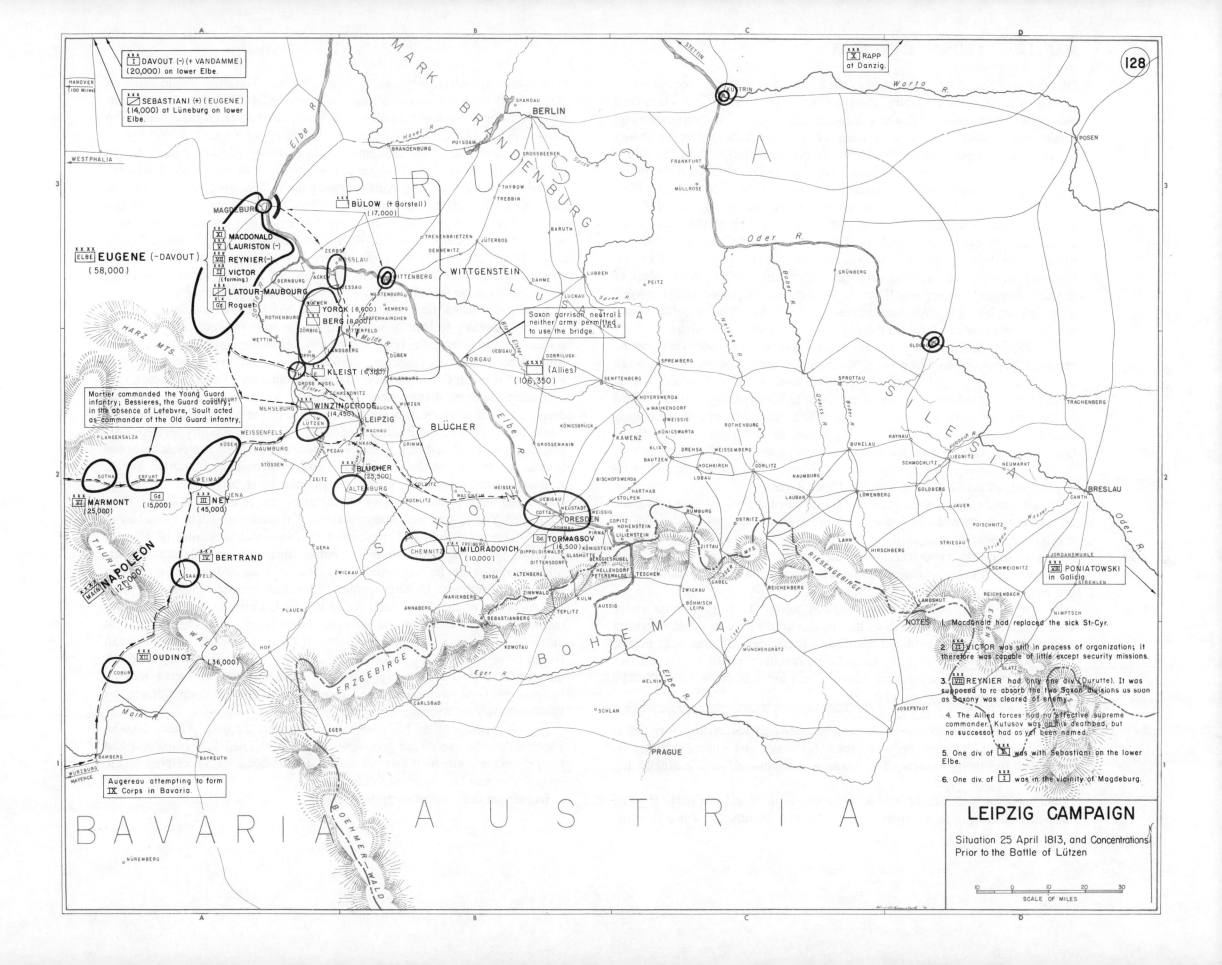

128

DAVOUT (−) (+ VANDAMME)
(20,000) on lower Elbe.

SEBASTIANI (+) (EUGENE)
(14,000) at Lüneburg on lower Elbe.

XXX RAPP at Danzig.

HANOVER (100 Miles)

WESTPHALIA

BERLIN

MARK BRANDENBURG

PRUSSIA

BÜLOW (+ Borstell) (17,000)

MAGDEBURG

XXXX ELBE EUGENE (−DAVOUT) (58,000)

XXX XI MACDONALD
V LAURISTON (−)
VII REYNIER (−)
II VICTOR (forming.)
LATOUR-MAUBOURG
Gd Roguet

WITTGENSTEIN

Saxon garrison neutral; neither army permitted to use the bridge.

YORCK (8,600)
BERG (8,000)

LUSATIA

XXXX (Allies) (106,350)

HARZ MTS.

KLEIST (6,300)

Mortier commanded the Young Guard infantry; Bessieres, the Guard cavalry, in the absence of Lefebvre; Soult acted as commander of the Old Guard infantry.

WINZINGERODE (14,450)

LEIPZIG

BLÜCHER

BLÜCHER (25,500)

SILESIA

BRESLAU

MARMONT (25,000)
Gd (15,000)
NEY (45,000)

THURINGIA

NAPOLEON (12,000)

BERTRAND

TORMASSOV (6,500)

MILORADOVICH (10,000)

DRESDEN

XXX VIII PONIATOWSKI in Galicia

WALD

OUDINOT (36,000)

ERZGEBIRGE

BOHEMIA

NOTES: 1. Macdonald had replaced the sick St-Cyr.

2. XXX II VICTOR was still in process of organization; it therefore was capable of little except security missions.

3. XXX VII REYNIER had only one div (Durutte). It was supposed to re absorb the two Saxon divisions as soon as Saxony was cleared of enemy.

4. The Allied forces had no effective supreme commander. Kutusov was on his deathbed, but no successor had as yet been named.

5. One div of XX was with Sebastiani on the lower Elbe.

6. One div of I was in the vicinity of Magdeburg.

Augereau attempting to form IX Corps in Bavaria.

BAVARIA

AUSTRIA

PRAGUE

BOEHMER-WALD

LEIPZIG CAMPAIGN

Situation 25 April 1813, and Concentrations Prior to the Battle of Lützen

SCALE OF MILES

On 30 April, Napoleon pushed across the Saale River and advanced in mass, driving Winzingerode's cavalry ahead of him. The one serious clash was near Rippach (*Map a, A2*), where Bessieres was killed while reconnoitering. Intelligence reports received at Lützen (1–2 May) indicated some enemy troops around Leipzig and a probable major concentration at Zwenkau (*B1*).

Despite the threat to his right flank, Napoleon intended to keep the initiative. Lauriston, supported by Latour-Maubourg, would seize Leipzig; Macdonald would advance to Markranstädt (*A2*), reconnoitering toward Zwenkau; Reynier would close up to Merseburg (*A2*). Ney would halt in the Lützen area to guard the French right flank, sending out reconnaissances in force toward Pegau (*A1*) and Zwenkau. Marmont would push toward Pegau; Bertrand must have his leading division in Tauchau (*A1*) by dark. Most of the Guard would remain near Lützen. So disposed, Napoleon could convert an attack on his right flank into a crushing defensive-offensive battle; if not attacked, he would not have been delayed in his march on Dresden.

The 25,000 Allied cavalry, though operating across a friendly countryside, reported Napoleon marching on Leipzig in one long column, with a weak flank guard at Kaja (*A2*), and a force of all arms south of Teuchern (*A1*). Thus misled, the Allied leaders ordered Kleist to hold Leipzig, and dispatched Miloradovich to Zeitz (*A1*) to cover their left flank. The rest of their army would be concentrated at 0700, 2 May, behind the low ridge south of Gross Görschen. As soon as their advance guard broke up the "weak flank guard" at Kaja, an all-out attack would seize the Weissenfels-Lützen highway, driving the French march column into the Elster River.

Wittgenstein's orders were long and complicated. Moving out at 0130, the Allied columns crossed and fouled each other; their leading brigades did not reach their assembly area until about 1100. Ordering an hour's rest, Wittgenstein sent staff officers to reconnoiter the French dispositions beyond Gross Görschen. Such French as were visible were busily cooking, apparently without outposts or patrols.

Ney himself had accompanied Napoleon toward Leipzig, without either concentrating his corps or making the required reconnaissances. His division commanders, though considered excellent officers, had not even sent patrols to the crest of the ridge to their front. Consequently, the Allies were left free to sort out their muddled advance. Meanwhile, Lauriston drove Kleist through Leipzig, clearing that city by 1300.

His staff officers having reported only some 2,000 French in the Gross Görschen–Kaja area, Wittgenstein sent Blücher and his cavalry forward at 1145, as shown. Caught open-mouthed, Souham's and Girard's conscripts scrabbled for their muskets. The surprise was mutual, and mutually unpleasant.

Napoleon was at Markranstädt, observing Lauriston's advance. Hearing massed artillery fire to his right rear, he listened intently for a few minutes, then issued his orders. Ney must hold at all costs. Marmont would form on Ney's right; Bertrand would attack the enemy's left, Macdonald his right. Lauriston would leave one division in Leipzig, countermarch his other two to Markranstädt. The Guard would concentrate north of Kaja.

Unexpectedly faced by Souham's whole division, Blücher paused to get his guns forward, allowing Souham to occupy Gross Görschen. At Starsiedel, Girard easily kept off the Allied cavalry until Marmont relieved him at 1300. Overwhelmed by concentrated artillery fire, Souham had been forced back, but now Ney arrived, gathered up his corps, and counterattacked furiously (*Map b*). Klein Görschen, Rahna, and Eisdorf changed hands repeatedly; massed Allied cavalry and artillery kept Marmont on the defensive around Starsiedel. Bertrand's leading division had reached Tauchau at 1300, but halted there on learning that Miloradovich was approaching Zeitz.

Napoleon reached the field at 1430 to find Ney's corps wavering. Ordering the Guard cavalry to form a straggler line, he rode forward, rallying Ney's shaken conscripts by voice, boot, and personal example, until they again drove Blücher back on Gross Görschen. Bertrand began marching forward through a cloud of Russian Guard cavalry; Macdonald appeared beyond Eisdorf.

Though both his flanks were threatened, Wittgenstein felt himself too deeply engaged to retire. Blücher was fought out, yet he hesitated to commit Yorck and Berg until the Russian grenadiers and Guard infantry arrived. (Alexander apparently had held them back for a theatrical final attack he would lead in person.) Upon their arrival at 1600, Wittgenstein committed Yorck, who surged clear to Kaja, only to be stopped by a brigade of the Young Guard and chased back to Gross Görschen by the rerallied III Corps. Berg reinforced Yorck, and the Allies recaptured Rahna and Klein Görschen at 1730. A tense lull followed, punctured by Macdonald's seizure of Eisdorf.

About 1800, Napoleon judged the battle "ripe." General Drouot (the artillery specialist among Napoleon's aides-de-camp) massed seventy guns from fresh units southwest of Kaja, pushed them into canister range, and blew the center out of the Allied line. At 1830, the Guard and the III Corps attacked, Marmont and Bertrand swinging in on their right. The Allies went hurriedly to the rear, a brief stand south of Gross Görschen by the Russian Guard being rolled up by Macdonald. Lacking cavalry, Napoleon could not pursue effectively. Late that night, clashes between Marmont's patrols and the Prussian rear guard produced a furious—but fruitless—counterattack by Prussian cavalry.

French losses seem to have been approximately 22,000; Allied, 20,000. Though the effective Allied propaganda system claimed that Napoleon had been completely surprised and practically defeated, the legend of Napoleonic invincibility was largely re-established.

During the day, Bülow recaptured Halle.

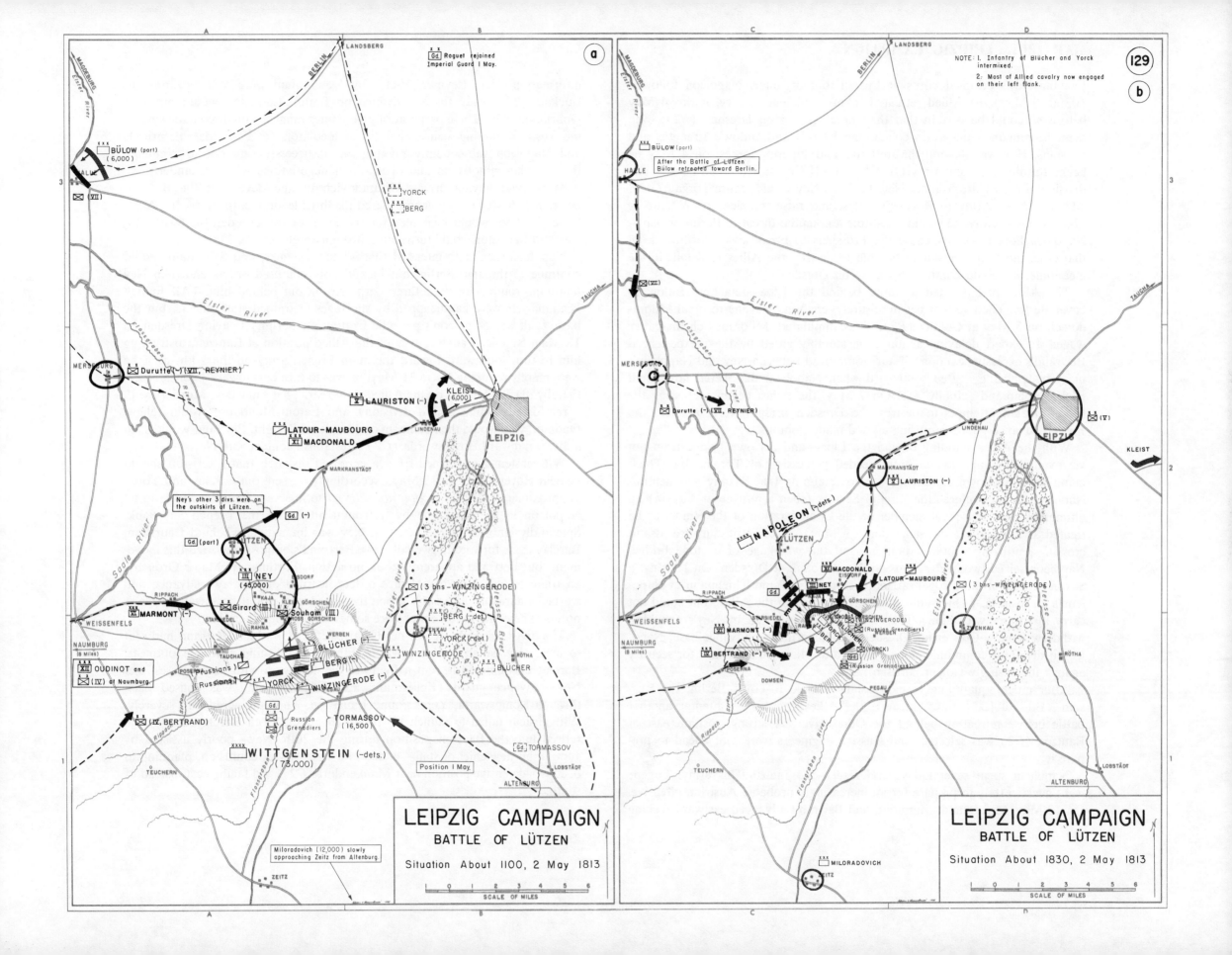

MAP a (left):

LANDSBERG

BERLIN

x x Gd. Roguet rejoined
Imperial Guard 1 May.

MAGDEBURG

Elster River

BÜLOW (part)
(6,000)

HALLE

⊠ (VII)

YORCK

BERG

TAUCHA

Elster River

MERSEBURG ⊠ Durutte (−) (VII, REYNIER)

Flossgraben River

KLEIST
(6,000)

LAURISTON (−)

LATOUR-MAUBOURG
MACDONALD

LINDENAU

LEIPZIG

MARKRANSTÄDT

Ney's other 3 divs. were on
the outskirts of Lützen.

Gd (−)

Saale River

Gd (part) LÜTZEN

NEY
(45,000)

RIPPACH

⊠ Girard (III)   KLEIN GÖRSCHEN Souham (III)

⊠ (3 bns—WINZINGERODE)

MARMONT (−)

WEISSENFELS

STARSIEDEL GROSS GÖRSCHEN

KAJA

RAHNA

WERBEN

BERG (−det)

YORCK (−det)

WINZINGERODE

RÖTHA

NAUMBURG
(8 Miles)

TAUCHA
Poserna
(Prussians)
(Russians)

BLÜCHER (−)
BERG (−)
YORCK
WINZINGERODE (−)

⊠ OUDINOT and
⊠ (IV) at Naumburg.

Gd
Russian
Grenadiers

TORMASSOV
(16,500)

Gd TORMASSOV

⊠ (IV, BERTRAND)

WITTGENSTEIN (−dets.)
(73,000)

Position 1 May.

TEUCHERN

ALTENBURG

LOBSTÄDT

Miloradovich (12,000) slowly
approaching Zeitz from Altenburg.

ZEITZ

LEIPZIG CAMPAIGN
BATTLE OF LÜTZEN

Situation About 1100, 2 May 1813

0 1 2 3 4 5 6
SCALE OF MILES

A   B

MAP b (right):

LANDSBERG

BERLIN

(129)

(b)

NOTE: 1. Infantry of Blücher and Yorck
intermixed.

2. Most of Allied cavalry now engaged
on their left flank.

MAGDEBURG

Elster River

BÜLOW (part)

After the Battle of Lützen
Bülow retreated toward Berlin.

HALLE

⊠ (VII)

TAUCHA

Elster River

MERSEBURG

⊠ Durutte (−) (VII, REYNIER)

Flossgraben River

MARKRANSTÄDT

LAURISTON (−)

LINDENAU

LEIPZIG

⊠ (V)

KLEIST

NAPOLEON (−dets.)
LÜTZEN

MACDONALD EISDORF LATOUR-MAUBOURG

(3 bns—WINZINGERODE)

Gd NEY

GÖRSCHEN

Saale River

RIPPACH

STARSIEDEL (WINZINGERODE)
(Russian Grenadiers)

BLÜCHER (−)
(YORCK)

MARMONT (−)

WEISSENFELS

KAJA RAHNA

TAUCHA

ZWENKAU

RÖTHA

NAUMBURG
(8 Miles)

BERTRAND (−)

POSERNA

DOMSEN

Gd
(Russian Grenadiers)

PEGAU

Rippach River

TEUCHERN

ALTENBURG

LOBSTÄDT

MILORADOVICH

ZEITZ

LEIPZIG CAMPAIGN
BATTLE OF LÜTZEN

Situation About 1830, 2 May 1813

0 1 2 3 4 5 6
SCALE OF MILES

C   D

Leaving Ney's crippled corps at Lützen to reorganize, Napoleon followed (0300, 3 May) the Allied retreat. Lacking sufficient cavalry, it was 4 May before he could be certain that they were retiring on Dresden (*B2*); even then, he remained uncertain concerning Kleist's and Bülow's strengths and missions. However, having the initiative and superior forces, on 4 May he began forming a second army (II, III, and VII Corps; Sebastiani's corps; one division of the I Corps) under Ney. Initially, Ney would secure Torgau (*B2*), add the Saxon Army to Reynier's corps, and raise the siege of Wittenberg (*B3*). Concurrently, he would constitute a potential threat to Berlin, which—Napoleon hoped—would cause the Prussians to break away northward. In that case, the Emperor should be able to destroy the Allies in detail; in the meantime, he would continue his drive on Dresden.

The Allies had decided to retire behind the Elbe, detaching Bülow to cover Berlin. Their retreat began leisurely, enabling Eugene to maul Miloradovich on 5 May at Colditz (*B2*). Thus stimulated, Miloradovich thereafter waged an expert delaying action (considerably aided by the inexperienced Bertrand's excessive caution). Lauriston moved between Ney and Napoleon's main body, being shifted southward when Napoleon discovered how small Kleist's command actually was. On 7 May, the Allies began recrossing the Elbe. Russian attempts to destroy the Dresden bridges were bungled, the French advance guard capturing a good many pontons.

With the Allies standing behind the Elbe—and his own bridge train not yet available—Napoleon urgently needed possession of Torgau, but Thielmann held that town against all comers, claiming that Saxony was neutral. Napoleon at once offered the King of Saxony (then a refugee in Austria) an ultimatum: Act as a loyal member of the Confederation of the Rhine, or be treated as a felon. At the same time (9 May), in brilliant, surprise assault crossings, utilizing captured pontons and the wreckage of a stone bridge, Napoleon seized two bridgeheads on the east bank at Dresden. On 10 May, a Saxon courier brought royal orders placing Torgau and Thielmann at Napoleon's disposition. (Thielmann promptly deserted to the Allies, but could not carry his troops with him.) The Allies, already worried by Ney's activities, withdrew tamely. Converting Dresden into his principal advance base, Napoleon ordered his communications westward to Mayence organized for security against increasingly violent partisan raids.

After much squabbling (the Prussians wanted to cover Berlin; the Russians, Breslau [*D2*] and Warsaw), the Allies decided to attempt another battle before retreating behind the Oder River. A strong position east of Bautzen (*C2*) was selected, and Russian engineers were sent ahead to prepare it.

Napoleon spent several days at Dresden reorganizing his army. Eugene went back to Italy to prepare for an increasingly probable Austrian offensive. On 12 May, Macdonald, Marmont, and Bertrand advanced eastward seeking information. Ney, Reynier, Victor, and Sebastiani were to concentrate at Luckau (*B3*) ready for an advance on Berlin. Lauriston would move to Dobrilugk (*B2*). These preparations were intermingled with diplomatic sorties, the Austrians hinting their availability as mediators (at a considerable price), and Napoleon subsequently making an unsuccessful attempt to eliminate the Austrian middleman and open direct negotiations with Alexander.

Macdonald having driven Miloradovich in and developed the Bautzen position (16 May), Napoleon ordered his three leading corps to fix the Allies there. Oudinot would beat the country south of the Dresden-Bautzen road; Ney and Lauriston would turn south through Spremberg (*C2*).

Napoleon seemingly intended that Victor, Reynier, and Sebastiani should continue to threaten Berlin, but inexplicably confused orders ended in Ney marching south with their three corps strung out behind him. (All French headquarters were handicapped by shortages of trained staff officers, but the basic fault was Napoleon's periodic fixation on Berlin.) Leaving Dresden on 18 May, Napoleon advised Ney of the Allied position at Bautzen, instructing him to turn southward toward the main French army on the 20th, as if he were merely rejoining it. On 21 May, he was to turn east toward Drehsa (*C2*), thereby placing himself on the Allied right rear. That same day, Mortier (with a reinforced Young Guard division) and Latour-Maubourg would relieve Oudinot, who would then come up on Macdonald's right. Bertrand would send a division toward Hoyerswerda (*C2*) to establish contact with Ney.

Wittgenstein had learned from a captured dispatch that Lauriston should be near Hoyerswerda on 19 May. Accordingly, he sent out Barclay and Yorck (approximately 24,000; *action not shown*) to intercept him, promising to fix Napoleon in the meantime by a frontal attack on the French left flank. Splendidly ignorant of the fact that Ney was immediately behind Lauriston, Barclay came forward in two columns. Bertrand's outposts reported this movement, but Bertrand apparently took no action. Fortunately, Major Grouchy, en route to Ney with Napoleon's orders, learned of Barclay's advance and warned Lauriston. Lauriston promptly halted and closed up, awaiting Ney's orders. These finally came, but were somewhat incomprehensible.

The division (composed of newly raised Italians) which Bertrand had sent to meet Ney halted at Königswarta without establishing adequate outposts. Barclay encountered it, sent it flying to the northwest with heavy losses, met Ney's advance guard (Kellermann and Souham), and was chased back through Königswarta. Yorck found Lauriston, who hammered him severely. Wittgenstein failed to launch his promised attack. Both Barclay and Yorck retired into the Bautzen position during the 20th. Ney—poorly assisted by Jomini, his new chief of staff—ended in a state of vast confusion, planning to occupy a defensive position near Maukendorf (*C2*), and facing east instead of south.

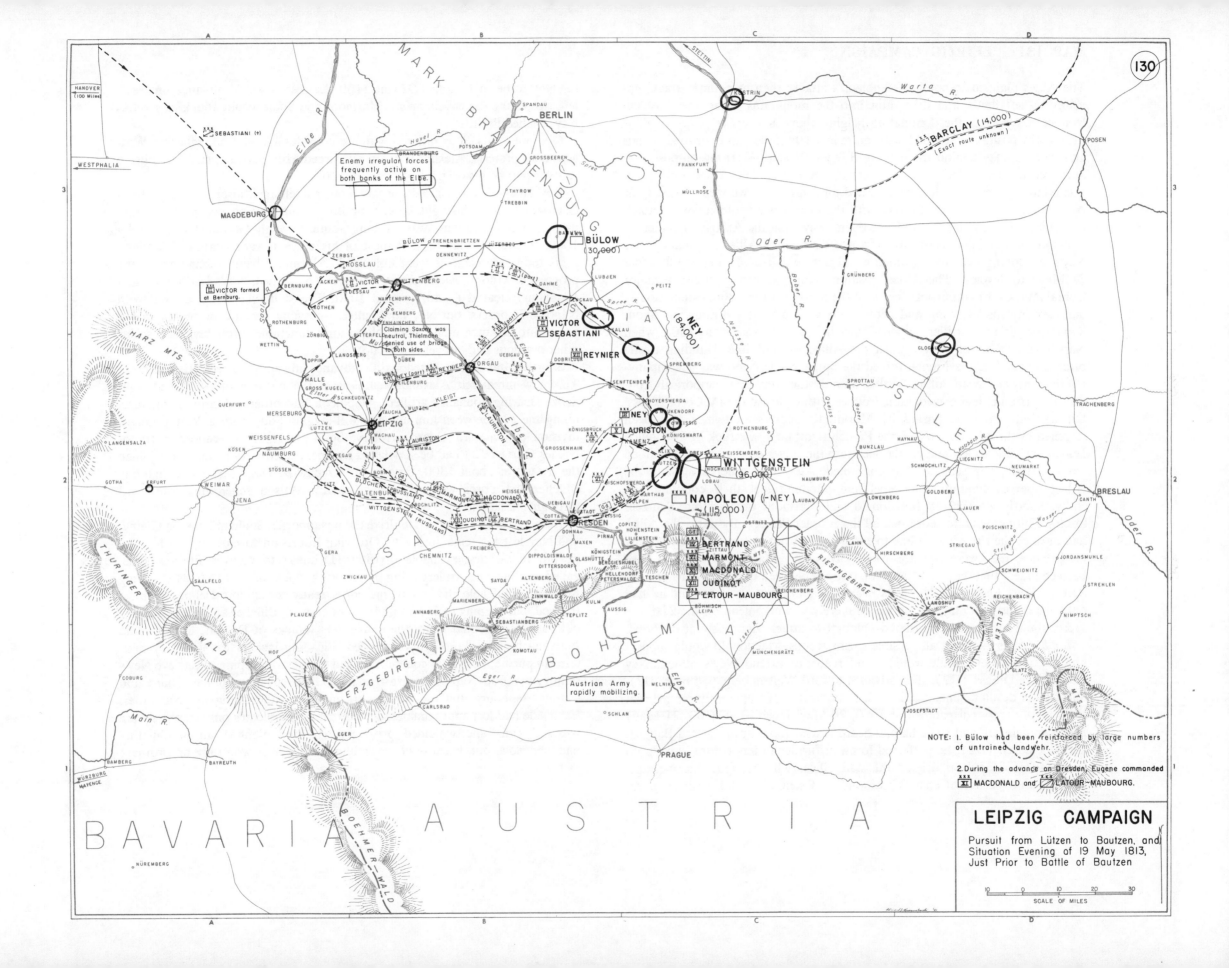

HANOVER
(100 Miles)

WESTPHALIA

MARK BRANDENBURG

BERLIN

PRUSSIA

STETTIN

KÜSTRIN

Warta R.

BARCLAY (14,000)
(Exact route unknown)

POSEN

Enemy irregular forces
frequently active on
both banks of the Elbe.

MAGDEBURG

BÜLOW
(30,000)

VICTOR formed
at Bernburg.

Claiming Saxony was
neutral, Thielmann
denied use of bridge
to both sides.

Oder R.

VICTOR
SEBASTIANI

NEY
(84,000)

SILESIA

REYNIER

GLOGAU

NEY
LAURISTON

LEIPZIG

WITTGENSTEIN
(96,000)

BRESLAU

NAPOLEON (-NEY)
(115,000)

DRESDEN

BERTRAND
MARMONT
MACDONALD
OUDINOT
LATOUR-MAUBOURG

HARZ MTS

THURINGER WALD

ERZGEBIRGE

SAXONY

BOHEMIA

RIESENGEBIRGE

EULEN
MTS.

Austrian Army
rapidly mobilizing.

PRAGUE

BAVARIA

AUSTRIA

BÖHMER WALD

Main R.

NOTE: I. Bülow had been reinforced by large numbers
of untrained landwehr.

2. During the advance on Dresden, Eugene commanded
MACDONALD and LATOUR-MAUBOURG.

LEIPZIG CAMPAIGN

Pursuit from Lützen to Bautzen, and
Situation Evening of 19 May 1813,
Just Prior to Battle of Bautzen

SCALE OF MILES

The Allies planned to contain Napoleon's attack; then to counterattack, envelop his left flank, and drive him into the mountains along the Austrian frontier. Except for the dominating heights above Kreckwitz (*Map a, B2*), their main position—studded with entrenched batteries and fortified woods and villages—lay behind the marshy Blösaer Wasser. A strong outpost line, anchored on the walled town of Bautzen, covered it. The Allied right flank was relatively open; the left flank rested on a tangle of wooded ridges. Czar Alexander, however, was obsessed with the idea that Napoleon would attack the Allies' left flank in order to force them away from the Austrian frontier.

Napoleon's main concern was to fix and distract the Allies long enough for Ney's enveloping maneuver (which could not be delivered in strength before 21 May) to develop. The Allied position being too strong to risk a major frontal attack for that purpose, he spent the morning of the 20th ostentatiously maneuvering his left wing and center into their assault positions. At about noon, the French artillery opened heavily, but it was after 1500 when Napoleon sent his infantry against the Allied outpost line. Building trestle bridges under fire, the French forced the Spree. Soult (who was accompanying the army as the still-ailing Berthier's understudy and now temporarily controlled Bertrand) had considerable trouble getting part of the IV Corps across, but was effectively supported by Marmont. Oudinot's advance had been screened by the hilly country on the French right; he now struck Miloradovich heavily, driving his left and center deep into the ridges on the left of the Allied main position. His pet fear thus confirmed, Alexander ordered most of the Allied reserves committed to repel him. Oudinot met their counterattack stiffly. Shortly after 1700, Macdonald and Marmont pinched out Bautzen, forcing Miloradovich to retire behind the Blösaer Wasser. By dark, the Allies had most of their reserves in line to extend their front southward. Thoroughly off balance, they were ripe for Ney's enveloping attack, but seem to have been confident that they had Napoleon trapped between their main line and the Spree. (They knew that Ney was near Klix [*B3*], but thought that he had only one corps with him, and so would merely join Napoleon on the 21st.)

For the 21st, Napoleon ordered Oudinot to attack vigorously at daybreak (*Map b*), so as to attract all possible enemy troops. Macdonald would support him; Marmont and Soult would stand ready to extend Ney's attack. Ney would seize Drehsa (*D2*), then advance toward Weissenberg (*off map, D2*). Subsequent developments are difficult to unravel. Ney apparently replied that since these orders (dispatched at 1600, 20 May; received at 0400, 21 May) had been delayed, and since he had heard considerable firing toward Bautzen and Hochkirch (*D2*), he preferred to await further orders before moving on Weissenberg. Napoleon briefed the staff officer who brought this message, pointing out the actual enemy positions, and sent him back with an order

for Ney to be in Preititz (*D2*) at 1100. Lauriston would advance on Ney's left, deepening the envelopment. Marmont and Soult would attack as soon as Ney reached Preititz.

Oudinot attacked as ordered, gaining considerable ground. Ignoring Wittgenstein's protests, Alexander again reinforced Miloradovich, enabling him to recover part of his original position by 1100.

Ney energetically snarled the situation, snatching Maison's division from Lauriston to cover his right flank, but failing to mass his own corps. Lauriston, though overly cautious, was pushing south through Gottamelde (*D3*) by 1000, forcing Barclay to shift most of his corps toward Baruth. (Barclay's pleas for reinforcements went unheeded, Alexander being fascinated by the progress of Miloradovich's counterattack.) Thus aided, Ney's leading division (Souham) cleared Preititz around 1030. The staff officer had arrived with Napoleon's orders, but Ney now halted—possibly because he feared that a premature advance might upset Napoleon's timetable, probably because his other divisions had not yet caught up.

Shortly after 1100, Macdonald's advance abruptly halted Miloradovich. This new threat left Alexander careless of the position of the Allied right flank. Hearing Souham's artillery, Napoleon had ordered Marmont forward, filling the gap between him and the still-lagging Soult with a Young Guard division and massed Guard artillery. Soult's bridging operations north of Nieder Gurig (*C2*) had been delayed by unexpectedly deep water. He joined the assault at about 1300, driving for Kreckwitz. Despite splendid fighting, Blücher and Yorck were steadily driven in, Maison penetrating southward through Plieskowitz.

However, Kleist managed to drive the unsupported Souham back on Gleina, and Ney lost his remaining wits. Ordering Lauriston to close up on his left, he put in his first available division (Delmas) to recover Preititz; then, galled by Blücher's artillery firing into his right flank, he sent Delmas attacking westward, and held the rest of his corps ready to support Delmas. Almost trapped, but keeping their men under tight control, Blücher and Yorck slipped out past Ney. Behind them, the converging attacks of Delmas, Maison, and Bertrand became thoroughly entangled. Pleading lack of cavalry, Ney hesitated to pursue; Lauriston countermarched fruitlessly. Hoping to retrieve Ney's failure, at 1600 Napoleon thrust at the Allied center with the Guard and Latour-Maubourg, but the Allies were already withdrawing in good order. Each side had lost approximately 20,000 men; Napoleon's only trophies were wrecked guns and wounded prisoners. He had planned an annihilating hammer blow, but, because of Ney's blunderings, had won only an ordinary victory.

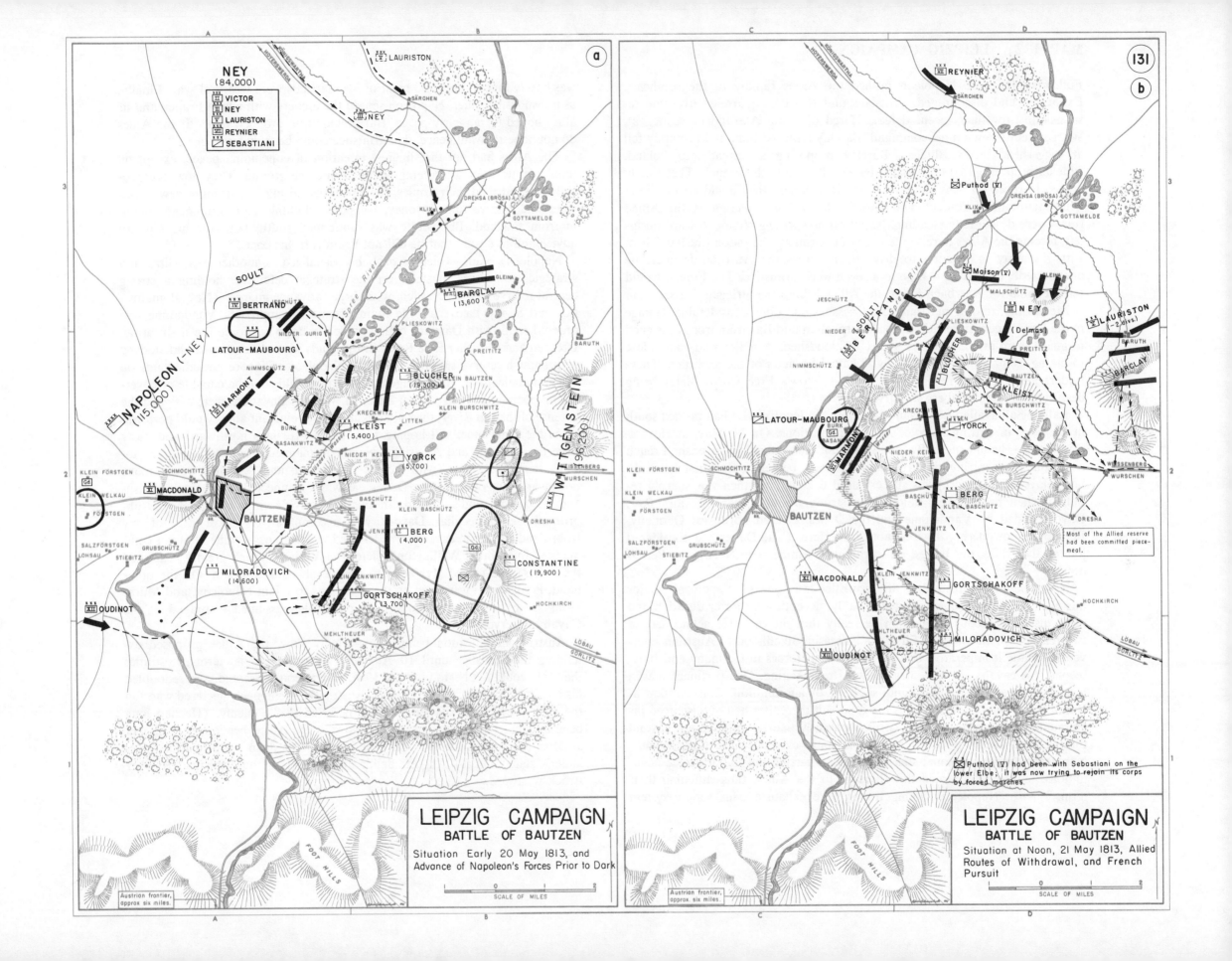

a

NEY
(84,000)

☒☒☒	VICTOR
☒☒☒	NEY
☒☒☒	LAURISTON
☒☒☒	REYNIER
▱	SEBASTIANI

☒☒☒ LAURISTON

☒☒☒ NEY

SOULT

☒☒☒ BERTRAND

▱ LATOUR-MAUBOURG

NAPOLEON (-NEY)
(115,000)

☒☒☒ MARMONT

☒☒☒ BARCLAY
(13,600)

☒☒☒ BLÜCHER
(19,300)

☒☒☒ KLEIST
(5,400)

WITTGENSTEIN
(96,200)

☒☒☒ YORCK
(5,700)

☒☒☒ MACDONALD

Gd.

☒☒☒ BAUTZEN

☒☒☒ BERG
(4,000)

Gd.

☒ CONSTANTINE
(19,900)

☒☒☒ MILORADOVICH
(14,600)

☒☒☒ GORTSCHAKOFF
(13,700)

☒☒☒ OUDINOT

FOOT HILLS

GÖRLITZ

Austrian frontier, approx six miles.

LEIPZIG CAMPAIGN
BATTLE OF BAUTZEN

Situation Early 20 May 1813, and
Advance of Napoleon's Forces Prior to Dark

SCALE OF MILES

b

131

☒☒☒ REYNIER

☒ Puthod (V)

☒ Maison (V)

☒☒☒ NEY

(Delmas)

☒☒☒ LAURISTON
(~2 divs.)

☒☒☒ BERTRAND (SOULT)

☒☒☒ BLÜCHER

☒☒☒ KLEIST

▱ LATOUR-MAUBOURG

Gd.

☒☒☒ MARMONT

☒☒☒ YORCK

☒☒☒ BARCLAY

☒☒☒ BAUTZEN

☒☒☒ BERG

WURSCHEN

Most of the Allied reserve had been committed piece-meal.

☒☒☒ MACDONALD

☒☒☒ GORTSCHAKOFF

☒☒☒ OUDINOT

☒☒☒ MILORADOVICH

GÖRLITZ

FOOT HILLS

☒ Puthod (V) had been with Sebastiani on the lower Elbe; it was now trying to rejoin its corps by forced marches.

Austrian frontier, approx. six miles.

LEIPZIG CAMPAIGN
BATTLE OF BAUTZEN

Situation at Noon, 21 May 1813, Allied
Routes of Withdrawal, and French
Pursuit

SCALE OF MILES

Following Bautzen, Napoleon pushed the Allies rapidly to the southeast. Exhausted and discouraged, Prussians and Russians quarreled over the responsibility for their recent defeats. Tired of being Alexander's scapegoat, Wittgenstein threw up his command. Barclay replaced him, and promptly fell at loggerheads with Blücher, Barclay proposing a retreat into Poland, Blücher protesting that this would abandon Prussia to the French. They finally agreed to retire on Schweidnitz (*inset map*), where they could cover Silesia while maintaining contact with Austria, for whose intervention the Allied rulers were desperately pleading. Napoleon now swung Victor forward on his left, forcing the Allies to raise the siege of Glogau and abandon Breslau. Then, with his army in position to drive them across the Austrian frontier, he unexpectedly agreed on 4 June to a seven-week armistice. The French would retire behind the Katzbach River, the Allies behind the Striegau Wasser.

Meanwhile, raiding partisans and Cossacks had done considerable damage to the French communications, the Westphalian and Bavarian troops assigned to guard them proving largely averse to bloodshed. A major raid came close to taking Leipzig on 7 June, but was halted by news of the armistice. These raiders also lost heavily, a major unit—Lützow's Free Corps—later being destroyed by Württemberg cavalry.

Rallying all available Prussian Landwehr, Bülow likewise had pushed south in the hope of cutting Napoleon's communications. On 28 May, at Hoyerswerda (*C2*), he unexpectedly found Oudinot (left behind to cover the French rear while reorganizing his corps) and was badly beaten. Unfortunately, Oudinot delayed following up his success until 6 June, and then was sharply repulsed when he attacked Bülow in a strong position near Luckau (*B3*). Davout, aided by Vandamme and the Danes, cleared northwest Germany, Bernadotte considering it wisest not to interfere. (The Danes had considered joining the Allies, but balked on learning they must cede Norway to Bernadotte.)

It is generally agreed that this armistice was one of Napoleon's major mistakes. Yet he obviously wanted it badly, accepting a shorter duration and more disadvantageous terms than he really thought wise. He acknowledged two reasons for this action: First, the increasing likelihood of Austrian intervention made it imperative that he build up his forces in Germany and Italy; second, his cavalry in particular needed strengthening. One pertinent reason he did not mention was his acute shortage of ammunition. Consumption at Bautzen had been heavy, and his rapid pursuit thereafter had outdistanced his ammunition trains. Two of his corps apparently had no ammunition beyond that in their men's pouches. (There is some evidence that Caulaincourt, Napoleon's trusted personal staff officer, who carried out the armistice negotiations, may have revealed this shortage to the Allies, thus stiffening their terms.) Also, Napoleon's young troops were exhausted, his supply system was barely functioning, and most of his marshals were weary of war. Finally, as a responsible ruler, Napoleon sensed the anxiety with which France and its allies hoped for an early peace. But premonition prodded him: "If the Allies do not honestly want peace, that armistice could be truly fatal for us."

The Allies had not the slightest intention of concluding peace, except on their own terms or after being whipped into the ground. They now energetically strengthened their armies, the Prussians raising and training new Landwehr and reserve units. Money, weapons, clothing, and equipment poured in from England. Bernadotte was summoned south, both for his military advice and to ensure that he did not again turn his coat.

Napoleon's plan—which he probably visualized as another Austerlitz, on a strategic scale—was to stand on the strategic defensive, holding a strong central reserve east of Dresden, with three "advance guards" (Ney, Poniatowski, and St.-Cyr) covering the main avenues of approach. Vandamme was ordered south with Davout's better-trained units to reinforce the main army. Dresden and the other Elbe River bridgeheads were strengthened and stocked with enough reserve supplies to enable Napoleon to ignore periodic raids on his communications. Also, Augereau's corps would soon be capable of covering his communications west of Dresden. Wrede's Bavarians were assigned the defense of the Inn River, the only mission these reluctant allies would perform.

At the same time, still hoping to pull the Prussians northward and away from the Russians and Austrians, Napoleon planned a converging attack toward Berlin. Oudinot (with Reynier, Bertrand, and Arrighi) would move northward, Davout and the Danes eastward, connected by a small Polish-French column under Girard. In this, Napoleon's employment of his subordinates seems peculiar. Davout, with a comparatively small force of raw troops and almost no cavalry, was left tied to Hamburg—while Oudinot commanded four corps! Wellington's victory at Vitoria (which greatly heartened the Allies) had forced Napoleon to send Soult back to Spain. On the other hand, Poniatowski was freed by the Austrians to rejoin Napoleon, and Murat —his Austrian intrigues temporarily put aside—assumed command of the Cavalry Reserve.

Austria's mobilization being unexpectedly slow, the Allies proposed extending the armistice until 10 August. (According to its terms, hostilities therefore could not begin until the 17th.) Napoleon consented, and redoubled his own preparations. On 12 August, Austria self-righteously declared war. On the 14th, Ney's chief of staff, Jomini, deserted to the enemy. (He had long been in contact with Russian agents. Now, at the Allied headquarters he met another renegade, Moreau, who had left his American exile to join Alexander's staff.) On 14 August, deliberately violating the armistice, Blücher struck westward.

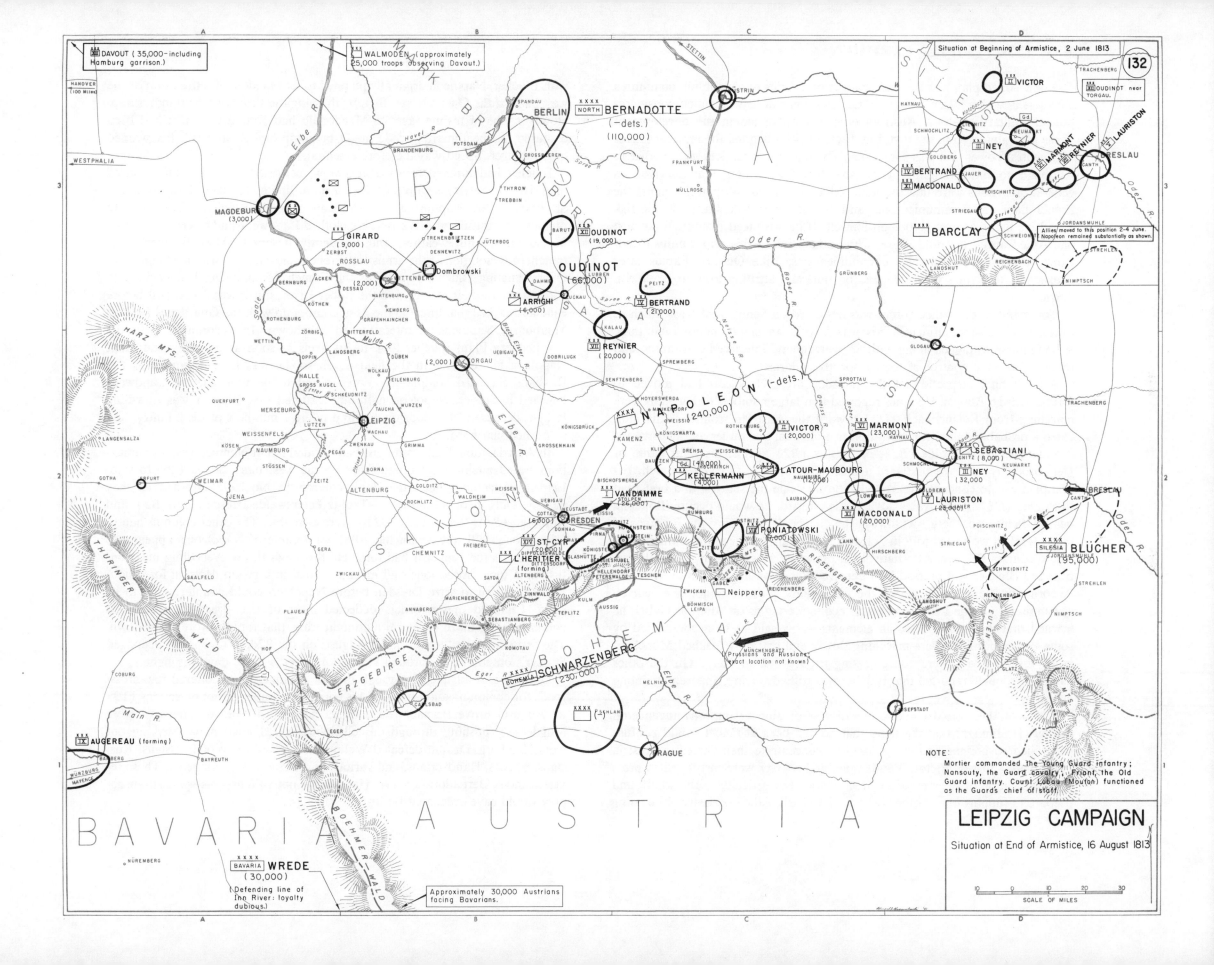

DAVOUT (35,000—including Hamburg garrison.)

WALMODEN (approximately 25,000 troops observing Davout.)

HANOVER (100 miles)

WESTPHALIA

LEIPZIG CAMPAIGN

Situation at End of Armistice, 16 August 1813

NOTE:
Mortier commanded the Young Guard infantry;
Nansouty, the Guard cavalry; Friant, the Old
Guard infantry. Count Lobau (Mouton) functioned
as the Guards chief of staff.

Situation at Beginning of Armistice, 2 June 1813

132

OUDINOT near TORGAU.

Allies moved to this position 2-4 June.
Napoleon remained substantially as shown.

NORTH BERNADOTTE (—dets.) (110,000)

GIRARD (9,000)

Dombrowski

(2,000)

OUDINOT XII (19,000)

OUDINOT (66,000)

ARRIGHI (6,000)

BERTRAND IV (21,000)

MAGDEBURG (3,000)

REYNIER VII (20,000)

NAPOLEON (—dets.) (240,000)

VICTOR II (20,000)

MARMONT VI (23,000)

SEBASTIANI (8,000)

NEY III (32,000)

KELLERMANN (4,000)

LATOUR-MAUBOURG (6,000)

LAURISTON V (25,000)

MACDONALD XI (20,000)

VANDAMME I (26,000)

PONIATOWSKI VIII (7,000)

BLÜCHER SILESIA (95,000)

DRESDEN

ST-CYR XIV (20,000)

L'HERITIER (forming)

Neipperg

BRESLAU

Munchengratz
(Prussians and Russians:
exact location not known)

SCHWARZENBERG BOHEMIA (230,000)

PRAGUE

(—)

AUGEREAU IX (forming)

WREDE BAVARIA (30,000)
Defending line of
Inn River; loyalty
dubious.

Approximately 30,000 Austrians
facing Bavarians.

SCALE OF MILES

Inset map:
VICTOR II
NEY III
BERTRAND IV
MACDONALD XI
MARMONT
REYNIER
LAURISTON
BARCLAY

The new Allied plan was the end product of a series of squabbling committee meetings in which international politics was given at least as much consideration as military strategy. Austrian officers participated in the development of the plan almost from the first, but discreetly—as befitted the representatives of a neutral power that was simultaneously offering its services as a mediator. Although no authentic copy of this so-called Trachenberg Plan survives, its general provisions were that the main Allied army would operate against the French flank and communications, and that no single Allied army would risk a decisive battle against Napoleon himself. If he advanced in strength against one Allied army, it would retire, while others seized this opportunity to advance, preferably against his communications. Like Quintus Fabius after Trasimene, the Allies would depend on time and attrition to wear Napoleon down.

Command of the Allied forces was bestowed on Schwarzenberg—much to Bernadotte's disappointment. This was largely an empty honor: All three Allied monarchs tagged along with Schwarzenberg, interfered constantly, and retained absolute control of their respective guards.

After a final inspection of the Dresden area, Napoleon had moved to Bautzen on 16 August. His spies reported that large numbers of Russians were marching from Reichenbach (D2) toward the Austrian frontier. This indicated a probable Allied concentration in Bohemia, and either an offensive via Zittau (C2), Peterswalde (B2), or Teplitz (B2) against his right flank, or (less probably) a drive westward against Nüremberg (A1) and Munich. His first plan was to concentrate around Zittau, astride the shortest and best road to Prague (C1). If the Allies advanced westward, he would occupy Bohemia behind them; also, there was always the chance of surprising the Russians as they marched westward to join Schwarzenberg. In the meantime, Macdonald would contain Blücher. Alternatively, if the entire Russian army entered Austria, and Blücher still pressed his offensive, Napoleon might turn on Blücher. Accordingly, he promptly seized the Zittau Pass, plus the minor one near by at Rumburg. On the 19th, personally reconnoitering as far south as Gabel, he learned that the leading Russian elements—now said to be accompanied by some Prussian units—were marching slowly and had only reached München-grätz; the Austrians were concentrating toward Schlan (B1). On the other hand, Macdonald reported that Blücher was still advancing, apparently aiming at Zittau.

Napoleon therefore decided to first dispose of Blücher and *then* advance on Prague. He thought that the news that he had been at Gabel would confuse the Allied sovereigns and cause them to concentrate their forces in Austria into a handy target. Victor, Vandamme, and St.-Cyr were instructed to press the fortification of their positions, reconnoiter energetically to the south, and prepare to support one another in case of an early Allied offensive. In dealing with Blücher, Napoleon originally planned to let Macdonald retire as far as the west bank of the Queiss River, thereby drawing the Prussians deep into a trap. However, one of his messages to Macdonald had gone astray; if it had been captured, his headquarters code might be compromised and Blücher warned of his danger. Speed was therefore essential.

Blücher had lurched forward in a slow, confused, generally mismanaged offensive. His relations with his Russian subordinates (Sacken, Langeron, and St. Priest) were sulphurous; his Prussian generals (such as Yorck) were politely unenthusiastic. His miserably clothed Landwehr and reservists suffered in the rainy, chill weather, and frequently deserted. After Blücher's first treacherous violation of the armistice, French rear-guard resistance toughened. Overestimating Blücher's strength, the French commanders had decided to concentrate to their rear behind the Bober River, but it was 20 August before Blücher reached that line. On the 21st, coming up with the Guard and Latour-Maubourg, Napoleon counterattacked as shown. In accordance with the Trachenberg Plan, Blücher took to his heels as soon as he was certain that Napoleon himself was in the field. Even so, he was heavily pounded. The Russians chorused complaints; Yorck asked to be relieved; the Landwehr deserted in droves. Napoleon naturally assumed that Blücher was unwilling to fight because of the poor quality and inferior numbers of his infantry, and so pushed him hard.

In Austria, the Allied sovereigns had decided to cut Napoleon's communications by advancing on a broad front up the west bank of the Elbe to seize Leipzig, detaching their right-flank column to blockade Dresden as they passed. Only two good roads—Teplitz-Peterswalde-Dresden (all B2) and Komotau (B1)–Marienberg (B2)—were available. The other columns had to follow rough hill tracks. On the 20th, word came of Napoleon's appearance at Zittau. As the Emperor had foreseen, this news threw everything into confusion. A long, uproarious staff meeting ended in a group decision for a bob-tailed offensive to seize Dresden before Napoleon could countermarch to its relief. Changed march orders deflected most of the already-weary Allied columns into a maze of lateral mountain trails that rapidly wore them down. The first skirmishes began on 21 August; on the 22d, Wittgenstein dislodged St.-Cyr's outposts from around Hellendorf after a hard, day-long fight.

Oudinot was advancing through broken country, which offered few crossroads for communication between his corps. A number of minor actions (19–21 August) drove Bernadotte's outposts northward. Girard came east from Magdeburg, pushing through miscellaneous Allied local units. Striking out from Hamburg, Davout defeated Walmoden's mixed force of Prussians, Russians, Swedes, Hanoverians, and various north German contingents. These reverses shook Bernadotte's nerve. Had Bülow not stiffened his spine, he probably would have evacuated Berlin.

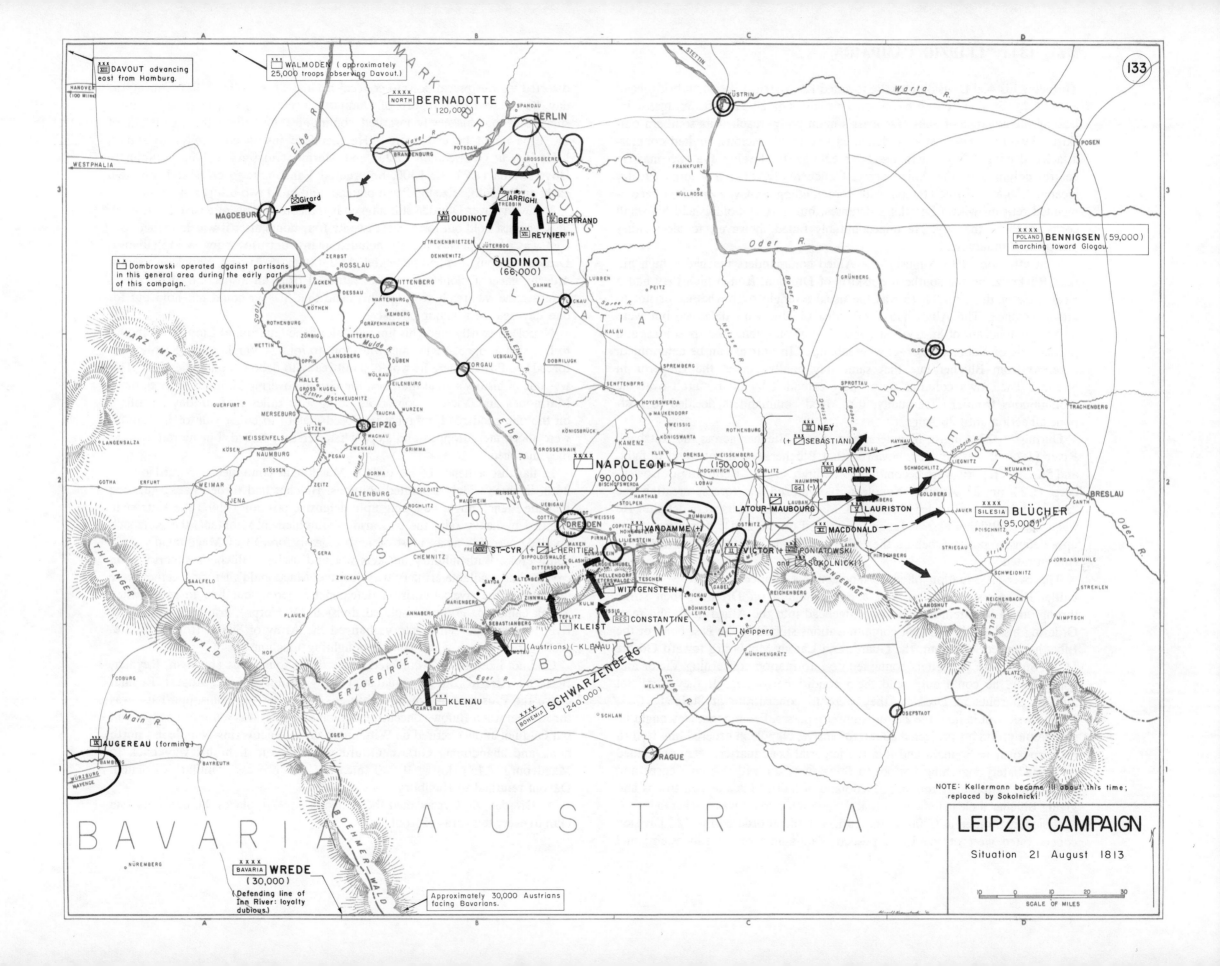

133

XXX DAVOUT advancing
east from Hamburg.

HANOVER (100 Miles)

WESTPHALIA

XXX WALMODEN (approximately
25,000 troops observing Davout.)

XXXX
NORTH BERNADOTTE
(120,000)

BERLIN

SPANDAU

GROSSBEEREN

POTSDAM

XXXX
POLAND BENNIGSEN (59,000)
marching toward Glogau.

MARK BRANDENBURG

BRANDENBURG

XX Girard

MAGDEBURG

XX Dombrowski operated against partisans
in this general part of this campaign.

ARRIGHI
TREBBIN
XII OUDINOT
XII REYNIER
IV BERTRAND

OUDINOT
(66,000)

TRENENBRIETZEN
JÜTERBOG
DAHME

ZERBST

ROSSLAU

ACKEN

DESSAU

KÖTHEN

WARTENBURG

WITTENBERG

KALAU

SPREMBERG

FRANKFURT

MÜLLROSE

Oder R.

STETTIN

KÜSTRIN

Warta R.

POSEN

P R U S S I A

L U S A T I A

Neisse R.

Bober R.

GRÜNBERG

GLOGAU

SPROTTAU

TRACHENBERG

S I L E S I A

Oder R.

BRESLAU

HARZ MTS.

QUERFURT

MERSEBURG

HALLE

LEIPZIG

TORGAU

WURZEN

EILENBURG

DÜBEN

KÖNIGSBRÜCK

KAMENZ

NEY
(+ SEBASTIANI)

MARMONT

BLÜCHER
(95,000)

SILESIA

NAPOLEON (−)
(90,000)

(150,000)

Gd. (−)
LATOUR-MAUBOURG

V LAURISTON

XI MACDONALD

DRESDEN

VANDAMME (+)

ST-CYR (+ L'HERITIER)

VICTOR (+ PONIATOWSKI
and SOKOLNICKI)

WITTGENSTEIN

KLEIST

RES CONSTANTINE

Neipperg

(Austrians) (−KLENAU)

SCHWARZENBERG
(240,000)

BOHEMIA

KLENAU

AUGEREAU (forming)

WÜRZBURG
MAYENCE

B A V A R I A

A U S T R I A

NÜREMBERG

BAVARIA WREDE
(30,000)
(Defending line of
Inn River; loyalty
dubious.)

Approximately 30,000 Austrians
facing Bavarians.

NOTE: Kellermann became ill about this time;
replaced by Sokolnicki.

LEIPZIG CAMPAIGN

Situation 21 August 1813

SCALE OF MILES

Throwing his 42d Division into the fortified Königstein-Lilienstein bridgehead area (*C2*), St.-Cyr retired easily on Dresden. On 23 August, Wittgenstein, leading the advance of Schwarzenberg's main body, reached its southern outskirts. Two days later, St.-Cyr delivered one of his vicious, limited counterattacks, driving Wittgenstein back far enough to develop the two massive central columns of the Allied army. Concurrently, St.-Cyr's corps cavalry located Klenau. Murat (temporarily commanding St.-Cyr's cavalry) recommended retiring within Dresden's defenses, but St.-Cyr boldly held his small corps south of the city. He unaccountably failed, however, to alert either Victor or Vandamme.

That afternoon (25 August), the Allied commanders reached a high hill near Räcknitz, on the southern outskirts of Dresden, from which they had a clear view of the city. There was the usual wrangle over whether or not to attack at once. The Allies had a fair idea of Dresden's defenses, but were amazingly ignorant of St.-Cyr's strength, Napoleon's general dispositions, and particularly of Napoleon's exact whereabouts. (Insofar as can be determined, a report from Blücher late that same day finally placed the Emperor in Silesia.) Their own columns were badly extended by their march over the mountainous frontier. Eventually, the Allied commanders decided to postpone all action until 26 August.

During 21–22 August, Napoleon had chased Blücher across the Katzbach River (*D2*). It was obvious, however, that Blücher would not stand to fight, and St.-Cyr's reports were becoming increasingly urgent. Returning to Löwenberg (*C2*) on 23 August, Napoleon reorganized his forces, creating the "Army of the Bober" under Macdonald. Macdonald's orders were definite: He was to drive Blücher east of Jauer (completed on the 23d), thereafter taking up a defensive position behind the Bober and being careful to keep his army concentrated.

The over-all situation offered Napoleon his chance for a truly decisive battle. His decision was to feint a countermarch on Dresden, then strike through the Lilienstein-Königstein bridgehead into the Allied flank and rear. Ordering his Leipzig-Dresden communications shifted to the east bank of the Elbe, he started Marmont, the Guard, and Latour-Maubourg toward Görlitz (*C2*). Since St.-Cyr's letters contained no information concerning Victor and Vandamme, he could only send them conditional orders: If they were not already en route to Dresden, they were to concentrate at Stolpen (*C2*). Poniatowski would hold the Zittau-Rumburg passes. Feeling that Ney might be best employed in his projected counteroffensive, Napoleon ordered him to turn his corps over to Souham and join the imperial headquarters. Ney responded by immediately marching hotfoot to Bunzlau (*C2*) with his own corps and Sebastiani, temporarily robbing Macdonald of half of his assigned troops and giving Blücher a clear indication that the French pursuit was slackening.

Reaching Stolpen at 0700 on the 25th, Napoleon ordered the 42d Division concentrated west of the Elbe; pushed Vandamme on to Lilienstein; and directed various precautions to conceal his arrival from the Allies. During the day, he received hazy reports of Oudinot's misadventures (described below), suggesting that his newly installed communications along the east bank of the Elbe might be endangered. He therefore instructed St.-Cyr to station L'Heritier at Grossenhain (*B2*), and Marmont to send a flying column to Hoyerswerda (*C2*). At 1500, he ordered Vandamme to cross at Königstein early on the 26th, seize the Pirna plateau, and build two bridges at Pirna.

But worry over Dresden still nagged Napoleon. For his offensive to succeed, St.-Cyr must hold out for at least twenty-four hours after it was launched. St.-Cyr was gloomy (his forces included many untrustworthy Westphalians); Dresden's population had panicked. At 2300 on 25 August, Napoleon's senior orderly officer, Colonel Gourgaud, returned from an inspection of Dresden's defenses; he was ready to wager his head that St.-Cyr could not hold out for one day against a major offensive.

Napoleon swiftly made his final decision: the Guard and Latour-Maubourg to Dresden at once; Victor and Marmont to follow; Vandamme (hastily reinforced) to Pirna, where he would stand ready to debouch on Hellendorf. This was one of history's great marches, the Guard covering 90 miles in three days; Marmont's and Victor's conscripts doing 120 miles in four days, artillery on the one good road, infantry in closed masses to either side of it. Rations were short, men dropped and slept whenever they halted, but morale rose as they marched.

In flat disobedience of his orders, Macdonald continued eastward on the 26th, in three widely separated columns. Blücher had turned back, guessing that the French might be taking up a defensive position behind the Katzbach. Blinded by heavy rain, the two armies stumbled into contact; the Katzbach flooded, sweeping away most of its bridges before all of Macdonald's army could cross. With infantry muskets wet and useless, Blücher's superiority in cavalry and available artillery was decisive. Macdonald's left and center were driven into the river; Lauriston defeated Langeron, but had to retire when Yorck came up. Puthod's isolated division (V Corps), trapped against the river, surrendered. This victory changed the Army of Silesia from a disintegrating rabble into a self-confident fighting machine.

Oudinot likewise had wandered forward, his four corps (his own, Reynier, Bertrand, Arrighi) out of mutual supporting distance. On 23 August, Reynier drove the Prussians out of Grossbeeren (*B3*), but—left unsupported—was thrown out when Bülow concentrated against him. It was a minor engagement but Oudinot at once retired on Wittenberg (*B3*), uncovering Napoleon's north flank and abandoning Girard. Girard was lucky to fight his way back to Magdeburg (*A3*) losing 1,000 men in the process. Similarly isolated, Davout returned to Hamburg.

At Dresden, St.-Cyr awaited the Allied assault; in places, he had only one man to every ten yards of front.

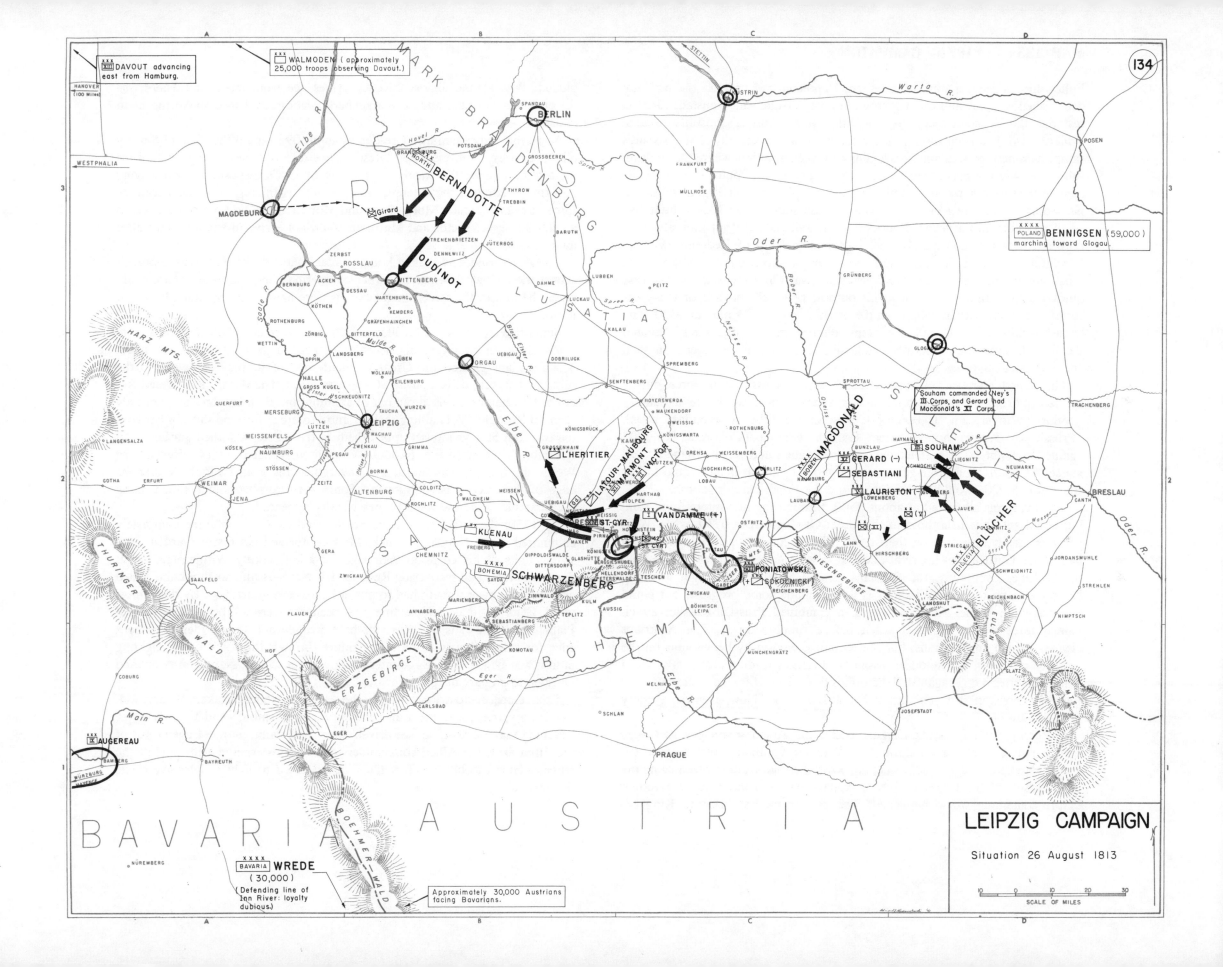

134

DAVOUT advancing east from Hamburg.

WALMODEN (approximately 25,000 troops observing Davout.)

BENNIGSEN (59,000) marching toward Glogau.

Souham commanded Ney's III Corps, and Gerard had Macdonald's XI Corps.

BERNADOTTE

OUDINOT

L'HERITIER

LATOUR-MAUBOURG
MARMONT
VICTOR

VANDAMME (+)

ST-CYR

KLENAU

SCHWARZENBERG

BOHEMIA

MACDONALD

GERARD (-)
SEBASTIANI

LAURISTON (-)

SOUHAM

BLÜCHER

SILESIA

PONIATOWSKI
SOKOLNICKI

AUGEREAU

WREDE
(30,000)
(Defending line of Inn River: loyalty dubious.)

Approximately 30,000 Austrians facing Bavarians.

LEIPZIG CAMPAIGN

Situation 26 August 1813

SCALE OF MILES

Following his reoccupation of Dresden, Napoleon had ordered the partially demolished rampart and ditch surrounding its Altstadt and Neustadt districts restored, the Neustadt sector to have priority. As Austria's hostility became evident, work had been started on the southern face of the city. The Altstadt's ramparts were repaired, and heavy guns emplaced at points where the built-up suburbs would not mask their fire. St.-Cyr improvised an outer line along the edge of the suburbs, walling up minor roads, loopholing houses and walls, and palisading major street entrances. Beyond the suburbs, he hastily built five small redoubts and a flèche. Redoubts I, II, and III were not mutually supporting; there was considerable dead ground in front of Redoubt IV. The Landgraben (*D2*), a drainage ditch, was a major obstacle that artillery could cross only by the main roads; the Weisseritz River (*B2*) was shallow, but rose quickly after a rain. St.-Cyr held his outpost line well forward of these uncertain defenses, withdrawing from the Strehlen area (*C2*) only at 0400. The terrain—cluttered with walled gardens, ditches, and small estates—favored the French, even the conscripts outclassing their veteran opponents in such "help-yourself" fighting.

The Allied plan vaguely provided for a reconnaissance in force during the late morning, followed by a major attack. There would be a demonstration (Wittgenstein, 10,000) just west of the Elbe, a secondary attack (Prussians, 35,000) on the Great Garden, another (Colloredo, 15,000) against Redoubt III. Chasteler would seize Pläuen and screen Bianchi's advance. At 1600, on a three-gun signal, a general bombardment would begin; Bianchi (35,000) would seize Löbtans and the Friedrichstadt suburb.

The Prussians advanced at about 0500, through fog and intermittent rain, but could get only a foothold in the Great Garden before 0730, when Wittgenstein tardily appeared on their right. His left flank helped gain the south half of the Garden, but his right and center were halted by French guns east of the Elbe. Eventually, the Russians cleared Striesen (*D2*), got a strong battery into position on Windmill Hill, and made some progress, but could not carry the flèche. At about 0900, a combined Prussian-Russian attack gained three-fourths of the Garden before running down. The Austrians cleared Pläuen and Löbtans, but the redoubts, backed by heavy guns on the Altstadt ramparts, withstood all assaults. Bianchi's leading elements reached Schusterhaüser (*B3*) against light opposition. By 1100, the Allies paused; they had driven in St.-Cyr's outpost line at heavy cost. Now, even the artillery fire died away.

Watching from Räcknitz Heights (*C2*), the Allied sovereigns had been increasingly aware of a stir throughout Dresden. Gradually, they learned the truth: Napoleon had arrived! Sweeping down the road from Bautzen came the dark masses of the Imperial Guard. Apparently, Alexander urged a retreat before something worse happened. The usually modest Prussian King ex-

ploded: Why should almost 200,000 Allies flee from one man? There was the customary debate, and Schwarzenberg was directed to suspend the main attack.

Napoleon had ridden into Dresden at about 0930, paid the King of Saxony a brief courtesy visit, inspected Dresden's western defenses, and gone forward for a close look at the enemy. Approving St.-Cyr's dispositions and leaving him free to conduct the defense, he set about organizing three counterattack forces, as shown, under Murat, Ney, and Mortier. The Old Guard remained as a central reserve. Victor and Marmont could not arrive in strength until after dark.

The Allied rulers had taken hours to reach their decision; Schwarzenberg's staff worked slowly. Before the order countermanding the main attack could reach the troops, the three signal cannons were fired, and the attack launched itself.

Supported by masses of artillery, the Allies stormed forward. Raked from across the river by increasing numbers of French guns, Wittgenstein failed. The Prussians cleared the Great Garden; west of it, they got close to the suburbs, but were driven off by St.-Cyr's reserves. The Austrians stormed Redoubt III when its garrison ran out of ammunition; their artillery momentarily silenced Redoubt IV, enabling their infantry to break into the suburbs between the two. But St.-Cyr mousetrapped them in the tangle of walled gardens, and Redoubt IV reopened fire. Redoubt V repulsed repeated attacks. Beyond the Weisseritz, Bianchi was stalled by converging fires from Redoubt V and the edge of the Friedrichstadt suburbs. Some Austrians worked forward along the Elbe, but withdrew when French cavalry appeared.

By 1730, the attack was at its height, and St.-Cyr's infantry completely committed. Then Napoleon struck. Mortier stormed the Great Garden, then swung units of his corps to their right and left, taking Wittgenstein front, flank, and rear, and recovering Redoubt III. Ney's assault so shook the Allied center that Schwarzenberg had to put in his reserve grenadiers. By dark, most of St.-Cyr's original outpost line had been recovered. The Austrians kept Pläuen, and Prussians and Russians held Striesen and the Garden's southern edge for several hours more. After riding through the thick of the fighting until it was evident that his counterattack was successful, Napoleon re-entered Dresden to prepare his plans for the 27th.

From emperors to drummer boys, the Allies were badly shaken. Weary, wet, and hungry, they heard the drums and cheers of Marmont's and Victor's corps. Learning that Vandamme had driven their right flank guard (Eugen) out of the Pirna area, the Allied commanders diverted Ostermann with part of the Russian Guard to block this menace, and decided to fight a defensive battle the next day.

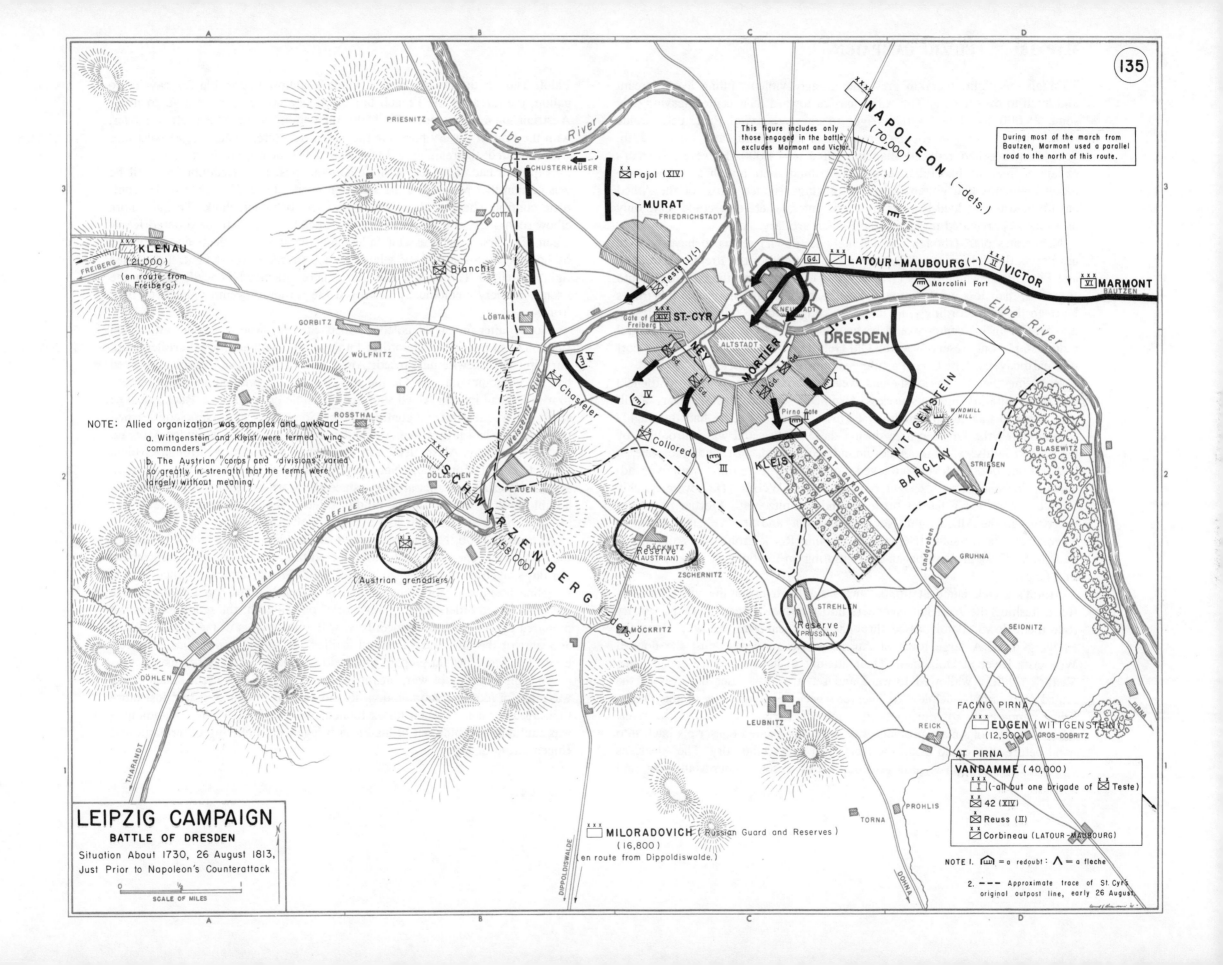

135

NAPOLEON (70,000)

This figure includes only those engaged in the battle; excludes Marmont and Victor.

During most of the march from Bautzen, Marmont used a parallel road to the north of this route.

PRIESNITZ

Elbe River

CHUSTERHÄUSER

Pajol (XIV)

MURAT

FRIEDRICHSTADT

KLENAU (21,000) (en route from Freiberg.)

COTTA

Bianchi

Teste (I)(-)

LATOUR-MAUBOURG(-)

Gd.

VICTOR

Marcolini Fort

MARMONT

BAUTZEN

Elbe River

LÖBTANS

Gate of Freiberg

ST.-CYR (-)

NEUSTADT

GORBITZ

WÖLFNITZ

V

Weisseritz River

NEY

Gd.

MORTIER

Gd.

Gd.

ALTSTADT

DRESDEN

Chasteler

IV

Gd.

I

ROSSTHAL

NOTE: Allied organization was complex and awkward:
a. Wittgenstein and Kleist were termed "wing commanders."
b. The Austrian "corps" and "divisions" varied so greatly in strength that the terms were largely without meaning.

Pirna Gate

Colloredo

III

WITTGENSTEIN

WINDMILL HILL

SCHWARZENBERG (58,000)

DÖLZSCHEN

PLAUEN

KLEIST

GREAT GARDEN

BARCLAY

BLASEWITZ

STRIESEN

TAHARANDT DEFILE

(Austrian grenadiers)

Reserve (AUSTRIAN)

RACKNITZ

ZSCHERNITZ

Landgraben

GRUHNA

(-dets.)

MÖCKRITZ

Reserve (PRUSSIAN)

STREHLIN

SEIDNITZ

PIRNA

THARANDT

DÖHLEN

LEUBNITZ

REICK

FACING PIRNA

EUGEN (WITTGENSTEIN) (12,500) GROS-DOBRITZ

AT PIRNA

VANDAMME (40,000)

I (-all but one brigade of Teste)

42 (XIV)

Reuss (II)

Corbineau (LATOUR-MAUBOURG)

TORNA

PROHLIS

DIPPOLDISWALDE

MILORADOVICH (Russian Guard and Reserves) (16,800) (en route from Dippoldiswalde.)

DOHNA

NOTE 1. [redoubt symbol] = a redoubt; ∧ = a fleche

2. - - - Approximate trace of St. Cyr's original outpost line, early 26 August.

LEIPZIG CAMPAIGN
BATTLE OF DRESDEN
Situation About 1730, 26 August 1813, Just Prior to Napoleon's Counterattack

SCALE OF MILES

Through the night, the rain grew increasingly violent, filling every stream and ditch to overflowing. The Allies massed toward their center, leaving only some 25,000 Russians on their right to cover the vital Pirna-Peterswalde road. Also, relying on Klenau's promise to be in line early on the 27th, Schwarzenberg had reduced Bianchi's force to 24,000. However, Klenau's exhausted recruits had fallen hopelessly behind their march schedule; only a few regiments had gotten within supporting distance. Most of the Allied cavalry had been added to their crowded center, where they could serve only as a much-appreciated target for the French artillery.

Napoleon's plan (though not definitely set down) seems to have been to envelop both flanks of the Allied army by seizing both the Freiberg-Komotau and Pirna-Peterswalde roads (*see Map 134*). These were the best routes into Bohemia; their loss would throw the Allies back on the miserable hill tracks between them. Accordingly, he made his wings strong (*this map*); Marmont and St.-Cyr in his center would be backed by the guns of the three central redoubts. His only reserve was the Old Guard infantry and his personal escort of Guard cavalry. The Guard artillery supported the French left.

Realizing that the furiously bad weather would dominate the battlefield and make infantry muskets useless, Napoleon scraped together every available horse to increase the mobility of his artillery. Also, he had thoroughly reconnoitered the Dresden area during the armistice and was untroubled by the poor visibility, while the Allies floundered in mud, mist, and ignorance.

At about 0600, Mortier attacked, followed by Nansouty, with Ney advancing in echelon to his right rear. Blasewitz Woods (*D2*) were quickly cleared. There was a harder tussle around Seidnitz, until Mortier and Nansouty turned the Allied right. Ney took Gruhna, and St.-Cyr seized Strehlen. Thereafter, the Russians fell back to the line Reick-Prohlis, and the attack paused. St.-Cyr's artillery began concentrating on Leubnitz (*C1*) and Zschernitz (*C2*).

Murat's attack came at 0630. Victor swiftly overran the villages to his front, flushing the Austrian defenders into the open where his corps cavalry rode them down. Pajol passed through Victor, sabering his way along the Freiberg road. A large force of Austrians was pinned against the flooded Weisseritz River at Dölzschen. Their attempt to hold the place ended when Victor's artillery wallowed forward and set it afire. Under the eyes of the Allied main army—helpless to intervene because of the loss of the Pläuen bridge, apparently to Marmont—the defenders were driven into the river. After that, Victor's main problem was to get his excited conscripts back into hand before they could drink the Dölzschen wine cellars dry. The Austrians opposite Murat's right were largely trapped by Teste, Latour-Maubourg, and Pajol. Though the muddy ground made it almost impossible for cavalry to gallop, the threat of the French horse artillery was usually enough to make Austrian squares surrender. By 1500, the action on the Allied left was over, with the French cavalry pursuing the survivors. Here, some 15,000 Austrians were captured; the remaining 9,000 were killed or hopelessly scattered.

Napoleon had remained at his command post near Redoubt IV until he was certain that Murat had the situation north of the Weisseritz under complete control. Then, at about 1000, he rode to his left flank. To gain more elbow room here, and to secure a strong anchor for his left, he ordered Reick taken. The first French assault failed, but the second—effectively supported by howitzer fire—carried the village after a savage bayonet fight. The Allied right retired to Torna, and the battle here practically ended, though the French artillery methodically destroyed the farmhouses and villages to their front.

Shortly after noon, Napoleon joined St.-Cyr, whose second attack on Leubnitz had just failed. He ordered a third one, with additional artillery support, but this likewise miscarried. Angered by this repulse, Napoleon started back to his command post. On the way, he casually ordered a French battery to toss a round into an Allied staff group visible on a hill near Räcknitz. The result was a square hit and confused flight. Some time later, Napoleon learned that this shot had just missed Alexander and had mortally wounded Moreau.

During the day, Alexander's staff planned a counterattack through Gruhna (*D2*) to cut off Mortier and Nansouty. Barclay objected that a repulse would cost the Russian army its artillery, since the worn-out gun teams would not be able to drag it back up the muddy ridges. About this time, Moreau was hit, and the three monarchs lost interest in offensive action.

At around 1600, Napoleon returned to Dresden. He did not yet consider the battle won. The Allies still outnumbered him; they might very well regard the day's fighting as merely an unsuccessful French attack on their strong ridgeline position. (St.-Cyr had failed in a fourth attack on Leubnitz.) He therefore issued orders for a "great battle" on the 28th; the redoubts must be prepared for last-ditch resistance; Ney, with one division of the Young Guard and part of the Guard cavalry and artillery, would take positions near Redoubt IV; Murat would prepare to envelop the new Allied left flank.

An Allied council of war, meanwhile, had decided to retreat. Their army was short of food and ammunition, its morale was dragging, it had lost more than 38,000 men. (French losses totaled barely 10,000.) Also, Vandamme was cautiously pushing out of his Pirna bridgehead, buffeting Ostermann and Eugen ahead of him.

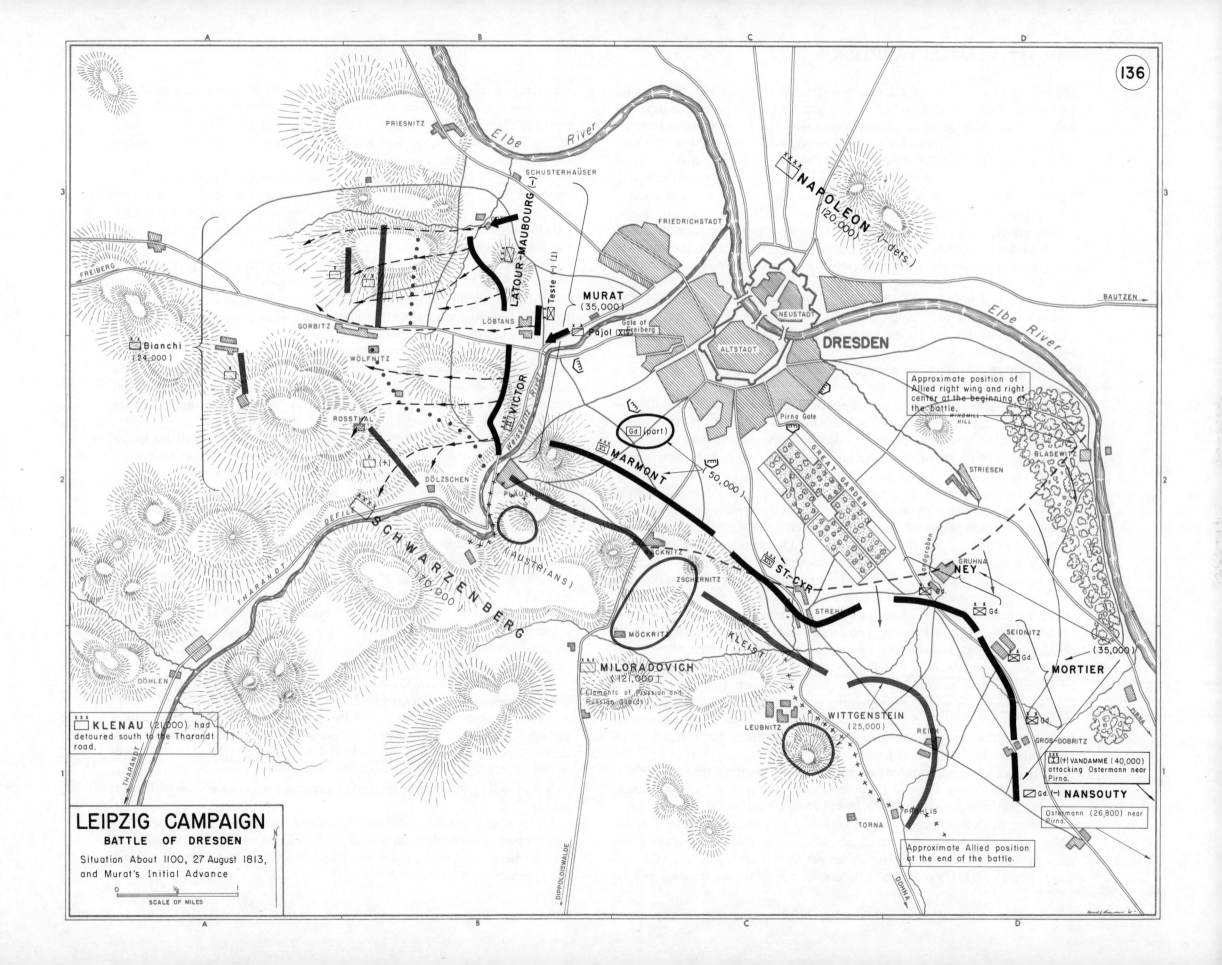

136

PRIESNITZ

Elbe River

SCHUSTERHAÜSER

FRIEDRICHSTADT

NAPOLEON
(120,000)
(-dets)

LATOUR-MAUBOURG

Teste (-) (1)

MURAT
(35,000)

FREIBERG

GORBITZ

LÖBTANS

Pajol XIV

Gate of
Freiberg

NEUSTADT

DRESDEN

ALTSTADT

Elbe River

BAUTZEN

Bianchi
(24,000)

WÖLFNITZ

VICTOR

Weisseritz River

Pirna Gate

Approximate position of
Allied right wing and right
center at the beginning of
the battle.

WINDMILL
HILL

ROSSTHAL

Gd (part)

(+)

DÖLZSCHEN

PLAUEN

MARMONT

(50,000)

GREAT GARDEN

STRIESEN

BLASEWITZ

DEFILE

SCHWARZENBERG
(70,000)

(AUSTRIANS)

ROCKNITZ

ZSCHERNITZ

ST-CYR

landgraben

GRUHNA

NEY

TATHARANDT

MÖCKRITZ

KLEIST

STREHL

Gd.

Gd.

SEIDNITZ

Gd.

(35,000)

MORTIER

DÖHLEN

MILORADOVICH
(12,000)
(Elements of Prussian and
Russian Guards)

LEUBNITZ

WITTGENSTEIN
(25,000)

REICK

Gd.

GROS-DOBRITZ

PIRNA

KLENAU (21,000) had
detoured south to the Tharandt
road.

TORNA

PRÖHLIS

(+) VANDAMME (40,000)
attacking Ostermann near
Pirna.

Gd (-) NANSOUTY

DIPPOLDISWALDE

DOHNA

Ostermann (26,800) near
Pirna.

LEIPZIG CAMPAIGN
BATTLE OF DRESDEN
Situation About 1100, 27 August 1813,
and Murat's Initial Advance

Approximate Allied position
at the end of the battle.

0   ½   1
SCALE OF MILES

The Allied plan of withdrawal assigned Barclay (Wittgenstein, Kleist, and the Prussian-Russian "Reserve" of guards, grenadiers, and heavy cavalry) the Dohna (C3)–Berggieshübel (C2)–Peterswalde (C2)–Teplitz (C1) route. Schwarzenberg would retire via Dippoldiswalde (B2)–Altenberg (C2)–Dux (C1); Klenau through Tharandt (B3)–Freiberg (B2)–Marienberg (A1)–Komotau (B1). Screened by storm, fog, and the heights they had occupied, the Allies moved out undetected after dark on the 27th. Klenau already had fled by the route shown, successfully evading both Napoleon's pursuit and Schwarzenberg's control. Barclay, fearful of being trapped between Napoleon and Vandamme, ignored his orders, sending his Reserve by the already-jammed Dippoldiswalde road, ordering Kleist through Maxen (C3) and Glashütte (C2), and authorizing Ostermann to rejoin him via Maxen, if Vandamme had blocked the Pirna (C3)–Peterswalde (C2) highway. The available roads were mere mountain tracks, still choked with the Allied supply trains. Stragglers fell out by the hundreds; whole battalions abandoned their weapons.

Early on 28 August, French patrols groped forward through the fog, and found only enemy rear guards. Napoleon galloped to Pirna, where he could observe the Allies ebbing back into the mountains; somehow, he got the impression that they were retreating toward Annaberg (A1). At 1600, learning that Vandamme had captured Berggieshübel, he ordered him to attempt to reach Teplitz (C1) ahead of the Allied main body, and destroy their trains. If Eugen opposed him, Vandamme should crush him. A ponton bridge would be moved from Pirna to Tetschen (D2), for easier lateral communication with Poniatowski. Mortier would halt at Pirna; Marmont would follow the Allied retreat. The Army of Bohemia had been damaged; if his corps commanders pushed their pursuit efficiently, it could be seriously crippled.

After issuing these orders, Napoleon returned to Dresden. He had received reports of Oudinot's misadventures, Girard's defeat, and Macdonald's rout; his major concerns now were Bernadotte's and Blücher's future movements, and the restoration of his west-bank communications with Leipzig.

On receiving Barclay's orders, Ostermann immediately proposed to retire on Maxen. Eugen protested that this would uncover the Allied rear. Ostermann gave in, on condition that Eugen accept full responsibility, but insisted on retreating first, to preserve his precious guardsmen from unauthorized combat. Vandamme was already pushing down a side road east of the highway to intercept them at Berggieshübel. Ostermann reached that point soon enough to break through Vandamme's leading elements, but Eugen's corps was caught and almost wrecked.

Early on 29 August, Napoleon ordered Murat to continue through Frauenstein (B2), Marmont through Dippoldiswalde, and St.-Cyr through Maxen, stressing that they should maintain lateral communication. St.-Cyr and Marmont were to change their routes as necessary to maintain contact with the Allies. At 1600, Napoleon warned Murat that Marmont had reported the enemy's main column to be definitely retreating through Altenberg (C2) toward Teplitz (C1). Vandamme's orders for the 29th are missing, but he

apparently received some directive, since he sent a detachment to Aussig (C2) that night to construct a bridge. During the day he had moved aggressively up the highway, completing the destruction of Eugen's corps in clashes at Hellendorf, Peterswalde, and Kulm. At Priesten, the last strong position above Teplitz, he finally found Ostermann.

The story of how Ostermann was persuaded to stand here reads like a romance. Quite possibly it is one. Reputedly, Ostermann had sent a courier to Teplitz to warn Alexander that he was retiring beyond the Eger River (D1). Only King Frederick William and the Emperor Francis were in Teplitz; the latter promptly ran, but Frederick William joined Ostermann and—pointing out that a further retreat would endanger the Czar—persuaded him to fight. Alexander and Metternich (who accompanied the Allied sovereigns) hustled all available troops toward Priesten. Vandamme attacked furiously, but Allied reinforcements built up too rapidly. Finally, outflanked by Allied cavalry, Vandamme slowly retired.

The other French corps, struggling up muddy passes, clogged with abandoned wagons, had fallen behind. Rebuffed in a clash with Kleist at Glashütte, St.-Cyr suddenly developed an amazing inability to regain contact, strayed off to his right rear, got entangled in Marmont's column, and finished by halting and requesting orders.

Resuming his march toward Teplitz, Kleist learned that all available routes, except the Pirna-Peterswalde highway, were hopelessly blocked by broken-down vehicles. His cavalry reported (erroneously) the highway empty of French troops, and found a hill track that led into it north of Kulm. Desperate, Kleist turned eastward, hoping to break through Vandamme before St.-Cyr again overtook him.

On 30 August, apparently after considering St.-Cyr's last report, Napoleon awoke to Vandamme's increasing isolation; Mortier was told to advance to Vandamme's support. Murat, Marmont, and St.-Cyr were to drive for Zinnwald (C2), the most difficult part of the Allied retreat, where they would be especially sensitive to pressure. Again, Vandamme's orders are missing, but it appears certain that he knew Mortier was advancing. A bold commander, anxious to win his marshal's baton, he chose to stand at Kulm, instead of retiring to a stronger position at Peterswalde.

To secure their retreat, the Allies concentrated 44,000 men against Vandamme. Vandamme (32,000) held his position against them, until Kleist (10,000) unexpectedly came out of the hills behind him. (Overconfident of prompt support, Vandamme had not outposted his rear.) Uncowed, Vandamme at once turned furiously against Kleist, trampling most of his corps underfoot. Kleist's rear guard finally blocked the pass near Peterswalde, but well over half of the French escaped. Vandamme was captured with his rear guard.

Meanwhile, Marmont had driven the Allied rear guard through Altenberg and Zinnwald, but St.-Cyr sat placidly throughout the morning. Mortier had reached Berggieshübel; on hearing of Vandamme's defeat, he initially retired, but later advanced to Hellendorf.

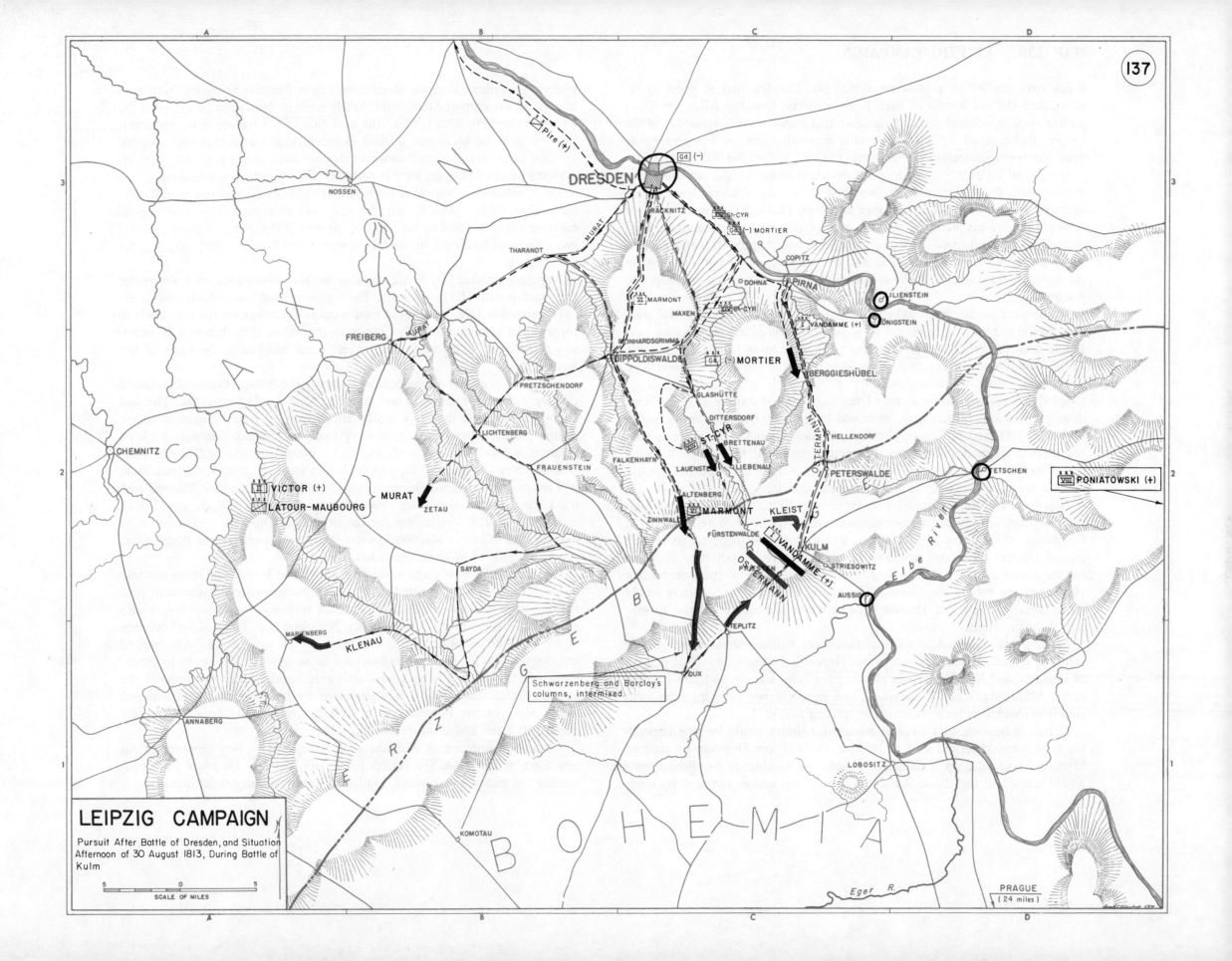

137

DRESDEN

Gd (−)

St-CYR
Gd (−) MORTIER

MARMONT

MAXEN

St-CYR

REINHARDSGRIMMA

DIPPOLDISWALDE

Gd (−) MORTIER

VANDAMME (+)

KÖNIGSTEIN

LILIENSTEIN

BERGGIESHÜBEL

GLASHÜTTE

DITTERSDORF

HELLENDORF

St-CYR

LAUENSTEIN
LIEBENAU

BRETTENAU

PETERSWALDE

OSTERMANN

FALKENHAYN

FRAUENSTEIN

ALTENBERG

LICHTENBERG

MARMONT

KLEIST

ZINNWALD

FÜRSTENWALDE

VANDAMME (+)

KULM

PRETZSCHENDORF

STRIESOWITZ

OSTERMANN

CHEMNITZ

II VICTOR (+)

LATOUR-MAUBOURG

MURAT

ZETAU

SAYDA

AUSSIG

TETSCHEN

VIII PONIATOWSKI (+)

Elbe River

TEPLITZ

MARIENBERG

KLENAU

DUX

Schwarzenberg and Barclay's
columns, intermixed.

NOSSEN

TarandT

MURAT

MURAT

FREIBERG

DOHNA

PIRNA

COPITZ

RACKNITZ

ANNABERG

KOMOTAU

LOBOSITZ

BOHEMIA

Eger R.

PRAGUE
(24 miles)

LEIPZIG CAMPAIGN

Pursuit After Battle of Dresden, and Situation
Afternoon of 30 August 1813, During Battle of
Kulm

5   0   5
SCALE OF MILES

Kulm gave the Allies a great emotional lift. Dresden had as good as re-established the old legend of French invincibility; now the Allies set about puffing their accidental success, claiming that "only some fragments" of the I Corps had escaped. (A factual count is impossible, but the French seem to have lost approximately 19,000 at Priesten and Kulm; the Allies, 11,000.)

During 30 August, Napoleon drew up an estimate of the situation confronting him, concluding that his two possible courses of action were an advance on Prague (*C1*) or an advance on Berlin (*B3*). The first he rejected: It would require his presence, with the bulk of his army on the extreme right of his overextended front; he would have to debouch through the mountains in the presence of a superior force; and Prague was not vitally important to the Allies. If Schwarzenberg chose to avoid combat, he could retire deep into Austria.

An advance on Berlin would enable him to maintain a more central position, would exploit the resources of a hitherto largely unforaged area, and should draw the Prussians and Russians northward, away from the Austrians. In this case, the Austrians could be held in check by the I, II, VI, and XIV Corps and Latour-Maubourg's cavalry. If the whole Army of Bohemia attempted another expedition against Dresden, it should require at least fifteen days' preparation. In that time, he would have taken Berlin, relieved Stettin (*off map, C3*), and broken up the Prussian mobilization. (His estimate does not mention Bernadotte, but he apparently considered that he could easily defeat his former marshal.) He could then reconcentrate his forces at Dresden, and win the campaign and the war together in one decisive blow.

Napoleon therefore planned to concentrate 25,000 men and 150 guns (largely from the Guard) at Grossenhain (*B2*) by the evening of the 31st. Combined with Oudinot's four corps, which Napoleon believed to be still around Luckau (*B3*), this would make approximately 80,000 men available for the Berlin offensive. Macdonald would hold the line of the Bober River (*C2*), retiring behind the Queiss if necessary. His own headquarters would move initially to Luckau. Davout likewise would advance on Berlin to support the main offensive.

These plans collapsed as soon as they were written. Vandamme's defeat seriously weakened one of the corps that Napoleon had assigned to the defense of Dresden, and Macdonald was pleading for help. Enemy partisans had got across Macdonald's communications, and he could not rally his men sufficiently to check Blücher's rather unenterprising pursuit.

Napoleon believed that an offensive against Berlin would become impossible if Macdonald retired west of Bautzen (*C2*). From Dresden, he ordered Macdonald to take up a defensive position at Gorlitz (*C2*). Poniatowski would remain in the Zittau-Rumburg area (*C2*), unless attacked by overwhelming numbers, to cover Macdonald's right flank. If necessary, Napoleon himself would support Macdonald. While waiting, Napoleon reorganized the I Corps, assigning it to Lobau (the new title of his former aide, Mouton), and concentrated his Guard around Dresden. Murat and Marmont mopped up their areas, Marmont subsequently slipping back out of line. All corps remaining south of Dresden were ordered to take up defensive positions.

On 2 September, Napoleon learned that Oudinot had retired into Wittenberg (*B3*). Stiffly rebuking him, he sent Ney to supersede him in over-all command, but left him at the head of his own XII Corps. Oudinot resented being replaced by Ney; both were high-stomached hotheads with no talent for cooperation.

Napoleon ordered Ney to march from the Wittenberg area on 4 September and reach Baruth (*B3*) on the 6th. The Emperor would move his headquarters to Hoyerswerda (*C2*) and would have a corps in Luckau on the 6th, ready to support him in an attack against Berlin on the 9th or 10th. It would be necessary to act quickly, before Schwarzenberg could reorganize the Army of Bohemia.

Napoleon promptly (2 September) started the Young Guard, the Guard cavalry and reserve artillery, and a bridge train for Hoyerswerda. The Old Guard infantry and the army headquarters' forward echelon were to follow on the 3rd. But then came another cry from Macdonald, tumbling back on Bautzen, his troops out of hand, and under increased pressure from Blücher. Warning Ney to expect no support from him until Blücher was driven back, and telling him to ask for Davout's help, Napoleon marched for Bautzen with the Guard, Latour-Maubourg, and Marmont. Victor, St.-Cyr, and Lobau were given explicit instructions for the defense of Dresden; gendarmes were sent forward to collect Macdonald's stragglers and deserters; and Poniatowski was to be ready to strike Blücher's left flank.

A large supply convoy was pushed ahead to meet Macdonald, who was told to get his army tightly concentrated so that Napoleon could inspect it in a half-hour. He was also to take the necessary measures to conceal Napoleon's approach from the enemy. Undoubtedly, Napoleon hoped to deal with Blücher as he had with Schwarzenberg, but the sight of Macdonald's demoralized command drove him into an unusual public fit of fury. Riding on to Hochkirch (*C2*), he saw Blücher's advance guard approaching, and ordered the nearest French units against it. Revitalized by his presence, these whipped men turned on the Prussians with such enthusiasm that Blücher rapidly guessed its cause and at once retreated.

Assuming command at Wittenberg on 3 September, Ney reorganized his new force and marched for Jüterbog (*B3*) on the 5th. He knew little concerning the enemy and, typically, failed to use his cavalry to learn more.

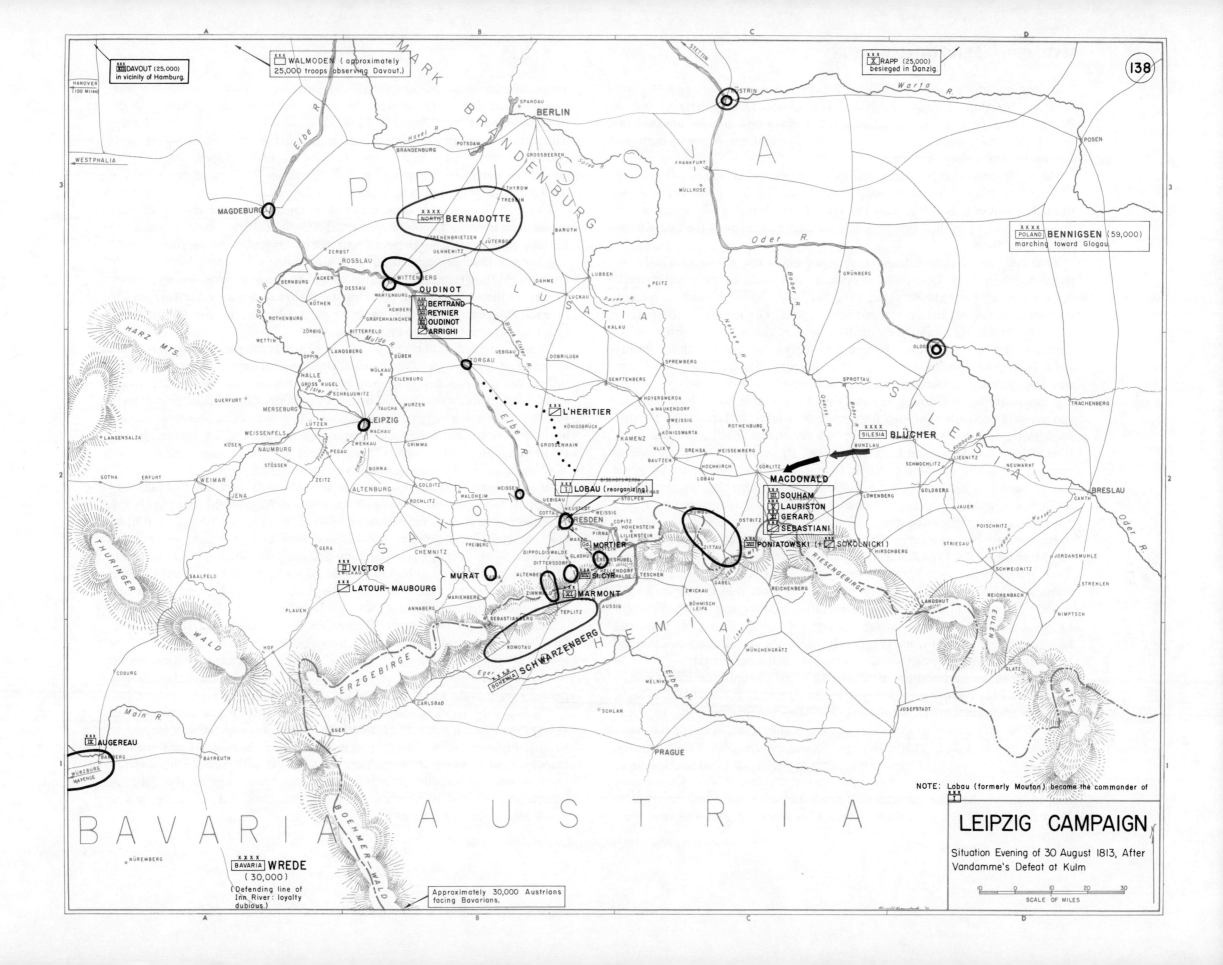

138

DAVOUT (25,000) in vicinity of Hamburg.

WALMODEN (approximately 25,000 troops observing Davout.)

RAPP (25,000) besieged in Danzig.

HANOVER (100 Miles)

WESTPHALIA

NORTH BERNADOTTE

POLAND BENNIGSEN (59,000) marching toward Glogau.

OUDINOT
BERTRAND
REYNIER
OUDINOT
ARRIGHI

L'HERITIER

SILESIA BLÜCHER

LOBAU (reorganizing)

MACDONALD
SOUHAM
LAURISTON
GERARD
SEBASTIANI

PONIATOWSKI (+ **SOKOLNICKI**)

MORTIER

VICTOR
LATOUR-MAUBOURG

MURAT

St.CYR

MARMONT

SCHWARZENBERG
BOHEMIA

AUGEREAU

WURZBURG
MAYENCE

NOTE: Lobau (formerly Mouton) became the commander of

BAVARIA WREDE
(30,000)
(Defending line of Inn River: loyalty dubious.)

Approximately 30,000 Austrians facing Bavarians.

LEIPZIG CAMPAIGN

Situation Evening of 30 August 1813, After Vandamme's Defeat at Kulm

SCALE OF MILES

Napoleon quickly realized that Blücher had no intention of fighting (*Map a*). Ordering Macdonald to drive Blücher east of the Queiss, he returned to Bautzen on 5 October. Here, his renewed preparations for the advance on Berlin were interrupted by a report from St.-Cyr that the Army of Bohemia was again threatening Dresden.

Having learned that Napoleon had moved against Blücher, Schwarzenberg had recrossed the Elbe with 60,000 Austrians, intending to drive north through Rumburg. Barclay, with the rest of the Army of Bohemia, would threaten Dresden. By late 6 September, Barclay had reached the line König-stein-Pirna-Dohna.

That same day, Ney blundered aggressively into a trap Bernadotte had contrived for him near Dennewitz. Reynier's skill and the fury with which the French came on almost saved him, but Ney—losing himself in leading Bertrand's corps—at the critical moment ordered Oudinot from the French left flank to the right. Fully aware that he was throwing the battle away, Oudinot obeyed. The French retreated to Torgau in great disorder, losing some 10,000 men to the Allies' 7,000. (Subsequently, Oudinot's XII Corps was deactivated, and Oudinot was given a Young Guard corps.)

After returning to Dresden and studying the situation there, Napoleon advanced on 8 September through Fürstenwalde, aiming at Teplitz. Barclay fell back through Peterswalde (*Map b*); Schwarzenberg hastily recrossed the Elbe, calling in Klenau and Lichtenstein. On 10 September, Napoleon came over the mountains just west of Kulm, to find Barclay frantically trying to get into position to meet him. In 1796, Napoleon would have attacked. Now, his artillery was unable to get into action over the ruined roads, and he would not risk his conscripts without it.

Increasingly bad weather made further major movements almost impossible. Meanwhile, the French troops around Dresden suffered on short rations. Their administrative service was incompetent, and Allied partisans—Thielmann, Mensdorf, Platov, and Czernitchew—constantly raided their communications. Napoleon strengthened his rear-guard garrisons, sent (11 September) Lefebvre-Desnoëttes with a strong cavalry column to sweep his rear, and brought flour in by boat from Torgau. His problems were further complicated by Macdonald's tendency to withdraw every time Blücher stirred.

After considering a variety of plans, Napoleon abruptly decided to retire west of the Elbe (*Map c*), retaining strong bridgeheads at Königstein, Pillnitz, Dresden, Meissen, Torgau, Wittenberg, and Magdeburg. This done, he would clear up his rear area, reorganize his communications, and wait for the Allies to come and be killed. This withdrawal began on the 24th. Coincidentally, after several successes, Lefebvre-Desnoëttes carelessly allowed himself to be surprised and defeated by Thielmann, Mensdorf, and Platov. Czernitchew slipped across the Elbe, frightened Jerome out of Kassel, and returned to Bernadotte. Napoleon thereafter converted his rear-area garrisons into coun-

terguerrilla columns and sent Poniatowski's Poles to purge the French rear.

Northward, Bernadotte bridged the Elbe at Rosslau and Acken, and the Elster River at Elster. Bertrand (24th–25th) broke up the Elster crossing, while Reynier defeated an Allied attempt to move south from Rosslau. However, Bernadotte managed to fortify both of his Elbe bridgeheads, and Ney lacked the necessary strength to reduce them. On 28 September, Napoleon shifted Latour-Maubourg and Marmont to Torgau.

The Allies likewise developed a new plan: Once Bennigsen arrived, Blücher would march north to join Bernadotte; Schwarzenberg would advance on Leipzig via Chemnitz. (There is no trace of any plan to coordinate their operations.) Blücher marched on the 25th, leaving a screening force opposite Dresden. At the first clash, L'Heritier retired to the west bank, losing contact. Sacken further screened this movement by an attack (unsuccessful) on the Meissen bridgehead. Moving south to meet Blücher, Bülow (Bernadotte) began constructing a bridge at Wartenburg.

Napoleon already had decided that Dresden was too close to the Bohemian mountains (behind which the beaten enemy could always take refuge) to be a satisfactory central position. Leipzig appeared a better one. Aware of Schwarzenberg's shift westward, he reinforced his own right flank. Blücher's maneuvers left him suspicious but uncertain until 4 October, when Marmont warned him that Blücher had forced the Elbe at Wartenburg the day before, driving Bertrand off after a hard fight (*Map d*). Bernadotte now began breaking out of Rosslau and Barby. Klenau approached Chemnitz.

Between 5 and 7 October, Napoleon sent Marmont and Latour-Maubourg to support Ney, following himself with Sebastiani, Macdonald, and the Guard. His plan was to cross to the east bank of the Elbe at either Torgau or Wittenberg and cut Bernadotte's and Blücher's communications. Murat would delay Schwarzenberg, keeping between him and Leipzig. With some reluctance, Napoleon left St.-Cyr and Lobau to hold Dresden, deciding he would need it for future operations against Schwarzenberg, once he had beaten Blücher and Bernadotte. Augereau would advance to Leipzig.

Learning on 8 October that Blücher was near Düben and Bernadotte at Dessau, Napoleon ordered Ney to follow the east bank of the Mulde River toward Düben. Reynier would follow the west bank; Bertrand and Sebastiani would advance through Mockrehna; Macdonald would follow Bertrand. Napoleon's main body would advance toward Eilenburg.

Weakened by short rations and bad weather, the French marched more slowly than usual. Blücher and Bernadotte, having lost contact with Ney, were angrily disputing the wisdom of proceeding farther. Suddenly confronted by Napoleon's converging columns, they chose (apparently on Blücher's initiative) to retire westward across the Saale, rather than recross the Elbe. A frantic scramble got Blücher clear, though Sebastiani cut up Sacken's rear guard and captured his trains.

Note: On Map 139b, Kustrin *(B2) should be* Küstrin.

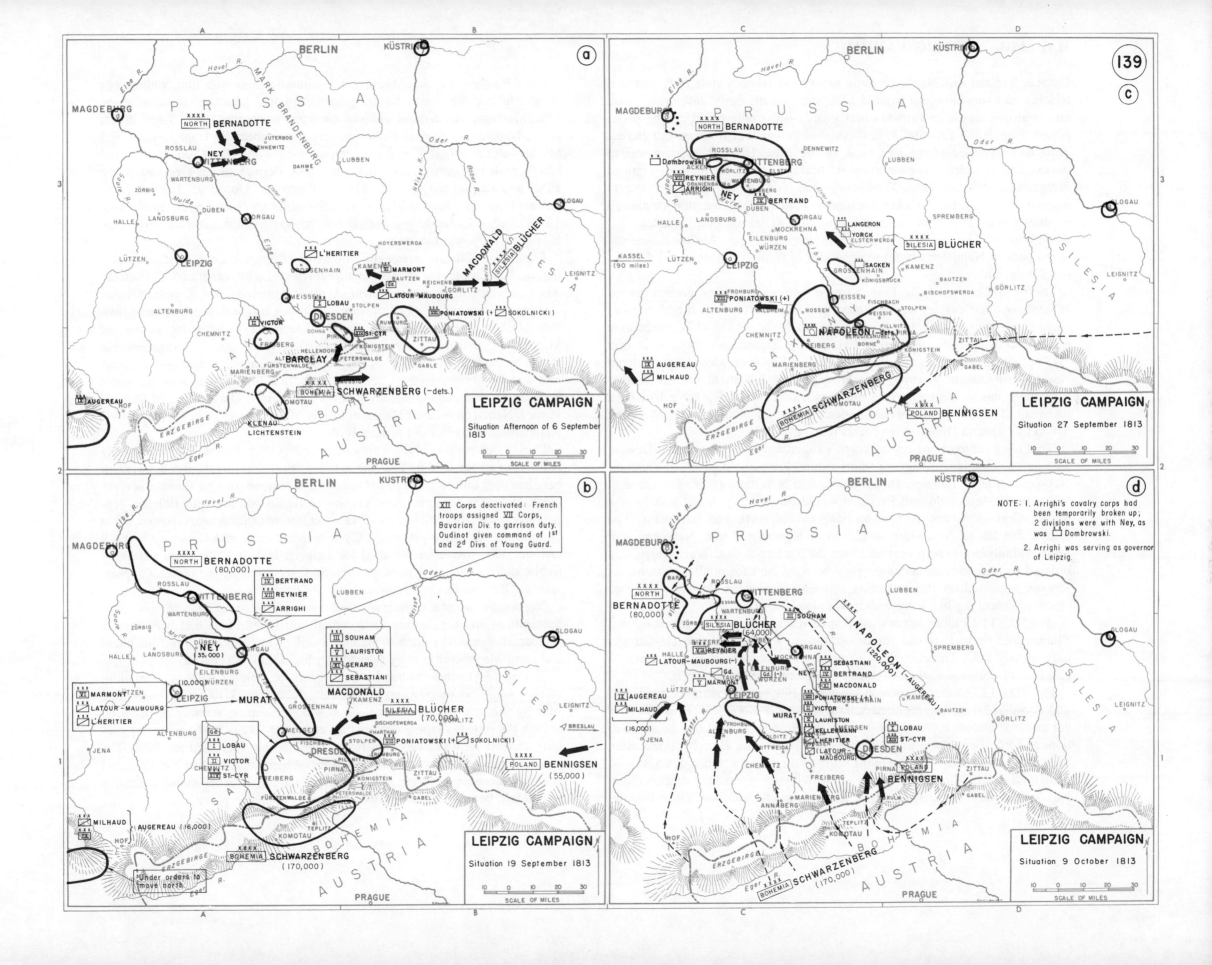

(a)

BERLIN KÜSTRIN

P R U S S I A

MAGDEBURG

MARK BRANDENBURG

NORTH BERNADOTTE

NEY WITTENBERG

ROSSLAU JÜTERBOG DENNEWITZ

WARTENBURG DAHME LUBBEN

ZÖRBIG DÜBEN Oder R.

HALLE LANDSBURG TORGAU

LÜTZEN LEIPZIG HOYERSWERDA

GROSSENHAIN L'HERITIER KAMENZ MARMONT BAUTZEN GÖRLITZ MACDONALD SILESIA BLÜCHER

MEISSEN LATOUR-MAUBOURG

I LOBAU STOLPEN

VICTOR DRESDEN REICHENB ZITTAU VIII PONIATOWSKI (+) SOKOLNICKI

FREIBERG DOHNA PIRNA SI-CYR RUMBURG LEIGNITZ

CHEMNITZ KONIGSTEIN GABLE

BARCLAY PETERSWALDE

MARIENBERG FURSTENWALDE

BÖHMEN SCHWARZENBERG (−dets.)

IX AUGEREAU

ERZGEBIRGE KLENAU LICHTENSTEIN

A U S T R I A

PRAGUE

LEIPZIG CAMPAIGN

Situation Afternoon of 6 September 1813

10 0 10 20 30
SCALE OF MILES

139

(c)

BERLIN KÜSTRIN

P R U S S I A

MAGDEBURG

NORTH BERNADOTTE

ROSSLAU DENNEWITZ

Dombrowski WITTENBERG LUBBEN Oder R.

REYNIER WORLITZ ELSTERWERDA

ARRIGHI NEY BERTRAND

ORANIENBAUM WARTENBURG DÜBEN LANGERON SPREMBERG

HALLE LANDSBURG TORGAU YORCK ELSTERWERDA SILESIA BLÜCHER GLOGAU

KASSEL (90 miles) LÜTZEN EILENBURG WÜRZEN MOCKREHNA SACKEN KAMENZ

LEIPZIG GROSSENHAIN KÖNIGSBRÜCK BAUTZEN GÖRLITZ

FROHBURG MEISSEN FISCHBACH BISCHOFSWERDA

VIII PONIATOWSKI (+) NOSSEN WEISSIG

ALTENBURG WALDHEIM PILLNITZ STOLPEN

CHEMNITZ NAPOLEON FREIBERG BORNE dets. PIRNA KÖNIGSTEIN ZITTAU

IX AUGEREAU MARIENBERG

MILHAUD KOMOTAU GABEL

BÖHMEN SCHWARZENBERG POLAND BENNIGSEN

ERZGEBIRGE Eger R.

A U S T R I A

PRAGUE

LEIPZIG CAMPAIGN

Situation 27 September 1813

10 0 10 20 30
SCALE OF MILES

(b)

BERLIN KÜSTRIN

XII Corps deactivated: French
troops assigned VII Corps,
Bavarian Div. to garrison duty.
Oudinot given command of 1st
and 2d Divs of Young Guard.

P R U S S I A

MAGDEBURG

NORTH BERNADOTTE
(80,000)

ROSSLAU IV BERTRAND

WITTENBERG VII REYNIER

WARTENBURG ARRIGHI

ZÖRBIG Oder R.

NEY TORGAU III SOUHAM LUBBEN
(35,000) V LAURISTON GLOGAU

HALLE EILENBURG XI GERARD

(10,000) WÜRZEN SEBASTIANI

LEIPZIG MURAT GROSSENHAIN MACDONALD SILESIA BLÜCHER
(70,000) LEIGNITZ

VI MARMONT KAMENZ BISCHOFSWERDA BRESLAU

LATOUR-MAUBOURG MEISSEN WARTHAU STOLPEN VIII PONIATOWSKI (+) SOKOLNICKI

L'HERITIER DRESDEN FISCHBACH

ALTENBURG Gd. LOBAU PILLNITZ

I LOBAU I VICTOR FREIBERG ZITTAU POLAND BENNIGSEN
JENA CHEMNITZ XIV ST-CYR KONIGSTEIN (55,000)

PIRNA GABEL

FÜRTENWALDE PETERSWALDE

MILHAUD (AUGEREAU (16,000) KOMOTAU TEPLITZ

BÖHMEN SCHWARZENBERG
(170,000)

ERZGEBIRGE Under orders to PRAGUE
move north Eger R.

A U S T R I A

LEIPZIG CAMPAIGN

Situation 19 September 1813

10 0 10 20 30
SCALE OF MILES

(d)

BERLIN KÜSTRIN

NOTE: 1. Arrighi's cavalry corps had
been temporarily broken up;
2 divisions were with Ney, as
was Dombrowski.

2. Arrighi was serving as governor
of Leipzig.

P R U S S I A

MAGDEBURG

BAR NORTH ACKEN
BERNADOTTE ROSSLAU DESSAU SOUHAM NAPOLEON
(80,000) WARTENBURG WITTENBERG (220,000)(−AUGEREAU) Oder R.

SILESIA BLÜCHER LUBBEN
(64,000)

ZÖRBIG BITTERFELD III

HALLE REYNIER MOCKREHNA SEBASTIANI GLOGAU

LATOUR-MAUBOURG Gd. TORGAU NEY IV BERTRAND

V MARMONT EILENBURG Gd.(−) WÜRZEN XI MACDONALD SPREMBERG

IX AUGEREAU LEIPZIG VIII PONIATOWSKI KAMENZ

MILHAUD LÜTZEN II VICTOR BAUTZEN

(16,000) JENA FROHBURG MURAT V LAURISTON

CHEMNITZ MITTWEIDA KELLERMANN I LOBAU
ALTENBURG COLDITZ L'HERITIER XIV ST-CYR

(LATOUR- DRESDEN
MAUBOURG) PIRNA POLAND ZITTAU

FREIBERG BENNIGSEN

HOF ANNABERG MARIENBERG KULM GABEL

TEPLITZ

KOMOTAU BÖHMEN
SCHWARZENBERG
Eger R. (170,000)

A U S T R I A

PRAGUE

LEIPZIG CAMPAIGN

Situation 9 October 1813

10 0 10 20 30
SCALE OF MILES

October 9 ended with Napoleon in an almost low-comedy state of frustration. Blücher had somehow just evaded him, and—in the early dark, rain, mist, and confused scuttle of Prussian rear guards—his route could not be determined. Napoleon's first and logical conclusion was that Blücher and Bernadotte had recrossed to the east bank of the Elbe. His first impulse was to pursue and complete their destruction. Basing himself on his well-supplied bridgeheads at Magdeburg, Wittenberg, and Torgau, he would be able to maneuver freely. Murat should attempt to hold Leipzig, but not let himself be drawn into battle with superior forces. St.-Cyr should hold Dresden, if it could possibly be done; if not, he should retire on Torgau. Always simmering in the back of Napoleon's brain was the idea of turning suddenly and destroying Schwarzenberg.

During 10 October, as the French sorted themselves out and pushed toward Wittenberg, their cavalry reported most of the enemy between the Mulde and Saale rivers. In fact, Blücher was moving on Halle (*A2*), while Bernadotte was withdrawing to Rothenburg (*A3*), leaving Tauenzien's corps at Dessau (*A3*) to cover the Acken and Rosslau bridges. Napoleon accordingly ordered Ney toward Dessau; Reynier, Dombrowski, and Sebastiani toward Wittenberg; Bertrand to Wartenburg to make sure that the bridge there had been taken up. The army trains would concentrate at Eilenburg (*B2*); Marmont would halt around Düben as a general reserve.

That night, at least one enemy corps (Tauenzien) was reported in Dessau, with an immense jam of baggage trains around Rosslau. At 0100, 11 October, Napoleon ordered Reynier, Dombrowski, and Sebastiani to cross at once at Wittenberg; Macdonald and Bertrand would follow. Ney would halt for the day at Gräfenhainchen (*B3*), observing to the north and northwest. The Guard and Latour-Maubourg would be at Kemberg. Later, Napoleon sent Latour-Maubourg to help Bertrand beat the country toward Wartenburg, and ordered Reynier to reconnoiter the right bank of the Elbe in all directions. As Reynier appeared on the east bank, the enemy division detached there to observe Wittenberg hurriedly withdrew toward Rosslau.

At 1500, 11 October, some trusted spies reached Napoleon, reporting that Blücher and Bernadotte had withdrawn toward Köthen and that Dessau was only weakly held. Directing Ney to send out a reconnaissance in force to check this information, Napoleon sent Oudinot to Gräfenhainchen.

By 0300, 12 October, Napoleon knew that Blücher had marched for Halle, and also that Murat had repulsed Schwarzenberg at Borna (*B2*) on 10 October and was under no great pressure. He therefore concluded that he still had time to force Bernadotte and Blücher back across the Elbe by threatening their communications. Reynier and Dombrowski would advance down its west bank on Rosslau; Macdonald would halt at Wittenberg, ready to support them; Ney would march on Dessau, where Bertrand would join him. Once Reynier

reached Rosslau, Ney would establish communications with him, while Ney's cavalry hunted the enemy trains. Sebastiani would beat the far bank of the Elbe; Marmont would move south of Bitterfeld to observe Halle. These orders given, Napoleon waited at Düben for reports—especially from Reynier and Murat—on the progress of these complex maneuvers. By 1500, he received news (probably from spies) indicating that Bernadotte had recrossed the Elbe, and so planned to mass Marmont and the Guard at Taucha (near Leipzig). Murat was to hold a position five miles south of Leipzig throughout 13 October, if humanly possible. If not, he was to shift eastward, extending his right flank toward Wurzen.

During the 12th, Augereau and Milhaud had reached Leipzig, after shattering, on 10 October, the slightly smaller force of Lichtenstein and Thielmann, who had been sent to intercept them. Another Austrian column, under Gyulai, occupied Weissenfels (*A2*), capturing a French hospital. Ney's leading division (Delmas) reached Dessau, caught Tauenzien withdrawing across the Mulde, and destroyed his rear-guard division. Once across, Tauenzien was joined by the Allied division that had been blockading Wittenberg—with Reynier and Dombrowski on its heels. In a short fight, Reynier sent the whole Prussian force streaming headlong north into Berlin. On learning of Delmas' victory, Napoleon ordered Marmont to join Murat, though still keeping strong reconnaissance parties out toward Halle.

During this period, Murat (ably seconded by Poniatowski and Lauriston) had waged an outstanding delaying action against Schwarzenberg. Schwarzenberg has been much criticized for requiring seventeen days to advance seventy miles. His main concern, however, was to regain contact with Blücher (apparently tenuously achieved on 12 October) without drawing Napoleon down on himself. Bennigsen pushed St.-Cyr's outposts back into Dresden (8 and 9 October) and thereafter marched for Leipzig, leaving Ostermann (20,000) to blockade Dresden. (A message from St.-Cyr, reporting Bennigsen's appearance at Dresden, reached Napoleon on 12 October.)

Napoleon's favorite techniques of maneuvering against his enemies' communications and threatening their capital had failed. This had been largely accidental, due in the main to Blücher's dislike for retreating, and his bland and complete refusal to obey Bernadotte, his technical superior.

During 13 October, Murat held out south of Leipzig without great difficulty, though his outposts were gradually forced back to an east-west line running through Wachau. Napoleon was concentrating steadily on Leipzig, though the rutted, slippery roads exhausted his empty-bellied troops. By evening, at least, he was aware that Bernadotte had not recrossed the Elbe. The situation was tightening, but he was still confident that he had the time and strength necessary to crush Schwarzenberg before Blücher could make his weight felt. Bernadotte, he felt, would merely "prance in place."

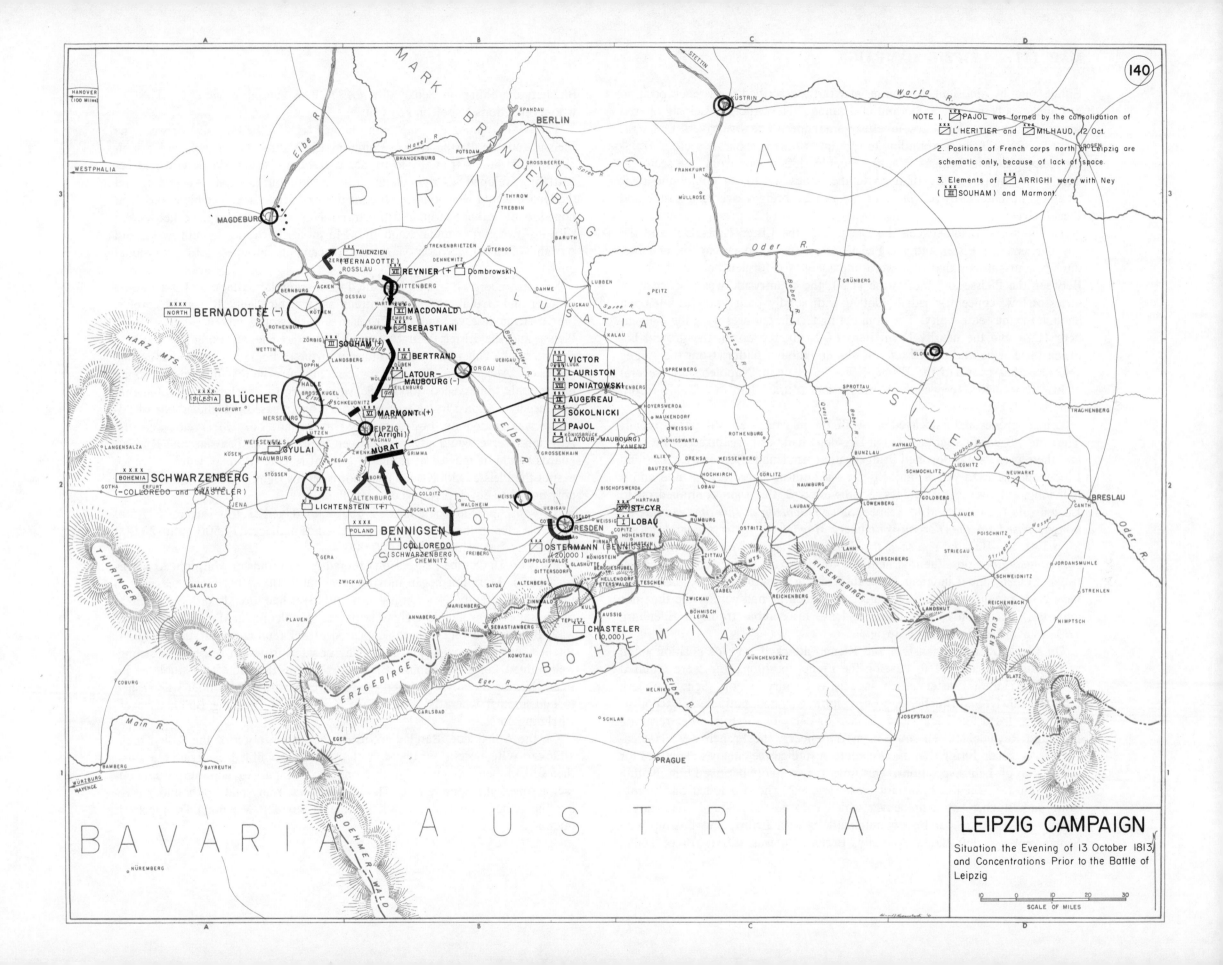

140

NOTE 1. ⊠⊠⊠ PAJOL was formed by the consolidation of ⊠⊠⊠ L'HERITIER and ⊠⊠⊠ MILHAUD, 12 Oct.

2. Positions of French corps north of Leipzig are schematic only, because of lack of space.

3. Elements of ⊠⊠⊠ ARRIGHI were with Ney (⊠⊠⊠ III SOUHAM) and Marmont.

HANOVER (100 Miles)

WESTPHALIA

MARK BRANDENBURG

P R U S S I A

L U S A T I A

S I L E S I A

HARZ MTS.

THURINGER WALD

ERZGEBIRGE

BÖHMER-WALD

B A V A R I A

A U S T R I A

B O H E M I A

RIESENGEBIRGE

EULEN

BERLIN

STETTIN

KÜSTRIN

Warta R.

Oder R.

Elbe R.

Boher R.

Neisse R.

Queiss R.

Main R.

Eger R.

Elbe R.

XXXX NORTH BERNADOTTE (−)

XXXX SILESIA BLÜCHER

XXXX BOHEMIA SCHWARZENBERG (−COLLOREDO and CHASTELER)

XXXX POLAND BENNIGSEN

XXX TAUENZIEN

XXX BERNADOTTE (−)

VII REYNIER (+ ☐ Dombrowski)

XI MACDONALD

☐ SEBASTIANI

III SOUHAM (+)

IV BERTRAND

☐ LATOUR−MAUBOURG (−)

VI MARMONT (+)

MURAT

☐ GYULAI

XX LICHTENSTEIN (+)

☐ COLLOREDO (Schwarzenberg)

XXX OSTERMANN (BENNIGSEN) (20,000)

XVI ST-CYR

I LOBAU

☐ CHASTELER (10,000)

XXX
II VICTOR
V LAURISTON
VIII PONIATOWSKI
IX AUGEREAU
SOKOLNICKI
PAJOL
(LATOUR−MAUBOURG)

LEIPZIG (Arrighi)

LEIPZIG CAMPAIGN

Situation the Evening of 13 October 1813, and Concentrations Prior to the Battle of Leipzig

SCALE OF MILES

Enlightened by hindsight, Marmont later tartly described the French position at Leipzig as being "at the bottom of a funnel." Nevertheless, Leipzig offered several advantages for a resourceful commander. The five rivers that converged there split the surrounding terrain into as many separate sectors. Holding Leipzig and its bridges, Napoleon could shift troops from one sector to another far more rapidly than could the Allies. (And, to compound their troubles, he had destroyed most of the nearby bridges over the Elster and Pleisse rivers.)

Two sectors—that between the Luppe and the Elster (*A3–B3*), and the one between the Elster and the Pleisse (*B2*)—were so cut up by marshes, ditches, and gardens that they were impassable for formed bodies of troops. Between the Pleisse and the Parthe (*C3*), the countryside was marked by a series of low, concentric ridges, dotted with solidly built villages, but open enough for massed cavalry. The dominating terrain features were the Galgenberg (*C2*) and the nearby Kolm Berg (*D2*). In the north, the ground between the Parthe and the Elster was similar, though flatter; from the Luppe (*A3*) southeastward to the Elster, it was level plain. Napoleon and several of his subordinates (especially Marmont and Murat) had thoroughly reconnoitered this entire area.

Leipzig proper had a decayed city wall, but its gates were still in fair repair. The outer edges of its suburbs (as at Dresden) had been organized for defense, and there was a small fortified bridgehead at Lindenau. Between Leipzig and Lindenau, the road was a major defile—a built-up causeway, a mile and a half long, cut by several bridges. Southwestward, this road continued on to Lützen (*A1*), Erfurt, and to France. *Since Napoleon at this time considered himself based on the Torgau-Wittenberg-Magdeburg fortress complex* (see Map 140, A3–B2), *he regarded this Erfurt road only as an alternate line of communication.* Consequently, he did not order extra bridges constructed between Leipzig and Lindenau. (Because of the swampy terrain, this would have been a major engineering project, for which he had neither the time nor material.) Napoleon further chose to leave his combat trains at Eilenburg (*B2*) to avoid encumbering Leipzig.

On 14 October, Wittgenstein and Klenau attacked Murat's position south of Leipzig in an attempt to develop the French positions, but were repulsed by French infantry after much indecisive cavalry action. Schwarzenberg marched slowly, and Blücher and Bernadotte remained motionless. Except for Ney, who closed late because of the loss or delay of the first order recalling him, and Reynier, still en route from Wittenberg, the French were concentrated. As usual, during that night Napoleon studied the enemy's campfires for indications of their dispositions. This time, they roundly deceived him. Noting a large cluster near Markranstädt (*this map, A2*), he concluded that Bernadotte and Blücher "by a maneuver which I do not understand" had moved south from Halle to cut his communications with Erfurt, and link up with Schwarzenberg's left flank. Actually, Bernadotte was still north of Halle;

Blücher, marching on Schkeuditz (*A3*). The campfires were Gyulai's, of whose operations Napoleon knew little.

Though outnumbered, Napoleon planned to take the offensive between the Pleisse and the Parthe rivers. Poniatowski, Victor, Lauriston, and Sokolnicki would attack frontally to fix Schwarzenberg, while Macdonald and Sebastiani enveloped his right flank. Latour-Maubourg, Pajol, Augereau, and the Guard would be held in reserve for the decisive attack, to which Napoleon hoped to add either Marmont or Bertrand. Ney would defend the other sectors with his own corps (under Souham), Marmont, Bertrand, Dombrowski, and Arrighi's Leipzig garrison (largely replacements grouped into provisional units).

Schwarzenberg's original plan called for a secondary attack on Lindenau by Blücher and Gyulai, and a main attack astride the Pleisse River: Meerveldt, the Austrian reserve, and the Prussian Guard would advance between the Pleisse and the Elster; Wittgenstein, Kleist, and Klenau along the Pleisse's eastern bank. This plan had the unusual virtue of being so bad that everyone protested. Alexander, "surprised beyond measure at this unanimity among his generals," intervened, forcing Schwarzenberg to develop a new plan that was largely designed to let everyone do as they pleased. Blücher's axis of advance was shifted northward to the Halle road; only Meerveldt and the Austrian reserve would advance between the rivers; the Prussian and Russian guards would be massed at Rotha in general reserve. Barclay would advance east of the Pleisse, with Klenau's big corps on his right. (Schwarzenberg probably hoped to envelop Napoleon's left flank.)

To sum up, Napoleon massed approximately 121,700 out of 177,500 available men in the decisive sector; the Allies managed 77,500 (plus 24,000 in reserve) out of more than 200,000.

Early on 16 October, Napoleon ordered Ney to transfer Marmont to Thonberg (*C2*). Marmont began moving at about 1000. What happened next is unclear. Apparently, Ney, on his own initiative, had already ordered Souham to continue on through Leipzig to reinforce Napoleon. As Marmont got under way, Blücher's advance guards appeared at Schkeuditz and Radefeld (*B3*). Pitched into a thorough quandary, Ney decided to retain Marmont's strong, well-trained corps to oppose Blücher, sending Bertrand to Napoleon instead. Having already evacuated his prepared position, Marmont was rushed to find another where he would have a chance of checking Blücher's overwhelming force.

On the Allied side, Barclay entrusted the organization of the Allied main attack to Wittgenstein. Wittgenstein thoroughly scrambled the available units, then spread them out on a six-mile front, too far apart to maintain visual contact across that rolling terrain. The morning was rainy and fog-bound, delaying the Allied attack until 0800, but also slowing Macdonald's approach march.

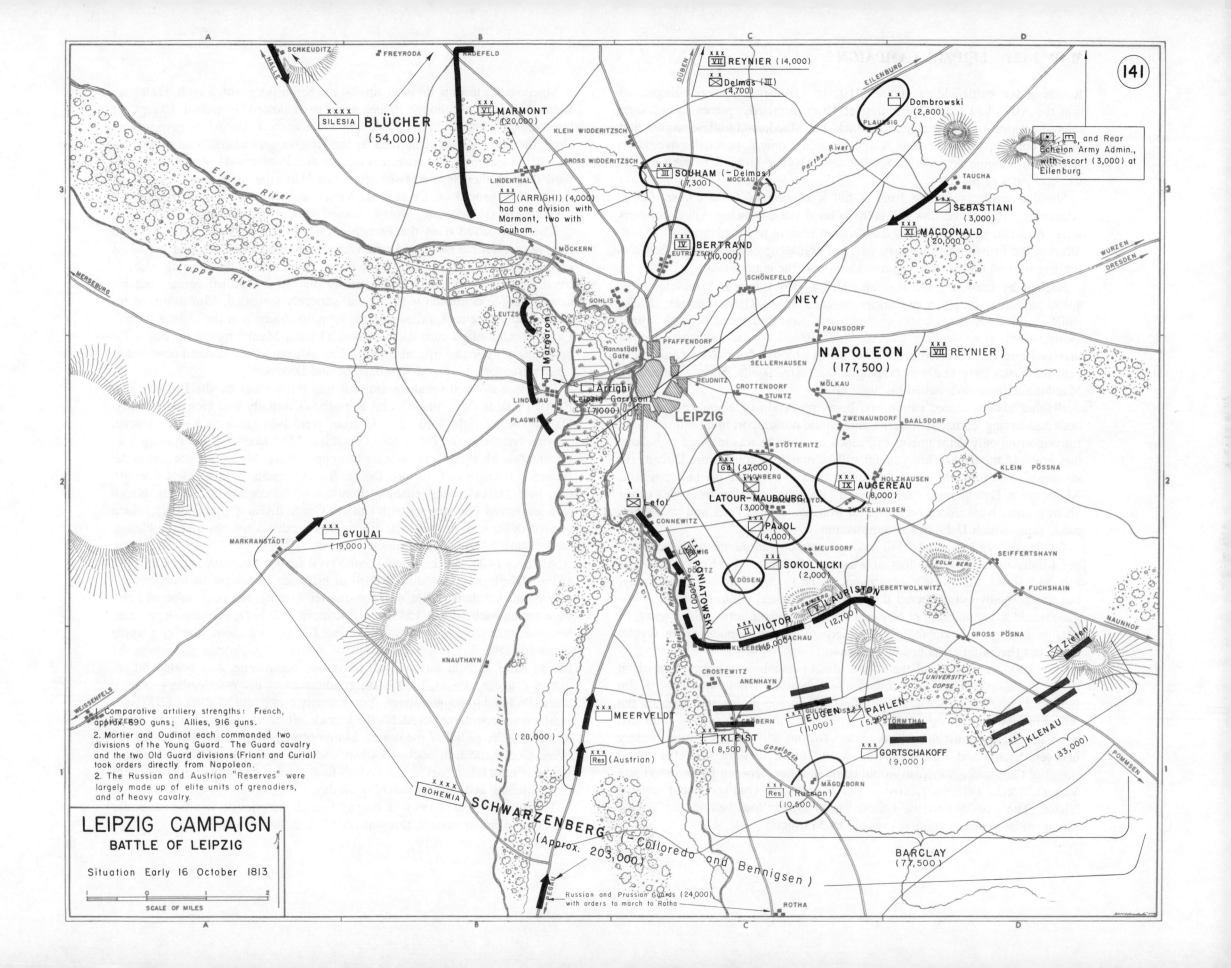

141

XXX VII REYNIER (14,000)

XX Delmas (III) (4,700)

XX Dombrowski (2,800)

XXXX SILESIA BLÜCHER (54,000)

VI MARMONT (20,000)

XXX III SOUHAM (−Delmas) (7,300)

XXX (ARRIGHI) (4,000) had one division with Marmont, two with Souham.

XXX IV BERTRAND (10,000) EUTRITZSCH

TAUCHA

XXX SEBASTIANI (3,000)

XXX XI MACDONALD (20,000)

XX ☀ ⅲ and Rear Echelon Army Admin., with escort (3,000) at Eilenburg.

NEY

NAPOLEON (− VII REYNIER) (177,500)

Margaron

Arrighi (Leipzig Garrison) (7,000)

LEIPZIG

XXX Gd (47,000) LATOUR-MAUBOURG (3,000)

XXX IX AUGEREAU (8,000)

XX Lefol

XXX GYULAI (19,000)

XX PAJOL (4,000)

XXX SOKOLNICKI (2,000)

XXX VIII PONIATOWSKI (7,000)

XXX II VICTOR (15,000)

XXX V LAURISTON (12,700)

X ZIETEN

XXX MEERVELDT (28,000)

XXX EUGEN (1,000)

XXX PAHLEN (6,500)

XXX KLEIST (8,500)

XXX GORTSCHAKOFF (9,000)

XXX KLENAU (33,000)

1. Comparative artillery strengths: French, approx. 690 guns; Allies, 916 guns.

2. Mortier and Oudinot each commanded two divisions of the Young Guard. The Guard cavalry and the two Old Guard divisions (Friant and Curial) took orders directly from Napoleon.

2. The Russian and Austrian "Reserves" were largely made up of elite units of grenadiers, and of heavy cavalry.

XXX Res (Austrian)

XXX Res (Russian) (10,500)

XXXX BOHEMIA SCHWARZENBERG (−Colloredo and Bennigsen) (Approx. 203,000)

BARCLAY (77,500)

LEIPZIG CAMPAIGN
BATTLE OF LEIPZIG

Situation Early 16 October 1813

SCALE OF MILES

Russian and Prussian Guards (24,000) with orders to march to Rotha

Reaching the battlefield at about 0910, 16 October, Napoleon discovered that the Allies had seized the initiative. Their disorderly, piecemeal advance offered an ideal target for a counterattack, but Macdonald and Sebastiani had not yet come up. Without them, Napoleon could only fight a defensive-offensive battle, moving Augereau, Oudinot, and Mortier forward to back up the weakest parts of his line.

Simultaneously, watching from a hill southwest of Güldengossa (C1), Alexander's staff noted how mutually isolated the advancing Allied columns were. Accordingly, they shifted the Russian reserve to Mägdeborn (C1), redirected the Prussian and Russian guards to Güldengossa, and urged Schwarzenberg to send the Austrian reserve to support the main attack.

Backed by massed guns, that attack straggled forward. Meerveldt took 4,000 casualties to get a precarious toehold in the Dölitz chateau. Kleist stalled in Markkleeberg; Eugen captured, and lost, Wachau. Lauriston caught Gortschakoff in an artillery trap, driving him off to the southeast. Klenau marched late; at 1100—with the other attacks bloody failures—he had occupied the Kolm Berg and was tapping at Liebertwolkwitz. Shortly thereafter, Macdonald's approach halted his timid attack.

Blücher also advanced cautiously, being uncertain of Napoleon's dispositions and having learned that Bernadotte would not support him until the 17th. Encountering only detachments of French cavalry, he was inspired to believe that much of the French army might still be marching south from Düben. He sat down to wait for it, giving Marmont time to organize his new position. About noon, Dombrowski came forward (whether on orders from Ney or on his own initiative is uncertain) to cover Marmont's right flank and the Düben road, along which Delmas was approaching.

Gyulai attacked at about 1030, taking Leutzsch and momentarily penetrating Lindenau itself, but failing at Plagwitz. Supported by French batteries around Leipzig, Margaron's detachment of the Leipzig garrison fought hotly, but was so badly outnumbered that Arrighi requested reinforcements. A brigade would have sufficed, but Ney sent Bertrand's whole corps, which was then passing through Leipzig to join Napoleon. Bertrand happily drove Gyulai back, but thereafter remained at Lindenau.

By 1120, seeing that all the Allied attacks had been repulsed, Napoleon began his counterattack. Macdonald and Sebastiani would storm the Kolm Berg and drive on to Seiffertshayn. This enveloping attack should draw the Allied reserves, which would thus be out of position when Napoleon launched his main effort against the Allied center. Drouot had massed a huge battery between Victor and Lauriston, and would move forward with the initial stages of the attack. Augereau would come into line between Poniatowski and Victor; Mortier between Lauriston and Macdonald. Oudinot would support Victor. The cavalry and the Guard would move close behind the French center, to be joined as soon as possible by Marmont.

Macdonald's leading division carried the Kolm Berg with a rush, scattering Klenau's right flank, though Pahlen and Zieten slowed Sebastiani. Except for bypassed detachments in Markkleeberg and elsewhere, the Allies gave way all along the front. Kleist, reinforced by the Russian grenadiers, tried a counterattack, but was cracked between Augereau and Poniatowski. As the Allies retired through their former assembly areas, Napoleon increased his pressure. Augereau advanced on Crostewitz; Victor and Oudinot against Anenhayn; Lauriston on Güldengossa; Mortier toward the University Copse.

Kleist was saved from the French cavalry by the arrival of the Austrian reserve cavalry, but renewed French assaults hustled Prussians and Austrians together into Cröbern (C1). In the center, there was a bewildering whirl of cavalry action. Latour-Maubourg nearly pierced the Allied center, but his attack fell into confusion when he was seriously wounded. Murat, out of his senses with excitement, failed to have supports ready, and the chance passed. Later, Bordesoulle's cuirassier division (Latour-Maubourg) rode down the remnants of Eugen's corps, almost reaching Alexander's command post, but—again unsupported—was driven back behind Drouot.

Lauriston stormed Güldengossa, but was thrown out by the Prussian and Russian guards. Macdonald's and Sebastiani's timidity had clogged Mortier. On Napoleon's right flank, the Austrian grenadiers came to Kleist's rescue, shoving Augereau and Poniatowski back into Markkleeberg, and forcing Victor to refuse his right flank. Seizing this opportunity, Meerveldt got across the Pleisse in strength and stormed Dölitz. But Augereau, fighting as at Castiglione, held Markkleeberg, enabling Poniatowski to contain Meerveldt. Napoleon reinforced Poniatowski with Curial's Guard division (*not shown*), which cleared Dölitz with the bayonet, driving Meerveldt's Austrians into the Pleisse, and capturing Meerveldt himself.

At about 1400, Blücher finally sent Yorck against Marmont, and Langeron against Dombrowski, holding a third of his army in reserve to meet any attack on his left flank. After wild, no-quarter fighting, the outnumbered Poles were forced back (about 1545) on Eutritzsch (C3). Delmas then appeared. Because of the large train he was escorting, Langeron mistook him for a whole corps and retired. Using his flank guard aggressively, Delmas got across the Parthe River without serious loss. Marmont, meanwhile, had beaten off repeated Prussian attacks, though the commander of his Württemberg cavalry brigade refused to counterattack. Yorck finally broke into Möckern (B3) and, as Marmont counterattacked, hit the French left flank with a desperate, head-on cavalry charge out of the sunset. Marmont was swept back, but rallied between Gohlis and Eutritzsch. (Souham's actions remain a mystery. One division may have taken part in Meerveldt's final repulse, but apparently Ney kept him marching and countermarching all day.)

The long day had ended with limited French victories on two fronts; under the existing circumstances, this was little better than defeat.

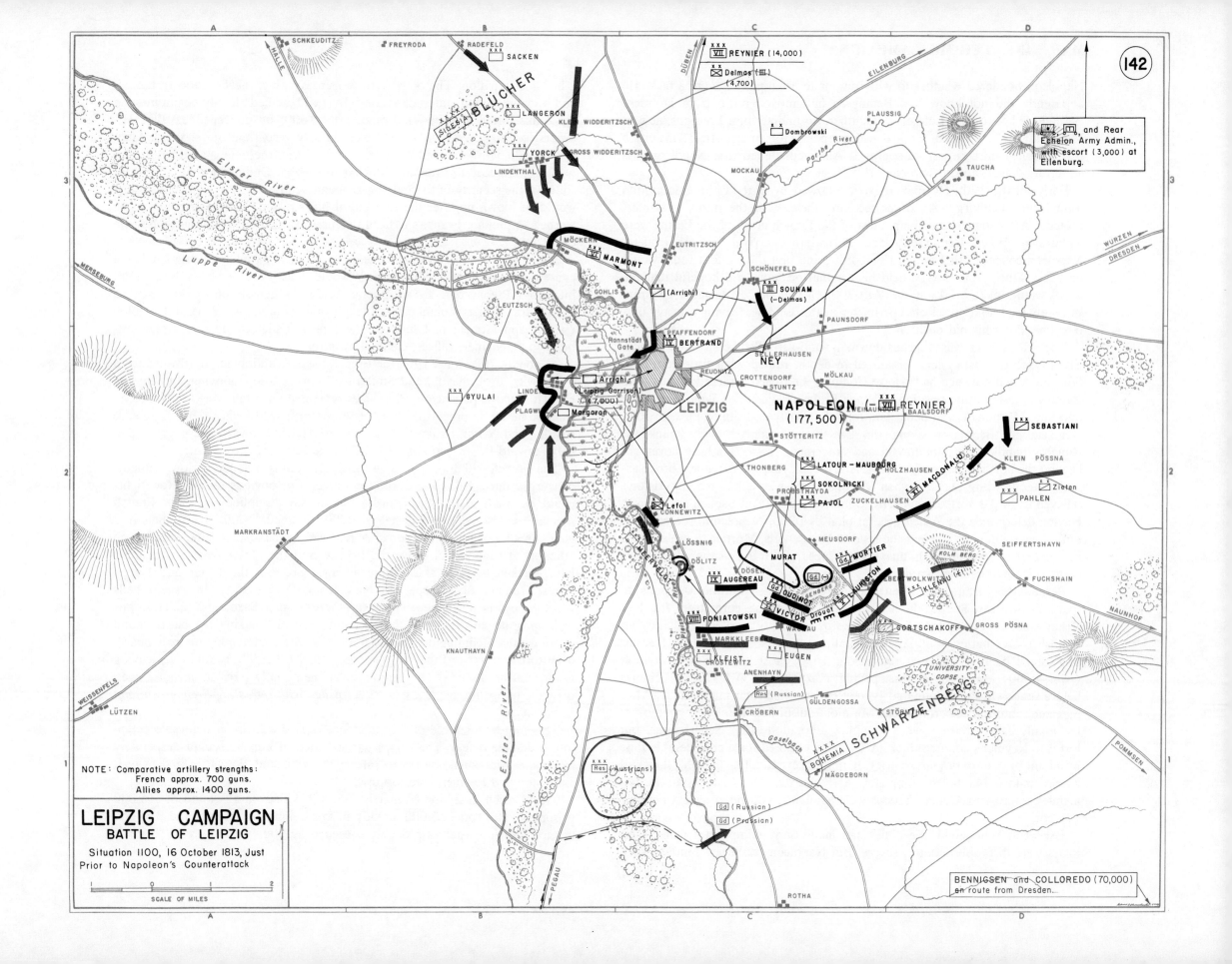

142

XXX REYNIER (14,000)
⊠ Delmas (III) (4,700)

⊠⊠, ⊞, and Rear Echelon Army Admin., with escort (3,000) at Eilenburg.

SCHKEUDITZ
FREYRODA
RADEFELD
XXXX SACKEN
BLÜCHER
Silesia
XXXX LANGERON
KLEIN WIDDERITZSCH
XXXX YORCK
GROSS WIDDERITZSCH
LINDENTHAL

PLAUSSIG
TAUCHA

Elster River
Luppe River
MERSEBURG
HALLE

MÖCKERN
MARMONT
EUTRITZSCH
GOHLIS
(Arrighi)
SOUHAM (−Delmas)
SCHÖNEFELD
PAUNSDORF
LEUTZSCH
Pfaffendorf
Rannstädt Gate
BERTRAND
SELLERHAUSEN
NEY
REUDNITZ
CROTTENDORF
STUNTZ
MÖLKAU

Dombrowski
MOCKAU
Partha River
EILENBURG
WURZEN
DRESDEN

GYULAI
LINDE
Arrighi (Leipzig Garrison) (17,000)
Margaron
PLAGW

LEIPZIG
NAPOLEON (− XXXX REYNIER) (177,500)
STÖTTERITZ
BAALSDORF
SEBASTIANI
KLEIN PÖSSNA
Zieten
MACDONALD
PAHLEN

MARKRANSTÄDT

Lefol CONNEWITZ
THONBERG
PROBSTHAYDA
LATOUR-MAUBOURG
SOKOLNICKI
PAJOL
HOLZHAUSEN
ZUCKELHAUSEN
MEUSDORF
SEIFFERTSHAYN
KOLM BERG
FUCHSHAIN

LÖSSNIG
DÖLITZ
MEERVELDT
MURAT
Gd MORTIER
Gd (−)
AUERSTON
WOLKWITZ
KLENAU (+)
UNIVERSITY COPSE
NAUNHOF

KNAUTHAYN
DÖSEN
AUGEREAU
Gd OUDINOT
VICTOR Drouot
GORTSCHAKOFF
GROSS PÖSNA

PONIATOWSKI
MARKKLEEBERG
WACHAU
KLEIST
CRÖSTEWITZ
EUGEN
ANENHAYN
Res (Russian)
GÜLDENGOSSA
CRÖBERN
STÖRMTHAL
SCHWARZENBERG
BOHEMIA

WEISSENFELS
LÜTZEN

Res (Austrians)
MÄGDEBORN
ROTHA
PEGAU
Gd (Russian)
Gd (Prussian)
POMMSEN

NOTE: Comparative artillery strengths:
French approx. 700 guns.
Allies approx. 1400 guns.

Goselbach

BENNIGSEN and COLLOREDO (70,000) en route from Dresden.

LEIPZIG CAMPAIGN
BATTLE OF LEIPZIG
Situation 1100, 16 October 1813, Just
Prior to Napoleon's Counterattack

1   0   1   2
SCALE OF MILES

Napoleon pondered whether to withdraw or to attempt one more attack. He apparently did not know that Bennigsen had moved north from Dresden. Bernadotte he scorned. Late on 16 October, for undetermined reasons, he sent Meerveldt to the Emperor Francis with proposals for an armistice. This was a psychological mistake; the discouraged Allies concluded that Napoleon was admitting defeat, and so hardened their hearts.

Early on the 17th, Reynier arrived, followed by part of the ammunition train from Eilenburg. (An order recalling the rest of the trains was intercepted.) After some skirmishing, most of the French north of the Parthe were withdrawn. When Bennigsen's and Bernadotte's arrival became evident, Napoleon conceded that he must withdraw, and that the western route would be safest. During the day he held his original position, still hopeful that the Allies would make a false move. At 0200, 18 October, he brought his army smoothly back to a preselected perimeter nearer Leipzig, leaving a heavy outpost line along his old position.

The Allied plan was a heads-down, go-and-get-killed, concentric attack. The French outpost system, organized in depth, ruined what little coordination the Allied advance had. Hesse-Homburg had been repulsed by the time Barclay at last got into position to attack Probsthayda. When Bennigsen came into line, Macdonald and Sebastiani retired expertly and linked up with Reynier, stalling Bennigsen along the line Zweinaundorf-Mölkau-Paunsdorf. Roughly handled by Poniatowski and Augereau, Hesse-Homburg never got beyond the northern edge of Lössnig. At Probsthayda, the defenders broke assault after howling assault; when Victor's corps was exhausted, Lauriston's relieved it. In the northern suburbs, Dombrowski beat off Sacken and Yorck. Having determined the Allied general plan by 0900, Napoleon ordered Bertrand, now reinforced, to clear the road to Weissenfels, Mortier to replace him in Lindenau. Striking with unexpected speed, Bertrand scattered Gyulai's corps and continued westward.

Bernadotte, meanwhile, leisurely maneuvered into position. Anxious to spare his own raw Swedes, he had wrangled Langeron's corps from Blücher. His advance on Paunsdorf was supported by masses of artillery, including an English rocket battery—initially demoralizing, but most inaccurate. Reynier was forced back on Sellerhausen; about 1630, most of his Saxon division (over 4,000) joined the Allies, opening a sizable gap in his front. Minutes before sundown, Bernadotte and Bennigsen launched their main attack. After repeated failures, Langeron forced Marmont out of Schönefeld. Ney retook it, but finally had to retire toward Reudnitz. Bernadotte took Sellerhausen, but lost it to Reynier's counterattack. After being checked for a considerable time by a feint by Nansouty (not shown), Bennigsen eventually gained Mölkau and Zweinaundorf, but failed completely at Stötteritz. The Czar's staff recommended reinforcing Gyulai. Troops were available, but the necessary courage was not.

Except at Schönefeld, the Allies had made only unimportant gains; their losses were disproportionately severe. But Napoleon could not continue such a battle of attrition. The odds were too unfavorable, the field too restricted, and his ammunition almost exhausted. By 1100, he had already begun moving his trains into Lindenau—followed, after 1600, by unneeded cavalry. His orders for the general withdrawal were largely verbal and unrecorded. Macdonald, Poniatowski, and Reynier would form the rear guard. Bertrand would push ahead to Freiburg, Mortier to Lützen. Oudinot would be responsible for the security of the Leipzig-Lindenau causeway; the Lindenau bridge would be blown up after the rear guard had crossed. Kellermann was to be warned to prepare France's eastern defenses, St.-Cyr to withdraw as best he could.

There was neither time nor means to build a parallel Leipzig-Lindenau causeway. Last-minute construction would only have revealed Napoleon's intentions. Preparation of the Lindenau bridge for demolition was entrusted to the Guard artillery commander, the grasping, unreliable General Dulauloy (whose appointment had shocked the army). Dulauloy delegated responsibility to an engineer officer, Colonel Montfort.

At about 0200 on the 19th, the French began withdrawing northward from Connewitz, Probsthayda, and Stötteritz. Hearing troops moving, but finding French outposts pugnacious, the Allies remained uncertain whether Napoleon was retreating or preparing an unpleasant surprise. Blücher sent his reserve cavalry and Yorck's ruined corps toward Halle. Schwarzenberg ordered a corps toward Pegau (off map, B1), then canceled the movement.

The French withdrawal grew increasingly confused as the various columns converged through Leipzig's crooked streets. For obvious reasons, few lights could be used, and traffic control and march discipline were not French specialties. The Allies advanced at 0700; at about 1000, the French rear guards withdrew into the suburbs. A renewed Allied assault, after vain Saxon attempts at negotiation, drove the French into the old city some two hours later. Sacken began a skirmishing advance between the Elster and Luppe rivers. Oudinot easily kept him back from the causeway, but spent balls whistling overhead frightened Montfort. Worse, some Saxon and Baden troops in Leipzig began firing into the retreating French, making the battle sound much nearer. Claiming that he did not know who commanded the rear guard, Montfort went off to Lindenau (not Leipzig), ostensibly to find out, leaving a corporal in charge of the demolitions. The equally terrified corporal soon blew the bridge up, *while it was still crowded with retreating Frenchmen, and in no danger.*

This murderous piece of incompetence turned a brilliant defensive action into a definite defeat. The troops left stranded in Leipzig fought desperately to escape. Macdonald swam to safety; the wounded Poniatowski drowned; Lauriston and Reynier were captured.

The French lost approximately 38,000 killed and wounded, 15,000 prisoners (plus some 15,000 already in the Leipzig hospitals), and 300-odd cannon. Allied casualties probably exceeded 52,000.

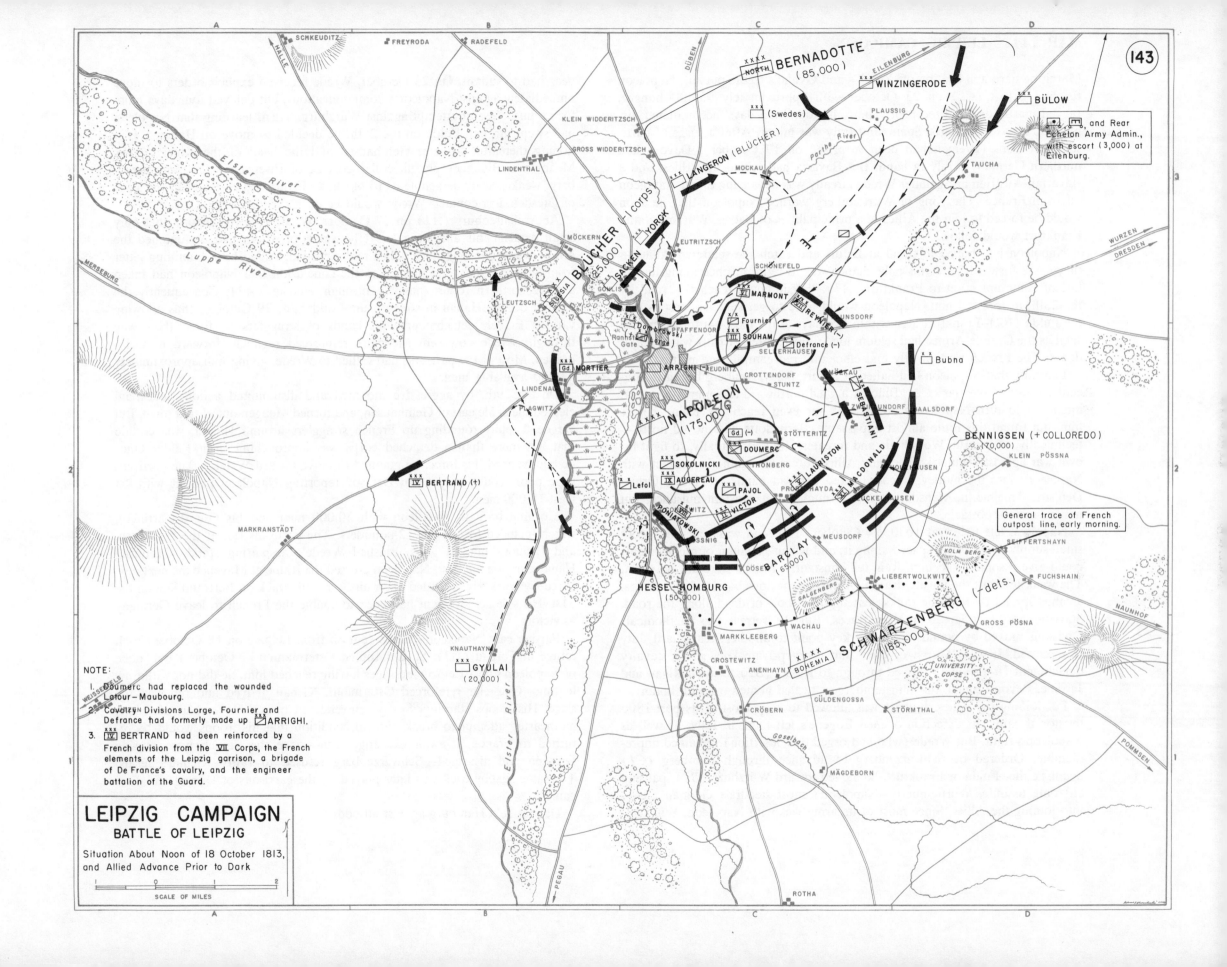

143

BERNADOTTE
(85,000)

NORTH

WINZINGERODE

(Swedes)

BÜLOW

•, 🏠, and Rear
Echelon Army Admin.,
with escort (3,000) at
Eilenburg.

LANGERON (BLÜCHER)

BLÜCHER
(85,000)

YORCK

SILESIA
SACKEN

MARMONT

REYNIER (–)

Fournier

SOUHAM

Defrance (–)

Bubna

MORTIER

ARRIGHI (–)

NAPOLEON
(175,000)

SEBASTIANI

BENNIGSEN (+ COLLOREDO)
(70,000)

DOUMERC

LAURISTON

MACDONALD

SOKOLNICKI

AUGEREAU

General trace of French
outpost line, early morning.

Lefol

PAJOL

VICTOR

PONIATOWSKI

BARCLAY
(65,000)

BERTRAND (†)

HESSE–HOMBURG
(50,000)

SCHWARZENBERG
(85,000)

GYULAI
(20,000)

BOHEMIA

NOTE:
1. Doumerc had replaced the wounded
   Latour–Maubourg.
2. Cavalry Divisions Lorge, Fournier and
   Defrance had formerly made up ⊠ ARRIGHI.
3. ⊠ BERTRAND had been reinforced by a
   French division from the VII Corps, the French
   elements of the Leipzig garrison, a brigade
   of De France's cavalry, and the engineer
   battalion of the Guard.

LEIPZIG CAMPAIGN
BATTLE OF LEIPZIG

Situation About Noon of 18 October 1813,
and Allied Advance Prior to Dark

SCALE OF MILES

Marching hard and beating off Yorck's and Gyulai's feeble pursuit, Napoleon reached Erfurt (*C2*) on 23 October with approximately 95,000 hungry, ragged, partly demoralized men. There, he found ten days' accumulated dispatches. News from Paris, Spain, and Italy was minor. After a surge of partisan operations (Bremen had been surprised on 17 October), Davout had northern Germany firmly in hand. But Bavaria had joined the Allies, and a Bavarian-Austrian army under Wrede already was advancing to cut Napoleon off from France. The King of Württemberg warned Napoleon that he soon would be forced to join the Allies; the principalities of Baden, Würzburg, and Frankfurt would follow.

Napoleon had hoped to stand at Erfurt and catch the scattered Allies as they came forward. Now, his only chance was to retire at once along his old line of communication to Frankfurt (*A1*). Wrede could reach this road by the 28th; to forestall him, Napoleon would have to get sufficient troops into the Fulda (*B2*)–Frankfurt area within five days at the most—a forced march such as the Grande Armée had seldom made. Fortunately, Erfurt was a major depot. The French were swiftly and efficiently reorganized and refitted.

Learning that Napoleon had halted at Erfurt, Schwarzenberg began to concentrate east of Weimar (*C2*). Blücher angled northward to Sömmerda (*C2*), intending to turn Napoleon's north flank, or even reach the Rhine before him, but found this route almost impassable. Bernadotte had moved north—technically, to overrun Westphalia and threaten Holland; actually, to fight his own war against Denmark. The only Allied forces remaining in contact with Napoleon were the motley, uncoordinated partisan bands of Platov, Orlov-Denisov, Thielmann, Mensdorf, and Czernitchew—a constant nuisance, but never a serious obstacle.

Napoleon left Erfurt at 1030, 24 October. The road was generally good; small supply depots were spaced along it; and Rigau's column of replacements could give it some protection. Rain fell constantly; rations were always short. The weak fell out; the unruly drifted off into pugnacious bands of marauders. Typhus spread through the ranks, leaving its dribble of dead along the road. Starving horses collapsed in their traces. But the retreat was methodical: Divisions moved by bounds from one key point to another; rear-guard duty was rotated. It was "March or die!" and every private knew it. A cavalry detachment (*not shown*) slipped through to Kassel (*B2*) to warn Rigau and Jerome. Beyond Fulda, the Württembergers turned homeward with honor.

For joining the Allies, Bavaria was allowed to keep most of its post-1805 territorial gains. Its defection opened Eugene's left flank in Italy, as well as Napoleon's right. But Wrede (who had urged this desertion) remained unpredictable. Ordered by Schwarzenberg to advance through Bamberg (*C1*) against either Fulda or Frankfurt, he moved toward Würzburg (*B1*), pausing en route to bully Württemberg—Napoleon's most steadfast German ally— into joining the Allies. Since most of its army was with Napoleon, Württem-

berg had to submit. On 23 October, Wrede received explicit orders to move immediately against Napoleon's communications, but delayed four days more for an unsuccessful attempt against Würzburg. Then, learning that Napoleon had swept through Fulda on the 25th, he decided to move on Hanau (*A1*), hoping thereafter to seize Gelnhausen and the head of the Kinzig defile. Meanwhile, Blücher's pursuit collapsed east of Eisenach (*B2*). Schwarzenberg, weakened by detachments to blockade Erfurt and re-establish the siege of Dresden, lost contact. Wrede would be on his own.

At Aschaffenburg (*A1*) on 27 October, Wrede received reports that only small detachments and stragglers (thousands of whom had outmarched the army) were following the Fulda-Frankfurt road. Aided by a bumbling letter from Schwarzenberg, he jumped to the conclusion that Napoleon had taken a more northern route—possibly through Wetzlar (*A2*). Consequently, he did not occupy Hanau in strength until midnight, 29 October, thus allowing various French detachments and bands of stragglers to force their way through. Wrede now sent Mengen's reinforced regiment forward to Gelnhausen. Most of the partisans had rallied to Wrede, giving him approximately 43,500 available men.

On the 29th, by aggressive mounted and dismounted action, Sebastiani cleared the defile east of Gelnhausen, and turned Mengen out of that town. But Wrede, happily rounding up French stragglers around Hanau, was certain that not more than a detached corps was approaching from Fulda. Once he had trapped this force, he planned to move toward Wetzlar. The partisans were poor scouts, only Orlov-Denisov reporting Napoleon present with "at least 18,000 men."

Morning brought Napoleon with 30,000 men and his Guard's artillery, which included forty-eight 12-pounders. The partisans ran at the first clash, and Drouot's massed guns smashed Wrede's despairing stand. Capturing Hanau early on the 31st, Napoleon crossed the Rhine at Mayence the next day. Wrede was gravely wounded in an unsuccessful attack on Bertrand late on the 31st. His sole achievement had been to enable the French to leave Germany as victors.

Farther east, Napoleon's trains (cut off from Leipzig on 18 October) took refuge in Torgau (*D3*). St.-Cyr routed Ostermann (17 October) but, none of Napoleon's post-Leipzig messages having reached him, he did not withdraw in time. Chasteler reinforced Ostermann; Klenau arrived and renewed the siege. His troops starving, St.-Cyr surrendered on 11 November, after one halfhearted attempt to break out, on condition that his troops would be returned to France to await exchange. But—once the French were outside Dresden and disarmed—Schwarzenberg refused to ratify Klenau's terms. The same shabby trick was later played on the garrisons of Danzig and Torgau.

Davout held Hamburg against all odds.

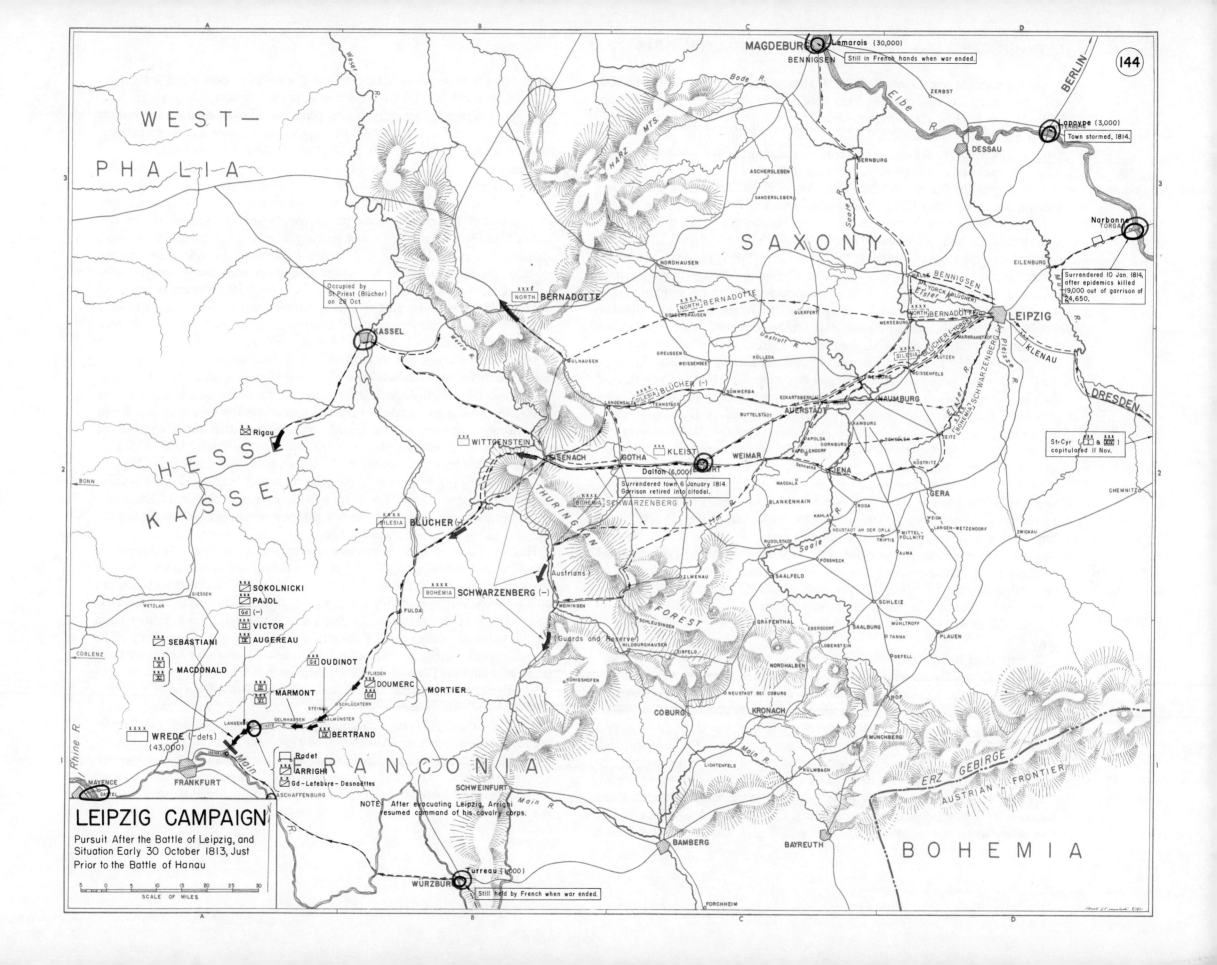

144

WEST-PHALIA

MAGDEBURG
Lemarois (30,000)
BENNIGSEN
Still in French hands when war ended.

BERLIN

Lapoype (3,000)
Town stormed, 1814.

SAXONY

Narbonne
TORGAU
Surrendered 10 Jan. 1814, after epidemics killed 19,000 out of garrison of 24,650.

XXXX NORTH BERNADOTTE

BENNIGSEN
HALLE
XX YORCK (BLÜCHER)

XXXX NORTH BERNADOTTE

LEIPZIG
KLENAU

DRESDEN

XXXX SILESIA BLÜCHER (YORCK)

XXXX BOHEMIA SCHWARZENBERG

St-Cyr (I & XIV)
capitulated 11 Nov.

KASSEL
Occupied by St-Priest (Blücher) on 28 Oct.

NAUMBURG
AUERSTÄDT

XXXX SILESIA BLÜCHER (-)

Rigau

WITTGENSTEIN

EISENACH GOTHA KLEIST WEIMAR

JENA

GERA

Dalton (6,000)
Surrendered town 6 January 1814. Garrison retired into citadel.

XXXX BOHEMIA SCHWARZENBERG (-)

BLÜCHER (-)
XXXX SILESIA

THURINGIAN

SOKOLNICKI
PAJOL
Gd (-)
VICTOR
AUGEREAU

SEBASTIANI

XXXX BOHEMIA SCHWARZENBERG (-)

Austrians

FOREST

OUDINOT
Gd

MACDONALD
V
XI

DOUMERC
Gd
MORTIER

(Guards and Reserve)

MARMONT
III
VI

BERTRAND
IV

WREDE (-dets)
(43,000)

Rodet
ARRIGHI
Gd-Lefebvre-Desnoëttes

FRANCONIA

MAYENCE

FRANKFURT

ASCHAFFENBURG

SCHWEINFURT

NOTE: After evacuating Leipzig, Arrighi resumed command of his cavalry corps.

BOHEMIA

ERZ GEBIRGE
AUSTRIAN FRONTIER

BAMBERG   BAYREUTH

LEIPZIG CAMPAIGN
Pursuit After the Battle of Leipzig, and Situation Early 30 October 1813, Just Prior to the Battle of Hanau

SCALE OF MILES

WÜRZBURG
Turreau (1,000)
Still held by French when war ended.

INTRODUCTION TO THE CAMPAIGN IN FRANCE, 1814

Napoleon brought approximately 80,000 effective soldiers, plus some 40,000 stragglers, back to France. He had left behind, in various Polish and German fortresses, more than 100,000 men (including a high percentage of invalids, recent conscripts, and dubious foreign units). The immediate problem was typhus, which now broke out in full epidemic among the famished, exhausted men, and required considerable time to control.

Fortunately for Napoleon, the Allies too were at the end of their rope. Despite protests from Blücher, Alexander, and the English, Schwarzenberg ordered a halt. A quick invasion of France might bring an equally quick victory, but he had only some 150,000 available men—ragged, worn out, wracked by typhus and dysentery. His trains were far to the rear, the roads ruined, canals frozen. Moreover, victory was bringing Allied national rivalries to a head, and these conflicting interests warped and stalled his planning. Still, by early December, after much livid argument, the Allies were ready. Blücher would attack directly west across the Rhine to fix Napoleon, while Schwarzenberg advanced through Switzerland to seize Langres, which the Austrian staff considered the key to eastern France. Bernadotte, leaving sufficient forces to contain Davout, would advance on Antwerp, raise the Dutch in revolt, and then turn south into France. A strong British expeditionary force would support him. These offensives would begin before the end of December, while the French were still weak. Napoleon's former German allies (Bavaria excepted) were stripped methodically of men, money, and supplies—far beyond any contribution Napoleon ever had required of them.

Metternich had already launched his own diplomatic psychological offensive to discredit Napoleon as much as possible in the eyes of the French people. As a diversionary, secondary attack, he blandly responded to the proposals that Napoleon had forwarded through Meerveldt during the battle of Leipzig. His language was intentionally vague: France must be content with her "natural frontiers"; Italy, Germany, and Holland must be "free"; Bourbon rule must be restored in Spain; the Allies did not wish to overthrow Napoleon, but felt, nevertheless, that he was the main obstacle to peace. (Not hinted was a long list of additional Allied objectives, which added up to unconditional surrender.)

Shortly thereafter, Metternich's main attack, embodied in an Allied manifesto, spread rapidly across France. It proclaimed that the Allies were animated only by the highest regard for France and her Emperor, and anxious only for an honorable peace; Napoleon, however—blinded by egotism, ambition, and folly—had refused their proffered friendship; therefore, for Europe's good, the Allies regretfully had accepted the war he forced upon them, but would wage it against Napoleon alone, and not against the French people.

During the harrying of Blücher's trains north of Leipzig (10–12 October), Napoleon had captured enough Allied diplomatic correspondence to know his enemies' actual intentions. Only a military victory could save him, but he was ready to haggle diplomatically if it would gain time or soothe French public opinion. The Allies having indicated a desire to deal through Caulaincourt, Napoleon made him his foreign minister, but deliberately gave him little freedom of action. Jerky negotiations followed. French diplomatic couriers were "accidentally" delayed by Allied outposts; Metternich had many excuses, but few definite proposals. His psychological campaign went on.

France was physically, financially, and emotionally drained by twenty-five years of almost constant war. Most common Frenchmen were still loyal, but subversive groups—Royalists, "liberals," Jacobins—were growing in strength and influence. Many influential personages, who had gained power and wealth from Napoleon, were ready to deny him to keep them. The military situation was poor. Berthier was very sick; Clarke, the war minister, had muddled his duties thoroughly enough to suggest something more than incompetence. Napoleon called up, or alerted, some 936,000 men in late 1813 and early 1814, but—because of a desperate shortage of horses and weapons, and an even more desperate one of competent regimental officers and noncommissioned officers—barely an eighth of these ever saw active service. To stiffen these new conscripts, Napoleon drew gendarmes, customs officers, and forest guards (mostly veterans) into their ranks, and recalled 15,000 veterans from Soult. Suchet furnished 10,000 more to form the backbone of a new "Army of the Rhone," under Augereau. Exploiting the excellent cadres and administrative services of his Guard, Napoleon drafted large numbers of conscripts into it, making it practically an army in itself. Diplomatically, Napoleon attempted to clear his flanks by returning the semicaptive Pope to Rome, and offering to restore the Spanish throne to Ferdinand, on condition that Spain become neutral. The latter agreement was signed on 11 December 1813, but thereafter hung fire, the Spanish provisional government being unenthusiastic about getting Ferdinand back.

Hostilities still flickered. Bernadotte gradually sent Bülow and Winzingerode into Holland, which was already in widespread, low-order revolt. In late August, an Austrian invasion and popular revolt had forced the French out of Illyria. Nevertheless, with an army of raw Italians, Eugene generally had retained the initiative until Bavaria's defection forced him to retire behind the Piave River. (He rebuffed Allied hints that he might rule Italy if he turned against Napoleon.) Murat, who had left Napoleon at Erfurt with the promise to support Eugene, finally appeared at Bologna late in December, but did nothing, having achieved an understanding with Metternich.

Meanwhile, Allied agents were busy in Switzerland. Switzerland had only some 35,000 troops; Napoleon could promise no support; the old "aristocratic" cantons were pro-Austrian. Swiss protestations of neutrality were smothered by the assertion that *this* was a war of humanity against the universal oppressor. After twisted political jockeyings, a sudden Austrian ultimatum on 19 December forced the Swiss to permit Allied passage through the Basel area.

The Campaign in France

"Against greatly superior forces it is possible to win a battle, but hardly a war." —NAPOLEON

"A people who have been brought up on victories often do not know how to accept defeat." —NAPOLEON

Burdened with political, financial, and military problems, Napoleon had hoped that the Allies would go into winter quarters long enough for him to rebuild France's defenses. His military planning was circumscribed by the overriding need to defend Paris—his capital, major arsenal, and principal communication and mobilization center. It was imperative to hold as much of France as he could, in order to draw conscripts from as wide an area as possible. He would therefore maneuver to cover Paris, seeking to catch and destroy the Allies in detail. It was reasonably certain that Blücher and Schwarzenberg would not pull smoothly together, and that disagreements between the Allied sovereigns might trip up their operations. Until mid-December, he expected that the main Allied offensive would strike directly across the lower Rhine, and so grouped his main strength accordingly (*Map a*). Fortresses on and behind the lower Rhine were given priority on repairs and supplies. Any Allied offensive through the Low Countries would be checked by this fortress system, backed by Maison's field army.

Initially, Napoleon planned to withdraw all French troops from northern Italy, leaving his Italian troops in that area's numerous fortresses to delay the Austrians as best they could. Eugene demurred: His "French" units had been filled up with Piedmontese conscripts, who were sure to desert if ordered northward; his Italian units were becoming increasingly unreliable. Any transfer of French troops therefore merely would open southern France to Bellegarde. Reluctantly, Napoleon agreed. As for Spain, Napoleon still hoped that his treaty with Ferdinand would take effect. If it did not, he could give Soult only "my confidence" and conscripts to replace the veterans he had taken from him. Suchet still kept the initiative in Catalonia, but—apparently to maintain pressure on Ferdinand—Napoleon was loath to withdraw him.

On 1 January 1814, Napoleon ordered qualified officers from the frontier areas detailed to their home districts to organize partisan units. This was too late to permit effective preparations, the frontiers already being partially overrun. Few weapons were available, the civil authorities were timid, and the population generally was apathetic. There was no existing social organization (such as the clergy in Spain) to inspire, stiffen, and coordinate such a rising. Various former Revolutionary hotheads whom Napoleon sent out on that mission proved largely ineffective.

Once the Allied dispositions became evident, Napoleon ordered (13 January) Marmont and Macdonald to operate against Blücher. Victor (then at Strasbourg [*D3*]) and Ney (at Metz [*C3*]) would check Schwarzenberg along the line Vosges Mountains-Nancy-Epinal-Langres (*D3–C2*); Mortier would move from Namur (*C3*) to Langres to support them. If finally forced back by superior numbers, the marshals must continue to cover Paris. Only Antwerp (*C3*) and Mayence (*D3*) were strongly garrisoned by first-line troops, the greatest possible use being made elsewhere of national guards, limited-service veterans, and conscripts. (However small, such garrisons would tie down considerable numbers of Blücher's and Schwarzenberg's armies until Landwehr units could be brought up from the interior of Germany.) Augereau would form a new army at Lyons (*C2*) for an advance to the northeast across Schwarzenberg's communications, once these were sufficiently exposed.

Crossing the Swiss frontier at Basel (*D2*) on 21 December, Schwarzenberg advanced on Langres with his main column, detaching Bubna toward Lyons to cover his left flank, and dropping another corps in Switzerland to support a revolt by its pro-Austrian "aristocratic" party. Blücher forced the Rhine against little or no opposition on 1 January, left a force to blockade Mayence, and pushed on across the Saar River. Winzingerode crossed a few days later, moving on Liege (*C3*) to assist Bülow and Graham, who had got thoroughly entangled among the Low Countries' fortresses.

Eastern France was quickly overrun (*Map b*), the open cities surrendering to handfuls of Allied cavalry. In part, this servile behavior resulted from Metternich's psychological warfare (reinforced by Schwarzenberg's proclamation that the Allies came in peace, friendship, and perfect discipline to liberate France), but the demoralizing behavior of several marshals contributed significantly. Macdonald dithered; Marmont retired in order, but with inappropriate speed; Victor scampered behind the Vosges, making no effort to defend Strasbourg; Ney did nothing. When his subordinates won early successes near Epinal, he did not support them, and ended by practically abandoning his corps to Victor. Only Mortier did his duty, fighting an aggressive, eighteen-day delaying action from Langres back to Bar-sur-Aube, with numerous minor victories. Seeing his defenses coming apart prematurely, on 19 January Napoleon sent Berthier to relieve Victor, place Marmont in command of all available troops, and organize a defensive line along the Meuse River. Berthier found the line of the Meuse already abandoned; with howling confusion everywhere, there was little he could do.

Finally getting governmental affairs into order, Napoleon reached Chalons on 26 January, leaving Joseph Bonaparte as his lieutenant in Paris. This was a major blunder, but in part unavoidable. Joseph was Napoleon's older brother, and so expected employment in some important capacity. If not so honored, he was perfectly capable of getting involved (as in 1805) in subversive intrigues. To complicate matters further, Paris still was practically unfortified, Napoleon having been reluctant to upset that volatile city by any such indication of possible danger.

At Chalons-sur-Marne (*B2*; hereafter referred to as Chalons), Napoleon learned that Blücher was approaching St.-Dizier; Schwarzenberg, Bar-sur-Aube. Both armies were considerably weakened by detachments left to blockade various fortified towns, but they were very close to establishing contact. If Napoleon was to catch either one separately, he must strike promptly. Blücher, advancing with the apparent intention of reaching Paris ahead of Schwarzenberg, was the nearer and weaker target.

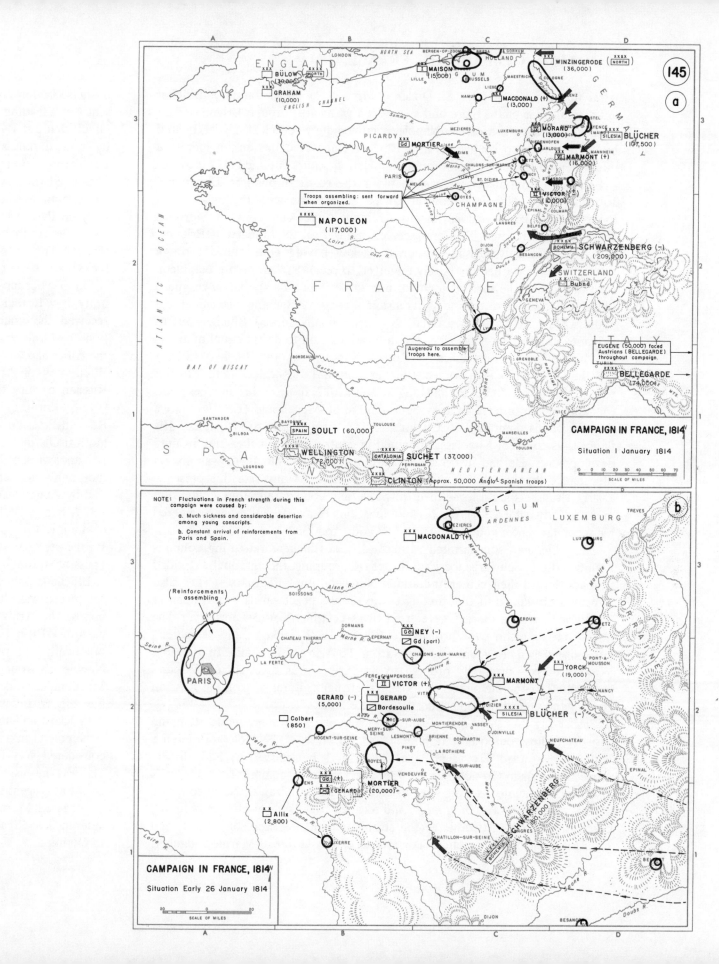

After flushing Victor from St.-Dizier (*Map a, C2*) on 26 January, Blücher left a small rear guard there and swaggered westward through Brienne (*C2*) to pick a fight with Mortier. Napoleon immediately seized St.-Dizier behind him. Poorly served by his cavalry, Blücher considered this action merely a minor demonstration against his communications, and continued on westward.

Sending Marmont farther east to block the roads through St.-Dizier and Joinville (*C2*), Napoleon now advanced on Brienne with the bulk of his forces, and ordered Mortier toward Arcis-sur-Aube. One copy of Mortier's orders was intercepted. Blücher received it early on 29 January at Brienne, where he had only Olssufiev's corps, Sacken having gone ahead through Lesmont. Thus warned, he barely managed to recall Sacken before Napoleon struck, and had the further good fortune to be joined by the advance guard (Pahlen, 3,000 cavalry) of Wittgenstein's corps. Attacking piecemeal (at about 1430) as his units arrived, Napoleon finally turned Blücher out of Brienne, French conscripts charging in unskilled fury to defeat equal numbers of Prussian and Russian veterans. (Losses: Napoleon, 3,000; Blücher, 4,000.) On the 30th, Napoleon forced Blücher out of La Rothiere, and Mortier reached Arcis-sur-Aube, establishing liaison with Napoleon through Lesmont. Macdonald was ordered to leave Sebastiani at St.-Menehould (*C3*) and move the rest of his command to Chalons (*B2*); Vitry was hastily fortified. His flanks thus covered, Napoleon remained in contact with Blücher and awaited developments. He had just missed destroying Blücher, but there was always the chance that the Allies would become rattled. At any rate, his presence east of Brienne should force them to pause and concentrate, thus giving him more time in which to press his mobilization. Heavy snowstorms hampered his reconnaissance, and he waited a few hours too long.

The Allies had concentrated haphazardly, as Blücher's retreating columns floundered into Schwarzenberg's advance. Regrouping, they gradually decided to mass toward their center and attack Napoleon on 1 February. (They also informed Caulaincourt that a congress to discuss peace terms would open at Chatillon-sur-Seine [hereafter referred to as Chatillon] on 3 February.) The attack on Napoleon was entrusted to Blücher, with Sacken's and Olssufiev's corps of his own army, and two corps from the Army of Bohemia. In addition, Wrede's corps—originally ordered to St.-Dizier—was diverted, on Wrede's suggestion, to operate against Napoleon's left flank. Barclay, with the Russian reserve and Guard, would support Blücher.

Suspecting that the Allies meant to fix him at La Rothiere while attacking Mortier (whose outposts were under Austrian pressure), Napoleon ordered a withdrawal toward Troyes (*B2*) at 0900 on 1 February. Ney had already moved off when Grouchy (now the army cavalry commander) reported Blücher advancing. Lacking time to complete his withdrawal, Napoleon took up the position shown (*inset map*) and recalled Ney. Blücher attacked blindly, concentrating on La Rothiere (the strongest point in Napoleon's line), and soon lost control of the action. Toward dark, Wrede forced Marmont danger-

ously back. Barclay reinforced Blücher, and La Rothiere finally fell. Napoleon sent Ney's leading division (Rottembourg) against La Rothiere in a counter-attack that put Barclay back on his heels, then expertly disengaged, covered by snow, darkness, and Drouot's guns. The exhausted Allies did not pursue. Each army lost approximately 6,000; Napoleon also had to abandon 50 guns.

Inflated with overconfidence at having defeated Napoleon on French soil, and certain he was no longer dangerous, the Allies decided to march immediately on Paris (*Map b, A2*). Blücher was to advance through Chalons and along the south bank of the Marne River to Meaux (*A2*); Schwarzenberg through Troyes and astride the Seine River; Wittgenstein and Seslawin's Cossacks (*not shown*) would advance between them to maintain contact.

On 3 February, Napoleon reached Troyes and began reorganizing his army, now further weakened by more than 4,000 desertions. (He was not well received, the inhabitants hoarding their food to meet expected Allied requisitions.) Morale was low; information concerning the Allies scanty. However, the Allies had lost contact with him on the 3d, when Marmont outmaneuvered Wrede east of Arcis-sur-Aube (*B2*), and Grouchy defeated an attempt by Russian cavalry to cut the Troyes-Arcis road. Yorck had found Vitry too strong to rush, and Schwarzenberg's left-flank corps crossed columns with the Russian-Prussian guards and reserves at Vendeuvre (*C2*), creating a mammoth traffic jam.

Napoleon sent Mortier southeast on a major reconnaissance in force, which thoroughly mauled Schwarzenberg's outposts in that direction, Already worried by Augereau's concentration at Lyons, and Platov's recent defeat at Sens (*B1*), Schwarzenberg became fearful of an impending offensive against his communications and decided to mass toward his left. Accordingly, he recalled Wittgenstein south of the Aube River; Seslawin (*not shown*) was ordered (possibly through error) to Schwarzenberg's extreme left flank.

Blücher's only reaction to Schwarzenberg's warning of Wittgenstein's shift southward was the joyful idea that Napoleon would be too hard-pressed to oppose the Army of Silesia. (He apparently was not told of Seslawin's departure.) By 6 February, Blücher's army was in four separate groups—all practically out of mutual supporting distance—plunging headlong across Napoleon's front in an attempt to destroy Macdonald. Yorck was pursuing Macdonald, while Sacken cut across country toward La Ferte (*B2*) to head him off; Olssufiev followed a day behind Sacken to maintain some contact with Kleist and Kapzevitsch.

Napoleon had contemplated attacking Schwarzenberg, whose position he considered very faulty. Blücher, however, was beginning to threaten Paris, and was the easier and nearer target. During 5–7 February, Napoleon concentrated at Nogent-sur-Seine (*B2*; hereafter referred to as Nogent); on the 7th, he ordered Marmont to Sezanne. The newly created VII Corps (largely veterans from Spain), which was forming at Nogent, was mistakenly entrusted to Oudinot.

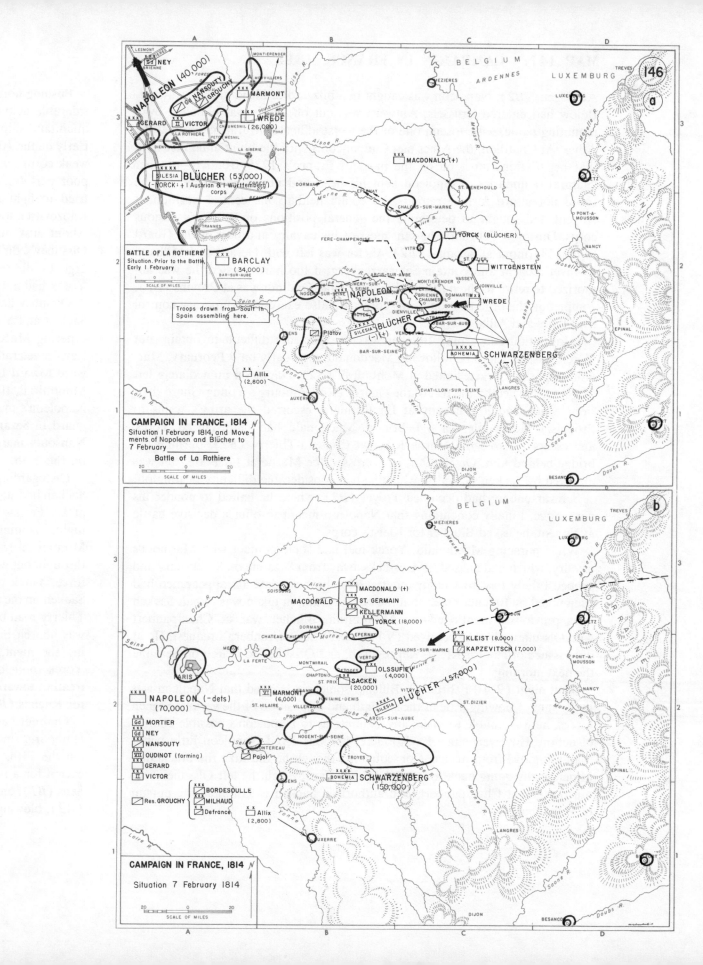

At Nogent (*B2*), Napoleon was caught in a blizzard of ill tidings. Northward, Bülow had entered Brussels; Antwerp was cut off. Paris was clutched by a mounting panic, with Joseph one of the worst afflicted. Murat had joined the Allies. At Chatillon, the Allies met Caulaincourt with the blunt announcement that negotiations must be on the basis of France's 1789 frontier—*not* her "natural boundaries." Napoleon kept his head and nerve. Realizing that he could not afford further retreats, he coolly held to his central position at Nogent and sought to determine the general positions of Blücher's various corps. During 8 February, he sent most of his cavalry and part of the Guard to join Marmont at Sezanne (*B2*). Victor was left with Gerard and Milhaud to cover Nogent and contain Schwarzenberg; if too hard pressed, he was authorized to retire to the north bank of the Seine. Oudinot was at Provins (*B2*), completing the organization of his corps. He also exercised temporary control over Pajol and Allix.

Information concerning Blücher was unexpectedly difficult to obtain, but Yorck was known to be following Macdonald, and, early on 9 February, Marmont reported Sacken halted at Montmirail (*B2*). Napoleon immediately left Nogent, followed by the rest of the Guard. (Rottembourg's Young Guard division, which had lost heavily at La Rothiere, escorted the army's trains to Provins.) Meanwhile, on 8 February, Macdonald had outdistanced Yorck and escaped across the Marne River at Chateau-Thierry (*B2*), burning the bridge behind him. On the 9th, he recrossed the Marne at La Ferte, but was attacked by Sacken's cavalry, which he had considerable difficulty beating off.

Schwarzenberg had occupied Troyes (*B2*), where he halted to ponder his next move. Finally concluding that Napoleon meant to offer a decisive battle at Nogent, he asked Blücher for Kleist's corps.

While pursuing Macdonald, Yorck had had some contact with Marmont's cavalry, which had chased his Cossacks away from Sezanne on 8 February and probed briefly toward Champaubert (*B2*) the next day. Its appearance had been noted by Blücher's staff, but the only precaution taken was to halt Sacken —as previously mentioned—at Montmirail. Blücher was at Champaubert with Olssufiev when he received (9 February) Schwarzenberg's request. He at once issued orders for Kleist, Kapzevitsch, and Olssufiev to march on Sezanne the next morning.

That night (9–10 February), Blücher somehow learned that Napoleon was in Sezanne. Knowing little of the strength and disposition of the various French forces, he was unable to make any estimate as to Napoleon's possible courses of action. However, since La Rothiere, he considered Napoleon little better than a fugitive from justice. Consequently, though he did take the precaution of personally going back to join Kleist and Kapzevitsch, he left Olssufiev very much alone at Champaubert, and authorized Sacken to continue the pursuit of Macdonald.

Pushing northward along roads "six feet deep in mud," Napoleon got considerable help from the local inhabitants, who, having enjoyed a brief acquaintanceship with Allied "liberation," turned out to help drag his guns along. Early on the 10th, French cavalry developed the isolated position of Olssufiev's weak corps (*inset map*). Olssufiev had been threatened with court-martial for poor performance at Brienne and La Rothiere; thoroughly sore-headed, he tried to fight and was squashed. Meanwhile, Blücher marched Kleist and Kapzevitsch toward Sezanne, placidly ignoring the sound of battle to the west. About dusk, near Fere-Champenoise (*main map, B2*), he finally learned of Olssufiev's disaster, and countermarched hastily to Vertus, sending off an urgent order recalling Sacken to Montmirail. Sacken had continued westward; Yorck had not budged from Chateau-Thierry.

Olssufiev having been disposed of, Napoleon swung westward to deal with Sacken and Yorck, sending Marmont to Etoges (*B2*) to watch Blücher, and ordering Macdonald to countermarch eastward. Oudinot was told to send Leval's veteran division (and, if possible, Rottembourg) from Provins northward toward La Ferte Gaucher. If Napoleon fought his expected battle near Montmirail, they were to march to the sound of his guns. Mortier, closing Napoleon's march column with an Old Guard division, was to leave a rear guard in Sezanne and establish contact with Leval. At 1900, 10 February, Nansouty marched for Montmirail, the rest of the army following at 0300 on the 11th.

Disregarding Yorck's suggestion that they concentrate at Chateau-Thierry, Sacken had started for Montmirail at 2100 on 10 February, burning the bridge at La Ferte-sous-Jouarre behind him. (Yorck himself made no move that night, claiming his troops were exhausted.) Encountering Napoleon west of Montmirail (*inset map*) the next morning, Sacken attempted to bull his way through, but was outmaneuvered and outfought by Napoleon's slightly smaller force. Yorck reached the field at about 1530, with part of his corps, to find Sacken on the point of collapse and Napoleon across the Montmirail–Chateau-Thierry road between them. His arrival saved Sacken from destruction, but he was himself promptly driven back toward Chateau-Thierry by Mortier. During the night, Sacken's shattered corps groped along woods roads to join Yorck; both corps commanders received orders from Blücher—himself retreating toward Bergeres (*main map, B2*)—to recross the Marne and make for Rheims (*B3*), where the Army of Silesia would reassemble.

Oudinot had dispatched Leval (*not shown*) as ordered, but retained Rottembourg, since Schwarzenberg had advanced from Troyes on 10 February. On the 11th, Wittgenstein and Wrede forced Victor back across the Seine, except for a rear guard left in Nogent. The Prince of Württemberg captured Sens (*B1*); on orders from Victor, Pajol retired behind the Seine at Montereau (*A2*), blowing up the bridge there.

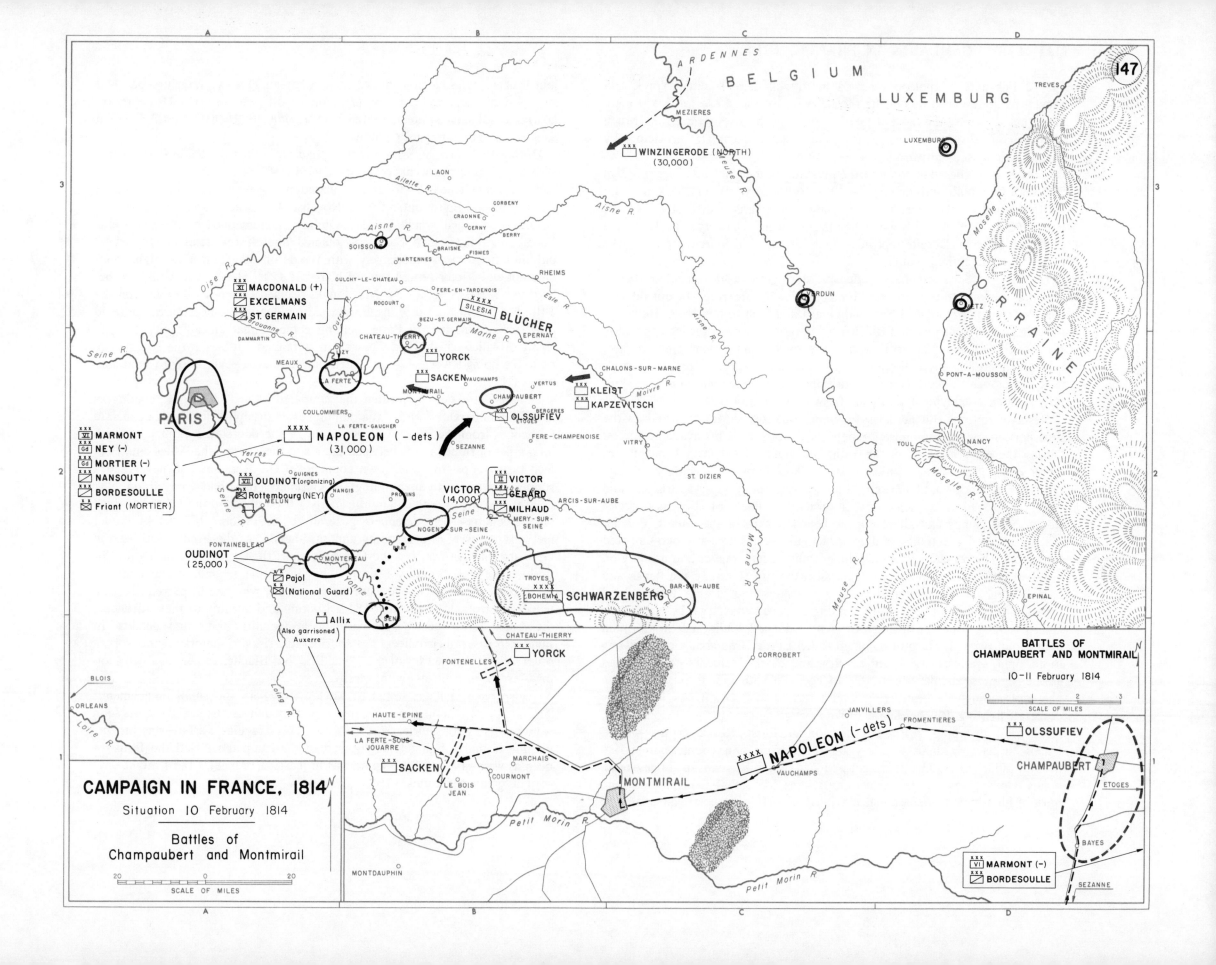

147

BELGIUM

LUXEMBURG

TREVES

ARDENNES

MEZIERES

LUXEMBURG

XXX WINZINGERODE (NORTH) (30,000)

LAON

CORBENY

CRAONNE

CERNY

BERRY

Aisne R.

Ailette R.

Aisne R.

Moselle R.

L O R R A I N E

METZ

SOISSO

HARTENNES

BRAISNE

FISMES

RHEIMS

OULCHY-LE-CHATEAU

FERE-EN-TARDENOIS

ROCOURT

XI MACDONALD (+)
EXCELMANS
ST. GERMAIN

BEZU-ST-GERMAIN

XXXX SILESIA BLÜCHER

Marne R.

EPERNAY

Oise R.

CHATEAU-THIERRY

Esle R.

Aisne R.

VERDUN

PONT-A-MOUSSON

Ourcq R.

Brouanne R.

DAMMARTIN

LUZY

LA FERTE

XXX YORCK

XXX SACKEN VAUCHAMPS

VERTUS

CHALONS-SUR-MARNE

XXX KLEIST
XXX KAPZEVITSCH

Moivre R.

MEAUX

COULOMMIERS

MONTMIRAIL

CHAMPAUBERT

BERGERES

XXX OLSSUFIEV
ETOGES

FERE-CHAMPENOISE

VITRY

TOUL

NANCY

Moselle R.

PARIS

VI MARMONT
Gd NEY (-)
Gd MORTIER (-)
NANSOUTY
BORDESOULLE
Friant (MORTIER)

XXXX NAPOLEON (-dets) (31,000)

Yerres R.

LA FERTE-GAUCHER

SEZANNE

ST. DIZIER

VII OUDINOT (organizing)

Rottembourg (NEY)
MELUN

NANGIS

PROVINS

VICTOR (14,000)

II VICTOR
GERARD
MILHAUD

ARCIS-SUR-AUBE

Seine R.

MERY-SUR-SEINE

Marne R.

NOGENT-SUR-SEINE

Meuse R.

FONTAINEBLEAU

OUDINOT (25,000)

MONTEREAU

BRAY

TROYES
XXXX BOHEMIA SCHWARZENBERG

BAR-SUR-AUBE

Yonne R.

Pajol
(National Guard)

Loing R.

Allix

(Also garrisoned
Auxerre)

BLOIS

ORLEANS

Loire R.

MONTDAUPHIN

CHATEAU-THIERRY

XXX YORCK

FONTENELLES

CORROBERT

EPINAL

BATTLES OF CHAMPAUBERT AND MONTMIRAIL
10-11 February 1814

0   1   2   3
SCALE OF MILES

HAUTE-EPINE

LA FERTE-SOUS-JOUARRE

XXX SACKEN

MARCHAIS

COURMONT

LE BOIS JEAN

JANVILLERS

FROMENTIERES

XXXX NAPOLEON (-dets)

XXX OLSSUFIEV

CHAMPAUBERT

ETOGES

VAUCHAMPS

MONTMIRAIL

Petit Morin R.

Petit Morin R.

BAYES

SEZANNE

XXX VI MARMONT (-)
XXX BORDESOULLE

CAMPAIGN IN FRANCE, 1814
Situation 10 February 1814
Battles of Champaubert and Montmirail

20   0   20
SCALE OF MILES

On 12 February, Napoleon renewed his attack, Ney leading. Yorck and Sacken barely escaped across the Marne, with over-all losses of 7,000 men, more than 20 guns, and most of their trains. French losses were 2,500. Much to Napoleon's disappointment, Macdonald failed to complete the victory by an energetic march eastward.

Mortier was ordered to continue the pursuit, but the Chateau-Thierry bridge could not be rebuilt until late on the 13th. By then, Yorck and Sacken—who had not stood on the order of their going—were safely north of the Ourcq River. (One of Napoleon's worst handicaps during 1814 was the lack of a small bridge train. Despite repeated orders, it was mid-March before Clarke produced some clumsy pontons.)

Learning of Schwarzenberg's offensive during the 13th, Napoleon began planning a concentration around Montereau (A2), ordering Macdonald (re-enforced by a newly arrived National Guard division) to that town. However, that night, Marmont reported Blücher again moving west. Blücher apparently had concluded that Napoleon would already be countermarching to meet Schwarzenberg; having collected some additional cavalry, he proposed to attack the Emperor's rear. Too weak to oppose this force, Marmont was skillfully fighting a delaying action back from Etoges (B2).

Resolved to teach Blücher a lesson, Napoleon ordered Marmont to draw the Prussian on toward Montmirail, where he concentrated his available forces. During the early morning of the 14th, Marmont retired from Fromentieres (inset map) to a strong position west of Vauchamps. Advancing carelessly, Blücher's advance guard (Zieten) attacked him there, but was trapped and largely destroyed as Grouchy burst in on its right flank. Meeting its fugitives east of Vauchamps and glimpsing the bearskin caps of the Guard, Blücher quickly ordered a retreat, though he actually seems to have outnumbered Napoleon. The retreat was initially in splendid order, wagons and artillery on the road, infantry in squares to either side, cavalry screening the flanks and rear. Though heavily pounded by Drouot's guns, the veteran Russian and Prussian infantry kept their ranks, beating off repeated charges by Nansouty's Guard cavalry. But, meanwhile, Grouchy led Bordesoulle and St. Germain along country roads north of the main route. East of Champaubert, he swung to his right, scattered the Allied cavalry, and blocked Blücher's retreat. Had Grouchy's horse artillery been able to keep up with him through the deep clay mud, Blücher's destruction would have been certain. As it was, by desperate fighting, Blücher finally broke through and made for Chalons (main map, B2), dropping a Russian division at Etoges to cover his retreat. Napoleon left Marmont to carry on the pursuit and countermarched to Montmirail. About 2030, Marmont pounced on the Russians in Etoges, practically wiping them out. In this action, Blücher lost 7,000 men, 16 guns, and most of his trains. Napoleon had 600 casualties. Farther north, advancing to join Blücher, who he thought was near Chateau-Thierry, Winzingerode had surprised and captured Soissons (B3) on 13–14 February. On 16 February, hearing of Blücher's defeat, he fell back rapidly to Rheims. Mortier herded Sacken and Yorck toward Chalons.

During 12 February, Schwarzenberg had got across the Seine River, when Wrede surprised the weak National Guard detachment at Bray (B2). His flank thus threatened, Victor had to abandon Nogent, though his rear guard (under General Bourmont, a former Royalist) had held his south-bank bridgehead against Allied assaults all day. Oudinot, handicapped by the absence of Leval's division (which Napoleon blamed himself for detaching), arrived only in time to clash indecisively with Wrede on the 13th. That night, both Oudinot and Victor retired toward Nangis (A2), intending to withdraw behind the Yerres River (A2). Macdonald reached Guignes (A2) late on the 14th, but provided no new inspiration. An unidentified officer hastily ordered the army's trains toward Paris, fanning panic in that unstable city. A long ripple of Allied cavalry and Cossacks now fanned out across the countryside up to the Loing River (A1–A2), their outriders even penetrating to Fontainebleau (A2).

A new factor now permeated the campaign. Allied claims of "coming as friends and liberators" and of maintaining exact discipline had been deliberate falsehoods from the start. Advancing out of the devastated Rhineland, with long miles of ruined roads between them and their bases, the Allies could not feed their troops from their own countries. (The Russians had never had a supply system worth mentioning; in Germany, they had foraged on ally, neutral, and enemy with equal informality.) From the first, the Allies had lived off the country—Schwarzenberg generally by requisition, Blücher by cruder methods. All were as demanding and hard-handed as the French had been in Germany and Austria, but the Cossacks and Prussians were outstanding for misbehavior and brutality—the first by habit, the second in the name of "vengeance." Almost as bad were the Bavarians, who had displayed identical tendencies from 1805 through 1812. Looting and burning as they advanced, the Allied forces became increasingly savage after their first defeats. In numerous cases, their officers ran considerable risks to maintain some sort of order. Yorck damned his men as "bandits," but Blücher rather regarded looting—except in Prussia—with approval.

Exasperated civilians began to waylay stragglers and small detachments. The Vosges Mountain passes became especially dangerous; heavy escorts soon were necessary for couriers and convoys. This irregular warfare was just beginning to make itself felt by the end of the campaign. "Had the Emperor been as well served in Paris as he was in [eastern France]," 1814 might have seen his greatest victories.

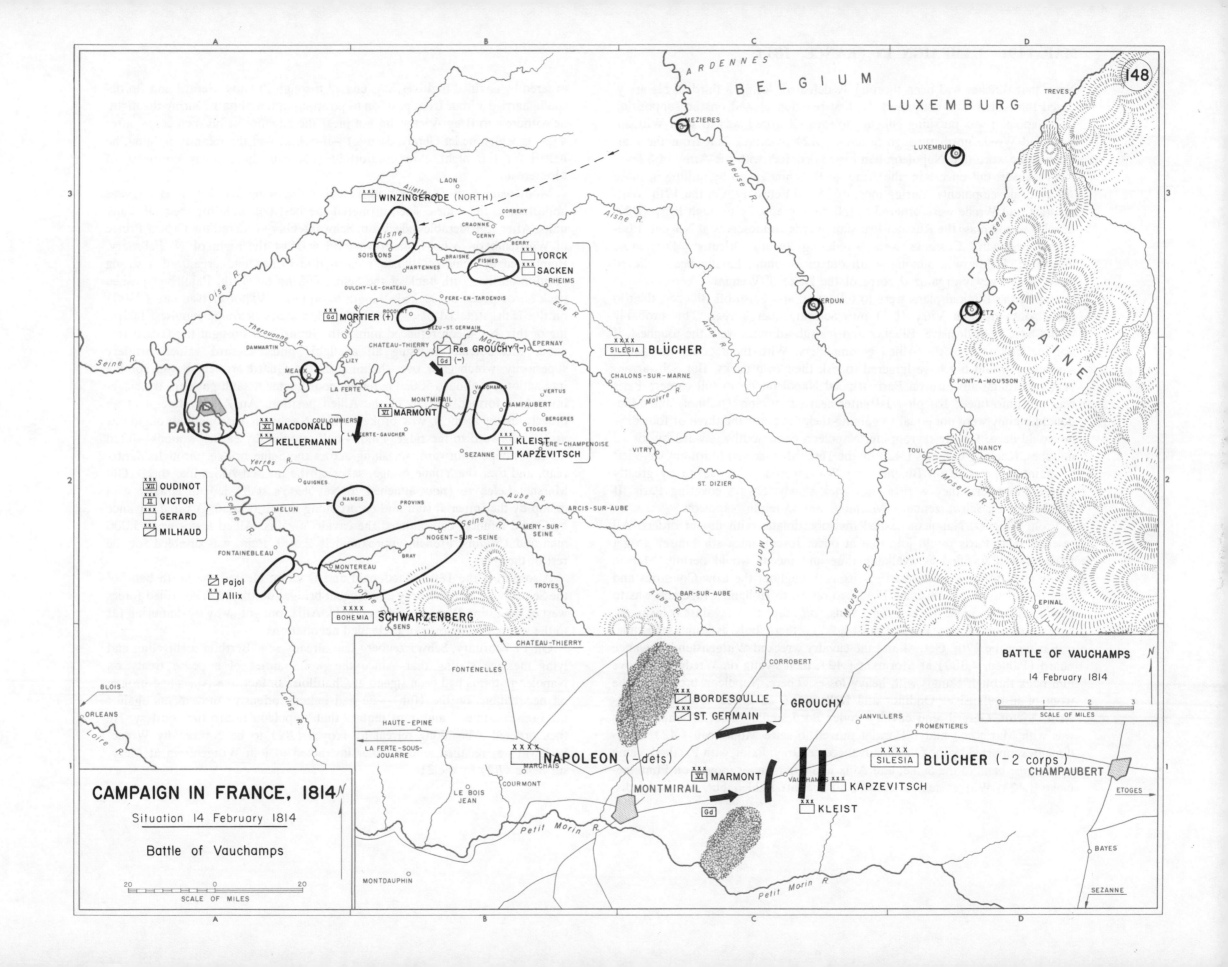

148

ARDENNES

BELGIUM

LUXEMBURG

TREVES

MEZIERES

LUXEMBURG

LORRAINE

LAON

Meuse R.

Moselle R.

WINZINGERODE (NORTH)
xxx

Aisne R.

CORBENY

CRAONNE

CERNY

Aisne

SOISSONS

HARTENNES

BRAISNE

FISMES

BERRY

YORCK
xxx

SACKEN
xxx

RHEIMS

VERDUN

METZ

PONT-A-MOUSSON

OULCHY-LE-CHATEAU

FERE-EN-TARDENOIS

Esle R.

MORTIER (+)
Gd xxx

ROCOURT

SEZU-ST. GERMAIN

Ourcq

CHATEAU-THIERRY

Res GROUCHY (-)

EPERNAY

Marne R.

BLÜCHER
SILESIA xxxx

CHALONS-SUR-MARNE

Moivre R.

TOUL

NANCY

Theorouanne R.

DAMMARTIN

LIZY

Gd (-)

VAUCHAMPS

VERTUS

Seine R.

MEAUX

LA FERTE

MONTMIRAIL

CHAMPAUBERT

BERGERES

ETOGES

PARIS

MACDONALD
xxx XI

KELLERMANN

COULOMMIERS

LA-FERTE-GAUCHER

MARMONT
xxx VI

KLEIST
xxx

KAPZEVITSCH
xxx

FERE-CHAMPENOISE

VITRY

ST. DIZIER

SEZANNE

OUDINOT
xxx VII

VICTOR
xxx II

GERARD
xxx

MILHAUD
xxx

GUIGNES

NANGIS

PROVINS

MELUN

Yerres R.

Aube R.

ARCIS-SUR-AUBE

MERY-SUR-SEINE

Seine R.

NOGENT-SUR-SEINE

FONTAINEBLEAU

BRAY

Marne R.

Meuse R.

Pajol
xx

Allix
xx

MONTEREAU

Yonne R.

TROYES

Aube R.

BAR-SUR-AUBE

EPINAL

SCHWARZENBERG
BOHEMIA xxxx

SENS

BATTLE OF VAUCHAMPS
14 February 1814

N

SCALE OF MILES

BLOIS

CHATEAU-THIERRY

CORROBERT

JANVILLERS

FROMENTIERES

ORLEANS

FONTENELLES

BORDESOULLE
xxx

ST. GERMAIN

GROUCHY

Loire R.

HAUTE-EPINE

SILESIA xxxx BLÜCHER (-2 corps)

CHAMPAUBERT

ETOGES

NAPOLEON (-dets)
xxxx

MARCHAIS

VAUCHAMPS

KAPZEVITSCH
xxx

LA FERTE-SOUS-JOUARRE

LE BOIS
JEAN

COURMONT

MARMONT
xxx VI

MONTMIRAIL

Gd

KLEIST
xxx

CAMPAIGN IN FRANCE, 1814

N

Situation 14 February 1814

Battle of Vauchamps

Petit Morin R.

BAYES

MONTDAUPHIN

Petit Morin R.

SEZANNE

SCALE OF MILES
20   0   20

News that Blücher had been thoroughly defeated, losing a third of his army, dazed the Allied high command. Its first reaction (based on the supposition that Napoleon was pursuing Blücher toward Chalons) was to send Wittgenstein and Wrede north through Sezanne (*B2*) to attack him from the rear. Then came word that Napoleon had broken contact with the Army of Silesia. Apprehensive but uncertain, the Army of Bohemia ended by milling in place "to await developments" during most of 15–16 February. On the 17th, Wittgenstein and Wrede were ordered to fall back gradually through Bray (*B2*). Barclay would mass the Russian-Prussian guards and reserves at Nogent. Elsewhere, Seslawin's Cossacks were wandering toward Orleans (*A1*); more important, Bülow was moving south out of Belgium, having been relieved there by the newly organized corps of the Duke of Weimar.

Napoleon's original plans were to follow up and finish off Blücher, then to move south through Vitry (*C2*) into Schwarzenberg's rear. This probably would have been decisive. Blücher and his subordinates were the toughest, if not the brightest, of the Allied commanders. With them gone, the Allied sovereigns would not have lingered to risk their own necks. But Schwarzenberg's fumbling advance on Paris tripped Napoleon up in full career: Paris was still unfortified; Joseph was butter-hearted; Victor, Oudinot, and Macdonald plainly were not equal to gaining their Emperor the three or four days he would need. Hastily regrouping, Napoleon came southwestward by forced marches, reaching Guignes (*A2*) on the 16th. Mortier and Marmont were left to maintain pressure on Blücher and Winzingerode; if attacked by greatly superior numbers, they were to fall back slowly, always covering Paris. If Blücher joined Schwarzenberg, Marmont was to rejoin Napoleon.

From Guignes, Napoleon lashed his subordinates with urgent orders. All reserves from Paris would join him at once; Joseph must stir himself to get Paris as well fortified as available time and means would permit. Maison would concentrate the scattered garrisons throughout the Low Countries and take the offensive, thus forcing Bülow to return to Holland. Augereau was to advance up the Saone River from Lyons (*off map, C1*) against Schwarzenberg's communications. Eugene must hold northern Italy as long as possible.

Early on the 17th, Gerard and the cavalry wrecked Wittgenstein's advance guard (Pahlen, 4,300) at Mormant (*A2*), then swung on Wrede and drove him back through Nangis with heavy losses. There, Napoleon broadened the front of his offensive: Oudinot and Kellermann advanced against Wittgenstein; Victor, Gerard, and cavalry under Bordesoulle (most of whose corps was with Marmont) and L'Heritier moved to seize Montereau (*A2*); Macdonald, supported by the Guard, advanced on Bray; Pajol, with Pacthod, came up the east bank of the Seine; and Allix and Charpentier moved on Fontainebleau (*A2*). Wittgenstein attempted to support Pahlen but, his ranks dis-

ordered by terrified fugitives, was chased through Provins. Gerard and Bordesoulle harried Wrede from position to position until nightfall. During the night, he withdrew to Bray. Victor did not press the advance of his own corps; after a day in which he let Gerard do most—if not all—of the infantry fighting, he halted for the night at a comfortable chateau three miles northeast of Montereau.

Montereau, with its stone bridges across the Seine and Yonne rivers, was important to the Allies, since it offered the best bolt hole for their left-flank units. After considerable indecision, Schwarzenberg ordered the Crown Prince of Württemberg to hold this town until at least the night of 18 February. Reinforced by some of Bianchi's corps, the Prince had organized a strong position on the north bank of the Seine. During the 17th, Pajol had pushed back his outposts, but lacked strength to do more. Victor arrived late (0900) on the 18th, attacked piecemeal, and took a series of rough repulses. Learning of this, Napoleon replaced him with Gerard and brought the Guard forward. Methodically massing all available guns, Gerard gained artillery superiority, which grew overwhelming as the Guard artillery began coming into action. At about 1500, a carefully coordinated assault got onto the ridgeline which formed the key of the Allied position. An Allied attempt at an orderly disengagement was broken when Napoleon personally brought his artillery forward to the ridge. Pajol—half-crippled by earlier wounds—lifted his raw troopers forward, smashing across the Seine bridge, through Montereau, and over the Yonne bridge, sabering the massed Allies like sheep. Old Marshal Lefebvre (now attached to Napoleon's staff) led an equally wild gallop by the Imperial staff and escort along the Bray road. A rapid advance by Guard infantry consolidated the cavalry's gains. Allied losses were 5,000 men and 15 guns; French, approximately 2,500. Pajol was disabled for the rest of the year.

Also during the 18th, Macdonald and Oudinot cleared the north bank of the Seine, but found the Bray and Nogent bridges destroyed. The Allied forces west of the Loing River were driven in by Allix, but got away by detouring far to the south, under cover of pretended negotiations.

On 17 February, Schwarzenberg had already sent Berthier a sniveling and lying message stating that—since the preliminaries of a peace treaty on Napoleon's terms had been signed at Chatillon (in fact, the Allies had broken off negotiations on the 10th)—he had halted "offensive movements against the French armies," and must request that Napoleon return the courtesy. He then ordered a headlong retreat to Troyes (*B2*) to be covered by Wrede. Seslawin was recalled, and Blücher instructed to join Wittgenstein at Mery-sur-Seine (*B2*) by the 21st.

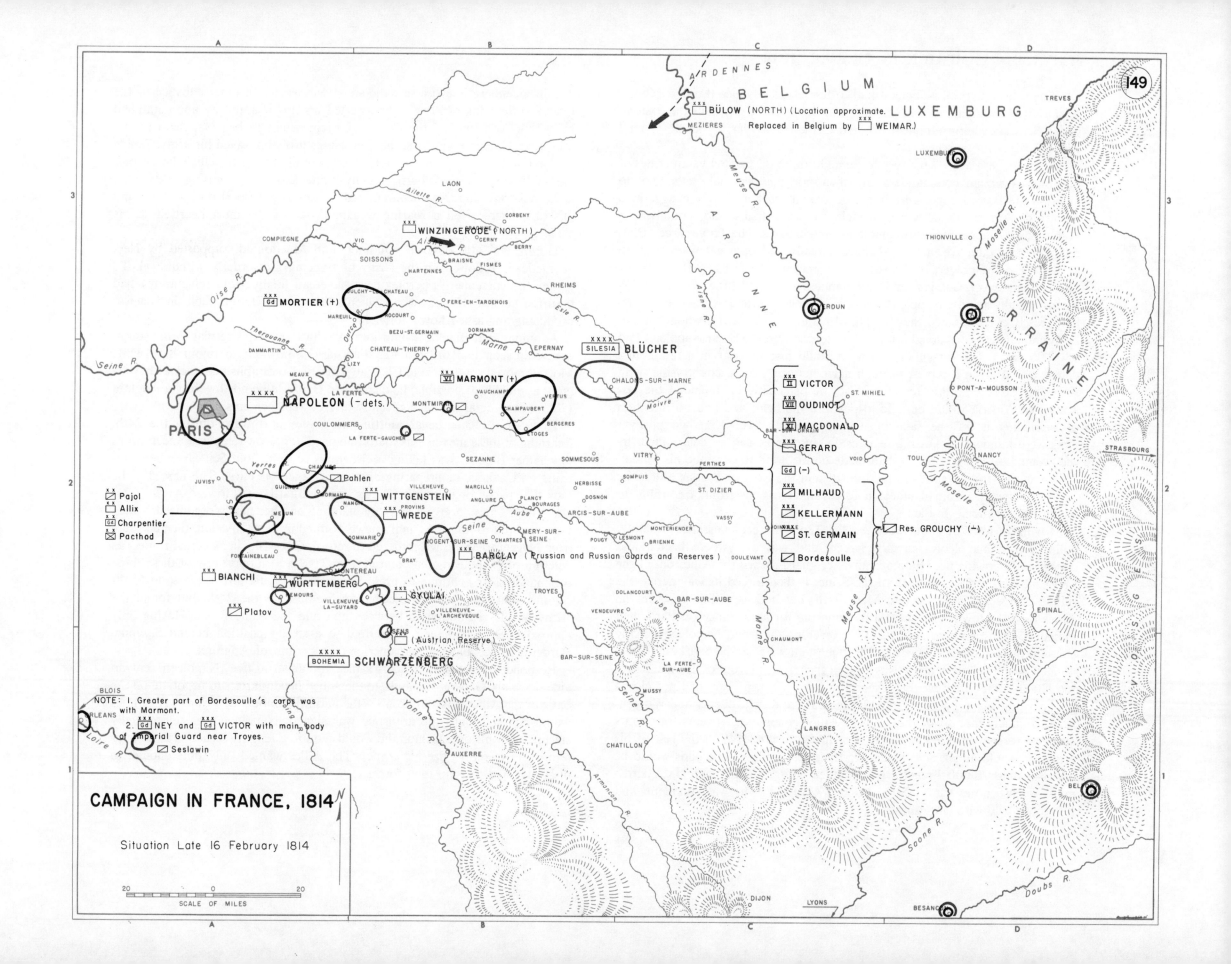

149

BELGIUM

ARDENNES

LUXEMBURG

TREVES

BÜLOW (NORTH) (Location approximate. LUXEMBURG
Replaced in Belgium by □□□ WEIMAR.)

MEZIERES

LUXEMBURG

LAON

CORBENY

THIONVILLE

Meuse R.

ARGONNE

Moselle R.

LORRAINE

COMPIEGNE

VIC

WINZINGERODE (NORTH)

CERNY

Ailette R.

Aisne R.

BERRY

SOISSONS

HARTENNES

BRAISNE
FISMES

RHEIMS

VERDUN

METZ

Oise R.

MORTIER (+)

OULCHY-LE-CHATEAU

FERE-EN-TARDENOIS

Esle R.

Therouanne R.

MAREUIL

ROCOURT

BEZU-ST.-GERMAIN

DORMANS

Ourcq R.

CHATEAU-THIERRY

Marne R.

EPERNAY

SILESIA BLÜCHER

PONT-A-MOUSSON

DAMMARTIN

LIZY

MEAUX

LA FERTE

VICTOR

ST. MIHIEL

OUDINOT

MACDONALD

MarneR.

MACDONALD

NAPOLEON (-dets.)

MONTMIRAIL

MARMONT (+)

VAUCHAMPS

VERTUS

CHAMPAUBERT

CHALONS-SUR-MARNE

Moivre R.

STRASBOURG

PARIS

COULOMMIERS

LA FERTE-GAUCHER

BERGERES
ETOGES

GERARD

Gd (-)

VOID

TOUL

NANCY

Moselle R.

JUVISY

Yerres R.

CHAUME

Pahlen

SEZANNE

SOMMESOUS

VITRY

PERTHES

HERBISSE

SOMPUIS

ST. DIZIER

MILHAUD

KELLERMANN

St. GERMAIN

Pajol
Allix
Charpentier
Pacthod

GUIGNES

DORMANT

NANGIS

VILLENEUVE

MARCILLY

PLANCY
BOURAGES

DOSNON

Aube R.

ARCIS-SUR-AUBE

VASSY

WITTGENSTEIN

WREDE

MELUN

PROVINS

Seine R.

MERY-SUR-SEINE

MONTERIENDER

Res. GROUCHY (-)

Bordesoulle

DOMMARIE

NOGENT-SUR-SEINE

CHARTRES

POUGY

LESMONT

BRIENNE

DOULEVANT

FONTAINEBLEAU

BRAY

BARCLAY (Prussian and Russian Guards and Reserves)

MONTEREAU

BIANCHI

WÜRTTEMBERG

GYULAI

TROYES

DOLANCOURT

BAR-SUR-AUBE

Platov

TEMOURS

VILLENEUVE
LA-GUYARD

VILLENEUVE-
L'ARCHEVEQUE

VENDEUVRE

Aube R.

CHAUMONT

SENS

(Austrian Reserve)

BAR-SUR-SEINE

LA FERTE-
SUR-AUBE

Meuse R.

MarneR.

VOSGES

EPINAL

SCHWARZENBERG
BOHEMIA

Yonne R.

Seine R.

MUSSY

LANGRES

BLOIS

NOTE: 1. Greater part of Bordesoulle's corps was
with Marmont.
2. NEY and VICTOR with main body
of Imperial Guard near Troyes.

ORLEANS

Loire R.

Seslawin

CHATILLON

Armancon R.

AUXERRE

BEL

CAMPAIGN IN FRANCE, 1814

N

Situation Late 16 February 1814

DIJON

LYONS

Soone R.

Doubs R.

BESANCON

20   0   20
SCALE OF MILES

Lacking a bridge train, Napoleon had to funnel his advance through Monte-reau until Macdonald restored the bridge at Bray. This delay, plus the haste in which Schwarzenberg retreated, resulted in the French largely losing contact with the Allies for two days.

Schwarzenberg needed the respite. In addition to the excited yammerings of his three sovereign commanders and their polyglot personal staffs (not to mention the English representatives), he was afflicted by highly exaggerated reports of Augereau's activities—which, so far, actually had amounted to nothing more than continuous complaints and excuses. The Troyes area (B2), relatively unproductive in normal times, already had been eaten up by both armies. Disease, hunger, bad weather, and recent defeats had left the Army of Bohemia shaky. Soldiers and commanders alike had little appetite for a stand-up fight against Napoleon, especially since recent intelligence reports had grossly overestimated the strength of his army. (Seslawin, whom the Allied commanders considered an accurate source, reported that Napoleon had 180,000 men!) Schwarzenberg knew he could lose the war in a few hours; defeat would mean a retreat through a vindictively hostile countryside, with Augereau advancing into his rear. Also, he personally commanded the last army that Austria would be able to put into the field, and had no intention of sacrificing it for the sake of temporary allies, whose known postwar aims were inimical to Austrian expansion. Insofar as can be determined, by the evening of 21 February he had made up his mind to continue his retreat. To screen it—from Napoleon, Alexander, and the King of Prussia alike—he ordered a heavy reconnaissance in force all across his front, ostensibly to locate the advancing French.

Moving forward at about noon on the 22d, this reconnaissance promptly collided with Napoleon's cavalry screen, and was everywhere beaten and driven in. Following up, Oudinot's advance guard rushed the Allies out of the Mery suburb on the west bank of the Seine. It then forced its way across the ruined bridge and stormed into Mery itself, but had to withdraw when the Allies fired the town. (Blücher, still clamoring for an advance on Paris, had joined Wittgenstein here on the 21st.) Reaching the front, Napoleon quickly assessed the situation: Blücher and Wittgenstein were on the east bank of the flooded Seine; Schwarzenberg was west of that river, in front of Troyes; it was too late to attack that evening, especially since his own army had not closed up. He would leave a part of Oudinot's veterans to watch Blücher and Wittgenstein, confident that it would take those Allied commanders twenty-four hours either to force a crossing at Mery or to find a new one. With the rest of his army, he would attack Schwarzenberg the next morning. The odds would be heavy—some 70,000 French, mostly green conscripts and national guardsmen, against more than 100,000 veteran Allies—but he was confident, and his troops wild with enthusiasm.

Schwarzenberg likewise saw the situation clearly. In quiet defiance of the Czar and the King of Prussia, he asserted his titular authority and continued his withdrawal, sending the Prince of Lichtenstein to beg Napoleon for an armistice. Though inglorious, these measures probably saved his army. Wrede was left with one division to hold Troyes until the 24th, which he accomplished by threatening to burn that city if attacked, but promising to evacuate it the next morning. Napoleon entered Troyes about 0600 on the 24th, and this time he received a roaring welcome, one of the most heartfelt in his career.

During the 24th, Gerard, Oudinot, and Macdonald, supported by Ney, energetically followed up the Army of Bohemia's disorderly withdrawal. To climax Schwarzenberg's perplexities, Augereau finally (and reluctantly) had bestirred himself. His advance elements had driven Bubna back on Geneva, producing anguished howls for help.

Assuming that Blücher would join in Schwarzenberg's retreat to the southeast, Napoleon had ordered (23 February) Marmont to rejoin him, while Mortier moved southward to Chateau-Thierry. To establish contact with Marmont as quickly as possible, he dispatched Bordesoulle northward via Anglure (B2) with a detachment of recently arrived replacements.

However, Blücher began shifting his forces northward during the 24th. Learning of these movements that same day, Napoleon remained uncertain as to whether Blücher was taking a circuitous route to join Schwarzenberg, retiring on Chalons, or preparing another advance on Paris. The next day, he took the precaution of sending Ney's Young Guard corps toward Arcis (B2), and Victor (now forgiven, and commanding another newly organized Young Guard corps) to Mery. Arrighi's newly formed infantry division, then en route from Nogent to Mery, was ordered to return. Once Blücher's actual route was determined, Napoleon could march from Troyes to support any of these three commanders, or continue to press Schwarzenberg. Reports were soon forthcoming. Marmont had advanced from Sezanne on the 24th, but found the Army of Silesia in strength between him and the Aube River. Having only approximately 6,000 men, he retired to a strong position behind Sezanne. Bordesoulle was blocked by superior forces south of Anglure.

Responding to Schwarzenberg's plea for an armistice, Napoleon sent an aide-de-camp, General Flahoult, to the Allied headquarters to negotiate on the basis of the Allies' first proposals—the natural frontiers of France. Hostilities would continue until the armistice was signed. Napoleon was undoubtedly sincere, after his own fashion; he would require a lengthy "truce" (as he later termed it) to reorganize his armies. The Allies wanted only time enough to disengage and regroup their forces.

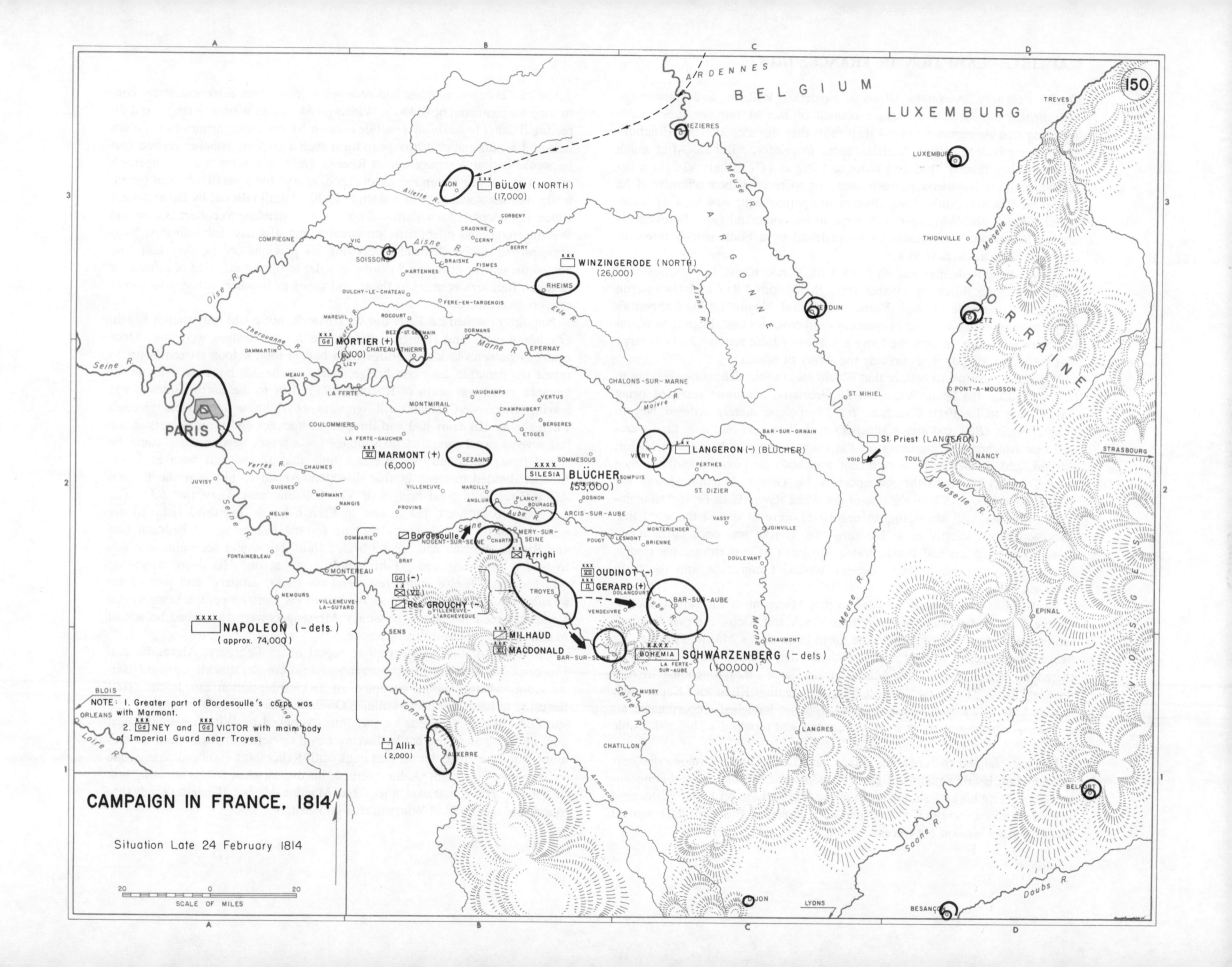

150

CAMPAIGN IN FRANCE, 1814

Situation Late 24 February 1814

NOTE: 1. Greater part of Bordesoulle's corps was with Marmont.
2. NEY and VICTOR with main body of Imperial Guard near Troyes.

SCALE OF MILES
20   0   20

On 25 February, Alexander, Francis, Frederick William, and Castelreagh (the British representative) held a council of war at Bar-sur-Aube (*C2*). Agreeing that Augereau menaced their rear, they dispatched Hesse-Homburg with the equivalent of two Austrian corps to reinforce Bubna. After much brawling, they further agreed to retire to Langres (*C1*), there to fight a defensive battle if Napoleon pursued them, or to resume their offensive if he turned on Blücher. Authorizing Blücher to operate as he saw fit, they transferred Bülow's and Winzingerode's corps to his command from Bernadotte's army. (Bernadotte's objections were squelched by a blunt British threat to drop him from their payroll.)

Blücher once more marched on Paris, with Yorck, Kleist, Kapzevitsch, and Sacken, ordering Bülow to advance through Soissons (*B3*) and Dammartin (*A2*); Winzingerode through Fismes (*B3*) and Meaux (*A2*). Langeron's corps, now approaching from Mayence, would cover his rear. Hoping to stimulate Schwarzenberg, he sent the latter a purposely false report (25 February) that Napoleon already was pursuing the Army of Silesia.

Napoleon was slow to believe that Blücher was again deliberately asking to be knocked on the head. When, on 26 February, Marmont reported being driven back to La Ferte-Gaucher (*B2*), Napoleon merely ordered Ney to cross at Arcis (*B2*) and attack Blücher's rear. The next morning, finally certain that Blücher was marching on Paris again, he sent Ney (with Victor, Arrighi, and Bordesoulle's detachment attached) in pursuit, and marched from Troyes (*B2*) with the remainder of his Guard. Macdonald was left 40,000 good troops to hold the line of the Aube River. Both he and Caulaincourt (who was still attempting to negotiate) were to spread the word that Napoleon would shortly be at Bar-sur-Aube. Clarke was once more vainly urged to provide a small bridge train; Augereau to concentrate his troops, and to either advance through Geneva toward Langres or join the main army via Dijon (*C1*).

Mortier had come boldly forward to join Marmont at La Ferte-Gaucher. On the 27th, under heavy pressure from Yorck and Kleist, the two marshals retired on Meaux, hoping to hold the north bank of the Marne. Finding that Sacken had reached Meaux ahead of them, they cleared him out. Blücher thereupon began crossing the Marne at La Ferte (*B2*), intending to turn their left flank. The marshals shifted north, defeating Kleist and Kapzevitsch around Lizy (*A2*) on the 28th. Furious, Blücher launched a coordinated attack across the Ourcq River on 1 March, but was repulsed with considerable loss.

Blücher planned to renew his attack on Mortier and Marmont the next morning but, hearing rumors of French troops near Sezanne, took the precaution of ordering his entire army north of the Marne. Late on 1 March, couriers from Tettenborn (whose Cossacks had been screening Blücher's left) warned that Napoleon was on his traces.

On 28 February, Blücher had received a letter from Schwarzenberg, confirming his command of Bülow's, Winzingerode's, and Weimar's corps, and directing Blücher to establish a mobile column between their armies to maintain liaison. Lacking sufficient troops to form such a column, Blücher replied that he would station Winzingerode at Rheims (*B3*) as a substitute. (Langeron's corps was still out of supporting distance, except for a small advance guard, while Weimar would have to remain in Holland until relieved by Bernadotte.) Blücher now ordered a withdrawal northward, intending to collect Bülow and Winzingerode, and offer battle on equal terms. His new subordinates, however, proved elusive. Instead of obeying his previous orders, they had concocted the scheme of taking Soissons in order to open a safe line of retreat for Blücher. Blücher's couriers to them, and theirs to Blücher, either went astray or were intercepted.

Napoleon reached La Ferte during 1 March, but could only snatch Blücher's last wagons and stragglers before the Marne bridges were cut. Once again, Napoleon's lack of a bridge train balked him; it took sixteen hours to repair the damaged La Ferte bridge. Early on the 3d, however, Napoleon's advance guard was north of Rocourt (*B3*). Just to the north, Blücher was leaving Oulchy-le-Chateau, still ignorant of Bülow's and Winzingerode's whereabouts. His army had had three night marches and three defeats in the last seventy-two hours, and no supplies for a week, beyond what could be seized from the countryside. Certain only that Bülow had been at Laon, Blücher decided to retire in that direction. Ahead of him was the flooded Aisne River, with good bridges at Vic, Soissons, and Berry (*all B3*). The first was too far west, the second in French hands, the third risky to use since Napoleon was obviously moving toward Fismes to cut between him and Rheims. Blücher had a good bridge train, but would need almost a day to bridge the Aisne and get his whole army across. His decision was to give his troops twelve hours' rest; send his trains, artillery, and part of his infantry through Berry; and cross the rest of his army by ponton bridges near Venizel (three miles east of Soissons). Messengers were dispatched broadcast in search of Bülow and Winzingerode.

On receipt of Blücher's deceptive report of 25 February, Alexander and Frederick William bullied Schwarzenberg into counterattacking toward Bar-sur-Aube, where Oudinot occupied an awkward position astride the river. Refusing to heed repeated warnings, Oudinot even ignored a premature, unsuccessful attack by Wrede on the 26th. Attacked by Wittgenstein the next day, he threw away the battle, leaving Leval's veteran division (*not shown*) alone without artillery on the east bank until Kellermann insubordinately rode to its rescue. That night Oudinot retired, his disheartened troops accusing him of treason. His withdrawal uncovered Macdonald, but the latter's advance guard managed to bluff Württemberg into halting.

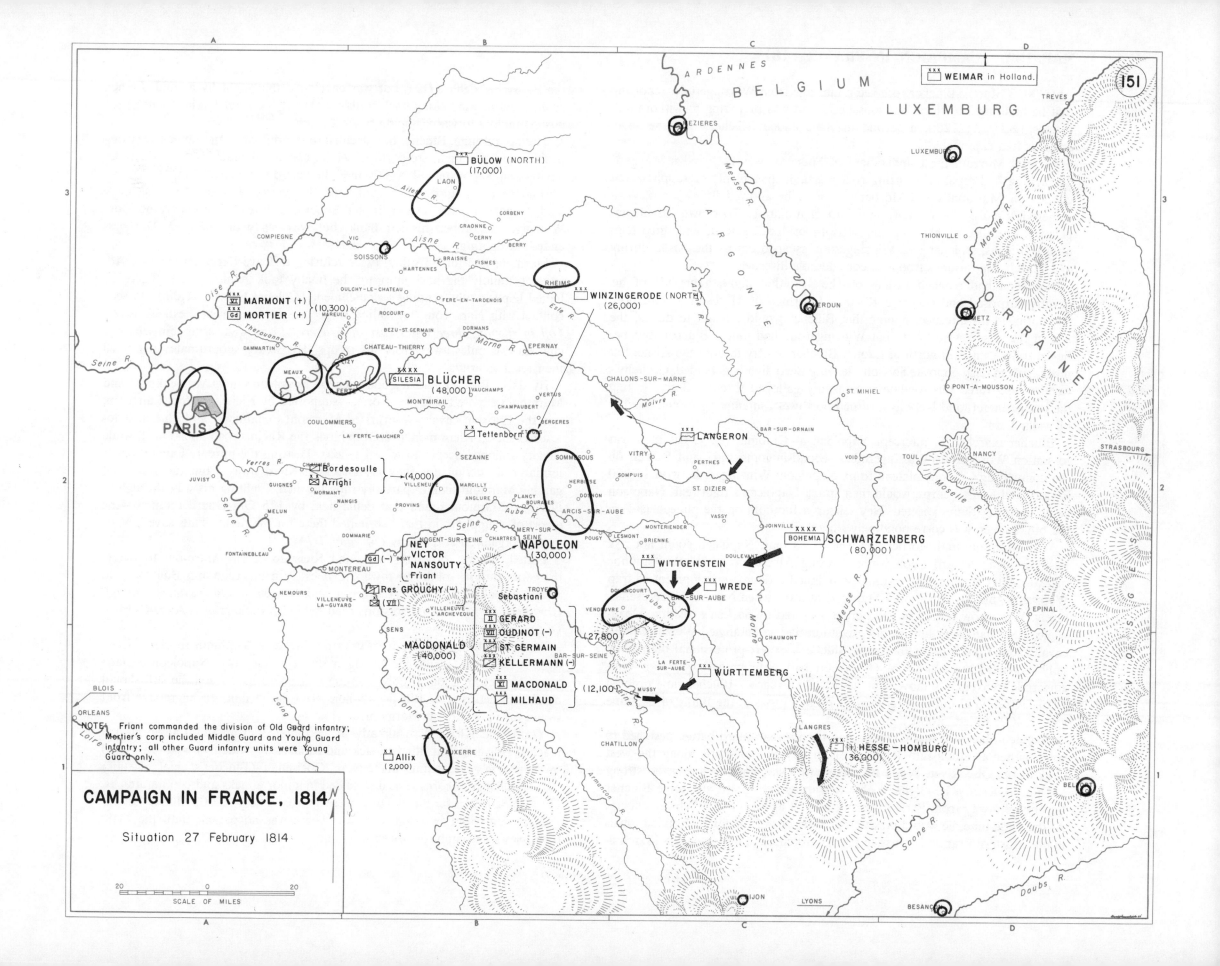

151

WEIMAR in Holland.

ARDENNES
BELGIUM
LUXEMBURG

BÜLOW (NORTH)
(17,000)

WINZINGERODE (NORTH)
(26,000)

MARMONT (+)
MORTIER (+)   (10,300)

BLÜCHER
(48,000)

LANGERON

Tettenborn

Bordesoulle
Arrighi   (4,000)

SCHWARZENBERG
(80,000)

NEY
VICTOR
NANSOUTY
Friant

NAPOLEON
(30,000)

Sebastiani

WITTGENSTEIN

WREDE

Res. GROUCHY (-)
(VII)

GERARD
OUDINOT (-)
ST. GERMAIN
KELLERMANN (-)

MACDONALD
(40,000)

(27,800)

WÜRTTEMBERG

MACDONALD
MILHAUD   (12,100)

HESSE-HOMBURG
(36,000)

NOTE: Friant commanded the division of Old Guard infantry;
Mortier's corp included Middle Guard and Young Guard
infantry; all other Guard infantry units were Young
Guard only.

Allix
(2,000)

CAMPAIGN IN FRANCE, 1814

Situation 27 February 1814

20   0   20
SCALE OF MILES

At 0700, 3 March, Blücher received a message from Winzingerode, reporting that he had failed to storm Soissons (*B3*) and was preparing to withdraw to Fismes (*B3*). At 1200, a second message ended Blücher's profane rage. Soissons had capitulated!

General Moreau, the commandant of Soissons, was lazy and a braggart. Though he had repulsed Winzingerode's assault, had plenty of supplies, and could hear Marmont's and Mortier's cannon, he allowed Bülow's and Winzingerode's emissaries to bully him into capitulating. To crown his incompetence, he failed to blow up the Soissons bridge. Using it, and three temporary bridges, Blücher and Winzingerode escaped across the Aisne during 4–5 March, the former's troops in considerable disorder.

Napoleon had reached Fismes on the 4th; that night, a brigade of his cavalry surprised and captured Rheims. Informed of Moreau's capitulation, he continued his advance, hoping that Blücher would attempt to defend the line of the Aisne. (He knew that Winzingerode had joined Blücher, but believed Bülow was still north of Laon.) Blücher did try to hold the Aisne, but mistakenly massed opposite Soissons, leaving Berry lightly defended. Grouchy's cavalry discovered this weakness; Nansouty galloped through Berry, seizing the bridge intact; and Napoleon turned northwest, attempting to cut Blücher off from Laon.

Blücher marched to intercept Napoleon at Craonne (*B3*). His plan was to station Woronzow (Winzingerode's second-in-command) and Sacken on the dominating Craonne plateau to fix Napoleon; Winzingerode, with 11,000 cavalry and Kleist's corps, would then attack Napoleon's right rear. Napoleon came up faster than expected, Ney seizing a foothold on the plateau late on the 6th. Sacken was correspondingly slow.

With Marmont and Mortier still well to his rear, Napoleon could not risk pushing ahead toward Laon while a strong Allied force held the Craonne plateau. After studying the terrain, he planned a double envelopment to trap Woronzow, but his attack on 7 March went awry when Ney advanced prematurely. Woronzow retired in good order, covered by Sacken's cavalry. Meanwhile, poor staff work and stupid execution had so entangled Winzingerode's cavalry and Kleist's corps that even Blücher's expert professional blasphemy only increased the confusion. (Napoleon had been prepared to trap Winzingerode's enveloping movement had it taken place.) Blücher now ordered a concentration at Laon (*inset map*). (French losses in the Battle of Craonne were 5,400; Allied, 5,000.)

Napoleon believed that Craonne had been a rear-guard battle, designed to cover either a retreat into Belgium or an advance on Paris along the west bank of the Oise River. While Blücher's army was now obviously too strong for him to destroy, he might be able to trap its rear guard and force Blücher far enough away from Paris to permit him to again turn on Schwarzenberg. At the same time, he would pick up the garrisons of the minor fortified towns in northeastern France. A Russian rear guard checked him late on 8 March at

the Etouvelles defile (*D2*), but was enveloped that night by a small French detachment moving along back trails and largely destroyed. The French then pushed rapidly forward, hoping to rush Laon.

Tired of running, Blücher had decided to stand there—an immensely strong position along a high, steep ridge, which concealed much of his army. Believing that Napoleon had 90,000 men, he feared some enveloping maneuver; Marmont's tardy appearance confirmed this worry. Finding Laon strongly held, Napoleon made several limited attacks to develop the enemy position. Winzingerode probed his left flank, but was easily discouraged. Darkness ended the fighting.

Marmont had turned sulky, twice refusing to leave Berry on the 8th. Advancing timidly the next morning, he finally took Athies (*D2*). There he halted haphazardly, sending a detachment (Colonel Fabvier, 1,000) to seek contact with Napoleon, but failing to secure the dangerous Festieux defile, (*off inset map, three miles east of Bruyeres*), and quartering himself in a chateau two miles away from his troops. His weary subordinates neglected their local security.

By dark, Blücher had a good idea of Napoleon's relative weakness and Marmont's exposed position. Yorck—supported by Kleist, Sacken, Langeron, and the Prussian cavalry—surprised Marmont's command and chased it toward Festieux. Kleist maneuvered to block the Rheims road ahead of it, while cavalry galloped deeper to seize Festieux. Hearing the uproar, Fabvier countermarched (*action not shown*), knocking Kleist away from the road and gaining Marmont time to partially rally his men. Fighting his way through to Festieux, Marmont found that defile held by 125 Old Guard infantry—the escort of a supply train that had halted there for the night! Thus saved, Marmont reorganized at Corbeny (*off map, D1*).

Elated, Blücher ordered Yorck and Kleist to pursue Marmont to Berry, thereafter turning southwest toward Fismes; Winzingerode and Bülow would attack Napoleon frontally; Langeron and Sacken would advance through Bruyeres (*D2*) to cut the Soissons road behind Napoleon at L'Ange-Gardien (*C1*).

At 0500, 10 March, two fugitives from Marmont's column reached Napoleon. A hasty reconnaissance having confirmed their story, Napoleon decided to remain before Laon. If only a strong rear guard held Laon, he still should be able to defeat it. If Blücher's whole army faced him, an aggressive front would take pressure off Marmont.

Yorck and Kleist were already at Festieux; Sacken and Langeron had reached Bruyeres. But Blücher, sick and exhausted, suddenly collapsed. Awed by Napoleon's threatening maneuvers, Gneisenau (Blücher's chief of staff) recalled these four corps. The day passed in minor attacks and counterattacks. (French casualties for the two days were approximately 6,000; Allied, 4,000.)

Napoleon withdrew after sundown. There was no pursuit until the 11th; then, Ney's first ambush cowed it.

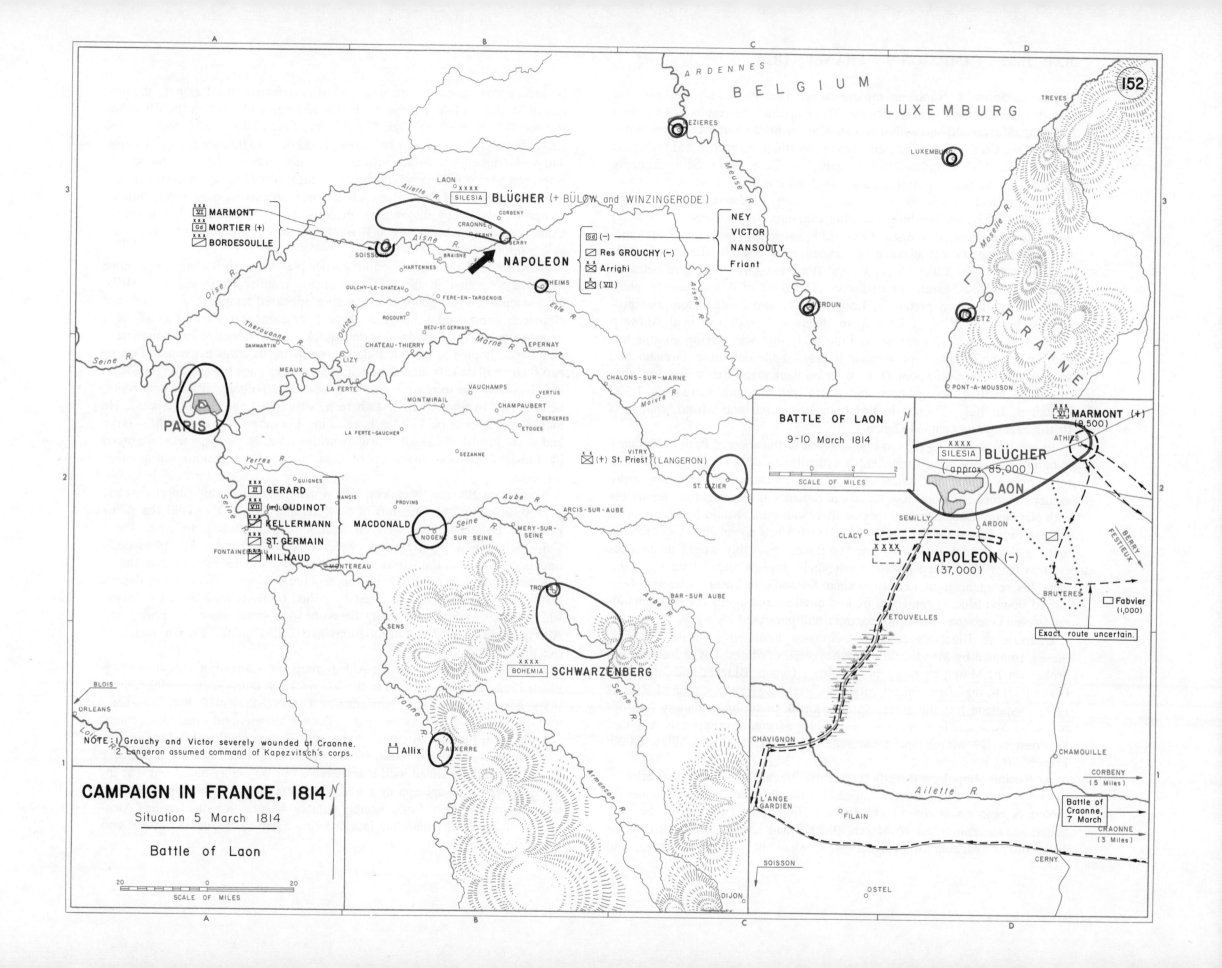

152

BELGIUM

LUXEMBURG

ARDENNES

TREVES

LAON XXXX
BLÜCHER (+ BÜLOW and WINZINGERODE)
SILESIA

XXX MARMONT
VI
Gd MORTIER (+)
BORDESOULLE

CORBENY
CRAONNE
CERNY
BERRY

SOISSO

Aisne R.
BRAISNE

HARTENNES

NEY
VICTOR
NANSOUTY
Friant

Gd (-)
Res GROUCHY (-)
Arrighi
(VII)

NAPOLEON

OULCHY-LE-CHATEAU

FERE-EN-TARDENOIS

HEIMS

VERDUN

METZ

LORRAINE

Moselle R.

Meuse R.

Oise R.

Therouanne R.

Ourcq R.

Marne R.

Esle R.

Aisne R.

LUXEMBURG

Seine R.

DAMMARTIN

ROCOURT

BEZU-ST-GERMAIN

CHATEAU-THIERRY

LIZY

EPERNAY

PONT-A-MOUSSON

MEAUX

LA FERTE

MONTMIRAIL

VAUCHAMPS

VERTUS

CHALONS-SUR-MARNE

Moivre R.

PARIS

LA FERTE-GAUCHER

CHAMPAUBERT

BERGERES

ETOGES

SEZANNE

XX (+) St. PRIEST (LANGERON)

VITRY
(LANGERON)

ST. DIZIER

BATTLE OF LAON
9-10 March 1814

SCALE OF MILES

XXX MARMONT (+)
VI (9,500)

ATHIES

XXXX BLÜCHER
SILESIA (approx. 85,000)

LAON

SEMILLY

ARDON

BERRY
FESTIEUX

GUIGNES

XXX GERARD
II
XXX OUDINOT
(-) VII
KELLERMANN
XXX ST. GERMAIN
MILHAUD

BANGIS

PROVINS

NOGENT
SUR SEINE

MERY-SUR-SEINE

ARCIS-SUR-AUBE

Aube R.

CLACY

XXXX NAPOLEON (-)
(37,000)

BRUYERES

Fabvier
(1,000)

Exact route uncertain.

MACDONALD

NOGEN

Seine R.

Seine R.

FONTAINEBLEAU

MONTEREAU

SENS

TROYES

BAR-SUR-AUBE

Aube R.

ETOUVELLES

BLOIS

ORLEANS

Loire R.

NOTE: 1. Grouchy and Victor severely wounded at Craonne.
2. Langeron assumed command of Kapezvitsch's corps.

XX Allix

AUXERRE

Yonne R.

XXXX SCHWARZENBERG
BOHEMIA

Seine R.

Armancon R.

CHAVIGNON

CHAMOUILLE

CAMPAIGN IN FRANCE, 1814

Situation 5 March 1814

Battle of Laon

SCALE OF MILES
20   0   20

L'ANGE GARDIEN

FILAIN

Ailette R.

CORBENY
(5 Miles)

Battle of Craonne,
7 March

CRAONNE
(3 Miles)

SOISSON

OSTEL

DIJON

CERNY

Halting at Soissons, Napoleon rapidly reorganized his little force. Most of his army commanders were in trouble. To compound the results of Oudinot's fumbling, Macdonald had withdrawn (6 March) his demoralized troops north of the Seine. On the 14th, much encouraged by Blücher's report that Napoleon "had sacrificed what remained of his army" at Laon (*B3*), Schwarzenberg broke across the Seine against an uninspired defense.

Augereau had complained away his opportunity to destroy Bubna. At the appearance of Hesse-Homburg's leading elements, he retreated (9 March) hastily toward Lyons (*see Map, 145a, C2*). Suchet still waited in Catalonia. Wellington's methodical advance had forced Soult back on Toulouse (*B1*); Bayonne (*A1*) was under blockade; and Bordeaux (*B1*) had been betrayed to the English (12 March) by its mayor. The Duke of Angouleme (nephew to the exiled Bourbon pretender, Louis XVIII) had landed there and proclaimed his uncle King of France. In Belgium, Carnot still held Antwerp (*C3*); Maison had had to retire on Lille (*C3*), but was waging an able hit-and-run campaign that kept Weimar largely on the defensive. Graham had broken into Bergen-op-Zoom (*C3*) by a brilliant night attack, but lost control of his men in the darkness, and was driven out with more than 2,500 casualties. In Italy, Eugene baffled both Bellegarde and Murat, though a British expedition occupied Genoa.

Joseph was neglecting the too-long-delayed fortification of Paris (*this map*) to babble for peace at any price. Diplomatically, the Allies had tightened their ranks by the Treaty of Chaumont (1 March), Castlereagh promising more money in return for more manpower and a pledge not to negotiate separately with Napoleon. Caulaincourt reported that "sacrifices" would be necessary to secure peace. From the previously mentioned Allied documents, captured before Leipzig, Napoleon knew these "sacrifices" probably would include his eviction from the French throne. Fortunately, he was allowed time to complete his reorganization and strengthen Soisson's defenses. Schwarzenberg moved slowly; Blücher remained ill, and quarrels among his corps commanders (whom Gneisenau could not control) half-paralyzed his army.

Unaware of Blücher's collapse, Napoleon hesitated to leave Soissons, though troubled by Macdonald's and Augereau's failures. His indecision was broken on 12 March by news that St.-Priest (whom Blücher had left at St.-Dizier [*C2*] to maintain contact with Schwarzenberg) had recaptured Rheims (*B3*). Napoleon had the great captain's knack of turning calamity into opportunity. Sweeping forty miles across Blücher's front, he completely surprised St.-Priest on 13 March and recovered Rheims. (Casualties: Allies, 6,000; French, 700.)

At Rheims, Napoleon directly threatened Blücher's left flank and Schwarzenberg's right. French morale rallied. To the shocked Allies, it seemed as though Napoleon was able to whistle fresh armies out of the earth. The news halted Schwarzenberg on 16 March. Blücher had lurched southward on the 13th, Bülow reaching Compiegne (*A3*), which he found too strong, and

Sacken approaching Soissons, where Mortier defeated him. Learning the next day of St.-Priest's fate, Blücher withdrew to Laon and went on the defensive, considerably heckled by French partisans. Bernadotte finally had reached Liege, but was refusing to enter France. (He hoped to become King of France, and so did not wish to overly irritate his possible future subjects. Also, should Napoleon finally win, he would be excellently placed to again turn his coat and recover Finland from Russia.) Napoleon seems to have subtly further compromised him by dispatching an emissary to "recall him to his duty." Consequently, Blücher regarded Bernadotte more as a threat to his rear than as a reinforcement.

At Rheims, Napoleon revived his earlier plan to crush Blücher, then move eastward to gather in the garrisons of his frontier fortresses, then strike Schwarzenberg's rear. Both enemy armies appeared temporarily stunned, but Napoleon considered Schwarzenberg dangerously near Paris. Instead of a major move eastward, he decided on a quick, limited offensive into Schwarzenberg's rear, hoping to catch and destroy some of his corps piecemeal. One or two such small defeats should send Schwarzenberg back toward Langres, leaving Napoleon free to move boldly into Lorraine. To gain initial elbow room, he sent Ney to seize Chalons (where he captured large supply depots). He himself left Rheims on 17 March, reaching Epernay (*B2*) that night. Clarke had at last furnished a small, unwieldy bridge train. Ney's corps was reinforced by Janssens' division, made up of detachments from various northeastern fortresses.

To contain Blücher, Napoleon left Mortier and Marmont (approximately 21,500, including the garrisons of Soissons and Rheims) to hold the Aisne River. If dislodged, they were to fight a delaying action to cover Paris. Caulaincourt now reported that peace could be secured only by unconditional acceptance of the Allied terms. Belatedly, Napoleon authorized him to offer enough concessions to keep the negotiations open. His courier, despite his diplomatic status, was detained by Allied outposts until the 21st. Meanwhile, on 19 March, with many breast-beating protestations of purity, the Allies had broken off the negotiations and called on the French nation to overthrow Napoleon.

Napoleon's approach sent the Allied command—already jittery over exaggerated reports of mass risings in the Vosges Mountains—into mental convulsions. Alexander panicked. Schwarzenberg reportedly issued three contradictory orders on the 16th alone, then collected his wits and ordered a general concentration between Arcis-sur-Aube and Troyes (*both B2*). Late on the 17th, however, he began redistributing his army to meet a possible offensive by Macdonald! He ended with it scattered along an eighty-mile front—as inviting a target as Napoleon ever had. Schwarzenberg himself then collapsed with an attack of gout. In this doubly vulnerable condition, the terrified Alexander managed to frighten him into ordering a general retreat on Troyes and Bar-sur-Aube.

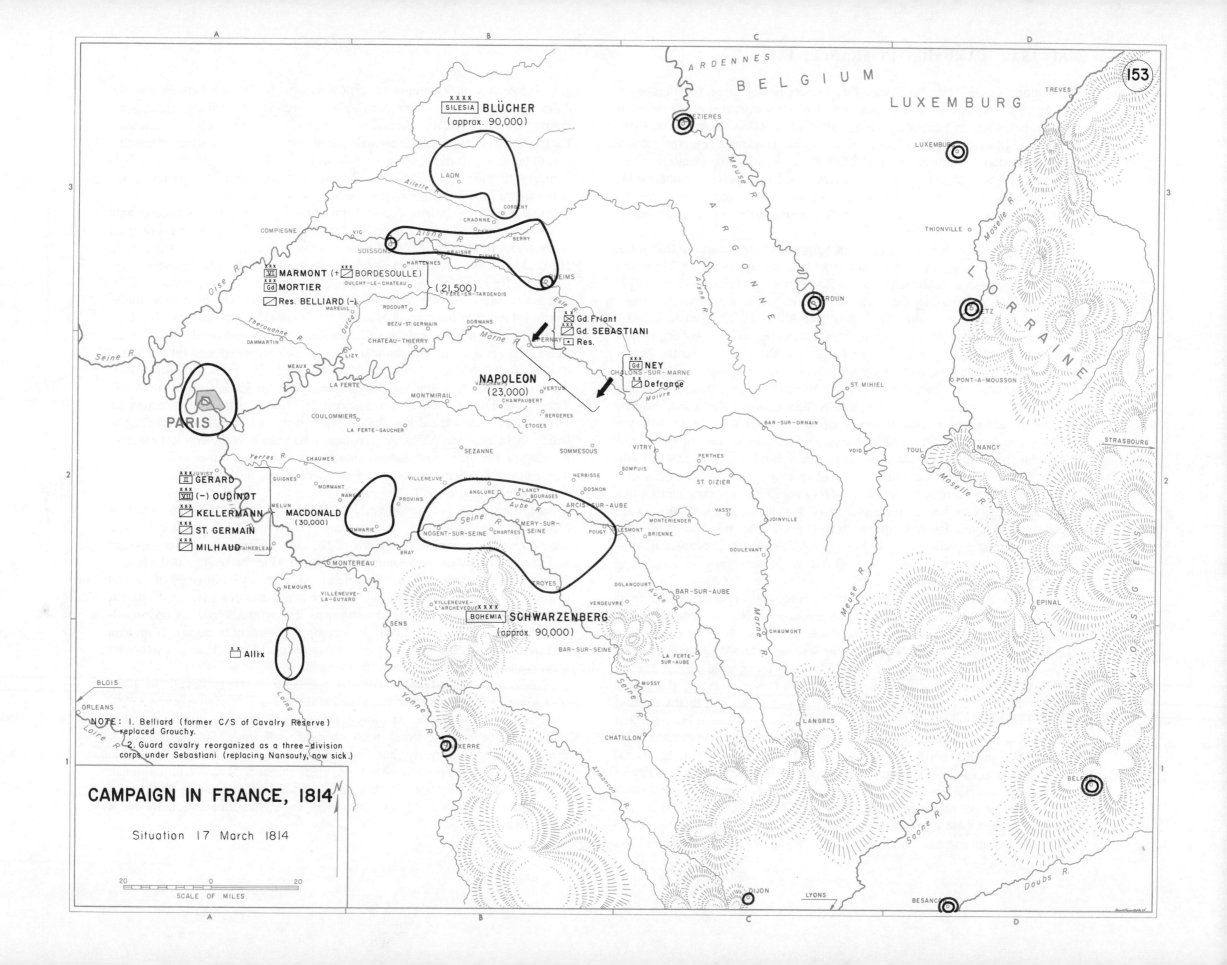

153

BELGIUM   LUXEMBURG

XXXX
SILESIA BLÜCHER
(approx. 90,000)

ARDENNES

LAON
CORBENY
CRAONNE
COMPIEGNE   VIC
Ailette R.
Aisne R.
SOISSONS   BRAISNE FISMES
HARTENNES
XXX
VI MARMONT (+ BORDESOULLE)
XXX
Gd MORTIER
Res. BELLIARD (-)
OULCHY-LE-CHATEAU
(21,500)
FERE-EN-TARDENOIS
ROCOURT
MAREUIL
BEZU-ST.GERMAIN   DORMANS
Gd. Friant
Gd. SEBASTIANI
Res.
XXX
Gd NEY
CHALONS-SUR-MARNE
Defrance

THERVANNE R.
DAMMARTIN
LIZY
CHATEAU-THIERRY
Marne R.
EPERNAY
VANDOEUVRE
VERTUS
NAPOLEON
(23,000)
CHAMPAUBERT
BERGERES
ETOGES

MEAUX
LA FERTE
MONTMIRAIL
COULOMMIERS
LA FERTE-GAUCHER
SEZANNE

PARIS

ARGONNE

LUXEMBURG
TREVES
THIONVILLE
Moselle R.
PONT-A-MOUSSON
ST. MIHIEL
BAR-SUR-ORNAIN
VOID
TOUL
STRASBOURG
NANCY
Moselle R.
LORRAINE

VERDUN
Meuse R.

XXXX Juvisy
II GERARD
XXXX
VII (-) OUDINOT
KELLERMANN   MACDONALD
XXX (30,000)
ST. GERMAIN
XXX
MILHAUD
FONTAINEBLEAU

Yerres R.
GUIGNES
MORMANT
NANGIS
PROVINS
MELUN
POMMARIE
MONTEREAU
BRAY
NEMOURS
VILLENEUVE-
LA-GUYARD
SENS

VILLENEUVE
ANGLURE
NOGENT-SUR-SEINE   CHARTRES
PLANCY
BOURAGES
Aube R.
ARCIS-SUR-AUBE
MERY-SUR-SEINE
POUGY
LESMONT
BRIENNE
TROYES
Seine R.
VILLENEUVE-
L'ARCHEVEQUE   XXXX
BOHEMIA SCHWARZENBERG
(approx. 90,000)

Esle
Aisne R.
Moivre
VITRY
HERBISSE
DOSNON
SOMMESOUS
SOMPUIS
ST. DIZIER
PERTHES
VASSY
MONTIERENDER
DOLANCOURT
Aube R.
BAR-SUR-AUBE
DOULEVANT
JOINVILLE
Marne R.
CHAUMONT
LA FERTE-
SUR-AUBE
BAR-SUR-SEINE
MUSSY
Seine R.
DOLANCOURT
VENDEUVRE

XX
Allix

BLOIS
ORLEANS
NOTE: 1. Belliard (former C/S of Cavalry Reserve)
replaced Grouchy.
2. Guard cavalry reorganized as a three-division
corps under Sebastiani (replacing Nansouty, now sick.)

Loire R.
Loing R.
Yonne R.
Armancon R.
AUXERRE

CAMPAIGN IN FRANCE, 1814

Situation 17 March 1814

20   0   20
SCALE OF MILES

CHATILLON
LANGRES
Meuse R.
Seine R.
Armancon R.
Saone R.
EPINAL
VOSGES
BELFORT
DIJON   LYONS   BESANCON
Doubs R.

Advancing through Mery-sur-Seine (*B2*) (where he destroyed Württemberg's rear guard), Napoleon found indications of a hasty retreat everywhere, and reverted to his former plan of marching eastward to collect his garrisons. Confident that Blücher would attempt no more independent offensives against Paris, he ordered Marmont and Mortier to rejoin him via Chalons. Contemptuous of Schwarzenberg, he himself marched on Arcis-sur-Aube (*B2*), Ney and Sebastiani moving south of the Aube. Paris would have to defend itself; he already had sent Joseph detailed instructions for its evacuation, should that become necessary.

Napoleon was overly contemptuous of Schwarzenberg. Learning that some French troops were south of the Aube, the Austrian advanced on Mery-sur-Seine, bringing on a haphazard clash (20 March) around Arcis-sur-Aube. Here Ney and Sebastiani—led with cold tactical savagery by Napoleon—whipped off twice their numbers. (Casualties: Allies, 2,500; French, 1,700.) Concluding that Napoleon was stronger than reported, Schwarzenberg retired that night, concentrating 80,000 men for a defensive-offensive battle. Napoleon first thought that he had encountered an unusually stubborn rear guard. Moving cautiously southward on 21 March to develop the situation, he found Schwarzenberg too strong to attack, and withdrew across the Aube, covered by a smart rear-guard action. He then continued toward Vitry (*C2*). Schwarzenburg attempted to follow (22 March), was repulsed, and relapsed into confusion. Southward, Augereau had managed (possibly deliberately) to lose Lyons. Northward, Blücher had moved out, seeking to rejoin Schwarzenberg, and collided with Marmont near Fismes (*B3*) on 17 March. Fearing that this was another drive on Paris, Marmont begged Mortier for support. Mortier reluctantly evacuated Rheims and marched west. The two marshals then received Napoleon's order to rejoin him. The Allies having reoccupied Rheims after Mortier's departure, the only suitable route remaining was the long detour through Chateau-Thierry.

Vitry now had a strong Russian garrison. Napoleon bypassed it, halting at St.-Dizier (*C2*), where he raided Schwarzenberg's communications while waiting for Macdonald, who—as usual—was a day late. Napoleon himself—the fond, middle-aged husband of a young wife—wrote Maria Louisa an uncoded letter, describing his latest plan. This was intercepted on 22 March, with corroborating dispatches, by Allied cavalry. So informed, the Allied commanders first contemplated a quick retreat southward, but finally decided to join Blücher, open up a new line of communication through Holland, and then seek a decisive battle between Vitry and Metz. Schwarzenberg accordingly began moving northward. During the night of 23–24 March, several dispatches from Paris to Napoleon were captured. These pictured that city as undefended and frightened; one stated that many of Napoleon's most influential domestic enemies were there. Alexander (who understood the uses of treason) studied these dispatches, then browbeat Schwarzenberg into ordering both Allied armies against Paris by way of Meaux. Winzingerode would fol-

low Napoleon with a column of light troops to make him believe that the Allies were still pursuing him. Moving westward, Schwarzenberg struck Marmont and Mortier, driving them through Fere-Champenoise (*B2*) in disorder. Pacthod's and Amey's tiny National Guard divisions, which were attempting to join the marshals there, were overwhelmed after an epic fight. The marshals withdrew through Provins to Paris. Rallying detachments and fugitives, Compans made a fighting withdrawal from Meaux.

At St.-Dizier, Napoleon found Schwarzenberg's movements increasingly puzzling. On the 26th, he routed Winzingerode, who had probed south from Vitry, and learned that the Allies were marching on Paris. Here was the crisis. He could hardly outstrip the Allies' advance on Paris, but he now could maneuver freely in their rear. The Thionville, Metz (*both D3*), Verdun (*C3*), and Strasbourg (*off map, D2*) garrisons were ready to join him; local forces controlled much of the Argonne, Ardennes (*both C3*), and Vosges (*D1–D2*) regions. Apparently, Napoleon still intended to move eastward, but his war-weary staff and corps commanders instinctively rebelled against the idea. Caulaincourt, radiating defeatism, had rejoined the French headquarters. Early on 28 March, Napoleon therefore marched for Paris via Bar-sur-Aube, Troyes, and Fontainebleau. At Doulevant (*C2*), an agent sent by Postmaster General Lavalette warned him that disloyal elements in Paris were plotting to betray that city to the Allies. At Troyes, on 30 March, Napoleon left Berthier to bring on the army, and dashed ahead with a small group of officers. That night, at a relay point eleven miles south of Paris, he learned that the city was in Allied hands.

Joseph had done practically nothing to organize Paris for defense until 29 March. At about 0400 the next morning, the Allies had begun a piecemeal attack against the northern outskirts of the city. Shortly after noon—though he knew that Napoleon was coming and that the Allies had not gained a foot—Joseph sneaked away, leaving the defense without any semblance of central control. After determined fighting, Mortier and Marmont gave up Paris (at 0200 on 31 March), and retired southward. Talleyrand seized his opportunities—charming Alexander, inventing a rump government to declare Napoleon dethroned, convincing Marmont that the latter could save France by turning traitor, and planning Napoleon's assassination.

Napoleon massed 60,000 troops at Fontainebleau. There were some 145,-000 Allies in Paris, but their communications were extremely sketchy. Paris itself was ready to explode. At Blois (*off map, A1*), the transplanted Imperial government began functioning with surprising efficiency. Soldiers and regimental officers stood ready, but the marshals and senior generals wanted a quick peace. Ney, Lefebvre, Moncey, Oudinot, and Macdonald mutinied. Marmont betrayed his corps to the Allies. After a vain effort to abdicate in favor of his three-year-old son, Napoleon abdicated unconditionally on 6 April, 1814.

154

ARDENNES

BELGIUM

LUXEMBURG

TREVES

LUXEMBURG

ZIERES

LAON

CORBENY

CRAONNE

CERNY

BERRY

BÜLOW

COMPIEGNE

VIC

SOISSO

BRAISNE

FISMES

RHEIMS

Aisne R.

Meuse R.

Moselle R.

THIONVILLE

Durutte (4,000)

LORRAINE

HARTENNES

OULCHY-LE-CHATEAU

FERE-EN-TAR

SILESIA BLÜCHER

Esle R.

VERDUN

METZ

MAREUIL

ROCOURT

BEZU-ST-GERMAIN

DORMANS

YORCK

KLEIST

CHATEAU-TH

EPERNAY

Marne R.

CHALONS-SUR-MARNE

ST. MIHIEL

Therouanne R.

DAMMARTIN

LIZY

LA FERTE

MEAU

VAUCHAMPS

VERTUS

R.

PONT-A-MOUSSON

Seine R.

Oise R.

MONTMIRAIL

Pacthod (1,300)

Amey

Moivre

BOHEMIA SCHWARZENBERG

WINZINGERODE

BAR-SUR-ORNAIN

Duvigneau

PARIS

COULOMMIERS

LA FERTE-GAUCHER

ETOGES

FERE-CHAMPENOISE

SOMMEPUIS

TRY

MACDONALD (-)

MILHAUD

VOID

TOUL

NANCY

STRASBOURG

Yerres R.

CHAUMES

SEZANNE

Compans (2,000)

MARMONT

MORTIER

Res (-) BELLIARD

HERBISSE

SOMPUIS

(16,600)

ST. DIZIER

NAPOLEON

JUVISY

GUIGNES

MORMANT

VILLENEUVE

MARGILLY

ANGLURE

BOURAGES

ARCIS-SUR-AUBE

ASSY

GERARD

NEY

Moselle R.

Seine R.

MELUN

NANGIS

PROVINS

Souham

Aube R.

MONTERIENDER

JOINVILLE

OUDINOT

Gd. Friant

DOMMARIE

NOGENT-SUR-SEINE

MERY-SUR-SEINE

POUGY

LESMONT

BRIENNE

DOULE VANT

ST. GERMAIN

TRELLIARD

Gd. SEBASTIANI

Defrance

Berckheim

Res.

FONTAINEBLEAU

CHARTRES

MONTEREAU

BRAY

TROYES

DOLANCOURT

VENDEUVRE

BAR-SUR-AUBE

Meuse R.

EPINAL

VOSGES

NEMOURS

VILLENEUVE-LA-GUYARD

VILLENEUVE-L'ARCHEVEQUE

Aube R.

CHAUMONT

SENS

Allix

Loing R.

Yonne R.

BAR-SUR-SEINE

Seine R.

LA FERTE-SUR-AUBE

MUSSY

Marne R.

LANGRES

Soone R.

BELF

NOTE: 1. Trelliard had replaced Kellermann.

2. Berckheim was a recently organized provisional unit.

AUXERRE

CHATILLON

BLOIS

ORLEANS

Loire R.

CAMPAIGN IN FRANCE, 1814

Armencon R.

Doubs R.

Situation 25 March 1814

Austrians had driven Augereau from Lyons, 20 March.

DIJON

LYONS

BESANC

20   0   20

SCALE OF MILES

Trafalgar (1805) permanently crippled the Spanish Navy, but the French soon recovered. Even as the English maneuvered to intercept Villeneuve, the Rochefort squadron put to sea in a long, destructive raid. Napoleon strengthened his Brest and Rochefort fleets, rebuilt the Toulon fleet, and began constructing a new one at Antwerp. Antwerp—a "pistol pointed at the heart of England"—was an ideal base for a cross-channel attack. The Boulogne flotilla was kept up until 1811; Napoleon also made considerable efforts to develop an effective Italian Navy, but without success.

Moreover, he sensed some of the basic weaknesses of the French naval service. He instituted permanently assigned ships' crews, and insisted on strict discipline and practical training for officers and men alike. Very little escaped his notice: He urged the use of the latest types of naval artillery; after the American frigate victories in 1812, he ordered the building of heavier frigates, similar to the American type. To develop senior naval officers capable of handling complex, unwieldy ships of the line in storm and battle, he was willing to risk the loss of ships on commerce-raiding cruises. By 1806, however, ships of the line had proved unsuitable for such operations. Frigates and lighter warships continued active, with varying success, but it took years for their commanders to gain the skills necessary to handle larger ships.

After Trafalgar, England continued its traditional policy of "subsidizing" (hiring) various Continental powers to do the land fighting, while her navy eliminated the enemy's merchant fleet and seized his colonies. But such operations, plus the protection of British shipping against enemy raiders, required a world-wide system of naval bases. Bases required units of the British Army for garrisons, as did captured enemy colonies. Many of these areas were horribly unhealthy. Furthermore, Trafalgar had left England with excess naval power. This, coupled with naval officers' appetites for prize money, led her into odd adventures, like the two unsuccessful expeditions against Buenos Aires in 1806 and 1807.

So weakened, the British Army was unable to concentrate sufficient forces for effective intervention on the Continent. (Wellington, in Spain, was the only exception, and his operations were a "near-run thing" for years.) Napoleon could campaign deep into Spain, Austria, and Russia, leaving his coasts lightly garrisoned by second-line troops, without much worry over a British invasion.

English naval power failed completely against the Turks at the Dardanelles in 1807. In 1808, the fleet and expeditionary force sent to help Sweden against Russian aggression proved powerless to prevent the Russian conquest of Finland. A British amphibious attack during 1807 did succeed in seizing the Danish fleet and occupying Heligoland Island as a base for English smugglers. But the Royal Navy's efficiency fell off from lack of enemy warships to fight— a factor that may have contributed to American naval victories in 1812. American privateers brought new troubles, which the handful of American frigates and sloops-of-war compounded.

Naval support was vital to Wellington's operations in Spain, yet it was late 1813 before he could secure proper naval cooperation in choking off French coastal shipping and protecting his supply ships from enemy privateers. One brilliant British joint operation in this theater was the crossing of the Adour River (southern France, 1814), when naval launches provided a bridge for Wellington's troops. Elsewhere, the British Navy prevented a French invasion of Sicily, though it failed to stop Murat's recovery of Capri by a sudden amphibious assault. In the Baltic, British naval operations had only the slightest effect on Napoleon's invasion of Russia, but British naval bombardments later had a major part in forcing the surrender of Danzig.

The other major mission of the British Navy was the blockade of Continental Europe, to prevent foreign trade with the Napoleonic empire. Napoleon replied by forbidding other nations to trade with England. It is impossible to state how badly this form of warfare hurt either nation. The British found new markets, while France was a remarkably self-sufficient nation which Napoleon made even more so. (For example, beet sugar replaced cane sugar.) It did break up the world's established trade systems, contributed greatly to French unpopularity throughout Europe, and embroiled England with every neutral nation that had a merchant marine.

British enforcement of this blockade was normally high-handed, frequently arrogant, and often stupid. (The French undoubtedly would have done as much had they been in England's place.) It involved constant impressment of citizens of neutral states into the primitively managed British Navy, violation of these states' territorial waters, and seizure of their shipping, frequently on the flimsiest of excuses. Such conduct contributed mightily to starting the War of 1812, which, except for the military incompetence of the Jefferson and Madison administrations, might well have cost England Canada.

In summation, the British Navy definitely kept Napoleon from invading England. And, so long as England remained unconquered, Napoleon's empire remained under siege. The Royal Navy easily kept control of the seas, but its effect upon the basically self-sufficient Napoleonic empire was limited to slow attrition. It was only after Napoleon overextended himself, from Portugal to Moscow, that he became vulnerable. Naval proponents maintain that this overextension was caused by his need to defeat England, and that it therefore was a direct result of British sea power. This would seem to be at least an oversimplification, the major cause of this expansion probably being Napoleon's burgeoning overconfidence.

Napoleon always overestimated the capabilities of his warships and sailors. Probably his worst handicap was his complete noncomprehension of the defeatist spirit that gripped his senior naval officers. He built a splendid navy, but could give it neither competent leaders nor a tradition of victory.

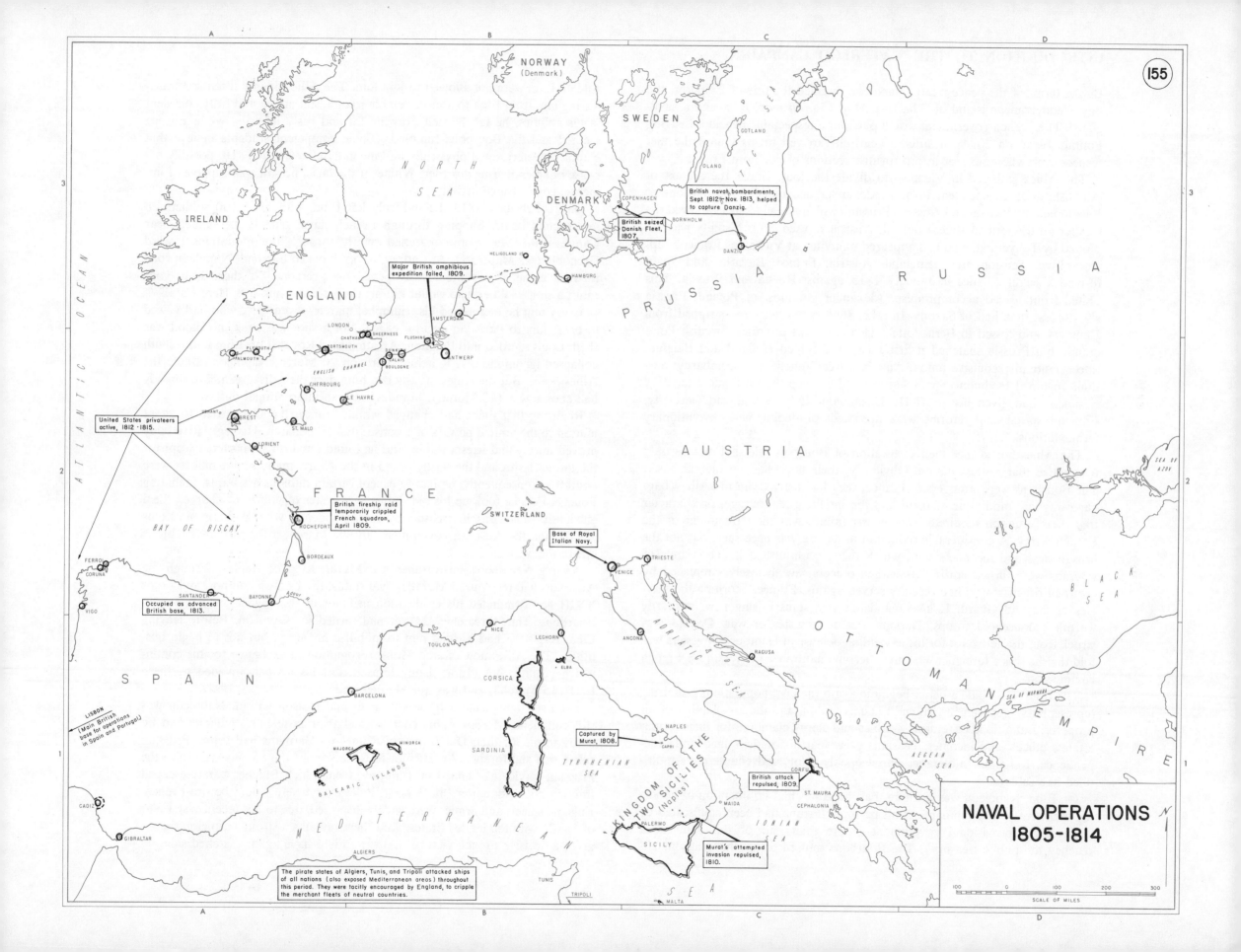

155

NORWAY
(Denmark)

SWEDEN

NORTH
SEA

DENMARK

COPENHAGEN

GOTLAND

OLAND

BORNHOLM

British naval bombardments,
Sept. 1812 – Nov. 1813, helped
to capture Danzig.

British seized
Danish Fleet,
1807.

DANZIG

PRUSSIA

RUSSIA

IRELAND

HELIGOLAND IS.

HAMBURG

ENGLAND

Major British amphibious
expedition failed, 1809.

LONDON
CHATHAM
SHEERNESS
PORTSMOUTH
DUNKIRK
CALAIS
BOULOGNE

AMSTERDAM

FLUSHING

ANTWERP

PLYMOUTH
FALMOUTH

CHERBOURG

LE HAVRE

United States privateers
active, 1812 - 1815.

USHANT
BREST

ST. MALO

FRANCE

AUSTRIA

SEA OF
AZOV

L'ORIENT

British fireship raid
temporarily crippled
French squadron,
April 1809.

SWITZERLAND

Base of Royal
Italian Navy.

BAY OF BISCAY

ROCHEFORT

BORDEAUX

TRIESTE

VENICE

BLACK
SEA

FERRO
CORUNA

SANTANDER

BAYONNE

Adour R.

OTTOMAN

SEA OF MARMARA

VIGO

Occupied as advanced
British base, 1813.

NICE

LEGHORN

ANCONA

ADRIATIC

SEA

RAGUSA

SPAIN

BARCELONA

TOULON

CORSICA

ELBA

TYRRHENIAN
SEA

SARDINIA

NAPLES

Captured by
Murat, 1808.

CAPRI

KINGDOM OF THE
TWO SICILIES
(Naples)

CORFU

British attack
repulsed, 1809.

ST. MAURA

CEPHALONIA

AEGEAN

SEA

EMPIRE

IONIAN

SEA

LISBON
(Main British
base for operations
in Spain and Portugal)

CADIZ

MAJORCA

MINORCA

BALEARIC ISLANDS

MEDITERRANEAN

MAIDA

PALERMO

SICILY

Murat's attempted
invasion repulsed,
1810.

GIBRALTAR

ALGIERS

The pirate states of Algiers, Tunis, and Tripoli attacked ships
of all nations (also exposed Mediterranean areas) throughout
this period. They were tacitly encouraged by England, to cripple
the merchant fleets of neutral countries.

SEA

TUNIS

TRIPOLI

MALTA

NAVAL OPERATIONS
1805-1814

N

100   0   100   200   300

SCALE OF MILES

INTRODUCTION TO THE WATERLOO CAMPAIGN

By the terms of the peace treaty, Napoleon retained the title of Emperor, the tiny Mediterranean island of Elba (*see Map 156, off map, B1*), and a small guard. The French government would pay him a respectable pension. Leaving Fontainebleau on 20 April, after a heartfelt farewell to his Guard, he met respect everywhere, except in pro-royalist sections of southern France.

The Allies gathered in Vienna—to divide the loot. Under the pretext of establishing an independent Poland, Alexander demanded those portions of Poland held by Prussia and Austria. Prussia (which already had swallowed the smaller north German states) agreed; Austria refused. This disunity was exploited by Tallyerand, who had appeared uninvited at Vienna as France's representative. Tension grew; England, Austria, France, Bavaria, and Spain formed a secret alliance in January 1815 against Russia and Prussia. This united front forced a compromise. Alexander got most of Poland, Prussia slightly less than half of Saxony. In other shuffles, Norway was stripped from Denmark and tossed to Bernadotte. (Denmark was promised Swedish Pomerania, but Prussia snatched it first.) England forced Holland and Belgium into a mutually repulsive union; Austria seized Venetia and Lombardy; Sardinia regained Piedmont. Spain was allowed to keep the Portuguese territory Napoleon had given her in 1801. Throughout Italy, Spain, and Germany, French-inspired civil reforms were uprooted, producing new revolutionary fermentations.

The Allies hoped that their restoration of Bourbon rule in France would tranquilize that restless nation. Obviously, their hope had no factual basis: The Bourbons were strangers to France; they had arrived "in the Allies' baggage wagons"; and none of them had the intelligence, courage, or character that their situation required. Their worst failure was their treatment of the French Army. A considerable reduction in its size was necessary, but not the brusqueness and meanness with which they accomplished it. Thousands of veterans were turned adrift. Discharged officers saw themselves replaced by returned royalists who had recently served against France. Scorning the services of the Old Guard, Louis squandered vast sums raising new, militarily worthless household troops. Dupont became minister of war. Davout was struck from the active list for his unyielding defense of Hamburg; Massena was told that he was a foreigner who must become naturalized to retain his French commission.

The Bourbons made a better beginning with the civil population, promising representative government, an end to conscription, and the inviolability of all property. But a flood of returning nobles and clergy clamored for their former estates, offices, and incomes. Peasants grew fearful for their land and independence. Religious intolerance flared openly. Plots and counterplots multiplied like rabbits.

On Elba, Napoleon was learning that the Allies had no intention of honoring their treaty. The remnants of his personal fortune had been confiscated by Talleyrand's provisional government (more than half of this sum never reached the public treasury). The Bourbons refused to pay his pension. His wife and son were not allowed to join him. The Allies openly discussed transferring him from Elba to a more remote island. Still active and fully confident in his abilities, he felt himself growing fat and rusty in exile, while Europe seethed and the Bourbons fumbled. (Some competent students believe that Napoleon deteriorated physically and mentally after about 1810, possibly because of an endocrine disorder. Whatever the facts, he still was capable of immense, concentrated activity.)

On 26 February 1815, he suddenly left Elba, with his 1,100 soldiers on seven small boats. Slipping through French naval patrols, he landed near Cannes on 1 March and marched swiftly through the mountains toward Grenoble (*see Map 156*). At Laffrey, troops blocked his road. Napoleon rode forward alone, dismounted, and opened his overcoat. "If there is in your ranks a single soldier who would kill his Emperor, let him fire. Here I am!"

Every unit he met joined his triumphal march—even Ney, who had vowed to bring him to Paris "in an iron cage." Not a shot was fired, no blood was shed. Louis scuttled into Belgium. An attempted Royalist uprising in the south collapsed ignominiously. Reaching Paris on 20 March, Napoleon offered the Allies peace. But the Allies, hastily patching over their disagreements, already had chosen war (13 March), branding him an international outlaw.

Realizing that times had changed within France, Napoleon tried to adapt himself to the limited powers of a constitutional monarch. His legislative body proved unruly and irresponsible, and he found few firm supporters except for the lower classes and the Army. Even in the Army, many senior officers were doubtful. Consequently, he had to accept certain dubious assistants, including Fouche. Fouche took up his old duties as minister of police, discharged them efficiently—and was in treasonous correspondence with Wellington, Louis XVIII, and the Austrian government. In late March, a Royalist revolt broke out in the Vendee.

Among Napoleon's misfortunes was Murat, King of Naples. Though the Austrians had recognized Murat's royal status, the English had not, and Louis XVIII had demanded his eradication in favor of the degenerate Neapolitan Bourbons. Thus threatened, Murat had turned to Napoleon. Before leaving Elba, Napoleon had warned him to mobilize his army, but not to begin hostilities. The Allies now offered Murat recognition in exchange for his continued neutrality. But Murat, being himself, lost his temper, invaded northern Italy (15 March), and was quickly defeated.

Even so, though faced by war without and treason within, Napoleon was still confident. Moreover, his enemies had their problems. Belgians had no desire to die for their Dutch prince; Rhineland Germans had found Prussian rule harsh and foreign. An attempt to force part of the Saxon Army into the Prussian service had ended in a mutiny, from which Blücher barely escaped through his headquarters' back door. Poles everywhere would be pro-French. England's fleets and armies were widely dispersed, due to her recent war (War of 1812) with the United States. And there remains a strong suspicion that—given a decisive French victory—Austria might have again switched sides.

The Waterloo Campaign

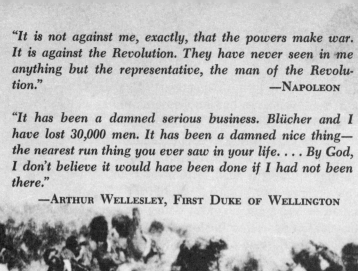

"It is not against me, exactly, that the powers make war. It is against the Revolution. They have never seen in me anything but the representative, the man of the Revolution."
—NAPOLEON

"It has been a damned serious business. Blücher and I have lost 30,000 men. It has been a damned nice thing— the nearest run thing you ever saw in your life. . . . By God, I don't believe it would have been done if I had not been there."
—ARTHUR WELLESLEY, FIRST DUKE OF WELLINGTON

Once more, all Europe marched against Napoleon.

Out of the 224,000 men the Emperor found on the French Army's muster rolls, hardly 50,000 were actually ready for field service. Morale was low, discipline shattered, organizations thoroughly scrambled by recent reductions and consolidations. There were dangerous shortages of clothing, equipment, weapons, and horses, and French businessmen were reluctant to risk money in supplying them. The frontier fortresses and the Navy had been completely neglected.

Seldom, in his whole amazing career, had Napoleon shown such sustained energy and imagination. Weapons designs were simplified, new workshops opened, clockmakers set to making musket locks. Paris was carefully fortified, and the eastern and northern frontier fortifications put into serviceable state. Lyons (A1) was organized as a base for the southern armies. Men on leave and retired veterans were recalled; deserters offered pardons; National Guard units mobilized; naval personnel transferred to the army. Voluntary enlistments filled several foreign regiments. Partisan units were organized along the frontiers. Plenty of competent officers were available to cadre new organizations, but there remained a serious shortage of individual replacements to fill existing regular units. It would be difficult to re-establish conscription, since its abolition had been the Bourbons' one universally popular act. After much hesitation, Napoleon finally got around this problem by decreeing that men of the class of 1815 (called up in 1813, but released after his abdication) were to be considered as being merely absent on leave, and so subject to recall. This announcement, however, was not made until late June, and these men were only entering their regimental depots when Napoleon marched northward.

Of the marshals, Marmont and Victor had joined the Bourbons; Augereau, Oudinot, St.-Cyr, Perignon, Kellermann, Moncey, Lefebvre, Serurier, and Murat (who had fled to France) were considered unsuitable for various reasons; Macdonald and Massena dodged duty on pretense of ill health. Ney displayed symptoms of severe emotional disturbance, and initially was trusted only with minor assignments. Jourdan was fit for nothing more than the command of the fortress city of Besancon (A2). Sickness crippled Mortier, just as the campaign opened. To fill their places, Napoleon recalled Brune (in disfavor since 1807) to active duty, and made Grouchy a marshal. Other corps commands went to experienced generals, many of them better soldiers than the marshals they replaced. Those given independent commands were chosen with special care. Planning for a protracted struggle, Napoleon made Davout his minister of war—undoubtedly a waste of his military skill, but a post for which his loyalty, zeal, and great administrative talent particularly fitted him.

The major weakness was the lack of a competent staff. Berthier died mysteriously in Bamberg (B2) on 1 June, seemingly while attempting to get back to France, after having escorted Louis to safety. His place was never properly filled, though Napoleon finally made Soult (who had understudied Berthier briefly in 1813) his chief of staff. Soult was able, but indolent, unfamiliar with staff work, widely disliked, and handicapped by a lack of trained assistants.

Napoleon had two possible courses of action: He could stand on the defensive, as in 1814, or he could take the offensive as soon as possible against Blücher and Wellington, attempting to destroy them before the other Allied armies came into action. His own talents and instincts were all for the latter course. The English and Prussian armies were his most dangerous enemies. With them destroyed, the Austrians, Bavarians, Piedmontese, and Spanish could be classed as minor annoyances; Barclay's Russians would find themselves far from home. Accordingly, he decided to advance suddenly through Charleroi (A2), wedge himself in between the methodical Wellington and the aggressive Blücher (whose differing temperaments promised differing reactions to his thrust), and defeat them in detail. That done, he would join Rapp and dispose of Schwarzenberg. This plan has been described as "desperate." Remember that it almost succeeded.

The Army of the North was one of the most formidable Napoleon ever led —devoted, hardened, eager veterans. Its larger units, however, were newly formed. Some of its generals were unknown to the men they led; the rank and file distrusted others because of their willing service under Louis. As a weapon, it was keen but brittle.

The smaller, defensive commands (Rapp's excepted) were composed in large part of national guardsmen and other second-line troops. Rapp (a stubborn, loyal Alsatian, popular in eastern France) was expected to delay Schwarzenberg as long as possible. Suchet had proved himself in Spain as an independent commander, and so was ideal for the dangerous, relatively unfortified Piedmontese frontier. Napoleon has been criticized for not withdrawing most of the regular troops from these armies, but the distances involved alone would have made this impossible in the time available. (Furthermore, national guardsmen would have been of doubtful value without a stiffening of regulars.)

Wellington's army was a slow-moving, clumsy, odd-lot collection. Most of his English and German troops had seen considerable service, but his Brunswick unit was raw and unsteady, and his Dutch-Belgian and Nassau troops were suspiciously unenthusiastic. His artillery was good, his cavalry splendidly mounted. Blücher's Prussians were generally well disciplined and willing, but half of his infantry and a third of his cavalry were poorly trained Landwehr, and his artillery and supply services were inefficient.

As Allied commander in chief, Schwarzenberg planned a concentric advance on Paris, beginning on 1 June (later postponed to 27 June), by Wellington, Blücher, Frimont, and himself. Kleist would link Schwarzenberg's army with Blücher's, and operate against the French frontier fortresses. Barclay would form the reserve. The Spanish, still mobilizing, would attack when they could.

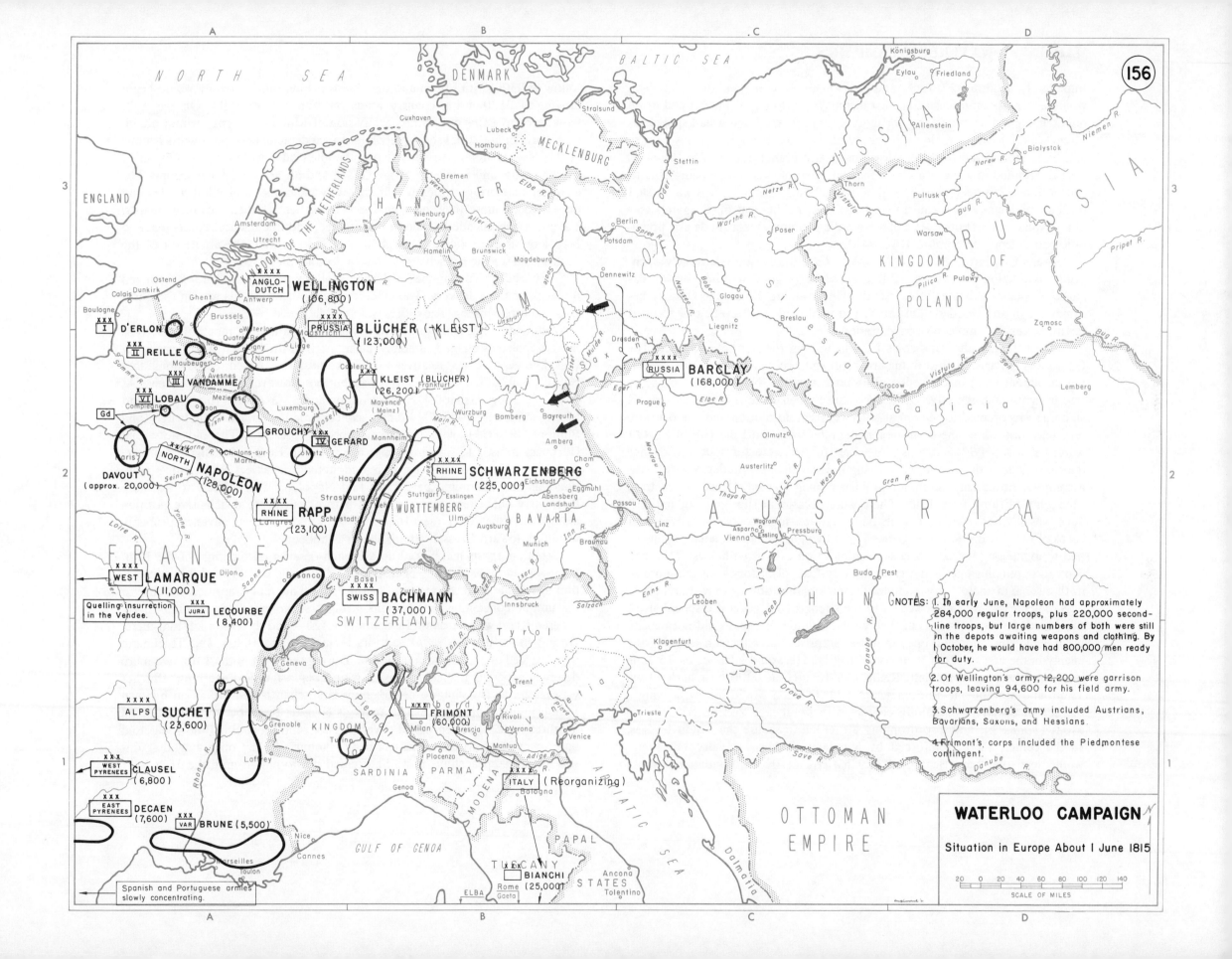

NORTH SEA

BALTIC SEA

DENMARK

ENGLAND

156

P R U S S I A

Königsburg
Eylau Friedland

Allenstein

Niemen R.

MECKLENBURG

H A N O V E R

Stralsund

Lübeck

Cuxhaven

Stettin

KINGDOM OF POLAND

Bialystok

Warthe R.

Netze R.

Vistula R.

Thorn

Pultusk

Narew R.

Bug R.

Amsterdam
Utrecht

Bremen

Nienburg

Hamelin

Aller R.

Elbe R.

Brunswick

Magdeburg

Berlin

Potsdam

Spree R.

Dennewitz

S A X O N Y

Dresden

Mulde R.

Eister R.

Bober R.

Glogau

Breslau

S I L E S I A

Liegnitz

Crocow

Poser

Pulawy

Pilica R.

Warsaw

Zamosc

Bug R.

Lemberg

G a l i c i a

Vistula R.

San R.

KINGDOM OF THE NETHERLANDS

XXXX
ANGLO-DUTCH | **WELLINGTON**
(106,800)

Ghent
Antwerp

Calais Dunkirk

Ostend

Boulogne

XXX
I | **D'ERLON**

Brussels
Waterloo
Quatre Bras

Louvain

XXX
II | **REILLE**

Charleroi Namur

Maubeuge

Avesnes

XXX
III | **VANDAMME**

Mezieres

XXX
VI | **LOBAU**

Gd

Compiegne

Aisne R.

Laon

Somme R.

XXX
GROUCHY | XXX
IV | **GERARD**

XXXX
NORTH | **NAPOLEON**
(128,000)

Paris

Seine R.

Chalons-sur-Marne

Metz

Marne R.

DAVOUT
(approx. 20,000)

XXXX
RHINE | **RAPP**
(23,100)

Langres

XXXX
PRUSSIA | **BLÜCHER** (-KLEIST)
(123,000)

Liege

Namur

Luxemburg

Coblenz

Moselle R.

XXX
KLEIST (BLÜCHER)
(26,200)

Mayence (Mainz)

Frankfurt

Mannheim

Hagenau

Strasbourg

Rhine R.

Schlstadt

Main R.

Wurzburg

Bamberg

Bayreuth

Amberg

Cham

XXXX
RHINE | **SCHWARZENBERG**
(225,000)

Eichstadt

Eggmuhl

Abensberg
Landshut

Stuttgart
Esslingen

WÜRTTEMBERG

Ulm

Augsburg

BAVARIA

Munich

Inn R.

Braunau

Passau

Linz

BARCLAY
(168,000)

XXXX
RUSSIA

Eger R.

Moldau R.

Prague

Olmutz

Austerlitz

Waag R.

A U S T R I A

Thaya R.

Gran R.

March R.

Wagram

Pressburg

Aspern
Essling

Vienna

XXXX
WEST | **LAMARQUE**
(11,000)

Dijon

Quelling insurrection
in the Vendee.

XXX
JURA | **LECOURBE**
(8,400)

Saone R.

Yonne R.

Loire R.

Besanco

Basel

Zurich

XXXX
SWISS | **BACHMANN**
(37,000)

S W I T Z E R L A N D

Geneva

Innsbruck

T y r o l

Salzach R.

Enns R.

Leoben

H U N G A R Y

Raab R.

Save R.

Klagenfurt

Drave R.

Danube R.

Danube R.

XXXX
ALPS | **SUCHET**
(23,600)

Grenoble

KINGDOM

Rhone R.

Laffrey

SARDINIA

Piedmont

Turin

Milan

L o m b a r d y

Brescia

Rivoli

Verona

V e n e t i a

Piave R.

Adige R.

Mantua

Venice

Trieste

A d r i a t i c   S E A

Dalmatia

XXXX
FRIMONT
(60,000)

XXX
WEST PYRENEES | **CLAUSEL**
(6,800)

XXX
EAST PYRENEES | **DECAEN**
(7,600)

XXX
VAR | **BRUNE** (5,500)

Nice

Marseilles

Toulon

Cannes

GULF OF GENOA

Genoa

PARMA

MODENA

Placenza

Bologna

ITALY (Reorganizing)

Ancona

TUSCANY

Rome

ELBA

Gaeta

Tolentino

PAPAL STATES

XXXX
BIANCHI
(25,000)

O T T O M A N
E M P I R E

Spanish and Portuguese armies
slowly concentrating.

NOTES: 1. In early June, Napoleon had approximately
284,000 regular troops, plus 220,000 second-
line troops, but large numbers of both were still
in the depots awaiting weapons and clothing. By
1 October, he would have had 800,000 men ready
for duty.

2. Of Wellington's army, 12,200 were garrison
troops, leaving 94,600 for his field army.

3. Schwarzenberg's army included Austrians,
Bavarians, Saxons, and Hessians.

4. Frimont's corps included the Piedmontese
contingent.

WATERLOO CAMPAIGN

Situation in Europe About 1 June 1815

20 0 20 40 60 80 100 120 140

SCALE OF MILES

Impatiently awaiting 27 June, and overweeningly confident that Napoleon would never risk an offensive against them, Wellington and Blücher had made only the vaguest arrangements for mutual support. Wellington had spread his forces widely to make their supply and billeting easier, relying on his cavalry and his espionage network to warn him of any French move. The Prussians were distributed in a more military fashion, each of their corps being able to concentrate on its headquarters within twelve hours. Zieten's corps was posted on the frontier as a covering force, but Zieten neither patrolled aggressively (his cavalry was stationed six miles behind his infantry) nor made any preparation to defend the Sambre River bridges.

Between Charleroi (*B1*) and Antwerp (*B3*), the terrain is a largely open, gently undulating plateau, passable everywhere in good weather, but an expanse of gluey mud after rains. South of the Sambre River, the country becomes rough and wooded. This broken ground, with its deep belt of fortified towns, screened Napoleon's concentration.

In early June, only Napoleon's I Corps was on the northern frontier. The Guard was in Paris, the rest of the army still undergoing reorganization. Selecting Beaumont (*B1*) as the center of his concentration, Napoleon fed his army into it swiftly and secretly. On 7 June, the French frontiers were closed; all shipping was ordered to remain at anchor; false information and rumors were broadcast, including one of an impending offensive from Lille (*off map, A2*) toward Brussels (*B2*). Troops along the frontier were forbidden to change their positions or daily routine. Arriving units bivouacked under cover. It was a complex movement, the major problems being Gerard's flank march from Metz and d'Erlon's from Lille. There were occasional slip-ups. Not until 12 June was it discovered that Soult had forgotten to issue orders to the four corps of the Cavalry Reserve. Grouchy got them together, but some regiments had to make long forced marches, coming in on exhausted horses. This concentration remains one of the great military feats of history—all the more so in that some of these corps completed their organization as they marched.

Napoleon was well informed as to the strength and general dispositions of the Allied armies, as well as of their casual attitude. His plans did not depend upon achieving complete, open-mouthed surprise, but rather on catching the enemy in the first stages of their concentration. He would advance on 15 June in three columns. On the left, Reille would march at 0300 on Charleroi via Thuin and Marchienne-au-Pont (*both B1*). D'Erlon would follow, leaving a brigade of cavalry to maintain contact with Maubeuge and observe toward Mons (*both B1*), and also dropping a division to secure the Thuin bridges. In the center, Pajol, reinforced by Vandamme's corps cavalry (Domon), would lead out from Beaumont to Charleroi at 0230; Vandamme would

follow at 0300, with Lobau and the Guard behind him. Grouchy would begin moving at 0530, using country roads on Vandamme's right. On the right flank, Gerard (plus one cuirassier division of Milhaud's corps) would march for Charleroi at 0300, keeping reconnaissance detachments out toward Namur (*C2*). Napoleon would ride with Vandamme's advance guard, accompanied by the sailors and engineers of the Guard and all army engineer troops. The engineer and bridge trains would follow Vandamme, and all three leading corps would mass their own engineer units behind their advance guards. Lateral communication would be maintained, and intelligence reports made to Napoleon at every opportunity. If this plan went well, the afternoon of the 15th would see the French army massed around Charleroi.

Soult sent off Vandamme's orders in single copy only, and never bothered to check on their delivery. The officer carrying them lost his way in the darkness and broke his leg. The orders were not delivered.

Wellington's spies had produced masses of information, much of it derived from Napoleon's planted rumors. The strength of the French Army was fairly well known, and its relative weakness bolstered Allied convictions that Napoleon would not attack. Its distribution, however, remained hazy. At 1500, 14 June, General Dörnberg, commanding a cavalry brigade around Mons, reported 100,000 French concentrated between Maubeuge and Philippeville (*C1*), with Napoleon probably present. (The old story that Dörnberg refused to forward a message from an English intelligence officer, warning of Napoleon's offensive, is undoubtedly a fable.) Wellington's reaction was that this might be so, but that Napoleon was unlikely to do more than carry out a few demonstrations before retiring to a defensive position along the Aisne River (*see Map 156, A2*). Any French advance probably would be toward Brussels from Lille or Maubeuge.

Zieten's outposts had picked up a French deserter on the night of the 12th, with word of the impending offensive, but Zieten did not forward this information to Namur until the morning of the 14th. This report aroused Blücher to the unique conception that Napoleon might strike east from Beaumont. He ordered Kleist westward into Luxemburg (*A2*)—and thereafter left him there. During the 14th (*this map*), rumors increased, and Bülow and Thielmann were warned to prepare to concentrate. During the night of the 14th, two more deserters reported that the offensive would begin the next morning. Blücher was asleep. Not wishing to disturb him, Gneisenau issued orders on his own responsibility. Thielmann would mass at Namur; Pirch between Namur and Sombreffe (*C2*); Zieten would cover this concentration. But Bülow was told only to move "into cantonments" near Hannut (*C2*). Concluding that this was a routine, peacetime move, he decided not to march until the 16th.

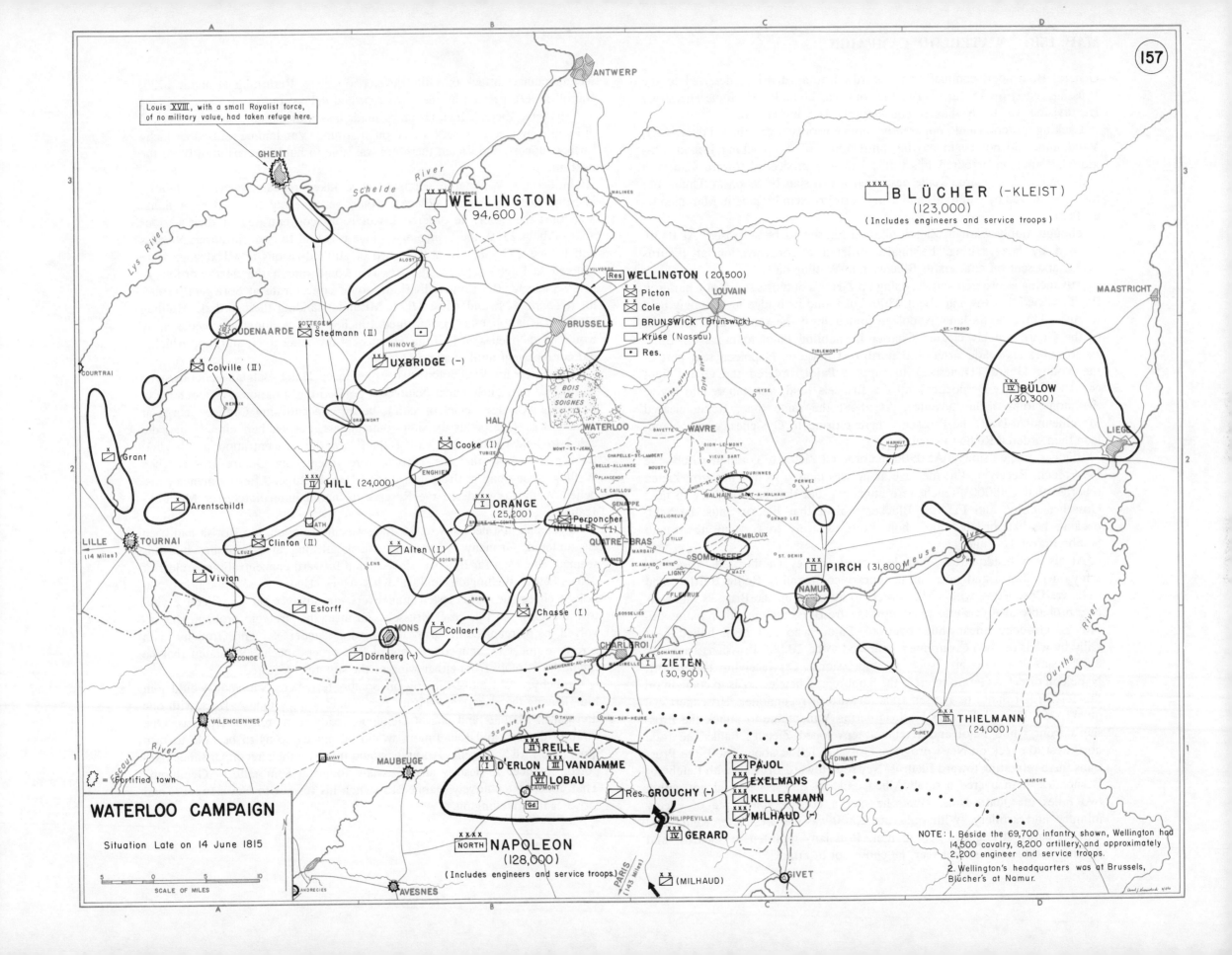

157

Louis XVIII, with a small Royalist force, of no military value, had taken refuge here.

GHENT

Schelde River

XXXX
WELLINGTON
(94,600)

BLÜCHER (-KLEIST)
(123,000)
(Includes engineers and service troops)

MAASTRICHT

Lys River

OUDENAARDE

SOTTEGEM

XX Stedmann (II)

NINOVE

XXX
UXBRIDGE (-)

BRUSSELS

Res WELLINGTON (20,500)

XX Picton
XX Cole
BRUNSWICK (Brunswick)
Krüse (Nassau)
Res.

VILVORDE

LOUVAIN

ST-TROND

COURTRAI

Colville (II)

RENAIX

BRAKMONT

BOIS DE SOIGNES

LIÈGE

XXX BÜLOW
(30,300)

HANNUT

Grant

HAL

Cooke (I)

TUBIZE

WATERLOO

WAVRE

BAVETTE DION-LE-MONT

VIEUX SART

LILLE
(14 Miles)

TOURNAI

Arentschildt

ATH

XXX HILL (24,000)

ENGHIEN

MONT-ST-JEAN

CHAPELLE-ST-LAMBERT

BELLE-ALLIANCE

PLANCENOIT

LE CAILLOU

XXX I ORANGE
(25,200)

BRAINE-LE-COMTE

GENAPPE

NIVELLES

XX Perponcher (I)

MELIOREUX

MONT-ST-GUIBERT

TOURINNES

PERWEZ

GRAND LEZ

Clinton (II)

LEUZE

XX Alten (I)

SOIGNIES

LENS

QUATRE-BRAS

TILLY

ST DENIS

XXX II PIRCH (31,800)

Vivian

ROEULX

XX Chasse (I)

GOSSELIES

SOMBREFFE

ST AMAND
LIGNY
BRYE

FLEURUS

GEMBLOUX

Meuse

Estorff

MONS

XX Collaert

Dörnberg (-)

CHARLEROI

MARCHIENNE-AU-PONT

SILLY

OGNATELET

XXX I ZIETEN
(30,900)

NAMUR

CONDE

VALENCIENNES

Sambre River

THUIN

HAM-SUR-HEURE

PHILIPPEVILLE

THIELMANN
(24,000)

CINEY

Ourthe River

MARCHE

MAUBEUGE

BAVAY

XX REILLE

XXX I D'ERLON

XXX III VANDAMME

XXX VI LOBAU

Res GROUCHY (-)

BEAUMONT

Gd

XXXX NORTH NAPOLEON
(128,000)
(Includes engineers and service troops.)

XXX PAJOL
XXX EXELMANS
XXX KELLERMANN
XXX MILHAUD (-)

DINANT

PHILIPPEVILLE

XXX IV GERARD

PARIS
(143 Miles)

XX (MILHAUD)

GIVET

AVESNES

ANDREGIES

= Fortified town

WATERLOO CAMPAIGN

Situation Late on 14 June 1815

SCALE OF MILES

NOTE: 1. Beside the 69,700 infantry shown, Wellington had 14,500 cavalry, 8,200 artillery, and approximately 2,200 engineer and service troops.

2. Wellington's headquarters was at Brussels, Blücher's at Namur.

General Bourmont, commanding Gerard's leading division, deserted to the Prussians early on 15 June. (Blücher told him he had half-canine ancestry.) His division was badly shaken, considerably delaying Gerard.

Lacking orders (and, apparently, any curiosity over their nonarrival), Vandamme did not begin moving until about 0700, blocking Lobau. Disgusted, Napoleon detoured this traffic jam and proceeded toward Charleroi with some of his Guard. Reille destroyed a Prussian battalion at Thuin, but then was slowed by bad roads and a stubborn Prussian brigade in Marchienne-au-Pont.

Though amply warned, Zieten allowed himself to be surprised. At 0430, aroused by heavy firing, he finally ordered a concentration at Fleurus (C2), and sent off couriers to Blücher and Wellington.

Advancing as ordered and snapping up Zieten's outposts south of Charleroi, Pajol reached that town at about 0800, but found its bridge too strongly held to rush. Three hours later Napoleon joined him; the sailors and engineers of the Guard quickly cleared Charleroi, enabling Pajol to move on Gilly. Establishing his headquarters just north of Charleroi, Napoleon sent part of the Young Guard (Duhesme) to support Pajol, ordered the Guard light cavalry (Lefebvre-Desnoëttes) up the Brussels road, and labored to revive the momentum of his advance. At about the same time, Reille cleared Marchienne-au-Pont, the Prussians there retiring to Gosselies, which Napoleon then ordered Reille to seize.

Blücher reacted slowly. At 0900, he ordered Zieten to continue to observe the French. Receiving this message as he was chased from Charleroi, Zieten reported that 120,000 French were attacking, but that he would try to hold Gosselies, Gilly, and Fleurus. Blücher replied that Fleurus must be held, because he had ordered the whole Prussian army to concentrate around Sombreffe on 16 June.

At his new headquarters, Napoleon received Ney (authorized to join the army on 11 June) and gave him temporary command of Reille, d'Erlon, and Lefebvre-Desnoëttes, with verbal orders to advance up the Brussels highway. Ney probably also was told to occupy Quatre-Bras, though this remains unproven. Grouchy, meanwhile, overtook Pajol, who had been halted near Gilly by what the two cavalrymen estimated to be 20,000 Prussians (actually 8,000, spread out to give such an impression). On receiving this report, Napoleon directed Gerard to cross the Sambre at Chatelet, so as to come in on this force's left flank; he himself rode forward to reconnoiter. His expert eye quickly saw through Zieten's bluff. Ordering Vandamme to attack the Prussian's front while Pajol and Exelmans enveloped Zieten's flanks, he rode northwest to check on Ney's progress. Gosselies fell at about 1600, the Prussians there retreating toward Fleurus. Ney rode toward Brussels with Lefebvre-Desnoëttes, maneuvered a small Allied unit out of Frasnes, and got within two miles of Quatre-Bras. Here, he met a considerable force of enemy infantry and artillery. With only his 2,800 cavalry available, Reille and d'Erlon badly strung out behind him, Prussians reported in Fleurus, and fighting audible to his right rear, he chose not to attack.

Vandamme's attack on Gilly developed slowly. Returning at about 1730, Napoleon, exasperated by the day's repeated delays, put in his cavalry escort and shattered Zieten's line. Grouchy made a skillful pursuit, but was checked at Fleurus by Zieten's reserves and rough ground. Vandamme refused Grouchy further support, and Zieten therefore was able to hold Fleurus until 0500 the next morning.

Until 1800, Wellington seems to have taken repeated warnings lightly, insisting that any French advance would be aimed at his own right flank. Sometime thereafter, he ordered his divisions concentrated in their various areas. About 2200, the Prince of Orange was told to concentrate at Nivelles and Braine-le-Comte (both B2); two of Hill's divisions and Uxbridge were ordered to Enghien (B2); the Reserve would march the next morning to Mont-St.-Jean (B2); other divisions would concentrate at Sottegem, Grammont (both A2), and Alost (B3). Misunderstanding these orders, Müffling (Blücher's liaison officer) informed Blücher that Wellington's whole army would be at Nivelles on 17 June. He missent this letter to Namur, and Blücher did not receive it until early on 16 June.

Fortunately for Wellington, two experienced Dutch-Belgian generals, who had served previously under Napoleon, grasped the situation. At about 1400, Rebecque (Orange's chief of staff), began concentrating Orange's corps at Quatre-Bras. One of his division commanders, Perponcher, already had decided to hold Quatre-Bras rather than join the concentration at Nivelles. Rebecque's report that the French were threatening Quatre-Bras reached Wellington at a ball in Brussels around 0100, 16 June. After momentary disbelief, Wellington ordered the Reserve to march immediately for Mont-St.-Jean.

Napoleon's first necessity on 16 June was information. No British had been encountered. Grouchy reported Prussians massing at Sombreffe, but this seemed rash, even for Blücher, since such a forward concentration would risk defeat before Wellington could aid his Allies. Under these conditions, Napoleon chose one of his tested maneuvers: an advance on an objective vital to the enemy—in this case, Brussels. To meet the strategic problem this involved, he reorganized his army in two wings, under Ney and Grouchy, with a reserve under his immediate control. His orders specifically stated that he might draw troops from either wing as the situation required.

Grouchy would move directly on Sombreffe, where Napoleon would join him, leaving the reserve at Fleurus. Ney would occupy Quatre-Bras, with one division at Marbais and one at Genappe, ready to march on Brussels. One infantry division and Kellermann would be placed so as to be able to turn quickly toward Sombreffe. All units would intensify their reconnaissance. Napoleon intended to destroy any Prussians found at Sombreffe or Gembloux. That done, he tentatively planned to switch his reserve to Ney's support and move against Wellington.

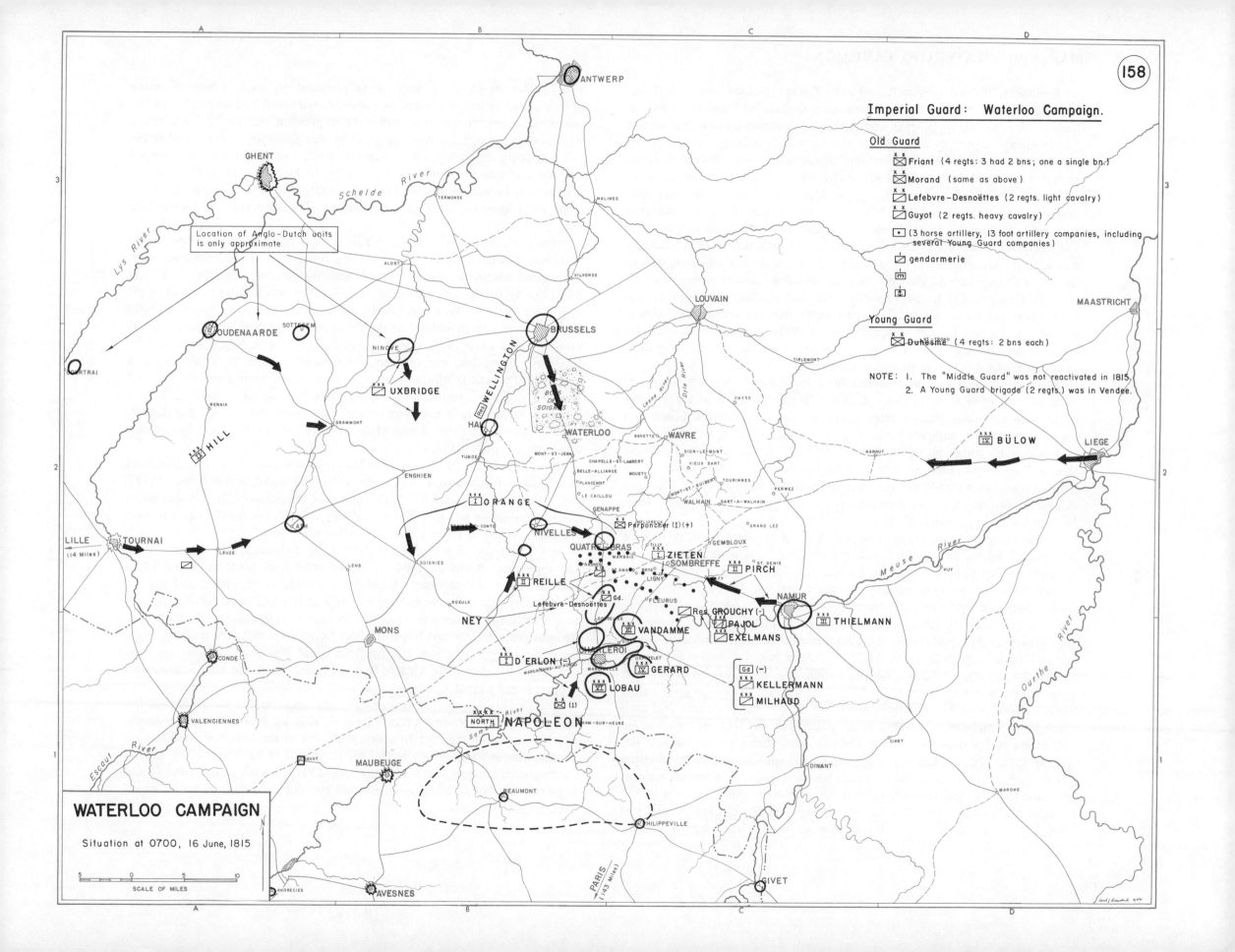

158

Imperial Guard: Waterloo Campaign.

Old Guard

☒ Friant (4 regts: 3 had 2 bns; one a single bn.)

☒ Morand (same as above)

◻ Lefebvre–Desnoëttes (2 regts. light cavalry)

☒ Guyot (2 regts. heavy cavalry)

⊡ (3 horse artillery, 13 foot artillery companies, including several Young Guard companies)

◻ gendarmerie

ⅿ

⚓

Young Guard

☒ Duhesme (4 regts: 2 bns each)

NOTE: 1. The "Middle Guard" was not reactivated in 1815.
2. A Young Guard brigade (2 regts.) was in Vendee.

ANTWERP

GHENT

Schelde River

Lys River

TERMONDE

MALINES

ALOST

VILVORDE

LOUVAIN

MAASTRICHT

OUDENAARDE

SOTTEGEM

NINOVE

BRUSSELS

Location of Anglo-Dutch units is only approximate

COURTRAI

RENAIX

GRAMMONT

ENGHIEN

⊠ UXBRIDGE

WELLINGTON

HAL

BOIS DE SOIGNES

WATERLOO

WAVRE

CHYSE

☒☒☒ BÜLOW

LIEGE

HILL

TUBIZE

MONT-ST-JEAN

CHAPELLE-ST-LAMBERT

BELLE-ALLIANCE

MOUSTY

PLANCENOIT

LE CAILLOU

DION-LE-MONT

VIEUX SART

TOURINNES

WALHAIN

SART-A-WALHAIN

PERWEZ

HAMNUT

Meuse River

LILLE
(14 Miles)

TOURNAI

ATH

ENGHIEN

SOIGNIES

LENS

GENAPPE

☒☒☒ ORANGE

NIVELLES

QUATRE BRAS

MELIORELA
☒ Perponcher (I)(+)

GRAND LEZ

GEMBLOUX

TILLY

☒ ZIETEN
SOMBREFFE

ST. DENIS

☒☒ PIRCH

HUY

ROEULX

MONS

☒☒☒ II REILLE

Lefebvre-Desnoëttes

☒☒ Gd.

FLEURUS

LIGNY

☒ Res GROUCHY (-)

☒☒ PAJOL
☒ EXELMANS

NAMUR

☒☒☒ III THIELMANN

Ourthe River

NEY

☒☒☒ III VANDAMME

CONDE

☒☒☒ I D'ERLON (-)

CHARLEROI

MARCHIENNE-AU-PONT

☒☒☒ IV GERARD

☒☒☒ VI LOBAU

[Gd] (-)
☒☒☒ KELLERMANN
☒☒☒ MILHAUD

VALENCIENNES

☒☒☒☒ River
☒☒ (1)

NORTH NAPOLEON

HAM-SUR-HEURE

CINEY

MAUBEUGE

GRAVAY

BEAUMONT

DINANT

MARCHE

Escaut River

PHILIPPEVILLE

ANDREGIES

AVESNES

PARIS
(143 Miles)

GIVET

WATERLOO CAMPAIGN

Situation at 0700, 16 June, 1815

SCALE OF MILES

At Sombreffe, Blücher originally had only Zieten's mauled corps. Pirch arrived at about 1100, Thielmann an hour later. Despite his belief that he faced Napoleon's entire army, Blücher was confident. Common sense might suggest a withdrawal—especially when Bülow proved to be hopelessly out of supporting distance—but Blücher's governing characteristic was unthinking pugnacity. Furthermore, he had Müffling's report (corroborated by an aide-de-camp who had contacted Orange at Quatre-Bras that morning) that Wellington was concentrating at Nivelles (*both off map, A3*). A withdrawal now, with Wellington obviously making superhuman efforts to support him, was repugnant to the old Prussian's concept of soldierly honor. His confidence was mightily strengthened at about 1215 by a letter from Wellington, stating that all of Orange's corps, the Reserve, and Uxbridge's cavalry would be in the Nivelles–Genappe–Quatre-Bras area by noon, and that there were few French near Quatre-Bras. This dispatch remains inexplicable: Its contents were almost entirely untrue, yet it seems impossible that Wellington (who allowed his subordinates considerably less latitude than did Napoleon) could have been so ignorant of the actual positions of his troops.

Wellington should have been thoroughly informed as to Ney's strength, the chief of staff of one of d'Erlon's divisions having deserted to the English during the morning. Shortly after noon, Wellington visited Blücher, but language difficulties hampered their interview. Gneisenau requested that part of Wellington's forces be shifted toward Brye (*C2*), and afterward claimed that Wellington promised an attack on Napoleon's left flank at about 1400. English tradition is that Wellington merely expressed disapproval of Blücher's defensive position along the forward slope of the low ridge extending from Brye to Le Point de Jour (*C2*).

The morning of 16 June found Napoleon in an excellent position. Despite unexpected delays, he had surprised, outgeneraled, and outmarched his opponents. At Ligny, he could concentrate almost 73,000 men against Blücher —odds large enough to practically guarantee victory. At Quatre-Bras, Ney outnumbered Orange's scratch forces six to one. (Also, because of Wellington's haphazard distribution of his forces, Orange had no cavalry except for fifty stray Prussians, and could expect reinforcements only in driblets.) Arriving at Fleurus sometime before 1100, Napoleon began a reconnaissance of the Prussian position. This was unusually difficult—the only good observation post, a mill on the northern edge of Fleurus, was too distant to give a clear view. Hedges, trees, and buildings concealed most of the Prussians. Not until Pirch's and Thielmann's columns came pouring in did Napoleon realize the full extent of his opportunity. But Gerard, badly behind schedule, did not appear until 1300. While waiting, Napoleon summoned Girard's division (II Corps), which he attached to Vandamme's corps; rode along his outpost line; and found a local surveyor to brief him on the terrain.

Blücher's position was quite strong. Though not large, Ligne Creek was steep-banked and marshy. The clusters of stone-built villages, walled gardens, and farmhouses along its north bank provided an ideal system of strong points, linked by hedgerows and orchards. Zieten's staff had originally studied this position, but at that time under the impression that any French attack would come through Le Point de Jour against Gembloux (*D3*). Either because of hurry, or tactical misconception, Pirch and Thielmann were hustled into the positions envisioned in that study. As Napoleon promptly realized, Blücher's right was in the air, his left overextended, and the irregular trace of his front line gave the French artillery excellent opportunities for enfilade fire.

Napoleon's plan was to envelop Blücher's right flank with troops drawn from Ney, combining this maneuver with a penetration of the Prussian center, to trap and destroy the greater part of the Prussian army. He wrote to Ney at 1400 that he would attack Blücher at 1430. Ney was to attack and drive off any enemy force on his immediate front, then turn and strike Blücher's right flank. If Napoleon should defeat the Prussians before Ney was successful, he himself would strike the left of the enemy engaged with Ney. Grouchy, with Exelmans, Pajol, and one of Gerard's divisions, would fix Thielmann and delay any Prussian reinforcements that might be en route from Namur (*off map, D2*). Gerard would storm Ligny, while Vandamme attacked Blücher's right. Between Gerard and Vandamme, guns were massed to rake the St. Amand salient. The Guard and Milhaud were held ready either to counterattack or to exploit the victory.

By mid-afternoon, the whole Prussian position was under attack. Napoleon called Lobau forward from his position south of Fleurus, and ordered (1515) Ney to maneuver against Blücher's right rear immediately. If Ney advanced promptly, Blücher was lost. The psychological impact of his destruction upon the Allies would be tremendous—all rested with Ney.

Ney had received his orders before 1100 to occupy the Quatre-Bras–Genappe area. Shortly thereafter, a second order from Soult had warned him that the enemy was reportedly building up around Quatre-Bras, and that he must concentrate and attack at once. These orders had been detailed enough to give Ney all necessary information on the over-all situation. Though Ney had not reported recently, Napoleon had heard no sound of a major engagement from Ney's direction. He therefore could logically conclude that Ney already had occupied the Quatre-Bras area and should be able to intervene around Brye by 1900.

Ney should have had the entire left wing concentrated by 0800, without the stimulus of Napoleon's orders. Instead, after an amateur reconnaissance, at 1400 he was straggling into action with part of Reille's corps, and had no definite idea as to where the rest of his troops might be. Even so, he grossly outnumbered Orange, who could only spread Perponcher's division widely and hope that the woods, farmsteads, and tall rye would conceal its actual weakness.

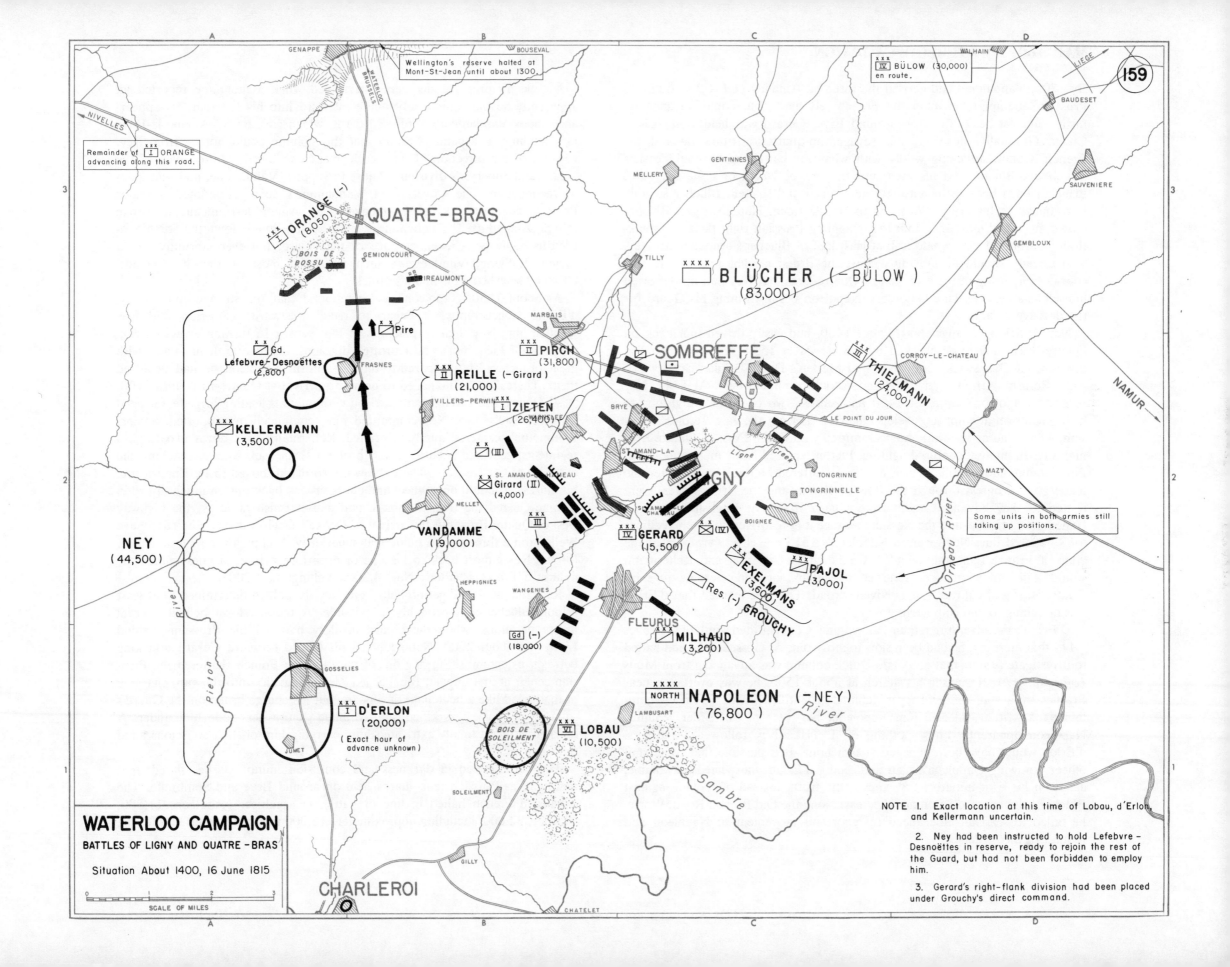

159

NIVELLES

GENAPPE

BOUSEVAL

WALHAIN

LIEGE

NAMUR

BÜLOW (30,000) en route.

BAUDESET

Wellington's reserve halted at Mont-St-Jean until about 1300.

Remainder of I ORANGE advancing along this road.

MELLERY

GENTINNES

SAUVENIERE

QUATRE-BRAS

ORANGE (−) (8,050)

BOIS DE BOSSU

GEMIONCOURT

TILLY

GEMBLOUX

CORROY-LE-CHATEAU

BLÜCHER (−BÜLOW) (83,000)

IREAUMONT

MARBAIS

Pire

Gd. Lefebvre-Desnoëttes (2,800)

Frasnes

SOMBREFFE

II PIRCH (31,800)

THIELMANN (24,000)

II REILLE (−Girard) (21,000)

VILLERS-PERWIN

I ZIETEN (26,400)

BRYE

LE POINT DU JOUR

KELLERMANN (3,500)

MELLET

ST-AMAND-LA-

LIGNE

Creek

TONGRINNE

MAZY

NEY (44,500)

III

St. AMAND-CHATEAU

Girard (II) (4,000)

VANDAMME (19,000)

III

IV GERARD (15,500)

IV

BOIGNEE

TONGRINNELLE

Some units in both armies still taking up positions.

EXELMANS (3,600)

PAJOL (3,000)

HEPPIGNIES

WANGENIES

Res (−) GROUCHY

FLEURUS

Gd (−) (18,000)

MILHAUD (3,200)

River

GOSSELIES

NORTH NAPOLEON (−NEY) (76,800)

LAMBUSART

I D'ERLON (20,000)

(Exact hour of advance unknown)

BOIS DE SOLEILMENT

VI LOBAU (10,500)

Sambre

JUMET

SOLEILMENT

NOTE 1. Exact location at this time of Lobau, d'Erlon, and Kellermann uncertain.

2. Ney had been instructed to hold Lefebvre-Desnoëttes in reserve, ready to rejoin the rest of the Guard, but had not been forbidden to employ him.

3. Gerard's right-flank division had been placed under Grouchy's direct command.

CHARLEROI

GILLY

CHATELET

WATERLOO CAMPAIGN

BATTLES OF LIGNY AND QUATRE-BRAS

Situation About 1400, 16 June 1815

SCALE OF MILES

By 1700, Vandamme had carried the three St. Amands (*C1–C2*), routing a Prussian attempt to envelop the French left flank, but could advance no farther against heavy fire from around Brye. Gerard was held along Ligny Creek. Gradually, however, this savage, no-quarter attrition favored the French. Counterattacking wildly with whatever battalions he could easiest snatch up, Blücher fed his men into the fire of Napoleon's massed guns. Prussian units became increasingly intermixed and shaken; Blücher steadily lost control of his army. Watching the battle ripen, Napoleon saw Blücher crowd more and more men into the struggling Prussian right flank. A breakthrough around Ligny would trap at least half of Blücher's army against Ney, who already should be moving against the Prussian right rear. There was considerable firing in the direction of Quatre-Bras, but Ney had not reported himself unable to execute his orders. Napoleon began forming his Guard for the decisive assault.

Ney, attacking Orange shortly after 1400, had easily driven him back on Quatre-Bras, only to be checked by the arrival at 1500 of Picton's English division, the Brunswick contingent, and Merlen's Dutch-Belgian cavalry brigade. Returning from Ligny, Wellington took command here. At 1545, Ney received Napoleon's order of 1400 and shifted two of Reille's divisions to his right for an attempt to envelop Quatre-Bras from the east. Jerome's division, which had arrived late, was committed west of the Frasnes–Quatre-Bras highway. In intense, confused fighting, Picton repulsed Ney's main attack, but Pire (commanding Reille's corps cavalry) scattered Merlen's cavalry, Jerome made good progress through the Bois de Bossu, and the Brunswickers were routed as they advanced south from Quatre-Bras. An English brigade, a Hanoverian brigade, and the Nassau contingent now arrived to patch Wellington's battered line. Ney received Napoleon's 1515 message, warning that the "fate of France is in your hands." Confident that d'Erlon and Kellermann would join him shortly, he renewed his attack, ordering Jerome to seize Quatre-Bras and cut the Namur-Nivelles road. Then, he learned that d'Erlon was marching to join Napoleon!

D'Erlon's misadventure remains an enigma. Concentrated south of Gosselies (*A1*) that morning, he had been slow to move out. At Gosselies, he had halted to investigate rumors that an Anglo-Dutch column was advancing from Mons (*off map, A1*). Resuming his march at about 1500, he was overtaken near Frasnes by a staff officer (never definitely identified) with (d'Erlon maintained) a written order to join Napoleon. No trace of this order remains; Napoleon apparently knew nothing of it. (Had Ney followed his orders, d'Erlon would have been engaged at that hour. It is possible that some staff officer, knowing Napoleon's plan and seeing d'Erlon unexpectedly available, acted on his own initiative.) Whatever the truth, instead of moving against Blücher's right rear, d'Erlon marched east along the Old Roman Road. Worse, he failed to send an aide ahead to report his movement to Napoleon and request further orders.

Napoleon's preparations were interrupted when Vandamme reported an apparently hostile column advancing eastward into his left rear. Its appearance shook Vandamme's hard-used corps, which gave up St. Amand-la-Haye in something of a panic. Certain that this column could not be from Ney, because of the direction of its march, Napoleon hastily shifted part of the Guard and Subervie's division (Pajol) to support Vandamme, and sent aides to reconnoiter. The wavering of Vandamme's corps stimulated a major Prussian counterattack. Zieten recovered St. Amand-le-Hameau and broke into St. Amand itself; Thielmann loosed a cavalry attack down the Sombreffe-Fleurus highway. The appearance of the Guard, however, abruptly halted Zieten. Rallying, Vandamme's men recovered most of the St. Amands; Grouchy smashed Thielmann's attack.

At about 1830, Napoleon's aides reported that the strange column was d'Erlon. Concurrently, it began to recoil westward. (D'Erlon said Ney recalled him; Ney, that Napoleon sent him back.) In turning away, d'Erlon dropped off Jacquinot's and Durutte's divisions, instructing them to act "with great prudence," but apparently did not inform Napoleon he had detached them. Thereafter, he managed to delay his arrival at Quatre-Bras until 2100.

At Quatre-Bras, Kellermann arrived with only his leading brigade. Gripped by a redhead's rage, Ney committed him, completely unsupported, against Wellington's center. Equally infuriated, Kellermann rode down two English regiments, captured a battery, and broke a Brunswick square, reaching the outskirts of Quatre-Bras. There, blown, disordered, boxed in by English fire, his cuirassiers could only wheel and cut their way back out, in much disorder. Jerome cleared the Bois de Bossu, and had skirmishers across the highway west of Quatre-Bras, but the arrival of Cooke's English division at 1815 gave Wellington a three-to-two numerical superiority. Wellington counterattacked, forcing Ney almost back to his line of departure before darkness ended the fight at 2100. (Casualties: Ney, 4,300; Wellington, 4,700.)

Realizing he would get no help from Ney, Napoleon determined to at least cripple Blücher as thoroughly as possible. A thunderstorm helped conceal his preparations, while the Guard artillery battered the Prussians behind Ligny. At about 2000, Napoleon led his Guard forward, Gerard attacking between its columns. Surging out of the rain, the French shattered the Prussian center at first impact. Blücher led Zieten's cavalry into the gap, charging at their head like a lieutenant of hussars, but his charge broke on the Guard's squares, his horse was killed, and Milhaud's cuirassiers rode him under. A devoted adjutant finally extricated him, carrying him off half-conscious amid the fugitives.

The battle ended in darkness and confusion; minor clashes flared until midnight, as Prussian rear guards held on around Brye and Sombreffe. The exhausted French halted in line of battle. (Casualties: Napoleon, 11,500; Blücher, 34,000, including approximately 12,000 men who deserted after the battle.)

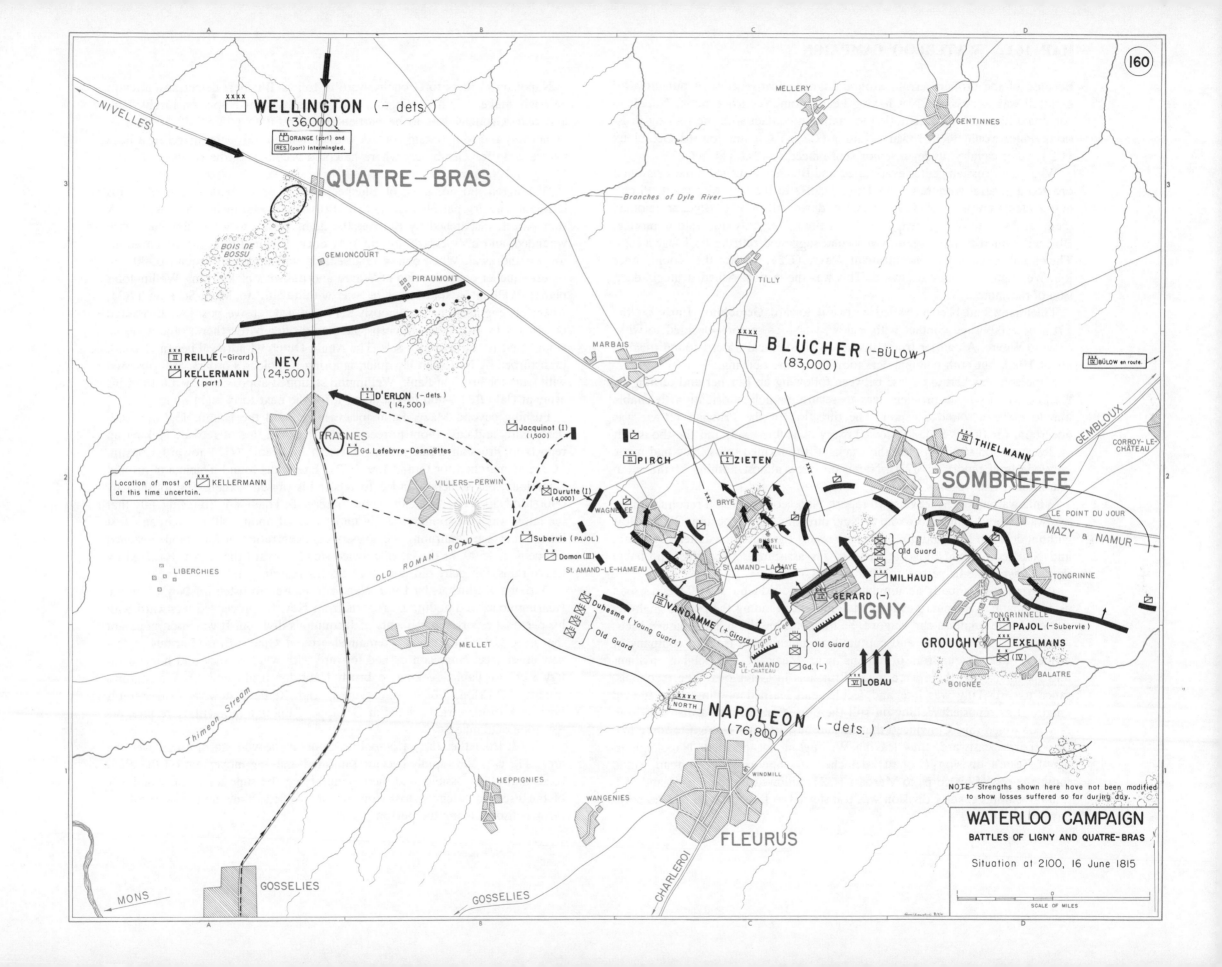

160

NIVELLES

WELLINGTON (-dets.)
(36,000)

XXXX

ORANGE (part) and
RES. (part) intermingled.

QUATRE-BRAS

MELLERY

GENTINNES

Branches of Dyle River

BOIS DE
BOSSU

GEMIONCOURT

TILLY

PIRAUMONT

MARBAIS

BLÜCHER (-BÜLOW)
(83,000)

XXXX

IX BÜLOW en route.

REILLE (-Girard)
II
KELLERMANN
(part)

NEY
(24,500)

XXX

D'ERLON (-dets.)
I
(14,500)

FRASNES

Gd. Lefebvre-Desnoëttes

Jacquinot (I)
(1,500)

PIRCH
II

ZIETEN
I

THIELMANN
III

SOMBREFFE

CORROY-LE-
CHATEAU

GEMBLOUX

Location of most of KELLERMANN
at this time uncertain.

XXX

VILLERS-PERWIN

Durutte (I)
(4,000)

WAGNELEE

BRYE

LE POINT DU JOUR

MAZY & NAMUR

OLD ROMAN ROAD

Subervie (PAJOL)

Domon (III)

St. AMAND-LE-HAMEAU

BUSSY
MILL

St. AMAND-LA-HAYE

Old Guard

MILHAUD

TONGRINNE

LIBERCHIES

Duhesme (Young Guard)

Old Guard

VANDAMME (+Girard)
III

Ligne Creek

GERARD (-)
IV

LIGNY

Old Guard

GROUCHY

TONGRINNELLE

PAJOL (-Subervie)
XXX

EXELMANS
XXX
IV

MELLET

St. AMAND
LE-CHATEAU

Gd. (-)

LOBAU
VI

BOIGNEE

BALATRE

NORTH
XXXX

NAPOLEON (-dets.)
(76,800)

HEPPIGNIES

WANGENIES

WINDMILL

NOTE- Strengths shown here have not been modified
to show losses suffered so far during day.

WATERLOO CAMPAIGN

BATTLES OF LIGNY AND QUATRE-BRAS

Situation at 2100, 16 June 1815

FLEURUS

MONS

GOSSELIES

GOSSELIES

CHARLEROI

Thimeon Stream

SCALE OF MILES

Because of the broken terrain around Ligny, effective cavalry pursuit after nightfall was impossible. Not having heard from Ney since noon, Napoleon contented himself with attempting to maintain contact with the retiring Prussions. Pajol would scout toward Namur (C2); Exelmans toward Gembloux (C2); other cavalry, under a senior staff officer, toward Tilly (C2).

When the Prussian center evaporated and Blücher vanished, Gneisenau had ordered a general withdrawal on Tilly. Thanks to the lack of pursuit, Pirch's and Zieten's corps recovered somewhat during the night. Blücher rejoined them at Melioreux, his reappearance helping mightily to restore morale. Blücher wanted to fight again; Gneisenau suggested retiring on Liege (D2). They finally decided to concentrate at Wavre (C2), whence they could either join Wellington or retire eastward. This was the critical Allied strategic decision of the campaign.

Thielmann had been crowded eastward toward Gembloux. Early on the 17th, he established contact with Bülow, who—as senior—decided to withdraw to Wavre. A courier from Blücher, with identical orders, found them at about 1020, but both commanders took their time obeying.

Napoleon now had to choose between following up Blücher and turning on Wellington. His basic problem was to secure enough information to enable him to make a sound decision. The direction of the Prussian retreat was uncertain, for fugitives had followed every available road, and the thousands of deserters and stragglers hid the tracks of the formed units. Ney had made only one brief report; at 0730, Napoleon knew almost nothing of the situation around Quatre-Bras.

While waiting for his cavalry to report, Napoleon ordered a reconnaissance westward from Ligny, and wrote to Ney, directing him to occupy Quatre-Bras without delay. If he could not, he was to report the fact immediately, in detail, and Napoleon would move at once to his assistance. (Napoleon probably should have gone in person to Quatre-Bras.)

Information gradually accumulated. Pajol had ridden out at 0230, as soon as Thielmann's rear guard evacuated Sombreffe. Finding the Namur highway cluttered with fugitives and wagons, he thought himself on Thielmann's heels. About 0530, he overtook and captured an ammunition train, a company of artillery, and a squadron of uhlans near Mazy (C2). Belgian civilians told Exelmans that there were many Prussians in Gembloux. The reconnaissance toward Tilly was late and feeble, and learned nothing; that toward Quatre-Bras reported Wellington still there in strength, and a dispatch from Ney confirmed this. Convinced that he had hurt Blücher enough to force him to withdraw eastward, thus leaving Wellington unsupported, Napoleon ordered Teste's division (Lobau) detached to support Pajol. Lobau would move the rest of his corps to Marbais (C2), followed by the Guard and Milhaud. Domon's cavalry division was transferred to Lobau (who had no corps cavalry).

Napoleon's orders to Grouchy were to follow Blücher, detect any attempt he might make to join Wellington, and generally cover Napoleon's right flank and rear. Grouchy was to be particularly careful to retain full freedom of maneuver, and to maintain contact with Napoleon. Grouchy marched a little before noon for Gembloux, where he could reconnoiter the roads to Wavre, Liege, and Namur.

Wellington did not learn of Blücher's defeat until about 0730, when his left-flank cavalry patrols reported the Prussians withdrawing northward. (A staff officer, dispatched by Blücher the night before to warn him, had been wounded, and his message mislaid.) At once, Wellington began preparations for a withdrawal. When one of Gneisenau's staff appeared around 0900—to report Blücher concentrating at Wavre and desirous of knowing Wellington's plans—Wellington stated that he was withdrawing to Mont-St.-Jean (B2), where his engineers had previously surveyed a defensive position. If assured of support by two Prussian corps, he would offer battle there; otherwise, he would have to retire on Brussels. The Anglo-Dutch withdrawal began at 1000, undisturbed by Ney, who lay quiet, ignoring Napoleon's orders. Still obsessed with fears for his right flank, Wellington stationed approximately a fifth of his army at Hal (B2)—and forgot about it for the next forty-eight hours.

Pushing beyond Mazy, Pajol meanwhile found the Namur highway suddenly bare, and cast about to recover the Prussian line of retreat. Picking up reports of Prussian trains moving through St. Denis (C2) toward Louvain (C3), he marched for Grand Lez (C2). Exelmans found Thielmann around Gembloux, but somehow failed to report his presence there (established by 0900) to Napoleon. As a climax, he "observed" Thielmann so negligently that the latter was able to march away undetected at about 1400. Exelman's first known message confirming the Prussian concentration at Gembloux reached Grouchy at 1500, as the latter crawled slowly toward that town. Battered by heavy rains, Grouchy did not speed up his march.

Arriving at Marbais by 1300, Napoleon paused to listen for Ney's cannon. Hearing none, and finding no reports from Ney, he proceeded westward with his personal escort and elements of Jacquinot's division. It was soon apparent that only Uxbridge's cavalry remained around Quatre-Bras. Furious at this new mischance, Napoleon dashed forward with what cavalry and horse artillery were available, seeking to brush Uxbridge aside and fix Wellington's infantry. D'Erlon, Lobau, the Guard, and Reille followed. Considerably hustled, Uxbridge tried a stand at Genappe, gaining a momentary respite, but was soon outflanked.

Almost from the start of Napoleon's pursuit, a wild storm burst over the area. The clay soil rapidly became saturated, making movement off the main roads almost impossible, and thereby nullifying the superior tactical mobility of the French. Attempts to follow side roads led many units badly astray, further disorganizing the pursuit.

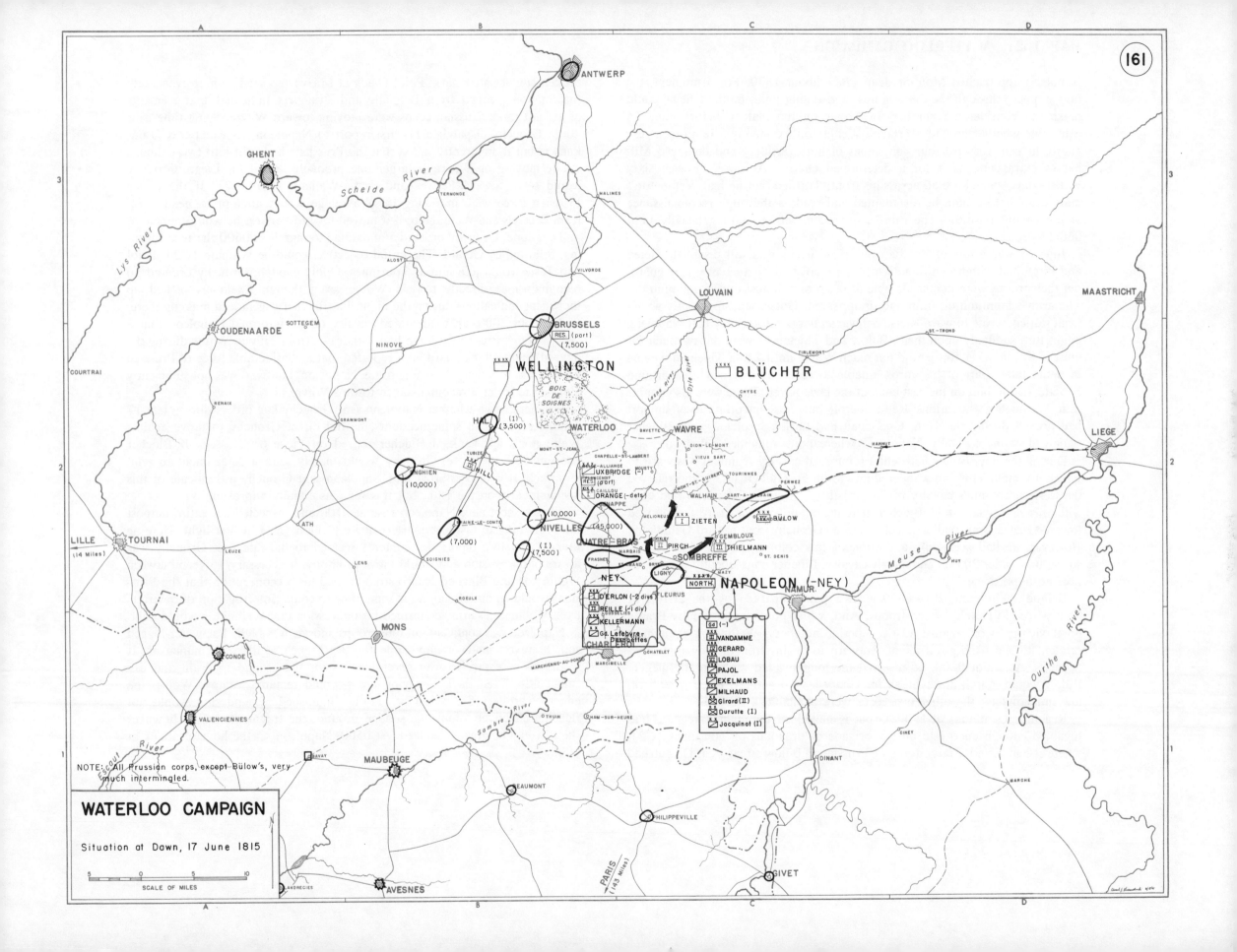

161

ANTWERP

GHENT

Schelde River

Lys River

TERMONDE

MALINES

ALOST

VILVORDE

LOUVAIN

MAASTRICHT

ST.-TROND

OUDENAARDE

SOTTEGEM

NINOVE

TIRLEMONT

COURTRAI

RENAIX

GRAMMONT

BRUSSELS
RES. (part)
(7,500)

XXXX
WELLINGTON

Leopa River

Dyle River

XXXX
BLÜCHER

CHYSE

BOIS
DE
SOIGNES

HAL
(1)
(3,500)

WATERLOO

MONT-ST-JEAN

BAVETTE

WAVRE

DION-LE-MONT

VIEUX SART

LIEGE

HANNUT

TUBIZE

III
HILL

CHAPELLE-ST-LAMBERT

LA-ALLIANCE
XXX
UXBRIDGE (-)

MOUSTY

ENGHIEN
(10,000)

GENDT
RES.
(part)

CAILLOU
XXX
I
ORANGE (-dets)

GENAPPE

MONT-ST.-GUIBERT

TOURINNES

PERWEZ

WALHAIN

SART-A-WALHAIN

LILLE
(14 Miles)

TOURNAI

BRAINE-LE-COMTE
(7,000)

(10,000)

NIVELLES

QUATRE-BRAS

MELIOREU

XXX
I ZIETEN

XXX
IV. BÜLOW

ATH

LEUZE

(1)
(7,500)

FRASNES

MARBAIS

GEMBLOUX

XXX
II PIRCH

XXX
III THIELMANN

Meuse River

LENS

SOIGNIES

SOMBREFFE

ST. DENIS

ROEULX

NEY

BRYE

LIGNY

MAZY

XXXX
NORTH

NAPOLEON (-NEY)

NAMUR

HUY

MONS

XXX
I D'ERLON (-2 divs)

FLEURUS

XXX
II REILLE (-1 div)

GOSSELIES

XXX
KELLERMANN

Gd Lefebvre
Desnoettes

CHARLEROI

Gd (-)

XXX
VANDAMME

III

XXX
GERARD
II

XX
LOBAU
VI

XX
PAJOL

XX
EXELMANS

XX
MILHAUD

Girard (II)

Durutte (I)

Jacquinot (I)

OCHATELET

MARCHIENNE-AU-PONT

MARCINELLE

CONDE

Sambre River

CIREY

MARCHE

Ourthe River

VALENCIENNES

O'THUIN

HAM-SUR-HEURE

NOTE: All Prussian corps, except Bülow's, very much intermingled.

BAVAY

MAUBEUGE

BEAUMONT

PHILIPPEVILLE

DINANT

WATERLOO CAMPAIGN

Situation at Dawn, 17 June 1815

5   0   5   10
SCALE OF MILES

PARIS
(143 Miles)

GIVET

Escaut River

LANDRECIES

AVESNES

David J. Eisenhauer N'44

Napoleon approached Mont-St.-Jean (*B2*) about 1830. For a moment, the rain stopped; through the evening mist and failing light, he thought he could make out considerable numbers of troops on the plateau before him. To determine whether he had overtaken Wellington, or merely a reinforced rear guard, he sent forward four companies of horse artillery and deployed Milhaud's cuirassiers, as if for a determined charge. At once, at least sixty British guns opened fire all across his front. Satisfied that he had Wellington's main army before him, he dismounted and made a thorough reconnaissance of the enemy position. The rains soon recommenced, falling heavily until 0600.

June 17 was a day of Prussian misery. Blücher was still disabled. Zieten and Pirch had withdrawn rapidly to Wavre, covered by a cavalry rear guard, but their troops were in considerable disorder and almost out of ammunition. The army's ammunition train had disappeared. Gneisenau, apparently somewhat rattled, wrote to warn Kleist, Schwarzenberg, and Barclay that Napoleon might turn suddenly upon them. Bülow and Thielmann were out of touch for most of the day. The former did not reach Wavre until 2200. Thielmann came in hours later; part of his corps, unable to reach its assigned area around Bavette, had to halt on the east bank of the Dyle River. There were also doubts as to Wellington's intentions. Remembering how false his promises of support had proved during the 16th, Gneisenau had turned suspicious, but Blücher remained staunch. Finally, Napoleon's whereabouts remained unknown.

During the day, Bülow had sent a reinforced cavalry regiment westward to screen his flank. This unit wandered into Mont-St.-Guibert (*C2*), and relieved the western column's cavalry rear guard there. A staff officer who had been with this rear guard told Blücher that the main French army had moved toward Quatre-Bras, with a detached force (Grouchy) out toward Gembloux. However, he had seen only a portion of this column, and so reported its strength as under 20,000 and mostly cavalry. Blücher consequently considered it of no importance.

Behind Wellington, Brussels was in a panic, sparked by the arrival of fugitive Anglo-Dutch service troops. And, while proclaiming Quatre-Bras a great victory, won against vastly superior numbers, Wellington thought it prudent to warn the governor of Antwerp to begin strengthening that city's defenses. At about 0200, he received the long-awaited reply from Blücher: Bülow would march at daybreak for Chapelle-St.-Lambert; Pirch would follow immediately; the other two corps were available if needed.

Reaching Gembloux at 1900, Grouchy halted for the night. Exelmans had regained enough energy to push a brigade of dragoons to Tourinnes (*C2*), where it had found a large force of Prussians (Bülow's rear guard), but had

broken contact after dark. Pajol (back at Mazy) reported Namur evacuated. Information gleaned from Belgians and stragglers indicated that elements of at least three Prussian corps were moving toward Wavre. Some time near 2000, Grouchy dispatched his first report to Napoleon. Its exact text is unknown, but it apparently stated that the Prussians had split into two columns —one moving on Wavre, a larger one probably bound for Liege. Grouchy would scout toward Perwez and Sart-a-Walhain (*both C2*). If the major Prussian force were marching for Wavre, he would attempt to head it off from Brussels and Wellington; if it moved toward Perwez, he would pursue it.

That done, Grouchy ordered Vandamme to march at 0600 the next morning, followed by Gerard. The initial objective would be Walhain (*C2*). Pajol and Teste would join him at Tourinnes. Oddly enough, Grouchy ordered no reconnaissance directly toward Wavre, even though Exelmans picked up increasing indications during the night that Blücher was indeed massing there.

At about 2000, an unidentified cavalry officer informed Napoleon that a "very strong" Prussian column had withdrawn from Tilly to Wavre during the day. Milhaud's flank guard later reported that a considerable force of Prussian cavalry was following that same route. Napoleon, however, was not sufficiently alarmed to order a reconnaissance toward Wavre.

It is not known whether Napoleon sent Grouchy any orders during late 17 June. According to some accounts, he did direct Grouchy to move against Wellington's left flank, if Blücher retired on Liege or Brussels. If Blücher concentrated at Wavre, Grouchy would merely send a detachment to feint an attack. It is also asserted that Napoleon sent Grouchy a duplicate of this dispatch early on the 18th, but this remains equally unproven.

After a short nap, Napoleon rose at 0100 and inspected his entire outpost line, returning to his headquarters at Le Caillou (*B2*) at first light. Here he found Grouchy's report. Its contents seemed to indicate that Grouchy was aware of his mission and would move promptly, if necessary, to keep between Wellington and Blücher. It also strengthened his preconception that the Prussians would be out of action for some time to come. Interrogation of deserters from Wellington's army confirmed his impression that Wellington would fight.

Napoleon was confident, and his troops' morale was high. The water-logged soil, however, made it impossible for the French artillery to maneuver. It would be necessary to wait several hours for the ground to drain and dry sufficiently. Even then, low-lying areas would remain swampy. Worse, the effect of artillery fire would be greatly diminished: Round shot would not ricochet effectively along the sodden ground; the fragmentation of howitzer shells would be greatly reduced. At 0500, Napoleon set the hour of attack at 0900.

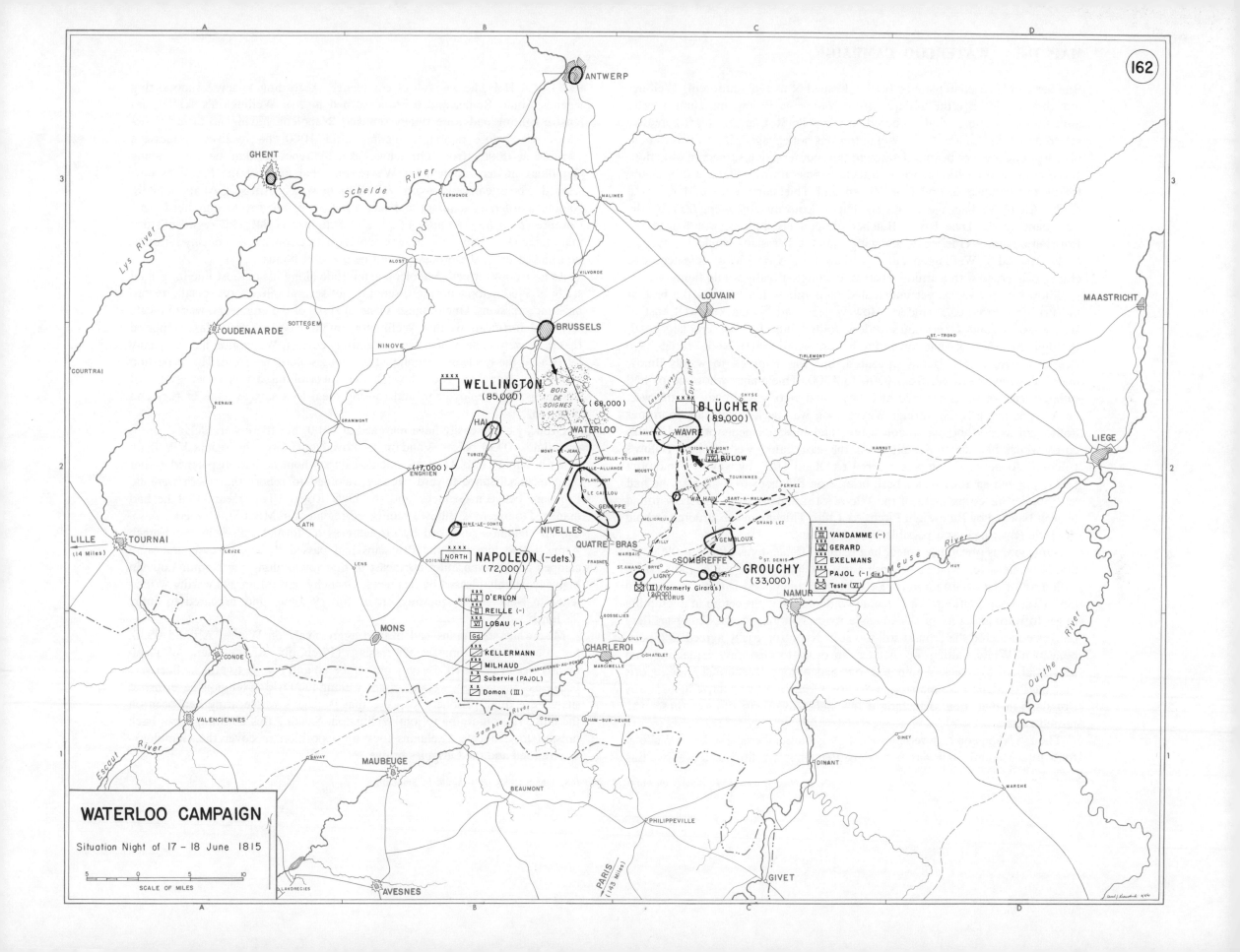

162

WELLINGTON
(85,000)

BLÜCHER
(89,000)

BOIS
DE
SOIGNES   (68,000)

WAVRE

III
IV BÜLOW

(17,000)
ENGHIEN

NORTH

NAPOLEON (−dets.)
(72,000)

NIVELLES

QUATRE-BRAS

GROUCHY
(33,000)

III	VANDAMME (−)
IV	GERARD
	EXELMANS
	PAJOL (−1 div)
	Teste (VI)

I	D'ERLON
II	REILLE (−)
VI	LOBAU (−)
Gd	
	KELLERMANN
	MILHAUD
	Subervie (PAJOL)
	Domon (III)

(II) (formerly Girard's)
(2,000)

LILLE
(14 Miles)

PARIS
(1.43 Miles)

WATERLOO CAMPAIGN

Situation Night of 17 – 18 June 1815

5   0   5   10
SCALE OF MILES

Blücher and Gneisenau planned boldly. Instead of merely reinforcing Wellington, they would seize the initiative from Napoleon. Bülow, marching shortly after 0400, 18 June, would proceed to Chapelle-St.-Lambert (*B3*; hereafter referred to as St.-Lambert). If Wellington was not engaged, Bülow was to hold his corps under cover behind that town, thus conserving his freedom of action. If the battle had begun, he was to attack Napoleon's right flank. Pirch would follow immediately behind him. Zieten and Thielmann were told to stand ready. All heavy baggage would be sent to Louvain (*off map, D3*) by the west bank of the Dyle River. Blücher, despite his injuries, would lead the Prussian advance. Gneisenau, knowing that the Prussians would be dangerously exposed if Wellington either withdrew or was quickly defeated, was chiefly concerned with learning whether Wellington really would fight.

Bülow's corps was as yet undefeated, and Bülow himself was the best of the Prussian corps commanders. However, he had bivouacked well east of Wavre (*C3*), and Gneisenau's orders routed him by one crooked road, through the heart of that town. Pirch, also on the east bank, could have cleared Wavre before Bülow appeared, but was required to watch Bülow march past, as it proved, from 0500 to 1300. Thielmann, whose corps had suffered least of those engaged at Ligny—and who was already on the west bank—was left placidly sitting. Wavre soon was packed with an enormous traffic jam as northbound wagon trains, and those elements of Thielmann's corps which had spent the night on the east bank, wedged into Bülow's columns. At noon, Zieten was ordered to Ohain (*B3*) by way of Froidmont (*B3*). Though he already had been briefed on Blücher's over-all plan, he had left most of his corps south of the Wavre–St.-Lambert road, and now found himself blocked by Bülow and Pirch. At 1300, Thielmann was ordered to hold the Dyle River against a possible French pursuit.

Napoleon, as previously noted, had planned to begin his attack at 0900. At that hour, however, Reille's sluggish corps was just passing Le Caillou (*A2*), with most of the Guard infantry, Kellermann, Lobau, and Durutte still behind him. (The Guard infantry had become scattered the night before in attempting to get forward along footpaths and side roads.) Moreover, the senior artillery officers considered the ground still too soft. Napoleon easily agreed to a postponement. While waiting, he dictated an order to Grouchy, explaining that he was about to attack Wellington, but had become concerned over reports that the Prussians were massing at Wavre. Grouchy was to move against any Prussians in that area, detaching a few light cavalry to observe those who retired eastward.

Though Napoleon believed himself slightly outnumbered (he knew Wellington's total strength, but was not aware that almost a fifth of it was waiting uselessly at Hal), he was full of confidence. According to several moralizing legends, Soult, Reille, and d'Erlon warned him of Wellington's skill in defensive fighting and were rudely rebuked, Napoleon having no taste for defeatist talk before action. Sometime after 1000, he received a message (written at 0600) from Grouchy. Grouchy reported that he was leaving Gembloux at that moment for Wavre, and that most of the Prussians now seemed to be attempting to join Wellington by way of Brussels. At about 1030, Napoleon ordered Jacquinot to detach a hussar regiment to reconnoiter Lasne, Couture (*both B3*), Mousty (*C2*), and Ottignies (*C3*). This regiment's primary mission probably was to seek contact with Grouchy; any enemy information picked up in the process would be a useful bonus.

As his troops formed, Napoleon again rode along his outpost line for a final study of Wellington's position, sending out several officers on specific reconnaissance missions. One of these, General Haxo of the engineers, was to locate any field fortifications that Wellington might have erected. Haxo reported that there were none, which was not entirely correct, Wellington having hastily barricaded the roads and loopholed the houses along his front. His inspection completed, Napoleon rode through the ranks of his army, supervising and hastening their deployment, and rousing them to a savage pitch of fury and devotion.

Grouchy could easily have marched at 0300, but there were delays, and it was almost 0730 before Vandamme moved out. Grouchy reached Walhain (*D2*) at about 1000. Here an aide-de-camp, whom he had dispatched earlier on a reconnaissance toward Mousty, rejoined to report that there were no Prussians between Grouchy and the Dyle River. (This meant that he had managed to overlook Bülow's reinforced regiment in Mont-St.-Guibert.) Also, a local civilian—described by Grouchy as a "former officer in the French Army"—told him that the Prussians had passed through Wavre and were camped about seven miles northeast of that town, along the Namur-Louvain highway. Highly pleased by this news, Grouchy sent off an awkwardly written letter to Napoleon, requesting orders for 19 June, and prepared to enjoy his lunch.

Meanwhile, Exelmans had pushed aggressively on Wavre. Around 0930, his scouts developed masses of Prussians (Pirch, plus stray elements of Thielmann) east of the town. Heavily outnumbered and unable to attack effectively because of the broken, wooded country along the Dyle, Exelmans nevertheless snatched enough prisoners to prove that Blücher's whole army had been on the move since morning to join Wellington. Sending this alarming news back hotspur to Grouchy, Exelmans took up a position to cover the Gembloux-Wavre road and the Ottignies bridge.

Note: On this map (and similarly on Maps 165 and 168), Ohain Creek (B3) should be Smohain Brook.

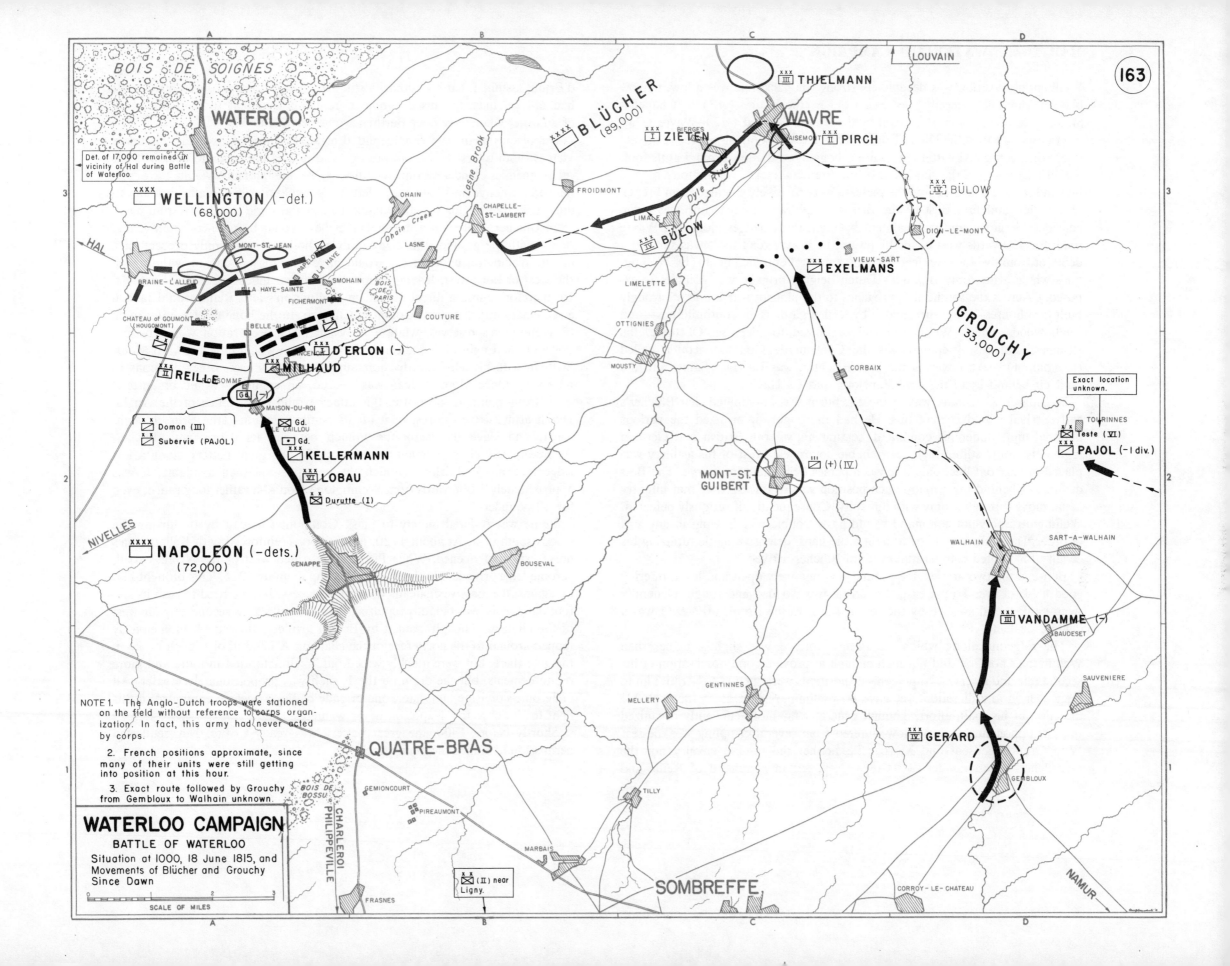

163

BOIS DE SOIGNES

WATERLOO

Det. of 17,000 remained in vicinity of Hal during Battle of Waterloo.

XXXX
WELLINGTON (-det.)
(68,000)

HAL

MONT-ST-JEAN

OHAIN

Ohain Creek

LASNE

Lasne Brook

PAPELOTTE
LA HAYE
SMOHAIN

BRAINE-L'ALLEUD

LA HAYE-SAINTE

FICHERMONT

BOIS DE PARIS

CHATEAU of GOUMONT (HOUGOMONT)

BELLE-ALLIANCE

COUTURE

XXX
I D'ERLON (-)

XXX
II REILLE

XXX
MILHAUD

Gd. (-)

MAISON-DU-ROI

Gd. LE CAILLOU

x x
Domon (III)

x x
Subervie (PAJOL)

Gd.

XXX
KELLERMANN

XXX
VI LOBAU

x x
Durutte (I)

NIVELLES

XXXX
NAPOLEON (-dets.)
(72,000)

GENAPPE

NOTE 1. The Anglo-Dutch troops were stationed on the field without reference to corps organization. In fact, this army had never acted by corps.

2. French positions approximate, since many of their units were still getting into position at this hour.

3. Exact route followed by Grouchy from Gembloux to Walhain unknown.

BOIS DE BOSSU

CHARLEROI
PHILIPPEVILLE

QUATRE-BRAS

GEMIONCOURT

PIREAUMONT

MARBAIS

FRASNES

x x
(II) near Ligny.

WATERLOO CAMPAIGN

BATTLE OF WATERLOO

Situation at 1000, 18 June 1815, and Movements of Blücher and Grouchy Since Dawn

SCALE OF MILES

LOUVAIN

XXX
III THIELMANN

XXXX
BLÜCHER
(89,000)

XXX
I ZIETEN

BIERGES

WAVRE

VAISEMONT

XXX
II PIRCH

FROIDMONT

LIMALE

Dyle River

CHAPELLE-ST-LAMBERT

XXX
IV BÜLOW

XXX
IV BÜLOW

DION-LE-MONT

LIMELETTE

VIEUX-SART

XXX
EXELMANS

OTTIGNIES

CORBAIX

MOUSTY

GROUCHY
(33,000)

Exact location unknown.

TOURINNES

XXX
MONT-ST-GUIBERT

III (+) (IV)

WALHAIN

SART-A-WALHAIN

XXX
Teste (VI)

XXX
PAJOL (-I div.)

XXX
III VANDAMME (-)

BAUDESET

MELLERY

GENTINNES

BOUSEVAL

SAUVENIERE

XXX
IV GERARD

GEMBLOUX

TILLY

SOMBREFFE

CORROY-LE-CHATEAU

NAMUR

Wellington's position was deceptively strong. Its backbone was a low, narrow plateau, running generally west-east from Merbe-Braine (*A2*) to Chapelle-St.-Jacques (*C3*), its crest marked by the Braine l'Alleud (*A2*)–Wavre (*D3*) road (usually called the Ohain Road). The plateau's south slope was relatively steep; this, combined with the fortuitous bogging of the low ground at its foot, would take much of the shock out of the French attacks. Wellington's second line and reserves, held behind the plateau, were relatively shielded from French observation and fire. East of the Brussels highway, his first line was given considerable cover and concealment by high, thick hedges along the Wavre road; for 450 yards west of the highway, the Wavre road itself was sunk to a depth of from five to seven feet, forming a natural entrenchment. (Of Wellington's whole army, only Bijlandt's Dutch-Belgian brigade was completely exposed.) Across the southern approaches to the plateau was a line of strongly built farmhouses—each surrounded by walled gardens and outbuildings—and small woods, which Wellington had organized for defense. Of these, the strongest and best prepared was the Chateau de Goumont (often called Hougomont); next, covering the British center, was La Haye-Sainte and the sand pit behind it; to the east, Papelotte and La Haye.

Wellington's left flank was in the air, but it was anticipated that Blücher's early arrival would correct this. He had thoroughly intermixed the various national units under his command, so that his veteran British and German regiments would stiffen their less reliable comrades. Most of his artillery was placed in his front line, only a few companies being held in reserve. The Bois de Soignes behind the Anglo-Dutch position was so thick-grown that infantry could move through it only with difficulty. Consequently, if seriously defeated, Wellington's polyglot command would have trouble withdrawing in any sort of order. He could only hope to fight a die-hard, defensive battle, utilizing his cavalry for limited counterattacks, until Blücher arrived.

Between the two armies, the ground was relatively open and level, offering good fields of fire. To the east, the terrain was wooded and rough. Generally steep-banked and swollen by the recent rains, Lasne Brook (*D2–D3*) was a definite obstacle.

The ridgeline along which the French formed was slightly higher than Wellington's position, but not high enough to provide good observation of his second line and reserves. Napoleon's dispositions were such as to permit him to maneuver in any direction, yet gave no preliminary hint as to the probable direction of his main effort. Though generally far more efficiently organized than its opponent, his army now suffered from several crippling weaknesses: With Grouchy absent and Mortier ill, neither the reserve cavalry nor the Guard had a commander of its own; Ney, left in command of Reille and

d'Erlon, assumed that his authority still extended to Kellermann's corps; Soult had not yet mastered his assignment, remaining content to send one copy of an order when "My poor Berthier would have sent six."

Napoleon's plan was simple and drastic. He needed a quick, complete victory, both to restore his old prestige and to free his hands to deal with his other enemies. Under normal conditions, he undoubtedly would have maneuvered to envelop Wellington's left flank, exploiting his greater mobility to thus strike Wellington's tactical flank and, at the same time, drive him away from Blücher. But such a movement at best would be time-consuming, and now—with the ground still boggy in every hollow—could only proceed at a crawl. Wellington undoubtedly would have warning enough to withdraw to the west or northwest, leaving Napoleon only an indecisive tactical success. He therefore chose a direct attack on Wellington's left. Reille would launch a secondary attack toward Goumont Chateau, in the hope of attracting some of Wellington's reserves, while a heavy artillery preparation would be put down on the English left and center. D'Erlon then would attack toward Mont-St.-Jean with his left-flank division, supporting it with his other divisions as necessary. Once Mont-St.-Jean was cleared, his engineers would organize it as a strong point. If successful, this attack would crush much of the Anglo-Dutch army, drive the rest of it off its communications (the Brussels highway), and leave the victorious French between its debris and Blücher. Approximately eighty cannon were massed in one great battery along a low ridge in front of d'Erlon. Though the best position then available, it was approximately 1,000 yards from Wellington's front—a rather long range, even for 12-pounders.

Reille was ordered merely to mask Goumont Chateau by occupying the woods south of it. At about 1120, his artillery (reinforced with Kellermann's horse artillery) opened. While Pire demonstrated west of the Nivelles road, Jerome led a brigade into the woods, clearing them by 1215. This brought him up against the massive chateau. Wild with success, Jerome tried to rush its six-foot park walls, was bloodily repulsed, then committed his second brigade west of the chateau. Though mauled by British artillery, this attack momentarily lapped around to the north face of the chateau. A handful of French broke in the gate there, but were quickly wiped out. Wellington fed in more and more reinforcements, but the drain on the French was proportionately greater. All of Jerome's division and, later, one brigade of Foy's became entangled in this fight for an objective Napoleon never wanted.

Shortly before 1300, the great battery was ready to fire. Ney requested permission to launch the main attack.

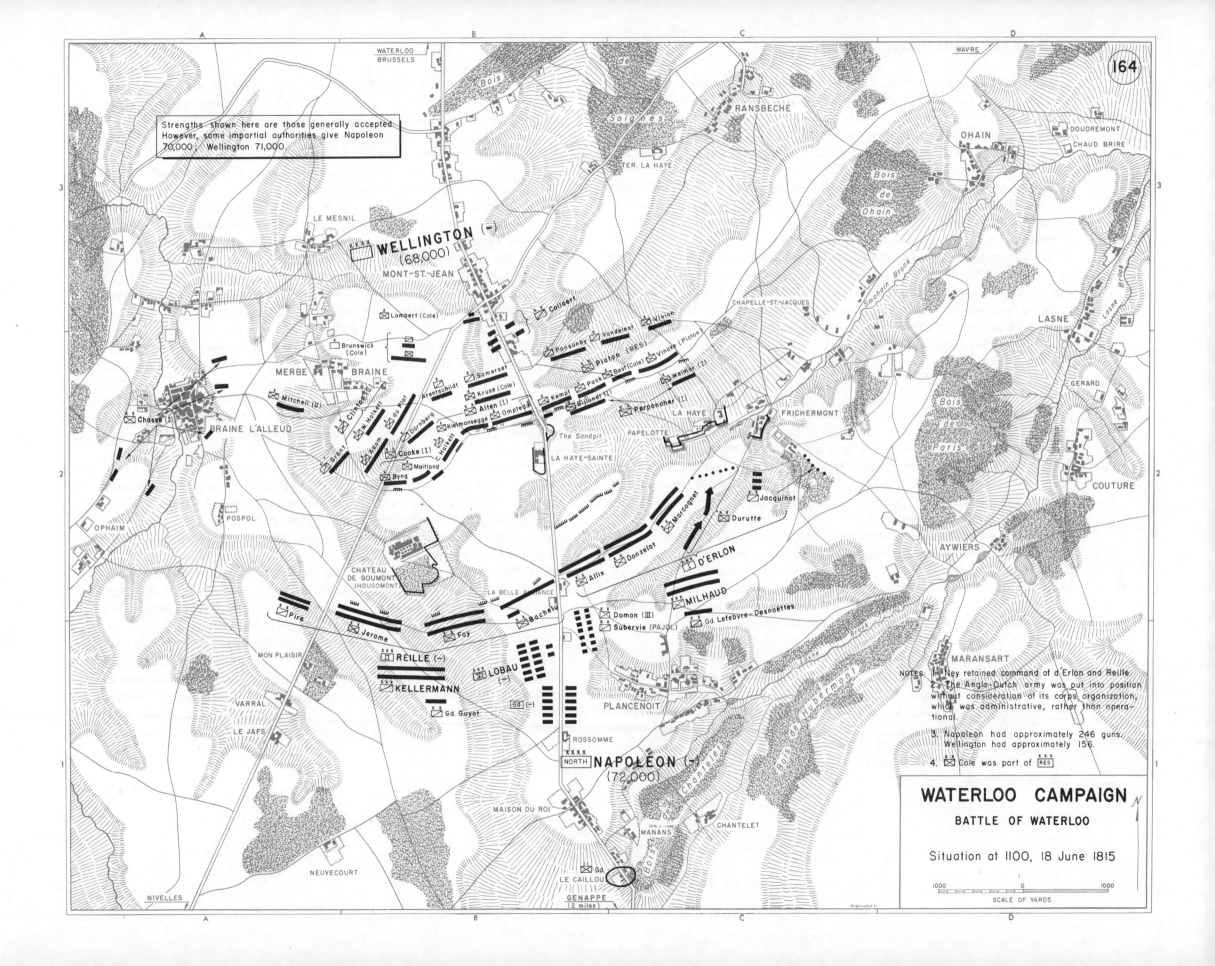

164

WATERLOO BRUSSELS

Bois
Saignes
de

RANSBECHE

WAVRE

OHAIN

DOUDREMONT

CHAUD BRIRE

Strengths shown here are those generally accepted
However, some impartial authorities give Napoleon
70,000 ; Wellington 71,000.

Bois
de
Ohain

LE MESNIL

TER. LA HAYE

CHAPELLE-ST-JACQUES

LASNE

WELLINGTON (-)
(68,000)
MONT-ST.-JEAN

Calisort

Lambert (Cole)

Vivian

Vandeleur

Ponsonby

Brunswick
(Cole)

Picton (RES)

Vincke (Picton)

Somerset

Pack

Best (Cole)

MERBE BRAINE

Arentschildt

Alten (1)

Kruse (Cole)

Kempt

Weimar

GERARD

Mitchell (II)

Dornberg

Kielmansegge

Ompteda

Bijlandt

Perponcher (1)

LA HAYE

Bois

Chasse (1)

W.Halkett

C.Halkett

Kruse (Cole)

PAPELOTTE

FRICHERMONT

de

BRAINE L'ALLEUD

Grant

Adam

du Plat

Cooke (1)

LA HAYE-SAINTE

The Sandpit

Paris

Byng

Maitland

COUTURE

POSPOL

Jacquinot

OPHAIM

Marcognet

Durutte

AYWIERS

CHATEAU
DE GOUMONT
(HOUGOMONT)

Donzelot

D'ERLON

Allix

MILHAUD

LA BELLE ALLIANCE

Pire

Bachelu

Domon (III)

Gd. Lefebvre-Desnoettes

Jerome

Foy

Subervie (PAJOL)

MON PLAISIR

MARANSART

REILLE (-)

LOBAU
(-)

NOTES: 1. Ney retained command of d'Erlon and Reille.
2. The Anglo-Dutch army was put into position
without consideration of its corps organization,
which was administrative, rather than operational.

KELLERMANN

Gd (-)

VARRAL

PLANCENOIT

3. Napoleon had approximately 246 guns;
Wellington had approximately 156.

LE JAFS

Gd. Guyot

4. Cole was part of RES

ROSSOMME

NAPOLEON (-)
NORTH
(72,000)

WATERLOO CAMPAIGN

BATTLE OF WATERLOO

MAISON DU ROI

MANANS

CHANTELET

Situation at 1100, 18 June 1815

NEUVECOURT

Gd

LE CAILLOU

NIVELLES

GENAPPE
(2 miles)

1000   0   1000
SCALE OF YARDS

Even as Ney requested orders, Napoleon's attention was called to an odd change in the appearance of the ridge around St.-Lambert (*B3*)—the whole area was darkening, as if a large body of troops were massing there. Some of his staff dismissed it as merely the shadow of a cloud, but cavalry was sent to make certain. If there were troops at St.-Lambert, they could only be enemy. The riddle was solved when Jacquinot's hussars brought in a group of Prussian prisoners and an intercepted message from Bülow to Wellington, revealing that Bülow was at St.-Lambert and Blücher's other three corps around Wavre (*C3*). Grouchy, the prisoners said, was not in contact with the Prussians.

The situation demanded a quick decision, which might determine the fate of France and Napoleon. The French army was fully deployed, but not committed, and so could still withdraw. Napoleon believed Wellington slightly stronger than himself; in addition, he now had a big Prussian corps on his right flank, with the rest of Blücher's army behind it. In 1814, Napoleon probably would have retired. Now, only quick and decisive victory would suffice. Even if he withdrew successfully and recalled Grouchy, he would find himself badly outnumbered by the combined armies of Blücher and Wellington, while other Allied armies were closing in all along France's frontiers.

Napoleon courageously chose the bolder course. Even if Wellington should be considerably reinforced, he was certain of his ability to beat both Wellington and Bülow. Also, Bülow plainly was not rushing to the rescue of his ally, and Grouchy should now be close enough to Wavre to have fixed a considerable portion of the Prussians there. Lobau, with Domon and Subervie, would cover the French right flank. Grouchy was warned that he must march at once to rejoin the main army and crush Bülow.

Bülow had marched slowly, apparently forgetting his orders en route. Arriving at St.-Lambert, he neither kept his troops under cover nor attacked. At 1500, with his corps fully assembled, he still was sitting bashfully in full view around St.-Lambert, unwilling to risk a crossing of Lasne Brook. A small Prussian detachment had entered the Bois de Paris (*B3*), but made no effort to establish contact with the French right flank. Blücher was back along the road from Wavre, urging his troops forward through the mud.

At Walhain (*D2*), Grouchy's lunch was interrupted at 1130 by the swelling sound of artillery fire off to the west. Local citizens placed it along the southern edge of the Bois de Soignes (*A3*). Gerard and several other senior officers immediately urged Grouchy to march to the sound of the guns. The discussion grew hot. Grouchy, disliking both the advice and the vehemence with which it was offered, stood stiffly on his orders—as he understood them—to "follow the Prussians," and refused Gerard's request to be allowed at least to take

his own corps westward. (Had he accepted this advice, Grouchy could have reached the outskirts of Napoleon's battle by 1900. His mere approach probable would have kept Blücher off Napoleon's right flank.)

At this point (about 1230), Exelmans' courier came in to report Wavre swarming with Prussians. Grouchy at once moved on that town with Vandamme and Gerard. Pajol now reported no trace of Prussians around Tourinnes; Grouchy ordered him to seize Limale (*C3*).

Fighting had already begun east of Wavre, the Prussian detachment from Mont-St.-Guibert having made a dash through Exelmans' outpost line to reach the town. Grouchy ordered Vandamme to seize the heights along the east bank of the Dyle, while Exelmans turned the left flank of the Prussian rearguard position there. He then rode briefly southward toward Limelette (*C3*) in hopes of getting a better idea of the constantly growing battle to the west. Returning, still unenlightened, he was overtaken by a staff officer with Napoleon's order of 1000, directing him to march on Wavre. Feeling thereby justified, Grouchy continued to Wavre, to find that Vandamme had, despite his orders, shoved his head into a sack. Attacking from march column, without reconnaissance or artillery preparation, Vandamme had quickly cleared the east bank, but lost heavily in repeated, unsuccessful attempts to rush the Wavre bridges. Caught under the plunging fire of Prussian batteries on the high west bank, his troops in the eastern suburb could neither advance nor withdraw.

Thielmann had received orders at about 1500 to march on Couture (*B3*), leaving two battalions to garrison Wavre. On attempting to march, he found the roads blocked by Pirch and Zieten until around 1600. Considering Exelmans no real threat, he then began moving off, but Vandamme's appearance forced him to halt and improvise a defense. His effort was somewhat haphazard. One of his brigades, ordered to retire into corps reserve, wandered off to Ohain (*B3*). Fortunately, one of Zieten's brigades (probably equally lost and confused) had remained at Limale. The fighting was hard, but indecisive. Grouchy made several attempts to cross above and below Wavre, but was thwarted by swampy terrain and the determined defense.

At St.-Lambert, Bülow gingerly began crossing Lasne Brook sometime after 1500. The slopes were steep, the bridge narrow, the troops weary; more important, Bülow was unenthusiastic. About 1600, an unexpected outburst of artillery fire from the direction of Wavre shocked the Prussians. But Blücher, seeing Wellington under heavy pressure, finally browbeat Bülow into continuing the crossing (1630). By 1800, all of his corps was across and ready for action.

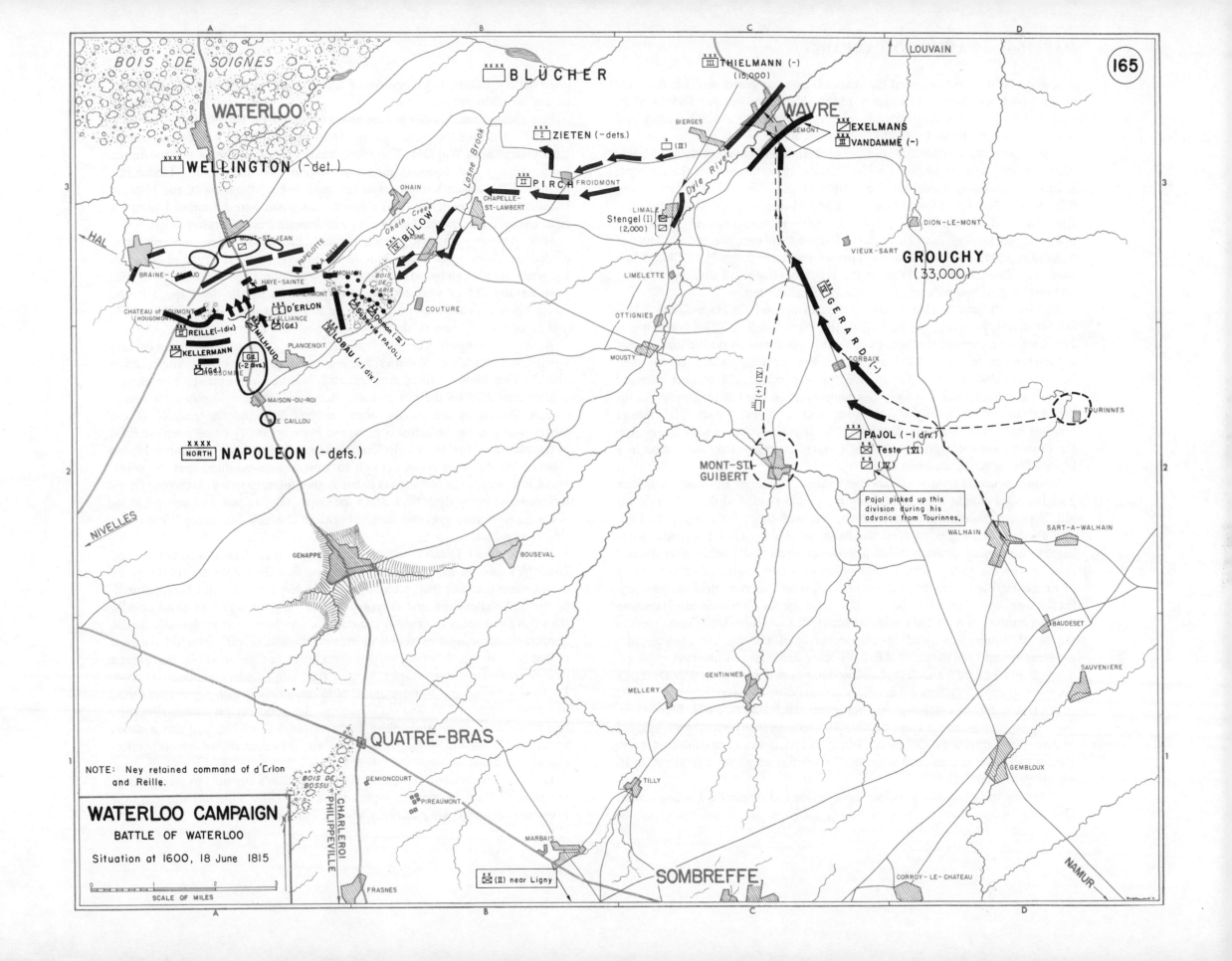

165

BOIS DE SOIGNES

WATERLOO

LOUVAIN

XXXX □ BLÜCHER

XXX III THIELMANN (-)
(15,000)

WAVRE

BIERGES

WELLINGTON (-det.)

XXX I ZIETEN (-dets.)

SEMONT

XXX EXELMANS
III VANDAMME (-)

OHAIN

XXX II PIRCH   FROIDMONT

CHAPELLE-
ST-LAMBERT

Lasne Brook

Dyle River

DION-LE-MONT

Ohain Creek

LIMALE
Stengel (I)
(2,000)

VIEUX-SART

GROUCHY
(33,000)

XXX BÜLOW
lX LASNE

MONT-ST-JEAN

PAPELOTTE

LA HAYE

LIMELETTE

PLANCENOIT bois
BOIS DE PARIS

LA HAYE-SAINTE

GERARD

BRAINE-L'ALLEUD

FRICHERMONT

D'ERLON
LA BELLE
ALLIANCE
(Gd.)

Durutte (III)
Subervie (PAJOL)

COUTURE

OTTIGNIES

CHATEAU of GOUMONT
(HOUGOMONT)

XXX REILLE (-1 div.)

LOBAU (-1 div.)

CORBAIX (-)

XXX KELLERMANN

MILHAUD

PLANCENOIT

Gd.
(-2 divs.)

MOUSTY

(Gd.)
MONTSOMME

(+) (IV)

MAISON-DU-ROI

LE CAILLOU

XXXX NORTH NAPOLEON (-dets.)

MONT-ST-
GUIBERT

XXX PAJOL (-1 div.)

Teste (VI)

TOURINNES

(IV)

NIVELLES

Pajol picked up this
division during his
advance from Tourinnes.

WALHAIN

SART-A-WALHAIN

GENAPPE

BOUSEVAL

BAUDESET

SAUVENIERE

MELLERY

GENTINNES

CHARLEROI
PHILIPPEVILLE

QUATRE-BRAS

BOIS DE
BOSSU

GEMIONCOURT

TILLY

GEMBLOUX

PIREAUMONT

NOTE: Ney retained command of d'Erlon
and Reille.

MARBAIS

WATERLOO CAMPAIGN
BATTLE OF WATERLOO
Situation at 1600, 18 June 1815

0   1   2   3
SCALE OF MILES

XX (II) near Ligny

SOMBREFFE

CORROY-LE-CHATEAU

NAMUR

FRASNES

The great battery had pounded the Anglo-Dutch left center and left flank for about a half-hour when (at roughly 1345) d'Erlon advanced. Thanks to its sheltered position, the Anglo-Dutch infantry (except Bijlandt's brigade) had suffered relatively little. Its artillery, however, had been hit hard.

The French came on swiftly, swarms of skirmishers covering their advance. Allix sent one brigade against La Haye-Sainte, his other against the sand pit. D'Erlon's remaining three divisions followed in echelon. For some reason, d'Erlon and Ney had formed Donzelot's and Marcognet's divisions into massive "columns of battalions," which the miry ground and tall grain soon clubbed into jostling crowds. Durutte followed, in two brigade columns of battalions, thus doubling his front. Travers' cuirassier brigade (Milhaud [*not shown*]) followed d'Erlon. West of the highway, Bachelu's division (Reille) and one of Kellermann's brigades covered d'Erlon's left.

The French quickly cleared the enclosures around La Haye-Sainte but—lacking artillery—could not break into the main buildings. The sand pit and Papelotte were captured; Bijlandt's ill-used brigade ran away. Wellington sent a battalion to reinforce La Haye-Sainte, but Travers rode it down, then hunted the skirmishers covering Wellington's center. Marcognet plunged across the Ohain road, but Donzelot halted just short of it to deploy. As his jumbled battalions struggled into line, Picton shouted Pack and Kempt forward in a counterattack. Staggered by English volleys and artillery fire, the French gave some ground, but then hung just below the Ohain road in a furious fire fight. Picton was killed.

Seizing the exact moment, Uxbridge charged. Somerset's brigade of British guard cavalry caught Travers crossing the Ohain road, and drove him downhill. Somerset then turned on Bachelu, but was thoroughly repulsed. Ponsonby's three regiments charged the flanks of Allix's, Donzelot's, and Marcognet's struggling divisions. Completely surprised, the French were herded back across the valley, losing 3,000 men and two eagles. Two companies of French artillery, caught in the stampede, were overrun. Brilliantly begun, the charge now ran wild. Seeing the great battery threatened, Napoleon ordered another of Milhaud's brigades forward; Jacquinot swung his lancers to the left. Ponsonby was killed, his brigade wrecked. Durutte had been advancing steadily until the defeat of d'Erlon's other divisions left his flank exposed. Though attacked by Vandeleur, he retired in fair order. Repulsed by Durutte's reserve regiment, Vandeleur was finally driven off by Jacquinot.

D'Erlon's shaken corps was not reformed until almost 1600. Meanwhile, Wellington reinforced La Haye-Sainte; Napoleon ordered howitzers employed against the Chateau de Goumont, where pointless brawling still continued. Shellfire soon set the chateau afire, but its reinforced garrison held out in its walled garden and chapel.

Assessing the situation, Napoleon now decided to smash the English center. Ordering Ney to clear the way by taking La Haye-Sainte, he reinforced the great battery, told Pire to demonstrate toward Braine l'Alleud, and began preparing his main attack.

Pire accomplished nothing. Ney again occupied La Haye-Sainte's grounds, but could not take the buildings. By 1600, the artillery duel reached an intensity surpassing Wagram. The more numerous French guns got the upper hand; Anglo-Dutch losses in men and cannon mounted rapidly. Under this pounding, Wellington's fraying line fell back behind the crest of the plateau; Lambert, the Brunswickers, and elements of Chasse were summoned from his right to rebuild his sagging center, as was Vincke from his extreme left.

Half glimpsing this withdrawal through the smoke, Ney excitedly concluded that Wellington was about to retreat. He ordered Milhaud forward. By some error, Lefebvre-Desnoëttes followed him. The beginnings of this great cavalry charge were hidden from Napoleon by the dead space in the valley below his command post. It was in full career when he first glimpsed it, and he could only remark that it was an hour too early.

Again Ney bungled. Veering erratically across the field, he sent the cavalry against Wellington's right center, the least-damaged part of the Anglo-Dutch line. Neither horse artillery nor infantry followed in support. The British artillerymen fired till the last minute, then took refuge in the nearest square or ran. Slowed by the muddy slope, artillery fire, and the passage of the Ohain road and the abandoned guns, the French cavalry came over the crest of the plateau to find the Anglo-Dutch infantry in two lines of squares, placed checkerwise. Without room enough to work up momentum, met by point-blank musketry, their best efforts to break that infantry failed. Uxbridge counterattacked, forcing them back down the slope. They rallied, and drove him in. Some English guns got into action between charges, but many cannoneers simply vanished.

Napoleon had Domon's report that Bülow was finally advancing, and Grouchy's message from Walhain, indicating that Grouchy was still far to the east. Grimly deciding that, premature or not, Ney's attack must be supported, he ordered Kellermann and Guyot forward. This actually was more cavalry than there was room to use, but their attack was bitter and prolonged. British accounts insist no squares were broken; nevertheless, several seem to have been thoroughly cut up. After a fourth unsuccessful charge at 1800, the French retired, shaken and discouraged, most of their commanders wounded or dead. Except for Vivian and Vandeleur, all of Wellington's British cavalry was used up; much of his artillery was out of action. Ney suddenly remembered that he had Bachelu's division and one of Foy's brigades available, and thrust them, unsupported, against Wellington's line. Caught in converging fire, this effort quickly crumbled.

Lobau meanwhile had repeatedly defeated Bülow's attempts to emerge from the Bois de Paris. However, exploiting their greatly superior numbers, the Prussians began working clumsily toward Plancenoit (*C1*).

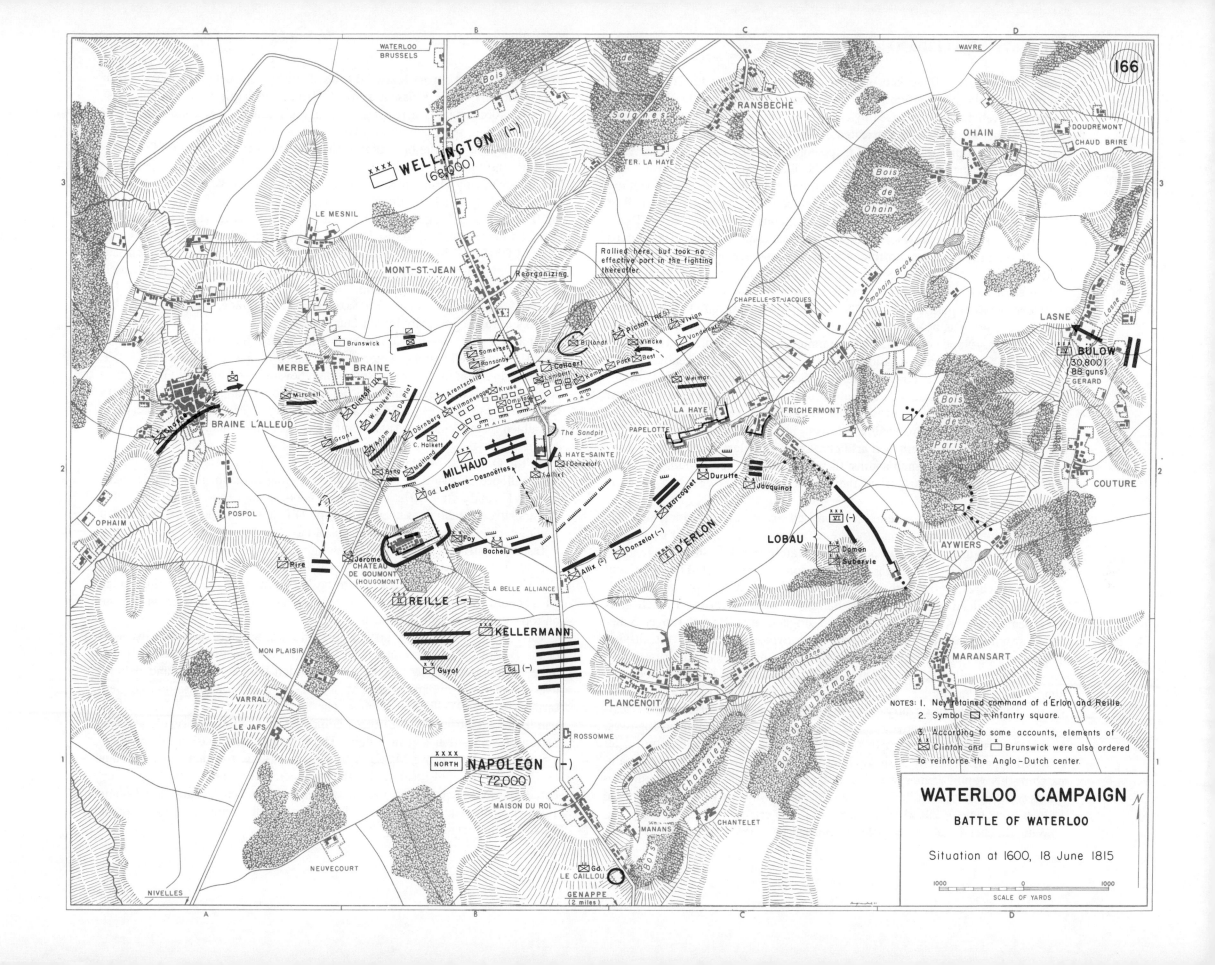

166

WATERLOO
BRUSSELS

WAVRE

WELLINGTON (-)
(68,000)

RANSBECHE

OHAIN

DOUDREMONT

CHAUD BRIRE

Bois de Saignes

Bois de Ohain

LE MESNIL

TER. LA HAYE

MONT-ST.-JEAN

Reorganizing.

Rallied here, but took no
effective part in the fighting
thereafter

CHAPELLE-ST-JACQUES

LASNE

MERBE BRAINE

Brunswick

Somerset
Ponsonby

Bijlandt

Picton (RK)

Vincke

Vivian

Vandeleur

Cotter?

Kempt

Pack

Best

Weimar

Mitchell

Ompteda
Arentschildt
Kilmansegge Kruse

Lambert

LA HAYE

FRICHERMONT

BÜLOW
(30,800)
(88 guns)

GERARD

Bois de Paris

Sharpe

BRAINE L'ALLEUD

Grant

Clinton
W. Halkett
Du Plat

Dörnberg

The Sandpit

PAPELOTTE

Adam

C. Halkett

HAYE-SAINTE
(Donzelot)

COUTURE

OPHAIM

POSPOL

Byng

Maitland

MILHAUD

Gd. Lefebvre-Desnoëttes

Allix

(Allix)

Gd. (-)

Durutte

Jacquinot

AYWIERS

Foy

Bachelu

Donzelot (-)

Morcognet

VI (-)

D'ERLON

LOBAU

Domon
Subervie

Pire

Jerome
CHATEAU
DE GOUMONT
(HOUGOMONT)

Allix (?)

LA BELLE ALLIANCE

MARANSART

II REILLE (-)

KELLERMANN

MON PLAISIR

Guyot

Gd. (-)

PLANCENOIT

VARRAL

LE JAFS

ROSSOMME

NOTES: 1. Ney retained command of d'Erlon and Reille.
2. Symbol ☐ = infantry square.
3. According to some accounts, elements of
Clinton and Brunswick were also ordered
to reinforce the Anglo-Dutch center.

NORTH

NAPOLEON (-)
(72,000)

MAISON DU ROI

MANANS

CHANTELET

WATERLOO CAMPAIGN

BATTLE OF WATERLOO

Situation at 1600, 18 June 1815

NEUVECOURT

NIVELLES

Gd.
LE CAILLOU

GENAPPE
(2 miles)

1000   0   1000
SCALE OF YARDS

French skirmishers had worked up close to the buildings of La Haye-Sainte, and the defenders' ammunition was running low. Two of Ompteda's battalions, sent to their relief, were surprised by cuirassiers. One was destroyed, the other badly hurt before Uxbridge extricated it. Having ridden along his lines to check the battle's progress, at 1730 Napoleon again ordered Ney to seize La Haye-Sainte. This time, there was heavy artillery support, directed at both La Haye-Sainte and the Anglo-Dutch positions behind it. Personally leading an infantry regiment and a company of engineers, Ney took his objective at 1800 in a furious, no-quarter assault. Simultaneously, Durutte retook Papelotte. French skirmishers swarmed through the sand pit; Ney got several guns into action on the knoll just north of La Haye-Sainte. Seeing Wellington's center definitely flinching, he called on Napoleon for infantry reinforcements.

Napoleon was fighting for his army's life against Blücher.

Blücher's enveloping attack finally had captured Plancenoit (C1). Prussian artillery fire was beginning to reach the French reserves along the Brussels highway—Napoleon's line of communication. Napoleon committed Duhesme's Young Guard division (4,000), recapturing Plancenoit. Bülow counterattacked, took a costly repulse, rallied, and attacked again—north, west, and south. Duhesme was mortally wounded; the Young Guard thrown out in disorder. Napoleon sent two Old Guard battalions, with orders to use the bayonet. Two battalions against fourteen, they flushed Plancenoit, chasing the Prussians back into their own artillery. Checked at last when Blücher concentrated every available man against their rush, they retired unpursued. Some 3,000 Prussian casualties marked their track. Lobau likewise had counterattacked successfully.

Though denied reinforcements, Ney pressed his attack. All along Wellington's left flank and center, clouds of French skirmishers, supported by aggressively handled guns, worked up onto the plateau in snarling, short-range fighting. A few cuirassier squadrons followed, forcing the Anglo-Dutch to stay massed in squares, or riding them down if they deployed. Kempt was battered; Ompteda was dead and his brigade shattered; Kruse wavering; French guns were demolishing Kielmansegge's ruined brigade at 100-yard range. Stalemated around Chateau Goumont, the French bypassed it to the west, driving in Clinton's right flank. Counterattacks by the Brunswickers and Kruse's Nassau contingent collapsed. Even English regiments faltered, having "fed death" almost beyond endurance. The British and German cavalry sacrificed itself vainly; Dutch-Belgian cavalry refused to charge; a Hanoverian hussar regiment ran away. The wounded, and growing numbers of unwounded fugitives, streamed northward. Through this gathering disaster rode Wellington, to all outward appearances icily unshaken, herding the Brunswickers forward again, patching his gaping center with his last reserve artillery. Further reinforcements were en route from his extreme right; meanwhile, it still would take the French some time to kill what remained of his veterans.

With Blücher repulsed, Napoleon returned at 1900 to his original battle.

From the smoking uproar eastward toward Wavre, Grouchy obviously was at grips with part of the Prussian army. In front, the battle was at high crisis: Some reinforcements had reached Wellington's center; Ney's guns, north of La Haye-Sainte, were being smothered; in places, the French were forced off the plateau. But Durutte had taken La Haye, and Wellington's right flank was sagging. Insofar as Napoleon could determine, Bülow was whipped, and Wellington's army so shattered that one more hard blow would finish it.

Prussian help was slow. Pirch began crawling across Lasne Brook at about 1830. Thielmann begged for reinforcements, which Gneisenau (ignorant of Grouchy's true strength) refused. It was 1800 before Zieten's advance guard reached Ohain. Wellington demanded that he reinforce the Anglo-Dutch left; Blücher ordered him to support Bülow. Both seemed unattractive lost causes. After considerable mental jiggling, Zieten finally moved against Durutte. His confused artillerymen opened on Saxe-Weimar's brigade, stampeding it, but Zieten's advance gradually forced Durutte back.

Napoleon had eleven battalions of Old Guard infantry available. Eight would attack Wellington's center, with a ninth detached to cover their left; two would remain in reserve at Rossomme. Several companies of Guard horse artillery would advance with them, and Ney would support them with every serviceable unit of Reille, d'Erlon, and the cavalry. Weary French artillerymen redoubled their pounding. Anglo-Dutch casualties mounted, but the survivors endured.

As the Old Guard battalions came forward, Napoleon turned them over to Ney, galloped eastward to rally Durutte's reeling division, then dashed back to press his main attack. He was too late. Ney—gone beserk—had committed the first five battalions as they came up. D'Erlon attacked once more, but Reille scarcely budged. Only a handful of cavalry joined the advance.

Instead of striking straight ahead, along the short, relatively sheltered route into Wellington's wrecked center, Ney led the five battalions northwestward along the same diagonal track where he had sent the cavalry. Anglo-Dutch guns behind Chateau Goumont enfiladed their advance. Ney moved with them, on foot, losing all control of the action.

Raked front and flank by artillery fire, the first battalion attacked just west of the Brussels highway, routing the Brunswickers and driving Halkett's battered troops. But Chasse, arriving with a Dutch-Belgian brigade and battery, overwhelmed it by a flank attack. Minutes later, the second battalion momentarily broke into Wellington's center. The third column (two battalions, which had linked up during their advance) collided with Maitland's brigade and was driven downhill after a savage fight. The fifth battalion, pushing through intense artillery fire, drove Maitland back, but was itself outflanked by Adam.

The Guard's repulse (around 2010) staggered the French. Wellington ordered his whole line forward. Zieten wedged in between Durutte and Lobau; Blücher again assailed Plancenoit. The panic cry of *"Sauve qui peut!"* spread from d'Erlon's right flank.

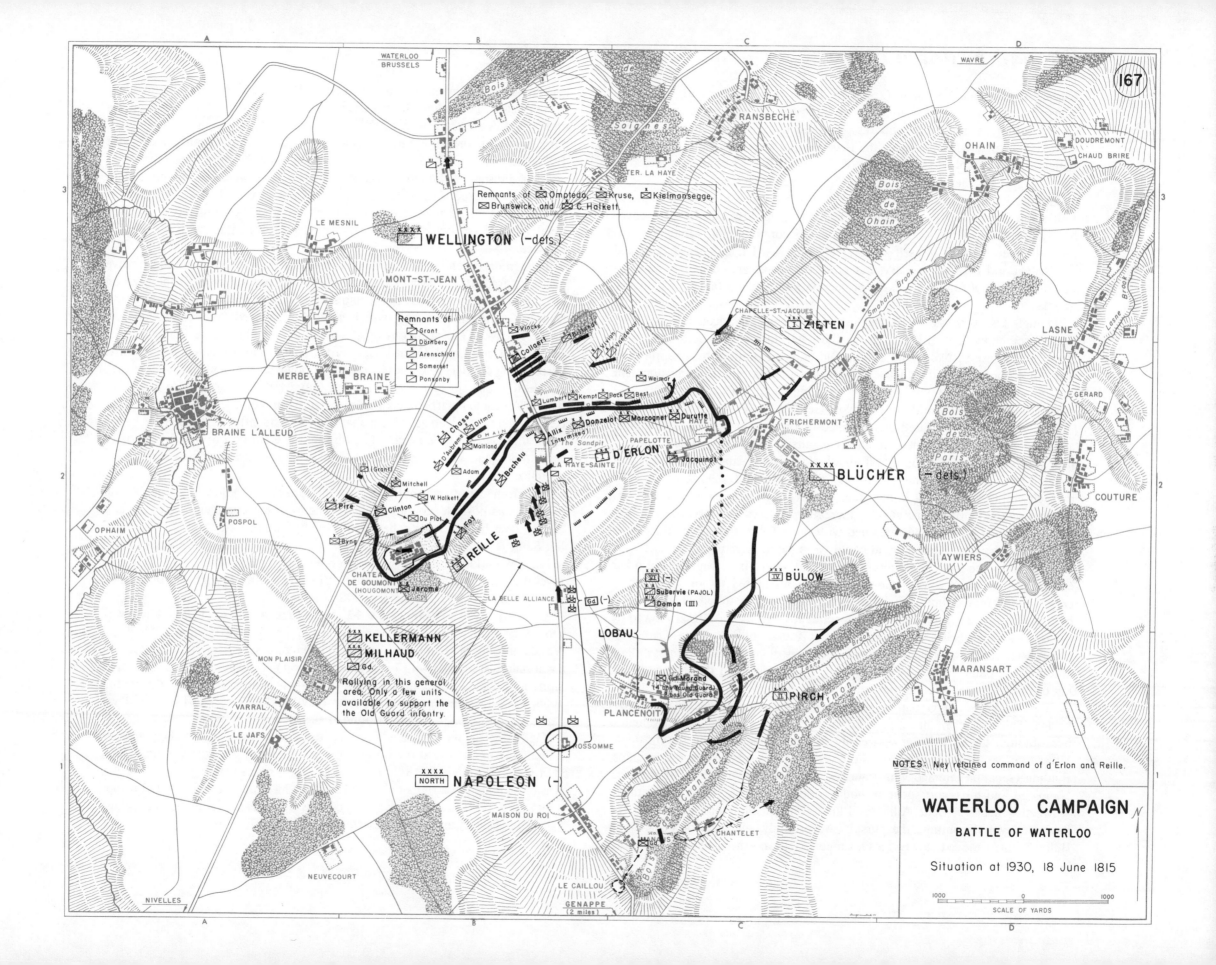

167

WATERLOO
BRUSSELS

WAVRE

Bois de Soignes

RANSBECHE

OHAIN

DOUDREMONT

CHAUD BRIRE

Bois de Ohain

Remnants of ⊠ Ompteda, ⊠ Kruse, ⊠ Kielmansegge,
⊠ Brunswick, and ⊠ C. Halkett.

LE MESNIL

TER. LA HAYE

XXXX WELLINGTON (-dets.)

CHAPELLE-ST-JACQUES

ZIETEN

LASNE

MONT-ST.-JEAN

Smohain Brook

Lasne Brook

GERARD

Remnants of
Grant
Dornberg
Arenschildt
Somerset
Ponsonby

MERBE BRAINE

Vincke
Colbert

Best
Vivian
Vandeleur

Weimar

FRICHERMONT

Bois de Paris

BRAINE L'ALLEUD

Chasse Ditmar
D'Aubreme Maitland
Adam
Bachelu

Lambert Kempt Pack Best
Donzelot Marcognet Durutte
Allix (Intermixed)
The Sandpit
D'ERLON
Jacquinot

LA HAVE

PAPELOTTE

COUTURE

XXXX BLÜCHER (-dets.)

Grant
Mitchell
W. Halkett
Clinton Du Plat
Pire
Foy
Byng

LA HAYE-SAINTE

AYWIERS

REILLE

IV BÜLOW

CHATEAU DE GOUMONT (HOUGOMONT)
Jerome

LA BELLE ALLIANCE

VI (-)
Subervie (PAJOL)
Damon (III)

Gd (-)

MARANSART

LOBAU

XXX KELLERMANN
XXX MILHAUD
Gd.

Rallying in this general area. Only a few units available to support the Old Guard infantry.

Gd Morand
(4 the Young Guard 8 bas Old Guard)

Lasne Brook

II PIRCH

PLANCENOIT

MON PLAISIR

POSPOL

OPHAIM

VARRAL

LE JAFS

NOTES: Ney retained command of d'Erlon and Reille.

Rossomme

XXXX
NORTH NAPOLEON (-)

Bois de Hubermont

WATERLOO CAMPAIGN

BATTLE OF WATERLOO

MAISON DU ROI

Bois de Chantelet

CHANTELET

Situation at 1930, 18 June 1815

NEUVECOURT

LE CAILLOU

Gd

1000   0   1000

NIVELLES

GENAPPE (2 miles)

SCALE OF YARDS

Napoleon did what he could (*see Map 167*). While his escort squadrons charged desperately to gain minutes, he stationed the four uncommitted Old Guard battalions in a line of squares below La Haye-Sainte. The two reserve battalions formed squares astride the Brussels highway, just south of La Belle Alliance (*B2*), flanked by a battery of Guard artillery. Lobau was told that he must hold Blücher until the army withdrew behind him.

Though some French batteries fought to the last, the Allied advance swept Reille and d'Erlon before it. Donzelot had a brigade firmly in hand to cover his withdrawal, but Ney wasted it in a hopeless counterattack—intended, apparently, merely to get himself killed. The four Guard squares easily checked the British and Prussian cavalry, but gradually disintegrated under the combined pressures of fugitives seeking protection and Allied infantry and cavalry attacks.

Though his corps slowly frayed away as Zieten advanced into its rear, Lobau somehow kept Blücher from the vital highway. The Guard sold Plancenoit house by blazing house, the Old Guard battalions bayoneting their way out at the bitter end. Blücher's one feeble attempt at a deep envelopment was routed by the Old Guard battalion covering Napoleon's headquarters, and a handful of stragglers rallied by Provost-General Radet.

Twilight and the confused convergence of the Anglo-Dutch and Prussian advances delayed any immediate effective pursuit. The Guard's two squares near La Belle Alliance shrugged off all attacks, withdrawing slowly, in perfect order. The Guard artillerymen there fired their last round, then stood stoically by their empty guns. Their bluff gained their comrades a few minutes. Reorganized remnants of Guard cavalry thereafter covered the retreat. Until the first crisis passed, Napoleon remained with one of the squares; he then (*this map*) rode ahead to see if a stand could be made at Genappe.

Covered by the remaining units of the Guard, intermixed fragments of other commands streamed toward Genappe. Reille attempted to join them by a cross-country march, but most of his remaining troops scattered when attacked by Prussian cavalry. Pire withdrew independently toward Nivelles, followed by some cuirassiers. The French had fought furiously, only to have victory repeatedly snatched from them. Their reaction was discouragement, indiscipline, and growing panic. (Also, being veterans, they understood the danger of being trapped between Wellington and Blücher, and saw no sense in lingering.) Real panic began in Genappe, where the main street ended in a narrow bridge. This was soon almost blocked by overturned and abandoned vehicles, but—though the Dyle River was easily fordable—men fought among themselves to cross it. Attempting to restore order, Radet was beaten unconscious. Finding Genappe jammed with fugitives, the Guard bypassed it to the east. Napoleon and his escort spent an hour working their way through the town.

Meeting near La Belle Alliance, Blücher and Wellington agreed that the Prussians would continue the pursuit. Accordingly, elements of Pirch's and Bülow's corps moved slowly on Genappe. At its northern edge, a few still-acrimonious Frenchmen held an improvised barricade until Prussian artillery demolished it. Thereafter, the Prussians sabered and shot the milling fugitives until fright drove them to ford the Dyle. Most of the Prussians then halted, but Gneisenau, ordering Pirch to aid Thielmann, himself pushed on with 4,000 men, harrying and slaughtering stragglers until exhaustion halted him south of Frasnes. (Though energetic, his operations were less effective than commonly believed. Organized groups were not molested; the hard core of practically every French regiment engaged withdrew successfully.) Bülow's cavalry joined Gneisenau the next morning, but all contact with the French had been lost.

Though dazed and exhausted, Napoleon had dispatched an administrative officer to evacuate the army's trains from Charleroi, and ordered the division at Ligny (formerly Girard's) to Quatre-Bras. Reaching Quatre-Bras at 0100, he learned that this division, which could have ruined Gneisenau's pursuit, had not arrived. The army obviously could not be rallied, especially since the Guard had continued toward Charleroi. There was no news of Grouchy. Dispatching couriers to warn Grouchy and other detachments, Napoleon proceeded to Charleroi (*off map, A1*), but found (0500) the town in wild confusion. A drunken garrison commander had hampered the administrative officer's attempts to organize the evacuation. Consequently, it had hardly begun when the fugitive horde engulfed it, turning the Charleroi bridge into another tumultuous jam. The Guard later restored order, but the army was further disorganized.

Napoleon continued southward to Philippeville (0900). Reorganization now became possible, contact with the enemy being completely broken, and the fugitives halting from exhaustion. Giving the necessary orders, Napoleon left Soult in command, and proceeded to Paris to organize a defensive campaign. (Waterloo casualties were approximately: Anglo-Dutch, 15,094, plus several thousand temporarily missing; Prussian, 7,000; French, 26,000 killed and wounded, 9,000 prisoners, 9,000 missing.)

Grouchy received Napoleon's 1330 message at about 1700. The ever-mounting thunder of artillery to westward emphasized its contents. Ordering Vandamme to maintain pressure on Thielmann, Grouchy directed Gerard (who had just arrived with his leading division) to divert his other two divisions to Limale. Either misunderstanding their orders or taking the wrong road, these divisions ended up opposite Wavre. All attempts to force the Dyle failed, Gerard being seriously wounded.

Gathering up the two newly arrived divisions, Grouchy led them toward Limale. There, he found the bridge already in French hands. Pajol had taken it at the dead run about 1845, riding down the Prussian battalion guarding it. Teste's panting infantry had cleared Limale. Thielmann quickly shifted troops southward, but Grouchy drove him off the ridge that dominated the village (2300). (Stengel apparently deserted Thielmann after dark.)

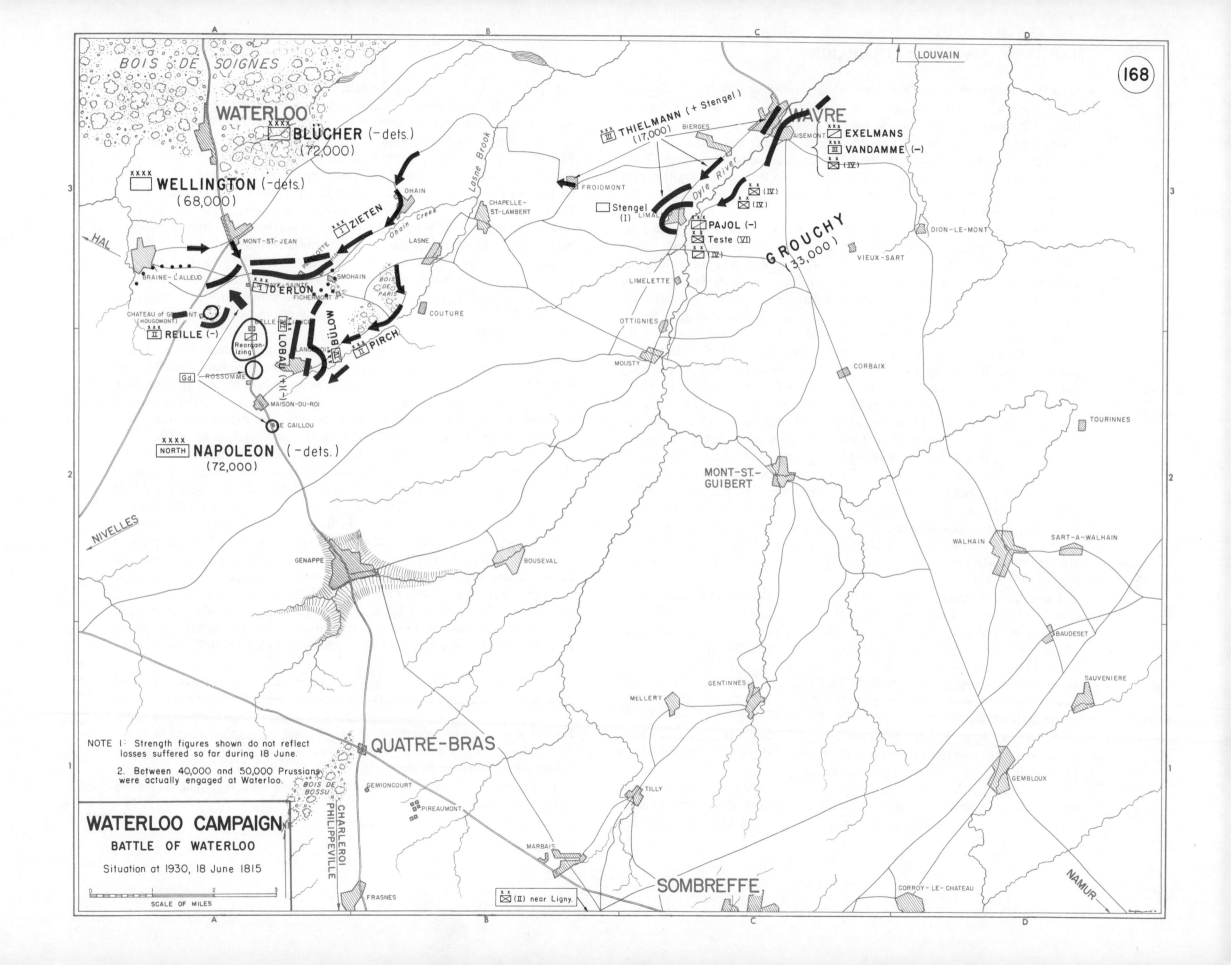

168

BOIS DE SOIGNES

LOUVAIN

WATERLOO

BLÜCHER (–dets.)
(72,000)

THIELMANN (+ Stengel)
III (17,000)

WAVRE

BIERGES

EXELMANS
III VANDAMME (–)
IV

AISEMONT

WELLINGTON (–dets.)
(68,000)

OHAIN

FROIDMONT

Dyle River

IV

DION-LE-MONT

HAL

ZIETEN
I

Ohain Creek

CHAPELLE-
ST-LAMBERT

Stengel
(I)

LIMAL

IV

PAJOL (–)
Teste (VI)

GROUCHY
(33,000)

VIEUX-SART

MONT-ST-JEAN

LASNE

LASNE

IV

BRAINE-L'ALLEUD

D'ERLON
I

SMOHAIN

FICHERMONT

BOIS
DE
PARIS

BÜLOW

LIMELETTE

CHATEAU of GO(HOUGOMONT)

COUTURE

OTTIGNIES

CORBAIX

REILLE (–)
II

Reorganizing

LOBAU

PIRCH
I

TOURINNES

Gd ROSSOMME

LANGO(?)

MOUSTY

MAISON-DU-ROI

DE CAILLOU

NAPOLEON (–dets.)
NORTH
(72,000)

MONT-ST-
GUIBERT

NIVELLES

WALHAIN

SART-A-WALHAIN

GENAPPE

BOUSEVAL

BAUDESET

SAUVENIERE

NOTE 1: Strength figures shown do not reflect
losses suffered so far during 18 June.

MELLERY

GENTINNES

2. Between 40,000 and 50,000 Prussians
were actually engaged at Waterloo.

BOIS DE
BOSSU

QUATRE-BRAS

TILLY

GEMBLOUX

GEMIONCOURT

PIREAUMONT

CHARLEROI
PHILIPPEVILLE

WATERLOO CAMPAIGN
BATTLE OF WATERLOO
Situation at 1930, 18 June 1815

MARBAIS

(II) near Ligny.

SOMBREFFE

NAMUR

FRASNES

CORROY-LE-CHATEAU

SCALE OF MILES

After thoroughly defeating Thielmann the next morning (19 June), Grouchy halted, uncertain whether to march on Mont-St.-Jean or Brussels. Warned at 1030 of Napoleon's defeat, he decided to retire through Namur (*C3*), rejecting Vandamme's proposal to march through Brussels and across the Allied rear. Sent ahead to secure Namur and its bridge over the Sambre Rriver, Exelmans reached that city about 1600; Grouchy's main body halted for the night northwest of Namur. Pajol, who had successfully bluffed Thielmann all day, caught up by a forced march.

Given hazy orders to operate against Grouchy (Gneisenau being too busy playing the dashing cavalry officer to attend to his proper duties as chief of staff), Pirch had wandered by moonlight to Mellery. He spent the 19th hiding there, his patrols having reported Thielmann routed and many French around Mont-St.-Guibert. Blücher sent neither orders, information, nor reinforcements. On 20 June, tardily undeceived, Pirch's and Thielmann's leading elements overtook Grouchy, but were repulsed. Pirch attacked again as the French withdrew through Namur, but lost 1,500 men to Teste's skillful rearguard defense. Blücher then recalled Pirch and Thielmann. Grouchy entered Philippeville (*B3*) late on 21 June with more than 25,000 undefeated soldiers.

Napoleon reached Paris at 0800 on 21 June, mentally and physically exhausted. The Chambers (national legislature) had panicked. Joseph and Caulaincourt advised capitulation. Davout, Carnot, and Lucian (his ablest brother) urged that he immediately use his legal powers to dissolve the Chambers, telling them that the danger to Paris made it necessary for them to reconvene in some more out-of-the-way city. But Napoleon wanted rest. While he slept, bathed, and lunched, Fouche raised the Chambers against him, using Lafayette (who combined idealism, prestige, and obtuseness) as his catspaw. The Chambers decreed that any attempt to dissolve them would be treason; Napoleon's too-late request for dictatorial powers was answered with demands for his abdication.

These actions, though unconstitutional, were accomplished facts. Only force would change them, and even Davout advised against the use of force. Still, it would be easy. Napoleon had 15,000 reliable troops in Paris, plus 17,000 "Federals" (volunteers). Moreover, he retained the savage loyalty of Paris' lower classes, being the first French ruler to worry greatly whether they ate or starved, and at the same time, in some sense, the inheritor of the French Revolution. One word from him, and the gabbling Chambers would be lucky to live an hour. But—"I have not come back from Elba to have Paris run with blood." On 22 June, finding the Chambers still hostile, Napoleon again abdicated. When they thanked him, he gravely reminded them that they had left France without an executive, in time of extreme peril.

Improvising a rickety provisional government by committee, the Chambers began excitedly debating a new constitution. Through this verbal tailspin, Fouche expertly slithered into temporary power, sabotaged Davout's and Carnot's preparations for further resistance, and looked about for the highest possible bidder. He had unwitting help from Ney, who deserted his command and returned to Paris, insanely insisting that France had no army left.

The military situation was not entirely hopeless. Soult had rallied some 55,000 troops, including Grouchy's command. The northern and eastern fortresses were solidly prepared and garrisoned. Wellington and Blücher were barely over the northern frontier. Suchet had invaded Piedmont and defeated Frimont. Lamarque had pacified the Vendee. There were approximately 170,-000 replacements available in the depots of northeastern France. News of Napoleon's abdication, however, caused many desertions.

Blücher and Wellington now advanced along the right bank of the Oise River, hoping to cut Soult off from Paris. Their march, however, was poorly coordinated, Wellington soon falling two days behind Blücher. Replacing Soult on 26 June, Grouchy brought the Army of the North into Paris by the 29th, fighting off Blücher en route.

Inspired by Waterloo, Schwarzenberg crossed the Rhine (23–26 June). Outnumbered and without orders, Rapp banged Württemberg soundly, then retired to a position near Strasbourg. Wrede moved on Nancy. Hohenzollern and Ferdinand enmeshed themselves in sieges of various frontier fortresses; Colloredo was expertly delayed by Lecourbe. Effective irregular warfare flared along the eastern frontier. Suchet and Frimont concluded an armistice.

On 30 June, Blücher assailed Paris' northern defenses. Repulsed, he began slipping his army westward, intending to attack from the south, where Fouche had delayed the construction of fortifications. Sohr's cavalry brigade was sent raiding ahead toward Versailles. Blücher was operating in a hostile countryside; Davout knew his every move. Wellington's half-crippled army was just approaching Paris, its columns considerably spread out. Blücher was sprawled to the southwest of the city. Davout was stronger than either Allied army, and possessed interior lines. But—though confident of victory—Davout saw no purpose in it. Disgusted with the maze of intrigue in which he was entrapped, he had decided that the only solution was to recall Louis XVIII, whose whole breed he hated. First, though, it would be necessary to moderate Blücher's fury. Davout loosed Exelmans, who quickly gobbled up Sohr (*action not shown*).

Blücher paused. Wellington whistled Louis XVIII back to Paris, buying off Fouche by making him Louis' minister of police. An armistice was improvised on 4 July, and the raging, half-mutinous French army retired behind the Loire. Davout had hoped to preserve it, to give France bargaining power in future negotiations, but Louis merely wanted to be King, regardless of humiliations. Under Allied pressure, he disbanded the army. France was completely occupied and thoroughly plundered. Many Frenchmen soon regretted not having risked one battle more.

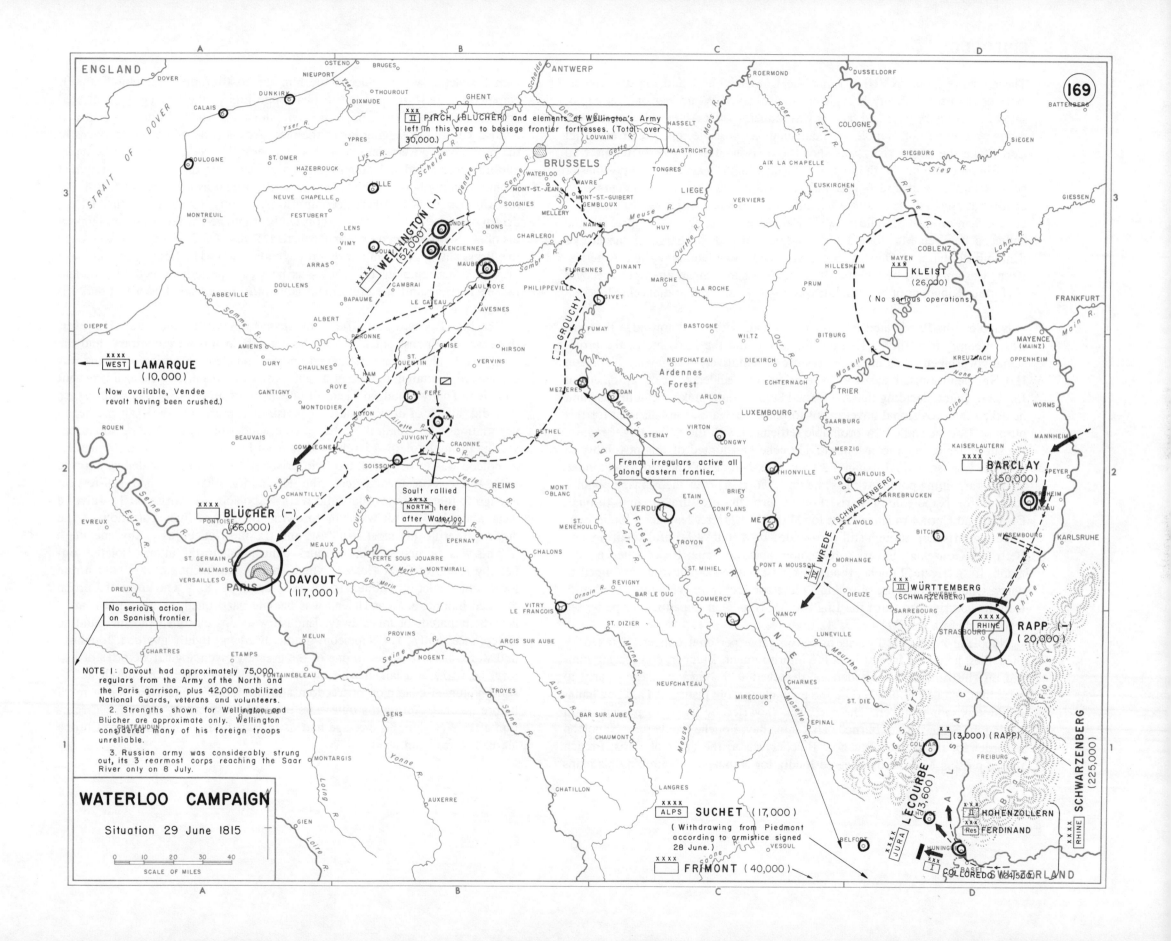

ENGLAND

169

xxx
II PIRCH (BLÜCHER) and elements of Wellington's Army left in this area to besiege frontier fortresses. (Total: over 30,000.)

STRAIT OF DOVER

xxxx
WELLINGTON (-)
(52,000)

xxxx
WEST LAMARQUE
(10,000)

(Now available, Vendée revolt having been crushed.)

xxx
KLEIST
(26,000)

(No serious operations)

French irregulars active all along eastern frontier.

xxxx
BARCLAY
(150,000)

Soult rallied
xxxx
NORTH here
after Waterloo.

xxxx
BLÜCHER (-)
(66,000)

No serious action on Spanish frontier.

xxxx
DAVOUT
(117,000)

xx WREDE (SCHWARZENBERG)

xxx III WÜRTTEMBERG
(SCHWARZENBERG)

xxxx
RHINE RAPP (-)
(20,000)

SCHWARZENBERG
(225,000)

NOTE I: Davout had approximately 75,000 regulars from the Army of the North and the Paris garrison, plus 42,000 mobilized National Guards, veterans and volunteers.

2. Strengths shown for Wellington and Blücher are approximate only. Wellington considered many of his foreign troops unreliable.

3. Russian army was considerably strung out, its 3 rearmost corps reaching the Saar River only on 8 July.

(3,000) (RAPP)

xxxx
JURA LECOURBE
(3,600)

xx II HOHENZOLLERN

xxx Res FERDINAND

xxxx RHINE

WATERLOO CAMPAIGN

Situation 29 June 1815

0 10 20 30 40
SCALE OF MILES

xxxx
ALPS SUCHET (17,000)

(Withdrawing from Piedmont according to armistice signed 28 June.)

xxxx
FRIMONT (40,000)

xxx I COLLOREDO (24,500) WITZERLAND

EPILOGUE

The return of Louis XVIII ("Louis the Unavoidable") and the dismemberment of the French Army brought on the so-called White Terror—an explosion of reactionary hate and fear. It was fanned by the Allies, who wanted the heads of as many of Napoleon's lieutenants as possible, but preferred to let Louis take the blame. Ney was shot for treason after a grossly unfair trial (Bourmont being one of the witnesses against him). Lavalette, the postmaster general and a loyal and honest public servant, was likewise condemned to death, but escaped, thanks to a gallant wife and some disgusted English officers. Other proscribed officers were warned in time, thanks to professional collusion between Macdonald (whom Louis placed in charge of the army's demobilization) and Davout. Soult vanished; Vandamme visited America; Brune was murdered by a mob; Murat made a harebrained attempt to recover his former Kingdom of Naples, but was quickly captured and executed.

Napoleon had abdicated in favor of his son, with full knowledge that this was an empty formality. (To calm the Army and the Paris mobs, the provisional government even made the gesture of tentatively recognizing Napoleon II.) Napoleon himself seems to have originally decided to seek retirement in England. Later, deciding that the United States would make a kindlier asylum, he asked the provisional government to place a frigate at his disposal for this purpose. Fouche stalled: A profitable settlement with the Allies might require the surrender of Napoleon himself. (Fouche had hinted of this possibility to both the English and Austrians.) At any rate, Napoleon's person should make a good bargaining point. At the same time, worrying over the growing popular support for Napoleon in Paris, Fouche brought pressure on him through Davout and Carnot to leave Paris for Malmaison. Here, Napoleon found himself a semiprisoner, though still surrounded by a staff of faithful subordinates: Bertrand, Gourgaud, Savary, Montholon, and Lavalette. He repeated his demands for a frigate; Fouche, though likewise nagged by Davout, continued to delay. Under the pretense of seeking a safe-conduct from Wellington for Napoleon, he contrived to warn the English that Napoleon hoped to escape by sea from Rochefort (*see Map 155, A2*).

Napoleon knew that he was in considerable personal danger. If taken by the Allies, he would face at least life imprisonment. Blücher, considering himself an "instrument of providence," detached (29 June) a raiding party to seize him, intending to "exercise the unchallengeable justice of God" by hanging him as soon as taken. The party was thwarted by Davout's precaution in having the Seine bridges burned. That same day, Fouche finally gave Napoleon an order for the frigate. But now Blücher was at the gates of Paris; French troops passing Malmaison cheered loudly for Napoleon. Examining his maps with Lavalette (whose office made him the best-informed man in France), Napoleon quickly grasped the tactical opportunity: the French concentrated around Paris; the Prussians strung out along the roads from Soissons and Senlis; the English lagging far to the rear. At once, he offered his services to the provisional government "not as an emperor, but as a general whose name and influence could still exercise a great influence on the fate of the nation. I promise, on my honor as a soldier, as a citizen and as a Frenchman, to leave for America, to finally there accomplish my destiny, the very day that I have driven out the enemy." Fouche, thoroughly frightened at the prospect, ignored his offer. Napoleon then left for Rochefort of his own free will (not to escape the Prussians, as contemporary propaganda claimed). Nothing could have prevented his rejoining the army—as he was repeatedly urged to do—and raising Paris against the provisional government, had he chosen to break his pledge to it.

Reaching Rochefort on 3 July, Napoleon found the frigate ready. However, there was an English squadron off the port, the winds were contrary, and the local naval officials were frightened and incompetent. A variety of plans was considered, including the use of a swift American vessel or a Danish brig, but Napoleon finally adjudged them all unworthy of an emperor—combining, as they did, a lack of dignity and a high risk of capture. On the 10th, he began negotiations with Admiral Maitland, commander of the blockading squadron. During the night of 14–15 July, orders from Louis XVIII reached Rochefort: Napoleon was to be seized and held prisoner (apparently for delivery to the Allies). However incompetent, the Rochefort authorities had self-respect enough to fumble these orders and warn Napoleon. At sunrise on 15 July, he went aboard a British warship, throwing himself on the protection of the "most powerful, the most steadfast, and the most generous of my enemies."

This was the first step in his quick banishment to the utterly isolated, unhealthy island of Saint Helena, where shabby treatment under a fourth-rate local commander contributed to his early death in 1821. The kings of Europe dreaded him alive. Saint Helena was heavily garrisoned, as were the nearest islands, hundreds of miles away. English warships patrolled the surrounding waters incessantly. Yet Napoleon, gradually dying, tightly guarded, fought—and won—his last battle. In one of the greatest psychological victories of history, he wrote and talked with masterful skill to apotheosize himself as the still-undaunted champion of freedom and the rights of man. He was a myth before he died. Across the dull years of regal, aristocratic, and clerical reaction after Waterloo, his message had its intended effect. The kings of Europe learned to fear him dead.

Biographical Sketches

"The man in the ranks is not a model of wisdom in every respect, but he is a mighty shrewd judge of his own commanding officer; no lying bulletin can throw dust in his eyes, no advertising swashbuckler can pass as a hero. The court-martial which sits round a bivouac fire may be very informal, but it has an 'instinct for reality.' I pin my faith to the judgment of the Grognards of the Old Guard. They spoke of him as 'l'Homme.'" —UNKNOWN

"Theirs was a case of the 'survival of the fittest' in a terribly hard school of selection. . . . Only born leaders of men could have survived such an ordeal. They may have been, indeed they often were, illiterate, rapacious, jealous and vindictive, but they all possessed that power which defied all examinations to elicit—viz. the power to get the last ounce of exertion and self-sacrifice out of the men under them, without recourse to legal formalities, or the application of authorized force." —FREDERICK N. MAUDE

BIOGRAPHICAL SKETCHES

The following biographical sketches are intended as a supplement to the text of this work. Readers seeking detailed information are referred to the Recommended Reading List.

Napoleon's Marshals

AUGEREAU, PIERRE FRANCOIS CHARLES (1757–1816). Duke of Castiglione. Born in Paris. His father was apparently a domestic servant, his mother German. Enlisted man in French Army (infantryman and dragoon), 1774–77. Entered Prussian service in 1777; deserted; returned to France in 1784, and enlisted in crack cavalry regiment, becoming a sergeant. In 1786, went to Naples as part of French military mission. Returned to France in 1790, entered the Paris National Guard, and from that the volunteers. Served in Vendee and Spain; general of division in late 1793. In 1797, became the commander of the Army of Germany. Marshal, 1804. In 1809–10, commanded the Army of Catalonia, in Spain. After Waterloo, Louis XVIII stripped him of all military rank and pay.

Augereau's life up to 1792 remains hazy. He is described as big and commanding—gaudy, but very immaculate in his dress. An iron drillmaster, stern disciplinarian, and good tactician, he looked after his men, but set them a poor example by his energetic looting. Though a braggart and always the shifty soldier of fortune, he was generally remembered as a good comrade, generous and friendly. By 1805, his health had begun to fail, and he suffered greatly from rheumatism.

"A fine, big man—handsome, large nose—has served in all countries, soldier with few equals, always bragging."—Desaix, 1797.

BERNADOTTE, JEAN BAPTISTE JULES (1763–1844). Prince of Ponte Corvo. Born in Pau. His father was a lawyer. Enlisted in 1780; sergeant by 1789. (His "Old Army" nickname was "Pretty-Leg.") Colonel in 1792, general of division in 1793. Served on the Rhine frontier until 1797, when transferred to Italy. Ambassador to Austria in 1798, but showed more swagger than sense. Briefly minister of war in 1799; worked hard, but accomplished little. Had hopes of seizing power in France, but was forestalled by Napoleon. Commanded in Vendee in 1800. Marshal, 1804. Repeatedly involved in plots against Napoleon. Thanks to his kindness to Swedish prisoners (1806), he was offered the succession to the Swedish throne in 1810, and speedily became Sweden's actual ruler as crown prince. Crowned in 1818 as Charles XIV. His rule was one of peace and prosperity, though his ultra-conservative views and secret police were widely detested. In 1798, he had married the sister-in-law of Joseph Napoleon, thus becoming a member of the Bonaparte clan—a fact of which both wife and husband took full advantage.

Extremely brave, tall, and dashing, Bernadotte was keen and intelligent, but always the "enemy of his superiors." Ambitious and constantly involved in intrigues, he was also oddly hesitant in their execution. At great pains to gain the affection of anyone who might be useful to him, he could be correspondingly cold when their usefulness had passed. It is impossible to determine how many of his apparent failures as a corps commander were actually intentional.

BERTHIER, LOUIS-ALEXANDRE (1753–1815). Prince of Neufchatel, Prince of Wagram. Born at Versailles. His father was a senior officer of topographical engineers. Berthier entered the same service early in 1766; later had infantry, cavalry, and staff duty. On Rochambeau's staff in America, 1780–83. Lieutenant colonel in 1789. General of brigade in 1792, but suspended from 1793 to 1795 because of noble birth. General of division in 1795. Served in Flanders, Vendee, and Italy. Minister of war, 1799–1807. Marshal, 1804. Held many imperial offices —grand huntsman, vice-constable, colonel-general of the Swiss contingent. Successful diplomatic mission to Spain after Marengo.

Short and stocky, with a sallow complexion, Berthier was immensely strong and tough, able to remain clear-headed after days without sleep. An expert rider, he loved hunting. Personal courage and calmness under fire outstanding. Originally an aggressive and imaginative officer, ended by completely subordinating himself to Napoleon. Treated subordinates with a mixture of brusqueness and courtesy; both a strict disciplinarian and thoroughly self-disciplined. Clean-handed. His work in staff organization and functioning still endures. His position, however, made him the butt equally of Napoleon's bad temper and the disappointments of the marshals. (Also, his reputation was methodically blackened by Jomini's malice.)

"Quite apart from his specialist training as a topographical engineer, he had knowledge and experience of staff work and furthermore a remarkable grasp of everything to do with war. He had also, above all else, the gift of writing a complete order and transmitting it with the utmost speed and clarity. . . . No one could have better suited General Bonaparte, who wanted a man capable of relieving him of all detailed work, to understand him instantly and to foresee what he would need."—Thiebault.

BESSIERES, JEAN BAPTISTE (1766–1813). Duke of Istria. Born at Prayssac. His father was a surgeon. Well educated. Enlisted in Louis XVI's short-lived Constitutional Guard in 1791. Reportedly aided in the attempted flight of the royal family; subsequently enlisted in cavalry. Service in Spain and Italy. Courage and steadiness led Napoleon to place him in command of his newly formed Guides in 1796. General of division, 1802; Marshal, 1804. Independent commands in Spain, 1808–9 and 1811. He normally commanded the cavalry of the Guard, but Napoleon frequently involved him in the Guard's general administration.

Physically impressive, Bessieres was a thorough soldier, and all soldier: honest, loyal, exact, reliable, even-tempered, gifted with a cold courage equal to all physical dangers. As an independent commander, he lacked decisiveness. He was much loved by his men, who felt that he was "a brother to every soldier"; his innate kindness and fairness made him respected even in Spain. He was the last man in the army to retain the old custom of wearing his hair powdered and in a queue.

"Bessieres lived like Bayard; he died like Turenne."—Napoleon.

BRUNE, GUILLAUME-MARIE (1763–1815). Born at Brive-la-Gaillarde. His father was a lawyer. While working as a printer in Paris, he became friendly with Danton and other revolutionary leaders. Edited a revolutionary newspaper; battalion adjutant of volunteers in 1791. Served in Flanders; being a "politically reliable" officer, he was involved in bloody counterrevolutionary operations around Bordeaux, in Paris, and in southern France. Staff colonel in 1792; general of brigade by 1793. Joined Napoleon in Italy in 1797. Occupied Switzerland in 1798; seized control of Piedmont, and defeated the Anglo-Russian invasion of Holland in 1799; pacified Vendee in 1800; commanded Army of Italy, 1800–1801. Marshal, 1804. In 1807, involved in an interview with the King of Sweden, garbled accounts of which—plus

BIOGRAPHICAL SKETCHES

Brune's stubborn refusal to clear himself—led Napoleon to relieve him. Not actively employed until 1815. Murdered by royalist terrorists after Waterloo.

Brune was tall and physically impressive. Brave and aggressive, a strict disciplinarian, he had a certain ability for irregular warfare, but could never overcome his lack of military training and experience. (*A la Brune* became a French version of "all fouled up.") Minor faults were a reputed tendency to loot, and the belief that he was a poet. Brune's sentiments were always republican; he aided some of the Revolution's cruelest police actions, but seems to have taken no pleasure in them. A model husband. Died sneering at his assassins' marksmanship.

DAVOUT, LOUIS NICOLAS (1770–1823). Duke of Auerstädt, Prince of Eckmühl. Born at Annoux of an old military family; noble, but poor. Entered military school in 1784; commissioned in cavalry in 1789. Expelled from army at beginning of the Revolution for insubordination. Commanded volunteer battalion in 1792. Staff colonel in 1793. Briefly retired, because of noble birth. General of brigade, 1794. Served on the Rhine; in 1798, accompanied Desaix to Egypt, where he came to Napoleon's attention. General of division, 1800. Marshal, 1804. Made all the major campaigns of the Grande Armee. Famous for his defense of Hamburg, 1813–14, surrendering only after Napoleon's first abdication. Inactive, 1814–15. Minister of war, 1815. Stripped of rank and titles, 1815–17.

Of all the marshals, Davout had the strongest character. He was obeyed by his subordinates—even Vandamme—but was respected rather than loved. Medium height, robust, severe features, prematurely bald. Very near-sighted, he wore special combat glasses that fastened at the back of his head. Cold, methodical, incorruptible, quiet, with an agile and open mind. An expert organizer; supervised the creation of the Duchy of Warsaw. His troops were always the best trained, equipped, and disciplined in the Grande Armee, and usually got the hardest assignments. Strict with his officers, he remembered and rewarded competence, and took responsibility for their mishaps when they had acted according to his orders. Had unusual skill in intelligence work. Although he was harsh in his dealings with civilians when it was necessary to feed his troops, he permitted no looting. Excellent tactician and strategist; never defeated. Soldiers called him "The Just."

GROUCHY, EMMANUEL (1766–1847). Born near Paris; his family belonged to the "old nobility." Entered Strasbourg artillery school in 1780. Cavalry captain, 1784; officer of bodyguard, 1786. Retired, probably for liberal views, in 1787. Volunteered in 1791. Colonel and general of brigade, 1792. Forced out of service as a noble, but returned in 1794. Badly wounded and captured at Novi (1799); exchanged in 1800, and distinguished himself as infantry division commander at Hohenlinden and elsewhere. Returned to cavalry in 1806. Badly hurt at Eylau. Too sick and crippled to serve in 1813. Marshal, 1815. Fled to America after Waterloo. Returned in 1819 and re-entered army. Marshal again, 1831.

Grouchy was an excellent cavalry general, but too often a "man of a single hour, a single maneuver, a single effort." A good administrator, clean-handed, and well liked by his men. Personally brave, taking twenty-three wounds in twenty-five years. Sensitive, complaining, and reluctant to assume responsibility, he was actually abler than he realized, as witness his superb performance after Waterloo.

JOURDAN, JEAN BAPTISTE (1762–1833). Born at Limoges. His father was a surgeon. Enlisted in 1778, serving in America. Small-scale linen merchant, 1784–90. Captain, National Guard, 1790. Lieutenant colonel, volunteers, 1791. Commanded Army of the North in 1793. Victories at Wattignies, Fleurus, Aldenhoven; subsequently, repeatedly defeated by Archduke Charles. Helped design 1798 conscription law. Promoted Marshal, 1804. Military adviser to Joseph in Naples and Spain, 1808–13. Joined Napoleon unenthusiastically in 1815; unfit for field service, was assigned command of Besancon. Refused to take part in the trial of Ney, but was not punished by Bourbons.

Squat and fat. Self-confident at first, and lucky for a while. In 1793, showed energy and talent as an organizer. Defeat made him increasingly irresolute. Amiable, moderate, unambitious. Little knowledge of tactics and none of strategy. Napoleon considered him "thoughtful, methodical," but "lacking vigor, and with too much of a reputation to be easily guided."

KELLERMANN, FRANCOIS CHRISTOPHE (1735–1820). Duke of Valmy. Born in Strasbourg. Entered army as a gentleman cadet in 1750; distinguished during Seven Years' War. General officer, 1784. Saved the Revolution at Valmy. Senatorial marshal,* 1804. Constantly employed by Napoleon along the Rhine (1806–7, 1809, and 1812–13) and at Bayonne (1808) to control the Grande Armee's rear area. Welcomed the Bourbons in 1814.

Vain and envious, with little ability as an army commander, Kellermann was nevertheless a highly capable organizer and administrator, devoted to the good of the service. Despite his age, he remained active, brave, and firm.

LANNES, JEAN (1769–1809). Duke of Montebello, Prince of Sievers. Born at Lectoure. His father was a poor farmer. As a boy, Lannes was apprenticed to a dyer. May have had regular service before the Revolution. Second lieutenant of volunteers, 1792; colonel, 1795; general of brigade, 1797; general of division, 1799; commander of the Consular Guard, 1800; Ambassador to Portugal, 1801; Marshal, 1804.

Small, agile, incredibly hardy, and the only real Gascon among the marshals, Lannes improved throughout his career. Truthful, kind, and generous. An active, driving, aggressive fighter; originally excitable, extravagant, and quarrelsome in everyday life, but calm and relaxed under fire. Learned to control violent temper; devoted several hours a day to professional study. Disciplinarian, drillmaster, and organizer. Relations with Napoleon frank, blunt, and loyal. Desaix described him in 1797 as "Bravest of the brave, young, well-made, features not particularly handsome, seamed with scars, elegant." The ideal advance guard commander—at once daring, careful, and stubborn.

"He was a swordsman when I found him, and a paladin when I lost him."—Napoleon.

LEFEBVRE, FRANCOIS JOSEPH (1755–1820). Duke of Danzig. Born near Colmar. His father was a miller. Enlisted in French Guards; sergeant, 1788. Early history obscure. May have retired and spent period as notary's clerk. Lieutenant-instructor, Paris National Guard. Served with a regular unit at beginning of Revolution. Gen-

---

* The grade of "senatorial" marshal was intended as an honor for distinguished soldiers, grown too old for active service, but capable of serving as members of the senate. Most of them subsequently saw considerable active duty.

eral of brigade, 1793; general of division, 1794; wing (corps) commander, 1797. Briefly retired after being badly wounded (1799), then given command of Paris garrison. Assisted Napoleon's *coup d'état* in 1799. Senatorial marshal, 1804. Usually employed with Imperial Guard. Depressed by death of his son in Russia in 1812. No command in 1814 or 1815.

Thoroughly simple, childishly pleased with the unexpected honors and prosperity that came to him late in life. Stern disciplinarian, but took excellent care of his men. Limited capability as independent commander, but an excellent "general of execution"—brave, a quick and able tactician, and a good leader of men.

MACDONALD, JACQUES ETIENNE JOSEPH ALEXANDRE (1765–1840). Duke of Taranto. Born near Bourges. His father was an army officer; his family Scottish refugees. In Dutch Army, 1785; gentleman cadet in French Army, 1787. Colonel, 1793; general of brigade, 1795; general of division, 1796. Commanded Army of Naples, 1798–99; Army of the Grisons, 1800–1801. Ambassador to Denmark, 1802. Fell into disfavor in 1803 for siding with Moreau. Not employed until 1809; Marshal after Wagram. Loyal to Bourbons after 1814.

Tall, well shaped, physically powerful, Macdonald had a natural air of authority and the knack of having his orders obeyed, even in a revolutionary army. Very proud and independent; extremely free and sarcastic in speech. Relatively clean-handed and careful of discipline, but something of an intriguer; frequently a "bad bedfellow," failing to support his comrades. Napoleon considered him "good and brave, but unlucky"—probably meaning that he lacked the mental flexibility to meet unforeseen dangers. Originally capable of independent command, his abilities declined after 1809. His ancestry has made him the pet, to a frequently undeserved degree, of English writers.

MARMONT, AUGUSTE FREDERIC LOUIS VIESSE (1774–1852). Duke of Ragusa. Born at Chatillon-sur-Seine. His father was a retired officer; his family petty nobility. Well educated; graduated from Metz artillery school in 1793. Met Napoleon at Toulon that year; became his aide-de-camp. Colonel, 1797; general of brigade, 1798; general of division, 1800. Artillery inspector-general, 1801–2. Marshal, 1809. During 1805–10, he was the military and civil governor of Dalmatia. In Spain, 1810–12; outmaneuvered Wellington for some time, but was defeated at Salamanca. Loyal to Bourbons after 1814; attempted unsuccessfully to suppress the final revolt against them in 1830. Died in exile in Venice.

Better educated and more intelligent than most of the marshals. An excellent organizer and administrator, showing imagination and energy, though not always clean-handed. Courageous, quick-witted, and cool; a neat, deadly tactician; understood strategy. He was, however, unsteady and apt to be seized, at exactly the wrong moment, by strange spasms of carelessness or depression. Suffered from an ingrowing vanity, which caused him to feel insufficiently appreciated.

"The ingrate. He will be much unhappier than I."—Napoleon (1814).

MASSENA, ANDRE (1756–1817). Duke of Rivoli, Prince of Essling. Born in Nice (then part of Piedmont). His father was a winegrower. Cabin boy when young. Enlisted in a French light infantry battalion in 1775; sergeant-major, 1784; retired in 1789. Settled in Antibes, became successful merchant-smuggler. Volunteered in 1792; general of division, 1793. Commander, Army of Rome, 1798; troops mutinied because of irregularities in their pay. Commander, Army of Switzerland,

1798–99; won great battle of Zürich over Austrians and Russians. Marshal, 1804. Inactive during 1815. Refused to take part in the trial of Ney.

Massena was short, lean, and lightly built; had a highly expressive Italian face, with the "look of an eagle"; head carried high and cocked slightly to the left. Dignified; outwardly the rough soldier, but also a cunning courtier. Moral and physical courage. A "general by instinct." Indolent and morose, he hated to read, and so never improved his military education. Consequently, he could not plan a campaign, but, once in the presence of the enemy, suddenly became resourceful, unrelenting, and indefatigable. Capable independent commander, but required a good staff. An industrious looter; enriched himself everywhere, from all sources. Neglected his men abominably, but could enforce an iron discipline, as at Genoa. Napoleon considered that he had great military gifts, but that he was entirely a slave to his love of money, which grew as he aged. Fell off physically and mentally after 1809. Never wounded.

"When Massena was opposed to me, and in the field, I never slept comfortably." —Wellington.

MONCEY, BON ADRIEN JEANNOT (1754–1842). Duke of Conegliano. Born in La Palisse. His father was a lawyer and landed proprietor. Educated for legal career, but enlisted in 1769. Father secured discharge, but Moncey soon re-enlisted. Bought discharge 1773; in Gendarmerie (then elite cavalry), 1774–76; dismissed for misconduct. Second lieutenant in a mercenary infantry regiment, 1779. Captain, 1791. Commander, Army of Western Pyrenees, 1794; largely responsible for Spanish request for peace. Inspector-general of the national gendarmerie, 1801. Promoted Marshal, 1804. Served in Spain, 1808–9. Opposed Russian expedition. Commanded Paris National Guard in 1814. Loyal to Bourbons thereafter, but briefly stripped of rank and honors for refusing to preside at Ney's trial. As governor of the Invalides, received Napoleon's body in 1840 on its return from St. Helena.

Tall, grand bearing, grave and stately manners, noble features. Kindly, sensitive, and conscientious; independent, but troubled by disapproval of others. A man of honor and decency, widely admired; won respect of Spanish. A slow, steady, methodical commander; excellent with young conscripts. Expert mountain fighter, never attacking anything he could outflank.

"An honest man."—Napoleon.

MORTIER, EDOUARD ADOLPHE CASIMER JOSEPH (1768–1835). Duke of Treviso. Born at Cateau-Cambresis. His father was a wealthy landowner and linen manufacturer. Offered commission as lieutenant of *carabiniers à cheval* in 1791, but preferred service with volunteers. Captain, 1792; colonel, 1795; general of division, 1799. Served in the north and along the Rhine; distinguished himself in Switzerland in 1799. In 1803, occupied Hanover. Marshal, 1804. Defeated Swedes in 1807. Noted for loyalty in 1814. Disabled by sickness in 1815. In disgrace until 1819. Killed by an assassin's bomb while escorting King Louis Philippe.

Very tall and strong; ordinarily slow-witted. Headlong and somewhat careless. In action, very calm; saw everything; orders very precise; undauntable courage. Easily influenced by subordinates. A loyal subordinate and good comrade. Could be trusted with minor independent commands. Spoke English fluently. Took care of his men, good disciplinarian and trainer.

"The big mortar [*mortier*] has a short range."—Anonymous.

BIOGRAPHICAL SKETCHES

MURAT, JOACHIM (1767–1815). Grand Duke of Berg, King of Naples. Born near Cahors. His father was a well-to-do farmer and innkeeper. Intended for the clergy, Murat was well educated, but enlisted in cavalry in 1787. Left regiment (cause unknown) in 1789; reinstated in 1790. Served briefly with Louis XVI's Constitutional Guard; apparently expelled; returned to his former regiment. Lieutenant, 1792; major, 1793. With Bonaparte in Paris, 1795; colonel and Bonaparte's senior aide-de-camp, 1796. General of brigade, 1796; general of division, 1799. Married Napoleon's sister Caroline, in 1800. Marshal, 1804. King of Naples, 1808; drove English out of Capri. Attempted invasion of Sicily failed in 1810. In 1813, began negotiations with Allies; turned on Napoleon in 1814. In 1815, defeated by Austrians and forced to flee to France. Captured in harebrained attempt to regain kingdom; executed.

Tall, handsome, an expert rider and swordsman. Delighted in amazing uniforms and fine horses. Thoroughly complex character—vain, rash, weak-willed, hot-tempered, naïve, ambitious, deceitful, and intriguing—but also generous, merciful, simple-mannered, good-humored, and courteous. Model husband, son, and brother. Bullied by his wife. Wonderful eye for terrain; noted for his ability to animate and carry along masses of men. Little tactical skill and no concept of strategy; never learned how to care for men and horses. Probably the bravest man in the world in battle, but without courage or judgment elsewhere.

"It would be better for us if he were less brave and had a little more common sense."—Savary (1807).

"[He] threw himself into the midst of the enemy in the strongest sense of the word."—Odeleben (1813).

NEY, MICHEL (1769–1815). Duke of Elchingen, Prince de la Moskova. Born at Sarrelouis. His father was a cooper and ex-soldier. Ney was trained as law clerk; then was superintendent of a small iron works. Enlisted in hussar regiment in 1788; sergeant major, 1792. Colonel, 1794; general of brigade, 1796; general of division, 1799. Successful diplomatic mission to Switzerland, 1803. Marshal, 1804. Served in all major campaigns; in 1811, relieved by Massena for insubordination in Spain, but soon given a new corps by Napoleon. Behavior after Napoleon's first abdication increasingly erratic. Arrested after Waterloo, tried by Chamber of Peers, shot as a traitor.

Ney "had nothing of a Frenchman about him." Red-headed (later bald), tall, broad-shouldered, powerful. Loved glory and fame; did not despise cash. An excellent drillmaster and—when he kept his head—a competent tactician. In action, a superb leader of men—energetic, quick-witted, the "bravest of the brave" (a title he shared with Lannes). Off the battlefield, weak and indecisive. Only moderately intelligent; showed much initiative, but frequently at the wrong time. Man of extremes, apt either to cling stubbornly to the exact letter of his orders or to ignore them entirely. His furious leadership in battle often led him to forget those units of his command that were not directly under his eye. Expert rear-guard fighter.

"Ney's best qualities, his heroic valor, his rapid *coup d'oeil,* and his energy, diminished in the same proportion that the extent of his command increased his responsibility."—Jomini.

OUDINOT, NICOLAS CHARLES (1767–1847). Duke of Reggio. Born at Bar-le-Duc. His father was a brewer. Enlisted service, 1784–87. Entered the National Guard in 1789. Major of volunteers, 1792; general of brigade, 1794; general of division, 1799. Chief of staff to Massena, 1799–1800. In 1805, commanded "Oudinot's Grenadiers," a big provisional division, made up of the elite companies of regiments remaining in France. Marshal, 1809. Sought a command during Hundred Days, but Napoleon refused to employ him. Thereafter, much favored by Bourbons.

Medium height, slim, aristocratic bearing, gentle face. Violent temper, but noted for many acts of kindness and decency. Apparently no knack for handling foreign troops. A highly capable infantry officer, but never mastered the employment of combined arms. Incapable of independent command. Personally brave; wounded thirty-four times.

PERIGNON, DOMINIQUE CATHERINE (1754–1818). Born near Toulouse. His family was minor nobility. Service, chiefly staff, with variety of provincial units, 1775–85. Magistrate, landowner, legislator. Appointed major of volunteers in 1792. Served on Spanish frontier. General of division, late 1793. Briefly commanded Army of Eastern Pyrenees, winning considerable success. Ambassador to Madrid, 1795. Wounded and captured at Novi in 1799. Senatorial marshal, 1804. Limited political-military assignments in Italy, 1804–8. During the Hundred Days, he attempted to organize resistance to Napoleon.

Courageous, determined, methodical, and modest.

PONIATOWSKI, JOSEPH ANTHONY (1763–1813). Born in Warsaw. His father was a Polish prince, serving as an officer in the Austrian Army. Poniatowski likewise served with Austrians against the Turks in 1788; recalled to Poland by his uncle, King Stanislaus, he helped reorganize the Polish Army. Appointed commander in chief of the Polish forces in 1791; defeated the Russians repeatedly. When uncle surrendered, went into exile. Returned to support Kosciuszko's unsuccessful revolt in 1794. Lived quietly in Warsaw until 1807, when he began the reorganization of the Polish Army. Minister of war of Duchy of Warsaw. Took part in campaigns of 1809, 1812, and 1813. Made Marshal and given command of rear guard at Leipzig; wounded three times, drowned attempting to escape.

A handsome, commanding Polish aristocrat with the ability to be a popular leader—as in 1809, when he raised Galicia in revolt and defeated a superior Austrian army with raw, half-armed volunteers. Administrative ability moderate. Wary and aggressive as a commander; loyal and honorable as a man.

ST.-CYR (properly Gouvion Saint-Cyr), **LAURENT** (1764–1830). Born at Toul. His father was a tanner. St.-Cyr was an artist at the beginning of the Revolution. Volunteered in 1792, but was soon placed on staff duty. Appointed general of brigade in 1793; general of division in 1794. Most of his service with Army of the Rhine. In Italy in 1799; his firmness saved French army after Novi; skill as defensive commander held Genoa. With Moreau in 1800. Appointed to Council of State, 1800–1801, to work on army reorganization. Ambassador to Spain, 1801–2. Commanded Army of Naples, 1803–6; Army of Catalonia, 1808–10. Disciplined for leaving army without permission. Marshal, 1812, after victory at Polotsk. Forced to surrender Dresden in 1813. Attempted to oppose Napoleon's return to France in 1815, and was "rusticated" to his estates as punishment. After 1815, served Bourbons several times as minister of war, but always clashed with reactionary elements.

BIOGRAPHICAL SKETCHES

Tall, square-built, strong-featured; dressed plainly. Thoroughly honest; strict disciplinarian. Independent in thought, speech, and action. Difficult subordinate. Extremely intelligent; waged war with detached calculation of a chess player. Napoleon entrusted him with independent commands in secondary theaters. Energy not equal to his skill; consequently, often accused of indolence. Contrary to tradition, he seems to have looked after his men fairly well. He regarded them, however, merely as tools of his trade, and made no effort to gain their affection. Courage of a chill, furious sort, seldom displayed, but always effective. Studied military history avidly; Frederick the Great, Montecuculli, and Machiavelli were his favorite authors. At his best with a relatively small command and a defensive-offensive mission. Nicknamed "The Owl."

SERURIER, JEAN MATHIEU PHILBERT (1742–1819). Born at Laon. His family was impoverished minor gentry. Appointed lieutenant in Laon militia in 1755; second lieutenant in regular infantry, 1759; lieutenant colonel, 1791. Distinguished himself in Germany (1758–60), Portugal (1762), and Corsica (1768). General of brigade, 1793; general of division, 1794. Health poor after 1796. Captured at Verderio in 1799; retired in 1802. Senatorial marshal, 1804. Governor of the Invalides, 1804–15.

Tall and straight; thin, pale face cut by a scar (a bullet broke his jaw in 1760, knocking out most of his teeth). Brave, well trained, good tactician. Modest, simple, a good husband, and a fond uncle. Adopted the daughter of an invalided NCO. Content with his pay; never sought to enrich himself; gave most of his estate away quietly and carefully. In semidotage by 1814.

"Honest and upright, praised by all; tormented by the fanatics, who accuse him of being an aristocrat, but supported by General Bonaparte who esteems him."—Desaix (1797).

SOULT, NICOLAS JEAN DE DIEU (1769–1851). Duke of Dalmatia. Born in southern France. His father was a notary and gave Soult a good education. Enlisted in 1785; sergeant by 1791. Went to volunteers as instructor in 1792, gaining commission. Appointed general of brigade in 1794; general of division in 1799. Service on Rhine, in Switzerland, and in Italy. Wounded and captured during a sortie from Genoa in 1800. Marshal, 1804. Overran Portugal in 1809; involved in peculiar effort to become its king; driven out by Wellington. In 1810, occupied Andalusia. Recalled to Grande Armee in 1813, but was soon sent back to Spain to delay Wellington. Minister of war, 1814–15. Napoleon's chief of staff during the Hundred Days. In exile until 1819. After the 1830 revolution, he reorganized the French Army, becoming "Marshal-General of France."

Short, bowlegged, one foot reportedly slightly clubbed; grew stout as he aged. Brusque, level-headed, imperturbable, intelligent. Highly self-sufficient, but with an odd touch of the courtier about him. Excellent administrator, disciplinarian, and instructor. Tactics excellent; little strategic sense, but was cautious enough to take care of himself on an independent mission. His ability and wisdom as civilian administrator (as in Andalusia) were reduced by his private plundering. Shared men's worst hardships to set an example. Soult appreciated the value of military intelligence, but was too indolent to be a chief of staff (as in 1815). As young officer, showed outstanding courage; by 1808, directed, rather than led, but still met emergencies with his old daring.

"The soldiers called him 'Iron Hand,' which described him exactly."—Ameil.

SUCHET, LOUIS GABRIEL (1772–1826). Duke of Albufera. Born at Lyons. His father was a wealthy silk merchant. Suchet volunteered in 1793. Appointed battalion commander that same year. Met Bonaparte at Toulon, but did not become particularly friendly. General of division, 1799. Service in Spain and Italy. Made all major campaigns. In 1809, given command of demoralized Army of Aragon. Series of victories brought him his marshal's baton in 1811. Conquered Valencia, 1811–12. Continued successes, 1813–14, during withdrawal from Spain. During the Hundred Days, defeated Austrians and Piedmontese.

Tall, handsome, cheerful. Very level-headed, patient, self-controlled, hard-working. Aggressive fighter; always exploited his successes. Orders clear and emphatic. Expert civil administrator; exploited separatist feelings in Aragon and Catalonia to develop those provinces as his base of operations. Clean-handed, just, and understanding; maintained discipline and morale of troops; got willing cooperation of inhabitants; comparatively little troubled by guerrillas.

"If I had had two marshals like Suchet, I should not only have conquered Spain, but have kept it."—Napoleon.

VICTOR, CLAUDE (properly Claude-Victor Perrin) (1764–1841). Duke of Belluno. Born in the Vosges area; his father was a well-to-do farmer. Musician in the La Fere Artillery Regiment, 1779 (never, as legend has it, a drummer); enlisted in 1781. Purchased discharge in 1791. Municipal employee, Valance; soon joined the volunteers. Appointed major in 1792; general of brigade in 1793; general of division in 1797. Served at Toulon, and in Spain and Italy. Commanded forces in Holland, 1801–5. (Appointed governor of Louisiana in 1802, but had no chance to actually occupy that office.) Chief of staff to Lannes, 1806. Corps commander, 1807; captured by Prussian raiding party; exchanged. Marshal, 1807. In Spain, 1808–12. After 1814, loyal to Bourbons; after Waterloo, member of commission to "purge" army.

An audacious combat officer, quick to see and strike the decisive point; at his best in a melee. Excellent tactician. Hesitant and uncertain on independent missions. Trained men carefully; maintained strict military discipline, but tolerated and protected excesses toward inhabitants that other marshals would punish. Some administrative ability. Moderate intelligence, weak character. Usually blamed mistakes on subordinates; unreliable comrade; occasionally insubordinate. Never particularly friendly toward Napoleon.

Outstanding French General Officers

CAULAINCOURT, ARMAND AUGUSTIN LOUIS (1773–1827). Duke of Vicenza. Born near Saint-Quentin of a noble family. His father was a general. Entered cavalry as gentleman cadet in 1787. Captain, 1792. Dismissed because of noble birth; re-enlisted as a private; restored by Hoche. Colonel, 1799. Employed on diplomatic missions; in 1801, sent to Russia and fell under influence of Czar Alexander. Named aide-de-camp to Napoleon in 1802; general of brigade in 1803; Master of Horse in 1804 (responsible for the Emperor's journeys, personal security on campaign, dispatch riders, and stables); general of division in 1805; Ambassador to Russia, 1807–11. Accompanied Napoleon on his return from Russia. Foreign minister, late 1813 and 1815. Proscribed after Waterloo, he was pardoned through Alexander's intervention. (His brother, a cavalry general, was killed at Borodino.)

BIOGRAPHICAL SKETCHES

As Master of Horse, Caulaincourt's energy and efficiency facilitated Napoleon's swift movements throughout his empire. It is difficult, however, to see any definite skill in his diplomatic services. Influenced by both Alexander and Talleyrand, he seems to have developed a thoroughly defeatist attitude. Napoleon trusted him—possibly too much.

DESAIX, LOUIS CHARLES ANTOINE (1768–1800). Born near Riom, of a noble but impoverished military family. A second lieutenant at the beginning of the Revolution; general of brigade, 1793; general of division, 1794. Probably the ablest general of the Rhine armies.

Desaix is described as tall and high-colored, with very white teeth and long black hair. A wound in the mouth gave him a troublesome lisp. Reckless on reconnaissance, at first careless of logistics, he improved constantly, being ready to learn from both defeat and friendly advice. Extremely intelligent and well educated. Very pure in speech and life; shy, with no social graces or interests; careless of hardship or appearance. Lived only for war and glory, but humane and chivalrous. Unusual appreciation of the value of military intelligence, which he impressed on Davout and Savary. Charming; once his reserve was penetrated, Desaix won the friendship of men as diverse as Napoleon and St.-Cyr.

"Nobody was braver—bravery of the modest sort which did not attach the price of being noticed. Man of conscience before all; man of duty, severe on self, an example to others, his kindness tempered his severity. . . . Esteemed by all who met him."—Marmont.

DROUOT, ANTOINE (1774–1847). Born in Nancy. His father was a baker. Graduated from the Metz artillery school in 1793. Came up through the artillery; in 1808, as a lieutenant colonel, was given the duty of organizing the foot artillery of the Guard. In 1813, general of division, imperial aide-de-camp, and aide-major (administrative chief) of the Guard. Accompanied Napoleon to Elba; wished to accompany him to St. Helena. Court-martialed by order of Louis XVIII, but acquitted. Would not accept half-pay from the Bourbons until well after Napoleon's death.

Drouot was a simple, honest, awkward gunner. An excellent organizer; a careful, strict commander; so deeply intelligent that he was dubbed the "Sage of the Grande Armee." Napoleon admired him and—had he won Waterloo—probably would have made him a marshal. Drouot was sincerely religious, studying his Bible every day.

"He disapproved always of the Emperor, but remained faithful."—Six.

EBLE, JEAN BAPTISTE (1758–1812). Born in Lorraine. His father apparently was an NCO. Eble entered father's regiment at age of nine. By 1785, he was an artillery lieutenant and member of military mission to Naples. General of brigade, 1793. By 1808, general of division. Appointed Westphalian minister of war in 1808; created the Westphalian army. In 1812, chief of ponton units of the Grande Armee; built the Berezina bridges; died of exhaustion at Königsberg at the end of the retreat.

Eble is repeatedly described as "having the appearance of an ancient Roman." Tall, taciturn, brusque, energetic, and persevering, he could make artillery units

and bridges alike out of the most unpromising materials. Superior as a man, a commander, and a technician. Few friends, but those he had were devoted. Universally admired. Called his soldiers "my comrades," but kept strict discipline—with his fists, if necessary.

"A man out of Plutarch."—Bernadotte.

EUGENE (BEAUHARNAIS) (1781–1824). Viceroy of Italy. Born in Paris. He was Josephine's son by her first husband, General Alexandre Beauharnais. Adopted by Napoleon, whom he served as aide-de-camp in Italy and Egypt. Officer of Consular Guard cavalry, 1800–1804. In 1805, made Viceroy of Kingdom of Italy; married to Princess Amelia Augusta of Bavaria. In 1814, retired to Bavaria; in semiarrest during Hundred Days.

Eugene was a hard worker, of moderate talents, but widely liked. Napoleon had great affection for him, coaching him constantly as a statesman and general. As a soldier, he was brave, cool, energetic, and a good comrade; harsh with inefficient administrative officers. Comparatively ineffective in 1809, he improved greatly by 1812, and, in 1813–14, handled impossible situations with competence, if not brilliance. Lacked the killer instinct of the true independent commander.

"Eugene never caused me the least chagrin."—Napoleon.

EXELMANS, REMI JOSEPH ISIDORE (1775–1852). Born at Bar-le-Duc. Volunteered in 1791; captain, 1799; colonel, 1805; general of brigade, 1807. On Murat's staff in Spain, 1808. Captured by English, but escaped, 1811. Master of Horse to Murat, 1811. Re-entered French service in 1812; general of division after Borodino. Tried, but acquitted, for "treasonable correspondence with Murat," 1814. Denounced Ney's execution (1815) and had to remain in exile until 1819. Restored to army in 1828. Marshal, 1851.

Exelmans seems to have been an excellent cavalry commander, but of uneven performance. He was outspoken, loyal, and personally reckless.

D'HAUTPOUL, JEAN JOSEPH ANGE (1754–1807). Born in Gascony, of an old but poor family. Almost uneducated. Entered army as a gentleman cadet in 1771. Rose rapidly during Revolution; when he was to be purged as a noble (1793), his regiment protected him: "No d'Hautpoul, no 6th Chasseurs!" General of brigade, 1794; general of division, 1796.

D'Hautpoul showed little talent, but had great self-confidence, courage, and dash, always leading in person. Some officers considered him fussy and pretentious, charging that he put more emphasis on appearances than on efficiency. Goodhearted and well liked by his men.

JUNOT, ANDOCHE (1771–1813). Duke of Abrantes. Born near Dijon. Law student; volunteered in 1792. His bravery at Toulon in 1793 impressed Napoleon, who made him his aide-de-camp. Colonel, 1796; general of brigade, 1798; general of division, 1803. While Ambassador to Portugal, he deserted his post in 1805 to join the army. Napoleon trusted him implicitly, leaving him in command in Paris in 1800 and 1806, much to Junot's disgust. Showed energy in the occupation of Portugal (1807), but lacked the administrative ability to consolidate his gains. Defeated by Wellington. Returned to France by Convention of Cintra; served under Massena in Spain, 1810–11. Governor of Illyria, 1812–13. Went insane and committed suicide.

BIOGRAPHICAL SKETCHES

Intelligent, hardy, and utterly brave, but lacked balance and self-control. His terrific rages and domineering manners were softened by his rough humor and oddly merciful disposition. Lacked a sound military education. Junot's plans—as at Vimiero—were usually basically good, but scrambled in execution. Devoted, out of all limits, to Napoleon. Insanity due to combination of severe head wounds, thwarted ambition, a vicious wife, an unduly amorous life, and worry over Napoleon's gathering misfortunes. Nicknamed "The Tempest."

KELLERMANN, FRANCOIS ETIENNE (1770–1825). Duke of Valmy. Son of Marshal Kellermann. Limited military service before the Revolution. Entered diplomatic service in 1791. Returned to army in 1793. Colonel, 1796. Served under Napoleon in Italy; general of brigade, 1797. General of division after Marengo. With Junot in Portugal; saw much service in Spain. Sick through 1812. Wounded at Waterloo. Broken from service thereafter.

One of Napoleon's best cavalry commanders; brave, skillful, and determined. Frequently involved in scandals and extortions, but always pardoned for the sake of his decisive charge at Marengo.

KILMAINE, CHARLES EDWARD JENNINGS (1751–99). Born in Dublin. His father was a doctor. Entered French cavalry in 1774. Served in America with Lauzun Hussars. Went from colonel to general of division (and temporary commander of the Army of the North), and was suspended as a "noble," during 1793. Returned to duty in 1795. Assigned to Army of England in 1798.

Kilmaine is described as tall, blond, cold, and wracked by disease acquired during tropical service. Well trained; capable of an independent command requiring alertness and common sense. Personally brave, but not the aggressive cavalry commander Napoleon required in 1796 to replace Steingel. A greedy, large-scale looter, arrogantly insubordinate when caught. The care with which he maintained connections with radical politicians in France made him difficult to discipline.

LASALLE, ANTOINE CHARLES LOUIS (1775–1809). Second lieutenant, 1793; colonel, 1799; general of brigade, 1805; general of division, 1806. Killed at Wagram.

Lasalle was the ideal light cavalryman—aggressive, courageous, high-hearted under hardship, always alert—but he was too reckless for high command. Extravagant and rakish, he was still a good friend, a good husband, and an excellent father. He collected maps and pipes.

"Only a saber, though truly well-tempered."—Six.

LATOUR-MAUBOURG, MARIE VICTOR NICOLAS, MARQUIS DE (1768–1850). Of noble family. Lieutenant of King's Bodyguard, 1789; colonel, 1792. Accompanied Lafayette when he went over to the Allies in 1792. Imprisoned by them; freed in 1797. Went to Egypt in 1798; thereafter rose steadily; general of division by 1808. Lost one leg at Leipzig; thereafter inactive.

A highly capable cavalryman; calm, active, courageous. Noted for his sense of discipline and the care he took of his men. Called "The Bayard of the Army" by the Germans who served under him in 1812. Told his weeping orderly at Leipzig, "What are you crying about, imbecile? You have one boot less to polish."

LAURISTON, JACQUES ALEXANDRE BERNARD LAW (1768–1828). Born in Pondichery, India, of Scottish family. Entered military school in 1784; captain, 1791; colonel of artillery, 1795. Became aide-de-camp to Napoleon in 1800; general of division in 1805. Ambassador to Russia, 1811. Captured at Leipzig in 1813. After 1814, he remained loyal to the Bourbons, becoming a marshal in 1823.

As Napoleon's aide, Lauriston was responsible for the defense of Ragusa against the Russians (1806) and for the artillery preparation for Macdonald's attack at Wagram. As a corps commander in 1813, he was at first slow, indecisive, and overcautious, but improved rapidly.

LOBAU. See Mouton.

MONTBRUN, LOUIS PIERRE (1770–1812). Born at Florensac. Enlisted in 1789. Colonel, 1799; general of brigade by 1805; noted for service in Silesia, 1806–7, and at Somo-Sierra, 1808. General of division, 1809. Killed at Borodino.

Very tall, imposing, bold-eyed, black-bearded. Expert horseman. Extremely brave, but prudent. Active, tireless, careful of the lives of his men. Demanded exact performance of duty. Violent temper. Possibly the most skillful of Napoleon's cavalry corps commanders.

MOREAU, JEAN VICTOR MARIE (1763–1813). Born at Morlaix. His father was a noted lawyer. Moreau served for a short period as an enlisted man. Well educated. Commanded volunteer battalion, 1791. General of brigade, 1793; general of division, 1794. Commanded Army of the Rhine, 1795–97. Stripped of command in 1797 for concealing pro-Royalist plotting of Pichegru, his old commander. Served in Italy in 1799, without distinction. Aided Napoleon's *coup d'état* in 1799. Commanded Army of the Rhine, 1800–1801. Jealous of Napoleon and involved—though apparently unwillingly—in Royalist plots against him. Banished to United States. Became Czar Alexander's military adviser in 1813; killed at Dresden.

About six feet, four inches tall; stout. Violent republican, even though his father was guillotined, but always touched with a suspicion of Royalist sympathy. Lazy and modest, but generally cold and inaccessible, except to his favorites. Took good care of his men; always loved by them. Normally cautious and slow; frequently indecisive; occasional flashes of brilliance. Extremely cool and collected in crises.

"Excellent soldier, personally brave, capable of handling a small army on the field of battle, but an absolute stranger to strategy."—Napoleon.

MOUTON, GEORGES (1770–1838). Count of Lobau. Born at Phalsbourg. Volunteered in 1791. Aide-de-camp to Joubert, 1798. With Massena in Geneva in 1800. Aide-de-camp to Napoleon, 1805. General of division, 1807. Distinguished himself at Aspern-Essling. Corps commander, 1813; captured at Dresden with St.-Cyr. Again captured, attempting to rally troops, at Waterloo. In exile until 1818. Marshal, 1831.

Big, honest, trustworthy; determined courage; a thorough soldier.

"My sheep [*mouton*] is a lion."—Napoleon.

NANSOUTY, ETIENNE MARIE ANTOINE (1768–1815). Born at Bordeaux of noble family. Student at Brienne military school. Captain of the Grey Musketeers before Revolution. General of division by 1808. Commanded the cavalry of the Imperial Guard, 1813–14. Loyal to the Bourbons thereafter.

BIOGRAPHICAL SKETCHES

Well educated, intelligent, excellent unit commander, good horseman. Served well and bravely, but lacked dash; not the man for a do-or-die charge. Rude and sarcastic to subordinates.

REYNIER, JEAN LOUIS EBENEZER (1771–1814). Born in Lausanne, Switzerland. Was a private at the beginning of Revolution. General of brigade, 1795; by 1796, general of division and chief of staff to Moreau. Lost favor in 1801 by advocating Egypt's evacuation. Defeated by English at Maida in 1806, but later subdued Calabria. With Massena in Spain, 1810–11. Supported Eugene, 1812–13, in reorganizing army after Russian campaign. Captured at Leipzig; refused the offer of a Russian commission; exchanged; died of exhaustion shortly thereafter.

Just, humane, brave; a rigid and conscientious Protestant of legendary honesty; cold and taciturn; not well liked. Difficult subordinate, self-sufficient and scornful of many of the marshals. An excellent planner (Napoleon rated him as superior to either Massena or St.-Cyr), he lacked the power to inspire his men. Consequently, did better with German than French troops.

"Reynier was a man of talent, but better fitted to [plan the operations of] an army of 20,000 or 30,000 men, than to command one of 5,000 or 6,000."—Napoleon.

SAVARY, ANNE JEAN MARIE RENE (1774–1833). Duke of Rovigo. Born in the Ardennes. Captain, 1793; aide-de-camp first to Desaix, then to Napoleon. General of brigade, 1803; general of division, 1805. Played a major part in the kidnaping of d'Enghien (1803) and in the arrest of the Spanish royal family (1807). In 1810, replaced Fouche as minister of police. (Fouche had deliberately destroyed the ministry's records and dispersed its staff.) Reconstructed, expanded, and improved the ministry. In 1814, overconfident and slow to utilize his forces properly for military intelligence missions. In 1815, replaced Moncey as inspector general of gendarmerie. Wished to accompany Napoleon to St. Helena, but was forbidden. In exile until 1819.

Though hated and feared as minister of police, Savary was kind-hearted and independent, speaking frankly to Napoleon whenever he thought him harsh or unjust. Personal devotion to Napoleon such that he willingly did the Empire's dirty work. Daring, expert light cavalry officer, with unusual understanding of intelligence work.

VANDAMME, DOMINIQUE JOSEPH RENE (1770–1830). Count of Unebourg. Born near Dunkirk. Reportedly had some military education. Enlisted in 1788; served in America, but apparently deserted in 1790. Re-enlisted in 1791; passed to the volunteers as an instructor. General of brigade, 1793; general of division, 1799. Service in the north, along the Rhine, and in Switzerland. In 1806–7, reduced Prussian fortresses in Silesia. Commanded big Württemberg division, 1809. Assigned the command of the Westphalian corps in 1812; relieved when he protested Jerome's mismanagement. Captured at Kulm in 1813; rebuffed by Bourbons on return to France. Joined Napoleon in 1815. After Waterloo, was refused refuge in Holland; lived in United States until 1824.

Highly intelligent and energetic, but so undisciplined that only Davout could control him, and he only with difficulty. Personally devoted to Napoleon. Thoroughgoing looter; brutal, violent, and high-handed. Language and manner rude. Maintained rigid discipline, but took good care of his men. Hated throughout

Germany for his exactions—but admired by his German soldiers. A driving, inspiring fighter—sometimes overly reckless—but brave and quick-witted. Much of his insubordination probably calculated, since (as in 1809) he thus gained independent commands.

"If I had two of you, the only solution would be to have one hang the other." —Napoleon.

WREDE, KARL PHILIPP (1767–1838). Born at Heidelberg. Educated for career as civil servant. In 1799, raised volunteer corps for service with Austrian Army. Austrian brigade commander at Hohenlinden. Lieutenant-general in the Bavarian Army after 1801. Initially pro-French, Wrede began turning against Napoleon by 1811. In 1813, headed the anti-French party; reorganized the Bavarian Army for a stroke at Napoleon's communications. Defeated and badly wounded at Hanau in 1813. Commanded Bavarian troops in France in 1814 and 1815. Active thereafter in Bavarian politics.

Brave, commanding, energetic, a good tactician and leader. No concept of strategy. Intensely ambitious; a thorough "guard-house lawyer." His French associates never trusted him; both in 1805 and 1809, there were suspicions that he was in the pay of the Austrian government. In Russia, however—despite all legends—he seems to have served loyally and ably.

"Poor Wrede. I made him a count, but I never could make him a general."—Napoleon (surveying Wrede's position at Hanau).

Foreign Military Leaders

BAGRATION, PETER (1765–1812). (Often called "Prince.") Descended from a noble Georgian family. Entered the Russian Army in 1782. Served in Caucasus, against Turks, and in Poland. In 1799, achieved considerable fame under Suvarov in Italy and Switzerland. In 1808, made daring march across the frozen Gulf of Finland to seize the Aland Islands from Swedes. In 1809, served against Turks. Mortally wounded at Borodino.

Normally taciturn and dignified, but with a violent temper that could erupt over trifles. No demonstrated strategic sense, tactical skill no more than moderate, unfitted for a large independent command. However, a furious, stubborn, inspiring leader of men, much like Ney. Personally fearless and reckless, equally good with advance guard or rear guard. Very ambitious and envious; bragged as energetically as he fought. Reports unreliable. Barclay found him a treacherous, unruly subordinate.

BARCLAY (properly Barclay de Tolly), **MICHAEL ANDREAS** (1761–1818). Born in Livonia (modern Lithuania-Estonia). He was descended from a Scots soldier of fortune who had settled there in the seventeenth century. Entered the Russian service while quite young; served against Turks, Swedes, and Poles. Colonel, 1798; general, 1799; lieutenant general, 1806; field marshal, 1814. During 1808, won several actions in Finland against the Swedes. Minister of war, 1810–13. Commanded Russian contingent in 1815. Died in Prussia.

A soldier of character: "calm, cool, possessed of a sense of order and discipline, and of great endurance." A stout fighter, able to keep his head in a crisis. Moderately good tactician; no real strategic sense. Had, as Russian command

BIOGRAPHICAL SKETCHES

went, considerable administrative ability. Could resist tremendous personal pressure and abuse. Not popular with his officers and men. (According to some accounts, Barclay never really mastered the Russian language.)

BENNIGSEN, LEVIN AUGUST (1745–1826). Born in Brunswick, Hanover. Page in the Hanoverian court; later, officer of foot guards. Left Hanoverian Army in 1764; entered Russian service as a field-grade officer in 1773. Served against Turks, Poles, and Persians with some distinction. Brigadier, 1787; general, 1802. Involved in murder of Czar Paul I. Served against Napoleon in 1806–7, 1812, and 1813. In 1814, commanded the forces operating against Davout (then at Hamburg), but achieved no success. Retired to Hanover in 1818.

"A pale, withered personage of high stature and cold appearance, with a scar across his face." Bennigsen had vague glimmerings of strategic ideas, but always flinched at the crucial moment. Clumsy tactician. Plans usually too complicated for successful execution. Physically brave. Thoroughly mercenary; untrustworthy as a subordinate; unreliable as a fellow commander; always intriguing.

BLÜCHER, GEBHARD LEBERECHT VON (1742–1819). Born at Rostock. Entered the Swedish Army in 1756; in 1760, captured by the Prussians and entered their service as hussar officer. Resigned in 1773, after being refused promotion to major. Farmer for fifteen years. Reinstated; won distinction in early clashes of Revolutionary wars. Lieutenant general in 1801. Member of war party, 1805–6. After capture, was exchanged (1807) for Victor. Relieved of command in 1812 for advocating an alliance with Russia. Field marshal, 1813. Retired in 1815.

Poorly educated, wild, frequently drunken; had no idea of strategy and possibly less of tactics, but was not without a certain low, foxy cunning. Loved fighting, had unusual powers to inspire men, hated Napoleon and everything French, never admitted defeat. By 1814, was weakening in body and mind, but still was more energetic than his allies and subordinates. Nicknamed "Marshal Forward." Said of himself, "Something could have been made of me if I only had had the sense to study."

CHARLES (Karl Ludwig) (1771–1847). Archduke of Austria. Born at Florence. A soldier from childhood; lieutenant field marshal, 1793. In 1796, given command of Allied forces on the Rhine frontier; defeated Jourdan and Moreau. Unable to check Bonaparte in 1797. Defeated Jourdan and Massena in 1799. Entrusted with reorganization of the Austrian Army after Austerlitz. Opposed war in 1809; retired at its end.

Handsome, frank, intelligent. As a soldier, Charles had a double personality. His early education (and subsequent writings) was in the formal eighteenth-century school, emphasizing strategic points, caution, and maneuver. As combat leader, he generally owed his successes to his personal courage, daring, and example. Health poor; subject to epileptic fits. Periods of indolence—possibly because of health, possibly because of lack of strategic inspiration. Excellent tactician; good strategist. Wellington reportedly thought him the best Allied commander of this period.

GNEISENAU, AUGUST WILHELM VON (1760–1831). Born in Saxony. His father was an impoverished Austrian noble, serving as a Saxon artillery officer. (Gnei-

senau reportedly was born during the retreat from the battle of Torgau.) Served first in Austrian cavalry; in 1782, went to Canada as a lieutenant of an Ansbach light infantry unit hired by British, but saw no active service. Transferred to the Prussian service, apparently as engineer officer; company commander in 1806. In 1807, transferred to general staff; played considerable part in reformation of Prussian Army. Resigned commission in 1809 because Prussia refused aid to Austria. However, employed on secret diplomatic missions to England and Russia. Joined Blücher's staff in 1813, becoming its chief after Scharnhorst's death. Held this position through 1814, and again in 1815, his association with Blücher resembling very much the later one of Ludendorff and Hindenburg. Liberal political views made him unpopular after Waterloo. Field marshal, 1828. Died of cholera in Posen during Polish revolt of 1831.

Gneisenau was willful, intelligent, and broad-minded. He is usually credited with planning Blücher's strategy, though this may have consisted largely of issuing the orders to implement Blücher's viscera-inspired decisions. Relations with Blücher were more correct than friendly. Always wanted an independent command, but—though energetic and courageous—does not seem to have possessed the requisite strength of character. Greatly improved the Prussian staff system, yet his staff operations during the Waterloo campaign would have horrified contemporary U.S. militia officers. Sincere patriot, champion of German unity.

KUTUSOV, MIKHAIL LARIONOVICH (1745–1813). Prince of Smolensk. Born at St. Petersburg; entered army in 1759 or 1760. Served in Poland, 1764–69, and against the Turks, 1770–74 and 1788–91. Was the favorite subordinate of Suvarov in these wars. In 1805, commanded Russian expeditionary force sent to aid Austria. Administrative posts, 1806–11; commander of army engaged with Turks, 1811. Recalled to supreme command against Napoleon in 1812. Made field marshal.

In youth, active, bold, and ruthless. By 1812, too fat and infirm to mount a horse. Possessed all the virtues necessary for success in Russian palace politics—shrewdness, craft, polish, vindictiveness. Both lazy and ambitious. Regarded as thoroughly "Russian." Showed no real tactical skill; strategic understanding still disputed.

MACK (properly Mack von Leiberich), **KARL** (1752–1828). Born in Bavaria of a lower-middle-class Protestant family. In 1770, enlisted in an Austrian cavalry regiment in which his maternal uncle was a squadron commander. Corporal, 1771; regimental staff sergeant, 1773; second lieutenant, 1777. In 1778, detailed (because of industry and skill as writer and draftsman) to accompany Austrian Emperor Joseph on frontier inspection. Transferred to the quartermaster general (operations) staff as captain in 1783. Ennobled in 1785. Distinguished himself in Turkish war; major and personal aide-de-camp to Emperor, 1788; colonel, 1789. In 1793, chief of staff to Austrian army in the Netherlands; responsible for most of Allied successes there that year. Lieutenant field marshal, 1797. Lent to Neapolitan government in 1798; but, failing to realize the worthlessness of Neapolitan troops, was defeated by Championnet. Took refuge with French to avoid being murdered. Escaped in 1800. Army quartermaster general, 1804; as a representative of the war party, quarreled with Archduke Charles. Tried by court-martial, 1806–7; broken from service; imprisoned until 1808. In 1819, Schwarzenberg secured his reinstatement.

BIOGRAPHICAL SKETCHES

History of hard service, repeated wounds, bad luck. Never fully recovered from a bad head injury during the Turkish wars. Mack's rise from the ranks on his own merits was most unusual in the Austrian service, in which higher grades customarily were reserved for (normally Catholic) nobility. Hard worker, frequently to the point where his health broke down; good organizer and administrator. Acquired an excellent military education, largely through own studies. Tendency toward pedantry; partially understood Napoleon's methods, but could not work out Austrian equivalent. High reputation for courage and sense of honor. As staff officer, highly regarded by a succession of commanders, won esteem of troops to unusual degree. As commander at Ulm, could not dominate high-born subordinates.

"With Mack, confidence, order, discipline disappeared from this army, which knew nothing further but reverses."—Langeron (1794).

MELAS, MICHAEL FRIEDRICH VON (1730–1806). Born in Moravia. Won early renown as a cavalry officer in the Turkish wars. Excellent service during the Seven Years' War and early Revolutionary wars. Commanded the Austrian forces under Suvarov in Italy in 1799. Suvarov himself credited Melas with much of the Allied success there. In 1806, presided over military commission that tried Mack.

Strategist of the old, deliberate, piecemeal Austrian school; generally considered a better-than-average tactician. A hard fighter, noted for personal courage and leadership.

SCHWARZENBERG, KARL PHILIPP (1771–1820). Prince. Began service in 1788. Distinguished himself in various cavalry actions during Turkish wars and early campaigns of French Revolution. Lieutenant field marshal, 1799; saved the Austrian right wing after Hohenlinden. Commanded a corps under Mack, 1805; escaped from Ulm with Archduke Ferdinand. In Russia, seeking aid, in 1808. Helped negotiate Napoleon's marriage to Maria Louisa. Napoleon requested him as commander of his Austrian auxiliary corps in 1812. Field marshal by 1813; commander in chief of Allied forces, 1813–15.

By 1812, quite fat. Intellectually active; letters show sense of humor. In 1812, strategically bold, tactically timid and clumsy. High order of personal bravery. In 1813–15, felt personally inferior to Napoleon; consequently overcautious. Considerable diplomatic ability, which sometimes declined into cheap trickery, as in his actions following St.-Cyr's surrender at Dresden.

WELLESLEY, ARTHUR (1769–1852). First Duke of Wellington. Born in Ireland; family wealthy and aristocratic. Entered army as ensign in 1787. Thanks to the system of "purchase" then customary, became a lieutenant colonel in 1793. Little regimental service during this period, since he was also aide-de-camp to the lord-lieutenant of Ireland. Took part in unsuccessful expedition to Holland, 1794–95. In India, 1796–1805; won several major successes over the Mahrattas; mastered art of military logistics. With abortive Hanover expedition in 1805; Copenhagen expedition in 1807. In 1808, began his famous peninsular campaign that ended in 1814 with the invasion of southern France. British Ambassador to France, 1814. After Waterloo, commanded the Allied army of occupation in France, 1815–18. Thereafter active in British politics and diplomacy, usually with little success.

Operating (1808–15) with a relatively small army, the loss of which probably would be fatal to the Allied cause, Wellington wrung maximum results from slender resources through patience, thorough preparation, plain common sense, and calm courage. Superior judge of terrain, expert tactician, past master of logistics, good understanding of strategy. Could be ruthless, as in his scorched-earth policy in Portugal in 1810. A thorough Anglo-Irish aristocrat, aloofly contemptuous of the rest of the world and its works; a "gentleman" only by the contemporary standards of his peers. Simple tastes, no liking for ostentation. No conscious effort to win his soldiers' affection, but gained respect through his efficiency. Kept his army under tight personal control, allowing even his best subordinates slight freedom of action. Ungrateful, vindictive, something of a toady and more of a snob, he was still a great captain who did more than his assigned duty.

WITTGENSTEIN, LUDWIG ADOLF PETER (1769–1843). His father was a Westphalian nobleman who had entered the Russian Army. Wittgenstein himself made his first campaign against the Poles in 1794–95, subsequently serving against Turks, Swedes, and French. Badly wounded at Bar-sur-Aube in 1814. Field marshal, 1823; retired because of ill health in about 1828.

A vigorous, aggressive officer, but without talents as either a strategist or tactician. Personally brave and willing to accept responsibility. Knew his own shortcomings, and willingly accepted a subordinate role after being defeated at Lützen and Bautzen. His after-action reports are remarkably unreliable.

WÜRMSER, DAGOBERT SIGISMOND (1724–97). Born in Alsace. Early service in French Army, 1745–47. Entered Austrian service in 1750; lieutenant general, 1778. Won distinction against the Prussians during the Seven Years' War, and against the French in Germany during the early Revolutionary wars.

Tough, courageous, and full of zeal; normally energetic, but (possibly because of age) subject to periods of inertia. Poor strategist; limited tactician; excellent, inspiring troop leader. Undaunted by defeat.

"[He] has not ceased to show a constancy and courage which History will record."—Bonapart (1797).

Major Political Figures

CARNOT, LAZARE NICOLAS MARGUERITE (1753–1823). Born in Nolay. His father was a lawyer. Educated at the famous Mezieres Engineer School. Commissioned in 1773; captain, 1783. Revolution drew him into politics. Served as a "Representative of the People on Mission" to the armies in the north, showing courage, but frequently hampering generals. Became a member first of the Committee of Public Safety, then of the Directory, discharging duties roughly equivalent to combined minister of war and chief of staff. Major of engineers, 1795. Internal intrigues of Directory drove him into exile in 1797. Napoleon made him minister of war in 1800, but Carnot resigned after Marengo. Living in retirement, he continued in public opposition to Napoleon; the latter, however, aided him by commissioning him to prepare a textbook on fortification. In 1814, he offered his services. Hastily promoted to general of division, he made a famous defense of Antwerp. Minister of interior, 1815. He opposed Napoleon's second abdication. Died in exile at Magdeburg.

Carnot was a sincere patriot, with strong republican convictions. Absolutely honest, he was easily taken in by accomplished rascals, such as Fouche. Author of many important works on mathematics, fortifications, physics, and balloons. His knowledge of strategy was very limited, but his powers as an organizer were extraordinary. As a captain in 1794, he directed fourteen separate armies. Called "The Organizer of Victory."

CLARKE, HENRI JACQUES GUILLAUME (1765–1818). Count of Hunebourg, Duke of Feltre. Of Irish descent, he entered the military school in 1781. General of brigade in 1793, but expelled from the service on suspicion of disloyalty. Reinstated by the Directory. He was sent to Italy to serve as Directory's agent in observing Bonaparte (under pretense of negotiating with Austria), but soon fell under Bonaparte's influence. Napoleon's confidential secretary, 1800–1804. In 1806, military governor of Berlin. From 1807 to 1814, minister of war. After 1814, he cast in his lot with Louis XVIII, who promoted him to marshal.

Clarke had much charm, was laborious and painstaking, but thoroughly stupid and not really military-minded. Much of a courtier, something of a coward. Extremely vain and conceited; harsh to subordinates and—after Waterloo—to former associates.

"An honest man, of mediocre talents, without character, and so addicted to flattering that one can never tell how much reliance to place on any opinion he may express."—Napoleon.

FOUCHE, JOSEPH (1759–1820). Duke of Otranto. Born near Nantes. His father was a sailor. Received a religious education, but took only minor vows, serving as a teacher. With the Revolution, he became an extreme Jacobin, responsible for large-scale butcheries at Lyons and elsewhere. He was involved in the attempt to abolish Christianity (1793), in the overthrow of Robespierre (1794), and in Napoleon's *coup d'état* (1799). Minister of police, 1799–1802 and 1804–10. In disgrace thereafter, he was given minor diplomatic posts. Welcomed the Bourbons in 1814, then plotted against them. Joined Napoleon in 1815, became his minister of police, and betrayed him. Louis XVIII retained him briefly, then exiled him. He died, immensely rich, at Trieste.

Fouche was ruled all his life by a complete mania for intrigue. He sold his God, his country, and every man who ever trusted or employed him—but never himself, remaining oddly independent of every human loyalty. Even his obscene and bloody fanaticism at the beginning of the Revolution probably was bogus. Yet he was intelligent, clever, and remarkably skillful in police work. Posing as a patriot, he played coldly and audaciously for power and fortune. However, he seems to have totally lacked ability as a leader; he could only serve as a lieutenant, and he was too ambitious to serve faithfully.

"Fouche needed intrigue like food. . . . [He was] always in everybody's shoes."—Napoleon.

MARET, HUGUES BERNARD (1763–1839). Duke of Bassano. Born at Dijon; educated as a lawyer. At the beginning of the Revolution, turned publisher and diplomat. Missions to England and Naples. Joined Napoleon in 1799 as secretary; later rose to secretary of state. Minister of foreign affairs, 1811–12. Served again as secretary of state, 1813–14 and 1815. Banished from France, 1815–20.

Maret accompanied Napoleon on most of his campaigns. He possessed good sense, great powers of work, and a cool head. Though capable of being a moderat-

ing influence, his great personal devotion to Napoleon made him too often unwilling to oppose actions he felt unwise.

METTERNICH (properly Metternich-Winneburg), CLEMENS WENZEL LOTHAR (1773–1859). Born at Coblenz. His father was a diplomat. Received an excellent education. In Strasbourg at the beginning of the Revolution; shocked by its excesses. Rose steadily in the Austrian diplomatic service; Ambassador to France, 1806. Urged Austrian declaration of war in 1809 because of exaggerated reports of French losses in Spain. Austrian foreign minister, 1809. His policy was directed toward strengthening Austria while retaining, insofar as possible, her international freedom of action. Favored marriage of Maria Louisa to Napoleon as a means to this end. From 1812 on, played a delicate game, seeking to make Austria the arbiter of Europe, curbing in turn French, Russian, and Prussian power. For years the most powerful European statesman. Personally conservative, and the servant of the stupidly reactionary Emperor Francis, he opposed all liberal movements. Driven from office by the Vienna revolt in 1848.

Handsome; "exquisite" manners; keenly, if narrowly, intelligent. Patient, patriotic, and courageous. Probably the most effective diplomat of his day, expert in the tangled intrigues and double-dealing that his position required. Occasionally, *too* clever.

TALLEYRAND (properly Talleyrand-Perigord), CHARLES MAURICE (1754–1838). Prince de Benevent. Born in Paris of noble family. Crippled through neglect in childhood, and therefore barred from his family inheritance and thrust into the church. Agent-general of the French clergy, 1780; bishop of Autun, 1789. Threw himself into the Revolution, leaving the church and entering the diplomatic service in 1791. Mission to England in 1792; thereafter, spent thirty months in the United States to escape the Reign of Terror in France. Returned to France in late 1795. Foreign minister, 1797; resigned in 1799. Supported Napoleon's *coup d'état* in 1799. Foreign minister until 1807; grand chamberlain and member of Napoleon's council of state until 1814. By 1807, actively engaged in plotting against Napoleon; set up rump provisional government in 1814 to declare Napoleon dethroned. Foreign minister, 1815; represented France at Congress of Vienna. Soon discarded as unreliable. Ambassador to London, 1830–34.

Sly-featured, untidy, limping, his unprepossessing appearance was, however, usually canceled by great personal charm, courtly bearing, and keen sense of humor. Highly intelligent, but indolent, immoral, and corrupt. Cool, supple, calculating; past master at awaiting events, without definitely committing himself. Used official position shamelessly to enrich himself (the famous "XYZ Affair" was a minor example). Worked indirectly and in secret, so that many of his activities remain problematical. No loyalties. Wanted a France that would permit him to live in luxury, untroubled by unseemly wars. His efforts (as at the Congress of Vienna) to ensure this have sometimes been mistaken for patriotism. Lack of energy and conviction reduced his effectiveness as a leader. To a soldier like Lannes, he was a "silk stocking full of [fresh manure]." Napoleon, who considered him "immorality personified," also said of him, "He judges things well. He is the most capable minister I ever had."

Recommended Reading List

"Old men forget: yet all shall be forgot,
But he'll remember with advantages
What feats he did that day . . ."
—WILLIAM SHAKESPEARE

"I know that it is much more easy to conceive and point
out the principles which ought to guide us in the construction of a machine than to put them into practice; for whatever passes through the hands of men participates of his
imperfections. We should not however despair; if the per-
fection we aim at is not attainable, to approach it is a great
merit, and will in some measure answer the end proposed."
—HENRY LLOYD

RECOMMENDED READING LIST

Of the perhaps quarter of a million books dealing with Napoleon, an amazing proportion are honest, valuable works, written by scholars and soldiers with their hearts in their work. No one can hope to read all of them; we have found the following books useful.

Introductory Material

BOURCET, PIERRE J. *Memories Historiques su la Guerre que les Francois Ont Soutenue en Allemagne 1757 Jusqu'en 1762.* Paris: Maradan, 1792. Bourcet was deeply impressed with the military efficiency of the Prussian system and favored adapting it for French use. He was also an expert on staff procedures and mountain warfare. Napoleon seems to have been considerably influenced by his works, which stressed careful preplanning and the advantages of the offensive.

CLAUSEWITZ, KARL VON. *On War.* London: N. Trubner & Co., 1873. Clausewitz's famous work is based on a devoted study of Napoleonic warfare. His bulky, often seemingly contradictory book (actually, only the draft of the complete work he contemplated) shows that he had grasped one great truth of those wars: the role of the human spirit and will—something that the neat-minded Jomini could not understand and so largely ignored.

COLIN, JEAN L. A. *L'Infanterie au XVIII Siecle: La Tactique.* Paris: Levrault, 1907. ———. *The Transformations of War.* Translated by L. H. R. Pope-Hennessy. London: H. Rees, 1912. Colin was one of the most thoughtful students of the Napoleonic period.

DU TEIL, JEAN. *De l'Usage de l'Artillerie Nouvelle Dans la Guerre de Campagne.* Paris, 1924. First printed in 1778, this was the authoritative work of its period on artillery. Du Teil preached the importance of mobility and of concentrated firepower. He and his older brother trained Napoleon as an artilleryman.

FEUQUIERES, ANTOINE DE PAS. *Memoires.* 4 vols. Paris: Rollin Fils, 1737. Feuquieres served during the early wars of Louis XIV, rising from private to lieutenant general. He was an aggressive, capable soldier. Napoleon approved of the sentiments expressed in his writings.

FOLARD, JEAN CHARLES DE. *Histoire de Polybe.* 6 vols. Paris: Pierre Gandouin, 1727–30. An experienced soldier, as well as a student of classical history, Folard urged a return to the use of massive columns and shock action. His ideas proved too extreme, but were the mental grandparents of Napoleonic infantry tactics.

FREDERICK THE GREAT. *The Instructions of Frederick the Great for His Generals.* Translated by T. R. Phillips. Harrisburg, Pa.: The Military Service Publishing Co., 1960. Originally written in 1747; revised in 1748. This slim book contains the essence of Frederick's careful, cynical, audacious mastery of the military art of his time.

GUIBERT, JACQUES A. *Essai General de Tactique.* Liege: C. Plonteux, 1775. Guibert had little practical military experience, but this early work was a sensation, and deeply influenced subsequent French doctrine. He recommended a national army, greater mobility, and a war of aggressive maneuvering.

———. *Oeuvres Militaires de Guibert.* Paris: Magimel, 1803. (Published by his widow.) Guibert's later writings partially retracted his earlier views. Fame made him conservative. He had come to favor professional armies and limited warfare. These later writings, however, had little influence compared to his *Essai.*

JOMINI, ANTOINE H. *Precis de l'Art de la Guerre.* Paris: Anselin, 1838. This immensely successful book summed up Jomini's years of experience and study. Considered the perfect summary of what officers should know, it established and defined many of the basic terms and concepts still used in the study of warfare. Its sources are probably less Napoleonic than eighteenth-century Prussian.

LLOYD, HENRY. *History of the Late War in Germany Between the King of Prussia, and the Empress of Germany and Her Allies.* 3 vols. London, 1766–81. Lloyd (1720–83), a too-little-known English soldier of fortune, was undoubtedly the most intelligent military student of the pre-Napoleonic period. His careful, modern-style study of Frederick's campaigns led him to deduce the initial "principles of war." This work includes an interesting opinion concerning the British campaigns against the American rebels: Lloyd believed that the Americans could not be subdued.

PHILLIPS, THOMAS R. *Roots of Strategy.* Harrisburg, Pa.: The Military Service Publishing Co., 1940. With its *Reveries* of Marshal Saxe, Frederick the Great's *Instructions,* and Napoleon's *Maxims,* this book handily traces the evolution—and the unchanging basic principles—of the art of war from prehistory through 1815.

QUIMBY, ROBERT S. *The Background of Napoleonic Warfare.* New York: Columbia University Press, 1957. A heavily researched review of the development of Napoleonic drill and tactics. As such, it forms a useful antidote to Oman's oversimplified theory of "column versus line."

SAXE, MAURICE. *Mes Reveries.* 2 vols. Amsterdam: Arkstee et Merkus, 1757. Saxe, a born soldier who had experienced all sorts of warfare, paused briefly to set down a few of the impressions gained from his whirling life. Some are fantastic, some prophetic, but most are hard common sense. He could detect "no principles" of war, but he suggested many practical improvements.

VAUBAN, SEBASTIEN L. P. *De l'Attaque et de la Defense des Places.* 2 vols. The Hague: Pierre de Hondt, 1737–42. The work of the master of fortification and siegecraft— the arts that characterized pre-Revolutionary warfare.

The United States and the Napoleonic Wars

ADAMS, HENRY. *The War of 1812.* Washington, D.C.: The Infantry Journal, 1944. This book shows the interrelationship of the American and European wars and their alternating effects on British military operations. It also remains the best history of American military operations, afloat and ashore.

BEIRNE, FRANCIS F. *The War of 1812.* New York: E. P. Dutton & Co., 1949.

CULLUM, GEORGE W. *Campaigns of the War of 1812.* New York: J. Miller, 1879. This book is particularly useful because of its emphasis on Engineer operations— that arm of the U.S. Army being much influenced by French doctrine.

ELLIOTT, CHARLES W. *Winfield Scott: The Soldier and the Man.* New York: The Macmillan Co., 1937. Scott visited France in 1815, shortly after Waterloo, to improve his professional knowledge. His reactions were frank and outspoken, based as they were on his own experiences in organizing and leading troops against the British.

ENGELMAN, FRED L. *The Peace of Christmas Eve.* New York: Harcourt, Brace, and World, 1962. A popular history of British-American diplomatic relations during the War of 1812. As such, it gives considerable insight into the pressures on the British government during this period. The United States was fortunate in possessing efficient representatives, but their best skills would have meant nothing without the last-ditch efforts of American military commanders.

FORESTER, CECIL S. *The Age of Fighting Sail.* Garden City, N.Y.: Doubleday & Co., 1956. An impartial history of the naval warfare of 1812–15, thoroughly integrated with European military and diplomatic events. A particularly interesting feature is the description of Wellington's dependence on American foodstuffs.

GILPIN, A. R. *The War of 1812 in the Old Northwest.* East Lansing, Mich.: Michigan State University Press, 1958.

JACOBS, JAMES R. *The Beginnings of the U.S. Army, 1783–1815.* Princeton, N.J.: Princeton University Press, 1947. An excellent study of the hungry first days of the American Army, showing the diverse influences that shaped it.

JAMES, MARQUIS. *Andrew Jackson, the Border Captain.* Indianapolis and New York: The Bobbs-Merrill Co., 1933.

MAHAN, ALFRED T. *Seapower in Relation to the War of 1812.* Boston: Little, Brown & Co., 1905. A classic statement of the importance of sea power.

MULLER, CHARLES G. *The Proudest Day.* New York: The John Day Co., 1960. A lively story of American operations on Lake Champlain.

PRATT, FLETCHER. *Preble's Boys.* New York: William Sloan Associates, 1950. A series of colorful stories of how the officers of the new U.S. Navy met the test of war.

SWANSON, NEIL H. *The Perilous Fight.* New York: Rinehart & Co., 1945. The British

RECOMMENDED READING LIST

attacks on Washington and Baltimore, stirringly told. Includes much useful information on British amphibious doctrine and equipment.

TUCKER, GLENN. *Poltroons and Patriots*. Indianapolis and New York: The Bobbs-Merrill Co., 1954. A popular history of the War of 1812 that brings out the interesting point that Napoleon's abdication in 1814 was heartily celebrated in many places in the United States, in childish obliviousness to the fact that England could now turn her whole strength westward. The author's attempts to make Monroe the hero of the war are less convincing.

———. *Dawn Like Thunder*. Indianapolis and New York: The Bobbs-Merrill Co., 1962. A good detailed history of United States naval operations against the Barbary pirate states during the Napoleonic era.

General Histories

ANDERSSON, INGVAR. *A History of Sweden*. Translated by Carolyn Hannay. New York: Frederick A. Praeger, 1956. Contains a good, brief account of how Sergeant "Pretty-Leg" Bernadotte, rabid revolutionist, became Charles XIV, reactionary King of Sweden. It also covers Swedish-French relations during this period.

BALLARD, COLIN R. *Napoleon: An Outline*. New York: D. Appleton & Co., 1924. A typical "John Bull" work of the better sort. Its scholarship is far from profound, its sources limited, and its grasp of the over-all history of the Napoleonic period only partial. The author, on the other hand, is an intelligent soldier who knows soldiers, and does his best to be fair and open-minded. Also, he surpasses many professional historians in his comprehension that contemporary gossip has more effect on the course of history than do the actual facts—laboriously reconstructed fifty years later.

BELLOC, HILAIRE. *Napoleon*. London: Cassell & Co., 1932. Belloc wrote from a special viewpoint—that of a passionate believer in a Europe united into a common Catholic civilization. For that reason—despite an occasionally slipshod handling of facts, plus a tendency to put Belloc reasonings into Bonaparte's head—this book deserves reading by all students of this period.

BERNARD, HENRI. *Lecons d'Histoire Militaire*. Vol. I. Brussels: Imprimerie Medical et Scientific, 1951. This is the competent textbook used in the Belgian Royal Military Academy for the study of the Napoleonic Wars.

BRYANT, ARTHUR. *The Years of Endurance, 1793–1802*. London: Collins, 1942.

———. *The Years of Victory, 1802–1812*. London: Collins, 1944.

———. *The Age of Elegance, 1812–1822*. London: Collins, 1950. This trilogy gives a full-flowing picture of England and her wars. Unsparing in describing domestic blemishes, the author becomes a trifle self-righteous abroad. His battle scenes have rare sweep and vigor—though he weights them heavily in favor of his countrymen. He understands and states the coiling intricacies of international jockeying for power, as well as the dead hand that party politics can drop upon the actions of soldier and diplomat alike.

CARLYLE, THOMAS. *The French Revolution*. New York: Modern Library, no date. Napoleon appears only occasionally in this classic work, which closes with his "whiff of grapeshot" that quelled Paris. Nevertheless, there are few better works for establishing the historical background of the Napoleonic period.

CHAIR, SOMERSET DE (ed.). *Napoleon's Memoirs*. New York: Harper & Brothers, 1949. A good English-language edition of the historical portions of Napoleon's own *Commentaires*.

DODGE, THEODORE A. *Napoleon*. 4 vols. Boston and New York: Houghton Mifflin Co., 1904. A massive, but well-organized review of all the Napoleonic campaigns. However, it is largely based on Jomini. Also, Dodge's usual tendency toward hero worship frequently becomes extreme.

DUMOLIN, MAURICE. *Precis d'Histoire Militaire, Revolution et Empire*. 3 vols. Paris: Maison Andriveau-Goujon, 1906. This is possibly the most studious French work on the Napoleonic campaigns—impartial, analytical, and packed with information. Unfortunately, it ends with the 1809 campaign. Its main fault seems to be the result of occasionally careless proofreading—some strength figures suddenly change in inexplicable ways, and (especially in the third volume) the names of various cavalry commanders are confused.

EARLE, EDWARD J. (ed.). *Makers of Modern Strategy*. Princeton, N.J.: Princeton University Press, 1943. An indispensable book, tracing the evolution of modern strategic concepts. The Napoleonic period is well represented by chapters on Clausewitz and Jomini—Napoleon's two self-appointed interpreters.

FALLS, CYRIL. *The Art of War from the Age of Napoleon to the Present Day*. New York: Oxford University Press, 1961. Contains an excellent, brief review of land and sea warfare of the Napoleonic period.

FLORINSKY, MICHAEL T. *Russia: A History and an Interpretation*. 2 vols. New York: The Macmillan Co., 1958.

FORTESCUE, SIR JOHN W. *History of the British Army*. 13 vols. London: The Macmillan Co., 1899–1930.

FULLER, JOHN F. C. *A Military History of the Western World*. 3 vols. New York: Funk & Wagnalls Co., 1955. Volume II covers the Napoleonic Wars, with due emphasis on Trafalgar. Fuller's ideas of history and its moving forces are very much his own; he is occasionally careless of details, but he tells a sweeping story of the great storms of empire.

———. *The Conduct of War, 1789–1961*. New Brunswick, N.J.; Rutgers University Press, 1962.

JOMINI, ANTOINE H. *Life of Napoleon*. Kansas City, Mo.: Hudson-Kimberly Publishing Co., 1897. This book, first translated into English by General Halleck, is one of the best-known reference works for this period. There are, however, several major dangers in using it. Jomini was so imbued with an appreciation for his own military talents that it is difficult at times to determine whether he is expressing Napoleon's opinions or his own. His statements as to enemy strengths and losses are almost always wide of the mark; he naturally exaggerates the role of Czar Alexander I, his second patron; and he credits himself with various deeds which do not seem to have happened. Finally, there is little evidence of any serious attempt at historical research behind his book—which has not kept it from becoming widely influential.

LANFREY, PIERRE. *The History of Napoleon the First*. 3 vols. London and New York: The Macmillan Co., 1871. This work, which unfortunately was not completed beyond 1810, was a deliberate attempt to "destroy the Napoleonic legend." The author was theoretically a liberal republican, but actually performed as a professional "anti" to all parties. As such, he makes a savage plea for the prosecution; his work is often a diatribe, not history in its proper sense.

NAPOLEON. *Correspondence de Napoleon Ier*. 32 vols. Paris: Henri Plon, 1858–1870. Published by order of Napoleon III, this material was carefully screened to prevent the publication of material that might diminish the glory of the Napoleonic legend. However, it still remains the major source of authentic Napoleonic expression, thoughts, and doctrine.

———. *Commentaires de Napoleon Premier*. 6 vols. Paris: Imprimerie Imperiale, 1867. Written at St. Helena by the exiled Emperor, who had no access to much necessary reference material. These books, therefore, must be used with caution. The last volume, dealing with the art of war, occasionally crackles with the traditional Napoleonic intelligence.

NICKERSON, HOFFMAN. *The Armed Horde, 1793–1939*. New York: G. P. Putnam's Sons, 1940. A popular history of the development and employment of mass armies. The author is an admirer of the warfare of the eighteenth century, when common people knew their places.

PHIPPS, RAMSAY W. *The Armies of the First French Republic, and the Rise of the Marshals of Napoleon I*. 5 vols. London: Oxford University Press, 1935–39. This splendid set of books covers all of the various campaigns through 1799, stressing the development of the future marshals and the appearance and fate of other promising military leaders who never achieved that grade. Carefully researched, well written, and full of valuable details.

PRATT, FLETCHER. *The Empire and the Glory: Napoleon Bonaparte, 1800–1806*. New York: William Sloane Associates, 1949. While not "history" in the strict sense, this book excels in projecting an idea of the atmosphere of the period described. Its characterizations frequently verge on caricature.

ROPES, JOHN C. *The First Napoleon*. Boston and New York: Houghton Mifflin Co., 1886. An extremely competent and concise book, which has been unaccountably overlooked by many writers in this field. Its hallmark is impartial common sense.

RECOMMENDED READING LIST

SAVANT, JEAN. *Napoleon and His Time*. Translated by Katherine John. New York: Thomas Nelson & Sons, 1958. An outstanding hatchet job, including selections from rather dubious sources, which will reinforce any pessimistic evaluations of Napoleon's character.

SHEPPARD, ERIC W. *A Short History of the British Army*. London: Constable & Co., 1950.

SKALKOWSKI, ADAM. *En Marge de la Correspondence de Napoleon I: Documents*. Warsaw: Gebethner and Wolff, 1911. A collection of Napoleon's letters and official documents, dealing with Polish and Lithuanian troops, from 1801 through 1815, complete with marginal comments and notations.

SLOANE, WILLIAM M. *The Life of Napoleon Bonaparte*. 4 vols. New York. The Century Co., 1915.

STEPHENS, H. MORSE. *Revolutionary Europe, 1789–1815*. London: Rivington's, 1900. An old book, but packed with sound and detailed chronological information.

Supplement a la Correspondence de Napoleon I. Paris: Bureau de l'Agence Polonnaise de Presse, 1908. This pamphlet deals with Napoleon's relations with Poland and the Poles.

THIERS, LOUIS A. *History of the Consulate and the Empire Under Napoleon*. 20 vols. London: Henry Colburn, 1845. This massive work, thoroughly authoritative in tone and appearance, is unfortunately as unreliable and overly dramatized as a gossip column. It does, however, have unusual value in giving the "big picture" of the Napoleonic period in its full scope.

THOMPSON, J. M. *Napoleon Bonaparte*. New York: Oxford University Press, 1952. A handy, modern history that puts overdue emphasis on Napoleon the administrator and reformer.

VALLAUX, CAMILLE. *Les Campagnes des Armees Francaises, 1792–1815*. Paris: Felix Alcan, 1899. A useful outline of these operations.

WARTENBURG, YORCK VON. *Napoleon as a General*. Edited by Walter H. James. ("The Wolseley Series.") London, no date. One of the better works on Napoleon's military career, though based on somewhat limited sources (chiefly the *Correspondence de Napoleon I*). The author writes as a patriotic Prussian and a professional soldier; the first quality occasionally trips up the second: For example, he states that making war support war is laudable, unless practiced in Prussia by an invading army. There is much Teutonic moralizing, which an uninspired translation does not improve.

WOERL, J. E. *Geschichte der Kriege von 1792 mit 1815 mit Schlachten Atlas*. Freiburg im Breisgau: Herber'fche Berlagshandlung, 1852. Brief surveys of the major battles of this period; valuable for its plentiful situation and strategic maps. The text is strongly German in viewpoint.

Battles and Campaigns

Italy, 1796–97

ADLOW, ELIJAH. *Napoleon in Italy, 1796–1797*. Boston: William J. Rochfort, 1948. A highly critical book, its value diminished by the limited character of its sources.

ANDREOSSY, ANTOINE F. *Operations des Pontonniers Francais en Italie Pendant les Campagnes de 1795 a 1797*. Paris: J. Correard, 1843.

BOUVIER, FELIX. *Bonaparte en Italie, 1796*. Paris: Librairie Leopold Cerf, 1899. Exhaustively detailed, but interestingly written, this book also contains a wealth of information on the various French, Italian, and Austrian commanders and rulers, as well as extensive order-of-battle material.

CLAUSEWITZ, KARL VON. *La Campagne de 1796 en Italie*. Translated into French by J. Colin. Paris: Librairie Militaire de L. Boudoin, 1899. This is both a terse analysis of the 1796 campaign and another battle in the author's running feud with Jomini.

FABRY, G. *Histoire de la Campagne de 1794 en Italie*. 2 vols. Paris: Chapelot, 1905. A good background book, showing Napoleon on his way up.

FERRERO, GUGLIELMO. *The Gamble: Bonaparte in Italy, 1796–1797*. Translated by Pritchard and Freeman. London: G. Bell & Sons, 1961. An Italian view of this famous campaign. This work was originally published in 1936, but was lost during World War II, therefore losing much of its originality, since subsequent authors rediscovered many of the facts unearthed by Ferrero. Ferrero insists that Bonaparte was little more than the obedient agent of the Directory, that his invasion of Austria was actually a military defeat, that his victories were impossible according to the properly established rules of warfare and so never should have happened. His main contribution is a deep sifting of the diplomatic archives; his major weakness a peculiar veneration for the morals and maneuvers of the eighteenth century.

HERIOT, ANGUS. *The French in Italy, 1796–1799*. London: Chatto & Windus, 1957. An account of the impact of the French Revolution on the Italian states, of which it gives a rich, compact description.

JACKSON, W. G. F. *Attack in the West*. London: Eyre & Spottiswoode, 1953. This book is of particular value in that it carries forward the lessons of Napoleon's first campaign for use in future clashes with larger armies, likewise striking from the East. In general, it is a first-rate book, though weak on the Austro-Sardinian command relationship.

JOMINI, ANTOINE H. *Histoire Critique et Militaire des Guerres de la Revolution*. 15 vols. and atlas. Paris: Anselinet Pochard, 1820–24. Covers operations from 1792 to 1803. Not too accurate, but valuable for its great scope and occasional sharp strategic insights.

PRATT, FLETCHER. *Road to Empire: The Life and Times of Bonaparte the General*. New York: Doubleday, Doran & Co., 1939. An excellently written popular work, full of inaccuracies and exaggerations, but told with a verve that carries the reader along with the tide of war.

WILKINSON, SPENSER. *The Rise of General Bonaparte*. Oxford: Clarendon Press, 1930. This splendid book—well supplied with good maps—takes Napoleon from his entry into the Brienne military school (1778) to the battle of Lodi (1796). The emphasis is on the training he received and the commanding officers, books, and events that shaped him for his first campaign. "The foundation of Bonaparte's military achievement was the training he received as a regimental officer."

Egypt and Syria

BERTHIER, LOUIS A. *Campagne d'Egypt*. Paris: Baudouin Freres, 1827. The unidentified editor has added some of Reynier's bitter comments on the latter part of the French occupation of Egypt.

ELGOOD, PERCIVAL G. *Bonaparte's Adventure in Egypt*. London: Oxford University Press, 1931.

JONQUIERE, CLEMENT E. DE LA. *L'Expedition d'Egypt*. 5 vols. Paris: Henri-Charles Lavauzelle, 1902. A massive, authoritative work.

MOOREHEAD, ALAN. *The Blue Nile*. New York: Harper & Row, 1962. This work begins with an account of Bonaparte's conquest of Egypt, and has an unusually good coverage of Desaix's operations on the upper Nile.

PRATT, FLETCHER. *Road to Empire: The Life and Times of Bonaparte the General*. New York: Doubleday, Doran, & Co., 1939. Popular-style work, inaccurate, but interesting.

WARNER, OLIVER. *The Battle of the Nile*. London: B. T. Batsford, 1960. One of British "Great Battles" series, easy to read, but well researched and generally impartial.

Marengo

DE CUGNAC, GASPAR J. M. R. *Campagne de l'Armee de Reserve en 1800*. Paris: Section Historique de l'Etat-major, 1900.

———. *Campagne de Marengo*. Paris: Chapelot, 1904. De Cugnac did valuable work in reviewing the available basic source material. Among other accomplishments, he corrected the chronology of that much-romanticized campaign. The first of these two publications—a collection of the official reports of both armies—is the more valuable for the serious student.

LANZA, CONRAD H. (ed.) *Marengo Campaign, 1800: Source Book*. Ft. Leavenworth, Kans.: The General Service School Press, 1922. A collection of background material, including detailed material on Fort Bard and a translation of De Cugnac's *The*

RECOMMENDED READING LIST

Campaign of the Army of the Reserve in 1800. Much of it is highly useful, but its coverage of the organization and equipment of the armies of this period is frequently incorrect.

SERGEANT, HERBERT H. *The Campaign of Marengo.* Chicago: A. C. McClurg & Co., 1897.

Ulm-Austerlitz

COLIN, JEAN L. A. *Surprise des Ponts de Vienne en 1805.* Paris: Chapelot, 1905.

MAUDE, F. N. *The Ulm Campaign.* London: George Allen & Co., 1912. A fairly good, brief review of this campaign, valuable as a study of the gradual development of Napoleon's generalship, and of Mack's qualities as a leader. Its value is decreased, however, by the author's hasty, sometimes careless, description of the actual operations. Maude was a prolific and fairly influential author; his conclusions are often stimulating.

OMAN, CAROLA. *Napoleon at the Channel.* Garden City, N.Y.: Doubleday, Doran & Co., 1942. This book deals chiefly with the effects of the threat of French invasion on everyday life in England.

Jena

DAVOUT, LOUIS N. *Operations du 3e Corps, 1806–1807: Rapport du Marechal Davout, Duc d'Auerstaedt.* Paris: Calmann Levy, 1896. No other book gives such an excellent picture of the internal organization and the tactical, strategic, and administrative functioning of a Napoleonic army corps.

HOUSSAYE, HENRY. *Jena et la Campagne de 1806.* Paris: Perrin, 1912. An outstanding, easily comprehended history of this campaign.

MAUDE, F. N. *1806: The Jena Campaign.* New York: The Macmillan Co., 1909. Maude was a stanch champion of the Prussian army, though his advocacy of it was based in large part on incomplete knowledge of its actual organization and functioning. As usual, however, he raises interesting speculations on the art of war in general. Contains a detailed order of battle of the Prussian army before Jena.

PERREAU, JOSEPH. *Iena, Eylau, Friedland.* Paris: Berger-Levrault, 1908.

PETIT, JEAN M. *Histoire des Campagnes de l'Empereur Napoleon, 1805–1806 et 1807–1809.* 3 vols. Paris: Ch. Picquet, 1843. This is a well-written book, but somewhat overly patriotic in its estimations of enemy strengths and losses. Its extensive annexes include detailed order-of-battle charts and the appropriate Napoleonic correspondence.

PETRE, F. LORAINE. *Napoleon's Conquest of Prussia, 1806.* London and New York: John Lane Co., 1907. Petre produced some of the better English-language books on the Napoleonic campaigns. Making "some conscience" of his work, he did much original research. Unfortunately, he did not fully understand the organization and tactics of that period. Also, he was an Englishman of the old school—Napoleon was a bloody tyrant, and that was that. Finally, he was inclined to exaggerate casualties—especially French casualties. He must be highly commended, however, for his unwillingness to accept the usual authorities at face value, and for his attempt to strike a balance between various accounts.

Eylau-Friedland

Bataille de Preussich-Eylau, Gagnee par la Grande-Armee, Commandee en Personne par S.M. Najoleon I, Empereur des Francais, Roi d'Italie, sur les Armees Combinees de Prusse et de Russie, le 8 Fevrier 1807. Paris: 1807. An excellent piece of Napoleonic propaganda, covering the campaign and battle of Eylau. It includes the various bulletins published by order of Napoleon during this period, plus a "relation" by an "eyewitness," reportedly translated from the German. It also contains several large maps: The troop dispositions depicted on them are thoroughly dubious, but the basic terrain map is excellent.

DAVOUT, LOUIS N. *Operations du 3e Corps, 1806: Rapport du Marechal Davout, Duc d'Auerstaedt.* Paris: Calmann Levy, 1896.

DERODE, M. *Nouvelle Relation de la Bataille de Friedland.* Paris: Bourgogne et Martinet, 1839. A clear, comprehensive account of this battle from the viewpoint of the French army—weakened only by a lack of definite information concerning the enemy. Derode was an unusually conscientious historian who wanted to unite "truth with style." He quizzed all the available French officers who had commanded units at Friedland, and made full use of available foreign sources.

GRENIER, PIERRE. *Etude sur 1807: Maneuvers d'Eylau et Friedland.* Paris: Henri-Charles Lavauzelle, no date. This book concerns itself completely with strategy. Battles are not discussed.

PARKER, HAROLD T. *Three Napoleonic Battles.* Durham, N.C.: Duke University Press, 1944. A review of Friedland, Aspern-Essling, and Waterloo. Very well written.

PERREAU, JOSEPH. *Iena, Eylau, Friedland.* Paris: Berger-Levrault, 1908.

PETIT, JEAN M. *Histoire des Campagnes de d'Empereur Napoleon, 1805–1806 et 1807–1809.* Paris: Ch. Picquet, 1843.

PETRE, F. LORAINE. *Napoleon's Campaign in Poland, 1806–1807.* London and New York: John Lane Co., 1907. Good, but possibly the weakest of Petre's books.

WILSON, ROBERT. *Brief Remarks on the Character and Composition of the Russian Army and a Sketch of the Campaigns in Poland in the Years 1806 and 1807.* London: T. Egerton, Military Library, 1810. Wilson came almost to love the Russian soldier, and his report therefore is one long apology. Nevertheless, he packed in as many facts as he could ascertain, though his statistics are inflationary whenever he deals with French losses. This edition is particularly valuable since it contains Russian, Prussian, and French reports for this period.

Spain

BALAGNY, DOMINIQUE E. P. *Campagne de l'Empereur Napoleon en Espagne (1808–1809).* 7 vols. Paris: Berger-Levrault, 1902–7. An exhaustive, analytical review of this campaign, with five volumes of text and two of maps. The author did considerable research in Spanish archives.

BELMAS, JACQUES. *Journaux des Sieges Faits ou Soutenus par les Francais dans la Peninsule de 1807 a 1814.* 4 vols. Paris: Didot Freres, 1836–37. A collection of all available pertinent official reports.

DANIEL, HAWTHORNE. *For Want of a Nail.* New York: McGraw-Hill Book Co., 1948. A good study of the influence of logistics on warfare, with chapters on the Peninsular War and the 1812 campaign.

FOY, MAXIMILIEN S. *Histoire de la Guerre de la Peninsule sous Napoleon.* 4 vols. Paris: Baudouin Freres, 1827. Foy's sudden death prevented the completion of this book, which was published in its unfinished state by his widow. Foy had a considerable and honorable part in the Peninsular War. The English receive the benefits of no doubts whatever in his writing, since Foy felt that soldiers should be trained to despise their enemies.

GOODSPEED, D. J. *The British Campaigns in the Peninsula, 1808–1814.* Ottawa: Queen's Printer and Controller of Stationery, 1958. A brief, handy account, produced by the Historical Section of the Canadian Army. The concluding chapter, assessing the Spanish campaigns in the light of modern principles of war, is quite good.

HIBBERT, CHRISTOPHER. *Corunna.* New York: The Macmillan Co., 1961. An interesting popular version of this campaign, based largely upon personal reminiscences of varying degrees of reliability.

KNOWLES, LEES. *The British on Capri, 1806–1808.* London and New York: John Lane Co., 1918. The little-known story of Murat's successful defiance of the Royal Navy.

MARTIN, E. *La Gendarmerie Francaise en Espagne et en Portugal.* Paris: Librairie Leautey, 1898. This is the history of those hard-bitten military police, who fought a constant, merciless war along the supply lines of the French armies—or took their place effectively in the line of battle.

MCGUFFIE, T. H. (ed.). *Peninsular Cavalry General.* London: George P. Harrap and Co., 1951. The correspondence of General Robert B. Long, who served in Spain under Wellington, 1811–13, as commander of a brigade of light dragoons.

NAPIER, WILLIAM F. P. *War in the Peninsula and in the South of France.* 5 vols. New York: A. C. Armstrong & Sons, 1882. This vivid, contentious book remains a basic history of the war in Spain, though written without access to many of the sources

RECOMMENDED READING LIST

later available to Oman. Napier was professional soldier enough to seek an impartial viewpoint; his work consequently ruffled feathers throughout Europe. He also was a man of strong feelings which at times may have misled him. But he had a distinguished part in many of the great events he describes, and the strong emotions of those battles and marches still flares in his written word.

OMAN, CHARLES W. C. *Wellington's Army, 1809–1814*. London: Edward Arnold, 1913. A complete and engrossing picture of that army and its campaigns and battles.

———. *A History of the Peninsular War*. 7 vols. Oxford: Clarendon Press, 1902–30. Undoubtedly the most detailed and studious English work on this subject, covering every operation in this long and doubtful campaign. Oman was, by his own lights, scrupulous; he was also pedantic and given to oversimplification. There is, however, no substitute for his work.

SUCHET, LOUIS G. *Memoires du Marechal Suchet, Duc d'Albufera, sur ses Campagnes en Espagne*. Paris: Anselin, 1834. Suchet was highly successful both as a commander and an administrator.

WARD, S. P. G. *Wellington's Headquarters: A Study of the Administrative Problems in the Peninsula, 1809–1814*. Oxford: Oxford University Press, 1957. A fascinating and authoritative little book, packed with concentrated information on all aspects of its subject.

WELLER, JAC. *Wellington in the Peninsula, 1808–1814*. London: Nicholas Vane, 1963. Written from English sources, with no particular understanding of the French side of the picture. Contains numerous photographs of various battlefields, and so gives an excellent feel of the battles described. The author's attitude toward Wellington is one of frank hero worship.

Austria, 1809

BONNAL, HENRI G. *La Manoeuvre de Landshut*. Paris: Chapelot, 1905. One of the author's numerous works on "The Spirit of Modern War," this book was intended as a study of Napoleon's strategy and psychological outlook from the middle of 1808 through April 1809. The study is interesting, but on the pedantic side; the author frequently becomes thoroughly oblivious to such vulgar considerations as muddy roads and exhausted soldiers of all grades. He also on occasion changes the wording of official texts.

PARKER, HAROLD T. *Three Napoleonic Battles*. Durham, N.C.: Duke University Press, 1944.

PETIT, JEAN M. *Histoire des Campagnes de l'Empereur Napoleon, 1805–1806 et 1807–1809*. 3 vols. Paris: Ch. Picquet, 1843.

PETRE, F. LORAINE. *Napoleon and the Archduke Charles*. London and New York: John Lane Co., 1909.

SASKI, CHARLES G. L. *Campagne de 1809 en Allemagne et en Autriche*. 3 vols. Paris and Nancy: Berger-Levrault, 1899–1900. This authoritative work is based on a close and detailed study of original documents.

Russia, 1812

BELLOC, HILAIRE. *Napoleon's Campaign of 1812 and the Retreat from Moscow*. New York: Harper & Brothers, 1926. A burning account, written by a man to whom Western civilization was a sacred thing. He may occasionally attribute his own ideas and opinions to Napoleon, but he also has shaped a mighty picture for the general reader.

BONNAL, HENRI G. *La Manoeuvre de Vilna*. Paris: Chapelot, 1905.

BOURGOGNE, ADRIEN J. *Memoirs of Sergeant Bourgogne, 1812–1813*. New York: Doubleday & McClure Co., 1899. A sergeant of the Young Guard, Bourgogne made no claim to military genius. His matter-of-fact story, however, does much to show why the invasion of Russia failed—and also how the indomitable cadre of the Grande Armee hewed its way home.

BURTON, R. G. *Napoleon's Invasion of Russia*. London: George Allen & Co., 1914. One of the better English accounts, but weakened by hasty writing and poor editing.

BUTURLIN, DIMITRII P. *Histoire Militaire de la Campagne de Russe en 1812*. 2 vols.

St. Petersburg: Librairie de la Cour, 1824. The author was one of Czar Alexander's aides-de-camp; his work was a semiofficial history. Although compelled to gild over the fumblings of the Russian leaders, he produced a modest, complete, and—within its natural limitations—reliable work. (Readers should note that his dates are those of the old Russian calendar.)

CAULAINCOURT, ARMAND A. L. *With Napoleon in Russia*. New York: William Morrow & Co., 1935. As an Imperial aide-de-camp and Master of Horse, Caulaincourt was in close contact with Napoleon from 1802 through 1815. Some doubt has been thrown on these memoirs, but this edition has been carefully checked. Be sure to read the introduction to understand Caulaincourt's opinions on Russia.

CHAMBRAY, GEORGES DE. *Histoire de l'Expedition de Russie*. 2 vols. and atlas. Paris: Pillet Aine, 1825. The author served with the French artillery during this campaign, and appears to have made every effort to write an impartial account of it. His book is still useful, but was based on very incomplete information.

CLAUSEWITZ, KARL VON. *La Campagne de 1812 en Russie*. Translated by Begouën. Paris: Librairie Militaire R. Chapelot, 1900. This book describes the howling confusion of the Russian command, and furnishes an eyewitness account of Yorck's defection. It is replete with sharp, frequently unkind, characterizations.

DANIEL, HAWTHORNE. *For Want of a Nail*. New York: McGraw-Hill Book Co., 1948. A good popular account of the logistical problems inherent in an invasion of Russia, and of how Napoleon's failure to solve them ensured his eventual defeat.

DUNDULIS, BRONIUS. *Napoleon et la Lituanie en 1812*. Paris: Alcan, Presses Universitaires de France, 1940. A complete, authoritative review of all aspects of the French occupation and attempted mobilization of Lithuania in 1812. It also gives largely impartial coverage to the various thorny aspects of Polish-Lithuanian relations and internal reactions within both of these countries.

FABER DU FAUR, CHRISTIAN W. VON. *Campagne de Russe, 1812*. Paris: Ernest Flammarion, no date. The eyewitness story of an officer of the Württemberg artillery, illustrated by sketches made during the campaign—a gripping combination.

FABRY, GABRIEL J. *Campagne de Russe (1812)*. 5 vols. Paris: Lucien Gougy, 1900–1912. A massive collection of material, requiring considerable study and sorting, but extremely rich in original sources: French, German, Austrian, Polish, and Russian. Unfortunately, it gives complete coverage only to the earlier parts of the campaign, there being fewer surviving original French documents after the campaign moved east of Smolensk. The coverage of events in French rear areas, and at the Beresina, however, is superb. In all, the best reference for this campaign.

FEZANSAC, RAYMOND A. P. J. DE. *Campagne de Russe en 1812*. London: Rivington's, 1896. This is actually an excerpt from the author's *Souvenirs Militaires,* but is complete in itself. From the beginning of this campaign until Borodino, Fezansac was one of Berthier's aides-de-camp; after the battle, he commanded a regiment in Ney's corps. This edition has been annotated by Granville Sharp, to make the translation easier.

GEORGE, HEREFORD B. *Napoleon's Invasion of Russia*. New York: New Amsterdam Book Co., 1899. Old, but good, especially on international politics. Its major fault is a too-literal dependence upon Wilson's *The French Invasion of Russia.*

GOURGAUD, GASPARD. *Napoleon et la Grande Armee en Russie*. Paris: Bossange Freres, 1825. One of Napoleon's orderly officers, Gourgaud wrote this book as a "critical examination of the work of Count Philippe de Segur." Though fanatically loyal to Napoleon, Gourgaud also wrote as a brave and level-headed officer; under his matter-of-fact pen, Segur's gaudy drama wilts away. (As a more direct form of literary criticism, Gourgaud also "called out" Segur and wounded him in a duel.)

JACKSON, W. G. F. *Seven Roads to Moscow*. New York: Philosophical Library, 1958. A reasonably competent review of the different invasions of Russia, including a good analysis of the 1812 campaign.

SEGUR, PHILIPPE-PAUL DE. *Napoleon's Russian Campaign*. Boston: Houghton Mifflin Co., 1958. This colorful book, roundly damned as a "romance" by many other veterans of this campaign, must be read with Segur's congenital tendency against allowing dull facts to spoil a good story firmly in mind. That considered, his book is a fair source of material on headquarters activities.

RECOMMENDED READING LIST

TARLE, EUGENE. *Napoleon's Invasion of Russia, 1812*. New York: Oxford University Press, 1942. History as translated into the Communist dialect. Actually, Tarle was a better historian than his environment permitted him to show himself, and his competence occasionally manages to shine through the party line.

WILSON, ROBERT. *Narrative of Events During the Invasion of Russia by Napoleon Bonaparte and the Retreat of the French Army, 1812*. London: John Murray, 1860. Wilson was the British representative at the headquarters of the Russian army. As such, he came to admire that army despite emphatic doubts about many of its generals. His book, though necessarily almost completely one-sided, is a valuable reference if used with care. Wilson had seen much service, and appreciated good soldiering by any army. His major weaknesses were his swallowing wholesale the Russian reports on actions he had not himself witnessed; a childlike faith in Russian statistics; and a somewhat inflated (though sincere) belief in his own importance. Apparently, he never realized that he was used as a cat's-paw in the various internal intrigues that rent the Russian army.

Germany, 1813

BEHAINE, LEFEBVRE DE. *Napoleon et des Allies sur le Rhin*. Paris: Librairie Academique, 1913. Much emphasis on political developments. Includes a detailed story of the battle of Hanau.

BERNADOTTE, JEAN B. J. *Proclamations de S.A.R. le Prince Royal de Suede et Bulletins Publies au Quartier-General de l'Armee Combinee du Nord de l'Allemagne Dupuis le Commencement des Operations Jusqu'au 10 Nov. 1813*. Gottingen: Henri Dieterich, 1813. Bernadotte's talents as a general may be disputed, but his ability to win battles in his bulletins is considerably superior to that even of Napoleon. Useful for information on the movements and general activities of the Allied "Army of the North."

CATHCART, GEORGE. *Commentaries on the War in Russia and Germany in 1812 and 1813*. London: John Murray, 1850. A useful work by a British representative with the Allied forces in Germany. Plenty of battlefield maps.

CLAUSEWITZ, KARL VON. *Le Campagne de 1813 et la Campagne de 1814 en France*. Translated by Commandant Thomann. Paris: Librairie Militaire R. Chapelot, 1900. This is far from being a balanced, studious work—such as might have been expected from the author of *Vom Krieg*. Clausewitz, however, was deeply involved in these campaigns—he does pause occasionally to critique the actions of both sides, but otherwise he writes merely as an exultant Prussian.

MAUDE, F. N. *The Leipzig Campaign, 1813*. London: Swan Sonnenschein & Co., 1908. As in his book on the Jena campaign, Maude is a thoroughly fervent and uncritical admirer of the Prussian army. He writes as an experienced soldier, but with incomplete knowledge of French organization and tactics or of the actual operations involved.

MINISTERE DE LA MARINE. *Historique de l'Artillerie de la Marine*. Paris: D. Dumoulin, 1899. Naval artillerymen, hastily converted into line infantry, formed the backbone of Marmont's VI Corps during this campaign.

ODELEBEN, ERNST O. *Circonstanciee de la Campagne de 1813 en Saxe*. Translation of 2d edition by A. de Vitry. Paris: Delaunay, 1817. A Saxon officer attached to Napoleon's headquarters during this campaign, Odeleben noted everything in great detail with intelligent impartiality. His book is a classic source of information on how Napoleon lived and worked in the field.

PETRE, F. LORAINE. *Napoleon's Last Campaign in Germany, 1813*. London and New York: John Lane Co., 1912.

SHANEHAN, WILLIAM O. *Prussian Military Reforms, 1786–1813*. New York: Columbia University Press, 1945. An excellent piece of historical writing, which plays hob and havoc with the usually accepted traditions about Prussia's 1807–12 rearming and her 1813 resumption of the war against Napoleon.

VAUDONCOURT, GUILLAUME DE. *Histoire de la Guerre Soutenue par les Francais en Allemagne en 1813*. (With atlas.) Paris: Chez Barrois, l'Aine, Librairie, 1819. An old book, and therefore lacking in accurate information on the Allies. However, it contains French orders-of-battle and situation maps, which can be valuable.

France, 1814

BEHAINE, LEFEBVRE DE. *Napoleon et des Allies sur le Rhin*. Paris: Librairie Academique, 1913.

BELLAIRE, J. P. *Precis de l'Invasion des Etats Romains par l'Armee Napolitaine en 1813 et 1814*. Paris: Librairie de Prince Royal, 1838. The brief story of Murat's turncoat war against Napoleon.

CAULAINCOURT, ARMAND A. L. *No Peace with Napoleon*. New York: William Morrow & Co., 1936.

CLAUSEWITZ, KARL VON. *La Campagne de 1813 et la Campagne de 1814 en France*. Paris: Librairie Militaire R. Chapelot, 1900.

HOUSSAYE, HENRY. *1814*. Paris: Librairie Academique Didier, 1899. Probably the classic work on this campaign. Houssaye had revised and expanded his original work for this edition (the thirty-first).

MAYCOCK, F. W. O. *The Invasion of France, 1814*. London: George Allen & Unwin, 1914.

PETRE, F. LORAINE. *Napoleon at Bay, 1814*. London and New York: John Lane Co., 1914.

WEIL, MAURICE H. *La Campagne de 1814*. 2 vols. Paris: Librairie Militaire, 1914. This is a detailed record of Allied cavalry operations, based largely upon official records.

———. *Le Prince Eugene et Murat, 1813–1814*. 4 vols. Paris: Librairie Thorin et Fils, 1902. An extremely detailed review of both military and political developments.

Waterloo, 1815

BECKE, A. F. *Napoleon and Waterloo*. London: Kegan Paul, Trench, Trubner & Co., 1939. Undoubtedly the best English-language account.

GARDNER, DORSEY. *Quatre-Bras, Ligny, and Waterloo*. London: Kegan Paul, Trench, & Co., 1882. Time has rather passed this book by. Today, at first reading, it has a thoroughly chauvinistic tone; however, the author was probably the first Englishman to attempt a scholarly—and badly needed—restudy of the campaign and battle. If he accepts many dubious personal claims, he still speaks far more bluntly about certain episodes of the battle than do more recent English writers.

GOURGAUD, GASPARD. *Campagne de Dix-huit Cent Quinz, au Relation des Operations Militaires Qui Ont Eu Lieu en France et en Belgique Pendant les Cent Jours*. Paris: P. Mongie Aine, 1818.

GUEDALLA, PHILIP. *The Hundred Days*. New York: G. P. Putnam's Sons, 1934.

HOUSSAYE, HENRY. *1815: Waterloo*. Kansas City: Franklin Hudson Publishing Co., 1905. A translation of that portion of Houssaye's works on the year 1815 which deals with Napoleon's Waterloo campaign.

———. *1815: Waterloo*. Paris: Librairie Academique Didier, 1899.

———. *1815: Les Cent Jours*. Paris: Librairie Academique Didier, 1905. Outstanding and authoritative works, which cover the events of the whole year, including the second restoration and the "white terror."

JAMES, W. H. *The Campaign of 1815, Chiefly in Flanders*. Edinburgh and London: William Blackwood and Sons, 1908. James gives more attention to the post-Waterloo operations than do most other English authors. An interesting book.

KELLY, W. HYDE. *The Battle of Wavre and Grouchy's Retreat*. London: John Murray, 1905. A well-written review of how Marshal Grouchy proved himself a resourceful and skillful army commander—exactly one day too late.

MACKINNON, DANIEL. *Origin and Services of the Coldstream Guards*. 3 vols. London: Richard Bentley, 1833. This famous old regimental history has an excellent account of the defense of Hougomont at Waterloo—but manages to have the English win that battle without any Prussian assistance whatever!

NAYLOR, JOHN. *Waterloo*. London: B. T. Batsford, 1960. A simple—frequently too simplified—version of this campaign. The major factors are generally well covered and there is much interesting anecdote, but the bulk of the material has been gathered from haphazard secondary sources.

PARKER, HAROLD T. *Three Napoleonic Battles*. Durham, N.C.: Duke University Press, 1944.

RECOMMENDED READING LIST

POLLIO, ALBERT. *Waterloo*. Translated from the Italian by General Goiran. Paris: Henri-Charles Lavauzelle, 1908. This comparatively recent history appears to be a model of impartiality and completeness.

PONTECOULANT, F. G. DE. *Napoleon au Waterloo*. Paris: Librairie Militaire, 1866. An analysis of the campaign by a former officer of the Imperial Guard.

PRATT, SISSON C. *The Waterloo Campaign*. London: Swan Sonnenschein & Co., 1907.

ROPES, JOHN C. *The Campaign of Waterloo*. New York: Charles Scribner's Sons, 1892. A careful and analytical study, thoroughly impartial.

WEBSTER, CHARLES. *The Congress of Vienna, 1814–1815*. New York: Barnes and Noble, 1963. Brief, but lucid and complete. An unusually useful book.

Memoirs, Biographies, and Autobiographies

ALDINGTON, RICHARD. *The Duke: Being an Account of the Life and Achievements of Arthur Wellesley, 1st Duke of Wellington*. Garden City, N.Y.: Garden City Publishing Co., 1943. The appendix contains an interesting study by Wellington of the French supply problem in Russia in 1812.

AUBRY, OCTAVE. *Napoleon*. Paris: Ernest Flammarion, 1936. A popular French biography, magnificently illustrated and well written.

BARRES, J. B. *Memoirs of a Napoleonic Officer*. New York: Dial Press, no date. An interesting book by an officer who had no amazing stories to tell, but much service honorably performed.

BELL, GEORGE. *Soldier's Glory*. London: G. Bell and Sons, 1956. The recollections of an English officer, who served through the nineteenth century, against the French in Spain and alongside them in the Crimea.

BIGARRE, AUGUSTE. *Memoires du General Bigarre; Aide de Camp du Roi Joseph*. Paris: Ernest Kolb, no date. Bigarre's account of his services under Joseph in Naples and Spain furnishes information on some of the lesser-known theaters of the Napoleonic wars. He also saw bloody fighting in the West Indies and the Vendee during the Revolution.

BLAZE, ELZEAR. *La Vie Militaire sous le Premier Empire*. Paris: Garnier Freres, no date. Blaze began his service as a *velite* in the Imperial Guard. He had a rare sense of humor, loved to hunt, and was a good officer. His book deserves wider reading.

BLAZE, SEBASTIEN. *Memoires d'un Aide-Major sous le Premier Empire*. Paris: Ernest Flammarion, no date. An excellent description of the war in Spain, 1808–14, by a medical officer whose chief interest makes *Forever Amber* read like a nursery tale.

BLYTHE, LEGETTE. *Marshal Ney: A Dual Life*. New York: Stackpole Sons. 1937. A book dedicated to the story that Ney actually died in South Carolina in 1846. Well worth reading.

BONNAL, HENRI G. *La Vie Militaire du Marechal Ney, Duc d'Elchingen, Prince de la Moskawa*. 3 vols. Paris: Chapelot, 1910–14. This very detailed work covers Ney's services only up to the beginning of 1812.

BOULART, BON. *Memoires Militaires*. Paris: Emile Colin, no date. An artillery officer's memoirs, including all the major campaigns. Boulart served with the Guard artillery from 1807.

BRETT-JAMES, ANTONY (ed.). *Wellington at War, 1794–1815*. London: The Macmillan Co., 1961. Wellington as self-portrayed from his sharply pointed official and personal correspondence. The man comes out better than through his biographies—as does the fact that he fought as bitter a war with an incompetent home government as with the French.

BURNE, ALFRED H. *The Noble Duke of York: The Military Life of Frederick, Duke of York and Albany*. London and New York: Staples Press, 1949. "The Noble Duke," an excellent soldier and army administrator, but a deplorable general, twice led the British Army to defeat, but made great improvements in its organization and effectiveness.

CASSE, A. DU. *Memoires de Prince Eugene*. 10 vols. Paris: Michel Levy Freres, 1859. This work includes Eugene's official correspondence. Consequently, it is both an invaluable supplement to Napoleon's correspondence, and an unequaled picture of the Kingdom of Italy.

———. *Le General Vandamme et sa Correspondance*. 2 vols. Paris: Didier Freres, 1870. Vandamme was the despair of most of his commanding officers, but an outstanding general for all that. His own account, unfortunately, kills off some of the wild stories with which other authors—such as Marbot—have decorated his career.

CASTELOT, ANDRE. *King of Rome*. Translated by Robert Baldick. New York: Harper & Brothers, 1960. The tragic history of Napoleon's son.

CHATEAUBRIAND, FRANCOIS A. R. *Memoirs*. Edited and translated by Robert Baldick. New York: Alfred A. Knopf, 1961. Chateaubriand, a French royalist of unusual talent and character, served First Consul Bonaparte briefly, in a minor capacity, but went into opposition after the execution of d'Enghien. His knowledge of Napoleon's subsequent campaigns and policies is largely hearsay, but he saw the Hundred Days from the side of Louis XVIII, and no man ever recorded his times with more effective language, or could sum it up in more pithy phrases. However, he was a poet at heart; his phrases were often more effective than accurate.

CHENIER, L. J. GABRIEL DE. *Histoire de la Vie Politique, Militaire et Administrative du Marechal Davout*. 2 vols. Paris: Cosse, Marechal, 1866. Useful for its pictures of the political-diplomatic problems faced in Poland; the task of maintaining the French army in Germany, 1807–12, under Napoleon's dual desires for increased strength and more economy; and the re-creation of the French Army during the Hundred Days.

CHUQUET, ARTHUR. *Quatre Generaux de la Revolution: Hoche et Desaix, Kleber et Marceau*. Paris: Fontemoing, 1911.

COMBIER, A. (ed.). *Memoires du General Radet*. Saint-Cloud: Imprimerie Belin Freres, 1892. Radet was a senior officer of the Imperial Gendarmerie, an iron man capable of introducing law and order into Naples, or of placing the Pope under arrest.

COURVILLE, XAVIER DE. *Jomini, ou le Devin de Napoleon*. Paris: Librairie Plon, 1935. A worshipful biography, written by Jomini's great-grandson, repeating many of the old fables, but dealing in a relatively just manner with Jomini's personality and its effects on his contemporaries.

CURRIE, LAURENCE. *The Baton in the Knapsack*. New York: E. P. Dutton & Co., 1935. A general history of Napoleon's marshals, remarkable for its simplicity and good sense.

DELDERFIELD, R. F. *The March of the Twenty-Six: The Story of Napoleon's Marshals*. A popular work, stronger on color than on strict historical accuracy.

DUNN-PATTISON, R. P. *Napoleon's Marshals*. Boston: Little, Brown & Co., 1909. Old, but undoubtedly the best popular book on this subject, the author having a sense of proportion, and no interest in mere sensationalism.

DUPARCQ, EDOUARD DE LA B. *Portraits Militaires*. 3 vols. Paris: Charles Tanera, 1853–61. Contains, among others, brief biographies of Hoche, Massena, Lannes, Ney, and Suchet.

FEZANSAC, RAYMOND A. P. J. (properly, Montesquieu-Fezansac). *Souvenirs Militaires de 1804 a 1814*. Paris: J. Dumaine, 1870. One of the most interesting and widely read memoirs of this period. Thanks to his own abilities, and family influence, Fezansac rose from an enlisted volunteer in 1804 to brigadier general in 1813. Though somewhat hazy in details which he did not personally witness, the author participated in a number of lesser-known actions, such as the battle of Kulm.

FOUCHE, JOSEPH. *Memoirs of Joseph Fouche, Duke of Otranto*. London: Gibbings & Co., 1894. The alleged memoirs of one of the ablest scoundrels known to mankind, who "always was true to one party—himself." His story is chiefly interesting for what he does not tell, and for its general indications of the twisted politics of this period.

GALLOIS, LEONARD. *Histoire de Joachim Murat*. Paris: Schubart et Heideloff, 1828. A rather disapproving little book. Like most of the marshals, Murat needs a new biographer.

GIVAULT, PHILIPPE-RENE. *Les Campagnes d'un Musicien d'Etat-Major Pendant la Republique et l'Empire, 1791–1810*. Paris: Societe d'Editions Litteraries et Artistiques, 1901. The wars as seen by a professional noncombatant.

GOUVION ST.-CYR, LAURENT. *Memoires sur les Campagnes des Armees du Rhin et de Rhin-et-Moselle de 1792 Jusqu'a la Paix de Campo-Formio*. 4 vols. Paris: Anselin, 1829.

GUEDALLA, PHILIP. *Wellington*. New York and London: Harper & Brothers, 1931.

RECOMMENDED READING LIST

HEADLEY, J. T. *Napoleon and His Marshals.* 2 vols. New York: Baker & Scribner, 1850. An early, inaccurate work, but of great interest as an example of the furious partisanship Napoleon could inspire.

HEROLD, J. CHRISTOPHER (ed.). *The Mind of Napoleon.* New York: Columbia University Press, 1955. A well-chosen collection of Napoleon's opinions on a wide range of subjects.

HUARD, ALBERT. *Connaissez-vous Cambronne?* Paris: Bloud et Gay, 1959. A modern biography of the famous *grognard,* who—it appears—was something more than a marching sword with a blistering vocabulary.

KIRCHEISEN, F. M. *Napoleon.* Translated by Henry St. Lawrence. New York: Harcourt, Brace, and Co., 1932.

KOCH, JEAN B. F. *Memoires de Massena.* 7 vols. and atlas. Paris: Paulin et Lechevalier, 1848–50. This work represents a careful editing of Massena's personal papers and all official records concerning him. The emphasis, though, is strictly military. Like modern official military historians, Koch went to great efforts to verify and extend his research through personal interrogation of officers of all grades. His work likewise includes many valuable official reports.

LANDRIEUX, JEAN. *Memoires de l'Adjutant General Jean Landrieux, Chef d'Etat-major de la Cavalerie de l'Armee d'Italie, Charge du Bureau Secret, 1795–1797.* Vol. I. Paris: Leonce Grasilier, 1893. Landrieux was excellently placed to see the seamy side of the Italian campaign. His spiteful and savage stories might carry more weight if not matched against his known prior career as an intriguer and "fantastic." He had failed twice as a regimental commander—once because of financial irregularities, once because of weakness as a leader and disciplinarian. Originally, three volumes of his memoirs were to be published; it would be interesting to know why the second and third never appeared.

LARCHEY, LOREDAN (ed.). *Les Cahiers du Capitaine Coignet.* Paris: Librairie Hachette, 1896. The simple story of an "old sweat" who raised himself up out of the ranks to a captaincy in the Imperial Guard. He was a good soldier and proud of it.

LARRY, DOMINIQUE J. *Memoir of Baron Larry, Surgeon-in-Chief of the Grande Armee.* London: Henry Renshaw, 1862. This heavily edited translation still brings out the problems facing the Napoleonic medical officer—and poses a challenge to his modern counterpart. Napoleon described Larry as the "most virtuous man I have ever known."

LECOMTE, FERDINAND. *Le General Jomini: Sa Vie et Ses Ecrits.* Paris: Tanera, 1860. A Swiss soldier's downright partisan appreciation of his fellow countryman.

LEJEUNE, LOUIS F. *Souvenirs d'un Officier de l'Empire.* Paris: Germain Bapst. Lejeune was an engineer officer who was for several years one of Berthier's aides-de-camp; he was also a military artist of considerable talent.

LIDDELL HART, BASIL H. (ed.). *The Letters of Private Wheeler.* Boston: Houghton Mifflin Co., 1952. A British infantryman's story, including Portugal, Spain, and Waterloo.

LUDWIG, EMIL. *Napoleon.* Garden City, N.Y.: Garden City Publishing Co., 1926. More "mood music" than biography, but interesting if only for that reason.

MACDONALD, JACQUES E. J. A. *Souvenirs du Marechal Macdonald, Duc de Tarente.* Paris: E. Plon, Nourvit, 1892. (An English translation by Stephen L. Simeon was published by Bentley in London, 1893.) For a soldier whose orders and letters were crisp and clear, these memoirs have an evasive quality. This may be due to the fact that he wrote them in 1825, when he was a favorite of the restored Bourbon regime, and had every reason to wish to further ingratiate himself. Obviously, there was a slippery substratum to his outwardly bluff and loyal personality. He shows it clearly in his tendency to blandly claim credit for actions where he was not present.

MARBOT, MARCELLIN DE. *The Memoirs of Baron de Marbot.* 2 vols. London: Longmans, Green & Co., 1892. These famous memoirs are an inextricable mixture of invaluable and colorful stories of army life—and of howling cock-and-bull inventions. Marbot saw much service. He was aide-de-camp to Bernadotte, Lannes, Augereau, and Massena, and commanded a cavalry regiment in 1812–13. Even some of his biggest whackers must have a small basis of truth—few Frenchmen have challenged them—possibly because they, too, had wonderful old-soldier stories to tell.

MARMONT, AUGUSTE F. L. V. *Memoires du Marechal Marmont, Duc de Raguse.* 9 vols.

Paris: Perrotine, 1857. The story of a brilliant man, trying to justify himself before a hostile generation—largely by throwing the blame on others. Marmont took an intelligent interest in soldering and the problems of command; his book remains a must for every student of this period, both for its professional content and for its unconscious self-portrait of a soldier who was too willing to listen to politicians and his own vanity. He remains, however, an untrustworthy witness, where his own conduct comes into question.

MASSON, FREDERIC. *Cavaliers de Napoleon.* Paris: Paul Ollendorff, 1896. The stories of the Grande Armee's great cavalrymen.

MAXWELL, HERBERT. *The Life of Wellington.* London: Sampson Low, Marston and Company, 1907. A sound work, well provided with maps.

NEY, MICHEL. *Memoirs of Marshal Ney.* 2 vols. London: Bull & Churton, 1833. Ends in 1805, but has a number of interesting appendixes, including his famous—but seldom encountered—*Instructions For the Troops Composing the Left Corps.*

NOEL, J. N. A. *Souvenirs Militaires d'un Officier du Premier Empire.* Paris: Berger-Levrault, 1895. Noel was an artillery officer, who served from Spain to Moscow.

PARQUIN, DENIS-CHARLES. *Souvenirs du Capitaine Parquin, 1803–1814.* Paris: Boussod, Valadon, 1892. One of the great personal memoirs of the period, as vivid as Marbot's—and considerably more accurate.

PERIN, RENE. *Vie Militaire de J. Lannes.* 2d ed. Paris: Delaunay, no date. Lannes is badly in need of a competent biographer. Perin's book lacks balance—for example, his description of Friedland allots paragraphs to Ney—and a few sentences to Lannes, the true hero of the day.

RAPP, JEAN. *Memoirs of General Count Rapp.* London: Henry Colburn & Co., 1823. Rapp, aide-de-camp to Napoleon, was one of the plain, honest men—frequently disapproving, but always loyal—who formed the Emperor's personal staff.

SAVARY, ANNE J. M. R. *Memoires du Duc de Rovigo.* 8 vols. Paris: A. Bossange, 1828. The story of a man who wanted to be—and was—an excellent combat general, but found his talents for intelligence and police work in greater demand.

SEGUR, PHILIPPE-PAUL DE. *An Aide-de-Camp of Napoleon.* New York: D. Appleton & Co., 1895. Segur, an impressionable young aristocrat, fell under Napoleon's spell in 1800 and served him loyally. This book covers his career until 1811. Segur was a perpetual romantic, always embroidering his stories and seeing many things much larger than life. At the same time, he was near the throne and privy to much that went on there.

SIX, GEORGES. *Les Generaux de la Revolution et de l'Empire.* Paris: Bordas, 1947. A definitive study of the French general officers, 1792–1814, tracing their origin, service, and general characteristics.

SOULT, NICOLAS J. DE D. *Memoires du Marechal-General Soult.* 3 vols. and atlas. Paris: Librairie d'Amyot, 1854. These three volumes cover only the first years of Soult's service after the Revolution.

STEININGER, J. *Memoires d'un Vieux Deserteur.* Paris: Ernest Flammarion, no date. By the time of the French Revolution, Steininger had served in—and deserted from—most of the armies of Europe. He served France loyally, however, like thousands of other German-born. He was a hard-case professional, whose one talent was drumming.

THIEBAULT, PAUL C. *The Memoirs of Baron Thiebault.* Translated and edited by Arthur J. Butler. New York: The Macmillan Co., 1896. Thiebault was an experienced soldier, an energetic and catholic hater, and an enthusiastic liar. His book reads like history written by a gossip columnist; it is full of clever and malicious little stories—some of which may be true. At the same time, he was a skilled staff officer, and his accounts of events in which he had no intense personal interest are considered highly factual.

THOMASON, JOHN W., JR. *Adventures of General Marbot.* New York and London: Charles Scribner's Sons, 1935. A condensed version of Marbot's memoirs, wonderfully magnified by Thomason's spirited sketches.

VIGIER, LE COMTE. *Davout: Marechal d'Empire.* 2 vols. Paris: Paul Ollendorff, 1898.

VILLARGENNES, ADELBERT J. D. DE. *Reminiscences of Army Life Under Napoleon Bonaparte.* Cincinnati: Robert Clarke & Co., 1884.

WATSON, S. J. *By Command of the Emperor.* London: The Bodley Head, 1957. A sympathetic biography of Marshal Louis-Alexandre Berthier. It is not first-class history, but does represent the initial effort to restore its much-abused subject to his rightful place among Napoleonic military leaders.

WATSON, THOMAS E. *Napoleon.* New York: Dodd, Mead & Co., 1926. A very partisan biography, seemingly written in indignation over various equally partisan—and hostile—English biographies. It is not thoroughly accurate, but does sing the praises of many of Napoleon's overlooked good deeds.

Unit Histories

BOPPE, PAUL L. H. *Les Espagnols a la Grande Armee.* Paris: Berger-Levrault. This work covers the fortunes of Romana's corps (1807–8) and the Regiment Joseph-Napoleon (1809–13).

BRANCACCIO, NICOLA. *L'Esercito Del Vecchio Piemonte (1560–1859).* Rome: Ministry of War, 1922. A brief, but complete history of the Sardinian-Piedmontese Army and its component units.

BRUNON, JEAN, and BRUNON, RAOUL. *Les Eclaireurs de la Garde Imperiale, 1813–1814.* Marseille: Collection Raoul et Jean Brunon, 1961. The history of these hastily created light cavalry units, which went into action before they were organized.

DETAILLE, EDOUARD, and RICHARD, JULES. *L'Armee Francaise.* Paris: Boussard, Valadon, 1885–89. A magnificent, wonderfully illustrated history of the French Army. Detaille's pictures have an accuracy and an authority all their own.

FIEFFE, EUGENE. *Histoire des Troupes Etrangers au Service de France.* 2 vols. Paris: Dumaine, 1854. A lavishly illustrated popular history of the role of the foreign soldier in France.

————. *Napoleon I et la Garde Imperiale.* Paris: Furne Fils, 1859. Illustrated by Raffet.

GAYDA, MARCEL, and KRIJITSKY, ANDRE. *L'Armee Russe Sous le Tsar Alexandre Ier, de 1805 a 1815.* Paris: La Sabretache, 1955 and 1960. A thorough study of all elements of the Russian service.

GROUVEL, R. *Les Corps de Troupe de l'Emigration Francaise, 1789–1815.* 2 vols. Paris: La Sabretache, 1957 and 1961. A series of competently illustrated unit histories, covering the French *émigré* (and related) units in the service of England, Austria, Holland, and Russia. A projected third volume is to cover those serving Spain and Piedmont.

LACHOUQUE, HENRY. *Napoleon et la Garde Imperiale.* Paris: Bloud et Gay, 1956. A wealth of detail about the Guard—including its history, officers, units, and music. (An English translation by Anne S. K. Brown, *An Anatomy of Glory: Napoleon and His Guard,* was published in 1961 by Brown University Press, Providence, R.I. Its text is slightly abridged, but its illustrations are magnificent.)

LOMIER. *La Bataillon des Marins de la Garde, 1803–1815.* Saint-Volery-sur-Somme: E. Lefebvre, 1905. These "sailors of the Guard" saw action on every front in every campaign, handily shifting from oar and sail to musket and saber, or hammer and saw. Their book contains a good chapter on Baylen.

MINISTERE DE LA GUERRE. *Historique des Corps de Troupe de l'Armee Francaise, 1596–1900.* Paris, 1900.

MINISTERE DE LA MARINE. *Historique de L'Artillerie de la Marine.* Paris: D. Dumoulin, 1889. This force, roughly corresponding to the U.S. Marine Corps, has a special place in French military history, especially in 1813-14.

MOLTZHEIM, A. DE. *L'Artillerie Francaise.* Paris: J. Rothschild, 1870.

PERNOT, A. M. *Apercu Historique sur les Service des Transports Militaires.* Paris: Henri-Charles Lavauzelle, 1894.

SAINT-HILAIRE, EMILE M. DE. *Histoire Populaire de la Garde Imperiale.* Paris: Adolphe Delahays, 1854.

Organization and Tactics

AMBERT, JOACHIM. *Esquisses Historiques des Differents Corps qui Composent l'Armee Francaise.* Samour: A. Degouy, 1835. This useful book covers the history of every arm and service in the French army of its time.

AVRIL, J. B. *Advantages d'une Bonne Discipline.* Paris: Migne, 1824. This oddly named book is a good history of the French infantry. It includes tables tracing the complicated reorganizations of the Revolutionary period.

CAMON, H. *La Bataille Napoleonienne.* Paris: Librairie Militaire R. Chapelot, 1899. An excellent, short analysis of Napoleonic strategy and tactics, which gives full value to the moral factors involved.

————. *La Guerre Napoleonienne.* Paris: Librairie Militaire R. Chapelot, 1903. A brief, competent outline and analysis.

CAMPANA, JR. *L'Artillerie de Campagne, 1792–1901.* Paris: Berger-Levrault, 1901.

COURTOT, A. *Quelques Notes sur l'Etat Militaire de France, de 1730 a 1830.* Paris: Victor Rozier, 1888

DE BRACK, ANTOINE F. *Avant-Postes de Cavalerie Legere.* Breda: Broese & Co., 1834. One of the great works of practical military literature. De Brack was a remarkable soldier, who was just beginning to establish his reputation by 1815. His remarks on outpost duty and reconnaissance have plenty of value for any aggressive war featuring dispersion and mobility.

DESBIERE, EDOUARD, and SAUTAI, MAURICE. *La Cavalerie Pendant la Revolution.* 2 vols. Paris: Berger-Levrault, 1907 and 1908.

————. *La Cavalerie sous le Directoire.* Paris: Berger-Levrault, 1910. Interesting in its coverage of both Hoche's and Bonaparte's efforts to improve cavalry organization.

DUSSIEUX, L. *L'Armee en France: Histoire et Organisation.* 3 vols. Versailles: L. Bernard, 1884.

HOHENLOHE-INGELFINGEN, KRAFT KARL. *Conversations on Cavalry.* London: J. J. Keliher & Co., 1897. Though written for contemporary cavalrymen, this book contains considerable useful information on the 1806–7, 1813, 1814, and 1815 campaigns.

LA ROCHE-AYMON, ANTOINE C. E. P. DE. *Des Troupes Legeres.* Paris: Magimel, Anselin, et Pochard, 1817. Written by a French *émigré*, who served in the Prussian Army and had considerable knowledge of the Russian service.

MENTION, LEON. *L'Armee de l'Ancien Regime de Louis XIV a la Revolution.* Paris: L. Henry May, no date.

PHILIP, RAYMOND M. A. DE. *Etude sur le Service d'Etat-Major Pendant les Guerres du Premier Empire.* Paris: Librairie Militaire R. Chapelot, 1900. An excellent reference work.

PICARD, LOUIS M. E. *La Cavalerie dans les Guerres de la Revolution et de l'Empire.* Saumur: Librairie Militaire, 1895.

QUIMBY, ROBERT S. *The Background of the Napoleonic Wars.* New York: Columbia University Press, 1957. The last chapter of this book contains an outstanding study of Napoleonic tactics.

THOUMAS, CHARLES A. *Les Transformations de L'Armee Francaise.* 2 vols. Paris: Berger-Levrault, 1887.

VIOLLET-LE-DUC, EUGENE E. *Annals of a Fortress.* Boston: James R. Osgood & Co., 1876. This book, liberally supplied with sketches and diagrams, provides an excellent picture of a siege during the Napoleonic wars. No student of military history should fail to read it.

Naval Operations

ALBERT, MARVIN H. *Broadsides and Boarders.* New York: Appleton-Century-Crofts, 1957. A hearty, popular history which covers—among other historical naval operations—Nelson's battles and the War of 1812.

CRESWELL, JOHN. *Generals and Admirals: The Story of Amphibious Command.* London: Longmans, Green & Co., 1952. Short but skillful pictures of the historic problems of amphibious operations, especially the Scheldt fiasco of 1809.

MACKESY, P. *The War in the Mediterranean, 1803–1810.* London: Longmans, Green & Co., 1957. This volume takes up a significant period of naval-amphibious warfare, which Mahan and other naval historians have oddly overlooked. It is especially valuable in that it shows the interplay of the naval, military, and political factors that

RECOMMENDED READING LIST

operated in the Mediterranean area, and underscores the limitations of naval power against a major, self-sufficient land power.

MAHAN, ALFRED T. *The Influence of Sea Power Upon the French Revolution and Empire*. Boston: Little, Brown & Co., 1892. The classic work on this subject, it must also be regarded as an expert piece of special pleading by an author who was fanatically convinced as to the justice of his theme.

PACINI, EUGENE. *La Marine*. Paris: L. Curmer, 1844.

POTTER, E. B. (ed.). *The United States and World Sea Power*. Englewood Cliffs, N.J.: Prentice-Hall, 1955. Excellent, detailed accounts of the Napoleonic naval operations and battles, somewhat weakened by an incomplete grasp of the land warfare and international politics of the period.

————, and NIMITZ, CHESTER W. (eds.) *Sea Power: A Naval History*. Englewood Cliffs, N.J.: Prentice-Hall, 1960. An updated version of the preceding book. It is, however, equally limited in its coverage of the Napoleonic period.

PRATT, FLETCHER. *Empire and the Sea*. New York: Henry Holt & Co., 1946. A serious effort to produce a good, popular work, covering naval operations, 1790–1805.

RICHMOND, HERBERT W. *The Invasion of Britain*. London: Methuen & Co., 1941. A brief, but sound "account of plans, attempts, and counter-measures from 1586 to 1918," which includes the various attempts made by the French during the Revolutionary and Napoleonic wars.

VAGTS, ALFRED. *Landing Operations*. Harrisburg, Pa.: The Military Service Publishing Co., 1946.

VARENDE, SEAN DE LA. *Cherish the Sea*. New York: Viking Press, 1956.

WARNER, OLIVER. *Trafalgar*. New York: The Macmillan Co., 1960. An excellent brief coverage of this campaign and battle, including a detailed order of battle of both fleets.

————. *The Battle of the Nile*. London: B. T. Batsford, 1960.

————. *The Glorious First of June*. London: B. T. Batsford, 1961.

Soldier Life, Statistical and Technical References, Miscellaneous

BAPST, GERMAIN. *Exposition Historique et Militaire de la Revolution et de l'Empire*. Paris: Galeriedes Champs-Elysees, 1895. A colorful, short account of Napoleon and the French Army on campaign during this period.

BONAPARTE, LOUIS N. and FAVE, ILDEPHONSE. *Etudes sur le Passe et l'Avenir de l'Artillerie*. 6 vols. Paris: Dumaine, 1846–71. Probably the best history of early artillery.

BREVILLE, JACQUES M. O. DE ("JOB"). *Tenues des Troupes de France*. Paris: Combet, 1913. This admirable book describes much more than the changing uniforms of the French army—namely, the men inside them through the centuries.

CHILLY, NUMA DE. *L'Espionnage*. Paris: Librairie Militaire de L. Baudoin, 1888. Provides a concise coverage of this aspect of Napoleonic military intelligence.

GARRISON, FIELDING H. *Notes on the History of Military Medicine*. Washington, D.C.: Association of Military Surgeons, 1922. This work contains a short, but informative, chapter on the Napoleonic period.

GRIMOARD, P. H. *Service de l'Etat-Major General des Armees*. Paris: Magimel, 1809.

HITTLE, J. D. *The Military Staff: Its History and Development*. Harrisburg, Pa.: The Military Service Publishing Co., 1961. This book contains, among other information, a fair picture of the organization of French staffs of the Napoleonic period. It is less reliable as regards personalities and actual staff functioning.

HOLTMAN, ROBERT B. *Napoleonic Propaganda*. Baton Rouge, La.: Louisiana State University Press, 1950. The author considers Napoleon the first modern propagandist, pointing out that he was the "first sovereign to talk to his subjects directly and frequently, partly through mediums such as the bulletins and orders of the day, which he was the first to exploit, and in his utilization of the machinery of the government, [by which] he took a pioneering step toward the systematic official propaganda activity of the type we know today."

HUNTINGTON, SAMUEL P. *The Soldier and the State*. Cambridge: Harvard University Press, 1957. This book briefly notes the Napoleonic era in the evolution of the interrelationship of army and nation.

KASTNER. *Manuel de Musique Militaire*. Paris: Didot Freres, 1848. The company's drums or trumpets and the regimental bands were important parts of the Napoleonic military machine.

MARTINIEN, A. *Tableaux par Corps et par Batailles des Officiers Tues et Blesses Pendant les Guerres de l'Empire (1805–1815)*. Paris: Henri-Charles Lavauzelle, no date. This book provides a ready and definitive check on unit participation in the various battles and campaigns.

MINISTERE DE LA GUERRE. *Dictionnaire Militaire, Encyclopedie des Sciences Militaires*. Paris: Berger-Levrault, 1894. An invaluable book for quick reference.

MORVAN, JEAN. *Le Soldat Imperial, 1800–1814*. 2 vols. Paris: Librairie Plon, 1904. A truly definitive work on every aspect of military life under Napoleon, with the emphasis on the shadows rather than the glory.

ODIER, P. A. *Cours d'Etudes sur l'Administration Militaire*. Paris: Anselin & Pochard, 1824.

OMAN, CHARLES. *Studies in the Napoleonic Wars*. New York: Charles Scribner's Sons, 1930. A meaty book that discusses a wide variety of subjects, among them, dueling customs in the British army in 1807, British secret-service operations within the Napoleonic Empire, the French cavalry, and the story of how Isaac Brock saved Canada. The author's fixation on some aspects of French tactics is its major weak point, though careful readers may find questionable statements—such as the bald assertion that the American declaration of war in 1812 against England "was being concerted in strict agreement with Napoleon."

PERNOT, A. M. *Apercu Historique sur les Service de Transports Militaires*. Paris: Henri-Charles Lavauzelle, 1894.

ROBIQUET, JEAN. *Daily Life in France Under Napoleon*. Translated by Violet M. Macdonald. New York: The Macmillan Co., 1963. An amusing and interesting background to Napoleon's rule.

SHIELDS, JOSEPH W., JR. *From Flintlock to M1*. New York: Coward-McCann, 1954. Readers wanting a quick, simplified description of nineteenth-century infantry weapons and tactics can find it here. American weapons of that period were very much like the French.

THIEBAULT, PAUL. *Manuel des Adjudans-Generaux et des Adjoints Employes dans les Etats-Majors-Divisionnaires des Armees*. Paris: 1803. Thiebault was vain, venomous, and intriguing, but he had a natural instinct for staff work and soldiering in general. His careful manual—one of the best ever published—still should be read by every staff officer.

VERNON, GAY DE. *Science of War and Fortification*. Translated by John M. O'Connor. New York: J. Seymour, 1817. This book was the official text of the Ecole Polytechnique during the Napoleonic era. After translation, it was the official textbook of the slowly budding United States Military Academy.

WATTEVILLE, H. DE. *The British Soldier: His Daily Life from Tudor to Modern Times*. London: J. M. Dent & Sons, 1954. There is no better brief picture of the men of the British armies, 1796–1815.

Magazines

Carnet de la Sabretache: Revue Militaire Retrospective. Paris: The Society of La Sabretache, 1893 to date. This magazine is a mine of invaluable information on all aspects of Revolutionary and Napoleonic warfare: personal memoirs, factual articles, and reproductions of official documents. Its editorial standards were particularly high during 1893–1914.

Journal: Royal United Service Institution. London: Whitehall 1, 1910 to date.

Journal of the Society for Army Historical Research. London: The Library, War Office, 1921 to date. Covering British military life in all times and places, the SAHR *Journal* usually can solve some part of any military researcher's problems.

Revue Historique de l'Armee. Paris: Ministere de Guerre, 1957 to date.

Revue de Paris. Paris: Bureau de la Revue de Paris, 1894–1940.

Revue de la Societe des Amis du Musee de l'Armee. Paris: Hotel des Invalides, 1956 to date.